PREPARATION FOR A REVOLUTION

STUDIES IN MIDDLE EASTERN HISTORY
Bernard Lewis, Itamar Rabinovich, and Roger Savory, General Editors

PREPARATION FOR A REVOLUTION

The Young Turks, 1902–1908

M. Şükrü Hanioğlu

UNIVERSITY PRESS

2001

OXFORD
UNIVERSITY PRESS

Oxford   New York
Athens   Auckland   Bangkok   Bogotá   Buenos Aires   Calcutta
Cape Town   Chennai   Dar es Salaam   Delhi   Florence   Hong Kong   Istanbul
Karachi   Kuala Lumpur   Madrid   Melbourne   Mexico City   Mumbai
Nairobi   Paris   São Paulo   Shanghai   Singapore   Taipei   Tokyo   Toronto   Warsaw

and associated companies in
Berlin   Ibadan

Copyright © 2001 by Oxford University Press, Inc.

Published by Oxford University Press, Inc.
198 Madison Avenue, New York, New York 10016

Oxford is a registered trademark of Oxford University Press.

Library of Congress Cataloging-in-Publication Data
Hanioğlu, M. Şükrü.
Preparation for a revolution :
the Young Turks, 1902–1908 / M. Şükrü Hanioğlu.
p.   cm.—(Studies in Middle Eastern history)
Includes bibliographical references and index.
ISBN 0-19-513463-X
1. Ittihat ve Terraki Cemiyeti.   2. Turkey—Politics and
government—1878–1909.   3. Opposition (Political science)—Turkey—
History—20th century.   I. Title.   II. Series: Studies in Middle
Eastern history (New York, N.Y.)
DR.5.H375   2000
956.1'015—dc21   99-35526

The art appearing on the title page
is the Ottoman Committee of Progress
and Union's coat of arms

1 3 5 7 9 8 6 4 2

Printed in the United States of America
on acid-free paper

For Arsev and Sinan

Acknowledgments

While engaging in the research and writing of this book, I have incurred numerous debts of gratitude to colleagues and others who have helped in various ways.

I owe a special debt of thanks to Professors Bernard Lewis and Abraham L. Udovitch for their consistent encouragement of this project over a period of many years. I must also express my heartfelt appreciation to the Chairman of the Department of Near Eastern Studies at Princeton, Professor András Hámori, who during the past three years created an atmosphere in which scholarship and collegial exchange flourished once again. Professors Michael A. Cook and András Hámori reviewed the successive drafts of the entire manuscript and made invaluable contributions on issues ranging from English usage to Arabic transliteration. Without their help this book would certainly have been the poorer. Professor Joshua Landis read two chapters and came forward with valuable suggestions.

I am also heavily indebted to a host of officials at the Turkish and other archives for courteous and faithful cooperation. I am particularly grateful to Mr. Necati Aktaş, Mr. İlhan Ovalıoğlu, Mr. İskender Türe, the late Mr. Veli Tola of the Başbakanlık Osmanlı Arşivi in Istanbul, and Ms. Penelope Tuson, formerly of the British Library. I also wish to thank Mr. Mustafa Aksakal, Dr. Phillip Allen, Professor Masami Arai, Professor Aydın Babuna, Ms. İffet Baytaş, Ms. Berrak Burçak, Ms. Anita L. P. Burdett, Professor Tufan Buzpınar, Professor Gökhan Çetinsaya, Mr. Roger E. Egan, Professor Khaled Fahmy, Professor Elizabeth Frierson, Professor François Georgeon, Dr. Maha Ghalwash, Professor Dimitri Gondicas, Mr. Şükrü Ilıcak, Dr. İsmail Kara, Professor Jacob M. Landau, Professor Hossein Modarrisi, Ms. Nancy K. Murphy, Ms. Kathleen A. O'Neill, Mr. Milen Petrov, Mr. Michael Reynolds, Professor Nader Sohrabi, the late Professor Tarık Z. Tunaya, Mr. M. Mehmet Ulucan, Professor Lucette Valensi, Professor Vakur Versan, Mr. David W. Wochner, and Professor Erik J. Zürcher, who all contributed to this study in various ways. I am also beholden to my wife, Arsev, for her devotion and to my son, Sinan, since the labor on this book deprived him of much of my time. Needless to say, while acknowledging the invaluable help of so many, the author takes full responsibility for any errors of fact and indiscretion of judgment.

Princeton, New Jersey　　　　　　　　　　　　　　　　　　　　　　　　　M. Ş. H
May 1999

Contents

Note on Transliteration, Place-names, and Dates

Names and titles in Ottoman Turkish are rendered according to modern Turkish usage and not by strict transliteration. The Arabic and Persian names and titles are transliterated according to a slightly simplified system based on that of *International Journal of Middle East Studies* (*IJMES*). The Greek names and titles are given in Greek script. The sources in Slavic languages—Bulgarian, Macedonian, Serbo-Croatian, and Russian—are transliterated according to the modified Library of Congress transliteration system. The titles of Russian works published before the 1918 orthography reform have not been modified. For example, "Politicheskiia partii" and not "Politicheskie partii" is the title of an article published before the orthography reform. Titles in Turkic languages written in Cyrillic alphabet are rendered according to current usage. There was no standard orthography for Albanian in Latin characters at the turn of the twentieth century; therefore the original usage found in the sources is preserved and not converted into modern Albanian usage. Since Ottoman intellectuals wrote their names differently when they published in languages written in Latin characters, one may find a single person's name written in two or more different ways. In this book the usage of the source is preserved. Thus we have Abdullah Djevdet and Ahmed Riza when they wrote in French, but Abdullah Cevdet and Ahmed Rıza when they wrote in Turkish.

For those geographical names frequently used in English language material, common English usage is preferred. Thus we have Salonica and Monastir, not Thessaloniki and Bitola. For all others, the names current within the Balkan and Middle Eastern states of today are used in order to avoid confusion. Thus we have Đakovica, not Yakova or Gjakovë. This usage has no implications for the ethnic origins or composition of the people now living in a given town or region.

In the period covered by this book, the Ottoman bureaucracy generally made use of two calendars. One was the purely lunar Hicrî (Hijrī) calendar, which used the traditional Arab months and counted the years from the Hijra (A.D. 622). The other was the Rumî (Malî) [Rūmī-Mālī] calendar, which combined the solar months of the Julian calendar with a divergent numbering of the years according to the Hijrī era. The Ottoman Foreign Ministry, however, used neither of these calendars, and instead dated its correspondence with Ottoman embassies and consulates in the Efrenci

(Gregorian) calendar. Ottoman periodicals of this period usually bore dates in two of these three calendars (either Hicrî and Rumî, or Hicrî and Efrenci); some are dated all three calendars. In order to avoid confusion, I have converted all Hicrî and Rumî dates found in the documents and periodicals to the Gregorian calendar, and given them in square brackets; I have omitted the original Hicrî and Rumî dates. Where a source provides a Gregorian date, I give this in parentheses.

When cataloging a document, Turkish archivists often incorporate its Hicrî date in its catalog number; I have not, of course, converted such dates to the Gregorian calendar.

With regard to the dates of publication of books, my practice in the endnotes is to give both the date that appears on the book and its Gregorian equivalent, the latter in square brackets. In the bibliography, however, only the Gregorian date is given.

Bulgarian, Greek, Serbian, and Russian documents and periodicals are normally dated according to the Julian calendar. Here I give the Julian date, accompanied by the Gregorian equivalent in square brackets.

Abbreviations

A & P	Accounts and Papers (State Papers)
ABCFM	Papers of the American Board of Commissioners for Foreign Missions
AE	Affaires étrangères
a.e.	arkhivna edinitsa
A.AMD.MV.	Âmedî-Meclis-i Vükelâ
A.AMD.NMH.	Âmedî-Nâme-i Hümayûn
A.DVN.MV.	Âmedî-Divan-ı Hümayûn Kalemi
A.MTZ	Âmedî-Mümtaze Kalemi
AN	Archives nationales
AQSh	Arkivi Qendror Shtetëror-Tirana
ASMAE	Archivio Storico del Ministero degli Affari Esteri-Rome
AYE	Αρχείον Υπονργείου Εξωτερικών-Athens
BBA	Başbakanlık Osmanlı Arşivi-Istanbul
BEO	Bâb-ı Âli Evrak Odası
BIA	Bŭlgarski Istoricheski Arkhiv-Sofia
BL	British Library
BM	British Museum
CAB	Cabinet Papers
CTF	Cerrahpaşa Tıp Fakültesi
CP	Correspondance Politique
CPU	Ottoman Committee of Progress and Union
CUP	Ottoman Committee of Union and Progress
CZA	Central Zionist Archives-Jerusalem
D	Dossier
DH.HMŞ.	Dahiliye Nezareti-Hukuk Müşavirliği
DH.MUİ.	Dahiliye Nezareti-Muhaberât-ı Umumiye
DH.SYS.	Dahiliye Nezareti-Siyasî
DUİT	Dosya Usûlü İrade Tasnifi
DWQ	Dār al-Wathā'iq al-Qawmiyya-Cairo
F	Fond
F.O.	Foreign Office
HH	Hatt-ı Hümayûn Tasnifi
HHStA	Haus-, Hof-u. Staatsarchiv-Vienna
HNA-TDA.	Hariciye Nezareti Arşivi-Osmanlı Belgelerinde Ermeniler Tasnifi

HR.MTV.   Hariciye Nezareti-Mütenevvia Kısmı Evrakı
HR.SYS.   Hariciye Nezareti-Siyasî
IJMES   International Journal of Middle East Studies
IMRO   Internal Macedonian Revolutionary Organization
IOR   India Office Records-London
Kopye Defteri   *İttihad ve Terakki Cemiyeti'nin 15 Teşrin- i sânî 1907–28 Mart 1908 Senelerine Ait Muhaberatının Kayıt Defteri*, Türk Tarih Kurumu Yazmaları, no. 130.
k.u.k   Kaiserlich und Königlich
MES   Middle Eastern Studies
MKT   Mektubî Kalemi
MS   Manuscript
Muhaberat Kopyası   *Osmanlı İttihad ve Terakki Cemiyeti Merkezi'nin 1906–1907 Senelerinin Muhaberat Kopyası*, Atatürk Library, Belediye Yazma, O. 30.
MV   Meclis-i Vükelâ Mazbataları
NL   Nachlaß
NS   Nouvelle Série
op.   opis
PA   Politisches Archiv
PAAA   Politisches Archiv des Auswärtigen Amtes der Bundesrepublik Deutschland-Bonn
PRO   Public Record Office-London
RM   Reichsmarineamt
ŞD   Şûra-yı Devlet
T   Turquie
T.B.M.M.   Türkiye Büyük Millet Meclisi
TFR.1.A.   Rumeli Müfettişliği-Sadaret ve Başkitabet Evrakı
TFR.1.AS.   Rumeli Müfettişliği-Jandarma Müşiriyet ve Kumandanlık Evrakı
TFR.1.İŞ   Rumeli Müfettişliği-İşkodra
TFR.1.KNS.   Rumeli Müfettişliği-Konsolosluk Evrakı
TFR.1.KV.   Rumeli Müfettişliği-Kosova
TFR.1.M.   Rumeli Müfettişliği-Müteferrik Evrak
TFR.1.MN.   Rumeli Müfettişliği-Manastır
TFR.1.SFR.   Rumeli Müfettişliği-Sefaret Evrakı
TFR.1.ŞKT   Rumeli Müfettişliği-Arzuhaller
TFR.1.SL.   Rumeli Müfettişliği-Selânik
TFR.1.UM.   Rumeli Müfettişliği-Umum Evrakı
TsDA   TSentralen Dŭrzhaven Arkhiv-Sofia
VGG(2)   Vilâyetler Gelen Giden (2) Kataloğu
YEE   Yıldız Esas Evrakı
YMGM   Yıldız Mütenevvî (Günlük) Marûzat
YP   Yıldız Perâkende
Y.PRK.GZT   Yıldız Perâkende Gazete
YSHM   Yıldız Sadaret Hususî Marûzat
YSRM   Yıldız Sadaret Resmî Marûzat

PREPARATION FOR A REVOLUTION

1

Introduction

This study is about the Young Turk opposition movement against the regime of Abdülhamid II between 1902 and 1908, with particular emphasis on the Committee of Progress and Union (CPU)/Committee of Union and Progress (CUP). This story has its climax in the Young Turk Revolution of 1908, which marked a watershed in Ottoman history and made a profound impact on the shaping of the modern Middle East and the Balkans.

The Young Turk movement can be traced back to 1889, when it emerged as intellectual opposition to the regime of Sultan Abdülhamid II, but it did not enter upon real political activity until the years immediately prior to the Young Turk Revolution of 1908. Until this change, it had possessed the peculiar characteristic of being a political opposition movement that had no clear political aims other than replacing the sultan's regime with a parliamentary one. Parliamentary government was not in itself the most important aspect of the Young Turks' ideal regime; indeed under the strong influence of European elitist theories of the late nineteenth century, they tended to look down on a parliament as a heterogeneous crowd. Thus Young Turk propaganda, which reflected a strong commitment to Social Darwinism, positivism, and elitism and promoted an ideal society based on these ideas, fell far short of convincing its sympathizers of the need for revolution. In the period between 1889 and 1902 the Young Turks' efforts did not go beyond palace putsch and military coup attempts, and the political debates in which the main Young Turk figures engaged were similar to the discussions between their mentors Carl Vogt and Ludwig Büchner, and Ferdinand Lassalle and Karl Marx, respectively.

In late 1901 Prince Sabahaddin, a nephew of the sultan who had joined the movement in 1899 along with his brother Lûtfullah Bey and his father Damad Mahmud Pasha, organized a congress to unite the various Young Turk factions that had ties to the CUP (the umbrella organization under which all these factions operated) with the organizations of the various Ottoman ethnic groups. At this congress, known as the First Congress of Ottoman Opposition Parties and held in Paris in February 1902, the leaders of the Young Turk movement for the first time debated substantial political issues, the most important of which was whether or not to accept the Great Powers' assistance in bringing down the Hamidian regime.[1] The congress served as a catalyst causing various Young Turks to take up political stands that had not been easy to identify amid the earlier intellectual discussions. As a result of a referendum on the issue of assistance from the Great Powers, two major fronts emerged: the "majority" and the "minority."Adding to the diversity of opinions at the congress, many small Young Turk groups and individual leaders decided to pursue their particular agendas independently.

The transformation of the Young Turk movement from an intellectual endeavor into a political one gained momentum in 1906; it bore fruit in the form of the rebellions which broke out in Eastern Anatolia and the Black Sea basin between 1905 and 1907 and ultimately in the Young Turk Revolution of 1908. The more the Young Turk organizations developed into political organizations, the more their focus on intellectual ideas diminished; despite their strong faith in these ideas, these organizations became pragmatic political committees. As a result, in contrast to the period between 1889 and 1902, the gap between the Young Turks' imagined ideal society and their pragmatic political agendas widened considerably between 1902 and 1908. Herein lies one of the main purposes of this study: to describe the difference between the Young Turks' ideal society as pictured in their intellectual writings and their pragmatic political preferences, resolving what at first sight appears to be a contradiction.

The book examines the inception of the two major fronts following the First Congress of Ottoman Opposition Parties. It covers the activities of the Young Turks, especially those of the coalition that emerged in 1902, comprising on the one hand the followers of Ahmed Rıza, the charismatic leader of the Young Turk movement between 1895 and 1902, and on the other the "activists" who strove to turn the Young Turk movement into an engine of revolution. It looks at the Osmanlı Hürriyetperverân Cemiyeti (Ottoman Freedom-lovers Committee), which had been formed by the so-called majority of the 1902 Congress and went on to attempt a coup d'état with the help of Great Britain in 1902–1903. It also covers the League of Private Initiative and Decentralization under the leadership of Sabahaddin Bey; this played an active role both in establishing a Dashnaktsutiun-Young Turk rapprochement and in fomenting the rebellions that broke out in Eastern Anatolia and the Black Sea basin between late 1905 and 1907. Considerable attention will be given to the CPU, which replaced the aforementioned coalition after the reorganization effected by Dr. Bahaeddin Şakir, who successfully converted an intellectual movement into a well-organized activist body, and to the Osmanlı Hürriyet Cemiyeti (Ottoman Freedom Society), which supplied revolutionary manpower to the CPU after the two organizations merged under the name of the latter. Relevant but brief information will be given about the activities of the less important Young Turk organizations and figures.

It should be remembered, however, that each of these organizations and figures could be the subject of a book; no single essay can include all the relevant details. This study should by no means be considered a history of all Young Turk activities. While the book attempts to describe a movement that was overflowing with committees, factions, coalitions, and alliances, it is important to remember that in each organization there were members who opposed the ideas and policies of the mainstream. Insofar as these opposing factions posed a serious challenge, they have been taken into consideration in this book, but it is not possible to discuss comprehensively the ideas of every individual or faction.

In addition, this study examines important events in the history of the Young Turk movement that took place during the period in question, with a special focus on the 1907 Congress of Ottoman Opposition Parties and on the Young Turk Revolution of 1908,[2] which resulted in the restoration of the constitutional regime in the Ottoman Empire after a 32-year interval. In order to give the reader a better understanding of the aftermath of the revolution and the performance of the CUP in power, an epilogue surveying the first year after the revolution is provided. This study, however, does not claim to analyze adequately either the events of the first year of the second constitutional period of 1908–1918 or the activities of the CUP and its opponents during that period.

This book also contains a chapter on the political ideas of the Young Turks. While not examining all their intellectual and political discussions between 1902 and 1908, the chapter focuses on the mainstream ideas that played a significant role in strengthening or altering the Young Turk *Weltanschauung* that had been shaped between 1889 and 1902.[3] In characterizing the Young Turk *Weltanschauung*, there is again the difficulty of taking into consideration all of the different factions as well as individuals who strayed from mainstream ideas. Many individuals who took part in the movement may have deviated from this *Weltanschauung* in one way or another; however, insofar as they share similarities rather than differences, they should be considered as those who internalized this *Weltanschauung*. In order to give an accurate and balanced portrayal of the policies and political ideas pursued by the various organizations and of the Young Turk *Weltanschauung*, all available Young Turk publications and private papers have been examined, and differences as well as commonalities have been taken into serious consideration.

The prominent actors of the Young Turk movement were members of the Ottoman intellectual, bureaucratic, and military elites. Their political ideas and the policies that they proposed were thus very different from those of the average person in the street. Undoubtedly, the strong censorship, which prevented the masses from obtaining any information on political discourse or familiarizing themselves with political ideas, widened the gap between the masses and an intellectual elite whose members were freely and avidly following the political and intellectual discussions taking place in European capitals and Egypt.

The readers of the Young Turk publications were members of the same elite within the Ottoman Empire. Much Young Turk material was made accessible to the illiterate masses in places outside direct Ottoman control, such as Bulgaria, Bosnia-Hercegovina, and Crete, through readings in coffee houses, but only members of the bureaucratic and intellectual elite could examine Young Turk publications smuggled into the Ottoman Empire. Ironically, almost all the letters published in the Young Turk journals were sent in by Young Turk sympathizers who were members of the elite. Hence, even if we accept the genuineness of these letters,[4] it is difficult to ascertain the impact of the Young Turk propaganda on the masses.

During the last phase of the Young Turk Revolution of 1908, the Young Turks finally succeeded in encouraging the masses in the European provinces of the Empire to engage in large demonstrations. These should be regarded, however, not as general popular support for the ideas promoted by the Young Turks, but rather as the Young Turks' successful manipulation of the masses, which they had long despised.

Similarly, the chapter on the activities of the League of Private Initiative and Decentralization attempts to uncover the political, economic, and social factors precipitating the rebellions in Eastern Anatolia and the Black Sea basin between late 1905 and 1907. Soviet historiography created the myth of a "popular constitutional movement deeply influenced by the Russian Revolution of 1905" and attributed to it all local uprisings and disturbances in this region. Such a popular and revolutionary constitutional movement never existed, although scholars have been misled into believing in it.

The Young Turk movement was not a popular movement; the ideas promoted by the Young Turks penetrated no deeper than the elite. This fact did not, however, mean that these ideas were unimportant. On the contrary, they played a very significant role in molding the CUP's policies during the second constitutional period, thereby shaping the future of the Middle East and the Balkans.

Between 1908 and 1918, former Young Turk groups and sympathizers constituted both the parties in power and the opposition in the Ottoman Empire. The ideas that had been discussed in Young Turk circles between 1902 and 1908 now acquired paramount importance. This was true of a variety of political issues: Ottomanism, relations between the Turkish element of the Empire and all the others, decentralization, and the role to be played by religion in Ottoman society. These issues were brought to the fore between 1908 and 1918 by the Young Turks, who used them to construct new political and intellectual discourses.

The Young Turk Revolution of 1908 also created an ancien régime in no uncertain terms. The destruction of the Hamidian regime was so complete that no serious opposition group expressed a desire for reinstituting it after the revolution; and in fact the opposition too strongly criticized it.

Although the roots of all the political discussions that took place between 1908 and 1918 lie in earlier debates among the various Young Turk groups, scholarship has blurred or downplayed this fact and exaggerated the novelty of these years. Also, without a knowledge of the history of the CUP and the opposition parties of this period, no real understanding of these organizations is possible. For instance, the most important characteristic of these parties, their conspiratorial nature, was a natural consequence of their past as outlawed, underground organizations.

The Young Turk Revolution of 1908 caused power shifts within the various Ottoman religious and ethnic groups that had been active as political opposition organizations before this event. The Dashnaktsutiun, which had been outlawed, now assumed a role of representation in the Armenian community as a political party with deputies; the sultan's loyal Muslim Albanian elite was replaced by one seeking to unite Albanians of all faiths under the flag of Skënderbeu in order to obtain autonomy; the right and left wings of the Internal Macedonian Revolutionary Organization (IMRO) became active participants in Ottoman politics with their clubs and deputies. Although these power shifts within the Ottoman communities were a fresh development, all these organizations were part of an opposition movement in which the Young Turk organizations had played an important role. The Young Turk Revolution did not merely bring Ahmed Rıza and Talât Bey to the Ottoman Chamber of Deputies, and make Sabahaddin Bey the honorary leader of the Ottoman opposition; it also brought members of the Dashnaktsutiun and İsmail Kemal (Ismail Qemali) to the Chamber of Deputies, and made Jane Sandanski a respected participant in Ottoman politics. This fact precipitated a renewal of old debates and struggles among these organizations and leaders. Anyone familiar with their disagreements before the 1908 Revolution will find the political discourse of the period between 1908 and 1918 a familiar continuation of the past.

This study relies on original papers of the Young Turk organizations and leaders in order to understand the real nature of their activities and agendas. The main flaw in the scholarship on the Young Turk organizations in general, and the CPU/CUP in particular, is undoubtedly its heavy dependence on official organs and their publications, and on the diplomatic papers of the various foreign ministries that collected information on them. It should be remembered that the significant Young Turk organizations, and the CPU/CUP in particular, had three distinct rhetorics: one for the Muslim-Turkish segment of Ottoman society, one for its other segments, and finally one for European public opinion. In addition, they had their own true agenda, which frequently conflicted with the other three. The diplomatic papers sometimes yield invaluable information, especially when they reproduce Young Turk material; however, they more often provide inaccurate information hastily assembled by third or fourth clerks of embassies. This study, while depending on original documents of the Young Turk organizations and leaders, attempts to use diplomatic documents to provide additional information and to serve as a source of critical analysis, without accepting the information they contain at face value.

In summary, this examination of the Young Turk movement and related issues is intended to achieve four primary objectives:

First, it aims to provide a detailed picture of the Young Turk movement between 1902 and 1908, by covering all significant organizations and the divisions between them.

Second, it attempts to demonstrate a continuity in the political and intellectual discourses that had existed in Ottoman expatriate circles prior to 1908 and that prevailed in the Ottoman Empire after the revolution. Therefore, despite what has been claimed by scholarship to date, while the Young Turk Revolution did constitute a deep rupture between the ancien régime and what followed, it did not lead to entirely new ideas and political and intellectual discourses. All the main political and intellectual issues of the second constitutional period had already been debated by the Young Turks.

Third, this analysis tries to provide the reader with a better understanding of the nature of the Young Turk Revolution of 1908, as well as the rebellions that took place in Eastern Anatolia and the Black Sea basin, thereby depicting the characteristics of the regime that the revolution brought into being in the Ottoman Empire.

Finally, this study seeks to portray the complex Young Turk *Weltanschauung* and the changes to which it was subjected between 1902 and 1908. Without an understanding of this *Weltanschauung*, which made a deeper impact on the Ottoman elite than did the political reverberations of the revolution, it is impossible fully to understand the second constitutional period and the developments that took place in its wake.

2

The "Majority" and Its Activities, 1902–1905

The 1902 Congress of Ottoman Opposition polarized the discord within the Young Turk movement, accelerating the rupture between two groups that had coexisted within the same movement in spite of their dissimilar viewpoints. This was in fact a schism among the leaders of the movement, not among the Young Turk sympathizers in the Ottoman Empire. As a matter of fact, Ali Fahri, who had advocated a convention for the purpose of creating a common front, spoke for many when he said, "Our compatriots within the empire kept telling us 'please convene this congress.' This is the essence of the matter."[1] European public opinion, having difficulty in discerning these differences, named the two factions as *Les Jeunes-Turcs républicains* and *Les Jeunes-Turcs midhatistes*.[2]

The schism that evolved within the congress was contrary to the expectations of those sympathetic to the Young Turk movement. The group proudly dubbing themselves the "majority" gave the immediate impression that they controlled the movement. But their campaign to institute an unrealistic program and carry out a coup d'état dissolved into so colossal a failure that its promoters lost active authority in the movement for many years. By contrast, the "minority" spent these years laying the groundwork for the expansion of the movement, and by the end of this period they had assumed control over it. Therefore, using the classification of the Ottoman ambassador to France, Münir Bey, it would be reasonable to assert that three main groups emerged following the congress:[3] the so-called majority, an alliance between the followers of Ahmed Rıza and the so-called activists, and finally the remaining members of the old CUP organization. The importance of the last category was minimal in comparison with the first two groups.

The Palace Action against the "Majority"

The palace launched an attack against the leaders of the "majority" immediately after the conclusion of the congress. First an arrest warrant was published in the newspapers for Sabahaddin and Lûtfullah Beys.[4] Later a grace period of ten days was offered to the princes if they would return and surrender, an offer that was also published in the dailies.[5] Then the two princes, along with Ali Haydar Midhat, Zeki Bey, and Abdülhakim Hikmet, were sentenced to death *in contumaciam*.[6] Şirvanizâde Mahmud Tahir, a former cadet of the Royal War Academy, and former Lieutenant-Colonel İsmail Hakkı received the same treatment.[7] This was the first time so many verdicts pronounced in absentia were published by the Ottoman press. Those who were sentenced and their sympathizers condemned the verdicts in various journals and attempted to exploit them to sway European public opinion.[8] Following this campaign, the palace banned the use of the title "Bey" for Sabahaddin and Lûtfullah Beys even in official correspondence.[9]

The second campaign was launched against Damad Mahmud Pasha, the most prestigious figure in the "majority" group. The efforts made by the Ottoman government against him had been set in motion prior to the congress and gathered momentum in its wake. By late January 1902 Damad Mahmud Pasha had realized that his situation in Rome was becoming dangerous, and he wanted to go to British-ruled Cyprus; however, he had been denied permission by the British authorities.[10] When he decided to go to Britain, where the central organ, *Osmanlı* (*Ottoman*), was published, the Ottoman authorities pressed the Foreign Office to deny him permission.[11] The British responded that they would not extradite the pasha but would put him under close surveillance.[12]

While these events were taking place under pressure applied by the Ottoman administration,[13] the Italians were bargaining with the Sublime Porte, demanding as a quid pro quo that the latter replace the anti-Italian governor of Iōánnina, Osman Pasha.[14] Before they had received a favorable answer, however, Damad Mahmud Pasha surmised that it was impossible for him to carry out any activities in Italy and left for Switzerland.[15] The Ottoman embassy immediately applied to the Swiss federal government,[16] but the latter granted the pasha conditional permission for residence.[17] Ottoman diplomats also applied to the Belgian government to prevent Damad Mahmud Pasha from engaging in political activities in the event that he went to his second residence in Brussels.[18] Under these circumstances the pasha was forced to lead a quiet life in Switzerland until he moved to Brussels when an illness from which he suffered became critical.[19]

In addition to these diplomatic maneuvers of Ottoman diplomats, Münir Bey succeeded in persuading a prominent French journalist to write an extremely critical article about Damad Mahmud Pasha and his sons in the prestigious French daily *Le Figaro*,[20] accusing them of working for their own benefit. The princes sent a strong but futile response.[21] The verdicts pronounced against the leaders of the "majority" had no effect on them, for they regarded these verdicts as a propaganda tool to influence European public opinion against the regime of Abdülhamid II. Damad Mahmud Pasha's inability to carry out activities in the centers of the Young Turk movement, however, caused great inconvenience to the new organization. In addition, the article in *Le Figaro* left no doubt about the real aims of Damad Mahmud Pasha and his sons and had a severe impact on their already low prestige.

After their success in forcing Damad Mahmud Pasha into inactivity, Ottoman officials turned their scrutiny upon the princes and their friends. On March 5, 1902, Münir Bey once again petitioned Théophile Delcassé, the French foreign minister, for their extradition. The Ottoman ambassador further claimed that Damad Mahmud

Pasha was serving British interests.[22] The French Ambassador Constans informed the Affaires étrangères that the sultan had been expecting the French government to extradite the Young Turks, whom he referred to as *maîtres chanteurs*, as did the Swiss government.[23] Following this, Münir Bey reapplied to Delcassé, presenting him with letters written by Damad Mahmud Pasha that he had intercepted. Those letters revealed the extreme pro-British proclivities of the pasha.[24] The Ottoman embassy in Paris also applied for the incarceration of the two Young Turks Hoca Kadri and Hüseyin Siyret, both accused of being anarchists.[25] The French authorities seemed to find themselves caught between their liberal values and Ottoman pressure.[26] Especially damaging to the position of the Young Turks was the claim made by the Ottoman diplomats that Hoca Kadri and Hüseyin Siyret were trying to obtain dynamite for an assassination. The French government refused the foremost demand of Münir Bey, notably the extradition of the princes, an action that they could not reconcile with their liberal tradition.[27] In the meantime, Hüseyin Siyret left France, and the new committee breathed a sigh of relief.[28]

A further measure taken by the Ottoman government was to cut the stipends of the students and officials who had been sent to Europe at government expense but who were instead helping the Young Turk cause. The Ottoman embassies were instructed to prepare lists of such officials and students.[29] As an additional measure, the property and assets of the Young Turks and their sympathizers were confiscated,[30] and their relatives were dismissed from their posts in the empire. The first dismissal was that of İsmail Kemal's son Mahmud Bey, an official at the Council of State.[31]

Following these actions the stipends of 39 students who allegedly had helped the Young Turk cause were slashed.[32] Afterward the Ottoman intelligence service attempted to collect information about the bank accounts of Young Turks at the Crédit-Lyonnais Bank.[33] At the same time, following the advice of Münir Bey, the stipends of all Ottoman students were suspended, and this action exacerbated the financial crisis the Young Turks were already facing.[34] Students complained about the matter to the Paris correspondent of *The Times*, denying any participation in Young Turk activities or in the 1902 Congress.[35] Since the Ottoman government feared such publicity, it restored the stipends for all who could be cleared by a security investigation. Nevertheless, by these measures the government had succeeded, first, in causing a financial crisis for the Young Turks and, second, in intimidating their sympathizers.

Immediately after the 1902 Congress, the newly established central committee undertook an initiative to construct a new organization. The initial plan was to form a "permanent committee" composed of Armenian, Greek, and Muslim former statesmen. The princes and İsmail Kemal, however, failed to procure direct support from the Armenians.[36] A meeting of "the permanent members" was held at the princes' house, and İsmail Kemal was appointed chairman. It was also claimed by the new committee that the remaining members of the old CUP organization had "bequeathed the journal [*Osmanlı*] to the new committee." Hüseyin Siyret was installed as the new editor of the journal and the princes donated Lt 1,250 so that it might be published on a regular basis.[37] Although it was claimed that the remaining members of the old society had bestowed "great honor" upon the new society by endowing it with the central organ, the vote of their representative Nuri Ahmed against the "majority" indicates that they were far from enthusiastic in their action.[38]

An additional development resulted in the collapse of their group: İshak Sükûti, who had made the publication of *Osmanlı* possible by his financial assistance and his anonymous articles, died in San Remo on the final day of the congress, February 9, 1902. His assistance and leadership alone had given life to the group composed of the remaining members of the old CUP organization, a fact acknowledged by all.[39] The "activists" grieved over Sükûti's death. He was the only member of the old CUP organization whom they respected.[40] But it was abundantly clear that they would not let the other members of this group, who had lodged a petition against them with the Swiss president and had labeled them "God-damn liberals," join their movement.[41] By publishing the shortest possible obituary note in *Mechveret Supplément Français*, Ahmed Rıza, who had treated the members of the old CUP organization as a group of *maîtres chanteurs*, made it very clear that he had no respect even for İshak Sükûti.[42] It was, therefore, inconceivable for them to approach the positivist leader. Their last chance was to make *Osmanlı* a mouthpiece of the khedive, and to this end initial negotiations had taken place between Nuri Ahmed and ʿAbbās Ḥilmī Pasha's spy Zeki Bey in July 1901.[43] The khedive, aware of their impotence, however, had paid no heed to their expectations.[44] Under the circumstances, the remaining members of the old CUP organization decided to hand over the central organ to the princes and asked for their protection. In this way they were transformed into a group of protégés of the princes.

İshak Sükûti's death brought about another problem for the members of the old CUP organization. He had worked as the archivist of that organization for almost seven years and accumulated a large number of papers related to the internal and organizational affairs of the CUP. Following his death, the sultan instructed the Ottoman diplomats to take possession of these papers, and they all were transferred to the imperial palace at his behest.[45] This move was undoubtedly a shattering blow to the members of the old CUP organization, since the Ottoman intelligence service now had this treasure chest in its hands.

The Activities of the New Committee

After its first meeting the newly established committee announced that it had adopted the name Osmanlı Hürriyetperverân Cemiyeti (Ottoman Freedom-lovers Committee). As described by one of the members of the new organization, this so-called Parti Libéral was the final link in the chain of successive political committees that first had been led by Murad Bey and since then had tried to secure foreign intervention.[46]

Shortly after the first meeting the central committee prepared the bylaws of the organization.[47] Compared with the previous CUP regulations, this document lacked any ideological coherence, merely underscoring the importance of "the union of all Ottomans."[48] As for the organizational framework described in the regulations, the new organization was to be strongly centralized with all decision-making powers assigned to the central committee in Paris. The central organ later announced that internal regulations for the organization were being prepared and were to be published soon in *Osmanlı*.[49] A month later a new announcement was made, claiming that this document was being published as an independent pamphlet.[50] It is unclear whether a document that framed the internal workings of the organization was actually prepared; one may easily suppose that there was no need for such a text, since the activities of the new committee were based solely upon the endeavors of its central committee members.[51] As a matter of fact, the French political police easily discovered that no activities were taking place at the address shown as the committee's center, which in reality was a residence rented by Lûtfullah Bey.[52] The sole ambition of this new committee now was to stage a coup d'état with the help of the British, and to realize this goal they decided to engage in high politics.

Once the central committee had structured its organization, it began to take the first steps toward realizing its primary goal. First, the proceedings and resolutions of the 1902 Congress were sent to the British,[53] French,[54] Italian,[55] and German Foreign Ministries.[56] These documents were further forwarded to Sir Nicholas R. O'Conor with the purpose of impressing the British ambassador in Istanbul, whose opinion might be sought for a prospective British endorsement.[57] Although it claimed to contain the official proceedings, the document actually presented the viewpoint of the "majority"; many critiques that had been advanced by the "minority" were omitted.[58] The British and French diplomats wrote marginal notes on or underlined those parts of the documents that dealt with the participation of the Armenians in the activities of the Ottoman opposition.[59] These minutes help us to discern the great efforts made by the leaders of the so-called majority to win over the Armenians, despite the latter's unwillingness to join in a common front against the regime of Abdülhamid II. The Ottoman government was further annoyed by the news that İsmail Kemal had acted as an intermediary between Damad Mahmud Pasha and the Armenian committees and had endeavored to encourage them to work together.[60] The available documents reveal that the Armenian committees did not actively take part in the ventures of the new organization. The official support given by the Armenians after the congress, however, was made much of by this new committee.[61]

The new central committee adopted a very different publication policy for the central organ. The main theme emphasized by the journal was that the present regime could be changed only with the intervention of the Great Powers:

> Abdülhamid is familiar enough with Ottoman history to know very well that all collective foreign interventions, occurring over the last seventy years, have resulted in the maintenance of the state and the preservation of its territorial integrity, and in some elements [ethnic/religious groups] receiving privileges.
>
> The sultan knows this and becomes upset when he thinks about the fact that, this time, the foreign powers have decided to act collectively in order to put an end to the oppressive rule and iniquity of the present absolutist regime, which has been the cause of the suffering of the people and has posed an obstacle to the progress needed in modern times, and has been presenting a permanent threat to the balance of power.
>
> Now all the different elements [of the empire], and the Turks first and foremost, would accept, with gratitude and a sense of obligation, the benevolent assistance and sincere recommendations [of the Great Powers] for the sake of acquiring freedom and preserving our independence. They will also roll up their sleeves to carry out these recommendations aimed at eliminating the unjust present regime that dishonors them.[62]

Later on, when it became abundantly clear that securing collective action by the Great Powers against the regime was far beyond their power, the members of the

new committee began to underscore the importance of procuring such an intervention on the part of Great Britain and France alone.[63] Delcassé's refusal to grant an
audience to İsmail Kemal made it clear that Great Britain would be the only power
likely to provide diplomatic support.[64] Thus in the pages of *Osmanlı* the allegedly
pro-Russian policy of the sultan was strongly denounced, and it was maintained that
the only choice for the Ottoman state was to reestablish the sound relations that had
formerly existed with Great Britain.[65] The superiority of the Anglo-Saxon social structure was also highly acclaimed,[66] and pro-British high-ranking Ottoman statesmen
were praised in the central organ.[67] In Sabahaddin Bey's own words, they "worked
systematically to prove to [their] fellow-countrymen the social superiority of the
Anglo-Saxon world, and the necessity of allying [themselves] with it."[68]

While the change in publication policy was striking, the leaders of the new organization realized that the effect of articles written in Turkish would be extremely limited with regard to the Great Powers. Thus they decided to publish similar articles in
the European press. As a beginning, the political testament of the late Fuad Pasha[69]
was published in a popular British journal,[70] and an Arabic translation was made
available by an Egyptian magazine.[71] The document had already been published by
a French journal in 1896,[72] and then Murad Bey published it in Turkish in Geneva as
a pamphlet, and also in *Mizan* in installments, while he was trying to impress the
British.[73] The English translation of the text was intended to cement the friendship
with Great Britain through the use of laudatory language.[74] This was also the reason
why the so-called minority members criticized it; however, they did so on the pretext of criticizing the document's comments on the Greek Orthodox Church.[75] The
editors of *The Nineteenth Century and After* made the following comment on the
objective of the new organization in publishing the text:

> This document, translated from an authentic copy and never before published in English,
> throws light upon the manner in which the Turkish Reform Party of the present day still
> view the affairs of their country.[76]

Other initiatives toward the same end were taken by a member of the central committee, Ali Haydar Midhat. He published articles in similar journals to prove that the
contemporary Young Turks were devotees of the *Tanzimat* bureaucrats who had tried
to reform the Ottoman Empire with the help of the British.[77] He also authored letters
to English dailies concerning the pro-British feelings of the Young Turks,[78] receiving favorable responses.[79]

A third attempt that aimed at obtaining support from the Great Powers in general,
and from Great Britain in particular, involved putting an entirely new focus on the
problems faced by the Christian groups of the Ottoman Empire. For instance, the
central organ informed its readership about the action taken by the Great Powers
against a governor who was accused of suppressing the Armenians:

> In a note that they presented to the Sublime Porte the ambassadors of the Great Powers
> required the dismissal of Enis Pasha, the governor of Aleppo, because of his oppression
> of the Christian population and the atrocities that he has perpetuated.
>
> Enis Pasha had been dismissed from the governorship of Diyar-ı Bekir due to a simi-
> lar demand [by the Great Powers]. The *Yıldız* does not appoint honest, adroit, capable,
> and just governors without intervention by [foreign] ambassadors. Isn't it strange?[80]

Interestingly, even the most pro-Armenian journals made no such comments, contenting themselves with information extracted from the French press on the subject.[81] Dr. Nâzım, a leading figure of the "minority," adopted an even stronger position by making furious remarks aimed at the members of the "majority" because they disparaged Enis Pasha.[82] The fact that Armenians were chosen by the new organization for their propaganda purposes was by no means a coincidence. İsmail Kemal had been aware of the fact that it was the Armenian crisis of 1895 that had brought the Great Powers to the brink of intervention. The central organ made this point very clear by revealing what the committee expected from the Armenians:

> The service that the Armenians are rendering to the Turks is that it would be easier to secure the moral support of the Western [Great] Powers should the Muslim and Christian elements [of our empire] demand the same reforms with one voice. The image of our compatriots working to secure reforms in Europe would be improved.[83]

The new committee exerted its best efforts to obtain this invaluable endorsement from the Armenians. In articles addressed to the Armenians, the committee gave its word that there was no difference between the various Ottoman ethnic groups in the eyes of its leaders.[84] Armenian responses characterizing Sabahaddin and Lûtfullah Beys as Ottoman "Washingtons" were proudly published in the central organ.[85] Similar treatment was given to İsmail Kemal by Armenian organizations.[86] Finally, Sabahaddin Bey took an unprecedented initiative and journeyed to Russian Armenia to negotiate with the Armenian committees. He was, however, arrested in T'bilisi by the Russian police on a charge of organizing an insurrection in Armenia. He was later brought to St. Petersburg and deported from Russia. Unfortunately, we lack further information about his venture or designs. The Young Turk and Armenian presses of the time did not even inform their readership of the event. Two western dailies provided a very small amount of information concerning the incident,[87] and Zeki Bey, in writing, merely informed the khedive that Sabahaddin Bey had left Paris on the pretext of going to London and that the news about the arrest was accurate.[88]

Another initiative by the new central committee was to organize joint activities with Albanian, Macedonian, and Armenian groups.[89] Immediately after the 1902 Congress, Armenian organizations and the IMRO had held negotiations toward joint action against the Ottoman government.[90] Sabahaddin Bey and his friends tried to seize the opportunity to benefit from these joint actions; however, these organizations' endeavors were aimed at winning over European public opinion—a mission that they subsequently accomplished—not at assisting the Young Turks.[91] The "minority" strongly denounced these activities.[92]

Another target selected by the new committee was the Albanians, unquestionably because of the prominent role played by İsmail Kemal in the new organization. Leading articles were published in *Osmanlı* warning Albanians that "Austria-Hungary and Italy have reached an agreement on the partition of Albania between themselves,"[93] as were readers' letters claiming that "Kâzım Pasha has the intention of selling out our fatherland [Albania] to Austrians, Montenegrins, Serbs, and Bulgarians."[94] The activities of those who were "working as intermediaries between the conspirators in Europe and their accomplices in Albania distributing banned publications and arms" reached a peak.[95] A good example is an Albanian named Xhemil Vlorë (Avlonyalı

Cemil), who worked in the region for İsmail Kemal.[96] Ottoman police stormed his house and uncovered a large number of "seditious publications."[97] Meanwhile, İsmail Kemal aided the leaders of the Albanian separatist movement, such as Jup Kastrati, by preparing their appeals[98] and taking the initiative to establish an Albanian council in Paris.[99] The journals supported by İsmail Kemal, furthermore, promoted autonomy for the Albanians.[100] Observing all these activities, the Ottoman administration concluded that "the sons of Damad Mahmud Pasha [were beginning] to direct Albanian provocateurs."[101] Similar allegations were made by the Ottoman embassy in Paris to the Affaires étrangères.[102] In order to deny these claims, the sons of Damad Mahmud Pasha were compelled to declare the following:

> Their Highnesses Sabahaddin and Lûtfullah Beys, the sons of Damad Mahmud Pasha, have stated that they by no means approve granting autonomy or independence to Albania. Besides, they have declared that they will exert all possible efforts for the sake of the territorial integrity of Turkey, and their intention has been simply to secure justice, freedom, and security in the Ottoman lands.[103]

These efforts aimed at winning over the Albanians to their cause bore no fruit for the new committee. First of all, during this period İsmail Kemal was far from being the leader of the Albanian movement abroad. A committee intending to make Albert Ghica Prince of Albania was founded in Paris by Derviş (Dervish) Hima (Maksud İbrahim Naci/Maksud Ibrahim Naxhi Spahiu), who had been a delegate in the 1902 Congress, and Dimitri Papazoglou, a Vlach captain.[104] This committee became very active in Romania,[105] underscoring the importance of an Albanian–Rumanian rapprochement, and adopted a strong anti-Greek and anti-Slav stand.[106] The Ottoman administration thought that Derviş Hima was a pawn of İsmail Kemal and Damad Mahmud Pasha.[107] This group had in fact established closer ties with certain pro-Austrian Albanian intellectuals such as Faïk Konica (Konitza). Thus, despite his good relations with Ghica, İsmail Kemal was in no position to orchestrate the Albanian movement because of his extreme pro-Greek and pro-British stand.[108]

In addition, İsmail Kemal was promoting a diplomatic solution for the establishment of an independent Albania, a position that elicited a cool rejection by the more active groups advocating guerilla activity against Ottoman rule.[109] Furthermore, the Greek members of the Ottoman Freedom-lovers Committee undoubtedly opposed the idea of procuring foreign intervention through Albanian affairs.[110] İsmail Kemal would have certainly preferred to have the Great Powers intervene in Ottoman politics on Albania's behalf, and this idea was the core of the accusations made against him by the "minority."[111] He too, however, was aware that such an intervention was highly unlikely.

It might thus be accurate to comment that all initial efforts made by the new organization were fruitless. There are four major reasons.

First, to secure a collective or at least a joint intervention by the Great Powers in Ottoman politics was far beyond the power of this new organization. Obviously, in this field the princes and İsmail Kemal were comparing themselves to the *Tanzimat* statesmen with little modesty.

Second, the fact that many of "the leading spirits of the organization [were] non-Turks"[112] made it a target of its Turkist opponents, who doubted that these leaders were "of the class which, owing to birth or long residence in Constantinople or the other large towns of the Empire, has retained only a vague consciousness of the varied origin of its members and developed a conception of a central patriotism."[113] They were accused of carrying out separatist activities at the expense of the Ottoman Empire's territorial integrity.

Third, the new committee could not obtain positive endorsement by the Armenian committees, something that was extremely important in securing the desired intervention. The members of the new central committee, invoking the vague wording used in the letters sent to them by the Armenians, always acted as if they were authorized by the Armenians. Their activities, however, were not sufficient to impress the Great Powers.

Fourth, although amicable relations with some Albanian organizations and leaders were established, those among the Albanian expatriates who were willing to help the Young Turks were far from having a firm grip over the Albanian nationalist movement. Besides, nothing but wishful thinking could have led the Young Turks to expect the Great Powers to intervene over the Albanian question alone.

The new committee therefore decided to explore other means to overthrow the regime of Abdülhamid II. Immediately after the 1902 Congress, the European press started to publish articles on an assassination attempt by the Young Turks.[114] This was undoubtedly an item on the Young Turks' agenda unchanged since the onset of their movement. According to Ottoman sources, Damad Mahmud Pasha and his sons had established sound links with certain European anarchists.[115] In the summer of 1902 Ottoman diplomats obtained information concerning a deal with two anarchists made by Sabahaddin Bey and his friends; this was accomplished through the mediation of a Polish anarchist.[116] According to Ottoman intelligence, a year earlier Damad Mahmud Pasha had sent an anarchist to Istanbul and, having failed in this scheme, he contrived a new plot and dispatched yet another anarchist to the Ottoman capital.[117] Anthopoulos Pasha applied to the British authorities without delay, requesting that they prevent the leaders of the new organization from persisting in such behavior.[118] Meanwhile, the Ottoman police apprehended three Italian anarchists in Istanbul and deported them.[119] Lord Lansdowne, the British foreign secretary, however, found the information presented him by Anthopoulos Pasha, who asked him to take the necessary measures against Damad Mahmud Pasha and his sons, "inadequate," and he told the Ottoman ambassador that "no British judge would consider the accusations made in the aforementioned documents seriously."[120] Later a similar plot by Damad Mahmud Pasha was also uncovered by the Ottoman intelligence service at its earliest stage,[121] and the efforts made by the new committee toward the assassination of the sultan ultimately bore no fruit.

The Coup d'État Attempt of 1902–1903

The members of the new committee were extremely confident of success in bringing down the sultan, and their failure in the initial undertakings gave rise to acute frustration. Thus while plotting to realize the typical Young Turk projects mentioned above, they also decided to carry out a new scheme. Sabahaddin Bey brought a proposal before the central committee that had been submitted by Colonel Şevket, a leader in the old CUP Tripoli of Barbary branch. This was a plan for a military coup d'état predicated on support from Receb Pasha, the governor and military commander of Tripoli of Barbary.[122] The central committee assigned Sabahaddin Bey and Ahmed Fazlı to prepare a report on the feasibility of the scheme.[123] After exchanging letters with Şevket Bey, they agreed to meet in Malta to discuss the details of the project.[124] Receb Pasha dispatched Colonel Şevket to Malta "under pretence of conferring with the Turkish Consul General at Malta as to measures to be taken for the prevention of smuggling."[125] There he secretly met with Sabahaddin Bey and Ahmed Fazlı. Colonel Şevket, on behalf of Receb Pasha, told the central committee members that they had initially planned to carry out a military undertaking in Albania but they feared that this would cause intervention by a foreign power, and therefore they decided to execute it at Dedeağaç (Alexandroúpolis). Sabahaddin Bey, with the claim that any military expedition outside the capital would allow the sultan to gain enough time to resist, asked Colonel Şevket to modify the plan.[126] The new scheme, prepared by Colonel Şevket, was as follows:

> The rising . . . was to have taken a form more or less analogous to that of the rising at Resne. On pretext of disorders in the interior among the Arabs, that portion of the army which was considered unreliable was to have been removed from Tripoli and ordered to Khoms or elsewhere, and the Khoms contingent, as more reliable, was to have been brought here wholly or in part. Before proclaiming the constitution, a number of troops with the Marshal at their head was to have left for the Dardanelles and Constantinople, as if they were time-expired men. Granted that transport difficulties by [İdare-i] Makhsussé or other steamers had been overcome, the Dardanelles, where under the former régime the passage of troops either up or down was always strictly watched and reported to Yıldız, represented the crucial point in the enterprise, and the force employed might have had to be sufficiently large to allow of the military occupation of the Straits taking place in case of a necessity, i.e., supposing any suspicion of the objects of the expedition had been excited there.[127]

Alvarez, the British consul in Tripoli of Barbary, when he heard this plan, claimed that "the odds against the success of the adventure at this point were . . . great."[128] Another problem, not mentioned in this report, also made success highly unlikely: a difficult military operation would have to be carried out by the worst equipped Ottoman army, the one positioned in Tripoli of Barbary.[129] Receb Pasha was the only general who volunteered his military services to the Young Turk cause at that point, and this fact compelled the central committee members to go forward with their plan.

Receb Pasha was one of the rare military leaders praised by both of the two newly emerged factions of the Young Turk movement,[130] and it was well known that the British also shared the Young Turks' view of this commander.[131] This fact was particularly important, since the new central committee planned to ask for British endorsement of the venture. Therefore, despite the weakness of the proposed plan from a military viewpoint, an agreement was reached between Colonel Şevket and Sabahaddin Bey. According to the arrangement, the military aspects of the venture were left to Receb Pasha and Colonel Şevket, and İsmail Kemal and Sabahaddin Bey were assigned to orchestrate the financial and diplomatic aspects and to purchase the two ships necessary for the plot.[132]

İsmail Kemal, who was assigned the most difficult part of the venture, kept a *pied-à-terre* in Paris and started political activities in his capacity as a high-ranking states-man in exile.[133] He also made frequent visits to London that annoyed the Ottoman administration, which could not discern his real agenda.[134] In his memoirs, İsmail Kemal stated that he had secured the support of Adolph Opper de Blowitz, the emi-nent Paris correspondent of *The Times*, and his assistant W. Morton Fullerton, "who both showed great and sympathetic interest in . . . [his] cause." In addition, de Blowitz recommended him to his adopted son Stéphane Lauzanne, who was then in charge of the offices of *Le Matin* in London.[135] Although the fact was not mentioned in his memoirs, in July 1902 İsmail Kemal traveled to London to obtain British support for the venture. A private letter from Sir Thomas Sanderson, the undersecretary of the Foreign Office, to O'Conor, the British ambassador in Istanbul, provides insights concerning the initial attitude taken by the Foreign Office:

> A certain Ismail Kemal Bey, with whose history you are well acquainted, is in London and has been asking Cromer whether he could not see L[ord] Lansdowne.
>
> Cromer discouraged the idea but said I could perhaps see him.
>
> I am not convinced that it is desirable. He is probably watched, and the Sultan will hear that he has been at the F[oreign] O[ffice].
>
> I don't quite see what advantage will result from the interview, but if I see him I rather think I had better ask him to call at my house in the morning. What do you say?[136]

O'Conor's note on this letter is "See him."[137] We do not know, however, whether İsmail Kemal had the chance to meet with Sir Thomas. Following this initiative, İsmail Kemal introduced himself to Sir Edmund Monson, the British ambassador to France, through de Blowitz. According to İsmail Kemal, he told Sir Edmund that "the suc-cess of this last attempt to assure the existence of Turkey depended on the interest that the British Government might show in it." Sir Edmund wrote "two personal let-ters on the spot, one for the Foreign Office and the other for Lord Onslow, then Under-Secretary for India."[138] Although İsmail Kemal maintained in his memoirs that he had left for London on the very same day, Zeki Bey, the spy of the khedive among the Young Turks, informed his "Auguste maître et Seigneur" five days before his departure for England that İsmail Kemal was "going to go to London in a couple of days and would journey to Egypt in the middle of November."[139] This information would seem to refute İsmail Kemal's statement that Sir Edmund provided him with two letters "on the spot" and that he left for London at once. Another letter by Zeki Bey reveals that İsmail Kemal spent his last hours before his trip with Sabahaddin Bey and Musurus Ghikis, the two other leading figures in the venture, and left for London on November 4.[140] Again something contradicts his version: İsmail Kemal handed over his letters to the Foreign Office and to Lord Onslow on November 8.[141] The next day Sir Thomas Sanderson invited him to come and see him at his private house. İsmail Kemal wrote the following about this private meeting:

> I gave him a detailed explanation of our proposed course of action and of the nature of the protection which we asked for from the British Government, which was simply to protect us against any action that Russia might bring to bear to prevent the success of our patriotic action. Lord [Sir Thomas] Sanderson promised to get into communication with his chief and let me know his decision. In less than two days I received a second

invitation from the Under-Secretary to go to his house, and he then read me the letter Lord Lansdowne had written him on the subject. This gave a promise of support which was worthy of the traditional policy of Great Britain, though it was surrounded with a natural reserve dictated by the fact that our coup was not yet a *fait accompli*. I was greatly encouraged, and with the consent of Lord [Sir Thomas] Sanderson I took a copy of the Minister's letter, which was in French, to show my co-workers. As I told Lord Sanderson I was going to Egypt, it was understood that Lord Cromer should be advised of my visit in order that he too might be put *au courant* of our enterprise, which would have an important effect on Eastern affairs generally, and give his advice.

I also saw Lord Onslow, but my interview with his colleague of the Foreign Office had given me the weapons I needed.[142]

At that point İsmail Kemal discussed the matter with Reşid Sadi, the chief clerk of the Ottoman embassy in London, who had secretly been helping the Young Turk cause since almost the beginning of the movement in Europe. He was asked by the new central committee to help them in their venture. Reşid Sadi and his father, who was a governor, were under British protection, and British diplomats had a high opinion of this young diplomat.[143] They were also aware of his Young Turk proclivities.[144] Although in the beginning he had secretly worked with Ahmed Rıza, following the 1902 Congress he criticized the latter's staunch opposition to foreign intervention, stating that he also "oppose[d] direct intervention by the Great Powers. [He had], however, no doubt that great advantages would be secured from their moral assistance."[145] His essay on reforms to be implemented in the Ottoman Empire also advocated good relations with the Great Powers.[146]

An invaluable letter written by Reşid Sadi provides detailed explanations of the venture. He gives the following information concerning the next step taken by him and İsmail Kemal:

> The British foreign secretary promised İsmail Kemal that his government would pay attention to the matter and would send a fleet to Beshika to protect Turkey against the probable Russian threat. Upon receiving this response from the secretary, I had to resign my post in order to work for the project, and I did so. Though I trusted İsmail Kemal, who was a clever person, to act prudently, I asked him to go to the undersecretary's house and obtain the promise, which had already been given, in written form. The next day we went to the undersecretary's house, and he made the text, which we had prepared prior to the meeting, more solid by altering some parts of it in his own handwriting. Following this, Sabahaddin, İsmail Kemal, and myself gathered at my apartment to discuss the final scheme. The military and political aspects of the venture were settled. Now, the remaining issue, which was of vital importance, was to procure money.[147]

This was the most difficult problem facing the leaders of the plot. When they took the initiative to convene the congress, Sabahaddin and Lûtfullah Beys were confident about the decisions to be reached there and had applied to a banker through a commissioner, asking for a two-year term loan at 4 percent interest "on behalf of the Ottoman people."[148] Many Young Turk leaders, including Ahmed Rıza, were aware that the princes were almost out of money after spending their final savings on the publication of *Osmanlı* and the assassination ventures.[149] The desperate princes took another initiative after the congress, when money became an issue of life and death for their plot. The details of this initiative were provided to the khedive by his spy.

The editor of *Écho de Paris*, assuming that Zeki Bey had an important position in the Parti Libéral Ottoman, invited and entreated the latter to furnish detailed information concerning the wealth and property of Damad Mahmud Pasha and his sons. Zeki Bey immediately perceived that the information requested was related to an *emprunt à conclure*. He gave some equivocal information to the editor, and after the interview he followed the editor and saw him meeting with a well-known banker, Siègler Pascal.[150] Zeki Bey later introduced himself to the banker and provided further information concerning the initiative taken by Damad Mahmud Pasha and his sons to the khedive.[151] Having failed in these initiatives, the princes implored Reşid Sadi to help them obtain money for the venture. Reşid Sadi again gives detailed information about his activities in this field:

> İsmail Kemal was intending to travel to Egypt to obtain money. Neither I nor Sabahaddin Bey trusted the khedive of Egypt. Therefore, we requested that İsmail Kemal convey nothing to the khedive concerning the project and we secured his word. . . . I decided to apply to Sir Edgar Speyer, a prominent figure in the world of finance. I went to his home and explained the matter in the utmost secrecy. He listened to me carefully, showed great interest, and asked questions about Sabahaddin and İsmail Kemal Beys. He then said, "Let me think about it tonight, and I shall give my response to you tomorrow at 10:00 a.m." The next day I went to his house, where he told me that he accepted my request in principle, but that he desired to discuss the matter with Sabahaddin and İsmail Kemal Beys. After this, in accordance with our [previous] decision, I sent a telegram to Cairo to İsmail Kemal, and a letter to Paris to Sabahaddin Bey and informed them of this development.[152]

Although a source close to Sabahaddin Bey claimed that £10,000 had been acquired from Sir Ernest Cassel, a banker who showed great interest in Ottoman affairs, Reşid Sadi's letter refutes this claim.[153] Speyer was the owner of a prominent banking company and had close ties with the Liberal party.[154] We might argue, however, that Sir Edgar was not the best person to work with, not only because the Young Turks were dealing with the Tories, but also because of his intimate relations with German diplomats and statesmen, through whom the sultan might easily have learned something of the venture.[155]

While these events were taking place in London, İsmail Kemal was trying to convince Lord Cromer "that the Turkish question was, if anything, more pressing than ever." He wrote in his memoirs that Lord Cromer "agreed with [his] view and he promised that he would reply to the Foreign Office in this sense."[156] Although he did not mention this in his memoirs, İsmail Kemal secretly met with the khedive in an effort to receive financial support for the venture. Despite the sultan's warnings requiring him not to support the Albanian statesman, the khedive dispatched £4,000 to an English bank to be used for the undertaking.[157] Furthermore, İsmail Kemal sent an Albanian confidant, Xhafer Berxhani, who was staying at an Albanian Bektashi *tekke* in Greece awaiting instructions, to Tripoli of Barbary to see Receb Pasha.[158] In late January 1903 İsmail Kemal returned to Paris, where he found the princes very much upset at the death of their father, Damad Mahmud Pasha; they nevertheless went to London to make the necessary financial arrangements for the venture.[159] The following events were described in detail by Reşid Sadi:

When I met with İsmail Kemal at my apartment, he asked me how much money we were going to borrow from E[dgar] Speyer, and told me that he had obtained £5,000 in gold from the khedive and would spend it when the scheme was put into action. He further implored me to say nothing about this sum, because Sabahaddin Bey had demanded that he convey nothing about the plot to the khedive before his departure. I told him that I was against having secrets among ourselves at the initial stage of such a consequential project, and when the three of us gathered, with the participation of Sabahaddin Bey, who had come from Paris, I informed the prince that the khedive had been informed of the venture. Sabahaddin Bey was extremely annoyed; however, it had already happened and we could do nothing about it. . . . The next day we were invited by E[dgar] Speyer to a luncheon at his office in the City. There he personally summoned me to his private room and asked me to provide him with information concerning the financial circumstances of Sabahaddin and İsmail Kemal Beys. Upon learning that only Sabahaddin Bey had real estate, he required detailed information concerning the project, and finally told us that he would loan the requested sum at an interest rate of 5 percent per year.[160]

A member of the new central committee wrote that the banker required Sabahaddin Bey and his comrades to inform him when the ships loaded with soldiers arrived in the Dardanelles.[161] This source and many others, giving contradictory information concerning the attempt, assert that the loan obtained from the banker was £10,000.[162]

The three masterminds of the plot then decided to work out the final details of their stratagem. İsmail Kemal was dispatched to Athens with £4,000 to purchase two vessels, and Reşid Sadi was sent to Tripoli of Barbary to give £3,000 to Receb Pasha for the expenses of the military campaign. Reşid Sadi again gives detailed information concerning his activities there:

While I was waiting for the person sent by Receb Pasha, who was supposed to recognize me, [Colonel] Şevket, aide-de-camp of the pasha, appeared at my hotel. Upon realizing who he was, I started to talk to him. Şevket Bey told me that the pasha had not given my friends any such promise, and still had not made a definite decision. This statement caused my utter amazement. I told him that I had no doubt that they were ready for the action, because Sabahaddin and İsmail Kemal Beys had assured me so; and that we had informed the British government and had dispatched İsmail Kemal to Greece to purchase the vessels. . . . The following night Şevket Bey came again . . . and I enjoyed the audience of Receb Pasha, accompanied by his aides-de-camp Şevket and Câmi Beys. I presented to them detailed information concerning our initiatives, which had been taken following their promise, and especially about the assurance given by the British government. . . .

The following night the same person came and took me to the pasha's house, and we commenced our discussion with the participation of Câmi and Şevket Beys. . . . The dangers foreseen by the pasha first concerned passage through the straits without being detected, and second the dispersion of the expeditionary force, which was to be dispatched to Istanbul, in case Abdülhamid continued to resist. It was my opinion that it was possible for the soldiers to pass through the straits without being detected, and an effective measure against the dispersion of the expeditionary force would be to storm the Topkapı Palace and seize the *sancak-ı şerîf* [the flag of the Prophet unfurled only for a holy war]. This might also help us to get the people to revolt. After lengthy discussion, the pasha finally decided to act decisively, and before I left them he told me, "I am trusting you with my military honor in this matter; so take all necessary measures and do not put me to shame."[163]

Before Reşid Sadi left Tripoli of Barbary, Colonel Şevket gave back the £3,000 that had been entrusted to him, saying that the expenses would be met directly by the pasha; he further asked Reşid Sadi not to doubt that the pasha would keep his word.[164] In the meantime, Damad Mahmud Pasha's secretary, Salih Bey, was dispatched to Cairo to give detailed information to the khedive about the new developments.[165] While these events were taking place in Tripoli of Barbary and Cairo, all other preparations were made, including the printing of a leaflet to be distributed when the expeditionary force landed in Istanbul. As usual, a heavy Islamic rhetoric was used:

[Soldiers] if you do not destroy [the palace] where Abdülhamid is residing today, crosses will be placed on the domes of the Ayasofya and Sultan Ahmed mosques which are on another hill [in Istanbul].[166]

Now the only remaining step to be taken before the venture was the purchase of the vessels, the tonnage and dimensions of which had been given to İsmail Kemal. The Albanian statesman maintains in his memoirs that "he found out that all that had been told [him] about th[ose] boats resolved itself into mere promises and vague suggestions."[167] The delay in purchasing ships caused all the central committee members to travel to Athens.[168] When Reşid Sadi arrived there, he was surprised at not seeing the large vessels that they had planned to purchase in the Piraeus harbor. He met Sabahaddin Bey and gave him information concerning the discussions in Tripoli of Barbary. Reşid Sadi later went to the house in which İsmail Kemal was staying and was once again astounded upon learning that İsmail Kemal was staying at the house of one of the aides-de-camp of the Greek king. İsmail Kemal told Reşid Sadi that he had been duped and that it was impossible to find suitable vessels in Greece. At the last moment, a sea captain named Godas appeared on the scene and asked the central committee to authorize him to purchase the vessels and sail to Tripoli of Barbary. Not hearing from him again, however, Sabahaddin Bey decided to go to Cairo to invite the khedive to buy or rent "a steamboat" for the venture. He went to Cairo, donned a hat as a disguise, and secretly met with ʿAbbās II. Although the khedive "tended to believe Sabahaddin Bey's statement," Aḥmad Shafīq, the *raʾīs* of the khidivial *dīwān*, and two other high-ranking officials who were called on by ʿAbbās II, found the plan impractical and even suspected that "maybe Sabahaddin was only intending to extort a few thousand pounds from His Highness and . . . luckily [the khedive] was convinced of their opinion and decided to have nothing to do with this activity."[169] Sabahaddin Bey's subsequent attempts through the mediation of an Egyptian notable bore no fruit.[170] Sabahaddin Bey quickly returned to Athens, and there he, Reşid Sadi, Musurus Ghikis, and İsmail Kemal convened for the last time. İsmail Kemal insisted on going to Naples to purchase vessels there. All the others, however, decided to extricate themselves from the venture.[171]

Various sources provide diametrically opposed information about the reasons for the failure. İsmail Kemal claims that because of the trouble he faced in Athens they "had to begin the work of getting the transports all over again, and this work and negotiations took such a long time that the period when Redjeb Pasha could take his troops out of the capital for maneuvers was past, the season would be too advanced."[172] A close friend of Colonel Şevket writes that some of İsmail Kemal's comments, such as "call on me when you arrive in Istanbul" and "to understand that the promised

British support was nothing more than no objection to the venture," compelled Receb Pasha to change his mind.[173] A source close to Sabahaddin Bey claims that İsmail Kemal seized the opportunity to profit from the venture for his own account.[174] Ali Haydar Midhat shared this view and made two additional claims in two independent books: that he left the new central committee when he learned that İsmail Kemal was on the Greek payroll and was working for Greek interests in Albania;[175] and that the Albanian statesman attempted to utilize this venture for his own designs on Albania.[176] İsmail Kemal does not make such a comment in his memoirs. He says, however, "If [Receb Pasha] seized Salonica with a portion of his army, he would draw to his side all his fellow Albanians."[177]

Some other individuals who worked for the opposition against the CUP after 1908 accused İsmail Kemal of being a crook and of purloining money from Sabahaddin Bey. They further claimed that İsmail Kemal had no interest whatsoever in the venture and was working only for his own interests.[178] Finally, the only source written by a member of the majority before 1908 made the most outrageous comment about the attempt:

> The permanent committee, which had emerged from the congress convened in Paris, collapsed without being able to achieve anything. Later a new committee was formed by the members of the defunct committee along with some diplomats [Reşid Sadi]; the *raison d'être* of this committee was to carry out a coup d'état under the command of a high-ranking Ottoman commander [Receb Pasha], and it was allegedly under the protection of a foreign power [Great Britain]. The members of this committee traveled to Athens to conduct the great revolution in the empire from a closer location, and at the time they convened there a dispute arose over the question of assassinating all the existing members of the [Ottoman] royal house who might ascend the throne, and enthroning a member of the committee in Europe, who was likewise a member of the royal house [Sabahaddin Bey]. Because of his [Sabahaddin Bey's] narcissism and other controversies this committee, too, collapsed.[179]

Though only one of many scenarios produced by various figures among the Young Turks, this stillborn plot is of great importance. For the first time in the history of the movement, the Young Turk leaders in exile secured support from high-ranking British statesmen, although the level of support received is still highly debatable. Therefore, it is worth putting this venture under a microscope for a more meticulous analysis.

Until now many historians have told the story by drawing on İsmail Kemal's memoirs without question.[180] One scholar believes in the genuineness of the letter allegedly written by Lansdowne but finds it "improbable" that Lansdowne also offered British naval cover for the enterprise.[181] In the light of later descriptions of Lansdowne's character, this scenario seems probable.[182]

It is better to begin by looking at the documents allegedly furnished by the British statesmen. In the light of İsmail Kemal's memoirs and Reşid Sadi's letter to Câmi Baykut, we may assume that there were two letters—one written by Lansdowne and presented by Sanderson to İsmail Kemal, and one prepared by İsmail Kemal and Reşid Sadi, on which Sanderson made alterations in his own handwriting. Receiving letters from the policy-makers of the Foreign Office itself was a great achievement for the Young Turks. As we have seen, Sanderson had been hesitant to meet with İsmail Kemal. Regarding the content of the letter, it might be argued that İsmail Kemal exaggerated the promised support and that the British statesmen provided the Young

Turks with no more than a letter of moral support with ambiguous wording. Reşid Sadi's account, however, seems accurate, and he had no reason to lie to Câmi Baykut in 1944.[183] Doing so would in any case have been extremely difficult, since the latter witnessed the former's activities in Tripoli of Barbary in his capacity as one of the aides-de-camp of Receb Pasha. According to Reşid Sadi, the second letter was prepared by the two prominent figures of the undertaking and therefore certainly contained the reference to the expected naval cover. Reşid Sadi makes it clear that the alterations made by Sanderson rendered the document "more solid." Regardless of the content, the British statesmen must have been aware of the seriousness of furnishing such a letter.[184] Any leakage concerning these letters would have had an irreparable impact on Anglo–Ottoman relations, and they might well have been used as propaganda material by the Young Turks.[185]

To my knowledge there are no available official British documents on this venture.[186] Two documents among the private papers of Sir Nicholas R. O'Conor, however, provide indirect information. A letter from Sanderson to O'Conor demonstrates that İsmail Kemal succeeded in elevating his own status from "a certain İsmail Kemal Bey," which is how Sanderson had referred to him before the first meeting, to "İsmail Kemal Bey," a more distinguished form of recognition. In fact, İsmail Kemal even discussed with Sanderson the situation of his son, who was exiled to Bitlis.[187] The second document is again a private letter from Sanderson to O'Conor, with a private dispatch from Cromer to the former enclosed. In this dispatch the British proconsul writes, "Musurus [Ghikis] Bey . . . called on me today. He is about to leave for voyage [*sic*] to İsmail Kemal. I did not like to cross question him but I gathered from what he said that he anticipates some early and important move on the part of [the] Young Turkish party."[188] Sanderson's comment on this is even more striking: "The enclosed rather coincides with my impression that İsmail Kemal is up to something, though whether it will really culminate in any serious attempt remains to be seen."[189] There is another document among the private papers of O'Conor that might be relevant. In April 1903 the British military attaché was required to prepare a memorandum on the Albanian troops in the garrison at the Yıldız Palace, and to comment on what would happen "should the Albanian battalions at Yildiz become mutinous."[190]

The examination of these documents clearly reveals that British statesmen were aware of İsmail Kemal's and his comrades' activities.[191] Another private letter exchanged between Sanderson and O'Conor provides riveting information concerning British statesmen's exploitation of the so-called majority's activities for their bargains with the Ottoman government and the sultan. Sanderson writes:

Anthopoulo[s] came here last Wednesday. . . . He is in a tremendous state of excitement about the possibility of Mahmoud Damad Pasha coming here and has been instructed to denounce him as an anarchist. . . . Luckily the individual has managed to hold his congress of reformers in Paris. . . . I told Anthopoulo[s] that if we had any more trouble about Kowait I thought L[ord] Lansdowne would offer Mahmoud the use of Lansdowne house for a meeting. He looked horrified.[192]

Using the Young Turks as a wild card in order to obtain concessions from the sultan was a more common form of political pressure. Presenting secret letters promising support for a coup d'état, however, was a direct action on the side of the British.

In regard to British relations with the Ottoman Empire, it might be plausible to assert that the former had many reasons to endorse a pro-British coup d'état attempt. As early as the time of the preparations for the 1902 Congress, O'Conor summarized the situation in the Ottoman Empire from the British viewpoint in the phrase, "things are going down hill."[193] About the time İsmail Kemal had started his maneuvers, even the Grand Vizier painted an extremely gloomy picture, and O'Conor, who called upon him, commented, "They seemed to be living only from day to day. How long the present system would endure it was impossible for him or for anyone else to predict, but there did not seem much chance of averting a political catastrophe in the end."[194] Also at the time of the preparations for the conspiracy, Lansdowne and the Foreign Office were facing deteriorating relations between Great Britain and Germany.[195] The award of the Baghdad Railway concession to Germany by the sultan during İsmail Kemal's maneuvers must surely have helped the Albanian statesman, since the British did their utmost to block this railway scheme beginning in late 1902, and especially after March 1903.[196] Lansdowne himself took a hostile position toward the scheme because of the lack of British participation.[197] Interestingly enough, Sir Edgar Speyer was representing one of the most prominent capital groups trying to participate in the railway project.[198] As was mentioned in the later official papers, the British gave up all hope until the sultan's death or dethronement:

> The life of the present Sultan is not likely to be prolonged. The Germans are well aware that the exceptional position they have succeeded in obtaining in Constantinople will probably not endure after the disappearance of Abdul Hamid. . . . There will apparently be no scope for diplomatic action in Constantinople until the death or deposition of the present Sultan.[199]

With this we may contrast what the British expected of the Young Turks:

> Germany's favourable position in Turkey is dependent to a great extent on the goodwill of the reigning Sultan. The Liberal party in Turkey views with alarm the preponderance of German influence at Constantinople and when opportunity occurs, its energies will no doubt be directed towards the frustration of German schemes.[200]

The replacement of the Hamidian regime by an extremely pro-British one, therefore, would certainly have helped them to fulfill their goals.

Naval cover against a possible Russian intervention was, for practical purposes, something easy for the British to offer, since they were preparing detailed plans for this at that very time.[201] In the light of all these factors, we may conclude that the circumstantial details are convincing and that the removal of Abdülhamid II from the scene would have been a great relief to the British.

As for the analysis of the other parts of İsmail Kemal's account, we have to start with his contacts in Paris. He claims, as we have seen, that he had established good relations with de Blowitz, William Morton Fullerton, and Stéphane Lauzanne, and in his memoirs he implies that through the help of the first he had the opportunity to meet with Sir Edmund Monson. De Blowitz had won fame through his famous interviews and articles on diplomatic affairs.[202] His interview with Abdülhamid II in 1883 had generated a great sensation, and despite his critical attitude, he had been decorated by the sultan.[203] He had, however, continued to disparage the Ottoman ruler and his regime. He had also taken part in many diplomatic intrigues during his long tenure[204] and was known for introducing people to prominent diplomats and states-men.[205] Unfortunately, I could not find a single document proving that he had con-tacts with İsmail Kemal. Two letters written by him, asking assistance for Ali Haydar Midhat, demonstrate that he had good relations with the members of the new central committee.[206] It is worth mentioning that he had helped Ahmed Rıza in 1896, during the Ottoman government's campaign against the central organ of the CUP.[207] De Blowitz's assistant Fullerton had a low opinion of the Young Turks and once wrote, "During more than ten years the present writer remained in contact, in Paris, with many of the conspirators who were destined to play a leading part in the Revolution of 1908. . . . He had no illusions as to the folly of the Foreign Offices of Europe in welcoming so effusively these sinister logicians, and on more than one occasion, in published utterances expressed the opinion that they would wreck their country. He gave them three years in which to prove their incompetence."[208] Without any doubt, however, he considered İsmail Kemal an exceptional character in the movement with a *revenu de beaucoup de choses*.[209] Stéphane Lauzanne had played a notable role in the anti-Hamidian campaign in the French press.[210] His good relations with İsmail Kemal had been criticized by a mouthpiece of the sultan in Paris for this reason.[211]

In regard to de Blowitz's relations with Sir Edmund Monson, the available British documents reveal that the former had furnished secret information to the latter on various occasions[212] and had helped people to receive assistance from the ambassa-dor.[213] It is therefore plausible that Sir Edmund treated İsmail Kemal well and paid heed to his scheme because of de Blowitz's introduction. Also, in the light of Sir Edmund's successful tenure in Paris and the high place he occupied among the Brit-ish ambassadors, it seems conceivable that, in his capacity as ambassador, he might have furnished two letters to İsmail Kemal, introducing him to Lords Lansdowne and Onslow.[214]

We may conclude that despite some minor inconsistencies, İsmail Kemal's account of the venture was quite accurate, and that the stillborn coup d'état attempt occupies a significant place not only in the history of the Young Turk movement, but also in the history of Anglo–Ottoman relations. This was the single most important case in which direct British support was obtained. Despite their success in securing such an important letter, however, carrying out such a coup was far beyond the power of the new organization. As a matter of fact, their failure also marked their collapse, and the name Ottoman Freedom-lovers Committee was quickly forgotten. It was also at this juncture that İsmail Kemal decided to cut all his ties with the Young Turks and pursue his hitherto hidden agenda openly. On August 16, 1903, he gave an interview to an Italian daily in his capacity as an "Albanian patriot,"[215] and he embarked on a new undertaking for the future of Albania.

Damad Mahmud Pasha's anticipated death on January 18, 1903, worsened the situ-ation of the group that deemed itself the "majority." This was a great loss for the movement's image.[216] The prestige he brought to the Young Turk movement was the reason behind the palace agents' and Ottoman diplomats' persistent attempts, down to Damad Mahmud Pasha's last hours, to persuade him to return to Istanbul.[217] The Young Turks resisted the palace's attempt to transfer the remains of the pasha to the Ottoman capital.[218] The influence of French public opinion in this matter caused an inconsequential Young Turk success,[219] and Damad Mahmud Pasha's funeral turned into a demonstration against the sultan, with the participation of all groups belonging to the movement.[220] This event was, however, nothing more than consolation for the leaders of a group who proudly called themselves "the majority" and who had such ambitious designs as we have seen. The fiasco also precipitated their financial bankruptcy. In consequence, *Osmanlı* was donated to a new central committee and ceased publication after the appearance of the 119th issue on March 15, 1903.[221]

A last noteworthy event concerning a leading member of the new committee was the arrest of Lûtfullah Bey on November 18, 1903. Some European dailies reported that he had been assigned to an important mission but was apprehended upon a tip from his friends.[222] The major Young Turk journals did not provide any information concerning the arrest; only periodicals of secondary importance supplied news of it to their readership.[223] A French newspaper claimed that Lûtfullah Bey had been promised an imperial pardon by Münir Bey and had attempted to enter the Ottoman Empire disguised as a European, only to be apprehended at once by the police.[224] Many years later Lûtfullah Bey professed that he had been arrested because of a betrayal, that he had been assigned to accomplish a mission, after which he had intended to return to Paris.[225] This statement made the event seem more cryptic than ever. Only in the light of a French political police report does the motivation behind this peculiar action and the so-called mission become clear:

> Prince Lûtfullah, who unlike his brother, likes to make merry and is always short of money, has followed the advice of Turkish emissaries and returned to Constantinople making honorable amends.
>
> Serious accusations have been directed against the former by the Young Turks of Paris, who openly accuse him of having revealed to the sultan all that he could have learned here regarding to Turkish refugees and diplomats accredited to European governments.[226]

The actual reason behind Sabahaddin Bey's decision, immediately after the 1902 Congress, to "devote himself to social and political science, the studies he felt he needed,"[227] according to one of his admirers, was not his infatuation with science, but the devastating failure that the group under his leadership had experienced. Thus it would be quite accurate to portray his and his so-called majority's activities during this period as a series of failures, and to share the judgment that the "Reform or Young Turkish Party [majority]" was not "a real party" but "merely a disorganized agitation for reform."[228]

The Coalition between the Followers of Ahmed Rıza and the Activists

First Activities of the "Minority" after the 1902 Congress

While the new central committee members were devoting their efforts to a quixotic coup attempt, Ahmed Rıza's followers and the activists were trying to strengthen their union and enjoying a relatively tranquil period. Although a source close to Sabahaddin Bey claims that members of this coalition had shown interest in taking part in the stillborn coup d'état,[1] other relevant sources and documents reveal that the coalition had not established meaningful relations with the "majority" of the congress. Ahmed Rıza gives the following as a reason for their inactivity during this period:

> Les travaux nouveaux exigent des mentalités nouvelles; l'ordre intellectuel est aussi nécessaire que l'ordre matériel pour assurer le progrès d'un État. Or, chez nous, rien n'est fait encore dans le domaine de l'enseignement public; les notions politiques les plus élémentaires, notions que tout citoyen doit posséder, ne sont pas enseignées. Tout le monde se déclare partisan de la justice et de la liberté; seulement il s'agit de savoir ce qu'on doit entendre par là et comment, et par quels moyens, on veut en garantir le bon fonctionnement. Par conséquent, avant de s'être assuré le concours volontaire de la majorité en faveur d'une doctrine sociale commune, il serait immoral d'appeler sur un terrain de combat mal préparé une nation qui prend les torches pour des flambeaux de la civilisation. . . .
>
> Un patriote ne doit jamais oublier qu'il est responsable, non seulement de tout acte de folie dont il a été l'instigateur, mais encore de toute parole imprudente pouvant exciter les passions des masses et amener une paralysie des fonctions vitales de la société. Toute insurrection n'est, certes, pas un crime, mais elle risque de devenir criminelle, si elle n'est pas inspirée par des conceptions de haute morale.[2]

Ahmed Rıza's explanation had three objectives: first, to emphasize that members of the coalition were seeking an evolutionary change and not a revolution, as Ahmed Rıza had consistently stressed since 1895; second, to deny emphatically the Ottoman administration's accusation of anarchism;[3] and third and most important, to conceal the inactivity of this group by recourse to a "scientific" positivist rhetoric, and thereby to calm the activist members in the empire who had been longing for decisive action. The so-called activists harbored a visceral hatred toward "evolutionary" theories, and soon after the reorganization of 1906 Ahmed Rıza himself began to promote an activist agenda, contradicting his own ideas as quoted above.

Immediately after the 1902 Congress, members of the "minority," who had predicted their minority status as an outcome of the congress, began to schedule organizational meetings. After lengthy discussion, the followers of Ahmed Rıza and leaders of various activist organizations agreed upon principles for common action. They decided to terminate the publication of all journals in Turkish printed by members of these groups and to publish instead a new central organ in Cairo.[4] They chose the Egyptian capital for two major reasons: they would prevent Münir Bey, the Ottoman ambassador in Paris, from using diplomatic channels against them; and in contrast to Paris or Geneva, they would have no difficulty in finding a typesetter for a Turkish journal in Cairo.[5] They also decided to publish *Mechveret Supplément Français* as the organ of the coalition in French, and to renew publication of *Kürdistan* in Kurdish as an organ of the new union.[6] Second, according to the agreement, Ahmed Rıza and his followers were to establish the center of the movement in Paris, activists were to form a branch in Geneva, and finally Ahmed Saib was to found a branch in Cairo.

As expected, Ahmed Rıza considered himself the natural leader of this new coalition. In fact, the first declaration made by the coalition announced that the offices of *Mechveret Supplément Français* were the "center for the committee" and that Ahmed Saib was the "director of the Egyptian branch."[7] Although Ahmed Saib was also given the title of editor of the new central organ published in Turkish, Ahmed Rıza made it clear that this post was on condition that "editorial matters and problems regarding publication policy would be entirely under his control."[8] Ahmed Rıza and the leaders of various activist organizations also agreed to send a prominent activist, former Captain Silistireli Mustafa Hamdi, to Cairo to balance Ahmed Saib's impact on the publication of the new central organ.[9] The activists in Geneva opted not to form a branch there because of Swiss government pressure, instead moving to Paris to join the new center founded by Ahmed Rıza and his followers.[10] Thereafter the activist movement in Switzerland ceased, leaving only the remaining members of the old CUP organization in Geneva.[11]

The activists also opposed the assignment of Ahmed Saib to the directorship of the Cairo branch of the prospective committee and required everyone other than Ahmed Rıza, who had charismatic authority among the members, to be equal within the organization.[12] They also urged Ahmed Rıza's followers to select a distinct name for the new organization. The names they proposed were Osmanlı Islahat Cemiyeti (Ottoman Reform Committee) and Terakki Cemiyet-i Osmaniyesi (Ottoman Committee for Progress).[13]

Ahmed Rıza and Ahmed Saib, however, opposed both suggestions. The latter had already written to Ahmed Rıza that unless he was granted the title of director of the Egyptian branch, he would not join the prospective organization.[14] Ahmed Rıza, on the other hand, intended to become the leader of the entire Young Turk movement, not of a separate and minor organization composed of untrustworthy activists. He refused to adopt a name for the coalition and insisted on publishing the new central organ as the "organ of the partisans of a constitutional regime." In order to soften the activists' opposition, he assured them that their proposals would be discussed during preparations for the adoption of new bylaws by the prospective organization.

The activists and the followers of Ahmed Rıza also discussed a proposal by Ahmed Rıza that only articles by the positivist leader, Khalīl Ghānim, and Hoca Kadri were to be published with signatures. All other articles were to appear anonymously. This was a precaution to prevent the palace from buying off those who might write for the central organ.[15] On the other hand, this precaution could have turned the journal into an organ of the followers of Ahmed Rıza, since all the signed articles were to be authored either by the positivist leader or by his closest associates. The organizers softened this rule because of opposition by the activists, and decided that all articles written by members of the new committee, other than the aforementioned three prominent leaders, would be published under pen names, while notes and open letters written by nonmembers would appear in the journal without any signature.[16] Through these steps the activists and the followers of Ahmed Rıza inaugurated a new phase of organizational activity in Paris.

This new movement, compared with the previous CUP networks, was remarkably weak from an organizational point of view. There were no branches in Europe other than the center. Also when the Ottoman authorities investigated "the Egyptian branch," which had been proudly advertised in the central organ, they uncovered the fact that there were only two Young Turks, Ahmed Saib and the former Captain Silistireli Mustafa Hamdi, publishing the central organ there.[17] Ahmed Saib succeeded in deluding foreign diplomats in Cairo into thinking that he was leading a significant movement;[18] but in organizational terms his endeavors were insignificant.

Despite its organizational weaknesses and problems, the coalition succeeded, in a very short time after the 1902 Congress, in publishing a central organ called *Şûra-yı Ümmet* (*Council of the People*). The first issue of this new journal appeared on April 10, 1902, and soon became a target of the Ottoman government.

The Ottoman administration, fearing that the coalition might construct a strong base for the movement, took exceptionally forceful measures against its publication of a central organ. In the case of the publications issued by the "majority," the Ottoman administration had contented itself with the usual precautions taken against "seditious" journals,[19] reserving its more serious efforts for hindering the leaders of the majority from carrying out their "conspiratorial" plans. The steps taken against the new organ, however, were much more vigorous. On May 23, 1902, the Sublime Porte instructed the Paris embassy to exhaust all possible means to halt the publication of *Şûra-yı Ümmet*.[20] Meanwhile, basing its claim on the fact that the journal was being smuggled into the empire through the French post offices in various Ottoman cities, the Sublime Porte also issued a note to the French embassy warning that "this development is intolerable."[21] On the very same day Tevfik Pasha, the Ottoman foreign minister, dispatched a circular to all Ottoman embassies and consulates, requesting them to take the necessary diplomatic measures to hinder the publications of the recently established coalition and impede the activities of Ahmed Rıza.[22] The Ottoman foreign minister reiterated the instructions in another circular three days later.[23] Münir Bey himself then took the initiative. He wrote to the Ottoman Foreign Ministry that it was "very difficult to stop the circulation and mailing of a journal which is being published outside France." He promised, however, to do his best against the journal and Ahmed Rıza.[24] On May 28 Münir Bey applied to Delcassé and, under-scoring the "revolutionary" themes trumpeted by *Şûra-yı Ümmet*, he beseeched the French minister to stop the circulation of the journal.[25]

Upon these importunate requests, the French Foreign Ministry decided to launch an investigation. First it asked Constans, French ambassador to the Sublime Porte, for the reasons behind the excessive Ottoman concern.[26] Constans replied that this concern was due to a maneuver on the part of Münir Bey, who wanted to strengthen his position in the eyes of the sultan.[27] Then the French government requested its diplomatic agent in Cairo and the French Ministry of the Interior to prepare memoranda concerning the new central organ and its editorial board.[28]

The French diplomatic agent in Cairo furnished a detailed memorandum in which he underscored the alleged support of the khedive for the new coalition and depicted the journal as "revolutionary."[29] The French Ministry of the Interior, however, did not find the publication radical and added further that nobody even knew the name of the journal in France, since it had not been circulated there.[30] Upon receiving these memoranda, Affaires étrangères rebuffed the application by Münir Bey.[31]

Despite this refusal, the Ottoman government continued with its diplomatic efforts. On July 30, 1902, Tevfik Pasha again dispatched a circular to the Ottoman embassies and consulates asking them to carry out all possible diplomatic action to prevent the journal from being smuggled into the empire through French post offices.[32] Münir Bey further petitioned Delcassé on August 2, 1902, officially demanding such an action. Affaires étrangères again asked the opinion of Constans, who informed his ministry that the journal was being smuggled into the Ottoman Empire through the French post office in Alexandria, and he accused Münir Bey of meddling with French policy.[33] On the basis of Constans's view, Delcassé refused the Ottoman requests.[34]

Upon this second refusal, the Ottoman administration concentrated its pressure on the khedive. The new central organ had started publication at a time when the relations between the sultan and the khedive were remarkably tense. ʿAbbās Ḥilmī Pasha had tried to ameliorate his relations with the sultan in order to settle the dispute between himself and the Ottoman administration over the status of the island of Samothrace. His efforts toward this end, however, bore no fruit, and he had received a cool reception by the sultan when he visited the Ottoman capital.[35] Meanwhile the palace gathered information concerning a separatist society called "The Union of the Arabs," which was allegedly subsidized by the khedive, and this made the relations between the two rulers tenser than ever.[36]

The khedive decided to use the Young Turks in Egypt as a wild card to appease the sultan. First, in April 1902, he closed down the printing houses that were publishing Young Turk propaganda material.[37] Following the presentation of this gift to the sultan, the Ottoman administration requested the khedive "to take necessary measures against the publisher and correspondents of the journal [*Şûra-yı Ümmet*]."[38] Terminating the publication of the journal, however, was beyond the power of the khedive, for as Gazi Ahmed Muhtar Pasha wrote to the Sublime Porte, it "depend[ed] on action by Lord Cromer."[39] Upon receiving this information, the Ottoman government immediately instructed the Ottoman chargé d'affaires in London to make a démarche at the Foreign Office.[40] The British, despite the "personal initiative" of Sir Thomas Sanderson, refused to meet Ottoman demands concerning the new central organ.[41]

Having exhausted all possibilities in Egypt, Münir Bey played his last card by accusing Ahmed Rıza of engaging in anarchist activities and publishing a "revolutionary" organ at the offices of *Mechveret*.[42] The French Foreign Ministry rebuffed this final application, and the Ottoman administration lost its war against the central organ of the new coalition. This turn of events can be regarded as the first success of that group.

The Organization of the Coalition

While the diplomatic campaign launched by the palace against their publication was unfolding, the members of the new coalition decided to pen bylaws for their unnamed organization. The first conclave toward this end was held in Paris with the participation of the followers of Ahmed Rıza and the activist leaders. According to the proceedings of this first gathering, the participants agreed to form a new society called the Hak Cemiyeti (Committee for Justice). In a final document they described the aims of this new organization as follows:

> The salvation of the fatherland from the present calamities, the securing of liberty and happiness for all Ottomans, the maintenance of the independence and territorial integrity of the Sublime State, the transformation of the absolutist arbitrary administration into a constitutional regime, the implementation of the Constitution dated 7 Zilhicce [Dhū al-Hijjah] 1293, the creation of an unfeigned union among the various Ottoman communities which would originate from patriotic and humanitarian feelings, the political unification of all Ottoman subjects, Muslim and non-Muslim, to secure the continuous existence of the noble Ottoman royal house upon the pillars of the caliphate and the sultanate.[43]

Ahmed Rıza had promoted these aims for almost a decade. The document, however, did not explain how these changes could be achieved. Other aims, also enumerated in the proceedings, seem like precepts of an educational society, as when the group vows "to exert its best efforts to promote education and moral improvement."[44] The dilemma that Ahmed Rıza and his followers had been facing for eight years seemed not to have been resolved by the establishment of the new coalition. They were quite successful in convincing their readership of the necessity of deposing the sultan and replacing his regime with a constitutional one, but they were not at all successful in identifying the means to bring about such changes.[45]

According to the proceedings, the organizers led by Ahmed Rıza agreed to appoint a central committee and to require this body to appoint one of its members as the director. The director was to be accountable to the central committee; however, he might make decisions without asking its opinion or consent. This provision demonstrates that Ahmed Rıza was quite influential during the preparation of the first draft of the bylaws.

It is clear from the proceedings of a second meeting that the founding members altered the first draft. Various members offered different names for the new committee and this issue could not be settled. Details of the organizational framework caused lengthy discussions. Also the founding members asked Ahmed Rıza to prepare an oath for the new members to take.

In the text of the proceedings, the remarks and comments made on various matters were noted along with the names of the members who made them. This record provides us with a list of the leaders who took part in laying the groundwork, namely Ahmed Rıza, Doctor Nâzım, Ahmed Ferid, Abdülhalim Memduh, Mahir Saʿid, and Hikmet Süleyman. It is interesting that with the exclusion of Khalīl Ghānim and Albert Fua, who had upheld the cause of the "minority" at the 1902 Congress, no non-Muslim played any role in this preparatory procedure.

Ahmed Rıza, having worked on the proceedings of the second meeting, penned a draft of the bylaws for the prospective committee. The main alteration he made was the removal of the name for the organization agreed upon at the meeting. He then sent two copies of this text to the activists. The activists, after examining the text, proposed a new name, Terakki Cemiyeti (Progress Committee). They also advised establishing major central branches in various regions of the empire and attaching small regional branches to those major ones. The activists further objected to the appointment of a director. They asserted that "in the event of an emergency a member would be given the title *représentant*, and when the emergency was over the title would be withdrawn."[46]

When Ahmed Rıza sent a copy of the draft of the bylaws to Cairo, he attached a note informing Ahmed Saib and former Captain Silistireli Mustafa Hamdi that he intended to publish a satirical opposition journal with the title *Nasreddin Hoca*, as well as a series of pamphlets.[47]

Both members carefully examined these texts. First Silistireli Mustafa Hamdi prepared a detailed memorandum commenting on every detail in the bylaws and sharing the activist opinion on the appointment of a director. Moreover, next to a clause in the text that read "by every means" he posed the critical question, "Including action or not?" He further reprimanded Ahmed Rıza's intervention in every matter concerning committee affairs and wrote that he found the project of publishing a satirical journal utterly absurd. After listing all these criticisms, he enclosed his letter of resignation with his response.[48]

Ahmed Saib sent two letters in response to Ahmed Rıza. In the first he strongly criticized the activists:

> I had no doubt then that things might come to this point. I did not find it acceptable and reasonable, however, to turn down your invitation to participate in the new committee, and I joined the ranks of the organization. But I did so only because of your invitation, for I had no relations with the other members, and furthermore to work with them was not something that I desired. . . . Anyhow, I participated. Although your presence was a guarantee I soon observed that our friends [the activists] were beginning to play their previous roles.[49]

Following this letter Ahmed Saib presented a detailed memorandum to the positivist leader. He insisted on the appointment of a strong director and begged Ahmed Rıza to fill this post. He further required the creation of a rank of "first-class members" and the appointment of himself and members like Khalīl Ghānim as such. This requirement was meant to hinder the activists from taking part in the decision-making.[50]

After receiving the responses of the activists and the two leaders in Cairo, Ahmed Rıza wrote the final version of the bylaws, and the founding members concluded the first phase of the establishment of a new organization. Although it was an important stage in the shaping of a new committee, the first disagreement between the activists, Ahmed Rıza, and his confidant Ahmed Saib had surfaced.

This dispute has two important aspects. First, Ahmed Rıza insisted on having a leadership position with prerogatives, and Ahmed Saib gave his full support to the positivist leader in this respect. In conjunction with this, Ahmed Rıza also wanted to extend his dominance over the new organization to its central organ published in Turkish. Second, in spite of all efforts made by the activists, the new bylaws were merely a restatement of Ahmed Rıza's principles and were far from addressing their longing for a more "active" organization.

Political Ideas Promoted by the Coalition

A careful eye might have seen that a similar struggle was taking place on the pages of the new central organ. Ahmed Rıza, Ahmed Saib, and a well-known literary figure, Sami Paşazâde Sezaî, who had fled to Europe and begun to publish his antirevolutionary articles in *Şûra-yı Ümmet*,[51] established a firm grip on the publication. The activists, however, although their contributions were outnumbered by the nonrevolutionary articles written by the aforementioned leaders, authored revolutionary columns contradicting the prevailing publication policy. The remarkable fact was that despite their disagreements on various matters, both sides were united against foreign intervention in Ottoman domestic politics and the economic penetration of the empire by the Great Powers. The marriage of the activists and the followers of Ahmed Rıza was a reaction to the interventionist group that had emerged at the 1902 Congress. As a matter of fact, the foreign diplomats underscored the anti-interventionist policy of the new coalition and described it as the engine of its activities.[52]

The article published following the introductory one in *Şûra-yı Ümmet* was devoted to the abhorrence felt against foreign intervention, and two points were highlighted. First, it was made very clear that members of the coalition saw foreign intervention from a Turkish viewpoint:

> Whenever the Great Powers intervened in our domestic affairs they concluded their intervention by separating an element [of the empire] from us, or obtained new privileges for profiteers and missionaries; to sum up, they always diminished the strength of the Turk.[53]

Second, in contrast to the position articulated by the "majority" of the 1902 Congress, members of the coalition labeled the Great Powers of Europe as "imperialist":

> As we observe, Europe, in every field, cares for her own interest. If she did not foresee a prodigious outcome for her own interest she would never help us. . . . Can we not see the fact that the smallest permission and privilege extended to foreign governments, even kindness and respect shown in a spirit of hospitality, later appeared as a prerogative in the treaties and capitulations? It is impossible to recall a privilege which was once granted even on a temporary basis. If Europe came to rescue us by accepting our invitation she would at first try to separate the Armenians and Macedonians from us.[54]

This theme of accusing the Great Powers of imperialism became one of the main theses of the new central organ.[55] Furthermore, "Western Imperialism" was castigated from a moral viewpoint:

The Europeans who emigrated to America from Europe plundered the natives and exterminated them there. There is no more wealth and property remaining in America to be looted and now they are wandering around. The Europeans now want to take advantage of the fear and madness of the sultan.[56]

Therefore the organs of the coalition claimed that the guarantees given to the Ottoman Empire by the Great Powers resulted from the power struggle among those states, and that to trust their word, as the members of the "majority" had done, was a great mistake:

> As the Great Powers had made up the principle of "the territorial integrity of the Sublime State" because they could not agree upon the partition of our country, now in order to prevent a single power from gaining dominance in the Orient, they have invented the formula of "the maintenance of the independence of [the Sublime State]."[57]

The central organ further claimed that the Great Powers' political and economic interference had tied the hands of the Ottoman state and that it was therefore the main cause of Ottoman decline:

> Our courts cannot pronounce a verdict against Russian subjects! Mr. Maksimov slaps our privates. Greek bishops function as Russian consuls. We cannot collect taxes from Greek subjects. When a [Greek] prostitute falls in love with a fireman and wants to convert to Islam to marry him, the dragoman of the Russian consulate intervenes and scolds the *mufti*.[58]

Mechveret Supplément Français adopted a similar rhetoric under the direction of Ahmed Rıza.[59] According to this discourse the Western *pénétration*, though seemingly *pacifique*, was a very dangerous one. Its consequences were apparent in what had happened to the native Americans, Sudanese, Boers, and Chinese; and the most distasteful part of this penetration was that it had depended on the presumption of a "superior race":

> C'est avec progrès de la civilisation, l'accroissement des cupidités et le perfectionnement des tartuferies politiques que l'idée vient aux hommes "race supérieure" de couvrir leur banditisme sous le vocable de "pénétration pacifique."[60]

The articles appearing in the French supplement were in a way rejoinders to the philosophers of Western imperialism, such as Rudyard Kipling and Ernest Psichari. The ideas put forward in these articles were undoubtedly diametrically opposed to Social Darwinist race theories and the ideas of Gustave Le Bon. Intellectual members of the "majority" group persisted in these theories and ideas even after the first Japanese victories over the Russians in 1904, referring to the "natural degradation of the Japanese race."[61] Members of the coalition, however, maintained that the Japanese people were "obliterating this slander against nature."[62]

According to many members of the coalition, Western assertions based on "superior race" would lead to significant political consequences, the most portentous of which was the idea of driving the Turks back to Asia from Europe:

> The government of Panama has prohibited the Chinese, the Syrians, and the Turks from entering Panama. This measure was taken in order to preclude the Asians, who are re-

garded as lower-class human beings by the foreigners, from immigrating there *en masse.*
Turks do not go to America for business. Here this term [refers to] the Armenians, etc.,
who when successful in commerce and industry say that they are Armenians, etc., claiming
that they had to leave the lands in our possession due to Turkish oppression allegedly
practiced by the government. At every opportunity, they deride and malign the Turks to
the foreigners. But whenever they commit a crime or an act of villainy they are considered Turkish because they are Turkish subjects. The humiliating treatment . . . of the
dark-complexioned and black races by the people of Western Europe and especially by
the English and the Americans is a well-known fact. Although most of the Turks are
racially European, it suits the desire of many powers to claim that the Turks do not belong to the white race and they are totally Asian, because in the future this claim would
be employed as an argument to drive us totally out of Europe and to preclude our rule of
Christian nations there.[63]

This viewpoint of members of the coalition was undoubtedly the major bone of
contention with their opponents who had gained a majority at the 1902 Congress.
For instance, while coalition organs accused Great Britain of occupying Egypt for
its economic and strategic interests and defined it as an imperialistic power,[64] *Osmanlı,*
under the administration of the "majority," depicted British rule there as a period of
prosperity under "the very zealous and courageous British administration."[65] Leaders of the "majority" group dreamed of the revitalization of the good relations with
Great Britain that had been established during the *Tanzimat* era and had borne fruit
during the Crimean War. According to these leaders, the only obstacle to this revitalization was the domination of the anti-British "Old Turkey party" in Istanbul. Ali
Haydar Midhat maintained:

> Sultan Abdul Hamid . . . for twenty-five years has done all in his power to bring dis-
> credit on the partisans of reform in Turkey. . . . And if this Liberal party remains in
> the shade it is because of the terror that reigns at Constantinople, and also grows in a
> direct ratio, and because not one partisan of reform is in power or protected by a friendly
> power. It [the Liberal party] is fighting the Government in the midst of the ignorance
> of the population.[66]

Leaders of the coalition, on the other hand, better discerned the change of balance
among the members of the Concert of Europe and the strong shift of British public
opinion to an anti-Ottoman stand. Hence they came to the conclusion that the idea of
overthrowing the current regime in the Ottoman Empire with the help of the Great
Powers was chimerical, and that the policy to be pursued by the Young Turks was an
anti-imperialist one.[67] They further added that Great Britain was "not only an enemy of our survival but also of our religion and nationality."[68] These strong con-
victions were found "ludicrous" by the prominent figures of the "majority," who
even criticized Ahmed Rıza for publishing the French supplement "in France, which
is an ally of Russia; and only in French."[69] It is true that the high politics pursued
by the "majority" leaders caused more of a sensation among the opponents of the
regime abroad;[70] however, as we have already seen, those leaders were a long way
from understanding the reality of the current politics.

With contributions by Ahmed Rıza, Hoca Kadri, and Khalīl Ghānim, Ahmed Saib
prepared the initial issue of *Şûra-yı Ümmet,* which promoted anti-imperialism.[71] There
was no significant participation by the activists, and the journal focused on the dan-

gers that might follow a foreign intervention in Ottoman politics. This became one of the oft-used themes in the new organ, indisputably with the consent of the activists.[72] Nevertheless, the prefatory article in the first issue, which explained the aims of the new coalition and its central organ, was nothing more than a repetition of the new regulations and thus was far from fulfilling the expectations of the activists.[73] Another article, published in installments in the first two issues, underscored the role played by an educated elite in a society; and contrary to the activist viewpoint, it presented the act of publication as the most important that can be undertaken by any group of political dissidents.[74]

The issues that followed repeated the themes employed by Ahmed Rıza and his followers since 1895, and these well-worn themes dominated the new central organ. But the activists, as at the time of the preparation of the bylaws, did not leave the arena to their positivist, nonrevolutionary allies. Gradually fierce articles written by activists began to appear in the journal. The first significant attempt was the publication of a warning by the activists on behalf of the new organization. They wrote:

> We have been receiving valuable articles through *Şûra-yı Ümmet*, written by individuals who intend to serve our country. In some of these, more than enough detailed theoretical information is given. Our fatherland, however, calls for help by saying "I have a fever, are you aware of that?" and expects an immediate cure from us.[75]

For those who had been reading the central organs of the CUP but knew nothing about the internal factions within the movement, this discourse was somewhat puzzling. Two antithetical rhetorics appeared in the central organ. To those who were aware of the internal division, however, this was its unavoidable consequence. For example, one article claimed that "they [the Young Turks] have never favored anarchism and bloody revolutions carried out in the streets;"[76] another, however, incited the Muslims to a bloody revolution.[77] Again, while some writers strongly denounced activities by revolutionary committees,[78] others praised the Russian revolutionaries[79] and urged Muslim Ottomans and especially Turks to emulate them.[80]

The most important disagreement between the two sides on organizational matters regarded the lack of a name for the new organization. This absence, and the vague title used by *Şûra-yı Ümmet*, "the organ of partisans of general reforms," were strongly criticized by the activists. In this field, however, Ahmed Rıza and his followers had the upper hand, and on May 1, 1904, they once again stated their pacifist policy:

> Our committee, too, has a well-arranged and definite program. Then is it appropriate to call our committee the "Young Turk Committee"? Surely not. Although the Ottomans have to unite and establish alliances, parties are surfacing like sinking and rising cormorants or sand dunes appearing according to the direction of the wind, due to the incitement of some people who are immoral or ignorant of political manners. Had there been no danger in announcing the establishment of our committee and proclaiming the names of its members, we would have refuted the lies and slanders of malicious people at once. . . . Besides having Ottomans from various ethnic groups and races such as Arabs, Greeks, Armenians, Jews, and Turks, the existence of more than five or six thousand people living in exile or imprisoned in dungeons proves that Young Turks do not compose a small party. . . . It would also be wrong to label us as innovators or as liberals, because those who desire to transform old-fashioned systems and customs are called innovators. We do not want, however, to alter anything. On the contrary we want the

admirable royal customs and present codes of the state, which are being trodden upon now, to be respected. . . . Consequently, until a name is found that will cause no inconvenience, contain all virtues, and above all be deemed praiseworthy by all Ottomans, members of our committee are called "partisans for constitutional government and general reforms," as is written under the masthead of *Şûra-yı Ümmet.*[81]

A similar remark was made in response to the criticism made by the activists that it was impossible to achieve anything by mere publication:

Those who opposed publication tell us of the importance of action instead of words. Action is not prior to words. Every action that comes before words is brigandage. The greatest idealists in the world are those who act according to ideas.[82]

When activist readers sent scolding letters complaining that they were sick and tired of repetitions in the journal, the editors responded that there was no other alternative.[83] This attitude derived from a belief in "irrevocable progress," frequently underscored by Ahmed Rıza and his followers.[84] The activists, on the other hand, were far from introducing any significant idea other than stressing the importance of "action." Ahmed Rıza and Sami Paşazâde Sezaî spearheaded the opposition against them. Both leaders authored leading articles for the new central organ and for the French supplement criticizing activism. Both also tried to reconcile Comte's ideas with Social Darwinism and claimed that "since the law of evolution is one of gradual progress," it was necessary to avoid sudden changes.[85]

Ahmed Rıza and Sami Paşazâde Sezaî, who dominated the central organ, also strongly opposed the propaganda against the Ottoman royal house so diligently spread by Abdülhalim Memduh, who had close contacts with the activists. They took an extremely conservative stand in this field. According to Ahmed Saib, "if the royal house is not maintained—this is between you [Ahmed Rıza] and me—we shall be overwhelmed at the hands of the Bulgarians, Greeks, and Armenians." Ahmed Rıza compared the republican criticism of the dynasty with the "barking of a dog at a horse."[86]

The interesting point here is that the strong resistance of the two leaders to this propaganda stemmed from their fear that opposition to the Ottoman royal house could become a radical and republicanist tool in the hands of the activists. It is striking that they had made no objection when Khalīl Ghānim, their closest associate, sharply criticized the Ottoman royal house.[87]

From this viewpoint the new central organ was undoubtedly as conservative as the previous one, *Osmanlı*; Max Freiherr von Oppenheim accurately commented that "the Young Turk party [the coalition] is not a revolutionary but a conservative one; it is the conservative party of the Ottoman Empire."[88] The only difference was that whereas *Osmanlı* had published many open letters, petitioning the sultan to put an end to his despotic regime, the new organ published only one such letter in which its antianarchist ideas were underscored and the accusation of anarchism was refuted.[89] Similarly, there was only a single example of a letter, in contrast to several published by *Mizan*, inviting reforming statesmen to take action against the regime.[90]

While Ahmed Rıza and his close associates were establishing their firm control over the new central organ, the French supplement remained a mouthpiece of his group. The positivist comments that had generated great difficulties for this group, especially between 1895–1897, were now made in a straightforward way by *Mechveret Supplément Français*. This journal claimed that Comte's ideas provided a solid basis for the Young Turk movement, and it condemned revolutionary organizations,[91] such as the Armenian committees, through its positivist rhetoric.[92] Furthermore, the French supplement praised the solidarity which existed among positivists, and it presented the support given by Mexican positivists to the Young Turks as an excellent example of this.[93] *Mechveret Supplément Français* had in fact been widely read by Latin American positivists, who expected the Young Turks to establish a positivist regime in the Ottoman Empire.[94] A Chilean positivist who wrote an open letter to Ahmed Rıza had previously expressed his appreciation of the latter's efforts even more clearly when he called Ahmed Rıza his "coreligionist."[95] Positivist activities also gave Ahmed Rıza opportunities to denounce the sultan's regime.[96] Despite the moral support it provided for Ahmed Rıza, however, the tribute paid by such positivists had no significant impact on the Young Turk movement.

In another field, however, Ahmed Rıza used positivist ideology as a means to censure European imperialism. He claimed that those Europeans who "allegedly defend peace" in reality aimed at driving the Turks from Europe.[97] Positivism served as a perfect base from which to refute such unacceptable ideas.

In brief, the group surrounding Ahmed Rıza had not accepted the ideas of the activists. Despite the disagreement between the two groups on a crucial matter, however, it is not difficult to comprehend the bases of the new coalition. Both sides admitted the urgency and necessity of the dethronement of Abdülhamid II. Both the French supplement and the new central organ published articles underscoring the importance of deposition, but in those articles written by Ahmed Rıza and his associates it was also made clear that this should not take place through a revolution.[98]

The disagreement hinged on the means of achieving this goal. Associates of Ahmed Rıza dreamed of creating a liberal "public opinion" and thereby changing the regime. The activists, on the other hand, asserted that they had no time to educate people and create such a public opinion.[99] They claimed that "a revolution to dethrone the sultan can be achieved only by high-ranking statesmen and the military."[100]

Despite this dispute, the two groups reached perfect accord on the Turkism that had flourished since the 1902 Congress. In truth, the real force that united the two groups was nothing other than a burgeoning Turkism. Their hatred of foreign intervention in Ottoman politics was another strong pillar of this ideology. Therefore efforts made by individuals such as Joseph (Yusuf) Fehmi (who claimed that "les Jeunes-Turcs légitimistes . . . ont la majorité, et détiennent l'appui tacite de la bourgeoisie à Constantinople"[101]) to revitalize the revolutionary faction by separating the activists from the followers of Ahmed Rıza, bore no fruit.

Yusuf Akçura, a leading figure among the members of the new coalition, later asserted that the articles published in the new organ were rudimentary, and they constantly repeated that "Sultan [Abdül]hamid is annihilating Turkey, that the utmost aim should be the [restoration] of the Constitution of Midhat Pasha, and that once it is promulgated the fatherland will be rescued"[102] ; nevertheless it would be unfair to underestimate the significance of the inclination toward Turkism displayed by the new central organ.

First, the journal extolled nationalism as a concept. For instance, it acclaimed the famous Hungarian nationalist Lajos Kossuth[103] and, more interestingly, Pávlos Melás, who had become a symbol of Greek nationalist activity in Macedonia. The central organ made it clear that Melás had combatted Ottoman interests; however, "since he was fighting for the sake of a nationalist ideology," he was an example to follow and to be treated as "a hero who had sacrificed his life for his nation."[104] In an article published in the French supplement, Ahmed Rıza denied the accusation of "being nationalist"; however, he did not necessarily conclude that nationalism was a negative ideology. In fact, he criticized only "anti-Semitism" and "hatred toward other nations" as negative aspects of existing nationalist movements.[105] As a matter of fact, when he later published an enlarged edition of this article in the central organ, in which he also commented on the al-Ḥizb al-Waṭanī ([Egyptian] National Party), he again denied the allegations. He defined this party, however, as "nonnationalist" but a "patriotic" organization similar to his coalition.[106]

A second characteristic of the new central organ was the frequent use of the term "Turk." This term replaced the word "Ottoman," which had been deliberately used by former CUP organs and had become the most oft-used term of Young Turk nomenclature. Besides referring to the Turkish element of the empire, the term "Turk" was used to allude to the average citizen. For instance, in describing those complaining about the regime, the phrase used was "Every thinking Turk complained about the government."[107] Similarly, *Şûra-yı Ümmet* portrayed Russia and the sultan as "the two united adversaries of the nationality and race of the poor Turk."[108] Finally, it referred to the Turks in Bulgaria as "our countrymen, compatriots,"[109] instead of using the phrase "our coreligionists," which had been employed by former CUP organs. More interestingly, the central organ and the French supplement candidly defended the Tatars against the Armenians and criticized the pro-Armenian Western press as an expression of brotherhood among the Turkic peoples.[110]

The most important admission made by the new organ, and one diametrically opposite to the previous Ottomanist rhetoric of the former journals, was that union with the non-Turkish opponents of the sultan was chimerical.[111] The central organ wrote:

> If there are among the Turks those who are hesitant to extend the right of citizenship to Christians, there are grounds for such hesitation. If a Christian happens to be a member of the Greek community, he looks toward Athens, if of the Bulgarian, to Sofia, and if he is an Armenian, he dreams about the establishment of an independent Armenia. Attempting to wrest from us a piece of our homeland, it was the Greeks who rebelled yesterday, and now the Bulgarians and the Armenians are engaged in armed rebellion. Turks are witnesses to all this, and naturally are saddened and feel that the Christians have hurt them.[112]

Şûra-yı Ümmet also declared that the non-Turkish ethnic groups' activities were "always against the Turks and directed to ethnic separatism."[113] The rhetoric of the central organ reflected a view held by many prominent Young Turks on the activities of these groups. For instance, Ahmed Rıza jotted the following in his notebook: "Christians acquired privileges when they rebelled [and] they desired to rebel when they acquired privileges."[114] When we compare this criticism with earlier claims that it was the policy of the sultan that resulted in activities damaging to fraternity among the Ottomans, the importance of this clear-cut accusation becomes clear. In fact, the central organ blamed the Ottoman administration for preventing the Turks from getting acquainted with nationalism:

> At the Armenian, Greek, and Bulgarian schools, the pupils' nationalist feelings are fomented against the Turkish administration, while at our schools the students are not allowed to pronounce the term "fatherland!" The negligent, ignorant, and treacherous absolutism of the present regime opens the doors of the country to violent attacks and to profiteering on the part of the foreigners. Isn't this a great fault, a crime?[115]

The members of the coalition asserted that a constant struggle had been taking place between the Turkish and non-Turkish elements of the empire. According to the central organ, all non-Turkish ethnic groups, especially the non-Muslim ones, had been trying to destroy a body which was defended only by the Turks. In order to legitimize this claim, a fictitious conversation between a Young Turk and a Greek who emigrated from Anatolia to France was published by the central organ.[116] Interestingly, the readers of the journal who wrote to comment on this dialogue adopted a more unusual approach. One reader wrote:

> We would have been surprised if a Greek who had fled to Paris with his fez donned and speaking in Turkish had uttered anything but accusations against the Turks at a time when everyone great and small was waiving his sword and dealing blows to the Turk and Muslim.
>
> Had Sultan Fatih [Mehmed II] used the same methods that the Russians adopted in the countries that they occupied, our Greek compatriot . . . in the [Bois de] Boulogne would have become a real Ottoman, and there would have been no difference between him and those whom he castigated, in religion and nationality. The grief is ours because this did not happen and because we, the Turks, have suffered losses. Our [Greek] compatriot mentions the unfair treatment of Christians by the ignorant classes of the people, in order to prove that there are no common values of citizenship between the Turks and the re'aya. [He claims that] in many towns to smoke a cigarette in a market during *Ramaḍān* might cause a Christian to be insulted! I have personally observed the shameless behavior of παληκάρια[117] when the *müezzin* called *Allāhu Akbar* from a minaret in Trikkala, a town recently taken from the hands of the Ottomans.[118]

Obviously, the strong nationalism that began to emerge and prevail among the people in the lands recently lost to the Christian nations also played an important role in shaping a new Young Turk conviction. Contrary to the earlier Ottomanist rhetoric that had been halfheartedly employed by former CUP organs, *Şûra-yı Ümmet* explicitly claimed that "it is the Turks and the Muslims who are meant when the term *Ottoman* is used, and reform of the Ottoman administration depends on a rebellion by the Turks, the dominant element in the empire, and not on insurrections by a bunch of Armenians or Bulgarians."[119]

According to the members of the coalition, the activities of non-Muslim groups could not be regarded as revolutionary movements, but rather seen as a war waged against the state. In this respect they reiterated the official Ottoman stance in the pages of a journal banned by the state:

> Putting obstacles in the way of those who have been smuggling guns, dynamite, and bombs over the Russian border is considered violent treatment of Armenians. . . . You

are accusing Turks. You don't have the right [to do so]. If the Turk, with whom you have lived together for centuries, had massacred you, you would not exist today. This is an absolute proof of the fact that he has never massacred you! Let's address this question to the entire world: Is there another nation that grants such magnanimous treatment to an ethnic group like the Armenians, who have done nothing for the maintenance of the common fatherland, and who have not shed a drop of blood to this end? Therefore, what is the reason behind the Armenians' revolt? What do they want? Autonomous administration in the lands which they dare to call Armenia? . . . If so, the revolt of the Armenians is not a rebellion but a war.[120]

When this previously unarticulated Turkism surfaced, the movement, for the first time since its inception, came to possess a political tenet in forming a revolutionary praxis. This newly unleashed Turkism had many important characteristics. First, as we have seen, it was highly critical of the non-Muslim ethnic groups of the empire, accusing their leaders of separatism. Second, for the first time it put the nationalist movements of the Muslim groups of the empire in the same category with those of the non-Muslims. For instance, just as the Albanian nationalist movement was castigated[121] and Albanian nationalists called "vagabonds,"[122] so too Arab nationalism was condemned by Young Turks, who now viewed the world with Turkish-tinted glasses. They responded to the Arabs, who described the Turks as a "fictitious nation,"[123] in fierce tones:

> The Arab gang . . . tries to deceive the reasonable Arabs who are willing to admit that the Arabs do not have among them men able to match the Turkish officers and governors, and that the Turks are superior to the other Muslims in the arts of war, administration, and law enforcement. . . . The present policy of the Arab gang is . . . to annihilate the power of the Turk in the Islamic lands. Essentially, this is the course that the nations who struggle to separate themselves from Ottoman rule adopt. The principal zeal of the Greek, Armenian, and Bulgarian revolutionary committees is directed at presenting the Turks as evil. In many articles published mostly by Syrians in Egypt and in Africa, the impotence of the Turk and the necessity of a restoration of the caliphate to the hands of the Arab is expounded. Friends residing at various locations in Arabia inform us that the authority of the Turk has been gradually diminishing. . . .
>
> If the Turks were only willing to look with open and worldly eyes to the Holy Ka'bah rather than with eyes half open and half closed five times a day, they would see the truth and understand why they turn their heads to the left and right and look around [during the prayers].[124]

According to the members of the coalition:

> [D]espite the Turk having done nothing but show respect and give good treatment to the Arab, the grudge of the Arab . . . originated from the fact that holy relics were in the hands of the Ottoman sultans who were not descendants of the Arabs. Just as Western imperialist powers employed Catholic and Protestant missionaries to separate Armenians from the empire, so various sheikhs and leaders of religious orders were employed by them to make the Arabs curse the Turks.[125]

Members of the coalition asserted, however, that Arabs did not possess the capacity to establish a state.[126]

Also the new central organ focused on the pre-Ottoman existence of the Turks, a theme that had never been used by former CUP organs:

Oh! [Poor] peasant working underfed, underdressed in Anatolia! You came from Transoxania.[127]

The Turkish nation has been among the most attacked and besmirched among the Ottoman nations because of the unceasing crimes of the Hamidian government. Stout-hearted Turks of strong character whose [ancestors] had come from Transoxania and had founded this great empire can still be found in some parts of Anatolia.[128]

Similarly, Sami Paşazâde Sezaî established a "literary section" in the central organ,[129] where articles belittled classical Ottoman literature and accused the most esteemed Ottoman literary figures of creating a poetry that looks Persian rather than Turkish. They also expressed a strong desire for the purification of the Turkish language.[130] The journal stated that it would publish all the letters that were sent by readers on this subject. The first criticism came from Hüseyin Siyret, a confidant of Saba-haddin Bey;[131] many Young Turk sympathizers, however, agreed with the Turkist view on the purification of the language. For instance, a reader who sent a letter from Bulgaria giving utterance to Turkist feelings claimed that to borrow words from Arabic and Persian, which were "Semitic" and "Aryan" languages respectively, would de-base Turkish, a Turanian language.[132] Later a leading article made it clear that the attention paid to this subject arose from a political concern:

Do not Magyars living in Austria, French living in Germany, and Poles living in Russia demonstrate that they are strong and vital communities that cannot be annihilated by becoming subjects of a foreign power? It is clear that a nation which has its science, literature, and language cannot be annihilated.[133]

By the same token the coalition's organs reproved the Muslim and non-Muslim Ottoman elements who were ignorant of the Turkish language.[134]

Another feature of the protonationalist Turkism expressed in the central organ of the coalition was its focus on national symbols and its desire to convert Ottomans into Turks. A striking example of the former is an article in which the author suggested that the Ottoman state have a "political-national anthem written in simple Turkish, giving utterance to nationalist feelings, and . . . similar to the *Marseillaise* of the French."[135] As to the latter, the central organ suggested the following:

Magyars do not show negligence in taking fruitful measures for the sake of increasing the political importance of the Hungarian nation, such as Magyarizing foreign elements through adoption. . . . In comparison to the patriotic endeavors and sacrifices that each and every nation makes, what are we . . . doing, not for the sake of progress, but simply to thwart the threats of annihilation and extermination to which we are subject, and to preserve the territories that still remain in our possession?[136]

The central organ proposed additional drastic means such as settling Turkish immigrants in Macedonia, as the Germans were doing in Poland and the Hungarians were doing in regions heavily populated by Slavs.[137] A letter scribbled by two officers and sent from within the empire gave utterance to Turkist feelings by expressing their trepidation concerning the change in the balance of population at the expense of the Turks, due to their burden of military service. This response suggests that the ideas promoted by the central organ reflected a widespread feeling prevailing among low-ranking Turkish officers.[138]

A final characteristic of the Turkism promoted by the coalition during this period was the use of Islam as a protonationalist device. The Young Turks, who had never considered that Islam might be used for such a purpose until 1902, had instead devoted their best efforts to accusing the sultan of harming Islam and to proving that rebellion against his tyrannical rule was in accordance with *sharī'a*. Such rhetoric was still employed by the central organ on occasion, but it was now used much less frequently. On a few occasions the sultan was accused of ordering the removal of some verses of the Qur'ān in editions prepared at his behest.[139] In a series of articles *Şûra-yı Ümmet* claimed that the reign of Abdülhamid II was one of the worst periods that Islam had ever gone through.[140] Once in the course of its long life the central organ published a single article that attempted to prove that a constitutional regime was, in fact, dictated by Islam.[141] In a similar vein, some members of the ulema gave a response to a query from the central organ, accusing the Istanbul dailies that were subsidized by the palace of deliberately misleading the people at the behest of the sultan.[142] Nonetheless, compared with the previous central organs, *Şûra-yı Ümmet*'s publication in this field was quite insignificant, and although the editor of the journal later claimed that all that was written in the pages of the periodical paid due respect to "the *sharī'a*,"[143] no special effort was made to secure this. The central organ further made it very clear that its main concern was the protonationalist role of Islam, and not Islamic faith and practice as such:

> It has been heard, unfortunately, that there are some fanatics, neither erudite nor farsighted, who claim that "as long as the religion has not been harmed, and worship has not been obstructed, it is not that important who rules in the fatherland, for example, Italy or Austria." The journals published to advocate Austrian and Italian interests and designs write that these two nations are in favor of the performance of prayers in Albanian. We do not suppose that the notables of Albania and Tripoli of Barbary would pay heed to these dimwitted promises.[144]

By contrast the members of the coalition frequently castigated Western anti-Islamic attitudes. When *Mechveret Supplément Français* commented that "l'Europe confond à dessein dans la question d'Orient les considérations politiques avec les considérations religieuses,"[145] and *Şûra-yı Ümmet* underscored an alleged Christian fanaticism,[146] the rhetoric adopted appears to be an Islamic one. Again when positivist French officials wrote to Ahmed Rıza that the French penetration into Africa played a significant role in the abolition of slavery,[147] or when they pointed out doubts concerning Islam's praise for work,[148] the rejoinders given can be viewed as Islamist responses. In these cases, however, Islam was defended not as a system of beliefs but as an anti-imperialist device to stir up the Muslim masses and a social tool for modernization. In fact, Catholic reformers such as Charles Jean-Marie Loyson (known as Père Hyacinthe) found the viewpoint of the French supplement very attractive. Loyson maintained that Islam did not provide suitable conditions for the progress of civilization, though he had also asserted that an understanding between Islam and Christianity should be realized.[149]

Nevertheless, the defense of Islam was nothing other than criticism of alleged Christian fanaticism against Turks. *Şûra-yı Ümmet* made the following comments when the Eastern Question was discussed as a perpetual struggle between Muslim Turks and Christians:

> The heir apparent Süleyman Pasha had advanced to the European continent along with sixty Turkish warriors during the reign of Sultan Orhan, and conquered Gallipoli. Since then the son of the Turk has not had a day's peace. . . . The provinces of Salonica, Iōánnina, Edirne, and Monastir have been filled with foreign schools and Catholic and Slavic churches. These schools are not content with teaching arts and sciences, they also teach Christian children that they should strive hard to separate themselves from the Turks, and work for the extinction of the Ottoman government.[150]

> The idea of driving all the Muslims out of European Turkey has become an idée fixe of all [the Christians,] since . . . the heir apparent Süleyman set foot in Bolayır. . . . We continuously work to denounce this loathsome idea, which originates from an old feeling of vengeance and fanaticism harbored by the allegedly civilized European governments, both in our articles in *Mechveret* [*Supplément Français*] and in our other publications.[151]

Interestingly, *Şûra-yı Ümmet* presented opposition to Islam as equivalent to being anti-Turkish. *Mechveret Supplément Français* further described European attitudes in these terms: "Si les Turcs exterminent la race bulgare ou massacrent les Arméniens, c'est qu'ils y sont poussés par le fanatisme musulman. Ce raisonnement paraît simple et logique à l'Europe chrétienne, parce qu'il satisfait sa passion et ses haines;"[152] however, "ce terme [fanaticisme] ne se définit, n'a sa raison d'être que lorsqu'il s'applique aux musulmans."[153] According to the French supplement, this alleged Christian fanaticism was the reason behind the "Turcophobia" found among the Europeans.[154] The coalition members also argued that the fact that the Turks did not possess a civilization similar to that of the Westerners did not necessarily mean that they were uncivilized, but rather indicated that they had a distinct and unique civilization.

As might be expected, however, members of the coalition attributed no particular importance to Islam as a religion. The central organ's criticism of those "who thought that Islam was nothing but the performance of the ritual prostrations in prayer five times a day or fasting from dusk to dawn for a month"[155] reveals that in the eyes of the members of the coalition, Islam had no value other than its social role. This opinion is also clear from their condemnation of the ulema, who, they claimed, received money and decorations from the sultan despite remaining idle.[156] Similarly, members of the coalition strongly criticized the sultan's Panislamist campaign. The French supplement wrote:

> Nous suivons cependant avec intérêt la campagne panislamique si bêtement dirigée par le Sultan Abdul Hamid, comme nous observons avec non moins d'intérêt l'agitation panslavique autrement dangereuse pour l'Orient et pour toute société civilisée.[157]

These comments unquestionably reveal that the members of the coalition viewed Islam as a protonationalist device and had no interest whatsoever in it as a religion. As long as it was useful to them as a device to accomplish their Turkist and modernizing goals, it would retain great value, and after the fulfillment of these aspirations it would be put aside. Good examples of using Islam for nationalist purposes are the criticism of the conversion of various mosques in Bulgaria, and the condemnation of similar events that took place in Crete. A strong Turkist tone can easily be discerned in these articles.[158]

In their efforts to influence European public opinion, the coalition adopted a different course from that of their opponents. Whereas the members of the "majority" tried to reconcile their theses with those of European public opinion, members of the coalition devoted their energies to the criticism of European imperialism and the separatist activities of various Ottoman nationalities. Selma Hanım, Ahmed Rıza's sister, described the aforementioned efforts as the struggle to make heard the voice of a nation, labeled as barbarous by almost all of Europe.[159] Unlike their opponents, they had apparently no interest in reconciling their ideas with those prevailing in Western Europe.

As the central organ stated, "the French supplement [was] utilized to castigate anti-Turkish ideas put before European public opinion by the Armenians, Bulgarians, and Greeks."[160] The coalition members expressed regret that their efforts did not produce significant results.[161] It is interesting that they did not disparage the similar propaganda put out by the palace but only remarked that this was unfortunately in the hands of "non-Turks" such as "Nicolaïdes or Abū Naẓẓārah [James Sanū'a]."[162]

Activities of the Coalition as a Political Organization

The coalition, with its claim to represent the Young Turk movement, was invited to the Peace Conference held in Monaco in 1902. Although no delegate could be sent because of the short notice given, the coalition forwarded an appeal to the meeting, accusing Armenian and Bulgarian revolutionaries of posing a great threat to peace, and once again they underscored the importance of general reforms but not of special ones for particular ethnic and religious groups.[163] Ahmed Rıza sent a similar letter to the Armenian Congress held in Brussels, although he had received no invitation.[164] The coalition's stand was made clear at the 1904 Anglo-Armenian Conference, whose organizers had invited Ahmed Rıza as the "Leader of the Young Turkey Party."[165] The coalition demurred on the ground that "they would not participate in a meeting at which the Turks and other Ottoman nations will be insulted, unless they will be permitted to give utterance to their own ideas on the subject."[166] The organizers initially accepted this condition; however, at the eleventh hour—on the very day that Ahmed Rıza departed for London—they informed the coalition that only the British, Italian, and French delegates would be given a turn to speak and that the positivist leader might be given a chance to address the delegates at the banquet after the meeting.[167] Although given only a limited time, Ahmed Rıza seized the opportunity to express his comrades' view. The central organ reported the subsequent events as follows:

> Ahmed Rıza described the situation in our fatherland in brief, and said that the measures taken by the foreigners harmed the fatherland and even the Armenians, and were not beneficial. While he was saying this the French and the Armenians began to grumble and to make a commotion. When Ahmed Rıza's observations shifted to the subject of provocations and criminal agitations by the Armenian and Bulgarian committees, the commotion grew. Monsieur [Francis de] Pressensé stood up in anger and vociferously said the following: "*Mechveret* [*Supplement Français*] has published many articles against

us. It has presented us as authors and servants of journals published with Russian money. We cannot let the editor of this journal reproach [us] here, on the same grounds." . . . When Ahmed Rıza began to discuss whether granting autonomy to the provinces inhabited by the Bulgarians in European Turkey and by the Armenians in Anatolia would be beneficial or hazardous to the entire population, and commented on the Muslims left in Bulgaria, and made a remark that forty thousand Muslims had been compelled to emigrate from Crete, the members of the Armenian, French, and Italian parties began to shriek, as if they wished to cut Ahmed Rıza into pieces, saying, "Entirely fallacious! Fallacious! Muslims fled because of their fear and because they did not like freedom. Ahmed Rıza defends the sultan. He is employing the language of the Sublime Porte. We do not want to listen to criticisms on this basis. Please give the floor to someone else. Please shut Ahmed Rıza up."[168]

Only Karl Blind defended Ahmed Rıza at the meeting, but "this honorable old gentleman was silenced by the commotion."[169] Learning about the events that took place at the conference, Anastase Adossidis, a Greek delegate who had participated in the Congress of Ottoman Opposition in 1902, also seized the opportunity to criticize Ahmed Rıza and the coalition, accusing them of endeavoring to subvert the rights of Christians guaranteed by international treaties, through the application of a constitution and the implementation of a program of centralization.[170] Adossidis further claimed that Ahmed Rıza had been exonerating the policies of the sultan.[171]

Their experience at the Anglo-Armenian Conference, and subsequent criticism levied by the Armenians, Greeks, and European liberals, showed the coalition members the great difficulty of their task. Until then, despite some criticism, the Young Turk movement had been viewed as a liberal movement by European public opinion. But the new coalition, with its strong Turkist stand, was beginning to be considered as a nationalist and anti-Christian organization.[172] It was therefore extremely difficult to reconcile their ideas with those prevailing in Europe on the Eastern Question, and members of the coalition had no desire to play down their strong Turkism. In a similar vein, Ahmed Rıza's efforts toward winning over European intellectuals bore no fruit. Even Georges Clemenceau, who had helped him during his trial in 1897, refused Ahmed Rıza's invitation to publish articles to exonerate the Young Turk cause. Clemenceau told Ahmed Rıza that he himself could have prepared a program similar to that of the coalition but he refused to give any support on the grounds that "Turks appreciate absolutism."[173] Other attempts in this field were also futile.[174] Upon their failure, the members of the coalition were predisposed to assert that behind a humanitarian mask, Europe craved only to maximize its financial interests.[175] But the ideas promoted by the coalition, such as general reforms for all Ottomans,[176] were branded as Turkish nationalism by their opponents: "Le parti jeune-turc reste nationaliste, royaliste, et musulman."[177] They further claimed:

M. A. Rıza ne reconnaît donc pas à un peuple le droit de disposer de lui-même, et de la forme de sa vie. Et si on se hasarde à lui dire que ce peuple ne trouve pas son bien-être dans le régime qu'on lui impose, M. A. Rıza, disciple d'un Auguste Comte et d'un Pierre Laffitte, répond superbement: "Qu'il l'y cherche!" Voyez-vous notre sultan Hamid Effendi, qui avec la même superbe, dirait à M. Rıza et à d'autres Jeunes-Trucs: "Vous voulez vivre dans le bien-être? Qu'à cela ne tienne, à condition toutefois que vous ne cherchiez ce bien-être que dans le régime que je vous offre."[178]

The leaders of the coalition responded to these accusations by asking if their European opponents were not promoting Western humanistic ideas among the Ottomans "[p]our leur faciliter, comme le désireraient les amis du progrès, la lecture de Voltaire et d'Auguste Comte? Point du tout; mais pour les mieux préparer à savourer la propagande évangélique."[179] In the same vein, Yusuf Akçura denied the allegations made by famous French historians accusing Midhat Pasha and his "parti national turc" of carrying out a nationalist and anti-Christian program "sous des apparences ultra-libérales et sous un certain vernis de civilisation européenne."[180] Thus at the end of this period Ahmed Rıza confessed that he had erred in not properly understanding the real aims of the Western world.[181] After their reorganization in 1906, the CPU members were to abandon the idea of appeasing European public opinion and devoted their best efforts to the fulfillment of an activist program.

It might be said that the coalition did not carry out any significant activity during this period. Their success, however, lay in the creation of a clear-cut ideology, one that was strongly anti-Western, was Turkist, and used Islam as a protonationalist device to appeal to the Muslims in general and the Turks in particular. The only remaining problem was the strong antiactivist stand of Ahmed Rıza and his close associates. A reason behind this was that the Young Turks, with the exception of the "activists," found the masses untrustworthy. According to the central organ, "the masses must be shown no blood and they should not become accustomed to bloodshed."[182] This stance was in perfect accordance with the evolutionary ideas of Ahmed Rıza and his followers in Paris. During the period in question the leaders of the coalition also made it crystal clear that their real fear of a bloody revolution was that it might propel foreign intervention. The central organ wrote that "the revolutionary committees" aimed at "provoking and agitating the Muslims until their patience was exhausted in order to goad them to massacre and plunder the Christians' homes and goods, and then to demonstrate to Europe such savage Muslim monstrosities and their own suffering." The real intention of these revolutionary committees, however, "was nothing other than securing the Great Powers' intervention."[183] The central organ constantly warned the Muslims not to be taken in by this trick.[184] To this end the pacifist group surrounding Ahmed Rıza asserted the following:

> The Turks had not taken part in the rebellions carried out by the Greek, Armenian, and Bulgarian committees, which aimed at separating themselves from the Ottoman state and dividing up the fatherland. By so abstaining they had done the right thing. We do not have an independent country immune to foreign intervention, like France or Russia. Jews and Armenians have been continuously slaughtered in Russia, yet the Great Powers say nothing and make no complaint. If such a general uprising took place in our country they would immediately send a fleet and invade our lands on the pretext of restoring order. The fault of the Turks is not that they did not participate in the rebellion, but that they paid no attention to it. Through these rebellions and insurrections, the rights and sovereignty of the Ottoman state have been assaulted. Why can the Turks not perceive this?[185]

This may have been an interesting point, but it provided little help for the coalition's main leaders in solving the problems arising from their lack of an activist agenda and of a well-organized committee. The "activists" suggested a more practical but also more naïve solution to these problems. They asserted that anarchist attacks on high-ranking statesmen, similar to those taking place in Russia, would be a less complicated solution:

> To achieve something through revolution in big cities, the populations of which are composed of people of different ethnic origins and affiliated with different faiths, is extremely difficult. The Russian freedom-lovers understood this through their own experience. They were persuaded that a self-sacrificing volunteer, who is dexterous in throwing a bomb and in shooting, could accomplish more than a revolutionary committee comprised of ten thousand individuals. They decided to cleanse their country of the dirt of the wicked bodies of the superior palace officials who were hazardous to the nation. . . . Instead of causing utter disorder in the country and foreign intervention, and shedding the blood of innocent people by a great revolution, it is much better to annihilate the bodies of a few shameless persons who are the real cause of wickedness and depravity, depending on the wisdom of *kullu muḍirrin yuqtal*.[186]

The point the activists were not able to recognize, however, was that they had no organization comparable to that of the Russian revolutionaries. Despite their success in creating a well-articulated ideology, from an organizational viewpoint members of the coalition were far from accomplishing anything of significance, primarily because they could not comprehend the importance of an organizational network and of effective propaganda. One activist leader who had grasped the significance of these issues was later to convert the coalition into an extremely effective organization, aimed at toppling the Hamidian regime, and based on the very ideology that had been shaped during the period 1902–1905.

Minor Young Turk Groups, 1902–1905

The 1902 Congress precipitated the formation of two major fronts by various Young Turk groups and marked the end of the CUP, which, as an umbrella organization, had dominated the movement since the outset. In a sense, the coalition between the followers of Ahmed Rıza and the activists now replaced the CUP. The new coalition, however, lacked the most significant characteristic of the old CUP, namely its role as an umbrella organization in which all groups worked together despite their conflicting agendas. The "majority" led by Sabahaddin Bey naturally attempted to counter the coalition's influence and prevent it from becoming a dominant force in the Young Turk movement. But it was the coalition's caustic and inflexible ideology that enabled Sabahaddin Bey and his followers to deny dominance to this body even during their period of inactivity following their ignominious defeat in 1903. Thus from 1902 onward the Young Turk movement displayed a polarized character.

The period between 1902 and 1905 also witnessed the gradual disintegration of several groups that could not join either of the two fronts that emerged after the congress. Worth mentioning in this regard are the activities of the various Young Turk groups in Egypt, in the Balkans, in the Ottoman capital, and in the other parts of the Ottoman Empire. Additionally a Turkish nationalist intellectual group, which published the journal *Türk* (*Turk*), developed in Cairo. Notable also were the activities of Ahmed Celâleddin Pasha, a former Ottoman Intelligence Service chief who had negotiated with the Young Turks in his capacity as the sultan's special envoy five years prior to his flight, but who in 1904 joined the ranks of the opposition with the intention of leading it.

The Remaining Members of the Old CUP Organization

The remaining members of the old CUP organization had no alternative but to bequeath the official organ *Osmanlı* to the new central committee under Sabahaddin Bey and İsmail Kemal. The new central committee set up by the "majority," however, had no desire whatsoever to work with this impotent group of intriguers. Thus the remaining members of the old CUP organization were once again compelled to embark on new machinations.

Tunalı Hilmi, a leading figure in the old CUP organization, took the first initiatives. He translated some parts of his treatise on "a new state model"[1] into French and published it in Geneva.[2] His choice of Geneva was by no means a random selection. Tunalı Hilmi believed that he could inaugurate pseudopolitical activity in this city by duping Ottoman diplomats and Swiss authorities. At this initial stage he succeeded in hoodwinking both of them.[3]

While working on the translation of his book, Tunalı Hilmi had already taken a more serious-looking initiative by publishing the second issue of his journal *Ezan* (the first issue had been published five years earlier) in late March 1902, and this attempt generated more positive attention.[4] The journal can be considered the climax of Islamist criticism against the sultan. In his ironic personal style Tunalı Hilmi exhorted Muslims to help the Turks against Abdülhamid II:

> Thank God that the Qur'ān is on the tongue, worry beads are in hand, hands are on the belly, eyes are looking to the ground, prayers are performed five times [a day], prayer is offered to God, *Ramaḍān* is observed for a month, pilgrimage is made during the season, alms, *fiṭrah*, sacrifices, soft words, smiling face, hearts are not disturbed, mercy is shown to humans, mercy is shown to animals, always the good side of everything is chosen, not an ant is hurt, if possible, the roads would be brushed and then walked on.
>
> How lucky for them. . . .
>
> How lucky for them that they do not care whether it is day or night, early or late, the depth of winter or extreme heat. The sun rises, the sun sets, they gather five times for prayer.
>
> How lucky for them that they breathe everywhere. As if a spiritual light of saintliness had blanketed the entire world, had spread over valleys, deserts, and sandy places, had reached to snowy hills, to the poles, infiltrated the dark forests and mountain caves. Everybody had observed this spiritual light of saintliness and had seen both himself and the Other, they all had become identical, they had formed the *ummah* of Muḥammad, a common name had been given to all of them, and they had been called Muslims. . . .
>
> Here are their [holy] books, mosques, here are *kibla* [i.e., the direction of Mecca], Kaʿbah, here is Mt. ʿArafāt. . . . Muslims unite! Please conceive of a means for giving brave assistance to your Turkish coreligionists, for the sake of both the religion and the caliphate. Imagine! Even the Europeans commiserate with these coreligionists of yours.
>
> Take warning.
>
> Politics is the greatest form of worship, it is justice. So much so that religion is politics. Because it is for humans. All that takes place among humans is politics. That is to say politics is one of the two pillars of the religion. No other religion involves itself in politics as much as Islam. . . .
>
> Today the divine command that is laid upon all Muslims by the Prophet is to save the caliphate from annihilation. Do not say "it is not my business." By doing so you would become accomplices of those who are annihilating the caliphate. . . .
>
> Oh my God, oh my God, how many lands were destroyed by the sword of an executioner, still being destroyed. . . . He says "I am God."
>
> *Jihād.*
>
> *Takbīr* [i.e., mentioning the formula *God is Great*] for *jihād*.[5]

Tunalı Hilmi's striking rhetoric must have bewitched the pilgrims to whom he distributed his journal free of charge in Suez;[6] however, he could not impress many

Young Turk sympathizers with the same polemical thrust. Tunalı Hilmi probably considered this extreme language the best mode of discourse, since he lacked any organizational ties with which to threaten the sultan. Otherwise this jargon contradicts the "humanist" and "Ottomanist" approach that he had expressed in previous writings,[7] and when he failed to deceive Ottoman diplomats with this rhetoric, he devoted himself to propagating Turkism.

Following the unsuccessful attempts by Tunalı Hilmi, Young Turk activities in Geneva began to decrease. The activists had already left town for Paris to work with the followers of Ahmed Rıza, and the remaining members of the old CUP organization were in no financial position to embark on fresh ventures. In fact, Eugène Regnault, the French consul in Geneva, underscored the point that Young Turk activities in that city had stemmed from the power struggle between Ahmed Celâleddin Pasha, still chief of the Ottoman Intelligence Service, and the Ottoman diplomats in Switzerland, Münir Bey, Baron Richtofen, and Haydar Bey, all of whom were trying to acquire more from the sultan in return for their efforts against his foes.[8] Accordingly they persuaded the palace to deliver a *coup de grâce* to the remaining Young Turks in Geneva. The sultan dispatched İbrahim Bey, an official in the First Chamberlain's office, to the German embassy. There he complained to the German diplomats that the measures that had been taken against the Young Turks had not produced satisfactory results, and he conveyed the sultan's message asking for diplomatic support through the German ambassador in Bern.[9] The Germans gave credence to the sultan's demands, and Reichskanzler Graf Ernst Bernhard von Bülow notified the Ottoman ambassador that the sultan's requirements would be seriously considered.[10] Further, the Auswärtiges Amt prepared a diplomatic note warning the Swiss authorities and underscoring the fact that their toleration of the anarchists' conspiratorial designs had been causing great anxiety.[11] Meanwhile the palace bought off some members of the old CUP organization, who subsequently left the movement.[12]

This diplomatic assault worsened the situation of the remaining members of the old CUP organization in Geneva. As a final undertaking, however, members of Albanian descent decided to publish a new bilingual journal, *İttihad-ı Osmanî— La Fédération Ottomane*, in Geneva. In order to give the impression that members of various Ottoman ethnic groups had established a new periodical, they set up an editorial board consisting of figureheads chosen from expatriates representing various ethnic groups.[13] The Swiss political police gathered detailed information concerning this publishing endeavor and asserted that it was led by three members of the old CUP organization: Ahmed Rıf'at, Derviş Hima, and Halil Muvaffak.[14] All three were Ottoman citizens of Albanian descent. Ahmed Rıf'at had not played a significant role in the movement. Derviş Hima had participated in the 1902 Congress as an Albanian representative, and Halil Muvaffak, who had been assigned significant duties by the CUP, was the son of an Albanian notable of Larissa.[15] The brain of the endeavor, however, was unquestionably Derviş Hima, who, after the Italians had shut down his journal *Albania-Arnavudluk*, planned to resume publication activities in Geneva.[16]

Following his plan of action, the first issue of *İttihad-ı Osmanî—La Fédération Ottomane* appeared on February 23, 1903, under Derviş Hima's editorship.[17] The initial article in the French section praised a federal type of administration, and not surprisingly the journal asserted that Albania was the most suitable region for the application of such an administration.[18] Other articles focused on general reforms for the empire.[19] In the Turkish section the prefatory article, as usual, underscored the importance of unity among the Ottomans; it additionally stated that all the letters written in the languages of the various Ottoman peoples would be answered in those tongues, and the same rule would apply to letters written in French, Italian, and Romanian.[20] Undoubtedly, those who were aware that Italy and Romania were two centers of Albanian nationalist activities readily understood the hidden message implied in the usage of the Italian and Romanian languages. It is plausible to consider this journal, therefore, a twin of the Turkish-Albanian journal published by Derviş Hima and Yaşar Sadık (Jashar Sadik) Erebera, another Albanian delegate at the 1902 Congress, on behalf of the Albanian nationalist society Shpresa.[21] There was, however, one difference. The former adopted a more meandering prose style to attract fellow Albanians. Hence, it is possible to conclude that although begun as a Young Turk venture, *İttihad-ı Osmanî—La Fédération Ottomane* soon turned into a vehicle of the Albanian nationalist movement; as such it could not last long because of the strict measures taken against Albanian opponents of the sultan by the Swiss authorities during this period.[22]

The resounding failure of the "majority" in carrying out their projected coup d'état furnished a new opportunity for the members of the old CUP organization. The temporary abandonment of the movement by Sabahaddin Bey and his comrades after this fiasco made the coalition the only organization to remain active on a significant scale. This was indisputably a great opportunity for those seeking to force the opponents of the coalition to unite under a single banner. As we have seen, the coalition, with its uncompromising Turkist ideology, could by no means hope to become an umbrella organization. Edhem Ruhi, the last CUP director, seized the opportunity and required Sabahaddin Bey to restore the central organ, *Osmanlı*, to him on behalf of the CUP. Having received the frustrated prince's reluctant approval, Edhem Ruhi tried to find a suitable place to publish the journal. Since the only possibility seemed to be Cairo, *Osmanlı* moved to the Egyptian capital as its fourth place of publication.[23] In order to fund the journal's publication, Edhem Ruhi found employment as a proofreader at the offices of a British commercial daily and as a translator at a local branch of a British company.[24] Another member of the old CUP organization who was active in Egypt, Necmeddin Ârif, helped him to publish the journal in Cairo,[25] and the 120th issue of *Osmanlı* appeared there on August 15, 1903. It was published in the name of the CUP, and the initial article, undoubtedly penned by Edhem Ruhi, indirectly criticized the so-called majority.[26] Despite this veiled criticism, however, it was avowed that the new editorial board had invited Sabahaddin Bey and his friends to join them in publishing the journal.[27] A letter of response by Sabahaddin Bey was also published in the same issue. Although he set out strong and detailed Social Darwinist views, he avoided making any remark on the new society, on the pretext of an illness that had allegedly prevented him from writing a more detailed note, and he promised to discuss the matter in another letter to be sent later.[28] It was thus made very clear that the "majority" had no intention of participating in this renewed publication of *Osmanlı*.

Under Edhem Ruhi's direction, the journal began to promote a Turkist policy. For instance, it strongly denounced "the Armenian quest for independence" in a manner

similar to *Şûra-yı Ümmet*.[29] It presented European control over Macedonia as a fla-
grant violation of Ottoman sovereignty and territorial integrity.[30] When *Osmanlı* commented on "European fanaticism," it adopted a rhetoric almost identical to that of
Ahmed Rıza,[31] and almost five years before the actual boycott of Austrian fezzes
initiated by the CUP in power in 1908 the journal made a plea for such action against
the Dual Monarchy.[32]

The journal made a more striking statement on the controversial issue of "foreign
intervention." When *Mechveret Supplément Français* published an article on the importance of dethroning the sultan and demanded that foreign statesmen facilitate this
mission,[33] *Osmanlı* seized the opportunity and criticized even the "minority" by
labeling it pro-interventionist:

> Unfortunately a liberal Young Ottoman journal, published in French, has joined the sec-
> tion of the foreign press that underscores the necessity of foreign intervention to solve
> the Macedonian Question. At the congress of the Young Ottomans, held in Paris, vari-
> ous solutions were discussed for the salvation of our fatherland. It was demonstrated
> that an intervention by the Europeans in favor of the Ottomans is unimaginable in
> Macedonia where intervention is made [on behalf of the Christians]. . . . If we do not
> depose the sultan, such an intervention may cause more damage than the existence of
> the sultan.[34]

In line with its extreme stand on foreign intervention, in its new phase of publication *Osmanlı* also underscored the pre-Ottoman achievements of the Turks, a subject totally ignored during the journal's long history in Europe:

> As is well known to the whole world, the Turks, who established our state, had been
> nomadic people who used to live in the deserts of Central Asia. . . . We advanced to
> Europe from Asia and conquered Macedonia, Istanbul, Albania, in effect the entirety of
> European Turkey and Hungary. Since we had no other intention besides robbery,
> marauding, and booty, however, we never contemplated how to impose our language,
> customs, and moral values on the inhabitants of the lands that we had conquered.[35]

The regrets expressed here are unquestionably a repetition of those earlier articulated by *Şûra-yı Ümmet*.

The main problem with such a discourse was that it was very unlikely to attract
many Young Turks. The central organ of the coalition had been promoting a similar
type of Turkism, and in the journal *Türk*, published in Cairo, a group of intellectuals
defended a more extreme nationalist program. From an intellectual viewpoint no
comparison can be made between the well-bred ideology promoted by the contributors to *Türk* and the vulgar protonationalist themes propagated by Edhem Ruhi and
his associates.

In any case, Edhem Ruhi faced financial difficulties immediately after starting publication. He succeeded in procuring small donations, but they were far from sufficient to meet all the expenses.[36] At that point Edhem Ruhi wisely realized that he
had two alternatives in order to continue his publication. The first was to create a
second wing within the Young Turk movement to oppose the coalition. The second
was to adopt an extreme "activist" course, since the real "activists" had been compelled to soften their language because of their compromise with Ahmed Rıza.

Edhem Ruhi decided to pursue both options. First he established contact with Muḥammad ʿAlī Ḥalīm Pasha, who was backing the coalition financially but had disagreements with Ahmed Rıza on crucial matters. Edhem Ruhi soon succeeded in impressing the Egyptian prince and became his private secretary. As was pointed out by Ahmed Saib, this situation posed a great threat to the coalition:

> The other day I met Muḥammad ʿAlī Ḥalīm Pasha. He is such a nice character. He could not properly decide, however, on a single course. Those who do not want *Şûra-yı Ümmet* here have exerted their best efforts to win over the royal princes. They have succeeded in making Edhem Ruhi a private secretary to Muḥammad ʿAlī Ḥalīm Pasha. Therefore, I recommend that you pay more attention to certain issues in your correspondence [with Muḥammad ʿAlī Ḥalīm Pasha].[37]

Having received the support of the Egyptian prince, Edhem Ruhi decided to carry out an assassination plan. He gave detailed information about this venture when he later confessed all his activities to Münir Pasha in 1905:

> When he was working as his private secretary, Muḥammad ʿAlī Ḥalīm Pasha had encouraged Edhem Ruhi and goaded him on by saying, "There is no blood flowing in the veins of the Turks, and feelings such as patriotism, sacrifice, zeal, and love of fatherland are all gone; all of them are poltroons like women. Swaggering is all they know, and in reality they cannot do anything, least of all in the field of action." In response, Edhem Ruhi had asserted that the Turks were ready to sacrifice themselves. . . . One day, when they were again debating and perversely opposing each other, the pasha told him, "If you can prove to me, in deeds, that what you have been saying is true, then I will help you [financially] as much as you ask." Upon this, Edhem Ruhi remembered Ârif Hikmet (who went by the pseudonym Ali Şakir), whose courage and wisdom he trusted. He took money from Muḥammad ʿAlī Ḥalīm Pasha and went to Bulgaria to coax Ârif Hikmet, who was then residing there. Ârif Hikmet was of Circassian origin and had previously fled to Bulgaria. At that time he was teaching at a school in Tutrakan. While these events were taking place, [Muḥammad] ʿAlī [Ḥalīm] Pasha was travelling in Europe along with the khedive of Egypt. Therefore, Edhem Ruhi took Ârif Hikmet to Europe to discuss the proposed action among themselves. In sum, they decided to obtain dynamite from Bulgaria and to smuggle it to Istanbul with the help of two or three persons, to assassinate some ministers and palace officials, to blow up some of the imperial offices with dynamite simultaneously, and by capitalizing on the panic which might ensue—we take refuge with God!—even to venture a greater and more execrable assassination [i.e., to liquidate the sultan.][38]

Edhem Ruhi's cohort later claimed that they had founded a local Young Turk nucleus in Tutrakan and had sent a letter to Sabahaddin Bey asking for his help through Edhem Ruhi. The latter, upon secretly opening the letter and reading it, decided to use this small organization for his own purposes and told Muḥammad ʿAlī Ḥalīm Pasha that he could carry out an assassination plot.[39]

Whichever account is accurate, Edhem Ruhi traveled to Trieste and invited Ârif Hikmet and another Young Turk, Mehmed Cemil (who went by the pseudonym Behzad), to meet him there. The two demanded that Edhem Ruhi go to Ruse, claiming that their organizational work was almost finished.[40] A secret meeting, described by *Osmanlı* as "a conference," was held on March 29 and 30, 1904.[41] The journal announced that "a Muslim notable presided over the meeting." The Swiss police inferred from this description that this person was an Egyptian prince desiring to gain importance in the eyes of the sultan.[42] If so, this could be none other than Muḥammad ʿAlī Ḥalīm Pasha.[43] It seems, however, very unlikely that the pasha traveled to Ruse and chaired a secret meeting there.

At the secret conclave the bylaws that had been prepared by the members of the nucleus were reexamined and a petition importuning the Egyptian prince to become the permanent director of the new committee was signed by the eight participants. The other important decisions taken were the following:

1. Behzad [Mehmed Cemil] would be appointed Secretary of the central branch.
2. The journal *Osmanlı* would be published in Egypt on behalf of the committee.
3. Edhem Ruhi, bearing a letter of credentials from the committee, would visit Bulgarian towns and other cities outside of the fatherland which are inhabited by Muslims, and would establish branches in accordance with the relevant clauses in the bylaws.[44]

Following the meeting Edhem Ruhi traveled within Bulgaria and then went to central Europe, and Mehmed Cemil was dispatched to Egypt as inspector.[45] The latter published the bylaws in Cairo,[46] and the Osmanlı İttihad ve İnkılâb Cemiyeti (the Ottoman Union and Revolution Committee) was born.

During the preparations for the establishment of this new organization, Abdullah Cevdet, who had been one of the original founders of the CUP at the Royal Medical Academy in 1889 and who had been appointed to the Ottoman embassy in Vienna as a medical doctor in 1899, gave a box on the ears to the ambassador, who was investigating his relations with his old friends.[47] The incident generated great interest in Austria and received extensive European press coverage. Coupled with an interpellation by a radical Austrian deputy,[48] it caused the Young Turk movement to become a topic of discussion.[49] Abdullah Cevdet, however, quickly understood the impossibility of remaining in Vienna, because of the heavy pressure of the Ottoman government on its Austrian counterpart, and went to Geneva with the intention of taking an active part in fresh Young Turk ventures.

At first, relying on his former role in the CUP, he wanted to approach the coalition directly.[50] Ahmed Rıza, however, wrote an article on the incident in the central organ, ridiculing Abdullah Cevdet.[51] The latter responded fiercely by publishing a pamphlet against Ahmed Rıza, and thereafter cut all ties with the coalition.[52] Abdullah Cevdet later established a publishing house in Geneva with the generous gifts of the khedive, Muḥammad ʿAlī Ḥalīm Pasha, and the former intelligence chief Ahmed Celâleddin Pasha.[53] Abdullah Cevdet was joined by Abdurrahman Bedirhan,[54] who once participated in the activities of the coalition but severed his connection with it when its members adopted a strong Turkist course. At the time Edhem Ruhi was traveling in Europe, Abdullah Cevdet intended to publish cultural works and translations of European classical masterpieces; however, the two old comrades decided instead to publish *Osmanlı* in its birthplace.[55] Muḥammad ʿAlī Ḥalīm Pasha, who endowed the publication handsomely, approved this decision, and the two members of the old organization started publishing *Osmanlı* as the central organ of the Ottoman Union and Revolution Committee. Although Edhem Ruhi tried to present this new organization as the natural heir of the CUP,[56] it was impossible for its leaders to establish any branches other than the one in Ruse. Mehmed Cemil, the so-called inspector, however, opposed the initiatives taken by Edhem Ruhi, stating on behalf of the branch in Bulgaria:

> The decision which had been taken by the executive committee was to publish *Osmanlı* in Egypt. Above all, according to the bylaws, we cannot work with individuals who have accepted money, decorations, ranks, and posts from the government.[57]

The publication of the bylaws by *Osmanlı*, despite the decision taken at the secret meeting, made relations even more strained.[58] For instance, a Turkish notable in Bulgaria who had donated FFr 1,000 to the new society protested this disarray at its onset by sending letters to both sides.[59] Although *Osmanlı* published messages addressed to five other branches, these must have been a spurious display intended to delude those who had donated money, and to deceive Ottoman diplomats.[60] Similarly the journal claimed that some swindlers were collecting subscriptions by using its name.[61] Ottoman diplomats, however, did not accept this tall tale and paid no heed to blackmail attempts by Abdullah Cevdet and Edhem Ruhi.[62] At last Edhem Ruhi made an announcement in the journal that the central organ would be published not under his editorship but under the full responsibility of the committee.[63] Again this step was to no avail.

An examination of the articles published by *Osmanlı* during this period makes it clear that anarchist themes were dominant. At that time Edhem Ruhi had already decided "to pursue terrorism,"[64] and Abdullah Cevdet had established ties with the Russian Nihilists.[65] *Osmanlı* openly praised shedding blood[66] and extolled the Russian Nihilists.[67] This publication policy made almost no impact on sympathizers of the Young Turk movement, and Edhem Ruhi accordingly decided to try something new:

> Edhem Ruhi dispatched Ârif Hikmet to Istanbul from the Piraeus aboard a Greek boat. Upon his arrival at Istanbul the latter set foot on land disguised as a Greek sailor. He later went to the house of one of their accomplices, this time disguised as a *muhacir*. Meanwhile, Edhem Ruhi had gone to Bulgaria, obtained dynamite, and taken a Romanian boat from Constanţa to Istanbul in disguise. He had remained on the boat and hidden the dynamite under straw in a chicken coop. He then passed it on to a sailor, who was supposed to deliver the dynamite to Ârif Hikmet in town. Although the sailor had promised to do this, when he came to the customs office, for some reason or other he left the coop before entering the inspection area, and the customs officials found the dynamite when they searched the coop. Meanwhile, the disguised Ârif Hikmet was unexpectedly identified by an old friend in Süleymaniye, while waiting for the dynamite, and upon the conveyance of this intelligence by this person, the police apprehended him. . . . The heir apparent, Reşad Efendi, was being continuously informed about the venture . . . and upon the recommendation of the khedive of Egypt, Edhem Ruhi had received help from the British consuls in Bulgaria and Constanţa.[68]

The documents presented by Edhem Ruhi to Münir Pasha reveal that the venture was a well-outlined undertaking, and the conspirators scheduled even the date of the bombing: September 21, 1904.[69] In an interview given after the 1905 assassination attempt by the Dashnaktsutiun, Abdullah Cevdet told a journalist that he and his friends had embarked on a similar enterprise eight months previously.[70] In October

1904 a Swiss daily published a telegram sent by the Young Turks in Ruse to the new committee in Geneva concerning the escape of a member who had earlier been arrested for smuggling dynamite.[71] Later, in 1905, dynamite and compromising documents were found in the houses of the Young Turks in Constanṭa, whence Edhem Ruhi had obtained explosives.[72] All this evidence proves that the attempt had not been a fake undertaking intended only to delude the Ottoman diplomats; however, its planners and financial supporters met with frustration.[73]

Just before the failure of the assassination attempt, Abdullah Cevdet started to publish his new journal, *İctihad*, devoted to an Ottoman cultural renaissance.[74] Its first issue appeared in Geneva on September 1, 1904, and with the exception of a few articles, the journal fulfilled the dreams of its founder by becoming the first Young Turk cultural organ.[75]

The palace, on the other hand, launched a campaign against this fresh Young Turk activity in Geneva. First Abdullah Cevdet was banned from public service.[76] Haydar Bey, the Ottoman consul in Geneva, bought off Mamas Efendi, the typesetter of *Osmanlı*,[77] and he hired a famous attorney to file a lawsuit against *Osmanlı* and *İctihad*.[78] He also employed a "capable sleuth," who was in the employ of the Swiss political police, to gather more information concerning the activities of Abdullah Cevdet and Edhem Ruhi.

Finally a plan, carefully sketched by the consul, was executed. The palace bought off Abdülhakim Hikmet, a Maronite Young Turk who had played only insignificant roles in the movement.[79] He submitted a manuscript to Abdullah Cevdet to be published by his publishing house. The obscene language in which the author referred to the sultan and various ministers was aimed at providing the attorneys of the palace with adequate grounds for a lawsuit.[80] Upon the insistence of the author, it was advertised as a literary supplement to *Osmanlı*.[81] In court the attorneys of the Ottoman consulate then petitioned for the interdiction of both *Osmanlı* and *İctihad* and for the expulsion of Abdullah Cevdet from Switzerland.[82] Edhem Ruhi claimed full responsibility for the publication of *Osmanlı*, but this declaration made no impact on the judge.[83] *Osmanlı*'s delayed 142nd issue was published on December 8, 1904, and marked the end of the seven-year publication of the journal in four different cities by three distinct organizations. Abdullah Cevdet was deported from Switzerland on November 2, 1904, and moved to Annemasse in France.[84] He sent notes to various dailies and journals to protest the event, blaming the Ottoman government. Thanks to his efforts, the last remaining members of the old CUP organization in Geneva gained the sympathy of Swiss public opinion,[85] but this support was not enough to enable them to continue publication in Geneva. Although Abdullah Cevdet published his journal in Geneva from Annemasse for seven months,[86] he finally decided to move his publishing house to Cairo and to participate in the Young Turk movement there. The ninth issue of *İctihad* appeared in Cairo in October 1905.[87]

This period also witnessed two other initiatives taken by Abdullah Cevdet in an effort to establish new organizations. In April 1905 *İctihad* proudly advertised that it had become a party organ under a new editorial board.[88] The party was named Parti de la Réforme et du Progrès Partout et Pour Tous.[89] This was obviously an endeavor aimed at impressing Prince Sabahaddin, who was striving for the publication of a new organ. Soon afterward, however, the prince established his own journal and this scheme of Abdullah Cevdet failed.

The second undertaking was another blackmailing venture. During his interview with Jean Longuet, Abdullah Cevdet asserted that the assassination attempt of 1905 might have been made by a Muslim.[90] This claim was further reiterated by his journal and underscored by *Pro Armenia*.[91] In late 1905 a German newspaper informed its readers of a memorandum presented to the ambassadors of the six Great Powers by a committee called the Ottoman Patriots' Freedom Committee, which had allegedly played a role in the assassination attempt.[92] Accordingly, a Young Turk appeal published in a journal in Egypt claimed that they "expressed [their] desire with a great roar on July 8, during the Friday prayers."[93] *Pro Armenia* further published an appeal dated August 20, 1905, that had allegedly been distributed by this committee, this time named Hurriet Organisation Patriotique Ottoman.[94] According to the appeal the organization had its headquarters in Istanbul and branches in Paris, London, Geneva, and Cairo.[95] It is not possible, however, to find any evidence of the existence of such a well-organized committee. Another European journal published an Islamist proclamation allegedly distributed about the same time in the mosques in Istanbul by Le Parti du Comité Révolutionnaire Ottoman to stir up Muslims.[96] Undoubtedly it was a trumped-up organization adopting various threatening titles for the purpose of negotiation with Ottoman diplomats.

Having been beaten on all fronts, Edhem Ruhi met with Münir Pasha and made a detailed oral confession to the ambassador. In return the palace gave him money and appointed him to a low-ranking position at the Ottoman Commissioner's office in Bulgaria.[97] Abdurrahman Bedirhan, who had helped Abdullah Cevdet in his publication, cut a deal with the palace and returned to Istanbul.[98] Thus the activities of the former members of the old CUP organization came to an end in Geneva.

Young Turks and the Zionists: Two Fascinating Schemes

We have examined many activities carried out by Abdullah Cevdet and other members of the old CUP organization aimed at extorting money from the Ottoman authorities and diplomats. Another noteworthy attempt by Abdullah Cevdet targeted Theodor Herzl, the leader and ideologue of the Zionist movement, who had been desperately seeking ways to strike a deal with the Ottoman government. Herzl's initial attempts to reach an understanding with the Ottoman government were fruitless.[99] During this period Herzl and other Zionist leaders viewed the Young Turk movement as a card with which to threaten the sultan.[100] Abdullah Cevdet, who had played significant roles in many Young Turk machinations and had become a master of intrigue, was one of the few Young Turks paying close attention to the Zionist movement. *Neue freie Presse*'s favorable review of one of Abdullah Cevdet's works of poetry gave him the opportunity for which he had hoped. He paid a visit to Herzl to thank him for the review, and he presented himself as a friend of the Jews and as one of the leaders of the old CUP organization. Herzl asked him to translate a letter into Turkish that he intended to submit to the sultan. In the course of the conversation

Abdullah Cevdet told Herzl that he could sketch out a plan through which the Zionist leader could reach a settlement with the Ottoman government. According to this outlandish scheme, Herzl was to distribute handsome bribes to various Ottoman cabinet ministers and lesser officials in order to receive formal approval for his designs for Palestine. Despite the extremely unrealistic nature of the plan, Abdullah Cevdet succeeded in convincing the Zionist leader that he would have no obligation to him until he received the formal approval. Herzl offered to pay Abdullah Cevdet the same amount that he would pay the cabinet ministers, and Abdullah Cevdet, as a proof of his sincerity, stated that he would be happy to receive less, declaring "his intention of collaborating *pour l'amour de la bonne cause*." Abdullah Cevdet further promised to write a letter immediately to Mehmed Memduh Pasha, the Ottoman Minister of the Interior.[101]

With the intention of impressing Herzl, Abdullah Cevdet sent him a note on the very same day, informing the Zionist leader of his early initiatives.[102] The next day Abdullah Cevdet introduced Herzl to Şükrü Pasha, the Ottoman military attaché in Vienna, who was also the son of the Ottoman Minister of War. Şükrü Pasha promised to send a favorable letter to his father, drafted by Abdullah Cevdet, regarding the Zionists.[103] Within a week Abdullah Cevdet sent two additional notes concerning his activities and set up meetings with Herzl.[104] In the meantime he told Herzl that he had corresponded with his friends and received important messages in response.[105] Herzl, who obviously had great expectations from the Young Turk intriguer, sent a note to Doctor Wellisch, his agent in Istanbul, and instructed him to call on Faik Bey, the private secretary of the Ottoman Minister of the Interior, with Abdullah Cevdet's card of introduction, and to reveal the bribery plan.[106] On March 16, 1903, Abdullah Cevdet passed on to Herzl a message, allegedly sent by one of his comrades in Istanbul, informing Herzl of possible success in bringing the matter before the sultan.[107] In response, Max Nordau conveyed messages from Herzl to Abdullah Cevdet,[108] who continued to tell Herzl concocted stories, claiming that his "relation avec le trône devient meilleure" and praising the Zionist leader as "un prophète de ce temps."[109] Abdullah Cevdet told similar stories to Nordau about his fictitious meeting with Ahmed Rıza, describing how he had proposed to the positivist leader "une alliance plutôt une fusion intellectuelle des turcs avec les juifs."[110] In June Abdullah Cevdet introduced Herzl to an Ottoman attorney who allegedly had "important relations with the Palace."[111] Although Herzl commented that Âdil Bey, the attorney, "makes an overly shrewd disagreeable impression," the next day he cabled the following message to his agent in Istanbul: "To the Constantinople attorney Âdil Bey— *if the Charter is obtained*—2,000 Turkish pds. Further, to Taik [Faik] Bey the Chamberlain [*sic*] £2,000 in that case."[112] The next month Abdullah Cevdet informed Herzl that his friend Âdil Bey had been asked by one of the assistant chamberlains to make the final payment in Istanbul.[113] In the meantime Âdil Bey sent a short message to the Zionist leader telling him that he did not have a clear plan; he would, however, work on the project of transferring properties in Palestine to Herzl.[114]

Two weeks later Âdil Bey forwarded a letter to Herzl claiming that he had been trying to win over Sheikh Abū al-Hudā al-Ṣayyādī to the Zionist cause.[115] At the same time Âdil Bey made his first inquiry about money, albeit in ambiguous language.[116] In September Abdullah Cevdet told Herzl that Âdil Bey thought that "le succès est à la fois très difficile et très facile et il s'agit de trouver un moment propice de S. M. I le Sultan."[117] The Young Turk intriguer sent another enigmatic message to Herzl two days later maintaining that "l'affaire semble avoir trouvé une route plus courte et sûre."[118] A letter by Âdil Bey to Abdullah Cevdet complaining that Herzl did not respond to any of his letters demonstrates that Herzl had begun to find the stories and vague promises less believable.[119] Afraid of a complete failure, Abdullah Cevdet even applied to Theodor Herzl's wife, Julie, and requested her to ask the Zionist leader to respond to Âdil Bey.[120]

When the Sixth Zionist Congress was convened at Basel on August 23, 1903, Abdullah Cevdet drafted two letters, an informative letter to the Ottoman Minister of the Interior, Mehmed Memduh Pasha, providing him with details about the congress, and a short note to Âdil Bey, who was supposed to convey the message concerning the goodwill of the Jews to important personalities in the Ottoman capital.[121] All these efforts, however, seem to have made very little impact on Herzl, who did not bother answering letters from Âdil Bey.[122] The incident at the Ottoman embassy in Vienna and Abdullah Cevdet's subsequent dismissal from government service seem to have influenced Herzl's opinion of him. In fact, Herzl did not even answer a telegram begging him to help Abdullah Cevdet.[123] The latter, however, continued telling stories to Herzl about his work for the possible immigration of "300 Jewish families to Palestine."[124] The last letter written by Abdullah Cevdet to Herzl says nothing about the bribery plan or about Âdil Bey.[125]

Meanwhile, Abdullah Cevdet had kept in contact with Nordau and now offered to help the Zionists by publishing favorable articles in the Young Turk journals.[126] Following the death of Herzl, Abdullah Cevdet asked Nordau to write articles on Zionism for his new journal, *İctihad*.[127] Nordau's article and Abdullah Cevdet's favorable comments on the Jews prove that both sides had agreed to keep the relationship alive.[128] Undoubtedly, this relationship was very little help to the Zionists; we lack further information on how Abdullah Cevdet benefited from it. It is very likely that small amounts of money had been extorted from Herzl before he understood the real nature of the project set before him. In the light of the history of the Young Turks in question, it is not difficult to discern that the money was not spent on any serious Young Turk activities.

Abdullah Cevdet was not the only Young Turk who offered a scheme to Herzl. An unimportant Young Turk, Ali Nuri (Gustaf Noring), who had played a minuscule role in the movement,[129] proposed an even more outlandish plan to Herzl almost a year later. Herzl jotted the following in his diary:

His proposal . . . comes to this: Sail into the Bosphorus with two cruisers, bombard Yildiz, let the Sultan flee or capture him, put in another Sultan (Murad or Reshad), but first form a provisional government—which is to give us the charter for Palestine.

A novel or an adventure?

The two cruisers will cost £400,000, the rest £100,000. The whole stroke would cost half a million pounds. If it fails, we would have lost the money and the participants their lives. . . .

The scheme could be carried out with a thousand men. Preferably during the *selamlik*.

The cruisers would pass through the Dardanelles at night and could bombard Yildiz by morning.[130]

Herzl responded that his "point of view has always been that [he] could only negotiate with the existing government of the land, not with a prospective one."[131] Yet interestingly, even such a bizarre scheme seemed conceivable to the Zionist leader. Ali Nuri paid other visits to Herzl and provided him with details about his quixotic plan.[132] Although Herzl planned to use Ali Nuri as a tool,[133] he later decided to reject "Ali Nuri's plan in [his] own mind."[134]

Following Herzl's death, Sabahaddin Bey, who took his early lessons in intrigue from well-experienced Young Turks, and always pursued high politics, tried to establish ties with the Zionists.[135] Undoubtedly his plan for decentralization was more attractive to the Zionists than was the burgeoning Turkism of the coalition members.[136] His initiative, too, was fruitless, however.

In summary it would not be inaccurate to say that the relations between the Young Turks and the Zionists were far from producing anything of significance and that the plots proposed by the Young Turks rivaled those in the most unrealistic spy novels.

The Young Turks in Egypt and the Journal *Türk*

The Young Turk movement in Egypt was already in disarray prior to the 1902 Congress, and the decision taken by the coalition members to publish their central organ in Cairo made very little difference. The fact that it was being published in the Egyptian capital did not enable the coalition to establish a strong base there. Prior to the 1902 Congress, Ahmed Rıza had complained that there was only one subscriber to his journal in Egypt,[137] and the renewed publication activity did not drastically alter this picture. During this period, Egypt became a center for promoting Turkist ideas and for petty as well as grand intrigue.

The Şafak Committee and the Conflict among Impostors

The only remaining Young Turk organization in Cairo, prior to the coalition's decision to found a branch there under Ahmed Saib, was the so-called Şafak Committee (the Dawn of Ottoman Union Committee). Bahriyeli Rıza, a master intriguer, and a negligible group of Ottoman refugees were fighting against each other over the inheritance of the CUP's Egyptian branch. These spendthrifts had no power whatsoever to make an impact on the course of events and on the Young Turk movement. As a matter of fact, even those who had an interest in the activities against the sultan faced difficulties in physically locating this so-called Dawn of Ottoman Union Committee.[138]

Internal intrigues among the members of this committee did, however, cause a diplomatic crisis. Lord Cromer provided an account of the events leading up to this crisis, which was followed by British intervention:

Early in 1899, a printing-office was opened in Cairo by two members of the Young Turk party named Khoja Kadri and Saleh Gamal [Salih Cemal] for the purpose of publishing a newspaper, "El-Kanoun el-Essassi," in the interests of their propaganda. . . . Shortly after its foundation, a certain Tonali Ali [Tunalı Hilmi] . . . put forward a claim to the printing-office, as having been purchased with the funds of the Young Turk society "El-

Ittehad" [CUP], in whose name he demanded restitution of the property. After a law-suit which lasted for a year, judgment was given in favour of the original founders.

Meanwhile, Saleh Gamal, fearing an adverse judgment, had signed a fictitious bond to a Russian subject employed in the office, whereby the latter was recognised as a part-ner in the undertaking; he giving to Saleh, at the same time, a document establishing the fictitious nature of the agreement. . . .

At some moment during the procedure in these cases, a "saise conservatoire" was made; and the Huissier affixed his seal to a desk which was said to contain a number of docu-ments highly compromising to many persons both in Turkey and abroad.

A short while after Khoja Kadri and Saleh Gamal had resumed possession of their printing office, the Russian subject (a certain Tewfik Mahrami) abstracted from Salih's pocket his own acknowledgement, and sold the original deed of partnership to a man named Bahari Riza [Bahriyeli Rıza]. This latter brought an action against the original partners, and demanded, in order to satisfy his claims, the liquidation of the concern. The Native Court gave judgment in favour of Bahari Riza. . . . Saleh Gamal appealed against this decision. Meanwhile, the official liquidator had taken possession of the plant etc. There only remained the desk containing the compromising documents. This was protected by the seal of the court.[139]

Although they paid great attention to these developments, the British were unaware that Bahriyeli Rıza had become an agent of the khedive and had done everything on instructions from the latter.[140] The khedive undoubtedly desired to exploit the papers of the CUP as a wild card in his bargaining with the sultan. Among the papers were full lists of all those implicated in the movement, code words, reams of correspondence, and documents relating to questions of money.[141] Had the khedive been able to seize them, the sultan would have paid an exorbitant price for their purchase.

The Young Turks then "hastily associated with themselves a French subject, named Guimbard, who went to the office with a dragoman of his Consulate and, as the *Hussier* of the court was about to remove the seals, declared himself a partner and demanded to withdraw certain papers, which were his private property. The *Hussier* took a note of the declaration, and suspended further proceedings." Two days later, however, the Young Turks learned that "Guimbard had been induced to renounce his claim, and that the liquidation would consequently go forward." On April 9 Mansfield, the head of the Cairo City Police, called on Cromer and stated that he had received information that "whilst the agents of the Khedive would hesitate at nothing to obtain the papers, the members of the Young Turk party were desperate, and should they see themselves and their friends—as they considered—irretrievably ruined, they would not improbably make an attack on the Khedive's person."[142] Under the circumstances Cromer did not hesitate: he ordered Mansfield to seize the papers and bring them to the former's house, which he did.[143]

Cromer later informed the Foreign Office of his action and took full responsibil-ity.[144] The Foreign Office found the action somewhat outrageous but nonetheless gave its approval:

I cannot imagine on what *legal* grounds the British Agent & Consul General can have seized papers belonging to Turks and retained them in the Agency. But Egypt being in British military occupation, I suppose we are justified in taking any exceptional mea-sures which we deem necessary for the preservation of order.[145]

At that point Bahriyeli Rıza hired an attorney, who sent a telegram of protest to the Foreign Office.[146] Sanderson favored the acknowledgement of the telegram and proposed that "enquiries shall be made."[147] Cromer vehemently opposed this action, stating that the attorney "Hanna Wahba is one of the worst types of the legal profession and a man of the lowest character."[148] Finally Lord Lansdowne overrode Sanderson's decision, the telegram was not acknowledged by the Foreign Office, and no answer was given to the attorney.[149]

This was the end of the British intervention; the heavy-handed action taken by Lord Cromer gave rise to sharp criticism in diplomatic circles.[150] The struggle over the printing press resumed. During the dispute over the papers, Salih Cemal died.[151] Colonel Şevket, the military strategist of the majority's coup d'état plan, wanted to procure the printing plant on behalf of the Young Turks in Tripoli of Barbary. Ottoman intelligence agents, however, intercepted his confidential letter being sent to an heir of Salih Cemal in the empire.[152] The governor of Cezaîr-i Bahr-i Sefîd Province, Âbidin Bey, proposed a government purchase of the printing press, but Mehmed Memduh Pasha, the Minister of the Interior, discouraged the idea, arguing that such a purchase would only help the Young Turks to accumulate money for their future ventures.[153]

As for the publication attempts of the members of the old CUP organization, the most significant undertaking was that of Süleyman Vahid, who had worked with Salih Cemal until the latter's sudden death. He started a journal called *Anadolu* (Anatolia) and obtained the help of Tarsusîzâde Münif Bey, who had once played an important role in the CUP branch in Cairo.[154] The latter authored a series of Turkist articles for the journal:

> Oh! Illustrious sultan. . . . Please look at the Turks, your servants. . . . They [the palace officials] swallowed the pill given by the spongers and totally ignored us, the Turks. . . . Pity, my sultan, pity! . . . Don't hang around with horse thieves and Arab vagabonds. . . . Trust the hearts of Turks and listen attentively to what they say.[155]

Another article on the Young Turk movement since the establishment of the CUP claimed that the most significant shortcoming of the movement had been its failure in carrying out "ventures."[156] This obviously illustrates the "activist" tendency of the group publishing the journal.

The palace was not long in launching a campaign against this new publication.[157] Later Süleyman Vahid was tried by a kangaroo court and sentenced *in contumaciam* to serve a life term.[158] Upon reaching an agreement with the sultan's agents, however, he was assured that the verdict would be considered annulled and that he would be granted an imperial pardon should he return to the empire.[159] His withdrawal from the struggle marked the end of publication activity on the part of the former members of the CUP branch in Egypt.

The Emergence of a Turkish Nationalist Press in Egypt and the Journal *Türk*

As we have seen, Cairo became a center for Young Turk publications immediately after the 1902 Congress. *Şûra-yı Ümmet* was published there as the central organ of the coalition; *Anadolu*, which was published by the former members of the CUP branch in Cairo, enjoyed a brief term of publication; later *Osmanlı*, until its move to Geneva, and *İctihad* starting in October 1905, were published in the Egyptian capital. The publication of an intellectual organ named *Türk*, however, can be considered a cornerstone in the molding of Turkish nationalist ideology.

The initial activities of the group of intellectuals involved with the organ, all of whom had played different roles in the movement, were identified by Ahmed Saib in a letter that he sent to Ahmed Rıza:

> In your previous letter you had required some information concerning the journal *Türk*, which is being published here. . . . Those who are publishing this journal are: Ali Kemal, Şerafeddin [Mağmumî], Necmeddin [Ârif], Es'ad Bey, and Celâl[eddin Ârif]. Unquestionably, they are publishing this journal against us. They perceived that they could not compete with us by publishing *Osmanlı*. . . . Their expenditure is Lt 21 a month. They have exerted great efforts to accumulate money. . . . Probably they have collected some money. They are speaking about Lt 300, but it is likely that they have accumulated only Lt 100. They cannot last for long with this money.[160]

Despite the fears of the director of the coalition's Cairo branch, the publishers made it clear that they had no intention of making their journal a committee organ.[161] As was explained in the maiden article, the founders aimed at promoting Turkish nationalism not as a distinct committee policy but as an ideology:

> *Türk* is a scientific, literary, and political journal, specifically established to defend the rights, to mend the manners and morals of the Turks, and to enliven their ideas. One day in the future, history, the eternal mirror of the truth of events, will precisely show that one nation that has been unjustly confronted with the entire world's enmity is the Turks. Now we conclusively know, not because we are Turks, but because we closely observe and perceive the actuality, that no injustice can be imagined similar to that of the West's disrespectful enmity toward the Turks. Is it not unjust to ignore the distinct native talents of a nation which has developed from a small tribe into a magnificent state, a nation which, starting from a remote corner of Asia, Söğüd, reached a shining center of Europe, Vienna, by relying on the sword? During that very era and on the very same continent, there lived many other nations, both Muslim and non-Muslim. Why is it that others were unable to exhibit the same level of miraculous native talent? If the British were in the position in which the Turks find themselves today, we are confident that they would be in a similar condition. The Turk has acquired all present harmful habits that he has from the East; and it is in the East that he has encountered all causes for his weakness and decline. Because of his innate strength, he has been able for six centuries to resist calamities which others could not have resisted for a hundred years. If he had entered Europe through the north instead of the south, and if he had settled in the west like his Hungarian brethren rather than settling in the east, then unquestionably today he would have outstanding governance, authority, prosperity, and independence. The Europeans err on the following point: They confuse Turks, who since the earliest days of their national existence have never experienced slavery and subjugation and have perpetually lived free and in a domineering position, with the impotent nations of the East, who have heretofore been oppressed under the yoke of degradation.[162]

This strong focus on nationalism and race and the indirect remarks on religion's alleged role in the backwardness of the Turks were the main pillars of the ideology promoted by the journal.[163] This strong nationalist focus was also the reason behind their receiving many letters "from towns in Transcaucasia, towns in mainland Asia, Bosnia-Hercegovina, Romania, and Asia Minor."[164] Even the founders were surprised that they could maintain publication for years despite the initial expectations of everyone that the journal would survive at most between three weeks and three months.[165] Other than Şerafeddin Mağmumî's nom de plume, "a Turk," all the authors contributing to the journal had chosen original Turkic pen names such as "Oğuz," "Uygur," "Özbek," "Tuğrul," "Turgud," "Kuneralp," and "Uluğ." It is these names that may have caused many Turks in Russia to send donations to the journal; similar contributions were also received from Bosnia and Crete.[166] The congratulatory letter sent by *Tercüman*, the journal that had been promoting a cultural union among Turkic peoples, was intended to express support by the Turks who were under Russian rule.[167]

In addition to its strong focus on nationalism and race, *Türk*, in the same vein as the coalition's central organ, praised nationalism in general[168] and castigated foreign intervention in Ottoman politics:

> We Turks should certainly understand this: How many times have the European Great Powers made treaties in order not to allow anyone even to touch our state's land; in any event, how many such treaties have they signed and approved with their official seals?! . . . Is there any power today which treats these treaties with respect? . . . Apparently the Europeans made all those treaties simply to make us heedless, to tie our hands gradually, and then to drive us out easily from our own country![169]

Türk also disparaged European economic penetration[170] and accused European powers of waging a crusade against the Turks.[171] Another interesting point was the journal's strong criticism of the members of the so-called majority because of their favorable attitude toward the Great Powers:

> The small Boer nation heroically fought against the British, who had been striving to usurp the gold mines in Transvaal. The sacrifices they made to prevent the independence of Transvaal being destroyed by the British were acclaimed by the entire world. Despite this, some of our people, who knew well what they were about, . . . went to the British embassy and expressed their hopes for a British triumph.[172]

Other objectives of the journal were formulated as "to make Turks known to the entire world" and "to refute the propaganda made by other [non-Turkish] Ottoman nations."[173] To achieve these goals, the founders of the journal once seriously considered publishing a French supplement to compete with *Mechveret Supplément Français*. Because of lack of financing, however, this project was not realized.[174]

The founders of the journal devoted no time to coming to terms with the other ethnic groups of the empire; they considered the Ottoman state a Turkish Empire. The great Ottoman victories such as Kosovo, Prut, and Plevna, which were frequently depicted as Turkish, were celebrated by the journal on their anniversaries.[175] The founders of the journal did not bother about Arab opinion when they celebrated Selim I's conquest of Egypt in Cairo.[176] Similarly, *Türk* launched a subscription campaign aimed at "the restoration of Sinan Pasha's tomb in Turkish architectural style" and succeeded in collecting a handsome sum.[177]

These examples unquestionably prove that no other group, including the coalition, could vie with *Türk* in promoting a version of Turkish nationalism that was extreme by the standards of the early years of the twentieth century. From an intellectual viewpoint, however, a more interesting matter was the journal's focus on race and its promotion of a Turkish nationalism based on it. Yusuf Akçura's submission of his famous article "Üç Tarz-ı Siyaset" (Three Political Systems)[178] to *Türk* was particularly significant, since he was on the editorial board of *Şûra-yı Ümmet* and had written all his earlier articles for the latter.[179] Although Akçura wanted *Türk* to pay more attention to the Turks living outside the Ottoman Empire, and criticized it for the lack of such a focus,[180] the article nevertheless fits hand in glove with the publication policy of *Türk*, which promoted an extreme Turkish nationalism. This fact was brilliantly pointed out by Georgeon:

> En fait, avec ce nouveau terme, Akçura veut caractériser une réalité nouvelle. Les termes utilisés traditionnellement pour distinguer l'élément turc, définissent les Turcs comme un genre (*cins*), un peuple (*kavim*) d'un ensemble qui est la nation islamique (*ümmet*). Par ırk, Akçura veut désigner un ensemble ethnique turc considéré en lui-même et non pas seulement par référence à l'islam.[181]

The significance of Yusuf Akçura's path-breaking article has been likened to that of the *Communist Manifesto* for the Marxists.[182] Akçura asserted that there were three alternatives before the Ottoman administration—Pan-Ottomanism, Panislamism, and Panturkism—and that the best choice would be "to pursue a Turkish nationalism based on race." The publication of his article was followed by prolonged discussion. Ali Kemal and Ahmed Ferid wrote letters criticizing Akçura's views. The former criticized his essay by claiming that no such policies had in fact ever been pursued and that Akçura had constructed them by reinterpreting historical evidence in accordance with his own personal view. Ali Kemal further found all three alternatives pinpointed by Akçura to be fanciful.[183] Ahmed Ferid began his response by attacking Ali Kemal and defending Akçura in a roundabout way. He went on to criticize Akçura by asserting that the best policy for the Ottoman state was an opportunist one, using Pan-Ottomanist and Panislamist policies for its interests. He claimed that there was no such thing as a Panturkist policy; however, in the long run one would probably be brought into existence in the event that "the Pan-Ottomanist policy preserves our national existence" and "when Panislamist policy sinks into the earth and disappears."[184] Undoubtedly the most arresting passage in Ahmed Ferid's response was his confession that "the term 'Ottoman' is an expression which has recently been given a new connotation to camouflage Turkish domination."[185]

Despite these critiques, the journal itself frequently stressed the importance of race, and nationalism based on race theories was asserted as a scientific superiority:

> According to some philosophers now working on heredity theories, the differences between nations are based on organic principles; so much so that if a French child were born and grew up among the Chinese or Africans he would still remain French! Let us put the following before the eyes of those who think that they can get rid of national sorrows by bragging: If the power of easily altering natural determinants, which rule us, had been placed in our hands, Heaven forfend, the life of nations . . . would have come to an end.[186]

Spencer's recommendation to the Japanese, advising them to eschew marriage with the Europeans in order to preserve their racial purity, was praised by the journal for similar reasons[187]—likewise the criticisms of "ignorant ulema" written by *jadidists*,[188] and articles avowing the impossibility of Pan-Ottomanism,[189] undoubtedly aimed at discrediting policies that could be seen as rivals to Turkish nationalism.

As might be expected, the journal showed great interest in underscoring the brotherhood of various Turkic groups, and Turkishness based on race was presented as a common bond:

> Placing Turkishness under the veil of oblivion, they proudly say that they are Tatars. We have met a couple of Muslims from the Crimea and the Caucasus and observed this regrettable attitude. Today a Pole, however, never overlooks his origins and his race. He always haughtily says that he is a Pole rather than a Russian [subject]. Is it the case that the past of the Tatars is less [glorious] than that of the Poles? The progenitors of the present-day Tatars distributed the conquered land to the vanquished owners, these Cossacks, on condition that tribute was paid to them.[190]

> Currently some learned Azerbaijanis comprehend that they are racially Turkish, and that sectarian differences, such as those between the Sunni and Shī'īte sects, had been widened in former times by Muslim rulers who intended to use them as tools for partisan maneuvers to serve their political ends.

> Therefore, they have attempted to alleviate the sectarian tensions among the people and have rolled up their sleeves to enlighten Azerbaijani Turks, concentrating on their national consciousness. Even the emergence of this much national consciousness among the Azerbaijani Turks has vexed some enlightened and educated Persians. They have started to claim that the Azerbaijani people are racially not Turkish but Persian![191]

The responses by readers of the journal made it clear that the ideas promoted had made quite an impact on them. Letters from "Young Tatars similar to the Young Turks" are also full of fierce criticism of the ulema.[192] Another Tatar letter demonstrates that *Türk*'s advocacy of Social Darwinism had made a strong impact.[193] With the exception of a polemic about Azerbaijani history that took place between the journal and Hüseyinzâde Ali, one of the first members of the CUP at the Royal Medical Academy,[194] the journal, in a short time, succeeded in establishing cordial relations with prominent intellectual figures of the Turkic world. Even while criticizing Hüseyinzâde Ali, the editors emphasized that "they did not exclude Tatars from the Turk[ish world] . . . and considered all the Turks in the entire world as brothers."[195]

Türk also paid great attention to linguistics, adopting a more radical course than the organ of the coalition in this field. To begin with, *Türk* asserted that Turkish was the most superior and advanced Oriental language;[196] when a letter was received criticizing some Young Turks for publishing articles in French and recommending that the Young Turks should employ only Arabic and Turkish,[197] one of the co-editors responded that their motto had been "we are Turkish, what we need is the Turkish language."[198] In addition, articles encouraging the purification of the Turkish language frequently appeared in the journal.[199] This radical attitude prompted Arminius Vámbéry to send a letter to the editor hailing his and his friends' efforts, recalling that when he had written his first articles in *Ceride-i Havâdis* a long time before, those who advocated the purification of the Turkish language had been mocked and ridiculed.[200] Many letters sent by readers supported the policy of purification; they presented Mehmed Emin's Turkish nationalist poems as the best products of this approach.[201] The journal further made two significant points in this field. The first was the importance of creating a standard Turkish to bond the Turkic peoples together:

> The reemergence of this dominant nation's language (which ranges from the borders of China to Bukhara, Khiva, Afghanistan, the province of Tabrīz in Persia, Kurdistan, Asia Minor, European Turkey, and Russia) with its present-day eloquence and perfection as the language of a civilized nation in Transoxania, its place of origin, can be considered a sign of awakening. It is an illustrious product of patriotism and holds out hope for cohesion and the ideal of solidarity rather than merely being a matter to be proud of.[202]

The second point was the importance of language as the dominant nation's device to maintain its hold on the various parts of the empire. We read:

> During the times of the former khedives the official gazette of the Egyptian government was published in the Turkish language. The late Mehmed Ali and İsmail Pashas promoted the propagation of our language and devoted time to increasing the currency of the mother tongue that they brought from their fatherland. This enthusiasm, this display of zeal, did not last too long. The initial tenacity gradually slackened. Finally, [subsequent Egyptian leaders] endeavored to find means to suppress morally a Turkish sovereignty, which had already disappeared materially, by abolishing our language in order to make our many compatriots residing in Egypt forget their origins.[203]

With regard to relations among the various peoples of the empire, the journal was highly critical of the non-Turkish ethnic groups, and this criticism gave rise to prolonged debates. *Türk* published special articles to address various Ottoman ethnic and religious groups. For instance, it warned the Armenians that they would damage their own interests[204] and render service only to the Western imperial powers if they continued their separatist activities.[205] *Türk* further stated that the struggle of the Armenians against the Turks with the help of radical Europeans would fail.[206] Later it used even stronger language, inviting Turks to boycott Armenian goods in an attempt to imitate the Indian boycott of British goods. The journal wrote:

> Why can we not do it? Why should we bow before these Armenians, who make us a laughingstock though we never deserve it? The fortunes that they have made, the arts that they have mastered all arise from the fact that they have lived at our expense. Let us display zeal, let us roll up our sleeves. Do not have any kind of relationship with the Armenians, and the number of our merchants and artisans will increase as a natural consequence.[207]

In an open letter addressed to the Jews, the journal stressed that "among the people of the world that have experienced suffering, injustice, and oppression, the Jews may perhaps come first," and it made the recommendation that "they [Jews living in the Ottoman Empire] should disseminate in their schools and in their homes the idea of a common interest with the Ottomans and Muslims."[208] The interesting point is that instead of appealing simultaneously to all components of the Ottoman population, the journal preferred to address them separately and from a Turkish viewpoint. Similarly, the journal made a point of avoiding the term "Macedonia," which was also banned by the sultan,[209] and replaced the expression *salade macédoine* with *Young Turk salad*, offering this dish at a banquet given on the 607th anniversary of the establishment of the Ottoman Empire.[210]

Regarding the Muslim elements of the empire, a debate between *al-Manār* and *Türk* provides insights. Years before the publication of *Türk*, Rashīd Riḍā had authored articles on relations between the Turks and the Arabs in *al-Manār*. In these articles Rashīd Riḍā commented on the caliphate, praised the Arabs, supported Abdülhamid II's "Islamist" policy, and finally criticized the Young Turks.[211] Şerafeddin Mağmumî, who made strongly Turkist remarks regarding the caliphate, belatedly responded to Rashīd Riḍā:

> It is the Arabs who see themselves as the natural candidates for assuming the caliphate. Arguing that the prophet comes from their lineage, that the Holy *Qur'ān* is written in their language, and invoking the Arab civilization that flourished after [they had accepted] Islam, they hold that to possess the caliphate is their true right. Above all they envy the Ottoman Turks, who had adopted Islam six or seven centuries ago, and never accept that they have produced caliphs. . . . In my opinion all these causes are without foundation, all these claims are baseless, and all these remarks are unjust. The *sharī'a*, intellect, and logic all dictate that the caliphate ought to be in the hands of that nation among the Muslims which is the most civilized, the strongest, and the most capable of withstanding attacks and encroachments from outside. If so, let us take a look at all of them: Can we identify any nation other than the Ottomans [Turks] who possess these characteristics? Never. . . . That the Christian world, even the Americans, have pestered the Turks and sought endless excuses to inflict harm on the Turks can be explained by the fact that Turks are the greatest and strongest pillar of Islam. For this reason all the blows aimed at Islam because of [Christian] fanaticism fall on Turkish heads. The responsibilities of the caliphate are not being discharged properly and as required. Sure enough. If there is someone who can do a better job, let him come forward. He should, however, prove himself in deeds, not in words. In such a case the Ottomans [Turks] are ready to turn over the holy relics immediately and to retire to their own corner of leisure. But the government [you say] is preventing the Yemenis, the Syrians, and the Iraqis from acting freely. But here are Moroccans, et cetera, et cetera. Do they not have a free hand?[212]

Al-Manār responded swiftly, refuting the claims put forth by *Türk* and warning the Young Turks that their attitude would be "the cause of an unnecessary rift among the Muslim rulers."[213] The language of the prominent Egyptian journal was in fact ambiguous. It claimed that Syrians and Egyptians had no claim to the caliphate and that those who made such assertions composed a small group of people receiving money from Istanbul and Cairo; yet when it came to the situation in Yemen, it commented that the Yemenis had been incited to rebellion by the oppression of Turkish rule and that had they not been ruled unjustly they would not have revolted. The journal based its claim that the Arabs were unjustly treated and therefore became rebellious on the "experiences of Muḥammad Bāshā 'Abd al-Wahhāb and the late Kawākibī." It branded the article that had been published in *Türk* as a "political" and not a religious one, and it further stated that it was not the Young Turk journal's claim but the *ḥadīth* related to this issue that was sound. From a religious viewpoint, *al-Manār* recommended that the Turks should choose and if necessary train someone from the tribe of Quraysh.

The journal further asserted that the Young Turk who had written the article knew well that the power of which he was so proud derived not only from Turks but also from the Arabs, the Kurds, the Albanians, and the other Muslim groups of the empire. Finally *al-Manār* stated that the Turks did not mention the title of caliph during their earlier conquests.[214] In addition to this criticism, a Syrian sent a letter directly to the editor of *Türk*, deprecating the claims made by Şerafeddin Mağmumî.[215] *Türk* now carried an open letter in response to Rashīd Riḍā's journal,[216] and another refuting its Syrian critic.[217] Thereupon *al-Manār* further castigated *Türk* on the pretext of chiding Khalīl al-Maṭrān, the editor of the journal *al-Jawā'ib*, who had accused both journals of instigating a problem but had come down in favor of the Young Turk opinion.[218]

A second refutation published by *Türk* emphasized that Islam had been protected by the Turks.[219] In addition, the journal published a follow-up article accusing Rashīd Riḍā of being anti-Turkish.[220] This long debate made it clear that the intellectuals in charge of this journal viewed the world through the tinted lenses of Turkish nationalism, and they suggested that a union even among the Muslim nations of the Ottoman Empire was unattainable. As was stated by Arminius Vámbéry, the single European intellectual who underscored the importance of this debate, this was an early but clear example of a series of controversial polemics between the Arab and Turkish nationalists:

> A periodical has recently appeared under the name of *Turk* [*Türk*], which in eloquent language preaches the necessity of national awakening, glorifying the founders of the Ottoman Empire, and placing the Turkish tribe even above the tribe of the Prophet—*i.e.*, the Arabs. All this is evident from the polemics between the Turkish paper, the *Turk* [*Türk*], and the Arab periodical *Al Monar* [*al-Manār*], appearing in Cairo. Such a controversy would formerly have been regarded as blasphemous, but now it has an elevating effect on the Moslem people.[221]

In the same vein, although *Türk* gladly informed its readership of the Japanese emperor's alleged conversion to Islam following the Japanese victory over Russia,[222] it strongly opposed Abdullah Cevdet's idea of offering the caliphate to the Japanese emperor,[223] on the grounds that the caliphate ought to be in the hands of the Turks.[224]

Türk also took a strongly critical stance against the pamphlet of Negib Azoury [Najīb 'Azūrī] entitled *Le réveil de la Nation arabe dans l'Asie turque*, and his purported organization Ligue de la Patrie Arabe.[225] Although many Young Turk journals did not even bother to answer the claims put forward by Azoury and his fictitious committee,[226] *Türk* participated in the campaign launched against Azoury and his ideas. In order to make the criticism appear more solid and less biased, *Türk* published a translation of a letter written by an Ottoman Arab attacking Azoury which had previously appeared in *al-Liwā'*.[227]

Another interesting aspect of the publication policy of *Türk* was its focus on modernization. As was later to be claimed by the modern Turkish republic, the journal maintained that in the Orient no ethnic group other than the Turks could modernize its society.[228] This ethnic entity, referred to in the journal as "the noble Turkish people," had been striving toward this end for two centuries, and there was no reason for even momentary skepticism about its future attainments.[229] As might be expected, *Türk* extolled pre-Ottoman Turkish customs. For example, with regard to the role that was to be played by women in a modern society, the journal commented that in times past, before the Turks had become acquainted with Islam, there had been women warriors among them, and that it was still possible to find such women warriors among Turcoman tribes "who are not purged of their Central Asian customs and have maintained our primal national virtues."[230] The significance of this attitude is that here for the first time a direct link was conceived between nationalism and modernization, a link which would later become a pillar of Turkish nationalism.

A further original approach of the journal was its strong criticism of all Western powers. Unlike many former CUP organs, *Türk* disparaged all the Western imperial powers without exception. Great Britain received the brunt of this criticism. The journal found Britain's policies toward the Eastern Question and toward the Orient to be extremely anti-Turkish.[231] The journals of Turkic groups living under Russian rule republished these criticisms, thus effecting an even wider impact.[232] At the same time *Türk* castigated the other Great Powers, such as the German Empire and the Dual Monarchy, in an attempt to demonstrate that all the Western Great Powers were imperialistic and were the enemies of the "Turkish nation."[233]

Although the Ottoman government took standard measures against the publication and distribution of the journal, it did not make the intense efforts it devoted to suppressing the coalition's organ, and in fact *Türk* faced very little pressure.[234] Despite similarities in their rhetoric,[235] the journal had disputes with the coalition and its organ. Ali Fahri, a leader of the "activists," strongly denounced Ali Kemal and described his articles in the journal as "articles reminding people of the Istanbul press of the old days."[236] *Türk* complained about the abundance of its foes by referring to the activists in the coalition.[237] In addition, later both sides accused each other of mendacity when commenting on an alleged corruption case regarding the purchase of a mansion by Gazi Ahmed Muhtar Pasha.[238] The CPU characterized *Türk* to new members of the organization as a "commercial journal being published under the protection of Ahmed Muhtar Pasha . . . whose title is *Gazi*."[239] Despite these disputes and accusations, however, no comparison can be made from an organizational viewpoint between the intellectuals who published *Türk* and the coalition; and the journal always had the disadvantage of being a political opposition journal without the support of any significant political society.

The members of the editorial board of *Türk* were not by any means unanimous in their support of the nationalist line, however. In November 1905 a strong disagreement surfaced, and those favoring the nationalist line left the journal.[240] Hüseyin Âlî, who now became editor, altered the publication policy without delay and published a petition to the sultan very similar to those that had previously been published by the old CUP organs.[241] This change, however, had such a negative impact on the readership that in June 1906 Hüseyin Âlî was forced to restore the journal to the former nationalist editorial board.[242] The members of this board described all these events as follows:

> We were saying that our affection and regard for Islam are complete; however, our century was a century of revolution. . . . Therefore, we could not make our journal merely a religious organ, we should not do so, and we could not adopt an explicitly religious rhetoric in our articles. . . . We should in any event devote our writings to the moral and

material progress of the Turkish world. What should we do, how should we work, that the Turks might never remain behind foreigners and Europeans in the struggle for survival? . . . These comments of ours were abhorred by some of our friends. They tried to find the remedy to all our grievances in attributing triumph in the struggle for survival to Islam. . . . They could not find it, however, and in the end they have become worn out and withdrawn. Once again it is our turn.[243]

This statement can be considered the first sign of the bitter struggle that was to take place between Islamists and Turkists during the second constitutional period. The journal again promoted Turkish nationalism and now adopted a more critical attitude toward religion.[244] Meanwhile, the lack of support from a political organization and the financial difficulties stemming from this caused further problems for the editorial board.[245] As a final attempt, Mahir Sa'id tried to establish sound relations with Sabahaddin Bey. Expressions of appreciation for Edmond Demolins's ideas[246] and praise for Sabahaddin Bey clearly show this effort.[247] It was, however, almost impossible to reconcile nationalism with Sabahaddin Bey's ideas of decentralization. Thus *Türk* disappeared from the scene in November 1907,[248] after making a significant impact on the development of Turkish nationalist ideology.

The Young Turks in the Balkans

During this period Ali Fehmi, the editor of the journal *Muvazene* (*The Balance*), published in Bulgaria, continued to carry out the most important Young Turk publication activity in the Balkans. At the 1902 Congress, Ali Fehmi had declared himself an impartial delegate and had done his best to remain so. He certainly had a liking for the anti-interventionist group; however, he could not join any faction in the movement openly, because the struggle among the factions in Paris, Geneva, and Cairo did not extend to the Balkans, and he wished to retain the support of all sympathizers.

His journal's "open letters" section reveals that he was corresponding with leaders belonging to various groups. These included Edhem Ruhi and Behzad [Mehmed Cemil], who were working for the assassination plot on behalf of the Ottoman Union and Revolution Committee; Kırımîzâde Ali Rıza, a representative of İbrahim Temo, the original founder of the CUP; Talât Bey, who was Ahmed Rıza's man in the Balkans; and various activists, such as Abdurrahman Bedirhan, Mahir Sa'id, and Hikmet Süleyman.[249] Similarly, *Muvazene* indiscriminately recommended *Osmanlı* and *Şûra-yı Ümmet* to its readers.[250] In order to underscore his impartiality, Ali Fehmi declared that his journal was "an independent gazette which did not belong to any domestic [Bulgarian] or foreign party."[251] Many readers in the region therefore addressed the journal as an "impartial" one, and *Muvazene* became the voice of all the Young Turk sympathizers in the Balkans.[252] The fugitive Ottoman schoolteachers who were tutoring at various secular Muslim schools in Bulgaria helped Ali Fehmi to carry his message to the Muslims there.[253]

Despite his prudence in avoiding issues involved in the internal factional struggle among the various Young Turk groups, Ali Fehmi made a point of republishing only Turkist articles that had appeared in Young Turks journals.[254] The journal's own publication policy was very similar to those of the coalition and *Türk*. Ali Fehmi claimed that "the reform of European Turkey means giving up the Edirne, Salonica, Iōánnina, and Monastir provinces of Turkey."[255] The fierce letters published in *Muvazene* that advised "protecting our values against the Europeans,"[256] and the recommendation made by the journal to the Albanian journals that "their journals' impact and weight would be increased should they publish a part of them in Turkish,"[257] demonstrate that this main Young Turk journal in the Balkans was on the same track as the coalition organ and by no means supported the efforts of the "majority." *Muvazene* also continued to criticize the conservative Muslim groups in the Balkans who remained loyal to the sultan.[258]

In order to prevent Ali Fehmi from publishing, the Ottoman representative in Varna filed a lawsuit on the grounds that the journal was guilty of "employing insolent language against the sultan," and the Bulgarian police then interrogated the editor.[259] Later Ali Fehmi moved his journal to Plovdiv, publishing the 263rd issue of *Muvazene* there on January 21, 1903.[260] The Turkist line adopted by the journal caused its editor to face violent attacks from Bulgarian and Macedonian nationalists. In March 1905 the building in which *Muvazene* had been published was set on fire by members of the Vŭrkhovist Committee.[261] Following this incident, the Bulgarian authorities deported Ali Fehmi; however, his brother Mehmed Sabri, with the help of Yunus Reşid and Talha Kemalî, started to publish the journal *Ahali* (*People*), the first issue of which appeared on April 9, 1905, in order to replace *Muvazene*.[262] The Bulgarian police arrested Mehmed Sabri and declared that they would not tolerate the publication of *Muvazene* under any title.[263] Moreover, Yunus Reşid was severely beaten by the Vŭrkhovist Committee members and hospitalized, while Talha Kemalî left town for Pazardzhik and became an elementary school teacher there.

The Bulgarian government also tried Mehmed Sabri and the contributors to the journal in a local court. In the trial, which lasted for eight months, the prosecutor accused them of "stirring up the subjects of the Bulgarian Principality" and of "trying to bring about foreign [Ottoman] intervention in Bulgarian domestic affairs."[264] At the end of the trial the court acquitted Mehmed Sabri. He and his two comrades, Yunus Reşid, who had recovered from his beating, and Talha Kemalî, who had returned to Plovdiv, succeeded in publishing the second issue of *Ahali* on November 4, 1906.[265] Meanwhile Ali Fehmi decided to join the Young Turks in Geneva, where he published the 374th issue of *Muvazene*;[266] however, failing to continue his publication in Switzerland, he went to Ṭūr Sīnā.[267] He later traveled to Afghanistan with his seven comrades[268] and engaged in "Panturkist" activities there.[269] During his time in Afghanistan as an advisor to the Afghan Ministry of Finance, he regularly corresponded with the CPU, and later the CUP central committee, and kept them informed of his activities.[270]

Although Ali Fehmi was in effect supporting the cause of the "minority" in the Balkans through his publication, Ahmed Rıza told one of his followers in Bulgaria, Talât Bey, to take the initiative toward the establishment of a new network in the Balkans. In his response to the positivist leader, however, Talât Bey gave a gloomy account of the situation in the Balkans. He wrote:

> The situation in Bulgaria has drastically changed. Especially in Ruse, with the exception of two or three individuals, everyone has turned away from us. . . . In sum, there had once been thirty, thirty-five people who openly worked [for us]; but nowadays it is not possible to find more than three individuals. Besides, each of these three defends a different idea.

Those in Ruse are fine. In Lom there is no one other than Şükrü Haşmet and İsmail Yürükov, who would do anything. You know about Plovdiv; there are also zealous and patriotic fellows in Varna and Dobruja. They, however, have commercial relations with Istanbul, and this hinders them from operating openly.

In some of the other towns there may be one or two individuals who might develop an interest in reading the newspapers, but it would be impossible to find anyone who would take part in committee activities. The reason why I provide all this information is to respond to your request, which you had put as "Please inform me if it is possible to establish a strong branch in Bulgaria." . . . Forget about a strong one today; it would be inconceivable even to establish a weak branch which would operate smoothly.[271]

The "majority" of the 1902 Congress engaged in high politics and made no effort to establish organizations in the Balkans. The only events worth mentioning were the activities of a person who introduced himself as İsmail Kemal. He toured many cities in Bulgaria, delivered speeches as if he were the Albanian statesman, and succeeded in deluding many Muslims.[272] Local Young Turks first protested the situation and claimed that it was a trick of Bulgarian and Macedonian committees.[273] They later discovered the real identity of the individual and made it public that he was Khristo Khristov, a former Muslim who had converted to Christianity a year before and was now working for the aforementioned committees.[274] The Ottoman government, which was more annoyed by these events than were the local Young Turks, dispatched two intelligence officers to Bulgaria.[275] After a secret bargain was struck, the Bulgarians handed over Khristov to the Ottoman intelligence service.[276]

Less significant was the publication activity carried out in Bulgaria by Mustafa Ragıb, who had played an important role in Young Turk activities in the Balkans and had represented the old CUP organization.[277] Mustafa Ragıb started publishing a journal called *Efkâr-ı Umumiye* (*Public Opinion*). The pressure applied by the Ottoman Commissioner in Bulgaria forced him to halt his publication for a while and join the group that was corresponding with the leaders of the coalition.[278] He employed a Turkist rhetoric in his journal during its early days.[279] Later he received financial aid and editorial support from Shahin Kolonja, the editor of the Albanian nationalist journal *Drita* (*The Light*) in Sofia,[280] and he restarted the publication of his journal in Bulgarian and Turkish.[281] The journal devoted many of its pages to articles on Albanian affairs[282] and published Albanian nationalist studies.[283] This new initiative compelled the Ottoman Commissioner in Sofia to summon Mustafa Ragıb and ask him to return to the empire.[284] The Ottoman Commissioner, Sadık el-Müeyyed Pasha, recommended that the Ottoman government grant amnesty to Mustafa Ragıb and appoint him to a position in the empire "to prevent him becoming a tool in the conspiracies of Shahin [Kolonja]."[285] But the Ottoman government did not follow this recommendation, and Mustafa Ragıb initiated a new bilingual journal in Bulgarian and Turkish and spearheaded a new committee, both named *Feryad* (*Cry*). The central committee of this organization included Mustafa Ragıb, Doctor Rıza, Ali İhsan, who had recently fled from the empire, and a Bulgarian medical doctor.[286] The committee solicited the help of İbrahim Temo, the leader of the Young Turk movement in the Balkans.[287]

An Ottoman military intelligence officer who investigated Mustafa Ragıb and his activities claimed that he had become a tool in the hands of the Vŭrkhovist Committee and had also published a Turkish journal named *Şark* under their auspices. According to this officer, both *Feryad* and *Şark* were distributed by the Vŭrkhovist Committee members, and the articles published in Bulgarian in *Feryad* aimed at a rapprochement between Bulgarians and Muslims living in Bulgaria.[288]

The so-called Feryad Committee had clear "activist" tendencies. For instance, it was claimed that "married individuals absolutely cannot become members of [their] activist committee."[289] The journal also adopted strongly Islamist language, published *fatwā*s against the sultan,[290] and criticized foreign intervention.[291]

Mustafa Ragıb's close association with the Bulgarian revolutionaries prevented him from receiving a warm response from the Muslims in Bulgaria.[292] He therefore published in his journal a committee decision averring that somehow the executive committee members had not seen the note reading "published at the Publishing House of Şark" at the foot of their journal. He further stated that his committee had no ties or relationship with the society publishing the journal *Şark*.[293] He later stopped providing a Bulgarian supplement and published his journal only in Turkish, levying strong nationalist charges against *Şark,* which was published under the auspices of the Macedo-Bulgarian revolutionaries.[294] In the meantime the Ottoman government appealed to its Bulgarian counterpart and requested the deportation of Mustafa Ragıb.[295] Despite all the measures taken by the Ottoman government and its commissioner in Bulgaria, however, Mustafa Ragıb refused to yield.[296] As a final attempt, the Ottoman authorities tried and sentenced Mustafa Ragıb *in contumaciam*, and he continued his unimportant publication activity in Bulgaria until the Bulgarian authorities deported him.[297]

While these events were taking place in Bulgaria, the main center of Young Turk activities in the Balkans, there were striking developments in Bosnia-Hercegovina, which was not a hotbed of the Young Turk movement.

The Austro-Hungarian diplomats, who constantly examined the articles in *Mechveret Supplément Français*, especially its comments on the Bosnian Muslims, decided to take advantage of the Young Turk movement to ruin relations between the sultan and the Bosnian Muslim leaders.[298] According to Austro-Hungarian documents, along with Dervishbeg Miralem, who had close ties with the Young Turks, many notables of Travnik were working for the Young Turk cause. A police report further reveals that one of the religious leaders of the Bosnian Muslim movement, Ali Fehmi Džabić, had relations with Abdullah Cevdet. Austro-Hungarian diplomats sketched out a plan according to which an article was to be published in *Le Figaro*, or in another prominent daily which was read at the Yıldız Palace, about the relations between Džabić and the Young Turk leaders.[299] Another Austro-Hungarian statesman proposed that it was a better idea to make the Young Turks publish such an article in *Mechveret Supplément Français*. He thought that it would be necessary to engineer this in order to establish contacts with the editorial board members of the French supplement, and to make all possible concessions to them.[300] Later Beni Kállay von Nagy Kállay, Reichsfinanzminister, informed Hugo von Kutschera, Civil Adlus, that he had found a way to publish such an article and that it would contain remarks against the Austro-Hungarian administration.[301] They were not able to carry out their plan, however.[302]

Austro-Hungarian documents further underscore Young Turk activities among the Bosnian Muslims. In one of his notes Kállay instructed officials to extradite the Young

Turk agents immediately, to refuse to allow them to have contact with the Muslims, and to demand some kind of compensation from the Ottoman Palace in return for their deportation.[303] A list enclosed with a manuscript prepared by a Young Turk provides us with the names of notables with whom the Young Turks had established contacts. The names of two prominent Hercegovinian notables stand out: Salih Efendi Alaybegović of Mostar and Ragib Bey Džinić of Banja Luka.[304] The Bosnian Muslims' lack of a political organization until 1906, however, prevented the Young Turks from becoming more active in the region, and their efforts were limited to collecting donations and distributing their journals. We shall see later how sounder relations between the Young Turks and the Bosnian Muslims were established following the foundation of the Muslimanska Narodna Organizacija in 1906.[305]

The two other countries in which the Young Turks were quite active during the period were Romania and Greece.

In Romania the conservative Muslims of Dobruja organized a demonstration to protest the participation of Sheikh Şevki Celâleddin in the 1902 Congress.[306] Following the rally, they presented a petition signed by 500 Muslims to the Ottoman consul in Constanţa.[307] Meanwhile the Ottoman Ministry of Justice filed a lawsuit against Sheikh Şevki Celâleddin.[308] In response the local Young Turks organized a secret meeting with all theYoung Turk leaders in Romania, together with Ali Fehmi, the editor of *Muvazene*, who traveled to Constanţa to join it.[309] The Young Turks further met with Armenian Revolutionary Committee leaders and discussed the formation of a common front.[310] Finally they founded a society named Cemiyet-i İslâmiye (The Islamic Society), under the leadership of Kırımîzâde Ali Rıza, which met with similar criticisms from conservative Muslims.[311] At the same time the Ottoman government requested its Romanian counterpart to treat the Young Turks as anarchists. The Romanians, despite their refusal of the Ottoman demand, promised that no Young Turk activities would be tolerated on Romanian soil. The undersecretary of the Romanian Foreign Ministry implied to von Kiderlen-Wächter, the German chargé d'affaires, that the delay in signing the Ottoman–Romanian commercial convention derived from the bargain on the Young Turks.[312] This secret agreement between the two governments meant that Young Turk activities in Romania had to be covert. In order to obtain support from the main Young Turk organizations and discuss prospective activities in the Balkans, İbrahim Temo traveled to Europe in late 1902 and met with the leaders of the two dominant fronts.[313]

In Greece the unorganized Young Turks increased their activities, especially in 1903, and published two journals. *Osmanlı* (*3*) was published by two activists, Fuad and Sadeddin Beys, who had come to Athens from Geneva; it adopted a radical line, even criticizing the Ottoman royal house.[314] The Ottoman government then put pressure on its Greek counterpart, and the two activists were forced to leave Greece for Alexandria in September 1903.[315] The second journal, *Islahat* (*Reform*), defended the Turkist cause.[316] Neither journal, however, lasted long.

The increased Young Turk activities in Greece caused the Ottoman government to dispatch additional intelligence agents to that country.[317] The Ottoman embassy, on the other hand, gave no credit to the Young Turks, whose aim was to extort money from the government.[318] In 1903 the Greek Prime Minister Rallis accepted the Ottoman demand for the extradition of the Young Turks who were active in Greece.

The German diplomats, however, in commenting on this, made it very clear that the Greek gesture was not sincere. In fact, one of the Young Turks, Hasan Rıf'at, aware of this insincerity, sent a letter to Rallis saying that "should the Greek government meet his travel expenses to Paris, he would gladly leave Greece."[319]

In addition to the Young Turk activities in Bulgaria and Greece, the ventures of Yaşar Sadık Erebera, who had participated in the 1902 Congress as a representative of the Balkan Young Turks, annoyed the Ottoman government. Erebera promoted both Young Turk ideas and Albanian nationalism in Serbia. In 1904 the Ottoman ambassador to Serbia reached a secret agreement with the private secretary of the Serbian king. According to this deal, the sultan was to grant an imperial pardon to the three Montenegrins previously arrested within the Ottoman Empire, and in return the Serbian government was to expel Erebera.[320]

In general it can be said that the Young Turks in the Balkans were far from carrying out any activity of importance, despite their efforts. This failure was undoubtedly due to the lack of strong organizational support from a well-organized committee.

Activities in the Empire

Following the 1902 Congress, the palace launched an open attack on the Young Turks. As we have seen, the dailies and *Ceride-i Mahakim-i Adliye* published the verdicts pronounced by kangaroo courts.[321] The government also applied extremely strict measures in order to prevent the Young Turks from having contacts with foreign diplomats. The intelligence service scrutinized even tourists, and the police confiscated all publishing materials on the grounds that these might be used by the Young Turks. In addition, the Ottoman authorities arrested many suspected individuals and took all possible precautions against the distribution of the journals and pamphlets published in Europe, Egypt, and Bulgaria.[322] As one diplomat commented:

> In view of the fact that the Turkish Government is opposed to meetings and gatherings of crowds of all kinds, frequently stopping small parties or dances when their own subjects were concerned, it is quite possible that were I to ask for permission, it would be either refused or the answer delayed indefinitely (which is generally their polite way of refusing).[323]

These strict measures not only were aimed at preventing the "majority" group of the Young Turks, who sought a coup d'état with the help of the Great Powers, from having contacts with foreign diplomats, but also stemmed from the government's discovery of a plan for a military coup.

According to İzzet Bey, one of the sultan's private secretaries and confidants, the intelligence service arrested Nâzım Pasha and many young officers who were accused of plotting against the regime.[324] Nâzım Pasha further revealed that Fuad Pasha, a leading military commander, was involved in the venture. İzzet Bey also told Marshall von Bieberstein that seditious proclamations had been found among the military divisions in Yemen.[325] The apprehension of officers in Yemen, who were accused of having corresponded with the Young Turks in Europe, confirms İzzet Bey's account,[326] and Fuad Pasha later confessed the existence of a well-organized committee.[327] A court martial chaired by Rauf Pasha tried Fuad Pasha and found him guilty on all counts.[328] Also many officers, including Nâzım Pasha, and a large number of Royal Military Academy cadets were banished. The disaffection in the army continued,[329] but the swift action taken by the palace did not allow the military sympathizers of the Young Turks to embark on new ventures.

Although foreign dailies portrayed these events as a "formidable armed uprising on the part of the Young Turks,"[330] the relations between the military adventurers and the main Young Turk groups in Europe were weak. Malaspina di Carbonara, the Italian ambassador to the Ottoman Empire, depicted the venture as a coup attempt aimed at the enthronement of the heir apparent, Reşad Efendi. He further underscored the arrest of the bankers, who sold gold to the heir apparent, and the apprehension of Damad Mahmud Pasha's sympathizers and friends in Istanbul. According to Malaspina di Carbonara, the sultan had told the Russian ambassador, Zinoviev, who had conveyed a personal message from the tzar requesting an imperial pardon for Fuad Pasha, that "Fuad Pasha [had given] weapons to his enemies."[331] Fuad Pasha presented the events as a plot against his person in the detailed petition which he succeeded in conveying to British authorities.[332] The French ambassador underscored the extremely exaggerated character of the intelligence reports that accused Fuad Pasha.[333] Similarly a French military attaché, who also praised Nâzım Pasha, depicted Fuad Pasha in his diaries as a person who was "absolument incapable de fomenter une révolution quelconque."[334] Furthermore the central organ *Osmanlı* commented on the events as if they were totally apolitical and, after criticizing Fuad Pasha by saying "we were and are not among those who appreciated Fuad Pasha," praised his very courageous action against the intelligence officers during his arrest.[335]

The verdict pronounced by the court martial was proclaimed after Fuad Pasha's banishment.[336] One of the sons of the pasha, İslâm Bey, applied to Paul Cambon, who had become the French ambassador to Great Britain, asking the latter to secure British help.[337] Cambon asked Delcassé to do something through the French embassy in Istanbul. This attempt, however, bore no fruit,[338] and when the palace received information about a second petition by the two sons of Fuad Pasha, presented to the Austrian ambassador, the intelligence service immediately apprehended them.[339] They were later dismissed from the army and exiled to Diyar-ı Bekir.[340] British documents reveal that 32 individuals, including two officials working in the First Chamberlain's office, were banished along with the sons of the pasha.[341] Likewise Nâzım Pasha secretly applied to the British from his exile in Erzincan, asking their help in saving his papers from being seized by the intelligence service.[342]

In summary, the stillborn coup plan of the officers had very little to do with the Young Turk organizations abroad, despite many of the low-ranking officers' sympathy toward the movement. The palace capitalized on the event to eliminate its opponents within the army.

Strict measures against the Young Turks continued after Fuad Pasha's case was closed. A main reason was that the new Grand Vizier, Mehmed Ferid Pasha (Vlorë), favored strong precautions against all possible Young Turk attempts.[343] Therefore very little organizational work could be done within the empire during the period, apart from smuggling in Young Turk propaganda. The activists had proudly announced before the 1902 Congress that they had "succeeded in forming a body that would distribute" Young Turk publications.[344] Most likely, publications, *Şûra-yı Ümmet* being foremost among them, were disseminated through this channel.[345] As a result a few officials in Syria donated money and sent letters to *Mechveret Supplément Français* and *Osmanlı*.[346] The impact, however, was very limited. Sami Paşazâde Sezaî's remark that "the last place where *Şûra-yı Ümmet* made an impact was Istanbul" speaks for itself.[347] In his much criticized pamphlet, Negib Azoury published a letter addressed to him by the Comité de la Jeune Turquie à Constantinople, dated October 10, 1904.[348] Even if such a letter existed and was not a fabrication of Azoury's, we have no further information about such a committee.[349] Similar claims were made about the mission of a Young Turk who secretly entered the empire from Europe and had an interview with the *Şeyhülislâm*.[350] This too seems very unlikely. Finally, following the Young Turk Revolution of 1908, various former dissidents claimed that they had established a strong Young Turk branch in Istanbul in October 1904, with the participation of many palace dignitaries, prominent Albanians, and members of the ulema. Available sources, however, provide no information to confirm the existence of such an organization in 1904.[351] Similarly other ventures attributed to the Young Turks had in fact very little to do with the movement.[352]

The Flight of Ahmed Celâleddin Pasha

Another event of interest that took place during the period was the flight of Ahmed Celâleddin Pasha, the chief of the Ottoman intelligence service. His participation in the Young Turk movement was undoubtedly one of the most unexpected developments in its history.

As early as 1900 a German daily drew its readers' attention to the power struggle between Ahmed Celâleddin Pasha and İzzet Bey, one of the private secretaries of the sultan, and commented that one of these two favorites of the sultan was going to be dismissed.[353] İzzet Bey, who had been expected to lose the sultan's favor, in fact continued to be a strong figure in internal politics.[354] French diplomats commented that Ahmed Celâleddin Pasha had lost his prestige when he rejected the demands that the intelligence service organize a plot against the life of Damad Mahmud Pasha.[355] On February 2, 1904, Ahmed Celâleddin Pasha was summoned to the Imperial Palace and questioned by İzzet Bey, his foremost rival. On February 7, agents of the intelligence service moved to put Ahmed Celâleddin Pasha under arrest. He became aware of this matter and immediately left his mansion, taking refuge at the French embassy.[356] The French diplomats asked Affaires étrangères to instruct them about the treatment of the pasha, and then they put him aboard *Vatour*, the *stationnaire* of the French embassy in Istanbul.[357] After an adventurous voyage, which was closely scrutinized by the French authorities, he reached Egypt, where he was assumed to be more influential because his wife was a member of the Egyptian royal house.[358] The sultan made all possible promises to the pasha to make him return, but to no avail.[359] In order to impress the opponents of the regime and to threaten the sultan, the pasha's men in the Ottoman capital published a manifesto on his behalf, denouncing the regime of Abdülhamid II and recommending decentralization for the Ottoman Empire. They also sent copies of this pronouncement to the foreign ministries of the Great

Powers.[360] With this Ahmed Celâleddin Pasha started his career as a Young Turk. The coalition, which had always taken an unfavorable view of his performance, castigated his final action.[361] The remaining members of the old CUP organization, scattered around Europe and Egypt, capitalized on this development, and Ahmed Celâleddin Pasha immediately put them on his pay list.[362] The roles that he was to play in the Young Turk movement will be discussed later.

In summary, the period in question witnessed many individual attempts or ventures carried out by minor societies; these were of very little importance from an organizational viewpoint. Although the same is true for the group that published the journal *Türk* in Cairo, their significant impact on the development of Turkish nationalist ideology is indisputable.

5

Sabahaddin Bey and His Leaque of Private Initiative and Decentralization, 1905–1907

Sabahaddin Bey and *Science Sociale*

Following the so-called majority's failure in staging a coup d'état with the help of the British in 1902 and 1903, its leader, Sabahaddin Bey, assumed a low profile for almost two years. As we have seen, Edhem Ruhi and Abdullah Cevdet could not induce Sabahaddin Bey to work with them. Apparently the prince had no desire to work with members of the old CUP organization and thus adopted a wait-and-see policy before launching a new campaign against both the Ottoman government and the coalition. In the meantime he became interested in the doctrine of *Science sociale*. He later provided one of his admirers with a detailed account of his exploration of this intellectual current:

> One day I was strolling along one of the renowned streets of Paris extremely tired and very upset, when Edmond Demolins's book entitled *A quoi tient la supériorité des Anglo-Saxons* caught my eye in the window of a book shop. I immediately entered the book shop and purchased the book. That night I read the book in a single sitting. In the response given by the author to the question "What is the reason for the Anglo-Saxons' superiority?" I noted the existence of a scientific method similar to the methods of the natural sciences that I had never come across in the sociological literature. The next day I went to the same book shop and bought all the works of Edmond Demolins. Upon reading these with great attention and interest, my conviction gained strength and I became certain that these studies follow a scientific train of ideas and possess a method of observation like that of the natural sciences. In the meantime, I was honored with the friendship of the great thinker Edmond Demolins . . . and I was convinced that it was feasible to make a sociological analysis of Ottoman society and to prepare the necessary reform program.[1]

Following his discovery of a "scientific" social theory, Sabahaddin Bey urged the editor of *Osmanlı*, then being published as the organ of the "majority," to pay attention to *Science sociale* and publish articles on it. The editor, however, responded that "nobody will read such articles and our people prefer receiving information to reading scientific articles."[2]

Despite his failure to persuade his Young Turk friends of the benefits that would ensue from using the theories of Demolins in their propaganda, Sabahaddin Bey did

82

not abandon his idea of preparing a reform program based on this "scientific" method, albeit the absence of a direct and obvious link between the *Science sociale* doctrine and Ottoman politics presented a problem for him. In order to overcome it, Sabahaddin Bey decided to frame a new program based on decentralization. The *Science sociale* literature in general, and the studies of Demolins in particular, frequently pointed to decentralization as one of the main reasons for the alleged Anglo-Saxon superiority. Sabahaddin Bey authored his first detailed essay on the subject in late 1905, under the title "Historical Analysis of Turkish Progress"; Demolins's *Comment la route crée le type social* heavily influenced his argument in the essay.[3] He maintained that a westernized Turkish elite had transformed Turkish society and lifted it to a new social stage, and that now at this stage a new generation of westernized Ottoman intellectuals could solve the Eastern Question by implementing a decentralized administrative system.[4] Later Sabahaddin Bey claimed that "decentralization" would also secure political unity alongside social diversity in the Ottoman Empire.[5]

Sabahaddin Bey was clever enough to realize that although these "scientific" analyses looked impressive on paper, by themselves they could do little to help him accomplish his mission. He decided, therefore, to try to woo to his side his former allies at the 1902 Congress of Ottoman Opposition. Sabahaddin Bey's confidant Ahmed Fazlı hinted at this new tactic in a letter to a French daily:

> Vous connaissez certainement le prince Sabahaddine qui vint en France en 1899 avec son père, Mahmoud pacha et son frère. Tous trois avaient quitté Constantinople pour protester énergiquement contre le régime actuel. Depuis, Mahmoud pacha est mort sur la terre d'exil; en 1903, le frère du prince tenta un voyage en Turquie; il y fut trahi et jeté en prison.
>
> Ces épreuves n'ont pas abattu l'énergie du prince Sabahaddine, qui poursuit courageusement la lutte pour la noble cause à laquelle il s'est voué. Abandonnant sa famille, son rang, sa fortune et malgré mille tentatives pour l'amener à rentrer en Turquie, il a réussi à l'interesser aux projets des libéraux turcs des hommes politiques éminents.
>
> Mais quelles sont les réformes qui demandent les libéraux turcs?
>
> Ils veulent, en premier lieu, une large décentralisation garantissant les intérêts moraux et matériels des différentes races vivant sur le territoire de l'empire. . . .
>
> La décentralisation aura pour effet de laisser au peuple, dans chaque province, la responsabilité de son développement économique et du maintien de l'ordre public. . . .
>
> L'étude sincère et approfondie que le prince Sabahaddine, quelques amis et moi avons faite de l'évolution des idées chez les nouvelle générations turques, nous mettent en mesure d'affirmer que de telles réformes seraient le point de départ d'une rénovation complète, dont l'Europe profiterait en même temps que la Turquie.[6]

Without delay, Sabahaddin Bey drafted an open letter to the Armenians. While condemning terrorism, he invited them to common action. The tone of the letter differed distinctly from the tone of the accusations made by members of the coalition against the Armenians:

> Au lieu de se livrer à une *propagande par le fait* nos compatriots arméniens agiraient donc dans un sens beaucoup plus favorable à leurs intérêts en faisant une *propagande par l'idée* dans les milieux turcs; ils y trouveraient des oreilles attentives et des cœurs d'autant plus sensibles qu'ils sont meurtris . . . par les mêmes souffrances, et qu'ils cultivent l'espoir d'une prochaine et définitive libération.[7]

A group of Armenian nationalists, who were allegedly active in Istanbul, responded favorably. Although they noted their disagreement with some of Sabahaddin Bey's ideas, they stated the following points:

> Avec quel enthousiasme l'Europe saluerait une action commune des libéraux turcs et arméniens pour remplacer le régime despotique du pays par un gouvernement libéral digne de l'époque ou nous vivons! En Russie, l'heureuse collaboration de la race dominante et des races dominées a réussi à obliger l'autocratie de se courber devant les exigences de l'esprit moderne. Pourquoi n'en serait-il pas de même en Turquie.[8]

One of Sabahaddin Bey's highest hopes from the first day of his participation in the Young Turk movement was for an enthusiastic European response to joint Young Turk-Armenian action. Pierre Quillard, an ardent supporter of the Dashnaktsutiun, viewed the letters exchanged between Sabahaddin Bey and some Armenian students as a promising start toward cooperation, likening them to the collaboration between Russian revolutionary leaders and those of the oppressed non-Russian peoples of Russia.[9] Sabahaddin Bey, who received the press coverage and attention he desired, expressed similar views during an interview given to Dikran Elmassian, a leading Armenian figure. The two sides disagreed on many issues during the interview; however, this interview made clear that Sabahaddin Bey was the only prominent Young Turk at that time proposing joint action with Armenians.[10] Indeed, during the interview, Elmassian strongly attacked Ahmed Rıza, the leader of the coalition, accusing him of being a defender of the present regime in the Ottoman Empire.[11] The interview in fact sparked a long-lasting debate among Armenians regarding the wisdom of cooperating with the Young Turks. This was, nonetheless, the first rapprochement between prominent Young Turks and Armenians since 1903;[12] in fact when the Armenians compared the ideas of Sabahaddin Bey to those of the coalition members, they must certainly have found Sabahaddin Bey's "liberalism" preferable to the Turkism of the coalition.[13]

The Armenians' sympathetic response encouraged Sabahaddin Bey to compose a new letter. After marshaling all the political, psychological, and economic reasons allegedly compelling the Young Turks and Armenians to carry out joint activities, he proposed the ultimate goal of such an alliance: establishment of a decentralized administrative system for the Ottoman Empire:

> La décentralisation, telle que nous la concevons, exige que chacun soit absolument maître chez soi, sous la direction générale d'une politique commune. . . .
>
> Je ne doute aucunement que les intérêts particuliers des Arméniens puissent s'harmoniser d'une parfaite manière avec les intérêts généraux de l'Empire Ottoman.
>
> Déjà les symptômes d'une collaboration de plus en plus consciente des peuples opprimés de la Turquie en vue du relèvement d'une Patrie commune nous fait prévoir l'aurore d'une ère nouvelle: La fusion de l'Orient, naguère immobile, avec l'Occident progressiste![14]

Following this exchange of letters, Sabahaddin Bey, fearing a hostile reaction from the coalition and the Turkist faction of the Young Turk movement, wrote a letter to U.S. President Theodore Roosevelt in response to an appeal from 400 Armenian and European intellectuals.[15] In his letter Sabahaddin Bey strongly criticized the Europeans' confusion of the Turks with the other Muslim ethnic groups of the Ottoman Empire. He stated that it was the Kurds who had been attacking Armenian villages and added that they had harmed Turkish villages in the region as well. The solution offered by Sabahaddin Bey, undoubtedly based on the analysis of Edmond Demolins, was to compel the Kurds to develop into a *société sédentaire*.[16]

Because of this defense of the Turks, the nationalist journals ran a translation of Sabahaddin Bey's letter.[17] The most important part of the letter, however, was the comment that the Turks and the Armenians had common interests since both had suffered from the encroachments of the nomadic Kurds:

> D'ailleurs, il existe, quoi qu'en disent les Arméniens, une parfaite solidarité d'intérêts entre eux et les Turcs. Ces deux éléments forment une société de travailleurs paisibles, qui rêvent d'ordre et de paix et qui sont exposés au même danger: l'agression périodique des tribus de nomades kurdes.[18]

Attacking the Kurds enabled Sabahaddin Bey to kill two birds with one stone. He initiated a rapprochement with the Armenians, whose support he deemed essential in order to secure the Great Powers' endorsement, and at the same time he defended himself against possible attacks by members of the coalition. In his own words, Sabahaddin Bey had created and implemented a new role of "moderation" for the Turkish element of the empire:

> Les Turcs qui sont stables "compacts" forment un élément de modération, d'harmonie entre tant de populations qui se déchirent. Mais l'utilité de leur rôle social d'aujord'hui ne peut se manifester d'une façon patente qui si on dote la Turquie d'un régime de décentralisation administrative qui seul pourrait répondre aux besoins variés de ses habitants.[19]

In comparison to the proposals of the coalition members and Turkists, assigning a dominant role to the Turks in the Ottoman Empire, Sabahaddin Bey's proposed "moderation" seemed much more attractive to the non-Turkish Ottoman elements.

The next step for Sabahaddin Bey was to found an organ to propagate and defend his ideas. In April 1906 a journal called *Terakki* (*Progress*) appeared in Paris, revealing in its maiden article that the committee publishing it had been established "to serve the following four objectives which until now have been neglected":

1. The advertisement of *Science sociale*, which promotes individual liberty and social prosperity among our compatriots. . . . The translation of important essays of the *Science sociale* literature into our language.
2. The gradual transformation of conflicts among various Ottoman elements into friendship.
3. The defense of the rights of the Ottomans against the developed nations and the creation of an intellectual current unremittingly favorable to the Turks.
4. The establishment of well-arranged organizations in necessary locations within the country.[20]

The editorial board of the journal further stated that their main goal would be clearly defined in the letter of Sabahaddin Bey which followed. This letter was published as the lead article.[21]

There was no other mention of the committee in the first issue other than the subheading under the masthead *Terakki*: "The journal propagating the ideas of the partisans of *Science sociale* and decentralization." Obviously this ambiguous wording referred only to Sabahaddin Bey and his cohort and not to a distinct, well-organized committee. As a matter of fact, the Ottoman embassy in Paris, after a thorough investigation, reached the partially inaccurate conclusion that the so-called society was in fact composed of only three persons, and that no other Young Turk had taken part in any of this organization's initiatives, including the publication of the journal *Terakki*. These three were Sabahaddin Bey, his foster brother Ahmed Fazlı, and Rıza Bey. Although Sabahaddin Bey had a group of adherents, the embassy's report was accurate in its claim that there was no serious organization during the early days of 1906.[22]

The prince opened his long letter, which defined the goals of his new organization, with a strong criticism of Ottoman society before the westernization movement.[23] He then inveighed against the Young Turks, charging that their publications contained no scientific arguments but were merely filled with repetitive assertions. He further alleged that "therefore the readership has become sick and tired of these publications, nobody has benefited from the publishing activities, and instead action has been favored." Sabahaddin Bey posed the rhetorical question: "How could a society that does not read and looks down on serious studies achieve progress and carry out a radical change?" This comment reveals that he was not fond of the so-called activists. The prince, however, also referred to a statement by Theodore Roosevelt that "under certain circumstances a revolution would become necessary," and he compared this necessity to that of surgery to cure certain illnesses; the analogy impressed many Young Turks.[24] In contrasting their aims and publication policies to those of the coalition and the CPU, Sabahaddin Bey remarked:

When I was living in Istanbul, I had frequently observed the following: Whenever somebody in the household had a bruise, a concavity caused by a blow, or even a broken bone, he/she was taken to a bonesetter at once. The bonesetter, after rubbing the bruise, took out a box from his pocket, which contained a red putty. The cure was the same regardless of the type of accident or its degree. Observing the application of this red putty for many years, I began to consider it a great elixir and to respect and appreciate the bonesetter who carried such a cure in his pocket. When I became mature, however, I began to compare the bonesetter to the medical doctor. This comparison caused my respect for the putty to decline, and I realized that the science of the bonesetter stemmed primarily from our ignorance, whereas the medical doctor's originated from the dissection and examination of the human body with the application of a [scientific] method. I then began to turn against the former and to favor the latter. Please excuse me for making the following comparison, but for the most part our publications are no different from the putty of the bonesetter. For twenty years a cry for help has been heard maintaining that the sultan is surrendering the country to the foreigners and that the nation is in a deep sleep. The articles authored to awaken the nation, however, cannot serve to do so, because none of them rests on a scientific basis. The following passage in the January 1, [1906] issue of *Mechveret* [*Supplément Français*] drew my attention: "Les actes et les jugements de notre parti consistent à faire de la propagande: ce qui hélas! N'a donné, jusqu'à présent, que de maigres résultats."[25] I was astonished because the red putty cannot perform a cure unless nature helps. To say that Sultan Hamid is a tyrant, or that a constitution[al regime] should replace the present administration, or even to make a thousand people believe this, will not help anybody to grasp the truth. In fact, nobody has grasped it so far.[26]

Sabahaddin Bey did not hesitate to cite some of the authors of such publications: Ahmed Rıza, the late Ali Şefkatî, and Murad Bey, all of whom had been prominent leaders in the Young Turk movement from its beginning.[27] According to the prince, the centralist administration was the heart of the tyranny, and in a country where such an administration prevailed, replacement of a king by a parliament composed of 500 individuals would not make much of a difference.[28] He and his disciples had found "the guide for which [they] had been searching for years in *Science sociale*, which possesses the key to the success of the civilized world."[29] This "guide" also provided them with the ability to claim to be "more scientific than thou," a claim which the Young Turks had frequently used. To impress the sympathizers of the Young Turk movement, Sabahaddin Bey and his disciples asserted the following:

> Our publication is based upon *Science sociale*. Under this rubric new works are published every day in the West, but most of them are no more than philosophical experiments. The school of sociology founded by [Frédéric] Le Play and continued by Edmond Demolins's group, however, has succeeded in elevating sociology to the level of the other sciences by the use of a scientific method.[30]

As its members' own words made clear, this new movement that Sabahaddin Bey inaugurated and that challenged the CPU was based in large measure on the *Science sociale* program. The *Science sociale* movement, which Frédéric Le Play had begun and which later gained strength under the leadership of Edmond Demolins and Abbé Henri de Tourville, had drawn the attention of Ottoman intellectuals following the publication of the journal *Science sociale*, Demolins's famous book *A quoi tient la supériorité des Anglo-Saxons*,[31] and his study of educational systems.[32] The book that explained the alleged superiority of the Anglo-Saxons won the instant attention and praise of the Young Turks.[33] There is no doubt that Demolins's pro-British views likewise impressed many Young Turks who had similar opinions on the same issues, such as the Transvaal War and its consequences.[34] After examining Demolins's works, Sabahaddin Bey concluded that the problems of the Ottoman Empire were rooted in its peculiar social structure and its educational system.

In 1904 Sabahaddin Bey became a member of the Société Internationale de Science Sociale through Demolins's introduction, and he later played a significant role in the scholarly activities of this organization.[35] It should be noted that Sabahaddin Bey was not the only Ottoman intellectual who had developed a strong interest in the *Science sociale* movement. Soon after him a certain Süha Bey who was an engineer in Istanbul, became a member, also introduced to the movement by Demolins.[36] In a letter he wrote to Demolins upon returning from al-Ḥijāz, Süha Bey stated that *Science sociale* had become his guide: "Je vous serais dès lors très reconnaisant de bien vouloir me guider, en me donnant votre avis sur le choix de l'étude la plus utile à la Science sociale, que je pourrais entreprendre dans ma région."[37] In Egypt Fathī Zaghlūl Pasha became a member of the society in 1906[38] and translated Demolins's book on the alleged superiority of the Anglo-Saxons into Arabic.[39]

Sabahaddin Bey was also not alone in his claim that the implementation of Demolins's theories could solve the problems besetting the Ottoman Empire. The organ of the coalition[40] and a journal published in the empire[41]—both published by opponents of Sabahaddin Bey—likewise accorded great importance to Demolins's ideas.

Thus Sabahaddin Bey encountered the same problem that faced Ahmed Rıza. Both Young Turk leaders had become disciples of nonrevolutionary theories—positivism and *Science sociale*—that lacked a revolutionary praxis. An additional problem for Sabahaddin Bey was that, in contrast to the positivists who criticized contemporary European values and departed from general European public opinion on the "Eastern Question," the members of the *Science sociale* movement were highly critical of the Ottoman establishment[42] and had a higher opinion of the non-Muslim components of the Ottoman Empire.[43] Moreover, the leaders of the *Science sociale* movement, far from proposing a revolutionary praxis, strongly denounced revolutionary activities.[44] *Terakki*'s publication of Demolins's work *A-t-on intérêt à s'emparer du pouvoir?* and the journal's promotion of the idea that seizing power in a society would make no difference as long as centralist administration prevailed, clearly reveal that Sabahaddin Bey agreed with the French thinker on that matter.[45] In his own words Sabahaddin Bey confessed that "*Science sociale* would not drive a country into a revolution; however, it shows the reasons behind the establishment of tyrannies and behind the eruption of revolutions."[46]

The transformation of the coalition into an activist and revolutionary committee finally provided Ahmed Rıza and his followers with a revolutionary praxis. Sabahaddin Bey, however, was left with no alternative but to present "decentralization" as a privilege to be accorded to the non-Turkish groups of the empire seeking autonomy.[47] This was quite different from what Demolins had defended in his works. In the realm of politics, however, Sabahaddin Bey's position provided a platform for the defense of the rights of the Ottoman Empire's non-Turkish elements.[48] Even this can be judged an achievement for Sabahaddin Bey, who earlier had been fairly criticized for "making holes in the water" by appealing only to the Great Powers during his initial years in opposition.[49]

In late 1905, when Bahaeddin Şakir led an attempt to establish a common front against the regime of Abdülhamid II, he appealed to Sabahaddin Bey.[50] The latter responded by sending him the political program of his so-called committee, which had originally been written in French, adding that he would join a common front only if his program were accepted. This reply indicates that Sabahaddin Bey did not consider the program, which *Terakki* published in its first issue, as his real political agenda. The important parts of the "political program" that he forwarded to Bahaeddin Şakir were the following:

1. The political reforms to be implemented in the Ottoman Empire are to be based upon the principle of the administration of the present provinces in accordance with the system of "Decentralization and Devolution," and this applies to all classes of people and subjects [of the empire] without distinction.
2. The municipalities, district councils, and municipal executive councils, all of which are to be formed through elections, are to participate in [decision-making] in the districts and provinces.
3. The partnership and relations between the present provinces and the central government . . . are to be strengthened.
4. Necessary measures are to be taken to resolve the disputes and strife that separate the [Ottoman] elements from each other and to provide proportional representation through members and delegates elected by all elements in the provinces.

5. All [citizens] are to enjoy equal rights and entitlement regardless of their ethnicity.
6. The peace and order of the country are to be guarded by a gendarmerie, and the privates serving in the gendarmerie are to be selected proportionally, based on the population of the various communities [in a given administrative unit]. In order to instruct and train the gendarmerie troops, foreign instructors and officers will be temporarily employed.
7. The governors, subgovernors, directors of the provincial financial administrations, directors of the tax registration offices, judges and prosecutors of courts of first instance and courts of appeal, and other government officials . . . are to be appointed by the governors proportionally from the various [Ottoman] communities.
8. The law enforcement personnel is to be under the supervision of the civil officials.
9. The tax [system] is to be altered.
10. The provisions of international treaties are to be inviolable.[51]

What is significant is that even the political program of Sabahaddin Bey and his disciples looked like an administrative schema. It lacked any reference to the policies to be pursued in order to overthrow the present regime. As was stated by Ahmed Rıza, it was "élastique, vague et obscur."[52] The "decentralization" and transfer of power to the provinces, however, had a clear political meaning, as was underscored by the leaders of the coalition who printed a special supplement to their chief publication in order to denounce Sabahaddin Bey's program. On behalf of the CPU, Bahaeddin Şakir made the following imputations to the prince:

> The aspect of the program which deserves the strongest criticism is its second article. . . . Who would be the local members into whose hands we should entrust the entire province along with full power? What would we do if these members were composed of those who are under the influence of the British in Arabia, the French in Syria, the Italians and the Austrians in Albania, the [Armenian] committee members in the six provinces, the Greeks in the [Aegean] islands, and the Bulgarians in Macedonia whose desires are made as clear as daylight by the weapons and guns in their hands and by their journals and pamphlets? Some Arabs would move to establish an Arab government by selecting the Sharif [of Mecca] or one of their sheikhs as caliph. The local councils in some parts of Albania would become an instrument of foreign aspirations, and in all schools in the provinces no language other than Albanian would be recognized. . . . On the other hand, is it possible to trust that the local councils in the [Aegean] islands would not strive to achieve a union with Greece based upon common religion, language, and ethnicity, as the Christians in Crete did? . . . The advantages that would result from this partition are ideal for those to whom we would grant it, but for whom would its detriment be tangible? Turks? You must be sure that no one among the many classes, from members of the royal house to peasants, would let this happen. . . . Eastern Rumelia and Crete are convincing examples of what this kind of decentralization would result in.[53]

Bahaeddin Şakir further added that the members of the CPU considered themselves "the real and legitimate owners of the fatherland that had been soaked with the blood of [their] martyred patriotic ancestors," and he maintained that Sabahaddin Bey's cure would cause a worse disease for the Ottoman Empire.[54]

The CPU leaders used even harsher language in their secret correspondence, accusing Sabahaddin Bey of being a traitor and a servant of the separatist committees and European imperialistic powers:

In order both to inflate his personal importance and to obtain material credit in the eyes of the Europeans by gaining the endorsement of the committees which advance the hazardous idea of separation from Ottomanness, Sabahaddin Bey has invented a program, that is to say, the proposal for "decentralization," which would never be accepted by a real Ottoman. Since supporting decentralization, as desired by Sabahaddin Bey, means working for the extinction of Ottomanness, it is beyond any doubt that no Turk who possesses even the smallest bit of patriotism and intelligence would ever consent to it. The Europeans would have to intervene collectively and by means of arms in order to apply a program that has not been and will not be accepted by the Turks in our country. Only if the parties trying to set themselves apart from Ottomanness, and Sabahaddin Bey, who has been serving the aspirations of those parties alone in exchange for moral and material interest, should succeed in bringing about such an intervention would the Turks, forced by necessity, acquiesce in the implementation of the decentralization program developed by Sabahaddin Bey.[55]

As Sabahaddin Bey himself confessed, his opponents' criticism made a strong impact on the Young Turks' sympathizers within the empire.[56] He responded to his Turkist rivals by asserting that his and his committee's single aim was to make it possible for the Muslims to enjoy the same privileges that the Christians had been enjoying for many years.[57] He further pointed out that *Mechveret Supplément Français* had also called for foreign intervention on many occasions.[58] Additionally, in a desperate attempt to refute the claim that they had no political program, the publishers of *Terakki* replaced the title under the journal's masthead—"the journal propagating the ideas of the partisans of *Science sociale* and decentralization"—first with "the journal propagating the ideas of the partisans of private initiative, the constitution, and decentralization," and later with "the journal propagating the ideas of the partisans of private initiative, a constitutional regime, and decentralization."

The CPU leaders acted swiftly to rebut Sabahaddin Bey's claims. First they accused him of taking what had been published in the French supplement out of context,[59] and then they published a new special supplement to the central organ *Şûra-yı Ümmet*, devoted to refuting the claims. The CPU opened its attack on Sabahaddin Bey with the charge that "decentralization [was] a policy the Europeans and Armenians desired to have implemented in order to annihilate Ottomanness."[60] Bahaeddin Şakir then stated that Sabahaddin Bey had been "applauding the committee members from the Christian elements [of the Ottoman Empire] who possess the madness of a self-declared greatness," and accused him of accepting intimations of Christian superiority over the Muslims. Following this accusation, the attack switched its focus to the Armenian committees with which Sabahaddin Bey had been trying to reach an agreement:

Everyone should know that the undeserved treatment which had been deemed proper for our Armenian compatriots, and which also provoked our lament and regret, had not stemmed from the necessities of the absolutist program that Sultan Hamid had implemented as Sabahaddin Bey maintains. The real authors of the disaster of our Armenian compatriots are some stupid people among the leaders who were running and administering [the affairs of] the Armenian community, the many vagabonds carrying out provocations under the title of committee members, and those merciless people known as European politicians. . . . In his memoranda Sabahaddin Bey portrays Armenian committee members as innocent children and places all the responsibility on the government. . . . As for the Armenian committee members, these individuals do not have independent ideas and they are nothing other than simple playthings in the hands of absolutist Russian Armenians who have money and have been controlling [the movement]. . . . As long as the Armenian committee members pursue a way [policy] that is hazardous to the Ottoman administration and Ottoman independence, and strive to harm our country's territorial integrity with the help and intervention of foreigners as they have done until now, we should be permitted to identify these people as a rebellious party and present them to our nation as such.[61]

In reaction to this harsh criticism from his Turkist rivals, Sabahaddin Bey decided to pursue two policies. The first policy, as he stated after the Young Turk Revolution of 1908, was to create an "organizational network from the west to the east of Asia Minor with agents who were dispatched there with great difficulty."[62] The second policy was to secure foreign intervention in Ottoman domestic politics. To this end, the prince authored open letters and memoranda addressed to the European powers and secretly met with influential European statesmen and intellectual and political figures.

Organizational Network of the League of Private Initiative and Decentralization and Its Role in the 1905–1907 Rebellions in Anatolia

Until 1905 Sabahaddin Bey had given little thought to the importance of creating a serious organization. Gradually, however, he came to recognize the need for a structured network of supporters and sympathizers. The CPU's continuous organizational efforts forced him to respond, and he accordingly moved to build up the league's presence in Eastern Anatolia and on the Black Sea coast.[63] The league set up branches in these two regions, and a newly established student organization in Istanbul became the league's Istanbul branch, though it remained only loosely affiliated with the Paris center.[64]

This student organization, called the Cemiyet-i İnkılâbiye (The Revolutionary Committee), merged with a secret society at the Royal Military Academy that had been founded by young cadets and attracted students from other colleges as well.[65] Like many other minor opposition societies formed within the empire, the Revolutionary Committee leaders attempted to establish ties to the major Young Turk organizations in Europe. Their first contact, Yusuf Fehmi, helped them to publish an appeal in a French daily.[66] Despite his claim to be a member of a central Young Turk Committee (which was literally nonexistent), he could not provide any further support.

The second door to knock on was obviously the CPU's in Paris. But when the CPU used the same form of address in its evasive response to their application that a high school principal uses for his pupils—"little brothers"—[67] the Revolutionary Committee members opted for a third possibility, Sabahaddin Bey. And when they received an affirmative answer from him, this society of young college students turned itself into the league's Istanbul branch.

Sabahaddin Bey had already distributed his propaganda material in Istanbul[68] and therefore must have had other connections there. The new branch, however, enabled the league to spread its propaganda more widely and more effectively.[69] Relations between Paris and Istanbul nonetheless remained extremely tenuous, and the branch's members obviously knew very little about Sabahaddin Bey's real aims and designs.[70] Despite this loose affiliation, the League of Private Initiative and Decentralization was encouraged by the development; it instructed the dissidents in the provinces to form branches themselves rather than wait for the initiative to come from the central committee in Paris.[71]

We know very little about the details of the organizational framework of Sabahaddin Bey's league, since no bylaws or regulations were ever published, and none are available.[72] All the information we have about its structure is from a letter sent by its executive secretary to a dissident in Sinob encouraging the latter to organize a branch of the league in that town. In this invaluable letter, which the Ottoman authorities intercepted, Ahmed Fazlı stated:

Although the details of our organization and rules are included in our internal regulations, we have felt it necessary to complete them by adding certain articles, and so they are not yet published. I summarize, for the time being, our main organizational framework in the eight articles given below:

First, each branch must have a director and two assistant directors. The responsibility for corresponding with the central committee is the director's.

Second, . . . [the branch] should strive to establish a new branch in the nearest district. . . .

Third, it should receive *Terakki* and distribute it within the empire.

Fourth, it should give detailed information to the central committee about social conditions in its region, that is to say, about the lifestyle of the people, the relations between people belonging to various faiths, the government's oppression, the people's reaction to this oppression, and current events.

Fifth, it should publish appeals in accordance with the ideas defended in *Terakki*. These appeals should highlight and enlarge upon the government's oppression and further the mission of [inviting] all the people, Muslim and non-Muslim, to work toward reopening the parliament by creating a union. A copy of each appeal should be sent to the central committee before distribution.

Sixth, members should establish relations with the most honest individuals among the people in order to increase the membership of the committee. They should read the constitution to the people and explain to them the meaning of the constitutional regime, telling the people that if such a regime is put into effect, the people of the province will be given the right to administer and look into local issues—this is what decentralization means. [Members] should also attempt to explain to the people that in this event, thanks to agriculture and industry on the one hand and the people's initiative on the other, and with the additional help of commerce, no trace of the present oppression will be seen in the future. The present misery will be replaced by prosperity and happiness.

Seventh, after the creation of a strong union covering several provinces, [the branch] should attempt to persuade the people not to pay any taxes to the government, and the government should be prevented from drafting anyone for military service.

Eighth, the local branches within a given province will be attached to the branch in the capital of that province. Also these branches will correspond with the central committee in Paris. In order to put correspondence in order, a branch should correspond with the central committee [in Paris] at least twice a month and with the central branch in Beirut at least once a month.[73]

Although Ahmed Fazlı claimed in this letter that there was a central branch in Beirut, Sabahaddin Bey and his league carried out their activities mainly in Eastern Anatolia and on the Black Sea coast. The existence of a significant Armenian movement in the very same region makes it difficult to believe that this was a mere coincidence. A report prepared by Sabahaddin Bey's followers after the Young Turk Revolution of 1908 underscores the role of the League of Private Initiative and Decentralization in the revolts that occurred in Eastern Anatolia. It also maintains that the CPU played no noteworthy role in these events:

> Mais le premier mouvement de révolte contre l'absolutisme du régime hamidien se manifesta dans le bassin de la mer Noire, en Asie Mineure, et notamment du côté d'Erzeroum, où "l'Union et le Progrès" ne joua aucun rôle.
>
>   Aussi, de fait que la révolution de Juillet 1908 eut lieu dans la zone d'influence attribuée à cette dernière fraction de l'opposition libérale, serait-il injuste de conclure à l'inactivité des autres.[74]

A French police report stresses the cordiality of relations between Sabahaddin Bey and the members of the Dashnaktsutiun while they were working together in Eastern Anatolia until the Young Turk Revolution of 1908.[75] Many other observers noted that the league and the Dashnaktsutiun had similar political platforms.[76]

A close confidant of Sabahaddin Bey made an interesting statement about the nature of the activities carried out by the league in Eastern Anatolia when he asserted that they aimed at a "union" of Muslims with non-Muslims.[77] This was also one of the most oft-cited themes of *Terakki*:

> Had the Muslims invited the Armenians to defend the rights of the Ottomans together, instead of going in haste to pillage Armenian villages, they would undoubtedly have rendered a greater service to their fatherland. At least we would not have been introduced to the civilized world as marauders. . . . It is clear that the present government seeks its strength in the feebleness of its subjects. Therefore, it desires that the people destroy each other. . . . Let us stop entombing our happiness with our own hands. The Muslims and Christians, who are the children of the same fatherland, should live in a harmony that would be appropriate for the children of the same fatherland.[78]

Unlike the CPU's organizational network, which tried to win over intellectuals, bureaucrats, and most important, military officers, Sabahaddin Bey's league targeted provincial leaders, through whom it hoped to persuade the masses in their theater of action. Sabahaddin Bey wanted to use the masses as a wild card, and he castigated the regime's treatment of them, comparing it to the treatment given "a flock of birds to be plucked."[79] He warned the masses against an alliance of "notables and government officials,"[80] and he decried heavy agricultural taxes.[81] The league's leaders went so far as to claim that the former Ottoman parliament had been a result not of the people's demands, but of the work of a small bureaucratic group. They further argued that the reopening of the parliament should result from the people's own will and that this was "a natural law of social progress."[82] Sabahaddin Bey reiterated that one of their main goals was to give the local people the right to administer their provinces.[83] In addition, the little known network of Sabahaddin Bey's league desired to build up an organization starting from the smallest administrative levels, villages, and small towns, in the provinces.[84]

Official Ottoman documents provide insight into the league's attempt to build an organizational structure in Eastern Anatolia and on the Black Sea coast. They reveal that the league sent instructions to the revolutionaries through a certain Mehmed, who was the Russian consulate's messenger in Erzurum. The league's center in Paris secretly corresponded with him through the Russian post offices in T'bilisi and Kars. From there the letters were forwarded to the Russian post office in Trabzon. When Ottoman intelligence intercepted a letter that had been sent by the league to this messenger but then mistakenly forwarded to the Ottoman post office, the Ottoman authorities cut this link.[85] Similar instructions sent by the league's secretary, Ahmed Fazlı, and intercepted by local authorities in Trabzon indicate that Sabahaddin Bey succeeded in forming some small branches on the Black Sea coast;[86] and an appeal issued by the Trabzon branch of the league immediately after the Young Turk Revolution in 1908 reveals that at least this branch survived.[87]

The league also succeeded in smuggling its publications into the region through the Austrian post office in İnebolu,[88] a port town very close to Kastamonu where an uprising had earlier taken place, and through the French post offices in Trabzon and Samsun.[89] In addition, with the help of Ali Haydar Midhat, the league sent *Terakki* and other propaganda materials to Bombay. From there some Indian Muslims smuggled them into Baghdad, surreptitiously enclosing them with the Persian journal *Ḥabl al-Matīn*.[90]

Thus a variety of league publications penetrated Eastern Anatolia from three directions. Additionally, numerous copies of Abdullah Cevdet's journal, which supported Sabahaddin Bey, were delivered to Salmās on the Iranian border and then smuggled into Eastern Anatolia.[91] In summary, Sabahaddin Bey's league was quite active in Eastern Anatolia and on the Black Sea coast.

The Eastern Anatolian Rebellions of 1905–1907

The historiography of the revolts that occurred in Eastern Anatolia between 1905 and 1907 divides into two major schools of interpretation. Early Turkish researchers, some of whom had the chance to interview former Young Turk leaders, maintained that the League of Private Initiative and Decentralization had organized and carried out the Erzurum revolt and other revolutionary movements in the region.[92] Later, Soviet historians adopted a different interpretation, asserting that these uprisings were popular constitutional movements inspired by the Russian Revolution of 1905;[93] they took the view that Sabahaddin Bey's league had played little if any role in these events.[94] This latter interpretation aimed at proving Lenin's assertion that the Persian, Young Turk, and Chinese revolutions of the early twentieth century were all stimulated by the Russian Revolution of 1905 and therefore displayed similar characteristics.[95] Although nonscholarly and highly political, this Soviet interpretation was accepted at face value by some dilettante Turkish scholars, who based their research on a combination of secondary material and essays of Soviet historians, which they did not wholly understand.[96] Both interpretations neglect almost entirely the role that the Armenians, and most important the Dashnaktsutiun, played in these uprisings.

It is therefore necessary to highlight the following matters in order to bring out the real nature of the uprisings in question: first, the Armenian and Young Turk initiatives toward rapprochement, and the negotiations between the Dashnaktsutiun and the League of Private Initiative and Decentralization; second, the activities of the Dashnaktsutiun, including those carried out by bogus Turkish revolutionary committees set up by the Dashnaktsutiun itself; third, the uprisings and revolutionary activities in Eastern Anatolia; finally, the role that the League of Private Initiative and Decentralization, the Dashnaktsutiun, and other Young Turk organizations played in these revolts.

Armenian and Young Turk Initiatives for a Rapprochement and Relations between Sabahaddin Bey's League and the Dashnaktsutiun

Although Sabahaddin Bey had started to pay more attention to the creation of a serious organizational structure, it nonetheless remained a secondary issue to him. This was so because he never wanted to seize power through a popular revolution; his intention was rather to use revolutionary activity as a device to secure foreign intervention. He believed that having a joint Armenian–Young Turk movement would be of inestimable value in impressing the Great Powers of Europe, and he therefore considered rapprochement between the two a *conditio sine qua non* for obtaining support from the Great Powers. Between 1905 and 1907, relations between the Young Turks and the Dashnaks improved, and as a result of Sabahaddin Bey's efforts, the two sides reached a serious agreement for the first time in the history of the Young Turk movement.

Sabahaddin Bey had wanted to reach an agreement with the Armenians ever since he first participated in the Young Turk movement. He accordingly launched his new campaign in 1905 with an appeal to them. As we have seen, this initiative led to an exchange of letters between Sabahaddin Bey and various Armenian individuals and intellectuals. Just as they had done in early 1902, during the preparations for the First Congress of Ottoman Opposition Parties in Paris, the Hncak party and its sympathizers turned a deaf ear to Sabahaddin Bey's proposals.[97] The prince was therefore left with only one possible alternative: a rapprochement with the Dashnaktsutiun.

As an initial step toward such a rapprochement, a Dashnak leader, Khachatur Malumian, who went by the pseudonym of Aknuni, gave an interview in May 1905 to Abdullah Cevdet, who had become a devotee of Sabahaddin Bey. The two discussed the problems facing the Ottoman and Russian opposition movements in very general terms.[98] Following this interview Abdullah Cevdet addressed an appeal to the Muslims of Caucasia, calling on them to come to terms with the Armenians.[99] This appeal received a warm response from the Armenians,[100] who distributed it in the Caucasus.[101]

Subsequently an Armenian intellectual, Tigrane Zaven, who had aided Abdullah Cevdet and İshak Sükûti when they were publishing *Osmanlı* in Geneva, acted to achieve an understanding between the Young Turks and the Armenian revolutionary organizations for a joint movement against the regime of the sultan.[102] His appeal to both sides provoked great anxiety among the Ottoman authorities.[103] The Dashnaktsutiun decided to support the initiative, while the CPU gave its standard response that a joint movement could be organized only if the other organizations complied with its terms.[104] Oddly enough, Sabahaddin Bey remained silent.

In the meantime a group of Armenian and Azerbaijani intellectuals began publishing a bilingual journal in Armenian and Azerbaijani Turkish called *Koč-Da 'vet* (*Invitation*).[105] This journal promoted the ideas of the Armenian-Azerbaijani League, which had been founded by the Armenian section of the Baku Committee of the Russian Social Democratic Labor party and the Azerbaijani Himmät party.[106] The publication of this journal likewise raised new hopes for reconciliation between the Young Turk and Armenian organizations.[107]

Finally, Sabahaddin Bey, because of accusations made against him by members of the coalition, made an offer to the Armenians through an unimportant Young Turk, Fuad Midhat Pasha, who claimed that Sabahaddin Bey was the head of their so-called association.[108] Fuad Midhat Pasha stated that "L'autonomie est possible, pourvu que vous apparteniez à un même empire, sous un même sultan modernisé et rendu constitutionnel."[109]

For propaganda purposes the CPU leaders highlighted the Armenian journals' claim that Sabahaddin Bey gave similar promises to Armenian organizations by quoting *Pro Armenia*.[110] They maintained that Sabahaddin Bey was "on good terms with the Macedonian committee under the administration of Sarafov, which wants to grab Macedonia from our hands and make it an independent country, and with Armenian committees that want to separate the six provinces located in the heart of the country in order to set up an Armenian government or principality, and [he] gave [such] promises to them."[111] Despite the CPU's outrage, *Droshak* quickly gave a favorable response to Sabahaddin Bey in the form of an invitation to all Ottomans. Later an appeal appeared in every issue of *Droshak* between September and December 1906, asking the Young Turks to form a joint revolutionary front and to clasp the Dashnaktsutiun's hand of solidarity.[112]

Although the Dashnaktsutiun officially declared itself in favor of "une solidarité avec les éléments révolutionnaires de Turquie" only at its 1907 General Assembly held in Vienna, its desire for a rapprochement with the Young Turks bore fruit before this formal declaration.[113] At that time the Dashnaktsutiun could expect nothing from the coalition. Indeed, the coalition's journals were describing all Armenian revolutionary committees in scurrilous terms, despite the fact that Bahaeddin Şakir, who was reorganizing the coalition, wanted to establish a tactical alliance with the Armenian organizations.[114]

The Dashnaktsutiun also tried to win over the Kurds for common action.[115] In July 1906, Ottoman intelligence received information about a joint Armenian–Kurdish anarchist action to be carried out in the Ottoman capital.[116] Around the same time, local authorities informed the central government of the efforts of the Armenians to form an alliance with the Kurds against the government in Eastern Anatolia.[117] Later, Ottoman troops found, on some Dashnaktsutiun members, appeals composed in Kurdish but written in the Armenian alphabet, describing the decisions taken at the 1907 Congress of Dashnaktsutiun and inviting the Kurds to revolt against the Ottoman government.[118] Despite the Dashnaktsutiun's efforts, the only positive response came from a Kurdish society named Azm-i Kavî (The Strong Determination), which merely asked the Kurds to treat Armenians well and not to obey the sultan.[119]

The Dashnaktsutiun's failure to achieve an effective alliance with the Kurds raised Sabahaddin Bey's value in the eyes of the its leaders. It also bolstered Sabahaddin Bey's call for the Armenians and the Turks to unite against the alleged Kurdish menace. Sabahaddin Bey maintained that "the Kurds and the government" were the two elements that caused "the sad Armenian incidents,"[120] while a military member of his league in Erzurum described the Kurds as a "nation . . . almost all of whom look like a band of brigands."[121] As stated in a British report, the Armenians' relations "with the Kurds . . . [were] merely a matter of paying them not to interfere."[122] Pro-Dashnak circles, who had previously acclaimed the "solidarité entre Arméniens et Turcs" against the "terrorisme kurde" in other regions,[123] shared Sabahaddin Bey's praise for a joint Armenian–Turkish counterattack against the Kurdish pillagers. Thanking the Dashnaktsutiun for its efforts to strengthen the union between the Turks and Armenians, Sabahaddin Bey presented this alleged incident as an example to follow.[124]

The Dashnaktsutiun and the League of Private Initiative and Decentralization thus made a secret deal to cooperate.[125] Both sides expected to benefit from cooperation. As an initial step and a gesture of goodwill, the Dashnaktsutiun smuggled a member of the League of Private Initiative and Decentralization into Eastern Anatolia to organize joint revolutionary activities. The person chosen for this dangerous task was Hüseyin Tosun, a former captain and French language instructor at the Military School in Tripoli of Barbary.[126]

Until his flight, Hüseyin Tosun had fulfilled important functions for the CUP's seventh branch in Tripoli of Barbary.[127] Next he joined the opponents of the coalition in Europe, publishing Abdullah Cevdet's journal *İctihad* in Geneva after the latter's expulsion from Switzerland.[128] It seems that Hüseyin Tosun had a genuine interest in theories of Anglo-Saxon superiority, and thus his participation in Sabahaddin Bey's camp was not a mere coincidence.[129] His activities in Eastern Anatolia are notable for two reasons. First, he received support from the Dashnaktsutiun. Second, he became the only Young Turk expatriate to play an important role in the Erzurum revolt and other revolutionary activities in Eastern Anatolia.

The Intermediary and Bogus Organizations Created by Sabahaddin Bey's League and the Dashnaktsutiun for Joint Action

Despite the fact that they were already working together to smuggle Hüseyin Tosun into Eastern Anatolia, neither Sabahaddin Bey nor the Dashnak leadership could allow their agreement to carry out joint revolutionary activities in Eastern Anatolia to become public knowledge. Accordingly, Sabahaddin Bey's league and the Dashnaktsutiun solicited help from intermediary organizations and set up bogus organizations to facilitate cooperation. This continued until the Second Congress of Ottoman Opposition Parties, after which the agreement between the Dashnaktsutiun, Sabahaddin Bey's League, the CPU, and numerous trivial and bogus opposition organizations was drawn up and made public.

The Ligue Constitutionnelle Ottomane

One such intermediary organization was established in Cairo under the name of Şûra-yı Osmanî Cemiyeti—Ligue Constitutionnelle Ottomane.[130] This committee was founded by well-known Arab intellectuals "with the participation of men from the other main Ottoman elements, with Turks, Circassians, and Armenians leading them. Among its founding members were the officer [Ahmed] Saib Bey . . . and the famous Abdullah Cevdet Bey, one of the founders of the original Committee of Union and Progress, who was the Turkish secretary of the committee. . . . [Rafīq al-ʿAẓm] became its treasurer, his cousin Haqqī [al-ʿAẓm] became its Arabic secretary, and [Rashīd Riḍā] became the head of its administrative board."[131] Rashīd Riḍā then asked Gazi Ahmed Muhtar Pasha for his permission to make his son, Mahmud Muhtar Pasha, the honorary director of the committee, but the Ottoman high commissioner rejected the offer.[132] It seems that Rashīd Riḍā and many prominent Arabs who became members of this society did not pay great attention either to its Turkish language propaganda or to its activities outside the Arab provinces of the empire. The Ligue Constitutionnelle Ottomane's early propaganda pamphlets and manifestos were sent to Eastern Black Sea ports, entrusted to the crews and travelers of Russian ships, and from those ports they were smuggled into Eastern Anatolia, where Sabahaddin Bey and the Dashnaktsutiun were active.[133] Also the Ligue's participation in the organization of an Armenian lottery to collect money for the Dashnaktsutiun led the Ottoman authorities to believe that the two societies were working together.[134]

The establishment of close ties between the Ligue Constitutionnelle Ottomane and Sabahaddin Bey became possible when Sabahaddin Bey's confidant, Abdullah Cevdet, assumed the post of Turkish secretary of the Ligue.[135] Sabahaddin Bey's admirers then offered the leadership of the organization to him, and he declared his acceptance by sending an official letter from Paris.[136] Although almost everyone in revolutionary circles was aware of this society's relations with Sabahaddin Bey, and the fact that its immediate aim was to achieve an understanding with the Armenian organizations,[137] the leaders of the Ligue Constitutionnelle Ottomane tried to give the impression of running a totally independent organization.[138] Ironically, *Pro Armenia* had published, and praised, the program of this new organization before it appeared in the central organ bearing the organization's own name.[139]

The CPU's note to the readers of *Şûra-yı Ümmet* labeling *Pro Armenia* a journal "hostile to the Turks and an enemy of Ottoman institutions," and underscoring the fact that such a journal had initially announced the establishment of the new committee without naming its founders, deserves attention.[140] Later the CPU harshly criticized this new organization's publications using language previously reserved for the Armenians and Sabahaddin Bey.[141] The CPU's criticism was supported by the Ottoman authorities' seizure of copies of this committee's organ in Eastern Anatolia,[142] and their interception of a letter regarding the circulation of Armenian journals in Egypt; this letter was being sent to the Ligue Constitutionnelle Ottomane by an Armenian working within the group led by Tigrane Zaven, which published the journal *Erkri Dzain* in T'bilisi.[143] Also *Şûra-yı Osmanî* was the only "Young Turk" journal that published appeals from various socialist organizations with close ties to the Dashnaktsutiun.[144]

It is interesting to note that the underground journals ostensibly published by Turkish committees in reality operated under Dashnaktsutiun supervision in Eastern Anatolia and reprinted articles and poetry originally published in *Şûra-yı Osmanî*.[145] A Dashnaktsutiun appeal enclosed with a journal published by one of the bogus "Turkish Committees" and sent to *Şûra-yı Osmanî* from Van leaves no doubt that the Ligue Constitutionnelle Ottomane and the Dashnaktsutiun had close ties.[146] The cooperation between Sabahaddin Bey's supporters and the Armenians in Egypt so alarmed the Ottoman government that the latter dispatched a special intelligence agent to Cairo to investigate "the Young Turk and Armenian conspirators in Egypt," even before they started publishing their journal.[147]

The Ligue Constitutionnelle Ottomane's central organ promoted several theses about which Sabahaddin Bey made indirect remarks. The most important theory espoused by this society was that a purely "Turkish revolution might cause the end of the existence of the state."[148] This is obviously related to Sabahaddin Bey's contention that common action and rapprochement among the various components of the Ottoman Empire were preferable to unilateral action by the Turks. The latter would necessarily be based on an exclusionary nationalist ideology and would thereby antagonize the Ottoman Empire's non-Turkish elements and so jeopardize the empire's existence.

The Ligue Constitutionnelle Ottomane and the Arabs

Because of this inclusive thesis, the Ligue Constitutionnelle Ottomane's activities and publication attracted many Ottoman dissidents of Arab descent residing in Cairo. Members of the Ligue also established branches of the League of Private Initiative and Decentralization in Damascus and in al-Lādhiqiyya, and helped the dissidents in Izmir to form another branch of the prince's organization there.[149] In response to the emergence of these new Arab supporters, Sabahaddin Bey started to focus on the alleged dissatisfaction of the Arabs, a subject hitherto neglected by the prince in his articles.[150] Sabahaddin Bey was not the only person who addressed issues important to the dissident Arabs. Another member of Sabahaddin Bey's League maintained that "the Yemenis were absolutely right to revolt against the Ottoman government."[151] This attitude was diametrically opposite to that of the CPU, and those who knew that the members of the Ligue Constitutionnelle Ottomane had hoisted black flags on their houses in Cairo two years earlier to protest the Ottoman military campaign against the Zaydīs in Yemen[152] easily understood the message. Sabahaddin Bey also proposed publishing an Arabic version of *Terakki* to appeal to his new sympathizers.[153]

Nonetheless, Sabahaddin Bey's interest in the Arabs remained relatively modest. He understood that the Arab opponents of the sultan could offer him little advantage in his political game, and so he maintained his focus on improving and maintaining relations with the Armenians.

The Bogus Organizations of the Dashnaktsutiun

Meanwhile the Dashnaktsutiun took a fascinating initiative to appeal to the Turkish populace.[154] As early as March 1904 the local Ottoman authorities obtained information about a new publication policy of "the Armenian committees to stir up the Muslim masses."[155] The Dashnaktsutiun, while carrying out revolutionary propaganda among the Armenians in the region,[156] also distributed appeals in Turkish inviting the Turks to common action.[157] In addition to these open activities, heretofore unknown Turkish and Muslim committees began to mushroom in Eastern Anatolia following the Dashnaktsutiun's rapprochement with Sabahaddin Bey. The activities and propaganda of these so-called Turkish committees have perplexed many historians.[158] Pro-Dashnaktsutiun organs praised the activities of these "Young Turk" organizations, actually created by the Dashnaktsutiun, and commented that "un sang nouveau circule dans les artères des Turcs, une nouvelle race surgit."[159]

The most important among these bogus organizations established by the Dashnaktsutiun was the so-called Turkish Allied Party. It published two journals in Turkish, *Sabah'ül-Hayr* (*Good Morning*) and *Rehber-i Umur-i Vatan* (*The Guide to the Affairs of the Fatherland*),[160] as well as a third bilingual (Turkish-Armenian) journal.[161] It sometimes operated under the name of the Ottoman Revolutionary Alliance Committee[162] and was referred to as Le Comité Turc Libéral d'Action,[163] Le Comité Libéral Turc d'Action,[164] or La Fédération Révolutionnaire Turque in the pro-Dashnaktsutiun journals.[165] Russian sources named it Musul'manskaia Federatsiia (Muslim Federation) or Federatsiia Osmantsev (Federation of Ottomans), maintaining that the people of Eastern Anatolia called it "The Popular Needs Party."[166]

The CPU moved swiftly to warn its readership about the real nature of this party that operated under various names, all indicating a Turkish or Muslim origin. It declared that "such a committee could never be Turkish or Ottoman. [Members of this committee] can only be people pursuing secret policies disguised under the veil of Ottomanness."[167] A confidant of Sabahaddin Bey provided information about relations between the prince and this bogus organization, which was carrying out active propaganda in Eastern Anatolia:

> Tout ce que je puis dire, c'est qu'on doit en partie à la *Ligue de décentralisation et d'initiative privée* ce mouvement inouï de résistance des musulmans, jusqu'alors passifs, contre l'oppression des pouvoirs. . . . *Sabah-ul-haîr* (Bonjour, ou Bon Matin), feuille volante, lithographiée, sans lieu ni date, dirigée par un "groupe d'Arméniens ottomans" et qui paraît en Arménie même. Cette feuille porte en épigraphe: "Nous sommes justes, nous repoussons le mensonge. Celui qui fait partie du Comité et en trahirait les secrets, qu'il prenne garde, sa vie est en danger." Dans un de ses premiers numéros, elle porte une appréciation favorable sur l'action du Prince Sabahaddine.[168]

A source who received information directly from Young Turk leaders, including Sabahaddin Bey, indicates that in reality this "appreciation" was nothing less than "disseminating the propaganda" of Sabahaddin Bey's League.[169] As a pro-Dashnak journal stated:

> Le prince Saba heddine [*sic*], fils de Mahmoud Pacha, qui supporte courageusement l'exil et vit en Europe avec une rare et parfaite dignité a exprimé à maintes reprises les intentions les meilleures au nom d'un parti réformateur.
>
> Il y a mieux, dans le pays même, des idées semblables se font jour et l'appel publié plus loin d'un Comité libéral turc d'action formule les principes d'une entente utile et satisfaisante.[170]

The term "allied" used in the original Turkish name of the party as it appeared in its journals, therefore, must have referred to the alliance between the League of Private Initiative and Decentralization and the Dashnaktsutiun. Indeed, an Armenian historian describes the organizations in question as "comités révolutionnaires arméno-turcs."[171] As for the Dashnaktsutiun's involvement in its publication activities, a note on one of the issues of the journal *Sabah'ül-Hayr* in the archives of the Dashnaktsutiun reveals that one of its publishers was an Armenian revolutionary figure named Dajad Terlemezian.[172] Terlemezian had been an "enrolled member" of the Dashnaktsutiun and had assassinated an Armenian informer in March 1908 in Van despite the committee's refusal of permission.[173] Also Ottoman documents reveal that copies of the main journal published by this party were found on Armenian revolutionaries killed in combat with security forces.[174]

Young Turk sources claimed that the publications of this party deeply influenced the Erzurum revolt and revolutionary movements in other provinces,[175] and a British consul commented that its main journal consisted of "inflammatory articles."[176] For example, the organ of this bogus committee asked local people to imitate the Iranians who had established local revolutionary committees (*anjuman*s).[177] It is difficult, however, to know whether they were widely distributed and read, even though the journals published by this bogus organization and pro-Dashnak periodicals made such claims.[178]

The party's program focused on "provincial administration" and was very similar to the program of Sabahaddin Bey's league.[179] The party's Dashnak members worked behind the scenes and exerted their best efforts to convince the people of the region that theirs was a brand new Turkish party.[180] They maintained that the foundation of the party had been the work of a handful of people in early 1907 and that more than a hundred members had later been enrolled.[181] Many articles were published under Muslim names,[182] and anonymous authors contrived to refer to their Muslim origins, for example by including recollections of their military service.[183] This bogus Turkish party further claimed that copies of its journal were being seized in Turkish houses by the gendarmes.[184] In order to strengthen the party's image as an entirely new Turkish organization, articles lamenting the fact that "half of our fatherland—Greece, Serbia, and Bulgaria—has separated from us" appeared in the main organ of the party.[185] The party also advanced and propagated theses to persuade Muslims that the revolts against the regime of the sultan had nothing to do with religion and did not stem from separatist tendencies:

> Arabs, Albanians, and Syrians are revolting too. Are these, too, enemies of religion? Isn't it true that those Arabs are the purest Muslims? Now what would our whorelike, ignorant, and oppressive government say? The inhabitants of Erzurum, Diyar-ı Bekir, Kastamoni, and pure Turks of other regions are revolting. Do they, too, oppose our religion, nation, and fatherland? O unbelievers and traitors who disguise yourselves with the masks of religion, nationality, and [love of] fatherland, and who do not recognize the nation, you are similar to cats. Every time you land on your four feet. . . . Therefore, the Christians [Hıristiyanlar], Yezidis, Jews, and Christians [Nasraniler] should be freed to worship by law their own God and to carry out their religious rituals. . . . The national question and fights among nationalities would then come to an end.[186]

Furthermore, the real object of the Dashnaktsutiun, a rapprochement between Turks and Armenians, became the most common theme in the Turkish Allied party's propaganda:

It was the Armenians who took the initial step toward liberty. Let us, the Turks, take the second step. The other nations will follow us. . . . Long live the union among nations! Long live liberty, fraternity, and equality![187]

What was the reason for the evil that fell upon the poor Armenians? Is it really true that they longed for a principality or a sultanate or that they desired to snatch our fatherland from our hands and hand it to the Russians or Europeans? Or did they really want to annihilate our religion? No! No! All of these are lies and slanders; our government wanted to rupture the hospitable relations that existed heretofore between us and the Armenians and make us fight against each other. But it should be admitted that the Armenians [understood] the oppressive attitude of the government before we did and strove to complain. The government, however, provoked us and our soldiers against them, instead of accepting their legitimate demands. And shame on us! We butchered them and never thought that they were the ones trying to show the path of happiness for the fatherland and demanding and claiming our liberty. Besides Armenians and Macedonians, Muslim Albanians and Arabs are revolting too.[188]

But the journals strongly opposed European intervention for the purpose of imposing the reforms, although securing such intervention had been one of the main designs of both the Dashnaktsutiun and its new ally Sabahaddin Bey:

European newspapers write that Russia and England have come to a mutual understanding to have reforms carried out within the six Armenian provinces. Who knows what kind of interests they are after? In order to clean up their [dirty] businesses, they left the poor Armenians riddled with holes like sieves. Russia, which oppresses its own subjects, cannot grant freedom to others. Nobody would believe this. If we do not want to lose our country, however, we should reform its administration. The foreigners would then not be able to act as a shampooer in a public bath [sticking their hands in everybody's business], and small people, too, would live in comfort and be free.[189]

The other interesting aspects of the propaganda spread by these bogus committees were its consistent appeal to soldiers to work with the revolutionaries[190] and its balanced language. Unlike the Young Turk journals published abroad, the organs of these bogus committees printed articles on topics ranging from sophisticated constitutional matters[191] to purely local matters explained in simple language.[192]

Besides publishing various periodicals, the bogus Turkish committees authored and distributed many appeals and pamphlets in the region.[193] These contained mainly complaints about government oppression and called for union among Ottomans.[194] When these materials were thrown into the quarters of garrisons[195] and left on the streets of the Muslim quarters in the towns of the region,[196] the Ottoman authorities reacted forcefully. First the local authorities declared that Armenians and not Muslims had been publishing and circulating the materials.[197] Then they discovered large numbers of "seditious publications" prepared by the Dashnaktsutiun in Van.[198] Later the local authorities uncovered the printing presses used by the Dashnaktsutiun to publish Turkish journals and appeals in the same town.[199] Meanwhile soldiers seized many Turkish pamphlets and journals on leading Armenian committee members killed during clashes.[200] Finally, the authorities arrested many Armenians involved with the revolutionary Turkish publications.[201]

Even in towns like Ankara, appeals against the governors were posted and distributed, and such activities caused uneasiness in places as far afield as Çorum.[202] Indeed the sultan himself paid attention to the activities and publications of the Dash-naktsutiun's pseudo-Turkish revolutionary committees.[203] He had the governors of the provinces in which Armenian committees were active informed of "a committee established to stir up people and prepare publications in Anatolia," and he required the governors to provide information about this organization.

Although the Dashnaktsutiun, the CPU, and Sabahaddin Bey's league decided to form a special committee and carry out joint activities at the Second Congress of Ottoman Opposition Parties in December 1907, the fact that the CPU had no presence in many parts of the area turned this common action into an extension of the former secret alliance. This time, however, both sides had the chance to speak openly about the alliance and present it as a union of all Ottoman ethnic groups. A leading member of the League of Private Initiative and Decentralization recommended the following to the Ottomans:

> Armenian compatriot[!] The Turk who would defend our common rights against the aggressors is not far away. From now on he will attack the butchers and face them together with you. Turkish compatriot[!] Do not think that you are alone in this great *gaza* of justice. Be sure that your Armenian compatriots, who would sacrifice their lives for you, are behind you. Bravely present a helping hand to them. . . . Soldier [!] From now on the *gazis* who would be targeted by your gun are the "self-sacrificing volunteers of the nation." There are no "Armenian bands" aiming at [the establishment of] an Armenian principality before you. From now on, Armenians will fight with us to save our fatherland from oppression. If the treacherous people who have turned our every day into the Day of Judgment will say "these are the enemies of the religion and the state," pointing to honest children of the fatherland, never believe them. The traitors are not they but those who say that they are traitors.[204]

The Dashnaktsutiun employed similar language in its appeals to Turkish people:

> Whoever is a supporter of the present administration, whoever plunders the poor by presuming that this government is good for his personal interests, whoever plants the seeds of hatred among brothers in soil, whoever becomes an enemy of liberty and justice . . . is an enemy of ours regardless of ethnicity and religion, regardless of whether he is Turkish or Armenian. Those who want justice and liberty are distressed because of the horrors of the oppressive government. These are our brothers, as are those who are working for a just Ottoman government, proclamation of the constitution, and establishment of the parliament and the constitutional regime. They are either under our banner now or will come under our banner.[205]

The strong measures taken by the government, along with the destruction of the lithographic printing house of the Dashnaktsutiun in Van, and the killing of many Dashnaktsutiun members there during the clashes of April 1908, prevented Sabahaddin Bey and his league from achieving any significant results.

This alliance, of course, could not have organized and carried out all the activities that occurred in the region between 1905 and 1907. It did, however, successfully turn dissatisfaction among various classes of people, which was rooted mainly in economic difficulties, into revolutionary movements demanding the reopening of the parliament and the restoration of the constitution. Although the revolutionary activities seriously challenged the government's authority in the region, the hopes of securing a foreign intervention through these revolts entertained by Sabahaddin Bey and the Dashnaktsutiun remained wishful thinking.

The various uprisings that took place in Eastern Anatolia and in the Black Sea basin are summarized below with special reference to the role played by Sabahaddin Bey's league and the Dashnaktsutiun. It should be remembered that providing a detailed study of each of these revolts is beyond the scope of this book.

The Kastamonu Uprising

Kastamonu province was an ideal place to organize revolutionary activities. It was an exile center, populated by many individuals who had participated in "seditious" activities and were banished to this province.[206] The Young Turk organizations had corresponded with the exiled dissidents in the province from the outset of the movement.[207] Many of these exiles were appointed under close scrutiny to civil and military posts within the province.[208] In addition to these Young Turks and their sympathizers, a large number of Albanian dissidents from Đakovica (Yakova-Gjakovë) and Prizren were also exiled to the town.

The activities of these groups in the town made the local administration uneasy.[209] For example, the Young Turks here dared to criticize the sultan's regime even to foreign travelers,[210] an action that very few people risked taking in the capital or in many other provinces. Ottoman documents also reveal that some of these exiles were distributing "seditious" publications[211] and that the Albanian exiles in Kastamonu played a significant role in agitating the people back in their homeland.[212]

The first "rebellious" activity in the province took place on December 9, 1905, in Sinob. More than 2,000 "Muslim and non-Muslim" inhabitants from the nearby towns and villages gathered in the town square and marched to the subgovernor's office. The crowd claimed that they had been victimized at the hands of the corrupt subgovernor, Kadri Bey, and his sons, and insisted that they would not disperse until the local council members, who had been summoned to the post office by the crowd, sent a telegram to the governor in Kastamonu. The alarmed governor immediately informed the Sublime Porte of the demonstration.[213] After discussing the matter with the Imperial Palace, the Sublime Porte fired the subgovernor and appointed the local commander as acting subgovernor.[214]

Encouraged by this demonstration and its successful outcome, the local guild wardens of Kastamonu submitted a petition to the governor on January 6, 1906, and requested exemption from the poll tax. Upon the governor's refusal of the petition, the wardens sent a similar telegram to the Grand Vizier.[215] The governor ordered that gatherings of the guild wardens in front of the post office stop. The guild wardens, however, succeeded in dispatching two additional telegrams to the sultan and the Grand Vizier. The governor, afraid that a new demonstration would be swelled by "ignorant people," maintained that it would be too risky to attempt to disperse the crowd. He suggested to the Sublime Porte that it summon a few guild wardens to Istanbul in order to calm the town.[216] Meanwhile the wardens invited the people to assemble in the main square in front of the post office and declared that either the governor or the Grand Vizier must have blocked the submission of their petitions to the sultan. Otherwise, they claimed, a favorable response would have been forthcoming, as in Sinob. They now sent a new telegram to the Minister of Justice asking him to pass the content of the telegram on to the sultan.[217]

The next day a group of local guild members gathered at the local post office and declared that they would not leave the building until they received an affirmative answer to their petition.[218] They decided to send a telegram via a foreign consulate to the First Chamberlain Tahsin Pasha informing him of their position. When Tahsin Pasha submitted the news to the sultan, the latter ordered the commander of the garrison in Kastamonu, Ali Rıza Pasha, to go to the post office and communicate with him directly. Then the sultan asked the commander, whom the crowd had allowed to enter the post office, whether the demonstration was a rebellion against the government and himself or was a mere protest against the governor, Enis Pasha. Upon receiving the answer that the only objective of the demonstrators was the dismissal of Enis Pasha, the sultan ordered his dismissal and appointed the commander of the town as acting governor.[219]

In the meantime the government instructed the local authorities "to accustom people to the poll tax gradually."[220] In contrast to its restrained and appeasing gestures vis-à-vis the masses, the government moved decisively against the leaders of the rebellion. It expelled the former assistant governor of the town to Tripoli of Barbary and sent the warden of the butchers' guild, Hacı Ali Efendi, to Ankara under strict police control. It also banished others to various provinces.[221]

The sultan and the government further instructed the new governor to seek out other individuals who had had a hand in the disturbances.[222] The new governor, accusing the remaining exiles of having organized the movement, took strong measures against them, such as deporting them to small towns within the province and quartering all bachelor exiles in bachelor houses under close scrutiny.[223] He further proposed that exiles who had established relations with locals be banished again. The government rejected this proposal, however, out of fear that news of it would spark new disturbances in the town.[224]

It is difficult to pinpoint the role played by Sabahaddin Bey's league and the Dashnaktsutiun in the demonstrations and subsequent activities in Kastamonu. The journal *Türk* devoted a detailed and informative article to the event and later published a letter that had been sent from Kastamonu. Both focused on the corruption allegedly prevalent in the province and presented the movement as a local phenomenon; they did not even insinuate Young Turk incitement or participation.[225] The journal *Hayat*, however, contended that "the crowd got excited because of the activity of the Young Turks."[226] This statement must have been a reference to the exiles and sympathizers of the various Young Turk organizations in the province. No evidence supports it. The later distribution of Sabahaddin Bey's journal within the province does indicate the league's desire to include the region in its sphere of activities. Here again there is no clear evidence of the league's direct involvement in the demonstrations. Although the participation of Armenians in demonstrations along with Muslims was quite unusual,[227] it is difficult to know whether local Dashnaktsutiun members played a role in this participation.

Demonstrations in Trabzon

The first demonstrations in Trabzon took place in October 1906. The demonstrators sent telegrams to the sultan asking him to dismiss the governor, İbrahim Pasha. When they received no response, they forced the governor to leave office. Trabzon had a history of mutinies because it was one of the main ports from which reinforcements were dispatched to Yemen,[228] and also because soldiers on some occasions had mutinied on failing to receive their pay.[229] Under the circumstances, the sultan formally dismissed the governor in order to avoid further complications.[230]

Opposition journals also reported that dissidents had affixed placards demanding the reopening of the parliament to the walls of the governor's office.[231] The reopening of the parliament, of course, was a matter beyond merely local concern.[232] The League of Private Initiative and Decentralization had a branch in Trabzon and frequently corresponded with dissidents there, and *Terakki* was widely distributed.[233] But again it is difficult to ascertain the extent of the league's role in these demonstrations. The same is true for the Dashnaktsutiun, which had one of its four Eastern Anatolian headquarters in Trabzon.

In December 1907, following new demonstrations against the governor[234] and the dispatch of telegrams to the *Şeyhülislâm* requesting him to intervene and halt the movement of reinforcements to Yemen,[235] Ottoman intelligence agents received information concerning secret correspondence between the Young Turks in Paris and exiled officers in Trabzon.[236] İshak Bey, who had hidden Bahaeddin Şakir in his house and helped him to flee to Europe, had led these officers until they were arrested and exiled to various towns in Eastern Anatolia.[237] Bahaeddin Şakir later attested that this was a shattering blow to the CPU central committee, since it took them a long time to reestablish a branch in Trabzon.[238] It is beyond any doubt, however, that the CPU branch in Trabzon played a commanding role in the revolutionary activities that took place there in late 1906 and during 1907 and 1908.

The complexity of the organizational frameworks of the three organizations— Sabahaddin Bey's league, the Dashnaktsutiun, and the CPU in Trabzon—prevents us from forming a clear idea about their respective roles in the demonstrations and other undertakings. It would not be inaccurate, however, to assume that all three organizations exerted their best efforts to foment antigovernment feelings and to turn local dissatisfaction that stemmed primarily from economic and social causes into political-revolutionary activity.

Unrest in Diyar-ı Bekir

Another town in which constant demonstrations and antigovernment activities took place during this period was Diyar-ı Bekir. Here the movement started as a reaction against pillaging and looting by a local Kurdish tribal leader, Milli İbrahim, whom the sultan had made a pasha in 1902. The Ottoman government for quite a while had been disturbed by İbrahim Pasha's violent attacks on villages in the region and had tried to take action against him, but to no avail.[239] Finally the local populace gathered to protest.

In early August 1905, following several days of demonstrations, a crowd occupied the post office and sent a telegram to the Sublime Porte complaining about İbrahim Pasha's aggression.[240] The *mufti* and the assistant-governor of the town supported the demonstrators, and they too sent telegrams and dispatches requesting government action.[241]

The government failed to respond affirmatively, and another mass demonstration took place in the town in November 1905. A new telegram in the same vein was sent to Istanbul.[242] This time the Ottoman administration, afraid of further and larger demonstrations, set up a commission to investigate the matter.[243] Despite the recommendation of the commission to court martial İbrahim Pasha,[244] the governor took no serious measures against him, with the result that İbrahim Pasha's depredations only increased.[245] Consequently, on January 27, 1906, a new demonstration took place during which hundreds of sheikhs, ulema, notables, merchants, and ordinary people dispatched yet another telegram to the Sublime Porte complaining about the situation.[246]

Although the local authorities assured the people that İbrahim Pasha would be punished and even banished, again no action was taken and the warlord continued his pillaging.[247] He even asked for British protection in the event that the government took serious action.[248] This situation caused the locals to occupy the post office once again for eleven days in November 1907 and to bombard the authorities in the capital with telegrams of protest.[249] Because of the circumstances, the Ottoman cabinet held an extraordinary meeting to discuss the measures to be taken against the warlord. It was decided that the pasha should be sent to Aleppo and kept there until a commission could prepare an investigative report on the matter, that the crowd that had occupied the post office should be assured that İbrahim Pasha would be placed under house arrest in Aleppo, and that troops would be rushed to Diyar-ı Bekir to put an end to the demonstrations.[250] The local administration promptly applied these measures and suppressed all demonstrations until the Young Turk Revolution of 1908.[251]

There is no information available concerning the participation of Sabahaddin Bey's league in the demonstrations in Diyar-ı Bekir. Although the Dashnaktsutiun had a small branch there, the town was by no means a hotbed of the Armenian movement, and there is no evidence of Dashnaktsutiun or Armenian participation in the demonstrations against Milli İbrahim Pasha.[252] In principle, a demonstration against a Kurdish warlord who was backed by the palace was in accordance with the understanding reached between Sabahaddin Bey's league and the Dashnaktsutiun. The former's nonexistence and the latter's weakness in the town, however, seem to have caused them to miss this golden opportunity for cooperation. The complaints, made in one of the telegrams signed by hundreds of Muslims, that İbrahim Pasha had also been helping Armenian revolutionaries to flee to Egypt and Europe instead of fighting against them, make it clear that neither Sabahaddin Bey's league nor the Dashnaktsutiun had a hand in the demonstrations.[253] The fact that Ziya Bey (Gökalp), who later became a leading ideologue of the CUP,[254] and other individuals such as Pirinçcizâde Ârif Bey, who had previously taken part in anti-Armenian activities, played leading roles in the organization of demonstrations further confirms their predominantly local character.[255] Finally, although the exiles in the town were quite numerous, none of them seems to have had close ties to Sabahaddin Bey's league.[256]

Revolutionary Activities in Van

Van, as the center of the Armenian revolutionary movement in the Ottoman Empire, was undoubtedly one of the most suitable towns for Sabahaddin Bey and the Dashnaktsutiun to make common cause.[257] All Dashnaktsutiun local committees in the region were subservient to the Van committee, and the town was also the printing and distribution center for both the Dashnaktsutiun and the bogus Turkish revolutionary committees. As a matter of fact, the Dashnaks carried out almost all their activities and propaganda in the town either openly or under the guise of Young Turks.

In April 1907, Dashnak leaders in Van held meetings with "mollahs and other Turks" and reached an "entente with the so-called Young Turks."[258] According to British representatives in the town, "if a Moslem employee etc. is condemned by the *fedaî* [the Dashnak revolutionaries] the sanction of the Young Turk committee is first obtained before assassinating him."[259] This so-called Turkish revolutionary party was "in close sympathy with the [Armenian] *fedaî*."[260]

No information was available about the identities of these "so-called Young Turks" mentioned in many British documents,[261] and it is therefore difficult to determine whether they were sympathizers of Sabahaddin Bey's league. Reports about the activities in Van reveal that the leaders of the movement demanded constitutional liberties and called upon the people not to pay taxes to the central government. The former demand was made by the "Young Turks" or individuals disguised as such.[262] As a matter of fact, pro-Dashnaktsutiun sources claimed that "déjà les turcs publient des feuilles et envoient des circulaires pour faire la propagande de la révolution."[263]

These "so-called Young Turks" and Dashnaktsutiun members initiated a campaign against Governor Âlî Bey and Assistant Governor Ermenak Efendi. British diplomats claimed that the governor had received threats both from the Dashnaktsutiun and the Young Turks.[264] Dashnak committee members assassinated Ermenak Efendi, whom they accused of being an informer, and the local Dashnaktsutiun branch and the "Young Turks" in the town drove out the governor. The Dashnaktsutiun central committee presented the assassination of Ermenak Efendi as the extermination of an individual who had been "trying to harm the union between the Armenian and Turkish communities and playing off one brother in soil against the other."[265] Scholars who have obtained information from reliable Armenian sources describe the campaign against the governor, Âlî Bey, as a Young Turk-Dashnaktsutiun operation.[266] Following their success against Governor Âlî Bey, the "so-called Young Turkey Party continue[d] to distribute their pamphlets, but they confine[d] their efforts to attacking the central government."[267]

Armenian organizations maintained that conservative Muslims in the town had formed a committee named "Friends of Islam" and distributed a pamphlet entitled "The Union of Muslims" as a riposte to these activities.[268] The Sublime Porte questioned the local authorities about the existence of such a committee, and the governor of Van responded that "for the time being there is no such committee in Van, nor are appeals [being distributed here]. A committee, however, had been formed five or six months ago to defend Islam against Armenian *fedaî*s, and an appeal had been distributed by this body."[269] The Grand Vizier used strong language against Osman Zeki Efendi, the judge at the court of appeal and the alleged leader of this anti-Armenian committee;[270] he threatened him and his fellow officers and officials with dismissal and banishment and warned them that they would "not ever be employed in the government service again," should they "interfere in Armenian matters."[271] The members of this anti-Armenian committee responded by persuading the local *mufti* and Muslim notables to send telegrams to Istanbul defending them and asking the government to take measures against the Dashnaktsutiun.[272] The Grand Vizier instructed the governor to tell these individuals that "since the government knows its duties well, they should occupy themselves with their own everyday affairs."[273]

The March 23, 1908 assassination of the Armenian informer David, who had caused the collapse of the Dashnaktsutiun network in the town, turned Van into a battleground.[274] The Dashnaktsutiun issued an appeal to the Turks stressing the "bon accord qui existe entre nous."[275] "Les Turcs libéraux de Van," on the other hand, sent a note of protest to the Affaires étrangères.[276] It is difficult to determine the real identities of these "liberal Turks of Van" who were able to convey such a note to Paris and have it published by pro-Dashnak journals.[277] One may nonetheless speculate that they must have had close contacts with the Dashnaktsutiun. The Van incident also caused the two major Young Turk organizations—the CPU and Sabahaddin Bey's league, which had decided to form a common front against the regime of Abdülhamid II by establishing an alliance with the Dashnaktsutiun in the Second Congress of Ottoman Opposition Parties held in December 1907—to demonstrate their solidarity.[278]

The Dashnaktsutiun Committee undoubtedly organized and carried out the revolutionary activities in Van. It also promoted Young Turk propaganda through bogus committees, propaganda that was in complete accordance with Sabahaddin Bey's program. While this propaganda promoted decentralization, it carefully avoided using phrases like "autonomy" and "federation," words that Sabahaddin Bey also carefully avoided; these terms appeared only in open Dashnaktsutiun propaganda.[279] In Van the burden of the "joint Young Turk-Armenian movement" fell on the Dashnaktsutiun,[280] and although it was claimed that the Dashnak revolutionaries were working toward "an armed rising against the government in conjunction with the Young Turk Party" and that they were "in communication with the Young Turk Party,"[281] most likely all these statements refer to Sabahaddin Bey's league, whose members in fact played a very insignificant role in this activity.

The Unending Rebellion of Erzurum, 1906–1907

The most important rebellion that took place in Eastern Anatolia during this period was undoubtedly the Erzurum revolt of 1906–1907. For many reasons Erzurum suited both Sabahaddin Bey's league and the Dashnaks. It was the most important city in Eastern Anatolia with a sizable Armenian community, and Ottoman official documents stated that the good order of the city depended on "measures to be taken against the attacks of the Kurds from outside."[282] In addition, "[a]lthough it was a pacific local branch and confined [itself] to spreading propaganda and collecting funds," one of the four local Dashnaktsutiun branches in Eastern Anatolia was in Erzurum.[283] Ottoman documents reveal that in general "Erzurum [was considered] a town that would go to an extreme in popular" movements.[284] Erzurum was also regarded as an ideal town to which to banish dissidents, most of whom were officers serving in the IV Ottoman Army.[285] All these reasons likely caused Hüseyin Tosun, who had been dispatched to the region by Sabahaddin Bey and had posed as a grocer in Erzurum, to form a branch of League of Private Initiative and Decentralization there, and to make the town his hub for revolutionary activities in the region.

The dissidents' first action in Erzurum was to submit a petition to the local judge, Osman Zeki Efendi, requesting exemption from the poll tax and the tax on domestic animals. As the dissidents anticipated, the judge refused.[286] Following this unsuccessful attempt, thirteen dissidents signed a new petition demanding exemption from these taxes and submitted it to the governor on March 5, 1906.[287] Not surprisingly, the governor ignored the petition.

On March 12, 1906, the governor alerted the Grand Vizier's office to "anxiety among the people and secret incitement and provocations against the payment of the tax on domestic animals" in the town. He further stated that in some neighborhoods people had obstructed officials engaged in posting tax lists. In an attempt to bolster his authority, the governor invited the leading members of the ulema and the notables to his office one at a time, and solicited their assistance.[288] The central government approved the governor's action and further advised him to find suitable ways to collect the taxes.[289]

Discontent mounted in the town, however, and the leaders of the antigovernment movement proposed the preparation of a round-robin to be signed by all male inhabitants over 18 years of age. The signatories demanded that no money be sent to the capital, that all local revenues be spent for local civil and military purposes, and that Erzurum be exempt from the poll tax and the tax on domestic animals.[290] The governor cabled Istanbul informing the central government of the local population's demand for exemption from both taxes.[291]

In the meantime, the leaders of the dissidents sent a telegram to the First Chamberlain's office for submission to the sultan.[292] As instructed by the imperial palace, the Grand Vizier paid no heed to the demands or to the governor's indirect approval of them; he once again asked the governor "to prevent seditious activities" by taking appropriate measures.[293] The next day the Grand Vizier's office cabled the governor requesting him to tell the people that "the aforementioned taxes were levied to protect the country and to defend it against enemies . . . and proposing their abolition contradicts patriotism." In addition, the Grand Vizier told the governor that the sultan had ordered measures to be taken against agitators if they would not listen to this advice and disperse.[294]

On the same day, however, a crowd marched to the post office, occupied it, and sent telegrams to the Grand Vizier's office and to the Ministry of Justice, stressing the governor's "absolutism" and pleading that attention be paid to their demands. They also conveyed a veiled threat of a large-scale uprising against the authorities.[295] The Grand Vizier's office instructed the governor to tell the "reasonable people" in the crowd that the taxes were statewide and no exception favoring a certain province could be made.[296] In response, the crowd sent a second telegram to the Ministry of Justice on March 24, 1906, demanding an imperial decree "to avert the rebellion that would otherwise take place."[297]

The next day a shorter telegram was sent to the sultan through the First Chamberlain's office.[298] The government's response of cutting back regular tax payments was too little, too late. Apparently the leaders of the rebellion had dispatched public criers to the markets and requested that all Muslims and non-Muslims close their shops,[299] and on March 29, 1906, they did so. Rebels blocked all the main avenues and streets, while the Armenian committee members posted in the Muslim neighborhoods an appeal reading "Our Armenian delegate from Erzurum gave his approval for the collection of the taxes recently levied, stating that our community could pay these [taxes]. Our community, however, craves money for bread. We do not recognize this delegate. Never."[300]

On March 31 the crowd severed the military telegraph wire, thereby cutting the local commander's communications with the IV Army Headquarters in Erzincan.[301] The troops that the governor dispatched to disperse the crowd took up positions in front of the post office but refused to open fire on their countrymen.[302] On April 3 the marshal of the IV Army informed the Ministry of War of restlessness among the Armenians in connection with the issue of the Armenian delegate, and he requested fresh troops.[303] On the same day, having heard rumors about a government decision extending the governor's term, all Muslims and non-Muslims once again closed their shops and gathered in front of the *medrese,* where the *mufti* of the town, Lûtfullah Efendi, taught.[304] In the meantime, at the behest of the sultan, the Ministry of War dispatched a divisional general from Erzincan to Erzurum and instructed him to start a thorough investigation pending the arrival of a special committee from Istanbul.[305] At this point the central government reached the conclusion that the movement that had manifested itself in petitioning against the governor and the new taxes had "originally stemmed from internal and external provocations."[306]

As a last resort, the Grand Vizier sent an ambiguous telegram to the *mufti* and the ulema of the town. On the one hand, it assured them that the commission that had been dispatched to Erzurum would investigate the matter and that the governor would be dismissed if such was warranted. On the other hand, it issued a stern warning to the dissidents by asking the *mufti* and ulema "to inform the notables and dignitaries of the town that the shops should be opened, and that everyone should occupy himself with his own work, cease engaging in rebellious activities against the orders and directions of the government, and become obedient and acquiescent without delay; otherwise it has been decided that the state will take strong action against the leaders of the movement."[307] In addition, in order to calm the crowd, the government dismissed the governor, Nâzım Bey, and appointed Divisional General Şevket Pasha as acting governor,[308] instructing him to stop counting animals for the new tax on domestic animals and to limit himself to counting the sheep for the regular *ağnâm* tax on sheep.[309]

All these gestures to appease the crowd were fruitless, however, and on April 30, 600 people signed and submitted to the authorities a fresh petition demanding the dismissal of twelve local officials.[310] Although the government had already decided to use military force against the protesters, the members of the special investigation commission who had recently arrived in town advised against excessive force because of the delicate situation.[311] Only the arrival of the new governor, Atâ Bey, and his oral promises of exemption from both taxes calmed the people. The utter humiliation of the former governor, who was forced to leave the town without any official ceremony and was not even saluted by the officers and soldiers at his departure, seems to have appeased the people and led them to believe that they had achieved an important success.[312]

The sultan and his government, however, had no intention of yielding to the demands of the revolutionaries in Erzurum. Even when the sultan issued an imperial decree ordering the appointment of a new commander and a new governor,[313] he still insisted on their taking all necessary measures to restore order, including declaring martial law if necessary.[314] Also the government instructed the new governor to find a suitable way to collect the new taxes.[315]

As a result, the new governor's honeymoon with the dissidents in Erzurum did not last very long. Under instructions from the imperial palace, he carried out a secret investigation of the officers who had helped the revolutionaries during the demonstrations. At the same time, the revolutionary movement assumed a more organized form under the strict control of a committee.[316] Subsequent to the investigation, the governor banished Major Safvet Bey—a leading officer among the revolutionaries—to Erzincan on September 12, 1906, on account of his "having relations with some stupid people and having participated in seditious activities."[317]

The governor's next initiative, however, triggered a second uprising in the town. After obtaining a favorable imperial decree,[318] the governor ordered the arrest and banishment of the three key figures behind the revolutionary activity—Mufti Lûtfullah Efendi, Pulcu Yusuf Efendi, and Tahsin Bey—three hours before midnight on October 22, 1906.[319] But the dissidents, who had gotten word of the governor's plan, retaliated swiftly. A crowd occupied the governor's office and captured the governor, who had hidden in a nearby house. He was wounded and held hostage at the İbrahim Pasha Mosque.

During and after the capture of the governor, clashes took place in which the mob lynched two police commissioners and seriously wounded two policemen and a gendarme. The revolutionaries declared that they would not free the governor until the three revolutionary leaders were returned safely to the town. Under the circumstances, the authorities decided to comply, and the crowd freed the governor in return.[320] The incident had the effect of expediting the revolutionaries' aim of replacing the civil authority and establishing a firm grip on the town's affairs.[321] The new governor, Nuri Bey, informed the government that with circumstances as they were, no punitive measures could ever be taken.[322]

The central government nonetheless instructed the governor and the commander in Erzurum to prepare a detailed investigative report on the event.[323] Upon receiving the report, the government set up a special commission composed of cabinet ministers and decided to replace the local officers and soldiers with personnel sent from other regions; the commission further resolved to banish two officers who had been dismissed from the army, Muhiddin Bey and Ali Faik, first to small towns in the province and then to other remote provinces.[324] In the meantime, in order to appease the people, the government promised to reduce the poll tax, declared a conditional amnesty to those who had taken part in the antigovernment activities,[325] and excused non-Muslims from payment for exemption from military service for one year.[326]

Although the promise of an amnesty appeased the people to a certain degree, the revolutionaries decided to compose two new documents: a note thanking the sovereign for the amnesty, and a petition demanding exemption from the tax on domestic animals. A huge crowd submitted both documents to the governor following a demonstration. The governor subsequently advised the Grand Vizier of "the impossibility" of collecting any taxes.[327] He added that if the government failed to take measures, its authority would be severely damaged. Thus he proposed abrogating the tax on domestic animals for good and levying the poll tax only on the wealthy.[328] These promises secured a temporary tranquility in the town, and soon after, the news of the abolition of both taxes throughout the empire reached Erzurum, causing great rejoicing among the masses.[329]

Having lost their main instrument for agitation, the dissidents now switched to two new issues. First, as the governor put it, "the Armenians in the villages have engaged in a conspiracy by attempting to renounce their [Ottoman] citizenship and by converting to Islam." The governor took swift measures against the conversions and averted any major disturbances. The second issue, however, brought the town once again to the brink of a general rebellion. All soldiers in the town, the reservists as well as those in uniform, demanded their unpaid salaries. Since 1881 the state had usually been paying wages only five or six times a year because of economic problems, and so the total amount of the unpaid salaries was extremely high and the government could never have met such a request. As a matter of fact, the soldiers had demanded the payment of salaries unpaid since 1884, in order to ensure that their demand could not be met.[330]

The governor's unfavorable response caused the dissidents to initiate a new revolt. They blocked the streets and even prevented the governor from entering his office.[331] During this new uprising, the dissidents, "acting under the orders of the revolutionary committee,"[332] circulated revolutionary publications.[333] Although the governor's later disbursement of small sums made little impact on the soldiers and people, the subsequent discontinuation of the disbursements due to the extremely limited sources at his disposal caused great resentment.[334]

From this point on, the revolutionary organization that "ha[d] taken the shape of a[n] . . . organization for the purposes of opposing the government" became the de facto local government of Erzurum.[335] As Sabahaddin Bey's journal stated, the government disappeared from the scene:

For fifteen days there has been no government in the country [province]! There has been, however, no time during which public order was as stable as this. All around the town the shops are open, trade is free. The absence of law enforcement officers such as policemen and gendarmes has not been noticed at all, since the nose of not one single individual, Muslim or Christian, has been bloodied. The political discipline of our people has also been appreciated by the European consuls.[336]

The local committee in Erzurum effectively filled the vacuum of authority. An Azeri journal likened the situation in the town to that in some Iranian cities under the administration of local *anjumans*. The local committee levied taxes on people,[337] it had the last word on all matters such as tax payments and local administration,[338] and it fixed market prices for goods and prohibited anyone from selling anything at a higher price.[339] The local committee also dismissed many officials. The Russian Consul General Skriabin observed that the remaining officials had done their best to appease the local committee.[340] The people too, applied to this body instead of the local government when they faced problems.[341]

The central government's response of changing officials had absolutely no effect on the local population.[342] When a grain shortage occurred in August 1907, the dissidents seized the opportunity to provoke new unrest.[343] The people gave the following ultimatum to the powerless governor: "if the government will not solve the problem, the profiteers causing this will be liquidated." Subsequently, on September 9, 1907, a mob lynched two "profiteers," one Muslim and one Armenian.[344] Afterward the dissidents organized several meetings among themselves and met with military commanders and the governor. They constantly accused the local government of causing all the disorder in town. The former director of the local revenue service, Uzun Osman, who claimed that he was "uttering the feelings of everyone," bluntly declared that "the government had not existed for eight months."[345]

Receiving this dire news, the sultan set up a military commission to address the crisis. In its report the commission recommended the ruthless suppression of the rebellion, if necessary by opening fire on the demonstrators. The sultan accordingly issued an imperial decree and he also requested that the authorities prevent any Muslim-Armenian strife.[346] The local military and civil authorities were informed of the decision at once.[347] Yet again a new governor, this time Abdülvahab Pasha, was dispatched to Erzurum from Mosul.[348] The new governor dismissed the leaders of the dissidents from their positions, the *mufti* being the most important among them.[349] The local committee took no retaliatory action.

The government, which had been secretly bolstering the police and gendarme forces in the province for almost a year,[350] sent in more reinforcements from other provinces to strike the long-awaited final blow.[351] With some of its members opposed to armed defense against the government forces, the local committee could not agree on how to act.[352] Then on November 25, 1907, the government forces entered the town and arrested all those who had taken part in the revolutionary activities after February 1906.[353] Under torture the imprisoned revolutionaries confessed their participation. They were later tried at the Erzurum Criminal Court of Appeal, and 69 individuals were sentenced to various terms.[354]

Thus one of the longest-lasting local revolutionary movements in the Ottoman Empire came to an end. For the purposes of this study, the most important aspect of this movement is its connections with the Young Turk organizations and with the Dashnaktsutiun.

The Role of the Young Turks and Dashnaktsutiun

Undoubtedly the most striking characteristic of this movement was the clear existence of an organizing committee that acted like an *anjuman* similar to those in Iranian towns in 1906. Various sources called this organization the Can Veren Komitesi (The Committee of Those Who Give Their Lives).[355] Almost all sources identified this committee as a Muslim organization, and the CPU called it a "Turkish Committee."[356] Although Soviet historians describe an organization composed of merchants,[357] the complete list of the arrested members of the committee includes many lower-middle and lower-class people such as drapers, bakers, butchers, porters, carpenters, and even many jobless individuals.[358] The participation of many butchers and drovers in the revolutionary activity unquestionably stemmed from the terrible consequences of the tax on domestic animals that stifled the local economy. Although some historians have described the movement as a "bourgeois revolt" based on the fact that notables and ulema led the movement, the active participation of the lower-and lower-middle-class people challenges this thesis.

An assertion made by the extremely conservative former court of appeals prosecutor of Erzurum, Osman Zeki Efendi, concerning the identities of those who took part in the movement also deserves attention. Osman Zeki told members of the investigative committee that he had obtained a handwritten and "extremely seditious" pamphlet prepared by the organizers of the rebellion that would provide invaluable information about the revolt.[359] He then submitted a "pamphlet advocating Shīʿism" to the governor of Van,[360] but he altered his testimony by saying that the pamphlet was only indirectly related to the rebellion.[361] Available Ottoman documents reveal that many individuals who had been exiled because of their unorthodox opinions "contradicting Islam" had been sent to Erzurum less than a year before the initial unrest,[362] and that the Ottoman government had resolved to build an elementary school in Erzurum "to correct the religious precepts of the Alawites and to thwart their conspiracy" during the revolt.[363] Such government policies undoubtedly further alienated the Alawites. Their participation in a movement led by orthodox ulema, however, seems very unlikely. Moreover, no other Ottoman documents suggest this possibility. Therefore, though we know very little about the attitude of the Alawites toward the local revolutionary movement, we may conclude that Osman Zeki Efendi's claim was a highly exaggerated one.

As for the relationship between the local Committee of Those Who Give Their Lives and opposition organizations abroad, the CPU had absolutely no ties to this organization, nor did it receive reliable information concerning the revolt. The CPU central committee did express a desire to establish an alliance with the leaders of the Committee of Those Who Give Their Lives, whose identities were unknown to them,[364] and attempted to distribute CPU publications in the region, especially in Erzurum. A piece of secret CPU correspondence written a month before the crushing of the revolutionary movement tries to persuade the addressee to smuggle CPU publications into Erzurum and other places in the empire from Kars, thus revealing the CPU's inability to disseminate its propaganda in Erzurum at the time.[365] Even as late as February 1908 the CPU central committee in Paris was still trying to obtain the names of influential individuals in Erzurum, Van, and Diyar-ı Bekir.[366] The CPU secret correspondence also indicates that one of the officers who took part in the initial disturbances, and who played a significant role "in this local activity's taking a political form," was banished during the early days of the unrest, first to Erzincan and then to Trabzon, where he became a member of the local CPU branch.[367] Apparently he had not received instructions from the CPU during the revolt.

Furthermore, although the CPU organs praised the revolutionary activities[368] and presented them as an example to be emulated,[369] their information was not original and was sometimes inaccurate.[370] Since the CPU central committee was badly misinformed about the events taking place in Erzurum, it decided to send a congratulatory letter to Marshal Mehmed Zeki Pasha, who it thought was helping the revolutionaries.[371] In fact, the marshal was exerting his best efforts to crush the revolutionary movement and demonstrate his complete loyalty to the sultan.[372] CPU members in Salonica reproached the CPU External Headquarters for its inability to establish ties with the revolutionaries and provide accurate information about the events.[373]

It was only after the Ottoman government had crushed the movement that the CPU External Headquarters succeeded in smuggling a former officer, Ömer Naci, who had participated in the Persian revolutionary movement, into Erzurum and Van to organize dissidents there. But it was too late. The region was no longer fertile ground for revolutionary activities, and accordingly Ömer Naci returned to Iran.[374] In summary, the CPU played no role in the genesis of the events and, its strong desire notwithstanding, it did not participate in the movement during its later phases.

Hüseyin Tosun and the Activities of the League of Private Initiative and Decentralization in Eastern Anatolia

In contrast to the CPU, the League of Private Initiative and Decentralization did play a significant role in the movement. The league dispatched Hüseyin Tosun from Paris, and he in turn participated in all the activities until his arrest. He first traveled to Caucasia with the help of the Dashnaktsutiun Committee.[375] He then went to T'bilisi and met with Azerbaijani socialists who were printing appeals drafted by Sabahaddin Bey and sending them clandestinely to Eastern Anatolia.[376] While he was in the Caucasus, he went by the pseudonym Sheikh Ali. His Armenian friends helped him obtain a Russian passport, and he penetrated the Ottoman border with the help of Dashnaktsutiun guerrillas.[377]

Various sources underscore Hüseyin Tosun's role in organizing revolutionary activities in Eastern Anatolia as a representative of Sabahaddin Bey's league. The most important among these are comments made by the two original founders of the CUP. Abdullah Cevdet relates the following:

> [Hüseyin Tosun] left Paris and entered Anatolia during the winter of last year to organize committees and initiate revolts. He traveled around the Anatolian provinces a couple of times. Most of the time he trekked through the snow-covered and misty mountains of Sivas on foot. He was setting hearts ablaze everywhere and inculcating in them the duties of soldiers and people. He prepared the Erzurum revolt. He created the organization. . . . He was a grocer in Erzurum. . . . I finish my words by quoting a passage from one of his letters sent from Sivas: "We are walking on snow and ice with torn and tattered boots. Customs guards besieged us assuming that we were tobacco smugglers. I thought that they understood who and what we were. I surmised that it was time to wrestle with Martini rifles and that the last moment of my mission had come."[378]

Upon setting foot on Ottoman soil Hüseyin Tosun was captured by an Ottoman military patrol and suspected of being an Armenian revolutionary. The commander of the troops who apprehended Sabahaddin Bey's agent, however, happened to be his classmate, and the following conversation took place between the two former cadets:

— I have established contacts with the Young Turks. I set forth on the journey with the help and under the instructions of the organization. I arrived in the Caucasus as a Russian subject. My intention is to go to Erzurum and create an organization [branch] there. . . .
— These things all sound very good; however, how can you conduct correspondence?
— Champan, the director of the Post Office at Kars in Russia, is a Russian courier. The letters and journals will be smuggled across the border with his help and given to the

director of the Erzurum Post Office. He, too, is a member of the organization. I shall open a shop to sell fur for headgear and Russian merchandise.[379]

With the help of the Armenians, Hüseyin Tosun was later appointed the Russian Consulate's mail carrier,[380] an assignment that must have helped him distribute banned publications and proclamations. Russian sources describe his initiatives as a good example of the joint actions undertaken by Armenian "bourgeois" organizations and Sabahaddin Bey's league.[381] We have in fact very little knowledge of Hüseyin Tosun's organizational activities. Ottoman documents state only that "he had joined the conspirators" in Erzurum.[382] Other sources provide conflicting information. While his Young Turk friends described him as the brain of the movement in Erzurum and in the region, and even portrayed him as "the soul of the Erzurum revolt,"[383] a local historian who collected information from the local people maintained that most of his revolutionary associates in the region did not share his views.[384] Nevertheless the fact that some locals joined Sabahaddin Bey's league suggests that Hüseyin Tosun not only participated in the revolutionary activities but also promoted Sabahaddin Bey's ideas.

Because Hüseyin Tosun bore a Russian passport, the Russians came to be involved. Under torture, Hüseyin Tosun confessed his real identity and repeated the confession in front of the dragoman of the Russian consulate.[385] Because of his unusual status, Hüseyin Tosun was separated from the other prisoners and sent to Istanbul, where he was incarcerated.[386]

Two other members of the League of Private Initiative and Decentralization whose names were provided by a confidant of Sabahaddin Bey to a scholar in 1951[387] became leading figures in the revolutionary movement. Sıdkı Efendi was arrested and charged with distributing revolutionary materials in March 1907.[388] The other member, Durak Bey, was one of the eight leaders apprehended and arrested on November 25, 1907.[389] He was later sentenced to perpetual detention along with seventeen other individuals who had led the movement.[390]

In addition to these two leaders, some officers who were members of the local committee sent letters to *Terakki,*[391] and these furnish the most accurate information about the revolutionary events. *Terakki* even hinted that the league's leaders knew the identities of the leaders of the local movement.[392] Finally, a confidant of Sabahaddin Bey, Abdullah Cevdet, even prepared an anthem for the revolutionaries of Erzurum to chant during the demonstrations.[393]

The Dashnaktsutiun and the Revolutionary Activities in Eastern Anatolia

The Dashnaktsutiun's role in these events is hard to pin down. At the outbreak of the disturbances in the town, Ottoman intelligence received information that "decisions had been taken by Armenian committees in Europe to carry out murderous acts in the provinces of Erzurum and Bitlis."[394] It appears that Armenian dissidents in Erzurum synchronized their activities with their Muslim counterparts, who were able to stir up much larger and more effective crowds. Şevket Pasha, who served as acting governor during the initial phase of the rebellion in 1906, underscored the joint—that is, Muslim-Armenian—character of the movement. He added that "this alliance [was] not something new. It materialized a couple of months ago and became visible in February 1906."[395] Armenians also made voluntary donations to the local committee, to the utter amazement of the Ottoman government.[396]

On three occasions, when tension between the government and the Muslim population was at a peak, Armenian committee members undertook actions that further exacerbated the situation for the Ottoman authorities. In March 1906, when the government was seriously considering armed intervention to crush the movement, the local Armenians challenged the authority of the Armenian representative to the local administration. They posted their manifestos in the Muslim quarters of the town and gave their full support to their fellow Muslim dissidents.[397] A Russian diplomatic report attested that in return the Committee of Those Who Give Their Lives made demands on behalf of the Armenians for such things as a reduction of the military exemption tax.[398]

In March 1907, again at a time of peak tension, the Armenians, according to the governor, worsened the situation by engaging in "a conspiracy by attempting to renounce their [Ottoman] citizenship and converting to Islam." Pro-Dashnaktsutiun sources mention joint Armeno-Muslim revolutionary declarations and comment that such an act was "unique dans l'histoire turque."[399] Still more interestingly, an Azeri journal praised such Armenian actions.[400] Pro-Dashnaktsutiun sources also emphasized the exceptionally good relations between the Armenians and Turks throughout the events.[401]

As for Armenian participation in the revolutionary movement, a British diplomatic report provides information about the arrest of an Armenian named Mĕgĕrdich Balasanian. The Ottoman authorities apprehended Balasanian in order to obtain information about "the revolutionary party's pamphlets."[402] A more interesting event, however, is the arrest of the aforementioned Sıdkı Efendi. Sıdkı Efendi, a member of the Erzurum branch of Sabahaddin Bey's league, active in the distribution of "seditious papers," was apprehended in connection with the bogus Turkish Allied Party's threat against an army contractor. *Sabah'ül-Hayr* accused this army contractor, Kâmil Efendi, of informing on its supporters to the local government and aiding in their arrest.[403] Following this threat, Kâmil Efendi received a threatening "seditious letter," which he immediately submitted to the governor of Van. After a short investigation, Sıdkı Efendi was found to be the person who had sent the letter and was immediately arrested.[404] As a result of Sıdkı Efendi's arrest, the Ottoman Minister of the Interior assumed that *Sabah'ül-Hayr* had been the organ of the "committee members who organized the Erzurum incident."[405] A Young Turk journal went one step further and claimed that *Sabah'ül-Hayr* had been the organ of the Committee of Those Who Give Their Lives that had conducted all revolutionary movements in the region.[406]

The agents of the so-called Fédération Révolutionnaire Turque, which was simply a front for the Dashnaktsutiun, also distributed revolutionary placards in Erzurum.[407] This committee, also called the Fédération Arméno-Turque by a pro-Dashnaktsutiun journal, worked actively to keep the union between Armenians and Turks in effect.[408] It is thus readily evident that members of Sabahaddin Bey's league and the Dashnaktsutiun worked hand in hand to agitate the masses. The Committee of Those Who Give Their Lives, which either was inspired by the Dashnak *fedaî* organization or adopted such a name to impress the Armenians, was supported by them. At the same time, bogus Turkish committees had the participation of members of Sabahaddin Bey's league. We nevertheless have enough evidence to conclude that it was an independent committee. There is no indication that any Armenians were members of this body.[409] As was stated by Osman Zeki, who was the prosecutor at the Erzurum court of appeals, in exchange for Armenian support the committee made demands on behalf of Armenians. He further claimed that "this committee was founded either to advocate Armenian aspirations by deluding the people through demanding the abolition of some taxes, or to pursue a secret policy along with the Armenians."[410]

Another interesting aspect of the local committee is its effectiveness within the districts and subdistricts of Erzurum. A joint Muslim-Armenian movement appeared in these small towns simultaneously with the one in the provincial center.[411] For example, on the very same day that the local committee in Erzurum submitted to the governor a round-robin with 600 signatures, more than 100 Armenians in Pasinler forced the Armenian representative on the local council to resign.[412]

Another example is what occurred in Hınıs. At the peak of the initial rebellion, on April 11, 1906, a petition decrying corruption among civil and military authorities was presented there on behalf of all the Muslims and Christians, "sealed by nineteen Armenians from fourteen Armenian villages." The local authorities prevented hundreds of villagers who had gathered at the district center from demonstrating, sending them back to their villages after "giving them the necessary advice."[413] People in small towns and villages asked for the dismissal of local officials simultaneously with the Erzurum committee's demands in the same vein.[414] Moreover, intercepted telegrams sent from the districts of Hınıs and Toprakkale to one of the leaders of the local committee in Erzurum leave no doubt that the movement in the districts was indeed the result of "provocations from the center town."[415] In another town, Bayburd, contemporary observers described the inhabitants' activities against officials[416] as the work of "the revolutionary committee branch" there.[417] The Ottoman government's subsequent investigations and its dismissal of local officials in the districts seem to have done little to placate the people.[418]

The propaganda of the Erzurum committee also merits attention. Although the committee's initial demands were of a local character, soon thereafter it started to employ a rhetoric that had never been used by any provincial organization. As the British consul commented, to assume "that the Erzurum mussulmans themselves will venture upon a general rising would seem to be extremely improbable in view of their isolated position. . . . [I]t is significant that the revolutionary documents and the pamphlets printed, I believe, in Europe, find their way here."[419] In Marshal Mehmed Zeki Pasha's words, "as a result both of perusing seditious, harmful papers published in Europe and Egypt and brought here, and of being deluded by foreigners and conspirators who are here as exiles, liberal ideas became popular among some people."[420] Indeed, the locals who had developed a keen interest in these "liberal ideas" read aloud the "seditious publications" to illiterate people during secret gatherings.[421]

Along with promoting ideas such as "constitution, parliament, and political participation," some of the local committee's leaflets employed a strongly Islamic tone. One appeal, for example, made the following statement:

O our brothers in religion! . . . We have appealed to you on many occasions; however, we could not discern even a little bit of your patriotism. Is this what the union of Muslims is all about? If you do not know, ask the *mufti*s and *hoca*s and learn. If our action is in accordance with the decree of God, then you, too, [should] join us. . . . This time, in order to put an end to this maladministration, and to secure that administration through consultation which is prescribed in divine statutes, Muslim practices, and rules derived from the Prophet's own habits and words, we demanded the acceptance of a constitutional regime and formation of a national assembly. . . . If the foreigners once intrude among us and intervene in our affairs, they will undoubtedly work for the interests of their own countries.[422]

Other appeals addressed to soldiers and compatriots included language such as "we obtained *fatwā*s from *hoca*s and *mufti*s avowing that our efforts are in conformity with the decrees of God and the Prophet,"[423] "defense of our fatherland and our religion," and "love for religion."[424]

Alongside these appeals with their decidedly Islamic rhetoric, however, were other manifestos in Erzurum that used a very different language:

O Mussulmans, Christians, Jews—all of you Ottomans! . . . . O Ottomans brothers in the soil! You are even as a family dwelling in one house. . . . Let us hold out the hand of comradeship to one another; let us love one another like brothers, and work together for the happiness of our country. Our government, as it now is, pays no heed to law, recks nothing of the general condition of the people; and until it is freed we shall see nor happiness nor wealth, nor peace. . . . Ottomans in order to escape from this horrible abyss, there is one way, and only one, and that is, through the ordering of the Empire even after the pattern of civilized lands, and the proclaiming of justice, equality, liberty, and right. . . . O Mussulmans, Christians, and Jews—all of you Ottomans! Your creeds ordain charity toward one another, living peaceably together in friendship and goodwill. Our land, which is the common heritage of us all, bids us unite and help each other. . . . O brothers in the soil! . . . Our need is a Constitution—liberty, justice, a parliament. Shout till you are hoarse! Make our voices heard on all sides and publish it in all the land![425]

Although these appeals all demanded "a constitution," they must have been prepared by various people. Available sources indicate that five groups were circulating propaganda material: the Committee of Those Who Give Their Lives, Sabahaddin Bey and his disciples in Paris,[426] Azeri dissidents in the Caucasus preparing appeals under Sabahaddin Bey's instructions, Ali Haydar Midhat, who exerted great efforts and spent his private fortune disseminating constitutional propaganda in Eastern Anatolia,[427] and finally the Dashnaktsutiun in the guise of the "Turkish Allied Party." The propaganda disseminated by these groups turned a local rebellion, originally stemming from provincial difficulties, into a constitutional movement. An Azeri journal claimed that after the Ottoman government arrested, interrogated, and investigated a certain dervish named Mehmed Ebulfezzan, it concluded that "the revolt in Erzurum did not indeed stem from economic reasons, that is to say, it was not carried out by the local people but was the work of a political party abroad."[428] It is impossible to know whether this interesting account is accurate. Nevertheless, we may confidently contend that the Young Turks abroad and in Eastern Anatolia were responsible for turning a regional disturbance into a fully-fledged constitutional movement.

The Revolutionary Activities: Centrally Coordinated or Spontaneous?

Foreign newspapers[429] and diplomats[430] likewise underscored the importance of the "constitutional movement" in Eastern Anatolia and attempted to find reasonable motives to explain this unexpected development. From the early days of the revolutionary activities in Eastern Anatolia and the Black Sea basin, diplomatic reports, press coverage, and later scholarly studies all focused on the shared aspects of the numerous revolts of 1905–1907. Foreign consuls, European diplomats, and foreign press coverage lumped together all the rebellions, demonstrations, and conspiratorial activities that took place in Eastern Anatolia and on the Black Sea coast.[431] All sources as well as all subsequent scholarship based on them have portrayed every mutiny led by unpaid soldiers or by privates who refused to serve in Yemen, every protest by officers against their superiors,[432] every mob demonstration against a local governor, and every round-robin signed by locals as a link in a revolutionary chain forged in the same center.

The rich Ottoman archival material, however, reveals that such expressions of discontent were quite common during the last three years of the Hamidian regime, and that most of them had nothing to do with any political opposition movement.[433] Rather they were all prompted by the general economic crisis and/or local and personal reasons. The sheer ubiquity of the disturbances argues strongly against the hypothesis that they were the result of a centrally directed plan.

For example, even in remote and isolated parts of Eastern Anatolia similar events occurred during the same period. In a town such as Çemişgezek people stormed the governor's office and prevented him from carrying out his duties.[434] In central Anatolia, in the subdistrict of Hacı Hamza in Çorum, an official at the local court, Rasih Efendi, and another at the mayor's office, Talât Bey, encouraged people for many years not to pay any type of tax to the government. Finally in 1906 the government ordered their arrest.[435] In Siird, people united under the leadership of the local mayor, Abdürrezzak Bey, against the alleged corruption of the local governor and officials.[436] In Bitlis, a mass movement forced the governor, Ferid Pasha, to take refuge with the military garrison and then leave town.[437] The participants, however, made no political demands.[438] None of these movements had a defined "political" character and no one iterated words such as "constitution" or "parliament" during them. It should also be remembered that despite the great efforts of the revolutionaries in Erzurum to undermine popular reverence for the sultan, whenever the sultan directly dismissed a governor or promised exemption from taxes, the crowds would shout, "Long live the sultan!" and pray for the sovereign in the mosques.[439] Each direct intervention by the sultan precipitated mass rejoicing and thereby compelled the revolutionaries to search for new issues with which to agitate the people.

The Russian and Iranian revolutions of 1905 and 1906 certainly inspired dissidents in their attempts to stir up the masses. Some Young Turk journals, too, maintained that "the Russian Revolution made an impact on the actions of the Muslim . . . Committee of Those Who Give Their Lives,"[440] and Ottoman officials in the region worried that "the events taking place in Russia cannot be kept totally concealed here because of the closeness" of Erzurum to Russia.[441] It is also true that many Young Turk journals gave high praise to the Russian revolutionaries, depicting their activities as examples for their readership to emulate. But these views do not necessarily mean that either the Young Turks or the people who took part in the revolutionary activities shared the ideas of the Russian revolutionaries, or were even aware of those ideas. Among hundreds of articles praising the Russian revolutionaries, some of which went as far as to assert that "the Russian revolutionaries worship God and not the shadow of God as we do,"[442] there was only a single article published by *Terakki* that offered an accurate assessment: "The Russian revolution is not a result of social progress, but the result of the heavy industry built in the country by the absolutist regime."[443]

As an antigovernment uprising, the Russian Revolution of 1905 obviously provided a solid example to the dissidents in the Ottoman Empire. But to describe the Eastern Anatolian revolts as exemplary of "Leninism's role in the awakening of the Asian peoples"[444] is, to say the least, far-fetched. Halil Halid, one of the few Young Turks who published articles on the revolutionary movement in Anatolia, made what were probably the most incisive comments on the similarities between the uprisings in Anatolia and the Russian Revolution of 1905:

> The origin of this pacific uprising in Turkey is traced by some persons to the revolutionary movements which are going on in Russia, and also to the agitations for constitutional government which have lately been carried on throughout Persia. This is mere conjecture. The fact that the risings are taking place in those provinces of Asiatic Turkey which are close to the frontiers of those two countries has perhaps led to the supposition that revolutionary ideas have been introduced into Asiatic Turkey through Russia and Persia. This is far from being the case. Indeed, the example of pacific opposition to the Sultan's bureaucracy was first set by the people of the Vilayet of Castamoni, which is situated much nearer to Constantinople than to any Russian or Persian town near the Turkish border; and here revolutionary steps had been taken by the Turkish population some time before the late Shah granted a constitution to Persia. Again, the Turkish methods of revolution bear no resemblance to those which are practiced in Russia.[445]

Halil Halid also asserted that "this pacific revolution [had] been planned entirely by the young Turkish exiles."[446] The press coverage of the time frequently, perhaps too frequently, emphasized the role played by the exiles.[447] Ottoman sources reveal that many exiles attempted "to incite people" against taxes even in small towns.[448] Other sources highlight the participation of Tatars in the revolutionary activity.[449] No account, however, comments on the vital role played by the alliance of Sabahaddin Bey's league and the Dashnaktsutiun.

Ali Haydar Midhat, who had firsthand information about the relations between the local revolutionaries and Sabahaddin Bey's league, asserted that the Young Turk expatriates in Paris had indeed conducted the uprisings in Eastern Anatolia and on the Black Sea coast. He even maintained that the Young Turks in Paris had been using a code word, "constitution," to commence the revolutionary movement in a given town.[450] He also underscored the importance of the solidarity between Young Turks and Armenians in the towns where revolutionary movements took place.[451]

Although assuming that the alliance initiated rebellions by sending code words from Paris is nothing more than romantic embellishment, Ali Haydar Midhat's testimony provides convincing evidence of the alliance's active participation in the revolutionary events. As Vámbéry stated, the peasants and artisans in Erzurum and Van had understandable reasons to hate the regime.[452] The people's demand for the reopening of the parliament, however, originated in the propaganda of the various nonlocal revolutionary groups, the alliance being foremost among them.

Research demonstrates that the various movements that made up the so-called revolutions of 1905–1907 neither stemmed wholly from the same reasons nor fully shared the same characteristics. On the one hand, some of them were of an entirely local character and had nothing to do with the others although they took place during the same time frame. Others, on the other hand, do appear to have been interlinked.

The Roots of Popular Dissatisfaction

There is no doubt that the general dissatisfaction among the masses of the empire resulted largely from deteriorating economic conditions,[453] and from the government's conscripting and dispatching of large numbers of troops from all provinces to the Yemen.[454]

Contrary to what many scholars have maintained, the two taxes that caused the greatest dissatisfaction were levied long before the revolutions[455] and had caused numerous local rebellions and tension throughout the empire.[456] In Erzurum the first protests and demands for exemption from the taxes took place two years prior to the initial rebellion, though the people then made no political demands.[457] Although the government in the beginning categorically refused to yield to the popular demands,[458] rebellions and strong resistance in many provinces[459] compelled it to grant exemptions to some provinces and towns,[460] to reduce the taxes, and to alter the regulations.[461]

The government was well aware of the fact that these taxes were providing the revolutionaries with an effective weapon for stirring up the angry masses, but the budgetary crisis, a crisis that the Yemeni campaign significantly exacerbated, left it no alternatives.[462] The alliance of Sabahaddin Bey's league and the Dashnaktsutiun seized the opportunity provided by fiscal grievances to exploit antigovernment sentiment in a region heavily dependent upon livestock.

Revolts against new taxes and governors, and signings of round-robins against them, were hardly unusual events in the Ottoman Empire.[463] As a result, the locals did not need an example from Russia. They had plenty of their own. The difference between the revolts in question and the earlier uprisings lies in the political character of the revolts. The evidence clearly indicates that the metamorphosis of these local disturbances into fully-fledged political movements demanding the reopening of the parliament was driven by the Young Turks in general, and the alliance of the Dashnaktsutiun and the League of Private Initiative and Decentralization in particular, and not by the Russian Revolution of 1905. As Sabahaddin Bey stated, "A l'instigation de la classe intellectuelle, les paysans commencent à prendre conscience de leurs devoirs et leurs droits."[464] It was not a mere coincidence that only in the provinces in which Sabahaddin Bey's league carried out extensive propaganda and in which the Dashnaktsutiun had strong branches did the uprisings evolve into "constitutional revolutions." The bogus Turkish committees, which may be likened to Piltdown Man, caused many scholars to imagine a purely local and popular constitu-

tional movement in Eastern Anatolia and on the Black Sea coast. The Dashnaktsutiun–
League of Private Initiative and Decentralization alliance, however, makes these
rebellions an important chapter in the history of the Young Turk movement.

Sabahaddin Bey and High Politics

Following his failure in carrying out his eccentric coup d'état plan in 1903, Sabahaddin
Bey continued pursuing "high politics" by establishing relations with prominent for-
eign statesmen.[465] His disappointing early relations with the British Foreign Office[466]
compelled him to establish ties with politicians and eminent political figures in
France.[467] He became a close friend of former French Minister of the Navy Jean-
Marie-Antoine de Lanessan, who was the political editor of the influential daily *Le
Siècle*,[468] and he succeeded in obtaining financial aid from the famous French financier Baron de Lormais in order to pursue his decentralization program.[469]

With the help of his influential French benefactors and of his secretary, Joseph-Remy
Denais, who was at the same time the secretary of the Association des Journalistes
Parisiens and had worked as the editor of various Catholic journals such as *Le Stéphanois*,
L'Écho de L'Ouest, *La Défense*, and *L'Observateur Français*, Sabahaddin Bey became
"a well-known figure in Paris."[470] He received extremely favorable press coverage.
Dailies, ranging from the extreme Catholic *La Croix* to the anticlerical *L'Action*, publi-
cized his ideas,[471] and these won positive evaluations from well-known intellectual figures such as Anatole France.[472] Sabahaddin Bey's inflated image in France provoked
wild speculations that he would become the new sultan of the Ottoman Empire.[473]

In addition to helping publicize his ideas, Sabahaddin Bey's Catholic friends pub-
lished a highly controversial study entitled *Constantinople aux derniers jours d'Abdul-
Hamid*, by a Catholic priest named Paul Fesch.[474] One of its chapters, entitled "La
Jeune Turquie," was the most detailed story of the Young Turk movement written
until then, and its use of extremely rare Young Turk material amazed its readers.[475]
Sabahaddin Bey's private papers in the Bibliothèque nationale in Paris reveal that
Abbé Fesch was not a stranger to him, and Fesch had also published *Terakki* on the
prince's behalf.[476] The chapter on the Young Turk movement panegyrized Sabahaddin
Bey, while through its adoption of the prince's own rhetoric it implicitly but harshly
attacked Sabahaddin Bey's opponents. The Ottoman authorities therefore assumed
that the name Paul Fesch was simply a pseudonym.[477] They judged the book "to have
been written in an extremely despicable manner" and banned it.[478] The work thus
ironically lent credence to Sabahaddin Bey's pretense of being the leader of the Young
Turk movement.[479]

As for political activities, Baron de Lormais, who was described as "le champion
de l'enseignement congréganiste et du prosélytisme papiste en Turquie,"[480] helped
Sabahaddin Bey to take an astonishing initiative. In March 1906 the two went to visit
Pope Pius X (Giuseppe Melchiorre Sarto) and Cardinal Raffaele Merry del Val,
the Vatican's Secretary of State, in order to secure the Pontiff's support.[481] The
Vatican's Finance Minister Spolverini, who was portrayed by a Vatican source as a
close friend of Sabahaddin and de Lormais, arranged a private audience. Prince

Sabahaddin introduced himself as a representative of the Young Turk party and, more important, as an emissary of the Ottoman heir apparent Mehmed Reşad Efendi.[482] On behalf of the heir apparent, Sabahaddin Bey offered radical changes in the Ottoman administrative system that would prove beneficial to the Catholic Church. These reforms were to be carried out after the inevitable death of Abdülhamid II.[483] According to the available documents, the Pontiff listened to Sabahaddin Bey carefully and refrained from making any comments on the current regime in the Ottoman Empire. The Young Turk leader was "satisfied" with the audience.[484] Unfortunately, the available Vatican documents say nothing of such a secret meeting.[485]

From Rome, Sabahaddin Bey intended to travel to Berlin to have an audience with the kaiser.[486] It is plausible that Pius X had advised this trip, as well as Sabahaddin Bey's subsequent applications to Fürst Ernst Bernhard von Bülow, with whom he had been on very good terms.[487] The plan came to naught, however, because of the German chancellor's hesitancy to meet with a Young Turk leader.[488]

Young Turk circles quickly got wind of Sabahaddin Bey's Papal visit, and the CPU expounded upon the prince's relations with the Catholic Church in propaganda material, accusing him of taking money from the Pope for his activities.[489] Although Sabahaddin Bey immediately denied the allegations, the rumors reduced his already low prestige even further in the eyes of many Young Turk sympathizers.[490] It is also highly questionable whether the Ottoman heir apparent had authorized Sabahaddin Bey to strike bargains with the Pope; more likely the young prince simply pretended to be an emissary. Reşad Efendi's later statement concerning Prince Sabahaddin's request for Lt 40,000 in gold to organize a coup against Abdülhamid II, and his own refusal, makes the latter alternative more likely.[491]

Still, Sabahaddin Bey's initiatives gained momentum after his Vatican visit. In response, the sultan, who had been annoyed by his nephew's new campaign, sent Lûtfullah Bey back to Paris to prevail on Sabahaddin Bey to return. The latter, however, turned down the sultan's offer.[492]

Sabahaddin Bey saw a chance to launch a new political campaign when Sir Edward Grey delivered a speech in the House of Commons after the Denshawai incident[493] and during the Ṭābā border crisis. In his speech Grey maintained that "a fanatical feeling in Egypt has been on the increase. It has not been confined to Egypt, it has been stretching along the north of Africa generally."[494] Sir Edward's speech, and subsequent comments on the subject by prominent British statesmen accusing the German government and Abdülhamid II of inciting Muslims against French and British rule in North Africa, drew great attention.[495]

In France two diametrically opposed reactions occurred. The first challenged Sir Edward and maintained that he had confused Egyptian nationalism with Panislamism.[496] Sabahaddin Bey's advisor, de Lanessan, led the second and positive reaction by publishing an article in a British daily. He claimed that the German Empire was backing the fanatical Panislamic movement and that "at the present time, wherever there are Mussulmans, there are also manifestations of fanaticism which seem likely to augment in the future."[497] De Lanessan continued his analysis by focusing on the need for a liberal regime in the Ottoman Empire, and he presented Sabahaddin Bey's ideas without mentioning his name:[498]

It is indispensable that a Liberal and honest régime should be substituted for the abominably despotic power to which the whole of Turkey is subjected. In this respect France and England can play a considerable part. Intelligent, well-educated Liberal elements are not wanting in the Ottoman Empire. Within the last twenty-five or thirty years a generation has come into existence which knows the West, has frequented its schools and colleges, and aspires to the liberties enjoyed by the European peoples. . . . The ideas of that laborious, honest, and Liberal element are shared by the natural heir to the throne of the Ottoman Empire. . . . If it be true that Abdul Hamid is an invalid, and even likely to succumb to his infirmities, it is indispensable that the Liberal Turks should be encouraged to secure as his successor the legitimate heir to the throne. . . . It is indispensable that England and France should return to the policy formerly followed by them in the Ottoman Empire.[499]

The British Foreign Office judged that de Lanessan's "article appears to merit perusal."[500]

Undoubtedly having awaited such an approbation, Sabahaddin Bey authored an open letter to Sir Edward. The Foreign Office commented that Prince Sabahaddin "[g]ives his views on the subject, showing the importance which has been recently attached to the Kaliphate by the Porte, and not so much out of sympathy with Panislamism as out of hatred to the liberal or 'Young Turkish' movement, which is gradually increasing in strength in Turkey."[501] But it declined to respond to the young prince.[502] Despite this neglect, Sabahaddin Bey managed to publish his open letter in *The Times*.[503] The most important characteristic of Sabahaddin Bey's missive was its extremely pro-European stance in contrast to mild essays by other Muslim intellectuals and scholars on the subject.[504]

In this letter Sabahaddin Bey first underscored that "Turkey . . . is the seat of the Kaliphate."[505] This emphasis was wholly intentional and purposeful. In England many well-known political figures and scholars had questioned the Ottoman sultan's claim to the caliphate in an attempt to promote an "Arab Caliphate." Sabahaddin Bey's adherence to this group would have been well received among the British authorities, but it would also have deprived him of an important bargaining chip: the prospect of a benevolent Panislamism friendly toward Great Britain and France under his party's future liberal regime.[506] In principle, Sabahaddin Bey's Panislamic policy would also appeal to Russian statesmen and to the Dashnaktsutiun leaders, both threatened by Abdülhamid II's alleged Panislamism, as well as to the Muslims of Russia, who strongly opposed the idea of the "Arab Caliphate."[507]

Following this point about the Ottoman sultan's right to the caliphate, Sabahaddin Bey responded to the allegations of the European statesmen in the following manner:

Panislamic policy is by no means what it is imagined to be, the outcome of . . . fanaticism, it is merely the expression of discontent caused by the gradual encroachments of the European Powers.[508]

After this remark, which would have been well received by his Turkist opponents in the Young Turk movement, Prince Sabahaddin delivered two important messages to European statesmen. The first had very little to do with the actual topic at hand, but Sabahaddin Bey deemed it necessary. He explained that the Armenians and the Young Turks were natural allies and that it was the policies of the sultan that had prevented them from working together:

The Armenians, unlike other Christian communities now separated from Turkey, do not form a compact aggregation at one extremity or other of the Empire. . . . Accordingly nothing could be more natural than that a direct understanding should come about between Turks and Armenians, who were alike dissatisfied with the existing *régime*. Had such an understanding once been effected between all the elements of the Empire suffering from the same oppression, and had they all combined for action, it would have meant certain death to the present Government. Such a peril had to be averted at any cost, and a recourse was had to a massacre of Armenians and the wholesale banishment of the Turkish Liberals. . . . Thus alas! The chasm was still more widened in time between two peoples whose duty was and is still the same life on terms of loyalty and of mutual esteem.[509]

Sabahaddin Bey's second message concerned the new form of "Panislamism" that would arise under a "liberal" regime in the Ottoman Empire:

Official Turkey has evolved in the sense of theocracy out of hatred to the Liberal movement, not out of sympathy with Panislamism. But such is the course adopted by social Turkey that it can hardly look favorably upon either theocracy or Panislamism. Its theocratic tendencies have made the present Government unpopular. It is obvious, therefore, that its successor will never be able to renew such a woful experiment; besides for the fact that it holds a considerable number of subjects belonging to non-islamic creeds, the Ottoman Empire must enjoy a fair and impartial, and consequently a secular and constitutional government. Turkey feels, moreover, the need of keeping on correct, if not on friendly, terms with all the Powers, and she could hardly advocate the formation of a league between Mussulman peoples without compromising her relations with those nations which have Mohamedan subjects. Such a policy would even go against the real interests of foreign Mussulmans. Thus we are estranged from Panislamism through reasons of internal as well as of foreign policy. With the triumph of liberal ideas in Turkey, the great moral influence which Constantinople possesses over Islamism at large is destined to assume an intellectual character. Such an influence would serve as a powerful agent of reconciliation between the two worlds.[510]

As expected, Sabahaddin Bey finished his essay by saying that England was "unquestionably of all European administrations the most favorable to the liberty of nations."[511]

This letter drew enormous interest in Europe and boosted Sabahaddin Bey's image as a leader of a serious movement that could replace the current regime in the Ottoman Empire.[512] Sabahaddin Bey also received favorable reviews from prominent British journalists[513] and pro-Dashnaktsutiun journals.[514] Because he failed to win the recognition and backing of the Foreign Office, however, his campaign to replace Abdülhamid II's objectionable Panislamism with his liberal, cultural, and benevolent Panislamism bore no fruit.[515]

Sabahaddin Bey found a second opportunity to gain international backing when Abdülhamid II allegedly attempted to alter the order of succession in the Ottoman Empire. The issue became a matter of great interest in diplomatic circles. European foreign ministries, especially those of Great Britain, France, and Russia, paid close attention to it out of fear of an increase in German influence in Istanbul.[516]

Like other Young Turks who wanted to pursue high politics, Sabahaddin Bey did not let this golden opportunity pass.[517] First he wrote a manifesto entitled *Usûl-i Verâset-i Saltanatın Tebdili Mes'elesi ve Millet* (The Question of Altering the Succession to the Throne, and the Nation),[518] which was later widely distributed throughout the empire.[519] Second, he had Baron de Lormais submit a memorandum he had written on the subject to the Auswärtiges Amt.[520] Sabahaddin Bey was not aware of his thick file in the Auswärtiges Amt, and interestingly enough in this memorandum, entitled *Note sur l'ordre de succession au trône en Turquie*, he emphasized the importance of German business enterprises in the Ottoman Empire and made the following remark: "D'autre part, il est peu probable que l'Angleterre et la France se désintéressent d'une question aussi grave. Des troubles à Constantinople, voir même dans plusieurs régions de l'Empire, pourraient éclater et provoquer l'intervention des Puissances étrangères hostiles au changement réalisé." Following this remark, Sabahaddin Bey solicited the help of the German kaiser to thwart Abdülhamid II's alleged initiative.[521] It is not known how the Germans reacted to this note, since they did not comment on it. Sabahaddin Bey's later harsh criticisms of Germany and her imperialist policies toward the Ottoman Empire, however, suggest that he did not receive an affirmative answer from the Auswärtiges Amt.[522]

During the last days of 1906, Sabahaddin Bey made a third attempt and submitted a memorandum to the chancelleries of the Great Powers under the title *Mémoire des libéraux Turcs relatif à la Question d'orient*.[523] In it he once again stressed that "the Turks [were] an unquestionable and indispensable element of equilibrium" in the Ottoman Empire. He then reiterated his explanation of the causes of the persecution of the Armenians:

> People object to us [on account of] the Armenian massacres; but the Armenians were persecuted for political reasons, which are not at all connected with religion. They were not oppressed because they were Christians. An attempt was made at suppressing them because they were the future allies of the Turkish Liberals; and to persecute them, recourse was had to the nomadic and warlike Kurds, whom Europe wrongly classes and confounds with the Turks.[524]

Finally, Sabahaddin Bey stated that a future liberal regime would solve the Eastern Question and transform Panislamism into a movement beneficial for the Europeans. A confidant of Sabahaddin Bey claimed that the prince also succeeded in obtaining a letter from the heir apparent Mehmed Reşad Efendi stating that "he [was] for the constitutional regime." Sabahaddin Bey informed Sir Edward Grey and Clemenceau of this promise and requested their help for the Young Turk cause.[525] De Lanessan also solicited the help of French and British statesmen for the "great designs" of Prince Sabahaddin and his Parti Libéral Ottoman.[526]

Despite de Lanessan's initiative, this final effort of Sabahaddin Bey failed as well. The young prince had always thought that the imperiled interests and political concerns of Great Britain and France in the Ottoman Empire would compel these two powers to endorse the pro-British and pro-French Ottoman liberals and to recognize him as their natural leader and spokesman. Having in mind the example of Anglo-French diplomacy in the *Tanzimat* era, Sabahaddin Bey believed that these two powers could install a liberal regime in the Ottoman Empire through diplomatic machinations.

He had failed, however, to discern two important points. First, in contrast to what had been the case during the *Tanzimat* era, Abdülhamid II had succeeded in instituting a regime that could resist foreign diplomatic pressure to a certain degree. Second, the two powers in question had no desire to back the expatriate nephew of the sultan in his intrigues. It is true, however, that Sabahaddin Bey received support and financial backing from prominent figures such as de Lanessan and de Lormais.[527] Indeed, Sabahaddin Bey's opponents accused him of taking loans at high interest from foreigners with the promise that the borrowed money would be repaid from the Ottoman treasury after he seized power in Istanbul.[528]

The prince did succeed in attracting non-Turkish, and especially Christian Ottoman, groups with his peculiar interpretation of the theories of Edmond Demolins. He failed, though, to secure direct support from the Foreign Office[529] and Affaires étrangères, and the support of the Christian elements could be of use only in securing foreign intervention, not for carrying out a revolution. It should also be remembered that, as one Young Turk stressed, Sabahaddin Bey's Catholic benefactors were "radical reactionaries"[530] who were on extremely bad terms with successive French governments, especially after the drastic secularist reforms of 1905. Their endorsement could have done little to help the prince secure French governmental support. Sabahaddin Bey's fantasy of changing the regime in the Ottoman Empire with the backing of the Pope and the Catholic Church, despite the limited role of the popes in early twentieth-century politics, reveals a striking failure to understand realpolitik.

Likewise, the prince's dispatching of speakers to international peace conferences and similar gatherings could have done little to help him gain the Great Powers' endorsement, since they paid no attention to those "usual victims" who turned such platforms into forums of complaint.[531] The frustration of Sabahaddin Bey and his benefactor de Lormais in seeking support from the Great Powers seems to have driven them to participate in an assassination plot in early 1908. Like their other maneuvers, this attempt did not produce any results.[532]

Those who were aware of Sabahaddin Bey's secret initiatives and followed his illustrious career in high politics were not at all surprised when they heard the rumors about his secret deal with the Greek patriarch in Istanbul following the Young Turk Revolution of 1908,[533] or when Sabahaddin Bey approached the Russians during the First World War,[534] or when he wrote letters to Amīr 'Abd Allāh stating that "this is the precious opportunity that the Arabs have been seeking for a long time, [for] their emancipation from Turkish tyranny."[535] The most accurate and summarizing comment about him came from a British intelligence officer who remarked that "in the bankruptcy of his own political fortune he is willing to join any and every party which offers him a temporary advantage."[536]

Many former Young Turk sympathizers who commented on the movement in retrospect claimed that "The League of Personal [*sic*] Initiative and of Administration . . . possessed a vitality superior to that of the preceding organization, and rose considerably above it due to the strong intellectual tone of its political and social program."[537] In reality, however, this "strong intellectual tone" was of little help to Sabahaddin Bey, and his opponents' simple patriotism and eschewal of the high politics that many members of the Ottoman intelligentsia, and more important the officer corps, typically regarded with disgust, made him the perennial loser in Ottoman politics from 1902 to 1922. Hence the words which a disciple of Sabahaddin Bey used to describe their opponents apply better to the prince and his adherents: "extinct animal species, eternal losers in the perpetual theater of the struggle for life."[538]

6

The Reorganization of the Coalition and the Emergence of the CPU

In June 1905 *Şûra-yı Ümmet* proudly announced that the coalition had received a sum of FFr 2,000, "sent by a generous person who had combined patriotism and sublimity in his soul."[1] Shortly afterward, the same journal informed its readership of the arrest of many officials in the entourage of Yusuf İzzeddin Efendi, the second Ottoman prince in the line of succession to the throne.[2] The private doctor of the prince was among those who were arrested and banished.

That doctor was Bahaeddin Şakir. Shortly after graduating from the Royal Medical Academy with highest honors, Bahaeddin Şakir became Yusuf İzzeddin Efendi's private physician,[3] and at about the same time he established close ties to Ahmed Celâleddin Pasha, the former intelligence service director and the new protector of the Young Turks. As a member of the old CUP organization, Bahaeddin Şakir was in contact with various members of the coalition, and he persuaded Yusuf İzzeddin Efendi, who was against absolutism and advocated parliamentary regime,[4] to make financial contributions to the coalition.[5]

Ahmed Rıza claimed that *Şûra-yı Ümmet*'s announcement had provoked an extensive intelligence investigation leading to the arrest and banishment of Doctor Bahaeddin Şakir, who in fact had dispatched the FFr 2,000 to Paris.[6] A left-wing Parisian journal, on the other hand, asserted that Bahaeddin Şakir had been accused of clandestinely sending it an article on the Ottoman imperial family.[7] Indeed, such an article had appeared in *Le Courrier Européen*. It was nothing other than a eulogy of Yusuf İzzeddin Efendi, providing detailed information about the prince's "high qualities" while introducing him to the European public as the best of the Ottoman princes in the immediate line of succession.[8]

How the Ottoman authorities uncovered Bahaeddin Şakir's secret relations with members of the coalition in Paris is unclear. His contacts in the capital, however, were influential, and thus he did not spend much time in Erzincan, to where the palace had banished him.[9] He fled first to Trabzon and then, with the help of some of the coalition's sympathizers in that town,[10] he secretly boarded a ship for Marseilles. The Ottoman government's subsequent relentless efforts to apprehend him on his way and later to have him extradited from France bore no fruit, and he arrived in Paris in September 1905.[11]

Bahaeddin Şakir was undoubtedly the individual most responsible for reshaping the coalition and transforming it into a well-organized activist committee.[12] His foes accused him of converting the Young Turk movement into a "nationalist" activity,[13] and they drew an extremely negative picture of him, portraying him as a "caractère très vindicatif, esprit très borné."[14]

Upon his arrival in Paris, Bahaeddin Şakir embarked on his new mission: to unite the Young Turks under a single banner and to form a revolutionary committee. He further hoped to reach an agreement with the Armenian committees for common action.

Bahaeddin Şakir began his mission as the emissary of Yusuf İzzeddin Efendi. The prince had also asked Diran Kelekian, a confidant, to work with Bahaeddin Şakir.[15] Before Bahaeddin Şakir's flight from the Ottoman Empire, Kelekian, who was residing in Cairo, convinced Ahmed Celâleddin Pasha to support their initiative of publishing a revolutionary organ once every ten days.[16] But since the coalition had no desire to participate in any activity led by Kelekian and financed by the former intelligence service chief, Kelekian asked Bahaeddin Şakir to stay in Paris and strike a bargain with the leaders of the coalition.[17] Bahaeddin Şakir held two meetings with the leading members of the coalition, the first of which took place on November 26, 1905. Bahaeddin Şakir succinctly described the meetings as follows:

> The organization was in the form of a nucleus of a committee with a couple of patriots in Paris and Egypt and some correspondents here and there. It was pursuing an "evolutionary" program. Upon joining my patriot friends in Paris, I informed them about the needs of the fatherland, and the expectations of the people from the committee. I also proposed the addition of "revolutionary principles" to the evolutionary program. . . . Thus upon their acceptance of switching from [passive] enlightenment to an active program, the committee was reorganized and reestablished according to the principle of the division of labor.[18]

Bahaeddin Şakir's swift success in persuading the leading members of the coalition to make such a decisive change is remarkable. Nonetheless, it should not be attributed solely to his great talents, for all that many of the leading figures of the coalition appreciated these.[19]

In the fall of 1905, when Bahaeddin Şakir began his difficult mission, the activities of the coalition had fallen to their lowest ebb. In January 1905 the Ottoman high commissioner in Egypt, Gazi Ahmed Muhtar Pasha, had complained to Lord Cromer and the local authorities about the official organ's use of words such as "vice," "shameless," "impudent," and "prevaricator" in reference to the sultan.[20] Thus Ahmed Saib, who had been publishing *Şûra-yı Ümmet* in Cairo, was arrested and the journal was closed down,[21] disrupting publication for a month.[22]

Later Lord Cromer had ordered Ahmed Saib's release, after he spent a few days in custody. The British high commissioner, however, insisted before freeing him that Ahmed Saib give his "word as an officer" not to use "insulting language and derogatory phrases" in regard to the sultan ever again.[23] This promise, not surprisingly, severed the delicate relations between the "activists," who to this point had halfheartedly supported the publication of the central organ which they found too moderate, and Ahmed Rıza, who had insisted on publishing a nonrevolutionary central organ. Ahmed Saib informed Ahmed Rıza of his decision that "despite the protests of my friends, I will never break my word and will employ a more balanced language, which in fact would help better our cause."[24]

Besides the new impasse over "activism" among the coalition members, Muḥammad ʿAlī Ḥalīm Pasha, whose financial aid had made the publication of the coalition's official journals possible, told Sami Paşazâde Sezaî that he would no longer help them in publishing *Şûra-yı Ümmet* and that they should confine themselves to publishing *Mechveret Supplément Français*.[25] Another difficulty facing Ahmed Rıza and the coalition was Dr. Nâzım's stay in Cambridge, where he replaced Halil Halid as an instructor of Turkish at the university for more than a term.[26] Dr. Nâzım impressed many young Cambridge students, who liked this "fiery, podgy" Young Turk,[27] and he found interesting information in the British press to be used in the coalition's central organ;[28] but his stay in England upset the organizational work in the Paris center, which was totally dependent upon his assistance to Ahmed Rıza.

All these factors must have helped Bahaeddin Şakir persuade the leading members of the coalition to make a drastic organizational change, since he soon received approval from all these leading figures. Even Dr. Nâzım, Ahmed Rıza's closest disciple, told the positivist leader that they had "formed a new committee and [he] may join [them] to work together."[29] This development enraged Ahmed Rıza, who had considered himself the natural leader of the entire movement, let alone the coalition, and who had insisted on being recognized as the leader.[30]

Bahaeddin Şakir's original plan was to include Ahmed Rıza merely as a member in his new committee, and to form an alliance with Sabahaddin Bey's league and Ahmed Celâleddin Pasha. In a letter to Yusuf İzzeddin Efendi he explained:

I have given you information about my initiative to combine the prominent Young Turks here and then to unite them with the party of Ziya Bey [Ahmed Celâleddin Pasha]. I achieved a union composed of Muḥammad ʿAlī [Ḥalīm] Pasha, [Sami Paşazâde] Sezaî Bey, Doctor Nâzım, and a young fellow named Murad Bey. Since all these people were sincere and have good intentions, the union was achieved without difficulty. My initiative to achieve a similar union with Sabahaddin Bey [and his followers], however, came to nought despite my relentless efforts. In fact, although it did not bear any fruit, it helped me very much to understand their ideas and agenda. Taking advantage of this opportunity, I succeeded in obtaining a statement from them. I discovered their ideas and intentions partly through the help of the content of this statement and partly through private meetings. We did not have great difficulties in comprehending that the aforementioned person has no goodwill either for the interests of the benefactor [Yusuf İzzeddin Efendi] or for the happiness of the country. Upon receiving this statement, I told him that the absence of a single word on the primary issues such as the type of regime [that they preferred] and the succession to the throne illustrates the defectiveness of this program. . . . Thus he attempted to give lackadaisical responses by stating that he had never thought of that point and that it was necessary to mention it, etc. I insisted by saying that at a time when Abdülhamid was proposing [a change in] the succession to the throne, this issue should be treated in a party program. Thus he was compelled to say: "I will think it over. If I find it appropriate then I will write [add] it." . . . Subsequently, we held a conference in which I, my friends, the prince [Sabahaddin Bey], and his followers Nihad [Reşad] and [Ahmed] Fazlı Beys participated, and there I criticized [their] program on behalf of my friends. . . . Naturally, I was not able to bring us together with a person whose goodwill is questionable and who is not trustworthy and scrupulous; thus we opposed each other's [programs]. He was extremely vexed because we unmasked him. . . . Therefore, we divided our work load amongst ourselves. [Sami Paşazâde] Sezaî Bey will direct publications on Turkey and on domestic matters along with Murad Bey, and the others will help them occasionally. Your servant will write on the news from Istanbul and publish letters coming from there. Prince Muḥammad ʿAlī [Ḥalīm] Pasha will become treasurer while Nâzım Bey works under him; your servant will administer the internal organization and affairs relating to the branches, having Nâzım Bey also working under me. In addition, I will work as an intermediary between this party and the party of Ziya Bey [Ahmed Celâleddin Pasha]. It is clear that the important segment will be in my hands and this is the reward for my relations with the committee over many years and my good behavior. Ahmed Rıza Bey was somewhat aloof toward us, but I presented him a final offer and he now inclines toward us. I am confident that I will include him too. In such a case we shall leave him foreign affairs and publications [in] foreign [languages]. . . . With a unanimous vote I abolished the chairmanship. Our master would [easily] divine to whom this chairmanship belongs, namely to Your Highness. I will unite the organization with the party of Ziya Bey [Ahmed Celâleddin Pasha], which pursues [an] activist [policy]. I informed Ziya Bey of my initial work. I informed him of this result yesterday. I am awaiting his answer. Bedri Bey [Diran Kelekian] has also exerted great efforts in every field.[31]

Giving up all hopes for including Sabahaddin Bey and his followers in the new committee,[32] Bahaeddin Şakir focused on wooing both Ahmed Rıza and Ahmed Celâleddin Pasha. The former's name and prestige[33] and the latter's financial resources made them indispensable for his envisioned organization. At this point Bahaeddin Şakir was still optimistic about a tactical alliance with the Armenian committees. In order to achieve these objectives, Bahaeddin Şakir and his close confidant Diran Kelekian initiated a new campaign.[34] One of Kelekian's letters to his comrade Bahaeddin Şakir provides insight into this:

In a letter that you sent upon your arrival in Europe you had stated that "28816 43613 89216 [Ahmed Rıza]'s claim to the leadership is ludicrous." I am by no means a supporter of 28816 43613 89216 [Ahmed Rıza], but I respect him very much because he manifested courage and I observed that he had succeeded in regaining their [the Young Turks'] prestige following Murad Bey's return to Istanbul. . . . What would be the basis of the alliance? If the intention is to do something serious, the existence of 41456 24173 [Ziya Bey=Ahmed Celâleddin Pasha] and his eccentric desires would prevent us from this. If, however, the aim is to win him over and receive his financial support for a plan that has already been prepared, I am not against it at all. On the contrary, I find it extremely appropriate.

I have heard that 94751 51225 52715 52616 [Ahmed Saib] intends to pursue an independent policy by separating himself from Ahmed Rıza. 94751 51225 52715 52616 [Ahmed Saib] is a person who could only follow somebody else. He cannot be a leader or a guide. We should scrutinize him to see whom he is going to follow. If a new journal is established (I cannot conceive of a journal the columnists of which reside in Paris but which has its publishing house in Egypt; this cannot be called a journal but only a basket for a dealer in second-hand clothes), who would determine its policies and political inclinations? I am of the opinion that an opposition journal should carry out the function of a banner, so that those who share the same ideas would unite around it. *Şûra-yıÜmmet* cannot perform this duty. The reasons for this are: first, that Ahmed Rıza does not know how to render services to a nation; and second, that nothing significant can be done without creating a serious organization and carrying out propaganda within the country. . . . *Şûra-yı Ümmet* is not an organ of a party but a liberal informative journal. What we need, however, is an "organe de parti." . . . Well, we are going to wipe out this organization. We shall also dismiss Ahmed Rıza. This is fine, too. But which new organization would be established by us to replace the former organization? Whose name would replace the name of Ahmed Rıza? All right, if it is possible to establish a serious organization with independence and a distinct policy, then this would be achieved. A new name is necessary, however.

Along with this name a person is needed to direct and guide a party organ with his political ideas, behavior, and zeal. If these are present, then do not hesitate for a minute to wipe out the organization, because the advantages that would stem from it are limited. But such an organization which would be more or less helpful should not be destroyed for nothing. In summary, I would like to submit to you that, in my opinion, on the one hand, 41456 24183 52616 [Ahmed Celâleddin Pasha] should never be offended, but on the other hand not an inch of the interests of the nation should be sacrificed to his bizarre designs. These two points must be the basic tenets of our policy. If it is plausible to do something good through secret activity let's do it. Otherwise, there is no need to exhaust ourselves for nothing.[35]

At this point Bahaeddin Şakir and Kelekian decided to win over Ahmed Celâleddin Pasha and to include him in the new organization. The two comrades assumed that they could lure the former intelligence service chief by striking a secret deal with him.

Like many secrets in the Young Turk movement, however, this one did not remain a secret. Members of the coalition who were strongly opposed to the scheme soon learned of it. Ahmed Saib met with Ahmed Celâleddin Pasha and required him to donate a handsome sum to the central committee in Paris prior to becoming a member. Ahmed Saib further stated that since sympathizers within the country either did not know Ahmed Celâleddin Pasha or had a very low opinion of him, his becoming the official leader of the new organization was totally out of the question.[36] This statement exasperated Ahmed Celâleddin Pasha, who described the coalition as a "committee composed of three people."[37]

Adding to this friction, Ahmed Celâleddin Pasha laid out four conditions for his full participation in the new committee: (1) The abandonment of the use of the term "La Jeune Turquie," which according to him had become a dishonored title. (2) The inclusion of the Dashnaktsutiun and Hncakian Committees in the union; the pasha claimed that his negotiations with these two committees would soon produce very productive results. (3) Limiting Ahmed Rıza to a regular membership and not entrusting him with a decision-making position. (4) The continuation of *Şûra-yı Ümmet* as the central organ, with the statement under its masthead that it was "the organ of the Committee of the Ottoman Covenant (Cemiyet-i Ahdiye-i Osmaniye), the name proposed by the pasha for the new organization.[38]

In addition, Ahmed Celâleddin Pasha asked Diran Kelekian to draft an appeal to be distributed as the first manifesto of the new organization laying out its program.[39] While editing the draft, Ahmed Celâleddin Pasha prepared an appeal inviting all opponents of the regime to unite under an umbrella organization. According to his blueprint, all participant organizations would remain semi-independent and could also retain separate policies that might not be in accordance with the policies of the others. As for its policies, the new committee was to prepare two contracts: one among all the Ottoman elements, and the other between the Ottomans and their sultan. These two contracts would replace the constitution of 1876, which would remain in effect until the preparation of the two contracts.[40]

The coalition's leading members strongly opposed Ahmed Celâleddin Pasha's peculiar scheme.[41] Although Bahaeddin Şakir persuaded Ahmed Celâleddin Pasha to donate a fixed amount of money to the central committee every month,[42] from this point on the former intelligence service chief embarked on new initiatives independently. Thus Bahaeddin Şakir once again started working toward achieving an understanding with the non-Muslim committees in general, and the Armenian organizations in particular. He prepared a memorandum to be presented to the Armenian organizations and again asked his comrade Kelekian's opinion on this issue. Kelekian responded in the following vein:

> Although this memorandum is quite different from Ahmed Rıza's program and more favorable toward the non-Muslim subjects, it is not adequate for the purposes of achieving a union. In order to achieve a union, more extensive decentralization will be needed. The provincial powers, which would not be political but within the limits of *autonomie locale*, should be extended, and more substantial rights in appointing officials, and in discussing and approving provincial budgets, should be granted to the provinces. On the other hand, while Turkish would be the official language of the country and official correspondence should be exclusively in Turkish, in the local governments' appeals to the people (i.e., in appeals prepared on behalf of the local government, in official provincial gazettes, etc.) local languages must be used. The other day you posed to me the question "what do you mean by saying the honor of various nations?" Here! By assuring equality among the nations by allowing them to use their own languages in official affairs without causing disorder in the government's administrative affairs, the honor of the aforementioned nations would be respected. The state grants such a privilege to the Greeks in the Aegean islands and Iōánnina, and to the Arabs in Beirut and Tripoli of Barbary. Those who do not benefit from this are Albanians and Armenians. . . . I am submitting this as an opinion. I am aware that your friends would not agree with this opinion. Events would demonstrate to them, however, that the country can only be saved by such a liberalism, and that nobody can be deceived by a liberalism based on the principle of Turkification. The non-Muslim subjects are ready to become Ottomans, because they hope that by preserving their nationality and making their nationality a component of Ottomanness they would become Ottomans. Becoming Christian Turks by gradually forgetting their racial [origins], however, would not be found beneficial by them. Despite this fact, even if this program was accepted, most of the discontent caused by [the publication of] *Mechveret [Supplément Français]* would disappear.[43]

Receiving these criticisms from Kelekian, Bahaeddin Şakir requested him to draft a memorandum to be discussed at a gathering of the leading coalition members in Paris. Kelekian agreed and authored a detailed memorandum on the subject in which he underscored the following points:

> The liberal initiatives would be based upon two principles: First: To establish an organization composed exclusively of Turks or Muslims.
> Second: To achieve participation of the non-Muslim subjects.
> Nobody could deny the right to establish committees exclusively for the Turks or Muslims, since Armenians, Greeks, Bulgarians, Arabs, and Albanians have such committees pursuing various policies. When we recognize the fact that even in France a

nationalism emerged at the end of the nineteenth century and demanded the withholding of certain rights from the Jews, it would not be very surprising to see that the Turkish nation, which has pursued a "dominant nation/religious community" policy since the establishment of the sultanate, wishes to base the freedom that it wishes for the country on this condition. . . . Then the offer by the Turks to the non-Muslim nations is simply inviting them to a union based on *égalité individuelle*. I wonder if the non-Muslim nations would accept such a union? The experience of the last ten years indicates that they would not. . . . If the Turkish nation deemed that the pursuance of a nationalist policy is in accordance with its interests, it should be carried out without hesitation. . . . Then the elements which find individual equality inappropriate and demand *égalité raciale et sociale* would naturally act as they wish. . . . [Putting an end to European intervention] would only be possible by basing domestic politics on maximal liberalism and unequivocal justice. . . . In order to be able to achieve this, it is necessary to regard the fatherland as common for all, to abandon the claims of superiority and hegemony, and to limit oneself to being a "partner" instead of a "superior."[44]

Not surprisingly, the coalition's leading members rejected the memorandum. Following this rejection, Bahaeddin Şakir asked Kelekian whether they could approach the Armenian committees by presenting them with the new regulations of the CPU. The latter answered that "to say that non-Muslim elements would join a Turkish committee under that program would be only to mislead you."[45] The CPU secret correspondence gives the impression that Bahaeddin Şakir intended to go first to Vienna and later to Bucharest to meet with Armenian committee members. It seems, however, that the other party decided to cancel the meeting at the eleventh hour.[46]

Following his failure to interest the Armenian committees, some of which were bargaining with Sabahaddin Bey at the same time, Bahaeddin Şakir decided to abandon his grandiose scheme of uniting all the Young Turks, Ahmed Celâleddin Pasha, and the Armenian committees in an organization that would in reality be under his control. On the one hand, he engaged in an assassination attempt against the sultan co-planned with Kelekian and financially backed by Ahmed Celâleddin Pasha and Yusuf İzzeddin Efendi.[47] On the other hand, he moved decisively to transform the coalition into a revolutionary committee.

The Committee of Progress and Union and Its Organizational Framework

Left with only the ineffective coalition, Bahaeddin Şakir focused on reshaping this organization, whose leaders in Paris were likened to a group of generals without an army.[48] After arriving in Paris, Bahaeddin Şakir began studying other revolutionary organizations.[49] Upon completing his study, he pinned down the coalition's two greatest shortcomings:

Whenever we appealed to a committee which was demanding independence [for an Ottoman element] or pursuing a policy of liberation [for an element], or whenever we examined [the organizational structure] of a party, two significant shortcomings of our [organization] always caught our eye: organization and propaganda. In fact, the bitter experiences which are the result of our work in the last twelve years clearly demonstrate to us that it is impossible to benefit from publication unless an organization exists. What advantages can be derived from publishing a journal, regardless of the seriousness of its content, if it is not made available to the people and read? . . . We observe every day that the zeal and power of three individuals who are organized overwhelm the power of thirty people who are not.[50]

In another secret letter Bahaeddin Şakir further stated that a strong organizational framework and revolutionary propaganda that could arouse the movement's potential sympathizers would be the two main pillars of their new program. This statement and his assertion that "in order to reach a desired point every suitable way is a shortcut" both indicate that his intent was to create an organization that would pursue revolutionary tactics and propaganda rather than develop an intellectual program. He wrote:

> What kinds of tools are to be used? In order to answer this [question] we had to examine the policies of the committees that could provide us with examples to follow, and take lessons from their experiences. We spent quite a long time carrying out this examination. Upon completing it we perceived that we need organization more than anything else. . . . An article written two or three years ago by Sarafov, who wants to separate Macedonia from our fatherland . . . could give us a modest idea about organization. Sarafov's article is very useful for us in all aspects since one better judges the rightness or wrongness of his program through his foes' criticism rather than through his friends' acclaim. Look what this person says in his article . . . : "You Young Turks do not possess an organization worthy of Europe's acclamation. To achieve that you must make many sacrifices. The accomplishment of this mission depends on great efforts over a long period. Everything starts with the education of minds. Therefore, it is necessary to carry out extensive written and oral propaganda. Minds educated by the same ideas secretly assemble under the same banner. In this way they establish branches throughout the country. These branches have recourse to various methods to multiply their members. In this field each branch should be granted a certain degree of freedom. This would also greatly assist in increasing the number of individuals favoring special action."[51]

The "activist" policies defended by many Young Turks from almost the outset of the movement always underestimated the importance of "organization"; to them this word did not mean anything more than a group of people purchasing dynamite together. With its focus on revolutionary training and propaganda, Bahaeddin Şakir's new "activism" differed considerably from the absurd "activism" that had challenged the conservative and positivist opposition program of Ahmed Rıza but had never gained the upper hand or become the mainstream ideology in the movement. While the aforementioned program's lack of a revolutionary praxis was apparent, until Bahaeddin Şakir's challenge nobody had seriously confronted this problem.

Bahaeddin Şakir's first step in implementing his new program was to prepare new regulations for the organization. As we have seen, although the coalition's leading figures formulated new regulations following the 1902 Congress, their disagreement on various issues, and especially on the name to be given to this new committee, had prevented them from publishing any such code.

The new regulations prepared by Bahaeddin Şakir, and published in Cairo in January 1906, provided the coalition with a name that was nothing more than a reversal in the word order of the old organization's title. This would enable the leaders of the new committee to make a claim to the heritage of the old CUP, which until 1902 had gathered many factions under its banner as an umbrella organization. As a matter of fact, the establishment of the new organization was described by its central organ as a reorganization, and the first section of the Ottoman Committee of Progress and Union's regulations, entitled "the aims of the committee," was an exact repetition of the ideas found in the unpublished program of the coalition prepared in 1902, ideas that obviously reflected Ahmed Rıza's beliefs.[52] Apparently, Bahaeddin Şakir, who focused his energies on reorganizing the committee, paid very little attention to its ideological basis and found the aforementioned section satisfactory. From an organizational viewpoint, the most important parts of the regulations were the sections on the "branches" and the "central committee." The branches were given significant autonomy by the ninth article of the regulations, which stated that "every branch that accepts the regulations of the committee will join the committee after its internal regulations have the seal [of approval] of the central committee," and by the tenth article, the first line of which stated that "branches are free in their internal and regional administration."[53]

According to the twentieth article, "[t]he central committee may elect one of its members as director, who would serve under the conditions that might be decided by the [central committee]. The director will act freely, but should act in accordance with the regulations and be responsible to the central committee." This rule, however, was not implemented because of Bahaeddin Şakir's opposition. The twenty-third article, the second line of which stipulated that "members [of the central committee] would divide their duties for the sake of convenience," enabled him to create four divisions within the central committee that could work independently.[54] A later addendum gave each division the privilege of sealing documents related to its own transactions. Central committee decisions were to be sealed by a special seal reading "Central Committee of the Ottoman Committee of Progress and Union"; this was to be kept in an iron strongbox.[55] Apparently the four divisions were conceived as virtually separate offices authorized to correspond with other individuals and organizations by sealing documents with their own seals.[56]

Bahaeddin Şakir was thus responsible for the creation of four independent divisions of the central committee, a fact that also helped him to gain the upper hand in the organization. After long discussions, the committee accepted his plan, and later *Şûra-yı Ümmet* announced it in these terms:

> Since the policy that has been pursued for eleven years by our committee was found acceptable by Ottomans who wish for the salvation and happiness of the fatherland, the number of our members is increasing every day. In tandem with this trend, the transactions of the committee are expanding, too. The leaders of the committee, who believe that order is the foundation for success in everything, have decided to divide the central committee into four divisions according to the 23rd article of the regulations of the committee. According to this decision:
>
> *Mechveret Supplément Français* and all transactions and relations with foreigners are entrusted to Ahmed Rıza Bey as they were before. Mahmud Bey, the grandson of Mustafa Fâzıl Pasha, is obliged to assist Ahmed Rıza Bey in this field. The duty of editing the publication of (*Şûra-yı Ümmet*), our organ in Turkish, belongs to Sezaî Bey, the son of the late Sami Pasha. A member among the leaders of the committee has been assigned to assist Sezaî Bey.

Doctor Nâzım Efendi will be in charge of financial affairs under the supervision of Prince Muḥammad ʿAlī [Ḥalīm] Pasha, the son of Mustafa Fâzıl Pasha.

Doctor Bahaeddin [Şakir] Bey and Doctor Nâzım Efendi are assigned to carry out transactions related to, and correspondence with, all the branches.

In order to inspect various divisions of the central committee, and to secure harmony and order among the branches of the committee, a position of inspectorship, which would be rotated every six months, has been created. For the time being this position is entrusted with an eminent Ottoman.

The central committee will convene on a determined day every week. The committee's clerk charged with the duty of recording the proceedings of [the central committee] meetings is Seyyid Kenʿan Bey.[57]

The creation of such divisions within the central committee made Bahaeddin Şakir the hidden leader of this new organization, while Ahmed Rıza became the new organization's director of correspondence in foreign languages and the editor of *Mechveret Supplément Français*. These new titles meant very little, since Ahmed Rıza had already been publishing *Mechveret Supplément Français* as the organ of "La Jeune Turquie" for almost nine years. Ahmed Rıza undoubtedly expected that his charisma would make him a natural leader in a committee that did not have a position of leadership. The new organizational schema, however, reduced his role from that of charismatic leader to eminent member, and he became merely a respected elder who played a very small role in decision-making and organization.

In order to achieve a balance of power within the new central committee, Ahmed Rıza insisted on the creation of a new position of inspectorship. Because of the positivist leader's persistent demands, the inspector was charged in the initial draft of the reorganization document with "bringing the benevolent warnings made by outside sources to the attention of the central committee."[58] Bahaeddin Şakir and other members of the central committee later required this phrase to be omitted because "it gave the power of a director to the inspector," and they deleted this line from the reorganization document.[59] Despite this action on the part of Bahaeddin Şakir, the remaining duties of the inspector sufficed to make him a powerful figure within the organization. This maneuver of Ahmed Rıza's, however, was thwarted by Bahaeddin Şakir's success in appointing Mehmed Saʿid Halim Pasha [Muḥammad Saʿīd Ḥalīm Pasha], the brother of Muḥammad ʿAlī [Ḥalīm] Pasha, to this powerful position.

Mehmed Saʿid Halim Pasha's expanding relations with the opponents of the regime had caused the sultan to order his deportation from Istanbul in 1905.[60] At the sultan's behest, the Ottoman Police Ministry secretly requested him to leave the Ottoman capital and never return.[61] This was the most that the sultan could do against a member of the Egyptian royal house who was at the same time a member of the Ottoman State Council. Still this action was nothing less than an expulsion.[62]

Seizing the opportunity, Bahaeddin Şakir invited the pasha to work with them. Like many other prominent figures in his family, Mehmed Saʿid Halim Pasha was known as a sympathizer of the Young Turk movement, but he had played no significant roles in the movement until that point. In Bahaeddin Şakir's eyes, the resources at Mehmed Saʿid Halim's disposal and the British authorities' praise for him[63] made the pasha an ideal candidate for the new position halfheartedly created on Ahmed Rıza's insistence. Mehmed Saʿid Halim Pasha could donate money to, and obtain prestige for, the new organization, but from Cairo he could play only a minuscule part in the decision-making of an organization that had its headquarters in Paris. Appointment of any prominent Young Turk to this post would have overshadowed the dominant position that Bahaeddin Şakir had obtained despite his moderate title.

In fact, the only inconvenience that stemmed from this appointment was Mehmed Sa'id Halim Pasha's insistence on keeping his participation secret. Many sympathizers of the movement assumed that the person defined as "an eminent Ottoman" was Ahmed Celâleddin Pasha and strongly protested against this.[64] Despite the central committee's intention to announce the real identity of the inspector,[65] Mehmed Sa'id Halim Pasha opposed such a public proclamation;[66] therefore the CPU was compelled secretly to inform members in various branches that the former intelligence chief had not become the inspector of the new committee. Bahaeddin Şakir and Dr. Nâzım informed Mehmed Sa'id Halim Pasha of new developments and schemes on a regular basis, and the central committee renewed his assignment once every six months.[67]

The two other members of the central committee, Muḥammad 'Alī Ḥalīm Pasha and Sami Paşazâde Sezaî, were well-known and prestigious figures, but they had no intention of participating in organizational affairs.[68] The new clerk, Seyyid Ken'an, was a former lieutenant who had fled to Sicily and published a short-lived journal called *Tercüme* (Translation) in Palermo.[69] This young lieutenant with strong "activist" tendencies, and his fellow lieutenant Mehmed Fazlı, were the first two former field officers to join the CPU. Both became strong supporters of the new policy-makers, Bahaeddin Şakir and Dr. Nâzım.

These two medical doctors were probably the least knowledgeable members of the Young Turk movement. Their political ideas and ideological commitments were nothing more than a strong nationalism, patriotism, and opposition toward the real or alleged separatism of non-Muslim groups; these arose from emotion and personal experience rather than from academic studies, lofty philosophies, or fashionable theories. In fact, Ahmed Rıza stated in his posthumously published memoirs that Bahaeddin Şakir "was a fanatical patriot" and that Dr. Nâzım "was not very clever."[70] It was not Ahmed Rıza but these revolutionary figures, however, who continued to occupy key positions in the CPU, and later in the CUP after the revolution.

Mardin likens the role of Bahaeddin Şakir in the CPU following this settlement to the role played by Joseph Stalin in the Bolshevik party.[71] Although Bahaeddin Şakir did not bear any grandiose title such as director, secretary general,[72] or executive secretary, from this point on until 1918, he, along with his colleague Dr. Nâzım, served as an *éminence grise* in the CPU and later in the CUP. These two medical doctors established a firm, controlling grip over the organizational affairs of the committee.[73]

Having secured reorganization of the center, Bahaeddin Şakir took the initiative of including in the committee Ali Haydar Midhat, who had been carrying out a one-man propaganda operation. On October 6, 1906, Bahaeddin Şakir and Doctor Nâzım invited Ali Haydar Midhat to the CPU's offices, where they persuaded him to become a member.[74] Bahaeddin Şakir did not appoint Ali Haydar Midhat to any permanent administrative position other than membership in subcommittees preparing memoranda for the perusal of the central committee. A letter written by Bahaeddin Şakir reveals that he and the other CPU central committee members were not very enthusiastic about Ali Haydar Midhat's participation. "This pathetic person," he wrote, "is a sick man who would be included in the category of unlucky people called 'imbécile' by the authorities of medical science. We accepted him among ourselves to save him from the deceitful hands of the Greeks and make him acquire some experience. We failed."[75]

Ali Haydar Midhat's high prestige among the Turkic population in the Caucasus and the Balkans obviously stemmed from his clever use of his father's charisma in his propaganda.[76] This, along with various CPU branches' demands for his inclusion in the CPU,[77] compelled Bahaeddin Şakir to invite him to join the organization. Later his objection to the publication of an article critical of British policies toward the Ottoman Empire in *Şûra-yı Ümmet* led to his resignation from the CPU.[78]

During the course of his short membership, the organization took advantage of his name and of his articles and letters published in local Young Turk journals,[79] and even in journals opposed to the CPU.[80] A British memorandum on the CPU pointedly noted that "the name of Midhat Pasha was used and widely circulated in Turkey and Egypt as being connected with the Comité."[81] Ali Haydar Midhat's brief tenure as a CPU central committee member, without his holding any offices, demonstrates the devalued significance of membership in the central committee. It also shows Bahaeddin Şakir's firm grip over committee affairs, which enabled him to make a prestigious figurehead into a central committee member.

The New Editorial Board of *Şûra-yı Ümmet* and the Publication Policy of the CPU

In the meantime another development helped Bahaeddin Şakir extend his domination to the publication policy of the CPU. Ahmed Saib, who had been publishing *Şûra-yı Ümmet* on behalf of the coalition since April 1902 and bore the title of "director of the Cairo branch," was left outside of the central committee by Bahaeddin Şakir. The latter told Ahmed Saib that he would become "the director of the Egyptian branch of the CPU," albeit under strict central committee supervision. Until then Ahmed Saib had been acting almost independently, editing the journal as he wished; he must have found both Bahaeddin Şakir's strict instructions and the appointment of Ahmed Ferid to help him publish the central organ very distasteful. In addition, Bahaeddin Şakir brought a letter of Ahmed Saib to Sami Paşazâde Sezaî, concerning the editing of the central organ, to the attention of the central committee. After discussing the letter, the central committee denied Ahmed Saib a free hand in refusing draft articles submitted to the committee and required him "to present his reasons for rejection" to the central committee.[82]

Despite this warning, Ahmed Saib published an article under his signature in *Şûra-yı Ümmet* in which he excoriated the Young Turks, comparing them unfavorably to the Russian revolutionaries.[83] This act precipitated a new central committee meeting on June 13, 1906. The central committee found the parts of the article about the Young Turks "inappropriate, deceptive, and counter to [its] program."[84] The committee admonished Ahmed Saib, informing him that he could publish only translations from other languages and that he, like all other members, must first receive approval from the central committee if he wanted to publish his own ideas in the central organ.[85] In response, Ahmed Saib tendered his resignation and requested that the resignation be announced in the next issue of the central organ.[86] The central committee accepted the resignation but refused to publish it,[87] and it appointed former lieutenant Mehmed Fazlı as a special emissary to take possession of all publishing material and documents in the possession of Ahmed Saib.[88]

Ahmed Saib did not give up, however; he maintained that as editor he had the right to publish the central organ as he wished. Mehmed Sa'id Halim Pasha met with him in Cairo under the central committee's instructions to settle the problem. Ahmed Saib threatened the committee that he would file a lawsuit and publish a second *Şûra-yı Ümmet* if they published the journal without his consent.[89] Bahaeddin Şakir immediately convened the available central committee members in Paris and obtained a ruling for the appointment of Ahmed Ferid both as the editor of *Şûra-yı Ümmet* and as the person responsible for the committee's affairs in Egypt.[90] At the same time Bahaeddin Şakir contacted Prince Muḥammad 'Alī Ḥalīm Pasha, Sami Paşazâde Sezaî, and the inspector Mehmed Sa'id Halim Pasha to solicit their opinions on publishing the journal without reaching a settlement with Ahmed Saib.[91] Bahaeddin Şakir also contacted a Young Turk leader in Bulgaria who could help publish the central organ in Bulgaria, if necessary, and tracked down a typesetter in Paris in case the committee was unable to publish the journal in any other place.[92]

Despite all Ahmed Saib's efforts to obstruct publication,[93] Ahmed Ferid and Mehmed Fazlı succeeded in publishing the 98th issue of *Şûra-yı Ümmet* on August 15, 1906 in Cairo.[94] This issue contained a notice prepared by the central committee announcing Ahmed Saib's resignation.[95] Ahmed Saib cut all ties to the CPU and began to republish his journal *Sancak (Standard)*, which he had closed down in 1902[96] and which favored Sabahaddin Bey.[97] He also became a founding member of the Ligue Constitutionnelle Ottomane, which supported Sabahaddin Bey.[98]

Ahmed Saib's resignation strengthened Bahaeddin Şakir's position against Ahmed Rıza within the central committee, because instead of a confidant of the latter, somebody much closer to the former became the editor of the central organ and the person in charge of committee affairs in Egypt. The resignation also provided Bahaeddin Şakir with a felicitous excuse to reopen discussion of the publication policy of the CPU. In October 1906 Bahaeddin Şakir outlined a new organizational framework to be published in the central organ. The only difference between this and the version that had been published in the 98th issue of *Şûra-yı Ümmet* was the addition that "two leading members of the committee would assist" Sami Paşazâde Sezaî in editing the journal.[99] CPU correspondence reveals that they were Ahmed Ferid in Cairo and Bahaeddin Şakir in Paris. In December 1906, after discussions that lasted for two weeks,[100] a subcommittee under the chairmanship of Sami Paşazâde Sezaî and composed of him, Ali Haydar Midhat, Bahaeddin Şakir, and Doctor Nâzım prepared a detailed organizational diagram for the journal and made *Şûra-yı Ümmet* the first and only Young Turk journal ever published according to a preconceived plan. The plan called for Sami Paşazâde Sezaî to write the lead articles and for the creation of sections entitled "Publications in the Islamic World," "What are the Europeans saying about us?" "What are the [separatist] committee members doing?" and a special section providing information about the activities of revolutionary committees within the empire. Bahaeddin Şakir was to be in charge of drafting the sections in which would be published excerpts from letters from the Ottoman Empire and information about the branches.[101] Bahaeddin Şakir hoped that this new plan would make *Şûra-yı Ümmet* superior to all other journals published abroad.[102]

Bahaeddin Şakir's settlement not only made the central organ a more activist journal, or "a journal of struggle" as he called it,[103] but also put him in charge of drafting the most important sections of it; the editor was reduced to a copy editor working under the strict supervision of the central committee members responsible for the journal.[104] As the person in charge of all correspondence, Bahaeddin Şakir also started receiving all the drafts before publication, and whenever he wished to add new information to or omit certain parts of draft articles, he brought these changes to the attention of the central committee, which made decisions accordingly. On many occasions Bahaeddin Şakir himself chose members to edit a given article under his instructions.[105] He did not hesitate to make autocratic decisions, declaring, for example, that "it would not be appropriate to publish articles in installments in revolutionary journals."[106] In 1907 a central committee decision to publish *Şûra-yı Ümmet* in Paris made Bahaeddin Şakir the de facto editor of the central organ.[107] As a final step in his gradual domination over the committee's publication affairs, Bahaeddin Şakir became the editor-in-chief of *Şûra-yı Ümmet* when the CUP decided to republish it in Istanbul after the Young Turk Revolution of 1908.

Another move that Bahaeddin Şakir took to strengthen his position within the organization was to rent an apartment for use as the CPU's offices.[108] He then had the apartment furnished "in a manner appropriate for a serious organization's bureau."[109] Thus for the first time, a Young Turk organization possessed independent offices. Until then the coalition's operational center had been Ahmed Rıza's private apartment, and all incoming letters were forwarded to his address. The establishment of new offices for the CPU was important both because it helped Bahaeddin Şakir to depersonalize the coalition that had hitherto been associated with the charismatic personality of Ahmed Rıza,[110] and also because it gave Bahaeddin Şakir and Doctor Nâzım the chance to receive all incoming correspondence. Although for a while members and sympathizers continued to send their letters and applications to Ahmed Rıza,[111] after strong warnings from Bahaeddin Şakir[112] it became standard to address all the correspondence to the "Internal Affairs and Correspondence division of the CPU."

The CPU Branches and Organizational Network from the Reorganization of the CPU to Its Merger with the Ottoman Freedom Society

Following the reorganization of the center, Bahaeddin Şakir focused on creating an effective network to execute the revolutionary program of the central committee. As he stated in official correspondence, his first duty was "to supervise the organization within the empire."[113]

Because of the disarray in which the coalition found itself by 1905, it did not have any branch in the real sense of the word. The so-called Egyptian branch was nothing other than Ahmed Saib's private apartment, and the official correspondence was nothing other than letters exchanged with Ahmed Rıza in Paris. To carry out any activity of significance within the empire was out of the question with such a network. In Bahaeddin Şakir's own words, "it is obvious that until the branches are established and perfected, the center will not achieve a major success."[114] He further stated that "the people of Diyar-ı Bekir evacuated the post office by chanting a prayer for the long life of the sultan. Such rebellious activities should be carried out by an organization and conducted by erudite and shrewd people."[115]

Bahaeddin Şakir's first tactical stroke in this field was to claim successorship to the old organization. In the official reorganization document he gave the following as the reason for the new settlement: "The program that our committee has pursued for eleven years must have been found agreeable by those Ottomans who wish for the salvation and happiness of the fatherland, because the number of our adherents continues to increase day by day."[116] This stratagem enabled the new committee to approach former sympathizers and request them to form organized branches. Whenever Ahmed Rıza brought Bahaeddin Şakir letters or postcards sent by various sympathizers, the latter first would reply to them that their letter sent to Ahmed Rıza had been received, and, since the central committee in Paris had been divided into four divisions (Publications in Foreign Languages, Publications in Turkish, Internal Affairs and Organization Correspondence, and Financial Affairs), in accordance with the principle of the division of labor, the duty of responding to their letter and any correspondence between them and the committee had been referred to him.[117] He would then ask them to gather at least three people and form a branch of the CPU in their region.[118]

The personal criteria for new branch members were changed significantly. Bahaeddin Şakir thought that "pessimistic" people and even those "married persons who care for and love their wives and children more than the fatherland" should not be accepted as members.[119] According to CPU correspondence instructing various individuals about branch formation, each branch was to have a director, a secretary, a treasurer, and a distributor of propaganda material.[120] One of the letters from the secret correspondence of the CPU includes the instructions for establishment of branches:

1. The printed regulations that had been previously sent to you will be used as a basis for the establishment of the branch.

2. After taking the written oath at the end of the regulations, you, our brotherly friend, and the others who will administer the branch there, should write the oath on a piece of paper and send it to the central committee, i.e., to us, after signing. All the members forming the central committee here are under oath. This oath is for the executive committee of the branch. As for the people who become members, the point about whether they are state officials or not is unimportant. It is, however, necessary to make them take an oath on their honor, integrity, and religion to serve the goals of the committee, rendering all services and sacrifices to the nation, the country, and the committee which has been working for them, and not betraying it. The signed or sealed documents obtained from them should be kept in your branch.

3. The members of the committee [branch] should not throw themselves into the field of battle, and they should conceal themselves from the people, the local government, and the office of the [Ottoman] Commissioner [in Bulgaria] as if they were carrying out organizational activities in Istanbul among the spies of Abdülhamid. One of the members of the committee [branch], especially the best-known, however, may conceal himself less than the others. But nobody must identify the others, because they may be employed to travel to Istanbul and to carry something.

4. A code book will be sent in order to keep special matters and the names of individuals and members secret by taking all possibilities into account.

5. Since the method of writing letters on one side of the paper is adopted for the letters to be sent to you from the central committee, these letters should be affixed to a copy notebook to be sent to you, by putting glue on the blank side of the letters. The letters to be sent to the central committee and to other branches, written upon receiving our notice informing you of such a necessity, should be written in copy ink and are to be sent only after they have been copied into the same copy book.

6. The acquisition of a round or oval medium-size seal written in *talik* or another style of writing that reads "   "[121] "branch of the Ottoman Committee of Progress and Union" is required.

7. The utmost care should be taken to safeguard the articles that might reveal the secrets of the committee, such as the seal, code book, and account book, which should be placed in a suitable strongbox under lock.

8. The branch is obliged to record income such as donations, money given by members and participants, journal subscriptions, and expenses in the aforementioned special notebook.

9. Each member of the executive council of the branch, being a unit leader, may induct individuals whom he knows well and whose integrity he trusts; however, in such a case only he should establish relations with such people, and they should be affiliated only with him and should not be introduced to other members. Each unit should have special numbers to be distributed to its members. Care should be taken not to introduce members to each other unnecessarily. A member should not know anyone but the person who made him a member and those whom he introduced to the committee [branch].

10. If it is difficult to acquire a seal there, one may be sent from here upon your request and the expense will be paid by the branch later. It should be quite easy to learn the technique of copying from a commercial firm there.[122]

In addition to these stipulations, the branches were required to send half of their revenues to the central committee,[123] and each member was obliged to send to it at least 45 *gurush*, the subscription fee for *Şûra-yı Ümmet*.[124] Initially the central committee assured the former sympathizers who were asked to form branches that it did not expect them to carry out extraordinary activities, but only to work in an organized fashion and to be in continuous contact with the central committee.[125] Branches established in various regions were given different code books so that they "could not understand the correspondence held with the other branches" and were in no position to communicate with each other.[126] According to the network plan, only after establishing several branches in a given region was the central committee supposed to establish a regional central branch to oversee all branches in its domain. CPU correspondence reveals that the central committee seriously considered establishing such regional central branches only in Bulgaria and Cyprus.[127] On certain occasions the central committee introduced branch directors to each other and requested them to exchange information or work together in carrying out tasks planned by the central committee.[128] Under normal circumstances, however, the branches were to correspond only with the central committee in Paris.[129]

The central committee aimed to establish two types of branches: "simple branches and branches for action." All those contacted were given the choice of forming one of these two types.[130] It seems that most of the branches established outside of the empire were simple branches, engaged chiefly in distributing CPU propaganda material and smuggling it into the empire. The branches within the Ottoman Empire, however, were mostly branches of action. The central committee also required the simple branches "to inform [it] of the existence of any real self-sacrificing volunteers who may put their lives and everything on the line."[131] All the branches were to "train young individuals and orphans who are capable of sacrificing" themselves for the CPU's ideals.[132] In other words, the branches were considered local organizations recruiting militants for the future activities of the central committee.

Regardless of their type, all CPU branches enjoyed a semiautonomous status. They administered their own affairs so long as their actions did not contradict the regulations of the CPU. In Bahaeddin Şakir's words, this autonomy followed from the need to establish branches in distinctly different regions of an enormous empire and in regions recently lost by it:

> Instructions regarding the establishment of committees [branches] are written based on our experience. Since the population of each region is of a different disposition, nature, and character, the establishment of branches is dependent upon the endeavors and efforts of the intelligent and upright people there. Because we cannot discern from here, for example, the [conditions of] the province of Trabzon adequately, we would be unable to take detailed decisions when necessary. We, by benefiting from the guidance and knowledge of the committee [branch] leaders, may attempt to unite the intentions of all provinces under a single banner, and to direct and instruct them so that the desired general union can be accomplished and all Ottoman dominions might suddenly arise and put the oppressors in their place.[133]

Again in Bahaeddin Şakir's words, the central committee did not "desire to redesign the 'idéal' . . . and therefore they asked [the branches] to start with a simple organization."[134] When the director of a branch apologized because he "could not write exquisite and well-written letters," Bahaeddin Şakir responded that "this is more than enough for you. Moreover, what is really needed in order to carry out a revolution is strength rather than the pen, exclusively strength."[135] Similarly, when one branch intended to send letters to the Grand Vizier to admonish him, the central committee denied permission for such an action on the grounds that it was "beyond the power of [a] branch."[136] The oath to be taken by members of the various branches was very vague, referring to the principles of the CPU in general terms.[137]

In other words, all opponents of the regime who accepted the general ideas mentioned in the first section of the CPU regulations could join it, and the central committee paid no attention whatsoever to the intentions and ideas from the branches. Bahaeddin Şakir apparently envisioned a revolutionary federation with a strong central committee and branch committees that could draw members from different backgrounds with distinct aims. As long as the branch committees served the central committee in carrying out revolutionary activities, the differences between them were of no importance. Because he frequently referred to his examination of other revolutionary committees, including the Armenian organizations, he must have been influenced by the organizational framework of the Dashnaktsutiun. In practice, because of the organizational framework of the CPU, the branches could by no means participate in decision-making, despite the rule mentioned in the regulations.[138] Besides recruiting militants for the central committee's activities, the second most important mission of the branches was to enroll as many members as they could and send agents disguised as "passengers, preachers, even beggars" to the towns and villages in their vicinity to organize more branches. Following the establishment of such a network of branches, "the people would rebel against this oppressive sultan and his oppressive government from all sides at a single order given by the central committee."[139]

Various branches sent their proposed internal regulations to the central committee for approval. Although they sometimes differed in technical matters, which were of no importance in the eyes of the central committee, the various branch regulations were quite similar. One set of regulations, that prepared by the Kazanlŭk (Kızanlık) branch, was extremely detailed and even included a clause banning "smoking or drinking coffee during meetings,"[140] but almost all the others simply reproduced the instructions given by the central committee to form a branch.[141] In order to demonstrate its power over the branches, the central committee made trivial changes in the internal regulations of the branches before approving them.[142] In a similar vein, the internal affairs and correspondence division of the central committee frequently admonished branches and questioned them as to whether they were having regular branch meetings and whether branch members' opinions were solicited before notes were sent to the central committee.[143]

Whereas the central committee had no director, the reorganizers assigned great importance to the directors of local branches because of their semiautonomous nature.[144] Later the central committee made detailed registers of branches, and for this purpose branches were required to send copies of their members' birth certificates to the central committee in Paris.[145] The central committee distributed code numbers to these members in addition to the code numbers given to them by their respective branches.[146]

The CPU Branches: Their Organization and Activities

Following the reorganization of the center, the great efforts exerted by the CPU Internal Affairs and Correspondence division under the direction of Bahaeddin Şakir, assisted by Dr. Nâzım, produced impressive results in a short period. An organizational network of which the coalition could not have dreamed was created. One may counter that this network was still not in a position to initiate a coup d'état before the CPU merged with the Ottoman Freedom Society in September 1907. Nonetheless, when compared with the coalition's nonexistent organizational network, the new network represented a momentous achievement. Most of the CPU branches that were revitalized or established during this period were in countries that were under nominal Ottoman suzerainty or that had recently acquired autonomy. In addition, the branches that were established within the empire, with the exception of those formed in the Arab provinces, aimed at carrying out revolutionary activities.

The CPU Branches Abroad

The CPU Network in Bulgaria

The first target in the CPU's campaign to establish a network was Bulgaria. With a well-organized network there, the central committee would be able to smuggle its propaganda material and publications into the Ottoman capital, into towns in the European provinces, and into Ottoman ports on the Black Sea. Also, since large numbers of Ottoman troops were stationed at posts on the Ottoman-Bulgarian border, branches in Bulgaria could be used to distribute such material to Ottoman officers.[147]

The CPU established its first Bulgarian branch in Kazanlŭk. A notable named İbrahim Rahmi Efendizâde Hayri had been corresponding with various Young Turks for a long time, and following the reorganization he began smuggling the CPU central organ and other propaganda material into various towns in the empire.[148] He did not know much about the factions within the Young Turk movement and was not even aware of the termination of the publication of *Osmanlı* a year and a half earlier. Bahaeddin Şakir asked him to establish a CPU branch in Kazanlŭk in accordance with the CPU regulations, as well as to smuggle materials into the empire and to act as a correspondent reporting from Bulgaria.[149] Upon receiving an affirmative answer and information about five individuals who intended to join the branch, the CPU provided him with the necessary instructions.[150] The central committee then instructed the branch to dispatch agents to towns in Bulgaria to disseminate propaganda and encourage Muslims to form CPU branches in other regions.[151]

When Edhem Ruhi, the former director of the old CUP organization and an ardent opponent of the coalition, learned of the CPU initiative, he attempted to disrupt the establishment of the branch by spreading a rumor that "Ahmed Rıza [was] an Armenian convert." The central committee thereupon assured the prospective branch director that the CPU "was a pure Turkish committee" and that "Ahmed Rıza was the person among the Turks whom the Armenians feared the most." It also provided him with a copy of a letter that Edhem Ruhi had sent to Ahmed Rıza while they were working together in the old CUP organization.[152] The members were mollified and began their work.[153]

The central committee formally approved the establishment of the branch on June 18, 1906, after receiving oaths written and signed by the director and members of the branch. Thus the first CPU branch in Bulgaria was founded.[154]

The branch worked with great enthusiasm. It sent the CPU charter to other towns,[155] provided the central committee with information about the Turks living in Bulgaria,[156] and on its own initiative made a Turkish teacher from Ruse a member by taking his oath in Kazanlŭk, sending him back to his home town to initiate activities there.[157] Most important, the branch smuggled large quantities of *Şûra-yı Ümmet* and other propaganda material into the Ottoman Empire.[158] By the time the branch completed its internal regulations, its membership had risen to eight.[159]

Although the branch members generally supported the decisions of the central committee,[160] they often discussed policies they believed the central committee should adopt. Research indicates, however, that their discussions of such policies as "unification with the Terakki Committee [the League of Private Initiative and Decentralization]," or the establishment of a new journal to replace *Şûra-yı Ümmet*, made no impact on the central committee.[161] Still, the strong activist and Turkist themes expressed in the branch's official correspondence,[162] along with letters in the same vein coming from other branches did push the central committee to sharpen the tone of its propaganda.

Because of Bulgaria's strategic importance for the CPU's smuggling operations in the empire, the CPU central committee sought to expand beyond the single branch in Kazanlŭk. In an early initiative in April 1906, Bahaeddin Şakir appealed to a former sympathizer of the coalition to form a branch in Sofia. This initiative, however, bore no fruit.[163]

In the meantime, the publications of the pro-Young Turk journals in Bulgaria kept their readership informed of the CPU's reorganization and provided them with the address of the new central committee. The result was a rapid increase in applications from various towns in Bulgaria to establish branches.[164] An active Young Turk who had worked for the old CUP organization, Talha Kemalî, corresponded with Bahaeddin Şakir, and under his instructions succeeded in establishing a small CPU branch in Dobrich (Dobriç).[165] This branch became very active in disseminating propaganda and availed itself of the town's many young Turkish students in this activity.[166]

Later Talha Kemalî was assigned to work as a CPU "traveling agent" to disseminate propaganda, establish more branches in Bulgaria,[167] and inform the central committee of the expectations of Young Turk sympathizers. Since these sympathizers were impatient for "real action," Talha Kemalî formed a "branch of self-sacrificing volunteers" composed of ten participants from Dobrich, Varna, and Shumen.[168] While traveling, he persuaded many in Plovdiv to join the movement, and so the central committee ordered him to set up a small branch there.[169] Upon Talha Kemalî's departure from Plovdiv, Hacı Ahmed Ağazâde Hasan Şevket was appointed the CPU special correspondent there and was charged with smuggling CPU propaganda material into the Ottoman Empire and providing intelligence about promising candidates for local branches.[170] A subsequent piece of correspondence, which instructed a member that "while in Shumen [he] should work within the [CPU] central branch in Bulgaria and while in Plovdiv [he] should administer the third division of the branch there," reveals that the Plovdiv branch eventually became relatively sophisticated.[171]

In August 1906 the CPU central committee approved a membership application from an individual from Balchik (Balçık). It first used this new member to smuggle CPU propaganda pamphlets into the Ottoman Empire. It then asked him to establish a CPU branch in Balchik.[172] Later CPU correspondence indicates that this individual succeeded in forming the branch and was able to distribute 28 copies of *Şûra-yı Ümmet* every month.[173] Following the Congress of Ottoman Opposition Parties in December 1907,[174] the central committee instructed the branch to increase its activities, including smuggling. The branch rendered the required services and provided the Paris center with intelligence as well.[175]

In a similar vein, a sympathizer in Burgas named Hamdi Aliev applied to the central committee for membership.[176] The central committee issued similar instructions to him as they had to the new member in Balchik, and accordingly he formed a CPU branch in Burgas. This branch later helped direct Ottoman officers who were CPU members on the Bulgarian border, and it also smuggled a flurry of CPU propaganda material into the Ottoman Black Sea ports of Ereğli and Zonguldak through a sea captain who agreed to work for the branch. This sea captain, named Mahir Efendi, utilized a fleet of barges to distribute CPU propaganda material in these ports.[177] The

Paris center also directed the branch to distribute CPU journals to the Ottoman officers on the border and to establish small CPU cells to work with them.[178]

In addition to these individual applications that resulted in the establishment of
branches in various parts of Bulgaria, an organization called the Islamic Youth Society of Vidin entreated the central committee to work with it. Bahaeddin Şakir provided them with the necessary instructions for establishing a branch.[179] Later CPU
correspondence indicates that this society transformed itself into the CPU Branch in
Vidin and provided important services to the central committee.[180]

Encouraged by the establishment of so many branches in Bulgaria in such a short
period of time, the CPU decided to place all the branches in Bulgaria under the administration of a central branch.[181] Because all the branch directors in Bulgaria had
established their branches on their own initiative, to make any of these individuals a
central branch director was logistically not possible. Although the central committee trusted Talha Kemalî, his employment as an agent traveling throughout Bulgaria
forced the CPU Internal Affairs division to contact Talât Bey, who maintained permanent residence in Shumen. Talât Bey was a loyal supporter of Ahmed Rıza, working for the old CUP organization and later for the coalition. While stopping in Bulgaria on his way back to Paris after a secret trip to Istanbul in May 1907, Bahaeddin
Şakir met with Talât Bey and authorized him to organize a branch in Shumen as the
CPU central branch in Bulgaria to oversee all other branches.[182] In a later letter
Bahaeddin Şakir referred to Talât Bey as the "Director of the CPU Central Branch in
Bulgaria."[183] In another letter, written for Talât Bey in January 1908, Bahaeddin Şakir
wrote that "all branches in Bulgaria will be placed under your administration and
oversight as stated during our meeting, and the Shumen branch will be given the title
of the central branch in Bulgaria."[184] Despite this style of address, however, it seems
that the branches in Bulgaria continued to work independently of each other, corresponding with the Paris center directly. Thus, despite its ostensible intention and its
use of the term "central branch," the CPU did not establish a real central branch to
oversee local branches in Bulgaria. In addition to those individuals who formed
branches throughout Bulgaria, many other people applied to the Paris center and were
subsequently provided with CPU publications.[185]

The CPU also enjoyed the positive coverage of the local Young Turk journals[186]
that favored the CPU over Sabahaddin Bey's league because of the CPU's Turkist
propaganda.[187] This coverage undoubtedly helped the CPU to expand its organization and propaganda activity in Bulgaria. Since no Young Turk journal directly
supported Sabahaddin Bey, and he had only a few sympathizers in Bulgaria,[188] the
internal Young Turk struggle in Bulgaria took place between the CPU's sympathizers and Edhem Ruhi in their respective publications.[189] Some CPU members went
as far as proposing the assassination of Edhem Ruhi, who was criticizing the CPU;
however, a lack of assassins prevented them from carrying out such an action.[190] It
appears that in this struggle the CPU's sympathizers received more support in Bulgaria and gained the upper hand. Despite their indirect support of the CPU, however, all these journals remained formally "impartial," and none ever became an official CPU organ.[191]

In response to the demands coming from the rapidly established network in Bulgaria, the CPU official organs began to attach more importance to the problems of

the Muslims and Turks in Bulgaria. They published appeals decrying the discrimination against the Muslims of Bulgaria,[192] as well as letters criticizing Bulgarian policies aimed at the assimilation and intimidation of Muslims.[193]

Besides establishing an effective network of vital importance in smuggling propaganda material into the Ottoman Empire, the CPU center undertook another, unexpected initiative in Bulgaria. In July 1907 Bahaeddin Şakir asked a Bulgarian high school teacher in Iambol named Nikola Manolov to disseminate CPU propaganda among Christians.[194] Undoubtedly the CPU's intention was to distribute its propaganda not only in Bulgaria but also in Macedonia. Manolov stated that it was quite difficult to carry out propaganda work among Bulgarians using journals in Turkish and French; he recommended that the CPU center establish ties and reach an understanding regarding cooperation with the liberal faction of the Bulgarian Socialist party,[195] and he offered to mediate between the two organizations.[196]

The central committee discussed Manolov's letter and accepted his recommendation. Bahaeddin Şakir further asked him to translate CPU appeals into Bulgarian.[197] The exchange of letters continued, and the CPU center in Paris provided Manolov with all available CPU pamphlets and journals.[198] The CPU center expressed its satisfaction when it received Manolov's translations of its material. The Bulgarian texts were apparently distributed in both Bulgaria and Macedonia. Bahaeddin Şakir also asked Manolov to work with his "Bulgarian compatriots, who are not members of the Bulgarian committees and are not dreamy castle-builders, but who comprehend reality and unite themselves with [the CPU]."[199]

In a similar vein, the CPU center appealed to Yürükoğlu İsmail to publish a journal and disseminate CPU propaganda among the Bulgarians in Macedonia. According to this plan, Yürükoğlu İsmail was supposed to translate lead articles from the Paris center and add other articles as long as they did not contradict CPU regulations. The CPU offered financial assistance in addition to all revenues to be received from the journal.[200] Yürükoğlu İsmail had previously published a Turkish-Bulgarian journal called *Şark* (*The East/The Orient*) until he was temporarily expelled from Bulgaria. Local Turkish journals supportive of the CPU were severely critical of *Şark*.[201] Available Bulgarian documents show that the local journals' criticism was well founded; they reveal that Yürükoğlu İsmail accepted friendly advice from the Bulgarian authorities.[202] He now accepted the CPU's offer to "promote our ideas and goals among our Bulgarian compatriots" and also offered to publish a Turkish journal on behalf of the CPU.[203] The central committee considered his offer and decided to entrust him with publishing a Bulgarian language journal and disseminating CPU propaganda in Macedonia.[204] This scheme, however, could not be put into effect because of financial problems.

In summary, the CPU's work in Bulgaria after the reorganization was a remarkable success story. The CPU had seven effective branches there, a substantial audience for its propaganda material, and significant contacts with Bulgarian intellectuals. The branches in Bulgaria provided invaluable assistance to the center, especially in smuggling propaganda material into the Ottoman Empire. The support given by Turks in Bulgaria to the Young Turk Revolution of 1908 may have startled many diplomats,[205] but for those who were aware of the new CPU network in this country, it was no surprise.

The CPU Organization in Romania

Following the reorganization, the CPU set about revitalizing Young Turk activity in Romania just as it did in Bulgaria. There were many Young Turks and local sympathizers in Romania, most of them residing in the Dobruja and subscribing to various Young Turk publications. They were not, however, involved in any organizational activities when Bahaeddin Şakir began working on reshaping the coalition.[206] Like its Bulgarian counterpart, the educated Muslim elite in Romania chafed under Romanian policies and therefore were extremely receptive to Young Turk propaganda. The CPU effort in Romania was also aided by the original founder of the old CUP organization, İbrahim Temo. He later became renowned throughout the Balkans, was very active in the Albanian movement,[207] and enjoyed close ties to the leaders of the Aromenis (Kutzo-Vlach) organization, which the Romanian authorities themselves supported.[208] In contrast to the situation in Bulgaria, however, activities in Romania had not entirely ceased before the reorganization. İbrahim Temo and his fellow Young Turk friends had continued their activities, although they were of no significance from an organizational viewpoint. Temo's combination of charisma and contacts made the revitalized branch invaluable to the CPU center in Paris.

While Bahaeddin Şakir was working on building up a CPU network in the Balkans, İbrahim Temo and the other leading Young Turk in Romania, Kırımîzâde Ali Rıza, were trying to establish ties to the Young Turk organizations in Paris in order to help thwart the sultan's alleged scheme to change the order of succession to the throne. They sent a letter to Sabahaddin Bey and asked him to provide them with a plan regarding his league's possible actions after the death of the sultan. They also offered to help the prince should he want to go to the empire and carry on his work there after the long-awaited death of Abdülhamid II.[209]

Two weeks later they sent a similar note to Ahmed Rıza, who passed it on to Bahaeddin Şakir. The CPU center assured İbrahim Temo and Kırımîzâde Ali Rıza that they would take their proposal into consideration and that the committee had prepared an appeal on the subject. The central committee also asked their help in smuggling CPU propaganda material into the empire and bade them "to revitalize their branch according to the new regulations."[210] In the meantime, Bahaeddin Şakir invited another subscriber to the CPU journals in Dobruja, Ali Sedad Halil, to join Temo and Kırımîzâde Ali in forming the branch.[211]

Following an exchange of letters between the CPU center and the three Young Turks, İbrahim Temo organized the three into a cell to conduct secret activities.[212] The cell was supposed to collect donations from sympathizers and distribute CPU propaganda material to them. It was not, however, supposed to inform them of secret operations.[213] The CPU center did not merely approve this plan, but in fact acclaimed it, declaring that "success lies not in the abundance of members, but in their being men of strong will and honor, and in their zeal."[214]

Immediately after the establishment of the cell, Mustafa Ragıb, who had been expelled from Bulgaria, became a teacher at a Turkish high school in Romania with the help of İbrahim Temo, and there the branch entrusted him with the distribution of propaganda material.[215] CPU secret correspondence reveals that the branch played an important role in smuggling propaganda material into the empire.[216]

The CPU branch in Romania also rendered an important service to the central committee by providing the latter with both original and fake Romanian passports.[217] CPU secret correspondence indicates that these passports were used to send agents to countries neighboring the Ottoman Empire.[218]

On his return from his secret trip to Istanbul, Bahaeddin Şakir stopped over in Constanţa in May 1907. There he met with İbrahim Temo and other CPU members and gave them instructions reflecting the new schemes of the CPU center.[219] The central committee asked the branch to smuggle an agent into Istanbul to work with the Istanbul branch in an assassination attempt. It also sought İbrahim Temo's assistance in order to thwart the undertakings of "İsmail Kemal and his cohort" in Albania,[220] and to correspond with Albanian notables in an effort to obtain help for an agent sent from Paris to Macedonia and Albania.[221] İbrahim Temo responded that the branch had found an agent who could collaborate with the CPU branch in Istanbul. He also commented that the only way to avoid further problems in Albania was through the "official recognition of the Albanian language by the government, like that of the Greek, Bulgarian, Romanian, and Jewish [Ladino] languages."[222]

Following the merger of the CPU and the Ottoman Freedom Society, the branch in Romania acquired the utmost importance, because the center deemed both an agreement with the Albanian committees and the support of the Muslim Albanian notables indispensable. İbrahim Temo was once again called upon to provide assistance in both efforts.[223]

In December 1907 the central committee invited İbrahim Temo to participate as a CPU delegate in the Congress of Ottoman Opposition Parties.[224] İbrahim Temo himself could not attend the congress; instead, the branch sent one of its members, Veliyullah Çelebizâde Mahmud Çelebi, who went under the pseudonym of Necati Bey.[225] He was the only CPU delegate coming from a CPU branch, a fact that clearly manifests the importance attached to the branch and its director by the central committee.

The center also asked the branch to smuggle an agent into the agent's hometown of Izmir so he could help Dr. Nâzım organize sympathizers there and could participate in joint CPU-Dashnaktsutiun activity.[226] The Ottoman authorities, however, apprehended the agent sent by Temo a day after he arrived in Izmir and met with Armenians.[227]

Taking advantage of his charisma among the local Young Turks in the Balkans, İbrahim Temo worked to revitalize the movement in Bulgaria and Albania. He frequently visited his comrades in Bulgaria "to encourage them," and he instructed his Albanian nationalist disciple Derviş Hima to contribute to the Young Turk journals there in order to achieve a rapprochement between Albanian opponents of the sultan and the Young Turks.[228] İbrahim Temo also donned his Albanian nationalist hat and authored articles making declarations like "as for the autochthonous people of Macedonia, neither Greeks, nor Bulgarians, nor Vlachs, nor Turks are Macedonian."[229]

The branch also made efforts to win over the Muslim population in Constanţa. To this end İbrahim Temo organized public lectures to enlighten the masses. Some were on scientific subjects, and some of these, such as one delivered by İbrahim Temo on "Viruses and the Struggle for Life," would have been of little direct use in propagandizing.[230] Others, however, such as Veliyullah Çelebizâde Mahmud Çelebi's lecture on "Ottoman Historical Geography," must have influenced their audience politically.[231]

Other branch members wrote inflammatory articles in order to incite local Muslims against the Ottoman government. One such article, for example, charged that "the Romanian government has been making all kinds of sacrifices for the Kutzo-Vlachs in Macedonia. What did we get from the Ottoman government? . . . We have not received from Istanbul as much as five *gurush* of assistance for our school. . . . You are working to unite the Muslims, and they work to divide the Muslims. One hundred thousand regrets!!"[232] Nonetheless these efforts failed to create a mass movement in Dobruja, and the uneducated populace refrained from joining the Young Turks.[233]

The CPU Organization in Crete

The third location where the CPU succeeded in establishing an effective network was Crete. Like their counterparts in Bulgaria and Romania, the educated Muslim elite of Crete were extremely receptive to Young Turk propaganda, and so the CPU center in Paris did not need to exert great efforts to establish branches on the island. The Muslim elite, extremely disheartened by the Ottoman government's inability to thwart foreign intervention, viewed the Young Turk movement as a last chance to save itself from Greek domination. A Cretan CPU member wrote:

> We are between life and death here. The Cretan Christians have decided to ruin us. Their success is in doubt. The *Yıldız* is an ally of the enemy [working] for our destruction! The days of the *Yıldız* are numbered. The nation, however, is being crushed and the sacred common fatherland is approaching a terrible abyss.[234]

Ekrem Bey, who had been very active in publishing letters in Young Turk journals about the situation of the Cretan Muslims,[235] was the first person from Crete to apply to the CPU center in Paris following the reorganization. He demanded "a special section in *Şûra-yı Ümmet* to defend the rights of the Muslims in Crete and to report on Christian acts of cruelty."[236] The CPU central committee unanimously accepted this proposal and devoted a section to Cretan affairs and the position of the Muslims on the island.[237]

Later a leader of the Muslim community, Yüzbaşızâde Ahmed Lütfi İbraki, established contacts with the CPU.[238] Influenced by the example of the Greek gendarmes' collection of donations for the Greek committees in Macedonia, he sent contributions to the CPU.[239] Another Cretan, Tahmiscaki Mehmed Cavid in Canea, offered services to the CPU such as providing detailed information about the situation of the Muslims in Crete. He furnished extremely detailed information, which the central committee used in preparing articles for the central organ and the French supplement.[240] The central committee highly appreciated these early contacts. Later it contacted a former confidant of Ahmed Rıza, Alyotîzâde Mustafa Tevfik, about forming a CPU branch in Canea in compliance with CPU regulations.[241] Upon accepting the CPU's invitation, Alyotîzâde Mustafa Tevfik asked Ahmed Lütfi İbraki to help him in forming the branch, and the Paris center provided both of them with the necessary instructions.[242]

Unlike other branches, the CPU branch in Canea favored having a periodical published by one of its founders as an unofficial journal. When Ahmed Lütfi İbraki informed the CPU center in Paris that he wanted to publish such a journal, called *Hilâl-i*

Ahmer (The Red Crescent), the CPU center advised him to publish a local journal in Crete and recommended that he purchase used publishing equipment to start the project immediately.[243] Ahmed Lütfi İbraki purchased a publishing house on behalf of the Muslim community in Canea[244] and started publishing a journal named *Sada-yı Girid* (The Voice of Crete) in April 1907. Mehmed Macid became the journal's main columnist.[245]

The journal adopted a strong anti-European, especially anti-British, rhetoric in accordance with the practice of the CPU's central organs.[246] It sharply criticized "Christian fanaticism,"[247] corresponded frequently with the Muslims in Central Asia,[248] and urged Muslim Ottoman elements such as the Albanians not to pursue separatist policies.[249] Like the CPU journals, *Sada-yı Girid* spoke very critically of separatist leaders. It called İsmail Kemal, for example, a "swindler and vagabond."[250] The CPU and the nationalist faction of the Young Turks praised the journal because of its publication policy and the ideas that it promoted.[251]

The CPU branch, composed of Arnaudoğlu İbrahim Fevzi, Yüzbaşızâde Ahmed Lütfi İbraki, and Suluzaki Hasan Tevfik, under the directorship of Alyotizâde Mustafa Tevfik, provided important services. Taking advantage of the island's strategic location and autonomous administration, the branch smuggled propaganda into Istanbul, Kalʿa-i Sultaniye (Çanakkale), and Tripoli of Barbary and enabled the central committee to send money to its agents in the empire.[252] The branch sent its clerk, who was fluent in Greek, to Greece in order to help former lieutenant Seyyid Kenʿan establish a branch on the Greek-Ottoman border. The central committee further required the branch to assign a member to work for the CPU in Greece[253] and to provide the names of trustworthy people who would work for the CPU in various towns in the empire.[254] The branch also kept the center posted regarding developments in Crete[255] that the CPU could exploit in its propaganda.[256]

A split, however, occurred in the branch in January 1908, when Ahmed Lütfi İbraki insisted on publishing a note to declare that the claims made in a letter published in *Şûra-yı Ümmet* against a certain Cretan Muslim were false.[257] Those who considered this an act of treason to the organization cut all ties to Ahmed Lütfi İbraki and moved to reestablish the branch with the consent of the CPU center in Paris.[258] The CPU External Headquarters approved the decision,[259] and the branch was reestablished on March 20, 1908, in accordance with the new internal regulations that were accepted following the merger of the CPU with the Ottoman Freedom Society.

In addition to its own members in Canea, the CPU was able to call upon many local sympathizers, thus making the town one of the most active centers of CPU propaganda.[260] Even before the Paris center initiated contact with Cretan Muslim intellectuals, CPU propaganda made extensive use of the example of Crete to illustrate "the double standards of the European powers" and "the suppression of Muslims at the hands of Christians." Once these contacts began, the branch undoubtedly forced the center to pay even more attention to the situation of the Muslims in Crete, and in turn the center helped the branch make the voice of the Cretan Muslims heard in Europe.[261] Following the Young Turk Revolution of 1908, the CPU branch in Canea became an open branch of the CUP.[262]

The Paris center also sought to establish a branch in another Cretan town, Candia. A sympathetic subscriber to the CPU organs suggested to the central committee that it ask Dr. Ali Rasih, who had participated in CUP activities on the island in 1895, to form a branch there. Bahaeddin Şakir and Dr. Nâzım accepted the advice, contacted Dr. Ali Rasih, and provided him with detailed instructions for establishing a branch in January 1907.[263] Although he worked very hard, Dr. Ali Rasih was unable to form a branch in Candia. As a result, the CPU center had no choice but to work with various individual sympathizers instead. One of the sympathizers, a man named Çiçekaki Hüseyin Salih, sent regular donations to the center and provided it with the names of individuals willing to work for the CPU.[264] He also distributed CPU propaganda material and journals in the town.[265]

With the encouragement of the Paris center, the sympathizers in Candia organized meetings on the anniversaries of Ottoman victories. The most important gathering was the celebration of the 455th anniversary of the Ottoman conquest of Constantinople, held on May 29, 1908. The CPU sympathizers, who addressed a large crowd of Muslims, expressed their desire to "expel the barbarian and bloodthirsty Greek invaders as [their] ancestors had ousted the Venetians."[266] Following the meeting they led the crowd in cheering "Long live our nation, long live our state, long live our committee [the CPU]."[267] After the Young Turk Revolution of 1908 Dr. Ali Rasih and other CPU sympathizers finally succeeded in establishing an open CUP branch in Candia.[268]

All in all, the CPU succeeded in establishing an efficient network in Crete, which rendered invaluable services to the CPU. Compared with the CPU networks in Bulgaria and Romania, however, it was of secondary importance.

The CPU Branches in Cyprus

The proximity of Cyprus to the Ottoman mainland coupled with British rule on the island made it a prime target of the CPU in its campaign to establish branches to smuggle propaganda into the empire. The Muslim intellectual elite in Cyprus, like those in Bulgaria, Romania, and Crete, were receptive to Young Turk propaganda. As one member of this elite stated in a letter to the CPU center, they considered the Young Turk movement the source of salvation from foreign domination and from the unification of Cyprus with Greece; in their eyes the sultan had failed in fulfilling this role:

> Your efforts for the salvation of the fatherland have been applauded by our compatriots here . . . because if the fatherland be snatched from our hands we shall be trodden upon by the filthy feet of the foreigners. Here is the example: your coreligionists [in Cyprus]. We have been oppressed under tyrannical British absolutism. Look! The Christians are insulting our elders day and night without missing an opportunity. They stone holy mosques and smear excrement on their doors. They prevent the *müezzin*s from performing the call to prayer. They drink wine on the tombs of our ancestors, and the government only looks on.[269]

As usual, when Edhem Safi, a subscriber to the CPU central organs, sent a letter to Ahmed Rıza and provided addresses in Izmir and Salonica to which propaganda material could be sent,[270] Bahaeddin Şakir seized the opportunity and asked him to work with Ali Sıdkı, İsmail Zeki, and Ahmed Rüşdi, who were known to the CPU center, toward establishing a branch in Cyprus.[271] Although he did not think highly of the Muslim Cypriots, Edhem Safi agreed to do so and established the first CPU branch in Nicosia. He further provided the center with new addresses in Larnaca.[272] Later the CPU center invited one of these sympathizers to form a branch in Larnaca and to distribute CPU material "to officers and notables in Adana, Aleppo, and towns on the Syrian coast."[273]

Finally Colonel Hacı Hamid and Aziz Mahmud officially formed a CPU branch in Larnaca in December 1907, with the help of a third sympathizer who was corresponding with the CPU center.[274] On account of the branch's large membership and suitable location, the center recognized it in January 1908 as the "central branch in Cyprus" and used it to smuggle propaganda material onto vessels going to Ottoman ports.[275] Nevertheless, when a schoolteacher in the same town independently offered to smuggle CPU propaganda material, the center set him to work as a correspondent in the town independent of the branch.[276]

In April 1908 Dr. Hafız Cemal, who had been very active in the island's Muslim intellectual circles, established ties with the CPU center.[277] He had founded a "Muslim Benevolent Society" in 1906,[278] calling upon the Muslims to unite and "to love the nation and work for it."[279] He had also published a journal urging Muslim Cypriots to pay more attention to education and progress. His journal adopted a tone that was respectful toward the sultan and overtly Islamic.[280] His participation in CPU activities, along with the two branches in Nicosia and Larnaca, enabled the CPU to disseminate its smuggled propaganda material and to correspond with Ottoman officers in Anamur and other Mediterranean towns.[281] But because the Muslim masses generally adopted a hostile attitude to "Young Turkism without understanding it,"[282] and because the local *mufti* opposed the CPU's activities, the Young Turks were prevented from carrying out extensive propaganda on the island.[283]

In order to overcome this opposition to its ideas, the CPU published letters from Muslim Cypriots explaining that the organization was not a radical body attacking the caliphate and the sultanate:

> My Cypriot compatriots should know very well that their children, who have been mesmerized by liberal ideas and have become lovers of these thoughts, are not the enemies of the caliphate and the sultanate, but of the sultan. And their enmity toward the sultan stems from their allegiance to the caliphate and sultanate.[284]

Despite these efforts, however, the CPU movement on the island did not become a mass movement, and outside the intellectual elite the majority of Muslims viewed Young Turk ideas with contempt.[285]

The CPU's revitalization of the Young Turk movement and its success in establishing two branches in Cyprus, despite the hostility of the Muslim masses, was an important success from an organizational viewpoint, and these branches unquestionably augmented the dissemination of center's propaganda. It was not until after the Young Turk Revolution of 1908, however, that banners were held high at Muslim Cypriot demonstrations in Cyprus reading "Long Live the Ottoman Committee of Union and Progress! Liberty! Justice! Fatherland!"[286]

The CPU Network in the Caucasus

The relative freedom enjoyed by the subject peoples of Russia after the decision to establish the Duma in 1905 facilitated the Young Turks' efforts to build a CPU network in the Caucasus. During this period of political awakening in the Caucasus, many Azerbaijanis and Tatars who had taken part in the Young Turk movement assumed leadership positions in their respective national and political movements. This fact undoubtedly helped the CPU to cooperate with the political organizations of these ethnic groups. The CPU expected to receive a warmer welcome in the Caucasus than in Bulgaria, Romania, Crete, and Cyprus because the question of loyalty to the sultan was not an issue, and because the large population of Shī'īte Muslims in the region did not recognize the Ottoman sultan as their spiritual leader.

The CPU expected the joint activity with these local organizations in the Caucasus to enable it not only to flood Eastern Anatolia and the Black Sea coast with propaganda, but also to disseminate its ideas through journals such as *Füyûzat*, *Hayat*, *İrşad*, *Tercüman*, and *Kaspii*, which were all widely read in these regions.

When some Caucasian Muslims sent a letter to Ahmed Rıza in March 1906 complaining about Armenian encroachments, Bahaeddin Şakir again seized the opportunity. He sent a letter in response on behalf of the CPU stating that "the authors of the detestable massacres are not you, but those Armenian revolutionaries who are enjoying themselves by offending humanity." He advised the Muslims in Caucasia "to provide their brothers with science and education instead of sword and rifle, taking into consideration the fact that [their] enemies are superior to [them] in wealth and education." In order to appease them, the CPU also promised to donate money to a fund for Muslim orphans and widows. Finally, in the letter's postscript, Bahaeddin Şakir expressed the CPU's desire to maintain regular correspondence with them.[287]

Subsequently the CPU sent a donation of FFr 250 to the Caucasian Muslims' fund for widows and orphans, despite the fact that it desperately needed every centime of this money. This example demonstrates the importance the CPU leadership attached to establishing strong ties with the Caucasian Muslims.[288]

In the meantime, the CPU leaders appealed to the leaders of the Muslim intellectuals to organize a common front. The first name on this list of intellectuals was İsmail Gaspıralı (Gasprinskii), who had pioneered the idea of the creation of a cultural union among the various Turkic groups. The CPU had been sending *Mechveret Supplément Français* and *Şûra-yı Ümmet* regularly to İsmail Gaspıralı. Bahaeddin Şakir and Dr. Nâzım in turn requested him to send his journal *Tercüman* to the CPU, explaining that "since [their] foremost duty is to achieve mutual friendship among various Muslim peoples," they would like to benefit from his journal.[289]

As a second initiative, *Şûra-yı Ümmet* republished a short story by Hüseyinzâde Ali (Turan), who had been very active in publishing journals in Baku since 1905 and had played various important roles during the early days of the Young Turk movement.[290] Hüseyinzâde Ali quickly responded by stating that he was ready to work together and that the pages of his journal *Füyûzat* were open to CPU propaganda.[291] He further offered to publish biographies of the "Young Turk warriors" in his journal.[292]

The CPU leaders appreciated this affirmative answer and instructed Sami Paşazâde Sezaî, the editor of the central organ, as follows:

> Have *Şûra-yı Ümmet* join the nationalist [campaign] of this person whose primary aim is to create a (Turkish Union) in the regions from the Adriatic Sea to the Chinese Sea and who does not miss the smallest opportunity to win over his compatriots to this aim, by taking advantage of the freedom of the press in Russia; and who believes that the first

step to be taken toward the realization of the aforementioned sacred aim is the unification of languages [i.e., the creation of a standard Turkish].[293]

Later the CPU approached Ahmed Agayef (Agaev-Ağaoğlu), the editor of *İrşad* and a leader of the Difaʿi movement in Azerbaijan. Agayef had met with Ahmed Rıza during the earliest stages of the Young Turk movement, and since then had remained a sympathizer.[294] As a gesture, the CPU center sent him FFr 50 when he was considering terminating his journal because of financial problems.[295] The CPU offered to work with Agayef, stating that "our ideas are directed to the same point. The same sun shines upon our paths. Let us achieve our aim by working together and being attached to each other."[296]

The CPU's initial contacts with the Muslims in the Caucasus, coupled with its revitalized ties with their intellectual leaders and the hospitable press that reissued many articles originally published in *Şûra-yı Ümmet* and *Mechveret Supplément Français*, resulted in the region's becoming a stronghold of the CPU. Many Muslims, individually or on behalf of their political organizations, established ties with the CPU and sent articles to be published in the CPU journals.

Most of these letters staunchly promoted the idea of "Panislamism." For example, one of them stated:

> O Muslim brothers in Paris! Our faith is in you. Tell our coreligionists in Turkey that we would turn the entire Caucasus into bloody arenas in order to make the souls of Muslim martyrs happy. They should lend us a hand then! O beautiful fatherland!!! You have been ruined! O Caucasus that we have inherited from our ancestors! O Caucasus that has red hills and whose sweet waters we drink! Do not fear! We did not lose you! Do not fear that spoiled Armenians [and] Russians may snatch you from our hands and possess you. We will make them drink blood from your fountains of cold running water! . . . Brothers! If the "Union of Muslims" is not realized, the Christians will massacre us.[297]

The CPU leaders responded to these letters by stating that "union" among the Muslims was the only way to save them from extermination. They wrote:

> The European Christian governments are very much afraid of even the term "Union of Muslims." Our enemies' fear is convincing proof of the necessity of a union for the Muslims. Northern Africa is inhabited by the Muslims from one extreme to the other. All regions from the Adriatic Sea to the Chinese Sea have a single faith. People living there speak a single language and belong to the Turkish race. Putting aside Africa and India, if only those who belong to the Turkish race were united, they would be able to establish the most majestic government in the world.[298]

The CPU, however, also strongly urged the Caucasian Muslims not to disclose any clue as to their Panislamism. Bahaeddin Şakir wrote:

> We find that overtly working for the "Union of Muslims" is not free of danger. As we mentioned above, Europe grasps the degree of danger that might derive from the "Union of Muslims," and so it crushes with all its force those who are working for this idea. Because we are certain that Ottoman greatness would be a starting-point for the salvation of all Muslims, we wish to devote all our power to transforming the Ottoman state into an orderly and normal one. Once the Ottoman state extricates itself from this palace of tyranny, enormous steps toward progress will be taken, and undoubtedly it will

extend its helping hand to its coreligionists and national brothers. For the time being our enemies are much more powerful than we. Making Europe suspicious would not be the appropriate course to follow at this stage of weakness. We should act like the Japanese. These Far Eastern heroes, although they are many times stronger than us, felt that they should act with caution in order to prevent the Europeans from getting excited. When a Japanese is questioned by a European, he does not say "Look, European! We are sick and tired of your inordinate desire to intrude. We shall break your fingers that intervene in our business by uniting ourselves with our Chinese brothers. We shall drive you out from the Far East." [Instead he] makes the Europeans swallow a disguised pill by saying, "The reason that we gained strength is because we adopted your education and civilization. Please do not fear us. Our aim is nothing but to implement the sciences and technologies that we learned from you. The yellow race's acceptance of your education and civilization will expand the relations and commerce you Europeans have in the Far East, and thus promote your interests there." We, too, shall [not] say, "O self-seeking people who are committing a thousand types of injustices behind the veil of humanity, the Muslims who have been crushed under your oppression and humiliation until now will not endure this oppression any more. Since discord has caused a disaster for Muslims, from now on all Muslims will unite and break the chain of slavery around their necks." Let us work quietly. Then it will be easy to carry the banner of union from one country to another.[299]

Therefore, although the CPU opened the pages of *Şûra-yı Ümmet* to the Muslims of the Caucasus,[300] it omitted passages advocating Panislamism when publishing letters from Caucasia.[301] The CPU also attempted to convince the European powers that it conceived of Panislamism as a cultural and humanitarian union among the Muslims and that this conception should not be confused with "the harmful idea of making 300 million Muslims unite in order to turn all of Europe upside down."[302] In order to be more convincing, the CPU assumed an allegedly neutral attitude toward the Muslim-Armenian strife in the Caucasus, declaring that "the Tatars [were their] brothers in religion and nationality, and the Armenians [were their] compatriots."[303]

What the CPU recommended to the Muslims in Caucasia should also be noted. Bahaeddin Şakir advised them: "to come to terms with the Armenians in order to drive out the stronger enemy, the Russians, together. Since the Muslims are in the majority, it would be then easy to persuade the Armenians."[304] The means of persuasion would be to "put an end to Armenian wealth and influence in the Caucasus."[305] He further urged the Muslims to "form committees in every town,"[306] "to pay more attention to education,"[307] "to ally themselves with revolutionary Poles and Jews,"[308] and "to hide the patriotic idea of unification with Turkey at the bottom of their hearts and to tell the Russians that [they] are loyal to the Russian government; do not harbor any enmity toward Christians in any way; that is to say, [they must say that they] are not carrying out a religious struggle but are engaged in a struggle against Armenians only because [they] have wearied of Armenian acts of aggression, outrages, and atrocities, and only in order to defend [their] property and honor."[309]

The CPU center also received personal applications from Azerbaijani individuals who offered services,[310] sent money, or asked help to obtain Turkish books.[311] All in all, the Caucasus in general, and Azerbaijan in particular, became a hotbed of CPU propaganda. Because of the popularity of the CPU journals, even booksellers started to purchase them.[312] They were read in public reading rooms in towns,[313] and many Muslims sought assistance from the CPU center to hire teachers for new schools to be opened in the Caucasus and requested help in preparing the curriculum.[314] This increasing popularity in the Caucasus was invaluable to the CPU for disseminating its propaganda on the Ottoman Black Sea coast.

In addition to Azerbaijani and Tatar leaders, the CPU targeted yet another group in the Caucasus. A large number of Ottoman subjects had left their hometowns in Eastern Anatolia and on the Black Sea coast to find better jobs in Abkhazia and Georgia or to escape conscription. One of them, Acaralı Hacı Raşidzâde Hasan Hüsni, contacted the CPU center in Paris in April 1907 and offered his services. He had taken part in the effort to organize the 60,000 Ottoman subjects living on the Russian Black Sea coast through the Teavün-i Osmanî Cemiyeti (Ottoman Mutual Assistance Society).[315] He and his supporters, however, had failed to turn this effort into pro-Young Turk activity.[316] Dr. Nâzım responded to his letter by providing him with a copy of the CPU's regulations and asked him to distribute CPU publications to the poor free of charge and to the wealthy at a reasonable price sufficient to cover the costs of transporting the journals to the Ottoman towns on the other side of the border. Dr. Nâzım also asked him to form a branch in Och'amch'ire in Abkhazia.[317] Hasan Hüsni succeeded in establishing a branch in Och'amch'ire with the participation of Uzun Osmanzâde Tevfik Fikri, Dede Alizâde İlyas Remzi, and Midillizâde Mustafa Âsım, and these four divided the branch's positions among themselves.[318] The branch leader smuggled CPU propaganda materials into Hopa, a small port on the Ottoman Black Sea coast, by hiding them in corn sacks loaded on barges. From Hopa the material was distributed to towns and villages in the region.[319] In the fall of 1907 the CPU center merged this branch with the CPU Lâzistan External branch in Of, and for the first time in the history of the Young Turk movement two branches, one outside and the other within the Ottoman Empire, merged and worked together.

In November 1907, when the CPU sent Ömer Naci to Eastern Anatolia to organize revolutionary activities there, the branch members, along with their comrades in Of, helped the center to dispatch money and instructions to Ömer Naci.[320] The Och'amch'ire branch, along with the non-Ottoman supporters of the CPU in the Caucasus, provided important services by way of smuggling and disseminating propaganda.[321] The latter's close contacts with the CPU made a very strong impact in molding the CPU's later anti-imperialist and Panislamist ideology.

The CPU Organization in Bosnia and Relations with the Bosnian Muslim Intellectuals

Following the CPU's reorganization, the ties between the Young Turks and the Bosnian Muslims grew stronger. During the same period the Bosnian Muslim movement gained momentum too, and with the founding of the Muslimanska Narodna Organizacija it acquired an organized form. The Muslim Bosnians' most important service to the CPU would be their smuggling of propaganda materials into the empire through the *Sanjak* of Yenipazar (Novibazar). The distribution of CPU propaganda in Sarajevo and other parts of Bosnia and Hercegovina would have been of very little help to the CPU since its impact would have been only slight. Setting up alliances with the Bosnian Muslim organizations that were active in Europe and Bosnia, however, would prove beneficial for the CPU.

When Bahaeddin Şakir commenced his work to win over influential Bosnian Muslims and form alliances with Bosnian Muslim organizations, he first established relations with those Bosnian Muslims who had already been corresponding with Ahmed Rıza and subscribing to *Şûra-yı Ümmet* and *Mechveret Supplément Français*. In March 1906 he asked Salih Borovac, who had sent him a draft article on land tenure in Bosnia for publication in *Şûra-yı Ümmet*, to help the CPU find Bosnian Muslims interested in reading the CPU central organs in Bosnia and willing to help smuggle them inside the Ottoman Empire.[322] Later Bahaeddin Şakir asked him to form a small CPU branch in Bosnia, stating that the branch should propagate the idea of "a common fatherland" in Bosnia, encourage youngsters to read and write in Turkish, and work toward "connecting the ideas and hearts of the Bosnians to the caliphate."[323]

Upon receiving an affirmative answer, the CPU center provided Salih Borovac with the regulations of the committee and warned him to keep all activities secret.[324] The CPU correspondence does not clearly reveal whether such a branch was indeed established in Sarajevo and whether it helped the CPU to disseminate propaganda material. A later letter sent by a Bosnian Muslim indicates that there was a CPU branch or cell in Bosnia; the writer asked whether the center had sent a special traveling agent to contact them. Most likely this was the unit formed by Salih Borovac.[325]

In the meantime, Mehmed Remzi Delić, a student at Zagreb University who translated works on Ottoman history into Serbo-Croatian, contacted the CPU in December 1906.[326] Bahaeddin Şakir immediately asked Delić to help set up a branch in Tašlığa (Plevlje), since Tašlığa's location made it a promising base for smuggling.[327] A later letter asking a Bosnian Muslim to help the CPU center establish a branch in Tašlığa indicates that this initiative must have failed.[328] It is difficult to know whether the CPU center actually formed a branch in this strategic town before the 1908 Young Turk Revolution.

By asking every Bosnian Muslim contact to provide it with new names, the CPU center succeeded in establishing a formidable network of sympathizers who sent donations, subscribed to the central organs, and provided information about the affairs of Bosnia and Hercegovina.[329] The foremost person who helped to establish this network was a student at the University of Vienna, Salih Muhiddin Bakamović.[330] Bakamović introduced many Bosnian Muslim intellectuals to the CPU center[331] and offered help in disseminating CPU propaganda among his compatriots. He set about preparing a detailed Ottoman Turkish—Serbo-Croatian lexicon for Bosnian Muslims to propagate "Ottomanism" and "the language of [his] principal fatherland" in Bosnia and Hercegovina, in accordance with the CPU's calls to make Turkish popular among the Bosnian Muslims.[332]

In addition to all these initiatives, the CPU center invited a Bosnian Muslim student organization in Vienna to enter into an alliance with it and work for the CPU in that city, where the "committee had for some time wanted to have an important branch."[333] Around this time the Bosnian student organization that had been formed in 1904 became very active and started supporting the autonomy movement and submitting memoranda to the Austrian authorities.[334] It is difficult to know whether this scheme for a Vienna branch was realized or even launched. The lack of further correspondence between the two organizations after February 1907, and the fact that the Austrians punished those students accused of taking part in "political activities,"[335] give the impression that the two organizations failed to form an alliance.

Overall the CPU succeeded in strengthening its ties with the Bosnian Muslim intellectuals. The CPU organs often published the appeals of Bosnian Muslim intellectuals[336] and publicly defended their cause.[337] As we shall see, their relations with them, and with other non-Ottoman Muslims, prompted the CPU to work toward the establishment of a society to create "fraternity among Muslims."

As in Bulgaria and Romania, endorsement of the Young Turks was confined to a group of intellectuals, while the masses, who held the sultan in high esteem, condemned these opponents of their spiritual leader.[338] In addition, Bosnian Muslim intellectuals who sympathized with the Young Turk cause paid very little attention to the internal Young Turk rivalries. As a result, when the CPU publications took a decisively revolutionary stand following the reorganization, Bosnian intellectual journals published revolutionary literary works of CPU rivals such as Abdullah Cevdet.[339]

While it is true that relations between the CPU and the Bosnian intellectuals increased significantly following the reorganization, from an organizational viewpoint the endorsement by the Bosnian Muslim intellectuals was of very little importance.

Efforts to Establish a Branch in Egypt

Egypt had been a center for Young Turk activities for more than a decade. The CUP and then the coalition had several real or nominal branches in Cairo until 1906. By this time, however, various factors that had formerly made Cairo extremely important in the eyes of the Young Turk leaders had lost their appeal. Although Cairo was the ideal place from which to mount a campaign to gain the ulema's backing, the reorganizers had no real desire to win the ulema's support, despite their use of an Islamic rhetoric. Moreover, the presence in the CPU of two Egyptian princes, one working as a central committee member and the other as the inspector, made it unnecessary for the new organization to have a branch in Egypt for contacting members of the Egyptian royal house. Finally, although Ottoman pressure on various European governments had compelled the coalition to publish its journal in Cairo, the reorganizers came to regard publishing a central organ in Cairo as more of a nuisance than a convenience. These changes notwithstanding, the CPU reorganizers still desired to maintain a branch in Egypt for financial reasons.

During the early days of the reorganization, Bahaeddin Şakir asked Ahmed Saib to turn the so-called Egyptian branch, which was nothing more than the latter's private apartment in Cairo, into a regular CPU branch.[340] But the plan stalled with Ahmed Saib's resignation. The center then appointed Ahmed Ferid, whom it had dispatched to Cairo to serve as the copy editor of *Şûra-yı Ümmet*, as its representative in Cairo.[341] Since the CPU reorganizers had only halfheartedly asked Ahmed Saib to form a new branch and did not want a regular branch, they did not make Ahmed Ferid a branch director. Thus for the first time since 1895 the main Young Turk organization had no branch in Cairo.

While Bahaeddin Şakir was working on the creation of a new CPU network, he asked Mehmed Saʿid Halim Pasha, the recently appointed inspector of the CPU, to organize a branch in Cairo for the purpose of collecting money:

Although we clearly value the degree to which these initiatives would increase the importance of our committee, our insufficient financial potential prevents us from putting them into effect. Therefore, we demand that you, whose patriotic feelings are known to us and are objects of our pride, should not hold back from taking initiatives with your relatives and your acquaintances in Egypt who admire your sagacity and patriotism, in order to achieve the patriotic aims.

Two members of our committee, His Excellency Kāmil Pasha and Mahmud Bey, are in Egypt. [Ahmed] Ferid Bey, who has been working with us for eight or nine years and who is a very trustworthy person from every viewpoint, and our paid official [Mehmed] Fazlı Bey are in Cairo too. We beg Your Excellency to initiate an exchange of ideas [with these people] toward the establishment of our committee['s branch in Cairo].[342]

The pasha's response, however, must have shocked Bahaeddin Şakir and the central committee in Paris. Mehmed Saʿid Halim Pasha maintained that the establishment of a branch in Cairo and the participation of Ottomans or Egyptians in this branch would not help the CPU. He stated:

As you know, every Ottoman in Egypt is a bizarre person who claims that only he is a reformer. If we include many of them in the branch, we shall one day reach a point wherein we cannot administer it any more. As for the local Egyptians, those who engage in politics and especially those who deal with Ottoman politics are a group of scheming and selfish conspirators educated in the schools of Hamid and ʿAbbās. Thus, in my opinion, the more members we have, the more trouble we face in the Egyptian branch.[343]

The pasha, however, promised financial support for the central committee's initiatives, while at the same time requesting Bahaeddin Şakir and Dr. Nâzım to articulate their reasons for establishing a branch in Egypt despite all these problems. Bahaeddin Şakir and Dr. Nâzım responded by putting forward these reasons:

Since the country of Egypt is a Muslim land adjacent to Turkey, and is known for its prosperity, our branch there would assist us and the fatherland in collecting cash donations and dispatching [propaganda] material to al-Ḥijāz, Syria, and the other Ottoman lands in the region. It is necessary that an Egyptian notable supervise the branch and that a few patriots who are influential and rich be among its members. . . . The branch's executive committee would know how to use Egypt for the salvation of the oppressed fatherland better than we do, because they know people's abilities. Another service expected of the Egyptian branch is the translation of our articles into Arabic and the publication of these translations and [other] appeals that would please Egyptians and Arabic-speaking Ottomans in one of the Egyptian newspapers or independently. . . . The only reason that the nation cannot manifest its power is its lack of moral strength. In order to revive this moral strength our committee should make shows of force for the sake of awakening [the people]. To raise our voice abroad, to smuggle people into the country, to establish face-to-face relations with our branch [leaders and members], to give a helping hand to those who are putting their life at risk for the fatherland—these are demonstrations that would revive the nation's moral strength. If the committee spends ten, fifteen thousand [French] francs on the initiatives put forth above, its strength and the services that it can therefore render to the fatherland will increase ten or fifteen times more. Since those who spend such a sum for their sexual desires in a single day are not rare among wealthy Egyptians, we hope that a part of Egypt's squandered wealth will be devoted to the honor and glory of the exalted fatherland and the Ottoman world through your efforts and mediation.[344]

The two CPU leaders forwarded to Ahmed Ferid a copy of their letter addressed to Mehmed Sa'id Halim Pasha, and they requested the former to work toward convincing the pasha of the necessity of establishing a branch in Cairo.[345] But when Mehmed Sa'id Halim Pasha met with Ahmed Ferid, he stoutly opposed both establishing a branch and publishing an Arabic supplement to *Şûra-yı Ümmet*, stating:

It is true that the Egyptians are rich and spend millions on their sexual desires. It is absolutely impossible, however, to receive any aid or to benefit from this type of Egyptian. Their character proves this. Dealing with the ignorant and vulgar Egyptians is impossible and futile. They do not have wisdom, money, and reasoning. The intellectual segment of Egyptian [society] is occupied with its own politics. These [politics] are to drive the British out of Egypt. In accordance with this policy, and despite our wishes, they rely on Turkey, the caliphate, and the sultanate. . . . Forget about branch meetings; even if all the Turks in Egypt, and not just three or four of them, should gather, they would not be able to do any good. They would become idle. For the same reasons publication in Arabic would not produce any fruit. It would not be useful to the non-Arabs, the vulgar Arabs would not understand anything from it, and the Arab elite is occupied with another political struggle. . . . Nothing can come of Arabic publications in Syria, al-Ḥijāz, Yemen, and Tripoli [of Barbary]. The Arabs of these provinces have more than enough enmity toward the [Ottoman] government due to maladministration, national ideas, and foreign encouragement. To explain to them that government and nation are two independent [entities] is more difficult than making a camel jump over a trench.[346]

Upon the pasha's second refusal, the CPU decided to work independently to establish a branch in Cairo and obtain money from rich Egyptians. Because the central committee intended publications to be in Arabic "not for the fanatical *fallāḥīn* but for the intellectual segment of Egypt[ian society], and primarily for [their] Arab compatriots in Turkey," it also decided to publish an Arabic supplement to *Şûra-yı Ümmet*, and appeals in Arabic as well.[347] In order to obtain money from Egyptian notables and put these decisions into effect, Ahmed Rıza went to Egypt. His visit, and the congenial coverage he received in the Egyptian press, helped the CPU to boost its image in Cairo;[348] Ahmed Rıza succeeded in securing FFr 1,500 from Egyptian notables, yet he failed in his attempt to establish a branch.[349] Furthermore, because of the CPU's gradual adoption of a more revolutionary program, the central committee decided to spend the money he had raised for "action," and not for publishing appeals in Arabic or an Arabic supplement to *Şûra-yı Ümmet* as originally planned.[350]

The CPU also obtained small sums of money from Egyptian notables and from the khedive through Mehmed Sa'id Halim Pasha's mediation.[351] It was compelled, however, to abandon the idea of having a regular, well-organized branch in Cairo. As a last resort, Ahmed Rıza met with Rashīd Riḍā and invited him and his Ligue Constitutionnelle Ottomane to work with the CPU. Rashīd Riḍā later asserted that he had rebuffed this offer by responding, "Yours is [a] Turkish [committee] and ours is Ottoman. We do not agree with you in general, except about fighting against tyranny and striving for a parliamentarian regime."[352] Therefore when the CPU moved *Şûra-yı*

Ümmet to Paris in July 1907, the central committee confessed that following this move they had "nothing to do in Egypt."[353]

The CPU's only consolation was the service offered by a certain Mehmed Efendi, a sailor on one of the Khedivial Line steamers in Suez.[354] He maintained that he and two of his fellow sailors could distribute CPU journals and propaganda material during their boat's excursions in the canal area. CPU correspondence does not provide further hints as to whether they rendered any such services.

Egypt, which was once a bastion of the Young Turks, thus played no role in the preparation and execution of the revolutionary activities of the CPU, other than that of being the residence of its inspector and providing small sums through him.

CPU Correspondents in Europe

Following the reorganization, the CPU also acted to set up branches in the main European capitals. As we have seen, it asked Reşid Sadi to form a CPU branch in London, and a Bosnian Muslim student organization to transform itself into a CPU branch in Vienna. Both initiatives failed, although the individuals in question continued to support the CPU cause.[355] The CPU's desire to form branches in important European capitals stemmed from its aspiration to follow the European press closely and to respond with letter campaigns to European newspaper and journal articles promoting the cause of separatist organizations or defending the non-Muslim Ottoman elements. The CPU believed such propaganda might help it to become the most important Young Turk organization in the eyes of European circles interested in Ottoman affairs, and also to impress their sympathizers.

In addition, as Bahaeddin Şakir stated, the CPU wished to exploit foreign language publications to bolster its own message:

> We want to introduce to our compatriots their friends and foes in Europe through *Şûra-yı Ümmet*. . . . If we tell them the British are our arch-enemies, they will not believe us. If we state, however, that "this is the verbatim translation or the summary of an article that appeared in *The Times* or another important newspaper, or such-and-such a discussion took place at this sitting of the parliament," then poor Turks who cannot differentiate friends from foes will come to recognize those who have been harming and want to harm them.[356]

Therefore, following their failure to establish branches in London and Vienna, the CPU asked two prominent Young Turks to become correspondents for the organization in Germany and England. Bahaeddin Şakir instructed Mustafa Refik, who had organized various early CUP activities in Berlin, to examine German language press and publications carefully and send translations for publishing in the CPU organs.[357] Similarly, Bahaeddin Şakir directed Halil Halid, who was a lecturer at Cambridge University, to render similar services to the committee from England.[358]

Thus both Young Turks became correspondents for the CPU and provided the desired material for publication. In addition, Mustafa Refik prepared pamphlets to be printed by the CPU.[359]

Despite having correspondents in Germany and England following the reorganization, the CPU did not have a single official branch in Western or Central Europe other than its center in Paris.

The CPU Branches Within the Ottoman Empire

The CPU Branches and Cells in Istanbul

Following the reorganization, the CPU's primary goal was to establish a strong organization in Istanbul, one that would enable its members either to assassinate the sultan or to execute a coup d'état. As the leading figures of the reorganization were well aware, this was a very difficult task because of the effectiveness of the sultan's spy network and the extraordinary precautions taken against "subversive activities" in the capital. Indeed, despite all initial efforts, the CPU failed to form a branch in Istanbul until 1907.[360]

There was a small cell in the Ottoman capital under the leadership of Silistireli Hacı İbrahim Paşazâde Hamdi, who went by the pseudonym Ağabey (Big Brother). He was assisted in his activities by two other Young Turks, Biraderzâde İbrahim Bey, who used the pseudonym Çoban (Shepherd), and another Young Turk, with the pseudonym Derya-dil (Great-hearted).[361] Their activities were limited to occasional correspondence with the Young Turks abroad; they owed their cell's miraculous freedom from government interference to this very low level of activity. During the reorganization Bahaeddin Şakir contacted them and asked them to transform themselves into a CPU branch in the capital in accordance with the new regulations.[362]

Upon accepting the invitation, this small cell became the first CPU branch in Istanbul. Despite its small size, it worked vigorously in distributing propaganda material. The CPU center even informed the other branches that this organization in Istanbul was a "device that could distribute four hundred appeals in two hours."[363]

Because the central committee attached the utmost importance to this branch in the capital, Bahaeddin Şakir decided to go secretly to Istanbul to reorganize it. He arrived in Istanbul in early May 1907, bearing a forged passport, and met with the representatives of various opposition organizations as well as with the Istanbul branch's members, in order to help the movement gain momentum in the capital.[364] He kept the central committee informed of his initiatives through open telegrams by using certain code words.[365] Bahaeddin Şakir succeeded in reorganizing the branch, prodding the branch members to take risks in order to carry out activities of significance, and promising them the central committee's support.[366]

Under instructions from Bahaeddin Şakir, and through distributing CPU propaganda material and journals, this small branch succeeded in forming small, independent cells. The branch informed the central committee that "it [was] quite easy to bring all these small societies under control; however, [they did] not find it appropriate to make themselves known to these people who [thought] that there [was] a major committee in Istanbul."[367] The central committee required the leaders of the Istanbul branch to work in the same manner by establishing small independent cells.[368]

The branch ventured to hold a secret gathering at Fenerbağçe in Istanbul. It also decided to publish an appeal addressing the inhabitants of the capital, and it asked the center to publish it for dissemination in Istanbul.[369] In every letter to Bahaeddin Şakir, the branch informed the center of the adherence of new individuals to their organization. In August 1907 a recently inducted member began to provide the branch with accurate information about events taking place in the Sublime Porte and at the

Imperial Palace. This person, who went under the pseudonym Istakoz (Lobster), further offered a contact close to the heir apparent.[370]

The rapid increase in the branch's operations also enabled the central committee to encourage members in other regions by stating that "the clamors that have been occasionally heard in Istanbul [were their] voice."[371] The branch, encouraged by its success, also urged the central committee to appoint a director to the organization in order to entice important figures. They stated:

> We have requested from the [central] committee the appointment of someone as director [of the CPU]. You have promised that you would give an answer upon correspondence [with other branches]. We are, however, in a difficult position. . . . You cannot imagine the desire of people [to join our branch]. We have been invited by someone beyond our wildest imagination who required us to describe to him the strength and vitality of our committee. As mentioned before, however, we cannot establish ties with these types of people until this directorship problem is solved. The time for tardiness is over. Let's take action. Let's demonstrate our strength and vitality to people.[372]

The CPU took measures to form further cells in the capital. With the help of Diran Kelekian, Bahaeddin Şakir succeeded in luring an Armenian to form a CPU cell in Istanbul. This person sent his oath to Bahaeddin Şakir and became "an instructed member." Bahaeddin Şakir and Dr. Nâzım told him that they wished "to take the Armenian nation from the whirlpool into which it was thrown by the [Armenian] committee members who lack sanity, into a valley of happiness and salvation" with the help of people like him.[373]

This Armenian introduced to the central committee another individual with whom he would work. Bahaeddin Şakir told him that their organizational plan for Istanbul was "to form numerous and independent parties [cells] to preserve the organization from the government's blows," and he invited him to form a small cell.[374] The CPU correspondence reveals that these two individuals formed a CPU cell in Istanbul and joined the stillborn assassination attempt planned by Bahaeddin Şakir and Diran Kelekian, which was financed by former intelligence service chief Ahmed Celâleddin Pasha and Yusuf İzzeddin Efendi.[375] This correspondence further indicates that the CPU had Lt. 500 (an amount called "red money" by the central committee, provided by Yusuf İzzeddin Efendi) in gold at its disposal, to spend for operations in Istanbul.[376]

Besides this cell, the only one formed by an Armenian, the CPU correspondence indicates that a cell called the "Ferdî party [cell] of the Istanbul branch" existed,[377] and that a correspondent named Edhem Bey provided intelligence about Istanbul to the central committee in Paris.[378]

Despite its many cells and correspondents in the capital and the handsome sum of Lt. 500 in gold reserved for "action," the CPU could not carry out any significant activities there. Following its merger with the Ottoman Freedom Society in Salonica, the CPU confessed that "though [it had] a few small groups there [in Istanbul], these could not be considered a significant and complete organization."[379] This comment itself indicates not the inherent weakness of the organization but rather the strength of the palace's security system. A comparable network of cells could carry out considerably more activities in many other parts of the empire, but in the well-protected capital such a network was simply not sufficient to strike a blow against the regime.

Because of their special organization, the CPU cells in the capital continued both to correspond with and receive instructions from the Paris center even after the CPU merged with the Ottoman Freedom Society, at which time it was decided to place all CPU branches within the empire under the administration of the latter, which assumed the title of CPU Internal Headquarters.[380] The Ottoman Freedom Society itself formed numerous cells in Istanbul. Its industrious organizer, Manyasizâde Refik, worked strenuously to establish a well-working organization in the capital and enjoyed considerable success.[381] Finally, prior to the revolution Adjutant-Major Kâzım (Karabekir) united all these cells under a single local organization and also achieved a merger between this local organization and the CPU branch under the direction of Silistireli Hacı İbrahim Paşazâde Hamdi. This new CPU branch in Istanbul had more than 70 members, most of them officers.[382] Because of the rapid CPU victory in Macedonia in July 1908, however, this branch did not play any role in the revolution.

The Twin CPU Lâzistan Branches

Although the CPU's primary aim was to form a branch for "action" in the capital that could stage a coup d'état and put an end to the Hamidian regime, it also worked to establish functioning branches in the other parts of the empire. The reorganizers regarded all the branches in the empire as organizations for "action." Obviously, actions outside the capital would not compel the sultan to change his regime unless they assumed a persistent and turbulent character.

The only CPU branch that carried out "action" before its merger with the Ottoman Freedom Society was one of its Lâzistan branches. The branch's inability to undertake further actions because of its limited membership permitted the government to cripple its operations.

When he started the reorganization of the branches, Bahaeddin Şakir sent his first letter to Trabzon, in which he asked Colonel İshak Bey and Ali Necib, an exiled official working in the local government, to form a CPU branch in Trabzon.[383] After exhausting and highly secret work, these two Young Turks formed a CPU branch there in November 1906 and named it the CPU Lâzistan branch. The center recognized it on November 25, 1906, and sent them a seal from Paris.[384]

The branch began its operations by distributing propaganda material and letters to officials and officers in the region. The local authorities swiftly retaliated with an extensive investigation and subsequently banished the branch's leader, Colonel İshak, to Erzincan in November 1906. The central committee, fearing the branch's collapse, sent a fiery letter to the remaining members warning them that "a lion launches an impetuous attack when it is wounded." The letter invited them to elect an acting director and work toward "securing the nation's happiness and avenging [their] friends."[385] Even before receiving this letter, Ali Necib, who had assumed responsibility over the branch's affairs, wrote fierce, threatening letters to the governor and the commander in Trabzon.[386] He further discussed the action to be taken against the local authorities with a young military member of the branch. He described the ensuing events as follows:

> On February 27 [March 12, 1907], which was a Tuesday, we were discussing the situation with the esteemed Naci Bey and a mutual friend. Naci stressed that the commander

should be assassinated. He stated that the commander had granted him many favors; however, because of his oppressive attitude toward the people and his betrayal, the commander should be killed. I told him that I was in favor of shooting a few people, and this must be considered carefully. We have a *hoca* here who gives us very beneficial recommendations on religious matters. We decided to discuss this matter with him. The *hoca* then issued a *fatwā* that the commander's assassination would be in accordance with the *sharī'a*. Subsequently, we decided to wait for a suitable time to seize the opportunity. Our self-sacrificing volunteer, however, pondered it well, and put the bullet in the commander's mouth, as I described to you previously, without giving us notice.[387]

During his interrogation the gunman did not give away the names of his comrades, claiming that he had assassinated the pasha out of personal hatred, and also because he had not been paid for two months and therefore his mother had been affected.[388] At the court martial, however, he made a bold statement: "I shot the commander in order to comply with the illustrious order of God asking us to kill seditious people and betrayers and eradicate the body of that traitor who thought of nothing but harming the state and the nation. If I succeeded I am happy, if I failed I am sorry."[389] He was executed in June 1907.

Upon receiving this news, the center sent another fierce letter telling the acting director that the commander and the governor had nothing left to use against the branch. The center also approved the acting director's previous action of sending threatening letters to the local authorities, but it urged him "to irritate their [authorities'] bodies instead of their souls" and urged "self-defense in the form of retaliation."[390]

This assassination of Divisional General Hamdi Pasha, the commander of Trabzon, by one of the CPU members, First Lieutenant Naci Bey, led everyone to believe that a more serious movement was imminent in Trabzon, and consequently the European press attached great importance to the event.[391] Despite the CPU center's encouragement, however, the branch was in no position to launch any further attacks.

In the meantime, Colonel İshak, the former director of the branch, who had been banished to Erzincan, wanted a certain major in the province to replace him as the new director. Since the major was assigned to a field post in Of, a town far from the provincial capital Trabzon, İshak Bey asked the approval of the central committee.[392] Seizing this chance, the Paris center asked this major to form a new branch in Of called "the CPU Lâzistan External Branch." The central committee's contact with the Lâzistan branch in Trabzon had been severed because of the arrests, and when a young artillery lieutenant reestablished it,[393] Bahaeddin Şakir informed the main branch in Trabzon of the formation of the new branch in Of and promised to introduce the two branches to each other.[394] But since the central committee wanted the branches to work independently and correspond only with itself, this promise was never fulfilled.

The CPU Lâzistan External branch in Of assisted the central committee in distributing much of its propaganda material in the region,[395] and the correspondence official of the branch extended his "hand" to the border of Erzurum. The central committee therefore assigned Ömer Naci to meet with the members of the external branch and work with them to disseminate CPU propaganda without waiting for instructions and material from Paris.[396] Also, thanks to its merger with the CPU branch in

Och'amch'ire, the branch became one of the largest CPU branches, having members both in the empire and abroad.[397] Fearing that the branch's affairs might spin out of control, the central committee warned the director "to conduct administration with consultation and in any case not to forget to submit adequate information to the central committee."[398] However, it also held this branch up as an example to emulate in their dealings with individuals who contacted the central committee.[399] Since the people of Of were considered the most pious people in the empire, the central committee employed an exceptionally strong Islamic rhetoric when it addressed these branch members.[400]

The CPU twin branches in Lâzistan were good examples of internal organizations working toward "action." In fact the central committee instructed the CPU Lâzistan branch "to choose [their] members from daring and upright individuals and not from pessimists."[401] The central committee prodded members in these branches to "action" by writing them fervent letters. It was the branches and not the central committee, however, that planned and carried out the operations in the region. The CPU drew the lesson from these actions that sporadic ventures could create only temporary excitement and that they needed an improved network to gain the upper hand against the local authorities in a region.

The CPU Izmir Branch

During the reorganization the CPU targeted Izmir, the most important Ottoman port on the Aegean, as a prospective branch center. A CPU branch in this city would enable the CPU to disseminate its propaganda through almost the whole of Western Anatolia. Establishing a branch in Izmir from Paris, however, was no less formidable an undertaking than establishing a branch in any other town in the empire.

Bahaeddin Şakir took the first step when an Ottoman merchant from Izmir came to Marseilles and sent a letter to the CPU asking them to provide him with CPU journals and pamphlets. Bahaeddin Şakir instructed the merchant to prepare a list of "honest patriots" in Izmir.[402] In the meantime the CPU received an unexpected letter from an opposition committee that had been established in Izmir. Its members stated in their letter that "some compatriots like the Armenians, Greeks, and others who are seeking to separate themselves from us are preparing to invite foreign intervention by exploiting the crisis over the succession to the throne." They thought "the nation's independence" was in danger and so formed a committee. They wanted to unite with the CPU in accordance with the Belgian motto "l'union fait la force."[403] They criticized the Young Turks in Europe for failing to conduct serious activities.

In response, Bahaeddin Şakir assured them that "their program [was] as comprehensive and extensive as their intentions," and he invited them to become the CPU branch in Izmir.[404] When he did not receive an answer, he sent another letter to this committee in which he stated that the CPU did not "have members who promise independence or autonomy to the Armenians here and there, or act like a Don Quijote by bragging, but is composed of patriotic and honest individuals such as Ahmed Rıza and [Sami Paşazâde] Sezaî Beys."[405] A secret CPU letter written in October 1907 reveals that this small committee did indeed become the CPU branch in Izmir. The center instructed the members of this new branch to throw propaganda material into gardens, in front of the doors of houses, and into the courtyards of mosques at night, and to establish ties with college students.[406]

Following the CPU's merger with the Ottoman Freedom Society, Izmir grew in importance for the CPU. The military members of the CPU knew that the palace would dispatch the first-class reserve divisions stationed in the province of Aydın as reinforcements in the event of an uprising in Macedonia. Since Macedonia became the hub of the CPU following the aforementioned merger, the CPU exerted its best efforts to carry out propaganda aimed at winning over reservists in Izmir, the capital of Aydın Province. Thus the central committee in Paris required everyone in the empire to provide them with names of "patriots" in Izmir.[407] The committee intended to strengthen the branch by recruiting many individuals for it.[408]

It was Dr. Nâzım, however, who conducted the real propaganda activity in Izmir on behalf of the CPU and succeeded in winning over many reservists who were subsequently sent to Macedonia at the peak of the revolutionary events there. His activities will be described in detail in the discussion of the Young Turk Revolution of 1908.

The CPU Branches in the Arab Provinces

The CPU did not consider the Arab provinces of the Ottoman Empire as an area of primary importance for carrying out operations. The leaders maintained that the reason was the fact that they "did not have any relations and especially any language affinity with Syria [and the other Arabic speaking] region[s]."[409] In spite of this, the CPU established branches and had correspondents in these provinces, but only for disseminating CPU propaganda. Most of the sympathizers who worked for the CPU in these provinces were Ottoman officials and officers. Only in Baghdad did some local notables become members of the CPU branch there.

In April 1906 Mehmed Macid, a leading member of the CPU branch in Canea, told Bahaeddin Şakir and Dr. Nâzım that he had a friend who worked at the bureau of education in Beirut[410] who would form a branch there.[411] In the meantime this low-ranking official, named Mes'ud Remzi, sent a letter to Ahmed Rıza stating that he would secretly distribute copies of *Mechveret Supplément Français* in Beirut. Bahaeddin Şakir invited him to become a CPU correspondent,[412] and Mes'ud Remzi started writing articles about Syria for *Şûra-yı Ümmet*, as well as distributing CPU journals.[413]

As a next step, Bahaeddin Şakir directed Mes'ud Remzi "to expand his activities" and establish a CPU branch for Syria.[414] Mes'ud Remzi accepted the offer but stated that he would form the Lebanon branch of the CPU by making a few officials at local offices CPU members.[415] Besides his activities in Lebanon, Mes'ud Remzi forwarded CPU propaganda material coming from Paris to Damascus.[416] The CPU's secret correspondence reveals that this person worked very actively in distributing CPU propaganda material. Still he failed to establish a branch in Syria or Lebanon, and CPU activities in these regions were limited to the circulation of a small amount of propaganda material.[417]

Despite the CPU's failure to establish a well-organized branch in Syria and Lebanon and its confinement to a simple correspondent in Beirut, its efforts to form a network of branches in Iraq and areas adjacent to it bore fruit. In Baghdad "six medical doctors, officers, and veterinary surgeons," along with "six local notable patriots," founded a branch[418] and took the initiative in setting up additional branches in Mosul and Diyar-ı Bekir.[419] CPU sympathizers agreed to establish a branch in Diyar-ı Bekir. Those in Mosul, however, offered to help solely by distributing CPU propaganda material.[420] Although the central committee was pleased with the activities of this new branch and encouraged its founders to expand their operations,[421] it is difficult to know to what degree these branches and sympathizers actually helped the CPU. Following the revolution, official CUP journals maintained that "more than thirty Kurdish *bey*s signed documents and took oaths a couple of months" before the Young Turk Revolution of 1908.[422] If this has any connection to the initiative of the Baghdad branch to establish a branch in Diyar-ı Bekir, it must be considered an important success.

Regardless of their activities, following the CPU's merger with the Ottoman Freedom Society, the branches in the Arab provinces lost their already limited importance in the eyes of the CPU leadership. While it is true that the Ottoman officers in Tripoli of Barbary established a CPU cell there following the merger, this cell, like the other branches and cells in the Arab provinces, was of no practical use to the CPU.

CPU Strategy and Ideology after the Reorganization

A peculiarity of the self-styled revolutionary coalition was its lack of a strong revolutionary praxis. The coalition confined itself to publications and awaited the moment when a few readers of these publications would carry out a miraculous revolution. Although the activist wing of the coalition continually protested against this languid course, they could not come up with anything other than bizarre assassination schemes to challenge Ahmed Rıza and his companions, who held the upper hand in the coalition.

The coalition's ideology crystalized between 1902 and 1905. It was strongly anti-European, anti-interventionist, and critical of the separatist desires of the Ottoman Empire's non-Turkish elements. At the same time, the coalition began to gravitate toward Turkism without entirely abandoning the idea of Ottomanism. The coalition's leaders, who were at pains to reconcile this nascent Turkism with Ottomanism, usually restricted themselves by claiming a dominant position for the Turkish element in the empire. When it came to defending this thesis at international platforms or during negotiations with various opposition committees, the coalition took a rigid stand and demonstrated absolute inflexibility. Ahmed Rıza offered just two alternatives to the other opposition groups: to accept the coalition's program without any discussion, or to work on their own and not expect any assistance from the coalition.

Examination of the available secret CPU correspondence reveals that, as a revolutionary committee attempting to destroy the regime, the CPU proposed common action to every one of the regime's opponents, employing not a single clear rhetoric but rather many conflicting rhetorics in order to lure diverse opposition groups and individuals to its cause.

For example, when corresponding with Turks in Bulgaria, the CPU declared:

No important matter of the committee may be left either to an Armenian enemy of the Turks or to anybody else. If an Armenian comes and says to us, "Look, I am an Ottoman too; I love Ottomanism and I want to serve Ottomanism in accordance with your program," we will then say to this Armenian, "Compatriot, welcome! This is the way if you indeed want to work toward the elevation of Ottomanism with us." We will draw his attention to this, because of the hospitality and generosity which are Islamic and Turkish characteristics. We will accept a non-Muslim Ottoman into our committee only under these conditions. Our committee is a pure Turkish committee. It will never be dominated by the ideas of those who are enemies of Islam and Turkishness.[423]

Another letter addressed to Muslims in Caucasia portrayed the revolutionary Armenians as "infidels who are enemies of Islam."[424] Also, in accordance with the coalition's approach, Bahaeddin Şakir stated the following:

Our fatherland and national independence are under absolute threat. . . . We should be certain that if we do not sacrifice ourselves, and continue to love life too much, we who are the children and grandchildren of the Turks, "who had produced a world-conquering state from a tribe," and of the Ottomans who maintained their national independence until now, would become a subject nation in a disgraceful manner. Instead of becoming a subject nation, and especially a subject nation as Turks and Muslims, it is better for us not to live.[425]

In other confidential letters CPU leaders underscored the feats of the Turks, such as "coming from Transoxania, establishing their metropolis in Europe, and protecting their fatherland against the assaults of internal and external crusades."[426]

When it addressed Armenians who showed interest, however, the CPU argued that "as you would agree, the wealth and happiness of all Ottomans may be achieved through the cooperation of all Ottomans composing the entire population without distinction of religion, faith, and ethnicity."[427] It stated that its aim was racial "equality and justice."[428] Finally, despite its claim to be a "pure Turkish committee," the CPU urged certain Armenians to form mixed branches composed of Armenians and Turks.[429] Bahaeddin Şakir also opened the pages of *Şûra-yı Ümmet* to Armenian sympathizers of the Young Turk movement.[430] It is true that the Armenian letters that appeared in the CPU central organ defended the Ottomanist thesis and criticized "Christian fanaticism." With the exception of Pierre Anméghian, who earlier had written articles to refute the Armenian committees' theses under the pseudonym Ottomanus in *Mechveret Supplément Français*, Armenians were writing for the first time for CPU journals.[431] Although Ahmed Rıza later underscored Bahaeddin Şakir's "enmity toward Armenians,"[432] it was Bahaeddin Şakir who exerted great efforts to establish ties with the Armenian organizations and who drafted Armenians as CPU branch members following the reorganization.

As we have seen, the CPU also welcomed cells established by the Armenians in Istanbul. Following the merger with the Ottoman Freedom Society, the CPU also worked seriously toward establishing a branch composed of Bulgarians in accordance with its regulations.[433]

Similarly, when Bahaeddin Şakir addressed a Bulgarian, he stated that "the origins of Bulgarians and Turks are the same, and with the help of the hand of destiny they have been compelled to live together. Since it is not possible to remove the necessity of living together and being neighbors, both sides' comfort and happiness depend on having good relations with each other. Look, our aim and organization are confined to this [principle]."[434]

When he addressed an Armenian, however, Bahaeddin Şakir stated that "everyone should fulfill his duties toward the fatherland in order to return to the glorious past of six hundred years ago, for the reinvigoration of the state, in order not to be downtrodden and humiliated by the Europeans, Greeks, and Bulgarians."[435] In another letter, however, the CPU leaders falsely claimed that "there [were] many Armenians and Greeks included in [their] committee."[436] In a letter to the Muslims in Caucasia it was stated that "the Armenians, Bulgarians, and Greeks who [were] jealous of the growing strength of [their] committee [were] making a thousand types of slanders" against them.[437]

The CPU's opinions on the issues of Turkism, the union of Turkic peoples, Ottomanism, and the role of Islam in their revolutionary movement also oscillated depending on their addressee. Even the style of address changed accordingly. While corresponding with Muslims and Turks the CPU frequently used the phrases "our coreligionists," "our brothers in religion," "our brothers," "we Turks," and "our fellow countrymen," whereas it used the standard phrases "our compatriots" and "we Ottomans" while exchanging letters with the non-Muslims. The CPU employed a heavy Ottomanist rhetoric when it addressed non-Turks and non-Muslims, maintaining that it was "working toward the happiness of all Ottoman elements such as the Albanians, Turks, Kurds, Armenians, Bulgarians, [and] Greeks."[438]

As we have seen, however, the reorganizers also strove "to make *Şûra-yı Ümmet* join" the struggle of Hüseyinzâde Ali, who was working to achieve "a (Turkish Union) in the regions from the Adriatic Sea to the Chinese Sea."[439] In this vein, the CPU journals quoted the most striking passages praising the Turks from the Turkic journals:

> The bread and idea should be ours. The Turkish nation exists and will exist. This great hero's head lies at the Chinese Wall and his legs reach to the Sea of Marmara and the Mediterranean. Turks exist and they will exist as they have existed for more than twenty centuries. Our ancestors, our fathers brought law and order to all of Asia and part of Europe and Africa by establishing many great states. . . . One of the greatest of nations is our Turkish nation.[440]

The CPU leaders exhorted Turkic groups to accept Ottoman Turkish as standard Turkish,[441] and they praised a Tatar *hoca*'s leading Friday prayers in Tatar instead of Arabic.[442]

As for the role of the Turkish element in the Ottoman Empire, notwithstanding the many articles on the advantages of Ottomanism, the CPU journals also often emphasized the dominant role of the Turks in Ottoman society. For instance, they maintained that

> In this fatherland the right of sovereignty belongs to those who have sacrificed their lives for the maintenance of the fatherland and the sovereignty of the nation for six hundred years. What a blessing that today those Muslims, the Turks who had come from Transoxania, and shed their blood from here to Transoxania, agree to have the Christians equal

to them in all rights in the fatherland. . . . It should be known that this majestic sultanate, this glory and honor enjoyed only by very few nations in the world, belongs to the Muslims, the Turks. As for the great pleas being made by the Christians to become soldiers, we hope that when the Greeks join the Ottoman armies, they will defend the fatherland more than they would defend Thessaly and Athens.[443]

When they addressed pious Muslims, however, the CPU leaders put the Ottomanist or Turkist rhetoric aside and adopted a strong Islamist discourse. For example, they claimed that

This man [the sultan] even allowed the Bulgarians to humiliate our exalted army. . . . Please demand [the application of] Islam, religious norms, and *sharī'a*. . . . As you know previously five or six former sultans were executed at the gallows because of small betrayals of the nation, and they thereby received their punishments. In those days, however, the *sharī'a* was the sovereign, the *sharī'a* was the sultan. . . . Every Muslim who dies for the salvation of the fatherland is a martyr. . . . The opening of the "National Assembly" would make the application of the sacred *sharī'a* of Muḥammad, justice, and freedom possible. . . . Please be a standard-bearer of freedom in the sacred *gaza* that will be carried out. As your virtuous soul knows, anyone who loves the religion of Islam, defends the Holy Qur'ān, this evident law, and saves his nation from the danger of extinction and enslavement is a man beloved of Almighty God, and descends from the most loyal *ummah* of our glorious Prophet."[444]

Further, they claimed that their committee was composed of "individuals who have devote[d] their lives both to the salvation of the Ottoman state and to enlightening the minds of [their] coreligionists in accordance with the meaning of '[innamā] al-mu'minūna ikhwatun.'"[445] The CPU also invited the ulema to give sermons against the sultan and to emulate Iranian constitutionalist ulema by using a similar rhetoric.[446]

In contrast to this Islamic rhetoric, the CPU explained its shortcomings in the field of action to an intellectual in Bulgaria by referring to a positivist and universal law of evolution allegedly pertinent to all secret societies, and by pleading that their "committee has not yet reached the final stage in this phase of evolution."[447]

Social and class differences also meant very little for the reorganizers. They thought that everyone should give something for the "daybreak" of the Ottoman Empire: the courageous their courage, the rich a "*zakāt* of their wealth," the wise "their ideas," and respected officials their "authority."[448]

For instance, the CPU urged a sympathizer who was influential among "capitalists" to collect money for the committee from his capitalist friends.[449] It required other sympathizers to provide information about "trade unions" in order to organize the workers.[450] Also when a Polish socialist revolutionary advised Dr. Nâzım and Bahaeddin Şakir to organize factory workers instead of peasants, they recommended to the CPU Internal Headquarters that they penetrate the factories and draft workers for the CPU:

As a matter of fact, it is not possible to concentrate the peasants as a body in a certain place. At a factory, however, the equivalent of a village population gathers. Whereas those who live separately are not aware of the world around them, those who live together naturally get used to thinking about the future of their country by learning everything quickly. . . . Therefore, the members of the committee should penetrate the factories and find sympathizers among the workers.[451]

In order to put this scheme into effect, the CPU even planned to make publications for workers.[452] This plan did not prevent the CPU, however, from establishing a "CPU peasant branch" just before the revolution in order to incite the peasants with promises of fiscal and agricultural reforms.[453] Also the CPU seriously considered making heavy agricultural taxes a central propaganda issue in their propaganda for Anatolia.[454]

Similarly, in order to obtain money, the CPU knocked on all available doors. Although the committee employed a populist rhetoric and frequently claimed that "freedom may not be gained as a favor granted by the upper classes but only through the work of the people,"[455] this populist approach did not prevent the CPU from instructing certain branches to establish ties with notables in order to win them over to the movement,[456] or from applauding the fact that "people from the upper classes" had begun to incline toward the CPU.[457] Indeed, the CPU officially appealed to the heir apparent Mehmed Reşad Efendi, Yusuf İzzeddin Efendi, and the Khedive ʿAbbās Ḥilmī Pasha, and solicited "cash" from all three of them.[458]

All these examples may cause one to conclude that the CPU did not have a clear-cut ideology, or any ideology at all, and that its leaders defended conflicting theses. This ideological elasticity, however, should be considered merely a revolutionary tactic. Rather than appeal to a small, limited group of individuals with a sharply defined and inflexible ideology, the CPU attempted to court all opponents of the regime with different rhetorics for different groups. In other words, it told diverse opposition groups whatever they wished to hear.

For Nikola Manolov and the Armenians who formed a CPU cell in Istanbul, the CPU was an Ottomanist committee working toward the happiness of all Ottomans. For those who thought that Turks should assume the dominant role that had been filled by the Muslim *millet* before the *Tanzimat*, the CPU was the organization that would fulfill their dreams. For Muslims and Turks in Bulgaria, Crete, and Cyprus, the CPU was a savior promising to reinvigorate the decadent Ottoman Empire and deliver it from foreign and Christian domination. For devout Muslims, it was a Muslim organization piously striving to change the regime in accordance with the *ḥadīth*s. And for many intellectuals, it was an organization under the guidance of positivist intellectuals. In a similar fashion, the CPU leaders also exerted their best efforts to win over bureaucrats, capitalists, factory workers, and peasants alike.

The CPU's success in drafting members from diverse social classes and ethnic and religious groups should not be underestimated. Through strenuous organizational work, the central committee succeeded in drafting low-ranking Turkish officials, Ottoman ambassadors, Egyptian princes, Anatolian notables, Bulgarian teachers, Armenian businessmen, Albanian medical doctors, ardent and devout Muslims, and free-thinking intellectuals, all of whom saw advantages in the replacement of Hamidian rule with a "Young Turk" regime.

In view of its success in drafting people from such varied social and ethnic groups, the CPU's failure to establish alliances with non-Turkish opposition societies is paradoxical. Other revolutionary committees such as the Dashnaktsutiun expressed no desire to merge with the CPU, regardless of the latter's rhetoric. They did not want to work under the CPU umbrella and made it clear that they would not accept anything other than a tactical alliance between independent committees.

Since the CPU welcomed everyone to its organization, the central committee was unable to carry out a single-faceted and clear-cut propaganda campaign. This does not mean, however, that the center itself did not have any ideological tendencies. When one examines all the CPU correspondence, its propaganda material, its secret documents, and its official publications, it becomes clear that the CPU followed the path taken by the former CUP and the coalition, leaning toward Turkism and a Turkish-led Panislamism. Inclination toward these ideas does not mean that the CPU abandoned all the other ideas embraced by its various members. Rather, it seems that the CPU was, in contrast to the coalition, extremely opportunistic. This opportunism was best summarized by Bahaeddin Şakir when he advised the Caucasian Muslims "not to express [their] real aims in letters."[459]

Thus not even the secret letters that the central committee sent to CPU branches and members can be considered as revealing the CPU's true aims. The semiautonomous status of the branches, and the presence of members from different backgrounds, social status, ethnic origins, and religious affiliations produced branches that had very little in common other than opposition to the existing regime. During this period the CPU functioned like a foreign ministry that possesses a long-term agenda but is forced to employ the short-term tactics of realpolitik. The CPU decision-makers did not discourage some of their members and allies from propagating certain policies just because they disapproved of these policies from an ideological standpoint. On the contrary, they evaluated these policies solely by considering their potential practical consequences, both short- and long term. For example, when the Cretan Muslims wanted to declare in the CPU journals that "in retaliation for the Cretan Christians' threatening the Muslims with a fully-fledged massacre, a reprisal against the Greeks in Izmir and other regions of the Ottoman lands will be put into effect," the CPU told them that this would be absolutely against the interests of the CPU and the Cretan Muslims.[460] The CPU's counsel was by no means a criticism of the idea itself, but rather a reflection of a practical assessment of the likely consequences of such a declaration. In Bahaeddin Şakir's own words, "subterfuge is permissible in war."[461] Similarly, although they themselves frequently employed a rhetoric promoting the union of Muslims, the CPU leaders told the Muslims in Caucasia that pursuance of such a policy "would not be in accordance with [their] interests."[462] The CPU leaders told both Cretan and Caucasian Muslims that they would give them a helping hand once they had toppled the Hamidian regime and strengthened the caliphate.

Following the reorganization, the CPU also adopted a very realistic approach toward foreign powers. In contrast to their arch-rival Sabahaddin Bey, who tried his best to convince the European public that the future Ottoman regime would follow European advice as the *Tanzimat* statesmen did, the CPU leaders adopted a defensive and extremely critical approach. Also lofty sociological theories played no role in the CPU's views on particular foreign powers.

In general, the CPU took an extremely anti-Western and anti-imperialist stand. As was stated in a secret letter, the CPU leaders wished "to understand the Europeans' progress in the sciences as the Japanese had done, and to see only this [scientific progress] realized in [their] country."[463] The CPU viewed Europe as a monolithic civilization that thought of "nothing but its economic interests."[464] According to CPU journals, in such a civilization, public opinion, manipulated by a press that is itself "capitalist," favored the exploitation of the Orient: "*The Times* itself is one of the greatest capitalists of Europe. England goes crazy when it sees money, as a tiger goes crazy when it sees blood."[465] The Europeans' "racial hierarchy" was a tool to exploit the "orientals" for their economic interests.[466] The Europeans' idea of "civilizing the Muslims" was nothing more than an instrument of political and economic domination.[467] The CPU leaders believed that the European "pénétration pacifique" that used economic devices had replaced the military and colonial conquests of the previous centuries.[468] As was reiterated by Ahmed Rıza, the European Great Powers were "high-quality anarchists" who were behind all catastrophic developments.[469]

The CPU leaders described the European Great Powers, which they labeled "ravens of civilization,"[470] with regard to their policies toward the Ottoman Empire as the guardians of "spoiled children named Bulgarians, Greeks, and Serbians," and maintained that these Great Powers' policy of "launching a crusade against the Turks" had been deeply rooted in their economic interests.[471] They further asserted that "if the Macedonian [Christians] who caused the present problems by inviting Europeans to intervene continue to pursue the same policy, they will become the servants of European capital in their own land."[472] As a reaction to this alleged exploitation, Ahmed Rıza proposed a general boycott of European goods to hinder European trade. This would be "the severest punishment for the money-worshipping Europeans."[473]

In accordance with this opposition to Europe as a whole and to its "capitalist-imperialist" policies, the CPU generally criticized the European powers. According to its leaders, "the present [European] civilization disguised as humanitarianism is carrying out atrocities."[474] In the same vein, the CPU organs bitterly opposed the European powers' use of the terms "indigène" and "native" when they referred to the Turks. In the eyes of the CPU leaders this guise of a civilizing mission was nothing other than a façade for their economic exploitation.[475]

Thus the CPU organs published articles criticizing all the European Great Powers without exception as representatives of a single barbarian civilization. As Ahmed Rıza pointed out, these provoked a strong reaction among the Europeans against the CPU, and so from a tactical understanding could be viewed as a mistake: "Notre tort est peut-être de nous plaindre à la fois des toutes les Puissances. Si nous nous attaquions à une seule d'entre elles, comme les Boers, nous serions également appuyés par les concurrents de la Puissance visée."[476]

For example, Italy and Austria-Hungary's efforts to secure autonomy for every ethnic group in Macedonia were "in plain Turkish" a scheme to "cut Turkey into pieces."[477] Italy and France were aiming at establishing a religious protectorate over the Ottoman Empire.[478] Russia's policy of Slavism was racist irredentism and a great threat to European peace.[479] Besides, Russia and the Dual Monarchy supported the status quo in the Ottoman Empire for the sake of continuing their "pénétration pacifique."[480]

The most striking feature of the CPU's new policy, however, was the exceptionally strong language it used against Great Britain. Previously, almost all Young Turk organizations had regarded Great Britain as an ally. Even as late as November 1906 the CPU censored paragraphs in a pamphlet castigating French and British policies toward the Ottoman Empire and the Muslims.[481] In January 1907, however, following a lengthy discussion, the CPU decided to attack Great Britain in its journals. Some members of the central committee were hesitant to launch a fully-fledged propaganda assault on Great Britain, but those who agreed that "the Turks are excused for not regarding the British, who provoked and prodded the Armenians yesterday and are provoking and prodding the Bulgarians and Arabs against [them] today, in the way that they used to," were the majority at the meeting in which the CPU's publication policy toward Great Britain was discussed.[482] Following this decision, which the Anglo–Russian *détente* of August 1907 only strengthened,[483] the CPU adopted a very critical policy toward Great Britain. Halil Halid's letters written under the instructions of the central committee,[484] and Bahaeddin Şakir's articles picturing British policy toward the Ottoman Empire as "a twentieth-century crusade" appeared in *Şûra-yı Ümmet.*[485] The French supplement joined the assault by publishing anti-British articles by 'Uthmān Ghālib, a positivist and a sympathizer of al–Ḥizb al-Waṭanī.[486]

Their leaders' own hatred of Western imperialism, bolstered by the grievances of Muslims under European administration, prompted the leaders of the CPU to form an Islamic fraternal society. It is remarkable that Ahmed Rıza, a staunch positivist, should have spearheaded this initiative. This fraternity was conceived first and foremost as a union against "Western imperialism," and Islam in this context was viewed by the founders of the organization as a culture and not a religion. Ahmed Rıza stated that the Christian West had been openly encouraging the rebellions in Crete with its claims that the Christian majority had wanted independence. He therefore posed the following questions: "Pourquoi ne pas admettre et tolérer le même principe, les mêmes droits chez les Musulmans de l'Egypte, de Tunisie, de l'Algérie, des Indes et de la Caucasie? Pourquoi traiter de fanatisme une idée de justice exempte de toute coterie religieuse?"[487] He further stated that it was not the Orientals who were seeking a fight, but the Europeans who wanted to thrash and pillage them in their own lands. Therefore Europe would receive the response she deserved: "Qui sème le vent récolte la tempête."[488]

Although the establishment of the "Islamic Fraternal Society" appeared to be a spontaneous development led by Muslim intellectuals, the facts that its offices were in Bahaeddin Şakir's private apartment[489] and that the CPU organs announced its establishment and published its bylaws[490] speak for themselves. Bahaeddin Şakir further claimed that the CPU administration had established ties with *Revue du Monde Musulman,* which provided favorable coverage.[491]

The CPU encouraged Muslims in Caucasia and in Bosnia to become members of this new organization,[492] and it sent the CPU organs to the Islamic Fraternal Society's members.[493] One should remember, however, that the CPU leaders always thought that the Ottoman state would play a vital role in shaping the future of Islam, and thus always envisioned this Islamic fraternity as centered around the Ottoman Empire.[494]

The CPU also strove to establish an alliance with the Iranian constitutionalists. During the Ottoman–Iranian border dissension of 1907–1908, the CPU protested the Ottoman military occupation of a disputed area by sending a letter to the Paris and Istanbul embassies of Iran and to the speaker of the Iranian parliament stating that "the strength to withstand and repel the foreign calamities that fall upon the Islamic world from all directions should be sought in fraternity and union."[495] The CPU also issued an appeal to the Ottoman officers and soldiers involved, exhorting them not to be misled by the maneuvers of the Europeans who were "striving to hasten the annihilation and eradication of the existing Islamic governments."[496] Later on the CPU also established close ties with the Anjuman-i Millī-i Tabrīz and the Iranian constitutionalists in their struggle.[497] Also Ömer Naci, whom the CPU central committee dispatched to Salmās in order to establish revolutionary branches in Eastern Anatolia, worked together with the Iranian constitutionalists.[498]

In general, the CPU wished to bring into its ranks all opponents of the regime in the Ottoman Empire. Accordingly, ideologies or rhetorics were nothing more than devices to leaders such as Bahaeddin Şakir. Therefore the CPU's conflicting announcements, instructions, appeals, and articles should be understood as parts of a coherent tactical plan, and not as the utterances of confused and perplexed minds. Beneath this quilt of conflicting ideas, the CPU's predilections were clear: anti-Europeanism, anti-imperialism, an Ottomanism granting dominance to the empire's Turkish element, and a Panislamism to be centered on the Ottoman Empire.

The CPU's policy toward the non-Muslim and non-Turkish Ottoman elements was a double-edged sword. It may be viewed as inclusive, because these elements were invited to common action insofar as they accepted the CPU's version of Ottomanism. For those who did not want to acquiesce in the CPU version of Turkish-dominated Ottomanism, however, the CPU's policies were exclusionist. For non-Turkish Muslim Ottomans the situation was more ambiguous because of the CPU's strong Panislamist rhetoric. In this case too, however, the CPU leaders assigned the pivotal role to the Turks, and thereby hindered their efforts to conclude alliances with organized Arab and Muslim Albanian societies. Besides these societies, the CPU also was unable to merge with organized non-Muslim opposition groups. Those non-Muslims who joined with the CPU as individuals and not as members of an organized group sooner or later broke with it.

The 1906 reorganization was a watershed event in the history of the Young Turk movement, not only because it created a well-organized and activist committee, but also because it finally armed this movement with a long-awaited strong revolutionary praxis. By harnessing resentment toward European political intervention and economic penetration into an active policy, adopting a Turkist discourse, and implementing a Panislamist rhetoric, the CPU succeeded in rallying Turks and Muslims, the two main actors of the Young Turk Revolution of 1908.

CPU Publication Policy and Propaganda after the Reorganization

Following the reorganization, the CPU made "propaganda" one of its two main objectives along with "organization." Because of the special importance attached to propaganda, the CPU drastically changed its publication policy and attempted to use new means of propaganda.

As was forthrightly explained by Bahaeddin Şakir, publication became a means rather than an end during this new phase of activity. The reorganized CPU anticipated that this new policy of publication would result in the recruitment of militants for future activities:

> In all the signed and anonymous letters sent to our committee, various methods have recently been proposed to us concerning this matter. If we want to summarize them, they all direct [us] to a single point: activity. [They write]: "Your committee has been work-

ing these many years; so many patriots have been sent into exile or thrown into dungeons. What good consequences have followed from all this for the fatherland? Do you not watch the Russians? Every day one of the traitors who is a tool of the [tzarist] tyranny is exterminated by a bomb." In another letter in the same vein the following is written: "For twelve years you have engaged in publication. Are you unable to see that this is a dead end? . . . To say 'We are not holding anybody's hand' cannot be an excuse for you."

If we want to find the force that provides an Ottoman Armenian who has never seen a gun in his life, or a Russian Jew, with the courage to play with bombs that can cut one hundred people into pieces in an instant, we can only find it in "political training."

In reality, publication means neither publishing a journal regularly nor publishing pamphlets. In order to win the title of publication, a journal or a pamphlet should be read by the masses, and this is possible only when supporters who would receive the publication are found in every corner of the country, read it, and then read it to those who are illiterate. These supporters should be attached to a single center as far as possible. This mutual assistance, this relationship, can only be achieved through "organization."[499]

In order to achieve its goal of using publication as a tool for "political training," the CPU leaders also decided to change the rhetoric that *Şûra-yı Ümmet* had been employing, and to replace the labyrinthine and intellectually abstract language it had used for many years with a basic emotional discourse that the people might more easily understand. Along these lines the CPU also established a satirical journal named *Lâklâk* [Twaddle] in Cairo, and published it as an independent periodical,[500] which publicly hinted at its ties with the CPU.[501] Mehmed Fazlı, the CPU official in Cairo, became the editor of this journal, and the CPU distributed it to its branches.[502]

In the reorganizers' own words, the essence of their "program can be found neither in the theories of sociologists nor in the books of socialists nor in the conference rooms of the Sorbonne," but rather in the souls of Ottomans and in the heart of the nation.[503] Since its new program was to be a mirror of the "souls of the people," the CPU decided to adopt a rhetoric appropriate for mass propaganda and to transform the central organ into "a Turkish soldier defending the fatherland."[504] A lead article in the official organ stressed this point:

Undoubtedly, the publications that will be read in Rumelia and Anatolia should be written in the style of the people in those lands, or to be more exact, in the language of those people. In various appeals *Şûra-yı Ümmet* employs this language. In its publications . . . it should follow this rule. . . . No benefit can result from echoing the theses, ideas, and opinions of Ma[r]x, [Be]rnstein, Proudhon, and Fourier to the people like a tiresome repetition.[505]

In addition to adapting the central organ's rhetoric to the new program, the CPU initiated extensive propaganda following the reorganization. It clearly differentiated between internal and external propaganda. The internal propaganda that was disseminated in the Ottoman Empire through appeals and leaflets had two objectives. First, it aimed at winning over the Turks and the Muslims to the struggle. Second, it attempted to provoke the elite to initiate a palace coup. The CPU Internal Affairs and Correspondence division prepared and spread propaganda material for both purposes under the directorship of Bahaeddin Şakir.

Ahmed Rıza was in charge of the preparation of the external propaganda. Here too the CPU set two main objectives. First, it sought to express to the Great Powers the CPU's opinion on international matters such as the future of Macedonia and Crete, which the CPU leaders regarded as domestic concerns of the Ottoman Empire. Thus it attempted to send letters and appeals to the foreign ministries of the Great Powers. Second, it carefully monitored the French press, while its correspondents in England and Germany followed their respective presses, with the result that it was able to send letters of protest to various European dailies when appropriate. The republication of these protests by the CPU organs and Turkish journals in the Balkans helped boost the CPU's prestige among its sympathizers.

The CPU's Internal Propaganda

Although regular publication of *Şûra-yı Ümmet* was essential if the CPU was to carry out its internal propaganda successfully, the organization faced great difficulties with this. The conflict that eventually led to the dismissal of Ahmed Saib from the editorship of *Şûra-yı Ümmet* resulted in a gap of almost three months between the 86th issue, published on November 12, 1905, and the 87th issue, published on February 9, 1906. Even after the problem of the editorship was resolved, the obstacles stemming from having the journal prepared in Paris and published in Cairo remained, disrupting its publication several times. In order to provide the readership with something to read during the long intervals, the CPU published two supplements to *Şûra-yı Ümmet*, in both of which Bahaeddin Şakir attacked Sabahaddin Bey's ideas on decentralization.[506]

Finally, in June 1907, the CPU decided to move the journal to Paris to simplify the publication process.[507] The 117th issue appeared in Paris on July 1, 1907,[508] and until October 15 of that year it was handwritten and reproduced by lithograph. Beginning with the 123th issue, the journal was published with a printing press brought from Bulgaria, and from then on the CPU had a regularly published central organ.[509]

The CPU started by printing 500 copies of *Şûra-yı Ümmet*, 100 of them on extremely thin paper for direct dispatch to addresses in the empire in letter-size envelopes.[510] In a short period of time, however, the CPU decided to increase the numbers to 750 and 250, respectively.[511] Although there are no publication figures available for the later period, it seems plausible that the establishment of many new branches lay behind the rapid rise in these numbers. In addition, these numbers should not be confused with the circulation figures for a standard and legally published journal; each smuggled issue of *Şûra-yı Ümmet* was read by many people through an underground network.

Following the reorganization, the CPU explored means of internal propaganda other than surreptitiously smuggling its central organ into the empire. The leadership considered distributing appeals to be the easiest and most effective means of internal propaganda. During this period the CPU issued two types of appeal. The first type was aimed at inviting the Ottoman elite to stage a palace coup against the sultan.

The sultan's alleged attempt to change the existing order of succession to the throne gave the CPU the issue it was waiting for with which to inflame the Ottoman elite. By carrying out such propaganda, the CPU leaders thought that they could spur palace cliques around both the heir apparent, Mehmed Reşad Efendi, and the second Ottoman prince in the line of succession, Yusuf İzzeddin Efendi, as well as the Sublime Porte bureaucrats whose hopes of reasserting the Sublime Porte's dominance at the expense of the palace system were in serious jeopardy because of the alleged plan to alter the order of succession.

In order to win over these groups, the CPU formed a bogus organization named Barika-i Reşadet Cemiyeti (Committee of the Flashing Sword of Truth) under the direction of Bahaeddin Şakir and Diran Kelekian. However, when the latter seized the opportunity to invite the Great Powers to intervene, the CPU leadership decided to terminate this organization and conduct the necessary work directly.[512]

The organs of the coalition were the first among the Young Turk press to initiate a campaign against the sultan's alleged scheme. As early as 1904 both journals of the coalition had published articles strongly opposing any changes to the order of succession.[513] Following the reorganization, when rumors about the sultan's serious illness were spreading, the CPU picked up the issue.[514] On August 13, 1906, the central committee decided to prepare an appeal on the illness and "hazardous" schemes of the sultan.[515] In the meantime it ran a hastily drafted appeal in *Şûra-yı Ümmet* exhorting all Ottomans to thwart the alleged scheme. The appeal voiced a strong will, stating, "Some traitors want to alter the succession to the throne. This cannot be done while we are alive." It ended with the cry of "Long Live Sultan Mehmed Reşad! Long Live the Fatherland!"[516] The Turkish press in Bulgaria republished the appeal and it was widely read.[517]

Following this appeal, the CPU prepared a still stronger manifesto entitled "Abdülhamid is Dying!" and distributed it throughout the empire and sent copies to the foreign embassies in Istanbul as well.[518] Foreign diplomats commented that "as it appears to have been widely distributed just before the commencement of *Ramazan*, it is sure to be very generally discussed during the coming month, and cannot fail to produce a certain disquieting effect."[519]

Since the appeal was sent to the foreign embassies, it had a strong Ottomanist tone and called all Ottomans to common action:

> If the chiefs and the leading men of the country do not pay attention to this appeal, then they will incur the responsibility for all the difficulties that will arise thereafter.
>
> Oh, non-Mussulman Ottomans! [W]e recognize you as our fellow countrymen. Neither as regards rights nor as regards responsibilities do we regard you as being in any way distinct from ourselves. Our desire is hand-in-hand to repair the evils that the Hamidian régime has wrought to you as well as to us. Come! [S]trive with us in this campaign of reform. . . . Oh, fellow-countrymen all! [L]et us unite! Let us not let this opportunity slip also. Let us live like human beings or die like heroes.[520]

The appeal caused a great stir in Istanbul's elite circles[521] and "increased the number of the people who were inclined toward the CPU."[522] The central committee even considered preparing an Arabic translation.[523]

On the heels of this appeal, the CPU decided to issue another manifesto on the same issue,[524] this one employing a stronger Islamic tone. Basing its argument on Islamic law, it declared the sultan unfit to make a decision on succession to the throne:

> La jurisprudence du Chéri définit les maladies mortelles de "maladies qui continuent sans interruption et tuent le patient avant le délai d'une année révolue."

Quand le malade se trouve en cette condition, il ne peut, d'aqrès [d'après] la loi du Chéri et la loi civile, donner que le tiers de ses biens, meubles, immeubles ou argent liquide. Aucun autre legs, aucun autre testament ne peut être valable.

En n'appliquant pas cette clause du Chéri et de loi civile á [à] Abdul-Hamid, qui est atteint d'une maladie mortelle, cette codification, par l'acceptation d'un pareil précédent, s'étendrait d'un ou de deux héritiers à des millions de sujets et de quelques maisons ou boutiques à tout un vaste empire.[525]

The Turkish press in Bulgaria also republished this appeal and thereby helped the CPU to reach a still greater audience.[526] Additionally, the CPU succeeded in distributing it in the capital in large numbers.[527] Finally, Bahaeddin Şakir penned an article reconciling Islamic law with the law of medicine in order to appease the CPU's intellectual sympathizers, declaring in it that the sultan's deposition was in accordance with all laws: Islamic, civil, and scientific.[528]

Besides the propaganda that targeted the elite and focused mainly on the issue of succession, the CPU disseminated extensive propaganda with a second type of appeal for winning over Turks and Muslims to their struggle. Bahaeddin Şakir and other CPU leaders prepared appeals and pamphlets directly addressing these potential supporters. These propaganda materials, written in a simple but fiery language, may be likened to the pamphlets and appeals that the CUP had drafted to incite Muslims in 1896–1897.[529]

One of them, prepared by Bahaeddin Şakir and enclosed with *Şûra-yı Ümmet's* 119th issue published in July 1907, stated:

In the name of God, the Most Merciful, the Most Compassionate!

O Turkish Sons! O Ottoman brothers, brave people of Anatolia and Rumelia! The time has come to rid the country of the oppressors who are spread all over the country because of our heedlessness. . . . Should we await our future at the hands of the Russians? [The fatherland] is in flames. Our villages have been ruined, our peasants have been starving. Our dearest sons, who had been the lights of our eyes, have been killed in the deserts of Yemen and in the mountains of Rumelia. . . . These people more treacherous than snakes, more vicious than beasts of prey . . . handed over our dominions that were as beautiful as paradise, such as Crete, Kars, Bat'umi, and [Eastern] Rumelia to the enemies. They let our coreligionists be trodden under the enemy's feet. They surrendered our sisters, for whose chastity and honor we live, to vicious rakes! O dear brothers! They disgraced and humiliated Islam and all Muslims. They installed bells in mosques, they drank wine at the tombs of our saints. They made Ottomanness, Turkishness . . . their prisoners. . . . O *ummah* of Muḥammad, which of our enemies is greater than the Russians and more treacherous than the Bulgarians? . . . It is the present government. . . . Is there any home today in which the echoes of wailing for a martyr who was killed in Yemen or Rumelia cannot be heard? O People! Open your eyes! This is not a time for sleeping. The fatherland is going to be lost. Do you assume that those who caused all these evils are only the ministers, governors, subgovernors . . . and gendarmes? Your weak eyes do not want to see the traitor hidden behind all these people. Do you know who this traitor is? It is Sultan Hamid who turned our country into ruins, our people into animals, and our country into a dungeon. . . . Did God create us so that we should become prisoners in the hands of these treacherous men? Do we not have an heir apparent who will ascend to the throne and become the father of the nation? Our heir apparent Reşad Efendi languishes in the dungeons in Istanbul. Even if we do not fear punishment on the Day of Judgment because of our laziness, we should fear being downtrodden under enemy feet like dogs, as happened in Kars and Bat'umi yesterday, and as is happening in [Eastern] Rumelia and Crete today.

Come along heroes! The time to save our fatherland has come. Chains are ill-suited to the neck of the lion. Brave people should not be deceived by the tricks of foxes. Come along heroes! Let us make our nation prosperous by taking our revenge! God is the Speaker of the Truth.[530]

It is extremely significant that during the Young Turk Revolution of 1908, the CPU branches redistributed this appeal to all the empire's Muslims in an edited form. Although some of the editing seems minor and cosmetic, it gives clear indications of the CPU's propaganda tactics. For instance, in the first line the address was changed from "O Turkish sons! O Ottoman brothers" to "O children of the Fatherland! O Ottoman brothers!" In addition, attacks against Christian elements of the empire were replaced by a passage reading, "You should understand that Bulgarians and Vlachs are not our enemies; on the contrary they are our confidants and our brothers." Finally, as expected, phrases expressing strong attacks against the sultan were omitted.[531]

Şûra-yı Ümmet continued to publish similar appeals to stir up the Muslims until the Young Turk Revolution of 1908.[532] In addition, with the help of local Turkish troubadours in Macedonia, Bahaeddin Şakir put together folk poems to provoke people.[533] One which was affixed to fountains in Macedonian villages in the fall of 1907 gives us a clear idea of this new means of propaganda:

In the name of God, the Most Merciful, the Most Compassionate
Muslims listen to my words
My eyes have become bloodshot because as I cried
I wonder what we had been and what we are now
We passed across the seas but drown in a rivulet
Our glory had made all things tremble
Where are our good old days?
We used to conquer lands by sacrificing lives
We used to think that we could keep them
Sultan Hamid delivers them one by one
The great nation is being lost in confusion
Our money, sons, all that we have
Those who are lost will not come back and our situation is hopeless
Orphans of the martyrs beg
Sultan Hamid makes fun of them
Money collected for the orphans
Sent from everywhere in knotted bundles
Exhibitions were opened the total donations increased
Tell me what is left to us
The sultan gobbled them all up
The share of the orphans is a wail
The *Yıldız* gang robbed our homes
What we have left in hand is a straw mattress
Our wives and daughters are stark naked

Our chastity has been downtrodden
Our sons are shot and in red blood
Our daughters are violated in the Balkans
We weep and groan all the time
We wail and lament before the government
They do not listen to us but repudiate us
They suffocate our words in our mouths
Beating us, they kick us out from the governor's office
All the people watch it from a distance
A gendarme comes and yells at the village
Summons all of us before him
He curses, beats, and apprehends
All villagers watch this lamely
This gendarme is the bastard Hasan
He is the one who slaughtered Ak Veli's kid
He enrolled as a gendarme when he was released from prison
I do not know why we are afraid of such a filthy man
Can we be called humans because of this?
Or vile and cowardly animals?
Those who deceive us are the ignorant *hoca*s
And idiotic, imbecilic, cowardly, and stupid elders
They call shabby Hamid the caliph
He is Yazīd's heir, and no mistake
The heirs of the Prophet were only four
Abū Bakr, 'Umar, 'Uthmān, and 'Alī
All who came after are shahs or sultans
Sultan means a cruel enemy
Compatriots! We have suffered enough
Let's roar like lions
Let's raze slavery to the ground
Let's cleanse the honor of Muḥammad
Let's dig out the eyes of the enemy
Let's get rid of jealousy and grudges among us
God orders us to unite
If we heroes go hand in hand
Mountains will tremble before us, the ground will groan
Who is Sultan Hamid? Who is this loathsome person?
Enemy of God, Enemy of Muḥammad
He wishes to hand over the fatherland to enemies
This home of religion cannot be surrendered as long as we are alive
Enough! Our lips are clenched
Our homes are destroyed because of silence
Let's abandon cowardice
There is a *fatwā* from the ulema for the execution of this traitor
We shall kill
We will obey Reşad Efendi
We sacrifice our heads for the sake of religion
We will color enemies with red blood
We are called brave sons of Turkistan

We are renowned as glorious Ottomans
We cry God and sacrifice our lives
We become martyrs for God
We should not be burned in this fire of oppression
We cannot stand this vileness any more
Consultation is the light of God's path
We either open the gate of consultation
Or spread red lights to the world
They hanged, slaughtered, flung us to our deaths
They sold us to the enemies of religion
Let's rely on the uniqueness of God
Let's awaken from sleep.[534]

The CPU Internal Affairs and Correspondence division also prepared pamphlets in a similar vein to stir up Muslims and Turks, and it disseminated them through a network established by Bahaeddin Şakir.[535] These pamphlets, such as the most important one entitled *Hayye-ale-l-felâh (Ḥayya ʿalā al-falāḥ)*, also displayed a very strong anti-Christian tone and had no similarities to the Ottomanist rhetoric implemented in appeals addressing all Ottomans.[536]

Finally, the CPU distributed appeals addressing soldiers and officers. The officers were invited "to join the *gaza* for freedom,"[537] while the soldiers were invited "to turn their weapons against high-ranking pashas, powerful governors who were selling the country to the Russians, the British, and the Germans."[538] In these appeals, too, a very strong Islamic tone was used.[539] This Islamic tone should not be confused with the implementation of an Islamist rhetoric. In the CPU propaganda Islam was used as a protonationalist device. For instance, the CPU declared that "in Macedonia it [was] the Muslims' natural right to reject and deny for the love of *Allāh*, and the protection of the fatherland, the encroachments and assaults perpetuated in the name of Christ by the Bulgarians and Greeks, who want to separate themselves from Ottomanness because of their Christian identity."[540] Therefore, when the ulema sent letters to the CPU criticizing it for not publishing Islamist articles, the CPU leaders responded that "since the journals [were] journals of struggle, they contained information on extraordinary events and developments, instead of religious issues."[541]

The CPU avoided a similar rhetoric in its official organs, however, because its leaders feared that their opponents might use this against them. The CPU leaders took warning from the heavy criticism levied by Armenian, Greek, and left-wing French journals in response to appeals addressing the Muslims. When these journals acquired copies of the appeals to Muslims that were distributed in early 1906, they used them to debunk the CPU's diametrically opposite propaganda targeting other groups.[542]

The CUP, too, faced problems following the Young Turk Revolution because of the appeals issued before the revolution. When one such appeal, employing strident anti-European language and using the motto "Turkey for the Turks," was discovered and republished by the European press in August 1908, it caused a considerable stir in European capitals.[543] In order to save the situation, the CUP first claimed that the appeal was a German fabrication.[544] Then it assured the powers that there was no relation between the Paris center that issued the appeal and the new committee in Istanbul.[545]

The CPU's External Propaganda

Following the reorganization, the CPU central committee assigned to Ahmed Rıza the task of carrying out external propaganda. The CPU's main instrument for this propaganda was *Mechveret Supplément Français*, edited by Ahmed Rıza. The CPU sent multiple copies of this journal to non-Muslim Ottomans and European politicians.[546] Therefore the journal employed a more balanced language than *Şûra-yı Ümmet*; although it too strongly criticized the separatist activities of the non-Muslim Ottoman elements, it made this criticism from an Ottomanist viewpoint. For example, while the Internal Affairs and Correspondence division was preparing the aforementioned appeals to Muslims, Ahmed Rıza was publishing appeals maintaining that under a constitutional regime all Ottomans would have equal rights.[547]

Besides editing *Mechveret Supplément Français*, Ahmed Rıza also penned manifestos for presentation to the representatives of the Great Powers. The activities of the CPU in this field should not be confused with those of Sabahaddin Bey. The CPU's aim was simply to oppose the policies of the Great Powers and express its own opinion on various matters, not to demand help from the Great Powers as did Sabahaddin Bey.

Some of the manifestos presented to the representatives of the Great Powers simply repeated the CPU theses on various issues such as the succession question.[548] Most of the others, however, underscored "the dangers" that might follow the implementation of the Great Powers' reform schemes, which favored Ottoman Christians at the expense of the Muslims,[549] and argued that instead of proposing such reforms, the Great Powers should favor the reestablishment of the constitutional regime.[550]

In addition to issuing these manifestos, Ahmed Rıza sent notes to European dailies challenging the assertions of their columnists. CPU correspondents monitoring the British and German language press helped Ahmed Rıza in this endeavor. For example, a British daily's correspondent in Istanbul asserted during the diplomatic crisis over the Ottoman-Egyptian border that "the Sultan is practically alone in opposing England's demands, and not a single Turk of any position or intelligence supports him. They all wish that England had come, not only to settle the Tabah question, but to occupy Turkey, and, as they say, save the country."[551] The CPU thereupon sent an immediate response refuting the claim. Although the daily did not publish the refutation, *Mechveret Supplément Français* did, and subsequent republication by the Turkish press in Bulgaria boosted the CPU's prestige in the eyes of its sympathizers.[552] Other prominent members of the CPU also helped Ahmed Rıza to influence European public opinion.[553] The CPU's primary objective, though, was merely to make its voice heard.

The CPU's propaganda during this period was the most extensive carried out since the beginning of the Young Turk movement. Like its secret correspondence and its publications, the CPU's propaganda seemingly lacked cohesiveness. Thus by using CPU propaganda material selectively, it is possible for one to picture "Ottomanist," "Turkist," and "Panislamist" committees. Again the apparent lack of coherence in the CPU propaganda does not reflect a corresponding lack of coherence in goals. On the contrary, it was totally in accordance with the CPU's general policy of winning over different groups pursuing divergent policies. It should also be remembered, however, that the core of the CPU's propaganda targeted the groups it considered most important: Turks and Muslims. As was stated in *Şûra-yı Ümmet*, "Muslims [were] the pure Ottomans" in the eyes of the reorganizers.[554]

In summary, the period between the initial attempts at reorganization and the CPU's merger with the Ottoman Freedom Society witnessed the emergence of a well-organized, effective, and activist committee carrying out extensive propaganda and opportunistically employing revolutionary tactics.

The CPU's activism should not be confused with radicalism. The CPU inherited and espoused the coalition's rather conservative ideology. The only difference was that for the sake of activism the CPU saw no problem with employing mutually contradictory rhetorics and propaganda efforts. Even while pretending to be something different, however, the CPU never became radicalized.

For example, the CPU always exalted the "state" and opposed any activity against it. As we shall discuss in detail in the chapter on the 1907 Congress of Ottoman Opposition Parties, the Dashnaktsutiun urged the congress to adopt a resolution calling upon all Ottomans to refuse conscription. The CPU, however, killed the proposed resolution, maintaining that the Ottoman armies must be stronger than ever because the country was surrounded by powerful enemies.

As for an understanding among the Ottoman peoples, the CPU leaders were never ready to embrace a radical slogan like *za naszą i waszą wolnosc* (for your and our freedom), as the Decembrists in Russia did to appeal to the ideals of the Polish nationalists. The maximum they offered non-Turkish elements, formal equality within the boundaries of Ottomanism, was found unacceptable by those elements since the CPU vision of Ottomanism assumed a dominant role for the Turks.

The CPU's innate conservatism seems to stem from an activist conservatism characteristic of the Ottoman opposition circles. It should be remembered that even Sabahaddin Bey, who for tactical reasons wanted to ally himself with the non-Turkish elements in the Ottoman Empire, did not want to speak on issues like "the nationalities question," as the Russian Social Democrats had done. In fact, he adopted an extremely defensive position, stating that his real aim was to make Muslims equal to the more advanced non-Muslim elements.

Bahaeddin Şakir's realization of the need to embrace this conservative activism is remarkable. The success of the reorganization of 1906, however, resulted from the CPU's effective use of opportunist revolutionary tactics. Beginning with the reorganization, the Young Turks gave greater emphasis to practical revolutionary tactics and actions at the expense of lofty "scientific" theories.

7

The 1907 Congress of "Ottoman Opposition Parties"

CPU Initiatives for a Tactical Alliance with the Armenian Revolutionary Organizations

Following the CPU's merger with the Ottoman Freedom Society,[1] the new CPU and the two other main opposition organizations, namely Sabahaddin Bey's League of Private Initiative and Decentralization and the Dashnaktsutiun Committee, organized a second congress of "Ottoman opposition parties" in order to unite all of these organizations in a program of revolutionary action. Although this meeting, which the organizers labeled a "congress," took place after the merger, the CPU central committee in Paris, now renamed the CPU External Headquarters, had in fact taken the first initiatives and had worked toward a congress on its own during the early negotiations. It was only during the final preparations for the gathering that the CPU External Headquarters received feedback from the CPU Internal Headquarters in the form of an approval of its action.

The preparations for the "Congress of Ottoman Opposition Parties" were made in the utmost secrecy; no organization made any public declaration on the subject. Thus it is not surprising that European governments of the time and scholars who later worked on the subject mistakenly credited the Dashnaktsutiun with spearheading a "congress" aiming at the establishment of a common front against the Hamidian regime. While the Dashnaktsutiun was clearly interested in such an arrangement, the available CPU documents provide adequate information to challenge the accepted view that the invitation came from the Armenian side.

When briefing the CPU Internal Headquarters, Bahaeddin Şakir stated that the CPU had set matters in motion by sending Ahmed Rıza to Geneva to approach the Dashnaktsutiun, which itself was attempting to bridge the gap that separated it from the Muslim opposition organizations. The Dashnaktsutiun, he continued, thereupon dispatched one of its leading members, Khachatur Malumian, who was a liaison between the Young Turks and their organization, to Paris to discuss the issue.[2] Although in the contemporary press coverage and in the secondary literature many authors characterized the congress as a Dashnaktsutiun initiative,[3] it would seem unlikely that the CPU External Headquarters would provide its counterpart in Salonica with false information. Examination of the CPU secret correspondence clearly reveals that the CPU center in Paris frequently and deliberately furnished inaccurate information to its branches in order to inflate its image. The CPU External Headquarters, however, always supplied precise and accurate information to the CPU Internal Headquarters. This congress should therefore be regarded as a CPU initiative.

It is true that during the same period the Dashnaktsutiun was ready to strike a tactical alliance with the Young Turks, having already cut a secret deal with Sabahaddin Bey for joint action in Eastern Anatolia. The decision to form an alliance with the CPU nevertheless provoked long-lasting debates among the Dashnak leadership because of the strong language used by the CPU against the Armenians, even after the CPU invitation to the Dashnaktsutiun to discuss the conditions of a future tactical alliance.[4] The CPU's gradual adoption of an activist program, however, seems to have convinced the Dashnak leaders; previously they had seen no benefit in a rapprochement with the coalition, since it was both highly critical of the Armenian revolutionary movement and dedicated to pursuing a purely evolutionary program.

To judge from the available documents, the first CPU overture to the Dashnaktsutiun must have been made in May 1907, prior to the CPU's merger with the Ottoman Freedom Society.

Available documents reveal that following its transformation into a revolutionary organization, the CPU secretly approached the Hnchakian Committee as well. The Hncakian Committee would have been an asset to a tactical revolutionary alliance because of the large number of militants in its ranks and its staunch revolutionary program. However, the Hncakists' insistence on the recognition of an "autonomous Armenia within the boundaries of Turkey, but under the guarantee of the European Great Powers" disappointed Ahmed Rıza, Bahaeddin Şakir, and Dr. Nâzım, who had met with the Hncakist leaders led by Stepan Sapah-Gulian to discuss the possibility of a tactical alliance.[5]

During the time that the CPU initiated a rapprochement with the Hnchakian party for tactical purposes, a Dashnak leader, Harutiun Shahrigian, sent an open letter to Sabahaddin Bey's journal *Terakki* strongly criticizing the Young Turks and accusing them of pursuing an Islamist policy, "despite the nonexistence of a Muslim nation." In his letter Shahrigian also spelled out the Dashnaks' conditions for a future Armenian–Young Turk alliance, including the recognition of "autonomous regions."[6] Other Dashnak leaders also joined this campaign by accusing the Young Turks of pursuing the same Panislamist policy as Abdülhamid II.[7]

Although Sabahaddin Bey attempted to refute the claims of the Dashnak leader with counterarguments,[8] he also stated that it was of "great importance to find grounds for union with various Ottoman elements."[9] The Turkist Young Turk intellectuals and the CPU, on the other hand, adopted stronger language in their responses to Shahrigian. An article in *Türk* enumerated "the things that can be given to the Christians in Turkey" in the form of 24 provisions, and it maintained that the Dashnak demands were totally unacceptable.[10]

The CPU employed harsh rhetoric, describing the Dashnak leader contemptuously as "traitor," "calumniator," and "buffoon." According to the CPU leaders, the Armenian leader's letter was "ludicrous," and the only way the Dashnak leader "could put his ideas and principles into effect would be if he entered Istanbul with a victorious army."[11] This exchange of allegations and the CPU's firm stand seem to have compelled the Dashnak leaders to soften their conditions for a tactical revolutionary alliance.

Hncakist sources claim that the CPU's failure to reach an understanding with the Hnchakian Committee caused it to approach the Dashnaktsutiun.[12] The available documents, however, make it seem more plausible that the CPU attempted a rapprochement with both Armenian organizations but received an affirmative answer from only one of them, which desperately wanted to reach an agreement with the Young Turks.

The CPU leaders maintained that the "the Armenians' situation [was] extremely bad. On the one hand Russia, and on the other hand the government of Abdülhamid, were destroying this nation. In addition, Iran has now proclaimed freedom [i.e., it was now a free society]. The Armenians, who [had] been squeezed among these three governments, [had] no other alternative but to ally themselves with us. They were shedding blood and getting killed for nothing."[13] Other sources who either witnessed the period or participated in the Armenian movement claimed that the gradual adoption of a noninterventionist stand by the Great Powers, and the CPU's evolution into a revolutionary committee, prompted the Dashnak intellectuals to make a last attempt to form an alliance with the Young Turks.[14]

During the early negotiations, Khachatur Malumian stated that "in their general [Fourth World] Congress held in May [1907], [they] had decided to find ways to work with the [Young Turks]," and Bahaeddin Şakir commented that "since the Armenians [were] seeking our hand for union it [was] hoped that the negotiations would result in" an agreement.[15]

In fact, the Dashnaktsutiun had sent a signal to the CPU when its representatives refused to sign a plea in late May 1907 "for aid in the war on Turkey." General Tchérep-Spiridovitch, who had traveled to the United States "to stir up the Armenian Colony of New York," had prepared the plea, and the Hnchakian Committee had endorsed it.[16] Prior to this event, pro-Dashnaktsutiun Armenians had sent letters to Turkic journals maintaining that the Armenians were not "traitors" as some claimed, and that the real traitor was the "Hamidian administration."[17]

When the CPU Internal Headquarters learned about the proposals for a meeting to unite the opponents of the regime, it demanded information about them. The CPU External Headquarters stated the following in response:

> It has been understood from the programs of the Christian Ottoman elements that have been presented to us that it would be impossible for an Ottoman to unite with that segment of the Christian Ottoman elements known as *komiteciler* [revolutionary committee members] in matters of policy and principle. In fact, we noticed the impossibility of this [union] at numerous meetings. With the hope that the union, which cannot be realized in theory, may be achieved in practice, the convention of such a congress has been approved and initiated.[18]

The CPU External Headquarters further reported to its counterpart within the empire that in a few days they were expecting a special envoy from the Dashnaktsutiun Committee to discuss the issue, and that additional information would be provided after the meeting with this envoy, after which the opinion of the internal headquarters would also be sought.[19]

Preparations for the Congress of "Ottoman Opposition Parties"

On November 30, 1907, the CPU External Headquarters sent a long letter to the CPU Internal Headquarters announcing the arrival of Malumian in Paris to discuss the details of a congress aimed at the creation of a revolutionary front against the sultan's regime. Bahaeddin Şakir stated that Malumian had "shown himself to be extraordinarily favorably disposed" to them; this extremely flexible and affable approach provoked suspicions among the CPU leaders, who consequently decided to act with "vigilance."[20]

The CPU leaders and Malumian agreed to establish a special mixed subcommittee to discuss matters and prepare the resolutions to be accepted by the congress.[21] It seems that both sides took lessons from the 1902 Congress, which, despite all hopes for union, had turned into a forum for internecine struggle. This time both sides agreed that the so-called congress should be nothing more than a social gathering and banquet at which a document prepared in advance would be unanimously approved.

Both sides also agreed to bring into this tactical alliance as many opposition organizations as possible. Malumian expressed a desire to include Sabahaddin Bey's league, and the CPU gave its approval. Subsequently the representatives of the three organizations decided to meet at the CPU and *Terakki* offices on alternate days. The mixed subcommittee formed by the three organizations and entrusted with the preparations for the meeting was composed of five individuals: Ahmed Rıza and Sami Paşazâde Sezaî as the CPU representatives, Ahmed Fazlı and Doctor Nihad Reşad as the representatives of the League of Private Initiative and Decentralization, and Malumian as the fully authorized representative of the Dashnaktsutiun.[22]

Before the first meeting, the members of the subcommittee had reached an agreement on the principles below, which all the participants were strictly to obey. They also required that all the invitees, including representatives of their own respective organizations, accept these stipulations:

1. The territorial integrity of the Ottoman state is to be recognized by all participating parties.
2. The order of succession to the throne is to be absolutely inviolable.
3. The first goal of the congress should be the destruction of the present absolutist administration. The second goal is to be the convening of the national assembly (the Chamber of Deputies).
4. The representatives participating in the congress should bear a certificate given to them by their own committees in an appropriate way.
5. Any committee that does not have an organization [within the Ottoman Empire] should not be allowed to participate in the congress.
6. The congress will convene in Paris.
7. A grace period should be given [to the CPU] to obtain the [CPU] Internal Headquarters' opinion on the decisions to be taken by the subcommittee.
8. All matters should be discussed here [at the subcommittee meetings] fully and in great detail and made ready [agreed upon] before the convention of the congress.
9. The proceedings of the congress should be held in utmost secrecy and nobody is to be informed of anything. On the day that the congress adjourns its meetings, however, those designated by the congress will announce the success of the congress to the press.
10. Upon the successful closure of the congress a mixed action or executive committee (*Comité d'ex[é]cution*) will be formed, which would be composed of members known

only to the chairman of the congress. They will be elected by secret ballot, and their identities will always be kept secret. This committee will be in effect until the convention of a second congress and it will supervise the implementation of the decisions of the [first] congress.

11. Although the committees will attempt to reach an accord in the field of action, each committee's activities and planning in this regard will be entirely separate.

12. Legal and revolutionary means will be used to achieve the goal (*Moyen [Moyens] legaux [légaux] et r[é]volutionnaires*):

First—It should be declared uniformly in journals and [published] appeals that none of the opposition parties wants the present government, and the reasons for this should also be explained.

Second—In the same way, it should be declared that the committees of various nations are uniting to destroy the present government and open the Chamber of Deputies.

Third—The fact that we absolutely reject foreign intervention should be declared by sending a joint memorandum to the powers, and it should also be disseminated through the press.

Fourth—The absolute rejection of "terrorism," which means to shock the country and set it aflame, and which is carried out either to invite foreign intervention or to destroy the administration.

Fifth—Although both individual actions and revolts can be employed in this field, a *sphere [sphère] d'action* should be delimited, and the Armenians especially should not participate in the revolt in Erzurum unless we [the CPU] approve it.[23]

At the first meeting the representatives of the organizing parties reached an agreement on the duties and responsibilities of the "comité permanent" which was to be established, and they charged Ahmed Rıza and Muḥammad ʿAlī Ḥalīm Pasha with drafting the invitation to the congress.[24] On the instructions of this subcommittee, and as a gesture of goodwill, they appealed to the Hncakian and Verakazmial Hncakian Committees, to a third Hnchakian faction, and to the Ligue Hellénique in Paris, inviting them all to participate in the forthcoming "congress."[25]

Despite this promising start, the members of the subcommittee ran into a disagreement on the term to be used for the Ottoman assembly that would be inaugurated following the anticipated revolution. The Armenians proposed the term *assemblée constituante* instead of *assemblée générale*, and Sabahaddin Bey gave his approval to this alteration. The CPU strongly opposed it, stating that "this word [had] a historical meaning" and that it did not want to have a "conflict in the future when the country would need absolute peace."[26]

The participating parties also agreed to establish a second subcommittee, composed of members from committees with organizations within the Ottoman Empire, and to discuss future plans of action.[27] Given the impotence of Sabahaddin Bey's league, this would necessarily be a joint CPU–Dashnaktsutiun undertaking.

The first subcommittee also prepared the issues for discussion at the three-day convention. On the first day the participants were to declare that they protested against the present administration. On the second day they were to speak about the virtues of the "r[é]gime repr[é]sentatif," and on the third day about the necessity for and types of action, though without "delving into the details."[28]

At the next meeting of the first subcommittee, a disagreement over what type of assembly should be formed in the capital after the revolution caused the parties temporarily to suspend the meeting. The Dashnaktsutiun declared that they supported using the term *assemblée constituante* to characterize the desired "régime représentatif" and insisted on acceptance of this term. The CPU's strong negative reaction compelled Malumian to request the Dashnaktsutiun central committee's opinion. It sent a telegram with the following offer to replace the term "national assembly" with "parliament": " . . . [le] r[é]gime actuel est [intéressé à] laisser à [l']avenir [la] question discutée et [à] ne s'occuper que les [des] points 1 et 3 de votre programme arrêté, d'après lequel aucun programme l[é]gislatif ne pourra être discuté. S'il y a impossibilité, remplacez assemblée national[e] qui pourrait donner lieu à dissentiment par mot parlement simplement sans entrer dans [les] d[é]tail[s]. Chaque parti se reservant ses vues et programmes."[29]

The representatives gathered after the CPU's conditional acceptance of this offer and discussed the legal and revolutionary means to be used against the government. The Dashnaktsutiun proposed the following:

    I. R[é]sistances armées ou non armées [*sic*]:
        1. To exhort the people not to yield to the illegal propositions and actions of the administration.
        2. To pay no taxes.
        3. To organize bands.
        4. To resist the draft.
    II. Insurrection générale.
    III. Grève général[e]:
        [1]. Strikes by policemen, mailmen, railway personnel, and government officials.
    [IV]. Terrorisme:
        [1]. Collective.
        [2]. Individual.[30]

The CPU disagreed on three important points, all of which Sabahaddin Bey had approved. First, the CPU asserted that the bands should act under strict regulations and thereby be differentiated from brigands. Second, the CPU strongly opposed the proposal to resist the draft. Its representatives claimed that while the country was "surrounded by enemies," the Ottoman armies must be better prepared for attacks than ever. Finally, the CPU required the Dashnaktsutiun to promise not to carry out "collective terrorism similar to that which had been carried out by Armenians in Istanbul [in 1895 and 1896] and by Bulgarians in Salonica [in 1903], and [it] proposed that the terrorist activities be confined to individual acts, that is, assassinations."[31]

The CPU further asked for a grace period to obtain approval from its internal headquarters. But because the Dashnaktsutiun insisted on a quick response, the CPU External Headquarters required its counterpart in Salonica to send a telegram reading "Merci lettre. Santé bonne" in the case of approval and reading "Remerciements attend lettre" in the case of disapproval.[32] Upon receiving approval from the CPU Internal Headquarters, the organizers decided that the foundation was laid and that the congress should meet on December 27, 1907.

It is interesting that all early negotiations turned into debates between the Dashnaktsutiun and the CPU, and that Sabahaddin Bey's representatives played a very insignificant role in them. It was the two committees that had internal organizations with which to put the decisions of the congress into effect that engaged in prolonged discussions on the wording of the agreement. For Sabahaddin Bey, who confessed that his league could not organize bands and execute "seditious people,"[33] but nonetheless hoped to derive benefits from the congress for his grandiose designs, these were mere technical, trivial details.

It should also be remembered that by spearheading an initiative toward a mutual understanding, both parties were taking significant risks. Given the Hncakist Committee's and the Armenian intellectuals' stern opposition to any kind of agreement with the Young Turks,[34] the Dashnaktsutiun was hard pressed to convince Armenian expatriates in Europe and the Armenian societies in Russia and the Ottoman Empire of the necessity of such a rapprochement. In addition, the Dashnaktsutiun did not raise any issues that might disrupt or terminate the negotiations, such as the application of the 61st article of the Berlin Congress of 1878, an issue that the joint Armenian delegation had raised at the 1902 Congress. The Dashnaktsutiun also accepted the CPU's anti-interventionist stand without further bargaining, and the Dashnak representative did not even bring up terms like "autonomy," "terms of international treaties," and "European intervention."

The CPU's position was relatively less conflictual. Because it was the single most important committee among the Young Turk organizations and had opposed any alliance with the Armenians for a long time, it experienced little real difficulty in convincing those who were suspicious of the real intentions of the Dashnaktsutiun that the CPU "would never be outwitted because of the agreement, and most probably would benefit from it." The CPU leadership made the following remark to convince their comrades in Salonica: "Let's first destroy the present administration and succeed in gathering the national assembly, then it will be easy to dissuade those who have the idea of obtaining administrative autonomy."[35]

The organizing parties also expected that the inclusion of other opposition organizations in this tactical alliance would yield benefits to all three committees. The CPU leaders thought that including more revolutionary organizations in the alliance would make it more powerful. For the Dashnak leaders it would be easier to sell the idea of a union of "Ottoman opposition parties" to Armenian public opinion than to promote a union with the Young Turks alone. Finally, Sabahaddin Bey thought that the only way to secure foreign intervention was to create an alliance of multiple Ottoman elements seeking a change of regime in the Ottoman Empire. It was because of these considerations that a rapprochement between the CPU and the Dashnaktsutiun, originally intended to form a tactical revolutionary alliance, now turned into a broader "Congress of Ottoman Opposition Parties."

Seeking the Participation of Other Opposition Groups

The representatives of the organizing parties worked to bring two different types of organizations into the alliance. The first was true revolutionary organizations. Their capabilities would certainly strengthen the alliance. The second was organizations whose activities were limited to publishing journals read only by a few people. Although their participation would have no tangible impact, it could serve as window-dressing to impress the Great Powers and to mollify an Armenian public opinion critical of any rapprochement with the CPU.

Contacts with the Genuine Revolutionary Organizations

The revolutionary organization whose participation was most desired by the organizing parties was undoubtedly the IMRO. The Dashnaktsutiun and the IMRO had revolutionary tactical alliances in both 1895 and 1903. During the early negotiations Malumian expressed his hope for IMRO participation in the congress.[36] Participating in an alliance with the Young Turks, however, was a totally different issue for the IMRO.[37]

Ahmed Rıza and Muḥammad ʿAlī Ḥalīm Pasha formally appealed to the IMRO on behalf of the mixed subcommittee and invited it to send delegates to the congress. In its invitation, the subcommittee stated that it honored only the IMRO with a proposal for talks, and that it dismissed the Greek and Serb committees as artificial propaganda movements maintained and directed by foreign states and favored by the sultan's government.[38] The IMRO, which was in total disarray because of the assassinations of Sarafov and Garvanov in November 1907, did not give a prompt answer and thus did not take part in the congress.[39] The CPU External Headquarters maintained that they had "invited the Bulgarian committee in Macedonia [the IMRO], and that despite its promise to participate it did not. Most likely the assassination of Sarafov prevented them from participating."[40] In fact, *Ilinden*, the organ of the right wing of the IMRO, confirmed that "the Macedonian revolutionaries were missing from the congress. We are attributing this lack of participation to an accident and would like to believe that, had it not been for the misfortune of November 28 [the murders of Sarafov and Garvanov], Macedonian participation might have been a fact."[41]

Even after the congress, the Dashnaktsutiun did not abandon hopes for the IMRO's inclusion in the tactical alliance,[42] and indeed the organizers planned to announce the IMRO's participation.[43] The IMRO organs, too, maintained that "even in the event that the Macedonian revolutionaries are entirely convinced that little or no practical result will come out of the action of the recently united organizations, even then, they are obligated to express solidarity with the resolution adopted at the common congress in Paris . . . there is no danger of any deviation from the principle of independence in supporting the resolutions of the congress."[44] The Dashnaktsutiun accordingly reproved the CPU for publishing articles critical of the IMRO. The CPU in response claimed that the semiofficial newspapers of the IMRO had already announced that they would neither disapprove of, nor take part in, a union with the CPU. In order to further this claim the CPU informed the Dashnaktsutiun representatives that during the congress an IMRO band had burned down a Muslim village in Macedonia. As a last word, the CPU leaders stated that despite the hopes of the Armenians, they could not see any prospect of establishing an alliance with the IMRO.[45] Following this strong statement the CPU continued to use highly critical language about the IMRO.[46]

The IMRO debated the matter at its Kyustendil Congress of March 1908. This congress was attended by Khristo Matov, Dr. Khristo Tatarchev, Petar Atsev, Efrem Chuchkov, Todor Chervarov, Khristo Shaldev, Petko Penchev, Petar Chaulev, Tanyu

Nikolov, Dobri Daskalov, Todor Aleksandrov, Milan Gyurlukov, Vasil Chekalarov, Kliment Shapkarev, Khristo Silianov, Ilia Biolchev, Mikhail Monev, and Angel Uzunov. Sandanski and his supporters from the Serres group, who were in a state of civil war with the other members of the organization after the assassination of Sarafov and Garvanov, did not attend. The congress considered the issue and unanimously decided to leave the mixed subcommittee's proposal unanswered, as the delegates led by Matov had wished.[47] The concerns of the delegates, known to us from the polemic exchanges of the columnists of the periodical *Ilinden* with the constitutionalists of *Odrinski glas* (Voice of Edirne), came down to the following:

> Our paths and those of the Young Turks do not meet. We want Macedonia to be autonomous as a separate region, and in fact the beginnings of such autonomy are already present, while the Young Turks have taken it as their task to wrest [Macedonia] from foreign control and place it under full Turkish domination. We have pushed our people on a path from which there is already no return, and we would commit a crime if we sacrificed its aspirations for alien daydreams of some kind of constitutional Turkey. The future of the Turkish state does not interest us, and we cannot tie the fate of our fatherland to that of the religiously and linguistically heterogeneous tribes, peoples, and races who inhabit the insecure Turkish possessions in Europe, Asia, and Africa. Our position is not at all as hopeless as that of Armenia, and we will not be caught in the Young Turk trap.[48]

Despite the IMRO's refusal to participate in the tactical alliance, the congress led to a rapprochement between the Young Turk parties and the so-called Macedonian constitutionalists publishing *Odrinski glas* and opposing the IMRO. They stated:

> Until recently the opposition movement in the Turkish empire possessed an exclusively national character; it was primarily a movement for the liberation of the nations under Turkish domination. . . . The Turkish despotism rests not simply on the general principle of a lack of national autonomy, but on the principle of a lack of autonomy for all [its] citizens, of common lack of rights for everyone who is not a part of the orbit of absolutist privileges. . . . That is why if the previous struggles against absolutism have been separatist in nature, without touching on absolutism itself, then from now on a struggle is possible and appropriate only if it is a struggle against the absolutism itself, and against the present system of government. Today we can joyfully welcome this new ray of liberation, without being bothered at all by the quarrels of the old historical traditions. The previous revolutionary national struggles dug the grave of the Turkish absolutism, but it will be the new type of struggle which will lay it to rest. . . . The expression of this movement is the first congress of the opposition parties of Turkey, which took place last month in Paris. The congress will remain a memorable event in the history of the new revolutionary movement in Turkey. . . . As can be seen from this list, only members of four nationalities—Turks, Armenians, Jews, and Arabs—participated. But this circumstance cannot prevent the congress from being considered an all-Turkish one, because it set the tasks of the future all-Turkish supranational movement, although it did not include representatives of all the empire's nationalities. It is that foundation of the future supranational movement that makes the congress a historical event.[49]

Pavel Deliradev, a socialist and a leader of the Macedonian constitutionalists, further commented that in examining the congress's declaration, he "cannot see the contradiction between the views it expresses and the views encompassed by the current

Macedono-Edirnian revolutionary thought so carefully preserved by the newly resurrected 'Vŭrkhovism' of [the] Ilindenists."[50]

The interest shown by the Macedonian constitutionalists later encouraged the CPU to come to an agreement with them during the period just prior to the Young Turk Revolution of 1908. The constitutionalists, however, would have been of very little assistance to the CPU and to the tactical alliance; they were nothing but a *quantité négligeable* in the Macedonian movement.

The organizing parties of the Congress of Ottoman Opposition Parties also discussed the Greeks' participation in the convention. As we saw, during the initial stages of the negotiations the organizers extended an invitation to the Ligue Hellénique in Paris, but this committee declined to respond. The CPU leaders were convinced that the Greeks in Paris were not for union but on the contrary "would do everything within their power to thwart the union."[51] Indeed after the congress, the Greek organizations in Paris criticized the way it had been organized.[52] In addition, Ali Haydar Midhat wrote a letter to the editor of *Le Siècle* lamenting the absence of the Greek element that formed such an important component of the Christian population in the Ottoman Empire. He accused Sabahaddin Bey, the Armenians, and the Bulgarians of working on a scheme of confederation.[53] The organizers, however, rebuffed the claim and stated that they had invited every element in the Ottoman Empire.[54]

Nevertheless, the organizers did not work as strenuously in the Greek case as they did in that of the IMRO but limited themselves to awaiting passively the Ligue Hellénique's answer. They did not attempt to contact the Greek committees that were active in Macedonia. As they stated in the invitation sent to the IMRO, they viewed these organizations as pawns in the hands of the Greek government.[55] From a tactical viewpoint the organizers must also have been aware of the fact that Greek participation in the congress would jeopardize participation by the IMRO, something they most eagerly desired, and also by the Kutzo-Vlach Committee and the Albanian Bashkimi Society.

The CPU External Headquarters also required the CPU Monastir branch to invite the "[Kutzo]-Vlach Committee" to the congress.[56] Because of the short notice, the invitation did not materialize, however, and the Kutzo-Vlach organization later struck a special bargain with the CPU.

In a similar vein the CPU demanded İbrahim Temo's help in inviting to the congress the Albanian Bashkimi Society, whose headquarters were in Bucharest.[57] Later the CPU sent a telegram to İbrahim Temo and demanded that he send a quick response concerning Albanian participation in the congress.[58]

The Bashkimi Society, a fusion of the three former Albanian societies—Ditiura, Drita, and Shpresa—was not a revolutionary committee in the strict sense of the word. It did, however, have relations with the newly formed Albanian bands active in Macedonia and Albania.[59] It also had sound ties with the Aromenis (Kutzo-Vlach) organization fighting mainly against the Greeks in Macedonia, thanks to the efforts of Nikolla Naço, the director of the Drita Society. For these reasons the participation of this committee would have been beneficial to the organizing parties. The CPU correspondence does not provide any information about the Albanian response to the invitation. The Albanians' nonparticipation, however, reveals that they turned the offer down.

Inclusion of Window-Dressing Organizations

The organizers' failure to entice any revolutionary committees to join the congress forced them to play up the participation of the insignificant organizations. To this end, the Dashnaktsutiun proposed incorporating the editorial boards of the Dashnak journals published in the United States and the Balkans as if they were independent organizations. The final document was signed by the "Rédaction du *Razmig* (*Combatant*), organe révolutionnaire (pays Balkaniques)" and the "Rédaction du *Haïrénik* (*Fatherland*), organe révolutionnaire (Amérique)."[60] In addition to these Dashnaktsutiun branches, the "Rédaction" of *Arménia* edited by Mĕgĕrdich Portukalian in Marseilles signed the resolutions. Portukalian was the founder of the Armenakan party, which scholars have considered to be the first Armenian political organization.[61] It is surprising that the leader of the Armenakan party signed the resolutions: the Armenakans' program did not promote "terroristic methods, although [this] policy was ignored by certain individuals," and they emphatically refused to work with non-Armenian groups.[62] In addition to these fundamental principles that would make its direct participation in the congress difficult, this organization had carried out its main activities in the late 1880s and had become quite insignificant by 1907. Therefore, instead of the Armenakan party, the "Rédaction" of *Arménia* signed the resolutions.

The CPU likewise obtained some extra "ghost" signatures for the resolutions. Bahaeddin Şakir's efforts to include the organization of the former intelligence service chief, the so-called Ottoman Covenant Committee, bore fruit. In the light of Ahmed Celâleddin's ties to European anarchist organizations and leading socialist-anarchist figures such as Jean Grave,[63] and his financial resources that allowed him to publish open letters in *The Times*, which had refused to publish the CPU's refutations, the signature of the pasha's bogus organization at the bottom of the resolutions seemed valuable.[64] For all practical purposes, however, the so-called committee was nonexistent.[65]

Another "committee" that was used to pad the list of signatures was the so-called Comité Israélite d'Egypte.[66] This committee too was nothing more than a one-man show, confined to the publication of the journal *La Vara* (The Truth/Stick).[67]

Abraham Galanté, who had written for the liberal Izmir daily *Hidmet*, whose editor joined the Young Turk movement in 1895, maintained close ties with the Young Turks after his flight to Egypt in October 1904.[68] He authored articles for *Mechveret Supplément Français*, *Şûra-yı Ümmet*, *Şûra-yı Osmanî*, and the Cairo-based Young Turk journal *Doğru Söz* (*The True Word*), in addition to co-editing *Le Progrès* of Cairo.[69]

In July 1905 Galanté founded his own journal, *La Vara*. Although in the maiden article he declared that its pages were "open to all those who suffer injustice in the [Ottoman Empire]," he described the main goal of the journal as "to improve the fate of our [Jewish] communities, to give a lesson to the new generation, and to describe the sad situation of the Jewish communities in Turkey."[70] Hence, although the journal had correspondents in various Ottoman towns as well as in Cairo and Alexandria,[71] it devoted all its publication to the affairs of the Jewish communities in the Ottoman Empire.

When Ahmed Rıza came to Cairo in March 1907, he "charged [Galanté] with organizing a committee of Ottoman Jews which will have a political program . . . representative of the Jewish population."[72] In July 1907 Galanté turned his network of correspondents into a committee and agreed to carry out activities "under the regulations of the Young Turk committee [the CPU]."[73] Ahmed Rıza invited Galanté to sign the forthcoming resolutions of the congress, and Galanté sent a telegram announcing his agreement on December 14, 1907.[74] Galanté then stated that Ahmed Rıza would represent the Comité Israélite d'Egypte at the congress.[75] At first the CPU wanted to publicize this fact. It later decided, however, that a bogus announcement of this organization's independent participation would be more useful.[76]

Thus the "Jewish participation" in the "Congress of Ottoman Opposition Parties," later deemed of great significance,[77] was in reality nothing more than a right of representation granted to Ahmed Rıza by Galanté on behalf of an organization composed of correspondents. In fact, a letter which Ahmed Rıza wrote to Galanté immediately after the closure of the congress reveals that the latter was not even aware of the resolutions signed on his behalf.[78]

A third "organization" that padded the signature list was the "Rédaction" of *Hilâfet -Khilâfa*, allegedly representing the Arab element of the Ottoman Empire. Virtually all Young Turk factions severely criticized this journal's early issues for directly challenging the sultan's rights to the caliphate and to the administration of the Arab provinces of the Ottoman Empire.[79] In 1901 a new group of Arab expatriates, who formed the so-called Türk Anarşist Cemiyeti (Turkish Anarchist Committee) in Paris,[80] established ties with Najīb Hindī. Hindī was involved in editing the sporadically published journal *Hilâfet-Khilâfa*, with the goal of revitalizing it.[81] When this end was achieved under a new editorial board in 1902, it "gave great offense to the sultan,"[82] and as a result the Ottoman representatives made interminable appeals to the British authorities to shut down the London-based journal[83] that was being smuggled into the Arab provinces.[84]

The CPU's opinion of *Hilâfet-Khilâfa* under its new editorial board remained as it had been. Bahaeddin Şakir warned CPU members about this journal that "serves the aim of planting the seeds of enmity between the Turks and Arabs."[85]

While the Dashnaktsutiun and the CPU desperately searched for organizations that could sign the resolutions, the CPU compelled *Hilâfet-Khilâfa*'s "Rédaction" to do so. During this period the organization that this journal represented sowed confusion. Contradictory claims surfaced to the effect that it was an "Arab journal" and a "Young Turk organ."[86] In fact, despite its name and its previous issues, in December 1907 it represented neither the Arab nor the Young Turk movement. Beginning with its 104th issue, dated February 15, 1906, *Hilâfet-Khilâfa* began to publish articles in Persian along with articles in Turkish; by the fall of 1906 it was devoting its coverage to the Iranian constitutional movement, and almost all articles were published in Persian with the exception of some special issues in Arabic and some short articles in Turkish. Hence it could be used only for window-dressing purposes, which the organizers did successfully.[87]

The organizers thus made use of the editorial boards of various insignificant journals and virtually nonexistent, one-man organizations to inflate the number of signatures. This ploy enabled them to make the bombastic claim of having accomplished a general union of "Ottoman opposition parties" and served as a shield against the attacks of opponents who rejected any rapprochement between the CPU and the

Dashnaktsutiun. These signatures were, however, of no help to the organizers in carrying out revolutionary activities.

The Congress of "Ottoman Opposition Parties"

Following the agreement among the three organizing committees and the drafting of the resolutions, the congress met in three sessions between December 27 and 29, 1907. As has been demonstrated, the subcommittee prepared every detail, including the topics to be discussed each day. Therefore, in contrast to what had taken place at the 1902 Congress, the discussions during the sessions in 1907 were not focused on the question of what resolutions to adopt. As with the 1902 Congress, there is no available document providing a comprehensive list of the participants' names. However, articles in various journals, along with the CPU secret correspondence, reveal the identities of those who participated in the meeting as representatives of the three organizations. Among them were the CPU's four central committee members: Ahmed Rıza, Bahaeddin Şakir, Muḥammad ʿAlī Ḥalīm Pasha, and Sami Paşazâde Sezaî. In addition, Veliyullah Çelebizâde Mahmud Çelebi (referred to as Necati Bey) represented the CPU Romania branch,[88] and Pierre Anméghian (referred to as Ottomanus) attended the congress as a columnist of *Mechveret Supplément Français*. The League of Private Initiative and Decentralization was represented by a delegation composed of its leader Sabahaddin Bey, Ahmed Fazlı, Dr. Mekkeli Sabri, and Dr. Nihad Reşad (referred to as Dr. Azmi). The Dashnaktsutiun was represented by Hratch, Harutiun Kalfaian (Vahram), Khachatur Malumian (E. Aknuni), Sarkis Minasian (Aram Ashod), the editor of the Dashnaktsutiun organ *Haïrenik*, Sarafian, and Ruben Zartarian (Aslan), the editor of the Dashnaktsutiun organ *Razmig*. Since no real balloting took place, the disproportionate representation of the component organizations was of no importance.

The congress was officially opened by Sami Paşazâde Sezaî. Then the representatives submitted the power-of-attorney documents prepared by their respective organizations to the subcommittee. After this the participants elected Sabahaddin Bey, Malumian, and Ahmed Rıza to preside over the sittings in turn as decreed by the subcommittee, and Pierre Anméghian was appointed secretary of the congress.[89]

Next Sabahaddin Bey, who presided over the first session, invited Dr. Nihad Reşad to read the subcommittee's report. The report called for the following:

1. The destruction of the present administration.
2. The establishment of constitutional administration (i.e., the restoration of the Chamber of Deputies and the Senate).
3. The search for peaceful or revolutionary means to accomplish these goals.

The first article includes compelling Sultan Hamid to abdicate. The members of the subcommittee have unanimously decided that disarmament will not take place until this objective is realized.

The second article is merely about the demand and wish for the formation of a constitutional government that would attain freedom, equality, and the rights of the nation. . . .

The members of the subcommittee have decided that a mixed and permanent executive committee will be established to put the decisions of the congress into effect.[90]

The subcommittee further proposed the following points to the congress, although Dr. Nihad Reşad stated that no details could be given about them because of the secret nature of the program:

1. General rebellion.
2. Armed and peaceful resistance (such as strikes) against the administration.
3. Nonpayment of taxes to the government.
4. The dissemination and propagation of these ideas within the army, that is to say, to win over the army [to work] toward our goals and against the present government; and to seek ways to keep the [army] from using arms against the children of the fatherland working for the salvation of the country and against rebels.[91]

Despite the arduous efforts of the subcommittee to prepare a program on which all three organizations could agree, two important confrontations took place during the congress between the CPU and Dashnaktsutiun members. During the first session, Ahmed Rıza called for the Armenian delegation's recognition of the Ottoman sultan's rights as caliph. The Armenian delegation objected that this demand had nothing to do with the work of the congress and thus brought the meeting to the brink of an unforeseen impasse.[92]

In order to reach an agreement on this issue, the participants formed a new subcommittee under Ahmed Rıza's direction. The conflicting parties could not reach an agreement, and Ahmed Fazlı accordingly replaced Ahmed Rıza as chairman of the subcommittee. Ahmed Fazlı, who was supported by Bahaeddin Şakir, succeeded in finding a compromise. Upon Ahmed Fazlı's suggestion, the Dashnak delegation declared that "the issues of the caliphate and the sultanate which have been considered sacred by [their] Turkish compatriots are of no interest to [them] and they are not against these institutions"; this statement caused Ahmed Rıza to abandon his obstruction.[93]

The second debate revolved around the use of revolutionary means, and it continued through the banquet that followed the meeting. On this issue the difference between the CPU and the Dashnaktsutiun was very deep, though both organizations spearheaded the initiative toward union among "the revolutionary committees." Despite the CPU's adoption of revolutionary methods following the reorganization, its ideology remained socially conservative, and in its leaders' eyes revolutionary tactics were just a form of activism. The Dashnaktsutiun, however, as a socialist organization and member of the Second International, was a revolutionary organization in the real sense of the word. Thus Malumian's accusation that the CPU was not being revolutionary enough illustrated a deep-seated ideological difference between the two organizations. Sami Paşazâde Sezaî responded to the criticism at the post-congress banquet by stating that they "could not become Reds."[94] Sabahaddin Bey too opposed the CPU's focus on assassinations as the main revolutionary tactic and proposed to strive to create "meaningful, national rebellions."[95] In order to find a middle ground, Pierre Anméghian argued that the Dashnaktsutiun's efforts to bring about a socialist order within the Ottoman Empire were superfluous, since "socialism very strongly exists in Turkey." He further asserted that "the Turk [was] a socialist without comprehending it. Had Molière been alive he would have said that the Turk is a socialist despite himself."[96] In order to illustrate the CPU's populism and thereby counter Malumian's rhetoric, Bahaeddin Şakir brought to the banquet pieces of some obscure substance in a box. When nobody could determine what they were, Bahaeddin Şakir told them that they had come from a loaf of bread eaten by poor peasants in the Ottoman Empire. He asked the participants to keep in mind while eating "high quality white bread and steaks at the banquet that the peasants feed on bread like this because of the poverty and destitution generated by Abdülhamid." He further asked the participants to publicize the sad situation of the peasants in the Ottoman Empire.[97] In the end these debates over being sufficiently revolutionary, over socialism, and over populism did not cause any impasse, nor did they make a significant impact on the results of the congress.

The congress unanimously decided to issue a declaration that included the following points:

1. To force Sultan Hamid to abdicate.
2. To change the present administration drastically.
3. To establish a system of *meşveret* (consultation) and constitutional [government].

This declaration also presented the final version of the revolutionary tactics to be implemented by the members of the participating organizations:

1. Armed resistance against the government's actions and operations.
2. Unarmed resistance. Strike[s] of policemen and government officials; their quitting of work.
3. Nonpayment of taxes to the present administration.
4. Propaganda within the army. The soldiers will be urged not to move against rebels.
5. General rebellion.
6. Other means of action to be taken in accordance with the course of events.[98]

The congress further decided to establish a mixed permanent committee as proposed by the subcommittee. This committee was also to take necessary precautions to "punish the traitors." Again the new propaganda that would be carried out by this mixed permanent committee would be in total accordance with the CPU strategy. First, appeals and pamphlets were to be written in "Turkish, Arabic, Kurdish, Albanian, Armenian, Bulgarian, and Greek" to disseminate "revolutionary propaganda." Second, similar publications were to be addressed to "peasants, government officials, soldiers and officers, the ulema, the governing elite, and to women." The first of these initiatives had been taken by the CPU after the reorganization. The second was clearly a repetition of Ahmed Rıza's idea on which he had been working since 1902.[99]

As a final act and on the insistence of the CPU, the congress sent a telegram of solidarity to the Iranian parliament expressing the Ottoman opposition groups' desire for collaboration between the future Ottoman constitutional government and Iranian constitutionalists.[100]

Before adjourning the congress, the three leaders addressed the participants one last time. Speaking first, Sabahaddin Bey presented Demolins's theories as a means to solve the problems besetting the Ottoman Empire. According to the prince, there were two basic problems. The first was that Ottoman social organization hindered individual initiative; thus a new social organization encouraging private initiative had to replace it. The second problem was the "Eastern Question." This problem, Sabahaddin Bey stated, should be solved in accordance with the desires of the "civilized" world:

En Angleterre, l'individu attend son salut de son seul effort personnel; il répudie autant que possible l'intervention de l'Etat dans ses affaires; aussi la vie privée y domine-t-elle toujours la vie publique.

Au contraire, dans l'Amérique du Sud, l'individu répugne à l'effort et à l'initiative; d'où, comme conséquence fatale, l'ingérance tyrannique de l'Etat dans la vie privée. . . .

Le monde civilisé doit souhaiter que la question d'Orient soit résolue par la consolidation et la régénération de l'empire ottoman car seule cette situation ne lèse aucun intérêt.[101]

After Sabahaddin Bey, Ahmed Rıza addressed the participants. As expected, he underscored the importance of "the existence of cold-blooded and truth-loving patriots along with fervent youngsters to maintain the balance and equilibrium of society." His positivistic themes were in character with his comparison of himself to a medical doctor adding water to a strong wine. He also emphasized the fact that the alliance was a tactical one and, accordingly, the participating committees would continue to pursue their own goals. Finally, he invited the Hnchakian, Verakazmial Hncakian, Greek, and Albanian committees, which had not participated in the congress, to join the tactical alliance.[102]

Malumian recommended extending "nationality" to all "humankind," claiming that thereby people would abandon religious and national hatreds and elevate themselves to a stage "beyond the human, as the great Nietzsche had said."[103] Apparently taking his cue from Nietzsche's attempt to transcend Christianity and its values, Malumian proposed "socialism" as a transvaluation of all values.

It is interesting that the leaders of the three main opposition committees could not find a common framework within which to incorporate their respective communities' political objectives; they thought that they could achieve this goal only by bypassing those irreconcilable ideals through the use of a transvaluative ideology. The proposed formulæ for changing the social structure in accordance with Demolins's theories, positivism, and socialism may have seemed workable to members of the elites such as Sabahaddin Bey, Ahmed Rıza, and Malumian. In practice, of course, they could do little to bridge the gap between the objectives of their communities.

On New Year's Eve Sabahaddin Bey's benefactor Baron de Lormais gave a banquet in honor of the participants, and all of them expressed their satisfaction with the successful completion of the congress.[104] The year 1908 thus opened with a tactical alliance in place among three opposition committees. For those who had witnessed the endless debates between the leaders of the Dashnaktsutiun and the CUP, the coalition, and finally the CPU, this seemed a considerable success.[105] It would, however, be of limited import for fomenting a revolution.

Consequences of the Tactical Alliance

Although the organizers portrayed their new tactical alliance as a union of all revolutionary Ottoman opposition groups, this was far from being the case. Malumian claimed that in addition to the union achieved between Arabs, Armenians, Jews, and Turks, "les comités révolutionnaires macédoniens étaient depuis longtemps d'accord avec le *Droschak*, leur adhésion est donc assurée. De même les Albanais et leurs

groupes vont adhérer. Quant aux Kurdes, ils manquent malheureusement de groupe-
ments politiques, mais nous sommes en rapport avec beaucoup des leurs et là aussi,
nous avons bon espoir."[106] But this statement was absolutely misleading.

First, as we have seen, the other signatories to the resolutions were in no position
to provide any assistance for a revolution other than publishing favorable articles
that might be read by a few people. Second, as Sabahaddin Bey himself confessed,
his league had spent all its resources following the government's obliteration of the
revolutionary movement in Erzurum in early December 1907; apart from appeals in
Terakki, it could do nothing to help any revolutionary movement. Third, despite favorable coverage by the Young Turk press in general,[107] almost all non-Turkish organizations adopted antagonistic stances toward the "union" of the three committees, and hence in a way formed a de facto opposition bloc against the tactical alliance.

The Hncakist party took the first step. The editor of the journal *Hnchak*, Stepan
Sapah-Gulian, authored an article strongly criticizing the very premise of the "alliance." The article summarized the feelings of the alliance's opponents so well that
they expressed their abhorrence of it by simply republishing this article. *Ilinden*'s
printing of a Bulgarian version of the article was an unambiguous signal of the
final refusal of the right wing of the IMRO to participate in the tactical alliance.[108]
L'Indépendance Arabe's publication of a French translation was less important, given
the CPU's hatred of the so-called Comité of Azoury.[109] These were, however, clear
signs that the tactical alliance would be confined to the signatories and that the
Dashnaktsutiun and the CPU would have to shoulder the burden of organizing joint
revolutionary activities by themselves.

The CPU papers and available Ottoman documents reveal that the joint CPU–
Dashnaktsutiun revolutionary activities were very insignificant and that the CPU never
trusted the Dashnaktsutiun. The CPU regarded the agreement as a tactical alliance
with a "deadly foe,"[110] restricted to "action," and it informed all its branches and correspondents accordingly.[111] Furthermore, the CPU External Headquarters assured the
branches that the tactical alliance would last only until the "reopening of the Chamber of Deputies, and thence forward each participating party would have the right to
pursue its own political program";[112] "once [they] toppled the administration and
opened the Chamber of Deputies, then naturally due to [their] dominant national power
[they] will not fear either a handful of Armenians, or even the government of Abdülhamid and the European governments."[113] In another secret letter Bahaeddin Şakir
stated that "an Armenian does not have courage like a Turk and will never have it.
Neither the Armenian nor any other person could be the heir of the bravery left us by
a glorious and honorable history of six hundred years."[114] The CPU central committee further instructed the members in the branches not to trust the Armenians, and to
scrutinize them closely, verifying whether or not they were violating the terms of the
tactical alliance.[115] The CPU also directed the Caucasian Muslims to be "very alert
there and not to put their weapons aside"[116] because of the agreement reached at the
congress. After the congress the CPU continued to portray Sabahaddin Bey's ideas
on "decentralization" as "seditious ideas"[117] and forbade its members to establish
ties with him.[118]

Even in its own journals the CPU expressed concern about the tactical alliance with
the Dashnaktsutiun. First, *Şûra-yı Ümmet* described Malumian as a follower of the

principle that "humanity is my nation and the world is my country."[119] Those who knew that Ahmed Rıza derisively criticized those who could "unfortunately" utter such a saying understood that the CPU did not think very highly of the Dashnak leader.[120] Although *Mechveret Supplément Français* did run some articles praising the "union,"[121] Ahmed Rıza was deeply disturbed by the friendly coverage of the congress in the socialist press,[122] and he soon attacked Malumian because of an interview published in *L'Humanité*, and Pierre Quillard because of his similar comments on the congress published in *Pro Armenia*.[123] Ahmed Rıza accused the Dashnak leader of presenting CPU members as "fougueux terroristes."[124] Quillard retaliated immediately by pointing out that the CPU too signed the resolutions calling for the use of revolutionary means.[125] The CPU dispatched a delegate from Paris to Geneva to discuss the matter with the Dashnaktsutiun leaders. The Dashnaks demanded that Ahmed Rıza not write provocative articles that could harm the "union," and they stated that they considered *Mechveret Supplément Français* to be the "official organ of a committee" with which they were allied.[126] Nonetheless, Ahmed Rıza continued his criticism.[127]

Despite these debates between the ideologues, those who were in charge of organization and propaganda in both committees worked together. The Dashnak propaganda claimed that "there was not a single Young Turk left among the Young Turks in Paris who oppose[d] the revolution and rebellion" and that Armenians and Turks in Anatolia were carrying out joint revolutionary activities.[128]

Although the CPU propaganda machine made only slight use of the tactical alliance with the Dashnaktsutiun, the CPU leaders sought its help in their activities. The Dashnaktsutiun distributed 50 copies of *Şûra-yı Ümmet* within the empire on a monthly basis.[129]

As for the joint revolutionary activities, available documents reveal that Dashnaktsutiun members in Tabrīz helped Ömer Naci, whom the CPU dispatched to Iran, during his dealings with the Iranian constitutionalists.[130] In March 1908, when the government launched a campaign of arrests against the CPU members in Salonica, the CPU External Headquarters asked whether the Dashnaktsutiun would help them to free the apprehended CPU members.[131] These initiatives, however, were far from being major revolutionary activities and are better described as gestures of goodwill and signs of a mutual understanding between the two organizations.

The only joint Muslim-Armenian mass movement after the congress took place in the town of Arapgir in the province of Ma'muret el-Azîz. A crowd composed of Muslim and Armenian women marched to the subgovernor's offices to demand the lowering of the price of wheat and the granting of credit to the poor. They broke the windows of the subgovernor's offices. Then an Armenian-Muslim mob consisting of men and women gathered and raided a wheat granary. It is difficult to know whether the tactical alliance had a hand in this rare overt, joint movement. The Ottoman documents underscored the importance of the joint character of the demonstration, and the central government ordered that the strictest measures be taken.[132] The governor of Ma'muret el-Azîz, however, maintained that the demonstration was against profiteers and stemmed from the devastating economic conditions prevailing in the province.[133]

Another interesting consequence of the congress was the achievement of socialist support for the "union." The support of the left-wing French deputies and *L'Humanité* would, however, be of little help to the organizing parties.[134] The CPU, as a conservative organization, found socialist support very distasteful and, as we have seen, Ahmed Rıza did not even hesitate to write articles criticizing the socialist intellectuals' comments on the union.

For Sabahaddin Bey this was a more serious problem. For a long time he had viewed a union with the Armenian organizations as a device to secure foreign intervention in general, and British intervention in particular. However, the fact that a member of the Second International played a leading role in the union, and the revolutionary ideas expressed in the final declarations of the congress, dashed all Sabahaddin Bey's hopes. When the Foreign Office received a copy of the declaration, the British foreign policy-makers simply jotted in the margin "no action."[135]

For the Dashnaktsutiun, the tactical alliance was at best a Pyrrhic victory. On the one hand, it worsened the Dashnaktsutiun's already unsatisfactory relations with the other Armenian organizations that strongly opposed any kind of rapprochement with the Young Turks in general, and the CPU in particular.[136] On the other hand, the tactical alliance forced the Dashnaktsutiun to work with a conservative activist organization that abhorred unfeigned revolutionary ideas and revolutionary socialism[137] and that wanted to implement revolutionary tactics only to the extent of bringing about a change of regime in the Ottoman Empire.

Although the Dashnaks[138] and many foreign observers attributed importance to the tactical alliance realized at the "1907 Congress of Ottoman Opposition Parties" and claimed that it played a significant role in the Young Turk Revolution of 1908,[139] the facts show the opposite: this tactical alliance played no role whatsoever in that revolution and was for practical purposes almost worthless. Malumian's prophecy that they would meet in Istanbul in eighteen months was indeed fulfilled even before the expected date. But this was so because of the CPU's independent initiative in the revolution and had nothing to do with the congress.[140]

8

The CPU at Work

The Preparation and Execution of the
Young Turk Revolution of 1908

The reorganization of the CPU created an effective Young Turk committee that adopted activist tactics and aimed at revolution. The leaders of the CPU set about creating a network of branches and correspondents that would enable them to spread extensive propaganda. Their success at this endeavor prompted them to take the second and final step: preparation for a revolution. Scholars have traditionally attributed the CPU's rapid success in carrying out a revolution in the summer of 1908 to the Hamidian regime's unpreparedness and to the fact that the palace was caught by surprise. Although these factors undoubtedly did play a role in the CPU's triumph, the Young Turk Revolution of 1908 cannot be fully understood without an examination of the CPU's own efforts to prepare it. This chapter will discuss these efforts. It will not, however, attempt to provide an evaluation of the revolution and its consequences as a whole.

The Ottoman Freedom Society and Its Merger with the CPU

Although the old CUP organization had succeeded in establishing a branch in Salonica in 1896, neither this city nor Macedonia became a center of Young Turk activities during the early days of the Young Turk movement.[1] The Ilinden revolt of 1903, and the subsequent application of the Mürzteg program, however, made "Macedonia" one of the most burdensome issues of European diplomacy, and a hotbed of Ottoman dissidents. The application of the Mürzteg program and the establishment of foreign control over the region provoked great resentment among the Muslim elites and masses in Macedonia. The Muslim masses reacted defensively. The people of various Muslim towns, who feared the extension of the program to their region, took oaths to "guard [their] weapons well and not surrender them to anyone, and in the event of an assault, to cut their ties with foreigners who [were their] deadly foes and enemies of [their] religion."[2]

In terms of the elite, the dissidents were mostly army officers who had been fighting against the nationalist bands of various ethno-religious groups. The Ilinden revolt of 1903 had profoundly affected them, and they seriously began to consider working with Young Turk expatriates in Europe and Egypt.[3] A British diplomat states in his memoirs that in August 1903 five local Young Turks "who were destined five years later to take a leading part in the Young Turk Revolution," namely Mustafa Rahmi (Arslan), Talât, Major Cemal, Mehmed Cavid, and Hacı Âdil Beys, requested a secret meeting with him and asked what he "thought were their prospects of success in carrying the people with them and obtaining some measure of foreign countenance and support." They stated that although they could count on many sympathizers, that sympathy was for the time being only platonic. The British diplomat then advised them "to put out of their minds all idea of an ill-timed revolt."[4] The leaders of the dissidents also corresponded with Ahmed Rıza and told him that they would like to establish a coalition branch in Salonica. Ahmed Rıza's response confessing the coalition's impotence and recommending that they should work independently disappointed and discouraged the dissidents.[5]

Various sources maintain that dissident activities aimed at establishing an organization in Salonica gained momentum during the course of 1905.[6] The movement, however, maintained its unorganized form and did not go beyond meetings at which dissident leaders reiterated the necessity of overthrowing the sultan's regime.

In the meantime, the reorganized CPU, recognizing Salonica's exceptional importance and receiving reports about the activities of the dissidents, attempted to establish a branch there. When a sympathizer sent a letter to the CPU central committee describing how "eight Bulgarians were killed, defending their national rights," Bahaeddin Şakir and Dr. Nâzım responded that "the Bulgarians sacrificed themselves because of the political edification given to them," and they asked the sympathizer to form a CPU branch in Salonica.[7] The fact that more than a year later the CPU asked another sympathizer, from whom the committee received a letter, to assist them in distributing materials in Salonica indicates the failure of the CPU initiative.[8]

In the meantime Captain Mustafa Kemal (Atatürk) had founded an embryonic opposition society named Vatan ve Hürriyet (Fatherland and Freedom) in Damascus in the summer of 1905, with three friends: Dr. Mahmud, Captain Müfid (Özdeş), and Mustafa (Cantekin), a former Royal Medical Academy student who had been banished to Damascus. Captain Mustafa Kemal now came to Salonica to establish a branch of their society.[9] There he met with leading dissidents such as Ömer Naci, Hakkı Baha, Hüsrev Sami, Mehmed Tahir, and İsmail Mahir, all of whom later joined the Ottoman Freedom Society.

It is difficult to discern whether Captain Mustafa Kemal actually succeeded in establishing a branch of his embryonic organization in Salonica. He later claimed that he did found a branch, which subsequently became the Ottoman Freedom Society and the internal headquarters of the CPU after the merger in September 1907.[10] Later official publications of the early Turkish Republic maintained that the founder of the Turkish Republic was also the founder of the Ottoman Freedom Society that successfully carried out the Young Turk Revolution of 1908.[11] This claim was seriously challenged by many of Mustafa Kemal's contemporaries.[12] More recently, in a meticulous study, Erik J. Zürcher has argued persuasively that these claims were part of the "personality cult" of Mustafa Kemal that was created during the early years of the Turkish Republic.[13] There is no question that the assertion that Mustafa Kemal was indeed the founder of the Ottoman Freedom Society was an inaccurate reconstruction by early republican Turkish historians and some of Mustafa Kemal's contemporaries.[14] Nevertheless, the first part of Mustafa Kemal's account—that he met with various dissidents and encouraged them to form a branch of his nascent society—seems quite plausible, since many independent sources referred to the society long before Mustafa Kemal became a pivotal figure in Turkish politics.[15]

The significance of the debates over the way in which the Ottoman Freedom Society was established has been much inflated by the tendency to downplay the CPU's role and give all the credit for the 1908 Revolution to the Ottoman Freedom Society. In the light of certain key facts, however, these debates lose their significance. First, despite what many members of the CUP later claimed, there were no sharp differences between members of the CPU and those of the Ottoman Freedom Society. Second, before its merger with the CPU, the Ottoman Freedom Society was unorganized and had no instruments of propaganda. By contrast, the efforts of Bahaeddin Şakir and Dr. Nâzım to organize the new committee after the merger, and the propaganda material disseminated by the CPU, played an invaluable role in the revolution. Without these the revolution could have not been realized for a long time to come.

Despite debates over who precisely took the first initiative, we can be certain that after many meetings and discussions presided over by various figures, the leading dissidents in Salonica decided in July 1906 to transform their scattered activities into an organized effort. Those involved were Major Bursalı Mehmed Tahir, the director of the Salonica Military High School; Major Naki Bey (Yücekök), instructor of French at the Salonica Military High School; Talât Bey (Pasha), chief clerk of correspondence at the Salonica post office directorate; Mustafa Rahmi, a businessman from the well-known, aristocratic, Salonican family of Evrenos; Midhat Şükrü (Bleda), director of the municipal hospital in Salonica; Captain Edib Servet (Tör), the Ottoman aide-de-camp of the Italian general Degiorgis, who was the commander of the gendarmerie in charge of Macedonian reform; Captain Kâzım Nâmi (Duru); First Lieutenant Hakkı Baha (Pars); and First Lieutenant Ömer Naci. At a secret meeting at First Lieutenant İsmail Canbolad's house these leading dissidents decided to assign the task of laying the groundwork for a secret society to a subcommittee composed of Talât Bey, Mustafa Rahmi, Midhat Şükrü, and İsmail Canbolad.[16] After two months of work, this subcommittee completed preparations for the establishment of a committee called Hilâl Cemiyeti (the Crescent Committee) on September 7, 1906.[17] At a second meeting, held in Midhat Şükrü's house on September 18, 1906, the dissidents changed the Crescent Committee's name to the Ottoman Freedom Society. They also recognized the ten who had participated at the first meeting as the society's founders.[18]

The ten founding members then elected a "High Council" composed of Talât Bey, İsmail Canbolad, and Mustafa Rahmi to oversee the administration of the newly formed committee.[19] In the meantime, Mustafa Rahmi drafted regulations.[20] According to these first regulations only Muslims could become members and even *dönme*s, the followers of Sabbatai Sevi, were to be excluded.[21] When founders began to recruit new members, they assigned them numbers at intervals of a hundred in order to boost the society's image in the new members' eyes.[22]

All the founding members but one, Major Mehmed Tahir, were (or became) Freemasons and members of the Italian Obedience of Macedonia Risorta and the French

Obedience of Véritas.[23] This fact helped the founders to meet secretly at Freemason lodges and clandestinely import and distribute publications from Europe and Egypt.[24] In a short period of time the new committee recruited 42 individuals in Salonica, most of them officers.[25]

In its early activities the society limited itself to recruiting as many individuals as possible. The founders made no plans for activities; at this stage their main problem seemed to be the lack of a journal with which to disseminate their ideas.

Immediately prior to the establishment of the Ottoman Freedom Society, a journal called *Çocuk Bağçesi* (The Children's Garden), for which First Lieutenant Ömer Naci wrote articles, became the voice of the Salonica dissidents. It conveyed opposition themes by publishing the works of the Turkish nationalist poet Mehmed Emin (Yurdakul). It also ventured to criticize the Hamidian press in a roundabout way,[26] and as a result the authorities temporarily suspended it.[27] Although the dissidents attempted to continue publication, the tight censorship limited the benefits that the journal could yield for a secret revolutionary organization. Under the circumstances it ceased publication with its 43rd issue on December 14, 1905.[28]

The founders were thus left with no press.[29] Accordingly, even during the early phases of the society's activities, they made use of CPU journals and propaganda material.[30]

It should be remembered that many founders of the Ottoman Freedom Society had been members of the old CUP organization. Talât Bey, while distributing CUP propaganda material as a member of the Edirne branch, had been arrested in 1896 and sentenced to three years imprisonment. He later continued corresponding with Ahmed Rıza. Midhat Şükrü had been a member of the CUP Geneva branch and returned to the empire after the so-called Contrexéville agreement between Mizancı Murad and Ahmed Celâleddin Pasha in 1897. Mustafa Rahmi had been a member of the CUP Salonica branch in 1897, when he was arrested in connection with his involvement in an assassination attempt. Kâzım Nâmi had belonged to the CUP Tirana branch until 1897. Many leading figures who joined the Ottoman Freedom Society had also had contacts with the CPU before their organization's merger with it.[31] Therefore, contrary to widespread belief, this new organization was not radically different from the CPU and was not founded by individuals who had nothing in common with the CPU.

It should thus come as no surprise that when two members of the Ottoman Freedom Soceity fled to Paris, they joined the CPU there.[32] One was First Lieutenant Ömer Naci, one of the founders of the Ottoman Freedom Society, identified as someone who "had been an officer but became a soldier for the *jihād*." He joined the CPU in May 1907 and immediately assumed the post of assistant editor of *Şûra-yı Ümmet* under Sami Paşazâde Sezaî.[33] Described as a "pure revolutionary,"[34] Ömer Naci also authored fierce propaganda pamphlets for the CPU, such as the famous *Hayye-ale-l-felâh*.[35] The other member, Captain Hüsrev Sami, who "preferred being a soldier fighting against tyranny to being an officer in the service of tyranny," joined the CPU in late August 1907. He immediately became the assistant director of the CPU Internal Affairs and Correspondence division under Bahaeddin Şakir,[36] and later he replaced Ömer Naci as the assistant editor of *Şûra-yı Ümmet* when the latter was dispatched to Iran by the CPU.[37] Thus the fusion of the Ottoman Freedom Society with the CPU should not be viewed as a merger of two committees pursuing different goals and possessing dissimilar agendas, but on the contrary as a merging of two very similar committees, both formed by individuals sharing the same ideas and directed toward the same goal.

While the Ottoman Freedom Society's founders were recruiting new members, the CPU decided to expand its activities in Macedonia. As an initial step, the central committee dispatched its official clerk, Seyyid Ken'an, to Greece and Montenegro to disseminate propaganda among the troops positioned on the Ottoman-Montenegrin and Ottoman-Greek borders.[38] Immediately after Seyyid Ken'an, the central committee dispatched another former officer, who traveled under the pseudonym of A. Raif, to Belgrade. From here he journeyed to the Ottoman-Serbian border, where he disseminated CPU propaganda among Ottoman officers and Albanians. His propaganda among the Albanians was especially successful, and he urged the central committee to print more copies of appeals inviting them to common action.[39]

In the meantime one of the founders of the Ottoman Freedom Society, most likely Talât Bey, sent a letter to Dr. Nâzım demanding the merger of the two committees. Bahaeddin Şakir scheduled a meeting in Budapest, but this plan fell through because the delegates of the Ottoman Freedom Society could not easily leave the empire.[40] Thus when Bahaeddin Şakir secretly traveled to Istanbul in May 1907, he met there with an attorney named Baha Bey, who had become the Istanbul representative of the Ottoman Freedom Society,[41] to discuss the proposed merger.[42] Bahaeddin Şakir also attempted to meet with Manyasizâde Refik, who had become a leading figure in the Ottoman Freedom Society, first in Istanbul and then secretly in Plovdiv. Although the two failed to meet, Bahaeddin Şakir stated that at that point, "it was discerned that both sides were pursuing the same goals and shared the same ideas, and that their organizations and initiatives were in complete accordance with each other."[43]

Thus the CPU center decided to dispatch Dr. Nâzım, a native of Salonica, to his hometown to discuss the merger with the leaders of the Ottoman Freedom Society. Dr. Nâzım secretly corresponded with Midhat Şükrü and with the latter's brother-in-law, who had contacts with the Ottoman Freedom Society.[44] One of the leaders of the society, Talât Bey, encouraged Dr. Nâzım to go to Greece and meet with the Greek revolutionary committee's representatives who were seriously considering working with the CPU against the Macedo-Bulgarian organizations. Following Talât Bey's advice, Dr. Nâzım went to Athens and entered into negotiations with the Greek revolutionary leaders. According to Dr. Nâzım's narrative, the Greek leaders broke their word and he was stuck in Athens for two months. While Dr. Nâzım was residing in Athens, a military member of the Ottoman Freedom Society, Captain Halil Bey, captured documents on a Greek band leader written by Lambros Koromilas, the Greek general consul in Salonica and the director general of all the Greek consulates in Macedonia. These documents clearly revealed Koromilas's involvement in the Greek armed struggle in Macedonia. The Ottoman Freedom Society offered the Greek committees the documents in return for their help in smuggling Dr. Nâzım into Macedonia.[45] The Greek revolutionary organization accepted the offer, and with the organization's assistance[46] Dr. Nâzım arrived at the lake of Yenice Vardar in mid-June 1907, disguised as a *hoca* aboard a fishing boat.[47]

Upon entering the empire, Dr. Nâzım was hidden in a farm by Greek committee members. He then went to Salonica, this time disguised as a peasant, to meet with the leaders of the Ottoman Freedom Society.[48] His first impression of this society was skeptical and pessimistic. In his first report to Bahaeddin Şakir he made the following points:

> People here do not pay any attention to being prudent. They have formed a society composed of eight or ten people. Among the members there are one or two officers (one of whom [Ömer] Naci knows, but this child is of no account) and a couple of officials. Look, we are not members of this society. But we know the identities of its members! The reason for this is the lack of cautionary behavior of the society. Tomorrow the government, too, will learn their identities. The occurrence of a mass arrest here for political reasons would not be in accordance with our policy. We are at the stage in our development of increasing the number of our members and the moral and material strength of our committee with the help of these people. We strongly feel the need to reach a total of four or five hundred members without attracting the government's attention. Until we reach that point we cannot waste any time on account of a government investigation. This incautious society, however, does things which would raise the government's suspicion, just to get three or five people to read some documents. They left a copy of the oath written on the last page of the regulations in an envelope on a table in a café. The method of recruiting members by making them sign this cannot work and will not work here. This method can be pursued only in places outside of Turkey. . . . It is absolutely impossible to trust them. Although there are patriotic and honest people among them, always keep in mind the proverb, "the green burns along with the dry." We know those who are useful and will gradually include them [in our committee]. To establish relations with all of them as a body, however, would not be to our advantage.[49]

In a second report Dr. Nâzım praised the "strong goodwill and passion" prevailing among the members of the Ottoman Freedom Society, while expressing his doubts about the "strength" of this organization.[50]

Because of Dr. Nâzım's reluctance to merge totally with the Ottoman Freedom Society, the negotiations took longer than expected. He did not reach an agreement in principle with the Ottoman Freedom Society leaders until late August 1907.[51] After long work on the details, Dr. Nâzım sent his final report to the CPU central committee on September 27, 1907, recommending the merger under certain conditions, together with a draft document setting out the conditions of fusion.[52] On October 16, 1907, the CPU central committee discussed the report and the draft at an extraordinary meeting at which Ahmed Rıza, Sami Paşazâde Sezaî, Bahaeddin Şakir, Hüsrev Sami, and Talha Kemalî were present. The central committee unanimously accepted the draft document and informed the CPU inspector Mehmed Saʿid Halim Pasha of their decision.[53] The merger document, dated September 27, 1907, made the following points:

> The Ottoman Progress and Union Committee with its headquarters in Paris and the Ottoman Freedom Society are united as of 19 Şaʿban [Shaʿbān] 1325/14 September [1]323/ 27 September 1907, under the name of the Ottoman Progress and Union Committee, and subject to the conditions enumerated below:
>
> 1. The committee will have two headquarters, one being internal and the other one being external, and of these the external headquarters will be in Paris and the internal headquarters in a proper place within [the empire]; both headquarters will have distinct seals.

2. The committee, the essential purpose of which is to bring about the implementation of the Constitution of Midhat Pasha proclaimed in 1292 [*sic*] [1293 = 1876], and to keep it in force, will have two independent charters, one internal and one external, to lay out the organization and the duties of members while taking their abilities and local requirements into consideration.

3. Although the headquarters are independent in administrative and financial affairs, they are required to assist each other in case of necessity.

4. Those branches within [the empire], and members with whom direct contact would be deemed dangerous, will be placed under [the authority of] the headquarters within [the empire], subject to the condition that correspondence with these [branches and members] will be carried on through the Paris headquarters.

5. The external headquarters will fulfill the duty of representing the committee to the outside [world], in addition to being the responsible authority for the branches outside [the empire]. The responsibility for relations with foreign governments and press will lie with the external headquarters, and the responsibility for initiatives and actions within [the empire] will be entirely with the internal headquarters.

6. The headquarters are authorized to interfere with each other's actions only in order to avoid [danger].

7. For the time being the committee's organs for disseminating its ideas are the journals *Şûra-yı Ümmet* in Turkish and *Meşveret [Mechveret Supplément Français]* in French. Since the external headquarters is required to take into consideration suggestions made by the internal headquarters regarding *Şûra-yı Ümmet* and all other publications in Turkish that are to be printed and published under the supervision of the external headquarters, the internal headquarters will share the responsibility for the [publications in Turkish]. Friday, 14 September [1]323 [September 27, 1907], 8 o'clock *ezanî* [the hour as reckoned from sunset] [2:02 P.M.].[54]

The merger of the two committees did not mean the absorption of one of the organizations by the other. Both continued to work as autonomous bodies. The fourth clause of the agreement, however, entitled the CPU External Headquarters to continue corresponding directly with virtually all the branches. Because of the palace's extensive spy network, it would have been extremely dangerous for the CPU Internal Headquarters to correspond with branches other than those in the European provinces. In addition, those strong branches that acted almost independently of the CPU Internal Headquarters, such as the CPU Monastir (Bitola) branch, corresponded directly with the CPU External Headquarters. Again, it should be remembered that the members of these headquarters and branches were not men of different ideas and were not pursuing different agendas. When we examine the CUP's lists of central committee members between 1908 and 1918, we note that all the main components of the movement received seats on this very important executive committee. Thus the CPU External Headquarters were represented by Bahaeddin Şakir, Dr. Nâzım, Ahmed Rıza, and Ömer Naci; the original founders of the Ottoman Freedom Society by Talât Bey and Midhat Şükrü; and quasi-independent branches by individuals such as Enver Bey (Pasha) of the Monastir branch and Eyüb Sabri of the Ohrid branch.

Despite this broad consensus, discussions on matters of detail continued through the exchange of memoranda. Bahaeddin Şakir implored the internal headquarters to pay more attention to secrecy and to use pseudonyms and the cipher code, which was to be sent by the external headquarters in their correspondence. He further demanded that the internal headquarters "adopt the method used by the committees of non-Muslim elements to swell the committee's resources, and to prepare and distribute propaganda material."[55] The CPU Internal Headquarters accepted these recommendations and requested a copy of the Dashnaktsutiun's printed program to be used as a model for revising the internal regulations, a draft of which had been prepared and forwarded to the CPU External Headquarters.[56]

With the merger, the CPU with its two headquarters entered a new phase. For only the second time in the history of the Young Turk movement, and for the first time since 1896, a Young Turk committee enjoyed a strong network concentrated in a particular region of the Ottoman Empire. It was now time for the leaders of the new CPU to draw up a redefined strategy toward fulfilling their long-deferred goals.

The CPU's New Activist Policies

Dr. Nâzım also urged the CPU Internal Headquarters to prepare new, activist regulations. He suggested that they adopt the internal regulations of the IMRO and the Dashnaktsutiun, and he provided them with detailed information about his and Bahaeddin Şakir's experience in this area.[57] The final product was deeply influenced by the IMRO and Dashnaktsutiun internal regulations and programs; foreign representatives likened the document to "the constitutions of Greek and Bulgarian committees" active in Macedonia.[58] At the same time, it reflected a clearly activist program.

As might be expected, the internal regulations underscored the importance of an "Ottomanist" union among the various Ottoman elements, and they opened membership to all Ottoman subjects regardless of faith and ethnicity, thanks to Dr. Nâzım's recommendation.[59] In addition, they stated that acting "to hinder those who work toward creating discord because of their racial and religious desires" was one of the "principal duties of the committee."[60] Thus for the first time in the history of the Young Turk movement, a committee officially adopted an aggressive position against "separatism" instead of merely inviting the others to "union."

The other new departure was the creation of branches of "self-sacrificing volunteers" (*fedaîs*). According to the 48th article of the internal regulations, "while all members who join the committee should sacrifice their lives for the sacred cause of the committee where necessary, those members who wish to be enlisted as self-sacrificing volunteers by their own will and for special actions should forward their names to the executive committee [of their branch] through the guide of the branch of which they are members."[61] The names of the self-sacrificing volunteers should be known only to the "executive committee members of a branch," and the "self-sacrificing branches" were not to be authorized to carry out any action without first informing the internal headquarters and receiving their approval. The volunteers were, however, entitled to propose actions to local executive committees.[62] Should a local committee's action need a single self-sacrificing volunteer, this person was to be chosen by drawing lots. Should the action need several self-sacrificing volunteers, it was to be carried out by a "self-sacrificing volunteers' branch."[63] The CPU was to be responsible for taking care of the family of any self-sacrificing volunteer killed in action, and also for publishing a pamphlet describing his self-sacrifice and for holding anniversary ceremonies at his tomb to pay tribute to his service.[64]

Besides these new branches of "self-sacrificing volunteers," the internal headquarters also authorized the executive committees of the branches to act as courts, pronouncing sentence on those "whose existence would endanger the fatherland or the committee."[65] The local executive committees were authorized to establish three types of guilt: "fault, serious offence, and crime."[66] When a branch found a suspect guilty of a crime, it was to obtain approval from the internal headquarters before carrying out the sentence. If a branch executive committee were to decide that the delay would endanger the committee's interests, however, it was entitled to carry out the verdict without seeking the internal headquarters' approval, thereby assuming all moral and material responsibility.[67]

In order to encourage members to carry out assassinations, the CPU went so far as to change its rules for enrollment. It presented two alternatives to the prospective candidates: either to serve for a year as a candidate and then become a real member, or "to offer a sacrifice to the committee" and thereby become a member immediately.[68]

Another innovation was a new oath-taking ceremony. The new oath itself was not very different from the old one,[69] but whereas the old ritual consisted in simply jotting down a text and sending it to Paris, the new ceremony was emotive and awe-inspiring.[70] The new internal regulations called for the establishment of "oath committees" to administer the oath-taking.[71] According to the 26th and 27th articles of the new internal regulations and their interpretation by the CPU External Headquarters, a candidate was to be brought blindfold to a house belonging to a committee member for the oath-taking ceremony. There he was to listen to a speech by the chairman of the "oath committee." Then he was to repeat the oath read by the chairman, holding one hand atop the sacred book of the religion he professed and the other hand atop a dagger and a revolver, or alternatively an Ottoman flag. When his blindfold was removed, the initiate was to see four masked members in red gowns.[72] By adopting this rather mysterious and arcane ritual, the CPU wished to add to the secret and mystic character of the committee. In this vein, with the adoption of the new regulations it was declared that the names of the CPU's central committee members and the place of its headquarters would "never be made public."[73]

Another notable innovation was the CPU's adoption of a coat of arms to underscore the importance of the juridical personality of the organization. This coat of arms recalled the Ottoman Imperial Coat of Arms, adopted in the second half of the nineteenth century. On top rested the constitution in the form of a book under a shining sun. Pennants reading "pen" and "weapon" hung from spears flanking the right and left sides respectively. From beneath each spear jutted a cannon. Unlike the cannon of the Ottoman Imperial Coat of Arms, however, this pair of cannons were being fired, symbolizing ideological dynamism. In the center stage stood a large upturned crescent reading "fraternity, freedom, equality." The word "justice" hung above the middle of the crescent. Below the crescent snaked a ribbon emblazoned "Ottoman Committee of Progress and Union," while at the bottom of the coat of arms, below the ribbon, two clasped hands symbolized mutual understanding among the Ottoman peoples.[74]

Encouraged by its internal counterpart's adoption of an activist program authorizing literally any branch to kill anybody it deemed "hazardous," the CPU External Headquarters informed the branches under its jurisdiction of its "merger with a committee, the former Ottoman Freedom Society," that had "more than a thousand members," that had been "founded for action," and that was "composed of our country's most elite individuals."[75] Only the CPU Istanbul branch questioned the claim that the Ottoman Freedom Society had more than a thousand members. It suspected that this number could not be accurate because of the efficiency of the palace's spy network.[76] The members of the CPU branch in Istanbul knew firsthand the difficulties of establishing even four-man cells inside the empire and found these grandiloquent boasts too good to be true. Indeed, such claims shook their trust in the center. Nonetheless, the merger and the CPU Internal Headquarters' adoption of an activist program provided the CPU External Headquarters with a long-awaited activist arm that could undertake sustained operations in a rather large region. Bahaeddin Şakir and Dr. Nâzım believed that a series of bold actions one after another might be enough to unleash the full range of the hitherto suppressed enmity toward the sultan and his regime; now "such a chance [was] at hand."[77]

Seeking to exploit this new capability to the full, the CPU External Headquarters did not leave its internal counterpart to act alone in finding "self-sacrificing volunteers" to carry out "action" within the empire. Bahaeddin Şakir had been deeply impressed by the large number of letter writers offering their service for such "action," and he accordingly announced "the preparation of a new generation of liberals" at the 1907 Congress.[78] In a letter sent to a prospective self-sacrificing volunteer, Bahaeddin Şakir and Hüsrev Sami wrote: "We need young and brave children of the fatherland. This is the time to render to the fatherland an honorable and glorious service. Please tell us what you feel in your heart and what services you can seriously undertake. Our committee has already entered the phase of action and execution."[79] Many other letters underscored the fact that the CPU had decided to undertake "action."[80] Bahaeddin Şakir also urged two Ottoman students at the chemistry department of Paris University to learn how to prepare "explosives" and to "keep this matter strictly secret."[81]

All of this clearly demonstrates that the CPU still considered the assassination of the sultan a serious option for toppling the regime. As a matter of fact, right up to the early days of the revolution, the CPU organs continued to encourage the dissidents to assassinate the sultan along with high-ranking civil and military officials and officers.[82] At the same time, the CPU leaders also felt it necessary to adopt more comprehensive tactics. A simple murder, or even a series of assassinations, would not be sufficient to foment and carry out the revolution.

In addition to striving to recruit as many self-sacrificing volunteers as possible, Bahaeddin Şakir and Dr. Nâzım gave much attention to the new strategy to be implemented through the help of these volunteers.

A New Invitation to the Military

One major concern of the leaders of the reorganized CPU was to create a strike force for the revolutionary movement. Although they still believed that the CPU should be open to all who wanted to join, they decided that it was absolutely necessary to limit membership in the strike force to young officers. Many such officers had become members of the CPU as a result of the merger.

The idea of officers being actively involved in revolutionary operations was not a new one. Many officers had even spoken of it in their letters to Young Turk journals.[83] Nevertheless, the creation of a revolutionary strike force under the command of young Ottoman officers, and modeled on the guerilla bands in Macedonia, led to the transformation of the CPU as a whole.

Even before the merger, Bahaeddin Şakir had underscored the importance of attracting zealous young officers. He stated that "if a committee limited itself to choosing as its members such and such a renowned pasha, or such and such *bey*, or such and such office director, as we have done so far, that committee would not find a single member ready to sacrifice himself to overcome the obstacles that it faces."[84] Thus, as Dr. Nâzım later attested, the CPU first started by recruiting lieutenants, and only then targeted higher ranks.[85] In order to attract officers, the CPU started publishing articles devoted to military affairs and the various Ottoman armies immediately after the reorganization.[86]

Two officers who joined the CPU as members of the Ottoman Freedom Society contributed their expertise to these articles. As was pointed out by one of them, Hüsrev Sami, "the armed forces would be a useful device in the hands of the low-ranking officers."[87] He addressed "his comrades in arms" in the following manner:

> Dear comrades in arms! We are the most responsible among the members of the nation. It is we who more than anybody provide protection for this source of tyranny, this soiled and abominable body of a sixty-seven-year-old. Although we possess the power and the means to annihilate and destroy this body in a momentary outburst, and to trample it under our feet like a rag, we still stand idle, loitering, and keeping silent. . . . Thus our duty becomes clear. The target is appointed! What is needed is only a sincere union, a union like a passionate love. Serving at the frontier and in the arena of the struggle for freedom are different matters. The former is a duty to the fatherland, but the latter is both a duty to the fatherland and a social duty.[88]

Şûra-yı Ümmet averred that the young officers "who should guide the people in the *gaza*"[89] were the "light of the eyes of our society and the darlings of the fatherland,"[90] and that "the highest commander of the army [was] the nation."[91] The central organ also emphasized that the CPU put its faith in the army, because "although all the national institutions have been shaken more or less during the world's great explosions in the times of crisis since we left Central Asia, the Ottoman sword has steadfastly maintained its glory and vigor."[92] In other words, the CPU leaders regarded the army as the only institution capable of carrying out a revolution. They also believed that the army was the only tool with which to thwart a most dreaded foreign intervention.[93] That Ahmed Rıza authored a pamphlet on the supposedly active role of the military during this period was no coincidence, but rather a clear signal from the CPU to the army to join the struggle.[94]

In order to entice junior officers, current CPU members from the military employed a rhetorical tone notable for its militancy. For example, Ömer Naci wrote:

The treaties prepared in order to give our fatherland to the Bulgarian are being signed before the tombs of Fatih, Selim I, Sokullu, Köprülü, and Barbaros Hayreddin. Let us not speak about Abdülhamid here. For the entire world knows that he is:

the *amīr* of the murderers,
the protector of the spies,
the helper of the Bulgarians,
the father of the Russians.[95]

Şûra-yı Ümmet gradually became a real revolutionary organ. It even downplayed the importance of words and theories. The military members of the editorial board were deeply influenced by Garibaldi, declaring that "a nation's salvation depends on the sacrifice it will make and the blood it will shed. Until now no nation has obtained the freedom that is its natural right through printing journals. In fact, theories are tools for preparing the way of evolution. Weapons, however, accelerate this evolution."[96]

These articles appeared in *Şûra-yı Ümmet* during the period immediately prior to the revolution and must have profoundly influenced the junior officers. For example, one of the military heroes of the Young Turk Revolution of 1908, Adjutant-Major Ahmed Niyazi, stated that *Şûra-yı Ümmet*, *Mechveret Supplément Français*, and Ahmed Rıza's pamphlet on the military "made an extraordinary impact in illuminating minds."[97]

In addition to publishing *Şûra-yı Ümmet*, the CPU printed a special pamphlet addressed to the officer corps. It called on army officers to take the lead against the sultan, who had no legitimacy according to *sharī'a*, and to demonstrate their patriotism by saving the country from foreign occupation.[98]

The New CPU Strategy: My Friend Ali Please Form a Band

The participation *en masse* of junior officers who were strongly motivated by CPU propaganda delighted the CPU leadership. Yet this leadership was also aware of the impossibility of moving large divisions against the administration with the help of low-ranking officers alone. This practical obstacle compelled the CPU leaders to consider seriously the option of establishing a network of bands in order to carry out a revolution. To create an effective band organization from scratch would be an extremely difficult task. The exceptional conditions of Macedonia, however, helped the CPU fulfill its goal in a very short time.

Contemporary European sources on Macedonia maintained in 1905 that the "Young Turkish party . . . has in fact but very small importance, and in Macedonia may be said to be non-existent."[99] The same sources, however, frequently spoke about the appearance of Turkish and Albanian bands as a new and significant factor on the Macedonian battlefield.[100] The Ottoman authorities persistently denied the existence of any Turkish or Muslim bands in Macedonia,[101] but beginning in 1905 their existence became impossible to deny. These bands, some of which could be traced back several years,[102] engaged in offensive operations and their existence became an indisputable fact.

Upon completing his initial survey of revolutionary operations in the region, Dr. Nâzım came to the conclusion that the Muslim bands would be an asset to the CPU and that they should be converted into CPU bands operating under the instructions of the CPU's military members. This was far from being a major innovation, involving as it did the simple emulation of the various band organizations operating under the command of Bulgarian, Greek, and Serbian officers in Macedonia.

The audacity of the Macedonian bands in general, and of the IMRO bands in particular, made a deep impression upon Ottoman officials who served in Macedonia.[103] They also grew to admire the bands and to think that perhaps a similar organization might stave off what they saw as the imminent collapse of the empire. Accordingly, military members of the CPU in Macedonia quickly embraced the idea of forming bands under their command. Some military members who discussed the matter with Dr. Nâzım told him that appropriating already existing bands would be an ideal way to create a sound and effective band network in a very short time. Since the Muslim bands were already active in Macedonia, the CPU could establish a band network "almost overnight" by winning over these bands. The officers involved informed Dr. Nâzım that they had earlier distributed rifles and revolvers to these Muslim bands to enable them to assassinate individuals whom they thought were working for the IMRO. In addition, they advised Dr. Nâzım that "since these bands [were] fighting to protect the defenseless Muslims from Christian bands, it would be very easy to convert them into bands fighting for the salvation of the fatherland from a foreign intervention that would result in the annihilation of Turkish rule in Europe."[104]

At the same time, appropriating these bands would help the CPU win popular support, since the Muslims in Macedonia viewed these bands as their saviors and protectors. For example, although on various occasions the local authorities arrested the famous bandit Gemici Hasan (Hasan the Sailor), nicknamed "the Butcher of the Bulgarians" by the Muslims and presented as an ideal example by Dr. Nâzım in his memoranda, they released him each time after taking his word that "he would not engage in seditious activities again."[105] As Dr. Nâzım stated in his memoranda, this leniency was due to popular pressure. The Muslim populace considered the bandit their protector and put pressure on the local authorities. In addition, the Muslim landlords and notables in Macedonia were supporting these bands financially because they protected their property against the attacks of the Christian bands.[106] Thus the CPU would not have to invest any money in creating and maintaining new band formations: their expenses would be met by the financial support of the landlords and the donations of the Muslim masses.

After conducting his first investigation and discussing the matter in detail with officers in the region, Dr. Nâzım sent a second memorandum to Bahaeddin Şakir underscoring the importance of the Muslim bands:

> In the struggle for Macedonia the Turks have not sat with their hands tied as you assumed. They provided invaluable services to Greek committees; Greek committees that did not have Turkish members were rare. Since the Turks who joined these bands received Greek money, what they did was not something to be proud of from the point of view of our nationalism. Since the Greeks' interest in this matter is similar to that of the Turks, however, the Turkish nation benefited directly from the efforts of those Turks. Moreover, the Turkish effort has not been confined to this. The Muslim population learned its lesson from

the events, united and formed its elite individuals into bands to patrol their districts. In districts such as Tikvesh and Doyran [Stari Toyran] they killed thirty or forty Bulgarians in retaliation for the killing of a single Muslim by Bulgarians. They took so great a vengeance that the Bulgarians in these districts would not dare to leave their houses. In addition, some patriotic officers who are our members established bands and armed these bands with rifles, sometimes with their own money. They had these bands patrol the Muslim villages, and they had seditious Bulgarians whom they could not arrest because of the lack of evidence to meet the burden of proof, assassinated by these bands. They used them also to secure the well-being of the Muslims and the orderliness [of their villages]. I know three such officers who have formed bands in this manner. Now there are four or five Turkish bands under the command of Hasan the Sailor, Martin Mustafa, Arab . . . ,[107] and others. These bands operate by killing at least five Bulgarians in retaliation for a single Turk killed by Bulgarians. When these bands kill a Bulgarian, they leave a letter addressed to the subgovernor of the subprovince reading: "Subgovernor *Bey*, the person who killed this infidel is Arab . . .[108] or Martin Mustafa. This person has been killed in order to avenge the Muslim killed at such and such place." Hasan the Sailor's program is as follows: to slay ten Bulgarians for each murdered Muslim. He does not differentiate in order to fulfill his goal. No Bulgarian, man, woman, old or young, can escape alive from the axe of Hasan the Sailor until he reaches the number of ten. Hasan the Sailor has become the god of a few districts and Bulgarians tremble when they hear his name. The government, pressed hard by [foreign] officers and civil agents, promises cash awards and two ranks to the officers for the killing of Hasan the Sailor. Yet he cannot be apprehended. The other day three or four members of Hasan the Sailor's band carried out an action which would have taken a Serbian band of a hundred members. The impact of these bands on the Bulgarians is greater than the impact of one hundred thousand troops dispatched by the administration, because these bands kill committee organizers who could not be arrested by the administration, and they thereby deliver shattering blows to the committees. Also, Bulgarians avoid killing Muslims, because they know very well that if they kill a single Muslim at least ten people from their village will be killed. . . . While the Muslims were in a deep sleep, that is to say during the initial phase of the Macedonian question, the [Christian] committees did indeed intimidate the Muslims. This intimidation did not last long, however, and Muslims were awakened in many regions and moved vigorously to avenge the Muslims who were murdered. . . . Please tell the esteemed Sezaî Beyefendi that the Turkish soldiers are the old lion-hearted soldiers that he knows. . . . The Turk's blood has not been frozen, and despite all the evil acts and conspiracies of the administration, the blood of his ancestors has been circulating in his veins.[109]

Shortly after this second memorandum, Dr. Nâzım sent a third and final memorandum on the subject to Paris. In it he stated that he had received approval from all the leading members of the CPU Internal Headquarters, and that a suitable member of the committee should announce the use of bands as a revolutionary tactic of the CPU in the official organ.[110]

The person whom Dr. Nâzım tapped was none other than Ahmed Rıza. The positivist leader wrote the suggested article in the form of an open letter to officers inviting them to establish bands. Many of the regular readers of the Young Turk journals must have been shocked when they saw Ahmed Rıza's signature at the bottom of such an article, since he had staunchly opposed these tactics since 1895. The open letter did no more than restate Dr. Nâzım's ideas as articulated in his memoranda in a more refined language. Ahmed Rıza wrote:

My brother Ali . . . we are aware of developments here that you cannot ascertain there. We know that secret treaties have been signed to partition Central Asia, to appoint a foreign prince to our provinces in Rumelia, to cede Tripoli of Barbary to the Italians. . . . The purpose of action, however, should be to restore the constitutional government. The problem is great, but it is not so difficult that it cannot be solved by a single individual. If a self-sacrificing volunteer comes forward and shoots the sultan to acquire merit in God's sight, the problem will be solved and ended at that moment. Also, by killing a couple of traitors who are Abdülhamid's instruments of crime, the solution of the problem can be facilitated. For such actions nobody should feel obliged to obtain any other person's recommendation or help. A person's finest guide and strongest assistant should be a conscience filled with love for the fatherland.

There is another way to solve this problem: a general rebellion. So far I have been opposed to this method, and I am still against it now. In a country the population of which is composed of elements that possess contradictory political ideas and are affiliated with different faiths, a revolution would only strengthen the tyranny and benefit the foreigners who are seeking a pretext with which to legitimize their intervention. . . . Under these conditions, the only measure that can be taken in order to solve the problem by force is the establishment of bands composed of ten or fifteen courageous Ottomans. . . . These bands will not have recourse to brigandage; on the contrary, they will attempt to rescue the people from their oppressors. You are an officer, and thus you know how to set up and dispatch a platoon. If there is a cunning and conscientious officer like you leading the band, then there will be no risk of its being unsuccessful. Every peasant who hears that a band has been established in a certain place and under the command of a certain officer with the good intention of protecting the property and the rights of the poor, and compelling the administration to comply with the terms of the *sharīʿa* and statutes, will naturally incline toward this band and join it. . . . The troops will not shoot at such a group which has taken up arms for the well-being of the people and the salvation of the state, even if the administration so orders them. Even if the law enforcement officers came upon it, they would act as if they had not seen it. The rich will feed [the members of the band] with pleasure. . . . If a given province were to be placed under the interim administration of eight or ten such bands, that is to say, eight or ten capable officers, then that province could be regarded as having been rescued from the oppression of Abdülhamid. Please give my greetings and regards to those of your comrades in arms whom you know and whose good character you trust, and tell them that in this field we are ready and able to aid them by all means. My dear Ali, please do not remain idle, but work.[111]

In the meantime, the CPU External Headquarters requested its internal counterpart to work toward incorporating the Muslim bands in Macedonia into the CPU organization.[112] Upon receiving this request, the CPU Internal Headquarters first "attached the Muslim bands in various places to the committee [CPU]" and then set up a commission to "attach them to a strong organizational structure in order to use them in accordance with our political ideas and put them under the command of our most suitable members."[113] This commission also prepared two documents setting forth the organization and activities of the CPU bands.

The first document was a memorandum most likely prepared by officers who knew band organizations and strategies well. This document focused on band organization and technical details of band activities such as setting up a base camp, ambush tactics, and night operations.[114] The second document contained the regulations for

CPU bands in action. The most important point in this document was its emphasis upon the political character of the bands. According to the band regulations, CPU members were to lead the CPU bands, to keep records of their actions, correspondence, and ammunition spent in action, and to maintain contact with the CPU branches.[115] The punishment proposed for band members who failed to carry out their duties provides a clear idea of the character of the band organization imagined by the CPU: "There is only a single punishment: execution."[116] In his memoirs Enver Bey stated that he had prepared more detailed regulations for the bands and paramilitary units while conducting band activity during the last days of the revolution.[117]

At the time when the internal and external headquarters agreed on the mobilization of bands in late March 1908, the CPU External Headquarters laid down five other general principles with which the CPU bands were to comply: (1) to act in a very just and humanitarian manner; (2) never to initiate attacks that would cause foreign complaints; (3) to encourage the rich to make cash donations and be generous; (4) to strive to promote the idea of union among the Ottoman elements and to propagate the idea of a parliament; and (5) always to work under the guidelines and instructions of the committee.[118] The CPU also once more underscored the point that the CPU bands were of a political nature and would work "for an honest political idea," and that they should be commanded by competent officers so as to demonstrate to everybody that the bands had no desire other than the implementation of justice and law.[119] Since the CPU Internal Headquarters wished to convert many Muslim bands into CPU bands and to organize new ones, it required its external counterpart to dispatch its military members—men such as Hüsrev Sami and Seyyid Ken'an—as potential commanders.[120] Since events developed very quickly, this scheme could not be put into effect. The CPU Internal Headquarters advised its external counterpart that the "political bands" that would operate under the regulations would be established in mid-June 1908, and that they anticipated significant results from their operations "for various sorts of action."[121]

Upon adopting this new revolutionary tactic, the CPU Internal Headquarters required all its military members to establish contact with Turkish and, if they were inclined to work with them, Muslim Albanian bands operating in Macedonia. A good example of the Muslim bands that became CPU branches and bands was the one formed in Ohrid.

Here a captain, Aziz Bey, who was a member of the Ottoman Freedom Society and the commander of the local troops, met with local notables and persuaded them to form a "Special Muslim Committee" that would operate under the principle of "damage against damage and blood for blood." The locals found this principle in accordance with *Kanuni i Lekë Dukagjini*, the northern Albanian customary law of the fifteenth century which favored retaliation. Captain Aziz Bey and local notables who took part in the venture formed the executive committee. This organization turned a local band, whose role had been to protect the Muslims against IMRO attacks, into its striking force. With the help of the subgovernor of Ohrid and various officers in Monastir, many members of the band were armed with rifles captured from IMRO members during clashes and placed in the military depots in Monastir. As its first activity, the Ohrid Special Muslim Organization's band ambushed and killed three IMRO band members on June 22, 1907, in retaliation for an IMRO attack on a Muslim ranch. The band left a document that read "This is the first initiative of the first Muslim band to do justice and to retaliate." The foreign consuls protested, stating that "a Moslem Committee in Ochrida, formed to counteract the Bulgarian revolutionary movement . . . is in itself a dangerous element . . . [and] [t]he present Kaimakam is believed to be not sufficiently vigilant" in restraining the organization.[122] But the Ottoman authorities did not take any serious action against the Ohrid Special Muslim Organization.

Major Enver Bey and Adjutant-Major Eyüb Sabri (Akgöl), the two leading CPU military leaders, thus turned the organization into a local branch of the CPU, and its band into the CPU band in Ohrid. By making all members take a new CPU oath, the CPU acquired a branch with forty members, most of whom were notables.[123] Fearing a fully-fledged government investigation, the CPU attempted to deny the claim made in the foreign press that the Special Muslim Organization had become a CPU branch.[124] Yet during the revolution Subgovernor Süleyman Kâni and Adjutant-Major Eyüb Sabri organized volunteers into the "CPU Ohrid National Regiment." Under the latter's command the "regiment" took to the mountains.[125]

The CPU also recruited Muslim "criminals and deserters" for its bands. Adjutant-Major Ahmed Niyazi stated in his memoirs that he "granted a pardon" to such criminals and deserters, whom he referred to as "vile blackguards" for their "past crimes," and included them in his band after they took their oaths.[126] Major Enver Bey too included in his band in Tikvesh a deserter who had been engaged in brigandage on the west bank of the Vardar River.[127]

Although the CPU chose Macedonia as its hub for conducting revolutionary activities through its bands, it also attempted to organize bands in Anatolia. Dr. Nâzım took the most important initiative in this field while propagandizing in Izmir. He decided to meet with the famous brigand Çakırcalı (Çakıcı) Mehmed Efe, who had compelled the government to recognize his sphere of influence, and whose power in this sphere was likened by the Ottoman authorities to that of the Zaydī Imāms, the de facto rulers of the mountainous parts of the Yemen.[128] By late 1907 the government resolved "to strike a final blow against Çakırcalı."[129]

In order to win over Çakırcalı Mehmed Efe to their struggle against the regime, the CPU leaders had published an article in *Şûra-yı Ümmet* praising the brigand and maintaining that the real brigand was the government and not Çakırcalı Mehmed Efe.[130] The article further described the brigand as somebody who was "busying himself with reforming certain districts of Aydın Province which had been brutally oppressed under the Hamidian tyranny."[131]

When Dr. Nâzım secretly met with the brigand, he told the latter that "the Europeans had decided to partition [the empire], and if [they] did not save the country, then faith, state, and Islam will be lost, and the chastity and honor of [the Muslims] will be trampled under enemy feet." Before he would join, however, the pious warlord insisted on a *fatwā* permitting him to participate in the CPU's activities against the "caliph." Hence Dr. Nâzım's efforts to recruit him bore no fruit.[132]

Following this failure, the CPU did not abandon efforts to persuade Çakırcalı Mehmed Efe; it continued to publish articles portraying the brigand as a "reformist."[133] With the hope of opening a new front in Western Anatolia during the last days of the revolution, Bahaeddin Şakir asked Edhem Safi, an important member in the

CPU Cyprus organization who knew the brigand, to write a letter to Çakırcalı Mehmed Efe warning him not to trust the government.[134] Edhem Safi drafted such a letter only two days before the repromulgation of the constitution and sent it to Bahaeddin Şakir.[135] The existence of the letter among the private papers of Bahaeddin Şakir reveals that the CPU did not see any point in sending the letter after its triumph.

Likewise in Bursa, the CPU contacted a small band under the command of two officers. During the earliest phases of CPU revolutionary activity, this band took to the mountains and went as far as the suburbs of Izmir.[136] In the turmoil, however, nobody paid any attention to its operations. It was only in Macedonia that significant revolutionary activities were conducted by CPU bands.

In summary, the CPU strategy and its implementation had crystalized by early 1908. The organization was to have a strike force led by junior officers from the ranks between first lieutenant and major. Following the example of the Christian bands in Macedonia, "political" CPU bands were to be established under the command of military members of the organization, and existing Muslim band members were encouraged to join these "political" bands. By winning over the Muslims, these bands were to establish de facto control over the Ottoman provinces in Macedonia. In the meantime, the CPU branches in the cities were to carry out a series of assassinations through the self-sacrificing volunteer branches at their disposal. These branches were given a free hand in killing anyone whom they deemed "seditious." Other branches within the empire were to carry out similar activities in various provinces, thus adding to the expected chaos. The CPU External Headquarters was to smuggle copious propaganda material through the CPU network and was also to counter the Ottoman government's propaganda initiatives in the European press. This propaganda aimed at convincing the European public that the rebellious activities were no more than mutinous actions or brigandage and that they were directed against Europe. There is no doubt that the CPU leaders envisioned a struggle that would last for months.

The main considerations of the CPU leaders following the adoption of the new strategy were threefold: first, to come to terms with the other revolutionary groups in Macedonia, or at least to neutralize them during their action, thereby preventing any Muslim–Christian strife that might trigger intervention by the Great Powers; second, to convince the Great Powers that the movement was not an anti-European and nationalist one; third, to win over the divisions that would eventually be sent against the CPU bands, and to induce the soldiers and officers of these divisions not to open fire on their comrades in arms.

The New CPU Revolutionary Organization

The CPU organization started recruiting both junior officers and civilians to serve in strike forces in the mountains and in the larger cities. The CPU assigned most of these individuals to self-sacrificing volunteer branches. They were to act immediately when given an assignment by their local branch. The membership figure—as many as 100,000—provided by the CPU leaders was far in excess of the true number enrolled.[137]

But there was no need for many thousands of people: the organization was successful in recruiting enough officers to start the intended revolutionary activity. In Salonica alone, the CPU Internal Headquarters recruited 505 members, 319 of whom were junior officers.[138] The total number of CPU members in all the European provinces was approximately 2,000, most of them officers.[139] Some of these officers assumed different posts in Macedonia after their service in a given town came to an end, thus helping the CPU to expand its network.

Many of these officers, like Major Enver Bey in Monastir, Captain Bekir Fikri in Grebená, Adjutant-Major Niyazi Bey in Resen, and Adjutant-Major Eyüb Sabri in Ohrid, possessed formidable authority among the Muslims of their respective regions. They could speak Albanian as well as Turkish and had no problems communicating with Muslims in Macedonia.[140] So when they took to the mountains they easily attracted many Muslim volunteers and secured the wholehearted support of the Muslim population. Major Enver Bey, for example, stayed at the houses of notables. These notables kissed his hands as a sign of their respect for the young major, who had saved them from the attack of an IMRO band a short while before.[141] The notables of Resen "made necessary sacrifices for [Adjutant-Major Ahmed Niyazi's] band"[142] and the Muslims of "Resen and villages surrounding it were all CPU members."[143] The Muslim notables of Chernovo, who welcomed the CPU band with the cry of "Thank God! Finally the nation has dispatched its troops," wanted to hug the commanding officers.[144] In Ohrid it was the notables themselves who organized Adjutant-Major Eyüb Sabri's band, named the "CPU Ohrid National Regiment."[145] Captain Bekir Fikri organized a large band in a couple of hours after making a short speech to the Muslims in Grebená. Those Muslims regarded him as their protector against Greek bands.[146]

In the cities, the CPU recruited junior officers to help carry out assassinations. By organizing these officers into small cells called "self-sacrificing volunteers' branches," the CPU created what it named the "CPU gendarme force."[147] This gendarme force was to retaliate for attacks on any member of the CPU or on the organization as a whole. It was to respond immediately to any attacks on CPU members by assassinating those who had killed or ordered the killing of those members. In the event of a fully-fledged attack aimed at the destruction of the CPU in a given region, all members in the locality were to strike back, because "the body of the committee [was] more sacred than anything."[148]

The CPU leadership also used this force "to annihilate traitors."[149] The self-sacrificing members of this so-called gendarme force were dauntless, fearless, and fanatic fighters ready to carry out any kind of assassination. A good example is Hamdi Efendi, a second lieutenant in the Salonica gendarme garrison and a self-sacrificing volunteer. After the revolution he committed suicide because of his grief that he "had not been able to render the fatherland and the nation any service in their achievement of freedom."[150]

In order to arm this gendarme force with effective weapons, the CPU branches asked the CPU External Headquarters to purchase a quantity of Parabellum shotguns. The CPU External Headquarters proceeded to discuss the matter secretly with Parabellum, but the CPU Internal Headquarters could not wait; it armed its self-sacrificing volunteers with Webley-Scott revolvers. Most of these, however, had defective bullets, and so the branches insisted on purchasing better shotguns for assassinations.[151]

Nonetheless, because of the quick turn of events, all assassinations were in fact carried out with weapons provided by the CPU Internal Headquarters.

The CPU also contacted some branches about using bombs to be sent by the CPU External Headquarters.[152] During the revolutionary activity, the CPU Monastir branch consulted the CPU External Headquarters regarding recourse to artillery bombardment in the event of resistance by the Ottoman authorities. The external headquarters gave its approval and stated that as long as government buildings alone were targeted, such a bombardment would not cause any outcry in Europe. It further instructed the branch that in the event of large-scale activity in the city, foreigners should be diligently protected, and no looting or plundering should take place that would result in complaints from the Christian Ottoman peoples.[153]

Expansion of the CPU Network

The CPU also succeeded in establishing an extremely effective network for carrying out its program of revolution. This expansion in the European provinces of the Ottoman Empire between the merger in September 1907 and the revolution in July 1908 was quite remarkable.

Before the merger the Ottoman Freedom Society had only a single branch, located in Monastir. Thanks to the strenuous work of Major Enver Bey and Captain (later Adjutant-Major) Kâzım (Karabekir) in this town, a branch was established that exceeded the CPU Internal Headquarters in both membership and activity.[154]

Largely as a result of the hard work of the CPU Internal Headquarters and its field officers, the CPU established centers in the cities of Edirne, Durazzo, Iōánnina, Monastir, Salonica, Scutari in Albania, Skopje, and Tirana. In the towns of the Balkans the CPU established significant centers in Chrisoúpolis (Sarışa'ban), Debar, Devin (Ropcoz), Dráma, Edessa (Vodina), Elasson (Alasonya), Elbasan, Elevtheroúpolis (Praviste), Filiatai (Filat), Firzovik, Flōrina, Gevgelija, Gianniza (Yenice Vardar), Gjirokastër (Ergiri), Gnjilane (Gilân), Gostivar, Grebená, Gusinje, Gyanikokastron (Avrethisar), Kačanik, and Karacaabad (north Gianniza). Additional centers were established in Karatova, Kassándra (Kesendire), Kastoria (Kesriye), Katerinē, Kavadarci (Tikveş), Kavála, Kićevo, Kílkis, Koćani, Kolonja (Erseke), Komanova, Kónitsa, Korçë (Görice), Kozánē, Krupišta, Kruševo, Langadas, Leskovik, Margarition (Margaliç), Melnik, Métsobon (Maçova), Mitrovica, Neapolis (Nasliç), Nevrekob, Ohrid, Paramythia (Aydunat), Petrich (Petriç), Pogradec (İstarova), Préveza, Prilep, Priština, Prizren, Ptolemais (Kayalar), Radovište, Razlog, Resen, Sarandë, Serres, Servia (Serfice), Stari Toyran (Doyran), Štip, Struga, Strumica, Tetovo (Kalkandelen), Tírnavos, Tomin bei Peshkëpijë (Debre-i Zîr), Veles (Köprülü), and Véroia (Karaferye).[155]

Among the centers located in cities, the most important were the CPU Internal Headquarters in Salonica, and the Monastir and Skopje branches. Among the centers in towns, the most significant were the Grebená, Ohrid, Resen, and Serres branches.

The CPU Internal Headquarters was composed of Talât Bey, Adjutant-Major Hafız Hakkı, Captain İsmail Canbolad, Manyasizâde Refik, and Major Enver Bey; it was in charge of all administration according to the agreement between the CPU External and Internal Headquarters and the CPU internal regulations.[156]

The Monastir branch played the most important role in the setting up and dispatching of the CPU bands. This branch was under the direction of an executive committee composed of Lieutenant Colonel Sadık Bey, Major Remzi Bey, Captain Habib Bey, First Lieutenant Tevfik Bey, First Lieutenant Yusuf Ziya, and Fahri Bey, the translator at the governor's office.

Even before the merger of the CPU and the Ottoman Freedom Society, the latter had approached the renowned Albanian notable Nexhib (Necib) Draga and asked him to form a branch in Skopje.[157] İbrahim Temo had made Draga a member of the old CUP during the early days of the Young Turk movement.[158] A CPU branch was formed later under the direction of an executive committee composed of Draga, Colonel Galib (Pasinler) Bey, Adjutant-Major Cafer Tayyar (Eğilmez), Mazhar Bey, who was the general secretary of the governor's office, Süreyya Bey, the first-clerk at the local court, and İslâm Bey, a local tax office director. With the inclusion of many Albanian notables it became an important center. The branch's membership exceeded 100 in April 1908, and it played a significant role in stirring up Albanians during the Firzovik (Ferizaj-Ferizović) gathering.[159]

The CPU External Headquarters also established town centers in Macedonia through correspondence. It asked these branches to operate under the CPU Internal Regulations as revolutionary groups.[160]

In addition to putting together an extensive revolutionary network in Macedonia, the CPU also established small cells composed of young civilians in large cities. The CPU gave them different and simple regulations composed of 18 clauses focusing on journal distribution and the collection of donations. Each cell was composed of five men, each assigned to a specific position; they were to enroll further "capable" individuals in their cells, and to disseminate CPU propaganda.[161] Similar cells that the CPU had established before the merger, some composed of young students[162] and others of CPU correspondents,[163] were attached to the CPU Internal Headquarters. These cells and correspondents worked independently of the revolutionary network, and their work was confined to propaganda.

Contingency Planning for the Ottoman Government's Counterrevolutionary Response

Once it became clear that the revolutionary movement had taken root in Macedonia, the CPU decided to disseminate active propaganda in Izmir. Military members of the CPU knew that in the event of unrest in Macedonia, the Ottoman administration would first attempt to use the troops available on the spot to halt the rebellion and would then send more reliable Anatolian troops from Izmir to Salonica by sea to crush the movement. The leaders of the movement confidently predicted that the divisions already in Macedonia would not fire on "national divisions" of volunteers under the command of renowned officers, who were to don special berets bearing the words "self-sacrificing volunteer of the fatherland." By contrast, the attitude of the Anatolian troops that might be sent to Macedonia was one of the greatest worries of the CPU.

The first troops that would be rushed to the region were the first-class reserve divisions in Aydın Province. In order to avoid an armed confrontation with the Anatolian troops, the CPU Internal Headquarters asked Dr. Nâzım to go to Izmir to disseminate active propaganda among the officers and soldiers of the regular and reserve troops in Aydın province.[164]

Under the instructions of the CPU Internal Headquarters, Dr. Nâzım arrived in Izmir in December 1907, aboard a Russian ship carrying pilgrims to Jerusalem.[165] In Izmir he met with one of the founders of the Ottoman Freedom Society, Major Mehmed Tahir. Dr. Nâzım reorganized the CPU branch in Izmir while opening a tobacco shop under the assumed identity of tobacco seller Yakub Ağa, and he constantly traveled in the region as a fortune-teller, porter, and street hawker. He also succeeded in meeting with many officers of the reserve divisions and winning them over. Meanwhile, Major Mehmed Tahir, who was the foremost Ottoman biographical encyclopædia writer, traveled in the region on the pretext of collecting old manuscripts, and likewise met with officers and soldiers.[166]

The CPU Internal Headquarters frequently informed its external counterpart of Dr. Nâzım's successes in carrying out his difficult mission.[167] On the basis of this information, when the CPU External Headquarters issued its communiqué declaring the commencement of the revolution, it commented that it strongly expected that "they [the Aydın reserve divisions] would not open fire on their brothers in religion."[168] Not only did these troops refuse to open fire on their comrades in arms, they actually joined the CPU. This response was clearly a result of Dr. Nâzım's active and successful propaganda and the CPU's long-term planning.

Although the CPU had already decided that it would commence the revolution in Macedonia, it continued its efforts to establish branches in the other parts of the empire. These branches were to assist the committee by taking various forms of action ranging from sending telegrams to the First Chamberlain's office to manifesting the power of the CPU throughout the empire.

In November 1907, some officers in Kalʿa-i Sultaniye (Çanakkale) formed an opposition cell and contacted the CPU External Headquarters, which offered to transform their cell into the Kalʿa-i Sultaniye branch of the CPU.[169] The officers accepted this offer.[170] The CPU then asked them to recruit junior officers in order to carry out revolutionary activities.[171] The branch provided the CPU External Headquarters with information about common complaints among officers and soldiers that could be stressed in CPU propaganda. It also proposed the establishment of an "insurance fund" to be used to support the dependents of the self-sacrificing volunteers, stating that such a fund would facilitate the enrollment of self-sacrificing volunteers.[172]

The CPU External Headquarters sent a traveling agent, Hasan Basri, who was the French correspondence official at the Ottoman Inspector General's Office in Salonica, to reorganize the branches in Northwestern Anatolia and to encourage them to establish small revolutionary cells in towns.[173] Likewise, the CPU Internal Headquarters attempted to establish such a cell in Bandırma in January 1908,[174] and on learning of the existence of dissidents in Bursa, it also attempted to organize them.[175] It did not, however, succeed in organizing a real branch or cell in this latter important city.[176]

In addition to such attempts to establish an effective network close to the capital in Northwestern Anatolia, the CPU External Headquarters asked a medical doctor who had been enrolled in Salonica but later banished to Tripoli of Barbary to found a branch there.[177] Doctor Captain Rauf Bey failed to set up a branch,[178] but under the protection of Receb Pasha, the governor of Tripoli of Barbary, he did form a cell to distribute CPU propaganda material.[179]

Because of strict government control and the weak structure of the branches and cells outside the European provinces of the empire, the CPU by and large failed to carry out any significant activity in these areas to help the revolutionary movement in Macedonia. The only assistance most cells or branches could render was to send telegrams to the First Chamberlain's office and other government offices, thereby helping to create the impression that the CPU possessed an organization throughout the empire and not just in Macedonia. But in contrast to the CPU branches in most of the Asiatic provinces of the empire and in Tripoli of Barbary, the CPU organization in Izmir under the administration of Dr. Nâzım played a key role in the success of the revolution by winning over the troops who were later to be sent against the CPU bands.

The strategy of the CPU organization concentrated entirely on revolutionary activity during this period. The nonrevolutionary branches, correspondents, and cells composed of intellectuals observed the revolution as bystanders. The CPU organization had now become strong enough to strike a major blow at the regime and trigger a revolutionary movement. As Talât Bey declared, in all the European provinces the CPU "has become expansive beyond any expectation"; he added that "the CPU has completed its childhood stage and is about to enter a new phase in which it will make sacrifices of all kinds."[180] Bahaeddin Şakir described the organization's strength as follows:

> We are not like what we were previously. We are working seriously. The present committee is very much stronger than the former committee. Our organization is extremely important. If we deem it necessary we will even use artillery. Our power in Istanbul, however, is not sufficient to bring about [a revolution]. All of us are working vigorously and putting our lives on the line. We are not contented with writing articles and penning empty words. Our self-sacrificing volunteers penetrate to the country's villages, our political bands are on patrol, our strength grows, and our network expands every day.[181]

In short, the CPU organization acquired a very different shape between September 1907 and the revolution of 1908. Until then, it had been a network of scattered branches, most of them outside the empire, that engaged in the distribution of propaganda material. The branches within the country were working against insuperable odds because of the sultan's effective spy network. The cells in Istanbul were thus in no position to assassinate the sultan. The few other domestic CPU branches possessing "self-sacrificing volunteers" could not carry out anything more than a single action. With a new organization and expanded recruitment, however, the CPU had acquired a true "strike force" with which to carry out its long-awaited revolutionary plans.

Factors Precipitating the Young Turk Revolution of 1908

The External Factors: The New Phase of the Macedonian Question

While the CPU was exerting its best efforts to enlist junior military officers to lead CPU bands in the Macedonian countryside and to carry out assassinations in Macedonian towns, new and drastic diplomatic developments took place beginning in late 1907 that helped the CPU leaders to muster more volunteers and to move the Muslim masses, who feared that a European intervention favoring the Christians or even aiming at the detachment of Macedonia from the rest of the empire was imminent.

The revitalized British and Russian interest in Macedonian reforms, the proposals for the replacement of the Mürzteg program with a more extensive and far-reaching reform scheme, and finally the so-called Railway Wars led by Austria-Hungary and Russia provided the CPU with a serendipitous pretext to invite those groups in Macedonia that were deeply anxious about these new developments to work with them to topple the regime, thwarting any foreign intervention.

Although the Liberal party's victory in 1905 had not led to a new British policy on Macedonian reforms,[182] and Sir Edward Grey, the British foreign secretary, had turned a deaf ear to the appeals by organizations such as the Balkan Committee demanding further British involvement,[183] a drastic change occurred during the last days of 1907. The mandates of the civil agents, the financial commission, and the gendarmerie, which were sanctioned by the Ottoman sultan's imperial decree, were about to expire. At this point the British for the first time took the initiative toward implementing reforms in Macedonia. Until then the reform program and its application had been a Russo—Austro-Hungarian initiative, in which the other Great Powers participated only in a secondary fashion.

On December 15, 1907, the ambassadors of the six Great Powers forwarded a joint note-verbale to the Sublime Porte requesting the Ottoman government to extend the duration of the duties of the European civil agents and the financial commission members.[184] The Ottoman response of the same day,[185] which said nothing about such an extension and proposed that the foreign agents of reform in Macedonia be taken into Ottoman service, led the ambassadors to forward an identic note pressuring the Ottoman government to the Sublime Porte on December 22, 1907.[186]

The Great Powers were, however, far from united. Before this second note-verbale was issued, Sir Edward had sent a memorandum to the ambassadors of the other five powers maintaining that "the Ottoman authorities have displayed an utter incapacity to maintain public tranquillity" in Macedonia. He proposed that

> General Degiorgis and the Foreign Staff Officers should be entrusted with a full measure of executive control [and that the powers] should represent to the Sublime Porte that the heavy charges on the Macedonian Budget in respect of the maintenance of the Turkish troops are out of all proportion to the services which, as shown by experience, they can render in the maintenance of public security; and that the only effective means of suppressing the bands lies in the increase upon a large scale of the gendarmerie, the formation of mobile columns of gendarmes, and granting to the officers-in-command executive power of a definite character.[187]

In response to this, a joint Austro-Hungarian and Russian memorandum was delivered to the Foreign Office on January 28, 1908, stating that the two architects of the Mürzteg program were "unable to find in it [the British proposal] any promise of an appreciable improvement in the situation."[188] This led many diplomats working on reform in Macedonia to believe they faced a new impasse.

There now developed a rift between the Austro-Hungarian and Russian Empires. The Dual Monarchy had been proposing a project for a railway from Uvać to Mitrovica, and succeeded in obtaining an imperial decree from the sultan for the construction of this railway.[189] This was a concession that would enable Austria to take advantage of Salonica as an outlet to the Aegean, and it ended Austro-Russian leadership in the Macedonian reform program.[190] The Austrians contended that their railway project was of purely economic significance and that it was covered by the 25th article of the Berlin Congress; they insisted that they had not given any concession to the Ottomans in connection with the Macedonian reforms.[191] Nevertheless, many politicians believed that it was "inconceivable . . . that Turkey should have given anything without something in return."[192] Although available documents do not reveal a secret deal between the Ottoman and Austro-Hungarian governments, the latter's unexpected move at a very critical juncture catalyzed a rapprochement between Great Britain and Russia regarding the Macedonian reforms.

Under the pressure of a furious public opinion fomented by the anti-German press, which was hinting at a German hand in the Austrian initiative, the Russian government took two important steps. On the one hand, it proposed a "Danube-Adriatic Railway" to challenge the proposed Austrian railway, and on the other, it moved to work more closely with the British toward a new reform scheme for Macedonia. As British ambassador Nicolson stated, "It is to Great Britain that the Russian public, and I might perhaps also add the Russian government, now look as being the coadjutor best adapted to further the cause of justice and of peace in Macedonia."[193]

The British position became clearer when a long discussion took place in the House of Commons. Some members of the Parliament argued that the most important result of the Austrian railway scheme "was that the Murzteg [*sic*] programme was killed," stating that the scheme itself was a "diplomatic bomb." These were strong accusations against the Ottoman administration.[194] Sir Edward Grey, who spoke like "a Gladstonian,"[195] made the most important statement:

> The situation in Macedonia in our opinion was so bad, and what is even more, the prospect of that situation was so bad, that it was absolutely necessary that some proposal likely to be effective in touching the real evil in Macedonia—the crimes of violence by bands— should be put forward without delay, and so we put it forward. . . . Everyone who has read the Press in the last fortnight will be aware that a new situation has arisen from the railway project which has lately received an Iradé from the Sultan. . . . In discussing the Macedonian question you are never far from the Turkish question. The Turkish question has more than once led to a European War. . . . If a Turkish Governor were appointed for a fixed term of years—a man whose character and capacity were accepted and recognized by the Powers—and if he had a free and willing hand and his position were secure, I believe that the whole Macedonian question might be solved. . . . I said a Turkish Governor, whose character and capacity were recognized and accepted by the Powers— I mean a Governor appointed with the consent of the Powers, irremovable without their consent, and secure in his appointment for a term of years.[196]

For those who knew that the insistence of the Great Powers' representatives on the appointment of governors with their consent had caused the failure of the Istanbul (Tersane) Conference in 1876–1877, and had precipitated the Russo-Turkish War of

1877–1878, Sir Edward's proposal was one that obviously would be found entirely unacceptable by any Ottoman government in office.

Sir Edward's new proposal as presented to the foreign ministers of the Great Powers also included the provisions that "[i]n order to render the Governor independent of the control of the palace, his pension should be guaranteed by the Powers," and that "the Turkish troops at present kept by the Macedonian Budget should be largely reduced in number."[197]

From this point until July 27, 1908, despite their differences on various details of the Macedonian reform program, Great Britain and Russia began to work together to draft a new and expansive reform scheme to be implemented in this sore spot of European diplomacy.[198] The most important aspect of this "diplomatic revolution" was the direct intervention of Great Britain in a matter in which it did not have any immediate self-interest. Many Ottoman diplomats believed that the transformation of the Anglo-Russian *détente* into a rapprochement, and the hints of its becoming an entente in the near future, would spell the beginning of the end of Ottoman rule in Macedonia. The sultan took a similar view of the Anglo-Russian rapprochement and was extremely alarmed. He accordingly issued an imperial decree on March 13, 1908, renewing the mandates of the foreign agents of reform in Macedonia until July 12, 1914,[199] hoping to prevent the British from turning the reform scheme into an Anglo-Russian undertaking.

The Mürzteg program, though hated by all Ottoman statesmen and intellectuals, had been a relatively conservative intervention, thanks to Austria-Hungary's leading role in it. It excluded those subprovinces of Kosovo and Monastir heavily inhabited by Muslims, as well as the entire provinces of Edirne and Iōánnina, which the Bulgarians and Greeks coveted for themselves. In addition, the status of the foreign agents was only an advisory one, and both the civil agents and the members of the Financial Commission were subordinated to an Ottoman inspector general. As a result, they were ineffective tools of reform in the face of evasive Ottoman tactics aimed at gaining time. In contrast to this relatively benign arrangement, a return to the Salisbury-Ignatiev line, with its demand for widespread reforms to resettle the "Eastern Question," would worsen the already unstable Ottoman position.

The diplomats in the European foreign ministries could not have anticipated that their discussions of "Macedonian reform" and the drastic change of leadership in this field, with Great Britain replacing Austria-Hungary, would provide the CPU with an effective propaganda weapon and thus help to precipitate the revolution of 1908. Ironically, it was the CPU more than any other political party in the Balkans that benefited from these changes in European diplomacy toward Macedonian reform.

The first European initiatives in November 1907 seemed alarming to the CPU External Headquarters. It discussed the matter with its internal counterpart. Since the CPU did not yet possess a band organization and had still to adopt the new activist program, the CPU External Headquarters' proposals were limited to mounting protests by organizing conferences in Paris; these were to demonstrate to the European public that "the civil agents did not protect the Muslim population," and to warn the Europeans "how the Muslims will retaliate against Macedonian independence."[200]

In March 1908, following Sir Edward's speech in the House of Commons[201] and the announcement of the British proposals for Macedonian reforms, the CPU External Headquarters organized a meeting of all central committee members and decided to take action against these proposals that aimed at "the partition and extinction of the Ottoman state and expulsion of Turks from Europe."[202] The CPU External Headquarters declared that the implementation of the British reform proposals would terminate Turkish existence in Europe:

Macedonia's independence means the loss of half of the Ottoman Empire and, therefore, its complete annihilation. As is known to our brother, without Macedonia in between, Albania will naturally be lost. Since our border will have to retreat to the gates of Istanbul, the capital cannot remain in Istanbul. The removal of our capital from Europe to Asia would exclude us from being among the powers of Europe and make us a second or even a third class Asiatic power. . . . If, Heaven forfend, we lose Rumelia, then because of the vastness of Anatolia, the fact that people are dispersed [throughout that area], and the lack of railways, we would need more than six months to transport troops to a given point. Thus Ottoman sovereignty will be reduced to the level of Iranian power. . . . Since the Macedonian Question is the Question of the Existence of the Turks, we presume that for a sincere government it should be preferable to take the chance of a great war instead of losing Macedonia [and] Rumelia. Alas! What can we expect from this filthy government? . . . Because today governments are controlled by parliaments and the life of the individual has gained enormous importance, no parliament would grant an authorization to a government for the killing of forty or fifty thousand Europeans.[203]

The CPU External Headquarters also developed a plan of action for Macedonia. The Muslims of Macedonia were to occupy post offices in various districts and were to tell the Ottoman administration that "they will not accept an independent governor either foreign or Muslim, and will never agree to their fatherland's partition and its placing under foreign administration." They were also to go to foreign consulates in the region and tell the diplomats that "they had decided to retaliate against the foreign governments' initiative to snatch their fatherland from their hands even if the Ottoman administration approves [such a plan]"; they were further to state to the diplomats that "the Ottomans who moved to Rumelia with seventy people will not leave Rumelia until they are reduced to that number," and that "it was foreign intervention that had caused the present massacres." The CPU External Headquarters also proposed that in the initial stages of the movement nobody should mention the term "constitution," and that in order to confuse the sultan and the government the popular motto should be "we will not give our fatherland to the enemy." The CPU External Headquarters also urged the officer members to fight against the bands with more enthusiasm, including the Greek bands which had been tolerated because they fought mainly against the IMRO bands.[204]

The CPU Internal Headquarters disagreed with its external counterpart on many points. The former assumed that implementation of the British proposals would take a long time because of squabbling among the Great Powers, and it felt that the CPU External Headquarters' plan was not practical. Talât Bey maintained that the occupation of the post offices and subsequent popular declarations against the Ottoman government would lead to the arrest of all the CPU provocateurs. He also opposed the idea of appealing to the foreign consulates, which, he claimed, would make the Ottoman administration more suspicious.

The counterplan of the CPU Internal Headquarters was as follows:

1. To eradicate the bodies with a revolver shot or a dagger thrust of various cursed government officials who are known for theft and corruption and are contaminated with villainy, and whose scandalous activities are also known to the European officials here, and to leave at the place of assassination an appeal with the emblem and the seal of the committee explaining the reasons for their assassination. By the application of this method the committee will make known its strong presence in Macedonia, and also no member of it will be arrested by the government. . . . Also, the execution of eight or ten [government] spies whose vileness is known to all in Salonica and its subprovinces will result in no such characters' setting foot here.

2. Following these executions, which will take place in important centers such as Salonica, Monastir, Skopje, and Serres, a *mémoire* will be composed against the speech of the British foreign secretary and the nonsense that a British member of Parliament uttered in the House of Commons against the Muslims. This *mémoire*, written on CPU letterhead which will also bear the seal of the committee, will be mailed to the aforementioned minister from one of the Macedonian cities, and copies of it will be sent to the Great Powers' prime ministers, foreign ministers, and ambassadors in Istanbul. . . .

3. To form mixed bands, for the time being composed of [Kutzo-] Vlachs and Muslims, and later to include Greeks and Bulgarians. . . .

4. To pursue the Greek and Bulgarian [the IMRO] bands with great vigor and annihilate them, and to find ways to get the Greeks and Bulgarians to join our committee. . . . One of our other decisions is to set up an organization of bands. We want this done immediately.

Since implementing these measures would not put any CPU members at risk, the CPU Internal Headquarters proposed that they be put into effect immediately. It insisted that the suggestions of the CPU External Headquarters be carried out only "when the Europeans move to pressure and threaten the Ottoman government."[205]

Had the Reval meeting of June 1908 between the Russian tzar and the British king not taken place, the CPU would have commenced its campaign to foment unrest at a relatively late date. This meeting, however, not only provided the CPU with the convincing propaganda thesis that a European intervention led by Great Britain and Russia was imminent, but also impelled the leaders and members of the CPU to risk all and start the revolution.

The Internal Factors: Disgust Toward Foreign Intervention, the Culture of Political Participation, and Mutinies in the Army

In early June 1908 the CPU was quite confident of its strike force, with its bands in the rural areas and mountains and its self-sacrificing volunteers in towns. This strike force was to set in motion the beginnings of the revolution in the region, to be followed by a CPU invitation to the people to join the movement and send telegrams to the capital demanding the reopening of the parliament and reinstatement of the Ottoman Constitution of 1876.

The CPU leaders had reason to expect that many Muslims would join a movement aimed at saving the fatherland from foreign intervention or from partition. Nevertheless, organizing populations of entire subprovinces and villages and leading them in demonstrations in favor of the constitution and other forms of protest demanded extensive propaganda work. The propaganda of the CPU did indeed play an important role in winning over the Muslims. The Christian population initially watched passively, but joined the demonstrations and telegram campaigns once the Young Turks seemed to have gained the upper hand against the overwhelmed local authorities. The CPU's success in striking deals with various Christian organizations and in neutralizing others, either by implicit threat or by explicit demonstrations of power, persuaded the Christian masses to join the movement at the hour of its triumph, or at least not to oppose it.

But the CUP's success in mobilizing Muslim and non-Muslim masses cannot be credited to its propaganda activity alone. Undoubtedly, the unique situation in Macedonia and Albania helped the CPU to achieve this quite complex and exacting goal. Unlike other provinces of the Ottoman Empire, Macedonia enjoyed relative freedom during the last years of the Hamidian era. The application of the Mürzteg program with the presence of foreign civil agents, officials, and officers collecting the complaints of the Christian elements, the widespread discussions of reform proposals, the emergence of bands that created safe havens, and the Ottoman government's response of dispatching large numbers of more capable but less loyal officers to the region, combined to create an atmosphere very different from that in the empire's other provinces.[206]

In Macedonia banned publications were openly read in cafés,[207] and officers had the prerogative of traveling almost anywhere they wanted, ostensibly in pursuit of the bands; thus they could easily disseminate propaganda. In other parts of the empire a banned newspaper was more dangerous than a time bomb, and no officer could obtain leave even to quit his garrison town. The opposition thus found exceptionally fertile ground in Macedonia. CPU propaganda foretelling foreign intervention or Christian domination reflected the uneasy feelings and deep-seated fears of the Muslim population in general, and of the officers in the region in particular. Foreign intervention, which was no more than an abstract idea in the capital, and not even an issue in the Asiatic provinces (except the so-called six-provinces in Eastern Anatolia), was embodied in the actual presence of foreign officers and officials in Macedonia. These foreigners were listening to the complaints of the local Christians and putting them before the Ottoman Inspector General in Salonica for rectification. The memoirs of the officers who led the CPU activities are accordingly filled with resentful comments expressing disgust toward "arrogant" foreign representatives "bossing them around in their own land."[208]

An unexpected result of the foreign intervention was its contribution to the creation of a peculiar type of political participation. The relatively prosperous Muslim population in Macedonia, encouraged by the example of the presentation of complaints on behalf of the Christian population to the inspector general, ventured to submit repeated local demands on various issues to the Ottoman authorities. To make such demands was unheard of elsewhere in the empire. As we saw during the initial stages of the Erzurum revolt, the Ottoman governor accepted a petition from the locals requesting their exemption from the new taxes only at gunpoint. In Diyar-ı Bekir and many other places, people could send telegrams to the authorities only after occupying the post offices. In Macedonia, however, sending petitions to the authorities on behalf of the entire population of a village, town, or sometimes even a large city like Monastir was quite a normal practice.[209] By capitalizing on this practice of lodging endless demands with the authorities, the CPU succeeded in motivating people to demonstrate and to send telegrams demanding the restoration of the Ottoman constitution. This aspect of the Young Turk Revolution has been almost totally ignored. An exception was a British diplomat who observed that the Young Turk revolution "was rather such a revolt as can be paralleled in Spanish-American politics—the revolt of a progressive and prosperous province against the spoliations and humiliations to which it is subjected by a corrupt clique in the capital city."[210]

Like Macedonia, Albania, too, enjoyed a relatively more open political environment. Although in 1881 the Ottoman government had put an end to the Albanian provisional administration that had virtually governed most provinces inhabited by Albanians, it was unable to reestablish full control over these regions. The sultan preferred to win over the Albanians, whom he considered a loyal and reliable force absolutely necessary for the maintenance of Ottoman rule in the European provinces,[211] through a policy of granting privileges, employing numerous Albanians in the central and local administrations, and showing greater tolerance. The midlevel local administrative and military posts mediating between the Muslim Albanian masses and the central government, such as those of the Albanian *bayrakdars*, served as a device to increase political participation for the Albanians. On many occasions the holders of these posts, who were encouraged by gatherings of Albanian notables, went so far as to demand that the central government leave the enforcement of law and the protection of the country to them. Although the central government rejected such demands, it never took strong measures against the Albanians who congregated and made such demands, and it limited itself to giving "necessary advice."[212] These meetings of Albanians, and their subsequent submission of demands to the Sublime Porte—or directly to the imperial palace for greater authority—were common events in the region. We shall see how the CPU exploited them.

Another internal development that aided the CPU's triumph was the intense uneasiness created among the troops by irregular payment, arbitrarily extended terms of service, and the refusal of applications for leave. Beginning in March 1908 the CPU resolved to incite the soldiers to organize meetings in order to demand their "legal rights."[213] As the French military attaché was later to comment, all these mutinies started and ended in the same manner. First the soldiers refused to obey their superiors; then they gathered in the nearest mosque, whence they marched to the local post office, occupied it, and sent a telegram to the sultan. The response was always the same: "Imperial greetings, and recognition and acceptance of their demands."[214]

The central government grew suspicious of these expanding mutinies as it attempted to find money to meet the demands and to compel the local authorities to halt the riots.[215] But by the time the local authorities finally uncovered the truth that these activities were organized under "secret instructions of the conspiratorial committee,"[216] it was too late. The CPU's clever stratagem for exploiting the tensions in the army helped the committee in two ways. First, as Adjutant-Major Ahmed

Niyazi remarked, the troops who received their payments and made their voice heard attributed their success to the power of the committee that had prodded them to mutiny. In particular, the committee's successful efforts to prevent the government from sending reservists from the European provinces to Mecca and Medina boosted its image.[217] Second, by stirring up large numbers of troops, the CPU created the illusion of having a strength far beyond its real power. The mutinies spread throughout Macedonia and Albania during the revolution and caused great confusion in the capital, where the central government could not distinguish between direct CPU actions and mutinies carried out by troops incited by CPU members.[218]

CPU Propaganda prior to and during the Revolution

Following the merger of the CPU with the Ottoman Freedom Society in September 1907, the new organization's propaganda activity gained momentum. *Şûra-yı Ümmet* and *Mechveret Supplément Français* remained the main organs of propaganda, and members in the branches had "a very strong desire to read them."[219] Any delay in publishing these journals or in smuggling them into the empire provoked the "rage" of members who considered them "nourishment for their souls."[220] For the first time since the onset of the Young Turk movement, two Young Turk journals enjoyed a steady, attentive, and enthusiastic readership. The CPU Internal Headquarters collected donations to publish *Şûra-yı Ümmet* more frequently and in a larger format, but the outbreak of the revolution disrupted this project.[221]

During this period *Şûra-yı Ümmet* came to focus entirely on the Macedonian question and attempted to stir up officers and Macedonian Muslims. According to the central organ, "the European intervention [had] caused massacres in Macedonia, and both the Hamidian administration and Europe [were] responsible for the blood that [had been] shed in Macedonia: the former [had] caused the [Macedonian] Question and the latter [had] stirred up the Christians."[222] The foreign gendarme was a creation of "Christian fanaticism" led by Great Britain and was in reality "a crusade gendarme."[223] *Şûra-yı Ümmet* further maintained that the Muslims "who have been the real and legitimate sovereign of Macedonia for centuries"[224] should go to war,[225] and it asserted that either Abdülhamid II would be deposed or Macedonia would be lost.[226] The CPU therefore invited all the Muslims of Macedonia to act according to its plan:

O unlucky Macedonian Muslims! What are we going to do about this disaster? To await our salvation from Abdülhamid and his ministers and viziers who are his accomplices in treason is as pointless and vain as crying before a tomb. The Bulgarians who compose one-fifth of our population in Macedonia gained a right of priority thanks to the gun that they used. The Greeks who observed this fact resorted to arms. Today Bulgarian and Greek elements have been recognized in Macedonia. Nobody even speaks about the Muslims who form the majority, and finally we shall be left in the hands of an administration which, by cutting all our ties with the Ottoman administration, will leave us in slavery. Only one alternative lies before us here. It is to demonstrate our existence. With mass assemblies we should tell the political agents of the Great Powers that neither England's intervention nor that of any other power in Ottoman domestic politics can be accepted. Because we are the sovereigns of this land. Enough now: demonstrate our existence.[227]

At the same time, the concession granted to Austria-Hungary to build a railway was denounced as a secret deal between the sultan and the foreigners: "Look! The foreigners are invading our fatherland through 'imperial decrees.' . . . Therefore, there are two things that we can do: either put Abdülhamid under restraint and dethrone him, or accept being the slaves of foreigners!"[228]

The great demand for revolutionary periodicals prompted the CPU to publish clandestinely a revolutionary journal in Monastir. The CPU Monastir branch obtained three lithograph publishing plants, and started to publish a journal called *Neyyir-i Hakikat* (The Sun of the Truth) as an official CPU organ.[229] Filled with fiercely worded and inflammatory articles written by officers, it deeply influenced its readers.[230] It was claimed that "reading a single issue of it was enough to move one against traitors, physically and materially."[231] Since this was the first CPU journal published within the empire, it boosted the CPU's efforts to disseminate propaganda, and also enhanced the image of the CPU. For a while, the Ottoman authorities had difficulty believing that a Young Turk journal was being published clandestinely in Monastir, and when they decided to take serious measures against its publication and distribution,[232] it was already too late. After publishing the first nine issues as an underground journal, the CPU Monastir branch started to publish *Neyyir-i Hakikat* openly as a CPU organ on the day after the restoration of the constitution.[233]

The CPU External Headquarters began to send propaganda pamphlets to Macedonia in bulk in order to encourage the large number of members there. Ömer Naci's fierce *Hayye-ale-l-felâh*, which invited Muslims in the European provinces to rebel in order to save their fatherland from falling under Christian domination, and Ahmed Rıza's *Vazife ve Mes'uliyet: Asker*, which begged the military to play a more significant role in society, began to pour into CPU branches in Macedonia.[234] The CPU External Headquarters also sent old CUP pamphlets such as *İmamet ve Hilâfet Risâlesi*,[235] challenging the sultan's authority on Islamic grounds, for the CPU Internal Headquarters to distribute to pious Muslims.[236]

In addition to journals and pamphlets, the CPU smuggled large numbers of appeals into Macedonia and distributed them during the revolution. "Taking the necessities of the time into consideration," separate appeals to Muslims and non-Muslim Ottomans that had been prepared by the CPU before the merger were distributed in large numbers.[237] As has already been seen,[238] wording attacking Christians was now omitted from the appeals addressed to Muslims. These edited appeals targeted different groups and thus had different themes. As a British consul stated, "in seeking recruits among Turks of lower orders, the League [CPU] announces its intention of restoring the Sheriat (Islamic Sacred Law), whereas in all appeals to the educated classes the intention is expressed of re-establishing the Constitution of 1876."[239] The CPU External Headquarters also prepared appeals to the peasants,[240] and members of the CPU Monastir branch who were familiar with "the morals and feelings of the Albanians"[241] edited appeals addressed to them. Right up to the triumph of the revolution, the CPU External Headquarters busied itself drafting different types of appeals and played a very significant role in the preparation of the propaganda material that was disseminated.[242]

During the period in question, October 1907 through July 23, 1908, the CPU distributed three types of appeals. Those addressing the Muslim population were edited versions of a widely distributed appeal drafted in the fall of 1907.[243] The second type, the general appeals addressing the population as a whole, headed *Umum Ahaliye* (To the entire population), were made available to officers, officials, townsmen, and peasants alike by the CPU organization. These appeals proclaimed that the CPU had "gathered all its brothers, sons of the same fatherland, under the banner of unity and friendship, and had made everyone love each other"; they called upon all to obey the committee, cautioning that "the punishment for those who act against the warnings and instructions of the committee will be severe and swift."[244] The third type of appeal addressed specific groups, such as Christians, peasants, or Macedo-Bulgarians; these were distributed to the relevant component of the population. For example, an appeal headed "To all our Christian compatriots" acknowledged the "righteous blood shed by all compatriots in the past ten, fifteen years," but at the same time it expressed the CPU's "deep regret" that the Christians had brought "religious grievances into play, and each of them had set out to pursue his national interest [by shedding] his brothers' blood." It averred that the CPU's purpose was "to wrest the constitution from the hands of the tyrants and robbers . . . and to sit together with representatives of [its] Christian brothers in the National Assembly."[245] When taken as a whole, these appeals, much like earlier propaganda, expressed contradictory themes.

All the propaganda material and appeals smuggled into Macedonia were distributed through an extremely effective network that worked like a sophisticated mail office system, with distribution branches in strategic locations.[246] This network enabled the CPU to distribute its propaganda material swiftly over a region extending from Scutari in Albania to Edirne.

The Negotiations between the CPU and Other Organizations in Macedonia

The 1907 Congress of Ottoman Opposition Parties had allegedly provided the CPU with the support of various Ottoman peoples for the purpose of revolutionary activity. The final agreement, however, represented nothing more than a tactical alliance between the CPU and the Dashnaktsutiun. All the other organizational signatories of the resolutions were mere window-dressing, giving the impression that a wide range of Ottoman elements had formed a common front against the current regime.

The CPU's choice of Macedonia as the center of revolutionary activity, and its plan to start the revolution there, rendered the tactical alliance with the Dashnaktsutiun obsolete. This alliance could be of very little help in a revolution in Macedonia, since few Armenians lived in the region, and the Dashnaktsutiun had no operational presence among them.[247] The CPU was well aware that for the sake of the revolution, and to prevent the European powers from intervening, it had to come to terms with the Christian band organizations operating in Macedonia. If it could not reach an understanding with these organizations, it at least had to be able to neutralize them during the revolution in order to avoid any clashes between its own bands and those of the Christians. Moreover, the CPU knew that it had to win over Albanians, and to receive support from other less important groups such as the Kutzo-Vlachs, if it was to prove to the European powers that its movement was not a Muslim rebellion but rather an Ottoman movement supported by a variety of groups. Though these goals looked straightforward on paper, they were extremely difficult to achieve in practice.

First, the CPU had come to terms with Macedo-Bulgarian, Greek, and Serbian band organizations that had categorically refused to work with the Young Turks or turned a deaf ear to the invitations of the Young Turk committees. Reaching an understanding with the first two organizations, the main actors in the so-called Macedonian struggle, was of the utmost importance to the Young Turks. The right wing of the IMRO had turned down the invitation to join the CPU-Dashnaktsutiun tactical alliance, and the Greek and Serbian bands had not even been invited to the Second Congress of Ottoman Opposition Parties on the grounds that they were pawns of the Greek and Serbian governments. The Ligue Hellénique in Paris, the only Greek organization invited to the congress, refused to participate. In addition, the Greek Patriarchate in Istanbul was opposed to Greek cooperation with the Young Turks.

Second, the CPU had to convince the Albanian organizations, bands, and notables, together with the Kutzo-Vlach organizations that the Ottoman government had backed against the IMRO, and the Greek and Serbian band organizations. Among all the organizations active in Macedonia, the Greek, Serbian, and to a certain degree Kutzo-Vlach organizations stood out as monolithic. An agreement with an authorized representative would bind all the respective band members. As for the other organizations, the CPU considered the IMRO the most important organization with which it should come to terms. The IMRO was torn by factionalism, and during the period preceding the Young Turk Revolution the factions were at each other's throats. This conflict enabled the CPU to secure the support of at least the left wing of the IMRO. Coming to a general understanding with all Albanian notables, opposition organizations abroad, and bands in the mountains was difficult, since they represented not a monolithic movement but groups with divergent and conflicting agendas.

Immediately after the merger between the CPU and the Ottoman Freedom Society, the CPU External and Internal Headquarters began to discuss the terms to be presented to the various organizations in Macedonia. The CPU Internal Headquarters proposed that the CPU offer the reinstatement of "Midhat Pasha's Constitution," thus guaranteeing equality to all Ottomans as a basis for any agreement with "the communities in Macedonia." The members of the CPU External Headquarters countered that this was "an ideal solution; however, the participation of the [Christian] committee members [on those grounds] was impossible." They therefore stipulated that, in the event that the band organizations refused to join the movement, the CPU should attempt to "win over the masses instead of the committee members."[248] The CPU adhered to this principle throughout its negotiations with the parties active in Macedonia. At the negotiations the CPU offered the representatives of these organizations equality under a constitutional regime that would replace the Hamidian autocracy and put an end to the sectarian and nationalist strife in Macedonia. As expected, the main organizations did not accept the CPU's offer. In the spring of 1908, however, no revolutionary committee could challenge the CPU on the ground.

Capitalizing on the weakness of these organizations, and exploiting the divisive power struggle within the IMRO, the CPU neutralized the right wing of the IMRO and struck a deal with Jane Sandanski, the leader of its left wing, commonly known as the Serres group. Sandanski had become the most wanted man in Bulgaria because of his comrade Panitsa's assassination of Boris Sarafov and Ivan Garvanov, and the CPU took advantage of this situation. The CPU also struck a deal with the so-called Macedonian constitutionalists publishing *Odrinski glas*. Although these groups were not very representative of the Macedo-Bulgarian organizations, the deals that the CPU was able to cut with them provided it with a weapon to use against the Greeks. The CPU's efforts toward a rapprochement with the Greek organizations did not bear any fruit because of the stiff opposition of the Greek Patriarchate in Istanbul and the Greek government in Athens. The patriarchate viewed such an alliance as a threat to "Hellenism," and the Greek government's hesitance stemmed from its skepticism regarding the strength of the Young Turks. A failed Young Turk revolt with Greek support would irreversibly harm the delicate Ottoman–Greek relationship. But by playing the Macedo-Bulgarian card and pointing to an alleged alliance with the Macedo-Bulgarians, the CPU was able to compel the Greek government and all the Greek bands to adopt a neutral stance and avoid any clash with the Young Turks.

By contrast, the CPU leaders undertook no serious negotiations with the Serbians; they did not do so because the latter were not capable of posing a threat to the CPU since they did not have the strength to confront the CPU bands or the Albanian supporters of the Young Turks. The Serbian organizations were surprised by the revolutionary developments, since the CPU had made no official overtures to them; they too adopted a neutral stance, and they were left with no alternative but to accept the *fait accompli*.

The CPU also succeeded in striking deals with certain Albanian bands, and some of these joined the CPU bands during the revolution. The CPU secured active support from a large number of Albanian notables and came to an understanding with the Albanian Bashkimi Society in Bucharest. The presence of Albanians on the side of the CPU made a very significant impact on the sultan when he finally decided to yield to the demands of the CPU in July 1908.

In addition to these ethnic groups, the Jewish community, with a sizable population in Salonica, had supported the Young Turks from the start of their movement. The Jewish support, however, was of less importance than the parts played by the aforementioned groups.

Negotiations Between the CPU and the Macedo-Bulgarian Organizations

The CPU attached great importance to reaching an understanding with Macedo-Bulgarian[249] organizations because they played the dominant role in band activities in Macedonia. The CPU viewed an understanding with them as a key determinant of the success of the revolution. It also attempted to convince the Bulgarian government, which had influence over the right wing of the IMRO, that its movement was not anti-Bulgarian but rather was aimed at reestablishing a constitutional regime in which Macedo-Bulgarians too would enjoy rights and liberties.[250] To this end the CPU Monastir branch kept in close contact with the Bulgarian Consul Nedkov, providing him with information on the development and goals of the movement.[251]

The decision of the right wing of the IMRO to refuse to participate in the tactical alliance between its longtime revolutionary associate Dashnaktsutiun and the CPU had been taken at its Kyustendil Congress in March 1908, and this led the CPU to believe that a rapprochement with the Macedo-Bulgarian organizations would be extremely difficult. The left wing of the IMRO was not represented at the Kyustendil Congress. The right wing, which had fallen under the control of the Vŭrkhovists and was backed by Bulgaria after the 1904 schism within the organization, had a dominant position at the congress, and it would not accept "Midhat Pasha's Constitution."[252] Such acceptance was the CPU's bottom line in its bargaining, and the basis for any negotiations about a common front. The strongest section of the left wing of the organization, the Serres group, had gradually become independent after the Rila Congress of 1905 and advocated socialist decentralization; this group was ready to accept the CPU's terms for a tactical alliance because of its extremely difficult situation at the time of the Young Turk Revolution. The left wing of the IMRO, with its claim to be the only genuine Macedonian organization defending the rights of Macedonians, as opposed to unification with one Balkan power or another, would be an invaluable ally for the CPU, since it would manifest the brotherhood of all Ottomans against the Hamidian regime.

When the CPU approached the IMRO, the latter was in total disarray. The assassination of Sarafov and Garvanov had put an end to all hopes for the establishment of a common front that would include all groups, and the Rila Congress, convened to reorganize the Macedo-Bulgarian movement, ended by denouncing and expelling Sandanski, the leader of the Serres group.[253] Although it proclaimed that "evolutionary tactics [were] absurd and must be declared alien to the Organization,"[254] the reasonable decision of the Rila Congress to halt band activities for a period and to replace the bands with "a number of instructors . . . to train the population" had the effect of giving the left wing's bands the upper hand. This decision was also in accordance with the policy of the new Bulgarian Foreign Minister General Stefan Paprikov, who for the moment opposed the presence of Macedonian bands in Bulgaria in order to show Bulgarian support for the British reform proposals. Despite its claims to absolute independence,[255] the right wing of the IMRO could not afford to enter into a serious conflict with Bulgaria. Thus in the two sections of Macedonia controlled by the right wing of the IMRO, Monastir and Skopje, the CPU did not face any real threat of armed confrontation from the IMRO.

A Serbian diplomatic report based on information provided by a reliable Young Turk stated that the Young Turks made a last attempt to come to terms with the right wing of the IMRO. According to this report the CPU sent Cevad [Mehmed Cavid] Bey to Sofia in April 1908; under the pretense of taking his wife for medical treatment, he met there with the representatives of the right wing, but the negotiations yielded no results. The right wing was not satisfied with the restoration of the constitution alone, since its goal was autonomy for Macedonia.[256] Although it is difficult to verify this account in its entirety, it is unquestionably true that the CPU understood the difficulty of coming to terms with the right wing of the IMRO, and thus it decided to strike a deal with the left wing of the movement, which was active in Serres, Salonica, and Strumica. Although there were other substantial bands in the two latter regions, the left wing's main military force was Sandanski's band in Serres.

The emergence of a new Macedo-Bulgarian group, the so-called constitutionalists, helped the Young Turks to reach an agreement with the left wing. This group started publishing the journal *Odrinski glas* on January 20 [February 2], 1908. Edited by Angel Tomov, this journal espoused a line similar to that of the left wing of the IMRO. The journal's praise for the Serres group's "open letter" clearly signaled an intention to establish close ties with the left wing.[257] However, the journal's strict antirevolutionary stance,[258] and its criticism of the left wing's assassination of Sarafov and Garvanov, delayed the establishment of stronger ties with the left wing in general, and Sandanski in particular.

Odrinski glas called the European concert "a tragicomedy,"[259] and in general it promoted the ideas of a young socialist, Pavel Deliradev, who claimed that neither foreign intervention nor unification with Bulgaria would solve the Macedonian problem. Deliradev believed that the problem should be solved by the democratization of the Ottoman Empire. He further stated that a union among the progressive elements of the empire, including the Young Turks, should be formed to achieve this democratization.[260]

The Second Congress of Ottoman Opposition Parties, held in Paris in December 1907, had given Deliradev a serendipitous opportunity to defend a union with the Young Turks more vigorously.[261] According to Deliradev, the activities of the right wing of the IMRO were "a revival of Vŭrkhovizm"; he argued that "the official patriots in Bulgaria, Serbia, and Greece have always tried to use [the guerilla movement] for their own purposes"[262] and that the right wing leaders' statements about "a war of liberation" were "meaningless talk."[263] As for the revolution, *Odrinski glas* proposed that a "new road" should be taken:

> First of all, this revolutionary movement absolutely cannot depend on foreign intervention, be it Bulgarian or European. The revolutionary movement must ally itself with the democratic elements. . . . It must be founded on broad democratic principles in order to be a broad revolutionary and cultural-educational movement. Attempting to serve exclusively the interests of the local Bulgarian populations as well as to act in unison with the common forces of revolution in Turkey, the movement must constantly define and redefine for itself a view of local and wider conditions . . . no bands, no artificial imposition from outside, no terror. . . . The revolutionary movement must be the intellect and the will of the Bulgarian population in its economic and cultural struggle, and it must, while performing the actions which are necessary today, also prepare for the coming revolution in Turkey, for the destruction of today's regime and the guaranteeing of the liberties and rights of the Bulgarian element.[264]

The publication of such ideas in *Odrinski glas* read like an invitation to the Young Turks to common action. It is no surprise that in May 1908 the journal published a Bulgarian translation of Doctor Mekkeli Sabri's pamphlet entitled *Vatandaşlarımıza* (To Our Compatriots), inviting all Ottomans to form a common front.[265] In connection with the publication of this translation, the journal commented that "the

Young Turk movement is purely revolutionary, and characteristically, its first act was to offer a hand to other revolutionaries for a common struggle."[266] Further, in a polemical debate with the right wing of the IMRO, *Odrinski glas* stated that "given the absence of a homogeneous national mass in Macedonia and the Edirne region, the revolutionary struggle against Turkish absolutism cannot be a struggle for the triumph of a particular national movement."[267]

A review of copies of *Odrinski glas* reveals that the group publishing it preferred the decentralist ideas of Sabahaddin Bey to those of the other Young Turk groups.[268] The absence of Sabahaddin Bey's league in Macedonia, however, forced the so-called constitutionalists publishing the journal to contact CPU branches. Forwarding copies of the articles that "they had written about the necessity and advantages of union" in their journal, they approached the CPU Monastir branch in early May and urged that the CPU contact Petŭr Poparsov, a confident of Sandanski who had fled to Macedonia after the assassination of the two leaders of the right wing of the IMRO in order to initiate joint action. The constitutionalists further stated that a Young Turk named Halil Bey, who had fled to Bulgaria and become an instructor at the Bulgarian Military Academy, should represent the CPU at secret negotiations with the left wing of the IMRO.[269]

Available documents provide no information about the negotiations.[270] While they were going on, Deliradev, whom the CPU had also contacted,[271] joined Sandanski's Serres group. On his initiative a federative solution to the Macedonian Question was debated at the left wing's joint Serres-Strumitsa Congress, which started in Bansko and continued in Pirin in May–June 1908. After long discussions, the congress decided to join forces with the Young Turks.[272] It is difficult to ascertain whether the congress discussed the basis of cooperation with the Young Turks, since the minutes of the meeting are not available. However, the fact that the members of the congress demanded that the two revolutionaries assigned to assassinate Hüseyin Hilmi Pasha, the Ottoman Inspector General in Salonica, should obtain the approval of the CPU for this action[273] suggests that there were contacts between the left wing and the CPU. In fact Deliradev told a Turkish journalist after the revolution that during their activities in the mountains he and other members of the Serres group had been reading the CPU organs *Şûra-yı Ümmet* and *Mechveret Supplément Français*, which were sent to them clandestinely by the CPU Internal Headquarters.[274]

During their excursion in Macedonia after the joint Serres-Strumitsa Congress, Sandanski and Deliradev propagated the "new idea" adopted by the congress of cooperating with progressive Turks.[275] Nevertheless, an actual agreement between the CPU and the left wing of the IMRO was reached only during the last days of the revolution.[276] Sandanski hinted at such an agreement by stating in his manifesto to "all nationalities in the empire," issued immediately after the triumph of the revolution, that "the revolutionary call to arms of our fraternal Young Turk revolutionary organization found a warm welcome in the hearts of the oppressed people."[277] Because of the rapidity of the CPU victory, the agreement between the IMRO's left wing and the CPU did not lead to any concrete results such as joint band activities. It did, however, provide the CPU with the invaluable trophy of an alliance with the Macedo-Bulgarian population of Macedonia.[278]

The CPU Bands and the Macedo-Bulgarians

During the revolution, the CPU Resen National Battalion under the command of Adjutant-Major Ahmed Niyazi made several overtures to the Macedo-Bulgarian population and invited them to join their movement. First one of the sisters of an IMRO *voyvoda* appealed to Adjutant-Major Ahmed Niyazi, who had annihilated her brother's band, for help in order to save her eight-year-old son, who had been kidnapped by a Serbian band. Adjutant-Major Ahmed Niyazi welcomed the appeal as a "blessing of God" and took a Serbian teacher from Resen as a hostage in order to force the Serbian band to release the boy. The teacher subsequently became a CPU sympathizer; he translated the adjutant-major's appeals into Bulgarian and Serbian and helped him to establish contacts with Serbian villagers and to force the Serbian band to free the child.[279] The recovery of the child boosted Ahmed Niyazi's image among the Macedo-Bulgarians in the region. For example, a local band leader who had been badly beaten by Adjutant-Major Ahmed Niyazi in 1906 told the latter: "Back then you beat me to death, but I did not die; but now I will die for you"; he then joined the CPU Resen National Battalion.[280] The CPU Monastir branch obtained information about an IMRO [right-wing] decree requesting the "Bulgarian villagers" to show hospitality to the "Muslim [CPU] bands," but not to join them in arms until a new decree was issued.[281]

On the heels of this incident, Adjutant-Major Ahmed Niyazi issued an appeal to the local "Bulgarians," in which he stated that "while there is a single Turk alive we will not let others rule [here] as you may think we would." He also placed the blame for the situation on "the government with its corrupt officials who keep causing bad things to happen." The appeal promised equality and justice to "Bulgarians," but it also tersely warned that "anyone who disobeys these orders will be hanged; if a band enters a village or town and the local people fail to inform the CPU authorities, the notables of the town will be executed."[282] The CPU Monastir branch approved Adjutant-Major Ahmed Niyazi's action but cautioned him against drafting "Bulgarians or other Christian" individuals into his band by force.[283]

This admonition of the CPU Monastir branch to Adjutant-Major Ahmed Niyazi reveals the organization's real intention. Whereas the participation of individual Macedo-Bulgarians in the movement would help the CPU for propaganda purposes, the coerced participation of large numbers would have caused problems. The CPU did not wish to have significant numbers of Christians joining its bands; such a development would have endangered the bands' position vis-à-vis the Muslim population in general, and conservative Albanians in particular, since the latter viewed the Young Turk movement in Macedonia as a defensive operation against foreign intrigues.

It was for this reason that, rather than having numerous Christians join its bands, the CPU formed separate multinational bands under the command of CPU officers. Anastas Mitrov gave detailed information about one of these volunteer bands formed in Kičevo (Kırçova); it was composed primarily of Macedo-Bulgarian youngsters but also included Turks, Albanians, and Kutzo-Vlachs. It was under the command of a CPU officer, Captain Hamdi Bey. When this band was sighted by IMRO members on its way to Monastir, the responsible IMRO *voyvoda* leader in the region, Milen

Matov, asked the Macedo-Bulgarians to leave the "Young Turks." To his utter amazement they refused.[284] Such bands, however, were of no practical use, primarily because they were not well organized but existed solely for propaganda purposes.

In its relations with the Macedo-Bulgarian organizations, the CPU had accomplished what it had desired before the revolution. Thanks to the internal problems of IMRO that tied its hands, and to the turn in Bulgarian policy toward Macedonian bands, the CPU was able to neutralize the right wing of the IMRO. The right wing "sent instructions to insurgent leaders in Macedonia to maintain a waiting attitude and to abstain for the present from giving the Young Turkish movement either direct or indirect support."[285] In addition, the CPU had struck a deal with the strongest part of the left wing of the IMRO led by Sandanski, and received popular support from Macedo-Bulgarians thanks to its propaganda. This was enough to enable the CPU to carry out its revolution.

The right wing of the IMRO had been very skeptical of the revolutionary movement until its triumph.[286] Its overtures to the CPU following the revolution and the subsequent negotiations with the Young Turks led everyone to believe that the CPU could obtain support from all Macedo-Bulgarian organizations.[287] The events following the revolution, however, quickly proved that the gap between the CPU and the right wing of the IMRO was unbridgeable.[288] This situation compelled the CPU to work with the left wing between 1908 and 1912. But for the CPU, which had no alternative, this relationship became an annoying burden after the initial period of cooperation in the fall of 1908.[289]

Negotiations between the CPU and the Greek Organizations

While the CPU was conducting its revolution, the Greek government was planning and controlling all Greek band activities in Macedonia.[290] Most of the band leaders were Greek army officers, and they were consequently in no position to initiate negotiations with any other group without instructions from the local Greek consuls who were organizing the bands behind the scenes. This fact compelled the CPU to approach the Greek consuls directly in order to obtain the support of the Greek organizations.

As was agreed between the CPU External and Internal Headquarters, the CPU offered the Greek representatives equality for Greek Ottomans under their prospective constitutional regime. Fearing a negative or evasive answer, the CPU also instructed local branches to approach the Greek population in certain strategic areas and to invite them—sometimes with threats and ultimata—to join CPU activities, or at least not oppose them.

At first glance, relations between the Greek organizations in Macedonia and the Young Turks would appear to have been cordial. Yet in truth these relations were no more cordial than the unwritten alliance between the Ottoman authorities and Greek organizations, both of which considered the Macedo-Bulgarian movement the greater menace. In fact, the Greek organizations' initial promise to smuggle Dr. Nâzım into Salonica made the Young Turks assume that a rapprochement with the Greeks would be easy. The Greek organizations, however, had no desire to see the Young Turks, whom they viewed as nationalists, come to power. In any case, they did not want to jeopardize their delicate relationship with the Ottoman government by becoming entangled in a semiunderground dissident network whose revolutionary triumph seemed highly unlikely. Hence Greek consuls hesitated to give assistance even to the local Young Turks who were cooperating with the Greek organizations. Always suspicious of the Young Turks' real aims, they thought that while "the Young Turks favored the Greeks because of their hatred of the current government," they were "fanatical and dangerous [and] will turn against us if they believe that our efforts are actually endangering Turkey and the Turkish race."[291]

Various Greek sources mention early meetings between the Young Turks and Lambros Koromilas, the Greek consul in Salonica, and tend to present these as an understanding between the Young Turks and the Greeks.[292] It is true that Koromilas was one of the Greek diplomats who agreed to work with the Young Turks against the Bulgarians, and so favored a secret alliance with the Young Turks insofar as it did not jeopardize relations between the Greek government and the Sublime Porte. Koromilas worked on cultivating initial relations with the Young Turks in Macedonia, but in February 1908 the Ottoman government, bowing to Russian and Bulgarian pressure, asked Koromilas to leave Macedonia.[293] Koromilas left Salonica on February 22, 1908, during the most crucial phase of the Young Turk movement; his successor, Kanellopoulos, and other Greek consuls in various towns in Macedonia advised the Greek government against adopting a conciliatory policy toward the Young Turks.

The Greek consuls were the first of the foreign representatives in Macedonia to get wind of the escalating Young Turk activities. On February 27, 1908, Kanellopoulos commented on some Ottoman officers' involvement in the "Young Turk party" and described the arrest of ten law students on charges of organizing secret meetings and distributing banned newspapers.[294] On May 1, 1908, Enialis, the Greek consul in Elasson, reported on "a conspiracy among officers of the imperial army in connection with citizens aimed at overthrowing the present regime in Turkey." The officer representing the CPU told him that the Greeks should not be afraid and, in order to convince the consul, pointed out that the CPU was working with Armenian committees. The consul mistakenly maintained that the center of the CPU conspiracy was Kozánē.[295] Around the same time the CPU organization in Kozánē approached local Greeks to win them over to the revolutionary movement, and the CPU branch in Elasson invited a Greek medical doctor named Brovas to participate in its activities.[296]

At almost the same point, Mustafa Rahmi, one of the leading figures of the CPU, visited the new Greek consul, Kanellopoulos, and spoke to him "about the need for a political change and how cooperation with the Greek element would be useful." Mustafa Rahmi complained about Bulgarian expansionism, giving it as a reason "why the Young Turks would like to cooperate with the weak Greeks."[297] Kanellopoulos, however, gave a vague and evasive answer to Mustafa Rahmi. This was a sign of the new consul's hesitance with regard to supporting the CPU. Other Greek consuls behaved similarly. For example, Dimaras, the Greek consul in Monastir, in commenting on Enialis's proposal for cooperation with the Young Turk officers, recommended that the Greeks be on good terms with the Young Turks but keep them at arm's length and be cautious. He thought that the Greeks had more to lose if the revolution failed.

He also considered the Turks incapable of organizing any political movement and believed that the Greeks should hate the Turks and not work with them.[298] On June 14, 1908, Sachtouris, the Greek consul in Serres, who expected that the Hamidian administration would soon be overthrown because everyone including the sub-governor and officers was talking freely about the coming change of the regime, reported that the Young Turks had promised to protect the Greeks in Serres. The consul expressed his opinion that the Young Turks had no interest in the Greeks and that they could not forge a national consciousness for Muslims. He further believed that the Young Turks' offer of equality under a constitutional regime was not enough to satisfy the Greek element.[299] The sultan's dispatching of agents to determine whether the Greeks in Salonica and Izmir were giving any support to the Young Turks further agitated the Greek consuls.[300] The CPU leaders claimed that the sultan had attempted to obstruct their movement by "uniting the Greek government and the Patriarchate" against them, and by sending Münir Pasha, his confidant and the Ottoman ambassador to France, on a mission to Athens.[301]

After evaluating all the reports from the consuls organizing Greek band activity in Macedonia,[302] Georgios Baltatzis, the Greek Foreign Minister, sent a circular to all Greek consuls on July 10, 1908, ordering them to prevent Greeks from getting involved in Young Turk activities.[303] Under the terms of these instructions no Greek band could enter into any negotiations with the Young Turks. Accordingly, the Greek band leaders turned down all the opportunities given them by the CPU leaders to join the CPU bands.[304] In the circumstances, the best that the CPU could hope to achieve would be the neutralization of the Greek bands.

The Greek Patriarchate in Istanbul, which had moral authority over the Greeks in the Ottoman Empire, was the other great obstacle to a rapprochement between the CPU and the Greeks in Macedonia. It even made the neutralization of the Greeks very difficult. The Greek Patriarch Iōakeim III was extremely suspicious of the Young Turks and thought that their success would jeopardize the Greek position in the Ottoman Empire.[305] His extreme dislike of the Young Turks later made relations between the new Ottoman government and the Greek population tense,[306] and although he "expressed his joy at the restoration of the Constitution,"[307] this statement could not have meant anything more than the sultan's own professions of happiness about the same development.

During the CPU's initial contacts with the Greek leaders in Macedonia, the CPU Monastir branch obtained information from "very reliable sources" that the "Greek Patriarchate, seeing that such a deal will be completely against the goals and designs of Hellenism, has strongly advised all bishops that the Greek community should make sacrifices and render assistance to the present government to secure its continued existence and that in the event of an armed action by the Young Turks, the Greeks should not participate in it at all, but rather take up arms against it, and thus make the Young Turks' liberal action appear to Europe as a sectarian attack by the Muslims on the Christians."[308]

Thus relations between the CPU and the Greek bands became extremely tense as a result of the opposition of the Greek government and the Patriarchate to any joint Young Turk–Greek activity. In April 1908 the CPU External Headquarters learned of a decision taken by the Greek band leaders to assassinate CPU members as they

had assassinated IMRO chiefs. The CPU related this decision to a recent clash between Ottoman troops and a Greek band in a village close to Monastir that had resulted in the killing of First Lieutenant Ali Efendi, a CPU member.[309] In the meantime, *L'Hellénisme* published a letter describing the secret missions of the CPU
members in the Caucasus and Macedonia.[310] The CPU External Headquarters viewed
this as a plot aiming to bring about the arrest of these members. The CPU then abandoned efforts to achieve agreement with the Greek committees through the Greek
consuls. Instead it decided to adopt a different policy. As the first sign of this new
policy, the CPU published a note in *Mechveret Supplément Français* strongly denouncing the activities of the Greek committees. The note accused the Greek committees of being controlled by Athens and of working against the interests of the Ottoman Empire.[311]

The CPU's new policy toward the Greeks was to exert all possible efforts to win
over the Greek masses and "to eradicate the band members with the help of the
masses." Winning over the Greek masses while simultaneously killing Greek band
members was obviously an absurd plan. The Greek consuls who opposed any rapprochement with the Young Turks freely acknowledged that many Greeks in many
towns were in favor of the Young Turk movement.[312] Those Greeks who favored a
rapprochement, however, did not want to enter into any negotiations with CPU members without the consent of their leaders abroad, who had close ties to the Greek
government.[313]

Consequently, the CPU felt it had no option available but to threaten the Greeks,
whose bands were continuing their activities and were engaging in clashes with Macedo-
Bulgarians and Muslims. In many towns the Young Turks gave ultimata to the Greeks
to join them or at least to remain neutral.[314] On July 13, 1908, at the peak of the revolutionary activity, Hasib Bey, a lawyer and a member of the CPU Monastir branch,
gave the dragoman of the Greek consulate a memorandum for the consul along with a
copy of the CPU program.[315] Despite this warning, which was a combination of both
sticks and carrots, the Greek bands rejected the offers made by the CPU and persisted in attacking Muslims and Exarchists.[316] In response, the CPU Monastir center
issued an ultimatum to the Greek committees and clerics. This document illustrates
the CPU's policy toward the Greek organizations:

As a matter of fact, our Bulgarian brothers have shown their inclination to and desire for
our sacred program by their actions and their goodwill. We beg from our Greek compatriots at least the manifestation of neutrality, if union cannot be achieved, and that they
should refrain in the name of humanity and civilization from shedding blood by attacking other elements. Let it be well known that by deviating from our sacred program and
serving the idea and dream of Hellenism, our Greek brothers [in Macedonia] have taken
a very dangerous path and are also treading under foot the happiness and the future of
the Greeks in Anatolia who are twice their number. . . . The secret discussions between
the *Yıldız* and the [Greek] Patriarchate on this matter will cause the devastation and destruction rather than the salvation of the Greek people. We request that Greek bands not
wander around shedding blood for the sake of sectarianism and nationalism, and we
request if possible their dispersal, or at least that they should keep the peace by adopting
neutrality for the time being. We especially do not want the Greeks to hire a few vulgar
and worthless Muslims and make them carry out atrocities. Such loathsome Muslims

naturally do not belong to our society . . . and therefore we will find and kill them if they do not leave the Greek bands.[317]

The CPU Monastir branch also forwarded a copy of this ultimatum to the consuls of the Great Powers and asked "au nom de l'humanité de vouloir bien user de votre influence en conseillant les archévêques d'être sages et dignes et de ne pas s'avilir et de devenir des instruments d'oppression du Palais en versant inutilement le sang des innocents."[318] Thus on July 22, 1908, many people who were aware of the developments believed a CPU–Greek clash to be imminent and thought that it would have a dire impact on the prospects of the revolution.

The exuberance and joy throughout Macedonia on the following day on account of the repromulgation of the constitution, the Greek masses' participation in those celebrations, and speech-making by prominent Greeks, who "until yesterday had strictly obeyed the Patriarchate's orders not to support the revolt,"[319] led everyone to believe that the Young Turks had succeeded in winning support from the Greek organizations. The reality, however, was just the contrary. The CPU had barely neutralized the Greek organizations at gunpoint with threats and the pretence of a fully-fledged rapprochement between the Macedo-Bulgarian bands and the Young Turks. Going against the counsel of the Greek government and the Greek Patriarchate, the "chief local Greeks," who were afraid of a boycott of Greek trade and harsher retributive actions by the CPU, halfheartedly declared their assent to the constitutional movement only a few hours before the repromulgation of the constitution.[320]

Following the CPU's triumph, the Greek Foreign Minister Baltatzis remarked that the Greeks did not play any role in the "recent events, but should be very careful because they [the Young Turks] suspect that the Greeks knew in advance" of the revolutionary movement.[321] The quick Young Turk victory on July 23, 1908, staved off clashes for the time being; but the tense standoff did not bode well for the CPU's future relations with the Greeks once it was in power. Subsequent events bore this fact out.

The CPU and the Serbian Organizations

Like the Greek bands, the Serbian bands carried out their activities in Macedonia under directions from a foreign capital, in their case Belgrade. Their activity was of secondary importance in comparison to that of the IMRO or the Greek organizations, and it could not pose a serious threat to the CPU so long as it was not aided by the IMRO or Greek bands.[322]

During the period when the CPU was preparing its final blow, the Serbian bands had just resolved a schism over the tactics to be employed by the *četniks*, as the members of the Serbian bands were called. Alimpije Marjanović (Lazar Mladenović) placed all the *četnik*s under a single authority that operated regional bands in northern Macedonia.[323] In the spring of 1908, *četnik* activity gained some momentum, especially against the IMRO bands. Nevertheless, the *četnik* organization was far from being able to carry out a fully-fledged offensive.

This weakness certainly played a significant role in relations between the CPU and the Serbian organizations. Nonetheless, it is interesting that the CPU, which attempted to come to terms with all organizations active in Macedonia, did not initiate any contacts with the Serbian organizations. Available CPU and Serbian documents reveal that the success of the revolution caught the Serbians completely off guard and that the first negotiations between the CPU and the Serbian organizations were not held until three days after the reinstatement of the constitution and dealt with the future of Serbian political prisoners. The Serbian diplomats who had been closely following the events had not believed the CPU to be capable of anything as momentous as overthrowing the Hamidian regime, and they were skeptical regarding the Young Turks' chances of success.[324]

As has been discussed, at the time when the CPU bands were active, Adjutant-Major Ahmed Niyazi exploited the opportunity presented by the participation in his "national battalion" of a Serbian teacher who had originally been taken hostage, seeking to impress the Serbian villagers with this fortuitous event.[325] But neither the CPU Internal Headquarters nor any significant branches of the movement addressed the Serbians of Macedonia or the Serbian committees through appeals or publications. In marked contrast to their relations with the Greek and Bulgarian consuls in Macedonia, they held no meetings with the Serbian consuls.

At first glance it might seem odd that the CPU should exclude the Serbian organizations from consideration as a potential ally. From a tactical point of view, however, the attitude of the CPU is understandable. The success of the revolution was dependent upon Albanian support, and the endorsement of the movement by the Gegs in Kosovo was thus a matter of life and death for the CPU. Accordingly, as Talât Bey stated, the CPU Internal Headquarters decided "to ignore the Serbian band [organization], and to threaten it with the use of strong force if it posed any danger to the success of the revolution, in order not to offend the Albanians."[326] During the first CPU–Serbian negotiations held after the triumph of the CPU, the Serbian consuls and band leaders demanded that the CPU exclude Albanians from the amnesty which was then being proclaimed; this demand proved to the CPU leadership that they were right in their fears, and that any negotiations with the Serbian organization would have been at the expense of the Albanians, whose support was deemed vital for the revolution. It was thus the belief within the Serbian government and political circles that "the greatest tragedy for the Ottoman Serbs lies in the frightening excesses of the fanatical Albanians"[327] which ultimately prevented the CPU from establishing any contacts with these Serbs before the revolution. The CPU military leaders knew that the Serbian *četnik*s posed no serious threat to their movement. Their plan was simply to halt them by violent force if they made any attempt to impede it. The plan worked well. The Serbian government and *četnik* organization adopted a neutral stand during the revolution and played no positive or negative role in the course of events.

The CPU and the Albanians

The CPU's overtures to the IMRO and the Greek committees aimed at a possible rapprochement with these organizations or, in the worst-case scenario, at neutralizing them for the duration of the revolution. As has been demonstrated, the CPU struck a deal with the left wing of the IMRO immediately prior to the revolution, and at the same time neutralized the right wing, which was in disarray, and cowed the Greek organizations with strong threats.

For the CPU, neutralization of the Macedo-Bulgarian and Greek organizations was sufficient as long as some non-Muslim elements gave their support to the revolutionary movement. These groups provided sufficient grist for the CPU's propaganda mill to enable it to describe its revolution to the European public as "a general uprising of all Ottomans regardless of race or faith." The Serres group's support and the participation of other non-Muslim groups in the revolutionary activities were thus welcomed by the CPU leadership, which feared that the Great Powers might react negatively on the pretext of defending the rights of the non-Muslims, or might obstruct the revolution for the sake of preserving the status quo.

In its relations with the Albanian notables, bands, and organizations abroad, the CPU's aims were quite different. The CPU was well aware of the fact that without the support of certain segments of the Albanian population,[328] which made up a considerable portion of the Muslim populace in the European provinces, success was impossible. Accordingly, the CPU was assiduous in contacting a variety of representatives of the Albanian population in order to persuade them to work for the movement.

Even before the merger of the CPU with the Ottoman Freedom Society, the former made great efforts to disseminate propaganda among the Albanians.[329] The fact that Macedonia had become the hub of the revolutionary activity compelled the CPU to redouble these efforts. Appeals addressed specifically to the Albanians promised them that the future constitutional regime would deliver them from unbearable taxes and from the despotism of corrupt local officials. They also accused the Ottoman government of doing nothing about Austro-Hungarian and Italian intrigues in provinces heavily inhabited by Albanians.[330]

Thanks to its active propaganda among Albanians and its practice of using officers of Albanian descent as mediators, the CPU had a relatively easy time winning over many Muslim Albanian notables. Its strongly anti-interventionist policy and propaganda appealed to the Muslim Albanians, who likewise loathed European policies and adamantly opposed any reforms that explicitly favored the Christians. In the oral and written propaganda directed at Albanians, the CPU avoided any negative references to the sultan, who was a father figure for the Muslim Albanians; instead it accused "the camarilla" surrounding him of responsibility for all misdeeds.[331] Through this propaganda and organizational work, the CPU enrolled large numbers of Muslim Albanians in its ranks. As we have seen, Nexhib Draga led the establishment of the CPU branch in Skopje, and in Ohrid Albanian notables spearheaded the establishment of a local Muslim organization that later transformed itself into the CPU Ohrid branch. In Resen the Albanian mayor, Hoca Xhemal (Cemal) Efendi, a member of a well-known local family, joined the CPU Resen National Battalion together with many other Albanian officials;[332] and while the "national battalion" was in the mountains, local notables such as "Kijanlı Ragıb Ağa" and "Kırkdölenceli Raif Ağa" joined it with their followers, helping it to become an armed force of 1,000 men.[333] At the same time the officers dispatched by the CPU Internal Headquarters to Albanian districts succeeded in turning large regions into CPU strongholds. The region called Çamëria (Çamlak), for example, which included the towns of Margarition

(Margaliç), Paramythia (Aydunat), and Filiatai (Filat), became one of these strong-holds and was ready to serve the purposes of the CPU in May 1908.[334]

In towns like Debar and Gjirokastër, local Albanian organizations became CPU branches while continuing to work for their own program.[335] Depending on their location, these organizations were either extremely anti-Greek or anti-Serbian, and they were heavily influenced by the CPU's anti-European rhetoric. In Kosovo, where the Albanian population feared an Austro-Hungarian or Serbian invasion, the CPU's success in winning over many local notables enabled it to gain control of an Alba-nian Geg crowd in Firzovik, which was protesting against alleged Austro-Hungarian military intervention, and to turn the gathering into a mass demonstration demand-ing the reinstatement of the constitution.

In its relations with the Albanian societies abroad, the CPU encountered more se-rious problems. The Albanian intellectuals leading these organizations were more nationalistic than the Albanian notables within the empire, and this stance made them wary of the CPU. In addition, some of these Albanian organizations were subsidized by the Greek, Austro-Hungarian, and Italian governments and had specific political designs for Albania's future. At the same time the CPU was unwilling to grant them any concession that could endanger the territorial integrity of the Ottoman Empire.

The CPU accordingly adopted a hostile stand toward Albanian leaders like İsmail Kemal, Faïk Konica, and Fan S. Noli, who were carrying out political activities with the help of outside powers. In particular, the CPU shunned İsmail Kemal be-cause of his secret understanding with the Greeks for a partition of the western parts of the European provinces of the Ottoman Empire.[336] Any rapprochement between the CPU and such Albanian leaders was out of the question, and the CPU attempted none.

The CPU did, however, contact expatriate organizations that were demanding Ottoman recognition of Albanian cultural rights. Some factions within these expa-triate organizations were quite radical, but the CPU nevertheless decided to con-tact the more moderate factions. In May 1908 the CPU engaged in long-lasting negotiations with one of the leaders of the Bashkimi Society in Leskovik, whom "they convinced of the necessity of Albanian support for the Ottoman Committee of Progress and Union." This leader promised to inform his committee center in Bucharest of his decision and to publish articles defending an alliance between the CPU, the Bashkimi Society, and other Albanians.[337]

The CPU's final target was the Albanian nationalist bands, most of which were composed of Tosks in southern Albania and Macedonia. The CPU easily won over the local Muslim Albanian bands active in Macedonia, and most of these bands freely joined the CPU "national battalions" during the revolution.[338] There were, however, some Albanian nationalist bands that were also active in the area. Reaching an under-standing with them was more difficult, since they were not fighting only against the Greek and Serbian bands but also against the Ottoman troops,[339] and they were in close contact with Albanian nationalist societies abroad. Moreover, though there were local Albanian bands composed entirely of Muslims, there were many Christian Albanians in these nationalist bands fighting for the Albanian national cause. There were even rumors about negotiations between them and the right wing of the IMRO regarding an alliance against the Greek bands.[340] Furthermore, the Albanian exile press praised nationalist Albanian bands' determination "to work for Albania and the Albanian language."[341]

The Albanian nationalist committees were preparing to launch a formidable offensive in Albania when the CPU initiated its revolutionary program, but the "Young Turks struck their blow and upset the plans of the Albanian nationalists."[342] Moreover, the CPU put the Albanian bands on the spot by initiating a revolution involving many Albanian officers and Muslim Albanian notables. During the revolution the CPU required all members of Albanian committees to enroll *en masse* in the CPU.[343] They were not to join individually.

In order to achieve this goal, Adjutant-Major Ahmed Niyazi sent a letter to the leader of the Tosk band organization, Çerçiz Topulli,[344] and invited him to a meeting to discuss the conditions of union.[345] The CPU Monastir branch likewise contacted Çerçiz Topulli and asked him to come to Monastir to discuss the matter.[346] In the meantime, Adjutant-Major Ahmed Niyazi met with Çerçiz Topulli's representatives in Korçë. The Albanian delegates accused the Turks of lack of commitment to Ottomanism, and asserted that it was this that had compelled the Tosks to struggle on their own to defend themselves against foreigners and rival Ottoman elements.[347] Adjutant-Major Ahmed Niyazi responded that the Turks had made strenuous efforts to promote Ottomanism and that the establishment of the CPU was proof of this effort.[348] Following this discussion, the Albanian representatives decided to accept the CPU's invitation to join *en masse*, and after an oath ceremony all of them were enrolled. The representatives promised to bring Çerçiz Topulli and other leading Albanian committee members to a final meeting to discuss the details of the agreement. A local Albanian notable, Hysrev Bey, was asked to arrange this meeting, which was to take place in Pogradec (İstarova).[349] Hysrev Bey also contacted the local Albanian Bektashi Sheikh Hysein Baba, who subsequently recommended his followers to support the CPU.[350]

Ahmed Niyazi did not provide any information about what happened afterward, stating simply that the meeting became less important because all Albanians in the region had already pledged allegiance to the CPU. The memoirs of Çerçiz Topulli's comrades, however, reveal that through the mediation of the local Albanian committees, Çerçiz Topulli, who had been pressed hard by his fellow Albanians, decided to meet with Ahmed Niyazi to discuss joint action. He and his band reached Pogradec on July 21, 1908.[351] They joined the combined CPU force composed of the CPU Ohrid National Regiment, the CPU Resen National Battalion, the CPU Monastir band under the command of Lieutenant Colonel Salâhaddin Bey and Major Hasan Tosun, and local armed tribal bands under the command of Albanian notables. The CPU Monastir branch had instructed this combined force to march on Monastir to abduct Marshal Tatar Osman Pasha and seize the town. Another Albanian band under the command of Adem Bey came from Kolonja (Erseke) and joined the force. The arrival of the forces of Çerçiz Topulli and Adem Bey turned an already heavily Albanian force into one that was overwhelmingly so.

The Key Significance of Albanian Involvement

The CPU's negotiations with various segments of Albanian society produced excellent results. Muslim Albanian notables lent their support from the outset of the movement, and districts heavily populated by Albanians became hotbeds of CPU band activity.[352] A gathering of Gegs in Firzovik terrified the Ottoman authorities in the capital. An understanding, albeit vague, was reached with the Albanian societies abroad; in the end, Albanian nationalist Tosk bands with close ties to the aforementioned societies joined with CPU bands and participated in delivering the final blow in Monastir.

In the course of his negotiations with Albanian committee members, Adjutant-Major Ahmed Niyazi made a striking remark when he stated that "most of the leaders and partisans of [the movement for] constitutional administration were not Turkish."[353] He was, of course, alluding to the significance of the Albanian role in the movement. When one considers the officers and privates in the CPU's so-called national battalions,[354] the local notables who supported the movement and fed those battalions, and the participants in the mass demonstration in Firzovik, this comment appears accurate.[355] In the available photographs of the "national battalions" and the local bands that had joined them, Albanians with white fezzes overwhelmingly outnumber all others. These people, including Adjutant-Major Ahmed Niyazi, did not occupy decision-making positions inside the CPU,[356] but it was they, and not the organizers such as Talât Bey and Bahaeddin Şakir, who were seen carrying out the revolution. Thus it was understandable that the Albanians considered the revolution an Albanian enterprise, and they expected special treatment in return.[357]

The question of what exactly the CPU offered Albanian organizations in return for this support is difficult to answer precisely. On paper it seems that the CPU offered nothing more than equality under a constitutional regime.[358] By contrast, the record of Albanian behavior in the first days after the revolution suggests that they viewed the restored constitutional regime as heralding a new era in which they were to be given a free hand to develop their cultural rights. In fact, the CPU labeled this separatism.[359] For many members of the Albanian intellectual elite who fought against the sultan's regime, this "was an era of freedom whose boundaries were very tightly drawn."[360] In a very short period of time the CUP's opposition to bestowing new cultural rights on Albanians, and its abrogation of the privileges that had been granted to the Muslim Albanians for the sake of making all citizens equal before the law, prompted the emergence of a strong anti-CUP sentiment among both the Albanian intellectual elite and the masses.

The CPU and the Kutzo-Vlach Organizations

The Kutzo-Vlach organizations had been cooperating with the Young Turks from the outset of the Young Turk movement.[361] Immediately prior to the revolution they struck a deal with the CPU to join the activities. The Aromenis movement was in fact directed principally against Greek propaganda and band activities. It supported the preservation of Ottoman rule in Macedonia, since the Kutzo-Vlachs did not form a majority in any particular province and thus found the prospect of remaining subjects of a multinational empire preferable to that of becoming a minority in a nation-state. They therefore cooperated with the Young Turk and the Albanian organizations in Macedonia. The leaders of the old CUP had hoped to transform the Aromenis movement into an active branch of their organization in Macedonia,[362] but their efforts toward this end produced no significant results.

The British proposals for a new and more extensive reform scheme for Macedonia prompted the Kutzo-Vlach committees, working under the instructions of the Societatea de Cultura Macedo-Română in Bucharest, to make overtures to the CPU. Talât Bey informed the CPU External Headquarters that Sir Edward's speech in the House of Commons had compelled the Kutzo-Vlachs to form an alliance with the CPU, and he opined that it would be wise to form mixed Muslim/Kutzo-Vlach bands.[363] The CPU External Headquarters approved this suggestion and recommended that these mixed bands be used against the Greek and IMRO bands if necessary.[364] The CPU External Headquarters hoped that an alliance with the Kutzo-Vlach organization would also put an end to the latter's cooperation with the Albanian nationalist organizations and would help the CPU to check the penetration of the Greek bands in Macedonia.[365]

During the negotiations between the CPU and the Kutzo-Vlach organization, the latter's propaganda director accepted all the conditions put forward by the CPU representatives and further agreed that the Kutzo-Vlachs would become members of the CPU and conduct their activities according to the CPU Internal Regulations.[366] The propaganda director was sworn in on March 25, 1908, and all members of the Kutzo-Vlach organization were informed of the alliance. Enver Bey's memoirs reveal that this propaganda director was Dr. Filip Mişea, who had been recruited by the CPU Monastir branch.[367] Another Kutzo-Vlach leader, Nicolae Constantin Batzaria, who was the supervisor and inspector of Romanian schools in the provinces of Salonica and Kosovo, also became a member of the CPU.[368] Both Mişea and Batzaria "worked wholeheartedly" for the committee.[369]

With the exception of the Jews, who lacked any band organization, the Kutzo-Vlachs were the only non-Muslim ethnic group from which the CPU recruited members. The strategy of the Kutzo-Vlach organization was simply to make common cause with the strongest group whose aim was to maintain a revitalized *Pax Ottomanica*, and thus to find an effective ally against the other nationalist organizations who posed a threat to the very national existence of the Kutzo-Vlachs in Macedonia. From the point of view of the CPU, the existence of a Christian ally that accepted the CPU version of Ottomanism was invaluable for propaganda purposes. Following the revolution Dr. Mişea became a deputy in the Ottoman Chamber of Deputies, and Batzaria became a member of the Ottoman Senate. In fact, the Kutzo-Vlach organization worked under the instructions of the CUP.[370]

Thus relations between the CPU and the Kutzo-Vlachs turned out to be a success for the former, which used this alliance as an example for other ethnic groups in Macedonia to follow. Those ethnic groups that could entertain separatist ambitions, however, expressed no desire to emulate the Kutzo-Vlach example.

The CPU and the Jews

Following the merger of the CPU with the Ottoman Freedom Society, the CPU Internal Headquarters began to enroll Jews as members, especially in Salonica. Before the revolution, prominent figures of the Jewish community in Salonica, such as Emmanuel Carasso, Nesim Matzliach, Nesim Ruso, and Emmanuel Salem, became CPU members and worked closely with the CPU Internal Headquarters.[371] These Jewish CPU members were at the same time influential Freemasons. They were thus able to render a great service to the committee by making their lodges available for secret meetings and for the storage of secret correspondence and records, the capture of which by the Ottoman authorities might have caused the collapse of the entire organization. Although the Freemasons' help was invaluable to the CPU, they had no role in shaping CPU policies.

Though limited in extent, the Jewish participation was symbolically important because of the need for visible support from non-Muslim communities, and CPU propaganda did not fail to exploit it.[372] The CUP's conservative opponents, however, overestimated the support of the various Jewish community leaders. They alleged that the revolution itself was a Jewish-Freemason-Zionist plot and that the CUP was nothing more than a façade for a cabal of Salonican Jews, Freemasons, and Zionists who supposedly ruled the empire from behind the scenes since July 1908.[373] Allied propaganda during the First World War exploited this idea in order to discredit the CUP and incite the Arabs to revolt against the CUP government.[374] In truth, the CPU had no desire to grant concessions to any ethnic or religious group, and it strongly opposed Zionism, which it viewed as a variant form of secessionism. When the Zionists, who thought that Prince Sabahaddin's "decentralization in Turkey . . . is of supreme interest for the Jewish people,"[375] made an approach to the CPU leaders, Dr. Nâzım gave them a clear answer:

Prinz Sabah Eddin ist tot; er existiert nicht mehr; sein Programm der Dezentralisation, der autonomen Nationalitäten und Provinzen ist verworfen. "Der Ausschuß Fortschritt und Einigkeit" (Progrès et Union) will Zentralisation und Alleinherrschaft der Türkischen [*sic*]. Er will keine Nationalitäten in der Türkei. Er will aus der Türkei kein neues Österreich machen. Er will einen einheitlichen türkischen Nationalstaat, mit türkischen Schulen, [mit] türkischer Verwaltung, [und] türkischer Rechtslage.

[Prince Sabahaddin is dead; he exists no more; his program of decentralization, of autonomous nationalities and provinces is abandoned. The Committee of Progress and Union wants centralization and a Turkish monopoly on power. It wants no nationalities in Turkey. It does not want Turkey to become a new Austria [-Hungary]. It wants a unified Turkish nation-state with Turkish schools, a Turkish administration, [and] a Turkish legal system.][376]

This answer, which also illuminates the CPU leaders' conception of an ideal society, illustrates unambiguously that the CPU as an organization desired to thwart the dissolution of the Ottoman Empire and had no intention of supporting movements that could threaten or complicate the empire's existence. CPU–Jewish relations did not go beyond the inclusion in the CPU of members from a non-Muslim community which was, for its own reasons, ready to accept the CPU version of Ottomanism. In addition, like the Kutzo-Vlachs, the Jews were not in a position to impose any terms on the CPU.[377]

CUP–Jewish and CUP–Zionist relations fluctuated after the revolution, as did the CUP's relations with all other communities in the empire. Still, even during the periods in which the CUP was more inclined toward having closer relations with various Jewish organizations, it still pursued its own agenda and policies.

In summary, the Young Turks' contacts and negotiations with the organizations of various ethnic and religious groups in Macedonia secured for them the support of Albanian notables, societies, and bands, the left wing of the IMRO, and especially the Serres group under Sandanski, Kutzo-Vlach organizations, and eminent figures of the Jewish community in Salonica. The CPU's other success was its neutralization of the organizations that opposed it. The support of Albanians in particular made the physical execution of the revolution possible, while support from the others helped the CPU to paint a picture of a broad "Ottomanist movement" seeking to restore a constitution under which all would be equal. The CPU leaders believed that a favorable image was as important as the actual revolutionary activity itself, because they feared that without such an image their movement's success would trigger a potentially catastrophic European intervention.

The Execution of the Young Turk Revolution of 1908

Beginning in 1908, the CPU began to contemplate seriously the opening of the last phase of its campaign to topple the Hamidian regime. Everything was now in place. It had an appropriate revolutionary program and a cadre of disciplined and zealous self-sacrificing volunteers. It had constructed a network of branches that covered the European provinces and enabled it to carry out propaganda campaigns with ease and effectiveness. Inside Macedonia the CPU was engaged in ongoing negotiations with all but one of the important active organized groups, while in Europe it had in place an external headquarters to inform, influence, and persuade European public opinion. In another important preparatory move, the CPU obtained a secret document from the heir apparent Mehmed Reşad Efendi, promising that he would remain loyal to the constitutional regime. This document would be used in the event of the dethronement of Abdülhamid II.[378] All that remained was to spark the revolution.

It is difficult to be certain whether the CPU leaders drew up a detailed plan of execution for their revolution, as the following remarks of Bahaeddin Şakir would suggest:

> The Sultan was evidently unaware that, in July 1908, the Macedonians had made every preparation to march on Constantinople, had amassed the fullest and most accurate data regarding the granaries, arsenals, wells, farm-houses &c. &c., all along the way, had noted down where the soldiers were Constitutionalist and where they were Hamnidia [*sic*], had, in short mastered all the problems involved in that great march with all the thoroughness that we should naturally expect from pupils of the Germans.[379]

There are various lists of officers among the private papers of Bahaeddin Şakir proving that the CPU did indeed enumerate officers who opposed them and would resist a CPU action, that the CPU branches did collect relevant data from national and regional yearbooks about officers and officials,[380] and that various CPU branches threatened the palace and the government with a march on the capital by an army of regular troops and volunteers during the last days of the revolution.[381] But there is no available itemized plan for revolution setting out the CPU's proposed action,[382] and it seems that the revolution was carried out by the CPU branches after the CPU External and Internal Headquarters had agreed to put everything on hold if foreign intervention seemed imminent.

As we have seen, the CPU External and Internal Headquarters settled upon a scheme envisioning a series of assassinations and the presentation of a *mémoire* to foreign consuls rejecting the application of a new reform plan for Macedonia. Although the CPU External Headquarters had favored organizing mass demonstrations and post office occupations, its internal counterpart argued for postponing all such actions that could lead to direct and open clashes with government forces, maintaining that in any case the Anglo-Russian initiatives would not produce any significant result in the short run.

There is also no clear information whether the CPU had fixed a date for the start of the revolution. Following the revolution, Enver Bey stated in an interview that they had scheduled their action for August 1908 but that circumstances had compelled them to start the revolution earlier.[383] Karabekir specified October 11, 1908, as the agreed date,[384] and a member of the special investigation committee dispatched by the palace to Salonica told the Greek consul in Mytilíni that "the Young Turk coup will take place on November 1, 1908."[385] Finally, Adjutant-Major Ahmed Niyazi told a journalist that they had acted before the predetermined day, but he did not name this date.[386]

Examination of the available CPU documents does allow us to draw the following picture: the CPU's swift expansion in the European provinces of the empire both boosted the morale of the headquarters and sizable branches, and made continuation of the strict secrecy in which the organization traditionally operated impossible. Even in Macedonia, where the spy network of the sultan was relatively less effective, no clandestine organization with more than 2,000 members could possibly operate secretly. The first local investigations were based only on spy reports, and thus the subsequent trials did little harm to the CPU. In June 1908, however, the situation grew critical. With the intention of crushing the movement, the palace called some of the military CPU leaders back to the capital and dispatched teams of investigators to Macedonia.

While the CPU deliberated about carrying out assassinations as a response to the investigations and the arrest of its members, rumors were floated of an agreement to partition Macedonia reached by Edward VII and Nicholas II in Reval (today's Tallinn) between June 9 and 12, 1908. These prompted the CPU to accelerate its plan to mobilize political bands. Deploying bands was apparently a way to save the military CPU members who were summoned to Istanbul for further investigation. The CPU Monastir branch gave a free hand to those in command of military units to form political bands and take to the mountains. When the first political band, the CPU Resen National Battalion, headed for the mountains on July 3, 1908, the CPU crossed the Rubicon. During the next twenty days the CPU "gendarme force" in various towns carried out a series of assassinations that sowed dread in government circles, and the Monastir branch assumed control of the military aspects of the uprising.[387] The available documents reveal that during these twenty days the branches worked on their own and risked everything. The CPU National Battalions increased their number with fresh recruits, some of them in the form of the intact forces of various Albanian feudal lords. The CPU Monastir branch also succeeded in persuading local Muslim bands and deserters in the mountains to join the "national battalions."

The situation grew more acute with the participation of Albanian nationalist bands and the Geg gathering in Firzovik. All the attempts of the palace to put down the rebellion proved futile, and on July 21, 1908, the CPU Internal Headquarters assumed command of the revolution's forces, instructing all branches to strike the final blow. In the event that the sultan refused to recognize the *fait accompli* by issuing an imperial decree, the plan was to march on Istanbul with an "Army of Liberation."

By this time the CPU had won over the left wing of the IMRO, which agreed to participate in such an operation although this operation never occurred.[388] When the rebels proclaimed the constitution in one town after another, the impotent sultan yielded, issuing an imperial decree reinstating the constitution of 1876, and inviting the parliament to convene in Istanbul.

The Government's Attempts to Crush the Movement and the CPU's Declaration of Its Existence

The Ottoman government had begun to receive information about the distribution of "seditious papers" in Macedonia as early as September 1907.[389] Reports on the circulation of subversive publications were nothing new for the regime, and it confined its reaction to taking standard measures. In February 1908 the Salonica police found CPU instructions to form cells and distribute propaganda material in the possession of two Salonica Law School students named Hüseyin Cudi and Ali İrfan.[390] The students were immediately tried and sentenced to imprisonment.[391] This arrest prompted a serious investigation. A great many CPU members who were "at the rank of lieutenant" were subsequently arrested along with civilians, on charges of being members of a secret society, corresponding with the "conspirators in Europe," and obtaining "seditious papers." The police, however, found no documents in their houses.[392] These developments alarmed the palace, which demanded more detailed information about those engaged in "seditious" activities and the individuals with whom they socialized, and ordered that strict measures be taken.[393]

The CPU External Headquarters proposed a raid to free the arrested members.[394] Its internal counterpart, however, counseled patience, maintaining that most of the members would be acquitted because of lack of evidence regarding their membership.[395] The court did in fact acquit all of the officers in late April.[396] It found guilty only one barber who had no relations with the CPU, sentencing him to five years in prison.[397]

The palace continued to receive intelligence reports from various parts of the European provinces concerning the activities of the CPU, and it did not cease to be worried by these.[398] But a further action taken by the CPU External Headquarters was soon to make the magnitude of the threat of the CPU activities clear to the government, manifesting the existence of a capable organization that intended to carry out a revolution in the near future. Confident of its own strength, the CPU External Headquarters sent a series of final warnings to the sultan, his cabinet ministers, and the Ottoman Minister of War Mehmed Rıza Pasha on May 13, 1908.

In the first warning the CPU stated that it harbored "no personal grudge and enmity" toward the sultan, but it warned Abdülhamid II that in the event of the postponement of the restoration of the constitution "blood will be shed and the dynasty will be in danger." It went on to claim that "since the blood is the blood of our compatriots, esteemed Muslim blood, its every drop is valuable in the extreme. The halting of such bloodshed is within His Majesty's power." The CPU further cautioned the sultan that he would be entirely responsible for any bloodshed arising from the revolution that the CPU would lead if it did not receive an affirmative answer in deeds rather than words.[399]

In its warning to the cabinet ministers, the CPU encouraged them to take action to save the empire from imminent chaos:

> If we leave to the Greeks and Bulgarians the three provinces which are our last connection with Europe and our final means of relating to the world of industry and progress, and go back to Anatolia, depriving ourselves of three hundred thousand soldiers, we shall sink to the level of an insignificant Asiatic power and even to that of a tribe. We shall be crushed amidst the economic penetration and dominance of the [Great] Powers. . . . In such a dangerous time a government that has lost the trust and confidence of the population gives the nation the right to find its salvation in other directions and to overthrow the present administration. . . . Therefore, changing the form of government and not surrendering the three provinces in Europe are not the duties but the sacred obligations of the cabinet ministers.[400]

The warning sent to the Minister of War was of a more aggressive nature. It demanded the minister's resignation with an open threat of assassination:

> Pasha! Look at this letter bearing the seal of the central committee of the Ottoman Committee of Progress and Union with all your attention and engrave our statement in your memory well. . . . Your soiled past and the fact that you possess the characteristic of being happy because you serve as a tool of destruction and annihilation are well known to us. Therefore, we recommend you to step down from the post to which you were raised up as a puppet. Otherwise, you will not be just stepping down, but will also become a target of the vanquishing and vindictive weapon of the nation.[401]

The palace responded by ordering a thorough search for "nonsensical documents coming from Paris and signed by Bahaeddin [Şakir] and [Hüsrev] Sami," and by listing measures to be taken against any new initiatives on the part of those same individuals.[402]

In addition to writing threatening letters to the authorities, the CPU External Headquarters publicly declared on the occasion of the sixth anniversary of the establishment of *Şûra-yı Ümmet* that the next anniversary, in April 1909, would be celebrated in Istanbul after the toppling of the regime.[403] All these acts suggest strongly that in May 1908 the CPU believed that it had reached a level of strength sufficient for it to initiate a revolution at any time it deemed propitious. Although it was planning to commence its uprising at a later date, developments both inside and outside the empire induced the CPU to start its revolutionary activities in June 1908.

The arrests in Salonica disrupted the CPU Internal Headquarters' contacts with its other branches. The larger branches, such as the CPU Monastir branch, accordingly asked the external headquarters to correspond directly with them and provide them with the necessary instructions.[404] The CPU External Headquarters told the Monastir branch's executive committee that it was difficult "to issue directives regarding the actions of self-sacrificing volunteers and attempts to free the prisoners . . . and the safest guide will be a thorough examination of events and developments."[405] In effect the CPU External Headquarters was telling the branches that they would be on their own once their activities began to escalate, and that it was on that basis that the revolution would go forward.

The CPU Action in Macedonia in May–July 1908

In April 1908 the CPU External and Internal Headquarters debated whether to present a *mémoire* to the European cabinets rejecting the implementation of new reforms in Macedonia. The external headquarters wanted to submit the memorandum from Paris, whereas its internal counterpart contended that it would make a stronger impact if delegations presented it to the British, French, Italian, and Austro-Hungarian consuls in Salonica, Monastir, and Skopje. The delegations were to make a short speech to the consuls explaining the goals of the CPU and telling them that the CPU did not fear the regime's reaction should the consuls violate diplomatic tradition and inform on them to the government.[406]

Accordingly, the CPU Internal Headquarters composed a draft *mémoire* and sent it to its external counterpart. After editing, it was sent back to the former for presentation.[407] Although the *mémoire* could not be delivered as planned, and the copies of the *mémoire* were simply left at a few consulates unaccompanied by any delegations,[408] the palace learned of the operation immediately after its execution.[409] The CPU's strength in Macedonia became more evident to both the palace and the foreign powers.

The *mémoire* was a strong denunciation of the European intervention in Macedonia. It vehemently attacked Russian policies[410] and asserted that the Macedonian Question was no more than a part of the general Ottoman Question; as such it could be solved only by the reinstatement of the constitution that made every Ottoman equal before the law. The most important passages were the following:

> L'œuvre réformatrice de l'Europe en Macédoine n'a abouti à aucun résultat et n'a contribué d'aucune façon à l'amélioration de la situation. Il y a plus. Les troubles ont augmenté, le problème macédonien est devenu plus compliqué, une confusion générale règne dans le pays. . . . Unie sous le nom de "Comité Ottoman d'Union et de Progrès" cette nation est décidée à écarter toute immixtion étrangère dans ses intérêts sacrés nationaux et, d'accord avec tous les fils de la patrie Ottomane—à l'exclusion de quelques traîtres qui profitent du despotisme du régime actuel—à reconquérir sa liberté individuelle et politique. . . . La Macédoine n'a conservé de son passé que son nom; elle n'est qu'une réminiscence historique, et rien [d']autre. Il n'y a pas de Macédoine, comme il n'y a plus de Macédoniens. La Macédoine est actuellement une partie intégrante et inséparable de l'Empire Ottoman dont on ne pourra la retrancher. . . . Les 3 Vilayets de Roumélie, dont vous avez fait une Macédoine fictive, partageront le sort, bon ou mauvais, des 27 autres Vilayets qui tous ensemble forment l'Empire Ottoman. Il n'y pas de distinction à faire. . . . C'est le despotisme du régime actuel qui est l'origine et la cause de tous les

maux dont se plaignent non seulement la Macédoine, mais toutes les autres provinces qui entrent dans la formation de l'Empire Ottoman.[411]

In the aftermath of this action, the CPU Internal Headquarters decided to assassinate the garrison commander of Salonica, Lieutenant Colonel Ömer Nâzım, who had regularly been sending spy reports to Istanbul about the committee.[412] The CPU Internal Headquarters had originally decided to assassinate the garrison commander in March 1908 but was forced to postpone the assassination because of Ömer Nâzım's visit to Istanbul.[413] On June 11, 1908, a CPU self-sacrificing volunteer, First Lieutenant Mustafa Necib, who belonged to the "CPU gendarme force," shot and wounded Lieutenant Colonel Ömer Nâzım in his house. In this condition, Ömer Nâzım was transferred to the capital the next day at the behest of the sultan, who ordered a more thorough investigation.[414]

Upon learning of the assassination attempt, the government ordered all governors, subgovernors, and military commanders in Macedonia to carry out a detailed investigation and uncover the CPU members.[415]

Meanwhile the palace sent a team to Salonica to prepare a special investigation and called some CPU leaders to the capital. The CPU Internal Headquarters suggested that two high-ranking CPU members who had recently joined the organization, Brigadier General Ali Pasha and Colonel Hasan Rıza, should go to Istanbul; it also, however, asked Major Enver Bey to go into the countryside to form a CPU band. Thus on June 26, 1908, Major Enver Bey, who was Lieutenant Colonel Ömer Nâzım's brother-in-law and had approved the committee's decision regarding the latter's assassination, left Salonica for Tikvesh to form a band under the instructions of the CPU Internal Headquarters.[416] The internal headquarters bestowed on Enver Bey the title of "CPU Inspector General of Internal Organization and Executive Forces."[417] In the meantime, on June 21, 1908, the CPU Monastir branch's gendarme force assassinated a police commissioner named Sami Bey, who had been dispatched to Kruševo by the Ottoman Inspector General to look into the CPU activities there.[418]

While the CPU was carrying out these assassinations, rumors emerged from the Reval meeting about an alleged Anglo-Russian partition plan. The CPU Internal Headquarters postponed taking any final action until it had more concrete information about this British initiative. Nonetheless, many CPU members thought that the time had come to act.[419] The Reval meeting seems to have served as a signal to certain CPU members to organize bands and carry out assassinations of whomever they found hazardous.[420] Meanwhile the Ottoman government, fearing a strong reaction to the Reval meeting, warned the civil and military authorities in Macedonia to tighten security as early as May 24, 1908.[421] But no authority could do anything against the escalating CPU activities,[422] and the rumors about the alleged Anglo–Russian agreement were so outrageous that they immediately catalyzed and accelerated the campaign planned by the CPU.[423]

The CPU Bands and "Gendarme Force" in Action

The CPU self-sacrificing volunteers who received the signal from Reval that the time had come decided to take immediate action. One such volunteer was Adjutant-Major Ahmed Niyazi, the commander of the Resen Reserve Battalion. He "was flushed with anxiety and excitement for three days and nights" when he heard the rumors about the Reval meeting, and "found salvation in sacrifice and death."[424] After a discussion with the local CPU members and the CPU Monastir branch, he decided to form a band and take to the hills. This was by no means an original idea, since the CPU External and Internal Headquarters had planned to mobilize bands in mid-June and had asked local branches to make the necessary preparations.

In fact, although Adjutant-Major Ahmed Niyazi wrote in his memoirs that he started to form a CPU band on June 28, 1908, he had actually been distributing weapons confiscated from Macedo-Bulgarian villages to his colleagues for some time before that.[425] The mayor of Resen, Xhemal Bey, who was also a CPU member, left for Monastir to discuss the details of action to be taken with the CPU Monastir branch. Upon receiving the branch's approval, the first CPU band set out from Resen on July 3, 1908, on the pretext of pursuing a Macedo-Bulgarian band. The rebels broke into the military warehouse and distributed rifles to volunteers. They also seized the money in the Resen Reserve Battalion's strongbox on behalf of the CPU and divided it among members of the band.[426] The band had reached a strength of 160 men when Adjutant-Major Ahmed Niyazi told the reservists and volunteers, the vast majority of whom were already aware of the ruse, that there was no Macedo-Bulgarian band and that they were taking to the mountains in order to force the Ottoman administration to restore the constitutional regime. Very few left the band, which was now named the CPU Resen National Battalion.

The CPU Monastir branch had readied everything for the CPU Resen National Battalion. Letters to be sent to the First Chamberlain's office, the inspector general, and the local civil and military authorities, had all been prepared ahead of time, together with contingency plans for a course of action for the band.[427]

The CPU Resen National Battalion roamed the hills and visited villages to recruit more members. Thanks to the participation of Albanian local notables, Muslim bands, army deserters, and other volunteers, its numbers increased every day. Adjutant-Major Ahmed Niyazi bombarded the authorities at all levels with letters, appeals, and ultimata on behalf of "two hundred self-sacrificing volunteers of the fatherland" and issued appeals addressing various Ottoman ethnic and social groups.[428] The local troops in Resen and Monastir categorically refused to pursue the "national battalion." This refusal was no great surprise to the government, which ten days before the CPU Resen National Battalion's sortie had appointed a new commander to the Third Army and instructed the governors in various Anatolian towns to call upon first-class reservists and send them as reinforcements to the Third Army region.[429] This move, however, was part of a long-term plan, and the government was well aware that assembling a large task force from the various towns and deploying it in Macedonia would take some time; it therefore wanted to rush trustworthy troops to the region before the flames of rebellion engulfed all of Macedonia.

The sortie of the CPU Resen National Battalion prompted the government to take two swift measures. First it instructed the governor of Aydın to dispatch hastily first-class reservists to Salonica by sea. Second, the sultan ordered one of his most trusted officers, Şemsi Pasha, an Albanian general, who though unschooled had rendered great services to the sultan during many previous Albanian rebellions,[430] to command the troops which were due to arrive from Anatolia. The First Chamberlain cabled

Şemsi Pasha, who happened to be in Prizren, to assemble local troops while waiting for the Anatolian divisions to arrive; he was then to march against the insurgents with this combined force.[431] On the heels of these instructions, just half an hour later the sultan sent a second cable to Şemsi Pasha ordering him to take as many battalions as he wished from the Mitrovica division, and also as many volunteers as he could on the condition that he put them in military uniform, and to move against the insurgents without waiting for the arrival of the Anatolian divisions.[432] Şemsi Pasha hastily ordered the two mobilized battalions from the Mitrovica division to board a special train to Monastir. He drafted a small number of Albanian volunteers by telling them that the Christians were massacring Muslims, and he said they would be going into action against the Christians.[433] He also telegraphed Albanian notables asking for their help against the insurgents.[434]

Şemsi Pasha's force of two battalions and a small number of Albanian volunteers arrived in Monastir by train on July 7, 1908. Although Şemsi Pasha could not obtain any hard intelligence concerning the whereabouts of the CPU Resen National Battalion, he decided to go to Resen to direct his operations.

An armed clash with Şemsi Pasha's forces would be detrimental to the CPU, since his force was superior to the CPU band, and a clash with a force composed of Albanian troops and volunteers would irreparably harm CPU–Albanian relations. The CPU Monastir branch therefore decided to assassinate Şemsi Pasha before he started his operation.[435] On the very day of his arrival, as he was leaving the post office where he had exchanged telegrams with the First Chamberlain's office and Albanian notables, and just before stepping into the carriage which was to take him to Resen, a CPU self-sacrificing volunteer, First Lieutenant Âtıf (Kamçıl), shot the pasha to death. Although the details are uncertain, First Lieutenant Âtıf Bey was wounded in the leg as he fled the scene.[436] Şemsi Pasha's Albanian guards had been won over by the CPU and therefore they merely fired their guns into the air. They then refused to pursue the self-sacrificing volunteer and fled themselves.[437]

The assassination of Şemsi Pasha was a shattering blow to the palace[438] and a big boost to the CPU. In fact, before Şemsi Pasha arrived in town, the CPU Monastir branch had posted many copies of an ultimatum, entitled "Memorandum to the Governor of Monastir for the Present Illegal Government," declaring the government unlawful.[439] A copy of the appeal was also hung on the door of the governor's house in an envelope with a bullet enclosed.[440]

On the same night, the CPU Monastir branch requested two officers, who had been ordered by the Third Army commander to go to Salonica, to form a new band. These officers, Lieutenant Colonel Salâhaddin Bey and Major Hasan Bey, were joined by two captains and three lieutenants and formed a band of 120 men armed with rifles. They named their band the CPU Monastir band and left for Prilep.[441]

On July 11, 1908, Major Enver Bey, who led a band of volunteers and deserters, sent an ultimatum to the inspector general demanding that the sultan issue an imperial decree within 48 hours for the release of CPU members who had been brought to Istanbul and arrested. Enver Bey warned that he would not take any responsibility for future developments if the inspector general did not comply with the ultimatum.[442] He also distributed a handwritten appeal in Tikvesh to his "esteemed compatriots," asking them to join him or at least remain neutral.[443]

The now panic-ridden government ordered Şemsi Pasha's son-in-law, Lieutenant Colonel Re'fet Bey, gendarme commander of Monastir, to pursue the insurgents with the forces assembled by the late pasha, completely unaware that Re'fet Bey was a member of the CPU.[444] The CPU Monastir branch instructed him to play for time. Now safely assured that Şemsi Pasha's forces would not mount an attack, the CPU leadership realized that the balance of power in Macedonia had shifted to their favor.[445]

On July 8, 1908, the palace ordered Marshal Osman Fevzi Pasha, who was known as Tatar Osman Pasha, to proceed to Monastir as extraordinary commander to direct operations.[446] He was given instructions to meet with the inspector general, Hüseyin Hilmi Pasha, and the commander of the Third Army, Marshal İbrahim Pasha. The sultan further directed these three pashas to use all possible methods to arrest and execute Şemsi Pasha's assassin as a warning to others.[447] After meeting on July 10, 1908, the three pashas decided to offer an amnesty to those officers who had fled and to hunt down the CPU Resen National Battalion as soon as the Anatolian reserve divisions arrived.[448]

Many of the officers and soldiers of the Aydın first-class reservist battalions had become members of the CPU, however, thanks to Dr. Nâzım's work in Izmir; they refused to go to Salonica unless their stipends were paid in full.[449] Two days later all the reservists gathered in their barracks and repeated their demands in a threatening manner.[450] The palace ordered that the demands of reservists be met at once.[451] Following the payment, the vessels carrying the reinforcements set sail from Izmir for Salonica. The first reservist battalions arrived on June 14, 1908, and further units from Aydın and other towns in Anatolia continued to arrive in Salonica harbor through July 22, 1908.[452] CPU members greeted the arriving troops disembarking at the harbor with provocative speeches and fiery oratory. A CPU delegation composed of ulema, officers, officials, and local notables at the Vodina (Edessa) train station exhorted the troops on their way to Monastir not to march against their coreligionists. Subsequently the troops, most of whom had already been won over in Izmir, refused to march against CPU National Battalions. Indeed, many of them later joined the insurgents.[453]

In the meantime, the advisory councils that were dispatched to the towns where rebellious activities were gaining momentum failed in their mission. For example, a delegation of sheikhs, ulema, and local notables was dispatched to Ohrid and Struga to admonish the local population,[454] but when some Albanians working for the CPU delivered a threatening letter to this delegation, its members quickly returned to their hometowns.[455] Many notables refused to serve in such delegations, either out of sympathy for the movement or because they were already members of the CPU.[456] Similarly, when the commander of the Monastir Region, General Osman Hidayet Pasha, assembled the officers in Monastir on July 17, 1908, to warn them to obey the orders of the sultan, an officer shot and wounded him while he was delivering his speech.[457] Marshal Şükrü Pasha, who was dispatched to Skopje to admonish junior officers, was luckier. When he asked the officers to obey the orders of the sultan, a first lieutenant interrupted his speech, shouting that they would not use their swords against people who were demanding their legal rights.[458] During the last days of the revolution, the CPU Skopje branch quickly expelled Divisional General Hüseyin Remzi Pasha from the town, handing him a letter from the CPU explaining the dangers that would arise from his continued stay in Skopje. He was forced to take the next train to Salonica.[459]

CPU branches also issued warnings to local governors, declaring that any official who did not obey CPU instructions would be executed by the committee.[460] In a joint action CPU and Albanian committee members expelled from Scutari in Albania the governor, Seyfullah Pasha, and his son-in-law, Kemal Pasha.[461]

The activities of the CPU gendarme force likewise increased during these days. A *mufti* of a regiment in Salonica who had provided information to the palace in Istanbul was shot by an officer on July 10, 1908.[462] Lieutenant Colonel Ahmed Naim, who had first been shot and wounded on July 19,[463] was once again shot by a private working for the "CPU gendarme force" dispatched by the CPU on July 21; although military police arrested the private, he escaped with the CPU's assistance.[464] On July 23 the subgovernor of Alasonya (Elasson), who had received a warning from the local CPU branch, was assassinated, and a first lieutenant was killed in Salonica by the "CPU gendarme force."[465]

In the meantime, to the utter amazement of the Ottoman authorities, the CPU propaganda divisions posted appeals calling for the restoration of the constitution all around the cities, towns, and Muslim villages near Monastir, Salonica, and Kosovo.[466]

The government, astounded by these unprecedented developments, attempted to undercut any foreign support to the CPU by portraying the movement to the Great Powers and the European public as mere brigandage. Ottoman Foreign Minister Tevfik Pasha sent circulars to Ottoman ambassadors explaining the events from the palace's viewpoint and accusing Adjutant-Major Ahmed Niyazi of organizing bands composed of subversives, deserters, and individuals seduced by such people. Ahmed Tevfik Pasha told them to inform the foreign press and governments accordingly.[467]

The CPU took swift action to counter the government's attempts to sway foreign opinion. On July 12, 1908, the CPU Monastir branch forwarded a memorandum to the consuls in that town. It made the following points:

Le but final et principal que la Ligue poursuit est d'obtenir l'application franche et sincère de la constitution de 1876 (1292) [sic]. . . .

Les Grandes Puissances en spécial ont l'occasion de donner une preuve de leurs bonnes intentions envers les peuples de la Turquie, en conseillant avec insistance le détenteur actuel du pouvoir, S. M. le Sultan, de céder aux demandes si bien fondées de ses sujets encore fidèles mais revoltés à cause de la situation honteuse créée à leur patrie.

La Ligue déclare solennellement qu'elle n'est nullement hostile aux non-musulmans. . . .

Pour donner une preuve encore du manque de scrupules du Gouvernement il suffit de citer le fait très-récent suivant; Chemsi Pasha, dans le but d'entrainer sa garde personnelle composée de Bachi-Bozouks, lui avait fait voir dans l'incident de Resna une surrection Serbe. L'emploi des Bachi-Bozouks, qui ne connaissent aucune loi et qui ne cherchent qu'à piller, ne constitue-t-il pas un mépris de[s] conseils amicaux que les Grandes Puissances ont donné[s] toujours au Gouvernement.[468]

Two days before its triumph, the CPU Internal Headquarters presented a second note to the consuls of the Great Powers in Salonica. It gave further assurances to the powers about the liberal character of the movement, and it vigorously denied the charges of the Ottoman government that the CPU had been attempting to incite Muslim fanaticism against the Christians. The CPU Internal Headquarters maintained that their work was not limited to the European provinces but covered the whole empire, and they averred that they had learned from European history a lesson regarding love of liberty, equality, and justice.[469]

While the CPU Internal Headquarters and branches were trying to refute the Ottoman government's claims concerning the nature of the revolution, the external headquarters issued a similar communiqué rebutting the same allegations for the benefit of the European press. The communiqué stated that the CPU respected all international treaties and that Jews, Christians, and Muslims had the same duties and rights.[470] The CPU circulated two more communiqués declaring that it would never accept foreign intervention, that the rebellion was an internal matter of the Ottoman Empire,[471] and that the CPU was not working for the interests of any Great Power.[472] In the interviews that he gave to European dailies, Ahmed Rıza also rejected the government's charges that the officers who were leading the movement in Macedonia were rebels.[473]

In sum, the CPU won all the battles on all the fronts. It started the revolution by sending out armed bands and carrying out assassinations. The government's every effort to check the revolutionary activity was in vain. The imperial government could not even mobilize a force to pursue the insurgents. The CPU paralyzed the civil administration in Macedonia and became a state within a state in the three provinces. Finally, by carrying out active propaganda, the CPU reassured the Great Powers that their movement was liberal, that it was not against Christians or Europe, and that everybody would benefit from a change of regime in the Ottoman Empire. Besides winning all these battles, the CPU skillfully exploited an Albanian Geg gathering, where it obtained a *besa* (besë) (solemn oath)[474] from the Albanians, who swore that no force would hinder them from working for the restoration of the constitution and the reopening of the parliament. With this result the CPU was ready to deliver the *coup de grâce* to the Hamidian regime.

The Firzovik Gathering and the CPU

While the CPU members were working hard to put CPU bands in the field, a special Austro-German school for the children of foreign railway workers in Skopje organized a rail excursion and a picnic at the gardens of a certain Hajrulah, an Albanian guard of the railway company, in the village of Saratishta near Firzovik. The government, which was on the alert because of the CPU's activities, ordered the local authorities to take all necessary precautions to prevent any Muslims from seizing the opportunity to hold a demonstration against foreigners. When some townspeople complained about the foreigners' picnic, the local authorities cancelled it. Nonetheless, "some conspirators" spread a rumor that Austrian troops were coming to take over Kosovo. The rumor inflamed[475] the already considerable anti-Austrian sentiment in the region.[476]

It is uncertain who these "conspirators" were and whether they had any relation to the CPU or the Albanian organizations. Nonetheless, despite the local authorities' announcements of cancellation, thousands of Albanian Gegs began to pour into Firzovik from other towns and villages in Gegëni. This mob refused to listen to an admonitory delegation composed of an *ʿalim*, some notables, and some law enforcement officers. It met only with the *'alim* and informed him that more people from other districts were coming.[477] The Ottoman authorities ordered the dispersal of the Albanian mobs in various towns,[478] but instead these mobs began to march on Firzovik. In the meantime the mob in Firzovik burned down the houses of two railway company guards who had invited foreigners to their gardens.[479] The Grand Vizier's office, fearing the emergence of a new crisis from the turmoil in Macedonia, directed Hüseyin Hilmi Pasha, the inspector general, to dispatch an official to find out the reason for the gathering and then to disperse the mob without use of force.[480] Upon receiving this order, the inspector general selected Colonel Galib, the commander of the gendarmes in Skopje, and dispatched him to Firzovik to carry out the mission. He did not know that Colonel Galib was a member of the executive committee of the CPU Skopje branch.[481] The branch instructed Galib Bey to stir up the Albanians by exploiting their fear of foreign threats and to obtain a *besa* from them demanding the restoration of the constitution. The CPU also succeeded in bringing three Albanian leaders to Firzovik, where they used their connections and ethnic credentials to help Colonel Galib stir up the crowd.[482] Two of them were Nexhib Draga, a member of the CPU Skopje branch who had close ties to the Albanian committees, and his brother Ferhad Draga. The third Albanian leader was Bajram Curri, a well-known and influential member of the Bashkimi committee.[483] The Albanian leaders played to the crowd by putting on their Albanian committee hats, and they provoked it by focusing on the most sensitive issue among the Muslim Albanians, the threat of "foreign intervention."[484] The Ottoman authorities were deeply dismayed when they learned that some "ignorant" people in the crowd were reading the journal *Drita*, the organ of the Bashkimi committee.[485]

While Colonel Galib attempted to persuade the Ottoman government to allow the Albanian notables and ulema to come to Firzovik on the grounds that doing so would prevent the mob from turning violent,[486] the three Albanian leaders did their best to persuade the Albanians to swear an oath to work for the restoration of the constitution. Meanwhile the crowd, now numbering 20,000, occupied the post office and began inviting Albanians in other provinces, including those in Monastir, to join them.[487]

In the end, the Albanians who had first gathered to protest a school picnic and then decided to take a *besa* to prevent internecine killings in Kosovo agreed to take a different *besa*, as a result of the work of Colonel Galib and the Albanian committee members. Brandishing the Holy Qur'ān before the crowd, a local *'alim* whom Colonel Galib made a CPU member declared in the Firzovik mosque after prayers that demanding the restoration of the constitution was equivalent to demanding the application of the *sharī'a*. Albanian ulema and notables confirmed this claim, and it was then decided to take a *besa* for the restoration of the constitution.[488]

In the course of all this, the government finally learned that Colonel Galib was not a "trustworthy person" and recalled him on July 19, 1908.[489] It was already too late. On the very same day Colonel Galib advised the authorities that the Albanians who gathered in Firzovik had taken "a very strong *besa*" demanding reforms.[490]

On July 20, 1908, the crowd sent two identical telegrams signed by 194 notables and ulema on their behalf to the Grand Vizier and the *Şeyhülislâm*, demanding that they in turn submit the telegram to the sultan. This telegram pleading for the restoration of the constitution was written in a highly respectful tone and adopted a markedly Islamic rhetoric.[491] When the CPU branches started bombarding the palace and government with telegrams demanding the restoration of the constitutional regime, Sudi Bey, the mayor of Priština, sent a new telegram to the authorities on behalf of the crowd, forcefully warning them that they would face dire consequences in the event that the crowd's demands were not met.[492] The sultan, it was said, asked İsmail Kemal for help as a last resort. İsmail Kemal allegedly responded that the only way to pacify the Albanians was to restore the constitution.[493] The Albanians' emphatic insistence on the reinstatement of the constitution was a clear sign that the days of the Hamidian regime were numbered.

The Declaration of *Hürriyet* (Freedom)

The events following Şemsi Pasha's assassination showed that the CPU had gained the upper hand in Macedonia and that nothing could be done to reverse that fact. The palace was in a panic, the government was powerless, and the local authorities were totally incapable of executing any instructions directed against the CPU. Among the high-ranking officials asked to submit their opinion, only the Ottoman Minister of War Mehmed Rıza Pasha advised the sultan "to apply the penal code" and punish the insurgents.[494] Almost all others recommended the implementation of swift reforms instead of "issuing warnings and using force and brutality which were too late to produce any positive results."[495]

In the meantime, the CPU branches decided to escalate their activities to deliver the final blow and create a *fait accompli* in Macedonia. On July 12, 1908, the Monastir branch sent a captain to the British consulate to tell the consul that "an extension of the rising to the town of Monastir is planned to take place in the course of a few days, that the intention is to take possession of the telegraph and most likely to cut the railway." The captain inquired how the British government would view the matter, "especially if some constitutional government could be set up [there] locally."[496]

On July 20, 1908, the CPU Monastir branch issued a directive banning anyone from using firearms in the town and stating that the CPU's "comité de salut public (Cemiyetin selâmet-i umumiye komisyonu)" was in charge of the town.[497] On July 21, 1908, the CPU Internal Headquarters sent sealed instructions to all branches directing them to commence the final revolutionary activities and to fulfill their task by Thursday, July 23, 1908. According to these instructions, a joint force of military units and volunteers would start marching on the capital on June 26, 1908, if the government continued to resist.[498]

Upon receiving these instructions, the new band of the CPU Monastir branch, called the CPU Ohrid National Regiment, left for the mountains on July 21, 1908, under the command of Adjutant-Major Eyüb Sabri and Second Lieutenant Mazhar Efendi.[499] On the same day, the Albanians who had gathered in Firzovik and been stirred up by CPU and Albanian committee members demanded special trains to go to Skopje, and they threatened to seize trains in the event that the government refused to supply them.[500] The commanders of the garrison in Skopje declared that they would not prevent the trains from entering the town.[501]

The next day Captain Bekir Fikri handed out rifles from the military warehouse in Grebená to his 390-man band and volunteers. To control the town, he left behind a well-armed reserve force composed of 410 locals.[502] He declared to the Ottoman authorities that this reserve force would take charge of the town.[503]

On the night of July 22, 1908, the CPU Monastir branch ordered the CPU Resen National Battalion, the CPU Ohrid National Regiment, and the CPU Monastir band to storm the town. A force of 2,300 men, including two Albanian bands, then entered Monastir and kidnapped Marshal Osman Pasha, the extraordinary commander appointed by Istanbul.[504] The CPU force next seized all government buildings, declaring that it was in charge of the town and that anybody who dared to dispute its authority or disobey its orders would be executed on the spot.[505] The CPU Monastir branch, now in complete control of the telegraph lines, sent telegrams to governors and high-ranking officials in other provinces telling them that the constitution would be put into effect by force on July 23, 1908, and bidding them to carry out their duties accordingly.[506]

Elsewhere the CPU branches began telegraphing the First Chamberlain's office through the inspector general. On July 22, 1908, a telegram on behalf of the entire population of Gevgelija was delivered to the inspector general asking for the reinstatement of the constitution.[507] The next day the CPU Monastir branch issued an ultimatum to the government demanding the restoration of the constitution by Sunday, July 26, 1908.[508] In the meantime, without waiting for the issuance of an imperial decree, the Monastir branch announced *hürriyet* with a 21-gun salute and declared the constitution of 1876 restored.[509] In Salonica during the early hours of the day, officers posted fliers asking the population to obey the CPU's orders. When the police attempted to tear down the fliers, the CPU countered with its own "gendarme force," which deployed the same policemen to protect the appeals.[510] Later in the day, in all the cities and even in small towns throughout Macedonia, crowds led by officers declared *hürriyet* with cannon fire. CPU leaders, CPU band commanders, notables, and religious leaders of various communities delivered thundering speeches. Even in the smallest towns, crowds incited by CPU members declared that the terms of the constitution would go into effect the next day.[511]

On the same day, July 23, 1908, the CPU branches bombarded the inspector general's office with telegrams to be submitted to the sultan and the Grand Vizier. All of these telegrams forcefully demanded the restoration of the constitutional regime, fixed as the deadline June 26, 1908, and threatened the palace with a march on the capital.[512] Some of them made trenchant threats, such as pledging a new oath of allegiance to the heir apparent,[513] and many crowds boasted that they would not disperse without receiving an affirmative answer to their demands from the capital, in the form of an imperial decree.

These developments prompted the sultan to take new measures. He dismissed Mehmed Ferid Pasha on July 22, 1908, and appointed Mehmed Sa'id Pasha as the new grand vizier. In the new cabinet, Kâmil Pasha, who had been dismissed because of his proposal advocating responsible government in 1895, became a minister without portfolio.[514] The next day the sultan required eleven select members of the cabinet and the director of the office of the general staff, Mehmed Şakir Pasha, to review all the telegrams sent from Macedonia and prepare a report on possible solutions to the political crisis. The sultan's appointment of Mehmed Saʿid Pasha was a clear sign of his expectation that the special commission would reject the idea of reopening the parliament. Mehmed Saʿid Pasha had persistently expressed his view to the sultan that "the nation is not ready for a constitutional regime."[515]

At the meeting of this special commission held at the Yıldız Palace, all the telegrams sent from Macedonia were read and a lengthy discussion was opened. The military members of the commission strongly denounced the officers who took part in the rebellion, while the civilian members wanted an investigation to find out who had provoked it. The ministers apparently feared submitting to the sultan a memorandum openly advocating the restoration of the constitutional system.

In the meantime the Grand Vizier sent telegrams to the various provinces and subprovinces that had made demands for the reopening of the parliament. He explained that the special commission was in session and asked them not to take any further action.[516] The Grand Vizier also sent a telegram to both the inspector general and the commander of the Third Army informing them that the cabinet was discussing the demands of the three provinces and that it would decide "whether the reopening of the parliament in the midst of such political problems would be hazardous to the state or not."[517]

As instructed by the CPU Internal Headquarters, the CPU branches responded immediately to these telegrams by asserting that it was the central government which created all those political problems, and that the nation had officially declared *hürriyet*. They also argued that the people had no need for "a decision by a cabinet that never cares for the interests of the country and the rights of the people."[518] They again threatened a march on the capital and a strict enforcement of the deadline.

This new flurry of telegrams compelled the sultan to send a messenger to tell the members of the special commission that "he was not against the reinstatement of the constitution."[519] The ministers, much relieved, immediately drafted a memorandum for submission to the sultan.[520] It employed very harsh language against the rebels but advised the sultan to reopen the Chamber of Deputies, which had been suspended "for a temporary period."[521] The sultan issued an imperial decree accepting the *fait accompli*.[522] The decree was rushed to the dailies and published on July 24, 1908.[523] The CPU's de facto declarations had acquired legal validity. The Young Turk movement had accomplished its long-awaited goal.

The Sultan's Last Attempts to Thwart the Movement

Although Abdülhamid II had yielded to the demands of the CPU at gunpoint, he did make a few final attempts to thwart the Young Turk movement's last operation. There is no doubt that the sultan saw constitutionalism as a threat to the very existence of the empire. He especially feared the emergence of party politics. It is also true that before the revolution rumors had circulated about his growing interest in some sort of representative government.[524] Indeed the available documents reveal that the sultan had started to collect information on the duties and responsibilities of the cabinet ministers of various countries to their rulers; but there is no evidence that he had any intention of reestablishing the parliamentary regime.[525] Thus it is no surprise that immediately before and after the revolution the sultan tried a few gambits to prevent the CPU from establishing a new regime based on party politics.

The first gambit was the so-called Münir Pasha and Kâmil Bey mission. It is difficult to be certain whether the sultan himself instructed these two officials, the Ottoman ambassador to France and the Ottoman commissioner in Bulgaria, to take such an initiative. It is unlikely, however, that these two carried out their exceptionally delicate mission on their own without the knowledge of the sultan.

Sources close to the CPU vigorously claimed after the revolution that Münir Pasha approached Stanchov, the Bulgarian diplomatic agent in Paris, and requested Bulgarian assistance in thwarting the Young Turk movement during the initial stages of the rebellion. These sources also stated that Münir Pasha offered new privileges to the Bulgarian principality in return for its help.[526] As a CPU member in Monastir told the Bulgarian consul:

> Given the rapid development of events, there was only one means left to the sultan to paralyze the Young Turk movement, namely to involve the army in a war with Bulgaria. The Greeks within the empire headed by their patriarch had agreed to participate in the plot . . . Münir Pasha was assigned the task of securing the neutrality of the other Balkan states. Fortunately we [the CPU leaders in Macedonia] received that information from our members in Paris and sped things up. Otherwise it would have been no surprise if the plot had succeeded and thereby put our work in grave danger.[527]

Münir Pasha sent notes to Ottoman dailies denying the charges and claiming that his mission was to form a Balkan alliance among the Ottoman Empire, Greece, Romania, and Serbia. But when he presented a memorandum at the end of his mission to the Ottoman Foreign Ministry, the dailies stood by their assertions, alleging that Münir Pasha had two different missions and that his secret mission was directed by the First Chamberlain's office.[528] Various diplomatic reports and accounts by journalists asserted that Münir Pasha took such actions against the Young Turk movement as securing the neutrality of the Balkan states during the rebellion,[529] and they underscored the tensions that had arisen between Münir Pasha and the CPU because of the pasha's alleged mission.[530] No source, however, furnished a clear picture of the mission.

In addition to Münir Pasha's efforts, Kâmil Bey, the Ottoman commissioner in Bulgaria, made a more explicit démarche. On June 25, 1908, Kâmil Bey requested an urgent secret audience with the prince of Bulgaria in order to convey a message from the sultan. Kâmil Bey "carefully avoided" divulging any details of the secret message even to the Bulgarian Foreign Minister Paprikov.[531] Kâmil Bey went to Varna for the secret audience on June 27, 1908.[532] We do not know anything, however, about the sultan's message or the prince's response to it.[533]

The Bulgarian documents indicate that the sultan's confidants continued making overtures to the Bulgarian government after the revolution. On August 31, 1908, Kâmil Bey made a new démarche and told Paprikov that "the sultan's situation is very precarious. He expects a revolution in Asia [Anatolia] as well." Kâmil Bey asked "whether [they] would not be disposed to do something to distract the armies' attention from Istanbul." Paprikov replied that "such a game would turn out to be even more dangerous both for the sultan and for the empire." Paprikov also made the following comment on the Ottoman commissioner's démarche: "I understood that the commissioner would like to push us in this direction [i.e., war], which would be very useful for the sultan and Turkey, but extremely dangerous for us."[534] Despite the Bulgarian foreign minister's refusal to engage in any secret dealings to help the sultan, Kâmil Bey continued his initiatives until he returned Istanbul.[535]

The Italian ambassador to the Ottoman Empire, Guglielmo Imperiali di Francavilla, who had served as the Italian diplomatic agent in Sofia before coming to Istanbul, commented that "a holy war against Bulgaria" would solve the problems that the sultan faced from the Young Turk movement[536] and would mobilize the Muslims in the European provinces against Bulgaria. Although we do not know the details of the scheme, the available documents provide enough circumstantial evidence for such a démarche and its failure.

Following his issuance of the imperial decree restoring the constitutional regime, the sultan made a second gambit to prevent the CPU from becoming the center of power in Ottoman politics and to impede the emergence of party politics in the empire. On July 24, 1908, the Grand Vizier, as ordered by the sultan, instructed the inspector general in Salonica to dissolve all political organizations and put an end to political demonstrations.[537] The CUP leaders categorically refused to accept this order; they told the inspector general that "it was not the Sultan who accorded but the Army which exacted the concession, and that the maintenance of the Committee [the CUP][538] was therefore essential until the parliament was duly constituted."[539] The inspector general accordingly advised the Grand Vizier that it was not possible to dissolve the CUP, since it had already emerged as the dominant actor in Ottoman politics, and that any such attempt would have very undesirable consequences.[540]

On the heels of this first postrevolution conflict between the palace and the CUP, the latter's organs published appeals labeling the CUP as "a national organization" and asserting that the continuation of its activities was more necessary than ever because of the delicate situation in the empire.[541] The CUP, according to these appeals, would safeguard the election process and make sure that honest individuals became members of the Chamber of Deputies and Senate.[542] The CUP's dominance in Ottoman politics now became clear to everybody.

Dissolution of all political organizations, including the CUP, would have enabled the sultan to remain supreme. It would have produced a parliament free of political parties, as was the case during the first constitutional period 32 years earlier. The CUP, however, had no intention of surrendering the political arena to the sultan and the Sublime Porte bureaucracy.

Extremely upset by the sultan's initiative and seeking to bolster its legal position, the CUP now demanded that the sultan cede the gardens known as the White Tower Gardens in Salonica to the CUP for a new headquarters.[543] The CUP branches immediately followed the example of the internal headquarters and demanded similar privileges from the sultan. The sultan's imperial decrees granting these favors meant recognition of the CUP. This recognition by the highest authority forced other authorities to follow suit and acknowledge the CUP's existence.[544]

This unprecedented recognition was a foretaste of the CUP's new political ascendancy, an ascendancy that lasted for ten years with only a short intermission. The Young Turk Revolution of 1908 not only forced the sultan to restore the constitutional regime, but also made the CUP the supreme force in Ottoman politics. Its victory was total; July 23, 1908, marked the dawn of a new era in Ottoman history.

The Young Turk Revolution was undoubtedly a watershed in late Ottoman history and had an undeniable impact on the future of the Middle East and Balkans. A close examination of the available material reveals conclusively that it was no mere bluff on the part of a handful of junior officers who took to the mountains to cajole the authorities. On July 23, 1908, the CPU had put a force of some 4,000 armed men in the field, not to mention the other CPU members in Macedonia. Soon thereafter it became clear that the CPU had the power to bring virtually all the important garrisons of the Third Army district over to its side should the sultan refuse to restore the constitution. By then it also had at its disposal at least 20,000 fully armed Albanian Gegs, the Serres and Strumica band network of the left wing of the IMRO, the Albanian Tosk bands, and those of the Kutzo-Vlachs. It should also be remembered that the first-class reservist battalions dispatched to Macedonia to march on the insurgents had gone over to the CPU cause. The number of troops of the Third Army alone, 70,000, exceeded the total number of troops of the First and Second Armies between Macedonia and the capital. No Ottoman sultan could risk a civil war between Ottoman armies, and Abdülhamid II's final decision reflected a realistic appraisal of the situation. It did not stem from his "suspicious character," as Turkish historiography has often asserted. As Karabekir made clear, these claims were made by people who did not know the real strength of the CPU, a power that was far greater than has been realized by later scholars.[545]

9

The CUP Consolidates Its Revolution

An Epilogue

On July 25, 1908, a Russian civil agent commented that the CUP and the Third Army controlled all the towns of Macedonia as if there were no government.[1] Nothing could better describe the situation in the Ottoman Empire after the revolution than this remark. In the three European provinces the CUP established de facto control, whereas the other regions of the empire were not even aware of the revolutionary movement, learning of it only after the restoration of the constitutional regime.[2]

Two centers of power—the CUP Headquarters in Salonica and the Sublime Porte—moved to compete with the palace for control of the empire in the days following the revolution. The battle for supremacy waged by these three authorities continued until April 1909, but never was it more bitter than in the period before the new parliament convened. In the midst of this three-way melee there were now masses proclaiming that *hürriyet* would sweep away all that was corrupt and unsatisfactory about the old regime.

The CUP, which naturally took great pride in its achievement, left no doubt from the first day of the new regime that it intended to take complete charge of everything, allowing only a limited sphere of influence to other political actors. The CUP leaders declared without false modesty that the CUP was "the soul of the state,"[3] that it "fear[ed] only God,"[4] and that to oppose it was "an expression of nescience."[5] The CUP referred to itself as the "sacred committee" (*cemiyet-i mukaddese*). Some regional branches even went so far as to carve this new and unabashedly exalted appellation into their seals.[6] The leaders of the revolution did not doubt that they were pursuing an unassailable and divinely appointed mission.

From the beginning of the revolution until September 18, 1908, when the CUP held its first legal, but still secret, congress, an *ad hoc* group composed of members of the former internal headquarters' executive committee and Dr. Nâzım directed the "sacred committee's" affairs. Dr. Bahaeddin Şakir joined this group upon his return from Paris. The CUP stuck to its principle of not appointing a director in order to avoid internecine conflict.[7] This precaution, however, did not mean that there were no such struggles. From the very first day of the new regime, there was friction between the CUP organizations in Salonica and Monastir, the strongest CUP organizations inside the empire.[8] Ahmed Rıza, who was the last CPU External Headquarters member to return, was disappointed to realize that he would not become the strong man of the CUP and that its leading figures ignored his memoranda.[9]

Nonetheless, during the first year the CUP did succeed in holding together almost all its factions. Under the new regime the intellectuals of the committee were gradually pushed aside. Although some of them assumed prestigious posts, the professional committee organizers, such as Talât Bey, Dr. Bahaeddin Şakir, and Dr. Nâzım, held the real power and indeed became more influential than cabinet ministers or even grand viziers. Remarkably, no definite information about the CUP's inner workings and leadership was leaked to the press, and the CUP leaders successfully kept the nature of their positions secret.

Following the revolution, the CUP lost no time in displaying its might and authority with a number of forceful demonstrations. In Macedonia when a corporal named Bilâl killed a CUP member, the CUP branch took matters into its own hands, declaring that "the assassin Bilâl's action was an assault on the sacred committee" and that it thus had the right to execute him. Even though the local court decided Bilâl's punishment was to be death, the local CUP branch members kidnapped Bilâl from jail and executed him by firing squad, denying him the chance to appeal.[10]

In many towns, such as Korçë, the CUP ordered residents to sign loyalty documents pledging their allegiance to the "sacred committee."[11] The CUP Edirne branch instructed the post offices in the province not to allow anyone other than foreign consuls to send coded telegrams unless the CUP branch had examined them first. Not even Ottoman state officials were exempted. The branch declared, "Anybody who dares to challenge this decision will be executed on the spot."[12] The Iōánnina branch of the CUP, which had been reading the telegrams between the governor and the imperial palace, instructed the governor of Iōánnina not to obey the orders given by one of the sultan's secretaries because the branch considered them unconstitutional.[13]

Later the CUP demanded that the Ministry of Communications ensure that all telegrams from CUP branches be sent without any delay whatsoever and that anyone found preventing a CUP telegram from reaching its destination be punished.[14] Other CUP branches bombarded the government with menacing telegrams threatening to execute telegraph operators who hesitated to send hostile telegrams to the Sublime Porte.[15] Fear of the CUP quickly spread throughout the ranks of the state bureaucracy, and in Salonica law enforcement personnel hesitated to arrest criminals for fear that the "crimes may have been ordered by the Ottoman Committee of Union and Progress." In order to make law enforcement work and to prevent complete chaos, the CUP central committee had to issue appeals demanding that policemen arrest criminals.[16]

In short, the CUP became a *comité de salut public* during the first days of the revolution, and it continued to play this role until the first elections and the convening of the new parliament.[17] The CUP took charge of everything. It scolded the Grand Vizier when he could not meet its deadline[18] and bluntly reproved him, adding dismissively that the CUP had known that "the present government would continue to administer the state arbitrarily and illegally."[19] Anybody who claimed to be a CUP member could order virtually anything he wished. For example, a confidence trickster who pretended to be a CUP member twice ordered a major to a hotel to call upon the governor of Hüdavendigâr province, and the major obeyed each time without questioning.[20] Elsewhere, impostors collected money by posing as members of the "sacred committee."[21] Finally, the CUP had to distribute appeals announcing that CUP members appearing before government offices on official business would be provided with special committee documents describing their mission. The appeals cautioned officials not to speak with professed CUP members without first determining that they carried the appropriate credentials.[22] Despite assurances by the CUP that it did not resemble the *comité de salut public* of the French Revolution and that it wanted to realize its humanitarian and social aims through peaceful means, it nonetheless did not hesitate to flex its muscle before its opponents in an unambiguous fashion during the early phases of the constitutional regime.[23]

In order to extend its virtually unassailable control from Macedonia to the capital and the non-European provinces, the CUP central committee dispatched official delegations to them. The most important delegation was of course that sent to Istanbul. Officially the CUP declared that it was sending the delegation to strengthen the trust and understanding between itself and the government.[24] The CUP central committee provided Mustafa Rahmi, the leader of this delegation, with a twenty-article agenda, which included demands for the appointment of foreign officials to reorganize the Ottoman customs, the dismissal of numerous Ottoman officials, the appointment of specific officials to various positions, and the settlement of the border dispute with Montenegro.[25] The document touched on all important domestic and foreign issues. Major Cemal Bey, a member of the CUP delegation, handed over an additional note to the acting Ottoman Minister of War dictating the appointments of the fourteen highest commanders in the Ottoman army.[26]

In a more significant move, the CUP forced the government of Mehmed Sa'id Pasha, which it judged unfit for office, to resign on August 4, 1908. There seemed to be nothing that the CUP could not achieve or was not involved in during the early days of the new regime. For example, it dictated the conditions of the amnesty to the government,[27] ordered the government to deploy military patrols for peace and order in the capital,[28] asked the inspector general to take necessary countermeasures against spying by the personnel of the Greek consulate in Salonica,[29] sent its members to advise local people to pay their taxes and fulfill other obligations to the state,[30] acted as a mediator between various Christian groups and the government,[31] and even granted permits for the performance of plays in theaters.[32] References to this authority of the CUP are numerous in the government's official correspondence; one document speaks of the need "to employ police commissioners Emin and Nazmi Efendis in Salonica or Kosovo because of the CUP's demand,"[33] while another speaks of "the dismissal of the present governor of Monastir and appointment in his place of Divisional General Fahri Pasha in accordance with the CUP's proposal."[34]

The CUP center set itself up in the capital in order to be able to give "advice" to the government and the various offices under the central committee's instructions. As a warning to the new cabinet, two members of the CUP branch in the capital met with the new Grand Vizier Kâmil Pasha; they enjoined him to take all necessary measures for public safety and order and to put an end to all appeals to the sultan, telling him that the CUP would provide as many members as necessary to join the law enforcement personnel. The Grand Vizier brought the communication to the cabinet ministers, who accepted the CUP's instructions.[35]

The CUP central committee in Salonica corresponded directly with the Grand Vizier's office by using the latter's cipher code, and it regularly issued orders in a way no cabinet minister would have dared to do. For example, when the CPU sent a delegation to Paris and London to meet with French and British statesmen, the central committee insisted that the Grand Vizier's office forward detailed information about the Ottoman government's assessments of diplomatic issues so that the delegation could discuss the matters in question with more competence.[36]

In the meantime, the CUP dispatched delegations or traveling agents to the Asiatic provinces and to Tripoli of Barbary. Their role was to explain the nature of the new regime to the people in these regions, to force local leaders to sign professions of loyalty to the constitutional regime,[37] and to set up CUP branches in every corner of the empire.[38] Here, however, the CUP faced an unexpected and unwelcome problem. As had happened before during the formation of the older CPU branches, the initiative came not from the center but from the regions, where notables, officials, and officers first formed CUP branches and only then sought the central committee's approval. Later the CUP confessed that "many local malefactors throughout the country . . . who wanted to use the committee's power for their own account had joined the organization."[39] The government constantly complained of interference in local politics by "ignorant" people who feigned affiliation with the CUP.[40] Some local CUP members even went so far as to levy wholly arbitrary taxes.[41] Many branches opened without the approval of the central committee in the provinces, and, acting as if they were receiving orders from a single center, every one of these branches urged the people of its district not to pay taxes. This situation caused a huge decrease in state tax collection,[42] and the government had to order local authorities to ignore the demands of CUP branches in regions other than the European provinces where the CUP had this and all other questions firmly under its control.[43] The CUP also distributed appeals imploring people to pay their taxes, explaining to them that "freedom" did not mean not paying taxes.[44]

The CUP also inserted itself into the fabric of local politics. CUP branches replaced institutions or bodies such as religious sects and notable households through which local demands had been made and local politics were transacted. In various places, such as Mosul, rival notables formed rival CUP branches that squabbled with one another over local political issues.[45] During the first year after the revolution it was everybody's ambition to be in control of the CUP branches, since they were universally dominant. Later, weaker groups in the provinces formed branches of the new parties which began to mushroom in the capital with the dawn of the new political system.[46]

Asserting their dominance, the CUP branches began to dismiss unpopular governors and officials, sometimes through violent demonstrations.[47] The CUP, however, wished to carry out a centrally planned purge of its remaining opponents, and it ordered its branches to put an end to their direct intervention in local government affairs and to stop dismissing officials. It urged local people to appeal to the central committee regarding suspected misconduct by important officials,[48] as when government authorities failed to conduct a necessary investigation,[49] or when obstacles were placed in the way of a popular petition.[50] Yet despite the central committee's instructions, many governors continued to accept the activities of the local CUP branches in "assisting the local government."[51] When the CUP branches called for the investigation of local officials, the latter usually complied by furnishing information to the Grand Vizier's office, and would also look into the matter and provide information to the CUP local branches as if these were properly authorized government offices.[52]

The CUP central committee knew very little about the members of these branches who were "assisting local governments,"[53] and it took more than two years to assert firm control over them. During the early years of the constitutional regime the CUP always worked with trusted officers that it knew in the local branches, and not with the locals themselves. It was some time before a local CUP network with the same goals and agenda as the center was in place. Until then the CUP invited only its trusted members to congresses and other important meetings, a practice that sparked protests in local branches.[54]

The CUP leaders did not intend their organization to be a decentralized one in practice, its written regulations notwithstanding. Accordingly, the CUP functioned as a strict hierarchy, with the central committee at the top and the periphery totally subordinated to the center whenever it was within its control. By dispatching to the provinces special delegations and inspectors empowered to discipline disobedient members and branches, the CUP was eventually able to build the provincial network it had always desired, that is, a network working obediently under the instructions of the central committee despite its semiautonomous character on paper.[55]

While the CUP and other party branches were mushrooming throughout the empire, former underground nationalist organizations of various Ottoman ethnic groups turned themselves into legal societies. Also, Ottoman ethnic groups that until then had lacked any societies, such as the Circassians, formed their own organizations.[56] The CUP, however, had no desire for a pluralist political system in which various parties and societies would pursue their particular agendas. Rather, its leaders envisioned an umbrella organization under which all ethnic, religious, and social groups would work together within limits carefully drawn by the CUP. CUP members expressed this vision on various occasions by answering the question, "Who are the members of the CUP?" with the response, "The entire Ottoman nation."[57] In order to achieve this vision, in appearance if not in reality, the CUP unilaterally and fictitiously declared the merger of their arch-rival Sabahaddin Bey's league with itself,[58] and it formed various specialized subdivisions such as the CUP ulema division[59] and the CUP women's division.[60] To mobilize professional groups such as the merchants[61] and keep them under its guidance, the CUP either set up special satellite organizations or co-opted already existing professional associations.[62]

Many praised the work of the CUP in inclusive terms: one admirer claimed that "everybody is a citizen belonging to the CUP and is ready to sacrifice everything for it;"[63] another averred that "all other organizations should work as CUP divisions."[64] Yet the CUP soon understood that assembling so many disparate groups under a single banner was an impossibility because of their inherently conflicting goals. It also realized that in a constitutional system it could not prevent its rivals from forming competing societies and political parties. Nevertheless, the CUP made its privileged position crystal clear. It forbade the government to accept any applications from other societies and ordered it to heed only CUP requests. The CUP further declared that "no other society has an official title"[65] and that they were merely unofficial societies. From a strictly legal point of view this was true. No organization, including the CUP, could technically be considered a society without government approval, since the Ottoman state lacked a law on societies at the time.[66]

Even after the new parliament was convened and the new regime had settled into its work, the CUP persisted in functioning as a kind of parallel government. It continued to interfere in all kinds of government affairs. For example, it asked the parliament to add an article to the "Press Law" banning the "smuggling and distribution of seditious papers published in foreign countries";[67] it warned the government about the situation in Iran and demanded the deployment of Ottoman troops in the event of Russian occupation of particular parts of Iran;[68] it called for investigations of corrupt officials,[69] asked for the appointment of new governors,[70] requested the government to support grape growers in the province of Aydın,[71] demanded that the Grand Vizier appease Sandanski,[72] and advised the government to grant property to Bulgarians in Anatolia to thwart the "machinations" of the Macedo-Bulgarian Committees.[73]

Despite the strong protests of its rivals,[74] the CUP did not cede an inch of its self-proclaimed privileged position until 1909, the year in which it officially became an ostensibly ordinary society in compliance with the new law of societies[75] and separated itself entirely from the parliamentary group of Union and Progress.[76] This change, however, was effected only on paper. The CUP continued as before to intervene in government affairs and to function as a parallel government in the Ottoman Empire.[77]

Despite its illusory nature, the division of the CUP into two separate, independent entities proved an extremely difficult process. First, the organization had a radical faction composed of self-sacrificing volunteers who virulently opposed even the appearance of the CUP's metamorphosis into a benevolent society and parliamentary group similar to other societies and parties. This faction pressured the organization to intervene more frequently and directly in the "nation's affairs." Some of the former self-sacrificing volunteers formed small secret societies to threaten other organizations or government officials. One of them, called the Red Axe Committee, blamed the principle of constitutional rights for tying the hands of the CUP.[78] Most of these militant CUP members remained within the CUP and, like the earlier activist factions of the various Young Turk organizations, they lobbied from within to encourage the committee to adopt a more radical, activist policy against its opponents.[79] Indeed, its new and allegedly tame character notwithstanding, the CUP retained many "self-sacrificing volunteers" for use against opponents. It was widely believed that these cadres participated in assassinations, especially of journalists who published articles critical of the "sacred society."

A second and perhaps more difficult problem for the CUP was that of abandoning the identity and mission it had assigned itself as the guardian of the constitutional regime. The impact of this self-imposed and openly proclaimed identity on the CUP was so profound that its members found being on equal footing with the other political parties unacceptable. As members of a patriotic organization that "had saved the fatherland" and thus become "sacred," they believed intensely in the absolute necessity of the CUP's political dominance for the sake of the empire. Thus from the beginning, relations between the CUP and opposition parties, relations inherently contrary to the ideals of the CUP, were tense and reciprocally destructive. It should be remembered that during the so-called second constitutional period between 1908 and 1918, despite the holding of elections, power changed hands only by force. In April 1909 the opposition carried out a coup known as the 31 March Incident, thereby evicting the CUP from power for two weeks. The CUP's response was to play the leading role in organizing the so-called Action Army, which marched on the capital from Macedonia and recovered power for the Committee. In June and July 1912 the opposition imitated the 1908 Revolution by dispatching small military units to the hills and delivering ultimata to the parliament. This effort coincided with the Albanian revolt and thus compelled the CPU-backed government to resign. The CUP's response was the so-called Sublime Porte raid of January 23, 1913, a successful bid to retake power. The opposition attempted to counter this with a futile coup attempt that began with the assassination of the Grand Vizier of the CUP-backed government, Mahmud Şevket Pasha, on June 11, 1913, thereby precipitating the CUP's establishment of a dictatorship that was to remain unchallenged until the end of the First World War.

As for its struggle against the two other power centers of the empire, the CUP was successful on both fronts. It forced Abdülhamid II, who had been wont to administer the empire through imperial decrees, to become a mere constitutional monarch.[80] Still, the strong personality of Abdülhamid II and his popularity among certain classes remained a primary concern of the CPU. His deposition on April 27, 1909, after the 31 March Incident, enabled the CUP to reduce the court to an insignificant factor in Ottoman politics.

The CUP's enthusiasm for Kâmil Pasha, who replaced Mehmed Sa'id Pasha as Grand Vizier in August 1908, turned to anger soon after. Kâmil Pasha was one of the last of the *Tanzimat* statesmen who believed in the propriety of the absolute power of the Sublime Porte. His expressed willingness to defend the concept of responsible government in 1895 had led to his dismissal from the grand vizirate and subsequent transfer to Izmir as governor.[81] Dreaming of reestablishing the Sublime Porte of the *Tanzimat* period, Kâmil Pasha resisted the CUP's constant interference in the affairs of government.[82] The CUP therefore turned against him.

The overwhelming victory of the CUP in the first elections held under the new regime in November–December 1908, and its consequent control over the parliament, gave the CUP a weapon with which to undermine further the government's role. The CUP deputies forced Kâmil Pasha to resign by handing him a vote of no confidence on February 13, 1909, and subsequent governments[83] never again dared to enter into a fully-fledged conflict with the CUP. Until June 1913 the CUP hesitated to form a government under a grand vizier belonging to the CUP, though at the same time it displayed no such hesitation in manipulating the cabinet. In retrospect one can see that the Sublime Porte did regain some of the power that it had lost to the palace during the Hamidian era. For example, governors could no longer correspond directly with the palace about important matters.[84] On the other hand, the new political actors—the CUP, the parliament under its control, and the army, which had been pushed into the background during the Hamidian era—left the Sublime Porte with only a sharply limited sphere of influence. The Sublime Porte's role in politics came to an end altogether in June 1913, when the CUP finally assumed direct control over the government too.

The CUP central committee in effect inherited the role formerly played by the Yıldız Palace, churning out thousands of central committee decisions in place of the old imperial decrees; in this way it kept the government in a relatively weak position in a manner similar to that of Abdülhamid II. The CUP possessed two additional assets that Abdülhamid II had lacked: a parliament under its effective control, notwithstanding the criticism of opposition deputies, and a large, active, and fanatically supportive segment of the army. As the CUP leaders had declared in the early days of the revolution, the army was the mainstay of CUP domination:

> The CUP fears only God, works for the salvation of our esteemed nation, and does not refrain from any sacrifice for the preservation of our constitution! In order to accomplish this important and sacred duty the CUP depends on the help of God, and on our army and navy which are the protectors of freedom! The two powers, the CUP and the Ottoman Armed Forces, which have been formed by the great majority of the Ottoman nation, can annihilate the supporters of tyranny at any time with a devastating blow.[85]

CUP domination of the active segment of the army did not go wholly unchallenged. In an attempt to win them over, Abdülhamid II granted promotions to the officers of the First, and even more so to the Second and Third Armies, which had played so important a role in the revolution.[86] Sabahaddin Bey gave a series of public talks at military clubs in Macedonia with a similar goal in mind. But these efforts of the CUP's rivals to make inroads into the army bore no fruit.[87]

Despite the protests of its opponents, and its own promise to restructure its relations with the army by drafting new (albeit secret) regulations on the subject,[88] the CUP never abandoned its military character. With its military clubs, thousands of officer members, and self-sacrificing volunteers, the CUP was a semimilitary organization. This feature was supposedly changed in compliance with revisions to the legal code made by the cabinet of Gazi Ahmed Muhtar Pasha in 1912, but this law, like so many others of the period, existed only on paper. Also, overlapping political and patriotic sentiments formed a bond between a great majority of junior officers and the CUP that no statute or organizational restructuring could break. This shared worldview was perhaps the main reason why the CUP's opponents made very little headway in their efforts to find support in the army.

The CUP was not content to control only the active segment of the army; it was determined to rebuild the entire bureaucracy. As was made clear by a memorandum sent to the CUP Monastir branch for submission at the first secret CUP congress, the CUP sought to fill key positions in the bureaucracy with loyal members of the committee. It stated:

> In order to fulfill our . . . goal we should try to ensure that the high-level law enforcement personnel, . . . the minister of education, all directors, professors and teachers at the university and all kinds of schools, the board of education, directors of education in the provinces, inspectors of education, the minister of the interior, governors, subgovernors, district directors, the minister of justice, judges, and the itinerant officials of the Ministry of Public Works and the Directorate of Forests should all be chosen from our loyal and self-sacrificing members.[89]

To create a new bureaucracy devoutly loyal to the party was a difficult goal to achieve, since the qualified bureaucratic elite was still quite small. As a result, the

CUP summarily dismissed those who were openly against it and placed its members in the best available positions, and it won over neutral bureaucrats by appointing them to better positions. The purges and reshufflings that the CUP central committee carried out in the bureaucracy following the revolution were pervasive, as an examination of the turnover rates for bureaucrats between 1906 and 1910 will demonstrate (see table 9.1).

Because of the small pool of trained civil servants, the CUP could not fill all the positions with bureaucrats who were loyal. But as these statistics reveal, it did create a

Table 9.1 Turnover Rates for Bureaucrats, 1906–1910

March 1906 to July 23, 1908[1]

Position	Total Number	Number of Changes	Percentage
Governors[2]	29	17	59%
Provincial Communications Directors	27	10	37%
Provincial Education Directors	27	7	26%
Ambassadors	16	2	13%
Chargés d'affaires	16	3	19%

July 24, 1908 to March 1910[3]

Position	Total Number	Number of Changes	Percentage
Governors[4]	29	29	100%
Provincial Communications Directors	27	25	93%
Provincial Education Directors	27	25	93%
Ambassadors	16	16	100%
Chargés d'affaires	16	15	94%

1. For the period between March 1906 and March 1908, this chart is based on the two Ottoman yearbooks, *1324 Sene-i Hicriyesine Mahsus Salnâme-i Devlet-i Aliyye-i Osmaniye* 62 (Istanbul 1322 [1906]) and *1326 Sene-i Hicriyesine Mahsus Salnâme-i Devlet-i Aliyye-i Osmaniye* 64 (Istanbul 1323 [1908]). For the period between March 1 and July 23, 1908 it is based on the appointments announced in Ottoman newspapers.

2. It should be remembered that the turnover rates during this period were atypical, since the sultan had been compelled to dismiss many governors because of rebellions in Eastern Anatolia.

3. The chart is based on comparison of the data of the two sequential Ottoman yearbooks, *1326 Sene-i Hicriyesine Mahsus Salnâme-i Devlet-i Aliyye-i Osmaniye* 64, and *Salnâme-i Devlet-i Aliyye-i Osmaniye 1326 Maliye* 65 (1326 Maliye [1910]).

4. Istanbul is not included in these data because there was no governor of the Istanbul region before the revolution. It may be added that out of 604 subgovernors and district directors (*mutassarrıfs* and *kaymakams*) who were in office before the revolution, only 11 remained in the same office in March 1910. (These figures do not include autonomous subprovinces and districts such as Kuwait and Qatar, where local leaders were recognized as Ottoman subgovernors.)

bureaucracy in which upward mobility was dependent upon its approval. Undoubtedly this fact forced bureaucrats to listen more attentively to the CUP's "recommendations."

As Bahaeddin Şakir proudly announced, the accomplishments of the CUP by the end of 1909 were proof of its success: "The CUP, with 360 centers throughout our country, more than 850,000 members, a majority in the parliament, and a government belonging to it, now comprises 'Ottoman Public Opinion.'"[90] During the same period the CUP had also succeeded in overcoming a counterrevolution, deposing a sultan, whom it still viewed as a serious threat, denying a dominant role to the Sublime Porte, and firmly establishing its mastery over Ottoman politics.

10

Political Ideas of the Young Turks, 1902–1908

From Intellectualism to Political Activism

Between 1902 and 1908 the political ideas of the Young Turks who occupied leading positions in major organizations shifted from grand theories aimed at reshaping the world order to simpler and more narrowly political doctrines and tactics. While the faith of the leading Young Turks in "science" endured as an underlying element, the more the Young Turk movement engaged in practical political activity, the less its earlier yearning for a society shaped by scientific doctrines is evidenced in its activities and propaganda. By 1908 these ideas were almost completely abandoned in favor of purely political doctrines and tactics. The object of these was initially to carry out a revolution and later to administer an empire, the maintenance of which was dependent on delicate political balances and not on grand theories of long-term global organization.

For example, the Young Turks who wrote for *Şûra-yı Ümmet* had believed that frequent use of such terms as "the fatherland" and "the nation" would reacquaint their compatriots with their lost natural instincts of patriotism and love for the fatherland. They believed that their compatriots, like Darwin's "Ceylon ducks which had forgotten how to swim," had forgotten their devotion to the homeland, and that only constant prodding was needed to revive their patriotism.[1] But when the CPU initiated its propaganda between 1907 and 1908 with the intent of carrying out a revolution, this Darwinist interpretation of patriotism was replaced by bold appeals to save the fatherland, to thwart foreign intervention, and to crush the separatist activities that had become widespread among various Ottoman ethnic groups. Similarly, the mainstream Young Turk journals had maintained that a revolution in the Ottoman Empire to replace the "outdated" Hamidian regime was inevitable because "life itself and the life of humankind were nothing other than a perpetual metamorphosis and an incessant transmutation in form and physique."[2] Yet when the CPU organized a "gendarme force" and "self-sacrificing volunteers," both its propaganda and the members of these units set aside all these lofty expressions that had seemed so convincing on paper.

It should nevertheless be remembered that even after the revolution, official and semiofficial periodicals of the CUP described the Young Turk Revolution as a stage in the evolution of "human society,"[3] reintroducing Darwinism to public opinion[4] and presenting "the natural law of the survival of the fittest" as a determining factor in the life of every human society, including the Ottoman.[5] In this respect, the Young Turk case was very different from that of China. There in 1912 Sun Yat-sen and his followers declared that the time of Darwinism and the applicability of Darwinist theory to Chinese society were over; they did this after following a Darwinist program over a long period and carrying out a revolution whose leaders were strong Social Darwinists. At the same time the attitude of the Young Turk leaders should not be confused with the ideas of thinkers such as Célestin Bouglé, Alphonse Darlu, and Jean Finot, who respected science but maintained that its impact in shaping society was trivial, and thought in terms of a moral philosophy free of science. The intellectual elite in the Young Turk movement still believed that science reigned supreme,[6] and it regarded Darwinism as an all-encompassing theory applicable to "every act of humanity."[7] The transformation of their movement into a merely political struggle founded on basic political themes, however, caused the leaders of major Young Turk organizations to sideline rather than abandon their grand theories. In fact, in journals supporting the CPU and in semiofficial branch organs several "scientific" theses appeared;[8] these included the interpretation of human history as a "struggle between religion and science,"[9] recommendations to the ulema to learn "psychology and sociology"[10] and examine the books of Spencer and Draper,[11] and fierce attacks on "superstitions."[12] Similarly, proposals to solve the problems of society by applying the organistic theories of Spencer[13] and Worms[14] appeared in journals of the nationalist faction or those supporting the CPU, but they did not have a place in the official CPU organs.

Despite the persistence of these "scientific" theories in the background, the CPU's transformation into a straightforwardly political organization was nearly complete by 1908. Its new program was purely pragmatic and political, unlike those of the early Young Turk organizations, in which an overwhelming number of the members despised true politics. This transformation began during the CPU's reorganization in 1906. As a result of the work of the committee organizers, the scientism of the Young Turk *Weltanschauung* was pushed into the background and played only a minimal role in CPU and later CUP propaganda. For example, a future Arab nationalist, Ṣāṭiʿ al-Ḥuṣrī, maintained that the science of "ethnography" had been used by the Christian committees in Macedonia to demonstrate the ethnic characteristics of the Macedonian people.[15] Likewise the CPU in its secret correspondence had made frequent references to the common ethnic and racial origins of Turks and Bulgarians.[16] Yet during the revolution this was no longer the case. CPU propaganda in Macedonia was restricted to such slogans as, "We are the real owners of this land" and "We will not surrender our fatherland to foreigners." Surprisingly, the CPU advanced no "scientific" claims to challenge the Macedo-Bulgarians and Greeks on an ethnographic basis. Similarly many Young Turks had developed a strong interest in Henry Thomas Buckle's ideas and his positivist interpretation of history.[17] Dr. Nâzım Bey, a leading figure in the CPU, had taken the view that an understanding of history in accordance with Buckle's thesis could help the Young

Turks to use "real history" in their writings.[18] To this end a leading member of the intellectual circle publishing the journal *Türk* had translated into Turkish some sections of Buckle's *History of Civilization in England*, in which religious fanaticism was strongly criticized.[19] In later CPU propaganda, however, the use of history did not go beyond celebrating former Ottoman military victories,[20] and Buckle did not become a hero of a generation as he had in Poland.[21]

The Young Turk *Weltanschauung* that had been shaped between 1889 and 1902 lacked a revolutionary praxis, and it played an insignificant role in the carrying out of the Young Turk Revolution of 1908. As Sohrabi's research demonstrates, it had a substantive impact on the CUP's efforts toward "building a scientific state" during the second constitutional period,[22] but it had little effect on the primary political ideologies used by the CUP. The impact of this *Weltanschauung*, however, was not limited to these efforts, which attracted little attention amid drastic domestic and international crises. It profoundly affected a section of the Ottoman intelligentsia, as later developments clearly showed. The impact of this *Weltanschauung* thus went far beyond the political changes that it marginally effected in 1908, as the CPU successfully transformed itself into an effective political organization pursuing well-defined and pragmatic political goals. The CPU was no longer envisioning the establishment of a new social order to prove the grand sociological theories venerated by many leading members of the organization. Prior to the revolution Bahaeddin Şakir had even criticized Sabahaddin Bey's claim to be a follower of a theory that the latter deemed "scientific," and he underscored the importance of comprehending realpolitik.[23]

Those Young Turks who could not cope with this important transformation left the main organizations to pursue their high ideals through their publications. Those who accepted this change adjusted themselves to the new CPU milieu. Ahmed Rıza was among them. After years of arguing that a revolution with all its attendant disruption would harm the empire, he changed his mind and called on junior officers to form bands and overthrow the government. Ahmed Rıza continued to make "scientific" references, as in his explanation of the idea of a fatherland, which he attributed to the fact that everyone derives the chemical compounds forming his or her body from the earth, water, and atmosphere where he or she is born.[24] Similarly Yusuf Akçura asked the Young Turks to pay more attention to the economic determinants of social developments, which he claimed were "natural laws" directly connected to the theory of evolution.[25] On the whole, however, these scientific references comprised a very small portion of the open writings of the leading CPU and later CUP members.

This change also helped political committee organizers and activists such as Bahaeddin Şakir, Dr. Nâzım, Talât Bey, Ömer Naci, and Enver Bey to assume prominence in the Young Turk movement, at the expense of the "grand theoreticians" of the preceding decade. It would be wrong to think that the main feature of the Young Turk *Weltanschauung* shaped between 1889 and 1902 had made absolutely no impact on the political thought of these activists, who, with the exception of Ömer Naci, have not left us much of a literary record. The writings and private correspondence of some of them indicate that they too shared many aspects of this *Weltanschauung*,[26] but their short-term objectives had very little to do with these lofty theories, and instead of striving to establish a new society they simply decided to deal with realpolitik.

They were remarkably successful in this process of transforming an intellectual movement, one that claimed it did not "want revolution in the streets but in the system of government administration, schools, science, and knowledge,"[27] into a political movement dispatching self-sacrificing volunteer squads to the streets to assassinate its opponents. It is no less astounding that such a movement, most of whose members perceived the Darwinist theory as the leading guide to understanding both organic and social life and who became adherents of Le Bon's theories, should nevertheless have chosen the motto "liberty, equality, and fraternity" and even engraved this slogan on the committee's coat of arms. The Social Darwinist theory, based as it was on the inequalities found in the social organism, had long discarded the tenet of "liberty, equality, and fraternity" as a metaphysical fantasy of the eighteenth century, an era which it viewed as a remote, prescientific, and obsolete past. It is also difficult to discern how the intellectual Young Turk leaders reconciled this motto with Le Bon's ideas as clearly expressed in his essay *La Révolution française et la psychologie des révolutions*, a work they admired.[28] For the planners of the revolution, who put these lofty scientific considerations aside, the motto could be used both as a slogan against the sultan's regime and as a device to win over various Ottoman ethnic groups to the cause of Ottomanism.[29] That it was an outdated slogan from a scientistic viewpoint did not matter to the leaders of the revolution.

This transformation is most obvious in the case of the main Young Turk organization that dominated the movement beginning in 1906. Yet at the same time the CPU's arch-rival, Sabahaddin Bey, was compelled to pay more attention to politics. Until 1906 Sabahaddin Bey's propaganda was based mainly on Demolins's theses and was aimed at establishing a new society through education; this approach would theoretically produce a new generation endowed with a revived work ethic and a yearning to take personal initiatives.[30] Sabahaddin Bey and his colleagues put their faith in "social progress," which they saw as subject to the same natural law that regulated biological processes;[31] thus instead of adopting a slogan like "equality" as embraced by the CPU, they focused on inequalities. In India, for example, according to their explanation, a handful of British officers could rule over 250 million Indians simply because they possessed "social skills" that the latter lacked.[32]

Despite their stronger faith in "science," Sabahaddin Bey and his League of Private Initiative and Decentralization began to focus more and more on decentralization in the period leading up to the revolution. This was a political vulgarization of Demolins's theory of a rather peculiar kind, since Demolins did not envision a decentralist administration in an empire like the Ottoman state but rather focused on the positive results of decentralized administration in the British Empire. By 1908 decentralization became the core of Sabahaddin Bey's program and won him the support of many non-Turkish organizations.[33] It was only this portion of his theory that survived the bitter political struggle that took place between 1908 and 1918. Demolins's name and the lofty theses of the *Science sociale* were quickly forgotten, and "decentralization" as a political thesis became simply the ideology of opposition in the Ottoman Empire.[34] From the beginning of the restored constitutional regime, the non-Turkish ethnic groups, for whom decentralization "was not . . . a mere ideological concept" but "a dire everyday necessity,"[35] made decentralization a key aspect of their programs.[36] They obviously paid no attention to Demolins's theories, perceiving decentralization from a strictly political and protonationalist viewpoint. Similarly, Sabahaddin Bey's rivals opposed decentralization, not because Demolins claimed that it had been a consequential factor in the alleged Anglo-Saxon superiority, but because in the Ottoman context it would be used as a means to pursue separatism. In discussing decentralization, Ahmed Rıza noted pointedly that in the Ottoman Empire "there is still feudalism; there are some separatist ethnic groups. These can be kept in hand only with the power of centralization. To give a little bit of power and credit to the separatists encourages them to detach themselves completely."[37]

When Sabahaddin Bey's disciples attempted to revitalize their movement in Republican Turkey, it had no impact as an intellectual current; it remained the obscure preserve of a very small group of intellectuals.[38] Sabahaddin Bey owed his great popularity among the opponents of the CPU, and later CUP, to the political interpretation of his thesis on decentralization, and not to the alleged scientific character of Demolins's theory.

During the period of transformation from an intellectual movement to a political one, the theorists among the Young Turks found that they had two alternatives. Either they could politicize their high ideals and readjust to the new realities of politics, or they had to break away from the mainstream movement and its politics to become full-time social critics and thinkers.

Intellectuals such as Ahmed Rıza deftly politicized the grand theories that they had championed. Ahmed Rıza had exploited positivism long before the transformation of the Young Turk movement by using it to defend the rights of the Turks in Macedonia.[39] At that time he was still hoping for a miraculous evolutionary change in the Ottoman Empire that would turn it into a society ruled in accordance with the "religion of humanity." By 1906, however, Ahmed Rıza had pushed positivism into the background of his writings until it was all but invisible. Ahmed Rıza now believed that positivism could be of use only when positivist leaders at the positivist meetings defended "la cause des Noirs, des Chinois, des Turcs contre 'leurs oppresseurs occidentaux.'"[40] Even after the revolution, instead of attempting to prove his fellow positivists' claims that the Young Turk Revolution was a positivistic one aimed at applying the religion of humanity,[41] Ahmed Rıza appealed to positivist organizations to help the Ottoman Empire in its struggle against Austria-Hungary, and to assist the CUP in its struggle against Abdülhamid II, whom he accused of secretly working against the revolution.[42]

Ahmed Rıza maintained his faith in positivism until his death. He believed it was the only solution for a world encumbered with insuperable problems following industrialization.[43] Nevertheless, while striving for and believing in the long-term success of positivism, he used it primarily to promote his political goals. Positivism, with its strong antipathy to nationalism and religion and its advocacy of the universal principles of humanity, was an effective tool for opposing the Ottoman Empire's enemies.[44] For example, the allied occupation of the Ottoman Empire against which Ahmed Rıza appealed to the positivist organizations in 1920, could easily be described as a *nouvelle croisade*, against which everybody who opposed egoistic nationalism and clerical militarism should stand up.[45] It is also interesting that like Bengali positivists, who, in reaction to British rule, understandably desired the development of India in accordance with its own indigenous propensities,[46] Ahmed Rıza, because of his strong anti-imperialist proclivities, aspired to a development in accordance with the Oriental culture and traditions of the Ottoman Empire.[47]

In short, Ahmed Rıza, who had dreamed of a "scientific" society where the "religion of humanity" would reign supreme, ended up using positivism to further his patriotic goals. His struggle to preserve the motto *ordre et progrès* as the maxim of the Young Turk movement was quickly forgotten, and after the revolution it never again became an issue among the leading CUP members.[48] While many Young Turks continued to believe that humankind was traveling along a course of irreversible progress, the immediate problems they encountered forced them to be pragmatic and calculating.

A regular reader of the Young Turk journals might have found this change dramatic and very distasteful if he had faith in such concepts as "science," "progress," and "natural laws," a belief many Young Turk leaders had held between 1899 and 1902. For the new CUP leadership, however, these concepts were nothing more than generalities that were of little help in resolving the great political problems they faced. These ideas, and the theories they were based on, could explain the long-term evolution of human society, but they could not help the Young Turk leadership solve the Ottoman Empire's immediate problems. Foreign observers erred in imagining that the problems the CUP leaders faced stemmed from their having made Comte and Spencer their prophets, thereby alienating themselves from their own culture.[49] Although the thinkers who had championed such ideas played an important role in shaping the Young Turk *Weltanschauung*, their role in CUP political decision-making after the Young Turk Revolution was negligible.

Another consequence of the CPU's shift to a pragmatic activism that paid very little heed to grand theories was a new role for the military in social and political life. The CPU leaders wanted the military to gain power "not to conquer lands," but to play an active role in society.[50] This idea was nothing other than a basic exegesis of Colmar von der Goltz's theory defended in his book *Das Volk in Waffen*,[51] which attributed a special role to the military in postindustrialized society. Von der Goltz's book was translated into Turkish and was recommended reading for all military cadets,[52] who embraced von der Goltz's theory, seeing in it a solution to Ottoman problems.[53] Following the revolution, the military members of the CUP argued that the army symbolized the Ottoman nation and that it was the army's task to lead Ottoman society on its path to progress. Von der Goltz's theory is evoked in the words of one CUP military member:

> The Ottoman army should become the Ottoman armed nation. This is a paramount objective that from now on must be engraved in the depths of the heart and conscience of every individual possessing the revered title of Ottoman. All endeavors, all efforts, all sacrifices, and all steps should aim at this sacred goal.[54]

Thus the CPU invited the military to play a new and more significant role in the society under its supervision. In practice, the military's affirmative answer provided the CPU not only with the only unchallengeable force, which had been kept under strict control by the sultan for many years, but also with an educated class of activists. The CPU, and later the CUP, as semimilitary organizations, in fact realized von der Goltz's theory.

The CPU undoubtedly owed its strong activism mostly to the junior officers who joined its ranks between 1907 and the revolution. In the Ottoman Empire, where the military had traditionally played a more significant role in policy-making than the militaries of many European states did, the reemergence of the military as a dominant power was a relatively easy transition.[55] Only those Young Turks who could cope with this military-based activism could remain in the decision-making positions of the CUP. Notably, these civilian CUP leaders also took on military or paramilitary positions with great enthusiasm. For example, after serving as Minister of the Interior of the empire, Talât Bey joined the army as a private during the Balkan Wars; Bahaeddin Şakir became one of the regional directors of the paramilitary Special Organization (Teşkilât-ı Mahsusa) during the First World War on his own initiative.

As might be expected, Sabahaddin Bey adamantly opposed the military activism of the CUP and the organization's desire to create an "Ottoman armed nation." As he saw it, the new role accorded to the military and its self-imposed duty of "being the guardian of the constitutional regime" under CUP domination was a clear sign of Ottoman society's "social defects."[56] Sabahaddin Bey's alternative to the CUP's approach—instituting schools that would apply Anglo-Saxon teaching methods and would produce men fitted for the "struggle for life" instead of passive, dependant individuals—may have looked better on paper. There is no doubt, however, that the CUP leaders had a firmer understanding of the realities of the Ottoman society they were attempting to change.

From Turkism to Political Opportunism

Between 1902 and 1905 the "coalition" adopted a strong Turkist line. The CPU had also espoused a Turkist ideology in its early days. As we have seen, until late 1907 CPU propaganda had strong Turkist or even Turkish nationalist themes. This propaganda undoubtedly helped the CPU to win over many Turkish groups that had become minorities in places like Bulgaria, and to establish sound ties with Turkic populations in the Caucasus. It also impressed many Turkish junior officers serving in Macedonia, since they had learned to admire the nationalist movements against which they were fighting.

This propaganda with its strong Turkist themes also provided the CPU with a revolutionary praxis for the first time since the inception of the Young Turk movement. As Yusuf Akçura later stated, having been deeply impressed by his professors at the École Libre des Sciences Politiques such as Albert Sorel and Émile Boutmy,[57] he had attempted to demonstrate the "power" of the concept of the "nation." In his articles published in *Şûra-yı Ümmet*, he deliberately avoided using the locution "Ottoman nation," instead employing expressions such as "various nations residing in the Ottoman country."[58] In his *mémoire de fin d'études*, entitled *Essai sur l'histoire des institutions du Sultanat ottoman*, which he submitted to the École Libre des Sciences Politiques, Akçura argued that it was "impossible to create a nation by uniting and blending various elements of the [Ottoman] Empire because of the development of the idea of the nation and because of the great degree of enmity among the various nations [in the empire], and especially between the two religions."[59] Although Akçura presented these ideas as uniquely his own, the coalition's publications and *Türk* contain many such articles underscoring the importance of the "nation" from a Turkist viewpoint; in fact between 1902 and 1907 the term "Turk" generally replaced "Ottoman" in these journals.

Nevertheless, just as they had pushed the earlier grand sociological theories into the background, the CPU, and later the CUP, sidelined their Turkist ideology, this time out of political opportunism. When we consider the Turkism that dominated the coalition circles between 1902 and 1905, and the early CPU propaganda (until late 1907), it is clear that relegating Turkist ideology to the background could not have been easy. By late 1907, however, the CPU leadership had comprehended the difficulty of carrying out a revolution with Macedonia at its center and of administering the Ottoman Empire while maintaining the strong Turkist ideology adopted by the coalition and more zealously defended by the journal *Türk*, for which many CPU members penned articles. Nonetheless, *Şûra-yı Ümmet* continued to publish articles underscoring the importance of the Turkish element of the empire; the CPU leaders praised Hüseyinzâde Ali for his goal of establishing a "Turkish Empire from the Adriatic to the Chinese Sea."[60] In an article written in defense of Albert Sorel, *Şûra-yı Ümmet* featured an imagined "Turkish fatherland" and stated that the only reason Sorel had been subjected to attacks accusing him of being a Turcophile was that "he ventured to recognize a 'Turkish fatherland' in the world."[61] In addition, the Turks' lack of "a national sentiment" continued to be a great disappointment to the CPU leaders.[62]

Despite their Turkist proclivities, the new leaders viewed Turkism, like Ottomanism and Panislamism, as a tool to be used to fulfill their supreme political goal: the salvation of the empire. By early 1908 the CPU had begun to employ Turkism, Ottomanism, and Panislamism interchangeably in its propaganda, sometimes simply replacing the term "Turk" with "Ottoman" in its appeals. As opposed to the coalition's explicit, caustic, and dogmatic Turkism, which had led to severed relations between the Young Turks and the leadership of other political organizations of the various Ottoman elements,[63] the CPU's fluid propaganda, which was frequently adjusted to accommodate a broad spectrum of beliefs and political objectives, helped the CPU to come to terms with many non-Turkish groups that had previously refused to work with the Young Turks. It should also be remembered that during this same period the CPU established strong contacts with the leaders of various Turkic groups by employing Panturkist, and sometimes Panislamist, rhetoric.

Despite having cordial relations with various Turkic groups, however, the CPU leadership did not actively support any idea that countered Ottomanism. On one occasion Hüseyinzâde Ali, a future CUP central committee member and someone who was extolled in the CPU organs, criticized the Ottoman Turks' use of the term "Ottoman," likening it to a German or a Frenchman calling himself a "Hohenzollern," "Bourbon," or "Bonaparte."[64] An intellectual Young Turk journal that opposed the Ottoman dynasty on the basis of Théodule Armand Ribot's heredity theory supported this criticism; the CPU, however, did not.[65]

When we take into consideration the number of committees and political organizations established between 1889 and 1908, it is remarkable that amid such widespread opposition activity no significant group defended republicanism. When

Hüsrev Sami praised the work of Giuseppe Mazzini, he carefully avoided any mention of the latter's strong republican views.[66] As has been demonstrated, the leaders of the coalition vehemently denounced anyone who dared to express even the faintest opposition to the Ottoman royal house.[67] Abdullah Cevdet launched the only campaign against the dynasty in 1906,[68] a campaign that was, however, based on the heredity theory of Ribot. According to Abdullah Cevdet, "since experiments on animals had proven that offspring born in captivity cannot inherit the racial characteristics of their fathers," the Ottoman royal house, a family composed of "degenerate and ill-bred" individuals,[69] ought to be deposed.[70] Although the campaign caused a stir in intellectual circles,[71] the CPU did not even comment on it; to recognize the movement would have given it credence and damaged Ottomanist policies.

The Young Turks' focus on race derived from "scientific" theories, but the placement of the Turks at the bottom of the racial schema with the yellow races prevented them from invoking racial theories in their analysis. The Japanese victory over Russia, however, gave plenty of ammunition to those Young Turks who wanted to apply to their political problems racial theories that were then "scientific."[72] As Yusuf Akçura pointed out, one of the choices before the Ottoman Empire was whether to pursue Turkish nationalism based on race,[73] and as a result, articles on race in general, and the Turkish race in particular, filled the pages of the journals *Şûra-yı Ümmet* and *Türk* between 1904 and 1907. Beginning in late 1907, however, the focus on race disappeared from the public propaganda of the CPU because of its incompatibility with Ottomanist propaganda. In the CPU's secret correspondence the common roots of Bulgarians and Turks were frequently mentioned, and Dr. Nâzım attributed the "five-hundred-year Turkish rule in Rumelia" to the fact that "among the others only the Turkish race proved the theory of the survival of the fittest because of its superior characteristics."[74] But these issues were never referred to in the open revolutionary propaganda, which shifted to Ottomanism in late 1907.

Ottoman intellectuals who discussed race theories after the revolution stated that it was impossible to apply such theories to the Ottoman Empire with its variety of ethnic groups and races, because "these peoples [forming the Ottoman Empire] in general have no similarities. Each of them has its special features, common characteristics, and racial peculiarities. Governing this mixture properly is extremely difficult."[75] The difficulty was obviously in the absence of an Ottoman "racial soul," a notion proposed by Gustave Le Bon, whose ideas seem to have been used as a foundation by these intellectuals.

The problem of propagating an ideology promoting an artificial "Ottoman nation" composed of different ethnic groups prevented the Young Turk leaders from making free use of the theories of Le Bon and Alfred Fouillée, which were based on the concepts of "racial soul" and "national character." The geographical makeup of the Ottoman Empire was an unavoidable obstacle to any attempt to come up with an artificial, unified race, such as the so-called Mediterranean race invented by Guiseppe Sergi. It is not coincidental, then, that the Young Turk leaders focused on the "crowd psychology" aspect of Le Bon's theories, and that Sabahaddin Bey, who regarded Fouillée as one of the foremost thinkers who influenced him,[76] drew only on the French thinker's ideas on psychology and individualism.

Because of its incompatibility with such "scientific" theories, Ottomanism was presented by Young Turk propaganda not in terms of such a theory, but rather as a mere political ideology with which to address the problems of a multinational state. For the main Young Turk organization, beginning in late 1907, this political aim of regulating a multinational state took precedence over the claims of science, which had for so long been regarded as vital by the Young Turks.

In the CPU's attempts to safeguard and preserve the empire, Ottomanism became enormously important as a tool for it, and later for the CUP leaders. Despite their strong proclivity for Turkism, the leaders also sought to use this ethnic appeal along with Panislamism, interchangeably when necessary. For instance, in 1909 the CUP central committee asked the Ottoman government to occupy Iranian Azerbaijan on the pretext of a border dispute, because "the Russian subjugation of the great and prosperous land of Azerbaijan, with its entire Muslim population of four million people composed of the warrior Turkish element, would cut our relations with, and devotion to, Central Asia."[77] Around the same time, the central committee asked the government to appoint Velpić Efendi to the Senate when the next Serb seat fell vacant, because he was "an ardent defender of Ottomanism" and "renowned for his love for Ottomanism."[78] Not surprisingly, at the same time the CUP dispatched delegates to Mecca during the pilgrimage season to appeal to the leading ulema of the Muslim world for their support for the new regime.[79] As these examples demonstrate, the same CUP leaders exploited Panturkist, Panislamist, and Ottomanist policies simultaneously. Scholars have too often tried to argue that the CUP adhered to one of these ideologies to the exclusion of the others, but such was never the case. This is not, of course, to deny that at certain times the CPU leaders appealed to one of these three ideologies more than the others under particular circumstances. For example, during and immediately after the revolution the CPU and CUP leaders sought to thwart foreign intervention in Macedonia. To achieve this goal, the CUP made bold Ottomanist gestures such as punishing Muslim Albanians and Turks who verbally or physically attacked Christians in various ethnic groups. Needless to say, the representatives of the Great Powers and the Balkan press appreciated this policy.[80] When, however, the CUP and the CUP-supported government wanted to come to terms with Imām Yaḥyā in order to quell the Zaydī revolt in the mountainous regions of the Ottoman province of Yemen, the CUP acquiesced in a rather outrageous demand of Imām Yaḥyā: to administer "the Jews [of Yemen] according to the peace contract of [the second Caliph] 'Umar."[81] This act was not only incompatible with the idea of Ottomanism, but also a clear violation of the eighth, ninth, and tenth articles of the Ottoman constitution, which granted equal individual rights and protection to all Ottoman citizens regardless of their religious affiliations.

The real and only CUP was not the Ottomanist CUP that punished Albanians and Turks in strict application of the principle of Ottomanism, nor was it the CUP and the government it supported that allowed a local leader to legally discriminate against the Jews in the area under his control. These measures were nothing other than pragmatic maneuvers to save the empire. The CUP's disparate policies, however, caused it to face a host of further problems. For instance, part of the Islamist opposition to the CUP attempted to refute the CUP's claim, put forth by leading ulema and the

Şeyhülislâm,[82] that an administration in which non-Muslims play a role in the decision-making process and an assembly with non-Muslim deputies are in absolute accordance with *sharī'a*; similarly they tried to refute the CUP's invocation of certain actions of the Prophet to legitimize this participation.[83] On another front, however, many non-Muslims argued that "the *sharī'a* absolutely denied constitutionalism and was incompatible with it."[84]

Undeniably, the leading members of the CPU, and later the CUP, had strong Turkist proclivities, and contrary to what scholarship has maintained until now, this had been the case long before the Balkan Wars of 1912 and 1913. Articles published in *Şûra-yı Ümmet* beginning in 1902, and in *Türk* beginning in 1903, leave no doubt regarding the CPU's predilection for Turkism. In many ways these articles defending the Turkist theses were no less exuberant than those in the Turkist journals of the second constitutional period such as *Genc Kalemler* and *Türk Yurdu*.[85] Nevertheless, upon its transformation into a political organization the CPU, whose priority was to save the empire, came to see Turkism quite simply as an instrument. The available CUP documents reveal that only in very late 1917 did the CUP decide to abandon Ottomanism totally and pursue a Turkist policy once Ottomanism had lost its utility for propaganda purposes. Despite this change, however, the CUP organs continued to publish articles praising Ottomanism.

Perhaps Ahmed Ferid best described the predicament facing the leaders of the CPU, and later of the CUP, who despite their Turkist tendencies used all available means for the sake of saving their empire. In his response to Yusuf Akçura, Ahmed Ferid stated that the best policy for the Ottoman State was an opportunist one, that is, to use Pan-Ottomanist and Panislamist policies to its own advantage. He also concluded that Panturkism would probably be useful in the long run in the event that "the Pan-Ottomanist policy preserves our national existence" and "when Panislamist policy sinks into the earth and disappears."[86] It would be only after such great changes that Turkism could become the principal policy. Although events took a slightly different course from what Ahmed Ferid had predicted, his prognostication became reality when, after much political turmoil, Turkism and Turkish nationalism became the single most dominant ideology.

Despite their practice of employing Ottomanist, Turkist, and Panislamist rhetoric interchangeably depending on the targeted group, the CPU leaders' Turkist inclinations had a profound impact on their interpretation of Ottomanism. In theory their version of Ottomanism viewed all Ottomans as equals. The CPU publications, however, attributed a dominant role to the Turkish element in the Ottoman empire by claiming that "reform of the Ottoman administration depends on a rebellion by the Turks, the dominant element in the empire, and not on insurrections by a bunch of Armenians or Bulgarians."[87]

The opponents of the CPU categorized this attitude as Turkism or even Turkish nationalism. Ahmed Rıza thought that "despite being Ottomans, these [elements] are not interested in the maintenance of this [Ottoman] government as Turks are. Most of them work together with the [European] consuls."[88] Yet when the CPU was bargaining with various nationalist organizations in Macedonia between early 1908 and the revolution, this widespread Turkist version of Ottomanism suddenly evaporated.[89]

It was publicly resurrected only some time after the revolution, when some Ottoman ethnic groups—the Greeks being the first—demanded a more privileged status and refused to accept the CUP's wholesale Ottomanism.[90]

The CUP-backed organizations that were formed to propagate the CUP's version of Ottomanism among the various Ottoman ethnic groups made very little headway.[91] The journals close to the CUP declared that "the dominant nation in Turkey is the Turkish one" and presented constitutional equality as a favor granted by the dominant nation to the rest.[92] The Panturkist journals too asked other elements to fall into line behind the dominant nation.[93] Later a CUP deputy reiterated this claim in more delicate and balanced language and presented it as a fact that should be accepted by everyone.[94] It should be remembered, however, that in secret meetings the CUP leaders were referring explicitly to a "Turkish monopoly on power" with the aim of never allowing the Ottoman state to become a new Austria-Hungary.[95] In retrospect, one may comment that despite their Turkist tendencies and secular propensities, the CPU and CUP leaders' formula of the "dominant nation" was similar to that of the "dominant Muslim religious community" in the pre-*Tanzimat* era; it may have had more in common with this than with more secular nationalist ideas, such as the Prussian notion of the *Herrenvolk* or Arkadii Prigozhin's idea of the *narod-patron*, which gave a dominant role to the Russians in the Soviet system. Many Young Turks took the view that, as with the Muslim community of the pre-*Tanzimat* era, the strengthening of the dominant Turkish element would help the state to become more powerful, thereby benefiting all other ethnic groups.

During the second constitutional period, it was the CUP's interpretation of Ottomanism, not its interest in developing relations with the Turkic world, that caused an outcry from its opponents and precipitated a struggle resembling the conflict between German centralists and Slav federalists during the early decades of the Austrian constitutional period.[96] The CUP's opponents viewed this version of Ottomanism, which aimed at the unification of various Ottoman elements in a melting pot full of Turkish symbols, as a "Turkification" process.[97] The CUP categorically denied these accusations while firmly opposing federalism and autonomy, which were offered as alternatives to the CUP version of Ottomanism.

It would be difficult to argue that the CUP's Ottomanism was more deleterious to the non-Turkish communities than was the interpretation of Ottomanism espoused under the Hamidian regime; this interpretation in any case lost ground to the Islamist policies of the sultan. It is true, however, that the main bone of contention between the CUP and the organizations representing the non-Turkish elements of the empire was the CUP's aggressive stand regarding Ottomanism. With the internal regulations which it accepted in early 1908, the CUP imposed on itself the duty of deterring those who wanted to separate from Ottomanism. This self-imposed duty gained prodigious importance when the CUP assumed power in the Ottoman Empire and attempted to prevent any activity that it deemed "separatism" or a deviation from the CUP version of Ottomanism.[98] Ahmed Rıza maintained that the Ottoman Empire must have a powerful army "in order to attach to the body of the state various elements who want to separate themselves from us with the idea of attaining autonomy."[99] This statement too was a very clear expression of the CPU's aggressive Ottomanism.

The negotiations between the CPU and various national organizations in Macedonia prior to the revolution demonstrated two important facts to the CPU leaders. First, despite the CPU's claim to represent all Ottomans, the non-Turkish organizations viewed the CPU, and later the CUP, as representing only the Turks in the empire; the presence of various non-Turks within the rank and file of the CPU and CUP did little or nothing to change this image. The nationalists among the Ottoman ethnic groups viewed these people as lackeys of the Turks or even as Turkified.[100] Thus despite the existence of many officers of Albanian descent working for the CPU, the leaders of the nationalist Albanian Tosk organizations viewed the bargaining process between themselves and the CPU representatives as a negotiation between the Albanians and Turks.

Second, the CPU/CUP leaders realized that the leaders of the non-Turkish ethno-religious organizations regarded their respective communities as well defined and distinct "nationalities" within a multinational empire.[101] Thus these groups had no desire to accept a wholesale Ottomanism, which would inordinately erode the ethno-religious characteristics of their respective communities by classifying them first and foremost as Ottomans.[102] Only very small ethno-religious groups such as the Jews and Kutzo-Vlachs, which could not entertain any notion of a viable separatism and preferred any sort of Ottomanism to becoming a minority in a nation-state, would accept such a version of Ottomanism. It is not surprising then that in the Ottoman parliament the representatives of such groups strongly opposed the non-Turkish elements' use of non-Ottoman symbols such as Greek flags or the Greek national colors of blue and white.[103] Even they, however, put their terms on the bargaining table during the negotiations with the CPU leaders prior to the revolution. Later CUP propaganda reveals that the CUP accepted the fact that various ethnic groups were nationalities within the empire. The CUP leaders still wished, however, to unite them under a more inclusive Ottomanism in which the several nationalisms were to be replaced by a common patriotism. They wrote:

What is a nation?

A nation is a people many of whom speak the same tongue, who have similar customs and morals, and who are subject to the laws of a government. For example, Turks and Arabs are nations, because each of them has a language, blood [ties], customs, and history.

What does the Ottoman nation mean?

The Ottoman nation is a body created by the incorporation of various peoples such as Turks, Arabs, Albanians, Kurds, Armenians, Greeks, Bulgarians, and Jews . . . who possess different religions and nationalities.

How is it that these peoples who have different languages, religions, and faiths are called the Ottoman nation? . . .

Although these peoples have different languages of their own their official language is the same. It is the Ottoman language.

Does the difference of religion and faith hinder the creation of a nation?

No, it cannot hinder the creation of a nation, because the question of religion and faith is a matter of the next world. In the affairs of this world, however, individuals cannot abandon their interests, and those who have common aims should unite. For example, a Muslim and a Christian merchant become partners to work together and earn together. . . .

What is the fatherland and why is it loved?

The fatherland is the land which a nation conquered with its sword and in whose conquest it shed its blood. The fatherland is loved because without a fatherland there will be no chastity and honor, no nation, no faith, no worship, and no salvation. The fatherland is loved because there will be no humanity without a fatherland. Look, the Gypsies have no credibility because they do not have a fatherland. Those who do not love the fatherland or fear dying for it have less importance than dogs.[104]

The main problem with this thesis, however, is that the "Ottoman language," despite its extensive Arabic and Persian vocabulary, was essentially Turkish, as were all Ottoman symbols.[105] The non-Turkish groups that could viably harbor centrifugal ambitions did not wish to accept such an Ottomanism in which Turks would play the dominant role. This difference over Ottomanism precipitated a bitter struggle between the CUP and organizations representing various ethnic groups in the Ottoman Empire, all of whom claimed to be Ottomanist, despite their defense of disparate theses.

The Young Turks and Anti-Imperialism

The CPU and the nationalist faction of the Young Turk movement sharpened their already strong anti-imperialist position during the period between 1902 and 1908. Following the revolution of 1908, anti-imperialism constituted one of the main pillars of the CUP ideology. In fact the emergence of the coalition in 1902, following the First Congress of Ottoman Opposition, was due to a schism over the issue of foreign intervention in Ottoman domestic politics. The CPU owed a large part of its triumph in the summer of 1908 to its sapient use of anti-imperialist themes in its propaganda. This played a consequential role both in winning over junior officers who viewed European intervention in Macedonia as a nauseating example of European imperialism, and in mobilizing the Muslim masses against the alleged intention of the European imperialist powers to partition their land.

As the writings of CPU members reveal, they viewed European policies directed against the Ottoman Empire as part of a general European imperialism that lacked moral values and idolized money.[106] They maintained that this imperialism had led to the massacre of the American Indians, plundered the entire African continent, and now targeted the Ottoman Empire.[107] They energetically refuted the alleged "scientific" character of European imperialism, especially after the Japanese victories over Russia, which they regarded as "obliterating the [European] slander against nature" that had placed the Turks along with the "yellow race" at the bottom of the racial hierarchy.[108] Along with European race theories and colonialist writing, European policies toward the Ottoman Empire exacerbated a feeling among many Ottoman intellectuals that something uniquely theirs was being threatened by the Europeans. Chinese intellectuals of the period felt the same.[109]

Beginning in 1902, anti-imperialist themes became the most frequently used in the organs of the coalition and the CPU and in the journal *Türk*. As has been shown, the CPU leaders viewed the "pillaging and disgusting administration" of the Great Powers "on the pretext of civilization and freedom" as a policy carried out absolutely at the expense of the Ottomans.[110] Even satirical Young Turk essays likened European imperialism with regard to the Ottoman Empire to a Nasreddin Hoca story in which bloodthirsty wolves were "eating a poor donkey whose owner had passed away."[111] The incessant conflicts between the Ottoman Empire and the Great Powers of Europe following the revolution sharpened the Young Turks' suspicions about the real aims of the European proposals for reform.[112]

Besides its alleged immoral character, CPU members maintained, European imperialism had a hidden Christian agenda. According to Ahmed Rıza, the European imperialism threatening the Ottoman Empire was an encroachment by a "modern crusade" with very strong religious overtones. He went on to write: "Wherever a shameful act or outbreak of disorder occurs in the Ottoman dominions, [the European statesmen] immediately put all the blame on the Turks and their religious fanaticism, thereby intervening in our domestic affairs on the pretext of safeguarding the Christians—as if the non-Christians were not human beings! They bombard towns with the cry of 'Turks are not capable of progress and reform, and the Ottoman state cannot be put into any kind of order,' and attempt to turn European public opinion against us."[113] Necmeddin Ârif remarked that European statesmen such as Clemenceau, de Pressensé, and Rochefort-Luçay, who deftly criticized their own religious leaders, were defending the Armenians in animated Christian tones, while European policies were nothing other than the implementation of a diplomatic and military crusade to drive out Muslims from everywhere in Europe and to seize their property.[114]

It is interesting that the CPU members and many Young Turks never realized that they were doing precisely the same thing as those European statesmen when they, having little respect for the religion itself, defended Islam against the Europeans by giving public lectures or publishing articles on it.[115] They believed this was not a defense of Islam as a religion from a theological viewpoint, but a refutation of the theses of European fanaticism:

> La doctrine d'Auguste Comte, loin de se constituer l'ennemi acharné de toutes les croyances, les considère comme des phases nécessaires et fatales dans la marche du Progrès humain, et si l'Islamisme est très souvent défendu par la plume d'Ahmed Riza, c'est plutôt contre les attaques injustes du fanatisme européen; d'ailleurs, cette défense n'est pas faite en vue d'une préférence ou d'une interprétation théologique, c'est l'exposé de la portée sociale et législative de cette religion mère d'une grande civilisation.[116]

Similarly, the CPU's spearheading of the establishment of the Islamic Fraternal Society stemmed not from a religious concern but rather from the CPU's disgust for European imperial policies. As Ahmed Rıza stated, "[l]es peuples orientaux, justement indignés, commencent à en avoir assez. En présence d'une humiliante croisade dirigée contre les institutions, les droits et les biens musulmans, il leur serait difficile de rester passifs, muets, et, surtout, de témoigner leur sympathie à ceux qui se plaisent à les ruiner."[117] Ahmed Rıza asked his positivist friends for help for this Islamic Fraternal Society,[118] and he even revitalized the campaign for the establishment of a mosque in Paris, an idea that Abdülhamid II had promoted initially in 1891.[119] Ahmed Rıza again enlisted the support of his positivist friends for this endeavor. His correspondence with them indicates that he dreamed of an institution that both would serve as an instrument to unify Muslims against imperialism and would give them a new ethic much as the positivist churches in South America did.[120]

The CPU also adopted a very strong posture against European claims that the Turks could not reform their decadent empire and that therefore European intervention was mandated. The leaders of the CPU thought that European colonial literature had created an "Orient of fantasy," which bore no resemblance to the real Orient. This, they assumed, was a great barrier to a true understanding between the Ottoman Empire and the European powers, whose policies toward the Ottoman Empire were based on this romantic, fictional perception of the Orient, of which the Ottoman dominions formed a considerable part.[121] A later influential CUP member wrote that the real Orient, from Tokyo to the Bosphorus, "which some occidental authors such as Lamartine, Byron, Disraeli, Hugo, Renan, and Loti represent only as sleeping under the caresses of the languid sun, rocked by the songs of the geisha, or sunk in nirvana or dreaming in the drunkenness of hashish," in fact provided "a vital force" and should be treated accordingly by the Western Powers.[122]

The Young Turks' idea of making the Ottoman Empire the "Japan of the Near East"[123] was a clear expression of their anti-imperialist feelings and their yearning to establish a modern state that could counter European imperialistic policies. After the initial Japanese victory, many Young Turks went so far as to apply to serve in the Japanese army.[124] To the Young Turks, the Japanese victory was a great joy because in their perception it was a direct show of force against the European imperialistic powers. Besides having dealt a blow to the then "scientific" race hierarchy, the Japanese victory provided the Young Turks with the example of a strong state that could resist European imperialism. They admired Japan while ignoring the differences between it and the Ottoman Empire.

The Young Turks' strong anti-imperialism, and their concept of international relations as an arena of the "struggle for life" in which they wanted to see the Ottoman Empire as a "vital force," were also in complete accordance with their "scientific" ideas. It is not surprising that the nationalist wing of the movement underscored the fact that the "strong engulf the weak," among nations as among individuals and races.[125]

The CPU organs also claimed that Japan became a great power because of its industrial strength and its military might, and that the Ottoman Empire should emulate the Japanese example rather than persisting in its eccentric desire to be recognized as a great power through diplomatic maneuvers.[126] As one military CUP member put it, "anti-militarism" was a dangerous idea[127] because it attempted to bypass some stages of "human evolution," and in the world of the early twentieth century, nations had no other alternative but to be ready for war in order to survive.[128] While the CPU and other Young Turk organizations did not go as far as Friedrich von Bernhardi, who believed that the "struggle for existence" and "survival of the fittest" in the arena of the struggle among nations provided a scientific justification for war, their anti-imperialism nevertheless assumed a constant struggle among nations and held that the Ottoman Empire should gain military strength in order to fight against the imperialist encroachments of the European Great Powers.

During the period between 1902 and 1908 the strongest faction within the Young Turk movement adopted anti-imperialism as a pillar of its ideology. Their principal opponent in this regard was Sabahaddin Bey, who, despite a strong belief in Darwinist theory, defended the diametrically opposite thesis of the need to reach an understanding with the Great Powers of Europe along the lines of that attempted by the *Tanzimat* statesmen. The journal *Terakki* of Sabahaddin Bey's league published absolutely no criticism of Western imperialism; it was not even a serious issue in the eyes of the prince and his disciples.

By 1908 the debate that had begun with a discussion over the acceptance or refusal of foreign intervention in Ottoman domestic politics had evolved into a polarization over the attitude to be taken in regard to European imperialism. One may comment that the debate over foreign intervention, which can be traced as far back as the pre-*Tanzimat* period, and the later struggle between the Young Ottomans and Âlî and Fuad Pashas, were a reflection of the dispute over the proper Ottoman response to European imperialism. The *Tanzimat* statesmen held the upper hand in this struggle for most of the *Tanzimat* period, despite the disapproval and opposition of the Muslim masses. Beginning in 1876, however, those who still viewed the Great Powers' imperial policies as "benevolent actions" had no chance of winning over public opinion in the Ottoman Empire. In the light of this situation, the CUP began to use bolder language and advocated retaliation by all possible means. The policies promoted by the CUP, nevertheless, remained very similar to those of Abdülhamid II, who, however, had carefully avoided using caustic language.

As with Turkism and Ottomanism, the CPU and subsequently the CUP regarded relations with foreign powers as a realpolitik game and a tool useful in helping them achieve their goal of saving the empire.[129] One might have expected the CUP to take a strong anti-British stand after the revolution in the light of the extreme and open criticism of British policies found in its official organs prior to the revolution; but in fact, the CUP showed great moderation in this regard following the revolution. In addition, the extreme anti-German sentiment which prevailed in Ottoman public opinion after the revolution because of the alleged German backing of the old regime had little if any impact on the CUP. Rather, the CUP contacted the German authorities and presented a letter to the kaiser making an appeal for his support in their attempt to make the sultan loyal to the constitutional regime.[130] Ahmed Rıza sent a similar letter to the British king, using similar language and requesting British support.[131] Shortly after, the CUP proffered to Great Britain an Anglo-Ottoman alliance, which was turned down by the British.[132] The standard view which sees a strong shift from an extreme pro-British to an extreme pro-German CUP foreign policy is erroneous. As was the case with CUP policies on Ottomanism and Turkism, the CUP leaders had individual preferences and ideas relating to the Great Powers. When the CUP set about saving the empire, however, its members put all their personal proclivities aside.[133]

The Young Turks and Religion

The Young Turk *Weltanschauung*, as it developed between 1889 and 1902, was vehemently antireligious, viewing religion as the greatest obstacle to human progress. Despite this strong negative sentiment, Young Turks from all factions attempted to use religion as a device for modernization.[134] For the Young Turks religion was to be the stimulant and not the opiate of the masses.

With the adoption of Turkism by the coalition, the main faction within the Young Turk movement began to pay much less attention to religion, and invitations were no longer issued to the ulema to lead the movement. What had been a principal theme in the Young Turk publications gradually disappeared from the organs of the coalition. These journals' rare references to Islam during this period were almost always in regard to anti-imperialism. Thus when ʿAbd al-Ḥaqq Ḥaqqī al-Aʿẓamī al-Baghdādī al-Azharī published a highly controversial essay criticizing general European views on Islam,[135] *Mechveret Supplément Français* presented it as an anti-imperialist treatise, even though this was only one of many themes discussed by the author.[136] The organ of Sabahaddin Bey's league, which resembled a French sociological periodical, showed even less interest in religious issues. When one considers the ideas of Frédéric Le Play, the founder of *Science sociale*, and the importance he attached to religion in theory, this fact becomes more startling. Obviously Sabahaddin Bey's faith in science compelled him to excise the religious element from Le Play's ideas; indeed, for Sabahaddin Bey religion was not an issue either in theoretical discussion or as a political device to stir up Muslims.[137]

The political opportunism adopted by the CPU following the reorganization of 1906 once again encouraged the frequent use of Islam as a protonationalist device in CPU propaganda. The CPU agitation carried out during this period was quite different from the CUP propaganda of 1895–1900, which had urged the ulema to lead an Islamic revolt against the sultan. In addition, shifting their focus to political goals, the CPU leaders ceased their pursuit of their grand scientific ideals and thereby put an end to their extensive use of Islam as a tool for modernization until they seized power in 1908.[138] They still believed that "faith is a personal matter,"[139] but this belief did not prevent them from using Islam as a propaganda tool. In their propaganda they never held Islam to be a "personal matter,"[140] and accordingly they were frequently accused of being "politically passionate Moslems."[141] Because of this, while Ahmed Rıza's Islamist opponents denounced him as an "atheist," secret foreign reports characterized him as a *panislamiste fanatique.*[142] CPU propaganda used Islam mainly for three purposes: first, as a protonationalist device to agitate the Muslim masses against the sultan; second, to attack European imperialism; and third, to delegitimize the sultan's position from an Islamic point of view.

By the time they seized power following the revolution of 1908, the CUP leaders had a better understanding of the functions that different forms of Islam had been playing in Ottoman society, and they were even obliged to form an ulema branch to demonstrate to the public that the constitutional regime was in absolute accordance with Islam.[143] Many Young Turks still believed that "religion was essential to nations in the past, but that it could not be allowed to affect the destiny of the world and its inhabitants to-day."[144] Despite this fact, the CUP was compelled to establish its own ulema branch, and many ulema who had detested Abdülhamid II's regime now published articles that legitimized the new regime.

Initially almost all leading ulema welcomed the Young Turk Revolution and the overthrow of the Hamidian system as a long-awaited miracle.[145] They too used the locution "sacred committee"[146] and many other honorific phrases in referring to the CUP.[147] They deftly penned pamphlets and articles[148] that supported the CUP and the constitutional regime, which they described as purely Islamic.[149] The CUP's semiofficial dailies and journals also joined this campaign, making claims that "the constitution is an exact repetition of the Qur'ān and is taken from God's book and the Prophet's *ḥadīths*,"[150] and admonishing those who took a hostile stand against religion.[151] Moreover Islamist journals that were taken in by the CUP's use of Islam exalted Young Turk leaders such as Ahmed Rıza and Abdullah Cevdet.[152] During this short-lived period of amiable relations between the leading members of the ulema and the CUP, the Cemiyet-i İlmiye, the society established by the ulema, not only was in line with the CUP but also presented itself as an association directly linked to it.[153]

Nevertheless, relations between the CUP and various ulema organizations and leading figures soon became strained, primarily because of statements made by many CUP members which revealed their true ideas about religion. For example, one CUP deputy remarked that the *sharī'a* had nothing to do with the rift among various churches in the Balkans over the use of languages other than Greek in the liturgy and in Christian holy books. Such statements swiftly ruined the CUP's positive image in the eyes of many ulema.[154] The emerging opposition accused the leading CUP members of being "positivists" in order to discredit them in the eyes of the believers.[155] Later the opposition called them enemies of Islam. This hostile propaganda was very damaging to the CUP.[156]

The Cemiyet-i İlmiye was the first important ulema organization that decided to detach itself from the CUP.[157] Even though the ulema publishing the influential journal *Sırat-ı Mustakim* (*The Straight Road*, i.e., the Islamic religion) continued to support the CUP, articles critical of the CUP began to appear even here a year after the revolution,[158] and from this point on the ulema gave only halfhearted support to the CUP.[159] Despite the growing opposition against the CUP in conservative circles, it continued to receive this halfhearted support primarily because it remained in power.

The end of its initially cordial relations with all leading members of the ulema prompted the CUP to develop its own religious propaganda. The CUP central committee assigned this task to its three clubs in Istanbul: Şehzadebaşı, Süleymaniye, and Sultan Ahmed. The Şehzâdebaşı Club published religious advice on issues such as "absolutism, freedom, national sovereignty, solidarity, equality, oppression, justice, union, and consultation"; very simple language was employed in order to propagate the CUP's ideas through the use of an Islamic rhetoric.[160] The Süleymaniye Club engaged in publishing a popular journal named *Işık* (Light), strongly Islamic in tone, and distributed it free of charge to peasants, soldiers, and sailors.[161] The journal attempted to explain concepts such as "Ottomanism, fatherland, constitution, freedom, equality, justice, brotherhood, union, and respect for the flag."[162] The Sultan Ahmed Club distributed leaflets made up of religious prayers to be posted in houses, supposedly to protect Muslims from pestilence.[163]

Besides these clubs which were dedicated to producing Islamist publications, the CUP's regional branches, which were not brought under central control for two years after the revolution, used a genuine Islamist rhetoric in all their correspondence and publications.[164] This strategy benefited the CUP by improving its image in the eyes of conservative people.

Despite Islamist publications designed to shield the CUP from conservative attacks, Ahmed Rıza was correct when he stated to his positivist friend Émile Corra that secularist efforts to reshape Ottoman society began in the Ottoman Empire with the Young Turk Revolution of 1908.[165] In line with this, the CUP gradually diminished the role of religion in many aspects of social life despite its use of Islam as a tool. For example, the limitation of the power of the *sharī'a* courts began with the imperial decree of June 13, 1909, which banned these courts from hearing cases of private law in which verdicts had been pronounced by regular civil courts;[166] it ended with the attachment of all *sharī'a* courts to the Ministry of Justice in March 1917.[167]

The CUP leaders' responsibilities as the administrators of the empire compelled them to adopt a balanced position vis-à-vis the ulema and religion. They had acquired a great deal of experience using Islam as a tool for modernization, and later inciting the Muslim masses against the Hamidian regime during their years in opposition. They also greatly benefited from using Islam for their anti-imperialist politics before, and even more after, the revolution. The support of the ulema for the revolution and their praise of all the Young Turks who had fought against the Hamidian regime created a very confusing scenario. Nowhere is this confusion more apparent than in Derviş Vahdetî's praise for Abdullah Cevdet, who was about to finish the translation of Reinhart Pieter Anne Dozy's *De Voornaamste Godsdiensten: het Islamisme*, a fervent attack on Islam and its prophet.

On the basis of its experience in opposition, the CUP knew well that in the fragmented world of Islamic groups and organizations, various orders, and ulema all defending somewhat contradictory theses, it would be able to receive support from certain elements among these groups in order to legitimize itself and the new regime from an Islamic viewpoint. Just as they hesitated to embrace a wholesale Turkism, so also the CUP leadership adopted a moderate secularization policy. There is no doubt, however, that their reforms paved the way for the more radical reforms in modern Turkey that attempted to make religion nothing more than a "personal" matter.

The Young Turks and Elitism

One of the most salient characteristics of the Young Turk *Weltanschauung* shaped between 1889 and 1902 was its elitism. In this respect the Young Turks depended largely on Gustave Le Bon's ideas, a vulgarized version of the theories of Tarde and Durkheim. These elitist ideas continued to fascinate the Young Turks even after the reorganization of the CPU. It is interesting that not only the more intellectual members of the CPU such as Ahmed Rıza,[168] but also leading military members of the organization like Ömer Naci,[169] Enver Bey,[170] and İsmail Hafız Hakkı,[171] had developed a great interest in Le Bon's ideas. Additionally, Abdullah Cevdet started to translate Le Bon's books into Turkish during this period and they became extremely popular in Young Turk circles.[172] Almost all important Young Turks seemed to share Abdullah Cevdet's view that those who wished to be the "social doctors" of a nation must be familiar with Le Bon's ideas, and that to make any attempt in this regard without understanding these ideas was akin to claiming to be a physician without knowing "anatomy and physiology."[173]

As an article in *Şûra-yı Ümmet* reveals, many Young Turks viewed society in accordance with Le Bon's pyramid, with the elite having the duty of molding the masses in accordance with requirements of general progress.[174] At the beginning of the Young Turk movement, John Stuart Mill's theories had helped bring about the leading Young Turks' awareness that this elite must be an intellectual one. They also buttressed this idea with the then popular phrenology and heredity theories, which maintained that an intellectual elite could gain biological superiority through education[175] and could transmit these characteristics to a new generation through heredity.[176]

Like many European social thinkers of the time, the intellectual Young Turks were unaware of August Weismann's findings distinguishing somatic and germ cells, thereby refuting these pseudoscientific, Darwinistic heredity theories that assumed the transmission of acquired characteristics from generation to generation. For many decades they continued to dream of the fruition of their ideal based on outdated theories of Lamarck, and later of Jean-Marie Guyau.

Besides their failure to perceive the key defects of their "scientific elitism," for a long time the Young Turks failed to develop ideas about a political elite and the qualities that it must possess. For years *Şûra-yı Ümmet* had presented an imagined struggle between the "crowned tyrants" and "Sorbonnes, Tolstois, and Hugos," as if the latter were political leaders,[177] and it reminded the intellectuals of their duty to enlighten the masses.[178] *Türk* further claimed that the elite's neglect of its duty was "one of the main reasons for the Orient's decline."[179] During the same period the Young Turk journals continued to despise the "masses" because of their inactivity and their refusal to accept enlightenment from the elite.[180]

Another interesting consequence of the Young Turks' strong elitist proclivities was their interest in ideas such as "reverence for great men." They developed a strong interest in Carlyle's theory of heroes. One CPU member planned to make a translation of Carlyle's *On Heroes, Hero-Worship, and the Heroic in History*;[181] however, this project never materialized.

Following the reorganization of the CPU, the focus shifted from the creation of an intellectual elite to that of a governing one. Such an elite had to be aware of scientific advances, but it also had to govern and rebuild the state. The Ottoman tradition of defining the elite simply as a "governing body" undoubtedly served as the basis for this imagined elite. The committee organizers swept away all the theories of phrenology, heredity, and transmission of acquired higher characteristics, which had long provided the Young Turks with utopian and unworkable devices to create an alternative elite, and replaced them with the concept of government by a young, patriotic, activist civil-military elite. *Şûra-yı Ümmet*'s ridiculing of Abdülhamid II's cabinet ministers was an effort to demonstrate to the people the need for such a new elite.[182] The CUP leaders nevertheless appreciated the difficulty of discarding the old elite and assuming direct control over governing positions, and as a result they confined themselves to acting behind the scenes until 1913. Despite the gradual nature of this shift in the elite, the CUP's success in this area should not be underestimated. Within five years a new governing civil-military elite, whose members could not have

dreamed of becoming bureau directors and division commanders under the old regime, had taken charge of the empire.

The CUP's attempt to create an alternative governing elite was by no means an
original idea. The originality lay in its use of a well-organized committee and later a
political party as a foundation for the creation of this governing elite.

During the first year after the revolution, foreign observers[183] and adversaries[184] likened the members of the CUP to Jacobins. Although this was a vague label, the most
striking similarity between the Jacobins and the CUP was undoubtedly the existence
of a well-organized minority bent on imposing its ideas on the masses.[185] Even when
Bahaeddin Şakir entered into a contest in populism with the Dashnaktsutiun representatives at the Second Congress of Ottoman Opposition Parties, the CPU did not want
to organize a popular revolutionary movement. The CPU leaders were frequently accused of not working for the "rough, rowdy, and illiterate people,"[186] and of having
concern only for the bureaucracy.[187] In point of fact, various leading Young Turks
told von der Goltz that if they had not carried out their revolution, the masses would
have rebelled and caused anarchy; their movement had thwarted just such a dangerous development.[188]

The CUP, which had no intention of allowing the people to participate directly in
decision-making, sent all the volunteers who had joined the CPU bands back to their
homes and requested its branches, many of which were led by bureaucrats and officers, to establish firm control over their respective regions. Young Turk propaganda
in general did not produce works and translations promoting a popular revolution.
The most important "revolutionary" essay that the leaders of the CPU Internal Headquarters supported was Jane Mendès-Catulle's *Le Roman rouge*,[189] which gives a
fair idea of their conception of revolutionary literature.[190]

While doing very little to actively promote a popular revolutionary movement, the
CPU leaders still despised the inactivity of the masses. For instance, *Şûra-yı Ümmet*
asked its readers the following question after Kâmil Pasha took refuge in the British
consulate in Izmir: "The rabble is in the palace, the governors are in the consulates,
Abdülhamid is on his death-bed, but where is the nation?!!"[191] As we have seen, the
masses, incited by the CPU members, participated in the movement by carrying out
demonstrations during the last days of the revolution; following the revolution, however, the CUP asked these crowds to put an end to their rallies.[192] It is not possible to
describe these masses as revolutionary mobs in the real sense of the word. As Mardin
has stated, the revolution "did not originate in the thrust of the masses," and there
were "no Turkish equivalents of the *tricoteuses* watching justice being carried out,
of castle-burning, and the revolutionary commune radicalizing the policy of the
Revolution."[193] Mass movements against detested officials sometimes became violent in the provinces, but they never turned into continuous, organized revolutionary
activities.

In a parallel vein to the interpretation of the term of *azādīkhvāhān* by masses in
Iran during the revolution of 1906, the masses in the Ottoman Empire interpreted
hürriyet not as revolution, but as a change intended to replace the arbitrary rule of
officials with justice. The CUP's program was directed at the new governing elite
that was charged with serving the people, a task that the Young Turk leaders viewed
as a virtuous activity; however, they never thought of making the masses a key fig-

ure in decision-making.[194] The Young Turks paid very little attention to the representative aspect of parliament, viewing it as an extension of the modern bureaucratic apparatus under the control of an enlightened governing elite. This attitude derived partly from the fact that they viewed society from the standpoint of the state and attributed the utmost importance to the interests of the state. As they saw it, deputies were agents of the state rather than representatives of the people. Thus in 1908 the CUP found it necessary to send party officials to the provinces "to help the people" elect the right men as deputies. In 1912, when its claim of being "sacred" was strongly challenged by its opponents, the CUP took oppressive measures to prevent undesirable individuals from becoming deputies. In short, the Young Turks did not believe in representation in the real sense of the word.

Parliamentary discussion was also very distasteful to the CUP leaders; after 1913 they totally bypassed the parliament and ruled the country through thousands of so-called temporary laws, issued by cabinet ministers and enacted through imperial decrees. The Young Turks' ideas about parliament also reflected the fact that they did not differentiate the various elements among the masses, despising them all. Early theoreticians of the elite theory, such as the members of the Italian School of criminal law, had used the term "masses" in a distinctly negative manner; in their works the "crowd" implied something inhuman, and crowd psychology was abnormal. Gustave Le Bon, who was deeply influenced by these scholars, especially by Scipio Sighele, considered a crowd an organized conglomeration capable of forming a collective mind. Le Bon did not make any distinction between "crowd" and "public" as Tarde did; instead he viewed an entire nation and a parliament as a "crowd" that forms a collective and "inferior" mind. It is not coincidental that many Young Turk leaders who became admirers of Le Bon viewed the voters as a "crowd" and the parliament as a heterogeneous crowd, just as their "genius" sociologist had done. Enver Bey viewed deputies as *les têtes moyennes* (*mittelmassig*), referring to Le Bon, and thought that their collective mind could become as dangerous as that of a despotic ruler.[195]

The Young Turks never desired the people's participation in decision-making or any real form of representation.[196] The CUP viewed itself as a "sacred committee" with the self-imposed duty of creating a governing civil-military elite to advance the nation on behalf of the people. Those deputies who were "smart enough" to understand the importance of this concept would be an asset to the CUP as the "representatives of the nation"; however, when they failed to comprehend their limited role and wanted to carry out functions of more consequence, the CUP leaders were ready to discount them as a "heterogenous crowd." In Ahmed Rıza's words, "silly people [*sebükmağzân*] should not be allowed to enter into politics; however, they have unfortunately even become deputies, and this is a defect of liberty that enables the masses [*avam*] to assume a role in the life and future of the state and nation."[197]

11

Conclusion

The 1908 Young Turk Revolution even though not a popular constitutional move-ment, was a watershed in the history of the late Ottoman Empire. It not only put an end to the long-lived Hamidian regime, but also identified an ancien régime in Otto-man politics in the strongest terms and attempted to replace old institutions and poli-cies with new ones. Abdülhamid II's carefully created regime, refined and revamped by its founder over more than three decades, simply vanished from the scene, and no one who possessed any weight in politics, even among the opponents of the CUP, either defended it or yearned for its return. The Young Turk Revolution not only es-tablished a new power center in Ottoman politics, namely the CUP, but also gave rise to a dynamic opposition that disputed the political program of the CUP. Another result of the revolution was the gradual creation of a new governing elite, which had consolidated and cemented its control over the Ottoman civil and military adminis-tration by 1913.

It was the CUP that created this new elite, and for the first time in Ottoman history an organized political party dominated politics. Like other parties of the period in different parts of the world, the CUP, with its self-imposed mission of saving the country, assumed the role of a "progressive" guide that did not want other political actors to criticize or even question its policies.

As with many similar parties that felt destined to change the very foundations of society, the internal divisions of the CUP began to grow in importance after its first year in power. For instance, when a journalist asked Talât Pasha the simple ques-tion, "What is the CUP?" the latter responded that it was "something of which the administration has been extremely difficult."[1] Despite the emergence of internal fac-tions and the rise of strong individual figures within the party, the CUP never fell under the domination of a single person; thus the party cult transcended individual personalities. In addition, although the delicate relations between the CPU/CUP and the army played a significant role in the organization's success in carrying out the revolution, and later in administering the country, the fact is that neither the com-ments describing the Young Turk Revolution as a simple *pronunciamento*,[2] nor the claims that the CUP was "under the patronage of the army,"[3] were accurate.

The CPU did take on a paramilitary character after its appeal to junior officers, but the Young Turk Revolution was the work of a broad political organization with far-reaching aims, and not the accomplishment of a small group of junior officers. After the reorganization in 1906, all important policy matters were discussed within the central committee, where the wishes of strong figures were frequently frustrated by other members. These individuals could to a certain degree manipulate the committee's decisions on general policies; however, no single person ever dominated this body, and even the strongest figures complied with decisions taken by their colleagues against their personal desires and wishes.

After the revolution, decisions of the CUP central committee grew in importance, since it became an *imperium in imperio*. Focusing on the policies implemented by the CUP, scholarship has hitherto accepted the Young Turk Revolution of 1908 as a starting point and has not paid due attention to its background. Yet a thorough examination of debates and political discussions among the Young Turks, and of the Young Turk *Weltanschauung*, leaves no doubt that all of the principal issues of the second constitutional period had been debated and discussed among the Young Turk expatriates. The CUP and its opponents had shaped their policies while fighting against their common enemy, the Hamidian regime, and they brought their ideas into the new era with the ultimate goal of implementation.

Because their contemporaries as well as later scholars identified the Young Turk Revolution as a constitutional movement and the Young Turks as constitutionalists, without paying heed to the goals they pursued and the ideas they embraced prior to 1908, many regarded the authoritarian character of the CUP regime as an unforeseen and surprising outcome, frequently attributed to the corruption of power or viewed as a response to external developments. Yet the examination of the Young Turk secret correspondence and publications, as well as the private papers of the leading members of their organizations, clearly reveals that they viewed themselves above all else as the saviors of an empire. They were not constitutionalists or advocates of the reinstatement of the constitutional regime for the sake of establishing a constitutional political system; rather they thought that having a constitution in effect would help them to overcome many of the internal and external problems of the empire.[4]

As empire-savers the Young Turks always viewed the problems confronting the Ottoman Empire from the standpoint of the state, placing little if any emphasis on the people's will. Thus the Young Turks' inclination toward authoritarian theories was by no means a coincidence. All the theories that the Young Turks developed and took particular interest in, such as biological materialism, positivism, Social Darwinism, and Gustave Le Bon's elitism, defended an enlightenment from above and opposed the idea of a supposed equality among fellow-citizens. In his *Système social*, Holbach, who was idolized by many Young Turks, maintained that true liberty consists in conforming to the laws that remedy the natural inequality of men; Comte's famous aphorism *ordre et progrès*, which many Young Turks wanted to see as the motto of their movement, presupposed a society in which duties preceded rights; the two icons of the intellectual Young Turks, Büchner and Vogt, found socialism and egalitarianism "unscientific"; Social Darwinism, the chosen guide of so many Young Turks, was based on the "inequality of men"; and finally, the advice of Le Bon, as the "greatest sociologist" in the eyes of the Young Turks, was simply to understand the psychology of the masses in order to make them support the work of the elite.

The Young Turks' mistrust of the masses also caused them to depend on already active forces within the society instead of on the complacent crowd, and to seek their alliance against the Hamidian regime. Before the reorganization of the coalition and the emergence of the CPU, *Şûra-yı Ümmet* had maintained that the Young Turks should replace what had been the two pillars of Ottoman society before the *Tanzimat*, the Janissaries and the ulema, with a free press and a parliament, respectively, in order to accomplish a new balance within the society.[5] It seems, however, that after the reorganization the CPU leaders abandoned this idea of substituting a free press for the Janissaries, instead deciding to depend on the army. The lower-ranking officers who became the backbone of the new organization gave the CPU control of the most active force in Ottoman society. This force shared the CPU/CUP's overall political conservatism and its rejection of any activity that challenged its version of Ottomanism. Therefore, despite carrying out a revolution that sought to destroy the Hamidian regime, the activist force within the CUP, because of its strong desire to maintain the empire, did not embrace any form of political radicalism. As many Young Turks emphasized, their revolution was far from being a radical one.[6]

The Young Turks' strong rejection of ideologies attacking the state stems partly from their aspiration to save the state and partly from the fact that they did not form an intelligentsia independent of the state. Like the *Tanzimat* statesmen who had been deeply impressed by *kameralismus*, the Young Turks admired authoritarian theories that defended a strong government and enlightenment from above. Ironically, they always underscored the inequality of men in their intellectual writings, despite their frequent use of the motto "equality" in their political propaganda. Interestingly, this term gained the peculiar political meaning of "equality among Ottomans from different ethnic and religious groups," rather than referring to equality among men in a general sense.

The Young Turks expected people to appreciate their implementation of a program intended to enlighten the masses and to carry out policies beneficial for them. The lack of enthusiasm on the part of the populace, and their continual demands of a local nature, only served to frustrate the Young Turk leadership even more; they had already been extremely displeased with the people's lack of interest in their propaganda during their early years in opposition. Despite becoming a political party with thousands of members and hundreds of branches throughout the empire, the CUP continued to be administered by a group of ideologues and committee/party organizers and did not allow the periphery to take an active part in decision-making. There was not a single CUP central committee member who had risen within the party as a local leader championing local interests.

Besides making the CUP the dominant actor in Ottoman politics, the 1908 Young Turk Revolution marked a strong shift in the organization of the elites of many ethnic and religious groups in the Ottoman Empire. For instance, the Dashnaktsutiun replaced the pre-1908 Armenian elite, which had been composed of merchants, artisans, and clerics who saw their future in obtaining more privileges within the boundaries of the state's version of Ottomanism. The loyal Muslim Albanian elite, who had greatly benefited from the Hamidian regime in return for their fidelity to the sultan, was replaced by an intellectual-nationalist elite, with members such as Bajram Curri, Nexhib Draga, and Myfit Libohova; all of these aimed at uniting Albanians of three different faiths under the flag of Skënderbeu and called for reforms for the benefit of all Albanians. In some communities, such as the Jewish one, reformist groups emulating the Young Turks ousted the conservative ruling elite and replaced them with a new reformist one.[7]

The changes that had brought the Young Turks' expatriate foes to power within their respective communities had the further implication that all the unsettled issues that had separated them from the Young Turks now returned to plague the new regime. The Young Turks and the expatriate organizations of the various ethnic groups had not been able to find common ground during their years in opposition; the most they could accomplish together was to strike tactical alliances to destroy the Hamidian regime. After the revolution their disagreements grew in importance, since they gained the upper hand in the administration of the empire and of community affairs. Under the Hamidian regime, loyal elites who were greatly benefiting from the existing system were able to coexist, despite the opposition they faced from active protonationalist, nationalist, and in some cases socialist elements; after the revolution, however, the new elites called for change and entered into a struggle with the new administration. The CUP's adoption of an aggressive Ottomanism, which its opponents considered tantamount to Turkification, strained relations even more.

In the best of all possible worlds, the emergence of all-encompassing political parties organized along lines that transcended national issues, and comprising different ethnic and religious groups regardless of their origins and affiliations, might have enabled the CUP and the representatives of other communities to find common ground. In actuality the political organization of the ethnic groups was dominated by nationalist committees and clubs through which they participated in politics, with the most hard-line autonomists and nationalists gaining the upper hand. This situation only sharpened the differences between the CUP and these organizations and made rapprochement impossible. It is unlikely that these organizations precisely reflected their communities' feelings and desires. In almost all cases strong opposition existed against the dominance of these nationalist-led groups; for example, the Geg notables and ulema in Kosovo supported the Arabo-Persian alphabet, the Armenian *amira* class evinced an intense dislike for nationalist-socialist party politics, and the Ottomanized Bulgarian community of Istanbul despised the IMRO and political bands. In each case, however, the upper hand was held by the overrepresented nationalist clubs and committees that dominated the communal presses and received support from many intellectuals.

The introduction of party politics to the Ottoman Empire also made burgeoning political parties, committees, and clubs the main actors in national and local politics. Other institutions—such as the local notable families, religious orders, and *tekke*s that had long served as a means of political participation and a device to convey local demands to the center—now lost their independence. They could survive the transition period only by incorporating themselves into the new political milieu. Thus intellectual and nationalist elites secured a gross overrepresentation at the expense of the unorganized masses who were strangers to new ideas, and of the old institutions which were pushed aside. Just as the CUP advocated avant-garde ideas embraced by a small percentage of the general population, so the various ethnic and religious groups came to be dominated by relatively radical intellectual elites.

The great schism in the Young Turk movement had occurred over the issue of foreign intervention in Ottoman politics. Two fronts had emerged, whose members were influenced by the same thinkers, such as Büchner, Comte, Darwin, Demolins, Fouillée, Le Bon, and Ribot. Shared influences did not prevent these Young Turks from entering into a bitter struggle with each other. This schism also marked the point where the Young Turk movement began gradually to transform itself from an intellectual milieu into a movement of political opposition. Sabahaddin Bey was propagating a program of decentralization in response to the CPU's and CUP's strong centralist tendencies and their aggressive Ottomanism; this attracted the elites of many non-Turkish ethnic groups that supported the prince's program in an attempt to obtain privileges for their communities.

With the support of the young and active segment of the army, the CUP became the dominant player in Ottoman politics, and Sabahaddin Bey's decentralization program could not gain ground except among the non-Turkish ethnic groups of the empire. CUP propaganda likened Sabahaddin Bey's program to a partition scheme, and this caused many intellectuals who had originally seen it as beneficial to the empire to distance themselves from it. Sabahaddin Bey, because of his self-declared intellectual superiority, looked down on his opponents and accused them of not understanding the realities of Ottoman society from a sociological and scientific viewpoint. It was the CPU's committee organizers, however, who better understood the basic political realities of the empire.

With the CPU's transformation into a real political committee following the reorganization of the former coalition between the followers of Ahmed Rıza and the "activists," this new body rapidly adopted more pragmatic and opportunist tactics. By making empire-saving their predominant task, the CPU, and later the CUP, attempted to entice other political groups to join them by adopting a plurality of different and sometimes conflicting theses.

The Young Turks' ideals and their policies therefore should not be confused with each other; the two were frequently at variance. For the sake of saving the empire, the CPU leaders pursued pragmatic policies designed to win over the opposition in an effort to topple the Hamidian regime, even though those policies conflicted with the CPU's ideals. When they seized power, the CUP leaders attempted to promote contradictory policies in order to satisfy various ethnic and religious groups, and despite their proclivities they did not implement a uniform and inflexible policy. CUP documents reveal that during the early years of the second constitutional period, the CUP simultaneously promoted Ottomanist, Turkist, and Islamist policies, together with a modernization program to build a "scientific" state.

Besides adopting such a complex program, the CUP leaders attempted to blend these policies ideologically. As early as 1907 Hüseyinzâde Ali advocated a policy of "being Turkish, Muslim, and European: possessing Turkish feelings, being affiliated with the religion of Islam, and being equipped with the present European civilization."[8] Hüseyinzâde Ali, like many Turkic intellectuals in Russia, had no hopes for Ottomanism; he made it clear that the Turkish component of this ideological blend was its dominant module. Yet despite the CUP's efforts to win over the Islamist intellectuals, many of them strongly opposed the dominance of Turkism.[9] All the efforts made by the CUP leaders, including the publication of an Islamist journal, made very little impact on the Islamist opponents of the CUP. This three-pronged ideology, best articulated by Ziya Gökalp in his essay *Türkleşmek, İslâmlaşmak, Mu'asırlaşmak*,[10] became a cornerstone of CUP policy, with a strong emphasis on the Turkish component.

Despite the CUP's implementation of a variety of policies and its attempts at reconciling other political ideologies with Turkism, this latter tenet always remained dominant in the CUP system; this stance reflected both its leaders' Turkist proclivities and the struggle among rival nationalist elites precipitated by the Young Turk Revolution of 1908.[11] As research reveals, the Young Turks had been inclined toward Turkism long before the Balkan Wars, but their self-imposed task of empire-saving for some time prevented the CUP leaders from unleashing their Turkism as a policy, since they had reason to avoid stimulating other nationalist and separatist movements within the empire. As empire-savers the CUP leaders found Turkism inoperable as an official state policy. The publications of the Turkish press in Cairo after 1902, and especially *Türk* and *Şûra-yı Ümmet*, leave no doubt about the existence of a Turkist ideology at the cultural level, and they show that it had been embraced by many Young Turks who were to occupy important positions in the empire after the Young Turk Revolution. At the same time the CUP was now joined by Turkic intellectuals from Russia such as Hüseyinzâde Ali and Ahmed Agayef, who had advocated Turkist policies in their journals *Füyûzat, Hayat, İrşad*, and *Kaspii* and had helped the CPU cause; as a result, Turkism became more dominant in the CUP inner circle during the later phase of the second constitutional period. This fact notwithstanding, the CUP continued to implement a diverse array of policies as long as it had any prospect of saving the empire and strengthening the various groups' allegiance to the center.

The Young Turk Revolution played a significant role in the reshaping of the Middle East and the Balkans. Because of it an area from Scutari in Albania to Basra became acquainted with political parties, nationalist clubs, elections, and the idea of constitutional rights.[12] The revolution's success made it one of the more momentous events of the first years of the twentieth century, causing many other movements to imitate the CPU/CUP. Immediately after the revolution, for example, some Greek newspapers encouraged the Greek military to carry out a similar revolution;[13] a Military League "founded . . . upon the model of the Turkish Committee of Union and Progress,"[14] carried out a coup in 1909.[15]

The revolution and the CPU/CUP's work made a stronger impact on Muslims.[16] The Persian community in Istanbul founded the "Iranian Union and Progress Committee";[17] more significantly, the Persian constitutionalist expatriates adopted for their own organization the CPU's regulations exactly as issued in 1908.[18] Indian Muslims imitated the CPU oath for joining the organization.[19] In Bukhara the *jadidist*s and the leaders of the Young Bukhara movement were deeply influenced by the Young Turk Revolution and saw it as an example to emulate.[20]

The revolution and the CPU/CUP's work remained for a long period a model for Muslims in many countries. For instance, in 1988 the Soviet authorities uncovered an underground organization in Zhambyl that allegedly aimed at organizing ties with "neo-fascist currents" in Turkey and at carrying out assassinations against the local Communist party leaders. The organizers had named their committee "Union and Progress."[21]

The real reason for the popularity of the CUP among Muslims throughout the world was its espousal simultaneously of the establishment of a modern state and the struggle against imperialism. While the CUP's attempt to establish a modern state as an expression of its *Weltanschauung* impressed Muslim intellectuals all over the world, it was its strong anti-imperialism that made it an icon of the Muslim populations under European rule. When Moussa-Mangoumbel, the grandson of the last king of Congo, appealed to the CUP for help against the "imperialist European invaders,"[22] he was naturally unable to secure the support that he desired, which was entirely beyond the capacity of the CUP. Such individuals, however, continued to view the "Young Turk Committee in Istanbul" as a power that could challenge the European imperialists. Later developments were to diminish the impact of the Young Turks on Muslim intellectuals. Moreover, the Chinese and Russian Revolutions of 1911 and 1917 diverted the attention of world revolutionaries from the Young Turk Revolution. Yet the impact of the Young Turk movement and its product, the Young Turk Revolution, was pivotal in the emergence of a new Middle East and Balkans, and it had far-reaching results that can be perceived even today. Finally, a knowledge of the Young Turk *Weltanschauung* is essential to any understanding of the changes that took place in the last years of the Ottoman Empire and the first years of the early Turkish Republic.

Notes

CHAPTER 1

1. For a description of the congress, see my *The Young Turks in Opposition* (New York, 1995), 173–99, and my "Der Jungtürkenkongress von Paris und seine Ergebnisse," *Die Welt des Islams* 33, no. 1 (1993), 23–65.

2. Another recent study that provides detailed information about the Young Turk Revolution of 1908 is Jusuf Hamza (Yusuf Hamza), *Mladoturskata revolucija vo Osmanskata Imperija-Osmanlı İmparatorluğu'nda II. Meşrutiyet'in İlânı* (Skopje, 1995).

3. A good analysis of the political ideas of the Young Turks can be found in Şerif Mardin, *Jön Türklerin Siyasi Fikirleri, 1895–1908*, 2nd ed. (Istanbul, 1983).

4. Especially in the period prior to 1906, the editorial board members of Young Turk journals became quite experienced in fabricating letters allegedly sent to them and supporting their views or providing information about developments. For an interesting example, see Rauf Ahmed to İshak Sükûti, Folkestone, May 4, 1901, AQSh, 19/106–6//242/1926.

CHAPTER 2

1. Ali Fahri, *Yine Kongre* (Paris, 1318 [1900]), 7.

2. "Les partis en Turquie," *Revue de l'Islam* 7 (1902), 121.

3. See Münir Bey to Tevfik Pasha, Paris, February 19, 1902/no. 15918-90, BBA–HR.SYS. 1792/1 (original. 503/61).

4. "Zübde-i Havâdis: Dahiliye," *Sabah*, February 13, 1902; "Dersaadet İstinaf Müdde'i-yi Umumiliği'nden," *Ceride-i Mahakim-i Adliye*, no. 36 (February 12, 1902), 1.

5. "Zübde-i Havâdis: Dahiliye," *Sabah*, February 20, 1902.

6. See Tevfik Pasha to Münir Bey, March 12, 1902/no. 46465-95, and the Ministry of Justice's note dated [March 10, 1902] and enclosed with the aforementioned dispatch, BBA–HR.SYS. 1792/1 (original. 503/61). See also "Zübde-i Havâdis: Dahiliye," *Sabah*, March 9, 1902.

7. See Şirvanizâde Mahmud Tahir's file in BBA–HR.SYS. 1796/7 (original. 502/48); "Zübde-i Havâdis: Dahiliye," *Sabah*, March 6, 1902; and "Dersaadet İstinaf Müdde'i-yi Umumiliği'nden," *Ceride-i Mahakim-i Adliye*, no. 49 (April 2, 1902), 1; and ibid., no. 64 (May 24, 1902), 1.

8. See "Midhat Pascha-Sohn contra Sultan," *Berliner Tageblatt*, February 20, 1902; "Yine Bir Cenâbet," *Osmanlı*, no. 103 (March 1, 1902), 5; "Mandats d'arrêt contre les Princes Loutfoullah et Sébaheddin," *Pro Armenia* 2, no. 7 (February 25, 1902), 56; and P[ierre] Q[uillard], "Nouvelles d'Orient," *Pro Armenia* 2, no. 9 (March 25, 1902), 70.

9. BBA–İrade-Hususî, Ra 1320/no. 59-340.

10. Damad Mahmud Pasha put his request to Blakeney, the British consul in Corfu. Sir Thomas Sanderson, under the instructions given by Lord Lansdowne, denied permission. See Sir Thomas's draft dated December 18, 1901; and Blakeney to O'Conor, Corfu, December 7, 1901/no. 7, enclosed with the draft, PRO/F.O. 78/5142. The same viewpoint was consistently displayed in the later correspondence relating to Damad Mahmud Pasha's travel to England. See Sir Thomas's draft to the Colonial Office dated January 10, 1902, and Cox to Sanderson, January 21, 1902/no. 1415 (confidential), PRO/F.O. 78/5211.

11. For detailed information, see BBA–YMGM, 236/70 (1320.Ş.12); BBA–İrade-Hususî, R 1320/no. 65-461 and no. 81-499. The sultan also required the help of O'Conor during an audience. See O'Conor's note "Friday, Audience of the Sultan" dated February 7, 1902, O'Conor Papers, Churchill College, Cambridge, 7/4/7.

12. The British explained their attitude to the Ottoman authorities twice, immediately after the 1902 Congress and later. See Murdoch to Sanderson, February 14, 1902/no. B.32482-15, PRO/F.O. 78/5211; the draft of the note sent to the Home Office, dated September 22, 1902 (confidential), PRO/F.O. 78/5212; and "Draft to [Abdülhak] Hamid," signed by Lord Lansdowne and dated October 7, 1902, PRO/F.O. 78/5209.

13. See the deciphers from Reşid Bey to Tevfik Pasha, Rome, February 21, 1902/no. 38 (decipher no. 204) and February 28, 1902/no. 44 (decipher no. 245); Tevfik Pasha to Reşid Bey, February 24, 1902/no. 46234-38 (decipher no. 38), March 10, 1902/no. 52 (decipher); the Grand Vizier's office's note dated [February 24, 1902], BBA–HR.SYS. 1792/1 (original. 503/61). For later developments, see Reşid Bey to Âsım Bey, Rome [May 23, 1902]/no. 80; and Tahsin Pasha to Hüseyin Hüsni Pasha [June 5, 1902]/no. 87, *Roma Sefaret-i Seniyesiyle Muhaberata Mahsus Defterdir*, BBA–YEE, 36/2468/141/XII; BBA–İrade-Hususî, Ra 1320/no. 14-289; Malaspina di Carbonara to Prinetti, Pera, March 8, 1902/no. 4; ASMAE, Affari Politici, Serie P. Politica (1891–1916), pacco 172; Tevfik Pasha to Reşid Bey, May 8, 1902/no. 47448-95 (decipher), May 11, 1902/no. 47490-96 (decipher), May 12, 1902/no. 47506-97 (decipher), May 13, 1902/no. 47524-98, May 17, 1902/no. 47585-101 (confidentielle); Reşid Bey to Tevfik Pasha, Rome, May 11, 1902/no. 122 (decipher), May 13, 1902/no. 124 (decipher), May 15, 1902/no. 131 (decipher), and the notes of the Grand Vizier's office dated [May 7, 1902] and [May 15, 1902], BBA–HR.SYS. 1792/1 (original. 503/61).

14. Malaspina di Carbonara to Prinetti, Pera, March 11, 1902/T. 403-5, *I Documenti Diplomatici Italiani* 6 (3rd Series, 1896–1906) (Rome, 1985), 172–73.

15. Reşid Bey to Tevfik Pasha, Rome, June 2, 1902/no. 151 (decipher) and June 3, 1902/no. 153 (decipher), BBA–HR.SYS. 1792/1 (original. 503/61); Prinetti to Basso, Rome, August 18, 1902/no. 39755-P.17 (confidenziale); Malvano to Lambertenghi, Rome, August 26, 1902/no. 40754-P. 1716 (confidenziale), ASMAE, Affari Politici, Serie P. Politica (1891–1916), pacco 172. It should be stated that the Italians agreed to send a warning to Damad Mahmud Pasha asking him never to return to Italy. See the first chamberlain's note to the Grand Vizier, dated [June 6, 1902], BBA–HR.SYS. 1792/1 (original. 503/61).

16. BBA–BEO/Hariciye Gelen, 160-5/16; 1112 (June 11, 1902); Tevfik Bey to Münir Pasha, June 7, 1902/no. 47864-17; and the latter to the former, Paris, June 10, 1902/no. 803, BBA–HR.SYS. 1792/1 (original. 503/61).

17. Müller to Münir Bey, Bern, June 30, 1902, Archives of the Turkish Embassy in Paris, D. 283. See also Münir Bey to Tevfik Pasha, Paris, June 28, 1902/no. 898 (decipher), BBA–HR.SYS. 1792/1 (original. 503/61).

18. Mihran Efendi to the Belgian Foreign Office, October 11, 1902/no. 254, Archives of the Turkish Embassy in Paris, D. 290.

19. Memorandum prepared by Sir Nicholas R. O'Conor and dated October 1, 1902/no. 425, PRO/F.O. 78/5193.

20. See R. Michelin, "La véridique histoire de Mahmoud-pacha," *Le Figaro*, March 17, 1902. For Münir Bey's efforts to publish such an article in the French daily, see Tevfik Pasha to Münir Bey, March 19, 1902/no. 46632-113; Münir Bey to Tevfik Pasha, Paris, March 20, 1902/no. 151-357; and Paris, March 29, 1902/no. 16027-164, BBA–HR.SYS. 1792/1 (original. 503/61); and BBA–YMGM, 227/140 (1319.Z.24). The event was criticized by the left-wing French press. See Pierre Quillard, "Le sultan et la Presse française," *L'Européen* 2, no. 16 (March 22, 1902), 4.

21. Loutfoullah et Sabahaddine, "A Monsieur le Directeur-Gérant du Figaro," *Le Figaro*, March 20, 1902.

22. AE–NS–T, 4 (1902–1904), 37–42.

23. Constans to Delcassé, Pera, March 4, 1902/no. 27, ibid., 43–44.

24. Münir Bey to Delcassé, Paris, March 9, 1902, ibid., 45–49. A copy of this letter is in BBA–HR.SYS. 1792/1 (original. 503/61), and enclosed with Münir Bey to Tevfik Pasha, April 12, 1902/no. 16091-208. Detailed information may also be found in a dispatch with nine enclosures that was sent to Tevfik Pasha from Münir Bey, dated Paris, March 7, 1902/no. 159561-116 (affaire des fils de Damad Mahmoud Pacha), BBA–HR.SYS. 1792/1 (original. 503/61).

25. Draft dated Paris, March 12, 1902/no. 60, AE–NS–T, 4 (1902–1904), 59–60.

26. See the drafts dated Paris, March 15, 1902/no. 64, and Paris, April 8, 1902/no. 93, ibid., 57, 58–60.

27. Delcassé to Münir Bey, April 5, 1902, Archives of the Turkish Embassy in Paris, D. 244.

28. The measures to be taken against them are described in the following documents: the Ministry of the Interior to Delcassé, Paris, April 28 [1902]; and the draft prepared by the Affaires étrangères dated Paris, April 30, 1902/no. 135, AE–NS–T, 4 (1902–1904), 91–92 and 92–93.

29. For the procedure and final lists prepared by the embassies, see BBA–YSHM, 446/154 (1321.1.29); 447/61 (1321.2.5); and 447/136 (1321.2.11); BBA–BEO/Dahiliye Giden, 101-3/50; 3849 [February 26, 1903]/150613; and the list entitled "Fransa'da Tahsilde Bulunub Bilâhare Maaşları Katʿ Olunduğu Halde Dersaadet'e Avdet Etmeyen Talebenin Esâmisi," and prepared by the Paris embassy, dated [March 7, 1903], Private Papers of Salih Münir Pasha.

30. See BBA–ŞD, Dersaadet XXI-30; 67 [November 3, 1902]/2723-45.

31. For the measures taken against him and other officials, see BBA–BEO/Hariciye Giden, 185-5/41; 135 [March 8, 1902]/135250, 135410, and 135495; BBA–BEO/Dahiliye Gelen, 49-3/100; 3606 [March 5, 1902]/135250; and BBA–İrade-Hususî, Za 1319/no. 98–975.

32. BBA–BEO/Dahiliye Gelen, 49-3/100; 3678 [March 9, 1902]/135410.

33. "Les perquisitions à Constantinople," *Le Petit Marseilles*, April 24, 1902.

34. See "Paris'deki Talebe-i Osmaniye," *Hilâfet*, no. 68 (April 15, 1902), [4].

35. "The Turkish Students in Europe," *The Times*, March 20, 1902. For the comments made by the Young Turks, see "Havâdis-i Hariciye," *Muvazene*, no. 231 [May 7, 1902], 4.

36. See M. Şükrü Hanioğlu, *The Young Turks in Opposition* (New York, 1995), 197–98.

37. "Tebşîr," *Osmanlı*, no. 103 (March 1, 1902), 4.

38. As a matter of fact, the original plan made by the members of the permanent committee who were not certain about the possible action to be taken by the editor of *Osmanlı* was to publish a new central organ in Manchester. See Münir Bey to Tevfik Pasha, Paris, February 28, 1902/no. 46285-72 (decipher no. 128), BBA–HR.SYS. 1792/1 (original. 503/61).

39. See "Pek Büyük Bir Zayâʿ," *Osmanlı*, no. 103, 1–3 and "Sene-i Devriye Münasebetiyle," *Osmanlı*, no. 127 (December 1, 1903), 1. His friends recorded İshak Sükûti's estate after his death and published the record later in order to prove that he had spent his own money in publishing the central organ *Osmanlı*. See "Büyük İftira," *Muhibban*, no. 6 [February 28, 1909], 46.

40. Ali Fahri, "Teessür-i Elîm: Doktor İshak Sükûti Bey Vefat Etdi!" *İntikam*, no. 50 (March 10, 1902), 3–4. Other groups within the so-called minority adopted a similar course. See "Zayâʿ-i Azîm," *Muvazene*, no. 223 [March 5, 1902], 3; Manastırlı Bahaeddin Sâî, "Mektub," *Muvazene*, no. 228 [April 16, 1902], 3; and "Zayâʿ-i Azîm," *Kürdistan*, no. 30 [March 14, 1902], 4.

41. See Hanioğlu, *The Young Turks*, 158, 161.

42. "Nécrologie," *Mechveret Supplément Français*, no. 127 (March 15, 1902), 4. See also the veiled criticism in "Avrupa'da Türkler," *Şûra-yı Ümmet*, no. 65 (December 8, 1904), 3.

43. Zeki Bey to the khedive, Folkestone, July 15, 1901, Abbas II Papers, Durham University, F. 40/39-43.

44. Nuri Ahmed to Abdullah Cevdet, Geneva, April 21, 1902, Private Papers of Abdullah Cevdet.

45. See the First Chamberlain's office's note dated August 15, 1902/no. 3602, BBA–HR.SYS. 1790/18 (original. 500/17).

46. I. Loutfi, *L'État politique de la Turquie et le Parti Libéral* (Paris, 1903), 6–7, 28.

47. "Osmanlı Hürriyetperverân Cemiyeti'nin Nizamnâmesi," *Osmanlı*, no. 104, 7–8.

48. Ibid., 7.

49. "İlân," *Osmanlı*, no. 105 (May 15, 1902), 8.

50. "İ'tizâr," *Osmanlı*, no. 106 (June 15, 1902), 8.

51. I have examined the sections in which the documents concerning the new committee might have been located in Archives nationales, namely F/7 (Police générale) and F7/12366-12376/B (Sociétés et associations du département de la Seine), but have come across no document giving any information about the Osmanlı Hürriyetperverân Cemiyeti.

52. Investigation report by Commissar M[aurice] Leproust dated May 7, 1902, Archives de la Préfecture de Police de Paris (Sabahaddine et Loutfoullah)/no. B. A (1653)-171154.

53. Enclosed with the letter dated Paris, February 20, 1902, PRO/F.O. 78/5211.

54. Enclosed with the undated letter sent to Delcassé, AE–NS–T, 4 (1902–1904), 30.

55. Enclosed with Sabahaddin Bey's visiting card and his letter dated Paris, February 20, 1902, ASMAE, Affari Politici, Serie P. Politica (1891–1916), pacco 172.

56. Enclosed with the letter dated Paris, February 20, 1902, PAAA, 733/3, Die Jungtürken, 198 (Bd. 4–5).

57. Enclosed with the note of Sabahaddin Bey dated March 8, 1902, PRO/F.O. 195/2129.

58. *Le congrès des libéraux ottomans* (Paris, 1902), 1–7.

59. The French diplomats who read the document underlined many sentences on the fifth page, in which Armenian participation had been discussed. They also put marks in the margin to underscore some phrases, AE–NS–T, 4(1902–1904). Lord Salisbury, on the other hand, jotted down the following: "The representatives of the Armenian Revolutionary Committees agreed to cooperate with the 'Young Turks' but made separate declarations." PRO/F.O. 78/5211.

60. See the dispatch by the Grand Vizier's office dated [March 2, 1902] and enclosed with the dispatch from Tevfik Pasha to Münir Bey, March 4, 1902/no. 46339-80; Tevfik Pasha to Anthopoulos Pasha, March 3, 1902/no. 46333-28 (decipher no. 132), BBA–HR.SYS. 1792/1 (original. 503/61); and BBA–İrade-Hususî, Za 1319/ no. 81-958.

61. It should also be stated that the Armenian and other non-Muslim groups had very different expectations from the "permanent committee." Anastase Adossidis, who had represented the Greek component of the Ottoman Empire at the congress, made the following comment: "Une dernière réunion doit avoir lieu prochainement, afin de procéder à l'élection d'un comité permanent, qui sera composé de musulmans et de chrétiens. Musulmans et chrétiens tiennent, en effet, à établir entre eux une étroite solidarité et à rechercher un terrain d'entente complète au sujet de leurs revendications respectives et de leurs communes aspirations." See G. Dorys [Anastase Adossidis], "Le congrès des libéraux ottomans," *L'Illustration* 119, no. 3077 (February 15, 1902), 112.

62. "Abdülhamid'in Meslek-i Siyasîsi," *Osmanlı*, no. 106, 1–2.

63. "Amerika Terakkiyâtına Bir Nazar," *Osmanlı*, no. 110 (August 15, 1902), 1.

64. Münir Bey to Tevfik Pasha, Paris, February 19, 1902/no. 15918-90, BBA–HR.SYS. 1792/1 (original. 503/61).

65. See "Rusya Dostluğu," *Osmanlı*, no. 112 (September 15, 1902), 1–2, esp. "İngiltere Dostluğu," *Osmanlı*, no. 111 (August 30, 1902), 1: "Since the friendly aims and recommendations of this freedom-loving government [Great Britain], which views the restoration of our country in accordance with modern civilization as beneficial to its interests, were perceived by the sultan as unsuitable for his tyrannical and absolutist regime, he gave currency to the old Nedimovian politics. . . . He reached the extreme point of exiling lovers of freedom who expressed the amity and gratitude that the Ottoman people have for Great Britain at the outset of the Transvaal War by going to the British embassy in Istanbul."

66. There were many examples of this. For a striking one, see "Londra Mektubu: Sulh," *Osmanlı*, no. 106, 7.

67. For such a letter praising Kâmil Pasha, see "Mekâtib: İzmir," *Osmanlı*, no. 110, 7.

68. See Sabahaddin Bey's letter to Lord Kitchener, dated Athens, September 28, 1915. Published in "The Destroyers of Turkey: A Letter from Prince Sabaheddine to Lord Kitchener," *The Near East* 10, no. 235 (November 5, 1915), 15.

69. The genuineness of this document has caused disputes among historians. Some hypothesize that the document was not genuine but was forged by Malkum Khān. For a detailed analysis of these discussions, see Roderic H. Davison, "The Question of Fuad Pasha's Political Testament," *Belleten* 23, nos. 89–92 (1959), 119–36. For another source which also gives valuable information, but tends to accuse Malkum Khān, see Hamid Algar, *Mīrzā Malkum Khān: A Study in the History of Iranian Modernism* (Berkeley, Cal., 1973), 72–77.

70. "The Political Testament of Fuad Pasha: Addressed to the Sultan Abdul Aziz in 1869, One Day before the Death of Its Author," *The Nineteenth Century and After* 53, no. 312 (February 1903), 190–97.

71. "Waṣiyyat Fu'ād Bāshā," *al-Muqtaṭaf* 28, no. 30 (March 1, 1903), 224–30.

72. Fuad Pasha, "Testament politique," *Revue de Paris* 3, no. 21 (November 1, 1896), 126–35.

73. See [Keçecizâde Mehmed Fuad Paşa], *Vasiyetnâme-i Siyasî* (Geneva, 1314 [1896]); and "Mizan'ın Tefrikası: Vasiyetnâme-i Siyasî," *Mizan*, no. 1 (December 14, 1896), 4 ff. Ahmed Rıza's faction on the other hand, had published extracts from the testament in which the reconciliation of Islam with progress was discussed. See "Testament politique," *Mechveret Supplément Français*, no. 24 (December 1, 1896), 7–8.

74. "Amongst our allies the British state is in the first rank. England's policy and friendship are as firm as her laws and rules. It would be impossible to disdain the great services that this state has rendered, and will render us. Whatever happens, the English people, with their tenacity and illustrious traditions in the world, will always be the first to have our alliance, and it is obvious that we, at any rate, will hold fast to that alliance to the last. To your slave it appears preferable, and more congruous, that we should relinquish our several provinces rather than see England abandon us." This quotation is taken from the version published by the Young Turks. See *Vasiyetnâme-i Siyasî*, 12. There are slight differences between this version and a version published after the Young Turk Revolution of 1908. See Mehmed Galib, "Tarihden Bir Sahife: Âlî ve Fuad Paşaların Vasiyetnâmeleri," *Tarih-i Osmanî Encümeni Mecmuası* 1, no. 2 [June 14, 1910], 78. These passages devoted to good relations with Great Britain were later published in Arabic and English by the British for propaganda purposes. See "The Last Charge of Fuad Pasha," *The Near East* 9, no. 227 (September 10, 1915), 529, and no. 228 (September 17, 1915), 560–61. It should be stated, however, that the laudatory language employed about Great Britain in the text made almost no impact on British statesmen. For instance Gladstone wrote the following after reviewing the testament: "I have read today the very curious paper called Fuad's Testament. The peccant part of it is, *me judice*, his view of his Greek fellow-subjects. I am glad to see there was a sentiment stirred up in Greece upon the first inkling of the meditated stroke." Gladstone to Clarendon, October 18, 1869, BM, Add MS 44537, f. 102.

75. "Balkanlar'da Mezheb Münaza'atı," *Şûra-yı Ümmet*, no. 9 (August 6, 1902), 4.

76. "The Political Testament of Fuad Pasha," *The Nineteenth Century and After* 53, 190/ n. 1. Contrary to the claim made by the journal, Davison writes that the document had been published in English by J. Lewis Farley in three different books. See Davison, "The Question. . . ," *Belleten*, 122.

77. Ali Haydar Midhat, "English and Russian Politics in the East," *The Nineteenth Century and After* 53, no. 311 (January 1903), 77–78. He proposes the following: "In making allusion to the support which England gave to such statesmen as Rechid, Fuad and Midhat, we cannot bring ourselves to believe that her friendship was altogether personal. Each of these men was the representative of an idea, a party. This liberal idea, this reform party (called Young Turkey) did not perish with the assassination of Midhat, but on the contrary liberal Ottomans have greatly increased in numbers." Ali Haydar Midhat, furthermore, initiated the publication of his father's biography in English to underscore the pro-British predilections of Ahmed Şefik Midhat Pasha and his colleagues. A detailed analysis of this publication is given in Roderic H. Davison, "The Beginning of Published Biographies of Ottoman Statesmen: The

Case of Midhat Pasha," *Türkische Wirtschaft und Sozialgeschichte von 1071 bis 1920: Akten des IV. Internationalen Kongresses* (Wiesbaden, 1995), 59–79; see esp. 66–67. Ali Haydar Midhat's book, *The Life of Midhat Pasha* came out in London in 1903 and caused anxiety in the Ottoman official circles. See Anthopoulos Pasha to Tahsin Bey, London [September 12, 1903], Archives of the Turkish Embassy in London, Box 383 (1).

78. See Ali Haydar Midhat, "The Young Turks and England," *The Standard*, June 7, 1902; and "The Decline of the British Influence in Turkey," *The Standard*, October 14, 1902.

79. "English and Russian Politics in the East," *The Daily News*, January 2, 1903.

80. "Havâdis," *Osmanlı*, no. 103, 8.

81. "Enis Pacha," *Pro Armenia* 2, no. 6 (February 10, 1902), 46–47. For the French press's comments, see "Turquie," *Le Temps*, February 5, 1902.

82. Dr. Nâzım to İshak Sükûti, undated [late January 1902], AQSh, 19/106–5//814/1384.

83. "New York Mektubu'na Cevab," *Osmanlı*, no. 108 (July 15, 1902), 5. The central organ also refuted the assertions against the Armenians by the "minority members." The following comment referring to a letter of Joseph Denais appeared in the journal: "I have heard that the aim of the Armenians is by no means the partition of the Ottoman state, as traitorously alleged." See "Brüksel Kongresi'ne Cevab," *Osmanlı*, no. 109 (August 1, 1902), 4. For the original letter, see in "Une lettre de M. Joseph Denais," *Pro Armenia* 2, no. 15 (July 10, 1902), 123.

84. "New York Mektubu'na Cevab," *Osmanlı*, no. 112, 2–3.

85. "Mekâtib: New York, 17 Mayıs [1]902," *Osmanlı*, no. 106, 5.

86. See İsmail Kemal to Dr. Loris Mélikoff, April 16, 1902, in "Le déjeuner de Pro Armenia," *Pro Armenia* 2, no. 10 (April 25, 1902), 80.

87. See "Russia: From Our Own Correspondent," *The Times*, June 7, 1902; and "Prince Sabaheddin Arrested: Charged with Organizing an Insurrection," *The New York Times*, June 7, 1902.

88. Zeki Bey to the khedive, Paris, July 25, 1902, Abbas II Papers, Durham University, F. 40/147.

89. A report dated Berlin, August 27, 1902, A. 12756 (Wien: 547), PAAA, 733/3, Die Jungtürken, 198 (Bd. 4–5). The Ottoman sources claimed that the "conspirators" from Paris, Corfu, and Geneva convened at l'Hôtel des Balkans in Vienna. See BBA–İrade-Hususî, R 1320/no. 14-399. An investigation, however, made it clear that there was no such hotel in Vienna. See BBA–YSHM, 432/55 (1320.4.16). For further claims on Damad Mahmud Pasha and his friends' relations with Bulgarian and Albanian revolutionary leaders, see Tevfik Pasha to Mahmud Nedim, October 19, 1902/no. 49824-256 (decipher), Cemil Pasha to Tevfik Pasha, Vienna, October 20, 1902/no. 380-1407 (decipher); and the note from the First Chamberlain's office dated [October 19, 1902], BBA–HR.SYS. 1792/1 (original. 503/61). Threats of joint Young Turk, Armenian, and Macedonian activities once again surfaced in 1904. See "Jeunes Turcs . . . et fumistes," *L'Orient* 16, no. 17 (April 30, 1904), 10. The members of the so-called majority, however, could never participate in joint Armenian–Macedonian activities that took place between 1902 and 1906.

90. For the first initiatives aimed at joint activities, see Duncan M. Perry, "The Macedonian Revolutionary Organization's Armenian Connection," *Armenian Review* 42, no. 1-165 (1989), 64 ff; and Louise Nalbandian, *The Armenian Revolutionary Movement: The Development of Armenian Revolutionary Parties through the Nineteenth Century* (Los Angeles, 1963), 175. For the negotiations led by Khachatur Malumian [Aknuni] and Boris Sarafov, see the detailed memorandum prepared by the Department of Justice and Police, dated June 19, 1902 (P.P. June 19, 1902/no. 75); and "Beilage 2: Jungtürken 1902," Bundesarchiv-Bern, E. 21/ 14'248. For further information, see "Pour l'Arménie et pour la Macédoine," *Pro-Armenia* 3, nos. 55–56 (February 10–March 1, 1903), 237–38; "Havâdis-i Hariciye," *Muvazene*, no. 226 [April 2, 1902], 2; and Général Mayéwski, *Les massacres d'Arménie* (St. Petersburg, 1916), 59–63. For the revolutionary activities planned by the two parties, see Whitehead to Lansdowne, Therapia, January 27, 1903/no. 42; Hampson to O'Conor, Erzurum, September 2, 1903, enclosed with the letter from O'Conor to Lansdowne, Constantinople, September 17, 1903/no. 571; and O'Conor to Lansdowne, Therapia, August 4, 1903/no. 438, PRO/F.O. 424/205.

91. See *Manifestations Franco-Anglo-Italiens: pour l'Arménie et la Macédoine* (Paris, 1904); and Anatole France, *Vers les temps meilleurs* (Paris, 1906), i–ii. The Ottoman government greatly feared the Young Turks' participation in these activities. For instance, strict orders were given to investigate whether "Muslims participated in the demonstrations in Milan." See BBA-BEO/VGG(2), Âmedî Kalemi: Marûzat-ı Hususiye Hülâsa Kayd Defteri: 290; [May 2, 1903]/no. 825, and [May 3, 1903]/no. 162. An interesting comment on the subject was made by the American ambassador in Istanbul, who stated, "It is altogether probable that there may be uprisings in Macedonia, and it looks very much as if the movements were being directed to a considerable extent by the joint committee of the Macedonians and Armenians, and the Young Turks who have their headquarters in Europe and in Paris and Geneva with a view of concentrated action should matters assume favorable shape." See Leishman to Hay, Pera, April 6, 1903/no. 384, Dispatches from United States Ministers to Turkey, 1818–1906, vol. 73.

92. "Perspective d'un congrès," *Mechveret Supplément Français*, no. 135 (December 1, 1902), 3–4; "Memâlik-i Osmaniye'de Makedonyalılar ve Ermeniler," *Türk*, no. 4 (November 26, 1903), 1; and Şekib, "Makedonya ve Ermeniler Konferansı," *İntibâh*, no. 5 (February 28, 1903), 3.

93. "Balkan Mesâili," *Osmanlı*, no. 105, 1–2.

94. "Mekâtib: İşkodra'dan," *Osmanlı*, no. 103, 8. For other articles focusing on taxation in Albania, see "Maktu'at-ı Cerâid," *Osmanlı*, no. 105, 5; and "Maktu'at-ı Cerâid," *Osmanlı*, no. 106, 7.

95. BBA–İrade-Dahiliye, Za 1320/no. 18-2053. In a cipher sent from Şakir Pasha to the First Chamberlain's office on February 12, 1903, it was stated that those who took part in the activities had been banished for good to intimidate others. For more information, see BBA–BEO/VGG(2): Takdim Evrakına Mahsus Defterdir: 1171; [October 21, 1903]/no. 4282/149953. Despite these claims, however, these people were given a pardon later. See BBA–İrade-Dahiliye, L 1322/no. 31-2181.

96. See BBA–BEO/Hariciye Gelen, 162-5/18; 4021 [February 21, 1904]; 4229 [March 13, 1904]/161610; and BBA–YSHM, 468/74 (1321.12.25). Rumors about Xhemil's meeting with İsmail Kemal were denied by the Ottoman consul at Corfu. See the translation of his telegram to the Ottoman Foreign Ministry dated March 12, 1904/no. 12 in the aforementioned file. For more detailed information, see his file entitled "Fugitifs: le fugitif Djémil (1903)," BBA–HR.SYS. 1797/5 (original. 502/66).

97. See BBA–İrade-Hususî, S 1320/no. 51-213; and BBA–BEO/Dahiliye-Giden, 101-3/50; 695-744/899 [May 25, 1902]/138955. He later fled to Bari (see "Dersaadet İstinaf Müdde'i-yi Umumiliği'nden," *Ceride-i Mahakim-i Adliye*, no. 155 (April 15, 1903), 1; and ibid., no. 264 (May 7, 1904), 1. He was later granted an imperial pardon and lived in Manisa, then was permitted to return to his native town of Vlora. See BBA–YMGM, 264/60 (1322.B.8); BBA–YSRM, 134/104 (1322.12.7), and 136/64 (1324.3.7).

98. See BBA–BEO/Dahiliye Giden, 102-3/51; 264 [April 3, 1903]/152708; BBA–BEO/VGG(2): Âmedî Kalemi: Marûzat-ı Hususiye Hülâsa Kayd Defteri: 290; [April 3, 1903]/no. 83, and [April 4, 1903]/no. 18.

99. BBA–BEO/Dahiliye Giden, 102-3/51; 288 [April 5, 1903]/152771.

100. "Vatan Tehlikede," *Arnavudluk Gazetesinin Üçüncü Numerosunun İlâvesi*, April 15, 1903, 1–2.

101. See Mahmud Nedim to Tevfik Pasha, dated Vienna, March 26, 1902/no. 99, Tevfik Pasha to Münir Bey, dated March 31, 1902/no. 46794-125, and the note from the Grand Vizier's office, dated [April 2, 1902], BBA–HR.SYS. 1792/1 (original. 503/61); BBA–BEO/Hariciye Giden, 186-5/42; 106 [March 29, 1902]/136297. This accusation was first made by *Neues Wiener Tageblatt* on March 26, 1902.

102. Münir Bey to Delcassé, Paris, April 2, 1902, AE–NS–T, 4 (1902–1904), 83–84. Detailed information about this initiative is given in Münir Bey to Tevfik Pasha, Paris, April 4, 1902/no. 190 (decipher), BBA–HR.SYS. 1792/1 (original. 503/61).

103. "Havâdis-i Hariciye," *Muvazene*, no. 230 [April 30, 1902], 3.

104. See Prince Albert Ghica, *L'Albanie et la Question d'orient: solution de la Question*

d'orient (Paris, 1908), 223–24; and Stavro Skendi, "Albanian Political Thought and Political Activity, 1881–1912," *Südost-Forschungen* 13 (1954), 168. For the activities of Ghica, who was mentioned as "vagrant Ghica" in Ottoman documents, see BBA–YSHM, 489/71 (1323.5.11), 490/18 (1323.5.20), 492/22 (1323.C.25), and 493/73 (1323.B.26); and BBA–BEO/Serasker Reft, 261-6/69; 1653 [September 10, 1905]/199581. For the role played by Hima and Papazoglou, see Elena Merlike Kruja, "La libertà Albanese e la politica Italiana dal 1878 al 1912," *Rivista d'Albania* 3, no. 3 (September 1942), 145. Around the same time, another group of intellectuals founded an organization seeking autonomy for Macedonia and Albania. See "Programme du comité pour l'autonomie de la Macédoine et d'Albanie," in Un non-Diplomat [Richard von Mach], *La question des réformes dans la Turquie d'Europe* (Paris, 1903), 58–61.

105. Nigra to Prinetti, Vienna, February 16, 1902/R.266-144, *I Documenti Diplomatici Italiani* 6, 109–10.

106. See Stavro Skendi, *The Albanian National Awakening, 1878–1912* (Princeton, 1967), 325. Anti-Greek themes employed by this committee were nothing other than a repetition of the ideas of Şemseddin Sami [Frashëri]. See Sami Bey Frasheri, *Was war Albanien, was ist es, was wird es werden? Gedanken und Betrachtungen über die unser geheiligtes Vaterland Albanien bedrohenden Gefahren und deren Abwendung*, trans. A. Traxler and A. Hölner (Vienna, 1913), 32 ff. This is a translation of the work from its Turkish version.

107. See BBA–YSHM, 429/116 (1320.2.27). Zeki Bey, however, accurately informed the khedive that it was Derviş Hima who, with the help of an Albanian leader who wished to become the prince of Albania [Ghica], had duped the princes. See his letter to the khedive, dated Paris, April 9, 1902, Abbas II Papers, Durham University, F. 40/71.

108. See the police report dated Paris, December 6, 1905/no. 8064, Archives de la Préfecture de Police de Paris, (Kémal Ismail Bey), B. A (1699)-216.335.5119.

109. This was İsmail Kemal's approach throughout his career in the Albanian movement. See "Intervista con Ismail Kemal bey capo del governo provvisorio d'Albania," *Il Giornale d'Italia*, April 2, 1913. This tactic, however, caused cool relations between him and hardliners advocating an armed national struggle. See M[ary] Edith Durham, *The Struggle for Scutari: Turk, Slav, and Albanian* (London, 1914), 68.

110. We know very little about the standpoint of the Greek members of the new organization. Interestingly, Musurus Ghikis, a member of the central committee, after dismissing the accusations that they were revolutionaries, made the following remark to a German journalist when he gave him an interview: "Eine Revolution könnte eine fremde Intervention veranlassen." See Bernhard Stern, *Jungtürken und Verschwörer; die innere Lage der Türkei unter Abdul Hamid II. Nach eigenen Ermittelungen und Mittheilungen osmanischer Parteiführer* (Leipzig, 1901), 234–35.

111. X.X., "Du club au trône," *Mechveret Supplément Français*, no. 128 (April 15, 1902), 4.

112. A. Rustem Bey de Bilinski, "The Situation in Turkey," *The Fortnightly Review* 72, no. 427 (July 1, 1902), 95.

113. Ibid., 95–96.

114. For the claims made by German dailies, see the memorandum prepared by the Foreign Press Department of the Ottoman Foreign Ministry dated March 10, 1902/no. 21, Tercüman Gazetesi Arşivi, D. 157 (1317). For those made in the French press, see Constans to the Affaires étrangères, Pera, February 26, 1902/no. 30, AE–NS–T, 4 (1902–1904), 36–37.

115. BBA–İrade-Hususî, R 1320/no. 81-499.

116. Tahsin Bey to Anthopoulos Pasha, July 15, 1902, Archives of the Turkish Embassy in London, Box 373 (2).

117. BBA–İrade-Hususî, R 1320/no. 65-41; BBA–BEO/Hariciye Giden, 186-5/42; 758 [July 16, 1902]/141383; Tevfik Pasha to Anthopoulos Pasha, July 16, 1902/no. 48475-140 (decipher); and the Grand Vizier's office's note dated [July 15, 1902], BBA–HR.SYS. 1792/1 (original. 503/61).

118. Anthopoulos Pasha to Tahsin Bey, London, July 19, 1902, Archives of the Turkish Embassy in London, Box 372 (2); Anthopoulos Pasha to Tevfik Pasha, London, July 20, 1902/

no. 259-1013 (decipher), August 7, 1902/no. 436-279, BBA–HR.SYS. 1792/1 (original. 503/61).

119. This information is gleaned from a dispatch from Şekib Bey to the U.S. State Department, dated July 17, 1902/no. 10174-4, Notes from the Turkish Legation in the United States to the Department of State, 1867–1908, 8–9 (July 2, 1895–July 2, 1906).

120. See Anthopoulos Pasha's dispatch to the Ottoman Foreign Ministry dated London, August 7, 1902/no. 436-279, BBA–HR.SYS. 1792/1 (original. 503/61). For the Turkish translation, see BBA–YSHM, 433/29 (1320.9.5). Lord Lansdowne further asked Anthopoulos Pasha to provide him with sufficient information about the reliability of the informants. An Ottoman intelligence document, enclosed with the aforementioned dispatch and dated July 16, 1902, reveals that even the Ottoman intelligence service found the main informer, named Ulmann, "unreliable."

121. "Résumé du télégramme de la Sublime Porte adressé à l'Ambassade impériale de Turquie à Londres," enclosed with a letter from A[bdülhak] Hamid to Sanderson, London, September 17, 1902, PRO/F.O. 78/5209. See also Tevfik Pasha to Hamid Bey, September 19, 1902/no. 49361-168 (confidentielle); Hamid Bey to Tevfik Pasha, London, September 17, 1902/no. 330-1268 (confidentielle-decipher), BBA–HR.SYS. 1792/2 (original. 503/61). It should be noted that a year later some Ottoman subjects allegedly participated in a secret anarchist conclave held in Paris and decided to dispatch 25 anarchists to the Ottoman capital. It is difficult, however, to be certain whether these Ottoman subjects were members of the "majority group." See the Ministry of the Navy to the First Chamberlain's office, July 2, 1903/no. 2442-11, Deniz Müzesi Arşivi, MKT. 765A/105/1.

122. Ali Fahri, *Emel Yolunda* (Istanbul, 1326 [1910]), 382–83.

123. Ahmed Bedevî Kuran, *İnkılâp Tarihimiz ve Jön Türkler* (Istanbul, 1945), 155.

124. Ali Fahri, *Emel Yolunda*, 383.

125. See Alvarez to Grey, Tripoli of Barbary, September 12, 1908 (confidential), PRO/F.O. 195/2271 and 371/546, file 32452. Alvarez received this information concerning the stillborn plot "from too reliable a source to be disregarded." Ibid.

126. See Ahmed Bedevî Kuran, *İnkılâp Tarihimiz ve Jön Türkler*, 155–56; and Cemil Cahit Conk, "Abdülhamid'i Meşrutiyete Döndürmek İçin Ne Yapacaktım?" *Yakın Tarihimiz* 4, no. 51 (February 14, 1963), 375.

127. Alvarez to Grey, Tripoli of Barbary, September 12, 1908 (confidential), PRO/F.O. 195/2271. Actually the situation was worse than Alvarez described in this dispatch. During that period an imperial decree had to be obtained for the passing of regular vessels and even for yachts belonging to the foreign embassies in Istanbul. See, for example, BBA–İrade-Hariciye, Ra 1320/no. 524 (2388); R 1320/no. 1-612 (2390); Za 1320/no. 10-2088 (2554); Z 1321/no. 4-2700 (2790); Z 1321/no. 6-2750 (2795). Damad Mahmud Pasha's secretary, Salih Bey, who provided detailed information to the khedive, claimed that the plotters were going to receive support from a high-ranking officer at Çanakkale, from the commander of the troops at Selimiye in Üsküdar, and from many officers in the Yıldız Palace. See Aḥmad Shafīq, *Mudhakkirātī fī nisf qarn* (Cairo, 1936), 9.

128. Alvarez to Grey, Tripoli of Barbary, September 12, 1908 (confidential), PRO/F.O. 195/2271. When the British authorities discussed measures to be taken against the Ottoman Empire during the Egyptian frontier question, however, they asserted the following: "Of all such measures, the appearance of British war ships before Constantinople would probably be most effective. . . . It is highly probable that two or three armored cruisers or a battleship could pass the Dardanelles by night with little danger, if the operation were undertaken at once." See "The Egyptian Frontier Question: Note prepared by direction of the Prime Minister," PRO/CAB. 38/11 (1906)/no. 27 (secret). A very similar comment was made in 1907, when the British authorities discussed a British intervention in the event of serious trouble in the Ottoman capital. Sir Nicholas wrote the following: "I was counting in great part on the moral effect which the propinquity of the British Fleet would have upon Turkey, and in assuming so much I do not think that I was mistaken. I believe it would act as a powerful restraint upon the Sultan if he were still alive and would be equally effectual upon whatever party held power at the

moment, especially so were it the Party of Reform, upheld by the people at large, who look to England for moral if not material support. . . . Speaking merely as a civilian I cannot help thinking that, should the Dardanelles Forts be no more effectively manned than they are at the present, the risk would not be great." O'Conor to Grey, Constantinople, March 5, 1907/ no. 148 (secret), PRO/F.O. 371/344, file 7897.

129. A scholar claims the opposite on the basis of Italian diplomatic documents. See Tomasz Wituch, *Tureckie przemiany: dzieje Turcji, 1878–1923* (Warsaw, 1980), 88.

130. Receb Pasha had been praised both in a pamphlet written by Reşid Sadi, who worked for the venture, and by the central organ of the "minority." See, respectively, Bir Diplomat [Reşid Sadi], *Usûl-i İdare ve Islahat* ([London]: 1319 [1902]), 9; and "Gazi Osman Paşa," *Şûra-yı Ümmet*, no. 19 (December 31, 1902), 3. In the articles written by some Young Turks after his death, Receb Pasha was presented as "not only a soldier but also a genius of politics." See "Receb Paşa," *Yeni Asır*, August 19, 1908. The sultan too was aware of Receb Pasha's enmity toward him and his regime. See *İkinci Meşrutiyet'in İlânı ve Otuzbir Mart Hâdisesi: II. Abdülhamid'in Son Mabeyn Başkâtibi Ali Cevat Beyin Fezleke'si*, ed. Faik Reşit Unat (Ankara, 1985), 10–11. See also "Redjeb Pacha," *Revue du Monde Musulman* 6, no. 9 (September 1908), 156.

131. For the praise by the British, see the memorandum by Adam Block dated May 1, 1900, and enclosed with the letter from O'Conor to Salisbury, Constantinople, May 2, 1900, PRO/ F.O. 78/5958.

132. Kuran, *İnkılâp Tarihimiz ve Jön Türkler*, 156.

133. *The Memoirs of Ismail Kemal Bey*, ed. Somerville Story (London, 1920), 308.

134. See Tevfik Pasha to Anthopoulos Pasha, March 3, 1902/no. 28, Archives of the Turkish Embassy in London, Box 377 (1). Also the Ottoman authorities closely scrutinized those who were allegedly working for İsmail Kemal. Some of these individuals were even court-martialed; however, no clue was found concerning the Albanian statesman's intentions. See the special court martial report dated November 1, 1904, BBA–YMGM, 267/116 (1322.Ş.24).

135. See Tevfik Pasha to Anthopoulos Pasha, March 3, 1902/no. 28, Archives of the Turkish Embassy in London, Box 377 (1).

136. Sanderson to O'Conor, July 16, 1902, O'Conor Papers, Churchill College, Cambridge, 6/1/34.

137. Sir Nicholas's action is by no means surprising since we know that he had conveyed secret messages to İsmail Kemal from Lord Rosebery. See Sanderson to Rosebery, Constantinople, November 23, 1899 (private), ibid., 4/1/17.

138. *Memoirs of Ismail Kemal Bey*, 309.

139. Zeki Bey to the khedive, Paris, October 31, 1902, Abbas II Papers, Durham University, F. 40/207.

140. Zeki Bey to the khedive, Paris, November 4, 1902, ibid., F. 40/210–11.

141. İsmail Kemal did not provide the exact date of this event. He said, however, that Lord Lansdowne happened to be in Sandringham with the king, who had as his guest the German emperor. Since this was on November 8 (see "German Emperor's Visit," *The Times*, November 10, 1902), we may assume that he handed over the letters on this day. İsmail Kemal's letter sent from London to his son in exile also bears the date November 8, 1902. [See Kuran, *İnkılâp Tarihimiz ve Jön Türkler*, 70.] Unfortunately Lord Onslow's diaries, which are now in the Surrey Record Office, reach only to 1892. His correspondence was collected and bound into a number of volumes, which have been itemized in list #173 and name-indexed. İsmail Kemal is mentioned only as appearing in letters concerning the London Peace Treaty of 1913 in which 5th Earl Onslow was involved. Surrey Record Office Guildford Muniment Room.

142. *Memoirs of Ismail Kemal Bey*, 310.

143. See Reşid Sadi to Currie, July 8, 1897, enclosed with the letter from Currie to Salisbury, July 16, 1897/no. 474 (confidential), PRO/F.O. 424/192. No marginal note, however, was written by the British diplomats on the document sent by the Ottoman ambassador concerning his appointment at the London embassy. See Anthopoulos Pasha to Lansdowne, December 16, 1901, PRO/F.O. 78/5140.

144. Sanderson describes him as "a violent and fanatical Young Turk." See Sanderson to O'Conor, April 1, 1902, O'Conor Papers, Churchill College, Cambridge, 6/1/3.

145. Reşid Sadi to Ahmed Rıza, London, March 2, 1902, Private Papers of Ahmed Rıza (1). His letter published following the Young Turk Revolution also reveals that he had disagreements with the viewpoint of Ahmed Rıza. See Reshid Sadi, "To the Editor of the Times," *The Times*, August 4, 1908. Despite these differences, however, he had been invited to constitute the London branch of the CPU. See the letter of Dr. Bahaeddin [Şakir] and Dr. Nâzım beginning "Hamiyetperver Efendimiz" and dated Paris, October 24, 1906/no. 180, *Muhaberat Kopyası*, 134–35.

146. [Reşid Sadi], *Usûl-i İdare ve Islahat*, passim. The book was published by the new central committee and recommended to the readership of the central organ. See "Matbuʿat," *Osmanlı*, no. 116 (December 1, 1902), 8, and "Matbuʿat-ı Cedîde: Usûl-i İdare ve Islahat," *Osmanlı*, no. 105, 5–6. The Ottoman government thought the book was written by İsmail Kemal and took measures against its distribution. See BBA–İrade-Hususî, Z 1320/no. 26-1130 and no. 148-1252; Tahsin Bey to Musurus Pasha, February 18 and 20, 1903, and Musurus Pasha to Tahsin Bey, London, February 22 and 25, 1903, Archives of the Turkish Embassy in London, Box 383 (1); and BBA–YEE–Kâmil Paşa Evrakına Ek I, 86/18, 1759 (1320.12.26). Interestingly, the pamphlet was later distributed by the CPU free of charge. See "Neşriyât-ı Cedîde," *Şûra-yı Ümmet*, no. 115 (June 1, 1907), 4.

147. Reşid Sadi to Cami Baykut, Istanbul, May 23, 1944. I am indebted to the late Professor Tarık Zafer Tunaya for allowing me to examine this six-page letter giving invaluable information about the venture.

148. Sabahaddin and Lûtfullah Beys' letter to Rueff, Cairo, March 2, 1901. This letter was provided by Münir Bey to the French authorities and enclosed with a letter sent to Delcassé from the Ministry of the Interior dated March 17, 1902, AE–NS–T, 4 (1902–1904), 63–65. Münir Bey also provided information concerning the princes' relations with British bankers. See Münir Bey to Tevfik Pasha, Paris, February 17, 1902/no. 96 (decipher no. 193), BBA–HR.SYS. 1792/1 (original. 503/61).

149. Zeki Bey to the khedive, Paris, April 9, 1902, Abbas II Papers, Durham University, F. 40/72. Also the mouthpiece of the sultan in Paris quoted the following from *Le Figaro*: "En effet, ils ont sollicité de divers côtés certains concours financiers auxquels ils promettent en rémunération des avantages, plus ou moins éloignés." The journal further made the following comment: "Ils ont accepté certains concours financiers et ils sont obligés de marcher de l'avant toujours de l'avant, vers la solution qu'ils rêvent par tous les moyens, accumulant autour d'eux scandales sur scandales, tandis que s'accentue la réprobation des honnêtes gens pour cette œuvre humiliante, que ces jeunes gens accomplissent contre leur patrie, d'accord avec ses pires ennemis." See "Quelques notes rétrospectives: la véridique histoire de Mahmoud Pacha," *L'Orient* 10, nos. 6–7 (February 7–14, 1903), 8–9.

150. Zeki Bey to the khedive, Paris, April 23, 1902, Abbas II Papers, Durham University, F. 40/82–85.

151. Zeki Bey to the khedive, Paris, May 14, 1902, ibid., F. 40/98–99.

152. Reşid Sadi to Câmi Baykut, May 23, 1944. Sabahaddin Bey was quite right to demand that İsmail Kemal say nothing to the khedive in the light of the khedive's hostile attitude toward them after the congress. See Zeki Bey to the khedive, April 2, 1902, Abbas II Papers, Durham University. F. 40/62–65.

153. See Kuran, *İnkılâp Tarihimiz ve Jön Türkler*, 159. The person referred to here as Danes Cassel must be Ernest Cassel. Two popular history essays reiterate this claim but mention no source; obviously they obtained their information from Kuran. See Sina Akşin, *Jön Türkler ve İttihat ve Terakki* (Istanbul, 1987), 46; and Cemal Kutay, *Prens Sabahattin Bey, Sultan II. Abdülhamit, İttihad ve Terakki* (Istanbul, 1964), 162–63.

154. For information about Speyer, see "Edgar Speyer," *The Universal Jewish Encyclopaedia* 9 (New York, 1943), 694; and "Sir Edgar Speyer," *The Dictionary of National Bibliography, 1931–1940*, ed. L. G. Wickham Legg (London, 1949), 828–29. For his company, Speyer and Co., see Thomas Skinner, *The London Banks and Kindred Companies and Firms, 1902–1903* (London [1903]), 353; Paul H[erman] Emden, *Money Powers of Europe in the Nineteenth and Twentieth Centuries* (London [1938]), 274–77; and Youssef Cassis, *Les banquiers de la City à l'époque Edouardienne, 1890–1914* (Geneva, 1984), 49, 127. For the

historical development of Speyer family institutions, see Alexander Dietz, *Stammbuch der Frankfurter Juden; geschichtliche Mitteilungen über die Frankfurter jüdischen Familien von 1349–1849* (Frankfurt am Main, 1907), 289–92. Sir Edgar's relations with the prominent members of the Liberal party are examined in the above-mentioned sources. For his views on economics, see Edgar Speyer, "Some Aspects of National Finance," *The Institute of Bankers* 26, no. 7 (October 1905), 361–96; and idem, *The Export of Capital* (London, 1911).

155. See von Bülow to von Holstein, Berlin, January 18, 1906; von Metternich to Auswärtiges Amt, London, February 20, 1906/no. 64 (streng vertraulich), *Die Große Politik der europäischen Kabinette, 1871–1914* 21/1, *Die Konferenz von Algeciras und ihre Auswirkung* (Berlin, 1925), 98, 187; von Bülow to von Metternich, Berlin, December 25, 1908 (Privatbrief-geheim); von Bülow to Tirpitz, Berlin, December 25, 1908 (geheim), *Die Große Politik* 28, *England und die deutsche Flotte, 1908–1911* (Berlin, 1925), 35–40; von Bethmann-Hollweg to von Metternich, Berlin, February 3, 1911 (Privatbrief), *Die Große Politik* 27/2, *Zwischen den Balkankrisen, 1909–1911* (Berlin, 1925), 668–69; von Bernstoff to Auswärtiges Amt, Washington, May 6, 1914/ no. 85 (Entzifferung), *Die Große Politik* 39, *Das Nahen des Weltkrieges, 1912–1914* (Berlin, 1926), 110; von Holstein to von Bülow, December 7, 1908, *Die geheimen Papiere Friedrich von Holsteins* 4, *Briefwechsel*, ed. Norman Rich and M. H. Fisher (Göttingen, 1963), 540–41; and Almeric Fitzroy [Fitz Roy], *Memoirs* 2 (London [1925]), 512. Because of his close relations with many leading German statesmen, Sir Edgar was later accused of being a German agent, and in 1914 he retired from the partnership first of the New York and then the Frankfurt branches of his bank. He was later accused of giving signals to German submarines from his mansion, and he left England for the United States after giving up his titles and posts. See "Edgar Speyer," *The Times*, October 7, 1914; E[dward] F[rederic] Benson, *As We Are: A Modern Revue* (London, 1932), 57, 247–51; Almeric Fitzroy [Fitz Roy], *The History of the Privy Council* (London, 1928), 299–300; and Jamie Camplin, *The Rise of the Plutocrats: Wealth and Power in Edwardian England* (London, 1978), 288–90.

156. *Memoirs of Ismail Kemal Bey*, 311.

157. Aḥmad Shafīq, *Mudhakkirātī fī nisf qarn*, 8.

158. Ibid. An unreliable source asserted that this person was a secretary to İsmail Kemal and described the role played by him differently. See Alexander Ular-Enrico Insabato, *Der erlöschende Halbmond; türkische Enthüllungen* (Frankfurt am Main, 1909), 278. Berxhani's participation in the venture brings up the Bektashi role in it. Although it was claimed that İsmail Kemal himself was a Bektashi (see Peter R. Krifti, "Introduction," in Baba Rexheb, *The Mysticism of Islam and Bektashism* [Naples, 1984], 19.), the late Rexheb Kadri Baba, with whom I had an interview in Detroit on March 20, 1990, told me that this claim was inaccurate and that a Bektashi intervention in the coup d'état attempt of 1902–1903 had never been discussed among the devotees of this order. On the other hand, there is no source providing information concerning Receb Pasha's relations with the Bektashis. The only reference I could find concerns his action against those who tried to attack the Bektashi convent in Karbalā' while he was serving in this town. His action was praised by the Bektashis. See A[hmed] Rıfkı, *Bektaşi Sırrı* 3 (Istanbul, 1328 [1910]), 160.

159. *Memoirs of Ismail Kemal Bey*, 311.

160. Reşid Sadi to Câmi Baykut, May 23, 1944. Unfortunately, I could not locate any financial record of Sir Edgar in any archives or in the hands of his relatives. There is a file on him in Hereford and Worcester County Archives; however, there I found nothing but his letters sent to Sir Edward Elgar.

161. Ali Haydar Mithat, *Hâtıralarım, 1872–1946* (Istanbul, 1946), 171–72.

162. See ibid., 170; Ular-Insabato, *Der erlöschende Halbmond*, 278; and Kuran, *İnkılâp Tarihimiz ve Jön Türkler*, 159.

163. Reşid Sadi to Câmi Baykut, May 23, 1944.

164. Ibid.

165. Aḥmad Shafīq, *Mudhakkirātī fī nisf qarn*, 8–9.

166. Ali Haydar Mithat, *Hâtıralarım*, 171. The text of the appeal is as recollected by Ali Haydar Midhat.

167. *Memoirs of Ismail Kemal Bey*, 311.

168. Sabahaddin Bey must have gone to Athens in July 1903. See Zeki Bey to the khedive, undated [July 1903?] letter, Abbas II Papers, Durham University, F. 40/336.

169. Aḥmad Shafīq, *Mudhakkirātī fī nisf qarn*, 9.

170. Ibid., 9–10.

171. All this information is given by Reşid Sadi. See his letter to Câmi Baykut, May 23, 1944.

172. *Memoirs of Ismail Kemal Bey*, 311.

173. Ali Fahri, *Emel Yolunda*, 383.

174. Kuran, *İnkılâp Tarihimiz ve Jön Türkler*, 162–63. A later description by Sabahaddin Bey of İsmail Kemal and his friends as "brigands" supports this claim. See Sabahaddin Bey's undated letter [1910?] entitled "Azizim" in Bibliothèque nationale, Supplément turc (1599): Papiers du Prince Sabahaddine, Box (1). In another letter that Sabahaddin Bey sent to a Cretan journal through Ahmed Fazlı, dated April 16, 1907, the prince characterized İsmail Kemal as "a shameless person who sells the country to foreigners for money." See "Sabahaddin Bey'in Mektubu," *İstikbâl*, no. 45 [April 29, 1909], 1.

175. Ali Haydar Midhat, *Menfa-yı İhtiyarî Hatırâtı* (Geneva, 1905), [3–4]. See also BBA–YSHM, 514/73 (1325.B.17). Many years later the following striking remark was made concerning this matter: "I saw the Bishop Garth of Wakefield. The point of the story is that the lady has, or thinks she has, knowledge that Kemal Bey, the Albanian, is a person by no means trusted since he is in the pay of one or the other of the foreign neighbors of Albania." Crewe to Grey, May 6, 1913. Sir Edward's statement on the subject is as follows: "We have already heard of the report referred to in it, and have been very guarded in all our dealings with Kemal." Grey to Crewe, May 8, 1913. Crewe Papers, University Library, Cambridge, C. 14. Also in a British official report, prepared in 1908, the following comment was made about İsmail Kemal: "He . . . is reproached by his enemies with a certain tendency to looseness in money matters." *Annual Report for Turkey for the Year 1908,* which is enclosed with from Lowther to Grey, Constantinople, February 17, 1909/no. 105 (confidential), PRO/F.O. 371/768, file 7053.

176. Ali Haydar Mithat, *Hâtıralarım*, 172. Upon learning this, he cut all his ties with the Albanian leader. Following the Young Turk Revolution Ali Haydar Midhat declared that "he had not had any kind of relationship with İsmail Kemal for approximately six years." See "Ali Haydar Bey'in Beyânâtı," *İkdam*, August 3, 1908.

177. *Memoirs of Ismail Kemal Bey*, 309. Insabato and Ular, too, speak about a landing in Salonica. See *Der erlöschende Halbmond*, 276. Unfortunately we lack information concerning Receb Pasha's attitude toward Albanian nationalists and about his relations with İsmail Kemal. Some interesting information was provided by Eqrem Bej Vlorë, who met with the pasha before the Young Turk Revolution. Eqrem Bej says that although the pasha had left his hometown of Mat 40 years ago, he was fluent in Albanian and considered himself an Albanian. He further writes that the pasha helped İsmail Kemal's son Tahir Bey flee to Europe from his exile in Tripoli of Barbary, and sent £1,000 in gold to his father. See Ekrem Bey Vlora, *Lebenserinnerungen* 1 (*1885 bis 1912*) (Munich, 1968), 183–84. For the flight of Tahir Bey, see BBA–YSHM, 427/28 (1320.1.6). Albanian nationalists criticized the European press for neglecting the ethnic origin of Receb Pasha in the articles written after his death. See Faik Konitza, "The Late Redjib Pasha: To the Editor of the Times," *The Times*, August 22, 1908. Modern Albanian sources, too, underscore Receb Pasha's ethnic origins. See Skënder Luarasi, *Ismail Qemali: jeta dhe vepra* (Tirana, 1962), 49.

178. Mevlânzâde Rıf'at, *İnkılâb-ı Osmanî'den Bir Yaprak yahud 31 Mart 1325 Kıyamı* (Cairo, 1329 [1911]), 12–13. Another author, who was informed by Reşid Sadi, agrees with Mevlânzâde Rıf'at. See Asaf Tugay, *İbret: Abdülhamid'e Verilen Jurnaller ve Jurnalciler* 1 (Istanbul [1961]), 185–86. For a similar accusation, see Ular-Insabato, *Der erlöschende Halbmond*, 282; and Pro-Islamite, "Turkish Revelations," *The Westminster Review* 62, no. 2 (August 1909), 125. Aḥmad Shafīq's recollections support this claim. He maintained that İsmail Kemal had succeeded in withdrawing £2,500 of £4,000 that was dispatched to an English bank, though the khedive had made any withdrawal conditional and required 'Abd al-'Azīz 'Izzat Pasha's permission. Later on the khedive had blocked the money and even wanted

to take steps against the bank that had disbursed it. He had changed his mind, however, fearing scandal and bad publicity. See Aḥmad Shafīq, *Mudhakkirātī fī nisf qarn*, 10. Strangely enough, the khedive continued to give large sums to the Albanian statesman. See ibid., 141.

179. Doktor Lütfi, *Millet ve Hükûmet* (Paris, 1906), 7–8. This part of the book was omitted in the second and third editions that appeared in Istanbul after the Young Turk Revolution of 1908.

180. See J[oseph] Swire, *Albania: The Rise of a Kingdom* (London, 1929), 80; and Peter Bartl, *Die albanischen Muslime zur Zeit der nationalen Unabhängigkeitsbewegung, 1878–1912* (Wiesbaden, 1968), 154.

181. Allan Cunningham, "The Wrong Horse? A Study of Anglo-Turkish Relations before the First World War," *St. Antony's Papers*, no. 17, *Middle Eastern Affairs*, no. 4 (1965), 66.

182. See Dudley Barker, *Prominent Edwardians* (New York, 1969), 154–57.

183. Unfortunately Câmi Baykut did not say anything about the venture in his unpublished memoirs, which focus on the events that took place during the Turkish War of Liberation. See *Câmi Baykut'un Anıları Defteri* 1–2, Türk Tarih Kurumu Arşivi, no. 1082.

184. The sultan himself thought that "the contemptible scoundrels called Young Turks" had been rendering services to the British day and night, and that some of his high-ranking state officials had been receiving money from the British. See Abdülhamid II's undated memorandum addressed to his confidant Ahmed Midhat, BBA–YEE, 9/2638/72/4.

185. It should be stated that even an article published by a former British diplomat and providing information about British endorsement of pro-reform Ottoman statesmen had caused great anxiety in Ottoman government circles and had compelled the Foreign Office to consult their law offices regarding possible penalties for such indiscretions. A memorandum written by Lord Lansdowne, who allegedly provided İsmail Kemal with a letter of support, reads as follows: "On the occasion of the publication by Sir Henry Elliot in 1888 of an article which caused great offence to the Sultan and the Turkish government, the law offices were consulted as to power of the Secretary of the State to attach pensions granted under 'The diplomatic salaries and c[onditions] Act 1869,' making the pension liable to forfeiture in case of those conditions being disregarded." See "Memorandum written by [Lord] L[ansdowne]," PRO/CAB, 37/63 (no. 160/1902). The article in question is Henry Elliot, "The Death of Abdul Aziz and of Turkish Reform," *The Nineteenth Century* 23, no. 132 (February 1888), 276–96.

186. Also there is no mention of this attempt among the private papers of Lansdowne and Sanderson kept in the Public Record Office and the India Office. See Lord Sanderson's Private Papers, PRO/F.O. 800/1–2, and Lansdowne Papers: Turkey, PRO/F.O. 800/143; and his papers in India Office Library MSS Eur D 558 (this collection consists only of his papers as Viceroy [1888–1894]). It should be stated, however, that the bulk of his Foreign Office papers are still in family hands.

187. Sanderson to O'Conor, February 2, 1903, O'Conor Papers, Churchill College, Cambridge, 6/1/35. His son had applied to O'Conor along with some Young Turks who had participated in the British embassy visit in November 1899. See the letter dated April 3, 1902, PRO/F.O. 195/2129.

188. Decipher from Cromer to Sanderson, Cairo, March 2, 1903 (private), O'Conor Papers, Churchill College, Cambridge, 6/1/37.

189. Sanderson to O'Conor, March 3, 1903 (private), ibid.

190. Memorandum prepared by F. R. Mannsell dated Constantinople, April 11, 1903, ibid., 6/1/32.

191. It should be stated, however, that later British documents about İsmail Kemal provide no hints about his initiatives taken in 1902–1903. For instance, when İsmail Kemal came up to London "avec le seul désir d'entretenir particulièrement votre Excellence [Sir Edward Grey] au sujet de la question du Chemin de Fer Danube-Adriatique, question qui intéresse en générale toute la Péninsule Balkanique et particulièrement mon pays natal, Albanie," the Foreign Office officials commented as follows, as Alwyn Parker minuted: "He explained his ideas very lucidly but acknowledge and inform him that Sir E. Grey will be happy to peruse any further written statement of his personal views but that he cannot assent to a personal interview." Western Dept. June 4, 1908. R. P. Maxwell altered the last part of the sentence

slightly from "but that" onward, saying that "but he regrets that the great pressure of official business precludes him from assenting to a personal interview." Herbert Norman minuted: "Ismail Kemal Bey is an educated and enlightened Albanian who was a member for Jerusalem in the Turkish Parliament [*sic*], which technically still exists. He was always very friendly to Great Britain and there was at one time a fear that he might take refuge in HM Embassy at Constantinople. I think he has now had to flee from Turkey. . . ." Louis Mallet minuted: "Acknowledge and say that pressure of official business will make it impossible for Sir E. Grey to see him." Sir Edward Grey's minute has no bearing on İsmail Kemal, PRO/F.O. 371/571, file 19138.

192. Sanderson to O'Conor, February 17, 1902 (private), O'Conor Papers, Churchill College, Cambridge, 6/1/32.

193. O'Conor to Lansdowne, June 4, 1901, PRO/F.O. Lansdowne Papers (Turkey), 800/143.

194. O'Conor to Lansdowne, Therapia, September 2, 1902/no. 390 (very confidential), PRO/F.O. 78/5192.

195. For the relations between the two countries during Lansdowne's term in office, see Lord Newton, *Lord Lansdowne: A Biography* (London, 1929), 246 ff; and Max Motlegas, "Lord Lansdowne," *Berliner Monatshefte für internationale Aufklärung* 9 (1931), 7–14.

196. See Edward Mead Earle, *Turkey, the Great Powers and the Baghdad Railway: A Study in Imperialism* (New York, 1923), 176 ff; G[rigorii] L['vovich] Bondarevskii, *Bagdadskaia doroga i proniknovenie germanskogo imperializma na Blizhnii Vostok, 1888–1903* (Tashkent, 1955), 265 ff; Maybelle Kennedy Chapman, *Great Britain and the Baghdad Railway, 1888–1914* (Northampton, 1948), 204–5; and N. F., "La Thèse anglaise sur le chemin de fer de Bagdad," *La Revue Politique Internationale* 9, no. 31 (1918), 123–25.

197. John B. Wolf, "The Diplomatic History of the Bagdad Railroad," *The University of Missouri Studies* 11, no. 2 (April 1, 1936), 40, 40/n. 22; "England und die Bagdadbahn," *Frankfurter Zeitung*, April 24, 1903; and "Lord Lansdowne über die Bagdad-Bahn und Persien," *Frankfurter Zeitung*, May 6, 1903. The British press, however, took a more hostile stand. See, for example, "The Baghdad Railway," *The Daily Graphic*, January 25, 1902: "Asia Minor now promises to become a Franco-German railway preserve. Almost all the existing and projected lines are in the hands of either French or German capitalists, and the new trunk line will virtually shut out all possibility of competition. It is curious to remember that the pioneers in this work were neither French or German but English." See also "Why Germany Is Courting France," *The Globe*, June 3, 1908.

198. See the "Memorandum by Sir Thomas Sanderson, July 28, 1905 (confidential)," PRO/F.O. 78/5449; von Mühlberg to von Bodman, Berlin, August 1, 1905/no. 126; and von Tschirschky to Marschall von Bieberstein, Berlin, May 19, 1906/no. 609, *Die Große Politik* 25/1, *Die englisch-russische Entente und der Osten* (Berlin, 1925), 188–89 and 200–201.

199. G. S. Clarke, "The Baghdad Railway—I: Memorandum prepared by the direction of the Prime Minister (January 26, 1905)," PRO/CAB. 38/8 (1905)/no. 5, 4.

200. "History of the Baghdad Railway Scheme to the End of 1904," ibid., 7–8. Similar comments were made on Germany's position in the Ottoman Empire by Constans, in a memorandum which he submitted to the president. See Constans to Loubet [December 1903], *Documents diplomatiques français*, 2ᵉ Série (1901–1911), 4 (Paris, 1932), 207–8.

201. See the undated [February 1903] secret report prepared by the director of naval intelligence in PRO/CAB. 38/2 (1903), no. 1 (Committee of Imperial Defence); and in O'Conor Papers, Churchill College, Cambridge, 7/4/12; PRO/CAB. 38/2 (1903)/no. 4 (Committee of Imperial Defence, Minutes of the Third Meeting, February 11, 1903); 38/2 (1903)/no. 6 (Report of the conclusion arrived at on the 11th February in reference to Russia and Constantinople [confidential]); and 38/2 (1903)/no. 41 (Papers regarding the defenses of Constantinople, submitted for the consideration of the committee of Imperial Defence, at the request of the Secretary of State for Foreign Affairs).

202. See William Dodgson Bowman, *The Story of "The Times"* (New York, 1931), 267–80; "The 'Times' from Delane to Northcliffe," *The Quarterly Review* 239, no. 474 (January

1923), 90–92; and Charles Lowe, *The Tale of a "Times" Correspondent* (London, 1927), 96–98.

203. For the details of the interview, see *Memoirs of M. de Blowitz* (New York, 1903), 242–69. It was originally published in *The Times*, November 12, 1883. The Young Turks used this interview for propaganda purposes, see "Le sultan et M. de Blowitz," *La Jeune Turquie*, no. 11 (May 2, 1896), [2, 4]. For his decoration by the sultan and his critical attitude, see M. de Blowitz, *Un course à Constantinople*, 3rd ed. (Paris, 1884), 266; Frank Giles, *A Prince of Journalists: The Life and Times of Henri Stefan Opper de Blowitz* (London, 1962), 149–54. Despite his criticisms of the policies of the sultan, de Blowitz confessed to one of the opponents of Abdülhamid II's regime that "in his opinion Abdul-Hamid was the most intelligent of reigning monarchs . . . possessing an intelligence amounting to genius." See Nicholas C. Adossides, "The Sultan of Turkey," *The American Magazine* 67, no. 1 (November 1908), 4.

204. For accusations made by the Germans, see von Bülow's notes written on May 14, 1875, *Die Große Politik* 1, *Der Frankfurter Friede und seine Nachwirkungen, 1871–1877* (Berlin, 1922), 278/fn., and 279–82; "Neuerscheinungen," *Berliner Monatshefte für internationale Aufklärung* 8 (1930), 897–98; Graf Herbert von Bismarck to Reichskanzler Fürst von Bismarck, London, January 7, 1882; von Bismarck to Münster, Berlin, December 5, 1884/no. 470, January 25, 1885/no. 31, *Die Große Politik* 4, *Die Dreibundmächte und England* (Berlin, 1922), 27, 89–90, 92, 94, and 106; Münster to von Bismarck, Paris, October 1, 1886/no. 255 (ganz vertraulich), *Die Große Politik* 6, *Kriegsgefahr in Ost und West: Ausklang der Bismarckzeit* (Berlin, 1922), 94; von Radolin to Auswärtiges Amt, St. Petersburg, August 8, 1899/no. 147 (entzifferung), *Die Große Politik* 13, *Die europäischen Mächte untereinander, 1897–1899* (Berlin, 1924), 278; and von Radolin to von Bülow, Paris, June 5, 1901/no. 195, *Die Große Politik* 18/2, *Zweibund und Dreibund, 1900–1904* (Berlin, 1924), 722–24. See also Werner Primke, *Die Politik der Times von der Unterzeichnung des Jangtseabkommens bis zum Ende der deutsch-englischen Bündnisbesprechungen* (Berlin, 1936), 16. For the French police's attitude toward de Blowitz's activities, see Jacques de Launay, *Police secrète, secrets de Police* (Paris, 1988), 135–37.

205. See Sidney Whitman, *Things I Remember: The Recollections of a Political Writer in the Capitals of Europe* (New York: [1916]), 200–2.

206. De Blowitz's letters to one of his friends dated April 7, [190]1 and June 26, [190]1, Blowitz Papers–The Times Archives.

207. Amin Arslan, "Un coup d'épée dans l'eau," *La Jeune Turquie*, no. 10 (April 17, 1896), [1]; see also "MM. Vernier et Blowitz," *L'Orient* 8, no. 16 (April 25, 1896), 5.

208. W[illiam] Morton Fullerton, *Problems of Power: A Study of International Politics from Sadowa to Kirk Kilissé* (New York, 1913), 133 n.1.

209. W[illiam] M[orton] F[ullerton], "Introduction," *Memoirs of Ismail Kemal Bey*, xvi.

210. See N. Nicolaïdes, "La Presse française et les Réfugiés ottomans—III," *L'Orient* 13, no. 3 (January 19, 1901), 5–7; and "La Presse française et les Réfugiés ottomans," *L'Orient* 13, no. 5 (February 9, 1901), 6. For Lauzanne's direct attacks on the sultan, see his article "Quo Vadis," *Le Matin*, March 16, 1901.

211. N. Nicolaïdes, "La Presse française et les Réfugiés ottomans II: Ismaïl Kémal Bey— Les Syndicats anglais," *L'Orient* 13, no. 2 (January 12, 1901), 5. Lauzanne later acclaimed İsmail Kemal's mastery in manipulation. See Stéphane Lauzanne, *Au chevet de la Turquie: quarante jours de guerre* (Paris, 1913), 206–10.

212. Monson to Salisbury, Paris, January 19, 1900/no. 29 (secret), in *British Documents on the Origins of the War, 1898–1914* 1, *The End of British Isolation* (London, 1927), 247–48.

213. Blowitz to Monson, dated Friday [?], E. J. Monson Papers 1900–1905, MS English History c. 1200, Bodleian Library, Oxford, 78.

214. For his successful tenure, see Beckles Willson, *The Paris Embassy: A Narrative of Franco-British Diplomatic Relations, 1814–1920* (London, 1927), 319–33.

215. See Vittorio Vettori, "La Questione d'oriente e l'Italia: colloquio con Ismail Kemal Bey," *Il Giornale d'Italia*, August 16, 1903. His initiative had caused anxiety among the

Ottoman statesmen. See Reşid Bey to Tevfik Pasha, Rome, August 17, 1903/no. 2874-503 (confidentielle), BBA–HR.SYS. 1795/20 (original. 502/47). A copy of the aforementioned interview and a French translation of it were enclosed with the confidential dispatch.

216. Underscored by the French press and his son Lûtfullah Bey, see Jean Longuet, "Aux pieds du grand assassin," *La Petite République*, January 24, 1903; Gaston Laporte, "Les obsèques de Mahmoud Pacha," *L'Intransigeant*, January 24, 1903; "Les obsèques de Mahmoud Pacha," *L'Aurore*, January 24, 1903; "Les obsèques de Mahmoud Pacha," *Écho de Paris*, January 24, 1903; "Obsèques de Mahmoud Pacha," *L'Éclair*, January 24, 1903; and A[hmed] Loutfoullah, "Au palais: un référé diplomatique," *Le Petit Temps*, January 28, 1903.

217. Decipher by Münir Bey dated November 28, 1902, BBA–YP, 26 Ş 1320/no. 950. Sabahaddin Bey denied the rumors that his father had decided to return. See "Hadisât-ı Siyasiye: *Muvazene*'nin Varna'dan Telgrafı, Cevabı," *Muvazene*, no. 259 [December 17, 1902], 1.

218. See BBA–YSHM, 440/74 (1320. 10.26), 440/79 (1320. 10.26), 440/81 (1320.10.26), 440/100 (1320. 10.26), 440/109 (1320.10.29), 441/1 (1320.11.1), 441/11 (1320.11.2), 441/14 (1320.11.3), and 441/17 (1320.11.3); and the draft dated January 28, 1903/no. 32, AE–NS–T, 4 (1902–1904), 138. See also the correspondence between Münir Bey and the Ottoman Foreign Ministry in BBA–HR.SYS. 1792/1 (original. 503/61). After the death of Damad Mahmud Pasha, Ottoman diplomats unsuccessfully tried to seize his private papers in Brussels. See the dispatch sent to Delcassé from Brussels, dated January 27, 1903/no. 12 (confidentiel), AE–NS–T, 4 (1902–1904), 136–37.

219. For the assistance provided by French public opinion, see "Le référé du sultan: Abdul Hamid perd son procès," *Le Matin*, January 28, 1903. See also "İlk Hür[r]iyet Kahramanı Ahmet Rıza," *Resimli Ay* 7, no. 2 (May 1930), 7.

220. See "Damad Mahmud Paşa," *Şûra-yı Ümmet*, nos. 22–23 (February 28, 1903), 1–2; "Sami Paşazâde Sezaî Bey'in Nutku," ibid., 2, "Ahmed Rıza Bey'in Nutku," ibid., 3; "Nutuklar," *Osmanlı*, no. 118 (February 15, 1903), 2–5; and "Voici la traduction des paroles prononcées sur la tombe de Mahmoud Pacha," *Mechveret Supplément Français*, no. 137 (February 1, 1903), 2–3. Some of the speeches delivered at the funeral were republished after the Young Turk Revolution with the purpose of proving that everyone had admired Damad Mahmud Pasha. See "*Şûra-yı Ümmet*' in 20 Numerolu Nüshasından," *Serbestî*, [December 14, 1908]; and "Damad Mahmud Paşa," *Yeni Gazete*, September 2, 1908.

221. [Edhem Ruhi], "Sebeb-i Te'ehhür," *Osmanlı*, no. 120 (August 15, 1903), 1.

222. See "Arrest of a Turkish Prince," *The Times*, November 21, 1903; "L'arrestation du Prince Loutfoullah," *L'Éclair*, November 22, 1903; and G. G., "Échos," *L'Européen* 3, no. 104 (November 28, 1903), 3–4.

223. See "Prens Lûtfullah," *Islahat*, no. 4 (December 14, 1903), [4].

224. "L'arrestation du Prince Loutfoullah," *Le Paris Nouvelles*, November 26, 1903.

225. *Prens Lûtfullah Dosyası*, ed. Cavit Orhan Tütengil and Vedat Günyol (Istanbul, 1977), 14.

226. Political police "rapport" prepared by Commissioner Soullière, no. 17.154 (Au sujet du Prince Sabaheddine), Archives de la Préfecture de Police de Paris (Sabaheddine et Loutfoullah). See also an undated report in Αρχείο Σουλιώτη, 9/263.

227. Demetra Vaka [Demetra Kenneth Brown], "Prince Sabahaddine as a Free Lance Liberal," *Asia* 24, no. 2 (February 1924), 122. See also Paul Fesch, *Les Jeunes-Turcs* (Paris, [1909]], 56.

228. "The Diary of a Turk," *The Athenæum*, no. 3948 (June 27, 1903), 814.

CHAPTER 3

1. Ahmed Bedevî Kuran, *İnkılâp Tarihimiz ve Jön Türkler* (Istanbul, 1945), 159–60. In fact, it was underscored by the new organ published by this coalition that they were going to organize an independent movement. See "Vatan'dan," *Şûra-yı Ümmet*, no. 12 (September 18, 1902), 3.

2. Ahmed Rıza, "L'inaction des Jeunes-Turcs," *La Revue Occidentale*, 2nd Series, 27,

no. 1 (January 1903), 95–96. Previously published by the French supplement; see *Mechveret Supplément Français*, no. 135 (December 1, 1902), 1–3.

3. "L'exploitation de la terreur," *Mechveret Supplément Français*, no. 143 (August 1, 1903), 2.

4. "Ahmed Saib Bey Efendi'ye," *Sancak*, no. 64 (March 5, 1902), 1. The closure of many journals published by the "activists" later caused European journals to comment that "the Young Turk propaganda had diminished." See "Les Jeunes Turcs," *Pro Armenia* 4, no. 83 (April 15, 1904), 478. Some diplomats, however, considered this new development as the emergence of a significant new movement as a result of the congress. See Basso to Prinetti, Geneva, May 3, 1902/no. 1246-55/026237, ASMAE, Affari Politici, Serie P. Politica (1891–1916), pacco 172.

5. Zeki Bey to the khedive, Paris, March 19, 1902, Abbas II Papers, Durham University, F. 40/109.

6. See "İhtar," *Şûra-yı Ümmet*, no. 1 (April 10, 1902), 4; and "Le 'Chouraï Ummett,'" *Mechveret Supplément Français*, no. 129 (May 15, 1902), 3.

7. "İhtar," *Şûra-yı Ümmet*, no. 1, 4.

8. "Rıza Bey Biraderimizin Yazdığı Mektub da Şudur," *Sancak*, no. 64, 1.

9. Ibid.

10. "Ahmed Saib Bey Efendi'ye," ibid., 1.

11. Department of Justice and Police to the Ministry of the Interior, April 30, 1902/ no. 175 (P.P. 75); and June 26, 1902/no. 296 (P.P. 75), Bundesarchiv-Bern, E. 21/14'252. Meanwhile the Swiss press reported on the new coalition. See "Jeunes-Turcs," *La Suisse*, April 29, 1902.

12. Memorandum dated March 18, 1902, signed by the activist leaders Abdurrahman Bedirhan, Ali Fahri, Mahir Sa'id, and Süleyman Hikmet and sent to Ahmed Rıza, Private Papers of Ahmed Rıza (1).

13. Ibid.

14. Ahmed Saib to Ahmed Rıza, Cairo, March 11, 1902, ibid.

15. Undated memorandum from Ahmed Saib to Ahmed Rıza, ibid.

16. Ahmed Saib to Ahmed Rıza, Cairo, March 3, 1902, ibid.

17. Grand Vizier's office to the Ottoman Foreign Ministry [October 18, 1902]/no. 962-151, BBA–BEO/Mısır Hidiviyet-i Celilesinin Tezâkir Defteri, 62, 1036-68/8; and BBA–BEO/Mümtaze Kalemi: Mısır, 15 B/119 (1320.8.17); decipher to Gazi Ahmed Muhtar Pasha [January 13, 1903]/no. 149, BBA–BEO/Mısır Hidiviyet-i Celilesinin Muharrerat Defteri, 71, 1032-68/4; BBA–İrade-Hususî, S 1320/no. 62-222; and Münir Bey to Tevfik Pasha, Paris, May 24, 1902/no. 719 (decipher), BBA–HR.SYS. 1796/1 (original. 502/45).

18. Rücker-Jenisch to von Bülow, Cairo, June 25, 1903/no. 98, A. 9743, PAAA, 733/3, Die Jungtürken, 198 (Bd. 4–5).

19. BBA–İrade-Hususî, S 1320/no. 108–273.

20. Tevfik Pasha to Münir Bey, May 23, 1902/no. 47667-192, BBA–HR.SYS. 1796/1 (original. 502/45); BBA–YSHM, 429/66 (1320.2.16) and 436/59 (1320.7.26); BBA–BEO/Dahiliye Giden, 101–3/50; 829 [May 23, 1902]; and BBA–YP, 14 M 1320/no. 72.

21. Tevfik Pasha to Münir Bey, July 30, 1902/no. 486-260 (decipher no. 531), BBA–HR.SYS. 1796/1 (original. 502/45); BBA–İrade-Hususî, S 1320/no. 41-197, no. 42-198, and no. 115-204; R 1320/no. 51-444; and BBA–YSHM, 429/66 (1320.2.16). For the efforts exerted by the Ottoman authorities to prevent publication, and the precautions taken against the circulation of the journal, see BBA–YSHM, 429/70 (1320.2.17); 430/1 (1320.3.1); and 436/59 (1320.7.26).

22. Circular dated May 23, 1902/no. 192, BBA–HR.SYS. 1796/1 (original. 502/45).

23. Circular dated May 26, 1902/no. 197, ibid.

24. Münir Bey to Tevfik Pasha, Paris, May 24, 1902/no. 719 (decipher) in BBA–HR.SYS. 1796/1 (original. 502/45); and BBA–YSHM, 429/66 (1320.2.16).

25. Münir Bey to Delcassé, Paris, May 28, 1902, AE–NS–T, 4, 93–94. A copy of it numbered 16234–303 is in BBA–HR.SYS. 1796/1 (original. 502/45).

26. Delcassé to Constans, May 29, 1902/no. 54 (telegram), AE–NS–T, 4, 99.

27. Constans to Delcassé, June 3, 1902/no. 78, ibid., 103–4.

28. See the draft of the dispatch sent to the French diplomatic agent in Cairo dated Paris, June 4, 1902 (Le Caire no. 81); and the telegram sent to the French Ministry of the Interior, Paris, June 18, 1902/no. 50194-67, ibid., 104, 108.

29. Cogordan to Delcassé, Cairo, June 24, 1902/no. 113, ibid., 110–12.

30. Police Général 4. Bureau to Delcassé, June 25, 1902, ibid., 112–13.

31. Draft of the letter sent by Delcassé to Münir Bey, prepared on June 27, 1902, ibid., 113. For the letter dated June 28, 1902, see BBA–HR.SYS. 1796/1 (original. 502/45).

32. Tevfik Pasha's circular dated July 30, 1902/no. 230-12371, Archives of the Turkish Embassy in Paris, D. 244.

33. Constans to Delcassé, Therapia, August 14, 1902/no. 139, AE–NS–T, 4, 120–21.

34. Delcassé to Münir Bey, September 18, 1902, Archives of the Turkish Embassy in Paris, D. 244. The draft of this letter is in AE–NS–T, 4, 121–22, and a copy is in BBA–HR.SYS. 1796/1 (original. 502/45).

35. L. Hirszowicz, "The Sultan and the Khedive, 1892–1908," *MES* 8, no. 3 (October 1972), 295. For the tense relations between the two rulers arising from the disagreement over Samothrace, see BBA–YSHM, 435/43 (1320.7.12), and the decipher from Lord Cromer, Cairo, October 14, 1902 (confidential), PRO/F.O. 195/2131.

36. Tahsin Bey to Anthopoulos Pasha, June 4, 1901 (telegram), Archives of the Turkish Embassy in London, Box 362 (4).

37. BBA–YSHM, 429/86 (1320.2.20); and BBA–İrade-Mısır Mesâlihi, [April 29, 1902]/no. 1762/241, and [May 8, 1902]/no. 1757/141.

38. BBA–BEO/Mısır Komiserliği Âmed: Mısır Fevkâlâde Komiseri Muhtar Paşa Hazret-lerinden Gelen Tahrirat Defteridir, 746-36/4; 950 [June 10, 1902]; Grand Vizier's office to the Foreign Ministry [October 18, 1902]/no. 962, and to Gazi Ahmed Muhtar Pasha [October 13, 1902] (decipher), BBA–BEO/Mümtaze Kalemi: Mısır, D. 15/B, S.119 (1320.8.17).

39. BBA–BEO/Mısır Komiserliği Âmed: Mısır Fevkâlâde Komiseri Muhtar Paşa Hazret-lerinden Gelen Tahrirat Defteridir, 746-36/4; 962 [October 18, 1902] (decipher); BBA–BEO/Mümtaze Kalemi: Mısır, D.15/B, S.116 (1320.8.14), and D. 15/B, 119 (1320.8.1); and BBA–YSHM, 429/109 (1320.2.26).

40. Grand Vizier's note to the Ottoman Foreign Ministry [November 18, 1902], BBA–HR.SYS. 1796/1 (original. 502/45). For the instructions given to the Ottoman chargé d'affaires in London and his démarche, see Tevfik Pasha to [Abdülhak] Hamid Bey, December 11, 1902/no. 50461-229 (decipher. 836); the latter to the former, London, December 13, 1902/no. 470 (decipher. 1695); and December 17, 1902/no. 481 (decipher. 1716), ibid.

41. Tevfik Pasha to the Grand Vizier's office, December 14, 1902/no. 3061, BBA–BEO/Mümtaze Kalemi: Mısır, D.15/B, S.127 (1320.9.15). Sir Thomas made the following comment on the subject: "The Turkish Ch[argé] d'affaires . . . said that there was a native newspaper in Egypt, the Shouraz Ummet [*sic*], which constantly attacked the Sultan and gave H.M. great annoyance. . . . [T]he matter was one to which the Sultan personally attached great importance, and . . . if a favourable answer could be given, it would have a most excellent effect on all our pending questions, some of which as you will know are sufficiently complicated." See Sanderson to Cromer, December 19, 1902/no. 9157 (confidential), PRO/F.O. 78/5240.

42. Münir Bey to Delcassé, December 10, 1902, AE–NS–T, 4, 124–25.

43. Private Papers of Ahmed Rıza (2).

44. Ibid.

45. For an excellent example, see M., "Déposition!" *Mechveret Supplément Français*, no. 144 (September 1, 1903), 1. See also "La déposition s'impose," *Mechveret Supplément Français*, no. 137 (February 1, 1903), 1; and Ahmed Riza, "La Perfidie russe," *Mechveret Supplément Français*, no. 139 (April 1, 1903), 1–2.

46. Memorandum by the activists signed by Süleyman Hikmet and Mahir Sa'id and dated September 12, 1902, Private Papers of Ahmed Rıza (2).

47. To "Ahmed Saib Bey in Cairo," Private Papers of Bahaeddin Şakir.

48. Captain Silistireli Mustafa Hamdi to Ahmed Rıza, October 8, 1902, and the enclosed letter of resignation dated October 31, 1902, Private Papers of Ahmed Rıza (1).

49. Ahmed Saib to Ahmed Rıza, October 18, 1902, Private Papers of Ahmed Rıza (2).

50. Ahmed Saib to Ahmed Rıza, October 30, [1902], ibid.

51. For his flight and his activities in Paris, see Sami Paşazâde Sezaî, "1901'den İtibaren Paris'de Geçen Seneler," *Servet-i Fünûn*, no. 1486-12 (February 5, 1924), 182–85; Fevziye Abdullah, "Samî Paşazâde Sezaî," *Türkiyat Mecmuası* 13 (1958), 17–18; and Filorinalı Nâzım, "Edebiyatımızın Büyük Bir Üstâd-ı Ebed-ı'karı Sami Paşazâde Sezaî Bey," *Süs*, no. 19 (October 20, 1339 [1923]).

52. Cogardan to Delcassé, Cairo, July 24, 1902/no. 113, AE–NS–T, 4, 111.

53. "Müdahale-i Ecnebiye," *Şûra-yı Ümmet*, no. 1, 1.

54. Ibid., 1–2.

55. "Nifak Neticeleri," *Şûra-yı Ümmet*, no. 40 (November 25, 1903), 2; "Aksa-yı Şark," *Şûra-yı Ümmet*, no. 46 (February 2, 1904), 1–2; "Trablusgarb," *Şûra-yı Ümmet*, no 63 (November 9, 1904), 3–4; and "Şundan Bundan," *Şûra-yı Ümmet*, no. 67 (January 7, 1904 [1905]), 3.

56. "Şundan Bundan," *Şûra-yı Ümmet*, no. 61 (October 10, 1904), 3.

57. "Boğazlar," *Şûra-yı Ümmet*, no. 13 (October 3, 1902), 1.

58. "Shcherbina'nın Vefatı," *Şûra-yı Ümmet*, no. 28 (May 13, 1903), 3. For similar themes, see "Namus ve Haysiyet-i Askeriye," *Şûra-yı Ümmet*, no. 39 (October 22, 1903), 1–2.

59. Ahmed Rıza was editing *Mechveret Supplément Français* with the help of an assistant, and almost all unsigned articles published in this journal were penned by Ahmed Rıza. See the letter of Dr. Bahaeddin [Şakir] and Dr. Nâzım, undated [February 1907]/no. 259, and beginning "Eâzz ve Ekrem Efendim," *Muhaberat Kopyası*, 254.

60. Ottomanus [Pierre Anméghian], "La 'pénétration pacifique,'" *Mechveret Supplément Français*, no. 165 (July 1, 1905), 1.

61. "Japonlar," *Osmanlı*, no. 134 (March 15, 1904), 1.

62. "Me'yus Olmalı mı?" *Şûra-yı Ümmet*, no. 62 (October 24, 1904), 1.

63. "Londra'dan," *Şûra-yı Ümmet*, no. 50 (April 1, 1904), 3.

64. "L'Angleterre en Orient," *Mechveret Supplément Français*, no. 146 (December 1, 1903), 3–4.

65. "Mısır el-Kahire'den," *Osmanlı*, no. 100 (January 15, 1902), 6–7.

66. Ali Haydar Midhat, "English and Russian Politics in the East," *The Nineteenth Century and After* 53, no. 311 (January 1903), 77.

67. "Cinquantenaire de Crimée," *Mechveret Supplément Français*, no. 149 (March 15, 1904), 1.

68. "İngiltere'de Türk Düşmanlığı," *Şûra-yı Ümmet*, no. 44 (December 21, 1903), 2.

69. Ali Haydar Midhat to Abdullah Cevdet, Nice, March 14, 1904, Private Papers of Abdullah Cevdet.

70. "Sultan Hamid Hakkında Türkler Ne Diyorlar [?] Müceddidîn-i Osmaniye," *Hilâfet*, no. 92 (August 20, 1903), 4.

71. Information about the preparation of the first issue is given in an undated note from Ahmed Saib to Ahmed Rıza, Private Papers of Ahmed Rıza (1); and in Sami Paşazâde Sezaî, "1901'den İtibaren," *Servet-i Fünûn*, no. 1486-12, 183–84.

72. See D., "Murakabe-i Ecnebiye," *Şûra-yı Ümmet*, no. 27 (April 29, 1903), 2–3; D., "Rumeli," *Şûra-yı Ümmet*, nos. 22–23 (February 28, 1903), 3; and "Osmanlı Mülkünde Hakimiyet-i Ecnebiye," *Şûra-yı Ümmet*, no. 49 (March 18, 1904), 3.

73. "İfade-i Mahsusa," *Şûra-yı Ümmet*, no. 1, 1.

74. "Erbâb-ı Kalemin Vazifesi," *Şûra-yı Ümmet*, no. 1, 4; no. 2 (April 24, 1902), 4. See also their critique of their opponents' criticism in "İfade," *Şûra-yı Ümmet*, no. [25] (March 30, 1903), 1.

75. "İhtar ve İ'tizâr," *Şûra-yı Ümmet*, no. 12, 4.

76. "Abdülhamid'e Atılan Bomb[a]," *Şûra-yı Ümmet*, no. 80 (August 16, 1905), 1; Cf. "Müfsidler," *Şûra-yı Ümmet*, no. 85 (October 29, 1905), 2.

77. "Ağlamayan Çocuğa Meme Vermezler," *Şûra-yı Ümmet*, no. 44, 2–3.

78. "Ermeni Konferansı," *Şûra-yı Ümmet*, no. 10 (August 20, 1902), 2; "Londra'da İngiliz ve Ermeni Konferansı," *Şûra-yı Ümmet*, no. 56 (July 29, 1904), 2. Also underscored by the French supplement. See Ahmed Rıza, "Confession publique," *Mechveret Supplément Français*, no. 171 (January 1, 1906), 1.

79. "Rusya'da Harekât-ı Fikriye," *Şûra-yı Ümmet*, no. 68 (February 6, 1905), 1; "Rusya İhtilâline Dair," *Şûra-yı Ümmet*, no. 82 (September 14, 1905), 2–3; and "Vazife-i Şahsiye," *Şûra-yı Ümmet*, no. 76 (June 4, 1905), 2.

80. "Okuyun İbret Alın," *Şûra-yı Ümmet*, no. 69 (February 19, 1905), 2–3; no. 72 (April 6, 1905), 2–3; and no. 74 (May 6, 1905), 2.

81. "İsim Mes'elesi," *Şûra-yı Ümmet*, no. 52 (May 1, 1904), 2.

82. "Yine Neşriyât," *Şûra-yı Ümmet*, no. 61, 1. Cf. "Neşriyât," *Şûra-yı Ümmet*, no. 39, 1. Ahmed Rıza's arch-rival, Sabahaddin Bey's journal, underscored the importance of publication in carrying out a revolution and criticized the activists who maintained that journals play an insignificant role in such a process. See L. K., "Rus Ordusu ve İhtilâlciler," *Terakki*, no. 8 [March 1907], 3.

83. "Tekrar," *Şûra-yı Ümmet*, no. 52, 1.

84. "Yine Neşriyât," *Şûra-yı Ümmet*, no. 61, 1; and "Mektub: Tunus'dan," *Şûra-yı Ümmet*, no. 76, 3.

85. See [Sami Paşazâde Sezaî] "İhtilâl," *Şûra-yı Ümmet*, no. 55 (July 15, 1904), 3; and [Ahmed Rıza], "Aux amis de la paix," *Mechveret Supplément Français*, no. 159 (January 1, 1905), 2.

86. Sami Paşazâde Sezaî to Ahmed Rıza, April 10, 1905, Private Papers of Bahaeddin Şakir. For Ahmed Rıza's comments, see [Ahmed Rıza], "Hanedân-ı Saltanat," *Şûra-yı Ümmet*, no. 63, 1–2. For other similar articles published in the central organ, see "Sultan Abdülhamid-i Sânî'ye Hitab," *Şûra-yı Ümmet*, no. 40, 1; "Mektub: İstanbul'dan," *Şûra-yı Ümmet*, no. 59 (September 11, 1904), 2; and "Aile-i Saltanat," *Şûra-yı Ümmet*, no. 79 (July 18, 1905), 2. For Abdülhalim Memduh's criticism of the dynasty, see A[bdülhalim] Memduh, "Autour des Réformes turques," *Le Courrier Européen*, no. 2 (September 18, 1904), 4; and idem, "Sur la mort de Murad V et la succession au trône," *L'Européen* 4, no. 148 (October 1, 1904), 3–4. In contrast with the sharp criticism made in the aforementioned private letter, the central organ published an obituary praising Abdülhalim Memduh. See "Te'essüf," *Şûra-yı Ümmet*, no. 83 (September 30, 1905), 2. The local Young Turk groups in Bulgaria who had close ties with the activists published an identical obituary. See "Merhum Abdülhalim Memduh Bey," *Tuna*, no. 206 [May 20, 1906], 3. A similar tone can be observed in an article written by Sami Paşazâde Sezaî long after the Young Turk Revolution. See "Paris'de Yedi Sene," *Servet-i Fünûn*, no. 1504 (June 11, 1925), 52.

87. See Halil Ganem, *Les Sultans ottomans* 1 (Paris, 1901), esp. his "Préface," i–ii. For the criticism made by the opponents of Ahmed Rıza, see [Ali Kemal], "Selâtîn-i Osmaniye," *Mecmua-i Kemal*, no. 1 (1901), 208–9.

88. Oppenheim's report, "Anlage zu pol. Bericht nr. 98," enclosed with the dispatch sent by Rücker-Jenisch to von Bülow, Cairo, June 25, 1903/no. 98, A. 9743, PAAA, 733/3, Die Jungtürken, 198 (Bd. 4–5).

89. "Sultan Abdülhamid'e Hitab," *Şûra-yı Ümmet*, no. 33 (July 26, 1903), 1–2.

90. For an invitation to Gazi Ahmed Muhtar, Mehmed Kâmil, and Mehmed Sa'id Pashas, see "İrtidâd-ı Siyasî," *Şûra-yı Ümmet İlâvesi*, no. 1 (August 28, 1902), 4.

91. "Aux amis de la paix," *Mechveret Supplément Français*, no. 159, 2. There is also an article in which positivism was praised in the new central organ. See "Memâlik-i Osmaniye'de Asayiş: Bulgar Prensi Kral Olmak İstiyor," *Şûra-yı Ümmet*, no. 74, 1.

92. Ottomanus [Pierre Anméghian], "Les Comités révolutionnaires arméniens," *Mechveret Supplément Français*, no. 152 (June 1, 1904), 2–3.

93. "Pierre Laffitte," *Mechveret Supplément Français*, no. 137, 3. For another endorsement of the positivists, see "Charles Ritter," ibid., 4.

94. See Agustin Aragon to Ahmed Rıza, Mexico, César 10, 117/May 2, 1905; and Homère 1, 118/January 29, 1906, Private Papers of Ahmed Rıza (2).

95. Juan Enrique Lagarrique, *Lettre à M. Ahmed Riza* (Santiago, 1901), passim. See also his letter to Ahmed Rıza, Santiago, 28 Shakespeare 116/October 7, 1904, Private Papers of Ahmed Rıza (2).

96. "Mesbityon Şenlikleri," *Hilâfet*, no. 74 (August 1, 1902), [4].

97. "Où sont les 'pacifistes'?" *Mechveret Supplément Français*, no. 170 (December 1, 1905), 3.

98. See M., "Déposition," *Mechveret Supplément Français*, no. 144, 1; and "Abdülhamid'in Hal'i," *Şûra-yı Ümmet*, no. [25], 3.

99. See "Efkâr-ı Umumiye," *Şûra-yı Ümmet*, no. 28, 1–2; and "Ermeni ve Makedonya Mitingi," *Şûra-yı Ümmet*, no. 41 (November 7, 1901), 2.

100. İ[smail] Hakkı, "Mekâtib: 12 Şubat 2[1]318, İstanbul'dan," *Şûra-yı Ümmet*, no. 26 (April 13, 1903), 2.

101. See Paul Audebert, "Le rêve des Jeunes-Turcs," *Le Soir*, July 30, 1905. In this article Joseph Fehmi also announced a seventeen-article program of the "Jeunes-Turcs révolutionnaires," a nonexistent organization.

102. Akçuraoğlu Yusuf, *Eski Şûra-yı Ümmet'de Çıkan Makalelerimden* (Istanbul, 1329 [1913]), 3. Obviously Akçura excluded his own articles from this generalization. He made a very similar comment much later, in 1932, in a preface to a book on the Young Turk movement, stating, however, that the importance of the movement stemmed from the fact that "the core of the Young Turks was composed of people who came to adhere to the idea of Turkishness either fully or partially." See his preface to [Feridun] Kan Demir, *Zindan Hatıraları* (Istanbul, 1932), 6–7.

103. "Kossuth," *Şûra-yı Ümmet*, no. 14 (October 18, 1902), 3–4. It is interesting to note that the Albanian committee sent a letter to the speaker of the Hungarian parliament praising Kossuth on the occasion of the one hundredth anniversary of his birth. See BBA–YSHM, 434/101 (1320.6.27).

104. "İbret," *Şûra-yı Ümmet*, no. 66 (December 22, 1904), 4.

105. Ahmed Riza, "Nationaliste," *Mechveret Supplément Français*, no. 155 (September 5, 1904), 4. A similar language was adopted by the CPU when corresponding with non-Muslim Ottomans. See Dr. Bahaeddin [Şakir]'s undated [August 1907]/no. 349 letter to Nikola Manolov, *Muhaberat Kopyası*, 396: "Our society is not a nationalist party caring only for its own nation's interests like the committees of other Muslim and Christian nations." See also the letter of Dr. Bahaeddin [Şakir] beginning "Muhterem Vatandaş" and dated Paris, September 3, 1907/no. 356, *Muhaberat Kopyası*, 404.

106. [Ahmed Rıza] "Mısır Vatanperverleri," *Şûra-yı Ümmet*, no. 109 (February 15, 1907), 2–3. Ahmed Rıza's description of Muṣṭafā Kāmil Pasha as a "grand patriote" elicited criticism from pro-Dashnak journals. See "L'Allemagne et l'islam," *Pro Armenia* 7, no. 151 (February 7, 1907), 1043.

107. "Za'af ve Cehl Numûneleri," *Şûra-yı Ümmet*, no. 12, 3.

108. "Makedonya," *Şûra-yı Ümmet*, no. 36 (September 7, 1903), 1.

109. "Bulgaristan'da Nüfûz-i Osmanî," *Şûra-yı Ümmet*, no. 7 (July 7, 1902), 2.

110. "Mektub: Bitlis'den," *Şûra-yı Ümmet*, no. 83, 2; and "Tatars et Arméniens," *Mechveret Supplément Français*, no. 168 (October 1, 1905), 3–4.

111. See "Nifak Neticeleri," *Şûra-yı Ümmet*, no. 40, 2.

112. "[Bois de] Boulogne Ormanında Bir Rum ile Muhavere," *Şûra-yı Ümmet*, no. 41, 3.

113. "Yemen İhtilâli," *Şûra-yı Ümmet*, no. 84 (October 14, 1905), 1.

114. Ahmed Rıza's undated note in his notebook, Private Papers of Ahmed Rıza (1).

115. "Ecnebiler İçinde Top Oynayor[sic]," *Şûra-yı Ümmet*, no. 30 (June 11, 1903), 1.

116. "[Bois de] Boulogne Ormanında Bir Rum ile Muhavere," *Şûra-yı Ümmet*, no. 41, 3–4.

117. This term refers to followers of a Greek military chief, especially during the Greek War of Independence (1821–1830). In Turkish colloquial usage the term is used in a derogatory way to refer to Greeks.

118. "Mekâtib: (Vatandaşlık): Kudüs-i Şerif'den Mektub," *Şûra-yı Ümmet*, no. 45 (December 19, 1904), 2.

119. "Küstahlık," *Şûra-yı Ümmet*, no. 75, 1.

120. [Sami Paşazâde Sezaî], "Ermeni Mes'elesi," *Şûra-yı Ümmet*, no. 57 (August 13, 1904), 1. Some parts of this article were also published by the French supplement. See "Pour les Arméniens," *Mechveret Supplément Français*, no. 158 (December 1, 1904), 2–3. For another article expressing a similar view, see "Akvâm-ı Osmaniye," *Şûra-yı Ümmet*, no. 51 (April 17, 1904), 1–2: "We cannot find any reasonable cause for the Greeks and the Armenians to complain of the Turks and to desire to separate themselves from the Turks. They ought to be grateful to their

Turkish compatriots for their existence at the moment. They have maintained their faiths, nationalities, and languages until now because they have lived amidst Turks." The first article was later presented as a clear example of the "Turkish nationalist policy" adopted by the coalition. See A[nastase] Adossidès, *Arméniens et Jeunes-Turcs: les massacres de Cilicie* (Paris, 1910), 141–42.

121. "Arnavudluğa Dair: Don Quijote," *Şûra-yı Ümmet*, no. 4 (May 23, 1902), 2–4.

122. "Arnavud İsyanı," *Şûra-yı Ümmet*, no. 28, 2.

123. "Şehid-i Zulm-i Hamidî ve Felâket-i Millet," *Hilâfet*, no. 85 (February 1, 1903), 1.

124. "Abū al-Hudā ve Avenesi," *Şûra-yı Ümmet*, no. 61, 2.

125. "Arab İsyanı," *Şûra-yı Ümmet*, no. 79, 2. For similar accusations against "separatist" Arabs, see "Yemen İhtilâli," *Şûra-yı Ümmet*, no. 84, 1. The French supplement, however, employed a different language to influence European public opinion. See "Les poussées d'insurrection au Yémen," *Mechveret Supplément Français*, no. 164 (June 1, 1905), 2. British documents reveal that the article had the intended effect. See Newmarch to the Secretary to the Government of India in the Foreign Department, Baghdad, November 27, 1905/ no. 941, BL, IOR: R/20/A/1256.

126. "Innamā al-mu'minūna ikhwatun," *Şûra-yı Ümmet*, no. 90 (March 26, 1906), 1. For a similar article in which the alleged British provocations were also denounced, see "Hilâfet ve Yemen," *Şûra-yı Ümmet*, no. 80, 3. It was further claimed that the problems in the Arab lands such as the Yemen originated from the Arabs' supposedly hostile attitude toward civilization and their ignorance. See "Yemen," *Şûra-yı Ümmet*, no. 78 (July 4, 1905), 1–2. A Young Turk organ published in the Balkans used similar language. See "Hilâfet Tehlikede!" *Rumeli*, no. 7 [January 19, 1906], 1–2.

127. "Millet-i Osmaniye'ye," *Şûra-yı Ümmet*, no. 41, 1.

128. "Abdülhamid–Devlet-i Aliyye," *Şûra-yı Ümmet*, no. 45, 1.

129. S[ami] [Paşazâde] S[ezaî], "Kısm-ı Edebî," *Şûra-yı Ümmet*, no. 35 (August 24, 1903), 3. For a letter of his written during this period and promoting similar ideas, see Sami Paşazâde Sezaî, "Bir Mektub," *Neyyir-i Hakikat Nüsha-i Mümtaze* [July 23, 1909], 16.

130. "Kısm-ı Edebî: Lisan," *Şûra-yı Ümmet*, no. 39, 3.

131. H[üseyin] S[iyret], "Kısm-ı Edebî," *Şûra-yı Ümmet*, no. 43 (December 7, 1903), 3.

132. M. M., "Lisan Bahsi," *Şûra-yı Ümmet*, no. 47 (February 18, 1904), 4.

133. "İfade-i Mahsusa," *Şûra-yı Ümmet*, no. 49, 1.

134. "Şundan Bundan," *Şûra-yı Ümmet*, no. 48 (March 3, 1904), 4.

135. "Millî ve Siyasî Şarkılar," *Şûra-yı Ümmet*, no. 18, December 15, 1902, 2–3. Special attention had been paid to national anthems in the previous central organs of the CUP. (For an interesting example concerning the Bulgarian revolutionaries' chanting of the Bulgarian national anthem on their way to exile, see "Havâdis," *Osmanlı*, no. 89 [August 1, 1901], 8.) Nobody, however, had written about a national anthem for the Ottoman Empire. It should be noted that the CUP could not achieve the goal of the adoption of a national anthem until sometime after its seizure of power, and in 1909 a new official song was composed for the new sultan. (See BBA–BEO/Re'sen İrade-i Seniye, 360-8/83; 7/8 [June 12, 1909]/268017.) Although the Union and Progress party adopted an Ottoman anthem much later, during the last days of its power in the empire, it was ironically put into effect only after the CUP leaders had fled to Europe in November 1918. See "Osmanlı Marşı," *Takvim-i Vekayi'*, no. 3302 [August 9, 1918], 1; and BBA–BEO/Dahiliye Giden, 118-3/67; 86 [January 22, 1919]/341354, and 215 [February 25, 1919]/341765.

136. "Milletimiz Ne Yapıyor [?]"*Şûra-yı Ümmet*, no. 5 (June 7, 1902), 4. Following the Young Turk Revolution of 1908, a British journal made this comment: "'The choice' they may say is between the Young Turks, on the one hand, who are certainly civilised and tolerant, but whose attitude towards other races begins to remind us unpleasantly of that of the Magyars towards the minorities in Hungary." See "The Turkish Reaction," *The Nation* 5, no. 3 (April 17, 1909), 77.

137. See "Rumeli'de Yapılması İcab Eden Şeyler," *Şûra-yı Ümmet*, no. 31 (June 27, 1903), 1–2, and "Avrupa-yı Osmanî," *Şûra-yı Ümmet*, no. 34 (August 9, 1903), 3. The later policies of the CUP in a way tried to fulfill the dreams of those who wrote these articles. Although

heavily dependent on Serbian diplomatic documents, an article by Gligor Todorovski provides worthwhile information on the CUP's policies on this matter. See Gligor Todorovski, "Prilog kon prašanjeto za sostojbata na muslimanskite iselenici (muadžiri) vo Makedonija po mladoturskata revolucija," *Glasnik* 26 (1982), 135–53. See also idem, "Srpski dokumenti za sostojbata na muadžirite vo Makedonija (1906–1911)," ibid., 197–218, for Serbian documents on the subject.

138. İki Asker, "Türklerde Tenâkus-i Zürriyet," *Şûra-yı Ümmet*, no. 86 (November 12, 1905), 4.

139. "Mekâtîb: Dahilden: Kütüb-i Diniye ve Fenniye-i İslâmiye Tahrib Ediliyor," *Şûra-yı Ümmet*, no. 49, 3–4; L., "Umum Âlem-i İslâmiyeti İkaz," *Şûra-yı Ümmet*, no. 78, 3–4; and "Abdülhamid Ahlâkiyyûnundan!" *Şûra-yı Ümmet*, no. 82, 1.

140. "Abdülhamid Devrinde İslâmiyet—I," *Şûra-yı Ümmet*, no. 15 (November 2, 1902), 1–3.

141. See "Meşrutiyet İdarenin Ezher-cihet Lüzûmunu İsbat Beyânındadır," *Şûra-yı Ümmet*, no. 36, 1–2.

142. For the query, see "Mebâhis-i Âtiyeyi Makale Zemini Olmak Üzere Haricden Mu'avenet-i Tahririyede Bulunacak Zevâtın Nazar-ı Dikkatlerine Arz Ederiz," *Şûra-yı Ümmet*, no. 8 (July 21, 1902), 3–4. For the response by some members of the ulema, see "Mukanna' Cevablar," *Şûra-yı Ümmet*, no. 11 (September 4, 1902), 4.

143. Sami Paşazâde Sezaî, "Vatana Hıyanet," *Selânik'de Şûra-yı Ümmet*, April 26, 1909, 1.

144. "Trablusgarb Elden Gidiyor," *Şûra-yı Ümmet*, no. 52, 4.

145. See "Influences religieuses," *Mechveret Supplément Français*, no. 147 (January 1, 1904), 3. For similar comments, see Ahmed Riza, "Protectorat religieux," *Mechveret Supplément Français*, no. 157 (November 1, 1904), 1–2; and idem, "Laïcisation du protectorat," *Mechveret Supplément Français*, no. 158, 1–2.

146. See "Avrupa Matbu'atı Niçün Türkler Aleyhinde ve Bulgarlar Lehindedir?" *Şûra-yı Ümmet*, no. 35, 1; and "Ermeni ve Makedonya Mitingi," *Şûra-yı Ümmet*, no. 41, 1–3.

147. A French official employed by the French administration in West Africa to Ahmed Rıza, Gorée (Senegal), September 19, 1905, Private Papers of Ahmed Rıza (2). The signature is illegible.

148. From the same official to Ahmed Rıza, Bafoulabé (Mali), February 20, 1906, ibid.

149. The ideas mentioned here are taken from a speech that was delivered by Loyson on May 27, 1895. See the text of the speech enclosed with the letter from Ziya Bey to Turhan Pasha, June 10, 1895/ no. 224-8919. See also Ziya Bey to Sa'id Pasha, May 27, 1895/no. 212-8889, Dışişleri Bakanlığı Hazine-i Evrak Arşivi, Siyasî: 226. See also Hyacinthe [Charles Jean-Marie] Loyson, *France et Algérie; christianisme et islamisme: conférences données à Paris dans le mois de Mai 1895* (Paris [1895]), passim. For Loyson's opinion concerning the French supplement, see his letter to Ahmed Rıza dated Rome, January 22, 1906, Private Papers of Ahmed Rıza (2). The French supplement had informed its readership about Loyson's activities. See "M. Hyacinthe Loyson à Constantinople," *Mechveret Supplément Français*, no. 106 (November 15, 1900), 3.

150. "Rumeli Elden Gidiyor," *Şûra-yı Ümmet*, no. 3 (May 9, 1902), 1.

151. "Avrupa, Hünkâr, Millet," *Şûra-yı Ümmet*, no. 42 (November 21, 1903), 1. The publication policy of the French supplement as described in the citation was hailed after the Young Turk Revolution by those members who had worked within the empire. See Âkil Koyuncu, "Ahmed Rıza Bey," *Bağçe*, no. 5 [August 31, 1908], 6.

152. "Fanatisme musulman," *Mechveret Supplément Français*, no. 145 (October 15, 1903), 3. For similar criticisms, see Ahmed Riza, "Informations partiales," *Mechveret Supplément Français*, no. 130 (June 15, 1902), 1–2; and "Tolérance chez les autres," ibid., 3–4.

153. O., "Fanatisme," *Mechveret Supplément Français*, no. 151 (May 1, 1904), 4.

154. "Turcophobie," *Mechveret Supplément Français*, no. 139 (April 1, 1903), 3.

155. "Parasızlığa Çâre," *Şûra-yı Ümmet*, no. 75 (May 20, 1905), 2. In addition, harsh criticisms were made against fatalism; it was claimed that there was no relationship whatsoever

between it and religion, and that those who could not comprehend this fact were unaware of the realities of Islam. See Lâ [Yusuf Akçura], "Kader," *Şûra-yı Ümmet*, no. 3, 2.

156. "Rusya'da Fikir ve Asker," *Şûra-yı Ümmet*, no. 71 (March 21, 1905), 1–2.

157. "Mouvement panislamique," *Mechveret Supplément Français*, no. 148 (February 1, 1904), 2.

158. See "Bulgaristan'da Nüfûz-i Osmanî," *Şûra-yı Ümmet*, no. 7, 1; and "Girid," *Şûra-yı Ümmet*, no. 9 (August 6, 1902), 1–2.

159. Selma Hanım to Joseph Reinach, Paris, November 27, 1903, Bibliothèque nationale (Paris), MSS. Occ. Correspondance de Joseph Reinach, 39, 247–48. She thanked Reinach for rendering such a service to the Turks.

160. "Ecnebilere Meram Anlatmanın Lüzûmu," *Şûra-yı Ümmet*, no. 66, 4. Also underscored in the CPU correspondence. See the letter of Dr. B. Server [Bahaeddin Şakir] to [Colonel Çerkes İshak and Necib Bey in Trabzon] beginning "Vicdanî ve Mihrabî Kardaşlarımız" and dated Paris, March 15, [1]906/no. 1, *Muhaberat Kopyası*, 1. This, however, made no impact on the Ottoman government, which continued to describe the journal as "nonsensical." See the Grand Vizier's office to the Foreign Ministry [October 9, 1904], BBA–BEO/Mahremâne Müsveddat, no. 209.

161. "Efkâr-ı Umumiye," *Şûra-yı Ümmet*, no. 28, 1–2.

162. Ibid., 2.

163. "Şuûnat," *Şûra-yı Ümmet*, no. 3, 4.

164. See "Ermeni Kongresi," *Şûra-yı Ümmet*, no. 10, 2. For the letters sent by the coalition and the responses given by the Armenians, see Ahmed Riza, "Affaires arméniennes au Congrès des arménophiles," *Mechveret Supplément Français*, no. 132 (August 20, 1902), 2–4. For further information about the congress, see "Brüksel'de Muhibb-i Ermeniyân Kongresi," *Anadolu*, no. 8 (August 6, 1902), 2–3.

165. The invitation sent by Edward Atkin to Ahmed Rıza, "M. le Président de la [du] Parti 'Jeune Turquie,'" provides no information concerning the format; Private Papers of Ahmed Rıza (2).

166. "Londra'da İngiliz ve Ermeni Konferansı," *Şûra-yı Ümmet*, no. 56, 2. See also Ahmed Riza, "La peur de la vérité," *Mechveret Supplément Français*, no. 153 (July 15, 1904), 1–3.

167. "Londra'da İngiliz ve Ermeni Konferansı," *Şûra-yı Ümmet*, no. 56, 2–3.

168. Ibid., 2–3. See also London Office of Pro Armenia, *Report of the International Conference on the Situation in the Near East* (held in London on June 29, 1904), 59; and "Incident Ahmed Riza," *Pro Armenia* 4, no. 90 (July 15, 1904), 550. Hoca Kadri had made nearly identical accusations at the 1902 Congress. He had said that "a European at the moment of the massacres had approached an Armenian woman and had asked that woman whether he could do something for her. She responded: 'Get out of here sir. All that has happened is because of the Europeans.'" See Zeki Bey to the khedive [April 1902], Abbas II Papers, Durham University, F. 40/103-104. Following the conference Ahmed Rıza sent a summary of the speech he had intended to make to the editor of the *Positivist Review*. For the summary and the editor's note defending Ahmed Rıza and his ideas, see "Paragraphs," *The Positivist Review* 12, no. 141 (September 1, 1904), 212–13.

169. See "Londra'da İngiliz ve Ermeni Konferansı," *Şûra-yı Ümmet*, no. 56, 3. For Blind's account, see Karl Blind, "The Far East and the Near East," *The Westminster Review* 161, no. 6 (June 1904), 609. Blind had defended the publication of *Mechveret Supplément Français* in articles written prior to the meeting. See Karl Blind, "Macedonia and England's Policy," *The Nineteenth Century and After* 54, no. 321 (November 1903), 746–47.

170. A[nastase] Adossidès, "Turcs, Grecs et Arméniens," *L'Hellénisme* 1, no. 9 (September 1, 1904), 11–12.

171. Ibid. Ahmed Rıza sent a letter in response to refute the charges and this caused Adossidis to make further accusations. See Ahmed Rıza's letter dated Paris, September 19, 1904, and Adossidis's comments in A[nastase] A[dossidis], "Turcs, Grecs et Arméniens," *L'Hellénisme* 1, no. 10 (October 1, 1904), 12–13. See also "A propos du philhellénisme," *Mechveret Supplément Français*, no. 164, 4. Armenian journals, on the other hand, accused Ahmed Rıza and

Karl Blind of "being notorious defenders of Bismarckist policies." See "Un article du 'Mechveret,'" *Pro Armenia* 8, no. 176 (February 20, 1908), 1242.

172. An interesting comment was made by Oppenheim, who wrote: "Young Turks fight against the sultan's policy when he tries to maintain peace at all costs, giving away Crete and maybe Macedonia. They wish to support the sultan by all means in maintaining the integrity of the Ottoman Empire." See his memorandum enclosed with the dispatch by Rücker-Jenisch to von Bülow, Cairo, June 25, 1903/no. 98, A. 9743, PAAA 733/3, Die Jungtürken, 198 (Bd. 4–5). The coalition's defense of the caliphate brought criticism from opposition groups who contrasted the *Tanzimat* statesmen and the members of the coalition: "Les réformateurs d'il y a trente ans proposaient la séparation de l'État d'avec la religion, innovation qui, avec une large décentralisation, constituait la seule chance de salut de la Turquie. Les modernes Jeunes-Turcs se présentent, eux aussi, avec de mirifiques promesses, avec une constitution et le califat. Mais ils ne nous expliquent point par quel tour de force ils parviendront à mettre d'accord ces choses disparates." See "Réformateurs Jeunes-Turcs," *L'Hellénisme* 3, no. 4 (April 1, 1906), 16.

173. "Sükûtun Mazarratı," *Şûra-yı Ümmet*, no. 57, 3. When Ahmed Rıza asked for his help during the crucial days of the Entente occupation in Turkey, Clemenceau rebuffed the former's demands on the very same grounds. See Ahmed Rıza's letter to Clemenceau, dated Constantinople, July 17, 1919, in *Échos de Turquie* (Paris, 1920), 61–62. See İsmail Ramiz, "Ahmed Rıza Beyle Mülâkat," *Vakit*, September 16, 1922, for Clemenceau's response.

174. "Menafiʿ-i Osmaniye Nokta-i Nazarından Avrupa'nın Hâl-i Hâzırı," *Şûra-yı Ümmet*, no. 58 (August 27, 1904), 2.

175. See "Pitoyable duperie," *Mechveret Supplément Français*, no. 144, 1; Ahmed Riza, "Affaires bulgares," *Mechveret Supplément Français*, no. 131 (July 15, 1902), 2–3; and "Nos pacifistes," *Mechveret Supplément Français*, no. 160 (February 1, 1905), 3.

176. For a good example, see Pax, "Aux chrétiens de Turquie," *Mechveret Supplément Français*, no. 152, 4.

177. Maurice Kahn, "Les Jeunes-Turcs," *L'Européen* 3, no. 103 (November 21, 1903), 12. For similar claims, see "La situation des partis en Macédoine," *La Revue* 54, no. 1 (January 1, 1905), 7–8. Another French daily accused the coalition of pursuing Panislamism. It referred to the coalition as "la fraction autoritaire et panislamique des Jeunes-Turcs." See "Bulletin de l'étranger: dans les Balkans," *Le Temps*, April 11, 1902. The leaders of the coalition, however, rebutted the charge. See "Une réponse au 'Temps,'" *Mechveret Supplément Français*, no. 129, 2.

178. Dikran Elmassian, "Une entente entre les Ottomans est-elle possible? Une conversation avec M. Ahmed Riza," *Le Courrier Européen*, no. 37 (July 21, 1905), 585. For similar accusations made later, see Diana Agabeg Apcar, *Betrayed Armenia* (Yokohama, 1910), 13–17; Tigrane Yergate, "Can Turkey Live?—III: Reforms," *The Armenian Herald* 1, no. 12 (November 1918), 649–50. For an exceptional and opposite evaluation of Ahmed Rıza's work before the Young Turk Revolution of 1908, see P. Risal [Joseph Nehamas], "Les Turcs à la recherche d'une âme national," *Mercure de France* 98 (July–August 1912), 679: "Ils désiraient la fusion franche des races. Leur sincérité était hors de doute. Partout ils essayèrent de réagir contre l'esprit de particularisme renaissant, et ils voulurent, pour cela, employer la persuasion, faire appel à l'idéal, aux sentiments. Des ligues de paix et d'entente, destinées à faciliter cette fusion, à l'accélérer, à abaisser les barrières qui les avaient séparées jusqu'alors. Ce fut la politique d'ottomanisme préconisée par le groupe jeune-turc de Paris, à la tête duquel se trouvait Ahmed Riza."

179. "Contre l'islam," *Mechveret Supplément Français*, no. 162 (April 1, 1905), 2.

180. Y[usuf] A[kçura], *Midhat-Pacha, la Constitution ottomane et l'Europe* (Paris, 1903), passim. Also published in the French supplement. See Y[usuf] A[kçura], "Midhat Pacha: La Constitution ottomane et l'Europe," *Mechveret Supplément Français*, no. 135, 4 ff.

181. Ahmed Riza, "Confession publique," *Mechveret Supplément Français*, no. 171, 1.

182. "İhtilâl," *Şûra-yı Ümmet*, no. 55, 3.

183. S [Yusuf Akçura], "Bir Tavsiye," *Şûra-yı Ümmet*, no. 15, 1. For similar comments, see "İntibâh," *Şûra-yı Ümmet*, no. 17 (December 1, 1902), 1.

184. See "Muharebe Olacak mı?" *Şûra-yı Ümmet*, no. 38 (October 6, 1903), 1.

185. "Fa-'tabirū yā ūlī 'l-abṣār," *Şûra-yı Ümmet*, no. 86, 1.
186. "Şundan Bundan," *Şûra-yı Ümmet*, no. 73 (March [April] 20, 1905), 4.

CHAPTER 4

1. Tunalı Hilmi, *Murad* (Geneva, 1317 [1899]), 43–139.
2. Hilmy Tounali, *Un projet d'organization de la souveranité du peuple en Turquie* (Geneva, 1902), passim.
3. See the Department of Justice and Police to the Ministry of the Interior, April 24, 1902/ no. 161 (P.P. April 25, 1902/no. 75), Bundesarchiv-Bern, E. 21/14'248.
4. See the Department of Justice and Police to the State Department, March 25, 1902/ no. 108 (P.P. March 26, 1902/no. 75), Bundesarchiv-Bern, 21/14'248.
5. [Tunalı] Hilmi, "Arafāt'dan," *Ezan*, no. 2 [March 1902], 1–8.
6. See the note by the Ministry of the Navy dated April 18, 1902, BBA–YMGM, 228/54 (1320 1.9).
7. See Tunalı [Hilmi], *Rezalet: Dördüncü Fasıl-Portekiz* (İhsanbol [Geneva], 1318 [1900]), 11–12; and idem, *On Birinci Hutbe: Türkiyalılık Osmanlılık; Osmanlılık Türkiyalılıkdır* ([Geneva], 1318 [1901]), passim.
8. Regnault to Delcassé, Geneva, March 17, 1902/no. 4 (confidentielle), AE–NS–T, 4 (1902–1904), 81–82.
9. Marschall von Bieberstein to Auswärtiges Amt, June 1, 1902/no. 201 (Telegramm-geheim), A. 8554, PAAA, 733/3, Die Jungtürken, 198 (Bd.4–5).
10. Draft dated Berlin, June 1902, A. 8554, ibid.
11. See the draft dated June 1902 and prepared by von Bülow, A. 8554, ibid.
12. For example, Âkil Muhtar, who played a significant role in the activities of members of the old CUP organization, was bought off by the palace and received a stipend. See BBA–YSRM, 112/15 (1319.1.10). He later claimed that there remained no organized committee activity in Europe at that point. See A. Süheyl Ünver, "Mektebi Tıbbiye Talebesi Arasında Hürriyet ve Serbest Fikir Cereyanları," *İstanbul Klinik Dersleri Aylık Tıp Dergisi* 8, no. 40 (March 1953), 12.
13. They succeeded in deluding the Swiss authorities who paid attention to this fact. See the note sent to the Department of Justice and Police, Bern, December 3, 1902 (P.P. December 4, 1902/no. 573), Bundesarchiv-Bern, E. 21/14'248.
14. Department of Justice and Police to the State Department, December 8, 1902/no. 537 (P.P. December 9, 1902/no. 573), ibid.
15. See İbrahim Temo to Karl Süssheim, Medgidia, September 2, 1933, 12, Nachlaß Süssheim, Staatsbibliothek Preußischer Kulturbesitz: Orientabteilung. This information contradicts the Swiss intelligence report that claimed he was from Salonica. See the note by the President of the Confederation to the Ottoman embassy, Bern, December 27, 1902, Archives of the Turkish Embassy in Paris, D. 283. See also Salâhi Bey to Münir Bey, Bern, December 30, 1902/no. 152–75, ibid. The Swiss authorities underscored Halil Muvaffak's role in the Albanian activities in Rome during the Greco-Turkish War of 1897 and his close relations with Damad Mahmud Pasha. See the Department of Justice and Police to the State Department, Geneva, December 14, 1902/no. 548 (P.P. December 16, 1902/no. 573), Bundesarchiv-Bern, E.21/14'248.
16. See "Havâdis-i Hariciye," *Muvazene*, no. 229 [April 14, 1902], 3. For the closure of the journal *Albania*, see Dervich Hima, "Ultime parole in Italia," *Albania*(2) 2, no. 2 (April 13, 1902), 1. The Ottoman authorities had claimed that the journal was nothing other than a revolutionary appeal. See the Ottoman ambassador's "note-verbale" to the Italian Foreign Ministry, Rome, July 13, 1901/no. 1979-11, ASMAE, Affari Politici, Serie P. Politica (1891–1916), pacco 121. This journal, as Hima later confessed, independently promoted Albanian nationalism, and he as the editor participated in international conferences. See

Derviş Hima, "Vatandaşlara İfademiz," *Arnaud*, no. 1 [January 13, 1910], 1. Hima later wrote that he had received support from Albanians within the Ottoman Empire for his publication activities. See Derviş Hima, "Muhterem Arnavud Vatandaşlarımıza ve Dostlarımıza," *Serbestî*, [January 28, 1909].

17. See Archives d'État-Genève/Chancellerie, B. 8, 77. The Ottoman authorities banned its entrance into the empire. See BBA–YEE–Kâmil Paşa Evrakına Ek I, 86/18, 1731 (1320.11.30).

18. "De l'utilité générale d'une Administration fédérale en Turquie," *La Fédération Ottomane*, no. 1 (February 23, 1903), [1].

19. See "Fédération ottomane et la Conférence armeno-macédonienne," ibid., [1]; and "A propos du livre jaune," ibid., [2].

20. "Gazetemizin Mesleği Hakkında Bir İki Söz," *İttihad-ı Osmanî*, no. 1 [1].

21. Sava Iancovici, "Relations Roumano-Albanaises à l'époque de la renaissance et de l'émancipation du peuple Albanais–I," *Revue des Études Sud-Est Européennes* 9, no. 1 (1971), 42 and 42/n. 143.

22. See J[ohann] Langhard, *Das Niederlassungsrecht der Ausländer in der Schweiz* (Zurich, 1913), 57.

23. *Ethem Ruhi Balkan Hatıraları-Canlı Tarihler* 6 (Istanbul, 1947), 28–29.

24. All this information was provided by Edhem Ruhi himself in January 1905, when he made a confession to Münir Pasha. See "Paris Sefaret-i Seniyesi'nin Mabeyn-i Hümayûn-i Mülûkâne Başkitabet-i Celilesi'ne İrsâl Olunan 25 Zilhicce [1]322 ve 20 Kânûn-i evvel [1]320 Tarihlû ve Bir Numerolu Tahriratın Kaydından Müstahrec Suretidir," BBA–YEE, 15/74-18-ç/74/15.

25. See BBA–BEO/Mısır Fevkâlâde Komiseri Muhtar Paşa Hazretlerinden Vürûd Eden, 747-36/5 [November 7, 1903]/no. 420. Necmeddin Ârif, on the other hand, claimed that the journal was being published under the sole responsibility of Edhem Ruhi. See BBA–BEO/ Mısır Hidiviyet-i Celilesinin Muharrerat Defteri (71), 1032-68/4 [November 21, 1903]/no. 544–102. The Ottoman High Commissioner's office could find no evidence of Necmeddin Ârif's participation, and he denied the accusations. See the draft of the note sent to the Otto-man Ministry of Justice, dated [November 15, 1903], and the note sent to the Grand Vizier's office, Alexandria [November 7, 1903]/no. 1056, BBA–BEO/Mümtaze Kalemi: Mısır, A. MTZ (05), 16/A, 43 (1321.8.25); and BBA–BEO/Mısır Komiserliği Âmed: Mısır Komiseri Muhtar Paşa Hazretlerinden Gelen Tahrirat Defteridir, 746-36/4; 1001-1056 [November 7, 1903].

26. [Edhem Ruhi], "Sebeb-i Te'ehhür," *Osmanlı*, no. 120 (August 15, 1903), 1.

27. Ibid., 2.

28. Sabahaddin, "Osmanlı İttihad ve Terakki Cemiyeti'ne," ibid., 2.

29. "Mısır'da Ermeni Konferansı," *Osmanlı*, no. 121 (September 1, 1903), 4.

30. "Balkanlar'da Avrupa Kontrolu," *Osmanlı*, no. 125 (November 1, 1903), 1.

31. "Avrupa Taassubu," *Osmanlı*, no. 126 (November 20, 1903), 1–2.

32. "Fes," *Osmanlı*, no. 125, 4.

33. M., "Déposition!" *Mechveret Supplément Français*, no. 144 (September 1, 1903), 1.

34. "Bir Mülâhaza," *Osmanlı*, no. 124 (October 15, 1903), 4.

35. "Bir Tarihçe," *Osmanlı*, no. 133 (February 20, 1904), 1.

36. See "İâne," *Osmanlı*, no. 121, 4.

37. Ahmed Saib's undated [late November 1903] letter to Ahmed Rıza, Private Papers of Ahmed Rıza (1).

38. BBA–YEE, 15/74–18–ç/74/15.

39. Mehmed Cemil, *Tarihçe-i Ahrardan Birkaç Yaprak: Ali Şakir, Kendim, Edhem Ruhi* (Ruse [1908]), 34–36. Later Muḥammad ʿAlī Ḥalīm Pasha expressed a similar opinion to Nihad Reşad (Belger), a member of the old CUP organization, and claimed that he had been duped and outwitted by Edhem Ruhi. See Nihad Reşad's letter dated November 2, 1904, in Türk İnkılâp Tarihi Enstitüsü Arşivi, 82/18329.

40. Mehmed Cemil, *Tarihçe-i Ahrardan*, 37.

41. Ibid., 38; and "Konferans," *Osmanlı*, no. 136 (July 15, 1904), 1.

42. "Beilage 5: Abdullah Djevdet," Archives de la Justice et Police-Genève.
43. Zeki Bey's spy report, too, confirms this. See Zeki Bey to the khedive, Paris, October 25, 1904, Abbas II Papers, Durham University, F. 40/554.
44. Mehmed Cemil, *Tarihçe-i Ahrardan*, 39.
45. Edhem Ruhi must have spent three months in Bulgaria under the pseudonym Egyptian Hikmet Bey. He also related that he had left the administration of *Osmanlı* to Doctor Mekkeli Sabri, a former administrator of the CUP in Istanbul. All this information is taken from Edhem Ruhi's letter addressed to "muazzez üstad" (honorable master) and dated April 18, 1904, AQSh, 19/106–2//40/724.
46. *Osmanlı İttihad ve İnkılâp Cemiyeti'nin Nizamnâme-i Dahilisi* ([Cairo], 1320 [1904]).
47. The ambassador treated him as suspect. See BBA–HR.MTV. 710/38 (1900.12.7)/no. 330; 710/41 (1901.4.29)/no. 82–30; and 710/45 (1903.5.10)/no. 163–88; Mahmud Nedim to Tevfik Pasha, Vienna, March 1, 1901/no. 25178-38, BBA–HR.SYS. 1793/9 (original. 504/80), and May 19, 1903/no. 27558-163, BBA–HR.SYS. 1790/19 (original. 500/17).
48. See the interpellation presented by Pernerstorfer and fourteen other deputies, dated September 25, 1903, Allgemeines Verwaltungsarchiv/k.u.k Innenministerium Präsidiale, zl. 6842/1903. For the answer (Interpellationsbeantwortung) given by the government, see ibid., zl. 7304/1903. For further information, see "Die Ausweisung Dr. Djevdet's," *Berliner Börsen-Courrier*, November 1, 1903.
49. For more information about the event and the European press coverage, see "Scene at a Turkish Embassy," *Daily Chronicle*, September 9, 1903; "Incidente all'ambasciata Turca a Vienna," *Il Messagero*, September 16, 1903; "Le cas du docteur Djewdet bey," *Journal de Marseille*, September 18, 1903; "Die Szene auf der türkischen Botschaft," *Deutsche Zeitung*, September 18, 1904; "Der geohrfeigte Botschafter," *Wiener Morgen Zeitung*, January 16, 1904; BBA–YSHM, 457/44 (1321.6.23); and BBA–HR.MTV. 710/48 (1903.9.14)/no. 343–173.
50. "Die Ausweisung Djevdet Bey aus der Schweiz," *Reichswehr*, November 3, 1904.
51. [Ahmed Rıza], "Şundan Bundan," *Şûra-yı Ümmet*, no. 38 (October 6, 1903), 3–4. For the official view of the CPU on Abdullah Cevdet and his activities, see Dr. Nâzım to Macid Bey, dated [Paris], May 10, [1]907/no. 292, *Muhaberat Kopyası* 307–8. The only article defending Abdullah Cevdet was published by members of the old CUP organization. See "L'incident de L'Ambassade ottoman," *La Fédération Ottomane*, no. 4 (October 19, 1903), [2].
52. Abdullah Cevdet, *Hadd-ı Te'dib: Ahmed Rıza Bey'e Açık Mektub* (Paris, 1903).
53. See Haydar Bey to Münir Pasha, Geneva, August 10, 1904/no. 184, Archives of the Turkish Embassy in Paris, D. 287.
54. Haydar Bey to Münir Pasha, Geneva, May 14, 1904/no. 142, ibid.
55. Haydar Bey to Münir Pasha, Geneva, July 18, 1904/no. 165, ibid. See also Zeki Bey to the khedive, Paris, April 16, 1904, Abbas II Papers, Durham University, F. 40/501–502.
56. See Edhem Ruhi, "Bir Hatve Daha!" *Osmanlı*, no. 136, 1; and Edhem Ruhi, "Ümid-i İnkılâb," *Osmanlı*, no. 142 (December 8, 1904), 1–2.
57. Mehmed Cemil, *Tarihçe-i Ahrardan*, 45.
58. "Nizamnâme-i Esasî," *Osmanlı*, no. 136, 2–3.
59. "Açık Muhabere: 'Âlem Yaldızlı Hab Yutmuyor' Diye Yazan Muâhîz-i Garib'e," *Osmanlı*, no. 138 (September 5, 1904), 4; and Mehmed Cemil, *Tarihçe-i Ahrardan*, 49.
60. See "Açık Muhabere," *Osmanlı*, no. 139 (September 20, 1904), 4: "To the acting director of the fourth branch Mr. Mehmed M.: You have unnecessarily hastened. The reason behind the detainment is portentous. The details are being written. . . . To the directorship of the third branch: The FFr 200 donation bestowed by member no. 2 had been previously received through Sebatî. . . . To the directorship of the second branch: What the hell are you doing? Is this the time for resting and pondering? Your response is important. Think it over carefully because the honor and the future of the committee is at stake. To the fifth and sixth branches: Why has no clear-cut answer been given?"

The sympathizers in Bulgaria, described as branch members by *Osmanlı* in an attempt to delude the Ottoman diplomats, soon after ceased sending donations to Geneva. There were six sympathizers in the so-called central branch in Ruse. See Mehmed Cemil, *Tarihçe-i Ahrardan*, 45, 49.

61. "İhtar-ı Mahsus," *Osmanlı*, no. 134, 4.

62. Haydar Bey made the following remark: "The aforesaid Abdullah Cevdet came here to carry out an outstanding blackmail plan by initiating various maneuvers ... and exerted his best efforts to demonstrate to us that he had established a new committee and had become the leader of this fictitious organization." See Haydar Bey to Münir Pasha, Geneva, August 21, 1904/no. 191, Archives of the Turkish Embassy in Paris, D. 287.

63. Edhem Ruhi, "İhtar," *Osmanlı*, no. 137 (August 12, 1904), 4.

64. *Ethem Ruhi Balkan Hatıraları-Canlı Tarihler* 6, 29–30.

65. Haydar Bey to Münir Pasha, Geneva, September 20, 1904/no. 209, Archives of the Turkish Embassy in Paris, D. 287.

66. "Edebiyat: Ey Ebnâ-yı Vatan!" *Osmanlı*, no. 136, 4. Republished in [Süleyman Nazif], *Gizli Figanlar* (Cairo, 1906), 16.

67. See, for example, "Sâ'ika-i İntikam," *Osmanlı*, no. 137, 4; and "Rusya'da Islahat," *Osmanlı*, no. 142, 4.

68. BBA–YEE, 15/74–18–ç/74/15. The Young Turks in Romania provided the dynamite. See İbrahim Temo, *İttihad ve Terakki Cemiyetinin Teşekkülü ve Hidemati Vataniye ve İnkılâbi Milliye Dair Hatıratım* (Medgidia, 1939), 156–57. Temo's account is quite different from Edhem Ruhi's.

69. The documents are a telegram by Muḥammad ʿAlī Ḥalīm Pasha asking Edhem Ruhi whether the assassination plan was carried out; a second telegram from the pasha dated September 20, 1904, reading "Is the surgery going to be applied to the patient?", and his two letters dated October 7 and October 22, 1904, respectively. See BBA–YEE, 15/74–18–ç/74/15.

70. Jean Longuet, "L'attentat contre le Sultan: l'auteur est un turc—entretien avec le docteur Abdullah Djevded—un représentant du parti libéral turc," *L'Humanité*, July 29, 1905. The Ottoman diplomats paid great attention to this interview. See Ahmed Tevfik Pasha to Âsım Bey, Berlin, August 10, 1995/no. 1446, *Umum Kayda Mahsus Defter*, BBA–YEE, 36/139–73–3/139/XIX.

71. "Genf," *Der Bund*, November 26, 1904. For the investigation made by the Swiss political police, see "Jungtürken 1902–P.P. 9a/54, October 26, 1904," Bundesarchiv-Bern, E. 21/14'248.

72. "The Attempt on the Sultan," *The Times*, July 29, 1905; "Plot to Kill the Sultan," *The New York Times*, July 29, 1905. The organ of the coalition described the organization in Constanţa as "the branch of the Turkish secret committee established by the opponents of the sultan in Constanţa." See "Abdülhamid'e Atılan Bomb[a]," *Şûra-yı Ümmet*, no. 80 (August 16, 1905), 1.

73. Muḥammad ʿAlī Ḥalīm Pasha, however, claimed that he had been duped and cajoled by Edhem Ruhi and lost Lt 500. See Nihad Reşad's letter dated November 2, 1904, in Türk İnkılâp Tarihi Enstitüsü Arşivi 82/18329. For Edhem Ruhi's account, see "İttihatçılığın Temelini Atanlar," *Yakın Tarihimiz* 2, no. 25 (August 16, 1962), 366–67.

74. For its establishment, see Archives d'État-Genève/Chancellerie, B. 8, 95. The Ottoman government took measures against its circulation. See BBA–YMGM, 289/57 (1324.B.21).

75. This was underscored by Abdullah Cevdet in the prefatory article. See Abdullah Cevdet, "İctihad," *İctihad*, no. 1 (September 1, 1904), 1; and La Direction, "Avant-Propos," *Idjtihad*, no. 1, 1. The European press also testified to this fact. See "Le docteur Djewdet Bey," *Écho de Paris*, September 20, 1904.

76. See BBA–Mahremâne Müsveddat, no. 168 [1904]; Grand Vizier's office's note dated [November 5, 1904], BBA–HR.SYS. 1790/24 (original. 500/17); the Ministry of Justice's note dated March 7, 1905/no. 245, enclosed with Tevfik Pasha to Münir Pasha, March 15, 1905/no. 311-5, BBA–HR.SYS. 1790/27 (original. 500/17); and BBA–BEO/Hariciye Giden, 187-5/43; 1318 [November 6, 1904]/183320; 6 [March 12, 1905]/189421. He was later tried by a court in Istanbul *in contumaciam* and sentenced to serve a life term. See "İstinaf

Müdde'i-yi Umumiliği'nden," *Ceride-i Mahakim-i Adliye*, no. 348 (March 4, 1905), 2. *İctihad* was banned too. See BBA–YMGM, 289/57 (1324.B.21).

77. Haydar Bey to Münir Pasha, Geneva, August 21, 1904/no. 191; and September 14, [1]904/ no. 207, Archives of the Turkish Embassy in Paris, D. 287.

78. Haydar Bey to Münir Pasha, Geneva, August 26, [1]904/no. 198, ibid.

79. For his role in the movement, see İbrahim Temo to Karl Süssheim, Medgidia, September 2, 1933, Nachlaß Süssheim. See also the draft of an Affaires étrangères note dated Paris, June 9, 1900, AE–NS–T, 3 (1899–1901), 202.

80. See Abdülhakim Hikmet, *Külliyat-ı Hikmet* 3: *Rüya veya Hudâ-negerde Hakikat-ı Müstakbele* (Geneva, 1904), esp. 31–32. Ironically the pamphlet was banned by the palace. See BBA–YEE–Kâmil Paşa Evrakına Ek I, 86/22, 2182 (1322.7.18). Abdülhalim Hikmet later continued to write for various opposition journals. See, for example, A[bdülhalim] Hikmet, "İran Terakkiyâtı," *Hilâfet*, no. 107 (May 1, 1906), 2–3. For further information about the event, see Nihad Reşad's letter dated November 2, 1904, in Türk İnkılâb Tarihi Enstitüsü Arşivi, 82/18329; and Zeki Bey's letter to the khedive dated October 26, 1904, Abbas II Papers, Durham University, F. 40/560 ff.

81. Alfred von Bülow to Graf Ernst Bernhard von Bülow, Bern, November 5, 1904/no. 66, A. 18559, PAAA, 733/3, Die Jungtürken, 198 (Bd. 4–5). See also "Vermischtes," *Thurgauer Zeitung*, November 2, 1904.

82. "Bravo La Suisse!" *Le Peuple de Genève*, October 18, 1904.

83. See Edhem Ruhi, "Abdülhamid'in Aleyhimize Da'vası," *Osmanlı*, no. 141 (November 15, 1904), 2; and "Choses de Turquie," *Tribune de Genève*, September 17, 1904.

84. BBA–YSHM, 482/27 (6.10.1322); BBA–HR.MTV. 710/54 (1904.11.15)/no. 9–30; 710/55 (1904.11.29)/no. 11; and 710/56 (1904.11.29)/no. 11–31; Münir Pasha to Tevfik Pasha, Bern, November 5, 1904/no. 315–9, BBA–HR.SYS. 1790/25 (original. 500/17); "L'expulsion du Dr. Djevdet," *Journal de Nyon*, November 2, 1904; "Les expulsions politiques," *Le Peuple de Genève*, November 3, 1904; "Genf," *Schweizer freie Presse*, November 3, 1904; "Le cas du Dr. Djevdet," *La Suisse*, November 3, 1904; "Bundesrat," *Täglicher Anzeiger*, November 5, 1904; and "Schweiz," *Frankfurter Zeitung*, November 9, 1904.

85. He collected the notes that he had sent to Swiss dailies in a pamphlet. See Abdullah Djevdet, *Droit d'asile en Suisse* (Geneva, 1905). It received positive reviews; see "Droit d'asile en Suisse," *Le Radical*, February 19, 1905. See also *Guguss*, no. 3 (December 5, 1904); and Djevdet (Dr.), *Réponse au Journal de Genève* (Geneva, 1904), 1–2. The declaration made by the members of the coalition, claiming that Abdullah Cevdet had not been a prominent figure in the movement and was not in the position of representing it, overshadowed this favorable approach. See "Die Ausweisung des Dr. Djewdet Abdullah," *Der Bund*, October 30, 1904.

86. The journal was published by Abdurrahman Bedirhan and Hüseyin Tosun. See Server Bediî [İlhami Safa], "Haftanâme," *İctihad*, no. 100 [April 16, 1914], 2261; and Abdullah Cevdet, "*Osmanlı İdaresi'ne*," *Osmanlı*, no. 141, 3. The First Chamberlain's office warned the Paris embassy about Abdullah Cevdet's possible publication activities in Paris. See Âsım Bey to Münir Pasha, August 1, [1]905, *Umum Kayda Mahsus Defter* (1321), BBA–YEE, 36/139-73-3/139/ XIX.

87. See Nuri Bey to the First Chamberlain's office, Cairo [September 8, 1905]/no. 1871, *Umum Kayda Mahsus Defter* (1321), BBA–YEE, 36/139-73-3/139/XIX; and the coded telegram to the First Chamberlain's office [September 8, 1905], BBA–BEO/Mısır Fevkâlâde Komiseri Gazi Ahmed Muhtar Paşa'dan Vürûd Eden, 746–36/5. For Abdullah Cevdet's explanation of the events, see Hey'et-i Tahririye, "Ka'rilerimize," *İctihad*, no. 9 (October 1905), 129–30. See also "Abdullah Cevdet 'İctihad'ı ile Mısır'da İctihada Başlıyor," *Hayat*, no. 59 (March 16 [29], 1906), 2.

88. "İhtar-ı Mahsus," *İctihad*, no. 4 (March 1905), 1.

89. "Avis," *Idjtihad*, no. 4, 1.

90. See *L'Humanité*, July 29, 1905, 1. The sultan too believed that the Young Turks had a hand in the attempt. See Whittall to O'Conor [Istanbul], September 20, 1905, O'Conor Papers, Churchill College, Cambridge, 6/1/53. The central organ of the coalition informed

its readership about this claim. See F[erid], "İşti'âl," *Şûra-yı Ümmet*, no. 81 (August 31, 1905), 3. This claim, however, was denied by other Young Turks, and those who had made it were accused of blackmail. See, for example, Hocazâde İzmirli Mehmed Ubeydullah, *Geçid* (Cairo, 1323 [1905]), 46. The members of the old CUP organization gave furious responses to these accusations. They used vague wording and could not prove that they had had a hand in the venture, however. See Döküntüler [?], *Uçurum* (Cairo, 1905), 10–12.

91. See "Attentat à la vie du Sultan," *Idjtihad*, no. 8 (July 1905), 129; and "L'auteur serait un Turc," *Pro Armenia* 5, no. 115 (August 1, 1905), 755. European dailies had informed their readers of such a possibility. See "The Attempt on the Sultan," *The Times*, August 10, 1905.

92. "Eine jungtürkische Denkschrift," *Vossische Zeitung*, December 31, 1905.

93. The translation of the petition was published in "Maktūb-i yakī az dānāyān: tarjumah-i 'ariża," *Ḥabl al-Matīn* 13, no. 38 (June 1, 1906), 19.

94. "Un document turc," *Pro Armenia* 5, no. 117 (September 1, 1906), 769. This journal later published another document allegedly authored by this committee. See "Une circulaire de l'association Hurriet aux ambassades," *Pro Armenia* 6, no. 125 (January 1, 1907), 834–35. The only reference to the organization in the Young Turk press was made by a Balkan Young Turk journal. See "İstanbul'da Hürriyet Komitesi," *Tuna*, no. 95 [January 5, 1906], 2.

95. Armenian journals attributed importance to this fictitious committee. See Pierre Quillard, "Victimes et bourreaux," *Pro Armenia* 6, no. 125, 830.

96. "Une proclamation révolutionnaire turque," *Le Courrier Européen*, no. 42 (August 25, 1905), 656; and Whittall to O'Conor [Istanbul], November 25, 1905, O'Conor Papers, Churchill College, Cambridge, 6/1/5.

97. BBA–YEE, 15/74–18–ç/74/15; BBA–BEO/Hariciye Giden, 187–5/43; 577 (mümtaze) [February 7, 1906]; BBA–BEO/Mümtaze Kalemi: Bulgaristan Evrakı II, A. MTZ (04), 135/49 (12.8.1323). He was given an additional FFr 2,000 as an imperial gift. See BBA–BEO/Dahiliye Giden, 104–3/53; 455 [April 22, 1905]/191247. See also his letter to Ali Şakir in Mehmed Cemil, *Tarihçe-i Ahrardan*, 50–51; and Bakkal Behzad, "Edeb," *Tuna*, no. 132 [February 22, 1906], 2–3. For Edhem Ruhi's own account, see Edhem Ruhi, "Harhara-i Ağraz," *Rumeli*, no. 11 [February 23, 1906], 2–4; and "Açık Mektub," *Balkan*, no. 111 [December 14, 1906], 1.

98. BBA–YMGM, 279/147 (1323.Ş.24); BBA–İrade-Hususî, B 1323/no. 657–17; and "Deux jeunes turcs," *Pro Armenia* 4, no. 89 (July 1, 1904), 535. Although he was later arrested by the Ottoman authorities, this incident was with regard to a Kurdish–Albanian feud in the capital and had nothing to do with the Young Turk movement. See Marschall von Bieberstein to von Bülow, Therapia, June 11, 1906, A. 10805; and Anl[age] II zu A. 4968 (Geneva, May 10, 1906), PAAA 943/5, Diverse Personalien, 159/4 (Bd. 1–2).

99. For these attempts, see Neville J. Mandel, *The Arabs and Zionism before World War I* (Berkeley, 1976), 9–16; Mim Kemal Öke, *Siyonizm ve Filistin Sorunu, 1880–1914* (Istanbul, 1981), 51–57; and David Vital, *Zionism: The Formative Years* (Oxford, 1982), 106 ff.

100. See *The Complete Diaries of Theodor Herzl* 3, ed. Raphael Patai, trans. Harry Zohn (New York, 1960), 889, 960; and Vámbéry to Herzl, August 24, 1900, and July 15, 1901, CZA, H VIII 870. Another Zionist leader who had been in touch with the Young Turks was Max Nordau. See Anna and Maxa Nordau, *Max Nordau: A Biography* (New York, 1943), 177, 193.

101. *Complete Diaries of Theodor Herzl* 4, 1417–18.

102. Abdullah Cevdet to Herzl, Vienna, February 16, 1903, CZA, H VIII 182/I.

103. *Complete Diaries of Theodor Herzl* 4, 1419. Abdullah Cevdet and Şükrü Pasha set up further meetings in March 1903 to discuss the matter. See Abdullah Cevdet to Herzl, Vienna, March 4, 5, and 7, 1902, CZA, H VIII 182/I.

104. Abdullah Cevdet to Herzl, Vienna, February 20 and 23, 1903, ibid.

105. Abdullah Cevdet to Herzl, Vienna, March 1, 1903. See also his undated note to Herzl informing him of his receipt of recent "news giving very good signals." Ibid.

106. *Complete Diaries of Theodor Herzl* 4, 1424.

107. See the note entitled "Extrait d'une lettre de Fr. de 16 Mars 1903 adressée au Dr. D[jevdet]" and written on *Die Welt* letterhead. CZA, H VIII 182/I.

108. Abdullah Cevdet to Herzl, Vienna, April 11, 1903, and London, May 9, 1903, ibid.
109. Abdullah Cevdet to Herzl, London, May 16, 1903, ibid. Many years later Abdullah Cevdet expressed a similar opinion on Herzl and his activities. See Abdullah Djevdet, "Büyük 'İdéaliste'ler: Dr. Th[eodor] Herzl," *İçtihat*, no. 300 (July 1, 1930), 5411–12.
110. See Abdullah Cevdet to Nordau, [Paris], May 29, 1903, CZA, A 119/133. Obviously during this period a meeting between Ahmed Rıza and Abdullah Cevdet was out of the question. Abdullah Cevdet made similar comments on the "Turco-Jewish cause" to Herzl. See Abdullah Cevdet to Herzl, Vienna, August 1, 1903, CZA, H VIII 182/II.
111. Abdullah Cevdet to Herzl, June 14, 1903, ibid.
112. *Complete Diaries of Theodor Herzl* 4, 1508.
113. Abdullah Cevdet to Herzl, Vienna, July 16, 1903, CZA, H VIII 182/I.
114. Âdil Bey to Herzl, Constantinople, July 22, [1]903, CZA, H VIII 5a/H 930.
115. Âdil Bey to Herzl, Constantinople, August 6, 1903, ibid.
116. Âdil Bey to Herzl, August [?], 1903, ibid.
117. Abdullah Cevdet to Herzl, Vienna, August 8, 1903, CZA, H VIII 182/II.
118. Abdullah Cevdet to Herzl, Vienna, August 10, 1903, ibid.
119. Âdil Bey to Abdullah Cevdet, Istanbul, August 18, 1903, passed on to Herzl by the latter, ibid. See also Âdil Bey's letters to Herzl, Prinkipio, August 8, [1]903, and Constantinople, August 14, 1903, CZA, H VIII 5a/H 930.
120. Abdullah Cevdet to Julie Herzl, Vienna, August 18, 1903, CZA, H VIII 182/II.
121. Both drafts were undated and must have been written on August 23, 1903, ibid.
122. See Abdullah Cevdet to Herzl, September 5, 7, 25, and October 10, 1903, ibid. Abdullah Cevdet continued using optimistic language: "Un avenir *proche* est à nous."
123. See the telegram from Reich to Herzl dated August 15, 1903/no. 48807, ibid. Abdullah Cevdet denied that he had sent a telegram asking for help. See his letter to Herzl, London, October 2, 1903, ibid.
124. Ibid.
125. Abdullah Cevdet to Herzl, Geneva, April 4, 1904, ibid.
126. Abdullah Cevdet to Nordau, Paris, March 24, 1904, CZA, A 119/177.
127. Abdullah Cevdet to Nordau, Geneva, September 11, 1904, ibid. Abdullah Cevdet maintained that his journal would become "l'organe de la [*sic*] parti modérée et constitutionelle en Turquie."
128. See J. M[ax] Nordau, "Le Sionisme," *Idjtihad*, no. 8, 128. For Abdullah Cevdet's favorable comments about the Jews, see Abdullah Djevdet, "Une profession de foi," *Ictihad*, no. 6 (May 1905), 88.
129. See M. Şükrü Hanioğlu, *The Young Turks in Opposition* (New York, 1995), 154.
130. *Complete Diaries of Theodor Herzl* 4, 1614–16.
131. Ibid., 1615.
132. Ibid., 1616–17.
133. Ibid., 1618–19: "I have sent Kahn and Levontin to Constantinople. If they return *bredouille* . . . , there will follow Tell's second arrow: Ali Nuri."
134. Ibid., 1619–21.
135. See de Lormais to Nordau on behalf of Sabahaddin Bey, January 30, 1906, CZA, A 119/177. Nordau met with Ahmed Fazlı, the secretary of Sabahaddin Bey's league. See Jacobson to Wolffsohn, Constantinople, February 12, 1909/no. 325, CZA, Z2/7.
136. Sabahaddin Bey's activities before the Young Turk Revolution of 1908 were praised by Zionist organs. See "Brief aus Konstantinopel: Prinz Sabahaddin," *Die Welt* 12, no. 37 (September 18, 1908), 8. Following the revolution, the Zionist leadership observed Sabahaddin Bey's activities with great interest. See Marmorek to Wolffsohn, November 21, 1908, CZA, W 94.
137. Ahmed Rıza's letter to the khedive, dated October 24, 1901, in Şerif Paşa, *İttihad ve Terakki'nin Sahtekârlıklarına, Denaetlerine Bülend Bir Sada-yı Lâ'netimiz* (Paris [1911]), 23.
138. Mohamed Farag, "To the Editor of the 'Egyptian Gazette,'" *Juhayna*, no. 24 (March 20, 1902), 8.
139. Cromer to Lansdowne, Cairo, April 14, 1902/no. 59 (confidential). Almost identical information is given in "Note sur l'Imprimerie 'Osmanieh,'" prepared by a certain Sfer for

H. Boyle and enclosed with the latter's letter to Cromer dated Ambleside, November 6, 1909, Cromer Papers, PRO/F.O. 633/11.

140. Gazi Ahmed Muhtar Pasha to the Grand Vizier's office, April 15, 1902/no. 997, BBA–BEO/Mümtaze Kalemi: Mısır, 15/B, 59 (1320.1.6). See also the note sent to both the Grand Vizier's and the First Chamberlain's offices, Cairo, April 15, 1902, BBA–YEE, 31/160-11/160/87.

141. See the "Memorandum about certain Turkish Papers left at the Agency in Cairo," by Cromer, dated August 1907 [1909?], and Boyle to Cromer, August 19, 1909, Cromer Papers, PRO/F.O. 633/11. Unfortunately, I could not find any clue about the fate of these papers. In the old F.O. indexes there is a reference reading "Question of papers left in Cairo re: Ottomans (16/5063A, 6381)." This can be converted to F.O. 371/659; however, as was stated by the British authorities (see PRO/F.O. 371/659, files 6831 and 5063: Gorst to Lowther, Cairo, February 13, 1909, enclosed with Gorst to Grey, Cairo, February 13, 1909/no. 13; and Lowther to Grey, January 29, 1909/no. 62) these were the personal papers of Gazi Ahmed Muhtar Pasha which the Ottoman police attempted to seize and which were sealed and sequestered by an order of an Egyptian court. A minute on the second document reading "Doubtless Muhtar Pasha's correspondence contains many interesting secrets but probably they will never see the light. L[ouis] M [allet] & R. P. M [axwell]" gives us a hint about what had happened to the papers of the Young Turks. Most likely these Young Turk papers did not reach London officially, even though the writer to Cromer refers to an F.O. bag. Given the glibness with which state papers were appropriated by high-ranking officials, Cromer may well have kept them.

142. Cromer to Lansdowne, Cairo, April 14, 1902/no. 59, PRO/F.O. 78/5226.

143. Cromer's "Memorandum about certain Turkish papers left at the Agency in Cairo," Cromer Papers, PRO/F.O. 633/11.

144. Decipher by Cromer, Cairo, April 11, 1902/no. 42, PRO/F.O. 78/5230. A copy of this decipher was sent to the British embassy in Istanbul. See PRO/F.O. 195/2129.

145. Sanderson to Cromer, April 12, 1902, PRO/F.O. 78/5229. Lansdowne's minute on Cromer's decipher no. 42 was as follows: "I approve of your action which was no doubt necessary in the public interest. For the present I think it better not to trouble you with questions but we may receive protests and you should be prepared to supply us with full information as to urgency employed and advice upon which you acted." PRO/F.O. 78/5229.

146. Ḥannā Wahba's telegram, dated Cairo, April 17, 1902, PRO/F.O. 78/5229.

147. See the draft of Sanderson's decipher to Cromer, April 17, 1902/no. 35, PRO/F.O. 78/5229.

148. Cromer's decipher, Cairo, April 18, 1902/no. 47, PRO/F.O. 78/5230.

149. The minutes on the telegram are as follows: "Copy to Cairo. Ack[nowledge] by post saying enquiries shall be made. THS [Thomas Sanderson]," and "No answer. See Lord Cromer's tel. 47." PRO/F.O. 78/5229. Lansdowne's minute on Cromer's decipher no. 47 read: "Leave Mr. Hanna Wahba's telegram unacknowledged. L[ansdowne]." PRO/F.O. 78/5230.

150. See the two dispatches sent by Cogordan to Delcassé on April 14, 1902, AE–NS–T, 4 (1902–1904), 88–89 and 90; and von Müller to von Bülow, Cairo, April 17, 1902/no. 40, A. 6522, and April 25, 1902/no. 45 (vertraulich); A. 6933, PAAA, 733/3, Die Jungtürken, 198 (Bd. 4–5). For the reaction by the Ottoman government, see the draft of the telegram sent by the Grand Vizier's office to Gazi Ahmed Muhtar Pasha, May 8, 1902/no. 870, BBA–BEO/ Mümtaze Kalemi: Mısır, A. MTZ (05), 15/B, 69 (1320.2.2).

151. See "Müessir Bir Zayâ'," *Anadolu,* no. 1 (April 24, 1902), 4; and Mehmed Kadri Nâsıh, *Sarayih* (Paris, 1910 [1911?]), 14–15.

152. Coded telegram from Âbidin Bey to the First Chamberlain's office, May 8, 1902, BBA–BEO/Mümtaze Kalemi Mısır, 15/B, 71 (1320.2.6). See also Avram Galanti, *Küçük Türk Tetebbu'lar* (Istanbul, 1925), 132. In another document it was asserted that "an individual named Convert Şevket [wanted] to reestablish the publishing house and republish *Kanun-i Esasî.*" See the khedive's coded telegram to the First Chamberlain's office dated [April 28, 1902] and enclosed with Tahsin Bey's note dated [April 29, 1902], and the Grand Vizier's office's dispatch to the Ministry of the Interior, BBA–BEO/Mümtaze Kalemi: Mısır, 38/17 (1325.4.1).

153. Memorandum by the Ministry of the Interior dated May 15, 1902, BBA–BEO/Mümtaze Kalemi: Mısır, A. MTZ (05), 15/B, 71 (1320.2.6).

154. See Hanioğlu, *The Young Turks*, 137.

155. [Tarsusîzâde Münif], "Bir Türk Kocası," *Anadolu*, no. 4 (June 7, 1902), 1–2. For similar themes, see "Bir Türk Karısından Oğluna," *Anadolu*, no. 5 (June 21, 1902), 1; and "Bir Türk Hocası," *Anadolu*, no. 8, August 6, 1902, 1. All these articles were later collected in a pamphlet. See [Tarsusîzâde Münif], *Türk Sözü Anadolu Ağzı* ([Cairo, 1904?]). He had previously published similar Turkist articles in the journals that he edited. For a striking example, see "Our programme," *Osmanlı* (2), no. 1 (December 1897), 8: "But we Turks, we who are members of the ruling race, we who know more than other peoples who compose our Empire, we of whom alone the government is formed."

156. "Biraz da Derdleşelim," *Anadolu*, no. 10 (September 18, 1902), 3–4.

157. BBA–YEE, Kâmil Paşa Evrakına Ek I, 86/17, 1610 (1320.6.14).

158. Gazi Ahmed Muhtar Pasha to the Grand Vizier's office, Cairo, February 5, 1903/no. 608-188, BBA–BEO/Mısır Hidiviyet-i Celilesinin Muharrerat Defteri (71)-1032–68/4. See also "Dersaadet Cinayet Mahkemesi'nden," *Ceride-i Mahakim-i Adliye*, no. 129 (January 1, 1903), 2.

159. Grand Vizier's office to Gazi Ahmed Muhtar Pasha, March 15, 1903/no. 788-203, BBA–BEO/Mısır Hidiviyet-i Celilesinin Muharrerat Defteri (71)-1032-68/4; and Ministry of Justice to the Grand Vizier's office [June 10, 1903]/no. 240, BBA–BEO/Mümtaze Kalemi: Mısır, A. MTZ (05), 16/A, 15 (1321.3.19).

160. Undated [November 1903] letter from Ahmed Saib to Ahmed Rıza, Private Papers of Ahmed Rıza (1). An article published after the Young Turk Revolution about the journal provided the following names as founders: Ali Kemal, Hasan Fehmi, Ali Su'ad, Şerafeddin Mağmumî, Necmeddin Ârif, and Celâleddin Ârif. See Hasan Fehmi, "Ali Kemal Bey—*Şûra-yı Ümmet*," *Serbestî*, [December 14, 1908]. A source close to the Young Turks in Cairo gives the names of Necmeddin Ârif and Şerafeddin Mağmumî. See Walī al-Dīn Yakan, *al-Ma'lūm wa al-majhūl* 1 (Cairo, 1909), 67. Halil Halid who wrote for the journal underscores the roles played by Necmeddin Ârif and Celâleddin Ârif in its publication. See Halil Halid, "Abdülhak Hamid Bey'in Gayr-ı Münteşir Mektublarından," *Mihrab* 1 [1908], 232–33.

161. "İfade-i Mahsusa," *Türk*, no. 10 (January 7, 1904), 1.

162. "*Türk*," *Türk*, no. 1 (November 5, 1903), 1. In many other articles Turks were described as "the British of the Orient." For an example, see Türkmen, "Fezâil-i Milliye," *Türk*, no. 65 (January 26, 1905), 1–2.

163. For the best examples, see "İstiklâl-i Osmanî: Altıyüz Beşinci Sene-i Devriye," *Türk*, no. 12 (January 20, 1904), 1; and "Hey'et-i İdaremizin Nutku," *Türk*, no. 15 (February 11, 1904), 1–2.

164. "*Türk*'ün Üçüncü Senesi," *Türk*, no. 104 (November 2, 1905), 1. For the letters sent to the journal by Cretan and Bosnian Muslims and by Turks residing in Bulgaria, see Akdağlı Ahmed,"Kahire'de Münteşir *Türk* Ceride-i Feridesine, an Hanya, 2 Nisan Sene 1320," *Türk*, no. 26 (April 28, 1904), 4; "İzzeddin Biçâregânı," *Türk*, no. 89 (July 13, 1905), 2; Doğan, "Ruscuk'dan," *Türk*, no. 51 (October 20, 1904), 4; and "Bosna'dan," *Türk*, no. 51, 4. The journal gave nationalist recommendations to the Cretan Muslims and the Turks residing in Bulgaria (see "Yine Girid İslâm Kardeşlerimiz İçin," *Türk*, no. 100 (October 6, 1905), 1; Oğuz, "Bulgaristan'da Müslümanlar," *Türk*, no. 39 (July 28, 1904), 1). It instructed the Turks in Bulgaria to establish a Turkish nationalist party instead of voting for various Bulgarian parties that had been trying to win them over (see Turgud, "Bend-i Mahsus," *Türk*, no. 31 [June 2, 1904], 1); and finally it told the Bosnian Muslims that their duty "is not to become Austrians but to stick to the Turks." See "Musahabe: Bosnalılara," *Türk*, no. 148 (November 29, 1906), 2.

165. "Matbaa-i Türk," *Türk*, no. 41 (August 11, 1904), 1.

166. For the checks sent by Fevzi Kemal from Bosnia and Barutçuzâde İbrahim from Canea (Crete), see "Açık Muhabere," *Türk*, no. 8 (December 24, 1903), 4. Mehmed Macid and Nesib Beys from Crete and İplikçi İzzet from Ruse subscribed to the journal. See "Açık Muhabere," *Türk*, no. 7 (December 17, 1903), 4.

167. "Teşekkür ve Tebrik," *Türk*, no. 10, 3. For the journal's impact on nationalist Tatar intelligentsia, see Zarevand [Zaven and Vartouhie Nalbandian], *Turtsiia i panturanizm* (Paris,

1930), 160. Interestingly, when Yusuf Akçura met with Tatar students in Cairo and questioned them about the journals they read, *Türk* was the only one they mentioned. See Musa bin Abdullah, "Mısır el-Kahire'den Mektub," *Hayat*, no. 49 (August 12 [25], 1905), 4. It seems, however, that other Young Turk journals were also read by these students. See "*Sancak* Gazetesi Müdîriyeti'ne," *Sancak*, no. 69 (February 15, 1907), 3.

168. The most striking example is the tribute paid to Pávlos Melás, who was also acclaimed by the coalition's organ. See Tuğrul, "Kıbrıs-Lefkoşe: Rumların Milliyetperverliği," *Türk*, no. 58 (December 8, 1904), 3. Similar articles dwelt upon Greek nationalism and presented it as an example to follow. See Vecdî, "Kıbrıs-Lefkoşe, 26 Nisan Sene [1]906: Yunanilerin Sene-i Devriye-i İstiklâlleri," *Türk*, no. 130 (May 17, 1906), 3–4; and *Türk*, no. 132 (May 31, 1906), 4.

169. Siyasî [Ahmed Kâmi], "Cehalet-i Siyasiyemiz," *Türk*, no. 17 (February 25, 1904), 2. For other articles in the same vein, see "İmtiyazât-ı Ecnebiye," *Türk*, no. 18 (March 3, 1904), 1; "Mes'ele-i Şarkiye–7: Hakk-ı Müdahale yahud Vazife-i Adem-i Müdahale," *Türk*, no. 22 (March 31, 1904), 1–2; and [Rıza Şakir], "Rumeli—Cihan-ı Beşeriyet," *Türk*, no. 175 (August 26, 1907), 1–2.

170. "Havâdis-i Dahiliye," *Türk*, no. 19 (March 10, 1904), 2.

171. "Yirminci Asırda Ehl-i Salib," *Türk*, no. 109 (December 14, 1905), 1.

172. "İzmir Hâdisesi ve İngiliz Gazeteleri," *Türk*, no. 155 (February 7, 1907), 1–2. In this article Damad Mahmud Pasha and Murad Bey were criticized as well.

173. Osmancık, "Avrupa Nazarında Türklük," *Türk*, no. 111 (December 28, 1905), 2.

174. "Açık Muhabere: Girid'de İbrahim Edhem Beyefendi'ye," *Türk*, no. 7, 4.

175. See "İstiklâl-i Osmanî: Altıyüz Beşinci Sene-i Devriye," *Türk*, no. 12, 1; "Hey'et-i İdaremizin Nutku," *Türk*, no. 15, 1–2; "Eyyâm-ı Mahsusa: Prut," *Türk*, no. 38 (July 21, 1904), 1; "Eyyâm-ı Mahsusa: Plevne," *Türk*, no. 40 (August 4, 1904), 1–2; "Eyyâm-ı Mahsusa: Kosova Muzafferiyeti," *Türk*, no. 1, 2–3, and no. 52 (October 27, 1904), 1; "İstiklâl-i Osmanî: Altıyüz Altıncı Sene-i Devriye Şenliği," *Türk*, no. 66 (February 2, 1905), 1–2; and "İstiklâl-i Osmanî: Altıyüz Yedinci Sene-i Devriye Şenliği," *Türk*, no. 116 (February 1, 1906), 1.

176. "Eyyâm-ı Mahsusa: Mısır'da Yavuz Sultan Selim," *Türk*, no. 20 (March 17, 1904), 1–2.

177. See "Zayâ'-i Elîm—Yâd-ı Mâzi," *Türk*, no. 110 (December 21, 1905), 2; and Münzevî, "Yâd-ı Mâzi," *Türk*, no. 115 (January 25, 1906), 3–4. The Turkish press in Bulgaria praised this initiative, see "Tebşîr ve Teşekkür-i Azîm," *Tuna*, no. 111 [January 25, 1906], 2; and "Yâd-ı Mâzi: Mısır'da Sinan Paşa Türbesi," *Tuna*, no. 127 [February 12, 1906], 2–3.

178. [Yusuf Akçura], "Üç Tarz-ı Siyaset," *Türk*, no. 24 (April 14, 1904), 1 ff. This article and responses to it were published as a pamphlet by the Young Turks. See Yusuf Akçura, *Üç Tarz-ı Siyaset* (Cairo, 1907).

179. He later sent information concerning the Tatars and other Turkic peoples in Russia to *Şûra-yı Ümmet*. See his letter to Ahmed Rıza, Kazan, September 19, 1905, Private Papers of Yusuf Akçura. In an earlier letter Yusuf Akçura wrote that he was contacted by a member of the editorial board of *Türk* and was asked to provide information concerning the Turkic peoples in Russia. See his letter to Ahmed Rıza dated Kazan, December 19, 1903, Private Papers of Ahmed Rıza (1).

180. Yusuf Akçura, *Üç Tarz-ı Siyaset*, 39–40.

181. François Georgeon, *Aux origines du Nationalisme turc: Yusuf Akçura, 1876–1935* (Paris, 1980), 26. Niyazi Berkes had challenged this view by claiming that Akçura had used the terms "nation" and "race" interchangeably and that there had been no specific term meaning nation in the Ottoman intellectual jargon. See Niyazi Berkes, "Unutulan Adam," *Sosyoloji Konferansları* 14 (1976), 198–99. Contrary to what Berkes claimed, however, the term *millet*, which for many centuries meant "religious community," was recoined in the midnineteenth century by Ottoman intellectuals to convey the sense of "nation." Even in the prefatory article in *Hürriyet* the phrase "Turkish nation" was used. See [Namık Kemal], "Ḥubb al-waṭan min al-imān," *Hürriyet*, no. 1 (June 29, 1868), 1. For further discussion and examples, see David Kushner, *The Rise of Turkish Nationalism, 1876–1908* (London, 1977), 21–26. Akçura, besides using this term, employed the phrase "the Ottoman Turks" in referring to them, and he further used the term *ırk* (race) in the modern sense when he spoke of "the unification of the Turks, who are spread out over a large part of the Asian continent and the eastern

part of Europe, and whose language, race, and customs and, for the most part, even religion, are the same." Yusuf Akçura, *Üç Tarz-ı Siyaset*, 36. An eminent linguist confirms that Akçura used the term *ırk* in the modern sense. See Louis Bazin, "Turc *irq* 'Race': une contamination Arabo-Tartare," in *Mélanges linguistiques offerts à Maxime Rodinson*, ed. Christian Robin (Paris, 1985), 103–7.

182. Zarevand [Zaven and Vartouhie Nalbandian], *Turtsiia i panturanizm*, 42.

183. See his letter dated May 26, 1904 and republished in Yusuf Akçura, *Üç Tarz-ı Siyaset*, 41–56. Both Ali Kemal and Yusuf Akçura used stronger rhetoric when they had a second debate on Ottomanism and Turkism later. See Ali Kemal's article "Atâlet-i Fikriye," *Peyam*, May 9, 1914; and Yusuf Akçura's response in T[ürk] Y[urdu] [Yusuf Akçura], "*Peyam*'a Cevab," *Türk Yurdu* 6, no. 6 (May 28, 1914), 2202–7.

184. See his response republished in Yusuf Akçura, *Üç Tarz-ı Siyaset*, 57–80. Ahmed Ferid's political ideas are well examined in Masami Arai, "A Note on the Life and Thought of Ahmed Ferid Tek: with Special Reference to His Activities in the Young Turk Era," *The Journal of Sophia Asian Studies*, no. 13 (1995), 109–29.

185. Yusuf Akçura, *Üç Tarz-ı Siyaset*, 78.

186. "İfade-i Mahsusa," *Türk*, no. 78 (April 27, 1905), 2.

187. "Musahabe: Spencer'in Japonlar'a Vasiyetnâmesi," *Türk*, no. 23 (April [7], 1904), 4.

188. Veled Müslim, "Mektub-i Mahsus: Rusya'dan 9 Temmuz 1904," *Türk*, no. 42 (August 18, 1904), 3.

189. See "Hem Cidâl Hem Hasbihâl," *Türk*, no. 34 (June 23, 1904), 1.

190. Oğuz, "Rusya," *Türk*, no. 5 (December 3, 1903), 2. See also "Türklerde ve Tatarlarda Terakkiyât-ı Kalemiye," *Türk*, no. 136 (July 5, 1906), 4. By the same token the journal condemned the Russian policy of forcing Turkic peoples to replace their names with Christian ones. See Oğuz, "Rusya'da Müslümanlar," *Türk*, no. 60 (December 22, 1904), 1.

191. "Azerbeycan Türkleri," *Türk*, no. 158 (March 14, 1907), 1. This letter was originally sent to *İrşad* and also published by the Ruse-based Young Turk journal *Tuna*. See *Tuna*, no. 413 [February 9, 1907], 2.

192. Esirzâde, "Sibirya'dan," *Türk*, no. 76 (April 13, 1905), 3–4.

193. Türkistanlı Bir Tatar Çocuğu, "Kazan'dan," *Türk*, no. 116, 3.

194. Hüseyinzâde Ali to Abdullah Cevdet, Baku, March 18, 1905, Private Papers of Abdullah Cevdet.

195. "'A. Turanî' İmzalı Mektuba Cevab," *Türk*, no. 59 (December 8[15], 1904), 1. For Hüseyinzâde's criticism, see A[li] H[üseyinzâde], "Vekayi'-i Âleme Bir Nazar," *Füyûzat*, no. 2 (November 13 [26], 1904), 2; and A. Turanî [Hüseyinzâde Ali], "Bakü'den," *Türk*, no. 71 (March 9, 1905), 3.

196. "Kısm-ı Edebî: Lisanımız, Edebiyatımız," *Türk*, no. 2 (November 12, 1903), 3.

197. Bir İhtiyar Türk, "*Türk* Gazetesi Müdîrliği'ne," *Türk*, no. 35 (June 30, 1904), 3.

198. "Hem Cidâl Hem Hasbihâl," *Türk*, no. 36 (July 7, 1904), 2.

199. See Y[usuf] A[kçura], "Kısm-ı Edebî: Lisanda Terakki Medeniyetde Terakkidir," *Türk*, no. 45 (September 9, 1904), 3; and Türkmen, "Kısm-ı Edebî: Türk Edebiyatının Noksanları," *Türk*, no. 59, 1.

200. [Arminius] Vámbéry, "*Türk* Mu'teber Gazetesi'nin Müdîri'ne," *Türk*, no. 49 (October 6, 1904), 1. He attributed great importance to certain articles published in the journal. See Arminius Vámbéry, *Western Culture in Eastern Lands: A Comparison of the Methods Adopted by England and Russia in the Middle East* (London, 1906), 314, 328–29, and 343–45.

201. "Ruscuk'dan," *Türk*, no. 165 (June 6, 1907), 3.

202. "Afganistan'da Türkce," *Türk*, no. 7, 1.

203. "Resm-i Tevzi': Bir Refik-i Şefik-i Muhteremimiz Tarafından Âzâ-yı Mü'essise Nâmına Okunan Nutk-i İftitâhîyi Derc-i Sütûn-i Mefharet Eyliyoruz," *Türk*, no. 2, 1. The authors of the journal spearheaded the establishment of a charitable fund for poor Turks residing in Egypt. See Mahmud Muhtar Pasha's spy report dated Cairo, February 3, 1904, BBA–YEE, 15/74–7/74/15.

204. "Ermeniler," *Türk*, no. 17, 1. Pro-Armenian sources strongly criticized *Türk*'s viewpoint on Armenians. See Pierre Quillard, "Les Arméniens et le Régime hamidien," *Pro Ar-*

menia 4, no. 75 (December 15, 1903), 413–14; and idem, "Les vrais ennemis de L'Empire turc," *Pro Armenia* 4, no. 78 (February 1, 1904), 437–38.

205. "Türkler-Ermeniler," *Türk*, no. 2, 2.

206. "Memâlik-i Osmaniye'de Makedonyalılar ve Ermeniler," *Türk*, no. 4, 1. See also "Havâdis-i Hariciye," *Türk*, no. 34, 2.

207. See Uluğ, "Ermeniler," *Türk*, no. 110, 2. For similar articles, see Bir Osmanlı, "Ermeniler ve Ermeni Metâlibi," *Türk*, no. 99 (September 28, 1905), 1–2; "Türkler—Ermeniler," *Türk*, no. 171 (August 1, 1907), 1; and "Türkler—Ermeniler," *Türk*, no. 186 (November 21, 1907), 1–2. It is interesting that even Hüseyinzâde Ali, who was promoting Turkism through the journals *Hayat*, *Füyûzat*, and *Kaspii*, and who had praised former articles published in *Türk* in this vein (see, for example, "Haricî Haberler," *Hayat*, no. 87 [October 25 (November 7), 1905], 4) strongly criticized *Türk*'s rhetoric on this matter and maintained that "*Türk* . . . foams at the mouth, vents its rage about the Armenian question, adopts an extreme course, and goes astray." See "Mısır'da Çıkan *Türk* Gazetesi," *Hayat*, no. 29 (February 5 [18], 1906), 4.

208. "Türkler—Yahudiler," *Türk*, no. 6 (December 10, 1903), 1. It should be noted that some Ottoman Jews had initiated attempts similar to those promoted by the journal. [See BBA–BEO/Dahiliye Giden, 99-3/48; 1032/555 (June 9, 1900)/110871, 112507, and 116253. They later asked for official recognition from the Young Turks. See BBA–TFR.1.KNS. 10/930 (1326.9.17)]. After the Young Turk Revolution of 1908, Jewish leaders tried to give assurances to the Young Turks in a similar vein. See D[r] T[rietsch], "The Revolution in Turkey and Jewish Activities in Palestine," *The Jewish Review* 2, no. 7 (May 1911), 22–23.

209. See BBA–İrade-Hususî, S 1320/no. 46-205 and M 1321/no. 64-55; and BBA–BEO/Dahiliye Giden, 102-3/51; 311 [April 7, 1903]/152863. The sultan ordered the use of the term "the three provinces" instead.

210. "İstiklâl-i Osmanî: Altıyüz Yedinci Sene-i Devriye Şenliği," *Türk*, no. 116, 1. Strikingly, the employment of the term "Macedonia" by Khristo Delchev, a Bulgarian deputy from Serres, in the Ottoman Parliament after the Young Turk Revolution of 1908, caused strong protests on the part of nationalist CUP deputies. One of them, Halil Bey, said, "There is no term like Macedonia. That is to say the term Macedonia cannot be uttered in our assembly." The speaker, Ahmed Rıza, required Delchev "to replace the phrase with that of the three provinces." See "Meclis-i Meb'usanın Zabıt Ceridesidir: On Dokuzuncu İctima'," *Takvim-i Vekayi'*, no. 110 [February 2, 1909], 9–10.

211. See "al-Turk wa al-'Arab (1)," *al-Manār* 3, no. 8 (May 20, 1900), 169–72; and "al-Turk wa al-'Arab (2)," *al-Manār* 3, no. 9 (May 29, 1900), 193–98. Rashīd Riḍā's comment on the Young Turks was as follows: "We thank God that our great sultan His Eminence Abdülhamid II, may God support him, is the second king (the first one being Sultan Selim Yavuz) who realized the harm of ethnic fanaticism, and but for the fanaticism of the Turks he would have reversed the [prevailing] conditions and changed the social structure of the state. And we are all aware of the 'Young Turkey' party which was constituted to oppose His Majesty because his policy is not satisfactory to them. The corruptness of this evil party occupied His Majesty's thoughts and took a great deal of his precious time. Had it not been for them, this time would have been spent for the benefit of the state and the nation." See ibid., 197. Rashīd Riḍā employed similar and even stronger language against the CUP after the Young Turk Revolution, when relations between CUP leaders and Arab intellectuals became tense. See J[acques] Jomier, *Le commentaire Coranique du Manâr; tendances modernes de l'exégèse Coranique en Égypte* (Paris, 1954), 263.

212. [Şerafeddin Mağmumî], "Düşündüm ki," *Türk*, no. 7, 1. Some articles of Şerafeddin Mağmumî were republished by Azerbaijani nationalist organs. See, for example, Bir Türk [Şerafeddin Mağmumî], "*Türk* Düşünüyor ki," *Hayat*, no. 178 (August 11[24], 1906), 4. Bir Türk [Şerafeddin Mağmumî], "Düşündüm ki," *İrşad*, no. 174 (July 25 [August 7], 1906), 4. All his articles published in *Türk* were later collected and published as a pamphlet. See Şerafeddin Mağmumî, *Düşündüm ki* (Cairo, 1913). Following the Young Turk Revolution of 1908, he continued publishing his articles under the same rubric in dailies opposing the CUP policies. See, for example, Şerafeddin Mağmumî, "Düşündüm ki," *Hukuk-u Umumiye*, October 11, 1908; and "Düşündüm ki," *Serbestî*, [February 3, 1909].

213. "Daʿwa al-khilāfa: taʿrīb maqālat nushirat fī jarīdat (Turk) al-gharrāʾ," *al-Manār* 6, no. 24 (March 3, 1904), 954–58. The article starts with an Arabic translation of the article that had been published in *Türk*.

214. Ibid., 956–58.

215. Suriyeli R. A., "al-Daʿwā al-Jāhiliyya," *Türk*, no. 25 (April 21, 1904), 3–4.

216. "*Al-Manār*'a Cevab: Hilâfet ve Türkler," *Türk*, no. 23, 1–2.

217. "*Türk*," *Türk*, no. 25, 4.

218. "Al-Khilāfa aw al-Turk wa al-ʿArab," *al-Manār* 7, no. 2 (April 2, 1904), 70–74.

219. "*Al-Manār*'a İkinci Reddiye," *Türk*, no. 24, 2.

220. "*Al-Manār* Gazetesi," *Türk*, no. 28 (May 21, 1904), 3. To my knowledge there is no source that dwelt upon the debate between the two journals. Studies of Rashīd Riḍā assert that he developed an interest in Arab nationalism either after the Young Turk Revolution or during the First World War. For the first thesis, see Eliezer Tauber, "Muḥammad Rashīd Riḍā as Pan-Arabist Before World War I," *The Muslim World* 74, no. 2 (April 1989), 103 ff. For the second thesis, see J[acques] Jomier, "Les raisons de l'adhésion du Sayyed Rashid Rida au Nationalisme arabe," *Bulletin de l'Institut d'Egypte* 53–54 (1971–1973), 57–58. Two years after the Young Turk Revolution Rashīd Riḍā himself made the following comment on the debate: "Yes, it was indeed written a few years ago in the journal *Türk* which used to be published in Cairo, edited by a small group of Turkish intellectuals like Ali Kemal Bey and Celâleddin Ârif Bey. That journal went far in praising the Turkish race, referring to them as the governing nation, and in doing so they degraded the Arabs. . . . I only wrote that response to the journal *Türk* in the journal *Manār* lest our silence encourage that journal to utter further boasts that might inspire in the Egyptians and others a hatred of the Sublime State and an aversion to it. . . . But the authors of the journal had one more boast after my refutation and then their voice faded." See "al-ʿArab wa al-Turk: waʿtaṣimū biḥabli allāhi jamīʿan wa-lā tafarraqū," *al-Manār* 12, no. 12 (January 11, 1910), 913. On the other hand, the Panturkists later accused *al-Manār* of serving British interests. See *Büyük Üstaz-ı Muhterem Reşid Efendi İbrahim Cenablarının Hatırâlarından İmlâ Kılınub: Tarihin Unudulmuş Sahifeleri* (Berlin, 1933), 14–15.

221. Vámbéry, *Western Culture in Eastern Lands*, 275. He further underscored it in the same study; see 348–49. See also A[rminius] Vámbéry, "The Revolt in Arabia," *The Contemporary Review* 88 (November 1905), 680–81.

222. "Rusya'da Münteşir al-ʿAlam al-Islāmī Gazetesinde Görülmüştür," *Türk*, no. 132, 1. See also "Mikado'nun Şeref-i İslâm ile Müşerref Olması Şayiʿası," *Hayat*, no. 89 (April 24 [May 7], 1906), 3.

223. "Rêve realisable," *İctihad*, no. 12 (June 1906), 179–82.

224. See "'İctihad'-ı Garib," *Türk*, no. 142 (October 4, 1906), 1–2.

225. The book was published in Paris in 1905. Azoury's book and activities are well examined in the following sources: Elie Kedourie, *Arabic Political Memoirs and other Studies* (London, 1974), 107–23; and Stefan Wild, "Negib Azoury and His Book *Le Réveil de la nation Arabe*," in Marwan R. Buheiry, ed., *Intellectual Life in the Arab East, 1890–1939* (Beirut, 1981), 92–104. For detailed information about Azoury, see Mandel, *The Arabs and Zionism*, 50–53.

226. For the appeals, see Townshend to Townley, Adana, February 1, 1905/no. 5, PRO/ F.O. 195/2187. Two appeals were enclosed with this document. For another copy of this document that does not contain the appeals, see PRO/F.O. 78/5392. See also Eugène Jung, *Les puissances devant la Révolte arabe: la crise mondiale de demain* (Paris, 1906), 22–29; "Une Proclamation arabe," *Pro Armenia* 5, no. 103 (February 1, 1905), 658; and "League of the Arabian Fatherland," *Armenia* 1, no. 8 (May 1905), 36–37. Some specialists considered Azoury's pamphlet and appeals to be an important expression of Arab nationalism. See, for example, René Pinon, "Le conflit Anglo-Turc," *La Revue des Deux Mondes* 34 (1906), 163–64. For other authors who did not mention Azoury's work but used his analysis, see Gervais-Courtellement, "Le réveil de la Nation arabe dans l'Asie turque: au directeur du Temps," *Le Temps*, June 23, 1905; Jean Imbart de la Tour, "Le Nationalisme arabe," *Annales des Sciences Politiques* 21 (1906), 1–11. For another example speaking about the "réveil arabe"

without mentioning Azoury, see James Bryce, "Le Turc et l'Europe," *La Revue de Paris* 12/ 3 (May 15, 1905), 291. These kinds of remarks were quoted even by Bulgarian dailies. See Ottoman Commissioner's office in Bulgaria to the Ottoman Ministry of the Interior [May 2, 1905], BBA–BEO/Mümtaze Kalemi: Bulgaristan Tasnifi Evrakı II, A. MTZ (04), 128/52 (1322.2.27); BBA–BEO/Dahiliye Giden, 104–3/53; 553 [May 2, 1905]. Although these appeals were dispatched to the embassies and consuls and "have caused quite a stir amongst the [local] government officials," the British chargé d'affaires commented that he was "not aware that they have been distributed in any number in Constantinople." See Townshend to Townley, Adana, February 1, 1905/no. 5, enclosed with Townley to Lansdowne, Constantinople, February 14, 1905/no. 113, PRO/F.O. 78/5392. For the criticism by the French supplement, see "Insurrection arabe," *Mechveret Supplément Français*, no. 162 (April 1, 1905), 4; and "Le réveil de la Nation arabe," *Mechveret Supplément Français*, no. 165 (July 1, 1905), 4. It should be stated that although no overt condemnation was made in the official organ of the coalition, a veiled criticism appeared in an article written against Imām Yaḥyā. See "Innamā al-mu'minūna ikhwatun," *Şûra-yı Ümmet*, no. 90 (March 26, 1906), 1–2; excerpts from a letter written by an Ottoman Arab and previously published by *Türk* are given in the aforementioned article.

227. Osmanlı Bir Arab, "Devlet-i Osmaniye ve Arablar," *Türk*, no. 105 (November 9, 1905), 1–2. The article accused Azoury of being a French agent and discredited all his claims. The themes employed by the author were very similar to those of Farīd Kassāb in his book *Le nouvel Empire arabe: la Curie romaine et le prétendu péril juif universel: Réponse à M. N. Azoury bey* (Paris, 1906); but they lacked a focus on and refutation of Azoury's ideas concerning Jewish immigration to Palestine and Syria. (It should be noted that the Zionists later accused Azoury of authoring anti-Semitic and anti-Zionist books. See Jacobson to Wolffsohn, Constantinople, June 1, 1910, CZA Z2/15.) Farīd Kassāb's book and his other activities are well examined in Stefan Wild, "Ottomanism versus Arabism, the Case of Farid Kassab (1884–1970)," *Die Welt des Islams* 28 (1988), 607–27. Farīd Kassāb was congratulated by a Young Turk leader in Paris "who prepared a Turkish encyclopædia and was an advocate of decentralization." See ibid., 611. This is most likely Sabahaddin Bey, although he had never prepared such a work. *Türk* had previously published another article written by an Ottoman Arab criticizing Azoury's articles published in *al-Muqaṭṭam*. See Osmanlı Bir Arab, "Hakayık Nasıl Kalbediliyor?" *Türk*, no. 98 (September 21, 1905), 1. See also Un Arabe, "L'Insurrection arabe," *Mechveret Supplément Français*, no. 168 (October 1, 1905), 2. Azoury's pamphlet and ideas were praised by pro-Armenian journalists. See P[ierre] Quillard, "La renaissance du Peuple arabe," *Pro Armenia* 5, no. 105 (March 1, 1905), 676.

228. "Avrupa, Müslümanlar ve Türkler," *Türk*, no. 137 (July 12, 1906), 1.

229. See "Kıbrıs Mektubu," *Türk*, no. 81 (May 18, 1905), 4; and "Türkler ve Terakki: Merhale-i Sâlise," *Türk*, no. 114 (January 18, 1906), 4. The ideas in the second article were originally Sabahaddin Bey's.

230. [Rıza Şakir], "Şecaât Nedir?" *Türk*, no. 163 (May 23, 1907), 2.

231. As a representative example, see "Türkiye-İngiltere," *Türk*, no. 108 (December 7, 1905), 1. An interesting example in this field is the denunciations of Halil Halid, who, in an interview given to an Italian journalist, asserted that "all reasonable Ottomans are pro-British" (see "Halil Halid Efendi Tarafından Vârid Olan Mektubdan Mülâhhasen," *Türk*, no. 131 [May 24, 1906], 3). Another example is Muṣṭafā Kāmil Pasha's criticism of the British. See Mustafa Kâmil Paşa, "İngiliz ve İslâm," *Türk*, no. 78, 2.

232. See, for example, "Türkiye ve İngiltere," *Tercüman-ı Ahvâl-i Zaman*, no. 25 (March 13 [26], 1906), 2; and "Devlet-i Aliyye-İngiltere: *Türk* Gazetesinden İstihracen," *Tercüman-ı Ahvâl-i Zaman*, no. 41 (April 21 [May 4], 1906), 2. *Türk*'s many articles criticizing British policy toward the Ottoman Empire were also republished by Azerbaijani journals. See, for example, "Haricî Haberler: İngilizlerin Devlet-i Osmaniye Hakkındaki Yeni Fikirleri," *Hayat*, no. 80 (October 9 [22], 1905), 4; "Haricî Haberler," *Hayat*, no. 25 (January 31 [February 13], 1906), 4; "Yine Akabe Mes'elesi Hakkında," *Hayat*, no. 107 (May 18 [31], 1906), 3; and "Matbuʿat-ı Hariciye," *Hayat*, no. 179 (August 13 [26], 1906), 4.

233. See "Memleketimizde Almanlar," *Türk*, no. 119 (February 22, 1906), 1; and "Türkiye'de Almanlar," *Türk*, no. 124 (March 29, 1906), 1. These articles were republished by the Mus-

lim press in Russia. See *"Türk* Gazetesinden: Memleketimizde Almanlar (Nemseler),*" Tercüman-ı Ahvâl-i Zaman,* no. 29 (March 22 [April 4], 1906), 1; and "Matbuʿat-ı Hariciye," *Hayat,* no. 74 (April 6 [19], 1906), 4.

234. For the measures taken against the journal, see Tahsin Bey to Gazi Ahmed Muhtar Pasha [August 7, 1905]/no. 1313, and August 18, 1905/no. 1424, *Umumî Kayda Mahsus Defterdir,* BBA–YEE, 36/139–73/139/XIX-3. In an undated [1904?] spy report, Mahmud Muhtar claimed that the Ottoman High Commissioner's office compelled the authors of the journal, by buying some of them off and threatening the others, to assume a low profile and not criticize the sultan's regime strongly. See Asaf Tugay, *Saray Dedikoduları ve Bazı Mâruzat* (Istanbul, 1963), 57–58.

235. After the Young Turk Revolution of 1908, Bahaeddin Şakir, while criticizing an article of Ali Kemal in *Türk* regarding succession in the Ottoman Empire, professed the following: "Yes, many signed and anonymous, useful, and patriotic articles had appeared in the journal *Türk."* See *Şûra-yı Ümmet-Ali Kemal Daʿvası* (Istanbul, 1325 [1909]), 66. Bahaeddin Şakir's criticism seems to be heavy-handed in the light of the articles written by Ali Kemal on the issue of succession. Although Ali Kemal asked for a change in the succession system, he also made the following statement: "We do not want, however, Burhaneddin Efendi to become the new sultan." See [Ali Kemal], "Hasta," *Türk,* no, 141 (October 4, 1906), 1. He further accused Burhaneddin Efendi of being under German influence. See [Ali Kemal], "Tebdil-i Verâset Mes'elesi," *Türk,* no. 145 (November 1, 1906), 1.

236. Ali Fahri, *Açık Mektub: Ali Pinhan Bey'e* (Cairo, 1904), 5–11. For further criticism by other Young Turks residing in Egypt, see "Dünya Ne Vakit Düzelir?" *Curcuna,* no. 1 (January 22, 1906), 1.

237. "İfade-i Mahsusa: Redd-i Ağraz," *Türk,* no. 77 (April 20, 1905), 1.

238. *"Al-Muqaṭṭam* Gazetesi'nden Aynen Tercümedir," *Şûra-yı Ümmet,* no. 91 (April 9, 1906), 3 (republished in *Tuna,* no. 184 [April 25, 1906], 3–4); "Dahiliye," *Türk,* no. 125 (April 5, 1906), 2; and Mehmed Kadri Nâsıh, *Sarayih,* 202. For more information on the purchase itself, see BBA–YEE, 5/2551/83/2 and 31/2096/160/87.

239. See the letter of Dr. [Bahaeddin Şakir] beginning "Aziz ve Muhterem Vatandaşımız" and dated Paris, September 6, 1907/no. 365, *Muhaberat Kopyası,* 414. In another letter, however, the CPU presented *Türk* as a journal whose only policy was "to defend Turkishness." See the letter of Dr. Bahaeddin [Şakir] and Dr. Nâzım beginning "Aziz Vatandaşımız" and dated September 24, 1906/no. [75], *Muhaberat Kopyası,* 124. Arminius Vámbéry made a similar comment concerning Gazi Ahmed Muhtar Pasha's alleged support of the journal. See Vámbéry to Sir Charles [Hardinge], Vorderbruck, June 9, 1906, Vambéry Papers, PRO/F.O. 800/33. The Ottoman High Commissioner did not include *Türk* in the list of "seditious journals" published in Egypt. See BBA–YSHM, 486/70 (1323.2.13).

240. "İfade-i Mahsusa," *Türk,* no. 106 (November 16, 1905), 1; and Hüseyin Âlî, *"Türk* Hey'et-i Müessise ve Tahririye-i Sabıkası," ibid. See also "Matbuʿat-ı Hariciye," *Hayat,* no. 121 (December 20, 1905 [January 2, 1906]), 3.

241. "Huzûr-i Maʿalinüşûr Hazret-i Hilâfetpenâhî'ye Açık Arzuhal," *Türk,* no. 107 (November 23, 1905), 1. Republished in "Matbuʿat-ı Hariciye: *Türk'*ün Sultana Arzuhali," *Hayat,* no. 14 (January 17 [30], 1906), 4.

242. Hüseyin Âlî, "[İhtar]," *Türk,* no. 134 (June 21, 1906), 1. The restoration of the journal to the former nationalist editorial board was praised by *Hayat.* See "Mısır'da Çıkan *Türk* Gazetesi," *Hayat,* no. 29, 4.

243. "Bir İfade," *Türk,* no. 134, 1.

244. The attitude taken by the journal was esteemed by Abdullah Cevdet. See "Matbuʿat-ı Cedîde: *Türk," İctihad* 2, no. 3 (November 1906), 262.

245. See "Bir Mektub," *Türk,* no. 157 (February 28, 1907), 1. As a response to this letter some subscribers and "friends" of the journal offered support. See "Beyân-ı Hâl," *Türk,* no. 159 (April 18, 1907), 1.

246. See M[ahir] S[aʿid], "Azm ü İrade," *Türk,* no. 146 (November 8, 1906), 2; M[ahir] S[aʿid], "Tasnif-i Cins-i Beşer," *Türk,* no. 154 (January 10, 1907), 1–2, and no. 156 (February 14, 1907), 1–2; M[ahir] S[aʿid], "Hakimiyet-i Şahsiye," *Türk,* no. 157, 1; and Mahir Saʿid, "Edmond Demolins," *Türk,* no. 174 (August 22, 1907), 4. Sabahaddin Bey praised Mahir Saʿid's

work in his journal. See "Nasıl Hıristiyanlar Vatanımızda Adem-i Merkeziyetden Müstefîd Olageldikleri Halde Müslümanlar Merkeziyetin Mahkûmu Oluyorlar?" *Terakki*, no. [6], [November 1906], 8/fn. 1. Mahir Sa'id continued to publish similar articles after the Young Turk Revolution. See Mahir Sa'id, "Adem-i Merkeziyet ve Teşebbüs-i Şahsî," *İkdam*, September 26, 1908.

247. See "Havâdis-i Dahiliye," *Türk*, no. 135 (June 28, 1906), 2; "Terakki," *Türk*, no. 157, 1–2. It should be noted that one of the prominent authors of the journal, who played a limited role in its publication policy during the final years of the periodical, later became an ardent supporter of Sabahaddin Bey and his thesis of decentralization. See Ali Kemal, "Sabahaddin Beyefendi," *İkdam*, September 2, 1908; and idem, "Teşebbüs-i Şahsî, Tevsi'-i Me'zuniyet," *İkdam*, September 5, 1908.

248. See the farewell note in the last issue: Rıza Şakir, "Nazar-ı Dikkate," *Türk*, no. 187 (November 28, 1907), 1; and "Muhtıra," enclosed with the note presented to the Grand Vizier's office, dated [March–April 1906], DWQ, Sijillāt 'Ābidīn-Turkī-Şādir talagrāfāt, S/5/52/10, folio 136.

249. "Açık Mektublar," *Muvazene*, no. 226 [April 2, 1902], 4; and *Muvazene*, no. 262 [January 14, 1903], 4.

250. "Matbu'at," *Muvazene*, no. 230 [April 30, 1902]; 4, "'*Osmanlı*' Gazetesi'nden," *Muvazene*, no. 277 [May 6, 1903], 4; and "Matbu'at," ibid., 4. It must be also stated that when the Ottoman Commissioner in Bulgaria seized the journals and pamphlets through the help of a certain Hüsni Efendi of Nakshik, he found journals and pamphlets that had been published by various Young Turk groups. See the list made by the the the Ottoman Commissioner and enclosed with a dispatch sent from the Minister of the Interior, Mehmed Memduh Pasha, to the First Chamberlain's office, BBA–YMGM, 261/168 (1322.5.28).

251. [Ali Fehmi], "Varna'da Vekâlethane-i Osmanî ve Şürekâsı," *Muvazene*, no. 244 [August 27, 1902], 2.

252. "Saraybosna'dan Mektub," *Muvazene*, no. 238 [July 16, 1902], 4.

253. "Filibe'den Mektub," *Muvazene*, no. 256 [November 19, 1902], 2.

254. See "*Anadolu* Gazetesinden Muktebesdir," *Muvazene*, no. 245 [September 3, 1902], 4; and "*Şûra-yı Ümmet*' in Neşr Etdiği Mühim Bir İlâveden Muktebesdir," *Muvazene*, no. 249 [October 1, 1902], 4.

255. "Hadisât-ı Siyasiye: Bu Millet Islah Olmaz Diyorlar," *Muvazene*, no. 242 [August 3, 1902], 1. For similar themes employed by the journal, see "Hadisât-ı Siyasiye," *Muvazene*, no. 259 [December 17, 1902], 1; and "Bulgaristan Havâdisi," *Muvazene*, no. 245, 1.

256. "Hamdi İmzasıyla Varaka-Ecnebilere Müdafaa," *Muvazene*, no. 264 [January 28, 1903], 1.

257. "Matbu'at," *Muvazene*, no. 238, 4.

258. See "Hafiyeler Haber Alıyorlar!" *Muvazene*, no. 238, 1; "Sözde İslâmiyetde Ruhanilik, Papaslık Yok," ibid., 2; "Bulgaristan Havâdisi: Nasihat (2)," *Muvazene*, no. 246 [September 10, 1902], 1–2; and "Şumnu'dan Mektub-i Mahsus," *Muvazene*, no. 249, 2.

259. "Varna'da Vekâlethane-i Osmanî ve Şürekâsı," *Muvazene*, no. 244, 2.

260. "İhtar," *Muvazene*, no. 263, 4. See also Ali Ferruh to the Grand Vizier's office [February 2, 1903]/no. 881, BBA–BEO/Mümtaze Kalemi: Bulgaristan Tasnifi Evrakı II, A.MTZ (04), 87/82 (1320.11.6).

261. "Mekâtib: Bulgaristan'dan," *Şûra-yı Ümmet*, no. 72 (April 6, 1905), 4.

262. "Tebrik," *Şûra-yı Ümmet*, no. 105 (December 1, 1906), 4.

263. For more information, see Petrov to Zolotovich, Sofia, May 30 [June 12], 1905/no. 380, TsDA, F. 176, op. 1, a.e. 2285, 5–6; Petrov to the cabinet, June 24 [July 7], 1905/no. 3993, TsDA, F. 176, op. 1, a.e. 2284, 3a; and Petrov to Nachovich, Sofia, July 20 [August 2], 1905/no. 4536, TsDA, F. 176, op. 1, a.e. 2284, 7.

264. See "Feyz-i Kanun ve Hürriyet," *Rumeli*, no. 4 [December 29, 1905], 3. This article provides us with the details of the defense advanced by Popov, the attorney of Mehmed Sabri and his friends, in court. For more details about the earlier events, see Ali Féhmi, "A Son Altesse le Prince Ferdinand de Bulgarie," *Muvazene*, no. 374 (June 21, 1905), [4]; "Bulgaris-

tan'dan," *Şûra-yı Ümmet*, no. 74 (May 6, 1905), 3; and "Le 'Roi' de Bulgarie," *Mechveret Supplément Français*, no. 163 (May 1, 1905), 3.

265. See "Arz-ı Merâm," *Ahali*, no. 2 [November 4, 1906], 1–2; "(*Sancak*) ve (*Ahali*) Gazeteleri," *Terakki* [no. 5] [October 1906], 12; and Sadık el-Müeyyed Pasha to the Grand Vizier's office [November 9, 1906]/no. 7886-282, BBA–BEO/Mümtaze Kalemi: Bulgaristan Tasnifi Evrakı II, A.MTZ (04), 150/46 (1324.9.20). For a survey of *Muvazene*'s publication activity in Bulgaria, see "Matbuʿat Arasında," *Sancak*, no. 68 (December 1, 1906), 4.

266. "İfade-i Merâm," *Muvazene*, no. 374, 1–2.

267. See BBA–YSHM, 517/16 (1325.Za.5); and BBA–İrade-Hususî, Za 1325/no. 70–1192.

268. See BBA–BEO/Mümtaze Kalemi: Mısır, A.MTZ (05), 18/B/137 (1325.11.18), and 18/B/143 (1325.11.28.); and BBA–BEO/Hidiviyet-i Celile-i Mısriyenin Tahrirat Defteri (78)-1033; 68/5 [January 2, 1908]/no. 1192–242.

269. His letter dated November 11, 1908, entitled "Afganistan'dan Bir Sada" and addressed to the Ottoman Chamber of Deputies, gives details about his ventures. See "Meclis-i Mebʿusan Müzâkeratı," *Takvim-i Vekayiʿ*, no. 75 [December 25, 1908], 1–2; and "Meclis-i Mebʿusanın Dördüncü İctimaʿı Müzâkerâtı: Afganistan'dan Bir Sada," *Şûra-yı Ümmet*, December 24, 1908.

270. See his letter to Bahaeddin Şakir dated Kābul, June 9, 1908, Private Papers of Bahaeddin Şakir.

271. M. Talât to Ahmed Rıza, [April 16, 1902], Private Papers of Ahmed Rıza (1). İsmail Yürükov [Yürükoğlu], whose name was mentioned in the aforementioned letter, was an agent of the Ottoman government. See Sadık el-Müeyyed Pasha to the Grand Vizier's office, Sofia, March 14, 1905, BBA–BEO/Mümtaze Kalemi: Bulgaristan Tasnifi Evrakı II, A.MTZ (04), 127/38 (1323.1.8).

272. Below-Rutzau to von Bülow, Sofia, June 14, 1902/no. 111, A. 9626, PAAA, 733/3, Die Jungtürken, 198 (Bd. 4–5).

273. "İsmail Kemal Bey," *Muvazene*, no. 231, 2.

274. "Muvazene İdaresi'ne," *Muvazene*, no. 232 [May 14, 1902], 2–3. For the similar information gathered by the Ottoman government, see BBA–YSHM, 426/137 (1319.12.29), 428/75 (1320.1.28), 429/36 (1320.6.2), and 437/37 (1321.3.22).

275. BBA–BEO/Mümtaze Kalemi: Bulgaristan Tasnifi Evrakı II, A.MTZ (04), 98/55 (9.4.1321), 98/95 (1321.5.6); and BBA–ŞD-Dersaadet XXI-30, 915 [August 6 1903]/2731–45.

276. Below-Rutzau to von Bülow, Sofia, June 14, 1902/no. 111, PAAA.

277. See Hanioğlu, *The Young Turks*, 90, 109, and 123.

278. Sadık el-Müeyyed Pasha to the Grand Vizier's office, June 11, 1904/no. 6615–287, BBA–BEO/Mümtaze Kalemi: Bulgaristan Tasnifi Evrakı II, A.MTZ (04), 117/118 (1322.3.29). The CPU, however, knew nothing about him and instructed its members in Bulgaria to gather information about Mustafa Ragıb. See the letter of Dr. Bahaeddin [Şakir] beginning "Vatanperver Biraderimiz" and dated Paris, April 2, [1]906/no. 7, *Muhaberat Kopyası*, 13.

279. "Hariciye: Efkâr-ı Umumiye," *Efkâr-ı Umumiye*, no. 3 [April 2, 1904], 4.

280. Sadık el-Müeyyed Pasha to the Grand Vizier's office, February 3, 1905/no. 8871–848, BBA–BEO/Mümtaze Kalemi: Bulgaristan Tasnifi Evrakı II, A.MTZ (04), 127/38 (1323.1.8).

281. İdare, "Beyân-ı Hakikat," *Efkâr-ı Umumiye*, no. 20 [March 11, 1905], 1.

282. "Albanski shovinizm i megalomaniia," ibid (Bulgarian section), 2.

283. Ibid, 1. The journal published a Turkish translation of Şemseddin Sami's pamphlet entitled *Shqipëria ç'ka genë, ç'esthë e ç'do bëhëte*. This Turkish version was translated by Shahin Kolonja and later published as a pamphlet. See Şemseddin Sami, *Arnavutluk Ne İdi, Nedir, Ne Olacak?* ed. Shahin Kolonja [Sofia?, 1904?]. An Albanian version had been published in installments in 1901 by Shahin Kolonja's Sofia-based journal *Drita*.

284. See the Grand Vizier's office to the Ministry of the Interior [February 9, 1905]/no. 71/187595, BBA–BEO–VGG(2): Dersaadet Giden: 424.

285. Sadık el-Müeyyed Pasha to the Grand Vizier's office, February 3, 1905/no. 8871–848, BBA–BEO/Mümtaze Kalemi: Bulgaristan Tasnifi Evrakı II, A.MTZ (04), 127/38 (1323.1.8).

286. He was referred to as "Doctor . . . ov." See İdare, "Yeni Yolumuz," *Feryad*, no. 6 [December 12, 1905], 1.

287. "İdare'nin Cevabları: Romanya'daki Doktor'a," ibid.

288. See Colonel Ali Hilmi's dispatch to the Ottoman Ministry of War, Sofia [December 2, 1905], enclosed with Minister of War Rıza Pasha's note to the Grand Vizier's office dated [December 14, 1905]/no. 2334, BBA–BEO/Mümtaze Kalemi: Bulgaristan Tasnifi Evrakı II, A.MTZ (04), 137/5 (1323.Ş.27). The Ottoman authorities banned both *Feryad* and *Şark*, see BBA–YSHM, 504/64 (1324.Ca.16).

289. "İdare'nin Cevabları: Varna'dan: M. D. Efendi'ye," *Feryad*, no. 6, 3. For articles using an "activist" language, see "Sultan Hamid Han ve İhtilâlcilik," *Feryad*, no. 6, 3; M[ustafa] Ragıb, "Rusya'da Meclis-i Meşveret," *Feryad*, no. 23 [May 16, 1906], 1; and Mustafa Ragıb, "Rusya'da Meclis-i Meşveret," *Feryad*, no. 24 [May 30, 1906], 1: "Freedom without blood[shed] may be likened to bread without salt." A Russian scholar pays great attention to the publication of *Feryad* and claims that this was the foremost journal that underscored the importance of rebellion against the regime of Abdülhamid II. See A[natolii] D[mitrievich] Zheltiakov, *Pechat' v obshchestvenno-politicheskoi i kul'turnoi zhizni Turtsii (1729–1908 gg.)* (Moscow, 1972), 284–85. See also *Bŭlgarski periodichen pechat, 1844–1944* 1 (Sofia, 1962), 42. It seems that *Feryad*'s publication was also appreciated by the Armenian press in Russia. See Kh. M. Tsovikian, "Vliianie russkoi revoliutsii 1905 g. na revoliutsionnoe dvizhenie v Turtsii," *Sovetskoe vostokovedenie* 3 (1945), 24–25.

290. See "Mektub-i Mahsus: İstanbul'dan: Teşrin-i sânî," *Feryad*, no. 5 [December 6, 1905], 1–2.

291. See "Makedonya Maliye Kontrolü ve Saray Eşkıyasının Miskinliği," *Feryad*, no. 5, 2–3.

292. Colonel Ali Hilmi's dispatch to the Ottoman Ministry of War, Sofia [December 2, 1905], BBA–BEO/Mümtaze Kalemi: Bulgaristan Tasnifi Evrakı II, A.MTZ (04), 137/5 (1323.Ş.27).

293. M[ustafa] Ragıb, "İlân," *Feryad*, no. 5, 1.

294. See M. R., "'Şark' Ceridesi'ne Hâb [Cevab] ve Tashih," *Feryad*, no. 24, 2–3.

295. Sadık el-Müeyyed Pasha to the First Chamberlain's office, Sofia [June 3, 1906]/ no. 6290–137, BBA–YMGM, 288/39 (1324. Ca.11).

296. See Mustafa Ragıb's letter to the Ottoman Commissioner dated Sofia, March 4, 1906, enclosed with the latter's note to the Ottoman Ministry of the Interior, dated [March 17, 1906]/ no. 2, BBA–YMGM, 285/69 (1324.10.2).

297. See "Dersaadet Ceza Mahkemesi'nden," *Ceride-i Mahakim-i Adliye*, no. 463 (April 18, 1906), 2.

298. For the Austro-Hungarian diplomats' interest in the articles published in *Mechveret Supplément Français*, see Arhiv Bosne i Hercegovine, Zajedničko ministarstvo finansija, odjeljenje za Bosnu i Hercegovinu, prezidialna, 1656/1900.

299. Kutschera to Kállay, Sarajevo, June 19, 1901, in *Borba Muslimana: Bosne i Hercegovine za vjersku i vakufsko-mearifsku autonomiju*, ed. Ferdo Hauptmann (Sarajevo, 1967), 154–55. Donia, who also focuses on this subject, presents the case entirely as a maneuver of Kutschera and Kállay, as if there were no relation between the Young Turks and the Bosnian Muslim leaders. See Robert J. Donia, *Islam under the Double Eagle: The Muslims of Bosnia and Hercegovina, 1878–1914* (New York, 1981), 165–66.

300. Henri Moseru's memorandum dated August 2, 1901, in *Borba Muslimana*, ed. Hauptmann, 161.

301. Kállay to Kutschera, Vienna, October 22, 1901, ibid., 195–96.

302. As a final attempt, Austro-Hungarian diplomats planned to send an issue of *Ostdeutsche Rundschau*, containing information about Young Turk publications in Geneva and Cairo and about the sultan's agents, to Džabić and other Muslim leaders who had frequently visited Istanbul and Bursa with the intention of securing the interception of these issues by the Ottoman intelligence service. See Kutschera to Thallóczy, Sarajevo, July 12, 1902, in *Borba Muslimana*, ed. Hauptmann, 323. In this document Kutschera refers to an article published in *Mechveret Supplément Français*. Since he suspected that the article had been written by an adherent of Džabić, it is certain that this was not the intended article.

303. Kállay to Kutschera, Vienna, March 3, 1902, in *Borba Muslimana*, ed. Hauptmann, 269–70.

304. Manastırlı Bahaeddin Sâî, *Güldeste-i Hatırât-ı Ahrar ve Eslâf—Refuge [Réfugié] Turc à Paris*, Hakkı Tarık Us Library, MS D. 38, 120. I was unable to figure out whether the Salih Bey mentioned in this list was Salih Efendi, who played a significant role in the publication of the journal *Gayret*. The fact that he was referred to as Salih Eff[endi] Aličehić in another document makes it unlikely that he was the same person. See *Kultura i umjetnost u Bosni i Hercegovini pod Austrougarskom upravom*, ed. Risto Besarović (Sarajevo, 1968), 363–64.

305. A detailed analysis of the establishment of this political organization is given in Mustafa Imamović, *Pravni položaj i unutrašnji politički raztivak Bosne i Hercegovine od 1878 do 1914* (Sarajevo, 1976), 134 ff.

306. "Un protest al musulmanilor," *Constanţa*, March 24, 1902, 4. See also Tevfik Pasha to Münir Bey, April 23, 1902/no. 47190-62 and April 23, 1902/no. 47212-155, BBA–HR.SYS. 1796/3 (original. 502/55). German press, too, covered the event. See Ahmed Tevfik Pasha to Tevfik Pasha, Berlin, May 3, 1902/no. 2623–89, ibid.

307. Kâzım Bey, the Ottoman General Consul in Constanţa, to the Ottoman Foreign Ministry, February 20, 1902, ibid.; see also "Informaţunị," *Constanţa*, March 24, 1906, 3. In the meantime Kâzım Bey seized the opportunity and threatened the Ottoman government that he would join the Young Turks unless he was given a salary raise. See Doktor [İbrahim] Temo, "Sorarız!" *Hukuk-u Umumiye*, September 22, 1908.

308. See the Ministry of Justice's note to the Grand Vizier's office [October 13, 1902]/no. 156; and Tevfik Pasha to Münir Bey, October 26, 1902/no. 49832–326, BBA–HR.SYS. 1796/3 (original. 502/55).

309. Tevfik Pasha to Kâzım Bey, June 28, 1902/no. 48645–174; and Ottoman General Consulate in Constanţa to the Ottoman Foreign Ministry [June 29, 1902], BBA–HR.SYS. 1796/2 (original. 502/43).

310. Ibid.

311. "Köstence'den," *Muvazene*, no. 268 (February 25, 1903), 4.

312. Von Kiderlen-Wächter to von Bülow, Bucharest, February 14, 1902/no. 11, A. 2893, PAAA, 733/3, Die Jungtürken, 198 (Bd. 4–5).

313. See Temo, *İttihad ve Terakki*, 166–87; the Ministry of the Interior to the Foreign Ministry, February 26, 1902/no. 1068; Mahmud Nedim to Tevfik Pasha, Vienna, April 5, 1903/no. 27468-110; and Tevfik Pasha to Mahmud Nedim, April 22, 1903/no. 52248-92, BBA–HR.SYS. 1796/2 (original. 502/43). In response the Ottoman government applied to its Rumanian counterpart requesting that necessary measures be taken, and tried and sentenced him *in contumaciam*. See Kâzım Bey to Tevfik Pasha, Bucharest, August 5, 1902/no. 19581-127 and December 12, 1902/no. 220, ibid., and İbrahim Temo, "İstanbul Muhakemat ve Mahakimine Cevab," *Balkan*, no. 342 [January 13, 1908], 1.

314. See "Muhtıra: Abdülhamid'e Hitab," *Osmanlı (3)*, no. 1 [August 11, 1903], 1. For the measures taken against the distribution of the journal in Western Anatolia, see BBA–YEE-Kâmil Paşa Evrakına Ek I, 86/19, 1877 (1321.5.21); 86/19, 1880 (3.6.1321); and Kâmil Pasha to Âsım Bey, August 15, 1903/no. 43, *Aydın Vilâyet-i Celilesiyle Muhaberata Mahsus Defterdir*, BBA–YEE, 36/2470-15/146/16. The journal was published in the Piraeus.

315. See BBA–YSHM, 456/7 (1321.6.10).

316. See "Rumeli de Elden Gitti," *Islahat*, no. 4 (December 14, 1903), 1.

317. Edhem Safi, "Atina'dan Mektub," *Muvazene*, no. 254 [November 5, 1902], 4. It should be stated that during the period in question the number of the Young Turks who fled to Greece increased dramatically. For interesting examples, see the following files: "Fugitifs: Athènes-Assaf bin Abdullah (1902)," BBA–HR.SYS. 1797/2 (original. 502/64); "Fugitifs: le Fugitif Irfan Kémal (1902)," ibid., 1797/3 (original. 502/62); "Fugitifs: Husseïn Sabri Eff[endi] et Béhaeddin Eff[endi] (1902)," ibid., 1797/4 (original. 502/63); "Fugitifs: Athènes-Fugitifs Ahmed Arif et Akif," ibid., 1797/7 (original. 502/68); and "Fugitifs: Fugitif Re'fet," ibid., 1796/11 (original. 502/58).

318. Ahmed Lütfi to Mehmed Ferid in Izmir, Athens [June 30, 1903], BBA–YEE-Kâmil Paşa Evrakına Ek I, 86/20, 1942 (1321.8.8).

319. Ratibor to von Bülow, Athens, October 29, 1903/no. 232, A. 16384, PAAA, 733/3, Die Jungtürken 198 (Bd. 4–5).

320. See İbrahim Fethi Pasha to the First Chamberlain's office, dated [October 30, 1904], BBA–YMGM, 280/1 (1323.N.1).

321. The foreign press, too, underscored the open attacks against the Young Turks. See "Der Sultan," *Der Tag*, March 10, 1902.

322. See BBA–BEO/Dahiliye Giden, 101–3/50; 2700 [October 26, 1902]/145511, and 3978 [March 11, 1903]/151394; BBA–BEO/Dahiliye Giden, 102–3/51; 113 [March 22, 1903]/ 151864, and 520 [April 25, 1903]/153875.

323. Leishman to Hay, Istanbul, July 9, 1902, Dispatches from United States Ministers to Turkey, 1816–1906, vol. 70. See also Bapst to Delcassé, Therapia, July 28, 1902/no. 127, AE–NS–T, 4 (1902–1904), 115–16. For similar comments made by Young Turks, see "Havâdis-i Hariciye," *Muvazene*, no. 223 [March 5, 1903], 3.

324. Nâzım Pasha later requested help from the British authorities to prevent the sultan from confiscating his private papers. See the translation of Nâzım Pasha's letter to Adam Block dated November 8, 1902, and the latter's memorandum dated November 28, 1902/no. 334, concerning the papers, PRO/F.O. 195/2124.

325. Marschall von Bieberstein to Auswärtiges Amt, March 13, 1902/no. 92 (Entzifferung), A. 4096, PAAA, 733/3, Die Jungtürken, 198 (Bd.4–5). See also "Weitere Verhaftungen in Konstantinopel," *Frankfurter Zeitung*, March 7, 1902. This could well be the reason behind the German naval attaché's interest in the trial of Fuad Pasha and his sending of newspaper clippings about the event to the Chef des Admiralstabes der Marine. One of these clippings, which is from the French edition of *Servet* of June 5, 1902, and entitled "Condamnation de Fouad Pasha," provides valuable information. See Bundesarchiv-Militärarchiv, RM 5 (Admiralstab der Marine)/1598: Türkei Politisches, Bd. 3–4.

326. Hüseyin Hilmi Pasha to the First Chamberlain's office [March 31, 1903]/no. 81, *Yemen ve Yedinci Ordu-yu Hümayun Müşiriyetiyle Muhaberata Mahsus Defterdir*, BBA–YEE, 36/ 247025/147/XIV. Despite these measures, the "seditious" publications continued to be sent to the divisions in Yemen. See BBA–BEO/VGG(2): Yemen ve Trablusgarb Giden: 371; 2 [March 15, 1903]/151546, 24 [March 25, 1903]/152049, 34 [April 11, 1903]/153066, 41 [May 14, 1903]/155048; BBA-BEO/VGG (2): Yemen Âmed: 367; 222 [March 6, 1903]; 1 [March 14, 1903]/150848; 62 [April 21, 1903]/153049, 153066, and 154143; 79 [June 7, 1903]/ 150848 and 153307. An Ottoman commander sent a note of protest to the French Supplement of the coalition and denounced the arrest on behalf of the Ottoman army. See Un Général Turc, "Une protestation," *Mechveret Supplément Français*, no. 127, 3.

327. See the Governor of Sivas, Reşid Âkif's detailed coded telegram to the First Chamberlain's office, dated [November 26, 1902], BBA–YEE, 15/2051/74/15.

328. For the comments made by foreign diplomats on the members of the court martial, see Constans to Delcassé, Pera, March 17, 1902/no. 37, AE–NS–T, 4 (1902–1904), 80; and O'Conor to Lansdowne, Pera, June 6, 1902/no. 266, PRO/F.O. 78/5191.

329. See Bapst to Delcassé, Pera, December 1, 1902/no. 221, AE-NS–T, 4 (1902–1904), 123. For the banishment of large numbers of officials and cadets, see BBA–BEO/Dahiliye Giden, 101-3/50; 1784 [August 6, 1902]/142317; 103-3/52; 2510 [November 5, 1904]/183158; 2513 [November 5, 1904]/183171; and 104-3/53; 2372 [October 19, 1905]/201640. Interestingly, the Grand Vizier's office asked the officials "not to provide information about the dissatisfaction of the army officers by open telegrams" and requested the use of "ciphers." See BBA–BEO/VGG(2): Haleb Giden: 297; 74 [September 23, 1903]/162493.

330. "Threatening Situation in Turkey," *The New York Times Magazine Supplement*, March 30, 1902, 16.

331. Malaspina di Carbonara to Prinetti, Istanbul, February 15, 1902/no. 134–58, *I Documenti Diplomatici Italiani* 4 (3rd Series), 108–9. For Zinoviev's efforts, see "Nouvelles de l'étranger," *Le Temps*, February 23, 1902. Another source claims that "Fuad Pasha was in communication with the 'Young Turkey' party." See Franklin E. Hoskins, "Triumph of a Turkish Exile," *The Independent* 65, no. 3120 (September 17, 1908), 649. I could not find any clear evidence of such a communication, however.

332. His petition entitled "İngiltere Devlet-i Fahîmesi Sefiri Asâletlû O'Conor Hazretleri'ne Ariza-i Âcizânemdir," PRO/F.O. 195/2154.

333. See Constans to Affaires étrangères, Pera, February 14, 1902/no. 26; and "Note au sujet du télégramme de Constantinople du 14 Février 1902, no. 26," AE–NS–T, 4 (1902–1904), 29. An interesting comment was made by O'Conor, who stated that Fuad Pasha "gave an opening to his enemies by taking of a house in Stamboul belonging to Mahmoud Pasha." See O'Conor to Lansdowne, Constantinople, February 14, 1902/no. 265, PRO/F.O. 78/5191.

334. Louis Rambert, *Notes et impressions de Turquie: l'Empire ottoman sous Abdul-Hamid II, 1895–1905* (Geneva, 1926), 161. The pro-palace journals, on the contrary, published articles concerning Fuad Pasha's "agissements révolutionnaires." See N[icolas] Nicolaïdes, "A propos d'un condamné," *L'Orient et L'Agence Ottoman* 14, no. 13 (July 5, 1902), 6; and "Réponse au 'Journal des Débats,'" *L'Orient et L'Agence Ottoman* 14, no. 15 (August 23, 1902), 5. The public prosecutor made similar accusations at the trial of the adventurers. See Mehmed Avnullah el-Kâzımî, *Son Müdafaa* (Istanbul, 1326 [1908]), 3 ff. See also BBA–YEE, 15/2051/74/14.

335. "Aferin Fuad Paşa," *Osmanlı*, no. 103 (March 1, 1902), 4–5. The French supplement of the coalition made a similar criticism. See X. X., "La série continue," *Mechveret Supplément Français*, no. 127 (March 15, 1902), 2. This prompted an Ottoman commander to protest against the Young Turks. See Un Général Turc, "Correspondance," *Mechveret Supplément Français*, no. 128 (April 15, 1902), 3–4.

336. "Tebligât-ı Resmiye," *Sabah*, June 5, 1902; "Mektub-i Mahsus: Şam'dan," *Şûra-yı Ümmet*, no. 16 (November 16, 1902), 4; and Constans to Delcassé, Pera, June 6, 1902/no. 83, AE–NS–T, 4 (1902–1904), 105.

337. See Cambon to Delcassé, London, September 1, 1903; and İslâm Fuad's letter, dated August 27, 1903, enclosed with it. Ibid., 143–44. Also Charles Allen, an M.P. of Gloucestershire, addressed a question, in which he praised Fuad Pasha, to Lord Cranborne, Undersecretary of State for Foreign Affairs, in the House of Commons. See *Hansard's Parliamentary Debates*, 4th Series, 103 (1902), col. 713.

338. "M. Constans Amb[assadeur] à Constantinople," no. 294, AE–NS–T, 4 (1902–1904), 144.

339. See the note written by O'Conor entitled "A Curious Story," which was dated 13/3/[190]2, O'Conor Papers, Churchill College, Cambridge, 6/1/31.

340. BBA–YMGM, 226/139 (1319.Za.28); Constans to Delcassé, Pera November 8, 1903/no. 188, December 22, 1903/no. 217; and to Delcassé, Diyar-ı Bekir, December 2, 1903/no. 3, AE–NS–T, 4, 144–48, 151–53.

341. O'Conor to Lansdowne, Therapia, August 4, 1903/no. 447 (confidential), PRO/F.O. 78/5267.

342. The translation of Nâzım Pasha's letter dated November 8, 1902, and Adam Block's memorandum entitled "Nazim Pasha's Papers" enclosed with it, PRO/F.O. 195/2124.

343. See his undated memorandum in BBA–YEE, 15/74-5-b/74/15. For the Young Turks' criticism toward Mehmed Ferid Pasha, see "Tebeddül-i Sadaret," *Şûra-yı Ümmet*, nos. 22–23 (February 28, 1903), 7; "Le nouveau Grand-Vizir," *Mechveret Supplément Français*, no. 137 (February 1, 1903), 1; "Sadr-ı âzâm ve Avrupa Matbu'atı," *Şûra-yı Ümmet*, no. 28 (May 13, 1903), 4; and "Hadisât-ı Siyasiye," *Muvazene*, no. 263, 1.

344. "Tevzi'-i Evrak," *İstirdat*, no. 17 (October 25, 1901), [3].

345. For the distribution in Izmir, see BBA–BEO/Dahiliye Giden, 101–3/50; 2828 [November 8, 1902]/145972; BBA–YEE, Kâmil Paşa Evrakına Ek I, 86/17, 1679 (1320.10.6). For the distribution in Hama and Homs, see Reşid Bey to Âsım Bey [January 14, 1903]/no. 24, *Beyrut Vilâyetiyle Muhaberata Mahsus Defter*, BBA–YEE, 36/139–68/139/XVIII. For the seditious publications discovered in the post offices in Istanbul, see BBA–BEO/Posta ve Telgraf Nezareti Giden, 579–17/4; 2 [March 17, 1903]/151211. In September 1902, documents entitled "Ottoman Union and Progress" were intercepted by the Ottoman intelligence service in post offices. See BBA–YMGM, 236/49 (1320.Ş.10).

346. Nâzım Bey to Âsım Bey, September 7, 1902/no. 1902, *Suriye [ve] Beşici Ordu ile [Muhaberata Mahsus Defter]*, BBA–YEE/36/2470-24/147/XVI; also an officer in Beirut was

accused of being "a member of the important conspiratorial committee of the Young Turks that has strong branches in Damascus, Hama, and Beirut." See Divisional General Mehmed Kâmil Pasha to the First Chamberlain's office [August 16, 1905]/no. 1579, *Umumî Kayda Mahsus Defterdir*, BBA–YEE, 36/139-73/139/XIX-3.

347. Sami Paşazâde Sezaî, "1901'den İtibaren Paris'de Geçen Seneler," *Servet-i Fünûn*, no. 12–1486 (February 5, 1924), 183.

348. Negib Azoury, *Le réveil de la Nation arabe dans l'Asie turque en présence des intérêts et des rivalités des puissances étrangères, de la Curie romaine et du Patriarcat œcuménique* (Paris, 1905), 249–54.

349. Two years earlier a journal, owners of which had close ties with Azoury, had published a manifesto allegedly issued by the Central Committee of Ottoman Liberals (Osmanlı Serbestiyânı Merkez Komitesi) in Istanbul. See "Hıtta-i Yemeniye," *Hilâfet*, no. 81 (June 1, 1902), [1].

350. Hercule Diamantopulo, *Le réveil de la Turquie* (Alexandria, [1909]), 27. Further underscored by Jean Larmeroux, *La politique extérieure de L'Autriche-Hongrie, 1875–1914* 2, *La politique d'asservissement, 1908–1914* (Paris, 1918), 31–32.

351. See Muhammed Adil, *Comment fut obtenue la Constitution ottomane* (Constantinople, 1908), 15–16; "The Origin of the Patriotic Movement," *The World To-Day* 15, no. 4 (October 1908), 990–91; "40,000 Turks Murdered," *The New York Times*, August, 27, 1908; and "Turkey," *The International Year Book 1908* (New York, 1908), 708. Âdil Bey's other claims concerning his activities before the revolution are as exciting as a detective novel, albeit totally baseless. See "Asrār Turkiyā al-fatāt wa ʿAkīf Bak," *al-Ahrām*, August 25, 1908. Despite the unrealistic nature of his stories, many European scholars took them seriously. See, for example, A. Wirth, "Zur Kritik der jüngsten Vorgänge in der Türkei," *Asien* 8, no. 12 (September 1909), 153.

352. For an event that was, as usual, initially attributed to the Young Turks, see Leishman to Hay, Pera, September 16, 1903, Dispatches from United States Ministers to Turkey, 1818–1906, vol. 74.

353. "Aus der Türkei," *Preußische Zeitung*, March 9, 1900.

354. Bernhard Stern provided interesting information on this; see Bernhard Stern, *Abdul Hamid II: seine Familie-sein Hofstaat* (Budapest, 1901), 169–70. Although there must be truth in what Stern wrote, it should be stated that his account was a highly exaggerated one. Walī al-Dīn Yakan claimed that Ahmed Celâleddin Pasha's success in persuading many Young Turks to return to the empire had been used by his enemies who insinuated a conspiratorial relationship and caused the sultan "to turn the page of Ahmed Celâleddin." See Walī al-Dīn Yakan, *al-Maʿlūm wa al-majhūl* 1, 168. Some of the Young Turks who returned to the empire began to work for the pasha, and this fact deepened the sultan's suspicion. See Aḥmad Shafīq, *Mudhakkirātī fī nisf qarn* (Cairo, 1936), 4.

355. Bapst to Delcassé, Pera, February 10, 1904/no. 24, AE–NS–T, 4 (1902–1904), 159.

356. All this information is taken from the dispatch from Bapst to Delcassé, Pera, February 10, 1904/no. 24, ibid. For more information, see "La fuite d'Ahmed Djelaleddin Pasha," *L'Européen* 4, no. 26 (April 30, 1904), 12–13; and "Policiers turcs," *Pro Armenia* 4, nos. 79–80 (February 15–March 1, 1904), 451.

357. See Bapst to Delcassé, Pera, February 7, 1904/no. 19, AE–NS–T, 4 (1902–1904), 154. The pasha and his wife sent letters to Delcassé and thanked the French authorities for their support. See Ahmed Celâleddin Pasha to Delcassé, Matarieh, March 16, 1904, and Princess Tosun to Delcassé, Matarieh, March 16, 1904, ibid., 187–88. Nevertheless, after the Young Turk Revolution, Harry H. Lamb, the British consul in Salonica, told Enver Bey and Dr. Nâzım, who were protesting against the British because of İzzet Pasha's flight aboard a British vessel, that many Young Turks including Ahmed Celâleddin Pasha "had found safety under" the Union Jack (see Lamb to Lowther, Salonica, August 2, 1908/no. 105, PRO/F.O. 195/2298). No British document written during the period in question mentions any such support provided to Ahmed Celâleddin Pasha.

358. For more information about the voyage, see Capdeville to Delcassé, Corfu, February 13, 1904/no. 1 (telegram), February 15, 1904/no. 2 (telegram); February 16, 1904/no. 2;

Delcassé to Capdeville, February 13, 1904/no. 1; and Affaires étrangères' note to Cairo, February 19, 1904/no. 17, AE–NS–T, 4 (1902–1904), 162–72.

359. "La fuite en Egypte," *Les Pyramides*, February 29, 1904.

360. See AE–NS–T, 4 (1902–1904), 180–89. Another copy is in PAAA, 733/3, A. 4534, Die Jungtürken 198 (Bd.4–5). For a detailed summary in English, see "Turkish Reform Memorandum," *The Times*, April 7, 1904. The daily asserted that the author of the manifesto was "a hand more or less familiar with the affairs of state."

361. "Mekâtib: İstanbul'dan," *Şûra-yı Ümmet*, no. 50 (April, 1904), 2.

362. Haydar Bey to Münir Pasha, Geneva, August 10, 1904/no. 184, and August 20, 1904/no. 194, Archives of the Turkish Embassy in Paris, D. 287; and the Khedive's office to the Ottoman Ministry of War, July 15, 1906, BBA–BEO/Mısır Hidiviyet-i Celilesinin Tezâkir Defteri, 63-1037-68/9; 170 [July 15, 1906].

CHAPTER 5

1. Nezahet Nurettin Ege, *Prens Sabahaddin: Hayatı ve İlmî Müdafaaları* (Istanbul, 1977), 36. Sabahaddin Bey underscored the importance of the application of the method of observation by *Science sociale* throughout his life. See, for example, [Mehmed] Sabahaddin, *Türkiye Nasıl Kurtarılabilir? Meslek-i İctimaʿî ve Programı* (Istanbul, 1334 [1918]), 18.

2. [Mehmed] Sabahaddin, "Genclerimize Mektublarım: Bizde Tenkid," *Terakki*, no. [2], [June 1906], 6.

3. Published in two volumes (Paris, [1901–1903]). The first volume was entitled *Les routes de l'antiquité*, and the second *Les routes du monde moderne*. The first volume was translated into Turkish after the Young Turk Revolution of 1908, by a disciple of Sabahaddin Bey. See Edmond Demolins, *Yollar: Asl-ı İctimaʿîyi Yol Nasıl Vücûda Getirir [?] Ezmine-i Kadime Yolları*, trans. Ahmed Sanih (Istanbul, 1329 [1913]).

4. See Sabahaddine, "Les Turcs et le progrès," *La Revue* 59, no. 24 (December 15, 1905), 433–48. An English summary was provided in Sabahaddine, "The Turks and Progress," *The Review of Reviews* 33, no. 193 (January 1906), 48. For Turkish summaries, see "Türkler ve Terakki," *Türk*, no. 112 (January 4, 1906), 4 ff; and "Matbuʿat Âleminde: Türkler ve Terakki," *Hayat*, no. 58 (March 15 [28], 1906), 4. The article attracted interest in diplomatic circles. See A. 17678, PAAA 733/3, Die Jungtürken, 198 (Bd. 4–5).

5. "Le neveu d'Abdul-Hamid: ce que veut S. A. I. le Prince Sabaheddine," *Le Radical*, January 26, 1906.

6. Fazli Bey, "A propos de l'attentat de Constantinople," *Le Siècle*, August 5, 1905.

7. Originally published in Sabaheddine, "Un manifeste du Prince Sabaheddine," *Le Siècle*, September 28, 1905. Republished in Sabahaddine, "Aux Arméniens ottomans," *Le Courrier Européen*, no. 51 (October 27, 1905), 3; and in "Documents: une lettre du Prince Sabahaddine," *Pro Armenia* 5, no. 120 (October 15, 1905), 796. A Turkish translation was published in "Şu Günlerde Yeniden Âsâr-ı Fiʿliyesi Görülen Ermeni Tahrikât-ı İhtilâlcûyânesi Üzerine Prens Sabahaddin Beyefendi Hazretleri'nin Osmanlı Ermenilere Hitaben Neşr Etdikleri Beyannâmedir," *Şûra-yı Ümmet*, no. 84 (October 14, 1905), 1–2. The appeal drew the attention of foreign diplomats. Two copies, one handwritten and one typewritten, are in A. 17678, PAAA 733/3, Die Jungtürken, 198 (Bd. 4–5). The original French text can also be found in Paul Fesch, *Constantinople aux derniers jours d'Abdul-Hamid* (Paris, 1907), 384–87.

8. Un groupe d'Arméniens ottomans, "L'appel du Prince Sabaheddine," *Le Siècle*, October 29, 1905. Republished in Un groupe d'Arméniens ottomans, "Réponse à S. A. le Prince Sabahaddine," *Pro Armenia* 5, no. 121 (November 1, 1905), 801–3. Summarized in "Libéraux turcs et arméniens: Réponse à S. A. le Prince Sabahaddine," *Le Courrier Européen*, no. 52 (November 3, 1905), 825.

9. Pierre Quillard, "Les deux méthodes," *Pro Armenia* 5, no. 121, 797–98. He reiterated similar views in "Et l'Arménie?" *Pro Armenia* 5, no. 122 (November 15, 1905), 807–8.

10. Dikran Elmassian, "Libéraux turcs et arméniens: interview du Prince Sabaheddine," *Le Courrier Européen*, no. 53 (November 10, 1905), 839–40.

11. Ibid. Ahmed Rıza sent a letter and protested the accusations that had been made against him. See his letter dated November 12, 1905, and published in *Le Courrier Européen*, no. 54 (November 17, 1905), 852. Elmassian, however, rebuffed Ahmed Rıza's claims.

12. For the discussion among the Armenians, see A. Tchobanian, "Le Peuple arménien," *Le Courrier Européen*, no. 54, 853–55; Elmassian's letter dated November 20, 1905, in *Le Courrier Européen*, no. 55 (November 24, 1905), 864; and Tchobanian's letter in response, dated November 26, 1905, in *Le Courrier Européen*, no. 56 (December 1, 1905), 881.

13. Pierre Quillard, "Un manifeste Jeune Turc," *Pro Armenia* 6, no. 130 (March 15, 1906), 870–72.

14. Sabahaddine, "Libéraux turcs et arméniens," *Le Courrier Européen*, no. 56, 877–78.

15. Important parts of this letter were translated into Turkish and published in the organ of the nationalist faction. See "Ermeniler Lehinde," *Türk*, no. 116 (February 1, 1906), 3. The letter sent to President Theodore Roosevelt was published in "Appel au Président Roosevelt," *Pro Armenia* 6, no. 127 (February 1, 1906), 845. For Roosevelt's answer, see "La réponse du Président Roosevelt," *Pro Armenia* 6, no. 130, 869.

16. Sabaheddine, "La régénération de la Turquie," *Le Matin*, February 5, 1906. A verbatim Turkish translation was published in Prens Sabahaddin, "Türkiya'da Devr-i Teceddüd," *Rumeli*, no. 10 [February 16, 1906], 1–2. Many years later Ziya Gökalp, one of Sabahaddin Bey's ideological arch-rivals and a father of Turkish nationalist ideology, made an identical comment about the Kurds. See [Ziya Gökalp], "Türklerle Kürdler," *Küçük Mecmua* 1, no. 1 [June 5, 1922], 9–10.

17. See "Türkiye'nin İntibâh ve Teceddüdü," *Türk*, no. 118 (February 15, 1906), 1.

18. *Le Matin*, February 5, 1906.

19. Paul Grez, "La Turquie et les puissances: l'éternelle et toujours dangereuse Question d'orient: interview du Prince Sabahaddine," *Le Petit Parisien*, January 3, 1906. See also M[ehmed] Sabahaddin, "Tenkidinizi Okurken," *Terakki*, nos. 19 and 20 [July 1908], 3.

20. Hey'et- Tahririye, "[Maksad]," *Terakki*, no. 1 [April 1906], 1. Also published in "Yeni Bir Türk Cemiyeti," *Hayat*, no. 146 (July 5 [18], 1906), 4; and in "Yeni Bir Osmanlı Cemiyeti," *Tuna*, no. 212 [May 29, 1906], 2. Following the Young Turk Revolution of 1908, Sabahaddin Bey commented that he and his followers had pursued three major goals: "(1) To demonstrate to the Turks and to the Muslim Ottoman elements that the absolutism originated from our way of life and social shortcomings, and not from one or a few individuals; to win over public opinion for reforming our national education, and to strive to establish linked centers of struggle and resistance to abolish the absolutism that prevented us from fulfilling the aforementioned goal. (2) To demonstrate to our Christian compatriots the necessity of cordial unity with the Muslims and to illustrate the absolute necessity of not pursuing policies for autonomous administration or independence for all Ottoman elements, without distinction of ethnicity and faith, such as Greeks, Armenians, Bulgarians, etc., who compose the Ottoman world. (3) To prove to the civilized world through decisive proofs that our nation had not deserved the unlimited oppression of the former regime, to make conscience-loving members of our nation known to it [the civilized world], and to win over at least a few Western intellectuals, almost all of whom were totally against our national cause." See Sabahaddin, "Bir İzah," *İkdam*, October 18, 1908; and M[ehmed] Sabahaddin, *Teşebbüs-i Şahsî ve Tevsi'-i Me'zuniyet Hakkında Bir İzah* (Istanbul, 1324[1908]), 6.

21. *Terakki*, no. [1], 1.

22. Coded telegram from Nâbi Bey to the First Chamberlain's office, dated Paris, May 29, [1]906, BBA–YMGM, 287/40 (1324.R.5). See also Nâbi Bey to Bourgeois, May 28, 1906, AE–NS–T, 5 (1905–1907), 38–39. In addition, Nâbi Bey asked the French authorities to deport Ahmed Fazlı. See the drafts dated Paris, May 31, 1906 (Justice-Constantinople 30), June 6, 1906 (Justice), and the coded telegram from Affaires étrangères to Constans, Paris, June 2, 1906/no. 69, ibid., 42, 48, and 44, respectively. There were other Young Turks, however, helping Sabahaddin Bey's activities. The most prominent were Doctor Rıf'at, Doctor Mekkeli Sabri, former Captain Hüseyin Tosun, and Doctor Nihad Reşad. See Tarık Zafer Tunaya, *Türkiyede Siyasi Partiler, 1859–1952* (Istanbul, 1952), 142; and Bedii N. Şehsuvaroğlu, "Prof. Dr. Nihat Reşad Belger (1881–1961)," *Medikal ve Trapötik Hidro-*

Klimatoloji Yıllığı 2 (1962), 7–16. Also three Ottoman Jews—Salih Gürcü, Albert Fua, and Benbassa—worked for Sabahaddin Bey's organization. See M[oiz] Kohen, "Musevî Vatandaşlarımız," *Yeni Asır*, September 5, 1908. The journal *Terakki* was banned by the Ottoman authorities. See BBA–BEO/Dahiliye Giden, 106–3/55; 1398 [July 30, 1907]/233381; and BBA–YSHM, 503/107 (1324.R.24), and 513/69 (1325.C.19).

23. M[ehmed] Sabahaddin, "Genclerimize Mektub: İntibâh-ı Fikrîmiz," *Terakki*, no. [1], 1.

24. M[ehmed] Sabahaddin, "Genclerimize Mektub: Neşriyât-ı Siyasiyemiz," *Terakki*, no. [1], 2. Republished in *Rumeli*, no. 24 [June 1, 1906], 1–2.

25. Ahmed Riza, "Confession publique," *Mechveret Supplément Français*, no. 171 (January 1, 1906), 1.

26. M[ehmed] Sabahaddin, "Genclerimize Mektub: Neşriyât-ı Siyasiyemiz," *Terakki*, no. [1], 2–3. The CPU organs swiftly retaliated by claiming that "the very extensive decentralization" which was invented as an "elixir instead of the putty of the bonesetter" by "some of our compatriots" did not help Crete. See "*Şûra-yı Ümmet*," *Şûra-yı Ümmet*, no. 95 (June 23, 1906), 3.

27. M[ehmed] Sabahaddin, "Genclerimize Mektub: Neşriyât-ı Siyasiyemiz," *Terakki*, no. [1], 4.

28. M[ehmed] Sabahaddin, "Genclerimize Mektub: Merkeziyet ve Adem-i Merkeziyet," *Terakki*, no. [1], 9.

29. M[ehmed] Sabahaddin, "Kendimizi Asrımıza Tanıtalım," *Terakki*, no. [1], 11.

30. M[ehmed] Sabri, *Adem-i Merkeziyet Cemiyeti Beyannâmesi* (1908), Türk Tarih Kurumu Yazmaları, no. 129, 10. For similar claims, see M[ehmed Sabahaddin], "Tenkidinizi Okurken: Terbiye-i Millîye ve Islahat-ı Şahsîye," *Terakki*, nos. 19 and 20, 7. (Republished following the Young Turk Revolution by a daily. See *Yeni Gazete*, September 6, 1908.) This is simply a repetition of the claims made by the devotees of the *Science sociale* theory. See, for example, Henri de Tourville, "La Science sociale: est-elle une science?" *Science sociale* 1, no. 1 (1886), 8 ff; and Paul Roux, *Guide pratique de Science sociale [La Science sociale* 28–II, no. 102 (March 1913)], passim.

31. (Paris, 1897). This book was translated into Turkish by two disciples of Sabahaddin Bey after the Young Turk Revolution. See *Anglo Saksonların Esbâb-ı Fâikiyeti Nedir?*, trans. A. Fuad and A. Naci (Istanbul 1330 [1912]).

32. Edmond Demolins, *L'Éducation nouvelle: l'École des Roches* (Paris [1898]).

33. See [Ali Kemal], "İngiltere'de Bulunan Paris Muhabirimizden İngiltere Mektubları," *İkdam*, August 28, 1898. For a relatively late praise, see A[bdullah] C[evdet], "Émile Boutmy," *İctihad*, no. 11 (April 1906), 165.

34. For the Young Turks' view on the Transvaal War, see M. Şükrü Hanioğlu, *The Young Turks in Opposition* (New York, 1995), 139, 149, 315, and 323. For Demolins's view on the same subject, see *Boers et Anglais: où est le droit?* (Paris, 1898).

35. "Nouveaux membres," *Bulletin de la Société Internationale de Science sociale*, no. 3 (March 1904), 26. For Sabahaddin Bey's later activities, see Paul Descamps, *La Sociologie expérimentale* (Paris, 1933), xxvii; and Descamps's letter to Sabahaddin Bey, dated Paris, March 10, 1910, among Sabahaddin's Bey's uncataloged papers in European languages in Bibliothèque nationale (Paris), Manuscrits occidentaux.

36. *Bulletin de la Société Internationale de Science sociale*, no. 6 (June 1904), 62.

37. Süha Bey's letter dated Constantinople, November 18, 1904, ibid., no. 9 (December 1904), 103.

38. Ibid., no. 21 (January 1906), 8.

39. For more information, see Tawfīq 'Alī Barrū, *al-'Arab wa al-Turk fī al-'ahd al-dustūrī al-'Uthmānī, 1908–1914* (Cairo, 1960), 57.

40. M., "Husûl-i İnkılâbda Ebeveyn," *Şûra-yı Ümmet*, no. 37 (September 23, 1903), 2–3. Another CPU member wrote after the Young Turk Revolution of 1908 that he had read Demolins's works with interest. See Selim Sırrı, "Terbiyede Oyunla İnkılâb," *Nevsâl-i Millî 1330* (Istanbul, [1912]), 386.

41. Ö[mer] Naci, "Kari'lerime," *Çocuk Bağçesi*, no. 37 [October 26, 1905], 4: "As Edmond Demolins stated in his book on the reasons for the superiority of the Anglo-Saxons, it is nec-

essary to detect *fécondité* in the creative power of the racial life instead of external motivations and phenomena."

42. See, for example, [Gabriel] Olphe-Galliard, *La morale des nations contemporaines* [*La Science sociale* 27, 2, no. 91 (March 1912)], 53.

43. See a later publication by Paul Descamps, *La formation sociale des Arméniens* (Paris, 1926).

44. Gabriel d'Azambuja, "A qui profitent les mouvements révolutionnaires?" *Bulletin* [*de la Société Internationale de Science sociale*], no. 32 (January 1907), 167–72.

45. The publication had started in the undated second [June 1906?] issue of *Terakki* and continued in the third and fourth issues. In the third issue a comment on Demolins's study was provided by the journal. See "Bir Tavsiye," *Terakki*, no. [3], [July 1906?], 1. A complete translation of Demolins's work was published after the Young Turk Revolution of 1908. See Edmond Demolins, *Mevki'-i İktidar*, trans. A. M. N (Istanbul, 1328 [1912]).

46. Sabahaddin, "Genclerimize Mektublarım: Bizde Tenkid," *Terakki*, no. [2], 4.

47. For example, a former member of the Sobranye made this remark about Sabahaddin Bey's program: "the latter contingency [federalist faction led by the sultan's nephew] would be far more favourable to the cause of the Christians in Macedonia." See Christian Rakowski, "Problems of the Turkish Revolution," *The International* 3 (August–November 1908), 174.

48. Sabahaddin Bey claimed that he had by no means intended political autonomy by decentralization. His ideas, however, were interpreted to mean this by non-Turkish groups of the empire. See Hüseyin Cahid, "Adem-i Merkeziyet," *Tanin*, [September 19, 1908]; M[ehmed] S[abahaddin], *Teşebbüs-i Şahsî ve Tevsi'-i Me'zuniyet Hakkında Bir İzah*, 6–7; "Sabahaddin Bey'in Konferansı," *İttihad ve Terakki*, October 20, 1908; "Die Zukunft der jungtürkischen Idee," *März* 3, no. 16 (August 17, 1909), 3; and Andrei Mandel'shtam, "Mladoturetskaia derzhava," *Russkaia mysl'* 31, no. 5 (May 1915), 90. Sabahaddin Bey's ideas on decentralization were presented as "political idea[s]" after the Young Turk Revolution of 1908. See "Osmanlı İttihad ve Terakki Cemiyeti ve Sultanzâde Sabahaddin Bey," *Yeni Gazete*, September 14, 1908; and Müştak, "Bir Muhavere," *Tanin*, [September 9, 1908].

49. See A. Rustem Bey de Bilinski, "The Situation in Turkey," *The Fortnightly Review* 72, no. 427 (July 1, 1902), 96–97.

50. Bahaeddin Şakir later confessed that his sole purpose was to benefit from Sabahaddin Bey's title of "the nephew of the sultan," which made him important in the eyes of ordinary people. See the letter of Dr. Bahaeddin [Şakir] beginning "Birader-i Azizim Efendim" and dated Paris, June 11, 1907/no. 298, *Muhaberat Kopyası*, 325.

51. "Fransızcadan Tercüme Edilerek Bize Verilen Program Şudur," *Şûra-yı Ümmet İlâvesi*, no. 95 (July 27, 1906), 1.

52. A[hmed] R[iza], "Réponse à quelques critiques," *Mechveret Supplément Français*, no. 172 (February 1, 1906), 7. He added the following: "Agissant sous la pression d'événements d'ordre extérieur, ils cherchent à se conformer servilement aux desiderata des Européens."

53. Bahaeddin Şakir, "[Cevab]," *Şûra-yı Ümmet İlâvesi*, no. 95, 2–4. Great importance was attributed to this criticism, and it was republished by *Hayat*. See "Genc Türklerde İttihad Gayreti," *Hayat*, no. 172 (August 3 [16], 1906), 2. The CUP organs employed similar language following the Young Turk Revolution of 1908. See, for example, Hüseyin Cahid, "Teşebbüs-i Şahsî ve Adem-i Merkeziyet Hakkında," *Tanin*, [March 9, 1909]: "Decentralization means preparing the ground for making Mytilíni and Khíos and other islands become another Crete and throw themselves upon the bosom of the Greeks." Despite these strong criticisms, Sabahaddin Bey and his friends continued to underscore the importance of providing municipal councils with power, both during their years in exile and after the Young Turk Revolution of 1908. They also stressed this issue when they tried to win over Christian groups in the Ottoman Empire. See "Le programme Jeune-Turc et les Grecs: une interview avec Ahmed Fazli Bey secrétaire général de la Ligue de Décentralisation administrative et d'Initiative privée," *Le Monde Hellénique*, August 13, 1908.

54. Bahaeddin Şakir, "[Cevab]," *Şûra-yı Ümmet İlâvesi*, no. 95, 4. Ahmed Rıza employed similar language when he accused Sabahaddin Bey and his friends of "flirting with separatist

revolutionary committees." See "Acte de contrition," *Mechveret Supplément Français*, no. 184 (February 1, 1907), 3. A confidant of Sabahaddin Bey, who was extremely annoyed by Ahmed Rıza's characterization of "vulgaires aventuriers et d'incorrigibles charlatans," authored a pamphlet against the positivist leader. See İsmail Hakkı, *Cidâl yahud Ma 'kes-i Hakikat* (Cairo, 1907).

55. Dr. Bahaeddin [Şakir] to Alyotîzâde Mustafa Tevfik, dated Paris, April 9, 1906/no. 276, *Muhaberat Kopyası*, 283. Sabahaddin Bey, on the other hand, strongly denied these charges made by the CPU and targeted the Muslims in Crete. See "Erzurum'daki Dolab Avrupa'da da Dönüyor!" *Terakki*, no. 14 [November 1907], 8.

56. Terakki, "Bir Te'essüf," *Terakki*, no. [6] [November 1906], 10.

57. "Nasıl Hıristiyanlar Vatanımızda Adem-i Merkeziyetden Müstefîd Olageldikleri Halde Müslümanlar Merkeziyetin Mahkûmu Oluyorlar?" *Terakki*, no. [6], 3–10. The same claim was made by Sabahaddin Bey after the Young Turk Revolution. See Sabahaddin, *Teşebbüs-i Şahsî ve Adem-i Merkeziyet Hakkında İkinci Bir İzah* (Istanbul, 1324 [1908]), 38. It should be stated, however, that Sabahaddin Bey's claim was far from convincing.

58. [Mehmed] Sabahaddin, "Genclerimize Mektublarım: Bizde Tenkid," *Terakki*, no. [2], 7–8.

59. "Müdahale-i Ecnebiye Mes'elesi," *Şûra-yı Ümmet*, no. 113 (April 15, 1907), 1.

60. Bahaeddin Şakir, "Kari'in-i Kirâmdam İ'tizâr," *Şûra-yı Ümmet İlâvesi*, no. 114 (June 1, 1907), 1.

61. Ibid., 4–6.

62. Sabahaddin, *İkinci İzah*, 30, 21/fn.

63. Despite this fact, the league distributed its propaganda material in various regions of the empire such as Salonica, Tekfurdağı, Banghāzī, and Aydın through foreign post offices. See respectively, the First Chamberlain's office's dispatch dated [May 25, 1906] and the Ministry of the Interior's note dated [March 2, 1906] in Dışişleri Bakanlığı Hazine-i Evrak Arşivi, Box İdarî, 198; BBA–BEO/Dahiliye Giden, 105–3/54; 3436 [March 8, 1906]/225515; BBA–YMGM, 299/112 (1325.Ca.15); and BBA–YEE, Kâmil Paşa Evrakına Ek I, 86–31/3056 (1324.10.14).

64. For more information, see Tunaya, *Türkiyede Siyasi Partiler*, 149–50.

65. See Ahmed Bedevî Kuran, *Osmanlı İmparatorluğunda İnkılâp Hareketleri ve Millî Mücadele* (Istanbul, 1959), 398–400; and idem, *Harbiye Mektebinde Hürriyet Mücadelesi* (Istanbul [1960?]), 49–56.

66. See "Jeune-Turquie," *Le Soir*, October 12, 1906.

67. "Our brotherly, maybe fatherly advice to you is that you should work toward [learning] the science and technology needed by the fatherland. The fatherland is in great need of you for roads, bridges, and railways that will make the fatherland prosperous." Dr. Bahaeddin [Şakir] and Dr. Nâzım to "Küçük Biraderler," dated Paris, December 9, 1906/no. 223, *Muhaberat Kopyası*, 194.

68. See, for example, "Turkey Slowly Awakening," *The World*, December 2, 1906.

69. Beginning in 1907 a great number of Sabahaddin Bey's appeals began to be distributed in Istanbul. See "Le Mouvement turc," *Pro Armenia* 7, no. 153 (March 5, 1907), 1055.

70. A good clue to the loose affiliation between the Paris center and the Istanbul branch established by young college students is the distribution of CPU organs by these youngsters. Obviously many of them did not differentiate one "Young Turk" publication from another. See Marshal Zeki Pasha's note to the First Chamberlain's office dated [June 19, 1908], concerning Ahmed [Bedevî Kuran]'s activities and arrest; BBA–YMGM, 311/94 (1326.6.20).

71. "Mülâhaza," *Terakki*, no. 16 [February 1908], 7.

72. It was maintained in *Terakki* that the league's "internal regulations are being prepared and would be distributed free of charge to those who order it." See "Anadolu Kıyamları," *Terakki*, no. 12 [August 1907], 8.

73. See the subgovernor of Sinob, Bekir Bey, to the Sublime Porte, Sinob [January 17, 1908]/no. 272-13393, BBA–BEO/VGG(2): Müteferrika 1323: 878. See also BBA–YSHM, 517/150 (1325.Z.15); and BBA–YMGM, 304/92 (1325.Za.13).

74. See the memorandum entitled "La situation politique de l'Empire ottoman," among

the uncataloged papers of Sabahaddin Bey in Bibliothèque nationale (Paris), Manuscrits occidentaux. A French political police report dwelt upon this very point: "Le parti du Prince Sabah Eddine, soit la Ligue Ottomane de Décentralisation et Constitution, déploie son activité révolutionnaire dans la Turquie d'Asie, c'est-à-dire en Asie-Mineure (Arménie, Anatolie, etc.)" See the police report dated Paris, July 16, 1908/no. 34513, Archives de la Préfecture de Police de Paris (Sabahaddine et Loutfoullah), B. A (1653)-171154. CPU secret correspondence also indicates the committee's inability to create an organizational network in the region. See Dr. Bahaeddin [Şakir] to the CPU Baghdad branch, dated Paris, October 22, 1907/no. 388, *Muhaberat Kopyası*, 447.

75. Police report dated Paris, October 12, 1908/no. 34153-17.154/14, Archives de la Préfecture de Police de Paris (Sabahaddine et Loutfoullah), B. A (1653)-171154.

76. A very interesting comment was made by a missionary who stated that "Sabah-ed-Dine is the leader of the Turkish Decentralization Party which has as its platform political reform on the principle of local management of local affairs, and social reforms of a moderate socialistic tenor. The Armenian Federative party has practically the same platform and was instrumental in bringing about the coalition between the Armenian and Turkish revolutionary parties which proved so important a factor in the present revolution." See Chambers to Barton, Izmit, September 24, 1908, ABCFM, Harvard University, vol. 30 [656].

77. Paul Fesch, *Les Jeunes-Turcs* (Paris, 1909), 58.

78. "Anadolu Kıyamları," *Terakki*, no. 12, 8. See also "Anadolu Kıyamları," *Terakki*, no. 7 [March 1907], 6; and "Suriye Mes'elesi ve Beyrut İhtilâlleri," *Terakki*, no. 11 [July 1907], 8/fn.1.

79. Sabahaddin, "Vilâyetler Ahalisine Bir Da'vet," *Terakki*, no. 12, 5.

80. See M. T., "Anadolu'da Tarz-ı İdare-i Hükûmet, Me'murlar ve Eşraf," *Terakki*, no. 10 [June 1907], 1–5. Another member of the league confessed that despite their approach, their "publications were mostly seen and read by local notables and honest government officials." See M. Salih, "Vilâyetler Ahalisine İkinci Bir Da'vet," *Terakki*, no. 14, 4. The CPU, on the other hand, always asked local government officials to fight against the notables. See "Küçük Himmetler," *Şûra-yı Ümmet*, no. 18 (December 15, 1902), 4.

81. M. T., "Âşâr İltizamı: Ahali ve Hazine-i Hükûmetin Soyulması," *Terakki*, no. 12, 1–3.

82. M[ehmed] Sabri, "Anadolu Kıyamları: Bir Milletin Müttehiden Zulme ve Erbâbına Mukavemeti Erbâb-ı Zulmün Teslim-i Hak Etmesini Müstelzim Âlî ve Meşru' Bir Kuvvetdir!" *Terakki*, no. 11, 1–2.

83. Sabahaddin, "Anadolu Kıyamları," *Terakki*, no. 10, 5.

84. Sabahaddin, "Vilâyetler Ahalisine Bir Da'vet," *Terakki*, no. 12, 6. See also "Anadolu Kıyamları," *Terakki*, no. 14, 5; and "Anadolu Kıyamları," *Balkan*, no. 156 [March 13, 1907], 1–2.

85. See BBA–BEO/Hariciye Giden, 187-5/43; 1430 [November 27, 1906]/224012 and 221193; BBA–BEO/Posta ve Telgraf Nezareti Gelen, 580-17/5; 140 [November 26, 1906]; BBA–BEO/Hariciye Gelen, 164-5/20; 3003 (mükerrer) [January 22, 1907]/224296. Ottoman authorities would examine all incoming letters before giving them to the Russian consulate in Erzurum. See BBA–BEO/Posta ve Telgraf Nezareti Gelen, 580-17/5; 101 [November 21, 1907].

86. BBA–BEO/VGG(2): Trabzon Giden: 193; 90 [January 18, 1907]/242274. The authorities in Samsun, however, denied the existence of a local branch in that town. See also the subgovernor of Sinob, Bekir Bey, to the Grand Vizier's office, Sinob, [January 17, 1908]/no. 272–13393, BBA–BEO/VGG(2): Müteferrika 1323: 878.

87. See the appeal Osmanlı Teşebbüs-i Şahsî Usûl-i Meşrutiyet ve Adem-i Merkeziyet Cemiyeti Trabzon Fırkası, "Umum Osmanlı Vatandaşlarımıza!" [1908] (a one-page handbill), Bibliothèque nationale, Supplément turc, no. 1599, Papiers du Prince Sabahaddine, Box 1.

88. See the draft of the Ottoman notes-verbales delivered to the ambassador of Austria-Hungary in Istanbul, dated March 10, 1907/no. 631-33, and March 28, 1907/no. 68288-10; the Grand Vizier's office to the Ottoman Foreign Ministry, dated March 24, 1907; Memduh Pasha to Tevfik Pasha, dated [March 25, 1907]/no. 16, Dışişleri Bakanlığı Hazine-i Evrak Arşivi, Box İdarî, 198. See also BBA–BEO/Dahiliye Giden, 105-3/54; 3441 [March 9, 1907]/225551.

89. See the coded telegram from the governor of Trabzon to the Ministry of the Interior, March 16, 1907, and the draft of the Ottoman note-verbale presented to the French ambassador in Istanbul, dated June 11, 1907/no. 69177-37, Dışişleri Bakanlığı Hazine-i Evrak Arşivi, Box İdarî, 198. The smuggling of "seditious" journals had caused the government to replace the officers at the ports of Trabzon and Samsun. This replacement, however, seems to have made very little impact. See BBA–BEO/Serasker Reft, 261-6/69; 739 [July 1, 1906]/ 214569.

90. See Ali Haydar Midhat, *Hâtıralarım*, 1872-1946 (Istanbul, 1946), 183–86. The government agents uncovered and stopped the smuggling of *Terakki* through this channel. Ali Haydar Midhat's further applications to the British authorities on this matter bore no fruit. See his "très confidentielle" letter to Edward Grey dated Paris, May 21, 1907; and O'Conor to Grey, Therapia, June 17, 1907/no. 349, PRO/F.O. 371/346, files 16734 and 19810, respectively.

91. The journal was made available in Salmās. See Türk Oğlu, "İstibdad," *İrşad*, no. 90, May 16 [29], 1907, 4. Many people in this region and those in Iranian and Russian Azerbaijan read Sabahaddin Bey's articles in *İctihad*, in which they were republished. See "Yeni Türk Matbu'atı," *İrşad*, no. 41 (March 29 [April 11], 1908), 4.

92. See Kuran, *Osmanlı İmparatorluğunda İnkılâp Hareketleri*, 393–94; Tunaya, *Türkiyede Siyasi Partiler*, 142; and Şükrü Kaya Gökozanoğlu, *Jöntürklerden Birkaçının Biyografisi* (Istanbul, 1936), 20.

93. See, for example, Kh. M. Tsovikian, "Vliianie russkoi revoliutsii 1905 g. na revoliutsionnoe dvizhenie v Turtsii," *Sovetskoe vostokovedenie* 3 (1945), 15–35; A[nna] M[ikhailovna] Pankratowa, *Die Erste russische Revolution von 1905 bis 1907* (Berlin, 1953), 247–48; A[natolii] F[ilippovich] Miller, "Burzhuaznaia revoliutsiia 1908 g. v Turtsii," *Sovetskoe vostokovedenie* 6 (1955), 29–45; idem, "Mladoturetskaia revoliutsiia," in *Pervaia russkaia revoliutsiia 1905–1907 gg. i mezhdunarodnoe revoliutsionnoe dvizhenie* 2 (Moscow, 1956), 313–48; idem, "Revoliutsiia 1908 g. v Turtsii i Mustafa Kemal," *Narody Azii i Afriki* 3 (1975), 54–55; A. D. Zheltiakov and IU[rii] A[shotovich] Petrosian, "Mladoturetskoe dvizhenie v trudakh turetskikh istorikov," *Narody Azii i Afriki* 5 (1965), 59–60; V. I. Shpil'kova, "Antipravitel'stvennye vystupleniia v vostochnoi Anatolii nakanune mladoturetskoi revoliutsii," *Narody Azii i Afriki* 3 (1971), 73–76; and S[emen] L['vovich] Agaev, "Iranskaia revoliutsiia 1905–1911 gg.," *Narody Azii i Afriki* 4 (1975), 66. This strand seems to have gained momentum after the Second World War. Earlier Soviet studies focused more on economic determinants of the Young Turk Revolution. For an example, see Kh. Gabidullin, "Problemy mladoturetskoi revoliutsii," *Revoliutsionnyi vostok* 3/25 (1934), 146–64.

94. See IU. A. Petrosian, *Mladoturetskoe dvizhenie* (*vtoraia polovina XIX-nachalo XX v*) (Moscow, 1957), 225.

95. See V. I. Lenin, *Collected Works* 18 (April 1912–March 1913) (Moscow, 1968), 163–64, 584–85; 19 (March–December 1913) (Moscow, 1968), 85–86; 20 (December 1913–August 1914) (Moscow, 1964), 406; 23 (August 1916–March 1917) (Moscow, 1977), 252; 25 (June–September 1917) (Moscow, 1964), 40; 30 (September 1919–April 1920) (Moscow, 1965), 160. See also V. I. Shpil'kova, "V. I. Lenin o mladoturetskoi revoliutsii," *Uchenie zapiski*, no. 370 (1970), 285–89. Leon Trotsky made similar claims. See, for example, *The War Correspondence of Leon Trotsky in the Balkan Wars, 1912–1913*, trans. Brian Pearce, ed. George Weissman and Duncan Williams (New York, 1980), 3. The article was originally published in *Pravda*. For obvious reasons, however, later Soviet historiography did not refer to Trotsky's comments.

96. See, for example, H. Zafer Kars, *Belgelerle 1908 Devrimi Öncesinde Anadolu* (Ankara, 1984). A worse example, however, is a recent book which has many factual errors and totally misunderstands and misrepresents the nature of the revolutionary activities that took place in Eastern Anatolia between 1905 and 1907. See Aykut Kansu, *1908 Devrimi* (Istanbul, 1995), 35 ff. Despite these amateurish essays, a serious study based on original sources provides insight. See Muammer Demirel, *İkinci Meşrutiyet Öncesinde Erzurum'da Halk Hareketleri* (Istanbul, 1990).

97. Pro-Hncak groups strongly criticized Sabahaddin Bey's proposals. See Uluğ, "Ermeniler," *Türk*, no. 110 (December 21, 1905), 1–2; "Mısır'da Çıkan *Türk* Gazetesi," *Hayat*, no. 29 (Feb-

ruary 5[18], 1906), 4. Also the idea of an alliance with the Young Turks was not popular among the Armenian intelligentsia and the European and American intellectuals who supported them. The following comment was made only eight months before the agreement reached by the CPU, Sabahaddin Bey's League, and the Dashnaktsutiun: "Your question . . . can[not] be settled by uniting with the Young Turkey party; religious differences deny that and, moreover, the Turk is not progressive." Christine Yetter, "The Inevitable," *Armenia* 3, no. 6 (April 1907), 5. See also "The Armenian Question in Its Present Phase," *Armenia* 2, no. 5 (February 1906), 3–7.

98. A[bdullah] Djevdet, "Une profession de foi," *Idjtihad*, no. 6 (May 1905), 87. For Abdullah Cevdet's admiration for Sabahaddin Bey and his ideas and the relations between these two Young Turk leaders, see "Térekki," *Idjtihad*, no. 11 (April 1906), 176; "Gazetelerimizden," *İctihad* 2, no. 5 (January 1908), 318; "Sabahaddin Bey," *İctihad*, no. 44 [April 14, 1912], 1061; Abdullah Djevdet, "Le Prince Sabahaddin Bey," *L'Express*, December 1, 1918; Abdullah Cevdet, "Prens Sabahaddin Bey," *Sabah*, December 8, 1919; Abdullah Djevdet, "Une opinion du Dr Abdullah Djevdet Bey," *Le Journal d'Orient*, October 20, 1921; and Abdullah Cevdet, *Cihan-ı İslâma Dair Bir Nazar-ı Tarihî ve Felsefî* (Istanbul, 1922), 11–12.

99. Abdullah Cevdet, *Kafkasya'daki Müslümanlara Beyannâme* (Geneva, 1905). Republished in "Beyannâme," *Rumeli*, no. 12 [March 2, 1906], 2–3. A French version was published in Ab[dullah] Djevdet, "Au musulmans de Caucase," *Idjtihad*, no. 10 (January [March 31], 1906), 146–48.

100. See "Ne Yazıyorlar [?]" *Hayat*, no. 68 (September 20 [October 3], 1905), 4. A Russian police report indicates that Abdullah Cevdet's pamphlet was found among the papers of an Azerbaijani dissident named Ali Asker Bey Hasmemedov and that it had been given to him by a Dashnak leader named Léon Mnatsakov. See G. Z [Hamid] Aliiev, "K voprosu o pomoshchi Azerbaidzhanskoi demokratii mladoturetskomu dvizheniiu," *Tiurkologicheskii sbornik* 5 (1973), 191. It seems that copies of the appeal were sent to Iranian Azerbaijan and from there smuggled into Russian Azerbaijan. See idem, *Turtsiia v period pravleniia mladoturok (1908–1918 gg.)* (Moscow, 1972), 90–91.

101. BBA–YSHM, 502/34 (1324.Ra.6). The Ottoman authorities further claimed that Abdullah Cevdet had authored the pamphlet "in order to help the Armenian cause and to deceive the Muslims in the Caucasus." See Tevfik Pasha to the Grand Vizier's office [April 29, 1906]/no. 452; and Mehmed Ferid Pasha to the First Chamberlain's office [April 30, 1906], ibid.

102. See his short biography and his letter to Vlakhof in "Tigrane Zaven," *La Fédération Balkanique* 4, no. 88 (March 15, 1928), 1821–23. See also "Entre Turcs et Arméniens," *L'Indépendance Arabe* 1, nos. 7–8 (October–November 1907), 124–25; and André Barre, *L'Esclavage blanc: Arménie et Macédoine* (Paris, [1908]), 90–91. For the journals' desire to unite Armenians under a single organization, see A. Ter-Arutiunov, "Politicheskiia partii v sovremennoi Turtsii," *Russkaia mysl'* 24, no. 9 (September 1908), 173. An Armenian scholar states that the co-editor of the journal *Yerkiri Tzaïn [Erkiri Dzain]*, Karékin G. Kozakian, had Hncakist affiliations. See Anahide Ter Minassian, "Le Mouvement révolutionnaire arménien, 1890–1903," *Cahiers du Monde Russe et Soviétique* 14, no. 4 (October–December 1973), 595–97. The journal paid great attention to the revolutionary movement in Erzurum. See Tsovikian, "Vliianie russkoi revoliutsii 1905 g.," *Sovetskoe vostokovedenie* 3, 32/fn.

103. BBA–BEO/VGG(2): Trabzon Giden: 193; 15 [May 9, 1906]/22481 (mühimme); and BBA–BEO/VGG(2): Erzurum Reft: 129; 21 [May 9, 1906]/22481 (mühimme).

104. See Ottomanus [Pierre Anméghian], "Aux Arméniens ottomans," *Mechveret Supplément Français*, no. 182 (December 1, 1906), 1–2.

105. Aliiev, "K voprosu o pomoshchi Azerbaidzhanskoi demokratii mladoturetskomu dvizheniiu," *Tiurkologicheskii sbornik*, 187–88. The CPU, on the other hand, required the authors of this initiative to accept its terms if they really wanted to reach an agreement. See Ottomanus [Pierre Anméghian], "Les intérêts arméniens," *Mechveret Supplément Français*, no. 177 (July 1, 1906), 3–4; and idem, "Aux Arméniens ottomans," *Mechveret Supplément Français*, no. 182, 1–2.

106. Alexandre Bennigsen and Chantal Lemercier-Quelquejay, *La presse et le mouvement national chez les musulmanes de Russie avant 1920* (Paris, 1964), 121; Tadeusz Swietochowski,

"The Himmät Party: Socialism and the National Question in Russian Azerbaijan, 1904–1920," *Cahiers du Monde Russe et Soviétique* 19, nos. 1–2 (January–June 1978), 123 ff. *"Da'vet ve Koç* Gazetesi'ne Tebrik," *Hayat,* no. 114 (May 28 [June 10], 1906), 3; and S. M., *"Da'vet-Koç," İrşad,* no. 111 (May 13 [26], 1906), 2.

107. See "Un heureux rapprochement," *Mechveret Supplément Français,* no. 178 (August 1, 1906), 4.

108. Fuad Medhat Pacha, "Jeune Turquie," *Pro Armenia* 6, no. 131 (April 5, 1906), 881.

109. Fuad Medhat Pacha, "Aux Ottomans," *Pro Armenia* 6, no. 126 (February 1, 1906), 852.

110. Dr. Bahaeddin [Şakir]'s letter to the CPU Baghdad branch beginning "Muhterem Meslekdaşım" and dated Paris, October 22, 1906/no. 388, *Muhaberat Kopyası,* 447–48.

111. See the letter of Dr. Bahaeddin [Şakir] beginning "Birader-i Azizim Efendim" and dated Paris, June 11, 1907/no. 298, *Muhaberat Kopyası,* 324. In another letter the following was stated: "He showed he preferred working with them to us by accepting the program of the separatist Armenians and by [proposing] an extensive decentralization." See the letter of Dr. Bahaeddin [Şakir] beginning "Aziz ve Muhterem Vatandaşımız" and dated Paris, September 6, 1907/no. 365, *Muhaberat Kopyası,* 415.

112. For more details, see J. Michael Hagopian, "Hyphenated Nationalism: The Spirit of the Revolutionary Movement in Asia Minor and the Caucasus, 1896–1910" Ph.D. diss., Harvard University (1942), 257–58.

113. For the official resolutions, see "Les résolutions du Congrès de la Fédération Révolutionnaire Arménienne," *Pro Armenia* 7, no. 160 (June 20, 1907), 1111; and "Résolutions de la Fédération Révolutionnaire Arménienne," *Pro Armenia* 7, no. 172 (December 20, 1907), 1207–8. They are also mentioned in the report prepared by the Dashnaktsutiun and submitted to the Socialist International Bureau. See "Les relations entre Arméniens et les musulmans de Turquie et de Russie," *Pro Armenia* 7, no. 167 (October 5, 1907), 1169.

114. For Armenian criticism of the CPU and its publication, see R., "Quelques thèses du 'Mechveret,'" *Pro Armenia* 4, no. 91 (August 1, 1904), 557–58; Pierre Quillard, "Un manifeste Jeune Turc," *Pro Armenia* 6, no. 130, 870; R., "Une circulaire des Jeunes Turcs aux ambassades," *Pro Armenia* 6, no. 145 (November 5, 1906), 993; P[ierre] Quillard, "Anniversaire," *Pro Armenia* 6, no. 146 (November 20, 1906), 999; Pierre Quillard, "L'impossible entente," *Pro Armenia* 7, no. 148 (December 20, 1906), 1015–16; "L'Allemagne et l'islam," *Pro Armenia* 7, no. 151 (February 5, 1907), 1043; "Une article du 'Mechveret,'" *Pro Armenia* 7, no. 155 (April 5, 1907), 1074; Pierre Quillard, "Turquie et Russie," *Pro Armenia* 7, no. 166 (September 20, 1907), 1158–59; and Pierre Quillard, "Dans l'Asie turque et à Paris," *Pro Armenia* 7, no. 168 (October 20, 1907), 1174–75. For the CPU's responses and countercharges, see Ottomanus [Pierre Anméghian], "Les Révolutionnaires arméniens," *Mechveret Supplément Français,* no. 176 (June 1, 1906), 1–2; and idem, "L'impossible 'programme,'" *Mechveret Supplément Français,* no. 185 (March 1, 1907), 1–2.

115. See Dickson to O'Conor, Van, March 2, 1908/no. 6, enclosed with Barclay to Grey, Pera, April 1, 1908/no. 163, PRO/F.O. 424/215 (confidential 9433).

116. Nuri Bey to İzzet Pasha, Cairo [July 16, 1906]/no. 1226, BBA–BEO/Umum Şifre Vârideli Kayıd Defteri, 691–28/2.

117. See BBA–BEO/VGG(2): Van Reft: 198; 105 [September 13, 1906]/237449; and BBA–BEO/VGG(2): Van Âmed: 195; 118 [August 27, 1906]/22654 (mühimme).

118. See Abdülvahab Pasha, the governor of Erzurum, to the Grand Vizier's office, Erzurum [June 12, 1908]/no. 296–13521, BBA–BEO/Şifre Telgraf Kayıd, Anadolu 1324 (1), 693/2. British consuls, and various journals too, obtained information concerning the Armenian committees' desire to establish friendly relations with the Kurds. See, for example, Shipley to O'Conor, Erzurum, March 7, 1907/no. 12 (confidential), enclosed with O'Conor to Grey, March 18, 1907/no. 177 (confidential), PRO/F.O. 424/212; "Kourdistan," *L'Indépendance Arabe* 1, no. 1 (April 1907), 15; "L'impôt personnel et le Mouvement turc," *Pro Armenia* 7, no. 155, 1069; and "Les musulmans contre Hamid," *Pro Armenia* 7, no. 161 (July 5, 1907), 1117.

119. See "Azm-i Kavî Cemiyeti'nden Kürdlere Beyannâme ve İstitrad," esp. 3–6, Abbas II Papers, Durham University, F. 24/1-6.

120. Sabahaddin, "On Üçüncü *Terakki*'de Tenkidinizi Okurken," *Terakki*, no. 15 [January 1908], 7.

121. Erzurum Cemiyet-i İttihadiyesinden Bir Zabit, "Kürdler," *Terakki*, no. 14, 5.

122. Dickson to O'Conor, Van, February 9, 1908/no. 3, PRO/F.O. 195/2283.

123. "Solidarité entre Arméniens et Turcs," *Pro Armenia* 7, no. 170 (November 20, 1907), 1189.

124. "Teşekkür," *Terakki*, nos. 19 and 20, 12.

125. The alliance seems to have lasted for a long time. For example, a memorandum prepared by Colonel Ali Hilmi reveals that even during the Young Turk Revolution of 1908, Sabahaddin Bey's appeals were smuggled into the empire with the help of the Dashnaktsutiun's Balkan branch. See Colonel Ali Hilmi's report presented to the Ottoman Commissioner in Bulgaria and dated [August 11, 1908]/no. 411-158, in BBA–BEO/Mümtaze Kalemi: Bulgaristan Tasnifi Evrakı II, A. MTZ (04), 170/45 (1326.2.8); and BBA–BEO/Bulgaristan Komiserliği Giden, 679–58/5; 770/89 [August 20, 1908].

126. For his flight and activities, see Tevfik Pasha to Münir Bey, April 8, 1902/ no. 139-46938; the Grand Vizier's office's dispatch dated [March 5, 1902]; Tevfik Pasha to Anthopoulos Pasha, April 30, 1902/no. 80-47315 (the original is in Archives of the Turkish Embassy in London, Box 377 [1]); and Münir Bey to Tevfik Pasha, April 17, 1902/ no. 222-16115, BBA–HR.SYS. 1796/14 (original. 502/57).

127. See Ali Fahri, *Emel Yolunda* (Istanbul, 1326 [1910]), 266 ff.

128. See [Abdullah Cevdet], "İhtar-ı Mahsus," *İctihad*, no. 4 (March 1905), 1; idem, *Hadd-ı Te'dib: Ahmed Rıza Bey'e Açık Mektub* (Paris, 1903), 56.

129. Abdullah Cevdet wrote that it was Hüseyin Tosun who gave him a copy of Émile Boutmy's book [*Essai d'une psychologie politique du Peuple anglais au XIXe siècle* (Paris, 1901)] and who had him translate the work into Turkish. See Abdullah Cevdet's dedication in Émile Boutmy, *İngiliz Kavmi* 1, trans. Abdullah Cevdet (Cairo, 1909), [5]. The work was translated into Turkish in three volumes, the second and third volumes published in Istanbul in 1911 and 1912, respectively.

130. The committee must have been founded in mid-1906, though it started publishing an organ in February 1907. Some researchers who misunderstood Rashīd Riḍā's introduction assumed that the Ligue Constitutionnelle Ottomane was established "sometime soon after 1897," which is obviously erroneous. See, for example, Zeine N. Zeine, *Arab-Turkish Relations and the Emergence of Arab Nationalism* (Beirut, 1958), 67.

131. See Muḥammad Rashīd Riḍā, "Rafīq al-ʿAẓm," in *Majmūʿat athār Rafīq Bak al-ʿAẓm* 1, ed. ʿUthmān al-ʿAẓm (Miṣr [Cairo], 1344 [1925]), iv–v.

132. Ibid., v. The pasha allegedly told the following to Rashīd Riḍā: "Reform does not come from the top, nor does it come from the statesmen; it rather comes from the lower and middle classes of the nation."

133. Rashīd Riḍā stated that "with the appearance of *Şûra-yı Osmanî*, [they] stopped writing leaflets." See ibid.

134. Coded telegram from Memduh Pasha, the Minister of the Interior, to the subgovernor of Jerusalem [December 24, 1907], Israel State Archives, RG. 83-1/ﬠ.

135. Abdullah Cevdet's biographer Karl Süssheim writes that "he was a member of the Young Turkish group known as Decentralists." See K[arl] Süssheim, "'Abd Allāh Djevdet," *El-Supplement* (1938), 57. For Abdullah Cevdet's praise of the new organization, see A[bdullah] C[evdet], "Matbuʿat-ı Cedîde: Şûra-yı Osmanî Cemiyeti ve Gazetesi," *İctihad* 2, no. 3 (November 1906), 262–63. The CPU strongly criticized Abdullah Cevdet's becoming a member of this organization. See the letter of Dr. Bahaeddin [Şakir] beginning "Muhterem Kardaşlar" and dated Paris, September 23, 1907/no. 372, *Muhaberat Kopyası*, 424–25. Ter-Arutiunov, in "Politicheskiia partii v sovremennoi Turtsii," *Russkaia mysl'* 24, no. 9 (September 1908), 170, further claims that Abdullah Cevdet's *İctihad* and Diran Kelekian's *Yeni Fikir* were published as the organs of this committee. There is no evidence, however, to support this claim.

136. "Türkiya'da İnkılâb," *Balkan*, no. 111 [December 15, 1906], 2.

137. See Diran Kelekian to Bahaeddin Şakir, Cairo, November 9, 1906, Private Papers of Bahaeddin Şakir.

138. For example, when the organ of this society published an article describing the opposition committees in the Ottoman Empire, it made the claim that Sabahaddin Bey's league and theirs were two independent organizations. See "Osmanlı Ahrarı, Cemiyetleri ve Gazeteleri," *Şûra-yı Osmanî*, no. 7 (May 1, 1907), 4–5.

139. See "La Ligue Constitutionnelle Ottomane," *Pro Armenia* 6, no. 146, 1003–4. For the original program, see "Cemiyetin Programı da Şudur," *Şûra-yı Osmanî*, no. 1 (February 1, 1907), 2. Armenian journals also praised the publication policy of the society. See "Le Mouvement libéral ottoman: un nouveau journal," *Pro Armenia* 7, no. 152 (February 20, 1907), 1048–49.

140. See "Komiteciler Ne Yapıyor?" *Şûra-yı Ümmet*, no. 107 (January 1, 1906 [1907]), 4. The new society and *Pro Armenia* denied the allegations. See "*Şûra-yı Ümmet* Gazetesi'ne," *Şura-yı Osmanî*, no. 1, 3; and Pierre Quillard, "L'impossible entente," *Pro Armenia* 7, no. 151, 1040. Sabahaddin Bey too praised the publication of the journal and recommended it to his readership. See "*Şûra-yı Osmanî*," *Terakki*, no. 12, 8.

141. For example, the new organization's appeal to all Muslims in the world, asking them to help their coreligionists in the Ottoman Empire (see "Bütün Dünyadaki Müslümanlar Gözlerini Açdı Yalnız Türkiya Müslümanları Henüz Uykuda: Ey Müslümanlar Türkiya'daki Mezhebdaşlarınızın İmdadına Yetişiniz," *Şûra-yı Osmanî*, no. 9 [May 31, 1907], 1–3) was strongly denounced by the CPU. See "Garib Bir İstimdad ve İmdad," *Şûra-yı Ümmet*, no. 122 (September 15, 1907), 1. The new organization responded in similar language. See "*Şûra-yı Ümmet*," *Şûra-yı Osmanî*, no. 19 (November 1, 1907), 2. For further criticism on their part, see "İslâm Matbu'atı," *İrşad*, no. 10 (January 22 [February 4], 1908), 4. Despite the CPU's strong criticism, the appeal in question attracted various Muslim groups. See, for example, its translation in *Musāvāt*, no. 1 (October 13, 1907), 4–7.

142. See the Minister of the Interior's two dispatches both dated [June 16, 1907] in BBA–YMGM, 299/30 (1325.Ca.5); and Marshal Zeki Pasha's letter submitted to the First Chamberlain's office, dated [October 1, 1907], BBA–YEE, 15/1504/74/14. The Ottoman authorities applied strict measures against the initiatives of the committee and against the smuggling and circulation of its journal. See the First Chamberlain's office to the Grand Vizier's office [February 9, 1907], and from the latter to the khedive and the Ottoman High Commissioner in Egypt [February 10, 1907]/no. 1107 (decipher), BBA–BEO/Mümtaze Kalemi: Mısır, A.MTZ (04), 18/A, 63 (1324.12.27); BBA–BEO/Hidiviyet-i Celile-i Mısriyenin Tahrirat Defteri, 78-1033-68/5; 1107/403 [February 10, 1907]; and BBA–BEO/İrade-Mısır Mesâlihi, no. 1859-1107/[February 9, 1907].

143. See the "Special Note" from the Ottoman Foreign Ministry to the First Chamberlain's office [June 10, 1907]/no. 246-915; and Fevzi Bey to Tevfik Pasha, T'bilisi, March 15/28, 1907/no. 128–32, BBA–TDA, End. M.T. Box 1220/no. 3.

144. See, for example, "İran ve Osmanlı: İran İctima'iyûn-i Amiyûn Mücahidîn Fırkası Tarafından Sureti Âtide Münderic Beyannâme Neşr Olunmuştur," quoted in *Balkan*, no. 291 [March 15, 1908], 4.

145. Abdullah Cevdet, "Yürekli Çiftci," *Sabah'ül-Hayr*, no. 8 (September 15, [1907]), 41.

146. On the copy of the appeal entitled "Uğurlar Olsun!" dated July 24 [1907] and signed by the "Central Committee of the Armenian Revolutionary Dashnak Party," a note reading "to *Şûra-yı Osmanî* journal" had been written in Ottoman Turkish. The appeal is in the Dashnaktsutiun archives, archival reference number 669–175. Similarly a Dashnak appeal was enclosed with *Sabah'ül-Hayr* and sent to a Young Turk journal. See Van Ermeni Daşnaksutyun İhtilâl Fırkası Merkez Komitesi, "Biz ve Bizim Düşmanlarımız," *Balkan*, no. 416 [April 14, 1908], 1–2; and "Türkiya'da İnkılâb Mukaddimeleri," *Balkan*, no. 416, 1. The appeal was originally distributed in Van. See Dickson to O'Conor, Van, March 2, 1908/no. 6, enclosed with Barclay to Grey, Pera, April 1, 1908/no. 163, and the French translation of the appeal entitled "Nous et nos adversaires," PRO/F.O. 424/215 (confidential 9433). There are differences between the Turkish version published in *Balkan* and the aforementioned French translation. Some sections were omitted in the former.

147. See BBA–BEO/Zabtiye Giden, 663–21/13; 150 [August 31, 1906]/217565; BBA–BEO/Hariciye Giden, 187–5/43; 1001 [August 31, 1906]/217547; and 1002 [September 1,

1906]/217564; BBA–İrade-Hususî, C 1324/no. 5–568 (543); BBA–BEO/Vilâyât-ı Muhtare ve Mümtaze Kalemlerine Mahsus Yevmiye Defteridir, 931–85/5; 341/2044 [October 31, 1906]; 342/2272 [November 6, 1906]; and 343/2393 [November 14, 1906].

148. *"Tercüman* ve *Şûra-yı Osmanî," Şûra-yı Osmanî,* no. 13 (July 31 [1907]), 1.

149. Tunaya, *Türkiyede Siyasi Partiler,* 143. Tunaya states that Mahmud Faiz, who was dispatched from Cairo, formed the branch in Izmir. This branch, however, was discovered and crushed by the Ottoman authorities early in 1908. See Heathcote-Smith to O'Conor, Izmir, February 17, 1907/no. 21, PRO/F.O. 195/2300; "Genc Türk Tevkifatı," *Balkan,* no. 254 [February 1, 1908], 4; "Le Mouvement turc," *Pro Armenia* 8, no. 175 (February 5, 1908), 1229; and "Contre Hamid," *Pro Armenia* 8, no. 181 (May 5, 1908), 1283.

150. See, for example, "Nasıl Hıristiyanlar Vatanımızda Adem-i Merkeziyetden Müstefîd Olageldikleri Halde Müslümanlar Merkeziyetin Mahkûmu Oluyorlar?" *Terakki,* no. [6], 7.

151. See M. Salih, "Vilâyetler Ahalisine İkinci Bir Da'vet," *Terakki,* no. 14, 1. Another article criticizing the CPU's propaganda about the Yemen uprising was published by a confidant of Sabahaddin Bey. See "Yemen'e Dair: Hususî Bir Mektubdan," *İctihad* 2, no. 4 (September 1907), 266.

152. Since the event took place before the official establishment of the Ligue Constitutionnelle Ottomane, in the Ottoman documents the individuals who carried out the protest were referred to as "the accursed Young Turks." See the coded telegram from the general secretary of the Ottoman Commissioner in Egypt to the Grand Vizier's office [August 27, 1905]/ no. 250-178/261, BBA–BEO/Mısır Hülâsa [Defteri], 1042-68/14. In Beirut some *hocas* who supported this campaign asserted that fighting against the Yemeni Muslims contradicts Islam. See Divisional General Mehmed Kâmil to the First Chamberlain's office, Beirut [June 24, 1905]/no. 761, *Umumî Kayda Mahsus Defterdir,* BBA–YEE, 36/139-72/139/XIX-2. Abraham Galanté, who had then worked closely with the aforementioned league, stated after the Young Turk Revolution that he "received a letter of thanks from Yaḥyā Ḥamīd al-Dīn, Imām of Yemen . . . demonstrating the great role that the founder of *La Vara* had played in the Young Turk movement through the efforts that he made in order to prevent bloodshed and the occurrence of a diplomatic complication." See "Abraham Galanté," *La Vara* 4, no. 65 (September 1908), 7.

153. See Sabahaddin Bey's letter dated November 23, [1]907 and addressed as "Azizim Birader," BBA–YEE, 15/1587/74/14. It should be noted, however, that Sabahaddin Bey employed critical language when discussing Azoury's ideas. See Sabahaddin, "On Üçüncü *Terakki'*de Tenkidinizi Okurken," *Terakki,* no. 15 [January 1908], 7.

154. Although this was the first serious and long-lasting policy of carrying out operations in the guise of Muslim committees, similar but more trivial initiatives may have been undertaken by Armenian organizations during their early activities. In fact, a British diplomat speaks about the arrest of Armenians by Ottoman authorities in 1893 because of the placarding of "seditious" appeals, although "there was nothing in these Yaftas to indicate an Armenian origin." See Robert Graves, *Storm Centres of the Near East: Personal Memories, 1879–1929* (London, 1933), 132.

155. See Nâzım Bey to the Grand Vizier's office, Erzurum [March 18, 1904]/no. 13-449, BBA–BEO/VGG: Anadolu [Telgrafı] Defteri: 909.

156. See, for example, BBA–BEO/VGG(2): Van Reft: 198; 15 [July 1, 1906]/22029 (mühimme); 35 [August 28, 1906]/22134 (mühimme); BBA–BEO/VGG(2): Van Vilâyeti Âmed: 195; 66/6 [October 16, 1906]/22134 (mühimme).

157. See, for example, BBA–BEO/VGG(2): Van Reft: 198; 9 [May 9, 1906]/22481 (mühimme); and the appeal Ermeni Daşnak İhtilâl Fırkası Merkez Komitesi, "Türk Vatandaşlarımıza," in PRO/F.O. 195/2251, folio 69, enclosed with Dickson to O'Conor, Van, August 4, 1907/no. 14, which ends with the following statement: "Good luck with the wish and the desire of the people! Death to the enemies of the people! Long live the alliance and union of the nations!" An Armenian version and a French translation of this appeal are available. See ibid., ff. 72, and 70–71, respectively.

158. See, for example, Petrosian, *Mladoturetskoe dvizhenie,* 226–27.

159. Quoted in "Une déclaration du *Droshag," Pro Armenia* 7, no. 169 (November 5, 1907), 1182.

160. A Russian source claims that both these journals were published as the organs of the same committee in Van and Erzurum. See Ter-Arutiunov, "Politicheskiia partii v sovremennoi Turtsii," *Russkaia mysl'* 24, no. 9 (September 1908), 173. Another scholar maintains that the second journal was published in Erzurum. See Tsovikian, "Vliianie russkoi revoliutsii 1905 g.," *Sovetskoe vostokovedenie* 3, 22.

161. A copy of this journal was received by a Plovdiv-based Young Turk journal. See "*Sabah'ül-Hayr*," *Balkan*, no. 260 [September 26, 1907], 3. See also "Turquie," *Revue du Monde Musulman* 4, no. 1 (January 1908), 155.

162. "Vatanda Tekâmül veya Mukaddime-i İnkılâb-2," *Balkan*, no. 310 [December 6, 1907], 1–2.

163. "Un appel aux Turcs qui veulent la liberté," *Pro Armenia* 6, nos. 142–43 (September 20–October 5, 1906), 974.

164. See Pierre Quillard, "L'union nécessaire," *Pro Armenia* 6, nos. 142–43, 969.

165. "La Fédération Révolutionnaire Turque," *Pro Armenia* 7, no. 171 (December 5, 1907), 1197.

166. Ter-Arutiunov, "Politicheskiia partii v sovremennoi Turtsii," *Russkaia mysl'* 24, no. 9 (September 1908), 171, 173. Another Russian source, however, speaks about a "Komitet liberalov" that made demands for the people. See Kh. Gabidullin, "Problemy mladoturetskoi revoliutsii," *Revoliutsionnyi vostok* 4/26 (1934), 113.

167. "Komiteciler Ne Yapıyor?" *Şûra-yı Ümmet*, no. 107 (January 1, 1906 [1907]), 4.

168. Fesch, *Constantinople*, 382–83.

169. See A[hmed] R[efik], *Abdülhamid-i Sânî ve Devr-i Saltanatı: Hayat-ı Hususiye ve Siyasiyesi* 3 (Istanbul, 1327 [1909]), 1104. *Terakki* recommended propaganda pamphlets published by this bogus committee to its readership. See "Yeni Kitablar: Sinekler ve Örümcekler," *Terakki*, no. 18 [May 1908], 8.

170. Pierre Quillard, "L'union nécessaire," *Pro Armenia* nos. 142–43, 969.

171. Hratch Dasnabedian, *Histoire de la Fédération révolutionnaire arménienne, Dachnaktsoutioun, 1890–1924* (Milan, 1988), 86/fn. 14. See also Albert Fua, "Histoire du Comité Union et Progrès," *Mècheroutiette*, no. 44 (July 1913), 38.

172. The note was written by Terlemezian on the sixth issue of the journal many years later in 1963. Archival reference 669–174.

173. Dickson to Barclay, Van, April 6, 1908/no. 9, PRO/F.O. 195/2283. See also BBA–BEO/VGG(2)/Van Reft: 198; 7 [March 24, 1908]/245795; Ali Rıza to the Sublime Porte, Van [March 23, 1908]/no. 24–11; [March 23, 1908]/no. 27-16; [March 28, 1908]/no. 42-23; [May 19, 1908]/no. 191-115, BBA–BEO/Şifre Telgraf Kayıd-Anadolu 1324 (1); the Grand Vizier's office to the Province of Van [March 24, 1908]/no. 70 and [March 24, 1908]/no. 75, BBA–BEO/Telgrafnâme-i Sâmi Defteri: 703-28/14. The informer named David caused the collapse of the Dashnaktsutiun branch in Van. The information provided by him was extremely valuable to the Ottoman government. [See BBA–YSHM, 518/78 (1326.M.13).] Thus after David's assassination the sultan issued a special imperial decree and granted a monthly stipend to the deceased informer's parents. See BBA–Yıldız Marûzat Defterleri, no. 15158 [March 29, 1908]/no. 2025 [March 28, 1908].

174. See the local police report dated [January 1, 1908]/no. 12 in BBA–Y.PRK.GZT. 64/16.

175. See "Türkiya'da Gizli Gazeteler," *Tercüman-ı Ahvâl-i Zaman*, no. 74 (November 16 [29], 1907), 2; "İnkılâb Emâreleri," *Balkan*, no. 302 [November 27, 1907], 3; and "La Presse clandestine en Turquie," *Revue du Monde Musulman* 4, no. 1 (January 1908), 190–91. See also Tsovikian, "Vliianie russkoi revoliutsii 1905 g.," *Sovetskoe vostokovedenie* 3, 22.

176. Dickson to O'Conor, Van, September 30, 1907/no. 20, PRO/F.O. 195/2251.

177. See "İran Dahi Uyandı!" Originally published in the fifth issue of *Sabah'ül-Hayr*, issued on July 12, 1907, and republished in *Balkan*, no. 260 [September 26, 1907], 2.

178. See Sabah'ül-Hayr, "Teşekkürât," *Sabah'ül-Hayr*, no. 6 (July 31, [1907]), 23; "Biz Ne Kazandık?" Ibid., 24; and "Entre Arméniens et Turcs," *Pro Armenia* 7, no. 167, 1165.

179. See "[Nizamnâme Mukaddimesi]," *Balkan*, no. 310, 1–2; "La Fédération Révolutionnaire Turque," *Pro Armenia* 7, no. 171, 1197; and "Les troubles d'Anatolie," *L'Hellénisme* 4, nos. 22–

23 (December 1–15, 1907), 7. Distributed in the form of a pamphlet. See "İnkılâb Emâreleri," *Balkan*, no. 302 [November 27, 1907], 3; and Edhem Ruhi, "Vatanda Tekâmül veya Mukaddime-i İnkılâb," *Balkan*, no. 309 [December 5, 1907], 1–2.

180. See, for example, "Biz Ne Kazandık?" *Sabah'ül-Hayr*, no. 6, 23–24.

181. Ibid., 23–24.

182. See, for example, the letter allegedly sent by a certain Abdullah who addresses the readers as "our coreligionists." See his letter dated September [15, 1907] in "İlânât," *Sabah'ül-Hayr*, no. 8, 44–45; and another letter allegedly sent by a certain Selâmet speaking about "lands soaked with the blood of our ancestors." See Selâmet, "Kûs-i Rihlet: Evlâd-ı Vatana," *Sabah'ül-Hayr*, no. 8, 42.

183. See Refik'ül-Rüfeka, "Sabrımız Ne Netice Verdi?" *Sabah'ül-Hayr*, no. 7 (August 31, [1907]), 34.

184. Refik'ül-Rüfeka, "Hâl-i Hâzıra Karşu Vazife ve Mesleğimiz," *Sabah'ül-Hayr*, no. 6, 29.

185. See "Maksadımız: 13üncü Nüshadan Maba'd," *Sabah'ül-Hayr*, no. 14 (December 15, [1907]), 77.

186. Ibid., 78. Also underscored in an appeal issued by the organization. See Le Comité Turc Libéral d'Action, "Un appel aux Turcs qui veulent la liberté," *Pro Armenia* 6, nos. 142–43, 974.

187. Refik'ül-Rüfeka, "Hâl-i Hâzıra Karşu Vazife ve Mesleğimiz," *Sabah'ül-Hayr*, no. 6, 29.

188. "Maksadımız: 7nci Nüshadan Maba'd," *Sabah'ül-Hayr*, no. 8, 43–44. For other examples underscoring the necessity of a union among the Ottoman elements, see "Umum Evlâd-ı Vatana," *Sabah'ül-Hayr*, no. 6, 25; and Muhibb-i Vatan Evlâdı M., "Vatan Mütercimi *Sabah'ül-Hayr*'a," *Sabah'ül-Hayr*, no. 14, 75. The journal's comments on a "nonsensical war" against Armenians were praised by a Pro-Dashnak journal, which attributed these remarks to Muslims. See Pierre Quillard, "Le seul salut," *Pro Armenia* 8, no. 178 (March 20, 1908), 1255–56.

189. "Vilâyât-ı Sâire Havâdisi," *Sabah'ül-Hayr*, no. 8, 45.

190. For the best examples, see R., "Hakk-ı Sarih mi? Sadaka mı?" *Sabah'ül-Hayr*, no. 6, 25; "Askerlerimiz," *Sabah'ül-Hayr*, no. 7, 34–35; and Fikret, "Ahlâkımızdan: Bedbaht Askerler," *Sabah'ül-Hayr*, no. 14, 76.

191. See, for example, "Hükûmet-i Hukukiye," *Sabah'ül-Hayr*, no. 14, 79 [80]; and "Notes et remarques," *Revue du Monde Musulman* 3, no. 8 (November–December 1907), 11–12.

192. See "Van'da Köpekler," *Sabah'ül-Hayr*, no. 14, 75–76; "Me'yus Köylü," ibid., 79; "Müslim ve Gayr-ı Müslim Arkadaşlarımıza Mahsus Arizadır," *Sabah'ül-Hayr*, no. 7, 36; "Hareket," quoted by *Balkan*, no. 261 [September 27, 1907], 2; and the appeal entitled "Van da Deprendi" by "The Central Committee of the Turkish Allied Revolutionary Party," dated [September 12, 1907]. This appeal was found on Dashnak revolutionaries killed in combat with Ottoman security forces. See BBA–Y.PRK.GZT. 64/16.

193. See BBA–BEO–VGG(2): Van Vilâyeti Âmed: 195; 42 [July 1, 1907, decipher]; and Âlî Bey to the Sublime Porte, Van [July 1, 1907]/no. 396–655, BBA–BEO/VGG(2): Anadolu Vilâyâtı Telgrafı Gelen: 911.

194. See the pamphlet *Örümcekler ve Sinekler* ([Van, 1907]), 2 ff. (Originally published in *Sabah'ül-Hayr*. Republished in "Örümcekler ve Sinekler," *Balkan*, no. 387 [March 12, 1908], 1–2.) See also the appeal entitled "Van Ahalisine," issued by the "Turkish Allied Party" in PRO/F.O. 195/2251, folios 79–80. (A French translation is also available. See ibid., folios 74–78.) Both enclosed with Dickson to O'Conor, Van, August 4, 1907/no. 14, PRO/F.O. 195/2251. Dickson too thought that there were independent Dashnaktsutiun and Young Turk committees in Van, not realizing that it was the Dashnaktsutiun carrying out all activities with the help of a few Muslim dissidents.

195. A copy of *Sabah'ül-Hayr* and "The Program of the Turkish Allied Party" were thrown into the military barracks of the cavalry regiment in Van. See Âlî Bey to the Ministry of the Interior, Van [May 13, 1907]/no. 23, BBA–YMGM, 298/113 (1325.R.23).

196. For example, the pamphlet entitled *Örümcekler İle [ve] Sinekler* was left in the Muslim quarters of Muş (see Safvet Bey, the subgovernor of Muş, to the Grand Vizier's office [December 18, 1907]/no. 272–26297, BBA–BEO/VGG(2): Müteferrika 1323: 878) and similar publica-

tions were left in the Muslim quarters of Van. See BBA–BEO/Serasker Reft, 261-6/69; 796 [July 11, 1906]/22045 (mühimme).

197. "Biz Ne Kazandık?" *Sabah-ül-Hayr*, no. 6, 24. The journal denied the charge: "No! No! All these are slanders! All Ottoman subjects, and Turks among them, too, are extremely dissatisfied with the present laws and regulations and especially with the administration of the government. . . . On this matter we Muslims are more anxious, because the government holds us up to scorn in the eyes of the world by using the term 'Turk' in its own interests."

198. See BBA–BEO–VGG(2): Van Reft: 198; 95 [August 29, 1907]/236648; and BBA–BEO/VGG(2): Van Vilâyeti Âmed: 195; 136 [August 31, 1907]/236648; Ali Rıza to the Grand Vizier's office, Van [May 20, 1908]/no. 198-7404 and Ali Rıza and Divisional General Mahmud Pasha to the Grand Vizier's office, Van [June 10, 1908]/no. 285-187, BBA–BEO/Şifre Telgraf Kayıd-Anadolu 1324 (1): 693/2. See also BBA–YSHM, 521/109 (1326.R.20).

199. See Ali Rıza to the Grand Vizier's office, Van [May 21, 1908]/no. 205-120, BBA–BEO/Şifre Telgraf Kayıd-Anadolu 1324 (1): 693/2.

200. See, for example, Safvet Bey to the Grand Vizier's office, Muş [January 2, 1908]/no. 262-30094; and Safvet Bey and Divisional General Salih Pasha to the Grand Vizier's office [January 3, 1908]/no. 262(mükerrer), BBA–BEO/VGG(2): Müteferrika 1323: 878.

201. See Shipley to O'Conor, Erzurum, January 6, 1908/no. 1 (confidential), PRO/F.O. 195/2283.

202. See Celâl Bey, the Subgovernor of Çorum, to the Grand Vizier's office, Çorum [July 9, 1907]/no. 73-321, BBA–BEO/VGG(2): Müteferrika 1323: 878. He maintained that the appeals posted in Ankara had not been prepared by "a committee." He made the following remark, however: "Since the Armenians had posted seditious appeals in Ankara during the earlier insurrections, the posting of the new appeals has caused murmuring among the people." For further information, see BBA–BEO/VGG(2): Ankara Vilâyeti Reft: 103; 19 [June 9, 1907]/230440; and BBA–BEO/VGG(2): Ankara Vilâyeti Gelen: 98; 44 [June 14, 1907].

203. Underscored by the Young Turk press. See "İstanbul'da Korku," *Balkan*, no. 291, 4.

204. M[ehmed] Sabri, *Vatandaşlarımıza* (Paris, 1908), 2–5. For a French translation, see K.-J. Basmadjian, "Deux brochures," *Revue du Monde Musulman* 5, no. 8 (August 1908), 742–44.

205. Van Ermeni Taşnaksutyun İhtilâl Fırkası Merkez Komitesi, "Biz ve Bizim Düşmanlarımız," *Balkan*, no. 416, 2.

206. For a late list, see BBA–BEO/Zabtiye Nezareti Âmed, 657-21/18; 71 [May 31, 1908]/249235.

207. For an early example, see "Açık Muhabere: Kastamoni'de (Lâ) Bey'e," *Mizan*, no. 24 (June 14, 1897), 4.

208. See, for example, BBA–YSHM, 486/158 (1323.2.28).

209. See, for example, BBA–BEO/VGG(2): Kastamoni Reft: 157; 1 [March 15, 1905]/189433; and 26 [June 29, 1905]/195797.

210. See, for example, Mark Sykes, *The Caliphs' Last Heritage: A Short History of the Turkish Empire* (London, 1915), 380. Sykes emphasized the role played by the "exiles" in the revolutionary movement after the Young Turk Revolution. See Mark Sykes, "Modern Turkey," *The Dublin Review* 144, nos. 288–89 (1909), 171.

211. BBA–BEO/VGG(2): Kastamoni Vilâyeti Gelen: 153; 17 [December 7, 1906, decipher].

212. Governor Enis Pasha made such an accusation in his dispatch to the Grand Vizier's office dated [January 6, 1906]/no. 68, and he presented the intercepted incoming and outgoing letters of the exiles to the government. One of the letters sent to a certain Hasan Ağa and dated [December 22, 1905] has detailed information about the popular resentment against the individual tax in Tetovo (Kalkandelen). See BBA–BEO/VGG(2): Kastamoni Reft: 157; 66 [January 16, 1906]/205692; and BBA–BEO/Kastamoni Vilâyeti Gelen: 153; 89 [January 3, 1906].

213. Enis Pasha to the Grand Vizier's office [December 9, 1905]/no. 464-29589, BBA–BEO/VGG(2): Anadolu Vilâyâtı Telgrafı Gelen: 910. See also BBA–YSHM, 496/83 (1323.L.13), and 496/111 (1323.L.16).

214. Grand Vizier's office to the governor of Kastamoni [December 9, 1905]/no. 1416, BBA–BEO/Şifre Telgrafnâme-i Samî, 701–28/12; Enis Pasha to the Grand Vizier's office [December 9, 1905]/466–29597; BBA–BEO/VGG(2): Kastamoni Reft: 157; 48 [December 9, 1905]/203688; 49 [December 10, 1905]/203826; 52 [December 17, 1905]/204016; and BBA–İrade-Dahiliye, S 1324/no. 50–402.

215. Enis Pasha to the Grand Vizier's office [January 8, 1906]/no. 511–32017, BBA–BEO/ VGG(2): Anadolu Vilâyâtı Gelen: 910.

216. Enis Pasha to the Grand Vizier's office [January 15, 1906]/no. 519–32942, ibid.

217. Enis Pasha to the Grand Vizier's office, and a copy of the telegram sent to Abdurrahman Pasha, the Minister of Justice, dated January 20, 1906/no. 427-33555, ibid.

218. Enis Pasha to the Grand Vizier's office [January 21, 1906]/no. 528–33558, ibid.

219. See Ziya Demircioğlu, *Kastamonu Valileri, 1881–1908* (Kastamonu, 1973), 87–90.

220. See BBA–BEO/VGG(2): Kastamoni Reft: 157; 67 [January 21, 1906]/205888; and BBA–BEO/VGG(2): Kastamoni Vilâyeti Gelen: 153; 103 [January 21, 1906]. See also BBA–YSHM, 498/114 (1323.Za.26).

221. See BBA–BEO/VGG(2): Kastamoni Reft: 157; 77 [February 16, 1906]/207123; 79 [March 6, 1906]/208066; BBA–BEO/Kastamoni Vilâyeti Gelen: 153; 120 [February 15, 1906]; 131 [March 4, 1906, decipher]; and [Acting] Governor Rıza Pasha to the Grand Vizier's office [February 15, 1906]/no. 555–35856, BBA–BEO/VGG(2): Anadolu Vilâyâtı Telgrafı Gelen: 910; and BBA–YSHM, 499/167 (1323.Z.18). The government also strengthened the police force in Kastamonu. See BBA–BEO/Serasker Reft, 261–6/69; 2665 [March 4, 1906]/ 207886.

222. See Ziya Demircioğlu, *Kastamonu'da Meşrutiyet Nasıl İlân Olundu [?]* (Kastamonu, 1961), 6–7.

223. See Rıza Pasha to the Grand Vizier's office [February 15, 1906]/no. 555–35856; [February 16, 1906]/no. 559–35889; and the detailed telegram dated [March 7, 1906]/no. 574–39958, BBA–BEO/VGG(2): Anadolu Vilâyâtı Telgrafı Gelen: 910.

224. See BBA–BEO/VGG(2): Kastamoni Reft: 157; 7 [March 27, 1906]/209303.

225. See "Kastamoni'de Hareket-i İhtilâlkârâne," *Türk*, no. 121 (March 8, 1906), 1–2 (a French summary of this article is given in Basmadjian, "Le Mouvement révolutionnaire en Asie Mineure," *Revue du Monde Musulman* 4, no. 4, 820–21); and "Kastamoni İhtilâline Dair," *Türk*, no. 123 (March 22, 1906), 1–2. The journal praised the movement in another article; see Münzevî, "Yaşasın Kastamonililer," *Türk*, no. 122 (March 15, 1906), 1–2. The articles published by *Türk* on the Kastamonu revolt were republished in "İktibas," *Rumeli*, no. 15 [March 23, 1906], 2 and 4; and "Kastamoni İhtilâline Dair," *Rumeli*, no. 18 [April 16, 1906], 1–3.

226. See "Kastamoni Vuku'atı," *Hayat*, no. 64 (March 22 [April 4], 1906), 3–4.

227. A Young Turk journal maintained that a few Armenians and Greeks had been arrested and charged with inciting the people against the government. See "Kastamoni'de Ahalinin Nümayişâtı," *Tuna*, no. 133 [February 22, 1906]. There is, however, no evidence to support this claim.

228. See, for example, "Le Mouvement turc," *Pro Armenia* 6, no. 145, 990–91.

229. See, for example, "Yine Askerimiz," *Şûra-yı Osmanî*, no. 16 (September 15, 1097 [1907]), 4.

230. See "Haricî Haberler," *Hayat*, no. 259 (November 8 [21], 1906), 4; and "İstanbul: 5 Receb 1325," *Şûra-yı Osmanî*, no. 14 (August 15, [1907]), 2.

231. "Les musulmans contre Hamid," *Pro Armenia* 7, nos. 158–59 (May 20–June 5, 1907), 1095.

232. "Erzurumla Bütün Türklük İftihar Eder Osmanlılık da Ümidvâr Olabilir," *Terakki*, no. [6], 12.

233. For the smuggling of *Terakki* into Trabzon and its circulation there, see the note-verbale presented by the Ottoman Foreign Ministry to the French ambassador in Istanbul, June 11, 1907/no. 69177–39; and the coded telegram sent by the province of Trabzon, dated [March 16, 1907], Dışişleri Bakanlığı Hazine-i Evrak Arşivi, Box İdarî, 198.

234. See "Osmanlı: Anadolu'da İğtişaş," *İrşad*, no. 123 (December 4 [17], 1907), 4.

235. Imperiali to Tittoni, Constantinople, December 9, 1907/no. 2359–835, ASMAE, Affari Politici, Serie P. Politica (1891–1916), pacco 123–24.

236. "Trabzon Müslümanları," *İrşad*, no. 16 (January 24 [February 6], 1908), 4; and "Le Mouvement turc," *Pro Armenia* 7, no. 149 (January 5, 1907), 1021.

237. Some of them were high-ranking officers. See Divisional General Hamdi Pasha to Âsım Bey [October 28, 1905]/no. 56, *Umum Kayda Mahsus Defter*, BBA–YEE, 36/139-75/ 139/XIX.

238. B[ahaeddin] Ş[akir], "Osmanlı İttihad ve Terakki Cemiyeti," *Haftalık Şûra-yı Ümmet*, no. 203 [January 13, 1910], 1–2.

239. See BBA–BEO/Serasker Reft, 261-6/69; 1099 [July 2, 1905]/195976; 1230 [July 20, 1905]/196908; 1239 [July 22, 1905]/196960; 1240 [July 21, 1905]/196961; 1285 [July 26, 1905]/197150; 1323 [August 1, 1905]/197419; 1353 [August 3, 1905]/197606; 1372 [August 4, 1905]/197728-197729; 1373 [August 5, 1905]/197716; 1382 [August 6, 1905]/197764; BBA–BEO/VGG(2): Diyar-ı Bekir Vilâyeti Reft: 121; 34 [July 20, 1905]/196909; 35 [July 22, 1905]/197037; 37 [July 26, 1905]/197035-197153; 43 [August 4, 1905]/197715; BBA–BEO/VGG(2): Anadolu Mutasarrıflığı Reft: 80; 38 [August 3, 1905]/197606; 41 [August 8, 1905]/197913; and BBA–YSHM, 490/13 (1323.5.20); 491/1 (1323.6.1).

240. BBA–BEO/Serasker Reft, 261-6/69; 1418 [August 9, 1905]/197940. A local newspaper that later commented on the event claimed that "thousands of people" occupied the post office and petitioned the sultan. See "Bedbîn Olmayalım," *Peyman*, no. 20 [November 15, 1909], 1.

241. For the *mufti* and his 25 friends' telegram, see BBA–YSHM, 491/26 (1323.6.6); for the assistant governor's dispatch, see BBA–YSHM, 491/53 (1323.6.9).

242. BBA–BEO/Serasker Reft, 261-6/69; 2082 [November 25, 1905]/203136; and 2247 [December 25, 1905]/20446. For further complaints, see ibid., 2109 [December 1, 1905]/ 202387.

243. See BBA–BEO/Serasker Reft, 261-6/69; 1411 [August 9, 1905]/197916; and the report prepared by this commission, 2247 [December 24, 1905]/204461.

244. See BBA–BEO/Serasker Reft, 261-6/69; 2041 [November 15, 1905]/203136; and 1595 [September 3, 1905]/199225; 1674 [September 12, 1905]/199712; 1827 [October 5, 1905]/200942; 1894 [November 16, 1905]/201494; and 1973 [October 31, 1905]/202236.

245. See BBA–BEO/Serasker Reft, 261-6/69; 1411 [August 8, 1905]/197916; 1428 [August 10, 1905]/198004; 1453 [August 14, 1905]/198231; 1483 [August 17, 1905]/198351; 1595 [September 13, 1905]/199225; 1971 [October 30, 1905]/202173; 1973 [October 31, 1905]/202236; 1994 [November 2, 1905]/202418; 1995 [November 4, 1905]/202415; and 2028 [November 14, 1905]/202696; BBA–BEO/VGG(2): Diyar-ı Bekir Reft: 121; 44 [August 5, 1905]/197712; 45 [August 7, 1905]/198817; 46 [August 9, 1905]/197906-196908-198402; 47 [August 9, 1905]/197493; 49 [August 9, 1905]/197995; 50 [August 10, 1905]/ 198107; 51 [August 13, 1905]/198117; 52 [August 13, 1905]/198125; and 57 [August 19, 1905]/198416; Grand Vizier's office to the IV Army [August 12, 1905]/no. 915, to the province of Diyar-ı Bekir [August 13, 1905]/no. 920, to the provinces of Diyar-ı Bekir and Aleppo [August 13, 1905]/no. 963, and to the IV Army [August 14, 1905/no. 1142], BBA–BEO/Şifre Telgrafnâme-i Sâmi (1321/2), 701-28/12; BBA–BEO/VGG: Haleb Reft: 298; 43 [August 12, 1905]/198116; 54 [August 18, 1905]/198489; 57 [September 22, 1905]/ 198630; BBA-BEO/VGG(2): Anadolu Mutasarrıflığı Reft: 80; 42 [August 10, 1905]/197991; 43 [August 12, 1905]/198116; 44 [August 18, 1905]/198402; and 46 [September 14, 1905]/ 199794.

246. BBA–BEO/Serasker Reft, 261-6/69; 2452 [January 27, 1906]/206265.

247. BBA–BEO/Serasker Reft, 261-6/69; 2608 [February 23, 1906]/207502; 2665 [March 3, 1906]/207851; 685 [June 25, 1906]/214273; 736 [July 1, 1906]/214592; 752 [July 3, 1906]/ 214718; 986 [August 10, 1906]/216596; 1190 [September 9, 1906]/217936; 1230 [September 14, 1906]/218158; BBA–BEO/VGG(2): Diyar-ı Bekir Reft: 121; 5 [March 31, 1906]/ 209572; and BBA–YSHM, 495/79 (1323.N.17), and 504/21 (1324.Ca.5).

248. Heard to O'Conor, Bitlis, August 26, 1907 (private), O'Conor Papers, Churchill College, Cambridge, 6/2/37.

249. For complaints, see BBA–İrade-Dahiliye, L 1325/no. 19-2605; BBA–BEO/Serasker Reft, 262-6/70; 1711 [November 21, 1907]/239121; BBA–BEO/VGG(2):Anadolu Mutasarrıflığı Reft: 80; 109 [November 17, 1907]/238927; van Limburg Stirum to Tets van Goudriaan, Pera, December 2, 1907/no. 523, Algemeen Rijksarchief: Tweede Afdeling: Kabinetsarchief Bu Za politieke rapportage (1871–1940): 50; Imperiali to Tittoni, Constantinople, December 9, 1907/ no. 2359-835, ASMAE, Affari Politici, Serie P. Politica (1891–1916), pacco 123–24; "Yeni Bir Haber-i Kıyam," *Şûra-yı Ümmet*, no. 126 (December 1, 1907), 2; and "Les troubles de Diarbékir," *Bulletin du Comité de L'Asie Française* 7, no. 81 (December 1907), 515–16. Two of the telegrams sent to the palace were published in Şevket Beysanoğlu, *Doğumu'nun 80. Yıldönümü Münasebetiyle: Ziya Gökalp'in İlk Yazı Hayatı, 1894–1909* (Istanbul, 1956), 156– 57. The commander of the IV Army, too, proposed to the government İbrahim Pasha's banishment. See BBA–BEO/VGG(2): Anadolu Mutasarrıflığı Reft: 80; 110 [November 19, 1907]/ 239135.

250. See BBA–Yıldız Marûzat Defterleri, no. 14925 (Milli Aşireti Re'isi İbrahim Paşa Hakkında Vuku'bulan Şikâyâtdan Dolayı İttihazı Muktazi Tedâbir Hakkında Encümen-i Vükelâ Mazbatası ve Tezkere-i Sâmiye Sureti—18 Şevval 1325 [November 24, 1907]) and Grand Vizier Mehmed Ferid Pasha's note dated [November 24, 1907]/no. 9975. See also BBA– İrade-Hususî, L 1325/no. 34-1023, L 1325/no. 43-1036, L 1325/no. 52-1043, and L 1325/ no. 56-1054.

251. See BBA–BEO/Serasker Reft, 262-6/70; 1734 [November 25, 1907]/239415; and BBA–BEO/VGG(2): Anadolu Mutasarrıflığı Reft: 80; 112 [November 21, 1907]/239232.

252. A reference was made in *Sabah'ül-Hayr*. It was claimed that "one of [their] companions in Diyar-ı Bekir" took a copy of the telegram allegedly sent to İbrahim Pasha by the Minister of War. See "Zulm Sahifesi: Vilâyet Havâdisi," *Sabah'ül-Hayr*, no. 14, 81. A pro-Dashnak journal maintained that "les Turcs invitaient les Arméniens à prendre part à leurs manifestations et ajoutaient: 'Ne craignez rien chrétiens, nous savons maintenant où est l'esprit du diable, nous sommes des frères du sol.'" See "Les événements de Diarbékir," *Pro Armenia* 8, no. 175, 1232.

253. See the petition submitted to the Grand Vizier's office and dated [January 3, 1906], BBA–BEO/Serasker Reft, 261-6/69; 2452 [January 27, 1906]/206265.

254. Ziya Bey later published an epic saga on the movement against Milli İbrahim Pasha. See Ziya Gökalp, *Şaki İbrahim Destanı*, ed. Cavit Orhan Tütengil and Nihat Gökalp (Istanbul, 1953).

255. See *Cumhuriyetin 50. Yılında Diyarbakır: 1973 İl Yıllığı* (Diyarbakır, 1973), 89–90.

256. For a list of 48 exiles providing details about their affiliations and the reasons for their banishment, see "List of Exiles in Diarbekir and Districts," enclosed with Graves to O'Conor, Diyar-ı Bekir, March 27, 1907 (separate), PRO/F.O. 195/2250.

257. As a matter of fact, a German report presented Van as the center of the revolutionary movement in Eastern Anatolia. See von Kiderlen-Wächter to von Bülow, Pera, December 16, 1907/no. 236, A. 19233, PAAA, 495/2, Allgemeine Angelegenheiten der Türkei, 134 (Bd. 22-23).

258. Dickson to O'Conor, Van, August 4, 1907/no. 14, PRO/F.O. 195/2251.

259. Ibid.

260. Dickson to O'Conor, Van, September 30, 1907/no. 20, PRO/F.O. 195/2251. See also P[ierre] Quillard, "Une Vendée kurde?" *Pro Armenia* 8, no. 190 (September 20, 1908), 1360.

261. See, for example, Dickson to O'Conor, Van, February 9, 1908/no. 3, PRO/F.O. 195/ 2283; and Van, March 2, 1908/no. 6, enclosed with Barclay to Grey, Pera, April 1, 1908/ no. 163, PRO/F.O. 424/215.

262. "Haricî Haberler: Türkiye," *İrşad*, no. 8 (January 17 [30], 1908), 4.

263. "Arméniens et musulmans," *Pro Armenia* 7, no. 169, 1181.

264. Dickson to O'Conor, Van, August 4, 1907/no. 14, PRO/F.O. 195/2251; and "Decipher from Captain Dickson," Van, July 29, 1907 (153 Erzurum), PRO/F.O. 195/2250.

265. Ermeni Taşnak İhtilâl Fırkası Merkez Komitesi, "Türk Vatandaşlarımıza." A copy of this appeal is in PRO/F.O. 195/2251.

266. See Ferdinand Winfrid, "Armenier und Türken," *Preußische Jahrbücher* 176 (June 1919), 378. An Armenian scholar made similar claims. See Dasnabedian, *Histoire*, 86.

267. Dickson to O'Conor, Van, December 31, 1907/no. 24 (confidential), PRO/F.O. 195/2251.

268. See BBA–BEO/VGG(2): Van Reft: 198; 78 [July 3, 1908]/251102; Grand Vizier's office to the governor of Van [July 3, 1908]/no. 847, BBA–BEO/Sadaretden Giden Şifre Kayd Defteri, 702–28/13. A pro-Dashnak journal published two appeals about this Muslim organization. See "Deux documents," *Pro Armenia* 8, no. 183 (June 5, 1908), 1297–98. See also the Dashnaktsutiun's letter to Clemenceau and Pichon dated Geneva, May 27, 1908, AE–NS–T, 6 (1908–1909), 9.

269. Governor Ali Rıza to the Grand Vizier's office [July 7, 1908]/no. 404-289, BBA–BEO/Şifre Telgraf Kayd: Anadolu 1324 (1), 693/2; and in BBA–BEO/VGG(2): Van Vilâyeti Âmed: 195; 100 [July 6, 1908]/251102.

270. Grand Vizier's office to the governor of Van [March 27, 1908]/no. 107, BBA–BEO/Telgrafnâme-i Sâmi Defteri, 703–28/14. Ironically, the next day the Şeyhülislâm's office petitioned the sultan to grant Osman Zeki the title of *İzmir pâye-i mücerredi*. It demonstrates that the Grand Vizier's opinion on the conservative judge was not shared by some other government offices. See BBA–Yıldız Marûzat Defterleri, no. 15158 [March 28, 1908]/no. 2044. The judge was removed from office after the Young Turk Revolution. See BBA–İrade-Adliye ve Mezâhib, S 1327/no. 27-275.

271. Grand Vizier's office to the governor of Van [April 2, 1908]/no. 148, BBA–BEO/Telgrafnâme-i Sâmi Defteri, 703-28/14. The British consul accused the same individuals of forming a clique. See Dickson to Barclay, Van, April 6, 1908/no. 9, PRO/F.O. 195/2251.

272. Grand Vizier's office to the governor of Van [March 28, 1908]/no. 109; and [June 3, 1908]/no. 571, BBA–BEO/Telgrafnâme-i Sâmi Defteri, 703–28/14. See also BBA–İrade-Dahiliye, S 1326/no. 21-201.

273. Grand Vizier's office to the governor of Van [March 28, 1908]/no. 109; and [June 3, 1908]/no. 571, BBA–BEO/Telgrafnâme-i Sâmi Defteri, 703-28/14.

274. For more information, see Dickson to Barclay, Van, April 6, 1908/no. 9, PRO/F.O. 195/2283. See also "Les tueries de Van," *Pro Armenia* 8, no. 179 (April 5, 1908), 1–2; and "Türkiye," *İrşad*, no. 40 (March 27 [April 9], 1908), 4.

275. "Les événements de Van," *Pro Armenia* 8, no. 180 (April 20, 1908), 1.

276. "Une Protestation turque," *Pro Armenia* 8, no. 185 (July 5, 1908), 1.

277. Shpil'kova, "Antipravitel'stvennye vystupleniia v vostochnoi Anatolii nakanune mladoturetskoi revoliutsii," *Narody Azii i Afriki* 3 (1971), 85, maintains that the movement in Erzurum was organized by those who went to Van from Erzurum, which seems very unlikely.

278. See "Havâdis-i Dahiliye," *Şûra-yı Ümmet*, no. 130 (February 15, 1908), 4; "Une protestation," *Mechveret Supplément Français*, no. 197 (March 1, 1908), 3; and "Genc Türklerin Protestosu," *Balkan*, no. 283 [March 7, 1908], 4.

279. See Ermeni İhtilâl (Revolüsyoner) Taşnak Fırkasının Merkez Komitesi, "Uğurlar Olsun!" (one-page handbill).

280. As a matter of fact, Sabahaddin Bey stated at the negotiations among the CPU, the Dashnaktsutiun, and the League of Private Initiative and Decentralization at the Congress of Ottoman Opposition Parties in December 1907 that his organization could not participate in an action program because it lacked any armed branch. See Dr. Bahaeddin [Şakir] to the director of the CPU [?] central branch, dated [Paris], January 29, 1908/no. 502, *Kopye Defteri*, 132. See also Dr. Bahaeddin [Şakir], "Osmanlı Terakki ve İttihad Cemiyeti Hey'et-i Merkeziye-i Dahilisi Cânib-i Âlisine Takdim Edilmek Üzere Sâî [Talât] Bey Efendi'ye," January [?], 1908/no. 501-8, *Kopye Defteri*, 122.

281. Heard to O'Conor, Bitlis, August 25, 1907/no. 4, PRO/F.O. 195/2251.

282. BBA–BEO/Harbiye Giden, 260-6/68; 906 [July 7, 1904]/177231. Delon, the French military attaché, made the following interesting comment about the reasons for the uprising: "Au cours de l'année dernière, une certaine agitation s'est, à plusieurs reprises, manifestée dans le vilayet d'Erzeroum, dont la population, mise en coupe réglée par les Kurdes et

succombant sous le fardeau des charges publiques, réclamait, comme mesure d'allègement à sa misère, la suppression de l'impôt personnel et de la taxe sur les animaux domestiques." Delon to the French Ministry of War, Constantinople, January 30, 1907/no. 65-294, Archives du Ministère de la Guerre, E.M.A et Attachés militaires, 7 N 1635.

283. Dickson to O'Conor, Van, March 2, 1908/no. 6, PRO/F.O. 424/215.

284. [Mehmed] Celâl, the governor of Erzurum, to the Grand Vizier's office [June 3, 1910]/ no. 47-10603, BBA–BEO/Şifre Telgraf Defteri, 698–28/9.

285. For a spy report about the distribution of "seditious papers" by exiled officers, see Major General İbrahim Rüşdi's undated [1906?] note presented to the First Chamberlain's office, BBA–YEE, 15/74-36-c/74/15. For the banishment of discharged cadets of the Royal Military Academy to Erzurum, see BBA–BEO/Dahiliye Giden, 103-3/52; 2513 [November 5, 1904]/183171.

286. See the handwritten memoirs of the bodyguard of Governor Nâzım Pasha, Barutçuzâde Tevfik, entitled "1320–1324 Erzurum İsyanı" and transliterated and published both in Orhan Türkdoğan, "1906–1907 Erzurum Hürriyet Ayaklanması II," *Türk Kültürü* 22, no. 256 (August 1984), 499; and in Önder Göçgün, "II. Meşrutiyet'e Öncülük Eden Bir Hareket: Erzurum İhtilâli ve Ona Dair Bazı Belgeler," *Türk Kültürü Araştırmaları* 23, no. 1–2 (1985), 268.

287. Mehmed Nusret, *Tarihçe-i Erzurum yahud Hemşehrilere Armağan* (Istanbul, 1338 [1920]), 58.

288. Nâzım Bey to the Grand Vizier's office [March 12, 1906]/no. 581-41889, BBA–BEO/ VGG(2): Anadolu Vilâyâtı Telgrafı Gelen: 910. The governor sent a similar telegram to the First Chamberlain's office on March 15, 1906. See Mehmed Nusret, *Tarihçe-i Erzurum*, 58. The date was erroneously given as March 15, 1905.

289. BBA–BEO/VGG(2): Erzurum Reft: 129; 136 [March 13, 1906]/208456 (decipher).

290. Orhan Türkdoğan, "1906–1907 Erzurum Hürriyet Ayaklanması İle İlgili Yeni Belgeler," *Türk Dünyası Araştırmaları*, no. 47 (April 1987), 28.

291. See Nâzım Bey to the Grand Vizier's office [March 20, 1906]; BBA–BEO/VGG(2): Erzurum Reft: 129; 4 [March 20, 1906]/208909.

292. Mentioned in the telegram sent by Mehmed Tevfik and his 108 fellows to the Ministry of Justice on [March 21, 1906], in BBA–BEO/VGG(2): Erzurum Reft: 129; 7 [March 29, 1906]/209436-208909. See also BBA–İrade-Hususî, M 1324/no. 103-91.

293. Decipher from the Grand Vizier's office to the province of Erzurum [March 20, 1906], BBA–BEO/VGG(2): Erzurum Reft: 129; 7 [March 29, 1906]/209436-208909.

294. BBA–BEO/Dahiliye Giden, 105-3/54; 119 [March 21, 1906]/209018-208909-208456; BBA–BEO/VGG(2): Erzurum Reft: 129; 5 [March 21, 1906]/209018 (decipher); and BBA–BEO/VGG(2): Erzurum Vilâyeti Gelen: 126; 1 [March 20, 1906, decipher].

295. BBA–BEO/VGG(2): Erzurum Reft: 129; 7 [March 29, 1906]/209436 and 208909.

296. BBA–BEO/VGG(2): Erzurum Reft: 129; 6 [March 23, 1906]/209134 and 209018.

297. See the telegram by Mustafa, Ali, an *'alim*, Hacı Osman, Süleyman, Veysel, and 205 other individuals to the Ministry of Justice, dated [March 24, 1906], in BBA–BEO/VGG(2): Erzurum Reft: 129; 7 [March 29, 1906]/209436 and 208909.

298. Mehmed Nusret, *Tarihçe-i Erzurum*, 59–60.

299. Ibid., 60; and BBA–YSHM, 501/32 (1324.S.4).

300. See a copy of the telegram sent from the commander of the Seventh Division in Erzurum to Marshal Zeki Pasha, Commander of the IV Army in Erzincan, dated [March 29, 1906], in BBA–BEO/VGG(2): Erzurum Reft: 129; 7 [March 29, 1908]/209436 and 208909. See also BBA–YMGM, 285/60 (1324.S.9); and BBA–YSHM, 501/64 (1324.S.9). The British consul maintained that only Muslims had closed their shops. See "decipher telegram from Mr. Shipley," Erzurum, March 29, 1906/no. 41, PRO/F.O. 195/2222.

301. Marshal Zeki Pasha to the Minister of War [March 31, 1906] in BBA–BEO/VGG(2): Erzurum Reft: 129; 7 [March 29, 1906]/209436 and 208909. See also BBA–YSHM, 501/72 (1324.S.10).

302. Mehmed Nusret, *Tarihçe-i Erzurum*, 60.

303. Marshal Zeki Pasha to the Minister of War [April 3, 1906] (decipher), in BBA–BEO/ VGG(2): Erzurum Reft: 129; 7 [March 29, 1906]/209436 and 208909. See also his coded

telegrams to the First Chamberlain's office, dated Erzincan [April 3, 1906]/nos. 173 and 183, and [April 4, 1906]/no. 190, *Umum Şifre Marûzat-ı Vâridenin Kayd Defteridir*, 1/1019, BBA–YEE, 36/139-76/139/XIX-1.

304. Marshal Zeki Pasha to the Minister of War [April 3, 1906], in BBA–BEO/VGG(2): Erzurum Reft: 129; 7 [March 29, 1906]/209436 and 208909. See also the decipher telegram from Mr. Shipley, Erzurum, April 3, 1906/no. 47, PRO/F.O. 195/2222.

305. See BBA–İrade-Dahiliye, S 1324/no. 6-249; the Minister of War, Rıza Pasha, to the Grand Vizier's office [April 4, 1906], in BBA–BEO/VGG(2): Erzurum Reft: 129; 7 [March 29, 1906]/209436 and 208909. See also BBA–BEO/Dahiliye Giden, 163–5/19; 280 [April 3, 1906]/209799. The special commission was composed of a State Council Court of Appeal judge, Mustafa Bey; a former subgovernor of Muş, Hüsni Bey; and a IV Army lieutenant-colonel, Âsâf Bey. See ibid., 1653 [July 29, 1906]/216021, 208546; and 2126 [September 24, 1906]/218626; and BBA–BEO/VGG(2): Erzurum Reft: 129; 12 [April 15, 1906]/210381.

306. Draft of the Grand Vizier's note to the commander of the IV Army, BBA–BEO/VGG(2): Erzurum Reft: 129; 7 [March 29, 1906]/209436, 209798, 209775, and 208456. See also BBA–BEO/VGG(2): Anadolu Mutasarrıflığı Reft: 80; 15 [April 28, 1906]/211131 and 16 [April 30, 1906]/211241. A Tatar journal made a similar comment. See "Osmanlı," *Tercüman-ı Ahvâl-i Zaman*, no. 38 (April 14 [27], 1906), 3.

307. BBA–BEO/VGG(2): Anadolu Mutasarrıflığı Reft: 80; 8 [April 3, 1906]/209800. Similar instructions were given to Marshal Zeki Pasha, the commander of the IV Army. See ibid., 7 [April 2, 1906]/209798. The government also initiated an investigation of gendarmes who refused to obey the governor's orders. See BBA–BEO/VGG(2): Erzurum Reft: 129; 6 [March 23, 1906]/209775 and 209134.

308. BBA–BEO/Dahiliye Giden, 105–3/54; 420 [April 14, 1906]/210293.

309. BBA–BEO/VGG(2): Erzurum Reft: 129; 8 [April 12, 1906]/210209.

310. BBA–BEO/VGG(2): Erzurum Reft: 129; 24 [May 1, 1906, decipher]/211246; and BBA–BEO/Serasker Reft, 261-6/69; 314 [April 30, 1906]/211262.

311. Coded telegram from Mustafa and Hüsni Beys, Erzurum [May 1, 1906, urgent], in BBA–BEO/VGG(2): Anadolu Mutasarrıflığı Reft: 80; 18 [May 2, 1906]/211381 and 211241; 20 [May 6, 1906]/211718.

312. Governor Nâzım Bey to the First Chamberlain's office, Diyar-ı Bekir [April 15, 1906]/no. 318, *Umum Şifre Marûzat-ı Vâridenin Kayd Defteridir*, 1/1019, BBA–YEE, 36/139-76/139/XIX-1. At this point the government feared that the former governor of Erzurum would renounce his citizenship and flee to Greece, where his brother was living. See BBA–BEO/VGG(2): Erzurum Reft: 129; 15 [April 14, 1906]/210499.

313. BBA–İrade-Hususî, Ş 1324/no. 27-767 (736); and no. 30-786(738).

314. See BBA–İrade-Hususî, Ş 1324/no. 28-772 (736). See also BBA–İrade Hususî, Ş 1324/no. 27-767; and L 1324/no. 12–826.

315. BBA–BEO/VGG(2): Erzurum Reft: 129; 39 [June 10, 1906]/213417.

316. See Bapst to Bourgeois, Pera, October 23, 1906/no. 213 and October 25, 1906/no. 216, AE–T–Politique Intérieure: Arménie, Anatolie, Cilicie XII (1905–1907): 82, [124–27].

317. Governor Atâ Bey to Âsım Bey at the First Chamberlain's office [September 12, 1906]/no. 1662, BBA–BEO/Umum Şifre Varidâtı Kayd Defteri, 691-28/2; and BBA–BEO/VGG(2): Erzurum Reft: 129; 104 [September 30, 1906]/218867.

318. BBA–İrade-Dahiliye, S 1324/no. 18-2023.

319. BBA–BEO/Dahiliye Giden, 105-3/54; 2309 [October 14, 1906]/219569.

320. Marshal Zeki Pasha to the First Chamberlain's office, Erzincan [October 23, 1906]/no. 1991, BBA–BEO/Umum Şifre Varidâtı Kayd Defteri, 691-28/2. For further information, see BBA–YSHM, 290/131 (1324.N.7); BBA–BEO/Serasker Reft, 262-6/70; 1492 [October 31, 1906]/220312; decipher telegrams from Mr. Shipley, Erzurum, October 23, 1906/no. 177, October 24, 1906/no. 178, and October 24, 1906/no. 179; Shipley to Barclay, Erzurum, October 27, 1906/no. 25 (confidential), PRO/F.O. 195/2222; Barclay to Grey, Pera, October 25, 1906/no. 718, PRO/F.O. 424/210 (confidential 8984); "Kıyam," *Türk*, no. 146 (November 8, 1906), 1; "Telgraf: Teşrin-i evvel 16: Türkiya Haberi," *Tuna*, no. 340 [October 30, 1906], 4; "Türkiya'da İnkılâb," *İrşad*, no. 264 (November 15 [28], 1906), 4; "Les événements

d'Erzeroum," *Pro Armenia* 7, no. 147 (December 5, 1906), 1005; and "Mahomedan Riot at Erzerum," *The Times*, October 27, 1906.

321. See the decipher telegrams from Shipley, October 24, 1906/no. 179; October 25, 1906/ no. 180; and October 29, 1906/no. 181, PRO/F.O. 195/2222. The central government, aware of the lack of civil authority, began to send instructions to the local military commander through the Ministry of War. See BBA–BEO/Seraskbr Reft, 262-6/70; 1492 [October 31, 1906]/ 220312.

322. See BBA–BEO/Serasker Reft, 262-6/70; 1818 [December 31, 1906]/223897. For the appointment of the new governor, see BBA–İrade-Hususî, N 1324/no. 30–786; and BBA–BEO/Dahiliye Giden, 105-3/54; 2430 [October 28, 1906]/220286.

323. BBA–BEO/VGG(2): Erzurum Reft: 129; 128 [November 25, 1906]/221146; BBA–BEO/Serasker Reft, 261-6/69; 1476 [October 28, 1906]/220267. The government later urged the governor and commander to prepare the report quickly (see the coded telegram sent to the governor dated [December 21, 1906], BBA–BEO/VGG(2): Erzurum Reft: 129; 140 [December 21, 1906]/222891) and went on to set up a special cabinet meeting to discuss the report. See BBA–İrade-Hususî, Za 1324/no. 93-1070.

324. See BBA–BEO/Serasker Reft, 261-6/69; 1291 [September 26, 1906]/218689; 262–6/70; 1948 [January 30, 1907]/223988; and BBA–YMGM, 294/53 (1324.2.23). See also Shipley to Barclay, Erzurum, January 28, 1907/no. 4, PRO/F.O. 195/2250.

325. See BBA–İrade-Hususî, M 1325/no. 76-95; and decipher telegram from Mr. Shipley, Erzurum, March 16, 1907, PRO/F.O. 195/2250.

326. BBA–BEO/VGG(2): Erzurum Reft: 129; 173 [March 10, 1907]/225946.

327. The authorities in Istanbul also received information about the fact that without the help of the military, only 50 percent of the regular taxes such as the sheep tax could be collected. See BBA–BEO/Serasker Reft, 262-6/70; 21 [March 18, 1907]/226039.

328. Governor Nuri Bey to the Grand Vizier's office, Erzurum [March 16, 1907]/no. 7-133, BBA–BEO/VGG(2): Anadolu Vilâyâtı Telgrafı Gelen: 911; and BBA–BEO/Dahiliye Giden, 105-3/54; 3285 [February 23, 1907]/224941; 3462 [March 11, 1907]/225945; BBA–İrade-Hususî, S 1325/no. 18-143. See also O'Conor to Grey, Constantinople, March 25, 1907/ no. 45, PRO/F.O. 424/212.

329. For the abolition of these taxes, see BBA–İrade-Maliye, S 1325/no. 11-124, and BBA–YSHM, 510/51 (1325.S.10); for the rejoicing of the people in Erzurum because of this, see the decipher telegram from Mr. Shipley, Erzurum March 26, 1907, PRO/F.O. 195/2250.

330. BBA–YSHM, 510/21 (1325.2.6).

331. Governor Nuri Bey to the Grand Vizier's office, Erzurum [March 19, 1907]/no. 12, BBA–BEO/VGG(2): Anadolu Vilâyâtı Telgrafı Gelen: 911. See also BBA–YSHM, 296/ 17 (1324.S.4).

332. Shipley to O'Conor, Erzurum, March 5, 1907/no. 10, enclosed with O'Conor to Grey, Constantinople, March 18, 1907/no. 169, PRO/F.O. 424/212.

333. O'Conor to Grey, Constantinople, March 3, 1907/no. 141, PRO/F.O. 424/212. The governor provided similar information about the distribution of "seditious papers." See Nuri Bey to Âsım Bey at the First Chamberlain's office [March 10, 1907]/no. 2862, *Umum Şifre Marûzat-ı Vâride Kayd Defteridir* 3 (2031–2892), BBA–YEE, 36/139-77/139/XIX-7.

334. Governor Nuri Bey to the Grand Vizier's office, Erzurum [July 31, 1906]/no. 532–16599, BBA–BEO/VGG(2): Anadolu Vilâyâtı Telgrafı Gelen: 911. The imperial palace had ordered the governor to pay the sums demanded by the soldiers (see BBA–İrade-Maliye, S 1325/no. 3-238); it was, however, totally out of the question to meet such a large request.

335. Shipley to O'Conor, Erzurum, February 15, 1907/no. 5 (confidential), PRO/F.O. 195/2250.

336. M. Sabri, "Anadolu Kıyamları . . . ," *Terakki*, no. 11, 5.

337. The local committee called this taxation "money collection for expenses." See BBA–BEO/VGG(2): Erzurum Reft: 129; 21 [April 18, 1906]/210786.

338. "Erzurum Vak'aatu [*sic*]," *İrşad*, no. 125 (December 8[21], 1907), 4. For similar information, see Shipley to O'Conor, Erzurum, July 1, 1907/no. 38, enclosed with O'Conor to Grey, Constantinople, July 17, 1907/no. 423, PRO/F.O. 424/213 (confidential 9305).

339. "Erzurum İhtilâli," *Türk*, no. 186 (November 21, 1907), 2.

340. A. M. Valuiskii, "Vosstaniia v vostochnoi Anatolii nakanune mladoturetskoi revoliutsii (po materialam Moskovskikh arkhivov)," *Turetskii sbornik* (1958), 55.

341. "Erzurum İğtişâşâtı," *Balkan*, no. 310 [December 5, 1907], 4.

342. See BBA–BEO/Dahiliye Giden, 106-3/55; 510 [May 1, 1907]/228290.

343. The governor had warned the central government more than a month before. See Nuri Bey to the Grand Vizier's office, Erzurum [July 12, 1906]/no. 460-14058, BBA–BEO/VGG(2): Anadolu Vilâyâtı Telgrafı Gelen: 911.

344. "Hükûmetin Yeni Bir İhaneti, Ahalinin Yeni Bir İttifakı," *Terakki*, no. 14, 7.

345. See the coded telegram from Marshal Zeki Pasha to the First Chamberlain's office, Erzincan [September 13, 1907], in BBA–YMGM, 302/28 (1325.Ş.7). The marshal later maintained that the civil authorities caused all the problems and did not take necessary measures. See his telegram to the Grand Vizier's office dated October 10, 1907/no. 172-43870, BBA–BEO/VGG(2): Müteferrika 1323: 878.

346. The military commission's report, cabinet proceedings, and the imperial decree all bear the same date, September 15, 1907, and are in BBA–YSRM, 149/78 (1325.8.7). In the same file there are two coded telegrams from Marshal Zeki Pasha, both dated September 15, 1907, expressing concern about a possible Muslim–Armenian clash. For the military commission's recommendations, see also BBA–İrade-Hususî, S 1325/no. 28.

347. BBA–BEO/Dahiliye Giden, 106–3/55; 1858 [September 16, 1907]/235963; and BBA–BEO/VGG(2): Anadolu Mutasarrıflığı Reft: 80; 98 [September 24, 1907]/238322.

348. He adopted a hard-line approach by accusing former authorities of not being tough enough. See BBA–BEO/VGG(2): Erzurum Reft: 129; 173 [March 11, 1908]/225946.

349. "Haricî Haberler: Türkiya," *Tercüman-ı Ahvâl-i Zaman*, no. 11 (November 6 [19], 1907), 3.

350. See BBA–BEO/Zabtiye Giden, 663-21/14; 230 [January 27, 1907]/223851; 247 [March 5, 1907]/225378; and 155 [September 26, 1907]/236495; and BBA–BEO/Zabtiye Nezareti Âmed, 657-21/18; 248 [March 11, 1907]; 60 [May 10, 1907]/211634; and 124 [August 24, 1907].

351. See BBA–BEO/Dahiliye Giden, 106-3/55; 1434 (mükerrer) [September 27, 1907]/236651-235963-236419, and 266419; and Delon to the French Ministry of War, Constantinople, December 2, 1907/no. 166-1608, Archives du Ministère de la Guerre, E.M.A et Attachés militaires, 7 N 1635.

352. Barutçuzâde Şevki's handwritten memoirs in Türkdoğan, "1906–1907 Erzurum Hürriyet Ayaklanması—II," *Türk Kültürü* 22, no. 256, 507.

353. Ibid., 507–8; BBA–YSHM, 516/151 (1325.L.20); Shipley to O'Conor, Erzurum, December 2, 1907/no. 79, enclosed with O'Conor to Grey, Constantinople, December 18, 1907/no. 772, in PRO/F.O. 424/213, and PRO/F.O. 195/2251; and "Erzurum Kahramanları," *Şûra-yı Osmanî*, no. 22 (December 15, 1907), 4.

354. The most accurate list is the one provided by Shipley and enclosed with his dispatch dated Erzurum, March 3, 1908/no. 5, PRO/F.O. 195/2283. See also BBA–YSHM, 518/25 (1326.M.9). A thorough investigation continued after the arrests (see the Grand Vizier's office to the governor of Erzurum [March 18, 1908]/no. 24, BBA–BEO/Telgrafnâme-i Samî Defteri, 703-28/14), and the most "dangerous conspirators" were imprisoned in the Sinob dungeon. See Abdülvahab Pasha to the Grand Vizier's office, Erzurum [April 8, 1908]/no. 274-12971, BBA–BEO/Şifre Telgraf Kayd: Anadolu 1324 (1).

355. See "Erzurum İsyanı," *Tuna*, no. 350 [November 12, 1906], 2; "Erzurum'da İhtilâl," *Şûra-yı Ümmet*, no. 104 (November 30, 1906), 4; "Exemples à suivre," *Mechveret Supplément Français*, no. 182 (December 1, 1906), 4; "Erzurum İhtilâli," *Türk*, no. 186, 2; "Can Veren Cemiyet-i İslâmiyesi," *Balkan*, no. 82 [November 4, 1906], 3; and "Les événements d'Erzeroum," *Pro Armenia* 7, no. 146, 998.

356. "Exemples à suivre," *Mechveret Supplément Français*, no. 182, 4.

357. Petrosian, *Mladoturetskoe dvizhenie*, 221. A Turkish scholar, basing his work on a partial list of those who were arrested, reaches a similar conclusion. See Orhan Türkdoğan, "1906–1907 Erzurum Hürriyet Ayaklanması—III," *Türk Kültürü* 22, no. 257 (September 1984), 575–79.

358. See the list enclosed with Shipley's dispatch dated March 3, 1908/no. 5, PRO/F.O. 195/2283.

359. Coded telegram from the Grand Vizier's office to the province of Van [May 17, 1906], BBA–BEO/Van Reft: 198; 9 [May 17, 1906]/212168-208456; and BBA–BEO/Van Vilâyeti Âmed: 195; 21/3 [July 14, 1906]/212168.

360. Governor Tahir Pasha to the Grand Vizier's office, Van [June 14, 1906]/no. 3, BBA–BEO/Van Reft: 198; 9 [May 17, 1906]/212168-208456.

361. See his marginal note dated [June 20, 1906] and enclosed with the governor's aforementioned dispatch. Ibid.

362. Governor Nâzım Bey to the Grand Vizier's office, Erzurum [March 20, 1905]/no. 11-611, BBA–BEO/VGG(2): Anadolu Vilâyâtı Telgrafı Gelen: 910; BBA–BEO/VGG(2): Erzurum Reft:129; 2 [March 21, 1905]/189773; BBA–BEO/VGG(2): Erzurum Vilâyeti Gelen: 126; 3 [March 20, 1905, decipher]/189773. The government sent these people to Erzurum, which it maintained was "a center of ulema." This was the traditional Ottoman policy that had been implemented for centuries. For an interesting example, see BBA–HH 25100; 25100 A; and 25100 B.

363. BBA–BEO/VGG(2): Erzurum Reft: 129; 28 [May 23, 1906]/193576.

364. Dr. Bahaeddin [Şakir] to the director of the CPU Lâzistan branch, dated Paris, November 25, 1906/no. 221, *Muhaberat Kopyası*, 189: "It has been understood from the information given in newspapers that there is a committee named 'Can Veren.' We expect your high authority to help us initiate some sort of contact with these people and to establish ties between our committee and theirs in order to elevate [our] power." He repeated the central committee's desire later. See Dr. Bahaeddin [Şakir] to the director of the CPU Lâzistan branch, dated Paris, July 30, 1907/no. 332, *Muhaberat Kopyası*, 372.

365. See Dr. Bahaeddin [Şakir] to Nazif Asbasizâde in Kars, dated Paris, October 30, 1907/ no. 397, *Muhaberat Kopyası*, 467. For the CPU's previous attempts, see Dr. Bahaeddin [Şakir] to the director of the CPU Lâzistan branch, dated Paris, July 30, 1907/no. 332, *Muhaberat Kopyası*, 372; Dr. Bahaeddin [Şakir]'s letter beginning "Muhterem Vatanperver Kardeşimiz" and dated [Paris, June 4, 1907]/no. 296, *Muhaberat Kopyası*, 317. Despite this, in order to impress those who were inclined to join their organization, the CPU falsely claimed that they had strong branches in Anatolia and "especially in Erzurum, Bitlis, Van, and Trabzon." See Dr. [Bahaeddin Şakir] to [Mesʿud Remzi] beginning "Muhterem ve Gayûr Vatandaşımız" and dated [Paris, November 27, 1907]/no. 443 [duplicate number], *Kopye Defteri*, 30.

366. See the letter of H[üsrev] Sami and Dr. Bahaeddin [Şakir] beginning "Refik-i Muhteremimiz" and dated [Paris], February 28, 1908/no. 535, *Kopye Defteri*, 188.

367. Dr. Bahaeddin [Şakir], "Osmanlı Terakki ve İttihad Cemiyeti Hey'et-i Merkeziye-i Dahiliyesi Cânib-i Âlisine Takdim Edilmek Üzere Sâî [Talât] Bey Efendi'ye," dated Paris, January [?], [1]908/no. 501–8, *Kopye Defteri*, 126–27.

368. See "Erzurum'da İhtilâl," *Şûra-yı Ümmet*, no. 104, 2–3; "Bravo, les provinciaux," *Mechveret Supplément Français*, no. 187 (May 1, 1907), 4; and "Les Patriotes musulmans d'Anatolie," *Mechveret Supplément Français*, no. 193 (November 1, 1907), 1.

369. [Ahmed Rıza], "Ne Yapmalı?" *Şûra-yı Ümmet*, no. 99 (August 31, 1906), 3; and "Bir Numûne-i İmtisâl," *Şûra-yı Ümmet*, no. 106 (December 15, 1906), 2.

370. See, for example, "Erzurum'dan," *Şûra-yı Ümmet*, nos. 96–97 (August 1, 1906), 6; and "Erzurum Haberleri: Bir Mektubdan Müstahrec," *Şûra-yı Ümmet*, nos. 128–29 (February 1, 1908), 8.

371. See the letter of Dr. Bahaeddin [Şakir] beginning "Vatanperver Efendim," sent to an officer known to some military members of the CPU, and dated Paris, October 30, 1907/ no. 397, *Muhaberat Kopyası*, 468. The letter to be submitted to the marshal was written almost a year earlier. This fact too demonstrates the CPU's inability to carry out activities in the region. See the unsigned letter beginning "Huzûr-i Âlî-i Müşîr-i Efhemilerine" and dated Paris, November 25, 1906/no. 214, *Muhaberat Kopyası*, 175. The CPU leaders later realized their misunderstanding and castigated the marshal. See Dr. Bahaeddin [Şakir], "Osmanlı Terakki ve İttihad Cemiyeti Hey'et-i Merkeziye-i Dahiliyesi Cânib-i Âlisine Takdim Edilmek Üzere Sâî [Talât] Bey Efendi'ye," dated Paris, January [?], [1]908/no. 501–8, *Kopye Defteri*,

127. Marshal Zeki Pasha's behavior stemmed from his dislike of the two governors of Erzurum (see, for example, Nuri Bey to the Grand Vizier's office, Erzurum [August 2, 1907]/no. 547-16902, BBA–BEO/VGG(2): Anadolu Vilâyâtı Telgrafı Gelen: 911; and Zeki Pasha to the Grand Vizier's office, Erzincan [October 10, 1907]/no. 172-43870, BBA–BEO/VGG(2): Müteferrika 1323: 878); this fact caused some foreign observers to believe that "he had joined the Young Turks." Some modern scholars have reiterated this claim without questioning it. See, for example, Shpil'kova, "Antipravitel'stvennye vystupleniia v vostochnoi Anatolii nakanune mladoturetskoi revoliutsii," *Narody Azii i Afriki* 3 (1971), 80.

372. See his coded telegram to the First Chamberlain's office, dated Erzincan [September 15, 1907], BBA–YSRM, 149/78 (1325.8.7).

373. See Sâî [Talât Bey] to [Bahaeddin Şakir], dated [Salonica], January 6, 1907 [1908], published in "Osmanlı İttihad ve Terakki Cemiyeti: Vesâik-i Tarihiyeden," *Haftalık Şûra-yı Ümmet*, no. 212 [March 17, 1910], 2.

374. See *Şûra-yı Ümmet-Ali Kemal Da'vası* (Istanbul, 1325 [1909]), 88–89; and "Mülâzım Naci Bey," *İttihad ve Terakki*, September 8, 1908.

375. See Ali Haydar Midhat, *Hâtıralarım,* 178.

376. Aliiev, "K voprosu o pomoshchi Azerbaidzhanskoi demokratii mladoturetskomu dvizheniiu," *Tiurkologicheskii sbornik*, 188. The Azerbaijanis who had helped Hüseyin Tosun had close ties with the Himmät party working toward an understanding between Armenians and the Azerbaijanis. Ömer Faik, who helped Hüseyin Tosun publish these appeals, maintained that "the appeals distributed among the Turkish soldiers and peasants had played a significant role in the preparation of the Erzurum revolt." See ibid.

377. See the coded telegram dated [December 14, 1907] from the province of Erzurum to the coded telegrams branch of the Grand Vizier's office, BBA–BEO/VGG(2): Erzurum Reft: 129; 122 [January 9, 1908]/241982; and BBA–BEO/VGG(2): Erzurum Vilâyeti Gelen: 126; 194 [January 8, 1908].

378. Abdullah Cevdet, "Hüseyin Tosun Bey," *İctihad* 2, no. 8 (July–August 1908), 308–9. See also Abdullah Cevdet, "Hüseyin Tosunu Gaybettik: Saltenetle [*sic*] Mücadele Tarihimizden Bir Sahife," *İçtihat*, no. 289 (January 15, 1930), 5323. Another founder of the CUP stated the following after the revolution: "The activities in the region of Erzurum were stronger. Hüseyin Tosun Bey . . . went to Anatolia from Europe in disguise and in two years he succeeded in enlightening the [people] by traveling all around [Eastern Anatolia]. With the zeal of Hüseyin Tosun and his friends, two years ago a plan similar to that of the recent revolt carried out by a military force that occurred in Rumelia [European Turkey] this last July had been prepared. Unfortunately it was discovered before it was put into effect." See Cevrî [Mehmed Reşid], *İnkılâb Niçin ve Nasıl Oldu* [?] (Cairo, 1909), 35.

379. Hüsameddin Ertürk, *İki Devrin Perde Arkası*, ed. Samih Nafiz Kansu (Istanbul, 1957), 62. The information given here confirms the Ottoman intelligence report, which relied on an intercepted secret letter sent by the league's Paris central committee to a certain Mehmed, who was the Russian consulate's messenger in Erzurum. supra pp. 93–94.

380. Coded telegram dated [December 14, 1907] from the province of Erzurum to the Grand Vizier's office, BBA–BEO/VGG(2): Erzurum Reft: 129; 122 [January 9, 1908]/241982; and BBA–BEO/VGG(2): Erzurum Vilâyeti Gelen: 126; 194 [January 8, 1908]. The local authorities were well aware of the Russian consulate's mail carriers' role in the distribution of "seditious publications." See Governor Nuri Bey to the Sublime Porte, Erzurum [April 24, 1907]/no. 90-3542 and [May 10, 1907]/no. 141, BBA–BEO/VGG(2): Anadolu Vilâyâtı Telgrafı Gelen: 911. The capitulations, however, tied their hands. See BBA–BEO/VGG(2): Erzurum Reft: 129; 145 [March 3, 1908]/244477; and BBA–BEO/VGG(2): Erzurum Vilâyeti Gelen: 126; 206/53 [January 21, 1908].

381. A. M. Valuiskii, "K voprosu o sozdanii pervykh mladoturetskikh organizatsii," *Uchenie zapiski Instituta Vostokovedeniia* 14 (1956), 221: "Hüseyin Tosun Bey was affiliated with the League of Decentralization and Private Initiative that apparently worked with the Armenian bourgeois organizations in this region."

382. See the coded telegram from the province of Erzurum to the Grand Vizier's office dated [December 14, 1907], BBA–BEO/VGG(2): Erzurum Reft: 129; 122 [January 9, 1908]/

241982; 120 [December 13, 1907]/240559; and BBA–BEO/VGG(2): Erzurum Vilâyeti Gelen: 126; 180 [December 14, 1907].

383. A[bdullah] C[evdet], "Erzurumluların Serdengeçdi Türküsü," *İctihad*, no. 42 [March 14, 1912], 1026–27; and Cevrî [Mehmed Reşid], *İnkılâb*, 35.

384. Mehmed Nusret, *Tarihçe-i Erzurum* , 68.

385. See BBA–BEO/VGG(2): Erzurum Reft: 129; 127 [January 9, 1908]/241812; 128 [January 9, 1908]/241981; 129 [January 11, 1908]/242178; 130 [January 14, 1908]/242210; and 139 [January 29, 1908]/242782; BBA–BEO/VGG(2): Erzurum Vilâyeti Gelen: 126; 194 [January 8, 1908]; 196 [January 13, 1908]; and 199 [January 15, 1908]; and BBA–BEO/ Hariciye Giden, 188-5/44; 1490 [January 11, 1908]/242179. When it referred to the political prisoners, a pro-Dashnak journal claimed that a Russian citizen was arrested. Undoubtedly this "Russian citizen" was none other than Hüseyin Tosun. See "Le Mouvement turc," *Pro Armenia* 8, no. 175, 1229.

386. Cevrî [Mehmed Reşid], *İnkılâb*, 35.

387. Tunaya, *Türkiyede Siyasi Partiler*, 142.

388. O'Conor to Grey, Constantinople, March 18, 1907/no. 169, PRO/F.O. 424/212.

389. Shipley to O'Conor, Erzurum, December 2, 1907/no. 79, PRO/F.O. 424/213. For Durak Bey's activities, see Miller, "Revoliutsiia 1908 g. v Turtsii i Mustafa Kemal," *Narody Azii i Afriki* 3 (1975), 56.

390. Shipley's list enclosed with his dispatch dated Erzurum, March 3, 1908/no. 5, PRO/ F.O. 195/2283.

391. See Erzurum Cemiyet-i İttihadiyesinden Bir Zabit, "Kürdler," *Terakki*, no. 14, 5–6. Other letters sent to *Terakki* and mistakenly received by the CPU central committee reveal that the league corresponded with revolutionaries in Erzurum. See the letter of Dr. Bahaeddin [Şakir] beginning "Muhterem Refikimiz" and dated Paris, January 3, [1]908/no. 468, *Kopye Defteri*, 62.

392. "There are indefatigable and industrious compatriots of ours who deserve everybody's respect leading the national movement." "Tebşir-i Azîm," *Terakki*, no. [6], 1.

393. See Harputlu Bir Türk [Abdullah Cevdet], "Erzurumluların Serdengeçti Türküsü," *Türk Yurdu* 1, no. [4], [1911], 122–23; A[bdullah] C[evdet], "Erzurumluların Serdengeçti Türküsü," *İctihad*, no. 42, 1026–27; and Mehmed Nusret, *Tarihçe-i Erzurum*, 56–57. In the first article Abdullah Cevdet stated that he had prepared the anthem on December 12, 1907, and that it had been smuggled into Erzurum from Egypt. Later Ahmed Celâleddin Pasha, who wanted to seize the opportunity, asked Ahmed Kemal "on behalf of all the Young Turks" to prepare an anthem for the Erzurum revolt. He promised that the poem would be sent to one of the most esteemed European composers, who would compose a melody. For his letter and Ahmed Kemal's poem, see "Erzurum Hürriyet 'Marşı'na Dair," *İrşad* , no. 26 (March 1 [14], 1908), 3.

394. BBA–BEO/Serasker Reft, 261–6/69; 400 [May 13, 1906]/21943 (mühimme); and BBA–BEO/VGG(2): Erzurum Reft: 129; 27 [May 13, 1906]/21943 (mühimme). See also BBA-BEO/Serasker Reft, 261-6/69; 250 [May 6, 1906]/21910 (mühimme).

395. Şevket Pasha's coded telegram to the Grand Vizier's office, dated [April 20, 1906], in BBA–BEO/VGG(2): Erzurum Reft: 129; 21 [April 18, 1906]/210786. Young Turk journals underscored the joint Armeno–Muslim activity. See "Haricî," *Balkan*, no. 272 [October 15, 1907], 3.

396. Coded telegram from the Grand Vizier's office to the acting governor of Erzurum, dated [April 18, 1906], in BBA–BEO/VGG(2): Erzurum Reft: 129; 21 [April 18, 1906]/ 210786.

397. Also underscored by the French chargé d'affaires. See Boppe to Bourgeois, Pera, October 23, 1906/no. 213, and October 25, 1906/no. 216, AE–T–Politique Intérieure: Arménie, Anatolie, Cilicie XII (1905–1907): 82.

398. Valuiskii, "Vosstaniia v vostochnoi Anatolii nakanune mladoturetskoi revoliutsii," *Turetskii sbornik*, 54.

399. "Les événements d'Erzeroum," *Pro Armenia* 7, no. 148, 1013.

400. "Osmanlı'da Hareket," *İrşad*, no. 293 (December 26, 1906 [January 8, 1907]), 4.

401. See "Les incidents d'Erzeroum," *Pro Armenia* 7, no. 151, 1037; "A Erzeroum," *Pro Armenia* 7, no. 153, 1053; "Solidarité entre Arméniens et Turcs," *Pro Armenia* 7, no. 172, 1205; and "Le Mouvement turc à Erzeroum," *Pro Armenia* 8, no. 175, 1230–31.

402. Shipley to O'Conor, Erzurum, January 6, 1908/no. 1 (confidential), PRO/F.O. 195/2283.

403. Governor Âlî Bey to the Ministry of the Interior, Van [May 13, 1907]/no. 32, BBA–YMGM, 298/113 (1325.R.23). An Armenian journal published an article on this subject. See "Osmanlu," *İrşad*, no. 103 (June 3 [16], 1907), 4.

404. BBA–YMGM, 298/113 (1325.R.23).

405. Mehmed Memduh Pasha to the First Chamberlain's office [June 5, 1907], ibid.

406. See "Türkiya'da İhtilâl," *Balkan*, no. 198 [June 14, 1907], 3.

407. "Les troubles d'Anatolie," *L'Hellénisme* 4, nos. 22–23, 7.

408. "Solidarité entre Arméniens et Turcs," *Pro Armenia* 7, no. 172, 1205.

409. *Sabah'ül-Hayr*, too, names this committee as *Türk İhtilâl Komitesi* (Turkish Revolutionary Committee), in order to differentiate it from their "Turkish Allied Party," and speaks about it as an independent organization. See "Zulm Sahifesi: Vilâyet Havâdisi," *Sabah'ül-Hayr*, no. 14, 81.

410. Osman Zeki's coded telegram to the Ministry of Justice, dated [April 16, 1906], in BBA–BEO/VGG(2): Erzurum Reft: 129; 21 [April 18, 1906]/210786.

411. Emphasized by Russian consuls. See Shpil'kova, "Antipravitel'stvennye vystupleniia v vostochnoi Anatolii nakanune mladoturetskoi revoliutsii," *Narody Azii i Afriki* 3 (1971), 77–78. See also Shipley to O'Conor, Erzurum, April 12, 1906/no. 7, enclosed with O'Conor to Grey, Constantinople, April 27, 1906/no. 284, PRO/F.O. 424/210.

412. BBA–BEO/Serasker Reft, 261–6/69; 120 [April 3, 1906]/21869 (mühimme).

413. BBA–BEO/VGG(2): Erzurum Reft: 129; 11 [April 14, 1906]/210316-208456. See also BBA–BEO/Adliye Giden [BEO Karton 1042]; 93 [April 18, 1906]/210566.

414. See BBA–BEO/VGG(2): Erzurum Reft: 129; 12 [April 15, 1906]/210381.

415. See the coded telegram from two members of the investigation committee, Mustafa and Mehmed Hüsni Beys, dated [April 29, 1906], in BBA–BEO/VGG(2): Anadolu Mutasarrıflığı Reft: 80; 16 [April 30, 1906]/211241.

416. "Entre Turcs et Arméniens," *L'Indépendance Arabe* 1, nos. 7–8, 124.

417. As is mentioned in the memoirs of the district governor; see Nedim Ulusalkul, *İstibdad Aleyhinde Türk Ulusunu[n] İlk Hareketi: "Erzurum İhtilâli" ve Siyasal Bilgiler Okulu Ailesinin Türk Ulusu Namına İstibdad Aleyhinde İlk İdarî Fedakârlığı* (Ankara, 1937), 27, 47–48.

418. See BBA–BEO/Dahiliye Giden, 105-3/54; 930 [June 10, 1906]/210377; and BBA–BEO/VGG(2): Erzurum Reft: 129; 44 (Dahiliye 1229) [June 19, 1906]/213976; 96 [September 9, 1906]/217915.

419. Shipley to O'Conor, Erzurum, February 15, 1907/no. 5 (confidential), in PRO/F.O. 195/2250 and 424/212.

420. Marshal Zeki Pasha to Âsım Bey, Erzincan [March 12, 1907]/no. 2873, *Umum Şifre Marûzat-ı Vâride Kayd Defteri* (2031-2892), BBA–YEE, 36/139-77/139/XIX-7.

421. Governor Nâzım Bey to the First Chamberlain's office, Erzurum [March 21, 1906]/no. 76, *Umum Şifre Marûzat-ı Vâridenin Kayd Defteridir*, 1/1019, BBA–YEE, 36/139–76/139/XIX-1.

422. An appeal issued by the "Cemiyet-i Mukaddese-i İslâmiye ve Osmaniye" (Sacred Islamic and Ottoman Committee). A copy of the original is in A. M. Valuiskii, "Novye arkhivnye dokumenty o narodnykh volneniiakh v Maloi Azii v period russkoi revoliutsii," *Kratkie soobshcheniia Instituta Vostokovedeniia* 22 (1956) [given as an enclosure between the 89th and 90th pages].

423. A French translation is given as an enclosure in Delon to the French Ministry of War, Constantinople, January 30, 1907/no. 65-294, Archives du Ministère de la Guerre, E.M.A et Attachés militaires, 7 N 1635; and in the dispatch sent to Pichon, dated Erzurum, January 14, 1907, AE–T–Politique Intérieure: Arménie, Anatolie, Cilicie XII (1905–1907): 82. A Russian translation is in Valuiskii, "Novye arkhivnye dokumenty o narodnykh volneniiakh v Maloi Azii v period russkoi revoliutsii," *Kratkie soobshcheniia Instituta Vostokovedeniia* 22 (1956), 89–90.

424. A French translation of this appeal is enclosed with the dispatch sent to Pichon, dated Erzurum, January 14, 1907, AE–T–Politique Intérieure: Arménie, Anatolie, Cilicie XII (1905–1907): 82.

425. Enclosed with O'Conor to Grey, Pera, November 19, 1907/no. 700, in PRO/F.O. 371/356, file 38758, and in PRO/F.O. 424/213. Originally sent from Young to O'Conor and enclosed with the dispatch dated Erzurum, October 12, 1907/no. 62, PRO/F.O. 195/2251.

426. Sabahaddin Bey's league, referred to as the "Ottoman Liberal Committee," distributed "revolutionary" manifestos in Istanbul and "in the provinces" demanding "a large degree of decentralization in the provinces." See "Agitation in Turkey," *The New York Tribune*, December 2, 1906.

427. See the one-page appeal by Ali Haydar Midhat, "Vatandaşlar!" [1907]. Also published in "Anadolu Ahvâline Dair," *Füyûzat*, no. 25 (August 13 [26], 1907), 408–9. This appeal asking Muslims and non-Muslims to unite against the sultan's regime was circulated all around Eastern Anatolia. See Ali Haydar Midhat, "Les troubles de l'Asie Mineure," *Le Siècle*, July 2, 1907; and "Les musulmans contre Hamid," *Pro Armenia* 7, no. 162 (July 30, 1907), 1125–26.

428. See "Osmanlu'ya Dair," *İrşad*, no. 133 (December 27, 1907 [January 9, 1908]), 4; and "Osmanlı'ya Dair," *İrşad*, no. 7 (January 15[28], 1908), 2. Another article provides somewhat different information about this event. See Basmadjian, "Le Mouvement révolutionnaire en Asie Mineure," *Revue du Monde Musulman* 4, no. 4, 822. See also Dr. Bahaeddin [Şakir] to [Ömer] Naci, dated [Paris], March 16, [190]8/no. 558, *Kopye Defteri*, 231.

429. See, for example, "Revolutionäre Bestrebungen in der Türkei," *Berliner Tageblatt*, December 7, 1907; and "Eine konstitutionelle Bewegung in der Türkei," *Neue freie Presse*, December 8, 1907.

430. To Constans, Erzurum, June 26, 1907/no. 38, AE–T–Politique Intérieur, Arménie, Anatolie, Cilicie XII (1905–1907): 82; Shipley to O'Conor, Erzurum, December 9, 1907/no. 80 (confidential), PRO/F.O. 195/2251; van Limburg Stirum to Tets van Goudriaan, Pera, December 11, 1907/no. 542, Algemeen Rijksarchief: Tweede Afdeling: Kabinetsarchief Bu Za politieke rapportage (1871–1940): 50; and von Kiderlen-Wächter to von Bülow, Pera, December 16, 1907/no. 236, A. 19233, PAAA, 495/2, Allgemeine Angelegenheiten der Türkei, 134 (Bd. 22–23); and 733/3, Die Jungtürken, 198 (Bd. 4-5).

431. See, for example, von Kiderlen-Wächter to von Bülow, Pera, December 16, 1907/no. 236, A.19233, ibid.; Imperiali to Tittoni, Constantinople, December 9, 1907/no. 2359-835, ASMAE, Affari Politici, Serie P. Politica (1891–1916), pacco 123–24; and Brown to Root, Constantinople, December 18, 1907/no. 515, Numerical and Minor Files of the Department of State, #717, NF 862 (Case numbers 10042-10044/95). For the foreign press coverage, see, for example, "Le mécontentement en Turquie," *Bulletin du Comité de L'Asie Française* 6, no. 66 (September 1906), 361; Eugène Jung, "Tout craque en Turquie," *L'Indépendance Arabe* 1, no. 4 (July 1907), 60; "Türkiya Ahvâli," *İrşad*, no. 265 (November 16 [29], 1906), 4; "Türkiye'de Fikr-i Meşrutiyet," *Terakki*, no. 16, 8; and "The New Era in Turkey," *The Edinburgh Review* 208, no. 426 (October 1908), 502–3.

432. See, for example, IU. A. Petrosian, "Iz istorii nelegal'noi propagandy mladoturok vo flote," *Narody Azii i Afriki* 5 (1973), 151–52. The pamphlet mentioned by Petrosian was written in 1896 and had nothing to do with the Young Turk propaganda during 1906–1907. Ottoman naval documents reveal that most of the mutinies or plans for "terrible riots" stemmed from nonpolitical reasons. See, for example, Deniz Müzesi Arşivi, Müteferrik-Divan-ı Harb, 54/38–39 [March 16, 1907]/no. 1176–1304; Gemiler, Erkân-ı Harbiye, Tersane, Limanlar, Daireler, 118/59 [April 29, 1905]; Şûra-yı Bahrî, 725/12A [November 24, 1906]; and MKT. 1630/2 [December 17, 1909]; 1645/5 [December 3, 1908]. See also O'Conor to Grey, Constantinople, December 19, 1906/no. 812, PRO/F.O. 371/157, file 43077; and "İstanbul'da Bahriyelilerin İsyanı," *Balkan*, no. 229 [August 3, 1907], 4.

433. This does not mean that similar movements did not take place before 1905. For an interesting example of a mass demonstration against the subgovernor of Dayr al-Zawr in Syria, see BBA–BEO/Serasker Reft, 258-6/66; 691 [September 18, 1899]/102852, and 711

[September 24, 1899]/103118. In this mass demonstration people closed down their shops and occupied the post office. Similar movements took place between 1905 and 1908.

434. See BBA–BEO/VGG(2): Ma'muret el-Azîz Vilâyeti Giden: 173; 56 [September 12, 1907]/235682; and BBA–YSHM, 515/106 (1325.Ş.21).

435. BBA–BEO/Zabtiye Giden, 663-21/14; 71 [April 20, 1906]/212223.

436. BBA–BEO/VGG(2): Anadolu Mutasarrıflığı Reft: 80; 33 [June 6, 1907]/231989; and 34 [June 6, 1907]/231983.

437. See BBA–YSHM, 512/51 (1325.5.11), and 512/68 (1325.Ca.13).

438. See the "Decipher from Mr. Shipley, April 29, 1907," PRO/F.O. 195/2250; Safrastian to Shipley, Bitlis, June 25, 1907, enclosed with Shipley to O'Conor, Erzurum, June 29, 1907/ no. 37, in PRO/F.O. 195/2250 and further enclosed with O'Conor to Grey, Constantinople, June 10, 1907/no. 411, in PRO/F.O. 424/213; Shipley to O'Conor, Erzurum, July 1, 1907 (confidential), PRO/F.O. 195/2250; to Pichon, Erzurum July 2, 1907/no. 9, AE–T–Politique Intérieure, Arménie, Anatolie, Cilicie XII (1905–1907): 82; "Trabzon Vali-i Cedîdi Ferid Paşa Bitlis'den Niçin Koğuldu [?]" *Terakki*, no. 16, 5–7; "Telgraf," *Şûra-yı Ümmet*, no. 118 (July 15, 1907), 1; and "Anadolu'da," *Şûra-yı Osmanî*, no. 15 (July 12, [1907]), 3.

439. See, for example, Mehmed Nusret, *Tarihçe-i Erzurum*, 62; and the report of the Russian consul Skriabin quoted in Valuiskii, "Vosstaniia v vostochnoi Anatolii nakanune mladoturetskoi revoliutsii," *Turetskii sbornik*, 53.

440. Erzurum İhtilâli," *Tuna*, no. 350, 2. See also "Les événements d'Erzeroum," *Pro Armenia* 7, no. 146, 998. Independent journals made similar claims before and during the Young Turk Revolution of 1908. See, for example, "Ne Yazıyorlar [?]" *İrşad*, no. 139 (June 14 [27], 1906), 4; "Inostrannaia khronika," *Kaspii*, no. 52 (March 7 [20], 1907), 2; and "Mladoturskoto dvizhenie," *Svobodno slovo*, no. 375 (July 2 [15], 1908).

441. Governor Nâzım Bey to the First Chamberlain's office, Erzurum [March 21, 1906]/ no. 76, *Umum Şifre Marûzat-ı Vâridenin Kayd Defteridir*, 1/1019, BBA–YEE, 36/139-76/ 139/XIX-1.

442. "Rusya Ahvâli," *İctihad*, no. 8 (July 1905), 123.

443. "Genclerimize Mektub: Rusya İhtilâlinin Ma'na-yı İctima'îsi," *Terakki* no. [1], 4.

444. Tsovikian, "Vliianie russkoi revoliutsii 1905 g. na revoliutsionnoe dvizhenie v Turtsii," *Sovetskoe vostokovedenie* 3, 34.

445. Halîl Hâlid, "A Pacific Revolution in Turkey," *The Orient Review* 1, 1 (January 1908), 23. See also A. L[e] C[hatelier], "Turquie," *Revue du Monde Musulman* 4, no. 2 (February 1908), 417.

446. Halîl Hâlid, "A Pacific Revolution in Turkey," *The Orient Review* 1, 1, 27.

447. See, for example, Pierre Quillard, "L'avenir prochain," *Pro Armenia* 6, no. 136 (June 20, 1906), 919; "The Unrest in Turkey," *The Times*, September 4, 1907; and A[nastase] [Adossidis], "L'effondrement d'un régime," *L'Hellénisme* 5, no. 15 (August 1, 1908), 15.

448. See, for example, the case of the Adjutant-Major Ferid Efendi, who had been exiled to Harput and who attempted to "stir up and provoke people." He was expelled from the army. See BBA–BEO/VGG(2): Ma'mûret el-Azîz Vilâyeti Giden: 173; 32 [July 10, 1906]/215099.

449. A[nastase] Adossidès, "Le Mouvement turc," *Le Courrier Européen* 4, no. 3 (January 18, 1907), 7. For an English translation of this article, see "The Turkish Movement," *Armenia* 3, no. 5 (March 1907), 29–32. The Young Turk press harshly criticized Adossides and claimed that he was strongly prejudiced against Muslims. See "Anadolu'da Harekât-ı Fikriye," *Tuna,* no. 407 [February 2, 1907], 1. For Tatar participation, see also Tsovikian, "Vliianie russkoi revoliutsii 1905 g. na revoliutsionnoe dvizhenie v Turtsii," *Sovetskoe vosto-kovedenie* 3 (1945), 18; and Governor Reşid Âkif Pasha to İzzet Pasha, Sivas [April 18, 1906]/no. 240, *Umum Şifre Marûzat-ı Vâridenin Kayd Defteridir*, 1/1019, BBA–YEE, 36/ 139-76/139/XIX-1.

450. He first provided this information in "Ali Haydar Midhat Bey über die Verfassung seines Vaters Midhat Pascha," *Neue freie Presse*, July 26, 1908. Many journalists later repeated this claim. See, for example, Heinrich Friedjung, "Die türkische Revolution," *Die Woche* 10/3, no. 31 (August 1, 1908), 1324. Imhoff, who later published a meticulous essay

on the Young Turk organizations, echoed Ali Haydar Midhat's claim. See Generalmajor z.D. Imhoff, "Die Entstehung und der Zweck des Comités für Einheit und Fortschritt," *Die Welt des Islams* 1, no. 3/4 (1913), 173–74.

451. "Die Aktion der Jungtürken: eine Unterredung mit Ali Haydar Midhat Bey Sohn Midhat Paschas," *Das freie Wort* 7 (April 1908–April 1909), 368. He also maintained that "modern ideas" made a strong impact in the provinces in question. See Ali Haydar Midhat, "Die Verfassungsbewegung in der asiatischen Türkei," *Illustrirte Zeitung* (Leipzig), no. 3397 (August 6, 1908), 218.

452. A[rminus] Vambéry, "Die türkische Revolution," *München allgemeine Zeitung*, no. 21 (August 22, 1908), 432.

453. In fact, a socialist Armenian researcher claimed that the economic problems of the empire played the decisive role in the Young Turk movement. See V. Totomiants, "Ekonomicheskaia pochva turetskoi revoliutsii," *Sovremennyi mir* 10 (October 1908), 15–20. Obviously, economic problems were a source of great dissatisfaction among the masses, as the author stated; nonetheless, this economic determinist thesis underestimates the importance of the political factors that in fact generated and shaped the revolution.

454. Thousands of documents on popular dissatisfaction, desertions, and mutinies in various provinces because of the Yemeni campaign are in eight boxes in the BEO collection. The boxes are numbered 767/1–767/8, and all the documents are merged under the general number 153295.

455. See BBA–İrade-Maliye, Ş 1321/no. 9–2206; "Vergü-yi Şahsî Hakkında Şûra-yı Devletin Meclis-i Vükelâdan Müzeyyel Mazbatası Suretidir [August 19, 1903]/no. 5365-183," and the addendum made by the cabinet and the imperial decree enclosed with it in BBA–Yıldız Marûzat Defterleri, no. 11488. See also BBA–İrade-Kavânin ve Nizâmât, L 1322/no. 1–2236(132); and Abdurrahman Vefik, *Tekâlif Kavâidi* 2 (Istanbul, 1330 [1912]), 237–39.

456. The taxes even provoked Iranian protests in objection to the Ottoman government's taxing of Iranian subjects. See BBA–BEO/VGG(2): Ankara Vilâyeti Reft: 103; 2 [April 2, 1905]/190496.

457. Âkif Bey to the Grand Vizier's office, Erzurum [March 14, 1904]/no. 2-2, BBA–BEO/VGG(2): Anadolu Defteri: 909.

458. See, for example, BBA–MV, 111/no. 17 [March 29, 1905]; 29 [April 30, 1905]; 30 [April 30, 1905]; 34 [May 7, 1905]. The government even turned down the demands made by the Hamidiye regiments' commanders and officers. See BBA–MV, 115/no. 3 [February 17, 1907].

459. For interesting examples, see BBA–TFR.1.MN. 36/3548 (1322.1.15); 39/3854 (1322.3.2); and 35/3462 (1322.1.4); BBA–TFR.1.İŞ. 7/672 (1321.7.5); 3/232 (1321.7.12); BBA–BEO/Harbiye Giden, 260–6/68; 1926 [September 26, 1903]/163303; and BBA–MV, 107/no. 77 [October 4, 1903]; BBA–MV, 108/no. 50 [February 7, 1904].

460. See, for example, the exemption of al-Hijāz, the province of Yemen [BBA–YSRM, 123/92 (1321.10.7); BBA–İrade-Maliye, C 1323/no. 34-1337 and B 1321/no. 29-1626], and Banghāzī [BBA–İrade-Maliye, Ş 1323/no. 43-1613]. In Scutari in Albania popular resistance forced the government to promise that the taxes collected would be spent for local purposes [see BBA–YSRM, 123/67 (1321.9.4)]. Later the provincial center and four subprovinces were "temporarily" exempted from the taxes. [See BBA–İrade-Maliye, L 1323/no. 23-2160; and BBA–YSRM, 124/21 (1321.11.13)]. In Priština, the governor ordered the taxes collected only from those who would pay them of their own will. (See BBA–İrade Maliye, S 1323/no. 16-148.) In Harran, because of the resistance, the government decided to ask for the payment of a flat tax. See BBA–MV, 108/no. 12 [November 12, 1903]. Finally an exemption was granted to Mosul. See BBA–MV, 107/no. 76 [September 30, 1903].

461. See BBA–YSRM, 123/108 (1321.10.14); 144/10 (1325.1.7); and 144/53 (1325.1.5); BBA–MV, 110/no. 96 [February 19, 1905]; 111/no. 50 [June 7, 1905]; 111/no. 70 [July 19,1905]; 112/no. 87 [May 16, 1906]; and BBA–İrade-Maliye, Ş 1321/no. 9-2206; and M 1324/no. 28-33.

462. Therefore immediately after the sultan's imperial decree abolishing the taxes, the

cabinet informed the sultan of the necessity of creating new revenues for military expenses. See "Gerek Hayvanat-ı Ehliye Resmi ve Gerek Vergü-yi Şahsî Afvolunduğundan Resm-i Mezkûrun Yerine Techizat-ı Askeriye Sanduğu İçün Münâsib Bir Vâridat Bulunması Hakkında Meclis-i Vükelâ Mazbatası Sureti" [March 27, 1907], and the Grand Vizier's note bearing the same date and enclosed with it. BBA–Yıldız Marûzat Defterleri, no. 14452.

463. Halil Sahillioğlu has published a recent article on a local revolt against a governor who attempted to levy taxes in Antioch in 1792. The people who refused to pay the taxes signed round-robins to be presented to the *divan*, but these did not prevent the governor from launching an attack which resulted in a battle between his troops and the local people. See Halil Sahillioğlu, "18. Yüzyıl Antakyası'na Ait Belgeler: Zulme Karşı Direnme," *Güneyde Kültür* 9, no. 96 (February 1997), 1–14.

464. Sabahaddine, *Mémoire des Libéraux turcs relatif à la Question d'orient* (Paris, 1906), [4].

465. For example, the khedive's spy attributed great importance to Sabahaddin Bey's visit to the former French premier Waldeck-Rousseau. See his report presented to ʿAbbās Ḥilmī dated Paris, May 13, 1904, Abbas II Papers, Durham University, F. 40/513.

466. See Hanioğlu, *The Young Turks*, 144–45. According to the Ottoman authorities, Sabahaddin Bey once again failed in meeting with prominent British statesmen. See the First Chamberlain's office to the London embassy, November 20, 1904, and from the latter to the former, London, December 1, 1904, Archives of the Turkish Embassy in London, Box 395 (1).

467. A later police report also indicates that Prince Sabahaddin continued to affirm "des sentiments francophiles." See the police report dated March 5, 1912/no. 880, Archives de la Préfecture de Police de Paris (Sabahaddine et Loutfoullah).

468. Ali Kemal, "Sabahaddin Beyefendi," *İkdam*, September, 2, 1908. De Lanessan also helped Sabahaddin Bey to receive good media coverage in France. See Fesch, *Constantinople*, 406. Bahaeddin Şakir, one of the leading opponents of Sabahaddin Bey, later claimed that de Lanessan had written an article about the Young Turks in *Le Siècle* on April 17, 1908, which criticized Sabahaddin Bey's faction by stating that their policy of decentralization would cause the annihilation and dismemberment of the Ottoman Empire (see *Şûra-yı Ümmet-Ali Kemal Daʿvası*, 125). There is, however, no such article about the Young Turks published in the aforementioned daily on the given date.

469. Imperiali to Tittoni, Constantinople, September 30, 1908/no. 2252-714, ASMAE, Affari Politici, Serie P. Politica (1891–1916), pacco 123–24. See also Marschall von Bieberstein to von Bülow, Therapia, September 14, 1908/no. 207, A. 15100: "Es fehlte nur an Geld. Dieses hat ihm ein Franzose vorgestreckt." PAAA, 943/5, Diverse Personalien, 159/4 (Bd. 1-2). Baron de Lormais was portrayed as "un ami dévoué du parti libéral ottoman" by the opponents of Abdülhamid II's regime. See "A Paris," *Pro Armenia* 8, no. 188 (August 30, 1908), 1347. De Lormais also made presentations at meetings organized by Sabahaddin Bey's faction. See, for example, his presentation on "Turkish women" in "Conférence sur la Turquie: préjugés et vérités," *Idjtihad*, no. 8, 113–18.

470. Frances Keyzer, "Paris Week by Week: An Enlightened Prince," *The Bystander*, October 24, 1906, 171.

471. See Fesch, *Constantinople*, 406. For a good example, see Camille Audigier, "Autour de l'homme malade," *Gil Blas*, October 1, 1906.

472. See Alfred Durand, *Jeune-Turquie, vieille France* (Paris, 1909), 58.

473. Finally, Sabahaddin Bey sent a letter to Camille Audigier and discredited the rumors. See his letter dated October 11, 1906, in "Situation politique en Turquie," *Gil Blas*, October 17, 1906. These rumors were started at a relatively early date and then gained momentum in 1906. For an early accusation against Sabahaddin Bey in this matter, see Mohammed Aga Schah-Tachtinsky, *Comment sauver la Turquie?* (Paris, 1901), 39.

474. Fesch's affiliation with the Catholic Church caused many scholars to speculate about the reasons this book was published. See Martin Hartmann, "Die neuere Literatur zum türkischen Problem," *Zeitschrift für Politik* 3 (1910), 171. Yusuf Fehmi, an opponent of Sabahaddin Bey, made the following interesting comment: "Avec le Prince Sabahaddine comme sultan, l'abbé Fesch comme cheik-ul-Islam, des accomodements étaient possibles." See Youssouf Fehmi, *La Révolution ottomane, 1908–1910* (Paris, 1911), 128.

475. See, for example, L. Bouvat, "La presse technique en Turquie," *Revue du Monde Musulman* 4, no. 2 (February 1908), 454. In reality the material used in the book had been provided by Ahmed Fazlı, Sabahaddin Bey's foster brother. See Ernest Edmondson Ramsaur, Jr., *The Young Turks: Prelude to the Revolution of 1908* (Princeton, 1957), 155–56.

476. Imprimerie Durand's letters dated February 26 and 28, 1906, and April 3, 1906, and its memorandum dated March 19, 1906, in Sabahaddin Bey's uncatalogued papers in European languages in Bibliothèque nationale (Paris), Manuscripts occidentaux.

477. See Münir Pasha to Tevfik Pasha, October 19, 1906/no. 296-900, and the latter to the former, October 28, 1906/no. 212-70863, Dışişleri Bakanlığı Hazine-i Evrak Arşivi, Box Siyasî 225. Later on, other publications of Fesch were banned by Ottoman authorities, however. See the Ottoman Foreign Ministry's note verbale presented to all ambassadors in Istanbul except the Italian and the U.S. ministers, dated April 29, 1907/no. 68724-71, Dışişleri Bakanlığı Hazine-i Evrak Arşivi, Box İdarî, 198. A prominent German scholar too maintained that the book had indeed been written by Sabahaddin Bey and published by Fesch. See Martin Hartmann, *Der islamische Orient: Berichte und Forschungen* 3, *Unpolitische Briefe aus der Türkei* (Leipzig, 1910), 41, 56. Sabahaddin Bey praised both the book and Fesch in the league's organ. See "Constantinople aux derniers jours d'Abdul-Hamid par P. Fesch," *Terakki*, no. 15, 12.

478. See the Ministry of the Interior's undated [1907] coded telegram to the subgovernor of Jerusalem, Israel State Archives, RG. 83-1/ט.

479. The chapter was considered the best source of information on the Young Turks, even following the Young Turk Revolution of 1908, and a translation of Fesch's chapter appeared in Turkish. See A[hmed] R[efik], *Abdülhamid-i Sânî* 3, 1062–1119.

480. See Youssouf Fehmi, *La Révolution ottomane*, 128. Sabahaddin Bey's secretary Denais too was described as "un catholique *militant*." See "Une lettre de M. Joseph Denais," *Pro Armenia* 2, no. 15 (July 10, 1902), 123.

481. Giovanni de Montel to [von Bülow] [October 1906]. The Italian original and the German translation of this long letter are in A. 17678, PAAA, 733/3, Die Jungtürken, 198 (Bd. 4–5), and enclosed with Kapp to von Bülow, London, October 19, 1906, A. 17678, ibid.

482. Giovanni de Montel to [von Bülow] [October 1906], A. 17678, ibid; and Rotenhan to von Bülow, Rome, March 8, 1906 (Entzifferung, AA. no. 24) (geheim), A. 4946, and Rome, March 23, 1906/no. 29 (geheim), A. 5955, ibid.

483. It should be remembered that because of Abdülhamid II's illness, which his opponents believed to be cancer, his death seemed imminent then. The European press succeeded in convincing the European public that the sultan was extremely ill. See "La maladie du Sultan," *Le Courrier Européen*, no. 10 (January 13, 1905), 1–2; no. 34 (June 30, 1905), 14; Camille Audigier, "Quand Abdul-Hamid mourra . . . ," *Gil Blas*, September 28, 1906; and idem, "Abdul-Hamid étant mort . . . ," *Gil Blas*, October 2, 1906. The illness, however, was a mere kidney infection. For a detailed article on the sultan's illness, see Rengin Bütün, "Sultan II. Abdülhamid'e 1906 Senesinde Yapılan Konsültasyon Reçetelerinin ve Sultan'ı Tedâvi Eden Hekimlerin Tanıtılması," *Yeni Symposium Dergisi* 1, no. 20 (1982), 1–19.

484. Giovanni de Montel to [von Bülow] [October 1906], A. 17678, PAAA, 733/3, Die Jungtürken, 198 (Bd. 4-5); and Rotenhan to von Bülow, Rome, March 23, 1906/no. 29 (geheim), A. 5955, ibid.

485. I conducted research in the Archivio Segreto Vaticano in the sections of Archivio della Casa Pontificia and Archivio delle Cerimonie Pontificie and did not come across any document on Sabahaddin Bey's visit or related subjects. During this research I also examined the list of visitors who met with Cardinal Raffaele Merry del Val, the Vatican's Secretary of State, between 1905 and 1907, and could not find Sabahaddin Bey's name in that list (Archivio Segreto Vaticano—Rubricelle Segretaria Stato). Also there is no mention of Sabahaddin Bey's visit in Cardinal Merry del Val's book on Pius X. See *Memories of Pope Pius X by Cardinal Merry del Val* (London: [1939]). For more information about Sabahaddin Bey's visit to the Vatican, see my "Prens Sabahaddin'in Katolik Kilisesiyle Olan İlişkileri," *İ.Ü. Siyasal Bilimler Fakültesi Mecmuası* 2 (1982), 99–119.

486. Rotenhan to von Bülow, Rome, March 8, 1906 (Entzifferung, AA. no. 24) (geheim), PAAA 733/3, Die Jungtürken, 198 (Bd. 4-5).

487. See *Memories of Pope Pius X*, 12. See also G[arreu] D[ombasie], "M. du Bulow au Vatican," *Le Siècle*, April 17, 1908.

488. See the drafts dated Berlin, March 13, 1906, A. 4946, and Berlin, March 17, 1906, A. 5073, PAAA 733/3, Die Jungtürken, 198 (Bd. 4–5). The following statement was made in the first document: "Die Pforte verfolgt den Genannten als staatsgefährlichen Revolutionär. Ein Empfang des Prinzen durch Seine Durchlaucht [von Bülow] kann hierauf nicht in Frage kommen."

489. The accusations were made by Ali Haydar Midhat. See the undated [March 1907]/ no. 265, letter of Dr. Bahaeddin [Şakir] and Dr. Nâzım to the director of the CPU Kazanlŭk branch, *Muhaberat Kopyası*, 264; the letter of Dr. Bahaeddin [Şakir] and Dr. Nâzım to Alyotîzâde Mustafa Tevfik dated Paris, April 9, 1907/no. 276, *Muhaberat Kopyası*, 284; and *Şûra-yı Ümmet-Ali Kemal Da'vası*, 33, 103–4. See also Ular-Insabato, *Der erlöschende Halbmond*, 174, 287; Hartmann, "Die neuere Literatur zum türkischen Problem," *Zeitschrift für Politik* 3 (1910), 171; and Youssouf Fehmi, *Les congréganistes de Turquie: ultramontanisme et concupiscence* (Paris, 1909), 2 ff.

490. "Bir Te'essüf," *Terakki*, no. [6], 10.

491. See *Sadrazam ve Harbiye Nazırı Mahmut Şevket Paşa'nın Günlüğü* (Istanbul, 1988), 41.

492. See "Jön Türkler-Sultan Hamid," *Tuna*, no. 224 [June 12, 1906], 2; "Sultanzâde Lûtfullah Bey'in Biraderini Kandırmak İçün Paris'e Gönderilmesi," ibid., 4; "Jön Türkler-Sultan Hamid Hazretleri," *Hayat*, no. 123 (June 7 [20], 1906), 4; and Fesch, *Constantinople*, 407.

493. The most important British documents concerning the impact of the incident on British policy have been published. For detailed information, see A & P (Cd.3086/1906), *Egypt* 3 (1906): *Correspondence Respecting the Attack on British Officers at Denshawai*; and (Cd. 3091/1906), *Egypt* 4 (1906): *Further Paper Respecting the Attacks on British Officers at Denshawai*.

494. *Hansard's Parliamentary Debates*, 4th Series, 160 (1906), col. 288.

495. The subject is well examined in Caesar E. Farah, "Great Britain, Germany, and the Ottoman Caliphate," *Der Islam* 66, no. 2 (1989), 264–88. See also "Le Panislamisme turc en Afrique et en Arabie et la Presse arabe," *Bulletin du Comité de L'Asie Française* 7, no. 71 (February 1907), 59–61; C. E. B., "Notes sur le panislamisme—IV," *Questions Diplomatiques et Coloniales* 28, no. 308 (December 16, 1909), 730–32. For the German point of view, see the following articles: "Panislamische Bewegung," *Tägliche Rundschau*, June 29, 1906; Hans Plehn, "Panislamismus," *Deutsche Monatsschrift für das gesamte Leben der Gegenwart* 11 (October 1906 to March 1907), 824–32; and Max Roloff, "Die muhammedanische Propaganda der Neuzeit," *Nord und Süd* 145, no. 164 (May 1913), 187 ff.

496. For best examples, see "Bulletin de l'étranger: le panislamisme en Afrique," *Le Temps*, August 23, 1906; and "Bulletin de l'étranger: la situation en Égypte," *Le Temps*, January 7, 1907.

497. "Mussulman Fanaticism by M. de Lanessan Ex-French Minister of Marine," *The Tribune*, July 12, 1906. A French version of this article was published by de Lanessan's daily (see J.-L. de Lanessan, "A propos du discours de Sir Edward Grey," *Le Siècle*, July 14, 1906) and was ascribed great importance. See G[arreu] D[ombasie], "Questions étrangères: affaires de la Turquie," *Le Siècle*, July 17, 1906. For *The Tribune*'s involvement in anti-Abdülhamid II propaganda, see C. E. B., "Notes sur le panislamisme," *Questions Diplomatiques et Coloniales* 28, no. 307 (December 1, 1909), 647. The articles published by the French press in the same vein are summarized in "Pan-Islamic Agitation: French Apprehensions," *The Times*, July 20, 1906. For further criticism toward German policies regarding Panislamism and toward the kaiser, see *Questions Diplomatiques et Coloniales* 28, no. 307, 646–47; C. Á. Court Repington, "Teuton and Turk," *The National Review* 49, no. 294 (August 1907), 871–72; J. Imbart de la Tour, "L'Allemagne en Asie Mineure," *Annales des Sciences Politiques* 21 (1906), 431–53; and Enrico Insabato, "La penetrazione della Germania in Turchia," *Rivista d'Italia* 11/2, no. 9 (September 1908), 348.

498. A comparison of the following paragraph with early writings of Sabahaddin Bey provides insight. The Prince had written the following: "Si, dans une société orientale, l'éducation européenne trouve un terraine propice à son développement, il lui faudrait élever au moins deux ou trois générations avant qu'un mouvement capable d'influencer les couches profondes de la société puisse s'établir péremptoirement. . . . Le successeur au trône impérial actuel, le prince Rechad . . . trouverait précisément dans la jeunesse ottomane un puissant auxiliarie . . . pour élever graduellement l'empire au sommet du monde civilisé. Cette génération est le produit direct de la réaction de l'Europe moderne sur la Turquie contemporaine." See Sabahaddine, "Les Turcs et le progrès," *La Revue* 59, no. 24 (December 1905), 441–43. Also a comparison between Sabahaddin Bey's early writings and another article by de Lanessan, information for which was undoubtedly provided by Sabahaddin Bey, would be informative. See J. L. de Lanessan, "L'Opposition ottomane," *Le Siècle*, February 7, 1908.

499. *The Tribune*, July 12, 1906. De Lanessan continued to ask France to work with the "liberal elements of Turkey." See J.-L. de Lanessan, "La succession d'Abdul Hamid," *Le Siècle*, October 20, 1906; idem, "La Turquie et le Parti libéral ottoman," *Le Siècle*, January 23, 1907; and idem, "La rôle de la France en Orient," *Le Siècle*, April 10, 1908.

500. See Sir Edward Grey's minute on the document entitled "Mussulman fanaticism—Egypt, Morocco and Turkey," PRO/F.O. 371/153, file 23706. De Lanessan's daily further encouraged the British to retaliate forcefully against the Panislamist agitation allegedly backed by the German and the Ottoman Empires. See G[arreu] D[ombasie], "Question étrangères: la leçon de Tabah," *Le Siècle*, July 18, 1906. Summarized in "The Pan-Islamic Agitation," *The Times*, July 19, 1906.

501. August 9, 1900, PRO/F.O. 371/153, file 27300. Sanderson too found the letter "rather remarkable." See Sanderson to O'Conor, August 13, 1906 (private), O'Conor Papers, Churchill College, Cambridge, 6/1/59.

502. "We do not acknowledge communications from 'Young Turks.'" RPM [R. P. Maxwell]," August 9, 1900, PRO/F.O. 371/153, file 27300.

503. "The Sultan and the Pan-Islamic Movement," *The Times*, August 13, 1906. A French version was published the next day by de Lanessan's daily. See "Une lettre du Prince Sabah Ed Dine sur le panislamisme et la Porte," *Le Siècle*, August 14, 1906. A Turkish translation was provided by the prince's journal. See "İttihad-ı İslâm," *Terakki*, no. 4 [September 1906], 1–3. Republished in a Ruse-based Young Turk organ. See "İttihad-ı İslâm," *Tuna*, no. 343 [November 2, 1906], 1–2, and no. 344 [November 3, 1906], 1–2.

504. For example, an Arab intellectual who worked closely with Sabahaddin Bey and authored a moderately critical essay on the subject spoke about "the European dailies' malicious coverage of Panislamism" and "the pervasive outcry of the Western statesmen on the prospective perils that might stem from it." He also gave advice to European diplomats. See Rafīq Bak al-ʿAẓm, *al-Jāmiʿah al-Islāmīyah wa Urubbā* (Cairo, 1907), 2 and 52–58.

505. Sabahaddine, "The Sultan and the Pan-Islamic Movement," *The Times*, August 13, 1906. Sabahaddin Bey continued to underscore his claim until the Young Turk Revolution of 1908. See, for example, Sabahaddin, "On Üçüncü *Terakki*'de Tenkidinizi Okurken," *Terakki*, no. 15, 5–6.

506. See "Le panislamisme est un péril imaginaire," *Le Matin*, August 14, 1906; and "Sabahaddin Bey'in Mektubu," *Tuna*, no. 276 [August 16, 1906], 3. In fact the Reverend Malcolm Mac Coll, one of the leaders of the "Arab Caliphate" doctrine in Great Britain, asserted that "[t]here [was] an error in the interesting letter of Prince Sabah-ed-din" concerning the Ottoman sultan's right to the caliphate. See Malcolm Mac Coll, "The Khalifate: To the Editor of the Times," *The Times*, August 18, 1906. [Mac Coll had formerly claimed that "reforms were not possible under Muslim rule." See Malcolm Mac Coll, "Are Reforms Possible under Mussulman Rule?" *Contemporary Review* 40, no. 2 (August 1881), 257–81. For an interesting response to his claims, see Moulaví Cherágh Ali, *The Political, Legal, and Social Reforms in the Ottoman Empire and Other Mohammedan States* (Bombay, 1883).] Arminius Vámbéry responded to this criticism by defending Sabahaddin Bey. See A. Vambéry, "The Khalifate: To The Editor of the Times," *The Times*, August 28, 1906. Mac Coll answered back (see Malcolm Mac Coll, "The Khalifate: To the Editor of the Times," *The Times*, Sep-

tember 7, 1906) and Vámbéry had the last word. See A. Vambéry, "The Khalifate: To The Editor of the Times," *The Times*, September 15, 1906. (In this issue another letter by Hosein [Ḥusayn] Kidmai [Qidwāī] was published in defense of the Ottoman sultan.) It should also be stated that although many prominent scholars and statesmen favored an "Arab Caliphate," in England and in various Western countries there were exceptions who claimed that "to go further, and to play off Mecca against Stamboul by reviving the Caliphate, would be an interesting but hazardous, experiment." See Lloyd Sanders, "The Sultan and the Caliphate: A Side-Light on Turkish Policy," *The North American Review* 176, no. 557 (April 1903), 552.

507. For Russian complaints, see G. Alisov, "Musul'manskii vopros v Rossii," *Russkaia mysl'* 25, no. 6 (June 1909), 36–37. For similar criticism by a Dashnak leader and a defender of the cause of the Dashnaktsutiun, see respectively Aknouni [Khachatur Malumian], *Les plaies du Caucase*, 339–41; and Pierre Quillard, "Autocratie et panislamisme," *Pro Armenia* 5, no. 112 (June 15, 1905), 727–28. For a socialist critique of "Panislamism" by the Armenians, see "Ermeni Matbuʿatı," *Hayat*, no. 71 (March 31 [April 13], 1906), 4.

508. Sabahaddine, "The Sultan and the Pan-Islamic Movement," *The Times*, August 13, 1906.

509. Ibid.

510. Ibid. Ironically Sabahaddin Bey made the following comment in a response to an Armenian leader: "How does it come about that a ruler who wants to see his governors incapable of repairing collapsed bridges would initiate the unification of a huge world composed of a few hundred millions?" See Sabahaddin, "On Üçüncü *Terakki*'de Tenkidinizi Okurken," *Terakki*, no. 15, 6.

511. Sabahaddine, "The Sultan and the Pan-Islamic Movement," *The Times*, August 13, 1906.

512. For a good example, see "Ueber das jetzige System in der Türkei und die Pläne der Jungtürken," *Deutsche Zeitung*, August 16, 1906.

513. For an open appreciation, see "Abdul Hamid, Sultan and Khalif and the Pan-Islamic Movement," *Blackwood's Edinburgh Magazine* 180, no. 1091 (September 1906), 309–10. For a veiled recognition, see Valentine Chirol, "Pan-Islamism," *The National Review* 48, no. 280 (December 1906), 649: "It may well be that Pan-Islamism in its present form will not survive. . . . None know better than the best class of Turks what Abdul-Hamid's policy has cost them, and none deplore more deeply the estrangement of British friendship." Republished in *The Eclectic Magazine* 148 (February 1907), 145–56. Also summarized in "The Pan-Islamic Revival," *The Times*, November 16, 1906.

514. Pierre Quillard, "Quand la bête sera morte," *Pro Armenia* 6, no. 140 (August 20, 1906), 952–53.

515. It is ironic that following the Young Turk Revolution of 1908, foreign journalists, assuming that Sabahaddin Bey was a leader of the movement, asked the Young Turks to fulfill the promises made by the prince in his letter to Sir Edward. See "La Jeune Turquie et l'avenir du panislamisme," *Questions Diplomatiques et Coloniales* 28, no. 301 (September 1, 1909), 265.

516. See Braham to Hardinge, January 17, 1907, PRO/F.O. 371/344, file 2783; Grey and Hardinge to O'Conor, January 29, 1907/no. 43 (secret), and Grey to Braham, January 29, 1907, PRO/F.O. 371/344, file 7897; Braham to Hardinge, Constantinople, January 29, 1907, PRO/F.O. 371/344, file 2866; O'Conor to Grey, Constantinople, February 5, 1907/no. 80 (secret), PRO/F.O. 371/344, file 4579; Gray to O'Conor, February 19, 1907 (secret), PRO/F.O. 371/344, file 4572; Edward Grey's "Memorandum for M. Cambon," dated March 10, 1907, PRO/F.O. 371/344, file 4572; O'Conor to Grey, Constantinople, March 5, 1907/no. 148 (secret), PRO/F.O. 371/344, file 7897; the "Note pour le Ministre," dated Paris, June 19, 1906; the draft of the Affaires étrangères note to Constans, Paris, June 21, 1906/no. 255 (confidential); Constans to Affaires étrangères, Therapia, July 22, 1906/no. 145; Bihourd to Bourgeois, Berlin, August 17, 1906/no. 174; "Extrait d'une lettre de M. P. Cambon, Londres, 27 Septembre [19]06"; "Extrait d'une lettre de M. P. Cambon du 3 Oct[obre] [19]06"; the "Note de la Division des Archives pour la Direction politique (28 Août 1906)"; the Affaires étrangères draft entitled "Au sujet de la succession au trône en Turquie," dated Paris, August 27, 1906; the

memorandum entitled "La Succession d'Abdul Hamid II," enclosed with Constans to Bourgeois, Therapia, September 1, 1906/no. 167 (confidentielle); the Affaires étrangères drafts dated Paris, September 13, 1906 (confidentiel) and September 21, 1906; Bihourd to Bourgeois, Berlin, September 22, 1906/no. 197; Cambon to Bourgeois, London, September 27, 1906/ no. 293 and October 3, 1906/no. 296; Boutiron to Bourgeois, St. Petersburg, October 6, 1906/ no. 132; the Affaires étrangères drafts dated Paris, October 8, 1906, October 11, 1906, October 12, 1906, October 23, 1906; the "Mémoire," presented by A. K.; Affaires étrangères drafts dated Paris, December 11, 1906, and December 19, 1906; Constans to Bourgeois, Pera, December 17, 1906/no. 258, AE–NS–T, 5 (1905–1907), 55, 56, 67, 73, 75, 78–82, 83, 84–85, 86–87, 88, 92, 94, 98, 102–3; 104–7; 108, 109, 110, 114, 117–18, 121, 122, and 123–24.

517. Another Young Turk who sent letters to European foreign ministries about this subject was Ali Haydar Midhat. See his letter to Lansdowne dated Paris, October 13, 1905, PRO/ F.O. 78/5422. See also "En Turquie," *Le Siècle*, December 12, 1907.

518. It was also published in two Young Turk journals in the Balkans. See "Verâset-i Saltanat-ı Seniyeye Dair," *Balkan*, no. 113 [September 25, 1906], 1–2, and "Usûl-i Verâset-i Saltanatın Tebdili Mes'elesi ve Millet," *Tuna*, no. 385 [December 28, 1906], 3 ff.

519. See, for example, [İbrahim] Halil Pasha to Âsım Bey at the First Chamberlain's office, Beirut [February 18, 1907]/no. 2695, *Umum Kayda Mahsus Defter*, 77, BBA–YEE, 36/ 139-77/139/XIX; *Terakki*, no. [7], 8; and "La succession au trône," *Le Siècle*, January 9, 1907.

520. Copy of de Lormais's letter to von Bülow dated Paris, October 1906, A. 17678, PAAA, 733/3, Die Jungtürken, 198 (Bd. 4-5). De Lormais claimed that the memorandum reflected the ideas of "hautes personnalités turques."

521. See *Note sur l'ordre de succession au trône en Turquie*, 7–8.

522. See M[ehmed Sabahaddin], "Almanya İmparatorluğu'nun Türkiye Hakkındaki Plânları," *Terakki*, no. [8], 1 ff: "If the present administration will allow this German flood of trouble coming from the East and West to continue for some time then it will be extremely difficult or impossible to resist it." See also A[hmed] Fazlı, "Rumeli Vilâyât-ı Selâsesi Mes'elesi ve Şimendöfer Politikası," *Terakki*, no. 18, 5.

523. The memorandum was also distributed as a pamphlet. See Sabahaddine, *Mémoire des Libéraux turcs relatif à la Question d'orient*. Two original copies are in HHStA, PA XII 190, Türkei, Varia 1907; and in PAAA 495/2, Allgemeine Angelegenheiten der Türkei, 134 (Bd. 22-23). An English version was sent to the Foreign Office. See "Memorandum of the Turkish Liberals with Respect to the Eastern Question: Prince Sabahaddine to 'Chancelleries,'" PRO/F.O. 371/157, file 43375. De Lanessan's daily published it verbatim. See "Mémoire des Libéraux turcs relatif à la Question d'orient," *Le Siècle*, January 2–3, 1907. An English translation was also published in "The Eastern Question," *The Times*, January 2, 1907. A pro-Armenian journal summarized and praised the memorandum. See "Un appel des Libéraux turcs," *Pro Armenia* 7, no. 149, 1025–26. For the Ottoman government's reaction, see BBA– YSHM, 508/101 (1324.Za.26).

524. "Memorandum . . . ," PRO/F.O. 371/157, file 43375. The CPU strongly criticized these claims. See Bahaeddin Şakir, "Kari'in-i Kirâmdam İ'tizâr," *Şûra-yı Ümmet İlâvesi*, no. 114, 5–6.

525. See Kuran, *İnkılâp Tarihimiz ve Jön Türkler*, 220.

526. J.-L. de Lanessan, "La Turquie et le Parti Libéral Ottoman," *Le Siècle*, January 23, 1907. De Lanessan continuously ignored the coalition and presented Sabahaddin Bey's group as the only Young Turk organization. For an early example, see J.-L de Lanessan, "La Turquie libérale," *Le Siècle*, October 10, 1905. Although he did not mention Sabahaddin Bey personally, de Lanessan maintained that the prince and his comrades had taken the place of the proreform statesmen led by Midhat Pasha. See de Lanessan's "Préface" in Ali Haydar Midhat Bey, *Midhat-Pacha: sa vie-son œuvre* (Paris, 1908), xxii–xxiii.

527. See Imperiali to Tittoni, Constantinople, September 30, 1908/no. 2252-714, ASMAE, Affari Politici, Serie P. Politica (1891–1916), pacco 123–24.

528. Sabahaddin Bey denied the allegations. See "Erzurum'daki Dolab Avrupa'da da Dönüyor!" *Terakki*, no. 14, 8. Halil Halid further claimed that one of Sabahaddin Bey's

close friends was "a *protégé* of a great financier well known in Europe." See Halil Halid, "The Origin of the Revolt in Turkey," *The Nineteenth Century* 65, no. 387 (May 9, 1909), 757.

529. As a matter of fact, his memoranda addressed to the Foreign Office had not been acknowledged. The following note was written on his memorandum on the "Eastern Question": "The writer is a 'Young Turk' & we do not acknowledge their communications." PRO/F.O. 371/157, file 43375.

530. See Doktor Lütfi, *Millet ve Hükûmet* (*Paris, 1906*), 12.

531. Santa Semo took the most important initiatives in this field. He had become a member of Sabahaddin Bey's league in late 1906. He gave a speech at the Cercle International during the Peace Conference of 1907. See "La liberté et la paix en Turquie: Santo-Semo au Cercle International," *Courrier de la Conférence de la Paix*, no. 84 (September 20, 1907), 3; and "Cemiyetimizin Diğer Bir Teşebbüsü: Monsieur Santo-Semo'nun La Haye'de Konferansı," *Terakki*, 15, 12. The conference was later found "prophetic" by the European press, and this reaction caused diplomatic circles to give undeserved credit to Sabahaddin Bey. See "Young Turks' Triumph," *The Daily Chronicle*, August 6, 1908; and Mensdorff-Pouilly-Dietrichstein to Aehrenthal, London, August 7, 1908/no. 36, HHStA, PA VIII 141, England Berichte 1908 (VI–XII). Sabahaddin Bey too sent a letter to William T. Steed thanking him for chairing Santo-Semo's conference in which he underscored the movement in Asia Minor. See "Prince Sabahaddine," *Courrier de la Conférence de la Paix*, no. 109 (October 20, 1907), 4. Santo-Semo had made similar presentations before the Peace Conference. See "En faveur du parlement," *Mechveret Supplément Français*, no. 183 (January 1, 1907), 3. His further initiatives, however, were thwarted by the Ottoman diplomats. See Tahsin Pasha to Fuad Hikmet, February 27, 1908 (Dossier: 1–agitateurs), Archives of the Turkish Embassy in Rome, Box 71 (1); BBA–İrade-Hususî, M 1326/no. 71-83; and BBA–YSHM, 520/118 (1326.3.28).

532. See Constans to Pichon, Constantinople, February 28, 1908/no. 43 (confidentiel), AE–NS–T, 6 (1908–1909), 8 (bis). The sultan complained about Sabahaddin Bey's and de Lormais's activities, and Constans, who considered the complaint serious, requested information about these. See also A. L[e] C[hatalier], "Dans les prisons," *Revue du Monde Musulman* 4, no. 3 (March 1908), 586.

533. Hüseyin Cahid, "İntihabât Entrikaları," *Tanin*, [December 9, 1908]. Other documents provide hints about Greek government support for Sabahaddin Bey. See, for example, an undated note among the papers of Athanasios-Souliotis-Nicolaides, Αρχείο Σουλιώτη, 9/250. The accusations about Sabahaddin Bey's alleged relations with the Greeks and the Greek Patriarchate continued despite his denials. See, for example, "Prens Sabahaddin Bey'in Beyânâtı," *İfham*, December 30, 1919; and "Prens Sabahaddin Bey'in Tekzibi," *İfham*, December 31, 1919.

534. See Bakherakht to Sazonov, Bern, 11/24 May 1916/no. 286 (Telegram), *Razdel aziatskoi Turtsii: po sekretnym dokumentam b. ministerstva inostrannykh del*, ed. E[vgenii] A[lexandrovich] Adamov (Moscow, 1924), 195. For more information about this attempt, see Bakherakht to Shturmer, 16/29 June 1916/no. 442, and 13/26 August 1916/no. 510, *Konstantinopol' i prolivy: po sekretnym dokumentam b. ministerstva inostrannykh del* 2, ed. E[vgenii] A[lexandrovich] Adamov (Moscow, 1926), 320–21. The leaders of this venture also addressed appeals to the Armenians inviting them to common action. See "Un appel de la Turquie libérale," *La Voix de l'Arménie* 1, no. 2 (January 15, 1918), 64–65.

535. "Letter from Prince Seba-ed-Din, Geneva, Ramazan 14, 1334 [July 15, 1916]," BL, IOR: L/P&S/10/657, f. 172/193.

536. Ibid., f. 173/195.

537. Salih Keramett Bey, "The Young Turk Movement," in *Modern Turkey: A Politico-Economic Interpretation, 1908–1923* (New York, 1924), 484.

538. M[ehmed] Sabri, "Anadolu Kıyamları: Bir Milletin Müttehiden Zulme ve Erbâbına Mukavemeti Erbâb-ı Zulmün Teslim-i Hak Etmesini Müstelzim Âlî ve Meşru' Bir Kuvvetdir!" *Terakki*, no. 11, 3.

CHAPTER 6

1. See "Teşekkür," *Şûra-yı Ümmet*, no. 76 (June 4, 1905), 4.
2. See "Havâdis-i Dahiliye: İstanbul'dan," *Şûra-yı Ümmet*, no. 80 (August 16, 1905), 4.
3. Following the Young Turk Revolution of 1908, Bahaeddin Şakir was reappointed private physician to Yusuf İzzeddin Efendi and served as a mediator between the CUP central committee and Yusuf İzzeddin Efendi, who became heir apparent on April 27, 1909. See Bahaeddin Şakir's deposition at the court investigating the suicide of Yusuf İzzeddin Efendi, which occurred on March 25, 1916, in BBA–DUİT, 86–2: Yusuf İzzeddin Efendi Evrakı, 23.
4. See Yusuf İzzeddin Efendi's personal notes dated [August 12, 1900], [November 4, 1900], and [September 29, 1900], BBA–DUİT, 86-1: Yusuf İzzeddin Efendi Evrakı, 5-6/4, 5-6/11, and 5/6/8, respectively. In one of his notes he also discussed the advantages of a "free press." See ibid., 5-6/5, dated [September 7, 1900].
5. This information is taken from the following sources: Bahaeddin Şakir, "İkdam Muharriri Ali Kemal Efendi," *Şûra-yı Ümmet*, December 14, 1908; and *Şûra-yı Ümmet-Ali Kemal Da'vası* (Istanbul, 1325 [1909]), 50.
6. Ahmed Rıza to Dr. Nâzım, Paris, July 15, 1905, Private Papers of Bahaeddin Şakir.
7. See "Déportation du médecin particulier de Youssouf Izzeddin," *Le Courrier Européen*, no. 38 (July 28, 1905), 592.
8. XXX., "La Famille impériale ottomane," *Le Courrier Européen*, no. 27 (May 12, 1905), 419–20.
9. He later claimed that he had carried out activities in Erzincan during his short stay. See the letter of Dr. Bahaeddin [Şakir] beginning "Aziz Refikim" and dated [Paris], March 28, [190]8/no. 565, *Kopye Defteri*, 246.
10. The coalition's leading sympathizers who later formed a CPU branch in this town were Colonel Çerkes İshak and Ali Necib. See B[ahaeddin] Ş[akir], "Osmanlı İttihad ve Terakki Cemiyeti," *Haftalık Şûra-yı Ümmet*, no. 203 [January 13, 1910], 1–2. Another Young Turk, Adjutant-Major Galib Bey, who was a harbor officer in Trabzon, assisted in Bahaeddin Şakir's flight. He was later apprehended during his own attempt to flee, however. See "Bir Zümre-i Hamiyet," *Yeni Asır*, August 6, 1908.
11. *Şûra-yı Ümmet-Ali Kemal Da'vası*, 129–30.
12. A former Young Turk made the following comment: "He sort of revitalized Young Turkism in Paris. In two years time he transformed it into a revolutionary committee [*komita*] and increased its membership." See Yahya Kemal, *Siyasî ve Edebî Portreler*, 2nd ed. (Istanbul, 1976), 122.
13. Albert Fua, "Ahmed Riza bey," *Mècheroutiette*, no. 39 (February 1913), 44.
14. Chérif Pacha, "Talaat Pacha," *La Revue* 119/12, no. 8 (August 1–15, 1917), 278.
15. Bedri [Diran Kelekian] to Bahaeddin Şakir, Alexandria, October 26, 1905, Private Papers of Bahaeddin Şakir.
16. Bedri [Diran Kelekian] to Bahaeddin Şakir, Cairo, April 12, 1905, Private Papers of Bahaeddin Şakir. In addition to this "revolutionary" organ, another more moderate journal was to be established according to the agreement reached between Kelekian and Ahmed Celâleddin Pasha.
17. Bedri [Diran Kelekian] to Bahaeddin Şakir, Cairo, October 10, 1905, Private Papers of Bahaeddin Şakir.
18. B[ahaedin] Ş[akir], "Osmanlı İttihad ve Terakki Cemiyeti," *Haftalık Şûra-yı Ümmet*, no. 203, 1–2.
19. Sami Paşazâde Sezaî stated the following: "I am indebted to you and most grateful that you have introduced a person like the doctor to me. What a blessed person he is. The present situation of the doctor is a disaster in the strongest sense of the word, not for himself, but for us, and indeed for the fatherland. How happy is that doctor, that person, because any harm to him is a disaster for the vast fatherland. . . . May God give His grace to you both and protect you both for the sake of the salvation of the fatherland. . . . You say that had the doctor remained in his former post he would have sent FFr 2,000 more and turned this subsidy into a monthly one. Had this project come to fruition, we would not have needed an Egyptian

to be able to publish our journals." See [Sami Paşazâde] Sezaî to [Dr. Nâzım], Paris, September 4, 1905, Private Papers of Bahaeddin Şakir.

20. All these phrases were used in "Abdülhamid'in Yeni Bir Tedbiri," *Şûra-yı Ümmet*, no. 65 (December 8, 1904), 3–4.

21. See [Sami Paşazâde] Sezaî to [Dr. Nâzım], February 13, 1905, Private Papers of Bahaeddin Şakir; Ahmed Riza, "Une nouvelle lâcheté," *Mechveret Supplément Français*, no. 160 (February 1, 1905), 1–2; idem, "Lèse-Majesté," *Mechveret Supplément Français*, no. 161 (March 1, 1905), 1–2; "Ahmed Saib Bey'in Mevkufiyeti," *Şûra-yı Ümmet*, no. 69 (February 19, 1905), 1; and "L'Angleterre et le sultan," *Le Courrier Européen*, no. 15 (February 17, 1905), 4.

22. "Sebeb-i Te'hir," *Şûra-yı Ümmet*, no. 68 (February 6, 1905), 1.

23. Ahmed Saib to Ahmed Riza, Cairo, February 18, 1905, Private Papers of Ahmed Riza (1).

24. Ahmed Saib to Ahmed Riza, Cairo, February 25, 1905, ibid.

25. [Sami Paşazâde] Sezaî to [Dr. Nâzım], Paris, September 4, 1905, Private Papers of Bahaeddin Şakir.

26. See Edward G. Browne to Dr. Nâzım, Cambridge, January 11, 1905, Private Papers of Ahmed Riza (1).

27. See Francis Toye, *For What We Have Received: An Autobiography* (New York, 1948), 70.

28. Dr. Nâzım to Ahmed Riza [Cambridge, February 6, 1905], Private Papers of Ahmed Riza (1).

29. "İlk Meclisi Mebusan Reisi Ahmet Riza Beyin Hatıraları (20): Doktor Bahaeddin Şakir ve doktor Nâzım Beyler," *Cumhuriyet*, February 14, 1950.

30. In fact Bahaeddin Şâkir informed Ahmed Ferid, who was asked to reorganize the Egyptian branch, that "the central committee—with the exception of one member—is against appointing a director for the time being." See Dr. Bahaeddin [Şakir] and Dr. Nâzım to [Ahmed] Ferid, dated Paris, September 3, 1906/no. 68, *Muhaberat Kopyası*, 105.

31. Bahaeddin Şakir to Yusuf İzzeddin Efendi, dated January 4, [19]06. The original letter is in BBA–YEE, 15/74–82/74/15. A copy is in İstanbul Üniversitesi Bedî N. Şehsuvaroğlu Tıp Tarihi ve Deontoloji Arşivi, file İttihad ve Terakki (İ.4). A member of Sabahaddin Bey's group later described the discussion that took place at this meeting as a "bitter debate." See Nihad Reşad [Belger], "İttihad ve Terakkinin Muhaliflerile Temasları," *Cumhuriyet*, November 22, 1946.

32. Bahaeddin Şakir sent an undated note to Sabahaddin Bey stating that "some of your principles are found entirely incompatible with our present social conditions." Private Papers of Bahaeddin Şakir.

33. Ahmed Riza's prestige was used extensively by the new organization to persuade various individuals to join the CPU. See, for example, the letter of Dr. Bahaeddin [Şakir] and Dr. Nâzım to [İbrahim Rahmi Efendizâde] Hayri, director of the CPU Kazanlŭk (Kızanlık) branch, dated Paris, June 2, 1906/no. 27, *Muhaberat Kopyası*, 47–49. Long after the Young Turk Revolution of 1908, even the local press in the Ottoman Empire continually underscored Ahmed Riza's endurance and sterling character and compared him with Mizancı Murad, who had returned to the empire in 1897. See, for example, "Ahmad Riḍā Bak," *al-Nafīr*, February 9, 1912.

34. For their early plans, see Bedri [Diran Kelekian] to Bahaeddin Şakir, Cairo, December 16, 1905; December 17, 1905; and December 25, 1905, Private Papers of Bahaeddin Şakir.

35. Bedri [Diran Kelekian] to Bahaeddin Şakir, Cairo, December 9, 1905, Private Papers of Bahaeddin Şakir. I decoded the number groups used in the confidential correspondence that took place between Kelekian and Bahaeddin Şakir by using a code book that I found among the private papers of Bahaeddin Şakir.

36. See Ahmed Celâleddin Pasha to Bahaeddin Şakir, undated [Cairo, March 9, 1906]; and Bedri [Diran Kelekian] to Bahaeddin Şakir, Cairo, March 4, 1906, Private Papers of Bahaeddin Şakir.

37. Ahmed Celâleddin Pasha to Bahaeddin Şakir, undated [Cairo, March 9, 1906], Private Papers of Bahaeddin Şakir.

38. Ibid.

39. Bedri [Diran Kelekian] to Bahaeddin Şakir, Cairo, March 9, 1906, Private Papers of Bahaeddin Şakir.

40. A manifesto (*beyannâme*), written in Ahmed Celâleddin Pasha's handwriting, Private Papers of Bahaeddin Şakir.

41. Bedri [Diran Kelekian] to Bahaeddin Şakir, April 9, 1906, Private Papers of Bahaeddin Şakir.

42. See Dr. Bahaeddin [Şakir] and Dr. Nâzım to [Ahmed] Ferid, dated Paris, December 12, 1906/no. 229, *Muhaberat Kopyası*, 204–5. The pasha, however, could not continue to pay this monthly subsidy because he lost a substantial portion of his fortune in the stock market. See the letter of Dr. Bahaeddin [Şakir] beginning "Birader-i Azizim Efendim" and dated [Paris], June 11, 1907/no. 298, *Muhaberat Kopyası*, 322; and the report submitted to the Grand Vizier's office, Cairo [March 4, 1908]/no. 195, DWQ, Sijillāt ʿĀbidīn-Turkī-Ṣādir talagrāfāt, S/5/52/10, folio 132.

43. Bedri [Diran Kelekian] to Bahaeddin Şakir, Cairo, April 9, 1906, Private Papers of Bahaeddin Şakir.

44. Undated memorandum [April 1906] drafted by Diran Kelekian, Private Papers of Bahaeddin Şakir. Kelekian later defended these ideas in his own journal. See [Diran Kelekian], "Saltanat ve Millet," *Yeni Fikir*, no. 1 (June 28, 1907), 3–4.

45. Diran Kelekian to Bahaeddin Şakir, Cairo, May 11, 1906, Private Papers of Bahaeddin Şakir.

46. Bedri [Diran Kelekian] to Bahaeddin Şakir, Cairo, September 18, 1906, speaking about a proposed meeting between the CPU delegates and the Dashnaktsutiun representatives. Bahaeddin Şakir's two letters provide information about a meeting between two organizations, although these letters do not mention the name of the other committee. See the letter of Dr. Bahaeddin [Şakir] beginning "Aziz Vatandaşımız Efendim" and dated Paris, September 12, 1906/no. 70, *Muhaberat Kopyası*, 107; and the letter of Dr. Bahaeddin [Şakir] and Dr. Nâzım beginning "Aziz Vatandaşlarımız" and dated Paris, October 19, 1906/no. 77, *Muhaberat Kopyası*, 130.

47. See Bedri [Diran Kelekian] to Bahaeddin Şakir, Cairo, April 9, 1906, and May 26, 1906, Private Papers of Bahaeddin Şakir. Later Kelekian sent Lt 1,000 that he obtained from Ahmed Celâleddin Pasha for this scheme, according to which bombs as small as cigarette boxes would be placed in the Yıldız Palace or in the Hamidiye Mosque. See Diran Kelekian to Bahaeddin Şakir, Cairo, June 7, 1906, Private Papers of Bahaeddin Şakir. The latter, however, later denied that he had received financial support from the pasha for this "bomb scheme." See *Şûra-yı Ümmet-Ali Kemal Daʿvası*, 131.

48. See Nicholas C. Adossides, "Abdul the Dethroned," *Cosmopolitan Magazine* 47, no. 2 (July 1909), 188.

49. Bahaeddin Şakir stated that they had "examined Armenian, Greek, and Bulgarian" organizations. See Dr. B. Server [Bahaeddin Şakir] to Vicdanî [Colonel İshak] and Mihrabî [Ali Necib], dated Paris, March 15, [1]906/no. 1, *Muhaberat Kopyası*, 26.

50. Letter of [Dr. Bahaeddin Şakir] beginning "Aziz Biraderimiz" and dated [Paris], May 29, 1906/no. 16, *Muhaberat Kopyası*, 32. Repeated in another letter by Dr. Bahaeddin [Şakir] beginning "Aziz Kardeşimiz" and dated [Paris], June 11, 1906/no. 19, *Muhaberat Kopyası*, 38.

51. Dr. Bahaeddin [Şakir] to Talha Kemalî, undated [May 1906]/no. 12, *Muhaberat Kopyası*, 21–22.

52. *Osmanlı Terakki ve İttihad Cemiyeti Nizamnâme-i Esasî* (Egypt [Cairo], 1323 [1906]), 3. Summarized in "Osmanlı Terakki ve İttihad Cemiyeti," *Tuna*, no. 221 [June 8, 1906], 1.

53. *Osmanlı Terakki ve İttihad Cemiyeti Nizamnâme-i Esasî*, 4.

54. See ibid., 6–7.

55. "Kararnâmeye İlâve [July 23, 1906]," *Muhaberat Kopyası*, 72.

56. See the letter of Dr. Bahaeddin [Şakir] beginning "Vatandaşlar" and dated [Paris], October 15, 1907/no. 383, *Muhaberat Kopyası*, 440.

57. "Osmanlı Terakki ve İttihad Cemiyeti'nin Tensikât-ı Dahiliyesine Dair Beyannâme, Paris, July 20, 1906/no. 45," in *Muhaberat Kopyası*, 69–70. A slightly different version was published in the central organ, including a notice that the regulations would be sent to every-one free of charge. See Hey'et-i Merkeziye, "Osmanlı Terakki ve İttihad Cemiyeti Hey'et-i Merkeziyesi'nin Tensikât-ı Dahiliyesine Dair Beyannâme," *Şûra-yı Ümmet*, no. 98 (August 15, 1906), 1.

58. Dr. Bahaeddin [Şakir] and Dr. Nâzım to [Ahmed] Ferid, dated Paris, September 3, 1906/no. 68, *Muhaberat Kopyası*, 105.

59. Ibid. It was Ahmed Ferid who warned Bahaeddin Şakir and the central committee about this phrase.

60. BBA–İrade-Mısır Mesâlihi, no. 1829–921 [December 6, 1905]. See also "Mısır Prensleri," *Tuna*, no. 110 [January 24, 1906], 3–4.

61. See BBA–BEO/Dahiliye Giden, 163–5/19; 1019/2801 [December 7, 1905]/203949.

62. See Zeki Bey to the khedive, Paris, January 29, 1906, Abbas II Papers, Durham University, F. 41/107.

63. For example, Cromer stated that: "Prince Saïd Halim is about the best of the Khedivial princes." See Cromer to Lansdowne, Cairo, March 23, 1905/no. 345 (private), Cromer Papers, PRO/F.O. 633/VI (Letters to Secretaries of State).

64. See "Tuna," *Tuna*, no. 329 [October 17, 1906], 2.

65. See Dr. Bahaeddin [Şakir] and Dr. Nâzım to [Mehmed Sa'id Halim Pasha] beginning "Muhterem Efendimiz" and dated Paris, October 24, 1906/no. 182, *Muhaberat Kopyası*, 138.

66. See Dr. Bahaeddin [Şakir] and Dr. Nâzım to [Mehmed Sa'id Halim Pasha] beginning "Muhterem Efendimiz" and dated Paris, October 29, 1906/no. 186, *Muhaberat Kopyası*, 145.

67. See the letter of Dr. Bahaeddin [Şakir] to [Mehmed Sa'id Halim Pasha] beginning "Marûz-i Bendeleridir," undated [July 1906]/no. [32], *Muhaberat Kopyası*, 54; the letters of Dr. Bahaeddin [Şakir] and Dr. Nâzım to [Mehmed Sa'id Halim Pasha], dated [Paris], Octo-ber 24, 1906/no. 186, *Muhaberat Kopyası*, 145; dated [Paris], November 7, 1906/no. 205, *Muhaberat Kopyası*, 156; and undated [November 1906]/no. 216, *Muhaberat Kopyası*, 182; the letters of Dr. Bahaeddin [Şakir] to Mehmed Sa'id Halim Pasha, undated [November 1906]/no. 209, *Muhaberat Kopyası*, 162–63; and dated [Paris], January 16, 1908/no. 490; *Kopye Defteri*, 107; and Mehmed Sa'id Halim Pasha to Bahaeddin Şakir and Dr. Nâzım, Cairo, November 8, 1906, Private Papers of Bahaeddin Şakir.

68. Necessary information is given concerning Sami Paşazâde Sezaî's participation in the movement. See *supra*, pp. 34 and 338. For Muḥammad 'Alī Ḥalīm Pasha, see Sami Paşazâde Sezaî, "Paris Hatırâtından," *Servet-i Fünûn*, no. 14/1488 (February 19, 1924), 214. The op-ponents of the CPU drew a different picture, however. See Mehmed Kadri Nâsıh, *Sarayih* (Paris, 1910 [1911]), 53, 189. See also "Makam-ı Sadaret'e Takrir [February 5, 1908]," DWQ, Sijillāt 'Ābidīn-Turkī-Ṣādir talagrāfāt, S/5/52/10, ff. 130–31.

69. BBA–YSHM, 486/52 (1323.2.10).

70. "İlk Meclisi Mebusan Rıza Reisi Ahmet Rıza Beyin Hatıraları (20): Doktor Bahaeddin Şakir ve doktor Nâzım Beyler," *Cumhuriyet*, February 14, 1950.

71. Şerif Mardin, *Jön Türklerin Siyasi Fikirleri, 1895-1908*, 2nd ed. (Istanbul, 1988), 207. In a similar manner Mandel'shtam wrote the following about Bahaeddin Şakir: "Béhaeddine Bey, un des agitateurs jeunes-turcs les plus en vue au début de la révolution, sorte d'aimable Marat, ne manquant pas parfois d'*humour*." André Mandelstam, *Le sort de l'Empire ottoman* (Paris, 1917), 17.

72. In September 1908 Bahaeddin Şakir and Talât Bey met with the British ambassador and presented themselves as "internal and external secretaries" of the committee. See Lowther to Grey, Therapia, September 14, 1908/no. 541 (confidential), PRO/F.O. 371/559, file 31787.

73. When a German journalist interviewed the CUP leaders during the First World War, he met with Bahaeddin Şakir and Dr. Nâzım as two members "of the triumvirate which pre-sides over the Committee." See Alfred Nossig, *Die neue Türkei und ihre Führer* (Halle [Saale] [1916]), 71. For an English summary of this interview, see "The Committee of Union and Progress at Home," *The Near East* 10, no. 258 (April 14, 1916), 651–52. For another source

posthumously representing Bahaeddin Şakir as "a leader of the Young Turk Committee of Union and Progress," see "Bahaeddin Schakir," *Das Interview* 8 (1922), 2 ff.

74. Ali Haydar Midhat, *Hâtıralarım*, 1872-1946 (Istanbul, 1946), 182.

75. Dr. Bahaeddin [Şakir] and Dr. Nâzım to Alyotîzâde Mustafa Tevfik in Crete, dated Paris, April 9, 1907/no. 276, *Muhaberat Kopyası*, 284. For similar accusations, see the letter of H[üsrev] Sami and Dr. Bahaeddin [Şakir] beginning "Aziz Refikimiz" and dated [Paris], January 29, 1908/no. 503, *Kopye Defteri*, 134.

76. Interestingly enough, three Balkan Young Turks challenged Halil Halid to a duel because he entered into a discussion with Ali Haydar Midhat. See "Mektub," *Tuna*, no. 247 [July 9, 1906], 3; "Halil Halid Efendi ve Üç Osmanlı," *Tuna*, no. 248 [July 10, 1906], 3; "Ali Haydar Midhat Efendi'nin Bir Mektubu," *Tuna*, no. 220 [June 7, 1906], 1–2; "Halil Halid Efendi," *Tuna*, no. 242 [July 3, 1906], 2; "Halil Halid Efendi'den Üç Osmanlı'ya," *Tuna*, no. 259 [July 22, 1906], 1–2; "Midhatpaşazâde Ali Haydar Bey Efendi'den Aldığımız Mektubdur," *Tuna*, no. 265 [August 12, 1906], 1–2; and "Halimiz Yamandır," *Balkan*, no. 12 [August 8, 1906], 1–2. Ali Haydar Midhat's distribution of propaganda appeals in the Caucasus, and his congratulatory telegram to the Russian Duma, won the appreciation of the Turkic peoples in the region whom the CPU targeted. See Ali Haydar Midhat, "Yaşasın Osmanlı'da Dahi Kanun-i Esasî!" *Hayat*, no. 106 (November 23 [December 6], 1905), 1; "Devlet Duması'na Yeni Türklerin Tebriknâmesi," *Hayat*, no. 127 (June 13 [26], 1906), 1; "Ali Haydar Bey'in Yeni Bir Kitabı," ibid., 4; "Ali Haydar Bey'in Duma Reisini Tebriki," *Tuna*, no. 207 [May 22, 1906], 4; "La Douma et la Jeune Turquie," *Idjtihad*, no. 11 (April 1906), 174–75; A[li] Hüseyinzâde, "Midhatpaşazâde Ali Haydar Bey," *Füyûzat*, no. 6 (December 29, 1906 [January 11, 1907]), 90–92; Ali Haydar Midhat, "Ali Haydar Midhat Bey'den Vârid Olan Makale-i Mahsusa," *Tuna*, no. 359 [November 27, 1906], 1, and the letter in response signed by 32 Muslims in the Caucasus, ibid., 1–2.

77. For the CPU branches' demand for his inclusion, see the letter of Dr. Bahaeddin [Şakir] and Dr. Nâzım to [İbrahim Rahmi Efendizâde] Hayri, the director of the CPU branch in Kazanlük, dated Paris, June 2, 1906/no. 27, *Muhaberat Kopyası*, 47. His participation was reported to the branches. See Dr. Bahaeddin [Şakir] to the director of the CPU Kazanlük branch, dated [Paris], November 24, [1]906/no. 211, *Muhaberat Kopyası*, 172.

78. See Dr. Bahaeddin [Şakir] to Ali Haydar Midhat, dated [Paris], February 7, [1]907/no. 257, *Muhaberat Kopyası*, 252; Dr. Bahaeddin [Şakir]'s letter to the director of the CPU Kazanlük branch, undated [Paris, February 1907]/no. 265, *Muhaberat Kopyası*, 263–65; and the letter of Dr. Bahaeddin [Şakir] beginning "Azizim Muhteremim Efendim" and dated [Paris], August 26, [1]907/no. 348, *Muhaberat Kopyası*, 394. Ali Haydar Midhat announced his resignation in the French press. He provided no details about the reasons for his resignation, however. See his letter to "Monsieur le Directeur du *Mémorial Diplomatique*" in *Le Mémorial Diplomatique* 45, no. 10 (March 10, 1907), 146. See also his note published in *Terakki*, no. [8], 8. He tried to bridge the gap with the CUP after the Young Turk Revolution, but his initiative bore no fruit. See "Ali Haydar Bey ile Mülâkat," *İkdam*, August 30, 1908.

79. See, for example, Ali Haydar Midhat, "Vükelâya ve Millete Açık Tebligat," *Tuna*, no. 340 [October 30, 1906], 1–2.

80. For example, his letter to Grand Vizier Mehmed Ferid Pasha was published in "Mektub," *Şûra-yı Osmanî*, no. 19 (November 1, 1907), 1–2. The CPU central committee did not publish it in the official organ and stated that it would be published by one of the CPU branches. Apparently the CPU leaders wanted him to publish his letters and articles in journals in which they could not publish anything. See Dr. Bahaeddin [Şakir] to [Ali Haydar Midhat] beginning "Aziz Vatandaşımız Efendim" and dated [Paris], October 22, 1906/no. 78, *Muhaberat Kopyası*, 131.

81. Memorandum entitled "Comité Ottoman d'Union et de Progrès," by Mr. Ovey, the third secretary at the British embassy in Paris, enclosed with Lister to Grey, Paris, February 20, 1907/no. 112, PRO/F.O. 371/346, file 6840.

82. Dr. Bahaeddin [Şakir] to [Ahmed Saib] beginning "Muhterem Refikimiz Efendim Hazretleri" and dated [Paris], May 21, [1]906/no. 15, *Muhaberat Kopyası*, 30–31.

83. Ahmed Saib, "Biz ve Onlar," *Şûra-yı Ümmet*, no. 94 (April [May] 24, 1906), 2–3.

84. Unsigned letter from Dr. Bahaeddin Şakir and Dr. Nâzım to [Ahmed Saib] beginning "Aziz Biraderimiz" and dated Paris, June 15, 1905 [1906]/no. 21, *Muhaberat Kopyası*, 42.

85. Ibid.

86. Dr. Bahaeddin [Şakir] to Ahmed Saib, dated [Paris], June 27, 1906/no. 24, *Muhaberat Kopyası*, 45.

87. Ibid.

88. See the CPU central committee decree dated [Paris], June 27, 1906/no. 25, *Muhaberat Kopyası*, 44; and Dr. Bahaeddin [Şakir] to [Mehmed Fazlı] beginning "Aziz Biraderimiz" and dated [Paris], June 27, 1906/no. 26, *Muhaberat Kopyası*, 46. See also Dr. Bahaeddin [Şakir] and Dr. Nâzım to [Mehmed] Fazlı, dated Paris, July 20, 1906/no. 41, *Muhaberat Kopyası*, 64.

89. Mehmed Saʿid [Halim Pasha] to Bahaeddin Şakir and Dr. Nâzım, Cairo, July 6, 1906, Private Papers of Bahaeddin Şakir.

90. Although this decision was signed by all central committee members, the letter sent to Muḥammad ʿAlī Ḥalīm Pasha on the same day and numbered 43 reveals that they signed the document at a later date. For the decision dated Paris, July 20, 1906/no. 42 and signed by Bahaeddin [Şakir], Ahmed Rıza, [Sami Paşazâde] Sezaî, Muḥammad ʿAlī [Ḥalīm], Seyyid Kenʿan, and [Dr.] Nâzım, see *Muhaberat Kopyası*, 65.

91. Dr. Bahaeddin [Şakir] and Dr. Nâzım to Muḥammad ʿAlī [Ḥalīm] Pasha and [Sami Paşazâde] Sezaî, dated Paris, July 20, 1906/no. 43, *Muhaberat Kopyası*, 66–67; and Dr. Bahaeddin [Şakir] and Dr. Nâzım to [Mehmed Saʿid Halim Pasha] beginning "Devletlû Efendim Hazretleri" and dated Paris, July 13, 1906/no. 36, *Muhaberat Kopyası*, 59.

92. Dr. Bahaeddin [Şakir] and Dr. Nâzım to Talha Kemalî, dated Paris, July 18, 1906/no. 39, *Muhaberat Kopyası*, 62; and Dr. Bahaeddin [Şakir] and Dr. Nâzım to [Mehmed Saʿid Halim Pasha] beginning "Devletlû Efendim Hazretleri" and dated Paris, July 18, 1906/no. 40, *Muhaberat Kopyası*, 63.

93. See the letters of Dr. Bahaeddin [Şakir] to Muḥammad ʿAlī [Ḥalīm] Pasha and [Sami Paşazâde] Sezaî, to [Mehmed Saʿid Halim Pasha], and to [Ahmed Rıza]; dated and numbered respectively, Paris, July 27, 1906/no. 51; no. 51 [duplicate number]; and no. 52, *Muhaberat Kopyası*, 78–80.

94. This issue was mistakenly given the number 98 instead of 96. Later an issue numbered 96 and 97 was published to fill the gap; however, it bears the date of August 15, 1906, as if it were published on the same day as the 98th issue. See Dr. Bahaeddin [Şakir] to Bedri Beyzâde İbrahim Et[h]em, dated Paris, August 27, 1906/no. 60, *Muhaberat Kopyası*, 101. For the preparation of the journal, see Dr. Bahaeddin [Şakir] and Dr. Nâzım to [Ahmed Ferid], dated Paris, July 20, 1906/no. 44; July 23, 1906/no. 46; July 27, 1906/no. 48, *Muhaberat Kopyası*, 68–69, 71, and 74–75, respectively. See also Dr. Bahaeddin [Şakir] and Dr. Nâzım to [Sami Paşazâde] Sezaî, dated Paris, August 6, 1906/no. 54, and to [Mehmed Fazlı] beginning "Arkadaşımız Efendim" and dated June 4, 1906/no. 31, *Muhaberat Kopyası*, 82–83 and 53, respectively; Ahmed Ferid to Ahmed Rıza, Cairo, June 27, [1906], Private Papers of Ahmed Rıza (1); and Ahmed Ferid to Bahaeddin Şakir, Cairo, August 6, 1906, Private Papers of Bahaeddin Şakir.

95. "İhtar," *Şûra-yı Ümmet*, no. 98, 1.

96. He did not give any significant reasons for his resignation from the CPU. See Ahmed Saib, "İfade-i Mahsusa," *Sancak*, no. 65 (October 1, 1906), 1.

97. See "Matbuʿat Arasında," *Sancak*, no. 65, 4. Sabahaddin Bey praised his journal in return. See "(*Sancak*) ve (*Ahali*) Gazeteleri," *Terakki*, no. [6] [November 1906], 11.

98. See Muḥammad Rashīd Riḍā, "Rafīq al-ʿAẓm," in *Majmūʿat athār Rafīq Bak al-ʿAẓm* 1, ed. ʿUthmān al-ʿAẓm (Miṣr [Cairo], 1344 [1925]), v.

99. Hey'et-i Merkeziye, "Osmanlı Terakki ve İttihad Cemiyeti Hey'et-i Merkeziyesi'nin Teşkilât-ı Dahiliyesi," *Şûra-yı Ümmet*, no. 101 (October 1, 1906), 1. Republished in "*Şûra-yı Ümmet* Refik-i Muhterememizden: Osmanlı Terakki ve İttihad Cemiyeti Hey'et-i Merkeziyesi'nin Teşkilât-ı Dahiliyesi," *Tuna*, no. 329, 2.

100. The commission was set up in late November 1906. See Dr. Bahaeddin [Şakir] to [Ahmed] Ferid, dated Paris, November 30, 1906/no. 220, *Muhaberat Kopyası*, 188.

101. "*Şûra-yı Ümmet* Gazetesi'nin Usûl-i Tensiki Hakkında Sezaî Bey Efendi'nin Riyasetinde Ali Haydar, Nâzım, Bahaeddin Beylerden Mürekkeb Komisyonun Tanzim Etdiği Program," dated [December 1906], in *Muhaberat Kopyası*, 195–98.

102. See the letter of Dr. Bahaeddin [Şakir] beginning "Muhterem Refikimiz Efendim" and dated [December 9, 1906]/no. 224, *Muhaberat Kopyası*, 198.

103. See the letter of Dr. Bahaeddin [Şakir] and Dr. Nâzım beginning "Efendim" and dated Paris, December 10, 1906/no. 225, *Muhaberat Kopyası*, 199.

104. See "İfade-i Mahsusa/no. 49," prepared for publication in *Şûra-yı Ümmet*, undated [August 1906], in *Muhaberat Kopyası*, 76.

105. For example, an article on Albert Sorel was sent to Sami Paşazâde Sezaî Bey for him to provide more information about Sorel. See Dr. Bahaeddin [Şakir] and Dr. Nâzım to [Sami Paşazâde] Sezaî, dated [Paris], July 23, 1906/no. 47, *Muhaberat Kopyası*, 73. Bahaeddin Şakir later sent the draft to Ahmed Ferid requiring him to work on this draft and provide more information about Sorel's conversion. See Dr. Bahaeddin [Şakir] and Dr. Nâzım to [Ahmed] Ferid, dated Paris, July 27, 1906/no. 48, *Muhaberat Kopyası*, 74. On another occasion Bahaeddin Şakir asked Sami Paşazâde Sezaî to write an article on "the succession to the throne" and to examine and edit an article by Ahmed Rıza. See Dr. Bahaeddin [Şakir] and Dr. Nâzım to [Sami Paşazâde] Sezaî, dated Paris, August 10, 1906/no. 58, *Muhaberat Kopyası*, 94.

106. See the letter of H[üsrev] Sami and Dr. Bahaeddin [Şakir] to [Mes'ud Remzi] beginning "Aziz Refikimiz" and dated Paris, January 16, 1908/no. 485, *Kopye Defteri*, 88.

107. Dr. Bahaeddin [Şakir] to Talât Bey, the director of the CPU central branch in Bulgaria, dated Paris, June 14, 1907/no. 299, *Muhaberat Kopyası*, 327.

108. See Dr. Bahaeddin [Şakir] to İbrahim [Rahmi Efendi]zâde Hayri Efendi, dated [Paris], April 25, [1]906/no. 10, *Muhaberat Kopyası*, 19; the letter of Dr. Bahaeddin [Şakir] beginning "Aziz Kardaşımız," dated [Paris], April 25, 1906/no. 11, and sent to Crete, *Muhaberat Kopyası*, 20; the letter of Dr. Bahaeddin [Şakir] and Dr. Nâzım beginning "Aziz Kardaşlarımız," and dated [Paris], May 10, 1906/no. 13, *Muhaberat Kopyası*, 25; and the letter of Dr. Bahaeddin [Şakir] beginning "Vatanperver Efendim" and dated Paris, June 15, 1906/no. 20, *Muhaberat Kopyası*, 41.

109. Dr. Bahaeddin [Şakir] and Dr. Nâzım requested the mediation of Sami Paşazâde Sezaî to persuade Kâmil Pasha to grant FFr 250 to buy "second-hand bargain" furniture for "the administrative offices of a committee that has the potential of becoming the greatest means of happiness for the future of the nation." See their letter to [Sami Paşazâde] Sezaî, dated Paris, August 6, 1906/no. 54, *Muhaberat Kopyası*, 83. Later pictures of the CPU central committee offices reveal that the furniture was purchased.

110. As a matter of fact, much later, when the CUP was in power, Dr. Nâzım related the following to a German journalist: "Das Komitee . . . lebt durch seine Prinzipien, nicht durch Personen. . . . Unser erster Grundsatz lautet: Das Komitee ist unpersönlich. Es existiert nur als Korporation und gestattet keinen Personenkultus." See Nossig, *Die neue Türkei*, 71–72. Following the Young Turk Revolution of 1908, this "committee cult" became the most acclaimed characteristic of the CUP. See, for example, Ahmed Ziya, *Meşrutiyet Uğrunda* (Istanbul, 1327 [1909]), 3: "Within the Committee of Union [and Progress] a juridical person has been personified. The honored Ottoman Committee of Union and Progress is a powerful guardian of its juridical personality."

111. Almost all the letters discussed at the central committee meetings before the publication of the reorganization program in the central organ were originally sent to Ahmed Rıza and brought to the attention of the central committee by him. (See, for example, the letter of Dr. Bahaeddin [Şakir] to the Muslims in the Caucasus beginning "Aziz Kardaşlarımız" and dated Paris, March 26, [1]906/no. 2; Dr. B[ahaeddi]n [Şakir] to M[ehmed] Cavid in Canea, dated [Paris], March 27, [1]906/no. 4; Dr. Bahaeddin [Şakir] to S[alih] Borovac in Sarajevo, dated Paris, March 29, [1906]/no. 6, *Muhaberat Kopyası*, 5–6, 8–9, and 10–11, respectively.) Following the reorganization of the branches, the number of such letters drastically declined. Even two and a half years after the reorganization, however, there were some sympathizers still sending letters to Ahmed Rıza. See, for example, the letter of H[üsrev] Sami and Dr. Bahaeddin [Şakir] beginning "Vatandaşımız" and dated [March] [190]8/no. 555, *Kopye Defteri*, 221.

112. See, for example, Dr. Bahaeddin [Şakir] and Dr. Nâzım to [Ahmed] Ferid, dated Paris, July 27, 1906/no. 48, *Muhaberat Kopyası*, 75.

113. See the letter of Dr. [Bahaeddin Şakir] beginning "Vatanperver Efendim" and dated [Paris], October 30, 1907/no. 397 [duplicate number], *Muhaberat Kopyası*, 470.

114. Dr. Bahaeddin [Şakir] to Talha Kemalî, dated [Paris], May 10, [1]906/no. 12, *Muhaberat Kopyası*, 22.

115. See the letter of H[üsrev] Sami and Dr. Bahaeddin [Şakir] beginning "Refik-i Muhteremimiz" and dated [Paris], February 28, 1908/no. 535, *Kopye Defteri*, 189.

116. See Hey'et-i Merkeziye, "Osmanlı Terakki ve İttihad Cemiyeti Hey'et-i Merkeziyesi'nin Tensikât-ı Dahiliyesine Dair Beyannâme," *Şûra-yı Ümmet*, no. 98, 1.

117. See the letter of Dr. Bahaeddin [Şakir] beginning "Vatanperver Biraderimiz" and dated [Paris], April 2, 1906/no. 7, *Muhaberat Kopyası*, 12.

118. Ibid., 13. See also the letter of Dr. Bahaeddin [Şakir] and Dr. Nâzım beginning "Aziz Vatandaşımız" and dated [Paris], January 7, 1907/no. 246, *Muhaberat Kopyası*, 230. Desperately needing new members, the CPU also accepted individual applications but asked those new members to form small branches in their towns. See, for example, the letter of Dr. Bahaeddin [Şakir] and Dr. Nâzım beginning "Efendim," dated Paris, November 29, 1906/no. 219, and sent to Balchik (Balçık), *Muhaberat Kopyası*, 185; and the letter of [Dr. Bahaeddin Şakir], beginning "Aziz ve Muhterem Vatandaşımız" and dated [Paris], September 6, 1907/no. 365, *Muhaberat Kopyası*, 414. The central committee also asked such individuals to join the nearest branch. See, for example, Dr. Bahaeddin [Şakir] and Dr. Nâzım to [Ahmed] Ferid, dated [Paris], December 19, 1906/no. 231, *Muhaberat Kopyası*, 210; and their letter to Ömer Sadi in Alexandria, dated [Paris], December 19, 1906/no. 232, *Muhaberat Kopyası*, 211. On another occasion an individual who had been asked to form a branch and responded that it was impossible to form a branch in his town was offered simple membership in the CPU. See the letter of Dr. Bahaeddin [Şakir] beginning "Muhterem Vatandaşımız" and dated Paris, December 13, 1907/no. 451, *Kopye Defteri*, 39.

119. Dr. B. Server [Bahaeddin Şakir] to Vicdanî [Colonel İshak] and Mihrabî [Ali Necib], dated Paris, March 15, [1]906/no. 1, *Muhaberat Kopyası*, 3.

120. See the letter of Dr. Bahaeddin [Şakir] and Dr. Nâzım beginning "Muhterem Vatandaşımız Efendim" and sent to Bosnia, dated Paris, December 10, 1906/no. 227, *Muhaberat Kopyası*, 201. Other letters specify four as the minimum number of members to form a branch. See the letter of Dr. [Bahaeddin Şakir] beginning "Aziz ve Muhterem Vatandaşımız" and dated [Paris], September 6, 1907/no. 365, *Muhaberat Kopyası*, 414; the letter of H[üsrev] Sami and Dr. Bahaeddin [Şakir] beginning "Muhterem Dindaşımız" and dated [Paris], December [January] 28, 1908/no. 499, *Kopye Defteri*, 120; and their letter beginning "Aziz ve Gayûr Arkadaşımız" and dated [Paris], February 6, 1908/no. 505, *Kopye Defteri*, 138. In only one letter did the center state that a branch should have three main officers, namely "director, secretary, and treasurer." See Dr. Bahaeddin [Şakir] and Dr. Nâzım to [Dr. Ali] Rasih in Candia, dated [Paris], January 5, 1907/no. 244, *Muhaberat Kopyası*, 227.

121. Left blank in the original text.

122. Dr. Bahaeddin [Şakir] to Talha Kemalî, dated [Paris], May 10, 1906/no. 12, *Muhaberat Kopyası*, 23–24. Similar instructions were given to İbrahim Rahmi Efendizâde Hayri in Kazanlük. See the letter of Dr. Bahaeddin [Şakir] dated [Paris], May 10, 1906/no. 14, *Muhaberat Kopyası*, 27–29.

123. See Dr. Bahaeddin [Şakir] and Dr. Nâzım to Teacher Mazhar Efendi in Vidin, dated [Paris], November 19, 1906/no. 208, *Muhaberat Kopyası*, 161.

124. Ibid.

125. See, for example, the letter of [Dr. Bahaeddin Şakir] beginning "Aziz Biraderimiz," dated [Paris], May 29, 1906/no. 16, and sent to Canea, *Muhaberat Kopyası*, 33; his letter entitled "Aziz Kardeşimiz" dated [Paris] May 29, 1906/no. 17 and sent to Kazanlük, *Muhaberat Kopyası*, 34; and his letter entitled "Aziz Vatandaşımız" dated [Paris], October 18, [1]906/no. 76, *Muhaberat Kopyası*, 129.

126. Dr. Bahaeddin [Şakir] and Dr. Nâzım to the director of the CPU Kazanlük branch, dated October 25, 1906/no. 181, *Muhaberat Kopyası*, 137. The CPU central committee re-

fused to help the director of the aforementioned branch communicate with the CPU branch in Canea. See ibid., 136–37.

127. In addition to these two branches, the phrase "central branch" was also used to refer to the Romanian branch, although the only branch in that country was in Constanţa. See Dr. Bahaeddin [Şakir] to the director of the CPU central branch in Romania, dated Paris, January 3, 1908/no. 465, *Kopye Defteri*, 57.

128. For example, İbrahim Temo, the director of the reorganized Constanţa branch, was introduced to the director of the CPU Lâzistan branch, who was required to work with the former in smuggling CPU propaganda from Constanţa into Trabzon. See Dr. Bahaeddin [Şakir] to the director of the CPU Lâzistan branch, dated Paris, November 25, 1906/no. 221, *Muhaberat Kopyası*, 190.

129. See the letter of Dr. Bahaeddin [Şakir] and Dr. Nâzım beginning "Muhterem Vatandaşımız Efendim," dated Paris, December 10, 1906/no. 227, and sent to Sarajevo, *Muhaberat Kopyası*, 201.

130. See the letter of Dr. Bahaeddin [Şakir] and Dr. Nâzım, beginning "Aziz Refikimiz," dated Paris, August 4, 1906/no. 57, and sent to Crete, *Muhaberat Kopyası*, 93.

131. Dr. Bahaeddin [Şakir] to the director of the CPU Kazanlük branch, dated [Paris], September 4, 1907/no. 363, *Muhaberat Kopyası*, 412.

132. Dr. B. Server [Bahaeddin Şakir] to Vicdanî [Colonel İshak] and Mihrabî [Ali Necib], dated Paris, March 15, [1]906/no. 1, *Muhaberat Kopyası*, 2.

133. See the letter of Dr. Bahaeddin [Şakir] beginning "Muhterem Vatanperver Kardeşimiz," undated [June 1907]/no. 296, and sent to Of, *Muhaberat Kopyası*, 316. In another secret letter the existence of various distinct ethnic groups within the Ottoman nation was given as the reason for the central committee's granting of autonomy to the branches. See Dr. Bahaeddin [Şakir] and Dr. Nâzım to Teacher Mazhar Efendi in Vidin, dated [Paris], November 19, 1906/no. 208, *Muhaberat Kopyası*, 160.

134. See the letter of Dr. Bahaeddin [Şakir] and Dr. Nâzım beginning "Aziz Refikimiz," dated Paris, August 6, 1906/no. 57, and sent to Shumen (Şumnu), *Muhaberat Kopyası*, 90–91.

135. Dr. Bahaeddin [Şakir] to the director of the CPU Lâzistan External branch, dated Paris, November 3, 1907/no. 406, *Muhaberat Kopyası*, 481.

136. [Dr. Bahaeddin Şakir] to the director of the CPU Kazanlük branch, dated Paris, August 27, 1906/no. 66, *Muhaberat Kopyası*, 102.

137. See Dr. Bahaeddin [Şakir] and Dr. Nâzım to Teacher Mazhar Efendi in Vidin, dated [Paris], November 19, 1906/no. 208, *Muhaberat Kopyası*, 161: "I will serve the aims of the committee, will not divulge the secrets of the committee, and will hand over my donations, which would be sent to the [central] committee, to the cashier of the branch."

138. *Osmanlı Terakki ve İttihad Cemiyeti Nizamnâme-i Esasî*, 5 (article 15).

139. See the letter of Dr. Bahaeddin [Şakir] beginning "Muhterem Vatanperver Kardeşimiz," undated [June 1907]/no. 296, and sent to Of, *Muhaberat Kopyası*, 316.

140. See "Osmanlı Terakki ve İttihad Cemiyeti Kızanlık Şu'besi Nizamnâme-i Dahilisi, [December 1906]," *Muhaberat Kopyası*, 209 (article 24).

141. See, for example, "Osmanlı Terakki ve İttihad Cemiyeti Vidin Şu'besi'nin Nizamnâme-i Dahilisi [January 1907]," *Muhaberat Kopyası*, 234–37.

142. See the letter of Dr. Bahaeddin [Şakir] and Dr. Nâzım beginning "Aziz Refikimiz Efendim" and dated [Paris], December 25, 1906/no. 234, *Muhaberat Kopyası*, 213; and their letter to the director of the CPU Vidin branch, dated Paris, November [January] 11, 1907/no. 251, *Muhaberat Kopyası*, 238.

143. See the letter of Dr. Bahaeddin [Şakir] and Dr. Nâzım to the director of the CPU Kazanlük branch, dated Paris, July 27, 1906/no. 50, *Muhaberat Kopyası*, 77. See also the letter of [Dr. Bahaeddin Şakir and Hüsrev Sami] to the CPU central branch in Cyprus, dated [Paris], January [?], 1908/no. 484, *Kopye Defteri*, 95.

144. See the letter of Dr. Bahaeddin [Şakir] beginning "Vatanperver Biraderimiz," dated [Paris], April 2, [1]906/no. 7, and sent to Bulgaria, *Muhaberat Kopyası*, 13.

145. Dr. Bahaeddin [Şakir] to the director of the CPU Kazanlük branch, dated [Paris], September 4, 1907/no. 363, *Muhaberat Kopyası*, 412.

146. Dr. Bahaeddin [Şakir] to Talât Bey, director of the CPU central branch in Bulgaria, dated Paris, June 14, [1]907/no. 299, *Muhaberat Kopyası*, 326–27; his letter beginning "Aziz Refikimiz," dated Paris, July 18, 1907/no. 312, and sent to the director of the CPU Kazanlŭk branch, *Muhaberat Kopyası*, 348; and his letter to Talha Kemalî, dated Paris, July 27, 1907/ no. 317, *Muhaberat Kopyası*, 361.

147. The CPU central committee asked its sympathizers in Bulgaria to help the CPU distribute propaganda material to the officers patrolling the border. See the letter of H[üsrev] Sami to Yürükoğlu [İsmail] in Bulgaria, undated [February 1908]/no. 504, *Kopye Defteri*, 136.

148. [Dr. Bahaeddin Şakir] to İbrahim [Rahmi] Efendizâde Hayri, dated [Paris], March [27], [1]906/no. 5, *Muhaberat Kopyası*, 9. This person later provided Bahaeddin Şakir with detailed information about his background and former activities, proving that very little was known about him before he had established the branch. See the CPU Kazanlŭk branch to Bahaeddin Şakir [July 18, 1906]/no. 3, Private Papers of Bahaeddin Şakir.

149. Dr. Bahaeddin [Şakir] to İbrahim [Rahmi Efendi]zâde Hayri, dated [Paris], April 25, 1906/no. 10, *Muhaberat Kopyası*, 18–19.

150. Dr. Bahaeddin [Şakir] to İbrahim Rahmi Efendizâde Hayri, dated [Paris], May 10, [1]906/no. 14, *Muhaberat Kopyası*, 26–29; and the letter of Dr. Bahaeddin [Şakir] beginning "Aziz Kardeşimiz" and dated [Paris], May 29, [1]906/no. 17, *Muhaberat Kopyası*, 34–35.

151. Dr. Bahaeddin [Şakir] and Dr. Nâzım to [İbrahim Rahmi Efendizâde] Hayri, dated Paris, June 2, 1906/no. 27, *Muhaberat Kopyası*, 47.

152. Ibid., 47–49.

153. See the CPU Kazanlŭk branch to the CPU Internal Affairs and Correspondence division [June 7, 1906]/no. 1, Private Papers of Bahaeddin Şakir.

154. Dr. Bahaeddin [Şakir] and Dr. Nâzım to the secretary of the CPU Kazanlŭk branch [Siporikozzâde Ali Rıza], dated Paris, July 18, 1906/no. 37, *Muhaberat Kopyası*, 60.

155. See the CPU Kazanlŭk branch to the CPU Internal Affairs and Correspondence division [June 7, 1906]/no. 1, Private Papers of Bahaeddin Şakir.

156. See the CPU Kazanlŭk branch to the CPU central committee [August 3, 1906]/no. 4, Private Papers of Bahaeddin Şakir; and Dr. Nâzım to the CPU Kazanlŭk branch, dated [Paris], January 7, 1907/no. 245, *Muhaberat Kopyası*, 229.

157. See the CPU Kazanlŭk branch to the CPU central committee [August 16, 1906]/ no. 5, Private Papers of Bahaeddin Şakir; and [Dr. Bahaeddin Şakir] to the CPU Kazanlŭk branch, dated Paris, August 23, 1906/no. 66, *Muhaberat Kopyası*, 102.

158. It seems that the Bulgarian local authorities, suspicious of the branch members' activities, intercepted some packages of *Şûra-yı Ümmet*. See Dr. Bahaeddin [Şakir] to the director of the CPU Kazanlŭk branch, undated [Paris, March 1907]/no. 265, *Muhaberat Kopyası*, 263; and Dr. Bahaeddin [Şakir] and Dr. Nâzım to the director of the CPU Kazanlŭk branch, dated [Paris], April 15, 1907/no. 280, *Muhaberat Kopyası*, 290. CPU correspondence reveals that the branch distributed the central organ throughout Bulgaria. See Dr. Bahaeddin [Şakir] to the director of the CPU Kazanlŭk branch, dated [Paris], September 4, 1907/no. 363, *Muhaberat Kopyası*, 412.

159. See the names of the branch members written at the bottom of the approved version of its internal regulations in *Muhaberat Kopyası*, 209.

160. See the CPU Kazanlŭk branch to the CPU central committee [August 18, 1906] (unofficial), Private Papers of Bahaeddin Şakir.

161. See the CPU Kazanlŭk branch to the CPU central committee [August 16, 1906]/ no. 5, Private Papers of Bahaeddin Şakir; and [Dr. Bahaeddin Şakir] to the CPU Kazanlŭk branch, dated Paris, August 23, 1906/no. 66, *Muhaberat Kopyası*, 102.

162. See especially the CPU Kazanlŭk branch to the CPU [central committee] [June 10, 1906]/no. 2; and [August 3, 1906]/no. 4, Private Papers of Bahaeddin Şakir.

163. See the letter of Dr. Bahaeddin [Şakir] beginning "Vatanperver Biraderimiz" and dated [Paris], April 2, [1]906/no. 7, *Muhaberat Kopyası*, 12–13.

164. See, for example, "Osmanlı Terakki ve İttihad Cemiyeti," *Tuna*, no. 221 [June 8, 1906], 1; and "Osmanlı Terakki ve İttihad Cemiyeti Hey'et-i Merkeziyesi'nin Teşkilât-ı Dahiliyesi," *Tuna*, no. 329, 2.

165. See Dr. Bahaeddin [Şakir] to Talha Kemalî, dated [Paris], May 10, 1906/no. 12, *Muhaberat Kopyası*, 21–24; and Dr. Bahaeddin [Şakir] to Talha Kemalî, "the founder of the Dobrich branch," dated Paris, July 11, 1906/no. 33, *Muhaberat Kopyası*, 55–56.

166. They published postcards picturing former Ottoman sultans and leading Young Ottomans. See "İlân," *Ahali*, no. 10 [November 14, 1906], 4; and Dr. Bahaeddin [Şakir] to Talha Kemalî, "the founder of the Dobrich branch," dated Paris, July 11, 1906/no. 33, *Muhaberat Kopyası*, 55.

167. See Talha Kemalî's postcard to the CPU Internal Affairs division, Varna, August 10, 1907, Private Papers of Bahaeddin Şakir; and Dr. Bahaeddin [Şakir] to Talha Kemalî, dated Paris, July 27, [1]907/no. 317, *Muhaberat Kopyası*, 361.

168. Talha Kemalî to the CPU Internal Affairs division, Varna, August 18, [1]907, Private Papers of Bahaeddin Şakir.

169. Dr. Bahaeddin [Şakir] to Talha Kemalî, dated [Paris], June 4, 1907/no. 293, *Muhaberat Kopyası*, 309.

170. Dr. Bahaeddin [Şakir] to Hacı Ahmed Ağazâde Hasan Şevket in Plovdiv, dated Paris, July 22, [1]907/no. 315, *Muhaberat Kopyası*, 357.

171. See the letter of Dr. Bahaeddin [Şakir] beginning "Muhterem Vatandaşımız" and dated [Paris], September 3, 1907/no. 362, *Muhaberat Kopyası*, 410.

172. See the letter of Dr. Bahaeddin [Şakir] and Dr. Nâzım beginning "Efendim" and dated Paris, November 29, 1906/no. 219, *Muhaberat Kopyası*, 185.

173. Dr. Nâzım's letters to the director of the CPU Balchik branch, dated [Paris], April 26, 1907/no. 282 and April 30, 1907/no. 287, *Muhaberat Kopyası*, 295 and 300, respectively; Dr. Bahaeddin [Şakir] to the director of the CPU Balchik branch, dated Paris, July 30, 1907/no. 330, *Muhaberat Kopyası*, 370; and Dr. Bahaeddin [Şakir] to the director of the CPU Balchik branch, dated [Paris], September 6, 1907/no. 360, *Muhaberat Kopyası*, 408.

174. H[üsrev] Sami and Dr. Bahaeddin [Şakir] to the CPU Balchik branch, dated [Paris], February 12, 1908/no. 514, *Kopye Defteri*, 160.

175. See the CPU Balchik branch to the CPU central committee, February 9[sic], 1908/no. 5, Private Papers of Bahaeddin Şakir.

176. Bahaeddin Şakir requested information about this individual from Talât Bey, who became the director of the CPU Bulgaria central branch in Shumen. See Dr. Bahaeddin [Şakir] to the CPU Bulgaria central branch, undated [Paris, July 1907]/no. 314, and his letter to [Talât Bey], beginning "Birader-i Azizim Efendim" and dated [Paris], August 20, 1907/no. 338, *Muhaberat Kopyası*, 355 and 379.

177. See the CPU Burgas branch to the CPU central committee, July 2, 1908/no. 8, Private Papers of Bahaeddin Şakir.

178. H[üsrev] Sami and Dr. Bahaeddin [Şakir] to the CPU Burgas branch, dated Paris, January 3, [1]908/no. 467, *Kopye Defteri*, 60–61.

179. [Dr. Bahaeddin Şakir], "Vidin Şübban-ı İslâmiyesi Hey'eti'ne," dated Paris, October 30, 1906/no. 202, *Muhaberat Kopyası*, 151.

180. See the letter of Dr. Bahaeddin [Şakir] and Dr. Nâzım to the CPU Vidin branch, dated Paris, November [January] 11, 1907/no. 251, *Muhaberat Kopyası*, 238; Dr. Nâzım to the CPU Vidin branch, dated [Paris], April 26, 1907/no. 283, *Muhaberat Kopyası*, 296; and Dr. Bahaeddin [Şakir] to the CPU Vidin branch, dated [Paris], October 30, 1907/no. 395, *Muhaberat Kopyası*, 465. The branch's approved internal regulations are in "Osmanlı Terakki ve İttihad Cemiyeti Vidin Şu'besi'nin Nizamnâme-i Dahilisi," *Muhaberat Kopyası*, 234–37.

181. Although the CPU center informed established branches of the formation of new branches, it did not provide them with any information about these new branches, nor did it want the branches to correspond without the mediation of the center. See, for example, Dr. Bahaeddin [Şakir] to Talha Kemalî, dated Paris, July 11, 1906/no. 33, *Muhaberat Kopyası*, 55: "We inform you that another branch has been formed in another region of Bulgaria. For the time being it is better if these branches work independently. Later on connections will be established between them."

182. Dr. Bahaeddin [Şakir] to Talât Bey, the CPU Bulgaria central branch director, dated [Paris], June 14, [1]907/no. 299, *Muhaberat Kopyası*, 326–27.

183. Dr. Bahaeddin [Şakir] to the CPU Bulgaria central branch, dated [Paris], August 20, [1]907/no. 314, *Muhaberat Kopyası*, 355–56.

184. H[üsrev] Sami and Dr. Bahaeddin [Şakir] to the CPU Bulgaria central branch, undated [January 27, 1908]/no. 495, *Kopye Defteri*, 114.

185. For example, the sweet-seller Necib Efendi in Haskovo (Hasköy) asked for *Mechveret Supplément Français* and the pamphlet entitled *Islahat Risâlesi* (see his letter dated [May 9, 1907] and CPU secretary Ken'an Bey's note indicating that he sent the requested material); Ahmed Mısrî in Silistra (Silistire) asked for the pamphlet entitled *Hayye-ale-l-felâh* (*Ḥayya 'alā al-falāḥ*) and, strangely enough, back issues of *Terakki* (see his letter dated September 6, 1907 and CPU secretary Ken'an Bey's note indicating that in response he sent a card, a copy of a *Şûra-yı Ümmet* supplement criticizing Sabahaddin Bey, and available pamphlets); Behrambeyzâde Eşref in Karnobat (Karinâbâd) wrote to the CPU Internal Affairs and Correspondence division asking for the pamphlets entitled *Hayye-ale-l-felâh* and *Usûl-i İdare ve Islahat* (see his letter dated [July 31, 1907] and Hüsrev Sami's note reading "what he asked for was sent"); and Hafız Mehmed Mutin in Tutrakan asked for the pamphlet *Vazife ve Mes'uliyet* (see Dr. Nâzım's letter to him, dated [Paris], July 2, 1906/no. 28, *Muhaberat Kopyası*, 50).

186. The Young Turk press in Bulgaria covered the most trivial CPU activity. See, for example, "'Terakki ve İttihad' Cemiyeti," *Tuna*, no. 337 [October 26, 1906], 2; and "Türkiya Haberleri," *Tuna*, no. 364 [December 3, 1906], 3. Also the local Young Turk journals republished many articles that had originally been published in the CPU organs. See, for example, "*Şûra-yı Ümmet* Refikimizden Muktebesdir," *Tuna*, no. 161 [March 27, 1906], 2; "*Şûra-yı Ümmet*'e Mektub," *Tuna*, no. 205 [May 19, 1906], 3; and "*Meşveret* Ceride-i Feridesinden Mütercemdir: Karadağ'ın Silahlanması," *Tuna*, no. 173 [April 10, 1906], 1. In return the CPU's central organ republished articles originally published in *Tuna*. See, for example, "Ruscuk'da Çıkan *Tuna* Gazetesi'nden: Tebeddül-i Verâset Mes'elesi," *Şûra-yı Ümmet*, no. 90 (March 26, 1906), 4; and "Bulgaristan'da Çıkan *Tuna* Gazetesi'nden," *Şûra-yı Ümmet*, no. 94, 4.

187. For example, while they praised the CPU program, the local Young Turk journals stated that they did not want to comment on Sabahaddin Bey's decentralization program. See "Osmanlı Terakki ve İttihad Cemiyeti," *Tuna*, no. 221, 1; and "Yeni Bir Osmanlı 'Cemiyet'i," *Tuna*, no. 212, 2, respectively. When they commented on decentralization they quoted a chapter on the subject written by an opponent of both Sabahaddin Bey and decentralization who recommended "la politique de spécialité" instead. See Doktor Lütfi, "Adem-i Merkeziyet Usûlü," *Uhuvvet*, no. 122 [September 19, 1906], 2–4. (Originally published in Doktor Lütfi, *Millet ve Hükûmet* (Paris, 1906), 12–18.) Similarly, when the CPU and Sabahaddin Bey's league distributed appeals protesting the alleged plan to change the order of succession to the throne, local journals provided detailed information about the CPU appeal, mentioning the CPU by name, but they did not say anything about the one authored by Sabahaddin Bey. See "Jön Türk Komitesi," *Tuna*, no. 326 [November 13, 1906], 3. See also "Jön Türklerin Protestosu," *Tuna*, no. 310 [September 25, 1906], 4. Moreover, when Sabahaddin Bey appealed to the chancelleries of the Great Powers, the local Young Turk press claimed that he had "requested foreign intervention." See "Son Telgraflar," *Ahali*, no. 65 [January 11, 1907], 4.

188. For an example of a rare sympathizer, Doctor Neş'et, who attempted to disseminate Sabahaddin Bey's propaganda, see Necmettin Deliorman, *Meşrutiyetten Önce Balkan Türkleri: Makedonya, Şarkî Rumeli Meseleleri, Hudud Harici Türk Gazeteciliği* (Istanbul, n.d [1943?]), 62–64. Young Turk journals in Bulgaria only rarely quoted from Sabahaddin Bey's journal. For an example, see *Ahali*, no. 57 [January 3, 1907], 3–4.

189. See "Bizde Yiğitlik, Erkeklik," *Tuna*, no. 73 [December 11, 1905], 1–2; "Bizde Yiğitlik, Erkeklik—4," *Tuna*, no. 77 [December 15, 1905], 1–2; İslâm Gencleri, "Anlamak İstiyoruz," ibid., 3; "İsbat el-Müsbet," *Tuna*, no. 82 [December 21, 1905], 2–4, and no. 83 [December 22, 1905], 2–4; "Açık Mektub: '*Rumeli*' Muharriri Edhem Ruhi Bey'e," *Tuna*, no. 120 [February 7, 1906], 3; "Edeb ve Haysiyet-i Matbu'at," *Tuna*, no. 121 [February 8, 1906], 1–2; Ebulrıza Namık, "Açık Mektub: Edhem Ruhi Efendi'ye," *Tuna*, no. 133 [February 22, 1906], 3; Damad Hasanzâde Mehmed Ferid, "Mektub: Tatar Pazarcık," *Tuna*, no. 167 [April 3, 1906], 3; "İftira," *Tuna*, no. 237 [June 27, 1906], 1–2; Letters of Kazaz İdris and Ali Rıza in "Şuûnât: Redd-i İftira," *Tuna*, no. 243 [July 4, 1906], 2; "Tebkit," *Tuna*, no. 248 [July

10, 1906], 1–2; "Tebkit—2," *Tuna*, no. 249 [July 10 [11], 1906], 1–2; "Tebkit—3: Rumeli'nin Âdiliği, Muharrir-i Tafrafurûşunun Cehalet-i Mürekkebesi," *Tuna*, no. 250 [July 12, 1906], 1–2; "Tebkit," *Tuna*, no. 251 [July 13, 1906], 1–3; and Silistre Ümid Kıraathanesi Encümen Hey'eti, "Herze de Hiç Çekilmez," *Tuna*, no. 351 [November 13, 1906], 3. For Edhem Ruhi's accusations, see "Feyz-i Kanun ve Hürriyet," *Rumeli*, no. 4 [December 29, 1905], 3; Ruscuklu Mehmed Ustazâde Mahmud, "Dahiliye," ibid., 4; Edhem Ruhi, "Fezâil-i Milliye'ye Dair: Edeb ve Haysiyet-i Matbuʿat," *Rumeli*, no. 9 [February 2, 1906], 1–2; idem, "Harhara-i Ağraz," *Rumeli*, no. 10, 2–3; idem, "İbret," *Rumeli*, no. 12 [March 2, 1906], 3–4; "Şumnu'dan Mektub," *Rumeli*, no. 10, 4; the letters of Hasan Basri, Hüseyin Nâzım, and Âkif bin Han in "Yine Silistre'den," *Rumeli*, no. 18 [April 16, 1906], 3–4; "Hakikat-i Hal," *Rumeli*, no. 28 [July 6, 1906], 2–3; and "Tehzîl-i Ağraz," *Balkan*, no. 5 [July 28, 1906], 1–2.

190. See the letter of Dr. Bahaeddin [Şakir] beginning "Vatanperver Biraderimiz" and dated [Paris], April 2, [1]906/no. 7, *Muhaberat Kopyası*, 12. Ironically, later "Edhem Ruhi . . . almost got strangled, before the Young Turk [CUP] government interceded for him to be set free." See Dimitrov and Radev to the tzar's consuls in Turkey, Sofia, March 17, 1912 (Ministry of the Interior [political no. 441]), TsDA, F. 336, op. 1, a.e. 110, 9.

191. The shoe-seller Mehmed Teftiş, the editor of *Tuna* and *Uhuvvet*, the most widely read Young Turk journals in Bulgaria during the period, had been the secretary of the old CUP organization in Ruse. (See *Ethem Ruhi Balkan Hatıraları-Canlı Tarihler* 6 [Istanbul, 1947], 29.) The CPU center stated in a letter that *Tuna* was an independent journal and had no ties with the CPU center. See the letter of Dr. Bahaeddin [Şakir] and Dr. Nâzım beginning "Aziz Vatandaşımız" and dated Paris, September 24, 1906/no. [175?], *Muhaberat Kopyası*, 125–26. See also "[Not]," *Şûra-yı Ümmet*, no. 85 (October 29, 1905), 4. The journal too declared its impartiality in its maiden issue. See Tuna'yı Yazanlar, "İlk Söz," *Tuna*, no. 1 [September 14, 1905], 1.

192. "Bulgaristan Prensi'ne Hitaben Gazetemizde Dercedilmek Üzere Gönderilen ve Birçok İmzayı Muhtevî Olan Varaka-i Müştereke-i İştikâ'iye," *Şûra-yı Ümmet*, no. 119 (July 30, 1907), 2.

193. See, for example, "Bulgaristan'dan," *Şûra-yı Ümmet*, no. 91 (April 9, 1906), 4; "Bulgaristan'dan," *Şûra-yı Ümmet*, nos. 96–97 (August 1, 1906), 6; and "Kızanlık'dan," *Şûra-yı Ümmet*, no. 99 (August 31, 1906), 4.

194. See Dr. Bahaeddin [Şakir] to [Nikola Manolov], dated [Paris, July 18, 1907/no. 313], *Muhaberat Kopyası*, 350. Most of the copy of this letter did not appear in the copy register of the Internal Affairs and Correspondence division. I could not find much about Manolov and his political affiliations and how and why he contacted the CPU in 1907. There is no mention of Nikola Manolov in the two books containing information on Iambol. See *Istoriia na grad Iambol*, ed. Zhecho Atanasov, Strashimir Dimitrov, and Boris Mataev (Sofia, 1976), which features detailed sections on schools, teachers, and cultural life in its chapter on the history of the town during the first decade of the twentieth century. Manolov is not among the names mentioned in these sections, nor is he mentioned among local activists of various political parties during the same period (1900–1910). See chapter VII (pp. 201–45). There is also no mention of a Nikola Manolov in a selection of miscellaneous documents, with a heavy bias toward socialist activities, on the history of Iambol and the surroundings of the town. See *Materiali za minaloto na Iambolskiia krai* (Iambol: Upravlenie "Narodna prosveta" pri ONS direktsiia "Okrŭzhen Dŭrzhaven Arkhiv," 1987).

195. Manolov must have been referring to the non-Marxist (broadly socialist) wing of the Bulgarian Workers' Social Democratic Party, which emerged after the 1903 schism under the leadership of Ianko Sakŭzov (publishing the journal *Obshto delo* as its organ) against the Marxist wing (narrowly socialist) led by Dimitŭr Blagoev and publishing the journals *Rabotnicheska borba* (1903–1908), *Rabotnicheska Bulgariia* (1908–1911), and *Narod* (1914–1918). It seems that the non-Marxist (broadly socialist) wing was for a "federation of Ottoman Empire and Bulgaria" and was critical of a "Bulgarian national ideal." However, it wanted to base such a federation on a union of the Bulgarian and Ottoman proletariats, something that cannot have seemed feasible to the Young Turks. See "Revoliutsiiata v Turtsiia," *Novo vreme* 12, nos. 8–9 (August–September 1908), 466–67.

196. Nikola Manolov to the CPU central committee, Iambol, August 7, [1]907, Private Papers of Bahaeddin Şakir.

197. Dr. Bahaeddin [Şakir] to Nikola Manolov, undated [Paris, August 1907]/no. 349, *Muhaberat Kopyası*, 395–97.

198. Ibid., and Dr. Bahaeddin [Şakir] to [Nikola Manolov] beginning "Muhterem Vatandaş" and dated [Paris], September 6, 1907/no. 361, *Muhaberat Kopyası*, 409.

199. Dr. Bahaeddin [Şakir] to Nikola Manolov, dated Paris, November 9, [1]907/no. 412, *Muhaberat Kopyası*, 492–93.

200. See the letter of Dr. Bahaeddin [Şakir] beginning "Aziz Vatandaşımız" and dated [Paris], August 12, 1907/no. 336, *Muhaberat Kopyası*, 377.

201. See, for example, "Refikimiz *Şark* Gazetesi'nde Görülmüştür," *Tuna*, no. 31 [October 19, 1905], 3–4; "*Tuna*," ibid., 4; and "Varna'dan Mektup," *Tuna*, no. 159 [March 24, 1906], 3.

202. See Petrov to Nachovich, Sofia, May 14, 1905/no. 1821, TsDA, F. 321, op. 1, a.e. 2589, 16. Petrov gave orders that the Bulgarian diplomatic agency in Istanbul subscribe to the journal. He stated: "I have good reason to believe that the editorial board of '*Şark*' is inclined to listen to [our] good advice." The Bulgarian authorities also tried to protect the journal's subscribers. See Nachovich to Petrov, Istanbul, June 27, 1906/no. 1095, TsDA, F. 176, op. 1, a.e. 2169, 12. See also Kâzım Karabekir, *İttihat ve Terakki Cemiyeti, 1896–1909: İttihat ve Terakki Cemiyeti Neden Kuruldu [?] Nasıl Kuruldu [?] Nasıl İdare Olundu [?]* (Istanbul, 1982), 169–70. As we have stated, Yürükoğlu İsmail was also working as an agent of the Ottoman commissioner. See supra p. 361.

203. See his letter to the CPU central committee, dated [Sofia], August 8 [21], [1]907, Private Papers of Bahaeddin Şakir.

204. See the letter of Dr. Bahaeddin [Şakir] to [Yürükoğlu İsmail], beginning "Azizim" and dated [Paris], September 23, 1907/no. 375, *Muhaberat Kopyası*, 429.

205. See the report entitled "Giovani Turchi in Bulgaria," sent to Tittoni by the Italian diplomatic agent, Sofia, July 22, 1908/no. 953–282, ASMAE, Affari Politici, Serie P. Politica (1891–1916), pacco 123–24.

206. For more information, see Müstecib Ülküsal, *Dobruca ve Türkler* (Ankara, 1966), 149–50. İbrahim Temo described the period prior to the reorganization as follows: "The branch that I had established in Dobruja with the additional help of the [former] naval officer Kırımîzâde Ali Rıza ten years ago has lost its dynamism during the last two years because of the despair that stems from the division and disorderliness that is seen everywhere." See İbrahim Temo to Bahaeddin Şakir and Dr. Nâzım, Constanţa, November 12, 1906, Private Papers of Bahaeddin Şakir.

207. For example, he spearheaded the preparation of appeals asking for Albanian autonomy issued by the Drita Committee. See "Pjesë nga thirrja drejtuar Fuqive të Mëdha, që t'i njihen popullit shqiptar disa të drejta kombëtare," dated Bucharest, October 14, 1903, in *Akte të rilindjes kombëtare Shqiptare, 1878–1912* (*memorandume, vendime, protesta, thirrje*), ed. Stefanaq Pollo and Selami Pulaha (Tirana, 1978), 154–57. A French translation is given in Georges Verdène, *La vérité sur la Question macédonienne* (Paris, 1905), 215–23.

208. İbrahim Temo later maintained that he worked toward achieving an understanding between the Turkish minority in Romania and the Romanians against Slavism. He did not state that such a policy accorded with policies pursued by mainstream Albanian organizations. See "Sărbătorirea d-lui Dr. Ibra[h]im Themo," *Dobrogea Junǎ*, April 13, 1935. For İbrahim Temo's relations with the leaders of the Aromenis movement, see M. Şükrü Hanioğlu, *The Young Turks in Opposition* (New York, 1995), 89, 169. The CPU's first demand from him was to propagate the organization's ideas among influential Albanians. See Dr. Bahaeddin [Şakir] to the director of the CPU Constanţa branch, dated [Paris], November 23, 1906/no. 212, *Muhaberat Kopyası*, 168.

209. İbrahim Temo and Kırımîzâde Ali Rıza to Sabahaddin Bey, dated [Medgidia], August 6, [1]906, AQSh, 19/31//97/444.

210. See the letter of Dr. Bahaeddin [Şakir] and Dr. Nâzım to [İbrahim Temo and Kırımîzâde Ali Rıza] beginning "Aziz Kardeşlerimiz" and dated Paris, August 27, 1906/no. 64. The original letter, which has a postscript informing the two Young Turks in Romania of the new CPU

address in Paris, is in AQSh, 19/59//19/120. A copy, which lacks this postscript, is in *Muhaberat Kopyası*, 100.

211. Dr. Bahaeddin [Şakir] and Dr. Nâzım to Ali Sedad Halil, dated [Paris], October 29, 1906/no. 187, *Muhaberat Kopyası*, 146: "Our happiness stems from once again working together with our brethren, whose religious and national zeal is incontestable and who are as strong as Turks."

212. İbrahim Temo to Bahaeddin Şakir and Dr. Nâzım, Constanța, November 12, 1906. (Some parts of this letter were written in Ruse), Private Papers of Bahaeddin Şakir; the undated written oath signed by these three Young Turks and sent to the CPU central committee, Private Papers of Bahaeddin Şakir; and Dr. Bahaeddin [Şakir] to Ali Sedad Halil, dated [Paris], November 24, [1]906/no. 213, *Muhaberat Kopyası*, 174.

213. İbrahim Temo to Bahaeddin Şakir and Dr. Nâzım, dated Constanța, November 12, 1906, Private Papers of Bahaeddin Şakir.

214. Dr. Bahaeddin [Şakir] to the CPU Constanța branch, dated [Paris], November 23, 1906/no. 212, *Muhaberat Kopyası*, 168.

215. İbrahim Temo, *İttihad ve Terakki Cemiyetinin Teşekkülü ve Hidemati Vataniye ve İnkılabi Milliye Dair Hatıratım* (Medgidia, 1939), 197–98.

216. See Dr. Bahaeddin [Şakir] to the CPU Constanța branch, dated [Paris], August 24, 1907/no. 345. The original letter is in AQSh, 19/59//19/24. A copy in which the name of a person who had sent a letter to the committee was omitted is in *Muhaberat Kopyası*, 391.

217. See H[üsrev] Sami to the CPU Romania branch, dated [Paris], May 9, 1908/no. 633, AQSh, 19/59//237/25; the letter of H[üsrev] Sami and Dr. Bahaeddin [Şakir] to the CPU Constanța branch, dated [Paris], June 1, 1908/no. 669, AQSh, 19/59//2311/26; and the letter of H[üsrev] Sami and Dr. Bahaeddin [Şakir] to the CPU branch in Romania, dated [Paris], June 17, 1908/no. 679, AQSh, 19/59//236/27.

218. See the letter of Dr. Bahaeddin [Şakir] and H[üsrev] Sami to the CPU Romania branch, dated [Paris], June 17, 1908/no. 679, ibid.: "This passport would be used abroad. . . . We do not need passports to enter the [Ottoman Empire]. The borders are open."

219. See Temo, *İttihad ve Terakki*, 200–202.

220. Dr. Bahaeddin [Şakir] to the CPU central branch in Romania, dated Paris, June 19, [1]907/no. 301. The original letter is in AQSh, 19/59//638/22, and its copy is in *Muhaberat Kopyası*, 330–31. It was also published in "Osmanlı İttihad ve Terakki Cemiyeti: Vesâik-i Tarihiyeden," *Haftalık Şûra-yı Ümmet*, no. 219 [May 5, 1910], 2. İsmail Kemal's name was omitted in the published version.

221. Dr. Bahaeddin [Şakir] to the CPU Constanța branch, dated [Paris], June 10, [1]907/no. 297, *Muhaberat Kopyası*, 319–20.

222. İbrahim Temo to Ahmed Rıza, Medgidia, July 1, [1]907, Private Papers of Ahmed Rıza (1).

223. Dr. Bahaeddin [Şakir] to the CPU Constanța branch, undated [Paris, December 1907]/no. 443. The original letter is in AQSh, 19/59//29/74, and its copy is in *Kopye Defteri*, 25; and the letter of H[üsrev] Sami and Dr. Bahaeddin [Şakir] to İbrahim Temo, dated [Paris], April 4, 1908/no. 584, AQSh, 19/59//996/28-10.

224. Dr. Bahaeddin [Şakir] to the CPU Constanța branch, undated [Paris, December 1907]/no. 443, in AQSh, 19/59//29/74, and in *Kopye Defteri*, 25.

225. Dr. Bahaeddin [Şakir] to the CPU central branch in Romania, dated Paris, January 3, 1908/no. 465, *Kopye Defteri*, 57.

226. See the letter of H[üsrev] Sami and Dr. Bahaeddin [Şakir] to İbrahim Temo, dated [Paris], April 4, 1908/no. 584, AQSh, 19/59//996/28–10; and Temo, *İttihad ve Terakki*, 205.

227. İbrahim Temo to Ahmed Rıza, dated Constanța, April 18, 1908, Private Papers of Ahmed Rıza (2). See also the letter of H[üsrev] Sami and Dr. Bahaeddin [Şakir] beginning "Aziz Arkadaşımız" and dated February 24, 1908/no. 533, *Kopye Defteri*, 184.

228. He wrote articles mostly for *Tuna* and sent letters to this journal. See İlhanî, "Bir Kıt'adır ki Sultan Hamid'e İthaf Olunur," *Tuna*, no. 174 [April 11, 1906], 1; Derviş Hima, "Abdülhamid-i Sâni ve İkinci Nikola," *Tuna*, no. 267 [August 6, 1906], 1–2, and *Tuna*, no. 268 [August 7, 1906], 1–2; and idem, "Türkiya Mirascıları," *Tuna*, no. 315 [October 1, 1906], 1.

229. İbrahim Temo, "Makedonya Komedyaları," *Balkan*, no. 344 [January 21, 1908], 1.

230. This fact is also true for the similar public seminars organized by İbrahim Temo to enlighten the masses in Babadag (Babadağ) in Dobruja. See Tahsin Gemil, "Asociaţia din România a 'Junilor Turci'," *Anuarul Institutului de Istorie şi Arheologie 'A. D. Xenepol'* 7 (1970), 190. Their secular focus must have annoyed the Muslim masses.

231. For more information, see Ramî, "Köstence'de Konferanslar," *Balkan*, no. 296 [November 19, 1907], 3–4; and Muverri-i Hicranî, "Köstence'de Harekât-ı Fikriye," *Balkan*, no. 403 [March 29, 1908], 1–2.

232. Naci, "Köstence'den Mektub," *Tuna*, no. 252 [July 14, 1906], 2–3. See also A. A., "Bir Nida-yı Millî: İstanbul'dan Dobruca Cemaʿat-i İslâmiye Müftisine Hitaben Yazılıyor," *Balkan*, no. 366 [February 15, 1908], 1–2.

233. See Veli Maksud, "Romanya Mektubları," *Bağçe*, no. 13 [December 18, 1909], 202.

234. Ahmed Lütfi İbraki to Bahaeddin Şakir, Canea, July [30], [1907], Private Papers of Bahaeddin Şakir.

235. For examples of his many letters published in Young Turk journals, see Ekrem, "Girid Mektubu," *Tuna*, no. 302 [September 15, 1906], 1–2; and idem, "Girid Mektubu," *Tuna*, no. 336 [October 25, 1906], 1–2.

236. Ekrem Bey to Ahmed Rıza, Canea, March 20, [19]06, Private Papers of Bahaeddin Şakir.

237. Dr. Bahaeddin [Şakir] to [Ekrem Bey] beginning "Aziz Kardeşimiz" and dated [Paris], April 25, [1]906/no. 11, *Muhaberat Kopyası*, 20.

238. Dr. B[ahaeddi]n [Şakir] to Ahmed Lütfi İbraki, dated [Paris], March 27, [1]906/ no. 3, *Muhaberat Kopyası*, 7.

239. Ahmed Lütfi İbraki to Ahmed Rıza, Canea, September 1, 1906, Private Papers of Bahaeddin Şakir.

240. Dr. B[ahaeddi]n [Şakir] to M[ehmed] Macid, dated [Paris], March 27, [1]906/no. 4, *Muhaberat Kopyası*, 8–9; and the letter of Dr. Bahaeddin [Şakir] and Dr. Nâzım to him dated Paris, June 2, 1906/no. 29, *Muhaberat Kopyası*, 51. It seems that though he did not become a member in the CPU branch in Canea, he worked as a CPU correspondent there. See his letters to Ahmed Rıza and to Bahaeddin Şakir and Dr. Nâzım, dated Canea, November 28, [1]906 and January 28, [1]907, respectively, Private Papers of Bahaeddin Şakir. See also the letter of Dr. Bahaeddin [Şakir] and Dr. Nâzım to him dated [Paris], December 10, 1906/no. 226, *Muhaberat Kopyası*, 200; and an unsigned letter by Dr. Bahaeddin [Şakir], dated Paris, April 3, 1907/no. 277, *Muhaberat Kopyası*, 286. Mehmed Macid later published a nationalist novel praised in the Young Turk circles. See Giridli Bir Türk [Mehmed Macid], *Firak* (Cairo, 1906). For an example of such praise, see "Firak yahud Girid Faciʿası," *İrşad*, no. 82 (May 4 [17], 1907), 4. For an example of Mehmed Macid's nationalist articles, see Firak Muharriri [Mehmed Macid], "Girid Tuhfesi," *Füyûzat*, no. 15 (April 13 [26], 1907), 229. The CPU center criticized Mehmed Macid because Abdullah Cevdet published his novel. See the letter of Dr. Nâzım to Macid Bey, dated [Paris], May 10, 1907/no. 292, *Muhaberat Kopyası*, 307–8. [Mehmed Macid further praised Abdullah Cevdet in the branch's unofficial journal. See [Mehmed] M[acid] "Havâdis-i Mahalliye," *Sada-yı Girid*, no. 2 (May [17], 1907, 3).] Despite the CPU center's strong criticism, Mehmed Macid continued to work for the CPU. See the letter of Dr. Bahaeddin [Şakir] to him, dated [Paris], August 22, [1]907/no. 341 (duplicate number), *Muhaberat Kopyası*, 386.

241. See the letter of [Dr. Bahaeddin Şakir] to [Alyotîzâde Mustafa Tevfik] beginning "Aziz Biraderimiz" and dated [Paris], May 29, [1]906/no. 16, *Muhaberat Kopyası*, 32–33. Alyotîzâde Mustafa Tevfik was an elected member of the Muslim community's executive committee in Canea. See "İntihab," *Sada-yı Girid*, no. 15 (August [15], 1907), 1.

242. See the unsigned letter of Bahaeddin Şakir and Dr. Nâzım to Alyotîzâde Mustafa Tevfik and Ahmed Lütfi İbraki, dated Paris, June 22, 1906/no. 22, *Muhaberat Kopyası*, 43.

243. Dr. Bahaeddin [Şakir] and Dr. Nâzım to Yüzbaşızâde Ahmed Lütfi [İbraki], undated [Paris, April 1907]/no. 273, *Muhaberat Kopyası*, 277–78.

244. See the letter of Ahmed Lütfi İbraki, dated Canea, July [30], [1907], Private Papers of Bahaeddin Şakir; and "İfade-i Mahsusa," *İstikbâl*, no. 1 [June 18, 1908], 1.

245. See [Mehmed] M[acid], "Sada-yı Girid," *Sada-yı Girid*, no. 1 ([April 9], 1907), 1–2. He resigned from this position in July 1907 because of a disagreement with Ahmed Lütfi İbraki. See Dr. Bahaeddin [Şakir] to [Mehmed Macid] beginning "Azizim Efendim" and dated Paris, July 30, 1907/no. 331, *Muhaberat Kopyası*, 371.

246. See, for example, "İngiliz Kavminin Türklere Olan Adavet-i Gayr-ı Muhikkaları Yine Taşmağa Başladı!" *Sada-yı Girid*, no. 33 (December [26], 1907), 4; and "Mezarımız Nasıl Kazılıyor [?]" *Sada-yı Girid*, no. 37 (January [30], 1908), 1–2.

247. See "Taassub-i Nasranî!" *Sada-yı Girid*, no. 39 ([February 14], 1908), 3; and "Tahkirât-ı Diniye!" *Sada-yı Girid*, no. 43 ([March 13], 1908), 2–3.

248. See, for example, Bekir bin İsfendiyar, "Türkistan'dan Mektub: İnkılâbât-ı Rusya," *Sada-yı Girid*, no. 33, 4; and "Buhara'dan Mektub," *Sada-yı Girid*, no. 47 ([April 9], 1908), 4.

249. See "Arnaudlar! Gözlerinizi Açınız," *Sada-yı Girid*, no. 42 ([March 6], 1908), 1–2.

250. "*Sada-yı Girid*," *Sada-yı Girid*, no. 16 (August [22], 1907), 3.

251. See "*Sada-yı Girid*," *Şûra-yı Ümmet*, no. 115 (June 1, 1907), 4; and "*Sada-yı Girid*," *Türk*, no. 164 (May 30, 1907), 3.

252. See the CPU Canea branch to the CPU Internal Affairs division, Canea, July 2, [1]907/ no. 13, Private Papers of Bahaeddin Şakir.

253. See the CPU Canea branch to Seyyid Ken'an in Athens, Canea, August 20, [1]907; and Ahmed Lütfi İbraki to [Seyyid Ken'an], Canea, [August 9], 1907, Private Papers of Bahaeddin Şakir.

254. See H[üsrev] Sami and Dr. Bahaeddin [Şakir] to the director of the CPU Canea branch, dated [Paris], January 19, 1908/no. 489, *Kopye Defteri*, 106.

255. See, for example, the CPU Canea branch to the CPU Internal Affairs and Correspondence division, Canea, November [28], [1]906/no. 9, and [January 1], 1906/no. 10; and Ahmed Lütfi İbraki to [Bahaeddin Şakir], Canea, July [26, 1907], Private Papers of Bahaeddin Şakir.

256. The CPU central organs published many letters sent by members of the branch. In addition, CPU members wrote articles based on the information provided by the Cretan Muslims. See "Hanya'dan," *Şûra-yı Ümmet*, no. 91, 4; "Hanya'dan," *Şûra-yı Ümmet*, no. 92 (April 25, 1906), 4; "Girid Müslümanları," *Şûra-yı Ümmet*, no. 94, 1; "Girid—Hanya'dan," *Şûra-yı Ümmet*, no. 95 (June 23, 1906), 3; "Lettre de Crète," *Mechveret Supplément Français*, no. 177 (July 1, 1906), 4; "Hanya'dan: Mektub," *Şûra-yı Ümmet*, no. 98, 4; "Girid'den," *Şûra-yı Ümmet*, no. 102 (October 15, 1906), 4; "Hanya'dan," *Şûra-yı Ümmet*, no. 103 (November 1, 1906), 3; "Paris'de Terakki ve İttihad Cemiyeti Hey'et-i Merkeziyesi'ne," *Şûra-yı Ümmet*, no. 111 (March 15, 1907), 3; "Girid'den," ibid., 4; "Girid," *Şûra-yı Ümmet*, no. 134 (May 15, 1908), 8; and "Girid, Hanya," *Şûra-yı Ümmet*, no. 137 (July 1, 1908), 4.

257. The note (see "Tekzib-i Muhikk," *Sada-yı Girid*, no. 36 [January 10, 1908], 4) was a strong denunciation of the letter allegedly sent from Tripoli of Barbary and published in "30 Teşrin-i sânî 1907, Trablusgarb," *Şûra-yı Ümmet*, no. 127 (December 15, 1907), 4.

258. See the CPU Canea branch to the Internal Affairs and Correspondence division of the CPU External Headquarters in Paris, February 8, 1908, Private Papers of Bahaeddin Şakir.

259. H[üsrev] Sami and Dr. Bahaeddin [Şakir] to the [CPU branch in Canea] beginning "Muhterem Arkadaşlar" and dated [Paris], March 10, 1908/no. 552, *Kopye Defteri*, 215.

260. Some names are given in M[ehmed] Macid, "Ağazâde Mehmed Behcet Bey," *İstikbâl*, no. 14 [September 17, 1908], 1.

261. For example, with the help of Halil Halid, members of the branch recounted the Cretan Muslims' situation in *The Times*, though the daily did not publish their letters verbatim but summarized them. See "İn'ikas-ı Sada-yı Mazlûmîn yahud Arz-ı Dîdâr-ı Hakikat," *Sada-yı Girid*, no. 27 (November [14], 1907), 1–2; and "The Mahomedans in Crete," *The Times*, October 21, 1907. See also Halil Halid's letter in "Greeks and Musulmans," *The Times*, June 3, 1908.

262. See the CPU Canea branch to Bahaeddin Şakir, dated [October 30, 1908], Private Papers of Bahaeddin Şakir.

263. Dr. Bahaeddin [Şakir] to Bedri Beyzâde İbrahim Et[h]em, dated Paris, August 27, 1906/no. 65, *Muhaberat Kopyası*, 101; and Dr. Bahaeddin [Şakir] and Dr. Nâzım to [Dr. Ali] Rasih in Candia, dated [Paris], January 5, 1907/no. 244, *Muhaberat Kopyası*, 227–28.

264. See his letter to the "*Şûra-yı Ümmet* Administration in Paris," dated Candia [August 9, 1907], Private Papers of Bahaeddin Şakir.

265. See Dr. Bahaeddin [Şakir] to Çiçekaki Hüseyin Salih in Candia, dated [Paris], August 22, [1]907/no. 342, *Muhaberat Kopyası*, 387.

266. See a copy of the address delivered by Şekerci Ali Efendizâde Ömer Şükrü and sent to the CPU central committee, dated Candia, May 29, [1908], Private Papers of Bahaeddin Şakir.

267. See a copy of the address delivered by Midhat Efendi, a teacher in Candia, and sent to the CPU central committee, dated Candia, May 29, [1908], Private Papers of Bahaeddin Şakir.

268. See the letter signed by Dr. Ali Rasih, Bedrizâde İbrahim Edhem, and Mazlumzâde Mehmed Şükrü and sent to Bahaeddin Şakir, dated [October 17, 1908], Private Papers of Bahaeddin Şakir.

269. Ağazâde Ali Sıdkı to Bahaeddin Şakir, dated Nicosia, May 14, [1]908, Private Papers of Bahaeddin Şakir. It should be stated that many conservative Muslims applied to the sultan asking help to thwart Greek aspirations. See, for example, "Kıbrıs Hakkında," *Tuna*, no. 232 [June 20, 1906], 1.

270. Edhem Safi to Ahmed Rıza, dated [Nicosia], October 12, [1]906, Private Papers of Bahaeddin Şakir.

271. Dr. Bahaeddin [Şakir] and Dr. Nâzım to [Edhem Safi] beginning "Aziz Vatandaş" and dated [Paris], October 31, 1906/no. 203, *Muhaberat Kopyası*, 152–53.

272. Edhem Safi to the CPU Internal Affairs division, dated Larnaca, November 15, [1]906, Private Papers of Bahaeddin Şakir.

273. See the letter of [Dr. Bahaeddin Şakir] to one of the CPU sympathizers in Larnaca beginning "Vatanperver Efendim," undated [November 1907]/no. 410, *Muhaberat Kopyası*, 489–90.

274. Edhem Safi to the CPU central committee, dated Nicosia, July 22, [1]908, Private Papers of Bahaeddin Şakir; and Dr. Bahaeddin [Şakir] to Mehmed Salih, dated Paris, July 30, [1]907/no. 328, *Muhaberat Kopyası*, 363–64.

275. See Dr. Bahaeddin [Şakir] to the director of the CPU central branch in Cyprus, dated [Paris], December 9, 1907/no. 447, *Kopye Defteri*, 34; and [Dr. Bahaeddin Şakir] to the director of the CPU central branch in Cyprus, dated [Paris], January [?], 1908/no. 484, *Kopye Defteri*, 95–96.

276. Ahmed Eyüb's undated [1907?] letter beginning "Huzûr-i Maarifperverîlerine," Private Papers of Bahaeddin Şakir.

277. See his letter to Bahaeddin Şakir, dated April 21, 1908, Private Papers of Bahaeddin Şakir.

278. Hafız Cemal, *Kıbrıs Cemiyet-i Hayriye-i İslâmiyesine Mahsus Ta'limatnâme* ([Nicosia], 1906). See also "Kıbrıs," *Tercüman-ı Ahvâl-i Zaman*, no. 83 [July 11, 1906], 3. He reorganized this society in 1912. See Hafız Cemal, *Kıbrıs Cemiyet-i Hayriye-i İslâmiyesi'nin Yeni Ta'limatnâmesi* (Nicosia, 1912), passim.

279. Hafız Cemal, *Sevgili İslâmlarım! Artık Uyanalım!* ([Nicosia], 1906), 1–2 and 11–12.

280. See, for example, "Mekâtib-i Sanayi'-i Şâhâne ve Sanayi'in Fevâidi," *İslâm*, no. 3 (May 2, 1907), 1; and "Ulviyet-i Din-i İslâm," ibid., 4.

281. Edhem Safi to the CPU central committee, dated Nicosia, July 22, [1]908, Private Papers of Bahaeddin Şakir.

282. Hafız Cemal, *Kıbrıs Osmanlılarına Mahsus Son Hediye-i Âcizânem veyahud Kıbrıs'da Geçen Dört Senelik Tarih-i Hayatım ile Kıbrıs Osmanlılarına Mahsus Parlak İstikbâl Programı* ([Nicosia], 1909), 25.

283. Edhem Safi to the CPU central committee, dated Nicosia, July 22, [1]908, Private Papers of Bahaeddin Şakir.

284. "Kıbrıs'dan," *Şûra-yı Ümmet*, no. 101, 3.

285. This provoked disappointment among the CPU leaders. See the letter of Dr. Bahaeddin [Şakir] and Dr. Nâzım to [Sami Paşazâde] Sezaî, dated Paris, August 6, 1906/no. 54, *Muhaberat Kopyası*, 82.

286. See "Velâdet-i Hümayûn," *İslâm*, no. 69 (September 14, 1908), 1.

287. See the letter of Dr. Bahaeddin [Şakir] beginning "Kafkasya Ahali-i İslâmiyesine: Aziz Kardaşlarımız" and dated Paris, March 26, [1]906/no. 2, *Muhaberat Kopyası*, 5–6.

288. See the letter of Dr. Bahaeddin [Şakir] and Dr. Nâzım beginning "Aziz Kardaşlarımız" and dated [Paris], May 10, [1]906/no. 13, *Muhaberat Kopyası*, 25.

289. Dr. Bahaeddin [Şakir] and Dr. Nâzım to [İsmail Gaspıralı] beginning "Hamiyetlû Efendim Hazretleri" and dated Paris, August 6, 1906/no. 53, *Muhaberat Kopyası*, 81. The CPU organs praised Gaspıralı's journal, *Tercüman*. See "Matbu'at-ı İslâmiye," *Şûra-yı Ümmet*, no. 109 (February 15, 1907), 2. İsmail Gaspıralı, for his part, republished articles that had originally been published in the CPU journals. He referred to the CPU organs as "our press." See "Bizim Matbu'at," *Tercüman-ı Ahvâl-i Zaman*, no. 60 (June 5 [18], 1906), 3.

290. See [Hüseyinzâde Ali], "Kaf ve Simürg," *Şûra-yı Ümmet*, no. 99, 3. The central organ later recommended *Füyûzat* to its readership. See "İlân," *Şûra-yı Ümmet*, no. 125 (November 15, 1907), 4.

291. Hüseyinzâde Ali to Bahaeddin Şakir, Baku, October 12, 1906, Private Papers of Bahaeddin Şakir.

292. Ibid.

293. See the letter of Dr. Bahaeddin [Şakir] and Dr. Nâzım to [Sami Paşazâde] Sezaî, dated Paris, August 6, 1906/no. 54, *Muhaberat Kopyası*, 82.

294. See Ağaoğlu Ahmet, "Ahmet Rıza Bey," *Vakit*, March 6, 1930.

295. See the letter of Dr. Bahaeddin [Şakir] and Dr. Nâzım, "*İrşad* Ceride-i Muhteremesi'ne," dated Paris, January 8, 1907/no. 249, *Muhaberat Kopyası*, 231.

296. See the letter of Dr. Bahaeddin [Şakir] to [Ahmed Agayef] beginning "*İrşad* Ceride-i Muhteremesi Sermuharrirliği'ne" and dated [Paris], July 3, 1907/no. 304, *Muhaberat Kopyası*, 336. The CPU central organ praised publication of *İrşad* too. See "Matbu'at-ı İslâmiye," *Şûra-yı Ümmet*, no. 109, 2.

297. See the unsigned letter to the CPU central committee in Paris dated [Baku] October 29, 1906, Private Papers of Bahaeddin Şakir. A European journalist stated that "Pan-Islamic proclamations had been published in Agaieff's paper *Heyat* [*sic*], and in a Young Turkish sheet published in Geneva called the *Ittiad* [*sic*]." See Luigi Villari, *Fire and Sword in the Caucasus* (London, 1906), 174.

298. See the letter of Dr. Bahaeddin [Şakir] beginning "Aziz Kardaşlarımız" and dated Paris, September 22, 1906/no. 74, *Muhaberat Kopyası*, 115–16.

299. See the undated [October 1906] and unnumbered letter of [Dr. Bahaeddin Şakir] to the Muslims in the Caucasus, *Muhaberat Kopyası*, 119–22. See also the letter of Dr. Bahaeddin [Şakir] beginning "Kafkasya'da Müslüman Kardeşlerimize: Aziz Kardeşlerimiz" and dated Paris, November 23, 1906/no. 215, *Muhaberat Kopyası*, 180–81: "The future Ottoman government will strongly hope that you will act in a manner that is in accordance with Islam and Turkishness. We would like to assure you that, if God pleases, it will not fail to do whatever it can for its brothers who share the same religion, language, and blood."

300. See, for example, "Kafkasya'dan Mektub," *Şûra-yı Ümmet*, no. 103, 3–4.

301. See the letter of Dr. Bahaeddin [Şakir] beginning "Aziz Kardeşlerimiz" and dated Paris, October 27, 1906/no. 184, *Muhaberat Kopyası*, 140. For the published version of the letter, see Türk Oğlu, "Gence'den," *Şûra-yı Ümmet*, no. 101, 3.

302. See "Mülkümüzde Me'muriyete İnhimakin Mehâziri: Çâre-i Selâmet," *Şûra-yı Ümmet*, no. 103, 3. The French supplement too repeated the following claim allegedly made by a Caucasian Muslim: "Le panislamisme n'existant que dans l'imagination de certains Européens qui n'emploient ce vocable de 'pan' que par pur snobisme." See Un Musulman du Caucase, "Lettre du Caucase," *Mechveret Supplément Français*, no. 168 (October 1, 1905), 4.

303. See "Kafkasya'dan Mektub," *Şûra-yı Ümmet*, no. 103, 3–4.

304. See the undated [October 1906] and unnumbered letter of [Dr. Bahaeddin Şakir] to the Muslims in the Caucasus, *Muhaberat Kopyası*, 123.

305. See the letter of Dr. Bahaeddin [Şakir] beginning "Kafkasya'da Müslüman Kardeş-lerimize: Aziz Kardeşlerimiz" and dated Paris, November 23, 1906/no. 215, *Muhaberat*

Kopyası, 180. In a roundabout way Bahaeddin Şakir also recommended an economic boycott against the Armenians.

306. Ibid., 178; and the letter of Dr. Bahaeddin [Şakir] beginning "Aziz Kardeşlerimiz" and dated Paris, October 27, 1906/no. 184, *Muhaberat Kopyası*, 141.

307. See the letter of Dr. Bahaeddin [Şakir] beginning "Aziz Kardaşlarımız" and dated Paris, September 22, 1906/no. 74, *Muhaberat Kopyası*, 118: "Do not forget that we strongly need the *medrese* before the mosque."

308. See the letter of Dr. Bahaeddin [Şakir] beginning "Kafkasya'da Müslüman Kardeşlerimize: Aziz Kardeşlerimiz" and dated Paris, November 23, 1906/no. 215, *Muhaberat Kopyası*, 178.

309. Ibid., 179–80.

310. See the letter of Dr. Bahaeddin [Şakir] and Dr. Nâzım beginning "Efendim Hazretleri" and dated [Paris], February 6, 1907/no. 254, *Muhaberat Kopyası*, 243–44.

311. Hüseyin Mollazâde Ahundova to the CPU central committee, Gäncä, April 3, 1907/no. 1000, Private Papers of Bahaeddin Şakir; and the letter of Dr. [Bahaeddin Şakir] in response, beginning "Gence Şehrinde Müslüman Kardaşlarımıza: Aziz ve Muhterem Kardaşlarımız" and dated [Paris], May 2, 1907/no. 288, *Muhaberat Kopyası*, 301–2.

312. Dr. Bahaeddin [Şakir] to Mir Abbas, the owner of the Ümid Library in Yerevan, undated [December 1907]/no. 458, *Kopye Defteri*, 46.

313. The reading room was opened in Bat'umi. See the letter of Dr. Bahaeddin [Şakir] beginning "Muhterem Dindaşımız" and dated Paris, January 3, 1907 [1908]/no. 464, *Kopye Defteri*, 56.

314. See the letter of Dr. Bahaeddin [Şakir] beginning "Muhterem Din Karındaşlarımız" and dated Paris, January 3, 1907 [1908]/no. 469, *Kopye Defteri*, 64–65.

315. See "Rusya'da Cemiyet-i Osmaniye," *Tuna*, no. 320 [October 6, 1906], 3.

316. Hasan Hüsni to the CPU central committee, Och'amch'ire [April 14, 1907], Private Papers of Bahaeddin Şakir.

317. Dr. Nâzım to [Hasan Hüsni] beginning "Vatanperver ve Muhterem Kardeşimiz" and dated Paris, April 26, 1906/no. 281, *Muhaberat Kopyası*, 293–94.

318. See the letter signed by these individuals and sent to Dr. Nâzım, Och'amch'ire, May 7, [1]907, Private Papers of Bahaeddin Şakir.

319. See the letter of Hasan Hüsni to [Dr. Bahaeddin Şakir and Dr. Nâzım], beginning "Saadetlû Vatanperverlerimiz" and dated Och'amch'ire [May 20, 1907]/no. 2, Private Papers of Bahaeddin Şakir.

320. See the letter of [Dr. Bahaeddin Şakir] beginning "Muhterem Vatandaşlar" and dated [Paris], November 23, 1907/no. 434, *Kopye Defteri*, 11; his letter beginning "Aziz Vatandaşımız," and dated [Paris], December 13, 1907/no. 455, *Kopye Defteri*, 43; and Dr. Bahaeddin [Şakir] to [Ömer] Naci, dated [Paris], March 16, [190]8/no. 558, *Kopye Defteri*, 231.

321. The CPU also asked its sympathizers in the Caucasus to smuggle its propaganda material into the Ottoman Empire. See the letter of Dr. Bahaeddin [Şakir] and Dr. Nâzım beginning "Muhterem Kardeşlerimiz" and dated Paris, April 9, 1907/no. 278, *Muhaberat Kopyası*, 287–88.

322. Dr. Bahaeddin [Şakir] to S[alih] Borovac in Sarajevo, dated [Paris], March 29, 1906/no. 6, *Muhaberat Kopyası*, 10–11.

323. Dr. Bahaeddin [Şakir] to [Salih Borovac] beginning "Aziz Vatandaşımız" and dated [Paris], October 18, [1]906/no. 76, *Muhaberat Kopyası*, 128–29. The Young Turk press in general encouraged the Bosnian Muslims to learn and use Turkish, and it acclaimed all efforts to this end. See, for example, "*Behar* Mecmua-i Edebiyesi," *Tuna*, no. 204 [May 18, 1906], 4; and "Boşnakların Huruf-i Osmanîyeyi Kabul Eylemeleri," *Tuna*, no. 307 [September 21, 1907], 2–3.

324. See the letter of Dr. Bahaeddin [Şakir] and Dr. Nâzım to [Salih Borovac] beginning "Muhterem Vatandaşımız Efendim" and dated Paris, December 10, 1906/no. 227, *Muhaberat Kopyası*, 201.

325. See the letter of Dr. Bahaeddin [Şakir] in response beginning "Hamiyetperver Efendim" and dated [Paris], August 24, [1]907/no. 343, *Muhaberat Kopyası*, 388–89.

326. See, for example, his translations from Ahmed Refik's work on Tiryaki Hasan Pasha in *Srpski Književni Glasnik* 17, no. 3 (August 1, 1906), 213–25, and no. 4 (August 16, 1906), 273–87.

327. [Dr. Bahaeddin Şakir], "Agram [Zagreb] Darülfünûnu Talebesinden Refikimiz Mehmed Remzi Bey'e," dated [Paris], December 28, 1906/no. 239, *Muhaberat Kopyası*, 220.

328. See the letter of H[üsrev] Sami and Dr. Bahaeddin [Şakir] beginning "Muhterem Dindaşımız" and dated [Paris], January 16, 1908/no. 491, *Kopye Defteri*, 108.

329. See, for example, Dr. Bahaeddin [Şakir]'s letter beginning "Aziz Vatandaş" and dated Paris, July 6, [1]907/no. 307, *Muhaberat Kopyası*, 340–41; and the letter of Dr. Bahaeddin [Şakir] beginning "Muhterem Kardeşimiz" and sent to a Bosnian Muslim introduced to the CPU by Salih Boravac, dated Paris, September 11, 1907/no. 367, *Muhaberat Kopyası*, 417.

330. He later published and translated works into and from Turkish, on subjects such as "Islamic morals" and "Panislamism and Panturkism." See Osman A[saf] Sokolović, "Pregled štampanih djela muslimana Bosne i Hercegovine na Srpsko-Hrvatskom jeziku od 1878–1948–III," *Glasnik Vrhovnog Islamskog Starješinstva* (1959), 8.

331. See, for example, the letter of Dr. Bahaeddin [Şakir] beginning "Muhterem Refikimiz Efendim" and dated Paris, September 11, [1]907/no. 366, *Muhaberat Kopyası*, 416.

332. See his letter to Bahaeddin Şakir dated Mostar, October 11, 1907, Private Papers of Bahaeddin Şakir. The CPU thanked him for his efforts. See Dr. Bahaeddin [Şakir] to [Salih Muhiddin Bakamović] beginning "Aziz ve Muhterem Vatandaşımız" and dated [Paris], November 10, 1907/no. 431, *Muhaberat Kopyası*, 499.

333. See the letter of Dr. Bahaeddin [Şakir] and Dr. Nâzım beginning "Aziz Vatandaşlarımız, Muhterem Kardeşlerimiz," undated [October 1906]/no. 179, *Muhaberat Kopyası*, 132–33. Bahaeddin Şakir sent a copy of the CPU regulations to this organization and asked for a copy of their bylaws in return. A later letter sent to the same organization reveals that the CPU did not receive a response. See Dr. Bahaeddin [Şakir] and Dr. Nâzım, "Bosna Şübban-ı İslâmiyesi Hey'et-i Muhteremesi'ne," dated [Paris], February 11, 1907/no. 261, *Muhaberat Kopyası*, 256.

334. See Ibrahim Kemura, *Uloga "Gajreta" u društvenom životu muslimana Bosne i Hercegovine, 1903–1941* (Sarajevo, 1986), 45; and idem, "Proglas muslimanske akademske omladine u Beču od 1907. godine," *Prilozi: Institut za Istoriju (Sarajevo)* 13 (1977), 334 ff.

335. Kemura, *Uloga "Gajreta,"* 45.

336. See "Bosna-Hersek Müslümanları," *Şûra-yı Ümmet*, no. 127, 2–3. Republished in "Bosna Hersek Müslümanları," *Balkan*, no. 335 [January 5, 1908], 1–2.

337. Ahmed Riza, "Pour 'Austroliser' la Bosnie-Herzégovine," *Mechveret Supplément Français*, no. 194 (December 1, 1907), 2–3.

338. See, for example, a letter from a Bosnian Muslim, sections of which were published in H. M., "Bir Cevab," *Tuna*, 398 [January 18, 1907], 1.

339. See, for example, Muhsin Rizvić, *Behar: književnoistoriska monografia* (Sarajevo, 1971), 361–62, 604. The pamphlet referred to on page 604, mistakenly attributed to Abdullah Cevdet, was originally written by Süleyman Nazif.

340. Dr. Bahaeddin [Şakir] to [Ahmed Saib] beginning "Muhterem Refikimiz Efendim Hazretleri" and dated May 21, [1]906/no. 15, *Muhaberat Kopyası*, 30–31.

341. See the letter from Dr. Bahaeddin [Şakir] and Dr. Nâzım to [Ahmed] Ferid, dated Paris, July 23, 1906/no. 46, *Muhaberat Kopyası*, 71.

342. Dr. Bahaeddin [Şakir] to [Mehmed Sa'id Halim Pasha], undated [November 1906]/no. 209, *Muhaberat Kopyası*, 162–63.

343. Mehmed Sa'id Halim Pasha to Bahaeddin Şakir and Dr. Nâzım, December 1, [1]906, Private Papers of Bahaeddin Şakir.

344. Dr. Bahaeddin [Şakir] and Dr. Nâzım to Mehmed Sa'id Halim Pasha, dated Paris, December 9, 1906/no. 222, *Muhaberat Kopyası*, 191–93.

345. Dr. Bahaeddin [Şakir] and Dr. Nâzım to [Ahmed] Ferid, dated Paris, December 12, 1906/no. 229, *Muhaberat Kopyası*, 204–5.

346. Ahmed Ferid to the CPU central committee, dated Egypt [Cairo], December 19, [1]906, Private Papers of Bahaeddin Şakir.

347. Dr. Bahaeddin [Şakir] to [Ahmed Ferid] beginning "Aziz Kardeşimiz" and dated Paris, January 11, 1907/no. 250, *Muhaberat Kopyası*, 232–33.

348. See, for example, "Mr. Ahmed Riza Bey," *Le Journal du Caire*, March 10, 1907. The CPU decided to publish a note of thanks in *Mechveret Supplément Français* because of this press coverage. See the letter of Dr. Bahaeddin [Şakir] and Dr. Nâzım to [Ahmed] Ferid, dated [Paris], March 6, 1907/no. 264, *Muhaberat Kopyası*, 261. For the note, see *Mechveret Supplement Français*, no. 185 (March 1, 1907), 1. A journal whose editor had close ties to Bahaeddin Şakir maintained that Ahmed Rıza went to Egypt "to reorganize the Cairo branch." See "Inostrannaia khronika," *Kaspii*, no. 52, 2. Bahaeddin Şakir and Dr. Nâzım merely stated that "Ahmed Rıza Bey went to Egypt for businesses related to the committee. He will be absent for a month." See their letter to Halil Halid, dated [Paris], February 7, [1]907/ no. 258, *Muhaberat Kopyası*, 253. See also the postscript in the letter from Dr. Bahaeddin [Şakir] and Dr. Nâzım to [İbrahim Temo] beginning "Azizimiz Efendim" and dated [Paris], February 1, [1]907/no. 253, AQSh, 19/59//975/20. The visit and Ahmed Rıza's initiatives caused uneasiness in Istanbul. See Gazi Ahmed Muhtar Pasha's dispatch to the Grand Vizier's office [November 24, 1907]/no. 214, BBA–BEO/Vilâyât-ı Muhtare ve Mümtaze Kalemine Mahsus Yevmiye Defteri, 931–85/5.

349. See the draft letter of Bahaeddin Şakir to Yusuf İzzeddin Efendi, undated [April 1907], Private Papers of Bahaeddin Şakir.

350. "İlk Meclisi Mebusan Reisi Ahmet Rıza Beyin Hatıraları (20): Doktor Bahaeddin Şakir ve doktor Nâzım Beyler," *Cumhuriyet*, February 14, 1950.

351. Note dated [February 4, 1908], and sent to the Grand Vizier's office, DWQ, Sijillāt ʿĀbidīn-Turkī-Şādir talagrāfāt, S/5/52/10, folio 130. The CPU officially applied to the khedive and demanded financial support. See the CPU central committee to the khedive, dated [Paris], October 30, 1906/no. 188, *Muhaberat Kopyası*, 147. The khedive told the sultan—who got wind of Ahmed Rıza's and Mehmed Saʿid Halim Pasha's activities—that they would not accomplish anything serious. See the khedive's dispatch to the First Chamberlain's office, dated [April 3, 1907], BBA–YEE, 30/1568/51/78.

352. Muḥammad Rashīd Riḍā, "Rafīq al-ʿAẓm," in *Majmūʿat athār Rafīq Bak al-ʿAẓm* 1, vi. Ahmed Rıza denied the allegation and stated the following: "Our committee is Ottoman, its bylaws do not distinguish between a Turk and a non-Turk. Its laws are just like the laws of Abdülhamid, and had Sultan Abdülhamid implemented the laws of the state I would not allow myself or anyone else to change the government." Rashīd Riḍā further maintained that they had decided to work cooperatively but independently.

353. See the letter of Dr. [Bahaeddin Şakir] beginning "Muhterem Vatandaşımız" and dated [Paris], February 27, 1908/no. 530, *Kopye Defteri*, 181.

354. Dr. Bahaeddin [Şakir] to Mehmed Efendi, dated Paris, July 6, [1]907/no. 309, *Muhaberat Kopyası*, 343.

355. According to a marginal note written on the letter that Bahaeddin Şakir had sent to Reşid Sadi, the latter "kindly refused the offer." See Dr. Bahaeddin [Şakir] and Dr. Nâzım to [Reşid Sadi] beginning "Hamiyetperver Efendimiz" and dated Paris, October 24, 1906/ no. 180, *Muhaberat Kopyası*, 134–35.

356. Dr. Bahaeddin [Şakir] and Dr. Nâzım to [Halil] Halid, dated [Paris], December 26, 1906/no. 235, *Muhaberat Kopyası*, 214.

357. [Dr. Bahaeddin Şakir] to Mustafa Refik in Berlin, undated [November 1906]/ no. 210, *Muhaberat Kopyası*, 164–65. The last page of this letter did not appear in the copy register.

358. Dr. Bahaeddin [Şakir] and Dr. Nâzım to [Halil] Halid, dated [Paris], December 26, 1906/no. 235, *Muhaberat Kopyası*, 214–15.

359. Dr. Bahaeddin [Şakir] and Dr. Nâzım to "Mustafa Refik in Berlin," undated [March 1907]/no. 267, *Muhaberat Kopyası*, 267.

360. Bahaeddin Şakir confessed this fact to İbrahim Temo. See Dr. Bahaeddin [Şakir] to [İbrahim Temo], dated [Paris], November 23, 1906/no. 212, *Muhaberat Kopyası*, 167–68. Dr. Nâzım maintained in his memoirs that "the first branch in Istanbul was founded in early October 1322 [mid-October 1906]." See "İttihad ve Terakki Cemiyet-i Muhteremesi'nin 10

Temmuz'dan Evveline Aid Tertibat ve İcraatına Dair: İzmir'de Tütüncü Yakub Ağa," *İnkılâb*, no. 9 [September 18, 1909], 133.

361. Silistireli Hacı İbrahim Paşazâde Hamdi to the CUP through Dr. Baha[eddin Şakir], Istanbul, September [14, 1908], Private Papers of Bahaeddin Şakir.

362. Ibid.

363. See Dr. Bahaeddin [Şakir] and Dr. Nâzım to [İbrahim Temo] beginning "Azizimiz Efendim" and dated [Paris], February 1, [1]907/no. 253, in AQSh, 19/59//975/20, and in *Muhaberat Kopyası*, 240–41.

364. See B[ahaeddin] Ş[akir], "Osmanlı İttihad ve Terakki Cemiyeti," *Bağçe*, no. [18], [September 9, 1908], 2; and Bahaeddin Şakir, "İkdam Muharriri Ali Kemal Efendi," *Şûra-yı Ümmet*, December 14, 1908.

365. *Şûra-yı Ümmet-Ali Kemal Da'vası*, 46.

366. See Bahaeddin Şakir's draft letter to be sent to Yusuf İzzeddin Efendi. The document bears no date but must have been written upon Bahaeddin Şakir's return to Paris in May 1907, Private Papers of Bahaeddin Şakir. See also Dr. Bahaeddin [Şakir] to Ağabey [Silistireli Hacı İbrahim Paşazâde Hamdi], "the director of the first division of the Istanbul branch," dated [Paris], August 21, [1]907/no. 341, *Muhaberat Kopyası*, 383.

367. Ağabey [Silistireli Hacı İbrahim Paşazâde Hamdi] on behalf of the CPU Istanbul branch to the CPU Internal Affairs division in Paris, dated Istanbul [September 1, 1907]/ no. 1, Private Papers of Bahaeddin Şakir.

368. See the letter of Dr. Bahaeddin [Şakir] to the director of the CPU [Istanbul] branch, dated Paris, September 27, [1]907/no. 377, *Muhaberat Kopyası*, 431.

369. Ağabey [Silistireli Hacı İbrahim Paşazâde Hamdi], on behalf of the CPU Istanbul branch, to the CPU Internal Affairs division in Paris, dated Istanbul [September 1, 1907]/ no. 1, Private Papers of Bahaeddin Şakir.

370. Undated [August? 1907] letter signed by the three leading members of the CPU Istanbul branch and sent to Bahaeddin Şakir, Private Papers of Bahaeddin Şakir.

371. See the undated [August 21, 1907]/no. 339 letter of Dr. Bahaeddin [Şakir] beginning "Azizim Efendim," *Muhaberat Kopyası*, 380. See also [Dr. Bahaeddin Şakir] to the acting director of the CPU Lâzistan External branch, dated [Paris], August 23, 1907/no. 340, *Muhaberat Kopyası*, 382.

372. Undated [August? 1907] letter signed by the three leading members of the CPU Istanbul branch and sent to [Bahaeddin Şakir], Private Papers of Bahaeddin Şakir.

373. See the letter of Dr. Bahaeddin [Şakir] and Dr. Nâzım to an Armenian in Istanbul, beginning "Muhterem Vatandaşımız Efendim" and dated [Paris], March 27, 1907/no. 270, *Muhaberat Kopyası*, 270–71.

374. See the letter of Dr. Bahaeddin [Şakir] beginning "Aziz Vatandaşımız" and dated Paris, July 7, [1]907/no. 310, *Muhaberat Kopyası*, 345–46.

375. See the letter of Dr. Bahaeddin [Şakir] beginning "Muhterem ve Mu'azzez Refikimiz Efendim" and dated Paris, June 17, [1]907/no. 300, *Muhaberat Kopyası*, 328–29.

376. See the letter of Dr. Bahaeddin [Şakir] beginning "Azizim Efendim" and dated [Paris] June 4, [1]907/no. 295, *Muhaberat Kopyası*, 311–12.

377. See the letter of Dr. Bahaeddin [Şakir] beginning "Aziz Vatandaşımız" and dated Paris, November 27, [1]907/no. 474 (duplicate number), *Kopye Defteri*, 12–13.

378. See [Dr. Nâzım] to Edhem Bey, dated [Paris], May 4, 1907/no. 290, *Muhaberat Kopyası*, 304; and Edhem Bey to Dr. Nâzım [Istanbul, May 20, 1907], Private Papers of Bahaeddin Şakir.

379. Dr. Bahaeddin [Şakir] to [Talât Bey] beginning "Refik-i Mu'azzezimiz Efendim," and undated [November 1907]/no. 433, *Kopye Defteri*, 7. See also "İttihad ve Terakki Cemiyet-i Muhteremesi'nin 10 Temmuz'dan Evveline Aid Tertibat ve İcraatına Dair: İzmir'de Tütüncü Yakub Ağa," *İnkılab*, no. 8 [September 11, 1909], 122.

380. See the letter of Dr. Bahaeddin [Şakir] beginning "Aziz Refikimiz" and undated [December 1907]/no. 459, *Kopye Defteri*, 47; H[üsrev] Sami and Dr. Bahaeddin [Şakir] to the director of the CPU Istanbul branch, dated [Paris], January 19, 1908/no. 488, *Kopye Defteri*, 102–4; and their undated letter [March 1908]/no. 545 to the director of the CPU Istanbul

branch, *Kopye Defteri*, 200. The central committee had informed the branch that "In the future you will be attached to the Internal Headquarters, though you will continue corresponding with us." See Dr. Bahaeddin [Şakir] to the director of the CPU Istanbul branch, undated
[November 1907]/no. 402, *Muhaberat Kopyası*, 475.

381. See, for example, Ahmed İhsan Tokgöz, "1908 İnkılâbında Eski Babıâli Yokuşu,"
Ülkü 5, no. 30 (August 1935), 406–7; and "Selim Sırrının İttihatçılığı," *Yakın Tarihimiz* 1,
no. 6 (April 5, 1962), 189.

382. See Kâzım Karabekir, *İttihat ve Terakki Cemiyeti, 1896–1909*, 306–7; and *Enver
Paşa'nın Anıları*, ed. Halil Erdoğan Cengiz (Istanbul, 1991), 88.

383. Dr. B. Server [Bahaeddin Şakir] to Vicdanî [Colonel İshak] and Mihrabî [Ali Necib],
dated Paris, March 15, [1]906/no. 1, *Muhaberat Kopyası*, 1–4.

384. Dr. Bahaeddin [Şakir] to [Colonel İshak], dated Paris, November 25, 1906/no. 221,
Muhaberat Kopyası, 189–90. The center held the seal and this letter until January 15, 1907,
because of the banishment of the branch's director, and forwarded the letter and seal enclosed
with a further letter and note written on the aforementioned date.

385. Dr. Bahaeddin [Şakir] and Dr. Nâzım to the members of the CPU Lâzistan branch
and the enclosure, dated [Paris], January 15, [1]907/no. 252, *Muhaberat Kopyası*, 239–40.

386. Unsigned letter by Ali Necib to Bahaeddin Şakir, Trabzon, December [22, 1906],
Private Papers of Bahaeddin Şakir.

387. X [Ali Necib] to Bahaeddin Şakir, undated [March 1907], Private Papers of Bahaeddin
Şakir.

388. See Governor Ziver Bey to the Grand Vizier's office, Trabzon [March 15, 1907]/
no. 2-176; [March 16, 1907]/no. 6-12; and [March 17, 1907]/no. 5-287, BBA–BEO/VGG(2):
Anadolu Vilâyâtı Telgrafı Gelen: 911; and BBA–BEO/Serasker Reft, 262-6/70; 11 [March
15, 1907]/225954.

389. X [Ali Necib] to Bahaeddin Şakir, undated [March 1907], Private Papers of
Bahaeddin Şakir. The French military attaché Delon suspected ties between the assassina-
tion and "l'esprit révolutionnaire" prevailing in the region, although he reiterated the rea-
sons given by First Lieutenant Naci Bey during his interrogation. See Delon's dispatch to the
French Ministry of War, March 16, 1907/no. 88, Archives du Ministère de la Guerre, E.M.A
et Attachés militaires, 7 N 1635. A Russian diplomatic report made a similar remark. See
G. Aliiev, "Iz istorii burzhuazno-revoliutsionnogo dvizheniia v Turstsii (konets XIX-nachalo
XX vv.)," in *Voprosy Turetskoi istorii-Turkije Tarikhi Meseleleri* (Baku, 1972), 66.

390. Dr. Bahaeddin [Şakir] and Dr. Nâzım to the CPU Lâzistan branch, undated [March
1907]/no. 269, *Muhaberat Kopyası*, 268–69.

391. See, for example, K.-J. Basmadjian, "Le Mouvement révolutionnaire en Asie Mineure,"
Revue du Monde Musulman 4, no. 4, 821; Pierre Quillard, "La peur de la liberté," *Pro Armenia*
7, no. 157 (May 5, 1907), 1088; and A. Le Chatelier, "Révolutions d'Orient," *Revue Bleue* 10,
no. 7 (August 15, 1908), 196.

392. Dr. Bahaeddin [Şakir] to the director of the CPU Lâzistan External branch, dated Paris,
March 24, 1907/no. 271, *Muhaberat Kopyası*, 272–73.

393. See the letter of Dr. Bahaeddin [Şakir] beginning "Muhterem Refikimiz" and dated
Paris, January 3, [1]908/no. 468, *Kopye Defteri*, 62; the letter of H[üsrev] Sami and Dr. Bahaeddin
[Şakir] beginning "Muhterem Efendim" and dated [Paris], February 26, 1908/no. 529, *Kopye
Defteri*, 180; and the letter of Dr. Bahaeddin [Şakir] beginning "Muhterem Vatandaşlar" and
dated [Paris], November 3, 1907/no. 405, *Muhaberat Kopyası*, 480.

394. Dr. Bahaeddin [Şakir] to the director of the CPU Lâzistan branch, dated Paris, July
30, 1907/no. 332, *Muhaberat Kopyası*, 372.

395. See [Dr. Bahaeddin Şakir] to the acting director of the CPU Lâzistan External branch,
dated [Paris], August 23, 1907/no. 340, *Muhaberat Kopyası*, 382.

396. Dr. Bahaeddin [Şakir] to the director of the CPU Lâzistan External branch, dated Paris,
October 14, [1]907/no. 384, *Muhaberat Kopyası*, 441–42.

397. The identification numbers given by the CPU central committee reveal the identities
of the members of this merged branch. They were Hasan Hüsni, Mehmed Kâmil, Tevfik Fikri
(secretary of the branch), Osman Nuri, Mustafa Midhat, İlyas Remzi, and Tevfik Fikret. See

Dr. Bahaeddin [Şakir] to the director of the CPU Lâzistan External branch, dated Paris, November 3, 1907/no. 406, *Muhaberat Kopyası*, 482. One of the members, Osman Nuri, was the assistant governor of the district of Of. See *1326 Sene-i Hicriyesine Mahsus Salnâme-i Devlet-i Aliyye-i Osmaniye* 64 (Istanbul 1323 [1908]), 882.

398. Dr. Bahaeddin [Şakir] to the director of the CPU Lâzistan External branch, dated Paris, November 3, 1907/no. 406, *Muhaberat Kopyası*, 481–82.

399. See the letter of H[üsrev] Sami and Dr. Bahaeddin [Şakir] beginning "Aziz Vatanperverler" and dated [Paris], March 7, 1908/no. 547, *Kopye Defteri*, 203.

400. See, for example, the letter of Dr. Bahaeddin [Şakir] beginning "Muhterem Vatanperver Kardeşimiz," undated [June 1907]/no. 296, and sent to Of, *Muhaberat Kopyası*, 313–18; and [Dr. Bahaeddin Şakir] to the acting director of the CPU Lâzistan External branch, dated [Paris], August 23, 1907/no. 340, *Muhaberat Kopyası*, 382.

401. Dr. Bahaeddin [Şakir] and Dr. Nâzım to the CPU Lâzistan branch, undated [March 1907]/no. 269, *Muhaberat Kopyası*, 269.

402. See the letter of Dr. Bahaeddin [Şakir] beginning "Aziz Vatandaş" and dated Paris, January 1, [1]907/no. 240, *Muhaberat Kopyası*, 221–22.

403. Dr. Bahaeddin [Şakir] to the Liberal party [Committee] of Izmir, dated [Paris], February 3, [1]907/no. 255, *Muhaberat Kopyası*, 245.

404. Ibid., 247.

405. See the letter of Dr. Bahaeddin [Şakir] beginning "Vatanperver Efendim," undated [July 1907]/no. 329, *Muhaberat Kopyası*, 368.

406. See the letter of Dr. Bahaeddin [Şakir] beginning "Aziz Refiklerimiz" and dated Paris, October 31, 1907/no. 398, *Muhaberat Kopyası*, 471.

407. See the letter of Dr. Bahaeddin [Şakir] beginning "Aziz Vatandaşımız" and dated Paris, November 27, [1]907/no. 474 (duplicate number), *Kopye Defteri*, 12; the letter of Dr. Bahaeddin [Şakir] beginning "Aziz Refikimiz" and undated [December 1907]/no. 459, *Kopye Defteri*, 47; the unsigned and undated letter [January 1908]/no. 473, *Kopye Defteri*, 73; and the letter of H[üsrev] Sami and Dr. Bahaeddin [Şakir] to Hacı Bey in Varna, dated [Paris], January 16, 1908/no. 487, *Kopye Defteri*, 101.

408. See the letter of H[üsrev] Sami and Dr. Bahaeddin [Şakir] beginning "Aziz Refikimiz" and dated January 29, 1908/no. 503, *Kopye Defteri*, 134.

409. Dr. [Bahaeddin Şakir] to [Mesʿud Remzi] beginning "Muhterem ve Gayûr Vatandaşımız" and dated [Paris, November 27, 1907]/no. 443, *Kopye Defteri*, 30.

410. He was made an inspector of education of the Province of Beirut after the Young Turk Revolution of 1908. See *Salnâme-i Devlet-i Aliyye-i Osmaniye* 65 (1326 Maliye [1910]), 592.

411. See M[ehmed] Macid to Bahaeddin [Şakir] and [Dr.] Nâzım, Canea, April 20, 1907, and April 27, [1]907, Private Papers of Bahaeddin Şakir; and Dr. Bahaeddin [Şakir] to [Mehmed Macid] beginning "Azizim Efendim" and dated Paris, July 30, 1907/no. 331, *Muhaberat Kopyası*, 371.

412. Dr. Bahaeddin [Şakir], "Şübban-ı Vatandan Beyrut'da M[esʿud Remzi] Efendi'ye," dated Paris, July 6, [1]907/no. 306, *Muhaberat Kopyası*, 339.

413. See, for example, Bir Osmanlı [Mesʿud Remzi], "Mekâtib: Beyrut, 25 Şubat [1]322," *Şûra-yı Ümmet*, no. 114 (May 1, 1907), 3–4; "Suriye Mektubları—2," *Şûra-yı Ümmet*, no. 116 (June 15, 1907), 6–8; and "Suriye Mektubları—3," *Şûra-yı Ümmet*, no. 119, 2–3.

414. Dr. Bahaeddin [Şakir] to [Mesʿud Remzi] beginning "Vatanperver Efendim" and dated Paris, July 21, 1907/no. 313, *Muhaberat Kopyası*, 352–54.

415. Mesʿud Remzi to the CPU Internal Affairs division, dated [Beirut], November 6, [1]907, Private Papers of Bahaeddin Şakir.

416. M[esʿud Remzi] to Bahaeddin Şakir, dated Beirut, December 25, [1]907, Private Papers of Bahaeddin Şakir.

417. See Dr. [Bahaeddin Şakir] to [Mesʿud Remzi] beginning "Muhterem ve Gayûr Vatandaşımız" and dated [Paris, November 27, 1907]/no. 443, *Kopye Defteri*, 30–31; and H[üsrev] Sami and Dr. Bahaeddin [Şakir] to [Mesʿud Remzi] beginning "Aziz Refikimiz" and dated Paris, January 16, 1908/no. 480, *Kopye Defteri*, 87–88. A missionary closely moni-

toring the events in Syria made the following comment: "There are no indications of the presence of the 'Young Turk' secret organization, but there is growing discontent with the present régime." See W. K. Eddy, "Islam in Syria and Palestine," in *The Mohammedan World of To-Day*, ed. S[amuel] M. Zwemer et al., (Chicago, 1906), 64.

418. One of them must be Salih Dilâver, a former medical student, who was exiled to Baghdad in 1905 and was praised by the CUP after his death in 1908. See "Vefat," *Şûra-yı Ümmet*, November 16, 1908.

419. See the CPU Baghdad branch to the "Internal Affairs division of the CPU central committee," dated Baghdad, January 27, [1907]/no. 3, Private Papers of Bahaeddin Şakir.

420. Ibid.

421. See [Dr. Bahaeddin Şakir] to the CPU Baghdad branch, dated [Paris], October 22, 1907/no. 388, *Muhaberat Kopyası*, 447–48; and Dr. Bahaeddin [Şakir] to the director of the CPU Baghdad branch, undated [November 1907]/no. 409, *Muhaberat Kopyası*, 488.

422. "Kürdler-Ermeniler," *İttihad ve Terakki*, August 25, 1908. The CPU central committee, too, recommended Ömer Naci to establish contacts with a *bey* of a Kurdish tribe and to benefit from his "mediation and protection." They advised Ömer Naci, however, not to disclose the real aim of the committee to the *bey*. See Dr. Bahaeddin [Şakir] to [Ömer] Naci, dated [Paris], March 16, [190]8/no. 558, *Kopye Defteri*, 232.

423. Dr. Bahaeddin [Şakir] and Dr. Nâzım to [İbrahim Rahmi Efendizâde] Hayri, dated Paris, June 2, 1906/no. 27, *Muhaberat Kopyası*, 48. Also, Bahaeddin Şakir assured the same person that they had "no relations with the Armenian committees." See Dr. Bahaeddin [Şakir] to İbrahim Rahmi Efendizâde Hayri, dated [Paris], May 10, [1]906/no. 14, *Muhaberat Kopyası*, 27.

424. See the letter of Dr. Bahaeddin [Şakir] beginning "Kafkasya'da Müslüman Kardeşlerimize: Aziz Kardeşlerimiz" and dated Paris, November 23, 1906/no. 215, *Muhaberat Kopyası*, 177.

425. Dr. Bahaeddin [Şakir] to the Liberal party [Committee] of Izmir, dated [Paris], February 3, [1]907/no. 255, *Muhaberat Kopyası*, 246.

426. See the letter of Dr. Bahaeddin [Şakir] and Dr. Nâzım beginning "Nur-i Ayn-ı İftiharımız," undated [February–March 1907]/no. 261, *Muhaberat Kopyası*, 257.

427. See the letter of Dr. Bahaeddin [Şakir] beginning "Vatandaşımız Efendim" and dated Paris, June 2, 1906/no. 30, *Muhaberat Kopyası*, 52. See also the letter of Dr. Bahaeddin [Şakir] and Dr. Nâzım to an Armenian in Istanbul beginning "Muhterem Vatandaşımız Efendim" and dated [Paris], March 27, 1907/no. 270, *Muhaberat Kopyası*, 270–71.

428. See the letter of Dr. Bahaeddin [Şakir] beginning "Muhterem Vatandaşımız" and dated Paris, September 3, 1907/no. 356, *Muhaberat Kopyası*, 404.

429. See the letter of Dr. Bahaeddin [Şakir] beginning "Aziz Vatandaşımız," dated [Paris], November 1, 1907/no. 399, and sent to an Armenian in the United States, *Muhaberat Kopyası*, 472. See also the letter of H[üsrev] Sami and Dr. Bahaeddin [Şakir] beginning "Gayretli Vatandaşımız" and dated [Paris], January 27, 1908/no. 494, *Kopye Defteri*, 112.

430. See the letter of Dr. Bahaeddin [Şakir] and Dr. Nâzım beginning "Aziz Vatandaşımız" and dated Paris, September 24, 1906/no. [?], *Muhaberat Kopyası*, 125–26.

431. See S. M., "Amerika'da Bir Ermeni Vatandaşımız[da]n Gelen Mektub: Vatan Nasıl Selâmetde Olur?" *Şûra-yı Ümmet*, no. 102, 4; and Mihran, "Mekâtib: Ermeni Vatandaşlarımızdan Bir Zât Tarafından," *Şûra-yı Ümmet*, no. 115 (June 1, 1907), 2–3. The second article was republished in "İslâm Matbu'atında," *İrşad*, no. 112 (June 15 [28], 1907), 3.

432. "İlk Meclisi Mebusan Reisi Ahmet Rıza Beyin Hatıraları (20): Doktor Bahaeddin Şakir ve doktor Nâzım Beyler," *Cumhuriyet*, February 14, 1950.

433. See the letter of H[üsrev] Sami and Dr. Bahaeddin [Şakir] to a Bulgarian beginning "Aziz Vatandaş" and dated March 14, [190]8/no. 556, *Kopye Defteri*, 222.

434. See the letter of Dr. Bahaeddin [Şakir] to [Nikola Manolov] beginning "Muhterem Vatandaş" and dated [September 6, 1907]/no. 361, *Muhaberat Kopyası*, 409. See also Dr. Bahaeddin [Şakir] to Nikola Manolov, undated [Paris, August 1907]/no. 349, *Muhaberat Kopyası*, 395–97; and the letter of H[üsrev] Sami and Dr. Bahaeddin [Şakir] beginning "Aziz Vatandaş" and dated [Paris], January 11, 1908/no. 475, *Kopye Defteri*, 76: "You should give information to those who do not know that the origins of the Turks, Bulgarians, Magyars,

and Tatars are the same. . . . Isn't it ugly that two Tatars, one who becomes Christian and the other Muslim, consider each other deadly foes?"

435. See the letter of Dr. Bahaeddin [Şakir] beginning "Aziz Vatandaşımız" and dated Paris, July 7, [1]907/no. 310, *Muhaberat Kopyası*, 345.

436. See the letter of Dr. Bahaeddin [Şakir] beginning "Muhterem Vatandaşlarımız" and dated Paris, September 3, 1907/no. 356, *Muhaberat Kopyası*, 404.

437. See the letter of Dr. Bahaeddin [Şakir] beginning "Aziz Kardeşierimiz" and dated Paris, October 27, 1906/no. 184, *Muhaberat Kopyası*, 140.

438. See the letter of Dr. Bahaeddin [Şakir] beginning "Aziz Vatandaşımız" and dated [Paris], December 13, 1907/no. 453, *Kopye Defteri*, 41.

439. See the letter of Dr. Bahaeddin [Şakir] and Dr. Nâzım to [Sami Paşazâde] Sezaî, dated Paris, August 6, 1906/no. 54, *Muhaberat Kopyası*, 82. See also "Rusya Türkleri," *Şûra-yı Ümmet*, no. 104, 1: "In our opinion the first concern of our press should be bridging the gap between the Ottoman Turks and the Turks in Russia, the two brothers having remained quite distant from each other."

440. "Ne Gerek Başına Ligue Var Olsun Türklük,"*Şûra-yı Ümmet*, no. 116, 4-5. See also "Matbu'at-ı İslâmiye: *İrşad*'dan," *Şûra-yı Ümmet*, no. 113 (April 15, 1907), 1.

441. See the undated [October 1906] and unnumbered letter of [Dr. Bahaeddin Şakir] to the Muslims in the Caucasus, *Muhaberat Kopyası*, 122. The CPU acclaimed the Caucasian Muslims' acceptance of this proposition. See the letter of Dr. Bahaeddin [Şakir] beginning "Kafkasya'da Müslüman Kardeşlerimize: Aziz Kardeşlerimiz" and dated Paris, November 23, 1906/no. 215, *Muhaberat Kopyası*, 176. See also "Tatarlarda Terakki," *Şûra-yı Ümmet*, no. 91, 2; "*Vakit* Gazetesi," *Şûra-yı Ümmet*, no. 106 (December 15, 1906), 4; and "Lisan Bahsi," *Tuna*, no. 213 [May 30, 1906], 3–4.

442. See "Matbu'at-ı İslâmiye," *Şûra-yı Ümmet*, no. 106, 3.

443. "Hıristiyanlardan Asker Almağa Dair," *Şûra-yı Ümmet*, nos. 96–97 (August 1, 1906), 3. See also "Kim Hükûmet Ediyor?" *Şûra-yı Ümmet*, no. 101, 1.

444. See the letter of Dr. Bahaeddin [Şakir] beginning "Devletlû Efendim Hazretleri" and dated Paris, November 3, 1907/no. 407, *Muhaberat Kopyası*, 483–85. For the employment of similar language, see the letter of Dr. Bahaeddin [Şakir] beginning "Muhterem Vatanperver Kardeşimiz," undated [June 1907]/no. 296, and sent to Of, *Muhaberat Kopyası*, 313–18.

445. See the letter of Dr. Bahaeddin [Şakir] beginning "Muhterem Dindaşımız" and dated Paris, January 3, 1907 [1908]/no. 464, *Kopye Defteri*, 56.

446. See "Ulemâmızın Nazar-ı Dikkat ve Himmetine," *Şûra-yı Ümmet*, no. 118 (July 15, 1907), 1–2; and "*Şûra-yı Ümmet*," *Şûra-yı Ümmet*, no. 126 (December 1, 1907), 3.

447. See the letter of Dr. Bahaeddin [Şakir] beginning "Vatanperver Biraderimiz" and dated [Paris], April 2, 1906/no. 7, *Muhaberat Kopyası*, 12.

448. See the letter of Dr. Bahaeddin [Şakir] to [Şerif Pasha, the Ottoman ambassador to Sweden], beginning "Pişgâh-ı Vatanperverânelerine: Muhterem Vatandaşımız Efendimiz Hazretleri" and dated Paris, November 9, 1907/no. 415, in Şerif Paşa, *Şûra-yı Ümmet yahud Numûne-i Denaet* (Paris, 1909), 8. The letter numbered 415 in the copy register (*Muhaberat Kopyası*, 495–96) does not fully correspond with this letter.

449. See the letter of Dr. Bahaeddin [Şakir] beginning "Muhterem Vatanperver Efendim," undated [December 1907]/no. 449, *Kopye Defteri*, 36–37.

450. See the letter of H[üsrev] Sami and Dr. Bahaeddin [Şakir] beginning "Aziz Birader" and dated [Paris], February 6, 1908/no. 509, *Kopye Defteri*, 143–44.

451. See the letter of H[üsrev] Sami and Dr. Bahaeddin [Şakir] to Sâî [Talât] Bey, dated [Paris], March 23, [1908]/no. 562–13, *Kopye Defteri*, 239–41.

452. See the letter of H[üsrev] Sami and Dr. Bahaeddin [Şakir] beginning "Aziz Refikimiz" and dated [Paris], March 28, [190]8/no. 568, *Kopye Defteri*, 248. For praise of the "working class," see Lâ [Yusuf Akçura], "Rusya İhtilâline Dair," *Şûra-yı Ümmet*, no. 82 (September 14, 1905), 3.

453. See Osmanlı Terakki ve İttihad Cemiyeti'nin Köylü Fırkası, "Ey Köylü Kardeşlerimiz, Ey Hemşehrilerimiz!" *Feyz-i Hürriyet*, no. 1 [August 17, 1908], 2–3. For similar themes, see

also the CPU appeal distributed in Serres during the revolution, enclosed with Semenov to Paprikov, Serres, July 11 [24], 1908/no. 406, TsDA, F. 176, op. 2, a.e. 96, 125.

454. See the letter of H[üsrev] Sami and Dr. Bahaeddin [Şakir] beginning "Muhterem Efendim" and dated [Paris], March 28, [190]8/no. 567, *Kopye Defteri*, 247.

455. See, for example, the letter of N. Bahaeddin Şakir dated Paris, April 8, [1]906/no. 8, *Muhaberat Kopyası*, 15.

456. See the letter of [Dr. Bahaeddin Şakir] to one of the CPU sympathizers in Larnaca beginning "Vatanperver Efendim," undated [November 1907]/no. 410, *Muhaberat Kopyası*, 489.

457. See the letter of Dr. Bahaeddin [Şakir] to [Şerif Pasha], beginning "Pişgâh-ı Vatanperverânelerine: Muhterem Vatandaşımız Efendimiz Hazretleri" and dated Paris, November 2, 1907/no. 415, *Muhaberat Kopyası*, 495–96.

458. See the CPU central committee to the Heir Apparent Mehmed Reşad Efendi, undated [September 1906], *Muhaberat Kopyası*, 111–12; to Yusuf İzzeddin Efendi, undated [September 1906], *Muhaberat Kopyası*, 113; and to the khedive, dated [Paris], October 30, 1906/ no. 188, *Muhaberat Kopyası*, 147.

459. See the letter of Dr. Bahaeddin [Şakir] beginning "Kafkasya'da Müslüman Kardeşlerimize: Aziz Kardeşlerimiz" and dated Paris, November 23, 1906/no. 215, *Muhaberat Kopyası*, 179.

460. See the letter of [Dr. Bahaeddin Şakir] beginning "Aziz İhvânımız" and dated Paris, August 31, 1906/no. 67, *Muhaberat Kopyası*, 104.

461. See the letter of Dr. Bahaeddin [Şakir] beginning "Kafkasya'da Müslüman Kardeşlerimize: Aziz Kardeşlerimiz" and dated Paris, November 23, 1906/no. 215, *Muhaberat Kopyası*, 179.

462. See the letter of Dr. Bahaeddin [Şakir] beginning "Aziz Kardeşlerimiz" and dated Paris, October 27, 1906/no. 184, *Muhaberat Kopyası*, 140.

463. Dr. Bahaeddin [Şakir] to İbrahim Rahmi Efendizâde Hayri, dated [Paris], May 10, 1906/no. 14, *Muhaberat Kopyası*, 27.

464. Dr. Bahaeddin [Şakir] and Dr. Nâzım, "Doktor . . . Bey'e," beginning "Mîr-i Muhterem" and dated Paris, April 19, 1907/no. 279, *Muhaberat Kopyası*, 289.

465. "Dinleyiniz!" *Şûra-yı Ümmet*, no. 119, 1. See also "Kim Hükûmet Ediyor?" *Şûra-yı Ümmet*, no. 81 (August 31, 1905), 1; "Dünya'da Mevki'imiz," *Şûra-yı Ümmet*, no. 91, 1; "Yarın," *Şûra-yı Ümmet*, no. 102, 2; and "Hypocrisies européennes," *Mechveret Supplément Français*, no. 190 (August 1, 1907), 2. Glubb Pasha, a witness of the Young Turks in power, made an astute comment on the "outstanding characteristics of the Young Turk mentality," and although he based his comment on the actions of the Young Turks in power, his observation can also be applied to the CPU's opinion on European powers: "After so glorious a past, the predatory attempts of the European powers to partition Turkey between them filled the Young Turks with bitterness. The constant threats and intrigues with which the European governments endeavored to circumvent one another and to gain concessions at the expense of Turkey's weakness, convinced the Young Turks that Europe was grasping, unscrupulous and materialistic." See John Bagot Glubb, *Britain and the Arabs: A Study of Fifty Years, 1908 to 1958* (London, 1959), 45.

466. "Zayâ'-i Elîm," *Şûra-yı Ümmet*, no. 131 (March 15, 1908), 2.

467. Ahmed Riza, "Pour civiliser les musulmans," *Mechveret Supplément Français*, no. 175 (May 1, 1906), 3. See also "İmtiyazât-ı Ecnebiye," *Şûra-yı Ümmet*, no. 98, 2–4.

468. Ignotus, "Boniment nouveau," *Mechveret Supplément Français*, no. 174, 1–2.

469. Ahmed Riza, "Les anarchistes d'en haut," *Mechveret Supplément Français*, no. 177, 2–3.

470. O., "Medeniyet Kargaları," *Şûra-yı Ümmet*, no. 98, 1–2; and O., "Les corbeaux de la civilisation," *Mechveret Supplément Français*, no. 177, 5–6.

471. Doktor S[er]v[er] [Bahaeddin Şakir], "Size Ey Sevgili Millet, Size Ey Kari'," *Şûra-yı Ümmet*, no. 116, 3.

472. See the letter of Dr. Bahaeddin [Şakir] beginning "Aziz Vatandaş," undated [August 24, 1907]/no. 344, *Muhaberat Kopyası*, 390.

473. Ahmed Rıza, "Frenk Meta'ı Almayalım," *Şûra-yı Ümmet*, no. 135 (June 1, 1908), 3.

474. Bahaeddin Şakir, "Yirminci Asırda Ehl-i Salib ve İngiltere Dostluğu!" *Şûra-yı Ümmet*, no. 132 (April 1, 1908), 2–3. See also "Makedonya Mes'elesi," *Şûra-yı Ümmet*, no. 134, 1.

475. See "Ecnebiler Bizim İçün Ne Diyorlar [?]"*Şûra-yı Ümmet*, no. 111, 4. For the importance attached to the matter, see the letter of Dr. Bahaeddin [Şakir] and Dr. Nâzım to [Ahmed] Ferid, dated [Paris], March 6, 1907/no. 264, *Muhaberat Kopyası*, 261. The CPU organs also republished articles that had originally been published in *İrşad*, maintaining that in the eyes of the Christians, Muslims were no different from African savages. See "Yine Mezkûr Gazete'den," *Şûra-yı Ümmet*, no. 113, 2.

476. Ahmed Riza, "Xénophobie," *Mechveret Supplément Français*, no. 173 (March 1, 1906), 7.

477. "*Şûra-yı Ümmet,*" *Şûra-yı Ümmet*, no. 107 (January 1, 1906 [1907]), 4.

478. "Le Protectorat catholique," *Mechveret Supplément Français*, no. 172 (February 1, 1906), 3–4. For further criticism of the French policy toward the Ottoman Empire, see "Religion ou politique," *Mechveret Supplément Français*, no. 175, 5–6.

479. Mahmoud, "Le Péril slave," *Mechveret Supplément Français*, no. 173, 3–4.

480. O., "Medeniyet Kargaları," *Şûra-yı Ümmet*, no. 98, 1–2

481. See the letters of Dr. Bahaeddin [Şakir] and Dr. Nâzım, beginning "Aziz Vatandaşımız" and dated [Paris], November 7, 1906/no. 206, *Muhaberat Kopyası*, 157–58; and beginning "Muhterem Vatandaşımız" and dated Paris, November 12, 1906/no. 207, *Muhaberat Kopyası*, 159.

482. See the undated [Paris, February 1907]/no. 265 letter of Dr. Bahaeddin [Şakir] to the director of the CPU Kazanlŭk branch, *Muhaberat Kopyası*, 264.

483. In a letter that was sent to the Anjuman-i Millī-i Tabrīz, the CPU portrayed England and Russia as "the eternal and real enemies of all Muslim nations." See the letter of Dr. Bahaeddin [Şakir] to the Anjuman-i Millī-i Tabrīz, dated [Paris], [November 16, 1907]/ no. 432, *Kopye Defteri*, 3.

484. See Dr. Bahaeddin [Şakir] to [Halil Halid], beginning "Muhterem Vatandaşımız Efendimiz" and dated [Paris], January 14, [1]907/no. 241, *Muhaberat Kopyası*, 223–24: "We request you to write an article, disguised as a letter coming from the country [Ottoman Empire], stating that the evil policies that have been carried out by England in the [last] 25 years are more hazardous than the devastation that the Russians caused by fighting for centuries."

485. See Lā Adrī [Halil Halid], "Londra'dan: Alman Dostluğu ve İngiliz Nifâkı," *Şûra-yı Ümmet*, no. 125 (November 15, 1907), 4; Bahaeddin Şakir, "Yirminci Asırda Ehl-i Salib ve İngiltere Dostluğu!" *Şûra-yı Ümmet*, no. 132, 2–3; and "Makedonya Mes'elesi," *Şûra-yı Ümmet*, no. 134, 1.

486. See, for example, Osman Ghaleb Bey, "L'Egypte et Lord Cromer," *Mechveret Supplément Français*, no. 187 (May 1, 1907), 1–2.

487. A[hmed] R[iza], "Le panislamisme," *Mechveret Supplément Français*, no. 179 (September 1, 1906), 3. See also "Grecs, Bulgares et l'Europe," *Mechveret Supplément Français*, no. 166 (August 1, 1905), 3; and "Solidarité musulmane," *Mechveret Supplément Français*, no. 171 (January 1, 1906), 6–7.

488. A[hmed] R[iza], "Le panislamisme," *Mechveret Supplément Français*, no. 179, 4.

489. See Dr. Bahaeddin [Şakir] to Ağabey [Silistireli Hacı İbrahim Paşazâde Hamdi], "the director of the first division of the Istanbul branch," dated [Paris], August 21, [1]907/no. 341, *Muhaberat Kopyası*, 384–85. The initiative came from Ahmed Rıza. Mahmūd Sālim also played a significant role in this undertaking. See "La Fraternité musulmane à Paris," *Bulletin de la Société Endjouman Terekki-Islam*, nos. 7–9 (October–December 1913), 373. Doctor Ḥusayn Pīrnia, the son of the well-known constitutionalist Muaẓid al-Salṭanah, writes that "his father was in direct contact with the Young Turks and worked with the nationalists and freedom-lovers of the Ottoman Empire, Iran, Egypt, and Morocco to create the organization named La Fraternité Musulmane." See *Mubarazah bā Muḥammad ʿAlī Shāh: asnādī az fa ʿaliyatˀhā-yi azādīkhvāhan-i Irān dar Urūpā va Istānbūl*, ed. Iraj Afshār (Tehran, 1359 [1980–81]), 2–3. Until the Young Turk Revolution of 1908, the CPU had a firm grip over the organization.

490. See "'Fraternité musulmane,'" *Mechveret Supplément Français*, no. 190, 2–3; "Uhuvvet-i İslâmiye Cemiyeti," *Şûra-yı Ümmet*, no. 122, 4; and "Fraternité musulmane," *Re-*

vue du Monde Musulman 3, no. 9 (August–September 1907), 159–60. A copy of the bylaws written both in French and Turkish is in AN 17/AS/23/dr 2.

491. See the letter of Dr. Bahaeddin [Şakir] and Dr. Nâzım beginning "Muhterem Efendim Hazretleri," undated [March 1907]/no. 266, *Muhaberat Kopyası*, 266.

492. For the CPU's encouragement of the Muslims in the Caucasus, see the letter of Dr. Bahaeddin [Şakir] beginning "Muhterem Kardaşlar" and dated [Paris], September 23, 1907/no. 372, *Muhaberat Kopyası*, 426. It seems that the Caucasian Muslims promised support for this new organization. See the letter of Dr. Bahaeddin [Şakir] beginning "Muhterem Din Karındaşlarımız" and dated Paris, January 3, 1907[1908]/no. 469, *Kopye Defteri*, 67. For the encouragement of the Bosnian Muslims, see the letter of H[üsrev] Sami and Dr. Bahaeddin [Şakir] beginning "Azizim" and dated [Paris], March [?], [190]8/no. 563, *Kopye Defteri*, 243–44.

493. See the letter of Dr. Bahaeddin [Şakir] beginning "İsmetlû Hanım Efendi Hazretleri," sent to a woman in Russia, dated Paris, December 9, 1907/no. 446, *Kopye Defteri*, 33.

494. See, for example, Ahmed Riza, "A quelque chose malheur est bon," *Mechveret Supplément Français*, no. 176 (June 1, 1906), 5.

495. See the CPU central committee to the Iranian embassies in Paris and Istanbul, and to the Speaker of the Iranian Parliament, dated [Paris], August 18, 1907/no. 337, *Muhaberat Kopyası*, 378. A Persian translation was given in "Savād-i maktūbīst kih az ṭaraf-i Hay'at-i Markaziya-i Jamʿiyat-i Ittihād va Taraqqī-i ʿUs̱māniyyah ziyad bih Majlis-i Shūrāy-i Millī-i Irān," *Musāvāt*, no. 1, 7–8.

496. See Osmanlı Terakki ve İttihad Cemiyeti, "Asker Kardaşlarımıza" [1907]. One-page appeal. Republished in *Haftalık Şûra-yı Ümmet*, no. 206 [February 3, 1910], 7–8.

497. See the letter of Dr. Bahaeddin [Şakir] to the Anjuman-i Millī-i Tabrīz, dated [Paris, November 16, 1907]/no. 432, *Kopye Defteri*, 1–4.

498. For his own account, see Ö[mer] Naci, "İran İnkılâbı Hatırâlarından," *Bağçe*, no. 42 [June 22, 1909], 244–45; and idem, "İran İnkılâbı Hatırâlarından—2: İlk Tevkif," *Bağçe*, no. 45 [July 13, 1909], 292. See also *Şûra-yı Ümmet-Ali Kemal Daʿvası*, 88–89; Rasim Haşmet, "Ö[mer] Naci," *Bağçe*, no. 24 [January 12, 1909] 8–9; "İran," *Bağçe*, no. 26 [January 26, 1909], 26; and Fethi Tevetoğlu, *Ömer Naci* (Istanbul, 1973), 96–103.

499. [Bahaeddin Şakir], "Teşkilât ve Neşriyâtın Lüzûm ve Faidesi," *Şûra-yı Ümmet*, no. 95, 2.

500. See, for example, *Lâklâk*, no. 4 (May 15, 1907), 2.

501. See "Neşriyât-ı Cedîde," *Şûra-yı Ümmet*, no. 115 (June 1, 1907), 4.

502. See, for example, Dr. Bahaeddin [Şakir] to the CPU Balchik branch, dated [Paris], September 6, 1907/no. 360, *Muhaberat Kopyası*, 408; and Ahmed Lütfi İbraki, the propaganda material distributor of the CPU Canea branch, to the administration of *Şûra-yı Ümmet* in Cairo, Canea, May 7, 1907, Private Papers of Bahaeddin Şakir.

503. "İlk Adım," *Şûra-yı Ümmet*, nos. 128 and 129 (February 1, 1908), 1.

504. "Kari'lerimize," *Şûra-yı Ümmet*, no. 123 (October 15, 1907), 1.

505. "İfade-i Mahsusa," *Şûra-yı Ümmet*, no. 133 (April 15, 1908), 1.

506. Dr. Bahaeddin [Şakir] to [Ahmed Ferid], beginning "Arkadaşımız Efendim" and dated Paris, June 4, 1906/no. 31, *Muhaberat Kopyası*, 53.

507. Dr. Bahaeddin [Şakir] to Talha Kemalî, dated Paris, June 4, 1907/no. 293, *Muhaberat Kopyası*, 309.

508. "Kari'lerimize," *Şûra-yı Ümmet*, no. 117 (June 1, 1907), 1. The CPU falsely claimed that the journal was being published in a place close to France.

509. See "Kari'lerimize," *Şûra-yı Ümmet*, no. 123, 1.

510. Dr. Bahaeddin [Şakir] to [Ahmed Ferid], beginning "Arkadaşımız Efendim" and dated Paris, June 4, 1906/no. 31, *Muhaberat Kopyası*, 53.

511. See the letter of Dr. Bahaeddin [Şakir] and Dr. Nâzım to Talha Kemalî, dated Paris, July 18, 1906/no. 39, *Muhaberat Kopyası*, 62.

512. See [Sami Paşazâde] Sezaî to Bahaeddin Şakir, Paris, March 11, [1]907, Private Papers of Bahaeddin Şakir. European sources thought that this was an independent organization. See Paul Fesch, *Constantinople aux derniers jours d'Abdul-Hamid* (Paris, 1907), 409–10.

513. See "İstanbul'dan," *Şûra-yı Ümmet*, no. 56 (July 29, 1904), 1; "Hanedân-ı Saltanat Tehlikede," *Şûra-yı Ümmet*, no. 58 (August 27, 1904), 1; "İzhar'ül-hakk lî-tenvîr'ül-halk," *Şûra-yı Ümmet*, no. 64 (November 23, 1904), 2; and "Succession au trône," *Mechveret Supplément Français*, no. 154 (August 15, 1904), 1–2.

514. See "Bir Teşebbüs-i Hainâne," *Şûra-yı Ümmet*, no. 89 (March 10, 1906), 1; "Bir Korkulu Rüya," *Şûra-yı Ümmet*, no. 90, 2; "Hérédité légitime," *Mechveret Supplément Français*, no. 173, 1; "Tebşir: Sultan Abdülhamid Hastadır!" *Şûra-yı Ümmet*, nos. 96–97, 1; "Maraz-ı Şâhâne," *Şûra-yı Ümmet*, no. 99, 1–2; "Abdülhamid'in Hastalığı, Verâset-i Saltanat," *Şûra-yı Ümmet*, no. 100 (September 15, 1906), 1–2; "Saltanat ve Hilâfet-i Osmaniye," *Şûra-yı Ümmet*, no. 102 (October 15, 1906), 1–2; "Artık Yeter," ibid., 3; and "İfade-i Kat'iye," *Şûra-yı Ümmet*, no. 107, 1.

515. See the letter of Dr. Bahaeddin [Şakir] and Dr. Nâzım to [Sami Paşazâde] Sezaî, dated Paris, August 13, 1906/no. 59, *Muhaberat Kopyası*, 95.

516. "Osmanlılar!" *Şûra-yı Ümmet*, no. 99, 1.

517. See "Sultan Mehmed Reşad Han," *Uhuvvet*, no. 121 [September 12, 1906], 2.

518. See the one-page appeal "Abdülhamid Ölüyor!" A copy of this manifesto is in AQSh, 19/60//819/7. The French supplement published a French translation, see "Proclamation," *Mechveret Supplément Français*, no. 181, November 1, 1906, 1–2. The CPU also informed the branches of the preparation of the appeal. See the letter of Dr. Bahaeddin [Şakir] and Dr. Nâzım beginning "Aziz Kardeşlerimiz" and dated Paris, [August], 27, 1906/no. 64, *Muhaberat Kopyası*, 100; Dr. Bahaeddin [Şakir] to Bedri Beyzâde İbrahim Et[h]em, dated Paris, August 27, 1906/no. 65, *Muhaberat Kopyası*, 101; and [Dr. Bahaeddin Şakir] to the director of the CPU Kazanlük branch, dated Paris, August 27, 1906/no. 66, *Muhaberat Kopyası*, 102.

519. Barclay to Grey, Pera, October 24, 1906/no. 216 (confidential), PRO/F.O. 371/155, file 36295.

520. This quotation is taken from the translation made by Harry Lamb, the first dragoman of the British Embassy in Istanbul. It was attached with Barclay to Grey, Pera, October 24, 1906/no. 216 (confidential), PRO/F.O. 371/155, file 36295.

521. For example, high-ranking officials sent letters to CPU members in Europe following the distribution of the appeal. See "Türkiya'da Verâset-i Saltanat Mes'elesi," *Tuna*, no. 330 [October 18, 1906], 1–2. See also "Mekâtib: 25 Teşrin-i evvel 1906," *Şûra-yı Ümmet*, no. 104 (November 30, 1906), 4.

522. See Dr. Bahaeddin [Şakir] to [Mehmed Sa'id Halim Pasha], undated [November 1906]/no. 209, *Muhaberat Kopyası*, 162. The Muslim press in Russia, too, praised the CPU because of this appeal. See "Türkiye," *İrşad*, no. 212, September 10 [23], 1906, 4.

523. Dr. Bahaeddin [Şakir] to [Ahmed] Ferid, dated Paris, November 30, 1906/no. 220, *Muhaberat Kopyası*, 187.

524. Ibid.

525. See the one-page appeal Osmanlı Terakki ve İttihad Cemiyeti, *Emr-i Şer'î ve Kanunî-De par le loi du Chéri et la loi civile* [1906], in Turkish and French. The French version also appeared in "Un Manifeste: de par le loi du Chéri et la loi civile," *Mechveret Supplément Français*, no. 182 (December 1, 1906), 1. An English translation is given in Argus Hamilton, *Problems of the Middle East* (London, 1909), 15–17. The CPU's claim was based on the *ḥadīth*s of the Prophet and the 393th and 1595th articles of the Ottoman civil code (*Mecelle*). [See Muslim ibn al-Ḥajjaj al-Qushayrī, *Ṣaḥīḥ Muslim* (Cairo, [1955–56]), 1250–53; Muwaffaq al-Dīn 'Abd Allāh ibn Ahmad ibn Qudāmah, *al-Mughnī* (Cairo, 1341 [1922–23]), 473–74; Abou Abdallah Mohammed ibn Ismaîl el-Bokhâri, *La recueil des Traditions mahométanes* 2 (Leiden, 1864), 186–87; *Mecelle-i Ahkâm-ı Adliyye* (Istanbul, 1308 [1890–91]), 108, 507–508; and Ali Haydar, *Dürer'ül-Hukkâm Şerh-i Mecellet'ül-ahkâm*, 2/1, *Şerh-i Kavâid-i Külliye*, *Kitab'ül-büyû* (Istanbul, 1310 [1892–93]), 1040–1042]; and 3/13 *Şerh-i Kitab'ül-ikrar* (Istanbul, 1314 [1896–97]), 442–446.] The *ḥadīth*s and the aforementioned articles of the Ottoman civil code, however, deal with private law, and their application to the succession problem seems inappropriate.

526. See Osmanlı Terakki ve İttihad Cemiyeti, "Emr-i Şer'î ve Kanunî," *Ahali*, no. 65 [January 11, 1907], 3.

527. See "Mekâtib: İstanbul'dan," *Şûra-yı Ümmet*, no. 105 (December 1, 1906), 3; "İstanbul 29 Kânûn-i evvel 1906," *Şûra-yı Ümmet*, 110 (March 1, 1907), 4; "Son Telgraflar," *Ahali*, no. 58 [January 4, 1907], 4; *Ahali*, no. 59 [January 5, 1907], 4; and *Ahali*, no. 62 [January 8, 1907], 4; and Cumberbatch to Barclay, Smyrna, January 18, 1907/no. 3 (confidential), enclosed with O'Conor to Grey, Constantinople, January 26, 1907/no. 62, PRO/F.O. 424/212.

528. Bahaeddin Şakir, "Bir Mes'ele-i Şa'ibe [Şer'îye] ve Tıb Kanunu," *Şûra-yı Ümmet*, no. 104, 2–3.

529. See, for example, *Neler Olacak!..* (Mısır [Cairo], 1314 [1896–97]), passim.

530. The appeal does not have a title and starts with the formula *Bismillâhirrahmanirrahim*, Private Papers of Bahaeddin Şakir. A copy can be found as enclosed with the 119th issue of *Şûra-yı Ümmet* in the collection of this journal at Dār al-Kutub (Cairo).

531. It seems that various CPU branches distributed this edited appeal throughout Macedonia during the revolution. See PRO/F.O. 371/544, file 25915; PRO/F.O. 294/46, ff. 125–27; PRO/F.O. 195/2297, ff. 810–12; TsDA, F. 331, op. 1, a.e. 334, 77–82; and *Krasnyi arkhiv* 6/43 (1930): *Turetskaia revoliutsiia 1908–1909 gg.* (Moscow, 1931), 18–20.

532. See, for example, "Köylü ve Şehirli Kardeşlerimize Mektub," *Şûra-yı Ümmet*, no. 122 (September 145, 1907), 4.

533. [Sami Paşazâde] Sezaî to Bahaeddin Şakir, September 10, 1907, Private Papers of Bahaeddin Şakir.

534. The appeal does not have a title and starts with the formula *Bismillâhirrahmanirrahim*, Private Papers of Bahaeddin Şakir.

535. See the letter of Dr. Bahaeddin [Şakir] beginning "Muhterem Vatanperver Kardeşimiz," undated [June 1907]/no. 296, and sent to Of, *Muhaberat Kopyası*, 317; and Dr. Bahaeddin [Şakir] to the director of the CPU Baltchik branch, dated [Paris], September 6, 1907/no. 360, *Muhaberat Kopyası*, 408.

536. See Osmanlı Terakki ve İttihad Cemiyeti Umur-i Dahiliye [Ömer Naci], *Hayye-ale-l-felâh* ([Paris], 1325 [1907]), 1–5: "O! Muslims take a lesson from your brothers, former compatriots who are wailing under the Christian fist. . . . Most of our mosques were destroyed and ruined, our ancestors' tombs were trampled. . . . In some places women were forced to convert to Christianity. . . . Our brothers in these lands are being humiliated and used for hard labor like animals. . . . If somebody slaps a Christian, an uproar will be created immediately. On the other hand the blood of thousands of Muslims is being shed, their properties are being snatched by the Christians, and the government is not lifting a finger. . . . In Kruševo the Bulgarians cut the veils of the Muslim women with daggers in the shape of a cross, they violated the Muslim women in front of their men; however, the government did not say a word, because Sultan Hamid and his government are the greatest enemies of Islam."

537. Osmanlı Terakki ve İttihad Cemiyeti Umur-i Dahiliye, "Namuslu Zabitlere" [1906?]. One-page handbill, Private Papers of Bahaeddin Şakir.

538. Osmanlı Terakki ve İttihad Cemiyeti Umur-i Dahiliye, "Askerlere" [1906?]. One-page handbill, Private Papers of Bahaeddin Şakir.

539. "By questioning them you would both obtain your rights and save the fatherland. Then both God and the Prophet will be pleased and your place will be heaven in both this and the next world. Come along my lions, may God help you!" Ibid.

540. "Makedonya Yunan Komitesine Dahil Olan Rumların İcra Etdikleri Tahlif Sureti," *Şûra-yı Ümmet*, no. 118, 4. The CPU organs on the other hand pointed to the nationalism of the Greeks as an example for the Turks to follow in Macedonia. See "Rumlardan İbret Alalım," *Şûra-yı Ümmet*, no. 108 (January 30, 1906 [1907]), 1.

541. See the letter of H[üsrev] Sami and Dr. Bahaeddin [Şakir] beginning "Faziletlû Efendim" and dated [Paris], March 20, [190]8/no. 560, *Kopye Defteri*, 235.

542. See "Un manifeste des Jeunes Turcs," *Le Courrier Européen*, no. 6 (February 9, 1906), 91–92; "Un manifeste Jeune-Turc," *L'Hellénisme* 3, no. 3 (March 1, 1906), 13; Pierre Quillard, "Un manifeste Jeune Turc," *Pro Armenia* 6, no. 130 (March 15, 1906), 870–72; and "Réformateurs Jeunes-Turcs," *L'Hellénisme* 3, no. 4 (April 1906), 15–16.

543. "Telgraflar," *İkdam*, August 17, 1908. According to a Baku-based daily Ahmed Rıza made a similar statement. See "Ahmed Rıza Bey," *Terakki* (2), August 7 [20], 1908.

544. "Telgraflar," *İkdam*, August 22, 1908.
545. "Osmanlı İttihad ve Terakki Cemiyeti'nden: Tashih-i Zehâb," *İkdam*, August 24, 1908.
546. We do not have circulation figures for *Mechveret Supplément Français*. A British confidential memorandum asserted a circulation between 400 and 500. This number, however, should be considered with caution, since the author attempted to downplay the importance of the CPU at the expense of Sabahaddin Bey's league. The author also claimed that *Terakki*'s circulation figure was between 4,000 and 5,000, which is absolutely out of the question. See the memorandum entitled "Comité Ottoman d'Union et de Progrès," PRO/F.O. 371/346, file 6840.
547. See Le Comité Ottoman d'Union et de Progrès, "Ce que nous voulons," *Mechveret Supplément Français*, no. 185, 1.
548. See "Circular addressed by the 'Comité Ottoman d'Union et de Progrès' at Paris to the Ambassadors of the Great Powers at Constantinople," enclosed with Barclay to Grey, Pera, October 28, 1906/no. 723 (confidential), PRO/F.O. 371/156, file 37169. See also "La succession du sultan et les Jeunes Turcs," *L'Hellénisme* 3, no. 10 (November 1, 1906), 13; and R., "Quand la bête sera morte: une circulaire des Jeunes Turcs aux Ambassades," *Pro Armenia* 6, no. 145 (November 5, 1906), 993. It was also distributed as an appeal. A copy of it is in AQSh, 19/60//166/22.
549. See, for example, the CPU circular dated Paris, January 16, 1907 and sent to the foreign ministers and ambassadors of the Great Powers in Istanbul. See PRO/F.O. 371/344, file 2026; and PRO/F.O. 371/344, file 3034. Also published in the French supplement. See "Un manifeste," *Mechveret Supplément Français*, no. 184 (February 1, 1907), 4.
550. See, for example, Ahmed Rıza's letter "pour le comité" to Sir Edward Grey, Paris, March 20, 1908, PRO/F.O. 371/540, file 9807.
551. "Sultan Yields to the British Demands," *The Daily Telegraph*, May 14, 1906.
552. See "Une rectification," *Mechveret Supplément Français*, no. 176 (June 1, 1906), 7; and "Tashihnâme," *Tuna*, no. 221, 1–2.
553. See, for example, the letter on the question of the order of succession originally published in *Le Figaro*, in "A propos du Prince héritier," *Mechveret Supplément Français*, no. 181, 2–3. It was praised by the Turkish press in Bulgaria and Turkic press in Russia. See "Verâset-i Saltanat," *Tuna*, no. 339 [October 29, 1906], 3.
554. "Makedonya Mes'elesi: Ne Bulgarların İstediği Gibi, Ne de 'Tittoni'nin Düşündüğü Gibi," *Şûra-yı Ümmet*, no. 112 (April 1, 1907), 4.

CHAPTER 7

1. See *infra* pp. 213ff.
2. Dr. Bahaeddin [Şakir] to the CPU Internal Headquarters, dated Paris, November 30, [1]907/no. 442–4, *Kopye Defteri*, 21. The fact that the first initiative was taken by Ahmed Rıza was underscored in another letter. See the letter of Dr. Bahaeddin [Şakir] beginning "Vatanperver Efendim Hazretleri" and dated [Paris], January 19, 1908/no. 502, *Kopye Defteri*, 132.
3. See, for example, "Abschrift einer Notiz der *Vossischen Zeitung*," in HHStA, PA, XII 197, Türkei, Varia 1908; Dikran Mardiros Bedikian, "The Silent Revolution in Turkey," *The World's Work* 16, no. 6 (October 1908), 10827; Melkon Krischtschian, "Türken und Armenier in Vergangenheit und Gegenwart," *Der Orient* 11, no. 3 (May–June 1929), 73–74; Kh [Hadzi] Z[agidullovich] Gabidullin, *Mladoturetskaia revoliutsiia: istoricheskie ocherki* (Moscow, 1936), 104; J. Michael Hagopian, "Hyphenated Nationalism: The Spirit of the Revolutionary Movement in Asia Minor and the Caucasus, 1896–1910" Ph.D. diss., Harvard University (1942), 263; Hratch Dasnabedian, *Histoire de la Fédération révolutionnaire arménienne, Dachnaktsoutioun, 1890–1924* (Milan, 1988), 87; and Richard G. Hovannisian, "The Armenian Question in the Ottoman Empire," *East European Quarterly* 6, no. 1 (March 1972), 17–18.

4. For the debate among the Dashnak leaders, see K[apriel] S[erope] Papazian, *Patriotism Perverted: A Discussion of the Deeds and the Misdeeds of the Armenian Revolutionary Federation, the So-Called Dashnagtzoutune* (Boston, 1934), 28–31. For the CPU's language against the Armenians, see, for example, M., "La Presse révolutionnaire arménienne et la Jeune-Turquie," *Mechveret Supplément Français*, no. 190 (August 1, 1907), 3–4.

5. All the information given here is taken from *Badmutiun S. D. Hncakean Kusaktsutiun* 1 (Beirut, 1962), 313–14.

6. Nitra [Harutiun Shahrigian], "Terakki Cemiyet-i Muhteremesi'ne," *Terakki*, no. 13 [September 1907], 1–6.

7. See [B. Andreasian], "Yeni Türkler, Panislâmizm," *İrşad*, no. 105 (June 6 [19], 1907), 2–3; and no. 106 (June 7 [20], 1907), 2–3.

8. Sabahaddin, "On Üçüncü *Terakki*'de Tenkidinizi Okurken," *Terakki*, no. 15 [January 1908], 1–9.

9. Sabahaddin Bey's statement in the footnote in *Terakki*, no. 13, 1.

10. "Türkiya Hıristiyanlarına Verebileceklerimiz," *Türk*, no. 180 (October 3, 1907), 1–2.

11. S[ami Paşazâde] Sezaî, "*Terakki*'de Tenkid," *Şûra-yı Ümmet*, no. 124 (October 31, 1907), 1–3.

12. *Badmutiun S. D. Hncakean Kusaktsutiun* 1, 314.

13. See the letter of H[üsrev] Sami and Dr. Bahaeddin [Şakir] beginning "Muhterem Arkadaşımız," dated [Paris], January [?], 1908/no. 483, and sent to a Muslim in Caucasia, *Kopye Defteri*, 92–93.

14. See André N. Mandelstam, *La Société des Nations et les puissances devant le Problème arménien* (Paris, 1925), 38; Mundji Bey, "The Regenerated Ottoman Empire," *The North American Review* 188, no. 634 (September 1908), 399. A Dashnak leader later made the following statement during an interview: "Both the Dashnaktzoutyoun and the Young Turks were revolutionary parties, and both wanted to see an end of Hamid's abuses. . . . If we could cooperate with the Young Turks . . . why shouldn't we try?" See Simon Vratzian [Kruzinian]'s interview in Sarkis Atamian, *The Armenian Community: The Historical Development of a Social and Historical Conflict* (New York, [1955]), 157.

15. Dr. Bahaeddin [Şakir] to the CPU Internal Headquarters, dated Paris, December 8, [1]907/no. 444–5, *Kopye Defteri*, 27.

16. "Pleads for Aid in War on Turkey," *The New York Times*, May 20, 1907. The importance of this event was also underscored by Armenian leaders such as Archbishop Mushegh. See Esat Uras, *Tarihte Ermeniler ve Ermeni Meselesi* (Ankara, 1950), 553–54. Spiridovitch continued his crusade against the Young Turks after the Young Turk Revolution of 1908. See A. Tchérep-Spiridovitch, *L'Europe sans Turquie: la sécurité de la France l'exige* (Paris, 1913), 101–2.

17. See S., "*Ülfet* Gazetesi Muharrirliği'ne," *Tuna*, no. 305 [September 19, 1906], 2–3.

18. Dr. Bahaeddin [Şakir] to the [CPU Internal Headquarters], dated [Paris], November 19, 1907/no. 433, *Kopye Defteri*, 9.

19. Ibid.

20. Dr. Bahaeddin [Şakir] to the CPU Internal Headquarters, dated Paris, November 30, [1]907/no. 442-4, *Kopye Defteri*, 21.

21. Ibid.

22. Ibid., 21–22.

23. Ibid., 22–24.

24. "Décision," written by Bahaeddin Şakir and signed by Aknuni [Khachatur Malumian], [Ahmed] Fazly [Fazlı], Bahaeddin [Şakir], N[ihad] Reşad, and S[ami Paşazâde] Sezaï [Sezaî], Private Papers of Ahmed Rıza (2).

25. Dr. Bahaeddin [Şakir] to the CPU Internal Headquarters, dated Paris, November 30, [1]907/no. 442-4, *Kopye Defteri*, 21–22.

26. Dr. Bahaeddin [Şakir] to the CPU Internal Headquarters, dated Paris, December 8, [1]907/no. 444-5, *Kopye Defteri*, 27.

27. Ibid., 26.

28. Ibid., 28.

29. Dr. Bahaeddin [Şakir] to the CPU Internal Headquarters, undated [mid-December 1907]/no. [461]-6, *Kopye Defteri*, 50–51.

30. Ibid., 52.

31. Ibid.

32. Ibid., 51.

33. Ibid., 52. See also the letter of Dr. Bahaeddin [Şakir] beginning "Vatanperver Efendim Hazretleri" and dated [Paris], January 16, 1908/no. 502, *Kopye Defteri*, 132: "Even Sabahaddin Bey and the others confessed their inability to participate actively in operations."

34. See, for example, "Can Turkey Live [?]—IV," *Armenia* 2, no. 4 (January 1906), 13–14; and "The Armenians and the Young Turks," *Armenia* 3, no. 7 (May–June 1907), 24–28.

35. Dr. Bahaeddin [Şakir] to the CPU Internal Headquarters, dated Paris, December 8, [1]907/no. 444–5, *Kopye Defteri*, 27.

36. Ibid., 28.

37. Although some sources hinted at relations between the Young Turks and the IMRO before the 1907 Congress of Ottoman opposition parties, these were connections of an entirely local character between local Young Turk sympathizers and the local IMRO organizations. See Jusuf Hamza, *Zaemnite odnosi meg'u progresivnite osmanski krugovi i makedonskoto revolucionerno dviženje vo vtorata polovina na XIX i početokot na XX vek* (Skopje, 1988), 152 ff; Mercia MacDermott, *For Freedom and Perfection: The Life of Yané Sandansky* (London, 1988), 322; and Stephen Fisher-Galaţi, "The Internal Macedonian Revolutionary Organization: Its Significance in 'Wars of National Liberation,'" *East European Quarterly* 6, no. 4 (January 1973), 468.

38. Khristo Silianov, *Osvoboditelnite borbi na Makedoniia* 2 (Sofia, 1983), 564.

39. Matov wrote in his memoirs that he had turned down the invitation. See Khristo Matov, *Khristo Matov za svoiata revoliutsionna deynost* (Sofia, 1928), 53. Also a Bulgarian daily's editor stated: "It [the IMRO], however, did not participate in the congress. What reasons caused the organization to abstain from participation, I do not know, but I think that its refusal was quite appropriate." See "Armeno-Turskiia sŭiuz i likvidatsiiata na turskiia rezhim," *Vecherna poshta*, December 29, 1907 [January 11, 1908].

40. See the letter of H[üsrev] Sami and Dr. Bahaeddin [Şakir] beginning "Aziz Vatandaş" and dated Paris, January 11, 1908/no. 475, *Kopye Defteri*, 75–76. A reliable Austrian daily reported from Sofia that the IMRO was invited and did not send delegates. See "Konferenz türkischer Revolutionäre im Ausland," *Neue freie Presse*, January 12, 1908.

41. Gr[igor] Vasilev, "Konstitutsiia v Turtsiia," *Ilinden* 1, no. 13 (January 12 [25], 1908), 2.

42. Dr. Bahaeddin [Şakir], "Osmanlı Terakki ve İttihad Cemiyeti Hey'et-i Merkeziye-i Dahiliyesi Cânib-i Âlisine Takdim Kılınmak Üzere Sâî [Talât] Bey'e," undated [late January 1908]/no. 478-7, *Kopye Defteri*, 81.

43. In the galley proofs of the 195th issue of *Mechveret Supplément Français* the line reading "Le Comité macédonien (empêché)" was omitted by Ahmed Rıza, Private Papers of Ahmed Rıza (2).

44. Gr[igor] Vasilev, "Konstitutsiia v Turtsiia," *Ilinden* 1, no. 13, 2–3. On the other hand, the IMRO organs expressed skepticism about the sincerity of the Young Turks: "Undoubtedly, the program embraced by the opposition parties is an excellent one: revolutionary means against the tyrannical regime are the only effective ones; the need for the rule of law is painfully felt in Turkey. But despite our efforts to overcome our concerns, we cannot hide a skepticism gnawing at us from within: the Young Turks are embittered mainly against the present sultan and not against the Turkish hegemony. This is why we must remain reserved in our assessment of the decisions of the congress. . . . The Young Turk ideal of the indivisibility of the empire is alien to the Christian population in Macedonia." See Dan[iel] Krapchev, "Konstitutsionnoto dvizhenie v Turtsiia," *Ilinden* 1, no. 12 (January 9 [22], 1908), 1–2.

45. H[üsrev] Sami and Dr. Bahaeddin [Şakir] to the "Droshak Committee," dated [Paris], February 6, 1908/no. 507-5, *Kopye Defteri*, 141.

46. Following the congress, the CPU organs used strong language against the IMRO. See, for example, "Un bon débarras," *Mechveret Supplément Français*, no. 195 (January 1, 1908),

7–8. It should be remembered that during the very period in which an offer was extended to the IMRO, the CPU organs were commenting on the "brigandage of the Bulgarian committees [the IMRO]." See "*Şûra-yı Ümmet,*" *Şûra-yı Ümmet,* no. 122 (September 15, 1907), 2. See also "Şûun-i Hariciye," *Şûra-yı Ümmet,* no. 127 (December 15, 1907), 4.

47. See V. I. Shpil'kova, "Pervyi proekt politicheskoi programmy Mladoturok," *Narody Azii i Afriki* 4 (1973), 62. See also Khristo Matov, *Mŭlchalivetsŭt ot Struga: ocherk za zhivota i deleto na makedonskiia revoliutsioner Khristo Matov* (Sofia, 1993), 117–18. Matov also played a consequential role in the IMRO's rejections of the offers made by Abdülhamid II's minister of the interior, Mehmed Memduh Pasha, in 1904 and by Talât Bey, a CUP central committee member, in 1912. Matov's answer was a standard one: "The organization will follow its revolutionary path and does not want to enter into any negotiations with you, the Turks." See the memorandum by Dimitrov and Radev, Sofia, March 17 [30], 1912/no. 440 (Top secret), TsDA, F. 336, op. 1. a.e. 110, 1, 5. During the negotiations in 1912 he stated that "the Young Turks have already spoken many lies, and will lie to us again." See Dimitrov and Radev to the tzar's consuls in Turkey, Sofia, March 17 [30], 1912/no. 441 (Top secret), TsDA, F. 336, op. 1. a.e. 110, 1, 7.

48. All the above information is taken from Silianov, *Osvoboditelnite borbi na Makedoniia* 2, 564–65. Silianov also stated: "These, however, are judgments of hindsight. At the congress itself . . . the delegates did not suspect that the Young Turk propaganda had already deeply infected the young Turkish officers, especially those from the Bitola [Monastir] and Salonica army corps, and that the coup d'état was imminent. Had Boris Sarafov, who maintained regular relations with the Armenian revolutionary committees, been alive, the congress would surely have been better informed." Ibid., 565–66. For Sarafov's "personal assistance" to the Dashnaktsutiun, see Dasnabedian, *Histoire,* 60. It could be assumed, however, that given Sarafov's extreme dislike of the Young Turks, the right wing of the IMRO would have acted similarly had he been alive. See, for example, B[oris] Sarafoff, "Macédoine: une lettre de Boris Sarafoff," *L'Européen* 5, no. 179 (May 6, 1905), 10; and "Réponse à Boris Sarafof," *L'Européen* 5, no. 184 (June 10, 1905), 12.

49. P. Bogdanov [Pavel Deliradev], "Opozitsionnoto dvizhenie v Turtsiia," *Odrinski glas* 1, no. 2 (January 20 [February 2], 1908), 1–2. See also "Iz sigurniia pŭt," *Odrinski glas* 1, no. 12 (March 30 [April 12], 1908), 1.

50. P. Bogdanov [Pavel Deliradev], "Opozitsionnoto dvizhenie v Turstiia," *Odrinski glas* 1, no. 4 (February 3 [16], 1908), 1–2.

51. Dr. Bahaeddin [Şakir], "Osmanlı Terakki ve İttihad Cemiyeti Hey'et-i Merkeziye-i Dahiliyesi Cânib-i Âlisine Takdim Kılınmak Üzere Sâî [Talât] Bey'e," undated [late January 1908]/no. 478–7, *Kopye Defteri,* 81.

52. "Échos: un congrès anti-Hamidien à Paris," *L'Hellénisme* 4, no. 1 (January 1, 1908), 5.

53. Ali Haydar Midhat, "Une lettre de Midhat-Bey," *Le Siècle,* January 12, 1908. Republished in "A propos du Congrès arméno[-]turc," *L'Hellénisme* 4, no. 3 (February 1, 1908), 8. See also "Un article de la 'Gazette de Francfort,'" *Pro Armenia* 8, no. 174 (January 20, 1908), 1224.

54. Un groupe du Congrès, "Les Partis d'opposition de l'Empire ottoman," *Le Siècle,* January 16, 1908.

55. The IMRO organs praised this view. See Gr[igor] Vasilev, "Konstitutsiia v Turtsiia," *Ilinden* 1, no. 13, 3: "And why is there no word on the Greek and Serbian revolutionary organizations, why did the committee organizing the congress not invite them to participate? . . . [B]ecause of chauvinistic feelings? We do not think so. But on the one hand, these organizations have yet to deserve the right to be regarded as fighters against the sultan's regime, and on the other hand, their participation was probably not thought to have any considerable importance. This is the naked truth."

56. Dr. Bahaeddin [Şakir], "Osmanlı Terakki ve İttihad Cemiyeti Hey'et-i Merkeziye-i Dahiliyesi Cânib-i Âlisine Takdim Kılınmak Üzere Sâî [Talât] Bey'e," undated [late January 1908]/no. 478–7, *Kopye Defteri,* 81.

57. Dr. Bahaeddin [Şakir] to the director of the CPU Constanţa branch, undated [early December 1907]/no. 443, *Kopye Defteri,* 25.

58. Dr. Bahaeddin [Şakir] to [İbrahim Temo], undated [second week of December 1907]/ no. 460, *Kopye Defteri*, 49. Most parts of the first page of this letter are illegible. There is a letter in French in the CPU's copy register of outgoing letters that invites an individual to participate in the congress and offers to meet half of his travel expenses. This looks like an invitation to the Albanian organization, but it is difficult to be certain. See Dr. Bahaeddin [Şakir]'s undated note [late December 1907]/no. 462, beginning "Mon cher ami," *Kopye Defteri*, 54.

59. For more information, see Stavro Skendi, *The Albanian National Awakening, 1878– 1912* (Princeton, 1967), 150–51.

60. The signing of the document by the editorial board of *Haïrenik* caused the American press to maintain erroneously that "Armenians, Turks, and Bulgarians in America were represented at the congress by delegates." See "Unite to Free Turkey," *The New York Times*, January 12, 1908.

61. See Louise Nalbandian, *The Armenian Revolutionary Movement: The Development of Armenian Revolutionary Parties through the Nineteenth Century* (Los Angeles, 1963), 95–105, 169– 72; and Christopher J. Walker, *Armenia: The Survival of a Nation* (London, 1990), 126–29.

62. Nalbandian, *The Armenian Revolutionary Movement*, 171–72.

63. For Ahmed Celâleddin Pasha's relations with the anarchist organizations and Jean Grave, see the Ottoman embassy's note to Affaires étrangères, Paris, May 29, 1906, AE-NS-T, 5 (1905– 1907), 40–41; the Sûreté générale's draft, Paris, June 3, 1906 (confidentiel), ibid., 43; the coded telegram from the Affaires étrangères to Constans, Paris, June 2, 1906, ibid., 45; Constans to Affaires étrangères, Pera, June 7, 1906/no. 75, ibid., 50; Nuri Bey to Âsım Bey at the First Chamberlain's office, Cairo [July 31, 1905]/no. 1249–1999, *Umumî Kayda Mahsus Defterdir* 2, BBA–YEE, 36/139–72/139/XIX-II; and Münir Pasha to the First Chamberlain's office, Paris [April 2, 1906]/no. 28, BBA–YMGM, 285/65 (1324.S.9). The Ottoman embassy in London also complained to the Foreign Office about Ahmed Celâleddin Pasha's relations with the anarchists and requested the British government to deport a certain Nuri who was allegedly an anarchist and working for the former intelligence service chief. The British, however, refused to meet the Ottoman demand. See PRO/F.O. 371/152, file 20537, and PRO/F.O. 371/153, file 23879.

64. See his letter in "The Condition of Turkey," *The Times*, October 4, 1907. For its impact, see "The Condition of Turkey: Ahmed Djelaleddin's Letter," *The Times*, October 15, 1907; and P[ierre] Q[uillard], "Sage prudence," *Pro Armenia* 7, no. 169 (November 5, 1907), 1187–88.

65. The following information is provided in "Osmanlı Ahrarı, Cemiyetleri ve Gazeteleri," *Şûra-yı Osmanî*, no. 7 (May 1, 1907), 4–5: "The Ottoman Covenant Committee: This committee was formed a few months ago. It does not yet have a journal. We have, however, seen its program in the appeal that was distributed by this committee. . . . We have heard that the leaders of the committee are people from the elite. The address of the committee is not known. It may be declared in the future."

66. It changed its name to "Comité Israélite Ottoman" after the Young Turk Revolution. See "Parti politique israélite ottoman," *Archives Israélites* 70, no. 32 (August 12, 1909), 251– 52; and "Le Comité Union et Progrès contre les Juifs," *Mècheroutiette*, no. 52 (March 1914), 19–20. Galanté later claimed that he had adopted the name "Comité Israélite d'Egypte" to avoid endangering those who were contacting him. See "Il rolo de los judios y la Jovina Turchia," *La Vara* 4, no. 65 (September 1908), 5.

67. For the journal and its publication, see Jacob M. Landau, *Jews in Nineteenth-Century Egypt* (New York, 1969), 102.

68. See Albert E. Kalderon, *Abraham Galante: A Biography* (New York, 1983), 28–31.

69. See his autobiography in "Abraham Galanté," *La Vara* 4, no. 65, 6.

70. Abraham Galanté, "Programa: nuestro escopo," *La Vara* 1, no. 1 (July 14, 1905), 1.

71. See Abraham Galanté, "Los colaboradores de La Vara," *La Vara* 4, no. 65, 7–8.

72. "Il rolo de los judios y la Jovina Turchia," *La Vara* 4, no. 65, 4.

73. See Avram Galanté to Ahmed Rıza, Cairo, July 15, 1907, Private Papers of Ahmed Rıza (1). Following the revolution, *La Vara* presented Galanté as a member of the CPU. See *La Vara* 4, 65, 1.

74. "Il rolo de los judios y la Jovina Turchia," *La Vara* 4, no. 65, 5.

75. Ahmed Rıza to Galanté, Paris, January 23, 1907. The original letter in Ottoman Turkish was published in Avram Galanti, *Küçük Türk Tetebbu'lar* (Istanbul, 1925), 46–47; and in Avram Galanti, *Türkler ve Yahudiler: Tarihî, Siyasî Tetkik*, 2nd ed. (Istanbul, 1947), 41–42. French translations can be found in Avram Galante, *Histoire des Juifs de Turquie* 8 (Istanbul, [1985?]), 17; and in Abraham Elmaleh, *Le Professeur Abraham Galanté: sa vie et ses œuvres* (Istanbul, 1946), 46.

76. In the galley proofs of the 195th issue of *Mechveret Supplément Français*, the line reading "Le Comité israélite du Caire, qui a prié Ahmed Riza bey de le représenter" was omitted by Ahmed Rıza, Private Papers of Ahmed Rıza (2).

77. See, for example, Ernst Simon, "Zur Geschichte des Zionismus; der Zionismus und die Jungtürken," *Jüdische Rundschau* 34, nos. 101–102 (December 24, 1929), 691.

78. See Ahmed Rıza to Galanté, Paris, January 30, 1907 in Galanti, *Küçük Türk Tetebbu'lar*, 47; idem, *Türkler ve Yahudiler*, 42; idem, *Histoire des Juifs de Turquie* 8, 17; and Elmaleh, *Le Professeur Abraham Galanté*, 46.

79. See M. Şükrü Hanioğlu, *The Young Turks in Opposition* (New York, 1995), 44.

80. The name of this so-called committee is somewhat confusing. For its separatist and Arabist appeal, see Türk Anarşist Cemiyeti'nin Naibleri Edhem ve Rüfekası, *Haremeyn Hâdimi, Zalim, Gaddar, Ahlakahu'l-lāh* [Paris, 1901], in Archives of the Turkish Embassy in Paris, D. 228.

81. Sanderson to Cromer, May 6, 1902, PRO/F.O. 78/5226.

82. See the Foreign Office draft to be sent to O'Conor, April 9, 1902/no. 113, PRO/F.O. 78/5187.

83. The place of publication of the journal also caused a debate between the Ottoman and British authorities. See Hamilton to Governor in Council in Bombay, London, August 15, 1902, PRO/F.O. 78/5212; and the Foreign Office draft dated April 11, 1902, PRO/F.O. 78/5224; the F.O. draft to be sent to Home Office, May 10, 1902 (confidential), PRO/F.O. 78/5211; and Cromer to Lansdowne, Cairo, April 25, 1902 (confidential), PRO/F.O. 78/5226. The Ottoman authorities banned the journal. See BBA–BEO/Dahiliye Giden, 101–3/50; 982 [June 1, 1902].

84. See Tevfik Pasha to Anthopoulos Pasha, June 3, 1902, Archives of the Turkish Embassy in London, Box 377 (1).

85. Letter of Dr. Bahaeddin [Şakir] beginning "Vatanperver Efendim" and dated Paris, June 15, 1906/no. 20, *Muhaberat Kopyası*, 40.

86. See "Matbu'at-ı Hariciye," *Hayat*, no. 62, March 19 [April 1], 1906, 4.

87. Later sources that wanted to downplay the CPU's role in the Young Turk movement attributed importance to the publication of this unimportant journal. See "Jön Türkler," *Hukuk-u Umumiye*, October 3, 1908.

88. In all documents, including the CPU's secret correspondence, he was referred to as Necati Bey to prevent the Ottoman government from being able to ask for his expulsion from Romania. See Dr. Bahaeddin [Şakir] to [İbrahim Temo], undated [second week of December 1907]/no. 460, *Kopye Defteri*, 48. The local Young Turk press too declared that he had gone to Paris for medical treatment. See "Köstence'de Harekât-ı Fikriye," *Balkan*, no. 403, 1.

89. See "Kongre," *Şûra-yı Ümmet*, nos. 128–29 (February 1, 1908), 1; "Kongre," *Terakki*, no. 16 (February 1908), 1–2; and "Le congrès," *Mechveret Supplément Français*, no. 195, 1.

90. "Kongre," *Şûra-yı Ümmet*, nos. 128–29, 1; "Kongre," *Terakki*, no. 16, 1–2; and "Le congrès," *Mechveret Supplément Français*, no. 195, 1–2.

91. See "Kongre," *Şûra-yı Ümmet*, nos. 128–29, 1; "Kongre," *Terakki*, no. 16, 1–2; and "Le congrès," *Mechveret Supplément Français*, no. 195, 2.

92. Ahmed Bedevî Kuran, *Osmanlı İmparatorluğunda İnkılâp Hareketleri ve Millî Mücadele* (Istanbul, 1959), 444–47. Other scholars repeated Kuran's account. See, for example, E[rvand] K[azarovich] Sarkisian, *Politika osmanskogo pravitel'stva v Zapadnoi Armenii i derzhavy v poslednei chetverti XIX i nachale XX vv.* (Erevan, 1972), 232.

93. Kuran, *Osmanlı İmparatorluğunda İnkılâp Hareketleri*, 446.

94. "Sezaî Bey'in Nutku," *Şûra-yı Ümmet*, nos. 128–29, 5.

95. [Mehmed] Sabahaddin, *İttihad ve Terakki Cemiyeti'ne Açık Mektublar: Mesleğimiz Hakkında Üçüncü ve Son Bir İzah* (Istanbul, 1327 [1911]), 52.

96. "Kongre'de Vazife-i Kitabeti İfa Eden Anméghian Efendi'nin Nutku," *Şûra-yı Ümmet*, nos. 128–29, 5.

97. *Şûra-yı Ümmet*, nos. 128–29, 6.

98. "Osmanlı Muhalifîn Fırkaları Tarafından Avrupa'da İn'ikad Eden Kongre'nin Beyannâmesi," *Şûra-yı Ümmet*, nos. 128–29, 3; "Muvaffakiyetle Neticelendiğini Tebşir Etdiğimiz Osmanlı Muhalifîn Kongresi'nin Beyannâmesi," *Terakki*, no. 17 [March 1908], 1–4; "Déclaration," *Mechveret Supplément Français*, no. 195, 3; "Haydararakir," *Droshak*, no. 1 (189), January 1908, 2–4; "Déclaration du Congrès des Partis d'opposition de l'Empire ottoman, réuni en Europe," *Pro Armenia* 8, no. 173 (January 5, 1908), 1214–15; P. Bogdanov [Pavel Deliradev], "Opozitsionnoto dvizhenie v Turtsiia—I," *Odrinski glas* 1, no. 3 (January 27 [February 9], 1908), 1–2; idem, "Opozitsionnoto dvizhenie v Turtsiia—II," *Odrinski glas* 1, no. 4 (February 3 [16], 1908), 1–2; "Osmanlı İnkılâb Fırkalarının İttihad Kongresi," *İrşad*, no. 20 (February 16 [March 1], 1908), 3; Edhem Ruhi, "Paris'de Müceddidîn-i Osmaniye Kongresi," *Balkan*, no. 343 [January 20, 1908], 1–2; "Osmanlı Hürriyetperverânı," *Tercüman-ı Ahvâl-i Zaman*, no. 3 (January 15 [28], 1908), 2; Jean Longuet, "La lutte contre le 'Grand Assassin,'" *L'Humanité*, January 12, 1908; and Alfred Durand, *Jeune Turquie, vieille France* (Paris, 1909), 39–43. Resolutions were also published in the form of an appeal to be sent to European statesmen. See *Déclaration du Congrès des Partis d'opposition de l'Empire ottoman, réuni en Europe* [Paris, 1908], in PRO/F.O. 371/534, file 677 and A. 352, PAAA, 734/1, Die Jungtürken, 198 (Bd.5–6). For Turkish versions, see Türk İnkılâp Tarihi Enstitüsü Arşivi, 82/18435 and 82/18437. For the Ottoman authorities' futile attempts to obstruct its publication in European dailies, see BBA-İrade-Hususî, Z 1325/no. 60–1275.

99. Ahmed Rıza, *Vazife ve Mes'uliyet* 1, *Mukaddime, Padişah, Şehzâdeler* (Cairo, 1320 [1902]), [27].

100. See "Kongrenin Kabûl Etdiği Tekâlif-i Mütenevvi'a," *Terakki*, no. 17, 4. This telegram was read at the Iranian Parliament on January 3, 1908. See *Majlis* 2, no. 16 (January 5, 1908); and *Rūznāmah-i Rasmī-i Kishvar-i Shāhanshahī-i Irān* (1908), 422.

101. "Discours du Prince Sabaheddine et de M. Ahmed Riza au Congrès des Partis d'opposition de Turquie," *Pro Armenia* 8, no. 174, 1225–26.

102. *Şûra-yı Ümmet*, nos. 128–29, 3–4; and *Mechveret Supplément Français*, no. 195, 5.

103. *Şûra-yı Ümmet*, nos. 128–29, 4; and *Terakki*, no. 17, 5.

104. "Ziyafet," *Şûra-yı Ümmet*, nos. 128–29, 4–6; and "Banquet," *Mechveret Supplément Français*, no. 195, 6–7.

105. The khedive's spy among the Young Turks, who had participated in the first congress in 1902, maintained in an intelligence report submitted to 'Abbās II that the Armenian participants could not possibly be Dashnaks because the CPU and the Dashnaktsutiun were using very strong language against each other. See Zeki Bey to the khedive, Paris, January 7, 1908, Abbas II Papers, Durham University, F. 41/229–30.

106. Malumian's interview in Jean Longuet, "Contre la 'bête rouge': Turcs, Arméniens, Kurdes, Macédoniens, Albanais et Arabes s'unissent contre Abdul-Hamid en un Congrès secret," *L'Humanité*, January 9, 1908. A large summary was given in "Gegen Abdul Hamid," *Berliner Tageblatt*, January 16, 1908.

107. See, for example, "Osmanlı Hürriyetperverânı," *Tercüman-ı Ahvâl-i Zaman*, no. 3, 2; "Türkler ve Ermeniler," *Tercüman-ı Ahvâl-i Zaman*, no. 11, February 12 [25], 1908, 3; "Matbu'at-ı İslâmiye: İslâm Matbu'atı," *İrşad*, no. 10 (January 22 [February 4], 1908), 4; and "Vatanda İnkılâb Ümidleri," *Balkan*, no. 369 [February 19, 1908], 1–2.

108. Sabakh Giuluian, "Turskata tiraniia i Mlado-Turtsite," *Ilinden* 1, no. 46 (May 19 [April 1], 1908), 2 ff.

109. S[tepan] Sapah-Gulian, "La Tyrannie turque et les Jeunes Turcs," *L'Indépendance Arabe* 2, nos. 11–12 (February–March 1908), 163–70. Furthermore, Azoury wrote an article in which he depicted the congress as a "fiasco." See N[egib] A[zoury], "Le fiasco des Jeunes Turcs," *L'Indépendance Arabe* 2, nos. 9–10 (December 1907–January 1908), 156–57.

110. H[üsrev] Sami and Dr. Bahaeddin [Şakir] to O[sman] Tevfik in Salonica, dated [Paris], February 25, [1]908/no. 529, *Kopye Defteri*, 177.

111. See, for example, Dr. Bahaeddin [Şakir] to the CPU Kal'a-i Sultaniye branch, un-

dated [early January 1908]/no. 466, *Kopye Defteri*, 58; to the CPU Burgas branch, dated Paris, January 3, [1]908/no. 468, *Kopye Defteri*, 60–61; the letter of Dr. Bahaeddin [Şakir] beginning "Muhterem Refikimiz" and dated Paris, January 3, 1908/no. 468, *Kopye Defteri*, 62–63; his letter beginning "Muhterem Vatandaş" and dated [Paris], January 9, 1908/no. 470, *Kopye Defteri*, 68–69; the letter of H[üsrev] Sami and Dr. Bahaeddin [Şakir] beginning "Aziz Refikimiz" and dated [Paris], January 11, 1908/no. 472, *Kopye Defteri*, 71–72; their letter beginning "Aziz Vatandaş" and dated [Paris], January 16, 1908/no. 479, *Kopye Defteri*, 86; their letter to [Mesʿud Remzi], beginning "Aziz Refikimiz" and dated Paris, January 16, 1908/ no. 480, *Kopye Defteri*, 87–88; their letter beginning "Gayûr ve Aziz Vatandaşımız," undated [January 1908]/no. 481, *Kopye Defteri*, 89–90; their unsigned letter to the CPU Cyprus central branch, dated [Paris], January [16], 1908/no. 484, *Kopye Defteri*, 95–96; their letter beginning "Aziz Vatandaşımız" and dated [Paris], January 16, 1908/no. 486, *Kopye Defteri*, 98–99; their letter to Hacı Bey in Varna, dated [Paris], January 16, 1908/no. 487, *Kopye Defteri*, 101; their letter to the CPU Canea branch, dated [Paris], January 16, 1908/no. 489, *Kopye Defteri*, 105–6; their letter beginning "Aziz Refiklerimiz" and dated [Paris], January 16, 1908/no. 492, *Kopye Defteri*, 109–10; their letter beginning "Aziz Birader" and dated [Paris], February 6, 1908/ no. 509, *Kopye Defteri*, 143; and their letter to the CPU Balchik branch, dated [Paris], February 12, [1]908/no. 514, *Kopye Defteri*, 160.

112. See the letter of Dr. Bahaeddin [Şakir] beginning "Vatanperver Efendim Hazretleri" and dated [Paris], January 19, 1908/no. 502, *Kopye Defteri*, 132.

113. See the letter of H[üsrev] Sami and Dr. Bahaeddin [Şakir] beginning "Muhterem Arkadaşımız" and dated [Paris], January [?], 1908/no. 483, *Kopye Defteri*, 92–94.

114. See the letter of Dr. Bahaeddin [Şakir] beginning "Aziz Refikimiz" and dated [Paris], March 28, [190]8/no. 565, *Kopye Defteri*, 245.

115. See the letter of H[üsrev] Sami and Dr. Bahaeddin [Şakir] beginning "Muhterem Arkadaşımız" and dated [Paris], January [?], 1908/no. 483, *Kopye Defteri*, 93. See also the letter of H[üsrev] Sami and Dr. Bahaeddin [Şakir] beginning "Aziz Arkadaşımız" and dated [Paris], March 10, 1908/no. 553, *Kopye Defteri*, 217.

116. See the letter of Dr. Bahaeddin [Şakir] beginning "Muhterem Din Karındaşlarımız" and dated Paris, January 3, 1907 [1908]/no. 469, *Kopye Defteri*, 67.

117. H[üsrev] Sami and Dr. Bahaeddin [Şakir] to the CPU Istanbul branch, dated [Paris] January 19, 1908/no. 488, *Kopye Defteri*, 103. See also the letter of H[üsrev] Sami and Dr. Bahaeddin [Şakir] beginning "Refik-i Muhteremimiz Efendim" and dated [Paris], February 27, 1908/no. 540, *Kopye Defteri*, 191–92.

118. See the letter of H[üsrev] Sami and Dr. Bahaeddin [Şakir] beginning "Aziz Refikimiz" and dated [Paris], January 28, 1908/no. 503, *Kopye Defteri*, 134.

119. *Şûra-yı Ümmet*, nos. 128–29, 4.

120. For Ahmed Rıza's criticism, see Ahmed Rıza, *Vazife ve Mesʾuliyet* 2, *Asker* (Cairo, 1323 [1907]), 42.

121. See, for example, Ottomanus [Pierre Anméghian], "Vers la fraternité," *Mechveret Supplément Français*, no. 196 (February 1, 1908), 1.

122. Besides *L'Humanité*, leading columnists of other left-wing journals such as Jean Bernard of *Le Radical* praised the resolutions adopted by the congress and the union between the Dashnaktsutiun and the Young Turks. See Khevenhüller-Metsch to Aehrenthal, Paris, February 8, 1908/no. 6, HHStA, PA, XII 197 Türkei, Varia 1908.

123. See, for example, P[ierre] Quillard, "Après le congrès," *Pro Armenia* 8, no. 173, 1218–19; and idem, "La guerre," *Pro Armenia* 8, no. 177 (March 5, 1908), 1247–48. These announcements also led the Ottoman diplomats to assume that the "Turkish subversive committee" had fused with the "Armenian revolutionary committee." See Şerif Pasha to Fuad Hikmet, Stockholm, March 2, 1908, Archives of the Turkish Embassy in Rome, Box 71(1).

124. A[hmed] R[ıza], "Prudence et modestie," *Mechveret Supplément Français*, no. 196, 3–4. *L'Humanité*'s favorable coverage caused the French authorities to think that "an anarchist congress" took place in Paris. See "Abschrift einer Note des französischen Ministeriums des Innern an das k.u.k. Polizei-Präsidium in Wien vom 5. März 1908," HHStA, PA, XII 197 Türkei, Varia 1908.

125. [Pierre Quillard], "Un article du 'Mechveret,'" *Pro Armenia*, 8, no. 176 (February 20, 1908), 1241–42. Here *Pro Armenia* also republished Ahmed Rıza's article for its readers. See also Albert Fua, "Histoire du Comité Union et Progrès," *Mècheroutiette*, no. 44, 43.

126. Letter of a CPU member, marked "confidential and personal," to Ahmed Rıza, Geneva, February 18, [1]908. The signature is illegible, Private Papers of Ahmed Rıza (2).

127. See "Encore un mot," *Mechveret Supplément Français*, no. 198 (April 1, 1908), 4.

128. See Colonel Ali Hilmi to the Ottoman Ministry of War, Plovdiv [July 2, 1908], enclosed with Ali Rıza Pasha to Mehmed Ferid Pasha [July 6, 1908]/no. 1030, BBA–BEO/ Mümtaze Kalemi: Bulgaristan Tasnifi Evrakı II, A. MTZ (04), 168/54 (1326.6.8); and BBA–BEO/Harbiye Giden, 228–6/36; 1316/1030 [July 6, 1908].

129. See the letter of H[üsrev] Sami and Dr. Bahaeddin [Şakir] to the "Droshak Committee," dated [Paris], February 6, 1908/no. 507–1, *Kopye Defteri*, 141–42; and their undated letter [February 1908]/no. 516–3, *Kopye Defteri*, 162.

130. Dr. Bahaeddin [Şakir] to [Ömer] Naci, dated [Paris], March 16, [190]8/no. 558, *Kopye Defteri*, 231.

131. See the letter of Dr. Bahaeddin [Şakir] beginning "Camarades" and sent to the Dashnaktsutiun central committee, undated [March 1908]/no. 554, *Kopye Defteri*, 218–20. A Turkish translation was published in *Haftalık Şûra-yı Ümmet*, no. 217 [April 21, 1910], 4.

132. Grand Vizier's office to the governor of Ma'muret el-Azîz [April 15, 1908]/no. 235, BBA–BEO/Telgrafnâme-i Sami Defteri, 703–28/14.

133. Governor Halid Bey to the Grand Vizier's office [April 16, 1908]/no. 801/86-2364; and [April 23, 1908]/no. 104-2759, BBA-BEO/ Şifre Telgraf Kayd: 693/2: Anadolu 1324 (1).

134. See Francis de Pressensé's letter dated January 9, 1908, and published in *Pro Armenia* 8, no. 173, 1217, and in *L'Humanité*, January 12, 1908. It is interesting to note that these left-wing deputies attributed great importance to this "congress" even after the 1908 Young Turk Revolution. See, for example, Pressensé's speech at the *Chambre des Députés* on December 27, 1908. Again the "applaudissements à l'extrême gauche" praising Pressensé's comments would be of very little help in securing French official endorsement. See *Journal Officiel: Chambre des Députés*, 9e législature-session ordinaire (1909), 3784.

135. The declarations were sent to the Foreign Office and received on January 7, 1908. The minutes are as follows: "No Action," A[lwyn] P[arker]. "A denunciation of the existing régime in Turkey." R. P. M[axwell], Louis Mallet, E[dward] G[rey], PRO/F.O. 371/ 534, file 677.

136. For instance, Arshak Chobanian wrote the following in the journal *Anahit* in 1908: "The last Congress in Paris . . . killed the Armenian question." Quoted in John S. Kirakossian, *The Armenian Genocide: The Young Turks before the Judgment of History* (Madison, 1992), 72.

137. It should be noted that Ahmed Rıza and many CPU members had no strong objections to utopian socialism and viewed it as a step in the long path of "indefinite progress." See Ahmed Rıza's interview in Jean Longuet, "Après la première victoire: La Jeune-Turquie: ce que dit Ahmed-Riza leader des Jeunes-Turcs," *L'Humanité*, July 26, 1908.

138. See, for example, Le Comité Responsable de Constantinople, "Proclamation de la Fédération Révolutionnaire Arménienne," *Pro Armenia* 8, no. 189 (September 5, 1908), 1350; "Taşnaksu[t]yun Ermeni Fırkası," *İttihad ve Terakki*, September 9, 1908; and P[ierre] Quillard, "En pleine révolution," *Pro Armenia* 8, no. 187 (August 5, 1908), 1338–39.

139. See, for example, Mundji Bey, "The New Constitution in Turkey," *The Independent* 67, no. 3315 (August 13, 1908), 363; "The New Spirit in Turkey," *The Nation* 3, no. 16 (July 18, 1908), 559–60; "La Révolution jeune-turque et la remise en vigueur de la Constitution de 1876," *La Vie Politique dans les Deux Mondes* 2 (1909), 338; and Georges Gaulis, "La chute d'Abdul Hamid," *Bulletin du Comité de L'Asie Française* 4, no. 98 (May 1909), 200.

140. For Malumian's statement, see "Contre la 'Bête-Rouge,'" *L'Humanité*, January 9, 1908. The Young Turk press attached great importance to it. See, for example, "Pek Dehşetli Bir Karar," *Balkan*, no. 349 [January 26, 1908], 4. The organs of the right wing of the IMRO made fun of the prophecy, which they attributed to Prince Sabahaddin. See Dan[iel] Krapchev, "Konstitutsionna Turtsiia," *Ilinden* 1, no. 41 (May 2 [15], 1908), 2.

CHAPTER 8

1. See M. Şükrü Hanioğlu, *The Young Turks in Opposition* (New York, 1995), 88–89.

2. The 105 residents of a village attached to Đakovica in the Province of Kosovo who signed this "ittifaknâme" also stated that they would oppose to the bitter end the appointment of non-Muslims as police and gendarme officers. They feared that the Mürzteg program's reforms might be extended to the *sanjaks* of the province of Kosovo, which were outside of the reform scheme of the Great Powers. See the undated [1321 (1903–1904)] written oath in BBA–TFR.1.M. 3/246 (1321). Not surprisingly, following the revolution the Albanians of Đakovica "expelled the Judicial Authorities, the police and three Christian gendarmes (two Serbs and a Catholic). The inhabitants of the town were notified by public crier that henceforth they would be governed and judged by the 'Sheri' law and there would be no other tribunals and European control." See Satow to Lamb, Skopje, August 15, 1908/no. 52, PRO/F.O. 195/2298. See also BBA–BEO/VGG(2): Vâride: Kosova Vilâyeti [1]324: 512; 3005 [August 30, 1908], and 3008 [August 31, 1908]; and I. G. Senkevitch, "Mladoturetskaia revoliutsiia 1908 goda. i Albanskoe natsional'noe dvizhenie," *Sovetskoe vostokovedenie*, 1958/1, 36.

3. See, for example, Ahmed Niyazi, *Hatırât-ı Niyazi yahud Tarihçe-i İnkilâb-ı Kebîr-i Osmanîden Bir Sahife* (Istanbul, 1326 [1908]), 26 ff; "Niazi Effendi and the Revolution," *The Times*, August 25, 1908; and Kâzım Nami Duru, *"İttihat ve Terakki" Hatıralarım* (Istanbul, 1957), 12–14.

4. Robert Graves, *Storm Centres of the Near East: Personal Memories, 1879–1929* (London, 1933), 200–201.

5. See Kâzım Karabekir, *İttihat ve Terakki Cemiyeti, 1896–1909* (Istanbul, 1982), 158.

6. See, for example, "Osmanlı İnkılâb-ı Kebîri Nasıl Oldu?" *Musavver Salnâme-i Servet-i Fünûn* 1 (Istanbul, 1326 [1910]), 84–85; "Osmanlı İttihad ve Terakki Cemiyeti," *Yeni Asır*, July 27, 1908; and Sami Kulle, "İttihad ve Terakki!" *Hukuk-u Umumiye*, December 23, 1909.

7. See the letter of Dr. Bahaeddin [Şakir] and Dr. Nâzım beginning "Hamiyetperver Vatandaşımız" and dated Paris, August 6, 1906/no. 55, *Muhaberat Kopyası*, 85–87.

8. See the letter of Dr. Bahaeddin [Şakir] beginning "Aziz Vatandaş" and dated [Paris], September 27, 1907/no. 379, *Muhaberat Kopyası*, 436.

9. He described his activities in detail in an interview that he gave to Ahmed Emin (Yalman). See "Büyük Millet Meclisi Reisi Başkumandan Mustafa Kemal Paşa ile Bir Mülâkat," *Vakit*, January 10, 1922. See also Âfet [İnan], "Atatürk'ü Dinlerken: Vatan ve Hürriyet," *Belleten* 1, no. 2 (April 1, 1937), 297–98; idem, "Atatürk'ü Dinlerken: Mukaddes Tabanca," *Belleten* 1, nos. 3–4 (October 1, 1937), 605–10; and A. F. Miller, "Revoliutsiia 1908 g. v Turtsii i Mustafa Kemal," *Narody Azii i Afriki* 3 (1975), 57–63.

10. "Büyük Millet Meclisi Reisi Başkumandan Mustafa Kemal Paşa ile Bir Mülâkat," *Vakit*, January 10, 1922.

11. See "Reis-i Cumhur Hazretleri'nin Tercüme-i Halleri," *1925–1926 Türkiye Cumhuriyeti Devlet Salnâmesi* (Istanbul, 1926), 50–51; *Tarih 3, Yeni ve Yakın Zamanlarda Türk Tarihi* (Istanbul, 1931), 141–42; and *Tarih 4, Türkiye Cümhuriyeti* (Istanbul, 1934), 18.

12. See, for example, Karabekir, *İttihat ve Terakki Cemiyeti, 1896–1909*, 176.

13. Erik Jan Zürcher, *The Unionist Factor: The Rôle of the Committee of Union and Progress in the Turkish National Movement, 1905–1926* (Leiden, 1984), 31–37.

14. See, for example, Hüsrev Sami Kızıldoğan, "Vatan ve Hürriyet=İttihat ve Terakki," *Belleten* 1, nos. 3–4, 619–25.

15. See, for example, Generalmajor z.D. Imhoff, "Die Entstehung und der Zweck des Comités für Einheit und Fortschritt," *Die Welt des Islams* I, no. 3/4 (1913), 174; P. Risal [Joseph Nehamas], *La ville convoitée: Salonique* (Paris, 1917), 309; and Faik Reşit Unat, "Atatürk'ün II. Meşrutiyet İnkılâbının Hazırlanmasındaki Rolüne Ait Bir Belge," *Belleten* 26, no. 102 (April 1962), 339–49.

16. See Karabekir, *İttihat ve Terakki Cemiyeti, 1896–1909*, 176; Duru, *"İttihat ve Terakki" Hatıralarım*, 13; [Halil Menteşe], *Osmanlı Mebusan Reisi Halil Menteşe'nin Anıları*, ed. İsmail Arar (Istanbul, 1986), 121; and Mithat Şükrü Bleda, *İmparatorluğun Çöküşü* (Istanbul, 1979), 21–22.

17. Karabekir, *İttihat ve Terakki Cemiyeti, 1896–1909*, 176.

18. Ibid.

19. Duru, *"İttihat ve Terakki" Hatıralarım*, 13.

20. Midhat Şükrü Bleda's interview given to Selâhaddin Güngör in "Talât Paşa'ya dair Hatıralar," *Cumhuriyet*, February 25, 1943. Bleda stated that "the committee left its first regulations as a draft with Süleyman Fehmi Bey."

21. Mentioned in Karabekir, *İttihat ve Terakki Cemiyeti, 1896–1909*, 176–77; and Hakkı Baha Pars to Câmi Baykut, Izmir, July 20, [1]941. I am indebted to the late Professor Tarık Zafer Tunaya for allowing me to examine this important letter providing detailed information about the establishment of the Ottoman Freedom Society.

22. Ibid.; and Karabekir, *İttihat ve Terakki Cemiyeti, 1896–1909*, 176.

23. See Angelo Iacovella, *Gönye ve Hilal: İttihad-Terakki ve Masonluk*, tr. Tülin Altınova (Istanbul, 1998), 38–39; and Tarık Zafer Tunaya, *Türkiye'de Siyasal Partiler* 3, *İttihat ve Terakki: Bir Çağın, Bir Kuşağın, Bir Partinin Tarihi* (Istanbul, 1989), 15.

24. Kemalettin Apak, *Ana Çizgileriyle Türkiye'deki Masonluk Tarihi* (Istanbul, 1958), 35–37.

25. Karabekir, *İttihat ve Terakki Cemiyeti, 1896–1909*, 177–79.

26. See "İhtar," *Çocuk Bağçesi*, no. 19 [June 9, 1905], 1.

27. "Tebligât-ı Resmiye," *Çocuk Bağçesi*, no. 22 [June 29, 1905], 1; and "Arz-ı İ'tizâr," *Çocuk Bağçesi*, no. 23 [July 20, 1905], 1.

28. "İfade-i Mahsusa," *Bağçe*, no. 1 [August 3, 1908], 1.

29. Many important members of the Ottoman Freedom Society were writing for a Salonican daily named *Yeni Asır* (*The New Century*) and would only initial their articles. [See Türkmen Parlak, *Yeni Asır'ın Selânik Yılları: Evlâd-ı Fatihan Diyarları* (Istanbul, 1986), 250–51.] Nonetheless, under the strict censorship the dailies could not even be used to make criticism between the lines.

30. See Karabekir, *İttihat ve Terakki Cemiyeti, 1896–1909*, 159–63.

31. For example, Bahaeddin Şakir advised Azerbaijani Muslims who wanted to send their children to Ottoman schools to contact Mehmed Cavid, who later became a leading figure in the Salonica organization. See Dr. [Bahaeddin Şakir]'s letter beginning "Gence Şehrinde Müslüman Kardaşlarımıza: Aziz ve Muhterem Kardaşlarımız" and dated [Paris], May 2, 1907/ no. 288, *Muhaberat Kopyası*, 301–2.

32. Kızıldoğan, "Vatan ve Hürriyet=İttihat ve Terakki," *Belleten*, 624.

33. "Teşekkür," *Şûra-yı Ümmet*, no. 115 (June 1, 1907), 2; Dr. Bahaeddin [Şakir] to Ağabey [Silistireli Hacı İbrahim Paşazâde Hamdi], "the director of the first division of the Istanbul branch," dated [Paris], August 21, [1]907/no. 341, *Muhaberat Kopyası*, 384.

34. See Rasim Haşmet, "Ö[mer] Naci," *Bağçe*, no. 24, 9.

35. Ahmed Niyazi, *Hatırât-ı Niyazi*, 32.

36. "Teşekkür," *Şûra-yı Ümmet*, no. 122 (September 15, 1907), 2.

37. See "Osmanlı Terakki ve İttihad Cemiyeti Hey'et-i Merkeziye-i Hariciyesi'nin Teşkilât-ı Cedîdesi," *Şûra-yı Ümmet*, nos. 128–29 (February 1, 1908), 8.

38. Dr. Bahaeddin [Şakir] to [Mehmed Sa'id Halim Pasha], dated Paris, August 26, [1]907/ no. 347, *Muhaberat Kopyası*, 393. See also *Şûra-yı Ümmet-Ali Kemal Da'vası* (Istanbul, 1325 [1909]), 88–89.

39. A. Raif to the CPU central committee, Belgrade, September 7, 1907, Private Papers of Bahaeddin Şakir.

40. B[ahaeddin] Ş[akir], "Osmanlı İttihad ve Terakki Cemiyeti: Vesâik-i Tarihiyeden," *Bağçe*, no. [18] [September 8, 1910], 2; and "Midhat Şükrü Bey'in Muhakemesi," *Cumhuriyet*, August 4, 1926.

41. For detailed information, see "İttihad ve Terakki Cemiyet-i Muhteremesi'nin 10 Temmuz'dan Evveline Aid Tertibat ve İcraatına Dair: İzmir'de Tütüncü Yakub Ağa," *İnkılâb*, no. 5 [August 21, 1909], 53–54; and no. 6 [August 28, 1909], 86–88.

42. B[ahaeddin] Ş[akir], "Osmanlı İttihad ve Terakki Cemiyeti: Vesâik-i Tarihiyeden," *Bağçe*, no. [18], 2.

43. Ibid.

44. See Midhat Şükrü Bleda's interview given to Selâhaddin Güngör in "Talât Paşa'ya dair Hatıralar," *Cumhuriyet*, February 25, 1943; and his interview given to the same journalist in "Bir Canlı Tarih Konuşuyor," *Resimli Tarih Mecmuası* 4, no. 40 (April 1953), 2172.

45. See the minutes of Dr. Nâzım's deposition at the "Ankara Independence Court" in July 1926, T.B.M.M. Arşivi, D. 239/31, Defter 8: Ankara İstiklâl Mahkemesi Zabıtnâmesi 1341, 5–6.

46. For the help of the Greek committees, see ibid., 3; Bahaeddin Şakir's note to the republished version of the letter from the CPU External Headquarters to Sâî [Talât] Bey, dated [Paris], April 6, [1]908/no. 585-14, in "Osmanlı İttihad ve Terakki Cemiyeti: Vesâik-i Tarihiyeden," *Haftalık Şûra-yı Ümmet*, no. 207 [January 10, 1910], 2–3. The information provided by these two sources is confirmed by Αλέξανδρος Δ. Ζάννας, *Ο Μακεδονικός Αγών: Αναμνήσεις* (Thessaloniki, 1960), 53–54. Zannas refers to Dr. Nâzım as Niyazi Bey.

47. For detailed information, see T.B.M.M. Arşivi, D. 239/31, Defter 8: Ankara İstiklâl Mahkemesi Zabıtnâmesi 1341, 6; "Nâzım Bey," *Yeni Asır*, July 28, 1908; "Doktor Nâzım Bey ve Hey'et-i Muhtereme'nin Şehrimizi Teşrifi," *İkdam*, August 10, 1908; "Doktor Nâzım Bey'in Selânik'e Muvâsalatı," *Sabah*, July 31, 1908; and "Nâzım Bey ile Mülâkat," *Sabah*, August 11, 1908.

48. See the minutes of Dr. Nâzım's deposition at the "Ankara Independence Court" in July 1926, T.B.M.M. Arşivi, D. 239/31, Defter 8: Ankara İstiklâl Mahkemesi Zabıtnâmesi 1341, 6.

49. Mehmed [Dr. Nâzım] to Şövalye [Bahaeddin Şakir], Salonica, undated [late June 1907?], Private Papers of Bahaeddin Şakir.

50. Şarliye [Dr. Nâzım] to Baha[eddin Şakir], Salonica, undated [late June–early July 1907], Private Papers of Bahaeddin Şakir. See also the minutes of Dr. Nâzım's deposition at the "Ankara Independence Court" in July 1926, T.B.M.M. Arşivi, D. 239/31, Defter 8: Ankara İstiklâl Mahkemesi Zabıtnâmesi 1341, 3.

51. The CPU central committee therefore informed the Istanbul branch of the merger more than a month before the actual agreement. See Dr. Bahaeddin [Şakir] to Ağabey [Silistireli Hacı İbrahim Paşazâde Hamdi], "the director of the first division of the Istanbul branch," dated [Paris], August 21, [1]907/no. 341, *Muhaberat Kopyası*, 385.

52. Dr. Bahaeddin [Şakir] to [Mehmed Sa'id Halim Pasha], dated Paris, August 26, [1]907/no. 347, *Muhaberat Kopyası*, 393.

53. [Dr. Bahaeddin Şakir]'s memorandum to the CPU Internal Headquarters, enclosed with a note to Mehmed [Dr. Nâzım], undated [October 16, 1907]/no. 390, *Muhaberat Kopyası*, 452–55; and Dr. Bahaeddin [Şakir] to the CPU Internal Headquarters, undated [October 25, 1907]/no. 391, *Muhaberat Kopyası*, 459–60.

54. Copies of this document are in "Hürriyet ve Osmanlı Terakki [ve] İttihad Cemiyetleri Arasındaki Mukavelenâme," no. 386, *Muhaberat Kopyası*, 444–45; and "Sûret," ibid., 487. There are minor discrepancies between the two texts, and the translation given here is based on the second document. A copy of the second document was sent to all branches and to the CPU Internal Headquarters. See, for example, the copy sent to the CPU Constanţa branch in AQSh, 19/58//962/18, enclosed with Dr. Bahaeddin [Şakir] to the CPU Constanţa branch, dated [Paris], November 1, 1907/no. 400, in AQSh, 19/58//962/17; and with Dr. Bahaeddin [Şakir] to the CPU Internal Headquarters, dated [Paris], November 1, 1907/no. 401, *Muhaberat Kopyası*, 474. Also published in "Osmanlı İttihad ve Terakki Cemiyeti: Vesâik-i Tarihiyeden," *Haftalık Şûra-yı Ümmet*, no. 204 [January 20, 1910], 2; and in B[ahaeddin] Ş[akir], "Osmanlı İttihad ve Terakki Cemiyeti: Vesâik-i Tarihiyeden," *Bağçe*, no. [18], 3–4.

55. [Dr. Bahaeddin Şakir]'s memorandum to the CPU Internal Headquarters, enclosed with a note to Mehmed [Dr. Nâzım], undated [October 16, 1907]/no. 390, *Muhaberat Kopyası*, 453. The CPU External Headquarters sent two sets of cipher code to the CPU Internal Headquarters on November 19, 1907.

56. Sâî [Talât Bey] to [Bahaeddin Şakir], October 19, [1]907/no. 1, in "Osmanlı İttihad ve Terakki Cemiyeti: Vesâik-i Tarihiyeden," *Haftalık Şûra-yı Ümmet*, no. 204, 2–3; and in B[ahaeddin] Ş[akir], "Osmanlı İttihad ve Terakki Cemiyeti: Vesâik-i Tarihiyeden," *Bağçe*, no. [18], 4–6.

57. Mehmed [Dr. Nâzım] to Şövalye [Bahaeddin Şakir], Salonica, undated [mid-October 1907], Private Papers of Bahaeddin Şakir.

58. See the report by the Italian adjoint respecting "the Turkish Revolutionary Society," enclosed with Barclay to Grey, Therapia, July 16, 1908/no. 392, PRO/F.O. 371/544, file 25303. A copy of it entitled "Association révolutionnaire turque" was enclosed with the note from Urbański to the Reichskriegsministerium, Skopje, July 15, 1908/no. 173 (Jungtürkenbewegung in Monastir) and is in Österreichisches Kriegsarchiv, Kriegsministerium Präsidial Register (1908). Another copy is in PAAA, 626/3, Mazedonien, 156 (Bd. 140-141). See also "L'œuvre de la 'Jeune Turquie,'" *Études* 118, no. 6 (January 20, 1909), 199; and René Pinon, "La Turquie nouvelle," *Revue des Deux Mondes* 47 (September 1, 1908), 151.

59. The 27th article of the regulations regarding the oath ceremony uses the phrase "while one of his hands is on the sacred book of the religion that he professes and the other hand is on a dagger and a revolver." *Osmanlı Terakki ve İttihad Cemiyeti Teşkilât-ı Dahiliye Nizamnâmesi* ([Paris], 1324 [1908]), 4–5 (article 27). The draft version of the CPU Internal Regulations is among the private papers of Bahaeddin Şakir.

60. *Osmanlı Terakki ve İttihad Cemiyeti Teşkilât-ı Dahiliye Nizamnâmesi*, 1 (article 2).

61. Ibid., 7 (article 48).

62. Ibid., 8 (article 52).

63. Ibid., 8 (article 50).

64. Ibid., 8 (article 55).

65. The section entitled "Usûl-i Muhakemât ve Mücazât Faslı," ibid. (Article 1 of this section).

66. Ibid.

67. Ibid., 10–11 (2nd article of this section).

68. See the letter of H[üsrev] Sami and Dr. Bahaeddin [Şakir] beginning "[Muhterem] Vatandaşımız" and dated [March 190]8/no. 555, *Kopye Defteri*, 221.

69. Despite this fact, the CPU External Headquarters required all members at the branches under their supervision to take the new oath. See the letter of H[üsrev] Sami and Dr. Bahaeddin [Şakir] beginning "Gayûr ve Aziz Vatandaşımız" and dated Paris, January 16, [1]908/no. 481, *Kopye Defteri*, 90; and their letter to the CPU Canea branch, dated [Paris], January 16, 1908/ no. 489, *Kopye Defteri*, 106.

70. For the strong impact of the oath ceremony on new members, see *Enver Paşa'nın Anıları*, ed. Halil Erdoğan Cengiz (Istabul, 1991), 60–61; Karabekir, *İttihat ve Terakki Cemiyeti, 1896–1909*, 184–85; and Ghulam Ambia Khan, "The Political Renaissance in Turkey," *The Hindustan Review* 19, no. 115 (March 1909), 239–40.

71. See *Osmanlı Terakki ve İttihad Cemiyeti Teşkilât-ı Dahiliye Nizamnâmesi*, 4–5 (articles 25 and 26).

72. Ibid., 5 (articles 27, 28, and 29); see also the letter of Dr. Bahaeddin [Şakir] beginning "Vatanperver Efendim" and dated [Paris], October, 30, 1907/no. 397 (duplicate number), *Muhaberat Kopyası*, 468–69; the letter of H[üsrev] Sami and Dr. Bahaeddin [Şakir] beginning "Aziz ve Gayûr Arkadaşımız" and dated [Paris], February 6, 1908/no. 505, *Kopye Defteri*, 138–39; and their letter beginning "Aziz Vatanperverler" and dated [Paris], March 7, 1908/ no. 547, *Kopye Defteri*, 204–5.

73. *Osmanlı Terakki ve İttihad Cemiyeti Teşkilât-ı Dahiliye Nizamnâmesi*, 1 (Article 3).

74. The new coat of arms was on the cover page of the new internal regulations. See also *Şûra-yı Ümmet*, no. 133 (April 15, 1908), 1, where the coat of arms was printed.

75. Dr. Bahaeddin [Şakir] to the director of the CPU Istanbul branch, undated [early November 1907]/no. 402, *Muhaberat Kopyası*, 475; Dr. Bahaeddin [Şakir] to the director of the CPU Lâzistan External branch, undated [early November 1907]/no. 408, *Muhaberat Kopyası*, 486; Dr. Bahaeddin [Şakir] to the director of the CPU Baghdad branch, undated [early November 1907]/no. 409, *Muhaberat Kopyası*, 488; Dr. Bahaeddin [Şakir] to the CPU Kazanlık branch, dated [Paris], November 26, 1907/no. 438, *Kopye Defteri*, 17; and Dr. Bahaeddin [Şakir] to the director of the CPU Canea branch, undated [late November 1907]/no. 440, *Kopye Defteri*, 18.

76. Ağabey [Silistireli Hacı İbrahim Paşazâde Hamdi] on behalf of the CPU Istanbul branch to the CPU Internal Affairs division in Paris, dated Istanbul [December 23, 1907]/no. 5, Private

Papers of Bahaeddin Şakir. In their letter of response, Bahaeddin Şakir and Hüsrev Sami insisted that the Ottoman Freedom Society had indeed more than a thousand members. See their letter to Ağabey [Silistireli Hacı İbrahim Paşazâde Hamdi], the director of the CPU Istanbul branch, dated [Paris] January 19, 1908/no. 488, *Kopye Defteri*, 103. The CPU Istanbul branch, however, was not fully convinced. See Ağabey [Silistireli Hacı İbrahim Paşazâde Hamdi] on behalf of the CPU Istanbul branch to the CPU Internal Affairs division in Paris, dated Istanbul [February 20, 1908]/no. 6, Private Papers of Bahaeddin Şakir. In later correspondence with the Istanbul branch the CPU center used the phrase "close to a thousand" instead of "more than a thousand" when referring to the number of the Ottoman Freedom Society's members. See [Dr. Bahaeddin Şakir] to the director of the CPU Istanbul branch, undated [March 1908]/no. 545, *Kopye Defteri*, 200.

77. Undated [August 1907] memorandum from Mehmed [Dr. Nâzım] to Şövalye [Bahaeddin Şakir], Private Papers of Bahaeddin Şakir.

78. [Bahaeddin Şakir], "Osmanlı İttihad ve Terakki Cemiyeti Paris Âzâsı," *Bağçe*, no. 3 [August 17, 1908], 13.

79. See the letter of H[üsrev] Sami and Dr. Bahaeddin [Şakir] beginning "Aziz Vatandaşımız" and dated [Paris], January 27, 1908/no. 493, *Kopye Defteri*, 111. Bahaeddin Şakir asked another individual whether he could "actively participate in rendering services to the fatherland." See the letter of Dr. Bahaeddin [Şakir] beginning "Muhterem Vatandaşımız" and undated [February 1908]/no. 523, *Kopye Defteri*, 176.

80. See, for example, the letter of H[üsrev] Sami and Dr. Bahaeddin [Şakir] beginning "Gayretli Vatandaşımız" and dated [Paris], January 27, 1908/no. 494, *Kopye Defteri*, 113; their letter beginning "Aziz Vatandaşımız" and dated [Paris], January 28, 1908/no. 498, *Kopye Defteri*, 119; and their letter beginning "Fâzıl-ı Muhteremimiz" and dated [Paris], February 13, 1908/no. 516, *Kopye Defteri*, 163.

81. See the letter of Dr. Bahaeddin [Şakir] beginning "Muhterem Biraderlerimiz" and dated [Paris], January 28, 1908/no. 500, *Kopye Defteri*, 121.

82. See, for example, "İstanbul 22 Teşrin-i evvel," *Şûra-yı Ümmet*, no. 126 (December 1, 1907), 3; "Portekiz Kralı'nın Millet Tarafından Katli," *Şûra-yı Ümmet*, nos. 128–29, 8; and "Portekiz Kralı'nın Katli," *Şûra-yı Ümmet*, no. 132 (April 1, 1908), 1.

83. See, for example, İ. Hakkı, "Mekâtib: İstanbul'dan," *Şûra-yı Ümmet*, no. 26 (April 13, 1903), 2; and "Bir Osmanlı Zabiti Tarafından Gönderilmiş Makale-i Mahsusadır," *Türk*, no. 90 (July 20, 1905), 2–3.

84. [Bahaeddin Şakir], "Küçüklerden Başlamalı," *Şûra-yı Ümmet*, no. 88 (February 24, 1906), 3.

85. "Les dessous de la Révolution turque," *L'Hellénisme* 6, no. 10 (October 1909), 287. See also Ahmed Ziya, *Meşrutiyet Uğrunda* (Istanbul, 1327 [1909]), 4.

86. See, for example, "Birinci ve İkinci Ordularımız," *Şûra-yı Ümmet*, no. 88, 4; "Dördüncü Ordu," *Şûra-yı Ümmet*, no. 89 (March 10, 1906), 3; "Osmanlı Ordusunda Kabiliyet-i İntizam," *Şûra-yı Ümmet*, no. 93 (April 9, 1906), 2–3; and "Mekteb-i Harbiye," *Şûra-yı Ümmet*, no. 105 (December 1, 1906), 2–3.

87. Bir Zabit [Hüsrev Sami], "Silah Arkadaşlarıma," *Şûra-yı Ümmet*, no. 116 (June 15, 1907), 2.

88. [Hüsrev Sami], "Silah Arkadaşlarıma—2," *Şûra-yı Ümmet*, nos. 120–21 (April 1, 1907), 2–3. For the use of a similar rhetoric, see "Asker Kardaşlarımıza," *Şûra-yı Ümmet*, no. 124 (October 31, 1907), 3.

89. H[üsrev] Sami, "Silah Arkadaşlarıma—4," *Şûra-yı Ümmet*, no. 126 (December 1, 1907), 1–2. See also "Malesh[evska planina] Balkanlarından," *Şûra-yı Ümmet*, no. 130 (February 15, 1908), 2.

90. "Şaşmaz mısınız [?]" *Şûra-yı Ümmet*, no. 123 (October 15, 1907), 2.

91. "Te'essüf-i Vatanperverâne," *Şûra-yı Ümmet*, no. 123, 2.

92. "*Şûra-yı Ümmet*," *Şûra-yı Ümmet*, no. 112 (April 1, 1907), 1.

93. [Hüsrev Sami], "Silah Arkadaşlarıma—3," *Şûra-yı Ümmet*, no. 125 (November 15, 1907), 1–2. See also "İstanbul Tehlikede," *Şûra-yı Ümmet*, no. 127 (December 15, 1907), 1–2.

94. Ahmed Rıza, *Vazife ve Mes'uliyet* 2, *Asker* (Cairo, 1323 [1907]).

95. [Ömer Naci], "İstanbul Kapularında," *Şûra-yı Ümmet*, no. 125, 1.

96. H[üsrev] Sami, "Silah Arkadaşlarıma—5," *Şûra-yı Ümmet*, no. 130, 2.

97. Ahmed Niyazi, *Hatırât-ı Niyazi*, 31/fn.

98. See Mehmed Ramih, *Berrî ve Bahrî Silah Arkadaşlarıma* ([Paris], 1326 [1908]), passim. A summary in French can be found in K.-J. Basmadjian, "Deux brochures," *Revue du Monde Musulman* 5, no. 8, 740–41.

99. Luigi Villari, "Races, Religions, and Propagandas," in *The Balkan Question: The Present Condition of the Balkans and European Responsibilities*, ed. Luigi Villari (New York, 1905), 134.

100. See, for example, the chapter on "Turkish and Albanian Brigandage" in Draganof, *Macedonia and the Reforms* (London, 1908), 181 ff; Gustav Hubka, *Die österreichisch-ungarische Offiziermission in Makedonien, 1903–1909* (Vienna, 1910), 93; O. Focief, *La Justice turque et les réformes en Macédoine: aperçu sur leur histoire et leur organisation, leur fonctionnement et leurs abus* (Paris, 1907), 264–72; and H. N. Brailsford, "Greece and Macedonia," *Contemporary Review* 88 (October 1905), 570–71.

101. See, for example, BBA–BEO/Mümtaze Kalemi: Bulgaristan Tasnifi Evrakı II, A. MTZ (04), 144/68 (1324.6.3); 158/74 (1325.5.20); 167/92 (1326.5.25); 168/31 (1326.6.5); and 169/23 (1326.6.20); BBA–YSHM, 493/17 (1323.B.17); BBA–TFR.1.SFR. 3/243 (1326.6.12); and BBA–TFR.1.A. 30/3804 (1326.6.16). For later denials, see BBA–DH.SYS. 74-4/2-50 (1330.3.8).

102. See, for example, the report dated 3/16 September 1901 and entitled "Bandes turques existentes dans le sandjak de Salonique," PRO/F.O. 297/2; and Louis Leger, *Turcs et Grecs contre Bulgares en Macédoine* (Paris, 1904), 30 ff. For examples of Turkish bands active during the period in which the CPU was attempting to organize a network of bands, see "Relevé des événements survenus dans le secteur Austro-Hongrois pendant le mois de Février 1908 (annexe au 311/Präs., 80-3); "Relevé des événements survenus dans le secteur Italien pendant le mois de Mai 1908 (Präs., 80-3/16)"; and "Relevé des événements survenus pendant le mois de Juillet 1908 n.s. dans le secteur d'Autriche-Hongrie (Präs., 80-3/29)," Österreichisches Kriegsarchiv, Kriegsministerium Präsidial Register (1908).

103. See, for example, Anastas Mitrev, *Memoari, ogledi, statii* (Skopje, 1974), 43–44; and Christ Anastasoff, *Tragic Peninsula: A History of the Macedonian Movement for Independence since 1878* (St. Louis, 1938), 322–23. Leading CPU military members maintained after the Young Turk Revolution of 1908 that they were deeply influenced by and imitated the band organizations in general and the IMRO in particular. See *Enver Paşa'nın Anıları*, 72; "Enver Pasha's Comments on the Work and Organization of the Macedonian anti-Ottoman Committees," *Balcania* 7, no. 1 (January 1973), 3–8; and Charles R. Buxton, *Turkey in Revolution* (London, 1909), 135. Freiherr von der Goltz, too, underscored the impact of band organizations in Macedonia on the Young Turks. See "Genc Türkiya ve Ordusu," *İttihad ve Terakki*, August 5, 1908. See also Alfred Rappaport, "Mazedonien und die Komitadschis," *Berliner Monatshefte für internationale Aufklärung* 8 (1930), 742.

104. Mehmed [Dr. Nâzım] to Şövalye [Bahaeddin Şakir], undated [August 1907?], Private Papers of Bahaeddin Şakir.

105. See BBA–TFR.1.ŞKT. 27/2667 (1321.10.21). His activities were closely scrutinized by the authorities. See, for example, BBA–BEO/Zabtiye Giden, 663-21/14; 247 [March 10, 1905]. He was sometimes referred to in documents as Gemici Hüseyin. The Austro-Hungarian adjoint in Monastir reported that the brigand had terrorized the Christians in three subdistricts. See Goiginger to the Austro-Hungarian Civil Agent Bureau in Salonica, January 22, 1908/no. 22, Österreichisches Kriegsarchiv, Kriegsministerium Präsidial Register (1908).

106. The claims made in the European press about the feudal landlords' support of the Young Turks missed this point, which was the real reason for their backing the Young Turk movement. See, for example, "The Young Turks," *The Times*, August 15, 1908.

107. Left blank in the original text.

108. Left blank in the original text.

109. Mehmed [Dr. Nâzım] to Şövalye [Bahaeddin Şakir], undated [early September 1907?], Private Papers of Bahaeddin Şakir.

110. Mehmed [Dr. Nâzım] to Baha[eddin Şakir], undated [mid- September 1907?], Private Papers of Bahaeddin Şakir.

111. Ahmed Rıza, "Çete Teşkili Lüzûmuna Dair Mektub," *Şûra-yı Ümmet*, no. 123, 3–4. The leading figures in the movement praised Ahmed Rıza's adoption of an activist stand. See Mehmed Saʿid [Halim Pasha] to Ahmed Rıza, Cairo, January 12, 1908, Private Papers of Ahmed Rıza (1).

112. Baha[eddin Şakir] to Mehmed Bey [Dr. Nâzım], dated Paris, November 1, [1]907, Private Papers of Bahaeddin Şakir.

113. Sâî [Talât Bey] to [Bahaeddin Şakir], dated January 6, [1]907 [1908], in "Osmanlı İttihad ve Terakki Cemiyeti: Vesâik-i Tarihiyeden," *Haftalık Şûra-yı Ümmet*, no. 212 [March 17, 1910], 2.

114. See the undated memorandum entitled "Bir Çetenin Kuvvet ve İktidarı Bundan İbaretdir," Private Papers of Bahaeddin Şakir.

115. See the draft of CPU band regulations in Private Papers of Bahaeddin Şakir.

116. Ibid.

117. *Enver Paşa'nın Anıları*, 111–13. There are many similarities but also many differences between the copy of the CPU band regulations found among the private papers of Bahaeddin Şakir and the regulations made by Enver Bey and sent to the CPU Internal Headquarters.

118. See A [Hüsrev] Sâî[Sami] and Dr. Bahaeddin Şakir to the CPU Monastir branch, March 28, 1908/no. 578, in "Osmanlı İttihad ve Terakki Cemiyeti: Vesâik-i Tarihiyeden," *Haftalık Şûra-yı Ümmet*, no. 210 [March 3, 1910], 2–3.

119. Sâî [Talât Bey] on behalf of the CPU Internal Headquarters to the CPU External Headquarters, April 7, [1]908/no. 16, in "Kabl el-İnkılâb Cemiyet'e Aid Vesâik-i Tarihiyeden," *Haftalık Şûra-yı Ümmet*, no. 200 [December 23, 1909], 7–8.

120. Sâî [Talât Bey] to the CPU External Headquarters, May 23, [1]908/no. 42-10, in "Osmanlı İttihad ve Terakki Cemiyeti," *Haftalık Şûra-yı Ümmet*, no. 215 [April 7, 1910], 2.

121. Sâî [Talât Bey], "Osmanlı Terakki ve İttihad Cemiyeti Haricî Merkez-i Umumîsi Cânib-i Âlisine," May 15, [1]908/no. 31-9, in "Osmanlı İttihad ve Terakki Cemiyeti: Vesâik-i Tarihiyeden," *Haftalık Şûra-yı Ümmet*, no. 211 [March 10, 1910], 2.

122. Heathcote to O'Conor, Monastir, February 15, 1908/no. 10, PRO/F.O. 195/2297.

123. All this information is taken from Süleyman Kâni İrtem, "Ohride [*sic*] İttihad ve Terakki Merkezi Nasıl Kuruldu?" *Akşam*, June 2, 1943. The author was the then subgovernor of Ohrid, who helped the organizers to arm their band in 1907. See also Süleyman Külçe, *Firzovik Toplantısı ve Meşrutiyet* (İzmir, 1944), 61–62.

124. Dr. Bahaeddin [Şakir], "Osmanlı Terakki ve İttihad Cemiyeti Hey'et-i Merkeziye-i Dahiliyesi Cânib-i Âlisine Takdim Edilmek Üzere Sâî [Talât] Bey Efendi'ye," dated [Paris], January [?], [1]908/no. 501–8, *Kopye Defteri*, 129.

125. Fazlı Necib, "Nasıl Oldu!—3," *Yeni Asır*, August 16, 1908.

126. Ahmed Niyazi, *Hatırât-ı Niyazi*, 109. The CPU Monastir branch too, sent "başıbozuklar" to join the CPU Resen National Battalion with a letter of introduction ordering their inclusion. See ibid., 196. Adjutant-Major Ahmed Niyazi made an interesting statement in his letter to the inspector general in which he admitted the participation of brigands in his band. He wrote: "We cannot be compared with Çakıcı because we are not marauders like Çakıcı." See "Suret," in Inspector General Hüseyin Hilmi Pasha to the Grand Vizier's office, Salonica [July 9, 1908]/no. 240–2964, BBA–BEO/Makam-ı Samî-i Hazret-i Sadaretpenâhîye Gelen Şifre Telgrafnâmelerin Kaydına Mahsus Defterdir, 981–61/15. See also Ahmed Niyazi, *Hatırât-ı Niyazi*, 117–19, which provides a slightly different version.

127. *Enver Paşa'nın Anıları*, 110.

128. See Ahmed İzzet Pasha's coded telegram to the Ottoman Ministry of War, Ṣanʿāʾ [November 27, 1911], BBA–A.DVN.NMH. 37/1 (1330.S.24/1336).

129. BBA–BEO/Serasker Reft, 262-6/70; 1757 [November 28, 1907]/239539. In the mean-

time the complaints about the brigand reached their peak. See ibid., 1937 [December 30, 1907]/
241375.

130. "Şakî Hangisi?!" *Şûra-yı Ümmet*, no. 112, 1–3.

131. Ibid., 1.

132. Zeynel Besim, *Çakıcı Efe: Şaki Çakırcalı Mehmedin Hayatı ve Mâceraları* (Izmir,
1934), 364–68. Dr. Nâzım's expressions as recorded by this popular historian seem to be an
exact repetition of the ideas expressed in the CPU propaganda material.

133. See "Şakî mi yoksa Islahat Müfettişi mi?!" *Şûra-yı Ümmet*, no. 135 (June 1, 1908), 3–4.

134. Edhem Safi to the CPU central committee, Larnaca, June 22, [1]908, Private Papers
of Bahaeddin Şakir.

135. Edhem Safi's letter beginning "Çakırcalı Oğlu Mehmed Efe'ye," signed "Kahraman-
lığınızın, yiğitliğinizin meftunu bir sadık dostunuz" and dated June [?], 1324 [July 1908],
Private Papers of Bahaeddin Şakir.

136. H[üsrev] Sami and Dr. Bahaeddin Şakir, "Osmanlı Terakki ve İttihad Cemiyeti Dahilî
Merkez-i Umumisi'ne Takdim Edilmek Üzere Sâî [Talât] Bey'e," April 6, [1]908/no. 585–
14, in "Osmanlı İttihad ve Terakki Cemiyeti: Vesâik-i Tarihiyeden," *Haftalık Şûra-yı Ümmet*,
no. 207, 2; and "Havâdis-i Dahiliye: 1 Nisan İstanbul," *Şûra-yı Ümmet*, no. 133, 3.

137. See Dr. Nâzım's claims in "Les dessous de la Révolution turque," *L'Hellénisme* 6,
no. 10, 288.

138. Karabekir, *İttihat ve Terakki Cemiyeti, 1896–1909*, 180.

139. *Enver Paşa'nın Anıları*, 97.

140. Adjutant-Major Ahmed Niyazi Bey was of Albanian origin. Adjutant-Major Eyüb Sabri
was from a mixed Albanian-Turkish family. Jäckh, who met with many Young Turk leaders,
described him as an Albanian. See Ernst Jäckh, *Im türkischen Kriegslager durch Albanien*
(Heilbronn, 1911), 192; and idem, "Mahmud Schevket Pascha," *Geist des Ostens* 1, no. 4 (July
1913), 202. Both of these officers spoke Albanian as their mother tongue. Enver Bey's mother
was from a mixed Albanian-Turkish family, and he could communicate in Albanian. (See İbrahim
Temo to Karl Süssheim, Medgidia, December 25, [1]933, Nachlaß Süssheim.) Captain Bekir
Fikri was from an Albanian-Turkish family and was trilingual, fluent in Albanian, Turkish, and
Greek.

141. Enver Bey to a German woman with whom he frequently corresponded, Köprülü
[Veles], May 4, 1911, Ernst Jäckh Papers, Yale University, MS 466, Box 1, Folder 37. Enver
Bey's successes against bands of the Christian ethnic groups were even echoed in the Turk-
ish press in Bulgaria. See, for example, "Makedonya'da Eşkıya Çeteleri," *Tuna*, no. 345
[November 6, 1906], 3.

142. Ahmed Niyazi, *Hatırât-ı Niyazi*, 68.

143. See the CPU Monastir branch to the CPU External Headquarters, July 9, 1908. This
letter must have been intercepted by Bulgarian intelligence agents, who made a verbatim translation of it. I have used this translated version in TsDA, F. 317, a.e. 37, 19–21. The letter was
also published in "Osmanlı İttihad ve Terakki Cemiyeti: Vesâik-i Tarihiyeden," *Haftalık Şûra-
yı Ümmet*, no. 209 [February 24, 1910], 2–3. The names and addresses omitted in the latter
can be found in the former copy.

144. Ahmed Niyazi, *Hatırât-ı Niyazi*, 162.

145. Süleyman Kâni İrtem, "Ohride [*sic*] İttihad ve Terakki Merkezi Nasıl Kuruldu?"
Akşam, June 2, 1943; and *Enver Paşa'nın Anıları*, 71.

146. Bekir Fikri, *Balkanlarda Tedhiş ve Gerilla: Grebene* (Istanbul, 1976), 22–23.

147. See the letter of H[üsrev] Sami and Dr. Bahaeddin [Şakir] beginning "Aziz Arkadaşımız"
and dated [Paris], February 24, 1908/no. 533, *Kopye Defteri*, 184–85.

148. A[Hüsrev] Sâî [Sami] and Dr. Bahaeddin Şakir to the CPU Monastir branch, March
28, 1908/no. 578, in "Osmanlı İttihad ve Terakki Cemiyeti: Vesâik-i Tarihiyeden," *Haftalık
Şûra-yı Ümmet*, no. 210, 2–3.

149. See the letter of H[üsrev] Sami and Dr. Bahaeddin [Şakir] beginning "Muhterem
Efendim" and dated [Paris], February 26, 1908/no. 528, *Kopye Defteri*, 180.

150. See the subgovernor of Serres to the inspector general in Salonica [July 30], 1908/
no. 101, BBA–TFR.1.SL. 193/19238 (1326.7.1).

151. See the CPU Monastir branch to the CPU External Headquarters, July 9, 1908, in TsDA, F. 317, a.e. 37, 19–21; and in "Osmanlı İttihad ve Terakki Cemiyeti: Vesâik-i Tarihiyeden," *Haftalık Şûra-yı Ümmet*, no. 209, 3.

152. A[Hüsrev] Sâî [Sami] and Dr. Bahaeddin Şakir to the CPU Monastir branch, March 28, 1908/no. 578, in "Osmanlı İttihad ve Terakki Cemiyeti: Vesâik-i Tarihiyeden," *Haftalık Şûra-yı Ümmet*, no. 210, 2.

153. Ibid., 3.

154. See Karabekir, *İttihat ve Terakki Cemiyeti, 1896–1909*, 163–207; and *Enver Paşa'nın Anıları*, 64–66.

155. These were the centers mentioned in the available CPU correspondence. During the last days of the revolution telegrams from many other towns in European Turkey were sent to the offices of the Inspector General and the First Chamberlain. It is difficult to know whether there were active CPU branches in all these towns. It should be noted, however, that in each case there must have been at least one sympathizer to go to the post office and send a telegram on behalf of a real or fictitious CPU branch.

156. *Enver Paşa'nın Anıları*, 77–78.

157. Sâî [Talât Bey] to Bahaeddin Şakir, October 19, [1]907/no. 1, in *Haftalık Şûra-yı Ümmet*, no. 204, 2–3. In the document Draga was referred to as "a notable from Northern Albania."

158. See Stavro Skendi, *The Albanian National Awakening, 1878–1912* (Princeton, 1967), 335.

159. The information about the branch is taken from the following sources: "Galib Paşa'nın Anıları," *Hayat Tarih Mecmuası* 2, no. 6 (July 1, 1966), 5–6; and Karabekir, *İttihat ve Terakki Cemiyeti, 1896–1909*, 209–10.

160. Sâî [Talât Bey] to the CPU External Headquarters, undated [early July 1908], in "Osmanlı İttihad ve Terakki Cemiyeti: Vesâik-i Tarihiyeden," *Haftalık Şûra-yı Ümmet*, no. 218 [April 28, 1910], 2.

161. A copy of these regulations was found on Hüseyin Cudi, a student at the law school in Salonica, written on various pieces of paper. It is in BBA–BEO/Rumeli Müfettişliği Gelen, 982-61/16; 12-1227 [March 17, 1908]/245393 and 240046.

162. Dr. Bahaeddin [Şakir], "Osmanlı Terakki ve İttihad Cemiyeti Hey'et-i Merkeziye-i Dahiliyesi Cânib-i Âlisine Takdim Kılınmak Üzere Sâî [Talât] Bey'e," undated [mid-January 1908]/no. 478-7, *Kopye Defteri*, 82.

163. H[üsrev] Sami and Dr. Bahaeddin [Şakir] to O[sman] Tevfik, dated [Paris], February 25, [1]908/no. 528, *Kopye Defteri*, 177.

164. See the minutes of Dr. Nâzım's deposition at the "Ankara Independence Court" in July 1926, T.B.M.M. Arşivi, D. 239/31, Defter 8: Ankara İstiklâl Mahkemesi Zabıtnâmesi 1341, 4.

165. He described his trip in "İttihad ve Terakki Cemiyet-i Muhteremesi'nin 10 Temmuzdan Evveline Aid Tertibat ve İcraatına Dair: İzmir'de Tütüncü Yakub Ağa," *İnkılab*, no. 15 [October 30, 1909], 229–30. Hoca Kadri maintained that Dr. Nâzım had been smuggled into Izmir with the help of "a Jewish committee." [See Mehmed Kadri Nâsıh, *Sarayih* (Paris, 1910 [1911])], 181. No other source, however, mentions such help.

166. For the activities of Dr. Nâzım in Izmir and adjacent towns, see "Doktor Nâzım Bey'in Selânik'e Muvasalâtı," *Sabah*, July 31, 1908; "Doktor Nâzım Bey ve Hey'et-i Muhtereme'nin Şehrimizi Teşrifi," *İkdam*, August 10, 1908; "Serbestî Gazetesi," *Şûra-yı Ümmet*, November 11, 1908; Ahmed Refik, *İnkılâb-ı Azîm: 11 Temmuz 1324* (Istanbul, 1324 [1908]), 69–71; *Halil Menteşe'nin Anıları*, 118–20; İsmet İnönü, *Hatıralar* 1, ed. Sabahattin Selek (Istanbul, 1985), 40; Lamb to Barclay, Salonica, July 28, 1908/no. 99, PRO/F.O. 195/2298; Camille Fidel, "Le Comité Ottoman 'Union et Progrès,'" *Questions Diplomatiques et Coloniales* 27, 440; Félicien Challaye, "La Révolution turque et la question de la Macédoine," *La Revue du Mois* 6 (July–December 1908), 502; and M. Kâmil Dursun, *İzmir Hatıraları*, ed. Ünal Şenel (Izmir, 1994), 45–46.

167. Sâî [Talât Bey] to the CPU External Headquarters, May 15, [1]908/no. 31–9, in "Osmanlı İttihad ve Terakki Cemiyeti: Vesâik-i Tarihiyeden," *Haftalık Şûra-yı Ümmet*, no. 211, 2; and Sâî [Talât Bey] to the CPU External Headquarters, May 23, [1]908/no. 42–10, in "Osmanlı

İttihad ve Terakki Cemiyeti," *Haftalık Şûra-yı Ümmet*, no. 215, 2. Dr. Nâzım's success greatly pleased the CPU External Headquarters. See Dr. Bahaeddin [Şakir], "Osmanlı Terakki ve İttihad Cemiyeti Dahilî Merkez-i Umumîsi Cânib-i Âlisine Takdim Olunmak Üzere Sâî [Talât] Bey'e," dated Paris, March 8, [1]908/no. 550-11, *Kopye Defteri*, 212.

168. Undated [July 1908] communiqué by the CPU External Headquarters, Private Papers of Bahaeddin Şakir.

169. Dr. Bahaeddin [Şakir] to [Captain Mehmed Edib] beginning "Vatanperver Efendim" and dated [Paris], November 25, 1907/no. 435, *Kopye Defteri*, 14.

170. Its members were Captain Mehmed Edib, Engineering officer First Lieutenant Salâhaddin Bey, Engineering officer First Lieutenant Osman Efendi, Engineering officer First Lieutenant Mehmed Efendi, Engineering officer Second Lieutenant Edib Nâzım, Artillery officer Second Lieutenant Mehmed Rüşdi, and Artillery officer Second Lieutenant Süleyman Şemseddin. See Captain Mehmed Edib to the CPU External Headquarters, April 27, 1908, Private Papers of Bahaeddin Şakir.

171. Dr. Bahaeddin [Şakir] to the director of the CPU Kalʿa-i Sultaniye branch, dated Paris, January 3, [1]908/no. 466, *Kopye Defteri*, 59; and H[üsrev], Sami and Dr. Bahaeddin [Şakir] to [the CPU Kalʿa-i Sultaniye branch] beginning "Vatanperver Kardeşlerimiz" and dated [Paris] March 7, 1908/no. 549, *Kopye Defteri*, 210.

172. Captain Mehmed Edib to the CPU External Headquarters, dated [February 19, 1908], Private Papers of Bahaeddin Şakir.

173. Ibid., Dr. Bahaeddin [Şakir] to the director of the CPU Kalʿa-i Sultaniye branch, dated Paris, January 3, [1]908/no. 466, *Kopye Defteri*, 59; and Captain Mehmed Edib to CPU External Headquarters, April 27, 1908, Private Papers of Bahaeddin Şakir.

174. Sâî [Talât Bey] to [Bahaeddin Şakir], January 6, [1]907 [1908], in "Osmanlı İttihad ve Terakki Cemiyeti: Vesâik-i Tarihiyeden," *Haftalık Şûra-yı Ümmet*, no. 212, 2.

175. Sâî [Talât Bey] to the CPU External Headquarters, May 23, [1]908/no. 42–10, in "Osmanlı İttihad ve Terakki Cemiyeti," *Haftalık Şûra-yı Ümmet*, no. 215, 2; and Hakkı Baha Pars to Câmi Baykut, Izmir, July 20, [1]941.

176. For the independent dissidents' activities, see Celâl Bayar's interview given to Kurtul Altuğ in "Meşrutiyet'ten Önce Gizli Teşkilât Kurduk," *Tercüman*, November 15, 1984; and Ziya Şakir, *Celâl Bayar: Hayatı ve Eserleri* (Istanbul, 1952), 18–19.

177. B. T. [Doctor Captain Rauf Bey] to Bahaeddin Şakir, Tripoli of Barbary, December 27, 1907, Private Papers of Bahaeddin Şakir; Sâî [Talât Bey] to the CPU External Headquarters, April [14, 1908], in "Osmanlı İttihad ve Terakki Cemiyeti: Vesâik-i Tarihiyeden," *Haftalık Şûra-yı Ümmet*, no. 213 [March 24, 1910], 2.

178. B. T. [Doctor Captain Rauf Bey] to [Bahaeddin Şakir], Tripoli of Barbary, April 28, 1908, Private Papers of Bahaeddin Şakir.

179. B. T. [Doctor Captain Rauf Bey] to [Bahaeddin Şakir], Tripoli of Barbary, June 16, 1908, Private Papers of Bahaeddin Şakir.

180. Sâî [Talât Bey] to the CPU External Headquarters, April 15, [1908]/no. 17–5, in *Şûra-yı Ümmet-Ali Kemal Daʿvası*, 80–82.

181. Bahaeddin Şakir to Hüseyinzâde Ali, undated [Paris, May 1908], Private Papers of Bahaeddin Şakir.

182. See Grey to O'Conor, December 22, 1905, Sir (Viscount) Grey's Private Papers, Turkey, 1905–1910, PRO/F.O. 800/79.

183. See G. P. Gooch, *Before the War: Studies in Diplomacy* 2, *The Coming of the Storm* (New York, 1938), 27; and Jacob Ruchti, *Die Reformaktion Österreich-Ungarns und Russlands in Mazedonien, 1903–1908; die Durchführung der Reformen* (Gotha, 1918), 91–92. The Balkan Committee's initiatives greatly irritated the sultan, although he found its proposals for Macedonian autonomy "utopian." See Marschall von Bieberstein to von Bülow, Pera, April 1, 1907/no. 68 (Entzifferung), A. 5547, PAAA 630/2, Das Verhältnis der Türkei zu Deutschland, 158 (Bd. 9-10).

184. "Joint note-verbale communicated to Sublime Porte," *A & P* (Cd. 4076), *Turkey* 3 (1908): *Further Correspondence Respecting the Affairs of South-Eastern Europe*, 179–81.

185. Ottoman note-verbale, ibid., 181–82. See also BBA–İrade-Hariciye, Za 1325/no. 8-2849(3730).

186. "Identic note communicated to Sublime Porte," dated Pera, December 22, 1907, *A & P* (Cd. 4076), *Turkey* 3 (1908): *Further Correspondence Respecting the Affairs of South-Eastern Europe*, 182–83. See also BBA–İrade-Hariciye, Za 1325/no. 9–2850 (3735).

187. Grey's memorandum to Cambon, di San Guiliano, Metternich, Beckendorff, and Mensdorff, dated December 18, 1907, *A & P* (Cd. 3958), *Turkey* 1 (1908): *Further Correspondence Respecting Proposals by His Majesty's Government for Reforms in Macedonia*, 1–2.

188. "Memorandum communicated by Austro-Hungarian and Russian Embassies, January 28, 1908," ibid., 2–3.

189. See BBA–İrade-Ticaret ve Nafiʿa, Z 1325/no. 8-552 (3133). See also BBA–İrade-Hariciye, Z 1325/no. 12-1244 (3756).

190. The important published documents regarding the Austrian railway project are in *Österreich-Ungarns Aussenpolitik von der bosnischen Krise 1908 bis zum Kriegsausbruch 1914* 1 (Vienna, 1930), 3 ff; *Die Große Politik* 25/2, *Die englisch-russische Entente und der Osten* (Berlin, 1925), 281–382; *British Documents on the Origins of the War, 1898–1914* 5, *The Near East* (London, 1928), 321–55; and *Amtliche Aktenstücke zur Geschichte der europäischen Politik, 1885–1914: Die belgischen Dokumente zur Vorgeschichte des Weltkrieges* 4, *Die Balkanprobleme, die bosnische Krise/Albanien, der Panthersprung nach Agadir, 1908–1911* (Berlin, 1925), 52–64. The following studies provide detailed information about and analysis of the Austrian project and its impact on the Macedonian reforms: Arthur J. Ray, "The Novibazar Railway Project," *The Journal of Modern History* 10, no. 4 (March–December 1938), 496–527; and Solomon Wank, "Aehrenthal and the Sanjak of Novibazar Railway Project: A Reappraisal," *The Slavonic and East European Review* 42, no. 99 (June 1964), 354–69.

191. A British document provides the following information: "M. Isvolsky . . . stated that in September 1907 he and Baron d'Aehrenthal had come to an absolutely full agreement upon a draft scheme of reforms, and that during its discussion not a word had been said of the Sanjak railway. A month afterwards, however, he (M. Isvolsky) had heard that Baron Aehrenthal was working secretly at Constantinople to obtain the concession for that railway, and was offering, in exchange for that Concession, to withdraw Austro-Hungarian support for the judicial reform scheme." See Goschen to Grey, Marienbad, August 27, 1908/no. 114 (confidential), PRO/F.O. 371/548, file 30143. Available Russian documents support the claim. See, for example, "Lettre confidentielle du Prince Ouroussoff, en date de Vienne, le 27 décembre 1907/9 janvier 1908," in *Au service de la Russie: Alexandre Iswolsky, Correspondance Diplomatique, 1906–1911* (Paris, 1937), 172–75; and Izvol'skii to von der Osten-Sacken, St. Petersburg, February 14/27, 1908, *Die Große Politik* 25/2, *Die englisch-russische Entente und der Osten*, 343–45.

192. Barclay to Grey, Sofia, February 19, 1908/no. 52 (confidential), *British Documents on the Origins of the War, 1898–1914* 5, *The Near East*, 340. The statement was made by Danev, leader of the Russophiles in Bulgaria, who went on to assert that what the Ottoman government received in return "must be to the cost of the welfare of the Christian population of Macedonia." British members of the Parliament made similar comments during the discussion on Macedonia. For example, Gooch stated that "[t]he concession which Austria asked for, though legal, was one which could not become operative until she had obtained the leave of the Porte, and it was obvious to anybody who knew Turkey or human nature that a Power could not press Turkey to give reform in Macedonia while at the same time she was asking for something for herself." *Hansard's Parliamentary Debates*, 4th series, 184 (1908), cols. 1673–74.

193. Nicolson to Grey, St. Petersburg, February 18, 1908/no. 85, *British Documents on the Origins of the War, 1898–1914* 5, *The Near East*, 232–33.

194. *Hansard's Parliamentary Debates*, 4th series, 184, cols. 1519 ff.

195. Gooch, *Before the War*, 31.

196. *Hansard's Parliamentary Debates*, 4th series, 184, cols. 1696–1705. See also *Speeches on Foreign Affairs, 1904–1914 by Sir Edward Grey*, ed. Paul Knaplund (London, 1931), 80–88.

197. Grey to Goschen, March 3, 1908/no. 29, PRO/F.O. 120/848, file 7462.
198. See Nicolson to Grey, St. Petersburg, March 4, 1908 (private); Grey to Nicolson, March 17, 1898 (private); and Hardinge to Nicolson, March 17, 1908 (private), *British Documents on the Origins of the War, 1898–1914* 5, *The Near East*, 233–36; "Aide-mémoire communicated to Sir E. Grey by Count Benckendorff," dated March 26, 1908," and "Memorandum communicated to Count Benckendorff by Sir Edward Grey," dated April 4, 1908, *A & P* (Cd. 3963), *Turkey 2* (1908): *Further Correspondence Respecting Proposals by His Majesty's Government for Reforms in Macedonia*, 2–9.
199. See BBA–İrade-Hususî, S 1326/no. 88-197 and S 1326/no. 93-202; and "Note communicated to Ambassadors by Sublime Porte," *A & P* (Cd. 4076), *Turkey 3* (1908): *Further Correspondence Respecting the Affairs of South-Eastern Europe*, 235–36.
200. Dr. Bahaeddin [Şakir] to [Talât Bey], beginning "Refik-i Mu'azzezimiz Efendim" and dated Paris, November 19, 1907/no. 433, *Kopye Defteri*, 10.
201. The CPU External Headquarters found the speech "terrible" and claimed that it had been "proclaiming that England would work extremely hard to make Macedonia obtain absolute independence." See H[üsrev] Sami and Dr. Bahaeddin [Şakir], "Osmanlı Terakki ve İttihad Cemiyeti Dahilî Merkez-i Umumîsi Cânib-i Âlisine Takdim Kılınmak Üzere Sâî [Talât] Bey'e," dated [Paris], March 8, [1]908/no. 550-11, *Kopye Defteri*, 214.
202. H[üsrev] Sami and Dr. Bahaeddin [Şakir], "Osmanlı Terakki ve İttihad Cemiyeti Dahilî Merkez-i Umumîsi Hey'et-i Muhteremesine Takdim Edilmek Üzere Sâî [Talât] Bey'e," dated [Paris], March 16, [190]8/no. 557-12, *Kopye Defteri*, 225.
203. Ibid., 226–27. The CPU employed similar language in a letter sent to the inspector general, Hüseyin Hilmi Pasha, immediately prior to the revolution. See the copy of the letter from H[üsrev] Sami and Dr. Bahaeddin [Şakir] to the inspector general, dated July 8, 1908/no. 707, Private Papers of Bahaeddin Şakir.
204. *Kopye Defteri*, 228–29.
205. Sâî [Talât Bey] to the CPU External Headquarters, March 23, [1]908, in "Osmanlı İttihad ve Terakki Cemiyeti: Vesâik-i Tarihiyeden," *Haftalık Şûra-yı Ümmet*, no. 208 [February 17, 1910], 2–3.
206. See [Ahmed Saib], "Bir Senelik İdare-i Meşruta," *Hakayık-ı Tarihiye ve Siyasiye*, no. 2 [July 28, 1909], 37–38.
207. See [Emmanuel] Carasso's undated spy report, BBA–YEE, 15/74-24/74/15.
208. For example, Enver Bey noted: "Die Reformen, welche die europäischen Staaten hier durchzuführen wünschen, werden nur die Trennung dieses Landesteiles von uns zur Folge haben . . . Jeder fühlte, dass das Vaterland sich immer mehr dem Abgrund näherte. Die von Europa durchgeführte Unterstützung der Christen im Lande hatte eine den früheren Verhältnissen ganz entgegengesetzte Ungleichheit hervorgerufen. . . . Ausserdem machten all die fremden Offiziere und Beamten eine schlechte Wirkung auf das Volk und erweckten in ihm einen Hass gegen den Staat." See Enver Pasha's autobiography in Ernst Jäckh Papers, Yale University, MS 466, Box 2, Folder 41. See also Ahmed Niyazi, *Hatırât-ı Niyazi*, 26–32; Duru, *"İttihat ve Terakki" Hatıralarım*, 13–14; Karabekir, *İttihat ve Terakki Cemiyeti, 1896–1909*, 62–65, 69; and Halil Paşa, *İttihat ve Terakkî'den Cumhuriyet'e: Bitmeyen Savaş: Kütûlamare Kahramanı Halil Paşa'nın Anıları*, ed. Taylan Sorgun (Istanbul, 1972), 28–29.
209. A list of demands handed over to the authorities between March 13 and June 29, 1908, on behalf of the entire populations of the towns where the CPU had branches, gives us a better idea:
   1. Yenice (Gianniza), March [13, 1908]/no. 10 (from the population): Subject: The appointment of a new educational board to replace the present educational board composed of individuals who cannot render any service to educational progress and who do not have the imagination to advance local education.
   2. Karacaâbâd (north Gianniza), March [21, 1908]/no. 62 (from the population): Subject: The subgovernor's confiscation of private lands by labeling them pasture. The people demand the appointment of an official to investigate the issue and that their rights be protected.
   3. Lankaza (Langadas), March [24, 1908]/no. 65 (from the population of the village of

Suha): Subject: Demand for the appointment of a capable teacher to their village who could teach according to the new method.

4. Kozánē, March [23, 1908]/no. 72 (from the population): Subject: Demand for retention of an assistant prosecutor who was appointed to another post in another district.

5. Monastir, March [16, 1908]/no. 74 (from the population): Subject: Demand for the postponement of the compulsory donation for "gendarme stations" to the end of September.

6. Monastir, March [16, 1908]/no. 137 (from the population): Subject: Demand for the postponement of the compulsory donation for "gendarme stations" to the end of September.

7. Kozánē, March [28, 1908]/no. 138 (from the population): Subject: Demand for the extension of the term of Religious Court Judge Hüseyin Nafiz Efendi.

8. Karatova, March [17, 1908]/no. 149 (from the population): Subject: Demand for the extension of the term of the mayor of Kumanova, Cavid Bey.

9. Gusinje, [April 2, 1908]/no. 203 (from the population): Subject: Demand for the retention of Registry of Births Office Clerk İsmail Efendi in his position.

10. Karaferye (Véroia), [April 8, 1908]/no. 219 (from the population): Subject: Demand not to take into consideration complaints made against Commander Adjutant-Major Ahmed Refik.

11. Priština [April 8, 1908]/nos. 248, 249, and 250 (from the population): Subject: Complaints about the local *Mufti* Mustafa Hamdi.

12. Priština, [April 5, 1908]/no. 293 (from the population): Subject: Same issue.

13. Flōrina, [April 9, 1908]/no. 328 (from the population): Subject: Demand for retention of Registry of Births Office Clerk Şerif Efendi in his post.

14. Vodina (Edessa), April [19, 1908]/no. 454 (from the population): Subject: The people's testimony to the fact that Mustafa Şevket Efendi, the local religious court judge who had been forced to resign, was a righteous and capable person.

15. Ropcoz (Devin), April [25, 1908]/no. 480 (from the population): Subject: Protesting the ban on lumbering by the local forest administration.

16. Dráma, [May 4, 1908]/no. 555 (from the population of Nusretiye village): Subject: Demand for publication of a corrective note in the newspaper *Yeni Asır*, which had falsely claimed that a trainload of beer had been brought from Salonica to be consumed at a circumcision ceremony.

17. Serres, April [30, 1908]/no. 576 (from the population): Subject: Demand for the extension of the term of Religious Court Judge Mehmed Sadık Efendi.

18. Gilan (Gnjilane), [May 3, 1908]/no. 580 (from the population): Subject: Demand for transportation of mail from Salonica and Skopje directly to Gilan without a stopover in Priština.

19. Krupišta, May [14, 1908]/no. 645 (from the population of the Revati village): Subject: Demand for the replacement of the present village headman and the village administrative council with other individuals who could meet the requirements for such posts.

20. Komanova, May [25, 1908]/no. 707 (from the population): Subject: Demand for the return of pastures being cultivated by other individuals.

21. Praviŝte (Elevtheroúpolis), May [22, 1908]/no. 921 (from the population): Subject: Demand of some individuals for the return of pastures being cultivated by others.

22. Praviŝte (Elevtheroúpolis), May [22, 1908]/no. 922 (from the population): Subject: Demand that reports by informers against Üveyiz Hasbi Efendi, the religious court judge, not be taken into consideration.

23. Görice (Korçë), [June 12, 1908]/no. 926 (from the population): Subject: Demand for permission to reopen the lime-kiln opened by a certain Tanash Kalfa and closed down by the authorities.

24. Vodina (Edessa), June [18, 1908]/no. 980 (from the population): Subject: Asking for the replacement of Mayor Mustafa Efendi.

25. Karaferye (Véroia), June [24, 1908]/no. 1035 (from the population): Subject: Protest against the forced contribution to road construction.

26. Melnik, [June 13, 1908]/no. 1040 (on behalf of the population of the villages): Subject: Demand to exempt drafted *medrese* students from military service.

27. Dráma, [July 12, 1908]/no. 1374 (from the population): Subject: Demand for the extension of the term of Religious Court Judge Mehmed Efendi.
BBA–BEO/VGG(2): Müstedʿiyat 1324: 830/1. I have left aside hundreds of personal demands on a great variety of issues made in places where the CPU had branches.

210. A Diplomatist [George Young], *Nationalism and War in the Near East*, ed. Lord Courtney of Penwith (London, 1915), 112.

211. See the sultan's undated memorandum on Albanians, BBA–YEE, 9/2637/72/4.

212. See, for example, the demands of the Lume (Kulat ë Lumës) and Prizren *bayrakdar*s and the government's rejection of these. See BBA–MV, 111/no. 73 [July 23, 1905]; BBA–YSHM, 485/126 (1323.24.1); the Grand Vizier's office to the inspector general in Salonica [July 25, 1905]/no. 775; and the Grand Vizier's office to the governor of Kosovo [July 25, 1905]/no. 776, BBA–BEO/Şifre Telgrafnâme-i Samî (1321-1322), 701-28/12.

213. For the CPU decision, see Ahmed Niyazi, *Hatırât-ı Niyazi*, 36. For the most important mutinies, see Ziver Bey, the governor of Edirne, to the Grand Vizier's office [March 22, 1908]/no. 18-1047; Hilmi Pasha, the governor of Iōánnina, to the Grand Vizier's office [May 24, 1908]/no. 159-8997; and Seyfullah Pasha, the governor of Scutari in Albania, to the Grand Vizier's office [June 19, 1908]/no. 285-386 and [June 20, 1908]/no. 206-397, BBA–BEO/ Rumeli 1324; 979-61/13. For an analysis of the military mutinies during this period, see Mehmet-Şehmus Güzel, "Prélude à la 'Révolution' Jeune-Turc: la grogne des casernes," *Varia Turcica* 13, *La Vie politique, économique et socio-culturelle de l'Empire ottoman à l'Époque jeune-turc* (Istanbul, 1991), 262 ff.

214. Delon to the French Ministry of War, July 7, 1908/no. 248 (mutineries et complot au 3ᵉ ordou), Archives du Ministère de la Guerre, E.M.A et Attachés militaires, 7 N 1635. He later underscored the uneasiness among the troops and gave it as one of the main reasons for the revolution. See Delon to the French Ministry of War, October 7, 1908/no. 253 (la Révolution turque et l'armée), ibid. This fact was also underscored by other foreign observers. See, for example, "The Turkish Rising in Macedonia," *The Economist* 67, no. 3386 (July 18, 1908), 114–15.

215. BBA–BEO/Harbiye Giden, 263-6/71; 352 [May 16, 1908]/248479 and 248483. See also the coded telegram from the Grand Vizier's office to the Ministry of War [May 16, 1908]/ no. 161, BBA–BEO/Rumeli Vilâyât-ı Şâhânesi Müfettişliği Gelen, 980-61/14; BBA–BEO/ VGG(2): Manastır Giden: 552; 1110 [July 18, 1908–telegram]; Grand Vizier's office to the inspector general [July, 5, 1908]/no. 854, BEO/Şifre Telgrafnâme-i Samîlerin Kaydına Mahsus Defterdir, 702-28/13; and BBA–İrade-Askerî, Ca 1326/no. 1-926.

216. Nuri Bey, the governor of Scutari in Albania, to the Grand Vizier's office [July 14, 1908]/no. 258-5902, BBA–BEO/Rumeli 1324, 979-61/13.

217. Ahmed Niyazi, *Hatırât-ı Niyazi*, 36.

218. These mutinies continued throughout the revolution. Even a few days prior to the restoration of the constitution the troops were rioting. For example, on July 21, 1908, the gendarmes in Durazzo took the chief accountant of the town hostage and demanded payment of their unpaid salaries. See Nuri Bey, the governor of Scutari in Albania, to the Grand Vizier's office [July 21, 1908]/no. 282-6228, BBA–BEO/Rumeli 1324, 979-61/13.

219. Sâî [Talât Bey] to [Bahaeddin Şakir], January 6, [1]907 [1908], in "Osmanlı İttihad ve Terakki Cemiyeti: Vesâik-i Tarihiyeden," *Haftalık Şûra-yı Ümmet*, no. 212, 2.

220. Sâî [Talât Bey] to CPU External Headquarters, April 15, [1908]/no. 17–5, in *Şûra-yı Ümmet-Ali Kemal Daʿvası*, 80–81.

221. Sâî [Talât Bey] to the CPU External Headquarters, May 23, [1]908/no. 42-10, in "Osmanlı İttihad ve Terakki Cemiyeti," *Haftalık Şûra-yı Ümmet*, no. 215, 2.

222. "Avrupa'daki Üç Vilâyetimiz," *Şûra-yı Ümmet*, no. 127, 3–4.

223. "Rumeli'ye Dair—2: Muhafaza-i Asayiş," *Şûra-yı Ümmet*, no. 135, 1.

224. "Makedonya Mes'elesi . . . ," *Şûra-yı Ümmet*, no. 112, 4.

225. "Makedonya Mes'elesi," *Şûra-yı Ümmet*, no. 134 (August 15, 1908), 1.

226. "Makale-i Mahsusa," *Şûra-yı Ümmet*, no. 137, 1–2. See also "Mütâlâat," *Şûra-yı Ümmet*, no. 134 (May 15, 1908), 7.

227. "İcmâl-i Haricî: Makedonya Gidiyor," *Şûra-yı Ümmet*, no. 131 (March 15, 1908), 4.

228. "Avusturya'nın Selâniğe İnmesine İrade Çıkdı!" *Şûra-yı Ümmet*, no. 130 (February 15, 1901), 3–4. See also "Rumeli'den: Saraybosna-Metroviçe Hattının Ehemmiyet-i İktisadiye ve Askeriyesi," *Şûra-yı Ümmet*, no. 131, 1–2.

229. H[üsrev] Sami and Dr. Bahaeddin Şakir, "Osmanlı Terakki ve İttihad Cemiyeti Dahilî Merkez-i Umumisi'ne Takdim Edilmek Üzere Sâî [Talât] Bey'e," April 6, [1]908/no. 585-14, in "Osmanlı İttihad ve Terakki Cemiyeti: Vesâik-i Tarihiyeden," *Haftalık Şûra-yı Ümmet*, no. 207, 2–3.

230. *Enver Paşa'nın Anıları*, 79.

231. Selânikli Faik, *Tarihçe-i Hürriyet ve Padişahın Efkârı* ([Istanbul], 1324 [1908]), 23–24.

232. See Memduh Pasha, the Minister of the Interior, to the Grand Vizier's office [July 12, 1908]/no. 1679 (müsta'cel), BBA–BEO/Dahiliye Giden, 107-3/56; 1097-1259 [July 13, 1908]/251600. A copy of this note is in BBA–YEE, 23/291/12/71/II (d-e). Ottoman documents provide information about another journal, *Ümid* (Hope), which was published in Macedonia and distributed during the revolution. See the Grand Vizier's office to the inspector general in Salonica [July 9, 1908]/no. 884, BBA–BEO/Şifre Telgrafnâme-i Samîlerin Kaydına Mahsus Defterdir, 702-28/13; and the inspector general to the Grand Vizier's office [July 9, 1908]/no. 237-2947, BBA–BEO/Makam-ı Samî-i Hazret-i Sadaretpenâhîye Gelen Şifre Telgrafnâmelerin Kaydına Mahsus Defterdir, 981-61/15. Austro-Hungarian sources provide information about a CPU organ named *Hürriyet* (Freedom) and distributed during the revolution. See Urbański to Reichskriegsministerium, Skopje, July 19, 1908/no. 194 (Jungtürken und Arnautenbewegung); and July 23, 1908/no. 201 (Jungtürkenbewegung), Österreichisches Kriegsarchiv, Kriegsministerium Präsidial Register (1908).

233. See "Bismillâhirrahmanirrahim: İfade-i Mahsusa: Hürriyet," *Neyyir-i Hakikat*, no. 10 (July [24, 1908]), 1.

234. Sâî [Talât Bey] to the CPU External Headquarters, April [14, 1908], in "Osmanlı İttihad ve Terakki Cemiyeti: Vesâik-i Tarihiyeden," *Haftalık Şûra-yı Ümmet*, no. 213, 2; and Sâî [Talât Bey] to the CPU External Headquarters, May 23, [1]908/no. 42-10, in "Osmanlı İttihad ve Terakki Cemiyeti," *Haftalık Şûra-yı Ümmet*, no. 215, 2.

235. This essay was originally published by the CUP branch in Cairo in *Kanun-i Esasî* 2, no. 11 [March 29, 1898], 2 ff. It was later reproduced as a pamphlet; see *İmamet ve Hilâfet Risâlesi* (Cairo, 1315 [1898]).

236. Sâî [Talât Bey] to the CPU External Headquarters, May 23, 1908/no. 42-10, in "Osmanlı İttihad ve Terakki Cemiyeti," *Haftalık Şûra-yı Ümmet*, no. 215, 2.

237. A[Hüsrev] Sâî [Sami] and Dr. Bahaeddin Şakir to the CPU Monastir branch, March 28, 1908/no. 578, in "Osmanlı İttihad ve Terakki Cemiyeti: Vesâik-i Tarihiyeden," *Haftalık Şûra-yı Ümmet*, no. 210, 2.

238. See supra p. 186.

239. Heathcote to Barclay, Monastir, July 15, 1908/no. 40 (confidential), PRO/F.O. 195/2297.

240. See the CPU Monastir branch to the CPU External Headquarters, July 9, 1908, in TsDA, F. 317, a.e. 37, 19–21; also in "Osmanlı İttihad ve Terakki Cemiyeti: Vesâik-i Tarihiyeden," *Haftalık Şûra-yı Ümmet*, no. 209, 3.

241. H[üsrev] Sami and Dr. Bahaeddin Şakir, "Osmanlı Terakki ve İttihad Cemiyeti Dahilî Merkez-i Umumisi'ne Takdim Edilmek Üzere Sâî [Talât] Bey'e," April 6, [1]908/no. 585-14, in "Osmanlı İttihad ve Terakki Cemiyeti: Vesâik-i Tarihiyeden," *Haftalık Şûra-yı Ümmet*, no. 207, 2–3.

242. Prominent members of the CPU External Headquarters were working on an appeal to address inhabitants of Scutari in Albania when they received a telegram informing them of the success of the constitutional movement. See Hüsrev Sami, "Menâkıb-ı İhtilâliyeden," *Bağçe*, no. 17 [January 1910], 256.

243. See Chapter 6, supra pp. 185–86, for this appeal and revisions made on it during the revolution.

244. A one-page CPU appeal entitled "Umum Ahaliye: Kardaşlar! Müjde!," Private Papers

of Bahaeddin Şakir. A copy of it, which was read to the public in Serres during the demonstration on July 23, 1908, was enclosed with Greig to Lamb, Serres, July 28, 1908/no. 27, PRO/F.O. 294/35. A slightly different version was distributed in Salonica and enclosed with Inspector General Hüseyin Hilmi Pasha's telegram to the Grand Vizier's office, Salonica [July 23, 1908]/no. 351-4029, BBA–BEO/Şifre Telgrafnâme-i Samîlerin Kaydına Mahsus Defterdir, 702-28/13. A copy of a slightly edited Bulgarian version entitled "Do vsichki Otomanski podanitsi" and bearing the CPU Salonica Center's seal was issued after the revolution on July 15 [28], 1908, and is in TsDA, F. 176, op. 2, a.e. 143, 23.

245. See the undated [July 23, 1908?] appeal in TsDA, F. 331, op. 1, a.e. 234, 121.

246. See the CPU Monastir branch to the CPU External Headquarters, undated [March 1908?], in *Şûra-yı Ümmet-Ali Kemal Da'vası*, 86–87; A[Hüsrev] Sâî [Sami] and Dr. Bahaeddin Şakir to the CPU Monastir branch, March 28, 1908/no. 578, in "Osmanlı İttihad ve Terakki Cemiyeti: Vesâik-i Tarihiyeden," *Haftalık Şûra-yı Ümmet*, no. 210, 2; and Sâî [Talât Bey] to the CPU External Headquarters, May 23, [1]908/no. 42-10, in "Osmanlı İttihad ve Terakki Cemiyeti," *Haftalık Şûra-yı Ümmet*, no. 215, 2.

247. It should be noted, however, that individual Armenians worked for the revolutionary activities in Macedonia. See, for example, BBA–BEO/VGG(2): Müşiriyet [1]324 Vâridesi: 639; 519 [July 20, 1908].

248. [Dr. Bahaeddin Şakir]'s memorandum to the CPU Internal Headquarters, enclosed with a note to Mehmed [Dr. Nâzım], undated [October 16, 1907]/no. 390, *Muhaberat Kopyası*, 455.

249. I use the convenient term Macedo-Bulgarian to refer to the IMRO, the Vŭrkhovist Committee, the so-called Constitutionalists, and the other related organizations active in Macedonia. The Ottoman sources and the CPU correspondence always refer to these organizations as Bulgarian organizations or committees. The term makes no claim as to the ethnic origins of the committees' members or the national characteristics of the organizations' members, which are controversial points of the existing nation-states in the Balkans.

250. See, for example, the note from Peev, the Bulgarian representative in Salonica, to Paprikov, Bulgarian Foreign Minister, dated July 21, 1908, in T. Vlakhov, "Bŭlgariia i mladoturskata revoliutsiia," *Godishnik na Sofiiskiia Universitet, Filosofsko-Istoricheski Fakultet* 59, no. 3 (1965), 41.

251. See Nedkov to Paprikov, Monastir, June 19 [July 2], 1908, BIA, F. 317, a.e. 37, 3–16. The CPU Headquarters too approached Shopov, the Bulgarian consul in Salonica, and expressed their wish to join forces with the IMRO. See Shopov to Paprikov, Salonica, June 27 [July 10], 1908, BIA, F. 317, a.e. 70, 54–57.

252. For an early refusal of the right wing of the IMRO to work with the Young Turks, see Sadık el-Müeyyed Pasha to the Grand Vizier's office, September 28, 1905/no. 2020-571, BBA–YSHM, 493/106 (1323.8.3).

253. "Wishing to preserve the integrity and discipline of the organization and to uproot the pattern of outrageous acts, and in view as well of the threats of further murders made in open letters, the congress unanimously decided that those who signed the open letter, as well as the actual murderers, are hereby expelled from the Organization and are to be considered its enemies." See "Deklaratsiia na obshtiia kongres na Vŭtreshnata Makedono-Odrinska Revoliutsionna Organizatsiia prez 1908 g.," *Ilinden* 1, no. 34 (March 28 [April 10], 1908), 1.

254. Ibid.

255. See, for example, the untitled editorial in *Ilinden* 1, no. 5 (December 12 [25], 1907), 1–2. They also criticize Sandanski's "acts as a defender of the principle of the Organization's independence."

256. Balugdžić to Milavanović, Skopje, July 24 [August 6], 1908/no. 685, in Gligor Todorovski, "Jane Sandanski niz dokumenti od Srpski izvori (1908–1910)," *Glasnik* 16, no. 3 (1972), 117. (Ottoman sources stated that Mehmed Cavid visited Sofia immediately after the revolution for negotiations with the right wing of the IMRO; see "Cavid Bey," *Yeni Asır*, July 30, 1908. It seems that the CPU chose him as its representative because of his early contacts with this group.) Although parts of the aforementioned Serbian report provide accurate information, the charges against Sandanski accusing him of being a Turkish agent and assas-

sinating Sarafov and Garvanov because of his agreement with the Young Turks (pp. 117–18) were entirely unfounded.

257. "Okritoto pismo na serchani," *Odrinski glas* 1, no. 7 (February 24 [March 9], 1908), 3.
258. See, for example, "Iz nov pŭt," *Odrinski glas* 1, no. 8 (March 2 [15], 1908), 1–2; and "Dolu chetnichestvoto!" *Odrinski glas* 1, no. 17 (May 4 [17], 1908), 1.
259. "Bŭlgariia i Makedonskata problema," *Odrinski glas* 1, no. 10 (March 16 [29], 1908), 1.
260. He defended his ideas in his pamphlet entitled *Makedonskiiat vŭpros i sotsialnata demokratsiia* (Sliven, 1907).
261. His articles praising the resolutions of the congress were mentioned in Chapter 7. See supra pp. 199–200.
262. P. Bogdanov [Pavel Deliradev], "Vŭzkrŭsvane na vŭrkhovizma," *Odrinski glas* 1, no. 5 (February 10 [23], 1908), 2.
263. P. Bogdanov [Pavel Deliradev], "Vŭzkrŭsvane na vŭrkhovizma," *Odrinski glas* 1, no. 6 (February 17 [March 2], 1908), 1–2. Sandanski used similar themes during an interview that he gave immediately after the Young Turk Revolution, accusing Serbia and Bulgaria and claiming that the slogan of "liberation of our brothers" became meaningless because of the reestablishment of the constitutional regime. See *Dokumenti za borbata na makedonskiot narod za samostojnost i za nacionalna država* 1 (Skopje, 1981), 502–3.
264. "Iz nov pŭt," *Odrinski glas* 1, no. 8, 1–2. This constitutionalist view was strongly criticized by the right wing. See W., "Za novite 'revoliutsioneri'," *Ilinden* 1, no. 39 (April 21 [May 4], 1908), 1.
265. "Iz mladoturskata revoliutsionna literatura," *Odrinski glas* 1, no. 17, 3–4.
266. Ibid., 3.
267. "Konstitutsionna Turtsiia," *Odrinski glas* 1, no. 18 (May 11 [24], 1908), 1–2.
268. See, for example, "Ilindentsi za mladoturtsite," *Odrinski glas* 1, no. 20 (May 25 [June 7], 1908), 2–3, defending Sabahaddin Bey's appeal to the Macedonian Muslims; see Sabahaddin, "Rumeli'deki Türk Vatandaşlarımıza Bir Da'vet," *Terakki*, no. 18, 5–6; this was republished in "Fransa'da," *İrşad*, no. 71 (May 20 [June 2], 1908), 3, and was severely denounced by the right wing of the IMRO. See *Ilinden*, 1, no. 44 (May 12 [May 25], 1908), 1–2; and no. 45 (May 16[29], 1908), 1.
269. See the CPU Monastir branch to the CPU External Headquarters, July 9, 1908, in TsDA, F. 317, a.e. 37, 19–21; also in "Osmanlı İttihad ve Terakki Cemiyeti: Vesâik-i Tarihiyeden," *Haftalık Şûra-yı Ümmet*, no. 209, 3. Halil Bey had been arrested in Skopje while working there as the translator of the Bulgarian consulate, charged with subscribing to illegal Young Turk publications, and he was freed thanks to the intervention of the Bulgarian diplomats. See Nedkov to Stanchov, Skopje, February 1[14], 1907/no. 91; Nedkov to Shopov, Skopje, February 2 [15], and February 5 [18], 1907/nos. 96 and 120; Shopov to Nedkov, Salonica, February 4 [17], February 8 [21], February 17 [March 2], and March 6[19], 1907/ nos. 109, 128, 174, and 256; Nedkov to Geshov, Skopje, February, 9 [22], 13 [26], 14 [27], 19 [March 4], March 14 [28], March 19 [April 1], and March 24 [April 6], 1907/nos. 139, 161, 172, 173, 176, 264, and 276, TsDA, F. 334, op. 1, a.e. 224, 1–31; and "Haricî," *Balkan*, no. 305 [November 30, 1907], 3.
270. A Serbian document underscored the clandestine relations between the Ottoman officers and Macedo-Bulgarian organizations during this period, but it did not provide any names. See Balugdžić to Milavanović, Monastir, July 24 [August 6], 1908/no. 497, in Gligor Todorovski, "Jane Sandanski niz dokumenti od Srpski izvori (1908–1910)," *Glasnik* 16, 114.
271. Sâî [Talât Bey]'s undated note [April–May 1908?] to Bahaeddin Şakir, Private Papers of Bahaeddin Şakir. A Young Turk officer allowed Deliradev to cross the border between Bulgaria and Macedonia to join Sandanski. See Mercia MacDermott, *For Freedom and Perfection: The Life of Yané Sandansky* (London, 1988), 323.
272. Ibid., 323–33.
273. Ibid., 338.
274. "Deliradef Efendi," *İttihad ve Terakki*, August 6, 1908.
275. MacDermott, *For Freedom and Perfection*, 333.
276. Heathcote to Barclay, Monastir, July 21, 1908/no. 42, PRO/F.O. 195/2298.

277. The manifesto was enclosed with Peev to Paprikov, Salonica, July 19, 1908 [August 1, 1908]/no. 665, and is in TsDA, F. 3, op. 8, a.e., 1256, 20–22. Another sign hinting at a prerevolution agreement was the very quick participation of the IMRO left-wing leaders Sandanski, Panitsa, and Khristo Chernopeev in the celebrations after the revolution. See Gorge Miljkovik', "Dva raritetni predmeti od vremoto na mladoturskata revolucija (1908) i revolucionernata dejnost na Jane Sandanski," *Istoria* 21, no. 1 (1985), 186–87.

278. This was the main concern of the CPU, which did not expect great military support from Christian bands. As a matter of fact, during the 1909 Counterrevolution, when the CPU decided to organize an "Action Army" to march on Istanbul and approached the left-wing leaders of the IMRO, it made it clear that it needed their support not for military reasons but to draw a picture of a multinational movement. See Alekso Martulkov, *Moeto učestvo vo revolucionernite borbi na Makedonija* (Skopje, 1954), 207–8.

279. Ahmed Niyazi, *Hatırât-ı Niyazi*, 71–72; and Nedkov to Paprikov, Monastir, June 21 [July 4], 1908/no. 506, TsDA, F. 176, op. 2, a.e. 110, 16–17.

280. See the CPU Monastir branch to the CPU External Headquarters, July 9, 1908, in TsDA, F. 317, a.e. 37, 19–21; also in "Osmanlı İttihad ve Terakki Cemiyeti: Vesâik-i Tarihiyeden," *Haftalık Şûra-yı Ümmet*, no. 209, 3.

281. See the CPU Monastir branch to the CPU Resen National Battalion through the CPU Ohrid branch, undated [July 12, 1908], in Ahmed Niyazi, *Hatırât-ı Niyazi*, 150.

282. Adjutant-Major Ahmed Niyazi Bey's appeal in Bulgarian, dated June 23 [July 6], 1908, and enclosed with Nedkov to Paprikov, Monastir, June 29 [July 12], 1908/no. 519, TsDA, F. 176, op. 2, a.e. 110, 36–37. Its Turkish translation, which provides the date of issuance as June 22 [July 5], 1908, appears in Ahmed Niyazi, *Hatırât-ı Niyazi*, 104–8. A French translation is in PRO/F.O. 195/2297.

283. See the CPU Monastir branch to Adjutant-Major Ahmed Niyazi, dated June 24 [July 7, 1908], in Ahmed Niyazi, *Hatırât-ı Niyazi*, 127.

284. Mitrev, *Memoari, ogledi, statii*, 45–46.

285. Buchanan to Grey, Sofia, July 23, 1908/no. 15-281 (decipher), PRO/F.O. 195/2292. See also Nedkov to Paprikov, Monastir, June 25 [July 8], 1908/no. 514, TsDA, F. 321, op. 2, a.e. 39, 8–10.

286. See, for example, "Mladoturtsizmŭt mezhdu Makedonskite voiski," *Ilinden* 1, no. 53 (June 14 [June 28, 1908]), 3.

287. See the address of the right wing of the IMRO to the "CUP in Salonica," in *Ilinden* 1, no. 58, 3.

288. See Peev to Paprikov, Salonica, August 6 [19], 1908/no. 733, TsDA, F. 176, op. 2, a.e. 116, 80; and Khristo Matov, *Khristo Matov za svoiata revoliutsionna deynost* (Sofia, 1928), 56–57. The IMRO insisted on "complete local autonomy for the various peoples of Turkey and their union or confederation into one State." See Pantchev's memorandum to the CUP on behalf of the right wing of the IMRO, enclosed with Lamb to Lowther, August 17, 1908/no. 112, PRO/F.O. 195/2298. See also Jacques Dorobantz, "Les Jeunes-Turcs et la Macédoine," *Questions Diplomatiques et Coloniales* 26, no. 277 (September 1, 1908), 281–82; "Pançef'in Beyânâtı," *İkdam*, August 13, 1908; and "Déclarations de M. Pintchef," *Le Temps*, August 8, 1908. Although the press communiqué of the right wing of the IMRO, addressing the CUP, seemed less radical, it too stressed the importance of strengthening local administration. See a copy of the address enclosed with Pára to Aehrenthal, Salonica, August 9, 1908/no. 169, HHStA, PA XXXVIII 409, Konsulat Saloniki, Berichte 1908 I–VIII. A slightly different version was summarized in a dispatch sent to Tittoni from Sofia on August 13, 1908/no. 1068-315, ASMAE, Affari Politici, Serie P. Politica (1891–1916), pacco 123–24.

289. During the early days of the revolution the CUP and the left wing of the IMRO went as far as to discuss attempts "to precipitate a revolution at Constantinople" to dispose of Abdülhamid II. See Buchanan to the British embassy in Istanbul, Sofia, August 2, 1908/no. 281 (confidential decipher), PRO/F.O. 195/2292. As for later relations, Hüseyin Kâzım Kadri, who had served as the subgovernor of Serres and later as the governor of Salonica during the period, gave an interesting account of the nature of the relationship between the CUP and Sandanski after the revolution. Despite his claim, complaints about Sandanski and the left

wing of the IMRO were common in CUP circles and not unique to him. See Şeyh Muhsin-i Fânî [Hüseyin Kâzım Kadri], *10 Temmuz İnkılâbi ve Netâyici: Türkiya İnkırazının Sâikleri: Makedonya, Ermenistan ve Suriye Mes'eleleri* (Istanbul, 1336 [1920]), 64–66.

290. For more information, see Douglas Dakin, *The Greek Struggle in Macedonia, 1897–1913* (Thessaloniki, 1966), 198 ff.

291. These comments were made by Koromilas, the Greek consul in Salonica, who asked the Greek authorities in Athens to look after a Young Turk named İshak Bey, a lawyer who defended accused Greek rebels in Salonica without charge, but not to give him any information. See Koromilas to Argyropoulos, Salonica, May 3, 1905, in Περικλής Α. Αργυρόπουλς, *Ο Μακεδονικός Αγών· Απομνημονεύματα* (Thessaloniki, 1957), 62–63.

292. See, for example, Ζάννας, *Ο Μακεδονικός Αγών*, 53.

293. Βασίλειος, Λαούρδας, *Το Ελληνικόν Γενικόν Προξενείον θεσσαλονίκης, 1903–1908* (Thessaloniki, 1961), 20–21.

294. Kanellopoulos to Baltatzis, Salonica, February 14 [27], 1908/no. 122-650, AYE.

295. Enialis's dispatch dated April 18 [May 1, 1908]/no. 148, enclosed with Kanellopoulos to Baltatzis, Salonica, May 12 [May 25], 1908/no. 425-2136, AYE.

296. Ibid., and Κωνσταντίνος Α. Βακαλόπουλος, *Νεότουρκοι και Μακεδονία* (Thessaloniki, 1988), 189.

297. A. J. Panayotopoulos, "Early Relations Between the Greeks and the Young Turks," *Balkan Studies* 21 (1980), 89.

298. Dimaras to Baltatzis, Monastir, May 27 [June 9], 1908/no. 575, AYE.

299. Sachtouris to Baltatzis, Serres, June 1 [14], 1908/no. 237, AYE.

300. See, for example, Karatzas, the Greek consul in Mytilíni, to Baltatzis, June 3 [16], 1908/no. 528-2628, AYE.

301. Ahmed Niyazi, *Hatırât-ı Niyazi*, 223. See also E. F. Knight, *The Awakening of Turkey* (London, 1909), 196. During his stay in Athens, Münir Pasha gave interviews to newspapers and attempted to downplay the importance of the Young Turk Revolution. See "Une interview avec Munir-Pacha ambassadeur de Turquie à Paris," *Le Monde Hellénique*, July 19, 1908; and A. Argyropoulo, "Les Jeunes Turcs," ibid.

302. Baltatzis earlier agreed with the line adopted by Dimaras and expressed in his dispatch of May 27 [June 9], 1908. See Baltatzis to Kanellopoulos, June 10 [23], 1908/no. 2628, AYE.

303. Confidential circular dated June 27 [July 10], 1908/no. 3006, AYE. Ottoman intelligence sources obtained this information soon thereafter. See BBA–BEO/Mümtaze Müteferrikası, 755/37-5; 54 [July 21, 1908]/285136.

304. For example, Stephanos turned down Adjutant-Major Ahmed Niyazi's invitation. See Dakin, *The Greek Struggle*, 379/n. 11. Talât Bey (Pasha) stated in his posthumously published memoirs that Greek intellectual leaders too had turned down the offer to join the CPU. See [Talât Paşa?] *Talât Paşa'nın Hâtıraları*, ed. Enver Bolayır (Istanbul, 1958), 12/fn.

305. See Potten to Baltatzis, Constantinople, July 18 [31], 1908/no. 3534 (telegram); and Griparis to Baltatzis, Constantinople, July 17[30], 1908/no. 694, AYE.

306. At one point even his deposition was discussed; see the undated [August 1908?] report signed by Papastephanapoulos in AYE. See also Ζάννας, *Ο Μακεδονικός Αγών*, 57. For his dislike of the Young Turks and the new regime, see Σία Αναγνωστοπούλου, *Μικρά Ασία, 19ος αι. -1919: Οι Ελληνορθόδοξες Κοινότητες* (Athens, 1997), 458–59, and 505/n. 15.

307. He made such a statement when he met with Mehmed Sa'id Pasha, the Grand Vizier. He also expressed his concerns regarding "imprisoned and mistreated Christians in Macedonia and Epirus." See Griparis to Baltatzis, Constantinople, July 17 [30], 1908/no. 694, AYE.

308. See the CPU Monastir branch to the CPU External Headquarters, July 9, 1908, in TsDA, F. 317, a.e. 37, 19–21; also in "Osmanlı İttihad ve Terakki Cemiyeti: Vesâik-i Tarihiyeden," *Haftalık Şûra-yı Ümmet*, no. 209, 3.

309. H[üsrev] Sami and Dr. Bahaeddin Şakir, "Osmanlı Terakki ve İttihad Cemiyeti Dahilî Merkez-i Umumisi'ne Takdim Edilmek Üzere Sâî [Talât] Bey'e," April 6, [1]908/no. 585-14, in "Osmanlı İttihad ve Terakki Cemiyeti: Vesâik-i Tarihiyeden," *Haftalık Şûra-yı Ümmet*, no. 207, 2–3.

310. "En Turquie: le mouvement révolutionnaire," *L'Hellénisme* 5, nos. 6–7 (March 15–April 1, 1908), 7. The information given by the journal was confidentially told to Adossidis by Dr. Nâzım before he left Paris for Salonica with the former's help to contact Greek committees. See H[üsrev] Sami and Dr. Bahaeddin Şakir, "Osmanlı Terakki ve İttihad Cemiyeti Dahilî Merkez-i Umumisi'ne Takdim Edilmek Üzere Sâî [Talât] Bey'e," April 6, [1]908/no. 585-14, in "Osmanlı İttihad ve Terakki Cemiyeti: Vesâik-i Tarihiyeden," *Haftalık Şûra-yı Ümmet*, no. 207, 2–3.

311. "Un bon conseil," *Mechveret Supplément Français*, no. 198 (April 1, 1908), 1–2.

312. Dimaras to Baltatzis, Monastir, May 27 [June 9], 1908/no. 575, AYE.

313. See the CPU Monastir branch to the CPU External Headquarters, July 9, 1908, in TsDA, F. 317, a.e. 37, 19–21; and in "Osmanlı İttihad ve Terakki Cemiyeti: Vesâik-i Tarihiyeden," *Haftalık Şûra-yı Ümmet*, no. 209, 3.

314. Βακαλόπουλος, *Νεότουρκοι και Μακεδονία*, 189.

315. Dimaras to Baltatzis, Monastir, July 2 [15], 1907/no. 711–3301, AYE.

316. See Heathcote to Barclay, Monastir, July 19, 1908/no. 170 (decipher), PRO/F.O. 195/2297; and July 21, 1908/no. 42, PRO/F.O. 195/2298; and the Austro-Hungarian report, Monastir, July 22, 1908/no. 49, in *Austro-Hungarian Documents Relating to the Macedonian Struggle, 1896–1912*, ed. F. R. Bridge (Thessaloniki, 1962), 393–94.

317. A copy of the original ultimatum, entitled "Manastır'da Rum Cemaati Reis-i Ruhanisiyle Rum Komitelerine Verilen Muhtıra Suretidir" and sealed with the seal of the CPU Monastir branch, is in PRO/F.O. 294/46. Another copy and its Bulgarian translation are in TsDA, F. 331, op. 1, a.e. 234, 99–101 and are republished in *Neyyir-i Hakikat*, no. 10, 3; and in Ahmed Niyazi, *Hatırât-ı Niyazi*, 223–26. See also Vlakhov, "Bŭlgariia i mladoturskata revoliutsiia," *Godishnik*, 41. The Greek bands also continued their attacks on Macedo-Bulgarian villages, adding to the tension between the CPU and Greek organizations. See René Pinon, "La Turquie nouvelle," *Revue des Deux Mondes* 78/47 (September 1, 1908), 151; and Heathcote to Barclay, Monastir, July 27, 1908/no. 47, PRO/F.O. 195/2298. An article that had been published in a local CPU journal provided detailed information about the Muslims serving in the Greek bands. See "Siyasî Fırıldaklar," *Sada-yı Girid*, no. 24 [October 17, 1907], 1–2.

318. See the CPU Monastir branch to the British consul in Monastir, dated July 22, 1908, originally enclosed with Heathcote to Barclay, July 27, 1908/no. 47, PRO/F.O. 195/2298. A second copy, with which an English translation of the ultimatum was enclosed, is in PRO/F.O. 294/46. Yet another copy of the letter to the consuls is in TsDA, F. 331, op. 1, a.e. 234, 101.

319. See Nedkov to Paprikov, Monastir, July 10 [23], 1908/no. 405, TsDA, F. 176, op. 2, a.e. 117, 91–92.

320. Heathcote to Barclay, Monastir, July 27, 1908/no. 47, PRO/F.O. 195/2298.

321. Baltatzis to Kanellopoulos, Athens, July 12 [25], 1908 (telegram), AYE.

322. The Ottoman authorities received information prior to the Young Turk Revolution that the Greeks and Serbians would launch an offensive against Macedo-Bulgarian bands. See BBA–BEO/VGG(2): Selânik Giden: 566; 44 [May 14, 1908]/248400. There were no plans, however, for a general Greek-Serbian offensive in the spring of 1908; this was to be no more than a local alliance against the Macedo-Bulgarian bands. See Austro-Hungarian reports, Monastir, May 24, 1908/no. 34; and June 3, 1908/no. 43 (telegram), in *Austro-Hungarian Documents*, ed. Bridge, 378–79 and 382.

323. See Wayne S. Vucinich, *Serbia Between East and West: The Events of 1903–1908* (Stanford, 1954), 159.

324. Gligor Todorovski, "Srpskite konzuli vo Makedonija za mladoturskata revolucija od 1908 godina.," *Glasnik* 9, no. 1 (1965), 194.

325. Ahmed Niyazi, *Hatırât-ı Niyazi*, 111–12.

326. Sâî [Talât Bey]'s undated note [April–May 1908?] to Bahaeddin Şakir, Private Papers of Bahaeddin Şakir.

327. Milan Vl. Đorđević, "Srbi i mladoturci," *Srpski Književni Glasnik* 23, no. 5 (1909), 346. The Serbian chargé d'affaires in London stated to Francis Bertie that "the reform movement in Turkey is illusory, and that nothing is to be hoped from the Turks." See Bertie to

Frank, July 30, 1908 (private), PRO/F.O. 800/180, The Private Papers of Sir (Lord) Francis Bertie, Confidential Series A (1899–1919).

328. Not necessarily by an "Albanian democratic bourgeois national liberation" movement, however, as was later claimed. See Manol Pandevski, "Razvitokot na političkiot život vo Evropska Turcija vo periodot na mladoturskoto upravuvanje (1908–1912)," *Istoria* 15, no. 2 (1979), 106.

329. See supra p. 214.

330. The appeal was quoted in I[rina] G[rigorevna] Senkevitch, "Mladoturetskaia revoliutsiia 1908 goda. i Albanskoe natsional'noe dvizhenie," *Sovetskoe vostokovedenie*, 1958/1, 33–34. The CPU distributed large numbers of these appeals, and by December 1907 the CPU External Headquarters told those who demanded copies of the appeals that they were out of print. See the letter of Dr. Bahaeddin [Şakir] beginning "Azizim Efendim" and dated [Paris], December 9, 1907/no. 448, *Kopye Defteri*, 35. Later, in April 1908, this appeal was edited and redistributed by the CPU Monastir branch. See H[üsrev] Sami and Dr. Bahaeddin Şakir, "Osmanlı Terakki ve İttihad Cemiyeti Dahilî Merkez-i Umumisi'ne Takdim Edilmek Üzere Sâî [Talât] Bey'e," April 6, [1]908/no. 585-14, in "Osmanlı İttihad ve Terakki Cemiyeti: Vesâik-i Tarihiyeden," *Haftalık Şûra-yı Ümmet*, no. 207, 2.

331. Sâî [Talât Bey]'s undated note [April–May 1908?] to Bahaeddin Şakir, Private Papers of Bahaeddin Şakir.

332. Underscored by Russian civil agents who, because of this fact, saw a scheme by the Young Turk party and the Albanian committees. See the report from Monastir dated July 6, 1908/no. 314, in *Krasnyi arkhiv* 6/43 (1930): *Turetskaia revoliutsiia 1908–1909 gg.*, 12–13.

333. Ahmed Niyazi, *Hatırât-ı Niyazi*, 197.

334. See Sâî [Talât Bey] to the CPU External Headquarters, May 23, [1]908/no. 42-10 in "Osmanlı İttihad ve Terakki Cemiyeti," *Haftalık Şûra-yı Ümmet*, no. 215, 2.

335. See I. G. Senkevich, *Osvoboditel'noe dvizhenie albanskogo naroda v 1905–1912 gg.* (Moscow, 1952), 92; Shukri Rahimi, *Vilayeti i Kosovës më 1878–1912* (Prishtina, 1969), 121; Peter Bartl, *Die albanischen Muslime zur Zeit der nationalen Unabhängigkeitsbewegung, 1878–1912* (Wiesbaden, 1968), 154; and Borbe Mikić, *Austro-Ugarska i Mladoturci, 1908–1912* (Banjaluka, 1983), 36.

336. The best source on İsmail Kemal's secret negotiations and agreement with the Greeks is Θάνος Αναγνωστόπουλος–Παλαιολόγος, *Ελλάς και Αλβαγία στις Αρχές του Εικοστού Αιώγα* (Thessaloniki, 1995), 35, 213–17, which provides the agreement document and all other related material. See also BBA–YSHM, 512/118 (1325.5.26), 513/83 (1325.C.21), and 518/80 (1325.B. 18); Timo Dilo, "Mbi të ashtuquajturën marrëveshje shqiptaro-greke midis Ismail Qemalit dhe Jorgo Theotoqis," *Studime Historike* 21/4 (1967), 112–13, 122; Basil Kondis, *Greece and Albania, 1908–1914* (Thessaloniki, 1976), 33–35; B.P. Papadakis, *Histoire diplomatique de la Question nord-epirote, 1912–1957* (Athens, 1958), 11–12; and Léon Maccas, *La Question gréco-albanaise* (Nancy, 1921), 58. For the CPU's severe criticism of İsmail Kemal on account of this agreement, see "Havâdis-i Dahiliye," *Şûra-yı Ümmet*, no. 117 (June 1, 1907), 4; "Trablusgarb Vali-i Esbakı İsmail Kemal Bey," *Şûra-yı Ümmet*, nos. 120–21, 4; and O., "Alliance Gréco-Albanaise," *Mechveret Supplément Français*, no. 191 (September 1, 1907), 2–3. For the criticism by the nationalist faction, see "İsmail Kemal'in Cemiyeti," *Türk*, no. 171 (August 1, 1907), 2.

337. Sâî [Talât Bey] to the CPU External Headquarters, May 23, [1]908/no. 42-10, in "Osmanlı İttihad ve Terakki Cemiyeti," *Haftalık Şûra-yı Ümmet*, no. 215, 2.

338. For example, Asamutlu Tevfik, Yisuçanlı Emin, and Nevesilli Kurtish joined the CPU Resen National Battalion with all their men. See Hüseyin Hilmi Pasha to the Grand Vizier's office, Salonica [July 9, 1908]/240-2964, and [July 9, 1908]/no. 245-1004, BBA–BEO/ Makam-ı Samî-i Hazret-i Sadaretpenâhîye Gelen Şifre Telgrafnâmelerin Kaydına Mahsus Defterdir, 981-61/15. See also Ahmed Niyazi, *Hatırât-ı Niyazi*, 117.

339. For these bands, see Shemsi Hajro, *Në gjirin e lëvizjes patriotike (kujtime nga vitet, 1888–1932)* (Tirana, 1962), 16 ff.; I. G. Senkevich, "Natsional'no-Osvoboditel'noe dvizhenie Albanskogo naroda v nachale XX veka," *Voprosy istorii* 6 (1956), 54 ff; Skendi, *The Albanian National Awakening*, 207 ff; Veselin Beševliev, "Aus der Geschichte der

Protobulgaren," *Études Balkaniques* 6, no. 2 (1970), 33; and Harry Lamb's memorandum entitled "Memorandum on course of events in Macedonia during 1908," enclosed with Lamb to Lowther, Salonica, February 6, 1909/no. 11, PRO/F.O. 195/2328.

340. Lamb to Barclay, Salonica, April 30, 1908/no. 51, PRO/F.O. 195/2297. Ottoman documents describe the most important Albanian band under the command of Çerçiz Topulli as "his cohort composed of fifty people, Muslims and Bulgarians." It is unclear, however, whether these Bulgarians were members of the IMRO or simply joined Çerçiz Topulli against the Greek bands. See BBA–BEO/VGG (2), Manastır Giden: 552; 926 [June 27, 1908– decipher]. Adjutant-Major Ahmed Niyazi too stated that in Ohrid, Bulgarian bands and Albanian Tosk bands under Çerçiz Topulli had been united. See Ahmed Niyazi, *Hatırât-ı Niyazi*, 43.

341. A translation of an article on the assassination of an Ottoman major by Çerçiz Topulli's band appeared in *Drita*, enclosed with Lamb to Barclay, May 26, 1908/no. 66, PRO/F.O. 195/ 2297. See also Hajro, *Në gjirin e lëvizjes patriotike,* 18–19; and idem, "Vrasja e bimbashit në Gjirokastër dhe lufta në mashkullorë," in *Kujtime nga lëvizja për çlirimin kombetar, 1878– 1912,* ed. Petraq Pepo (Tirana, 1962), 136–39.

342. *The Albanian Struggle in the Old World and New* (Boston, 1939), 44–45. See also I[van] S[tepanovich] Galkin, *Diplomatiia evropeiskikh derzhav v sviazi s osvoboditel'nym dvizheniem narodov Evropeiskoi Turtsii v 1905–1912 gg.* (Moscow, 1960), 111–12. Ottoman documents confirm these claims. See, for example, BBA–BEO/VGG(2): Manastır Giden: 552; 851 [June 18, 1908]. For Çerçiz Topulli's increasing activities immediately prior to the CPU's revolutionary drive, see the Grand Vizier's office to the governor of Iōánnina [June 27, 1908]/no. 798; and [July 1, 1908]/no. 827, BBA–BEO/Şifre Telgrafnâme-i Samîlerin Kaydına Mahsus Defterdir, 702-28/13; Hilmi Pasha to the Grand Vizier's office, Iōánnina [July 13, 1908]/no. 253-15630; BBA–BEO/Rumeli 1324, 979-61/13; BBA–İrade-Hususî, Ca 1326/no. 6-1010; and BBA–YSHM, 523/118 (1326.C.19).

343. Ahmed Niyazi, *Hatırât-ı Niyazi*, 160.

344. For biographical information about Çerçiz Topulli and about his activities, see N. Mermet, "Revolucioner shpyptarë-Disá heroj t'indipendences shqyptare—II: Qerqiz Topulli," *La Fédération Balkanique* 2, no. 37 (February 1, 1926), 545.

345. Ahmed Niyazi, *Hatırât-ı Niyazi*, 95.

346. Ibid.

347. Ibid., 163–64. An Albanian committee member made almost identical remarks at a café in Salonica and was subsequently arrested. See Niyazi Bey, the police director of Salonica, to the inspector general [July 13, 1908]/no. 131, BBA–TFR.1.SL. 191/19019 (1326.6.13).

348. Ahmed Niyazi, *Hatırât-ı Niyazi*, 163–64.

349. Ibid., 164–66.

350. Ibid., 167. Hajro, *Në gjirin e lëvizjes patriotike*, 59–60, underscores the role of Sheikh Hysein Baba as a mediator between Adjutant-Major Ahmed Niyazi and Çerçiz Topulli. See also idem, "Pritja e Bajos dhe e Çerçizit në Gjirokastër," in *Kujtime nga lëvizja për çlirimin kombetar, 1878–1912,* 160.

351. See Mihal Grameno, *Vepra* 2, *Kryengritja Shqiptare* (Priština, 1979), 200 ff; idem, "Kujtim nga malet: Rëfenjë: Abaz Nivica," in *Mendimi politik e shoqëror i rilindjes kombëtare shqiptare* 2 (1908–1910), ed. Zihni Haskaj (Tirana, 1976), 179; Esat Minarolli, "Një mbledhje në Manastirin e shën naumit," in *Kujtime nga lëvizja për çlirimin kombetar, 1878–1912,* 151; and Sadik Zhari, "Njaziu dhe Shqiptarët," ibid., 153–54;

352. The British military attaché in Istanbul emphasized this point. See Surtees's memorandum to Barclay, entitled "Program of Young Turk Movement in Macedonia" and dated Constantinople, July 15, 1908/no. 28, PRO/F.O. 195/2290.

353. Ahmed Niyazi, *Hatırât-ı Niyazi*, 164.

354. The sultan himself told Pallavicini, the Austro-Hungarian ambassador, that the officers participating in the movement were limited to those of Albanian descent. See Pallavicini to Aehrenthal, Constantinople, July 18, 1908/no. 9764-201, HHStA, PA XII 195, Türkei, Berichte, 1908 VI–VII.

355. An important exception was Major Enver Bey, whom the Albanians viewed as an officer with a close affinity to them.

356. He did not even know the identities of the members of the CPU Monastir branch's executive committee. See Ahmed Niyazi, *Hatırât-ı Niyazi*, 325–26.

357. Various neutral observers shared this viewpoint. See, for example, "Copie d'une lettre de M. Vernezza, Directeur de la Banque Ottomane à Uskub à M. Auboyneous, du 9 Juillet 1908," AE, T, Politique Intérieure: Macédoine 38 (Juin–Sept., 1908): 58, [62]. For an Albanian letter asking that the Albanians be credited for the revolution, see Bir Arnavud, "*Yeni Gazete*'ye Samimî Bir İhtar," *İkdam*, October 24, 1908. See also "*Yeni Asır*'dan: Arnavutluk'da Efkâr-ı Milliye," *İkdam*, August 30, 1908. Albanian committees later stressed this fact. See the appeal issued by the Central Albanian Committee on May 1, 1911, in *Albania*, ed. Historical Section of the Foreign Office (London, 1920), 93: "[W]e lent the Young Turk movement our aid, and to us its success was due."

358. An Austro-Hungarian diplomatic report claimed that the CPU had promised the Albanians the right to publish journals in Albanian. See Pósfai to Aehrenthal, Monastir, June 5, 1908/no. 36 (vertraulich), HHStA, PA XXXVIII 395 Konsulat Monastir, 1908. Aischin and Bartl maintain that Adjutant-Major Ahmed Niyazi, in the course of his negotiations with the Albanian committee members, accepted the Albanian proposal for an autonomous Albania administered by a governor appointed by the sultan. See Mohamed Aischin, *Die Freiheitsbewegung in der Türkei* (Berlin, [1908]), 84–85; and Bartl, *Die albanischen Muslime*, 155, respectively. See also "The Revolution in the Turkish Empire," *The Economist* 67, no. 3388 (August 1, 1908), 207.

359. See, for example, the memorandum of M[ary] Edith Durham, who was in Korçë during the restoration of the constitution: "Memorandum on the Albanian Question," in Aubrey Herbert Papers, Somerset Record Office (Taunton), DD/DRU 47, 5–6; idem, *Twenty Years of Balkan Tangle* (London, 1920),190–91; Pósfai to Aehrenthal, Monastir, July 31, 1908/ no. 50, HHStA, PA XXXVIII 395 Konsulat Monastir, 1908; Šukri Rahimi, "Albanci u borbi za nacionalnu emancipaciju posle mladoturske revolucije," *Jugoslavenski Istorijski Časopis* 1–2 (1970), 73; Kristaq Prifti, "Le mouvement politique et culturel en Albanie à la veille du Congrès de Monastir," *Studia Albanica* 6, no. 1 (1969), 44; Albert Ghica, *L'Albanie et la Question d'orient: solution de la Question d'orient* (Paris, 1908), 284, 290; and Senkevich, *Osvoboditel'noe dvizhenie albanskogo naroda*, 104. The most detailed list of the Albanian organizations' demands from the CPU immediately after the revolution is given in a long memorandum prepared by the Greek consul in Iōánnina and presented to Baltatzis. The memorandum is dated July 27 [August 9], 1908, and is in AYE.

360. Derviş Hima, *Devr-i Hürriyetde Zindandan Bir Sada* (Salonica, n.d. [1908?]), 14. He was arrested on charges of Albanian separatism. For more information, see Summa to Lowther, Scutari, September 24, 1908/no. 11, PRO/F.O. 195/2298; Summa to Lowther, Scutari, September 12, 1908/no. 9, PRO/F.O. 294/49; Summa to Lamb, Scutari, September 14, 1908/ no. 10, ibid.; Lamb to Lowther, January 20, 1909/no. 5, PRO/F.O. 295/19; "Dervish Hima," in *Mendimi politik e shoqëror i rilindjes kombëtare shqiptare* 2 (1908–1910), 143–45; and "La voie du mouvement révolutionnaire de Cossovo," *La Fédération Balkanique* 6, nos. 138–39, (August 1, 1930), 2970.

361. See Hanioğlu, *The Young Turks*, 89, 169.

362. [Tunalı Hilmi], *Makedonya: Mazi-Hâl-İstikbâl* (Cairo, 1316 [1898]), 14.

363. Sâî [Talât Bey] to the CPU External Headquarters, March 23, [1]908, in "Osmanlı İttihad ve Terakki Cemiyeti: Vesâik-i Tarihiyeden," *Haftalık Şûra-yı Ümmet*, no. 208, 3.

364. Sâî [Talât Bey] on behalf of the CPU Internal Headquarters to the CPU External Headquarters, April 7, [1]908/no. 16, in "Kabl el-İnkılâb Cemiyet'e Aid Vesâik-i Tarihiyeden," *Haftalık Şûra-yı Ümmet*, no. 200, 8.

365. A[Hüsrev] Sâî [Sami] and Dr. Bahaeddin Şakir to the CPU Monastir branch, March 28, 1908/no. 578, in "Osmanlı İttihad ve Terakki Cemiyeti: Vesâik-i Tarihiyeden," *Haftalık Şûra-yı Ümmet*, no. 210, 2.

366. Sâî [Talât Bey] to the CPU External Headquarters, March 23, [1]908, in "Osmanlı İttihad ve Terakki Cemiyeti: Vesâik-i Tarihiyeden," *Haftalık Şûra-yı Ümmet*, no. 208, 3.

367. *Enver Paşa'nın Anıları*, 79.
368. See Kemal H. Karpat, "The Memoirs of N. Batzaria: The Young Turks and Nationalism," *IJMES* 6, no. 3 (July 1975), 282.
369. *Enver Paşa'nın Anıları*, 79.
370. See Max Demeter Peyfuss, *Die aromunische Frage: ihre Entwicklung von den Ursprüngen bis zum Frieden von Bukarest (1913) und die Haltung Österreich-Ungarns* (Vienna, 1974), 108–9. Batzaria became the Minister of Public Works in 1913, and served as a mediator between the CUP and the Romanian government. See Take Jonescu [Ionescu], *Some Personal Impressions* (New York, 1920), 192.
371. M[oiz] Kohen, "Musevî Vatandaşlarımız," *Yeni Asır*, September 5, 1908.
372. See, for example, the note that the CPU Iōánnina branch presented to the consuls on July 24, 1908, enclosed with Camicia to Lamb, Iōánnina, July 28, 1908/no. 19, PRO/F.O. 294/32. A translation of it was published in "La nuova Turchia," *Nuova Antologia di Lettere, Scienze ed Arti* 136, no. 220/880 (August 16, 1908), 659.
373. See, for example, Mehmed Kadri Nâsıh, *Sarayih*, 133, 197–98, 216; Ali Necati, *İttihadın İç Yüzü: Cinayât-ı İttihadiyeden Bir Nebze* (Trabzon, 1328 [1912]), 47; and Şerif Paşa, *İkaz: Millet-i Osmaniye Bir Hitabe* (Paris, 1914), 15. For a foreign source underscoring the alleged role of the Freemasons, see "La puissance de l'islam: ses confréries religieuses," *Le Correspondant* 237, no. 4 (November 25, 1909), 632–35.
374. See, for example, *Turkey in Europe and Asia, Oxford Pamphlets 1914*, no. 38 (Oxford, 1914), 14; and "Enemy Portraits: (I) Enver Pasha," *The New Europe* 1, no. 5 (November 16, 1916), 149. Even more scholarly works published during the war stressed these claims. See, for example, R. W. Seton-Watson, *The Rise of Nationality in the Balkans* (London, 1917), 134–35.
375. "New Turkey and Jewish Prospects," *The Jewish Chronicle*, August 21, 1908, 7; for the view that "the constitution is equal to the charter for Jewish settlement for which Dr. Herzl fought" and similar claims, see "The Turkish Constitution and the Jews," *The Missionary Review of the World* 31/21 (October 1908), 783.
376. Nordau to Wolffsohn, Paris, November 25, 1908, CZA, W 96/I.
377. A good overview of Young Turk relations with Jews and Zionists is provided in Robert Olson, "The Young Turks and the Jews: A Historical Revision," *Turcica* 18 (1986), 219–35.
378. Karabekir, *İttihat ve Terakki Cemiyeti, 1896–1909*, 272–75.
379. Francis McCullagh, *The Fall of Abd-ul-Hamid* (London, 1910), 19. See also "The Secret of the Turkish Revolution," *The Living Age* 40, no. 258 (July–September 1908), 817.
380. Sâî [Talât Bey], "Osmanlı Terakki ve İttihad Cemiyeti Haricî Merkez-i Umumîsi Canib-i Âlisine," May 15, [1]908/no. 31–9, in "Osmanlı İttihad ve Terakki Cemiyeti: Vesâik-i Tarihiyeden," *Haftalık Şûra-yı Ümmet*, no. 211, 2.
381. Karabekir notes the importance that the CPU military organizers attributed to having a strong CPU branch in Edirne in the event that "the Third Army sent an 'Army of Liberation' to Istanbul." See Karabekir, *İttihat ve Terakki Cemiyeti, 1896–1909*, 268.
382. Obviously, this does not mean that no such plan was made. Unfortunately, the CPU documents about the last phase of the revolutionary activity are very limited. Also, as Adjutant-Major Ahmed Niyazi stated, certain plans providing their executors with details were burned according to strict orders by branch executive committees. See Ahmed Niyazi, *Hatırât-ı Niyazi*, 197.
383. Σπύρος Μελάς, *Η Επάγαστασις του 1909* (Athens, 1957), 65.
384. Karabekir, *İttihat ve Terakki Cemiyeti, 1896–1909*, 299.
385. Karatzas to Baltatzis, Mytilíni, June 3 [16], 1908/no. 528-2628, AYE. This person named Hakkı Bey was wounded by the CPU "gendarme force" while he was carrying out his investigation in Salonica. See Lamb to Barclay, Salonica, July 7, 1908/no. 84 (confidential), PRO/F.O. 195/2297.
386. "Sŭbitiiata v konstitutsionnata Turtsiia," *Mir*, August 8 [21], 1908. A list of dates given by foreign journalists and scholars is found in Ernest Edmondson Ramsaur, Jr. *The Young Turks: Prelude to the Revolution of 1908* (Princeton, 1957), 133/fn. 94.

387. Bahaeddin Şakir later stated that the "CPU Monastir branch was the center that struck the final blow." See B[ahaeddin] Ş[akir], "Osmanlı İttihad ve Terakki Cemiyeti," *Haftalık Şûra-yı Ümmet*, no. 203, 2.

388. The left wing of the IMRO again agreed to participate in a similar plan in April 1909; it eventually was carried out.

389. Lieutenant Colonel Ömer Nâzım, Salonica garrison commander, to the First Chamberlain's office [September, 25, 1907], BBA–YEE, 15/74-11-a/74/15.

390. Ahmed Şefik Pasha, the Minister of Police, to the Grand Vizier's office [March 13, 1908]/no. 273, BBA–BEO/Rumeli Müfettişliği Gelen, 982-61/16; 12-1227 [March 16, 1908]/ 245393 and 246046; BBA–BEO/Zabtiye Nezareti Âmed, 657-21/8; 273 [March 13, 1908]. For more information about this arrest, see Tırhalalı Vefik, "'Hürriyet Çelebi' İmzalı Makaleye Cevab," *Bağçe*, no. 5 [September 1, 1908], 13–14; and Alasonyalı H[üseyin] Cudi, "Komiser 'Vefik'e," *Bağçe*, no. 7 [September 15, 1908], 7–9.

391. "Rumeli," *Şûra-yı Ümmet*, no. 132, 4.

392. Es'ad Pasha, the acting commander of the Third Army, to the First Chamberlain's office [February 24, 1908]/no. 620 (decipher); and [March 8, 1908]/no. 577 (decipher), BBA–YEE, 15/74-9-a/74/15 and 15/74-9-b/74/15, respectively.

393. Tahsin Pasha, the First Chamberlain, to the acting commander of the Third Army [February 28, 1908], BBA–YEE, 15/74-11-b/74/15.

394. See the letter of Dr. Bahaeddin [Şakir] beginning "Camarades," sent to the Dashnaktsutiun central committee, undated [March 1908]/no. 554, *Kopye Defteri*, 218–20.

395. H[üsrev] Sami and Dr. Bahaeddin [Şakir], "Osmanlı İttihad ve Terakki Cemiyeti Dahilî Merkez-i Umumîsi Cânib-i Âlisine Takdim Olunmak Üzere Sâî [Talât] Bey'e," dated [Paris], March 8, [1]908/no. 550-11, *Kopye Defteri*, 211.

396. See BBA–BEO/VGG(2): Müşiriyet [1]324 Vâridesi: 639; 204-637 [May 5, 1908]; and BBA–BEO/VGG(2): Müşiriyet 1324 Sadırası: 651; 193 [May 8, 1908].

397. See Sâî [Talât Bey] to the CPU External Headquarters, May 23, [1]908/no. 42-10, in "Osmanlı İttihad ve Terakki Cemiyeti," *Haftalık Şûra-yı Ümmet*, no. 215, 2. His apprentice distributing CPU journals, however, was found not guilty by the court. See ibid., and Es'ad Pasha, the acting commander of the Third Army, to the First Chamberlain's office [February 24, 1908]/no. 620 (decipher), BBA–YEE, 15/74-9-a/74/15.

398. See, for example, Sadık Rıza Pasha's spy report about the activities of the assistant prosecutor of Préveza who was a CPU member. BBA–BEO/VGG(2): Rumeli Müteferrikası: 445; 136 [May 3, 1908]; for another spy report from Prilep by a lawyer named İbrahim Efendi, see BBA–BEO/VGG(2): Manastır Giden: 552; 873 [June 22, 1908].

399. A copy of this letter, entitled "Huzûr-u Şâhânelerine" and dated April 30, 1324 [May 13, 1908], was given in "Osmanlı İttihad ve Terakki Cemiyeti," *Haftalık Şûra-yı Ümmet*, no. 201 [December 30, 1909], 2–3. A somewhat inaccurate French translation was published in "Ultimatum du Comité 'Union et Progrès' à Abdul-Hamid," *Correspondance d'Orient* 3 (May 15, 1910), 127–28.

400. "325 [1324] Senesi Nisanının Gâyesinde Abdülhamid Vükelâsının Yedlerine İsâl Edilen 'Ültimatom' Sureti," in "Osmanlı İttihad ve Terakki Cemiyeti: Vesâik-i Tarihiyeden," *Haftalık Şûra-yı Ümmet*, no. 202 [January 6, 1910], 2.

401. "İlân-ı Hürriyetden Evvel Osmanlı İttihad ve Terakki Cemiyeti Merkez-i Umumisi'nden Serasker-i Esbak Rıza Paşa'ya Hitaben Yazılub Gönderilen Mektubun Suretidir," *Sabah*, September 2, 1908.

402. BBA–BEO/Dahiliye Giden, 107-3/56; 561 [May 18, 1908]/248618; and BBA–İrade-Hususî, R 1326/no. 36-337.

403. "İfade-i Mahsusa," *Şûra-yı Ümmet*, no. 133, 1.

404. See the CPU Monastir branch to the CPU External Headquarters, undated, in *Şûra-yı Ümmet-Ali Kemal Da'vası*, 86–87.

405. A[Hüsrev] Sâî [Sami] and Dr. Bahaeddin Şakir to the CPU Monastir branch, March 28, 1908/no. 578, in "Osmanlı İttihad ve Terakki Cemiyeti: Vesâik-i Tarihiyeden," *Haftalık Şûra-yı Ümmet*, no. 210, 2.

406. Sâî [Talât Bey] on behalf of the CPU Internal Headquarters to the CPU External

Headquarters, April 7, 1908/no. 16, in "Kabl el-İnkılâb Cemiyet'e Dair Vesâik-i Siyasiye," *Haftalık Şûra-yı Ümmet*, no. 200, 8.

407. See Sâî [Talât Bey] to the CPU External Headquarters, May 23, 1908/no. 42-10, in "Osmanlı İttihad ve Terakki Cemiyeti," *Haftalık Şûra-yı Ümmet*, no. 215, 2; and Karabekir, *İttihat ve Terakki Cemiyeti, 1896–1909*, 297–99.

408. Lamb to Barclay, Salonica, May 31, 1908, PRO/F.O. 195/2297; and Heathcote to Barclay, Monastir, June 3, 1908/no. 25, PRO/F.O. 195/2297.

409. [Mehmed Saʿid Paşa], *Saʿid Paşa'nın Hatırâtı* 2/2 (Istanbul, 1328 [1912]), 407.

410. The *mémoire* was addressed to all the Great Powers but Russia, which it strongly denounced.

411. *Mémoire*, dated Turquie, May 25, 1908, and enclosed with Heathcote to Barclay, Monastir, June 3, 1908/no. 25 (confidential), PRO/F.O. 195/2297. Published in "Mémorandum aux Puissances," *Mechveret Supplément Français*, no. 201 (July 1, 1908), 1–4. The CPU External Headquarters also distributed a Turkish translation entitled "Osmanlı Terakki ve İttihad Cemiyeti Tarafından Düvel-i Muʿazzama Vekillerine Dahilden Takdim Olunan Lâyihanın Tercümesidir." This text was given in Ahmed Niyazi, *Hatırât-ı Niyazi*, 51–61; and in *Kırmızı Kitab: İttihad ve Terakki—Adem-i Merkeziyet*, ed. M. Bedri (Istanbul, 1330 [1912]), 19–41.

412. When Ömer Nâzım later denied spying on CPU members, the CUP published his notes inviting officers to extract information from CPU members. See Ömer Nâzım, "Muharrerat-ı İkdam," *İkdam*, August 21, 1908; and Abdüllâtif, "Cevab-ı Müskit, Bürhan-ı Müdhiş," *İkdam*, August 23, 1908. See also Enis Avni, "Nâzım Bey'e Cevab," *İkdam*, August 29, 1908.

413. Sâî [Talât Bey] to the CPU External Headquarters, March 23, [1]908, in "Osmanlı İttihad ve Terakki Cemiyeti: Vesâik-i Tarihiyeden," *Haftalık Şûra-yı Ümmet*, no. 208, 3.

414. For the details of the assassination attempt, see *Enver Paşa'nın Anıları*, 79–84; Ahmed Niyazi, *Hatırât-ı Niyazi*, 37–39; and Lamb to Barclay, Salonica, June 12, 1908/no. 73, PRO/F.O. 195/2297.

415. BBA–BEO/VGG(2): Rumeli Vilâyâtı Giden: 465; 201 [June 11, 1908, decipher].

416. See the CPU Monastir branch to the CPU External Headquarters [July 9, 1908] in "Osmanlı İttihad ve Terakki Cemiyeti: Vesâik-i Tarihiyeden," *Haftalık Şûra-yı Ümmet*, no. 209, 3.

417. Sâî [Talât Bey] to the CPU External Headquarters, undated [June 1908], in "Osmanlı İttihad ve Terakki Cemiyeti: Vesâik-i Tarihiyeden," *Haftalık Şûra-yı Ümmet*, no. 218 [April 28, 1910], 2.

418. *Enver Paşa'nın Anıları*, 85; Nedkov to Paprikov, Monastir, June 11 [24], 1908/ no. 477, TsDA, F. 176, op. 2, a.e. 110, 13.

419. Apparently no concrete plan was drafted at Reval regarding Macedonia. See Charles Hardinge's memorandum, "Visit to the Emperor of Russia at Reval in June, 1908," dated June 12, 1908, in Sidney Lee, *King Edward VII: A Biography* 2, *The Reign* (New York, 1927), 590–97; and in *British Documents on the Origins of the War, 1898–1914* 5, *The Near East*, 237–45. For the Russian account of the meeting, see Izvol'skii to Benckendorff, June 5–18, 1908, ibid., 245–46. [These were only summaries of the many hours of conversation, as stated in Wade Dewood David, *European Diplomacy in the Near Eastern Question, 1906–1909* (Urbana, 1940), 62–63.] Furthermore, the fact that people widely considered the meeting a historically significant watershed in a "diplomatic revolution" overturning all balances in Europe prompted everyone to believe that it would lead to drastic changes in the short run. [See, for example, von Bülow to the kaiser, Berlin, June 17, 1908 (geheim), *Die Große Politik* 25/ 2, *Die english–russische Entente und der Osten* (Berlin, 1925), 466–67.] It should be remembered that the meeting implied so drastic a change in British foreign policy that even many British MPs strongly opposed Edward VII's visit to Russia. See their petition to Grey dated May 29, 1908, PRO/F.O. 371/577, file 18567. The sultan himself expressed his deep concerns about the meeting in Reval to the acting German ambassador. See von Kiderlen-Wächter to von Bülow, Therapia, June 18, 1908/no. 95, *Die Große Politik* 25/2, *Die english–russische Entente und der Osten*, 497–98.

420. The use of the Reval meeting in CPU oral propaganda also helped the organization attract more members. For the increase in members during the period following the arrival of

the news in Macedonia, see Ahmed Saib, *Tarih-i Meşrutiyet ve Şark Mes'ele-i Hâzırası* (Istanbul, 1328 [1912]), 57–58.

421. See the Grand Vizier's office to the inspector general, May 24, 1908/no. 482, BBA–BEO/Telgrafnâme-i Samî Defteri, 703-28/14; BBA–BEO/Rumeli Vilâyât-ı Şâhânesi Müfettişliği Gelen, 980-61/14; 177 [May 26, 1908, decipher]; 178 [May 27, 1908, decipher]; BBA–İrade-Hususî, S 1326/no. 54-162; Ra 1326/no. 4-223; and no. 33-260.

422. Local Ottoman records concerning Salonica reveal that, although the authorities increased their security searches and discovered ammunition on various Muslims, they were in no position to take any measures against the CPU. See, for example, the proceedings of the Salonica Provincial Council, dated May 26 [June 8, 1908]/no. 72-1021, Selânik Vilâyeti Meclis-i İdare Kalemi, Mazbata Müsvedde Paketi, 1/1324, Ιστορικό Αρχείο Μακεδονίας (Salonica).

423. It should be remembered that CPU members like Major Enver Bey were receiving information about world events through *Neue freie Presse* (see *Enver Paşa'nın Anıları*, 108), which was claimed to be "notoriously inspired from Berlin" and to have "published a series of articles in the manner peculiar to that journal when its object is to arouse and excite public opinion" on the Reval meeting. See Goshen to Grey, Vienna, June 12, 1908/no. 80 (confidential), PRO/F.O. 371/577, file 20489. For the daily's provocative language, see "Wien, 9. Juni," *Neue freie Presse*, June 10, 1908.

424. Ahmed Niyazi, *Hatırât-ı Niyazi*, 63.

425. Grand Vizier's office to the commander of the Third Army [June 24, 1908]/no. 372, BBA–BEO/VGG(2): Müşiriyet [1]324 Sadırası: 651.

426. For the story of the band's sortie, see Hıfzı Pasha, the governor of Monastir, to the Grand Vizier's office [July 4, 1908]/no. 229-18581, BBA–BEO/Rumeli 1324, 979-61/13; BBA–TFR.1.AS. 63/6236 (1326.6.6); "Résumé des évènements qui constituèrent le Mouvement révolutionnaire ottoman du mois de Juillet 1908 à Monastir," in PRO/F.O. 297/2; and Ahmed Niyazi, *Hatırât-ı Niyazi*, 68 ff. Coded messages exchanged between Adjutant-Major Ahmed Niyazi and First Lieutenant Osman Efendi concerning the activities of the "national battalion" are in BBA–YEE, 23/2046/12/71.

427. See the CPU Monastir branch to the CPU External Headquarters [July 9, 1908] in "Osmanlı İttihad ve Terakki Cemiyeti: Vesâik-i Tarihiyeden," *Haftalık Şûra-yı Ümmet*, no. 209, 3. Adjutant-Major Ahmed Niyazi, however, stated that he himself prepared the letters and appeals, a claim that seems inaccurate. See Ahmed Niyazi, *Hatırât-ı Niyazi*, 81.

428. Adjutant-Major Ahmed Niyazi's appeals can be found in his memoirs. See Ahmed Niyazi, *Hatırât-ı Niyazi*, 83 ff. Translations of these appeals can be found in the following sources: enclosed with Heathcote to Barclay, Monastir, July 15, 1908/no. 40, and with Lamb to Barclay, Salonica, July 13, 1908/no. 86 (confidential), PRO/F.O. 195/2227; enclosed with van der Does de Willebois to Tets van Goudriaan, Pera, July 15, 1908/no. 350, Algemeen Rijksarchief: Tweede Afdeling: Kabinetsarchief Bu Za politieke rapportage (1871–1940): 50; enclosed with Nedkov to Paprikov, Monastir, June 21 [July 4], 1908/no. 506, and June 29 [July 12], 1908/no. 519, TsDA, F. 176, op. 2, a.e. 110, 16–17 and 36–37; *Archives Diplomatiques* 109/1, nos. 1-3 (1909), 219–20; and *Dokumenti za borbata na makedonskiot narod za samostojnost i za nacionalna država* 1, 500.

429. See the Grand Vizier's office to the governors of Ankara, Kastamoni, Hüdavendigâr, Kangırı, Sivas, Trabzon, Erzurum, Ma'muret-el-Azîz, Adana, Beirut, and Syria [June 23, 1908]/no. 761, BBA–BEO/Şifre Telgrafnâme-i Samîlerin Kaydına Mahsus Defterdir, 702-28/13. The total number of first-class reserve battalions that had been ordered to Macedonia from Anatolia was twenty-eight. Marshal İbrahim Pasha was appointed as the new commander of the Third Army on June 30, 1908.

430. See Süleyman Külçe, *Osmanlı Tarihinde Arnavutluk* (Izmir, 1944), 288–90, 306–8, and 318 ff. The sultan frequently decorated him for services rendered. See, for example, BBA–BEO/Serasker Reft, 261-6/69; 367 [May 6, 1906]/211670.

431. Tahsin Pasha to Şemsi Pasha [July 3, 1908], in Külçe, *Firzovik Toplantısı*, 26–27.

432. Tahsin Pasha to Şemsi Pasha [July 3, 1908], ibid., 30–31.

433. Many CPU leaders underscored this claim. See, for example, Ahmed Niyazi, *Hatırât-ı*

Niyazi, 133; and the CPU Monastir branch to the CPU External Headquarters [July 9, 1908], in "Osmanlı İttihad ve Terakki Cemiyeti: Vesâik-i Tarihiyeden," *Haftalık Şûra-yı Ümmet*, no. 209, 3. However, Şemsi Pasha's son and his aide-de-camp, who was a CPU member, strongly denied that the pasha had made such a statement. See Müfid Şemsi, *al-Ḥaqq ya 'lū wa-lā yu 'lā 'alayh* (Istanbul, 1919), 11; and Külçe, *Firzovik Toplantısı*, 75.

434. Ibid., 42–43.

435. Later Âtıf Kamçıl claimed that he had decided to assassinate Şemsi Pasha on his own as a member of the CPU Monastir branch's self-sacrificing volunteer division. He also stated, however, that he had asked the branch to provide him with a revolver and discussed the issue with the CPU Monastir branch's guide, Süleyman Askerî. The CPU Monastir branch's director, Lieutenant Colonel Sadık Bey (Şehreküştü), adamantly maintained that he had "given the *fatwā* for removal of Şemsi Pasha." See Âtıf Kamçıl's letter to Süleyman Külçe, dated December 5, 1940, in Külçe, *Firzovik Toplantısı*, 48–49; and Sadık Şehreküştü to İsmet İnönü, Hârşova, October 31, 1940. (The original letter is in Professor Vakur Versan's collection. I am indebted to Professor Versan for allowing me to examine this important letter.) In a telegram sent to a daily to explain how the CPU assassinated Şemsi Pasha, the CPU Monastir branch stated that the self-sacrificing volunteer himself demanded the duty. See "İttihad ve Terakki Cemiyeti Manastır Merkezi'nden Matbaamıza Keşide Edilen Telgrafdır," *İkdam*, September 3, 1908.

436. The best sources describing the assassination are the detailed telegram sent to Inspector General Hüseyin Hilmi Pasha from Monastir and enclosed with his coded telegram to the Grand Vizier's office, Salonica [July 7, 1908]/no. 221-2841; additional cables from him to the Grand Vizier's office, Salonica [July 7, 1908]/no. 223-2859; no. 224-2873; [July 8, 1908]/no. 230–2911; and [July 9, 1908]/no. 236-2944; BBA–BEO/Makam-ı Samî-i Hazret-i Sadaretpenâhîye Gelen Şifre Telgrafnâmelerin Kaydına Mahsus Defterdir, 981-61/15; Hıfzı Pasha to the Grand Vizier's office, Monastir [July 7, 1908]/no. 232-19189 and no. 233-19360, BBA–BEO/Rumeli 1324, 979-61/13; Heathcote to Barclay, Monastir, July 8, 1908/no. 37, PRO/F.O. 195/2297; Bedi N. Şehsuvaroğlu "İkinci Meşrutiyet ve Atıf Bey," *Belleten* 23, no. 90 (April 1959), 307–32; and Halim Cavit Arcak, "7 Temmuz ve Âtıf Kamçıl," *Ulus*, July 7, 1947.

437. Hıfzı Pasha to the Grand Vizier's office, Monastir [July 18, 1908]/no. 268-20721, BBA–BEO/Rumeli 1324, 979-61/13; and Ahmed Refik, *İnkılâb-ı Azîm*, 41.

438. Foreign diplomats who had close contact with the palace underscored this fact. See, for example, von Kiderlen-Wächter to von Bülow, Therapia, July 9, 1908/no. 110, PAAA 638/3, Der Sultan und seine Familie, 159/1 (Bd. 11-12).

439. A copy of the original appeal posted on walls is in TsDA, F. 331, op. 1, a.e. 234, 51–52. Republished in "23 Haziran [1]324 Tarihinde Esvâka Ta'lik Edilen Beyannâme," *Neyyir-i Hakikat*, no. 11 [July 27, 1908], 1; in "Rumeli Harekât-ı İhtilâliyesinden Mukaddem Osmanlı Terakki ve İttihad Cemiyeti Manastır Hey'et-i Merkeziyesi Tarafından Neşr Olunan Beyannâme," *Şûra-yı Ümmet*, no. 139 (August 1, 1908), 1–2; and in Ahmed Refik, *İnkılâb-ı Azîm*, 45–51. A French translation entitled "Memorandum remis par le Comité Ottoman d'Union et Progrès au Vali de Monastir, chef du Gouvernement illégal actuel," enclosed with Heathcote to Barclay, Monastir, July 15, 1908/no. 40 (confidential), is in PRO/F.O. 195/2297. Another French translation is in TsDA, F. 331, op. 1, a.e. 234, 47–48.

440. Hıfzı Pasha to the Grand Vizier's office, Monastir [July 6, 1908]/no. 921-19125, BBA–BEO/Rumeli 1324, 979-61/13; BBA–BEO/Rumeli Müfettişliği Gelen, 982-61/16; 281/53 [July 7, 1908]/251856 and 251858; and BBA–YMGM, 312/63 (1326.C.9).

441. See the CPU Monastir branch to the CPU External Headquarters [July 9, 1908], in "Osmanlı İttihad ve Terakki Cemiyeti: Vesâik-i Tarihiyeden," *Haftalık Şûra-yı Ümmet*, no. 209, 3.

442. Major Enver Bey's ultimatum was enclosed with Hüseyin Hilmi Pasha's telegram to the Grand Vizier's office, dated Salonica [July 11, 1908]/no. 255-3113, BBA–BEO/Makam-ı Samî-i Hazret-i Sadaretpenâhîye Gelen Şifre Telgrafnâmelerin Kaydına Mahsus Defterdir, 981-61/15.

443. A copy of his appeal is given in Şevket Süreyya Aydemir, *Makedonya'dan Ortaasya'ya Enver Paşa* 1, *1860–1908*, 2nd ed. (Istanbul, 1972), 528–29.

444. Marshal İbrahim Pasha to Osman Hidayet Pasha, Salonica [July 7, 1908–telegram], in Ahmed Niyazi, *Hatırât-ı Niyazi*, 219–20.

445. See the CPU Monastir branch to the CPU External Headquarters [July 9, 1908], in "Osmanlı İttihad ve Terakki Cemiyeti: Vesâik-i Tarihiyeden," *Haftalık Şûra-yı Ümmet*, no. 209, 3.

446. BBA–BEO/Harbiye Giden, 263-6/71; 739(mükerrer) [July 8, 1908]/251330.

447. Tahsin Pasha to Hüseyin Hilmi Pasha [July 9, 1908], in Ahmed Niyazi, *Hatırât-ı Niyazi*, 211–12.

448. Coded telegram from Osman [Fevzi], İbrahim, and Hüseyin Hilmi Pashas to the First Chamberlain's office [July 10, 1908], ibid., 212–13.

449. Faik Bey, the governor of Aydın, to the Grand Vizier's office, Izmir [July 9, 1908]/no. 313-8704, BBA–BEO/Müteferrika-Sadarete Gelen Şifre: Anadolu, 693/2.

450. Faik Bey to the Grand Vizier's office, Izmir [July 11, 1908]/no. 324-830, ibid.

451. Faik Bey to the Grand Vizier's office, Izmir [July 12, 1908]/no. 426-837; and [July 14, 1908]/no. 435-856, ibid.

452. Faik Bey to the Grand Vizier's office, Izmir [July 20, 1908]/nos. 456–97; 458–925; and 455–927; and [July 21, 1908]/no. 461-931, ibid.; BBA–BEO/İrade-i Hususiye, 385-8/108, 572 (mükerrer) [July 10, 1908]/251710; BBA–İrade-Hususî, Ca 1326/no. 34-552 and no. 35-556; and Barnham to Barclay, July 22, 1908/no. 75 (confidential), PRO/F.O. 195/2300.

453. For detailed information, see Ahmed Refik, *İnkılâb-ı Azîm*, 66–69; Hüseyin Hilmi Pasha to the Grand Vizier's office, Salonica [July 23, 1908]/no. 343-4002, BBA–BEO/Makam-ı Samî-i Sadaretpenâhîye Gelen Şifre Telgrafnamelerin Kaydına Mahsus Defterdir, 981-61/15. The local authorities decided to use them against bands of the Christian ethnic groups. See Hüseyin Hilmi Pasha to the Grand Vizier's office, Salonica [July 22, 1908]/no. 324-3969, ibid.

454. Hüseyin Hilmi Pasha to the Grand Vizier's office, Salonica [July 10, 1908]/no. 274-3689, ibid.

455. The letter sealed by the CPU Ohrid branch asked the members of the delegation to return to their homes immediately or they would be executed and their property confiscated by the committee. See Hüseyin Hilmi Pasha to the Grand Vizier's office, Salonica [July 12, 1908]/no. 289–3757, ibid. See also Hıfzı Pasha to the Grand Vizier's office, Monastir [July 18, 1908]/no. 268–20721, BBA–BEO/Rumeli 1324, 979-61/13; and BBA–YSHM, 523/125 (1326.C.19).

456. Hilmi Pasha to the Grand Vizier's office, Iōánnina [July 16, 1908]/no. 262-16048, BBA–BEO/Rumeli 1324, 979–61/13.

457. Hüseyin Hilmi Pasha to the Grand Vizier's office, Salonica [July 17, 1908]/no. 280-3718, BBA–BEO/Makam-ı Samî-i Sadaretpenâhîye Gelen Şifre Telgrafnâmelerin Kaydına Mahsus Defterdir, 981-61/15; and Hıfzı Pasha to the Grand Vizier's office, Monastir [July 17, 1908]/no. 265-20603, BBA–BEO/Rumeli 1324, 979-61/13.

458. Hüseyin Hilmi Pasha to the Grand Vizier's office, Salonica [July 22, 1908]/no. 322-3967, BBA–BEO/Makam-ı Samî-i Sadaretpenâhîye Gelen Şifre Telgrafnâmelerin Kaydına Mahsus Defterdir, 981-61/15. (A copy of this telegram is in BBA–YEE, 23/291/12/71.) See also Satow to Lamb, Skopje, July 16, 1908/no. 41, PRO/F.O. 195/2297.

459. Hüseyin Hilmi Pasha to the Grand Vizier's office, Salonica [July 23, 1908]/no. 350-4024, BBA–BEO/Makam-ı Samî-i Sadaretpenâhîye Gelen Şifre Telgrafnâmelerin Kaydına Mahsus Defterdir, 981-61/15. See also Satow to Lamb, Skopje, July 24, 1908 (decipher), PRO/F.O. 195/2298; and Lukes to Aehrenthal, Skopje, July 23, 1908/no. 71, Österreichisches Kriegsarchiv, Kriegsministerium Präsidial Register (1908).

460. See the CPU warning sent to Süleyman Kâni, the subgovernor of Ohrid, who was in fact a member of the CPU, enclosed with Hüseyin Hilmi Pasha's telegram to the Grand Vizier's office, Salonica [July 15, 1908]/no. 272-3665; and the warning sent by a certain Âbidin, who was a member of the CPU Monastir band, to the subgovernor of Kičevo, enclosed with Hüseyin Hilmi Pasha's telegram to the Grand Vizier's office, Salonica [July 17, 1908]/no. 285-3743, BBA–BEO/Makam-ı Samî-i Sadaretpenâhîye Gelen Şifre Telgrafnâmelerin Kaydına Mahsus Defterdir, 981-61/15.

461. Undated [July 1908] CPU External Headquarters communiqué, Private Papers of Bahaeddin Şakir. See also Kolushev to Paprikov, Cetinje, June 10 [23], 1908/no. 160, TsDA, F. 339, op. 1, a.e. 30, 7–8.

462. Hüseyin Hilmi Pasha to the Grand Vizier's office, Salonica [July 10, 1908]/no. 242-2987, BBA–BEO/Makam-ı Samî-i Sadaretpenâhîye Gelen Şifre Telgrafnâmelerin Kaydına Mahsus Defterdir, 981-61/15; and Lamb to Barclay, Salonica, July 10, 1908/no. 85, PRO/F.O. 195/2297.

463. Hüseyin Hilmi Pasha to the Grand Vizier's office, Salonica [July 19, 1908]/no. 296-2823, BBA–BEO/Makam-ı Samî-i Sadaretpenâhîye Gelen Şifre Telgrafnâmelerin Kaydına Mahsus Defterdir, 981-61/15.

464. Hüseyin Hilmi Pasha to the Grand Vizier's office, Salonica [July 21, 1908]/no. 320-3946, ibid., BBA–YSHM, 523/136 (1326.C.20); and Lamb to Barclay, Salonica, July 22, 1908/no. 93, PRO/F.O. 195/2298. His son, a military cadet at the Royal Military College in Monastir and a CPU member, wrote the following in a letter to his father before the latter's death: "I have heard that you were one of those vile traitors . . . and were shot by a self-sacrificing volunteer of the nation. I extol that hero and curse you. From now on you have no relation to our family." See "Bir Hiss-i Ulvî ve Muhibb," *Yeni Asır*, August 2, 1908.

465. Hüseyin Hilmi Pasha to the Grand Vizier's office, Salonica [July 23, 1908]/no. 330-3088, BBA–BEO/Makam-ı Samî-i Sadaretpenâhîye Gelen Şifre Telgrafnâmelerin Kaydına Mahsus Defterdir, 981-61/15.

466. Hüseyin Hilmi Pasha to the Grand Vizier's office, Salonica [July 13, 1908]/no. 262-3584; [July 14, 1908]/no. 266-3624; [July 19, 1908]/no. 298-3824; [July 19, 1908]/no. 294-3821; [July 19, 1908]/no. 295-3822; [July 19, 1908]/no. 298-3824; [July 20, 1908]/no. 310-3889; and [July 23, 1908]/no. 351-4029, ibid.

467. Tevfik Pasha to "Haridjié," July 11, 1908/no. 68, and July 12, 1908/no. 74, Archives of the Turkish Embassy in Paris, D. 277; Tevfik Pasha to Mustafa Reşid Pasha, July 12, 1908/no. 74; and July 21, 1908, and the enclosed circular, Archives of the Turkish Embassy in Rome, Box 71 (1). See also the draft of the note prepared for the foreign press by the Ottoman embassy in Paris, July 12, 1908, ibid., and "Το Νεοτουρκικό κίνημα," *Χρόνος*, July 1 [14], 1908, for a press declaration made by the Ottoman embassy in Athens. The Grand Vizier's office also asked the Ottoman diplomats to refute the claims made by European journals. See the Grand Vizier's office to the Ottoman Foreign Ministry [July 18, 1908], Archives of the Turkish Embassy in Paris, D. 277.

468. The original document sealed by the CPU Monastir branch is in PRO/F.O. 294/46, and a copy was enclosed with Heathcote to Barclay, Monastir, July 15, 1908/no. 40 (confidential), PRO/F.O. 195/2297. Another copy was enclosed with van der Does de Willebois to Tets van Goudriaan, Pera, July 15, 1908/no. 350, Algemeen Rijksarchief: Tweede Afdeling: Kabinetsarchief Bu Za politieke rapportage (1871–1940): 50. An English translation is in Heathcote to Barclay, Monastir, July 13, 1908/no. 39 (confidential), PRO/F.O. 195/2297. See also BBA–BEO/Rumeli Vilâyâtı Müfettişliği Gelen, 980-61/14; 351(mükerrer) [July 18, 1908]. The European press in general praised the document. See, for example, "Les Jeunes-Turcs," *L'Italie*, July 22, 1908.

469. The CPU memorandum presented to the consuls on July 21, 1908. Copies of it were enclosed with Lamb to Barclay, Salonica, July 21, 1908/no. 91, further enclosed with Barclay to Grey, Therapia, July 28, 1908/no. 421, PRO/F.O. 371/544, file 26954, and PRO/F.O. 195/2298; and another copy is in HHStA, PA, XXXVIII Konsulat Saloniki, Berichte 1908, I–VIIII. It was also published in *Archives Diplomatiques* 109/1, nos. 1–3 (1909), 216–18.

470. See Ahmed Riza (pour la Comité Ottoman d'Union et de Progrès), "Déclaration de M. Ahmed Riza—Paris Juillet 11, 1908," *Pro Armenia* 8, no. 186 (July 20, 1908), 1326; and "Révolution turque en Macédoine," *Le Siècle*, July 12, 1908. Ahmed Rıza continued to give similar assurances following the triumph of the revolution. See "Eine Erklärung des Präsidenten des Pariser jungtürkischen Komitees," *Neue freie Presse*, July 26, 1908.

471. "Rumeli Harekât-ı İhtilâliyesi Üzerine Bazı Devletlerin Umur-i Dahiliyemize Müdahale Edecekleri Şüyu' Bulmasıyla Cemiyetimiz Tarafından Avrupa Matbu'atına Gönderilen Reddiye," *Şûra-yı Ümmet*, no. 139, 2–3.

472. "Osmanlı Terakki ve İttihad Cemiyeti Âtideki Notu Matbu'at-ı Ecnebiyeye İrsâl Eylemişdir," *Şûra-yı Ümmet*, no. 139, 3.

473. See, for example, "Le Mouvement jeune-turc en Macédoine: interview de M. Ahmed Riza," *Le Siècle*, July 14, 1908.

474. For the historical origins, of *besa* and its importance in Albania, see Syrja Pupovci, "Le formalisme et la 'Besa' dans le droit des obligations du Coutumier de Lek Dukagjine," *Studia Albanica* 2 (1968), 143–49; and Skender Rizaj, "Osmanlı ve Batı Kaynaklarına Göre Arnavutlarda Besa," *II. Milletlerarası Türk Folklor Kongresi Bildirileri* (Ankara, 1982), 235–39.

475. İsmail Pasha, the subgovernor of Priština, to the inspector general, Firzovik [July 5, 1908]/no. 552 (telegram), BBA–TFR.1.KV. 206/20501 (1326.6.24). See also Satow to Lamb, Skopje, July 11, 1908/no. 40, PRO/F.O. 195/2297.

476. In order to capitalize on the anti-Austrian feelings of Muslim Gegs, opponents of the Young Turks spread a rumor that the Young Turk movement had been subsidized by Austria-Hungary. See August Urbański, "Die jungtürkische Revolution 1908 und der Weltkrieg," *Berliner Monatshefte für internationale Aufklärung* 7 (March 1929), 201–2.

477. İsmail Pasha to the inspector general, Firzovik [July 5, 1908]/no. 537 (telegram), BBA–TFR.1.KV. 206/20501 (1326.6.24); and Hüseyin Hilmi Pasha to the Grand Vizier's office, Salonica [July 6, 1908]/no. 216–4853, BBA–BEO/Makam-ı Samî-i Sadaretpenâhîye Gelen Şifre Telgrafnâmelerin Kaydına Mahsus Defterdir, 981–61/15.

478. See, for example, the Grand Vizier's office to the governor of Kosovo [June 27, 1908]/no. 801, and [June 28, 1908]/no. 806, BBA–BEO/Şifre Telgrafnâme-i Samîlerin Kaydına Mahsus Defterdir, 702-28/13.

479. Telegram of the Grand Vizier's office, marked "extremely urgent," to the governor of Kosovo [July 10, 1908]/no. 1764, BBA–TFR.1.KV. 206/20501 (1326.6.24).

480. Grand Vizier's office to the inspector general [July 7, 1908]/no. 866, BBA–BEO/Şifre Telgrafnâme-i Samîlerin Kaydına Mahsus Defterdir, 702-28/13; BBA–YSHM, 523/101 (1326.C.16); and BBA–YMGM, 312/74 (1326.C.10).

481. Hüseyin Hilmi Pasha to the Grand Vizier's office, Salonica [July 8, 1908]/no. 226-2888, BBA–BEO/Makam-ı Samî-i Sadaretpenâhîye Gelen Şifre Telgrafnâmelerin Kaydına Mahsus Defterdir, 981–61/15. For Colonel Galib's mission, see "Galib Paşa'nın Anıları," *Hayat Tarih Mecmuası* 2, no. 6, 8–11; "Nasıl Oldu?" *Yeni Asır*, August 6, 1908; Selânikli Faik, *Tarihçe-i Hürriyet*, 25–26; and Süleyman Külçe, *Mareşal Fevzi Çakmak* (Istanbul, 1953), 39.

482. Âtıf, "Şimalî Arnavudluk Kahramanları," *İkdam*, August 11, 1908; A[bdülgani] Seni, "Kahraman Arnavud Kardeşlerimize Karşı İkmâl-i Vazife-i Şükran ve Tarihce-i Hürriyetimize Aid Bir Sahne," *Sabah*, August 12, 1908; [Fevzi Çakmak], "Mareşal Hayatını Anlatıyor," ed. Bahadır Dülger, *Tasvir*, October 2, 1947; Ahmed Ziya, *Meşrutiyet Uğrunda*, 22; and Jäckh, *Im türkischen Kriegslager durch Albanien*, 25–26.

483. Albanian sources noted his role in the meeting. See Rahimi, *Vilajeti i Kosovës*, 122. For detailed information about Curri, see M. Jasa, *Bajram Curri: patriot revolucionar i shpellës së Dragobisë* (Tirana, 1958); Skënder Drini, *Bajram Curri* (Tirana, 1983); and "Baïram Tzouri, héros de l'indépendance albanaise," *La Fédération Balkanique* 1, nos. 18–19 (April 30, 1925), 243–44.

484. Müfid Şemsi, *al-Ḥaqq ya'lū wa-lā yu'lā 'alayh*, 27. See also Marcelle Tinayre, "Notes d'une voyageuse en Turquie (Avril-Mai 1909)," *Revue des Deux Mondes* 54 (November 1, 1909), 812: "Un sentiment commun unissait les Albanais et les Jeunes-Turcs: l'horreur des 'réformes.'"

485. Colonel Galib to Mahmud Şevket Pasha, the governor of Kosovo, enclosed with the latter's telegram to the inspector general [July 16, 1908]/no. 765, BBA–TFR.1.KV. 206/20501 (1326.6.24).

486. See his responses to the questions from the inspector general, enclosed with the latter's coded telegram to the First Chamberlain's office, Salonica [July 9, 1908]/no. 495, BBA–TFR.1.KV. 206/20501 (1326.6.24).

487. Telegram from the province of Kosovo to Hüseyin Hilmi Pasha, enclosed with the latter's telegram to the Grand Vizier's office, Salonica [July 9, 1908]/no. 234-2398, BBA–

BEO/Makam-ı Samî-i Sadaretpenâhîye Gelen Şifre Telgrafnâmelerin Kaydına Mahsus Defterdir, 981-61/15; BBA–BEO/VGG(2): Müşiriyet Vâridesi: 639; 486/1448 [July 8, 1908].

488. Külçe, *Firzovik Toplantısı*, 59.

489. See the Grand Vizier's office to the inspector general [July 19, 1908]/no. 960, BBA–BEO/Şifre Telgrafnâme-i Samîlerin Kaydına Mahsus Defterdir, 702-28/13; and the Grand Vizier's office to the Commander of the Third Army [July 20, 1908]/no. 489; BBA–TFR.1.KV. 206/20501 (1326.6.24).

490. Galib Bey's telegram, enclosed with Hüseyin Hilmi Pasha's telegram to the Grand Vizier's office, Salonica [July 19, 1908]/no. 300-3837, BBA–BEO/Makam-ı Samî-i Sadaretpenâhîye Gelen Şifre Telgrafnâmelerin Kaydına Mahsus Defterdir, 981-61/15. See also BBA–BEO/VGG(2): Müşiriyet 324 Vâridesi: 639; 516/5882 [July 20, 1908]; BBA–BEO/VGG(2): Müşiriyet [1]324 Sadırası: 651; 489 [July 20, 1908]; and BBA–YSHM, 523/142 (1326.6.21).

491. The full text of the telegram is given in Ahmed Refik, *İnkılâb-ı Azîm*, 88–89; and in Külçe, *Firzovik Toplantısı*, 60–61. The *besa* adopted by the crowd included the points stated in this telegram. The main points of the *besa* were sent to the inspector general on July 23, 1908, by telegram (no. 783), BBA–TFR.1.KV. 206/20503 (1326.6.10). See also "Die Forderungen der Albanen," *Neue freie Presse*, July 26, 1908. The full text of the *besa* was published in "Ahd ü Misâk: Şimalî Arnavutluğun 'Besa'sı," *İkdam*, August 11, 1908; *Yeni Gazete*, August 23, 1908; and *Mizan*, [August 25, 1908]. An English translation entitled "Solemn Compact and Agreement" was enclosed with Satow to Lamb, August 21, 1908/no. 53, PRO/F.O. 195/2298.

492. Ahmed Refik, *İnkılâb-ı Azîm*, 89–90.

493. *The Memoirs of Ismail Kemal Bey* (London, 1920), 316; Ismail Kemal Bey, "Albania and the Albanians," *The Quarterly Review* 228, no. 425 (July 1917), 150; and *Ismail Kemal Bey Vlora: Il pensiero e l'opera attraverso i documenti Italiani*, ed. Renzo Falaschi (Rome, [1985]), 23. It was also claimed that the sultan requested the help of Isa Boletin, a famous Albanian chieftain, to disperse the Firzovik meeting. See René Pinon, "La Question albanaise," *Revue des Deux Mondes* 54 (1909), 812; and Külçe, *Firzovik Toplantısı*, 73. Tahsin Pasha, however, denied this claim. See Tahsin Paşa, *Abdülhamit Yıldız Hatıraları* (Istanbul, 1931), 268–69.

494. Ibid., 249–50, 259. Mehmed Rıza Pasha, however, wrote in his memoirs that he had "asked the application of the constitutional law." See Rıza Paşa, *Hülâsa-i Hatırât* (Istanbul, 1325 [1909]), ii and 71.

495. Hıfzı Pasha to the Grand Vizier's office, Monastir [July 18, 1908]/no. 268-20721, BBA–BEO/Rumeli 1324, 979-61/13. After this warning Hıfzı Pasha demanded his appointment to another province, stating that since the government did not pay attention to his counsel he did not want to be responsible for the "inescapable tragedy that will take place." See his telegram to the Grand Vizier's office, Monastir [July 20, 1908]/no. 273-21931, ibid.

496. See Heathcote's decipher and dispatch to Barclay dated Monastir, July 12, 1908, and July 13, 1908/no. 30 (confidential), respectively, PRO/F.O. 195/2297.

497. A one-page appeal entitled "İlân" and sealed by the seal of the CPU Monastir branch, Private Papers of Bahaeddin Şakir.

498. This information is taken from a letter from Colonel Sadık to Bahaeddin Şakir [August 29, 1908], Private Papers of Bahaeddin Şakir. An identical description was provided by Ahmed Ziya, *Meşrutiyet Uğrunda*, 25–26. See also *Enver Paşa'nın Anıları*, 121.

499. Hüseyin Hilmi Pasha to the Grand Vizier's office, Salonica [July 21, 1908]/no. 314-3909, BBA–BEO/Makam-ı Samî-i Hazret-i Sadaretpenâhîye Gelen Şifre Telgrafnâmelerin Kaydına Mahsus Defterdir, 981-61/15.

500. Hüseyin Hilmi Pasha to the Grand Vizier's office, Salonica [July 21, 1908]/no. 318-3930, no. 319-3936; [July 22, 1908]/no. 321-3966, ibid.

501. Hüseyin Hilmi Pasha to the Grand Vizier's office, Salonica [July 22, 1908]/no. 322-3967, no. 323-3968, ibid.

502. Hüseyin Hilmi Pasha to the Grand Vizier's office, Salonica [July 22, 1908]/no. 325-3972, ibid. This document provided the figure of 1,000 men for the band. The figures given in the text are taken from Bekir Fikri's memoirs. See Bekir Fikri, *Grebene*, 22–23.

503. See his declaration enclosed with Hüseyin Hilmi Pasha to the Grand Vizier's office, Salonica [July 22, 1908]/no. 325–3972, BBA–BEO/Makam-ı Samî-i Hazret-i Sadaretpenâhîye Gelen Şifre Telgrafnâmelerin Kaydına Mahsus Defterdir, 981-61/15.

504. See Hüseyin Hilmi Pasha to the Grand Vizier's office, Salonica [July 23, 1908]/no. 331-3977/no. 337-3993, ibid.; Süleyman Kâni to the inspector general, Ohrid [July 23, 1908]/no. 3135, BBA–TFR.1.MN. 174/17359 (1326.6.23); Ahmed Niyazi, *Hatırât-ı Niyazi*, 197 ff.; "Müşir Paşa Hazretleri'nin Cemiyet-i İttihadiye Tarafından Suret-i Misaferetleri," *Neyyir-i Hakikat*, no. 10, 2–3; and "Nasıl Oldu—2," *Yeni Asır*, August 11, 1908.

505. See Hüseyin Hilmi Pasha to the Grand Vizier's office, Salonica [July 23, 1908]/no. 331-3977, BBA–BEO/Şifre Telgrafnâme-i Samîlerin Kaydına Mahsus Defterdir, 981-61/15. See also Colonel Taki to the Ministry of War [July 23, 1908]/no. 2237, and [July 23, 1908]/no. 2231, BBA–YEE, 23/291/12/71.

506. See, for example, Hilmi Pasha to the Grand Vizier's office, Iōánnina [July 23, 1908]/no. 296–11599, BBA–BEO/Rumeli 1324, 979-61/13.

507. Enclosed with the telegram from Hüseyin Hilmi Pasha to the Grand Vizier's office, Salonica [July 22, 1908]/no. 324-3969, BBA–BEO/Şifre Telgrafnâme-i Samîlerin Kaydına Mahsus Defterdir, 981-61/15.

508. Hüseyin Hilmi Pasha to the Grand Vizier's office, Salonica [July 23, 1908]/no. 333-3981, ibid., and Marshal İbrahim Pasha to the Ministry of War, Monastir [July 23, 1908]/no. 239, BBA–YEE, 23/291/12/71.

509. Hüseyin Hilmi Pasha to the Grand Vizier's office, Salonica [July 23, 1908]/no. 339-3997, BBA–BEO/Şifre Telgrafnâme-i Samîlerin Kaydına Mahsus Defterdir, 981-61/15; Póstfai to Aehrenthal, Monastir, July 23, 1908/no. 48, HHStA, PA XXXVIII 395, Konsulat Monastir, 1908; "İlân-ı Hürriyet ve İcra-yı Merâsim-i Mahsusa," *Neyyir-i Hakikat*, no. 11, 1–2; and "Manastır'dan Mektub," *İkdam*, August 10, 1908.

510. Hüseyin Hilmi Pasha to the Grand Vizier's office, Salonica [July 23, 1908]/no. 338-3996, no. 343-4002, and no. 353-4033, BBA–BEO/Makam-ı Samî-i Hazret-i Sadaretpenâhîye Gelen Şifre Telgrafnâmelerin Kaydına Mahsus Defterdir, 981–61/15.

511. See, for example, BBA–TFR.1.SL. 192/19180 (1326.6.23).

512. For the demands made during the demonstrations and by local CPU branches and populations, see the telegrams from various local authorities, forwarding telegrams prepared on behalf of local populations, which were enclosed with Hüseyin Hilmi Pasha to the Grand Vizier's office, and the inspector general's telegrams to the Grand Vizier's office, Salonica [July 23, 1908]/no. 334-3982, no. 335–3985, no. 340-4001, no. 341-4004, no. 346-4017, no. 354-4034, BBA–BEO/Makam-ı Samî-i Hazret-i Sadaretpenâhîye Gelen Şifre Telgrafnâmelerin Kaydına Mahsus Defterdir, 981-61/15; BBA–TFR.1.M. 21/2094 (1326.6.24); BBA–TFR.1.KV. 205/20403 (1326.6.24); 205/20489 (1326.6.23); BBA–TFR.1.MN. 174/17355 (1326.6.23); 174/17356 (1326.6.23); 174/17357 (1326.6.23); 174/17358 (1326.6.23); 174/17360 (1326.6.23); 174/17361 (1326.6.23); 174/17366 (1326.6.23); BBA–TFR.1.SL. 192/19175 (1326.6.23); 192/19178 (1326.6.23); 192/19206 (1326.6.23); and copies of the telegrams sent from various towns in BBA–YEE, 23/291/12/71. Republished versions of some of these documents can be found in Ahmed Refik, *İnkılâb-ı Azîm*, 90 ff; and in İsmail Hakkı Uzunçarşılı, "1908 Yılında İkinci Meşrutiyetin Ne Suretle İlân Edildiğine Dair Vesikalar," *Belleten* 20, no. 77 (January 1956), 168–72.

513. See, for example, the subgovernor of Petrich's telegram to the inspector general, BBA–TFR.1.SL. 192/19176 (1326.6.23); and a telegram sent by the entire military personnel and people of Serres [July 23, 1908], in "Menâkıb-ı Hürriyet," *Bağçe*, no. 25 [December 19, 1908], 9.

514. BBA–BEO/Re'sen İrade-i Seniye, 360–8/83; 654 [July 22, 1908].

515. See Tahsin Paşa, *Abdülhamit Yıldız Hatıraları*, 259; and [Mehmed Cemaleddin], *Şeyhülislâm-ı Esbâk Cemaleddin Efendi Merhumun Hatırât-ı Siyasiyesi* (Istanbul, 1336 [1920]), 8.

516. See, for example, the telegram sent to the subgovernor of Serres [July 23, 1908], BBA–YEE, 23/1794/12/71.

517. See the telegram dated [July 23, 1908], BBA–YEE, 23/1794/12/71. The inspector general forwarded this message to all administrative units in Macedonia.

518. See, for example, the CPU Alasonya (Elasson) branch to the inspector general [July 23, 1908], BBA–TFR.1.M. 21/2094 (1326.6.24).

519. [Mehmed Kâmil Paşa], *Kâmil Paşa'nın Âyân Re'isi Sa'id Paşa'ya Cevabları* (Istanbul, 1327 [1911]), 50; and Mehmed Memduh, *Esvât-ı Sudûr* (Izmir, 1328 [1912]), 80.

520. [Mehmed Sa'id Paşa], *Sa'id Paşa'nın Hatırâtı* 2/2, 443–47.

521. See the special commission's memorandum dated [July 23, 1908], BBA–YEE, 23/1715/12/71. Also published in *Düstûr*, 2nd Series, vol. 1 (Istanbul, 1329 [1911]), 1–2.

522. Ibid., 2.

523. See "Tebligât-ı Resmiye," *İkdam*, July 24, 1908.

524. See, for example, Halîl Hálid, "A Pacific Revolution in Turkey," *The Orient Review* 1, no. 1, 27. Many admirers of the sultan claimed that the sultan's granting of the constitution was a result of his own intentions as discussed in that article. See, for example, Ghulam Haider, "The Sultan and the Turkish Constitution," *The Indian Review* 9, no. 8 (August 1908), 574.

525. See, for example, Âsım Bey at the First Chamberlain's office to Fuad Hikmet, August 20, 1907; and from the latter to the former, Rome, August 23, 1907, Archives of the Turkish Embassy in Rome, Box 81 (7). Immediately after the revolution the German authorities provided the sultan with information about the clauses of the German constitution regulating ministers' responsibilities to the kaiser. See Holstein to von Bülow, July 29, 1908, *Die geheimen Papiere Friedrich von Holsteins* 4, *Briefwechsel*, ed. Norman Rich and M. H. Fisher (Göttingen, 1963), 491.

526. See "Münir Paşa'nın Me'muriyeti," *İkdam*, August 10, 1908; "Mühim Bir Haber," *Yeni Asır*, August 11, 1908; and "Munir Pacha et la Bulgarie," *Le Progrès de Salonique*, August 10, 1908. Bulgarian dailies reiterated the same accusations. See "Nova misiia Munir Pasha," *Vecherna poshta*, July 7 [20], 1908; "Munir Pasha," *Kambana*, July 12 [25], 1908; "Priedlozheniiata na Munir Pasha do Bŭlgariia," *Vecherna poshta*, August 2 [15], 1908; and *Nov zhivot*, August 16 [29], 1908.

527. Nedkov to Paprikov, Monastir, July 11 [24], 1908/no. 554, BIA, F. 321, op. 1, a.e. 1835, 164–65.

528. See "Münir Paşa," *Yeni Asır*, August 26, 1908; and "Sefir-i Sabık Münir'in Zât-ı Şâhâne'ye Bir Arizası," *İkdam*, August 28, 1908. Münir Pasha's final report about his diplomatic mission was republished in Galip Kemali Söylemezoğlu, *Hariciye Hizmetinde Otuz Sene, 1892–1922* 1 (Istanbul, 1950), 131–32. The pasha mentions nothing about his initiatives against the Young Turks in this report.

529. See Tschirschky to von Bülow, Vienna, July 24, 1908/no. 173, PAAA 641/3, Türkische Staatsmänner, 159/2 (Bd. 9-10); and Buxton, *Turkey in Revolution*, 63.

530. See, for example, Pallavicini to Aehrenthal, Yeniköy, August 5, 1908/no. 53 (vertraulich), HHStA, PA XII 196, Türkei, Berichte 1908 VIII–IX; and "Sefir Münir," *İttihad ve Terakki*, August 6, 1908.

531. Coded telegram from Paprikov to Prince Ferdinand, June 12 [25], 1908, TsDA, F. 3, op. 8, a.e. 1216, 61.

532. Paprikov to Dobrovich in Prince Ferdinand's residence in Evksinograd near Varna, July 14 [27], 1908, TsDA, F. 3, op. 8, a.e. 1216, 63.

533. Maurice Paléologue, the French chargé de l'agence, asserted the following: "Le commissaire ottoman à Sofia demandait au Gouvernement bulgare de provoquer une crise extérieure qui permettrait au Sultan d'étouffer la révolution. En revanche, il reconnaîtrait l'indépendance de la Bulgarie. Cette dernière se refusait à tenter cette aventure." See *Documents diplomatiques français*, 2ᵉ Série (1901–1911), 11 (Paris, 1950), 732/n. Kâmil Bey did not mention anything about his démarche in his memorandum about his meetings with Paprikov and other foreign representatives in Sofia to discuss the effects of the restoration of the constitutional regime in the Ottoman Empire. See Kâmil Bey's memorandum to the Grand Vizier, Sofia [August 16, 1908]/no. 84, BBA–BEO/Mümtaze Kalemi: Bulgaristan Tasnifi Evrakı II, A. MTZ (04), 170/18 (1326.7.10). Following his démarche, Kâmil Bey went to Istanbul to present information about his proposition. See ibid., 169/84 (1326.7.23).

534. Coded telegram from Paprikov to Prince Ferdinand, Sofia, August 19/September 1, 1908, in *Dokumenti po obiaviavane na nezavisimostta na Bŭlgariia 1908 godina: iz tainiia kabinet na kniaz Ferdinand*, ed. TSv. Todorova and El. Statelova (Sofia, 1968), 18–19.

535. Paprikov wrote: "Kâmil Bey in his desire to help the sultan in these difficult and grave times wanted very much to lead us along this slippery road [i.e., war]. He has not yet abandoned these ideas of his. I keep telling him that we would not take even one step which could complicate the situation. In doing so we are indirectly helping His Majesty [the sultan], who we hope would be grateful to us for that.... Kâmil Bey, however, is not satisfied with that.... He keeps insisting that it would be a good thing if we enter into an agreement with the sultan." See coded telegram from Paprikov to Prince Ferdinand, Sofia, August 25 [September 7], 1908, ibid., 22–24. The new government dismissed Kâmil Bey from his post on August 26, 1908. Thus while making his final initiatives he had no official title. See BBA–İrade-Bulgaristan, B 1326/no. 1768. Later the government, backed by the CUP, started to investigate him because of financial irregularities during his term in office as the Ottoman commissioner in Sofia. See BBA–İrade-Hariciye, B 1327/no. 21-1027(4130).

536. Imperiali to Tittoni, Therapia, July 22, 1908/no. 1574-516, ASMAE, Affari Politici, Serie P. Politica (1891–1916), pacco 123–24.

537. Grand Vizier's office to the inspector general [July 24, 1908]/no. 1012, BBA–BEO/ Şifre Telgrafnâme-i Samîlerin Kaydına Mahsus Defterdir, 702-28/13.

538. The committee began to use the title of Ottoman Committee of Union and Progress again following the revolution.

539. Lamb to Barclay, July 24, [1908]/no. 95 (telegram), PRO/F.O. 295/18. Local CUP branches made similar declarations. See, for example, Greig to Barclay, Serres, July 26, 1908 (decipher), PRO/F.O. 294/45.

540. See Hüseyin Hilmi Pasha to the Grand Vizier's office, Salonica [July 28, 1908]/ no. 74 (381-4169), in BBA–DUİT, Kavânin ve Nizâmât, 49/11; and in BBA–BEO/Makam-ı Samî-i Sadaretpenâhîye Gelen Şifre Telgrafnâmelerin Kaydına Mahsus Defterdir, 981–61/ 15.

541. "Umuma İhtar," *İttihad ve Terakki*, August 9, 1908.

542. "Açmadan Kapamak," *Neyyir-i Hakikat*, no. 14 [August 10, 1908], 1.

543. See BBA–BEO/VGG(2): Rumeli Müteferrikası: 445; 172 [July 25, 1908]; BBA–BEO/ Rumeli Vilâyât-ı Şâhânesi Müfettişliği Gelen, 980–61/14; 362 (mükerrer) [July 28, 1908]; and "Enver'in Bir Fikr-i Münevveri," *Yeni Asır*, July 30, 1908.

544. The formalities took time and the CUP acquired the aforementioned gardens in Salonica only in November. See BBA–BEO/VGG(2): Selânik Giden: 566; 73 [November 11, 1908]; and BBA–DH.MUİ. 14–1/4 (1327.N.7). In the meantime, the sultan granted property to other CUP branches. See, for example, BBA–BEO/İrade-i Hususiye, 385-8/108; 678-4466 [August 25, 1908]/254827.

545. Karabekir, *İttihat ve Terakki Cemiyeti, 1896–1909*, 327. See also "İnkılâb," *Şûra-yı Ümmet*, no. 139, 1.

CHAPTER 9

This epilogue provides only an overview of the CUP's first year in power after the Young Turk Revolution of 1908. It is by no means a detailed account of that year, much less of the CUP organization and activities during the second constitutional period.

1. Petriaev's report dated July 25, 1908/no. 369, *Krasnyi arkhiv* 6/43 (1930): *Turetskaia revoliutsiia 1908–1909 gg.* (Moscow, 1931), 33.

2. During the revolution the Ottoman administration attempted to ban all European newspapers providing information about the Young Turk movement. See BBA–BEO/Dahiliye Giden, 107-3/56; 1131 [July 16, 1908]/251834; BBA–BEO/Zabtiye Giden, 663-21/14; 1051 [July 16, 1908]/251834; and BBA–BEO/İrade-Hususî, C 1326/no. 47-572.

3. "İttihad ve Terakki," *Şûra-yı Ümmet*, September 6, 1908.

4. "Osmanlı İttihad ve Terakki Cemiyeti ve Osmanlı Ordusu!" *Şûra-yı Ümmet*, October 19, 1908.

5. "Osmanlı İttihad ve Terakki Cemiyeti ve Mu'arızları," *Şûra-yı Ümmet*, December 30, 1908.

6. See, for example, the seal of the CUP branch in Lanja that reads "Osmanlı İttihad ve Terakki Cemiyeti al-Muqaddas," on a document giving information regarding the founders of the branch; see BBA–YEE–Kâmil Paşa Evrakına Ek II, 86/31, 3094 (1324.9.12) [*sic*].

7. See "İhvân-ı Cemiyet'e," *İttihad ve Terakki*, August 6, 1908.

8. See *Câmi Baykut'un Anıları Defteri* 2, Türk Tarih Kurumu Arşivi, no. 1082, 45.

9. Ahmed Rıza to Şerif Pasha, Istanbul, September 10, 1908, in Şerif Paşa, *İttihad ve Terakki'nin Sahtekârlıklarına, Denaetlerine Bülend Bir Sada-yı Lâ'netimiz* (Paris [1911]), 25–26.

10. BBA–TFR.1.MN. 176/17506 (1326.7.17).

11. See, for example, Phineas B. Kennedy's dispatch, dated Korçë, August 18, 1908, ABCFM, Harvard University, vol. 15 [637].

12. See BBA–BEO/VGG(2): Edirne Giden: 483; 56 [July 28, 1908]/252717; and BBA–YSHM, 524/16 (1326.7.1).

13. "Selânik: Güzel Bir Numûne-i İntizam," *Yeni Asır*, July 30, 1908.

14. "Tebliğ," *İkdam*, September 26, 1908.

15. Grand Vizier Mehmed Sa'id Pasha to Hüseyin Hilmi Pasha [July 28, 1908]/no. 925 (telegram), BBA–TFR.1.UM. 26/2524 (1326.7.8).

16. See "İlân-ı Resmî," *Yeni Asır*, July 29, 1908; and "İlân-ı Resmî," *İkdam*, August 2, 1908. See also "Polislerde Tereddüd," *Yeni Asır*, August 25, 1908.

17. The press supporting the CUP praised it for this. See, for example, Sermuharrir, "Meclis-i Meb'usan ve İttihad ve Terakki Cemiyeti," *Meram*, no. 5 [December 24, 1908], 130–31.

18. See the CPU Internal Headquarters to the Grand Vizier, July 31, 1908 (telegram), BBA–TFR.1.UM. 26/2524 (1326.7.8).

19. See the CPU Internal Headquarters to the Grand Vizier's office [July 31, 1908]/no. 25291 (telegram), ibid.

20. *İkdam*, August 17, 1908.

21. "Osmanlı İttihad ve Terakki Cemiyeti," *İkdam*, September 12, 1908. See also "Yeni Usûl Dolandırıcılık," *Tanin*, [August 21, 1908].

22. See Osmanlı İttihad ve Terakki Cemiyeti, *Tebliğât*. One-page appeal dated [August 6, 1908], Private Papers of Bahaeddin Şakir.

23. Camille Fidel, *Les premiers jours de la Turquie libre: lettres d'un témoin* (Paris, 1909), 54.

24. "Selânik'den Matbaamıza Vârid Olan Telgrafnâmedir," *İkdam*, August 3, 1908; "Rahmi Bey," *İkdam*, August 2, 1908; and "Tanin İdarehânesi'ne," *Tanin*, [August 3, 1908].

25. See the undated memorandum entitled "Cemiyet Tarafından Dersaadet'e İ'zam Kılınan Rahmi Bey'in Hükûmet Nezdinde Tervicini Ta'kib ve İcrasını Taleb Edeceği Mevadd," Private Papers of Bahaeddin Şakir.

26. See BBA–A.AMD.MV. 90/1 (1326.B.11). See also BBA–BEO/Harbiye Gelen, 228-6/36; 1634/715 [August 8, 1908].

27. See BBA–YEE, 15/74–84/74/15; BBA–BEO/Dahiliye Giden, 107-3/56; 1251 [July 28, 1908]/252528; and BBA–YSHM, 523/184 (1326.6.28).

28. "İttihad ve Terakki Cemiyeti İstanbul Merkezi'nden Tebliğ Olunmuşdur," *Tercüman-ı Hakikat*, August 11, 1908.

29. See the CUP Salonica center to the inspector general, BBA–TFR.1.SL. 202/20126 (1326.12.17).

30. See BBA–TFR.1.SL. 195/19426 (1326.7.29).

31. See, for example, BBA–TFR.1.MN. 178/17727 (1326.8.25).

32. "Osmanlı Tiyatrosu," *Tanin*, [August 7, 1908].

33. See BBA–TFR.1.MN. 179/17863 (1326.9.21).

34. See BBA–TFR.1.MN. 182/18175 (1326.11.24). See also the note of the CUP Serres branch to the CPU Monastir branch, enclosed with Heathcote to Lowther, Monastir, Decem-

ber 19, 1908/no. 68, PRO/F.O. 294/46. A German officer made the following comment about the governor of Beirut in 1909: "Der *Wali* ist schwach, und ein Spielball der verschiedenen Parteien. So stellt das sogenannte 'Comit[é] [d]'Union et Progrès' besondere Forderungen auf und bildet eine Art Nebenregierung." See "Militärpolitischer Bericht über den Aufenthalt Eurer Majestät Schiff 'Lübeck' und die Lage in Beirut," written by Müller aboard the man-of-war on May 6, 1909, Bundesarchiv-Militärarchiv, RM 5/5868 (Admiralstab der Marine): Türkei: Unruhen im Jahre 1909, Bd. 1, 197.

35. BBA–MV, 119/no. 3288 [August 9, 1908].

36. See the CUP central committee to the Grand Vizier's office, Salonica [November 1, 1908]/no. 190-49583, BBA–BEO/Sadarete Gelen Şifre: Müteferrika: 1324, 692-28/3. It should be noted that the CUP secretly negotiated with the Austro-Hungarian authorities to resolve the crisis resulting from the Dual Monarchy's unilateral declaration of its annexation of Bosnia and Hercegovina on October 5, 1908. See HHStA, PA XII 351, Türkei, Liasse XXXIX/1b (Verhandlungen anläßlich der Annexion Bosniens und der Herzegowina mit dem jungtürkischen Komité in Saloniki, 1908–1909).

37. See, for example, Pernale to Tittoni, Banghāzī, November 28, 1908/no. 690-374, ASMAE, Affari Politici, Serie P. Politica (1891–1916), pacco 123–24, describing how the CUP delegation forced the local notables to sign loyalty documents.

38. See "Selânik: Bir Tedbir-i Celîl ve Mühim," *Yeni Asır*, August 6, 1908; "Adana İttihad ve Terakki Cemiyeti'nden Matbaamıza Suret-i Mahsusada Keşide Kılınan Telgrafnâmedir," *Tercüman-ı Hakikat*, August 6, 1908; "Bir Tedbir-i Celîl ve Mühim," *İkdam*, August 9, 1908; "Şuûnât-ı Dahiliye," *Sabah*, August 31, 1908; "Şuûn," *Tanin*, [September 7, 1908]; and Yemen Seyyar Me'muru Mehmed Selim, "Yemen Mektubu," *İttihad ve Terakki*, November 18, 1908.

39. "Osmanlı İnkılâb-ı Kebîri Nasıl Oldu?" *Musavver Salnâme-i Servet-i Fünûn* 1 [1910], 102–3.

40. See, for example, subgovernor of Jerusalem, Ali Ekrem, to the subgovernor of Haifa [August 10, 1908], Israel State Archives, RG. 83-1/ﺏ; BBA–DH.MUİ. 10-1/64 (1327.Ş.29); BBA–BEO/Dahiliye Giden, 107-3/56; 2760 [December 7, 1908]/258672 and 257913; Sharif Ḥusayn to the Grand Vizier's office, Mecca [March 6, 1909]/no. 179, BBA–BEO/Müteferrika [1]325, 699-28/6; and BBA–BEO/VGG(2): Yemen Vilâyeti Âmed: 368; 50 [March 2, 1909, decipher].

41. See, for example, the complaint about the secretary general of the subprovince of Acre, Hakkı Bey, who "exploited the CUP's power so much as to levy a poll tax of 20 *para*s (half a *gurush*) on every sheep brought to Acre." Subgovernor Edhem Bey to the Grand Vizier's office [July 16, 1909]/no. 130-206, BBA–BEO/Sadarete Gelen Şifre, Arabistan 1325, 697-28/8.

42. See, for example, Acting Governor Nailî Bey and Director of the Financial Department Edhem Bey to the Grand Vizier's office [August 10, 1908]/n. 491-21413, BBA–BEO/Sadarete Gelen Şifre, Müteferrika Anadolu 1324, 693-2, 28/4. See also BBA–A.AMD.MV. 90/43 (1326.8.29); BBA–BEO/Maliye Gelen, 463-10/64; 1302 [September 9, 1908]/254527; and BBA–BEO/Maliye Giden, 503-10/104; 2117 [September 10, 1908]/254527.

43. Grand Vizier's office to "all provinces and autonomous subprovinces other than those in Rumelia" [September 10, 1908], BBA–BEO/VGG(2): Umum Defteri: 880; 57 [September 10, 1908]/255022 and 254527.

44. Osmanlı İttihad ve Terakki Cemiyeti İstanbul Merkezi, "Beyannâme," a one-page hand-bill dated [August 16, 1908], Private Papers of Bahaeddin Şakir. The pro-CUP newspapers also published articles encouraging the people to pay their taxes as due. See, for example, "Vergü Verecek miyiz?" *Tanin*, [August 25, 1908].

45. Governor Zeki Pasha to the Grand Vizier's office, Mosul [October 1, 1908]/no. 390, BBA–BEO/Sadarete Gelen Şifre, Arabistan: 1324, 693-28/4. See also Acting Governor Zühdi Pasha to the Grand Vizier's office, Mosul [April 2, 1909]/no. 23-794, BBA–BEO/Sadarete Gelen Şifre, Arabistan: 1325, 697-28/8; and Ramsay to the Government of India, Baghdad, September 14, 1908, enclosed with Lowther to Grey, Therapia, October 13, 1908/no. 662, PRO/F.O. 424/217.

46. See, for example, the case of Baghdad as explained by Acting Governor Nâzım Pasha

to the Grand Vizier's office, Baghdad [October 17, 1908]/no. 392-29829; [October 18, 1908]/ no. 393-29975; and Governor Mehmed Fâzıl to the Grand Vizier's office [November 1, 1908]/ no. 397-30867, BBA–BEO/Sadarete Gelen Şifre, Arabistan: 1324, 693-28/14. See also Ghassan R. Atiyyah, *Iraq, 1908–1921: A Socio-Political Study* (Beirut, 1973), 52–53.

47. See, for example, BBA–BEO/VGG(2): Kastamoni Reft: 157; 66 [August 15, 1908]/ 253166; BBA–BEO/VGG(2): Müşiriyet [1]324 Vâridesi: 639; 584 [August 8, 1908]; BBA– BEO/Harbiye Gelen, 228–6/36; 1652/730 [August 10, 1908]; BBA–BEO/VGG(2): Kastamoni Gelen: 153; 130 [July 30, 1908]; 131 [August 3, 1908]; 132 [August 4, 1908]; 133 [August 3, 1908]; and 140 [August 15, 1908]; Major General Şahin to the Grand Vizier's office, Rhodes [August 2, 1908]/no. 236 (telegram), BBA–BEO/VGG (2): Rumeli Müteferrikası: 445; Subgovernor Nusret Bey to the Grand Vizier's office, Mytilíni [August 1, 1908]/no. 115-2572; Subgovernor Neş'et to the Grand Vizier's office, Lemnos [August 8, 1908]/no. 118-1907, BBA–BEO/Sadarete Gelen Şifre, Müteferrika 1324, 692-28/3; BBA–BEO/Dahiliye Giden, 107-3/56; 1260 [August 3, 1908]/252580; and "Hususî Telgraflar: Medine 10 Ağustos," *Yeni Gazete*, September 2, 1908.

48. See the CUP communiqué dated [August 20, 1908] and published in *Yeni Gazete*, September 6, 1908.

49. "Osmanlı İttihad ve Terakki Cemiyeti Tarafından İlân," *Neyyir-i Hakikat*, no. 14 [August 10, 1908], 4; and "İlân," *Yeni Edirne*, August 19, 1908.

50. "Osmanlı İttihad ve Terakki Cemiyeti Tarafından Vârid Olan Beyannâme Suretidir," *Tanin*, [August 5, 1908].

51. Acting Governor Mahmud Pasha to the Grand Vizier's office, Van [September 14, 1908]/ no. 18851 (telegram), BBA–BEO/VGG(2): Umum Defteri: 880; 57-1273-1269 [September 14, 1908]/254527 and 254528. The governor of Erzurum made a similar comment later. See "Hükûmet ve Cemiyet," *Tanin*, [March 26, 1909].

52. See, for example, the CUP Bursa branch's application to the Grand Vizier's office dated [October 1, 1908]/no. 240 (telegram), and the government's response dated [October 2, 1908] (telegram), BBA–BEO/Umum Muhaberat-Bursa, 255618.

53. Some of these branches even appealed to the First Chamberlain's office, an act that the CUP central committee denounced in the strongest terms. See, for example, the CUP Zeytun branch to the First Chamberlain's office [October 28, 1908], BBA–İrade-Hususî, L 1326/ no. 82–904.

54. See, for example, "Bir Mukayese," *Takdirat*, December 26, 1911.

55. This important issue was discussed during Ziya [Gökalp]'s testimony at the special court martial in 1919. See "8 Mart Sene [1]335 Tarihinde İrade-i Seniye-i Hazret-i Padişahî'ye İktiran Eden Kararnâme ile Müteşekkil Divan-ı Harb-i Örfî Muhakematı Zabıt Ceridesi: İkinci Muhakeme, 4 Mayıs 1335," enclosed with *Takvim-i Vekayi'*, no. 3543, May 8 [1919], 23–24. As Hohler stated, early delegations dispatched by the committee during the first days of the revolution made very little headway. He wrote: "No one knows exactly who are the credited organs and committees of the League, and delegates sent from Salonica to see unauthorized branches have been suppressing and reforming them all over the place. Some of these delegates have been most unwise. It is all very well, but nice modern ideas straight from Paris and London do *not* suit well Kurdish and Arab chiefs, at places like Baghdad and Van." See T. B. Hohler to Cromer, Constantinople, October 25, 1908, Cromer Papers: Foreign Correspondence (1907–1910), PRO/F.O. 633/14. The Swedish ambassador to the Ottoman Empire made a similar comment: "The Young Turk Committee's efforts to alleviate the struggle between conflicting interests and open the eyes of Ottoman citizens, irrespective of race and religion, seem to have had some success in the European part, the capital, the larger urban centers of Turkey, and the coastal areas of Asia Minor. In the inner parts of Asiatic Turkey, in Aleppo, Urfa, Mardin, Diyar-ı Bekir, Mosul, and Baghdad, however, a situation exists which cannot be described as anything but more or less anarchy." See the ambassador's dispatch to Ehrensvärd, Constantinople, August 12, 1908/no. 103, Riksarkivet, Utrikesdepartementet, 1902 ars dossieringssystem, vol. 7, Redogörelsen fran Beskickningen i Konstantinopel 1908, s 12/8. See also Edwin Pears, "The Future of Turkey," *Yale Review* 4, no. 1 (October 1914), 169–70.

56. See Çerkes İttihad ve Teavün Cemiyeti, "Beyannâme" [1908]. A one-page appeal. See also "Varaka," *Şûra-yı Ümmet*, November 4, 1908.

57. See "Âlî Bir Sâniha," *Sabah*, July 29, 1908; "Bir Hafiyenin Cür'eti," *Tercüman-ı Hakikat*, July 29, 1908; and "İlân-ı Resmî," *İkdam*, August 11, 1908.

58. "Osmanlı İttihad ve Terakki İstanbul Merkezi'nden," *Sabah*, August 23, 1908.

59. See the testimony of the former *Şeyhülislâm* Musa Kâzım Efendi at the special court martial in 1919, in "8 Mart Sene [1]335 Tarihinde İrade-i Seniye-i Hazret-i Padişahî'ye İktiran Eden Kararnâme ile Müteşekkil Divan-ı Harb-i Örfî Muhakematı Zabıt Ceridesi: Birinci Muhakeme, 3 Haziran 1335," enclosed with *Takvim-i Vekayiʿ*, no. 3571 (June 10, 1335 [1919]), 133.

60. See "Les femmes patriotes," *Mechveret Supplément Français*, no. 202 (August 1, 1908), 6; "Les Dames turques," *Le Journal de Salonique*, July 30, 1908; Osmanlı İttihad ve Terakki Cemiyeti Kadın Şuʿbesi Nâmına Emine Semiye, "İsmet Hakkı Hanımefendiyle Bir Hasbihâl," *İkdam*, August 29, 1908; "The Young Turkish Woman," *The Guardian*, November 25, 1908; Felice de Chaurand de St-Eustache, "L'esercito nel movimento costituzionale della Turchia," *Rivista d'Italia* 11, no. 2/10 (October 1908), 526; and Demetra Kenneth Brown, "Women in the Young Turk Movement," *The Atlantic Monthly* 103 (May 1909), 696–701. Claims regarding the active participation of women in the revolutionary activities were, however, baseless. For such claims, see Mary Mills Patrick, "The Emancipation of Mohammedan Women," *The National Geographic Magazine* 20, no. 1 (January 1909), 42.

61. "İttihad ve Terakki Cemiyeti'nin İtimadnâmesi," *Sabah*, September 4, 1908.

62. For example, the CUP formed a society named "League for Peace and Solidarity" under the control of Dr. Nâzım and Fâik Bey, to unite left-wing organizations and workers' societies. See Spiridon Blagoev, "Narodnoto dvizhenje vo Makedonija po mladoturskata revolucija: spored materijalite od arhivot na nadvorešnata politika na Rusija," *Istoria* 15, no. 1 (1979), 141.

63. Hazerzâde Rüşdi, "İttihad ve Terakki Cemiyet-i Muhteremesi'ne," *Ceride-i Vakfiye*, no. 3 [January 11, 1909], 1.

64. A. Y. Musa, "Cemiyetlerimiz ve Milletin Arzusu," *Metin*, [August 14, 1908].

65. See "İttihad ve Terakki Cemiyeti ve Diğer Cemiyetler," *Şûra-yı Ümmet*, December 11, 1908; and BBA–DH.HMŞ. 19/3 (1326.12.25).

66. The Ottoman Law for Societies was issued on August 16, 1909. See *Düstûr*, 2nd Series, vol. 1 (Istanbul, 1329 [1911]), 604–8. Although the Constitution's thirteenth article acknowledged the right of Ottoman citizens to form societies, an imperial decree issued in 1889 made the establishment of societies conditional upon government permission. Thus no society could be legally established without the government's permission, and hence all the organizations that mushroomed after the revolution were of a de facto nature.

67. See the CPU central committee decision [August 8/9, 1909]/no. 630, Private Papers of Ahmed Rıza (1).

68. See the CUP central committee decision [July 6/7, 1909]/no. 437, ibid.

69. See the CUP central committee decision [June 15, 1909]/no. 293, ibid.

70. See, for example, the CUP Diyar-ı Bekir branch's memorandum to the CUP central committee [June 18, 1909]/no. 3, ibid.

71. See the CPU Izmir branch to the CPU central committee [June 28, 1909]/no. 379, ibid.

72. See the CUP central committee decision [June 30/July 1, 1909]/no. 403, ibid.

73. See the CUP central committee decision [June 9–10, 1909]/no. 271, ibid. The central committee believed that the Macedo-Bulgarian peasants would not go to Anatolia even if the government granted the property but that, by making such an offer, the government could frustrate the efforts of the Macedo-Bulgarian committees which were promising land to the peasants.

74. See, for example, "Serbestî," *Serbestî*, [November 28, 1908]; "Bugünkü Meşrutiyet ve Cemiyet-i İttihadiye," *Hukuk-u Umumiye*, December 24, 1908; "İttihad ve Terakki İzmir Şuʿbesi Ne Yapıyor?" *Serbest İzmir*, [February 14, 1909], 2–3; and Rıza Nur, "Görüyorum ki İş Fena Gidiyor," *İkdam*, March 13, 1909.

75. The CUP was officially recognized as a benevolent society by the State Council in 1910. The sections about the goals of the committee in the later regulations of the CUP, how-

ever, remained unchanged. See *Osmanlı İttihad ve Terakki Cemiyeti'nin Nizamnâmesi: 1327 Senesi Umumî Kongresince Tanzim Olunmuşdur* (Salonica, 1327 [1911]), 2.

76. See "Umum Vilâyât ve Elviye-i Gayr-ı Mülhakaya Tastîr Olunan Telgrafnâme-i Samî Sureti," *Tanin*, [March 23, 1909]; and Hüseyin Cahid, "Fırkanın İçinde," *Tanin*, [November 19, 1909].

77. For an example, see the CUP central committee's note to Talât Bey signed by CUP General Secretary Hacı Âdil (Arda), discussing the policies to be pursued by the government in Yemen and dated [February 1, 1911]/no. 2052, in BBA–DH.SYS. 38/1 (1331.7.10). The cabinet took issues mentioned in this note into serious consideration. See BBA-MV, 149/ no. 768 [February 28, 1911].

78. "Kırmızı Balta Cemiyeti," *Hürriyet* (2), no. 4 [January 10, 1908], 13–14.

79. Their journals were full of threats against the CUP's opponents. See, for example, "Dilini Keserler, Anasını Bellerler," *Top*, no. 7 [April 24, 1911], 4; "Çok Uluyanlar ya Kudurur ya Geberir," *Silah*, no. 196 [April 30, 1911], 2–3; and "Bir Hitab," *Top*, no. 17 [July 5, 1911], 1. See also Top, "Top Nerede Patlamalı?" *Top*, no. 7, 1: "On this Day of Judgment the vile people who shamelessly dared to propose the annihilation of the fatherland should be shot, the criminals who put a lancet in the pure bosom of the fatherland should be hanged. . . . It [the cannon] should roar on this Day of Judgment, a day of rescue and deliverance. That is where salvation lies." The publications of these activist factions disturbed the CPU-backed governments and local governors. See, for example, BBA–DH.SYS. 57-1/26 (1329.7.25).

80. Before the revolution the sultan had been issuing approximately ten to fifteen imperial decrees a day, and many files requesting imperial decrees had been submitted to the imperial palace. The records in the registers reveal a great decrease in the files submitted to the imperial palace. For example, the register of the files that were submitted officially by the Grand Vizier's office indicates that no files had been submitted between July 21, 1908 (file #BBA–YSRM, 158/56) and August 5, 1908 (file #BBA–YSRM, 158/57).

81. See M. Şükrü Hanioğlu, *The Young Turks in Opposition* (New York, 1995), 62–64.

82. See Yusuf Hikmet Bayur, *Türk İnkılâbı Tarihi* 2/4 (Ankara, 1952), 203–8; and Hilmi Kâmil Bayur, *Sadrazam Kâmil Paşa: Siyasî Hayatı* (Ankara, 1954), 244 ff.

83. The governments of Gazi Ahmed Muhtar Pasha and Kâmil Pasha between July 1912 and January 1913 were obvious exceptions to this rule. These cabinets were formed during a short period in which the CUP found itself in an unaccustomed role of opposition, and they pursued strong anti-CUP policies aimed at putting an end to the CUP domination.

84. BBA–BEO/Dahiliye Giden, 107–3/56; 410 [May 6, 1909]/265634.

85. "Osmanlı İttihad ve Terakki Cemiyeti ve Osmanlı Ordusu!" *Şûra-yı Ümmet*, October 19, 1908. The opponents of the CUP strongly criticized the close relations between the CUP and the army. See, for example, "Armée et politique," *Mècheroutiette*, no. 48 (November 1913), 54.

86. See BBA–BEO/Re'sen İrade-i Seniye, 360-8/83; 4355 [August 7, 1908]; 4410 [August 10, 1908]; and 5090 [December 7, 1908]. These imperial decrees ordered the promotion of officers in the First and Second Armies. Karabekir claimed that the officers in the Third Army turned down this reward. See Karabekir, *İttihat ve Terakki Cemiyeti, 1896–1909* (Istanbul, 1982), 327.

87. Although some officers praised Sabahaddin Bey (see, for example, Mecdeddin, "Sabahaddin Bey," *İkdam*, October 24, 1908), the CUP carried out extensive propaganda to thwart his efforts. Sabahaddin Bey's attempt to win over Adjutant-Major Ahmed Niyazi and use this move for propaganda purposes was blocked by the CUP central committee, which stated that "the decentralist's efforts have been thwarted." See the CUP central committee to Dr. Nâzım and Ahmed Rıza [November 9, 1908], Private Papers of Ahmed Rıza (1). Rumors about Ahmed Niyazi's interest in Sabahaddin Bey's ideas were again afloat in 1909; however, the CPU succeeded in keeping this "hero of the revolution" in its ranks. See Geary to Lamb, Monastir, March 12, 1909/no. 10, PRO/F.O. 195/2328.

88. This was one of the important decisions of the first secret CUP congress. See "Osmanlı İttihad ve Terakki Cemiyeti Kongresi," *Şûra-yı Ümmet*, November 13, 1908.

89. Draft memorandum submitted to the CUP Monastir branch to be forwarded to the congress, dated Monastir [October 4, 1908], Private Papers of Bahaeddin Şakir.

90. "Osmanlı İttihad ve Terakki Cemiyeti," *Haftalık Şûra-yı Ümmet*, no. 203, 2.

CHAPTER 10

1. "Ḥubb al-waṭan min al-imān ve Japonya-Rus Seferi," *Şûra-yı Ümmet*, no. 52 (May 1, 1904), 3. For praises for Darwin and Social Darwinism, see respectively "Ye's," *Şûra-yı Ümmet*, no. 50 (April 1, 1904), 1; and "Mısır ve Mısırlılar," *Şûra-yı Ümmet*, no. 32, (July 11, 1903), 2.

2. "İkdam Gazetesi Lisana Gelmiş," *Şûra-yı Ümmet*, no. 73 (March [April] 20, 1905), 1. The CPU organs also claimed that ruling a country by absolute monarchy was comparable to using pigeons instead of the telegraph in modern times. See "İran," *Şûra-yı Ümmet*, no. 104 (November 30, 1906), 3.

3. "Endişe-i Menfaat, Meslek-i Siyaset," *İttihad ve Terakki*, September 1, 1908. See also M. A., "Tekâmül ve Terakki," *Tanin*, [August 16, 1908].

4. See Doktor Nâmi, "Charles Darwin," *Bağçe*, no. 33 [March 16, 1909], 106–8; and no. 34 [March 23, 1909], 117–22.

5. Halid[e] Salih, "Beşiği Sallayan El Dünyaya Hükm Eder," *Tanin*, [August 6, 1908]. See also Ahmed Şuʿayib, "Kanun-i Tekâmül," *Tanin*, [August 7, 1908]; and "İran Ahvâli," *İttihad ve Terakki*, August 30, 1908.

6. See Victor Bérard, "L'éternelle Turquie," *La Revue de Paris* 3 (June 15, 1909), 893.

7. S[ami Paşazâde] Sezaî, "Paris Kongresi–Gülhane Hatt-ı Hümayûnu," *Şûra-yı Ümmet*, no. 92 (April 25, 1906), 1; and [Yusuf Akçura], "Yer, İnsan ve Nizaʿ," *Tercüman-ı Ahvâl-i Zaman*, no. 10 (February 8 [21], 1908), 1–2. See also Ahmed Rıza's note on Darwin, among his scattered notes in AN 17/ AS/10/dr 7.

8. See, for example, "Hayat ve Meyl-i Füyûzat," *Füyûzat*, no. 1 (November 1 [14], 1906), 1; "Mendeleev ve Kimya," *Füyûzat*, no. 10 (February 20 [March 5], 1907), 148–51; and A[li] H[üseyinzâde], "Perde İniyor: Son Temâşâ," *Füyûzat*, no. 32 (October 23 [November 5], 1907), 474.

9. "Kırmızı Karanlıklar İçinde Yeşil Işıklar," *Füyûzat*, no. 5 (December 18 [31], 1906), 66.

10. See, for example, A[li] Hüseyinzâde, "İntikad Ediyoruz, İntikad Olunuyoruz," *Füyûzat*, no. 27 (September 26 [October 9], 1907), 373.

11. Ibid. This journal also published a Turkish translation of Draper's essay *The Intellectual Development of Europe*. See John W. Draper, "Avrupa'nın İnkişâfât-ı Fikriyesi," *Füyûzat*, no. 30 (October 19 [November 1], 1907), 440 ff.

12. See, for example, Z., "İtikâdât-ı Bâtıla," *Sada-yı Girid*, no. 6 (May 31 [June 13], 1907), 1–2.

13. See "Makale-i Mahsusa: Herbert Spencer," *Türk*, no. 9 (December 31, 1903), 2; and Mahir Saʿid, "Mektub-i Mahsus: Herbert Spencer," *Türk*, no. 15 (February 11, 1904), 3–4.

14. Doktor Vedîd, "Biraz da Fen ve Siyaset!" *Doğru Söz*, no. 12 (September 13, 1906), 4–5.

15. M[uṣṭafā] Sâtiʿ [al-Ḥusrī], *Etnografya—İlm-i Akvam—Ahvâl-i Umumiye-i Beşer, Ahvâl-i Umumiye-i Akvâm, Ahvâl-i Hususiye-i Akvâm* (Istanbul, 1327 [1912?]), 13. A more "scientific" approach applied after the Balkan Wars, when those who had massacred Muslim civilians were presented as "specimens who would qualify for [Cesare] Lombroso's gallery!" See Ahmed Cevad, *Kırmızı Siyah Kitab: 1328 Fecayiʿi* 1 (Istanbul 1329 [1913]), 125.

16. See, for example, Dr. Bahaeddin [Şakir]'s letter to [Nikola Manolov] beginning "Muhterem Vatandaş" and dated [September 6, 1907]/no. 361, *Muhaberat Kopyası*, 409. See also Dr. Bahaeddin [Şakir] to Nikola Manolov, undated [Paris, August 1907]/no. 349, *Muhaberat Kopyası*, 395–97; and the letter of H[üsrev] Sami and Dr. Bahaeddin [Şakir] beginning "Aziz Vatandaş" and dated [Paris], January 11, 1908/no. 475, *Kopye Defteri*, 76. Abdullah Cevdet also made an interesting statement in one of his poems: "Nos yeux graves et doux miroitent

la même âme/D'un père étant deux fils le Turc et le Magyar." See Abdullah Djevdet Bey, *Magyar-Turc* ([Budapest, 1901?]). One-page leaflet. The poem was also published in *Budapesti Hírlap*, December 25, 1900.

17. See A[bdullah] C[evdet], "Buckle: Henry Thomas Buckle," *İctihad* 2, no. 10 (March 1906), 154. The ideas discussed in this article were taken from the "General Introduction" section of Henry Thomas Buckle, *History of Civilization in England* (London, 1857).

18. Dr. Nâzım to Ahmed Rıza, undated [1907?], Private Papers of Ahmed Rıza (1).

19. H[enry] T[homas] Buckle, *İngiltere Tarih-i Medeniyeti Medhalinden İspanya Faslı: Taassub, Fazla İtaat ve Cehalet Aleyhindedir*, trans. Mahir Sa'id (Cairo, 1325 [1907]). See also its review in A. F., "Cehl!" *Terakki*, no. 16 [February 1908], 3–5.

20. See, for example, "Mazi ve Tarih," *Şûra-yı Ümmet*, no. 117 (June 1, 1907), 3–4.

21. See Stanislaus A. Blejwas, *Realism in Polish Politics: Warsaw Positivism and National Survival in Nineteenth Century Poland* (New Haven, 1984), 68 ff. Dillon underscored Buckle's impact on the Young Turks. See E. J. Dillon, "A Clue to the Turkish Tangle," *The Contemporary Review* 95 (June 1909), 743.

22. See Nader Sohrabi, "Constitutionalism, Revolution and State: The Young Turk Revolution of 1908 and the Iranian Revolution of 1906 with Comparisons to the Russian Revolution of 1905." Unpublished Ph.D. diss., University of Chicago (Chicago, 1996), 499 ff.

23. Bahaeddin Şakir, "Kari'in-i Kirâmdam İ'tizâr," *Şûra-yı Ümmet İlâvesi*, no. 114 (June 1, 1907), 4.

24. Ahmed Rıza, *Vazife ve Mes'uliyet* 2, *Asker* (Cairo, 1325 [1907]), 40. For a very similar but more poetic reference, see S[ami Paşazâde Sezaî], "Fas," *Şûra-yı Ümmet*, no. 88 (February 24, 1906), 1. Ahmed Rıza's private writings contain more examples of such "scientific" correlations. For example, he wrote that "Turks are like gas. If they are let free they cause no harm because they evaporate; however, if they are suppressed they burn and may cause accidents." See Ahmed Rıza's note among his scattered notes in AN 17/AS/10/dr 7.

25. Lâ [Yusuf Akçura], "Mes'ele-i Şarkiye'ye Dair," *Şûra-yı Ümmet*, no. 17 (December 1, 1902), 1.

26. For an interesting comment of Dr. Nâzım, see "İttihad ve Terakki Cemiyet-i Muhteremesi'nin 10 Temmuz'dan Evveline Aid Tertibat ve İcraatına Dair: İzmir'de Tütüncü Yakub Ağa," *İnkılâb*, no. 15 [October 30, 1909], 230.

27. "Ahmed Saib Bey'in Mevkufiyeti," *Şûra-yı Ümmet*, no. 69 (February 19, 1905), 1. See also "İhtilâl," *Şûra-yı Ümmet*, no. 55 (June 15, 1904), 3: "The law of evolution is a gradual progress. All the acts and activities that do not depend on science, philosophy, and an ideal, like the present-day Bulgarian and Armenian rebellions and Abdülhamid's massacres, are brigandage."

28. It should be remembered that Mazzini, whose works were praised by the CPU members, had regarded the French Revolution unfavorably.

29. This absolutely did not mean that "the . . . movement is of French origin," as was claimed by many observers. [See, for example, J. C. Roome, "The Nationalist Movement in Persia," *The Modern Review* 7, no. 1/37 (January 1910), 47.] The CPU and CUP leaders attributed different meanings to the motto.

30. See [Mehmed] Sabahaddin, *Türkiye Nasıl Kurtarılabilir? Meslek-i İctima'î ve Programı* (Istanbul, 1334 [1918]), 100–101. As was stated earlier, Demolins's theories on education deeply influenced Sabahaddin Bey. Most of Sabahaddin Bey's remarks in this field were taken from Edmond Demolins, *L'Éducation nouvelle: l'École des Roches* (Paris [1898]). Sabahaddin Bey never differentiated between the English, French, and Ottoman societies, and he and his admirers defended the establishment of a new educational system based on Demolins's example. [See, for example, Abdullah Cevdet, *Dimağ ve Melekât-ı Akliyenin Fizyolociya ve Hıfzısıhhası* (Istanbul, 1335 [1919]), 359.] Disciples of Demolins in other countries seem more cautious. For example, in the preface to the Russian translation of Demolins's book, Pobedonostsev states that "the construction of schools proposed by the author [Demolins] modeled on the English colleges undoubtedly cannot serve as a universal model for every society, for all conditions, and for every economy, and of course Russia offers the worst conditions for the adoption of this model." See [Edmond Demolins],

Novaia shkola, trans. K[onstantin] P[etrovich] Pobedonostsev (Moscow, 1898), 3–4. For criticisms of Sabahaddin Bey for not taking differences between the Anglo-Saxons and Turks into consideration, see M. Fazıl Reşid, *Son İzah Münasebetiyle Sabahaddin Bey Efendi'ye Açık Cevab* (Istanbul, 1329 [1912]), 22–24.

31. M. Sabri, "Anadolu Kıyamları. . . . ," *Terakki*, no. 11 [July 1907], 3. See also Lûtfullah Bey's statements in Seniha Sultan ve Damad Mahmud Paşazâde Ahmed Lûtfullah, "İstikbâlden İstikbâle," *İkdam*, August 2, 1908.

32. M. Sabri, "Anadolu Kıyamları. . . . ," *Terakki*, no. 11, 3. This is reminiscent of Kipling's idea that it had been the higher administrative skills of the British, and not racial superiority, that had led to British domination.

33. See, for example, "Le Prince Sabaheddine et son programme politique," *L'Hellénisme* 5, nos. 18–19 (September 15–October 1, 1908), 9.

34. See, for example, Ahmed Midhat, "Adem-i Merkeziyet," *Takvimli Gazete*, [December 23, 1912] and Baha Tevfik, "Memleket Nasıl Islâh Olunur," *Takvimli Gazete*, [December 25, 1912]. See also Ali Birinci, *Hürriyet ve İtilâf Fırkası: İkinci Meşrutiyet Devrinde İttihat ve Terakki'ye Karşı Çıkanlar* (Istanbul, 1990), 57. The CUP was hostile to the idea of making decentralization a pillar of opposition. See, for example, Osmanlı İttihad ve Terakki Cemiyeti'nin Bursa Hey'et-i Merkeziyesi, *Selâmet-i Vatan İçin: İrşad* ([Bursa], 1328 [1912]), 27–28.

35. See J. Michael Hagopian, "Hyphenated Nationalism: The Spirit of the Revolutionary Movement in Asia Minor and the Caucasus, 1896–1910." Unpublished Ph.D. diss., Harvard University (1942), 354. See also Manastırlı N[ikola] Rizof [Rizov], *Türkiya Nasıl Teceddüd Edebilir [?] Ahmed Rıza Bey'e Açık Mektub* (Istanbul, 1325 [1909]), 18 ff.

36. See, for example, "Rumların Programı," *Sabah*, September 2, 1908.

37. Ahmed Rıza's notebook. Private Papers of Ahmed Rıza (1), n.p.

38. For more information, see Z. Fahri Fındıkoğlu, *İçtimaiyat 2, Metodoloji Nazariyeleri* (Istanbul, 1961), 360–61; and Nurettin Sazi [*sic*] Kösemihal, "L'école de Le Play et son influence en Turquie," *Recueil d'études sociales publié à la mémoire de Frédéric Le Play* (Paris, 1956), 44–47.

39. See M. Şükrü Hanioğlu, *The Young Turks in Opposition* (New York, 1998), 205, 355.

40. "Une Fête internationale," *Mechveret Supplément Français*, no. 192 (October 1, 1907), 2.

41. See, for example, E. S. Beesly, "The Turkish Revolution," *The Positivist Review* 16, no. 189 (September 1, 1908), 204–5; Frederic Harrison, "The Turkish Reform," *The Positivist Review* 17, no. 194 (February 1, 1909), 42–43; and "Ahmed Riza," *Menschheitsziele* 3 (1909), 98–99.

42. Edward Atkin, "The Turkish Reformers," *The Positivist Review* 18, no. 201 (September 1, 1909), 208–10. For Ahmed Rıza's efforts during the Italo-Ottoman war over Tripoli, see his letter to Harrison, Constantinople, October 9, 1911, Harrison Papers, R/S.R/C. 2, 1/99, 30–31, in British Library of Political and Economic Science, London School of Economics, London. Ahmed Rıza also appealed for positivist support for the Ottoman government against the Italian invasion of Tripoli. See his letters to Corra, dated Constantinople, October 5, 1911; October [?], 1911; May 11, 1912; July 3, 1912; and August 11, 1912, AN 17/AS/10/dr 7.

43. See, for example, "Comité positif occidental: avis de M. Ahmed Riza," *La Revue Positiviste Internationale* 26, no. 5 (September 1, 1921), 65–68. See also Ahmed Rıza to Corra, Constantinople, March 29, [19]10, AN 17/AS/10/dr 7.

44. Various CUP organs republished and praised the positivist organizations' pro-Ottoman appeals criticizing European imperialistic policies. See, for example, "'Pozitivist' Cemiyeti ve Buhran-ı Şark," *Şûra-yı Ümmet*, November 25, 1908.

45. Ahmed Rıza's letter dated May 7, 1920, in "Comité positif occidental: avis de M. Ahmed Riza," *La Revue Positiviste Internationale* 24, no. 5 (September 1, 1920), 62–64.

46. Geraldine Hancock Forbes, *Positivism in Bengal: A Case Study in the Transmission and Assimilation of an Ideology* (Calcutta, 1975), 154.

47. Ahmed Riza, "Die neue Ära," *März* 2, no. 3 (August 1908), 259.

48. This did not, however, prevent Ahmed Rıza from representing to his positivist friends the early activities of the CUP after the revolution as the application of the motto *ordre et*

progrès. See Ahmed Rıza to Corra, dated Constantinople, August 17, 1912 (personelle), AN 17/AS/10/dr 7.

49. H. N. Brailsford, "The Counter-revolution in Turkey," *The English Review* 2, no. [6] (May 1909), 369.

50. Ahmed Rıza, *Vazife ve Mes'uliyet* 2, *Asker*, 67.

51. Ahmed Rıza referred to von der Goltz's work in his essay on the military. See ibid., 19.

52. [Colmar] von der Goltz, *Millet-i Müsellaha: Asrımızın Usûl ve Ahvâl-i Askeriyesi*, trans. Mehmed Tahir (Istanbul, 1301 [1884]).

53. See the answer given to an American scholar by a former cadet, Fehmi Bey, who graduated in 1902, in Merwin Albert Griffiths, "The Reorganization of the Ottoman Army under Abdülhamid II, 1880–1897," unpublished Ph.D. diss., University of California (Los Angeles, 1966), 176. For von der Goltz's influence among the Ottoman elite, see Ottomanus, "Das Streben der Türkei nach wirtschaftlicher Selbständigkeit und die Stellung des deutschen Handels," *Der neue Orient* 1, nos. 11–12 (September 15, 1917), 503.

54. Ali Fuad, "Ordu ve Millet," *Asker* 1, no. 1 [September 3, 1908], 16. A CUP member further claimed that the CPU's revolutionary activity was an example of "the Ottoman armed nation." See Ahmed Refik, *İnkılâb-ı Azîm 11 Temmuz 1324* (Istanbul, 1324 [1908]), 33. Von der Goltz's theory impressed many nonmilitary intellectuals in the Ottoman Empire as well. Even those who criticized the application of von der Goltz's theory to the Ottoman case acknowledged its authority. See, for example, Hakkı, *Millet-i Gayr-ı Müsellaha* ([Istanbul], n.d.), 7–8.

55. De Bilinski stated that "To-day the principle upon which the military establishment of Turkey was reared has become almost universal. The 'armed nation' idea is only an extension of it." See A. de Bilinski, "The Turkish Army," *The Contemporary Review* 92 (September 1907), 405.

56. Sabahaddin, *Türkiye Nasıl Kurtarılabilir?*, 81.

57. See Muharrem Feyzi Togay, *Yusuf Akçura'nın Hayatı* (Istanbul, 1944), 40. For the impact of Sorel on students, see René Dollot, *Souvenirs de l'École Libre des Sciences Politiques, 1895–1905* (Paris, 1947), 9–14. For the school, see Andrew D. White, *European Schools of History and Politics* (Baltimore, 1887), 56–67; and Pierre Rain, *L'École Libre des Sciences Politiques* (Paris, 1963), passim.

58. Akçuraoğlu Yusuf, *Türk Yılı 1928* (Istanbul, 1928), 400. Despite Akçura's claim that he was the only person to use such phrases, these locutions had, in fact, become standard expressions in the articles that appeared in *Şûra-yı Ümmet*. See, for example, S[ami Paşazâde] Sezaî, "Rusya'da İhtilâl Niçün Hâlâ Muvaffak Olamıyor?" *Şûra-yı Ümmet*, no. 87 (February 9, 1906), 2: [This is] "a fatherland filled with different nations. At present, each of these nations finds separation a way of salvation for itself because of the enmities and personal interests of those who lead it."

59. Akçuraoğlu Yusuf, *Türk Yılı*, 401.

60. Akçura considers Hüseyinzâde Ali the first "Pan-Turanist" because of his publications during this period. See ibid., 414.

61. "Albert Sorel," *Şûra-yı Ümmet*, nos. 96–97 (August 1, 1906), 4. The nationalist faction also praised Sorel. See "Albert Sorel," *Türk*, no. 137 (July 12, 1906), 3.

62. "Şuûnat," *Şûra-yı Ümmet*, no. 89 (March 10, 1906), 3.

63. Many Young Turks confessed this fact in their writings. See, for example, F., "Bir Musahabe," *İctihad*, no. 1 (September 1, 1904), 9.

64. Turanî [Hüseyinzâde Ali], "Türk Dilinin Vazife-i Medeniyesi," *Füyûzat*, no. 9 (February 6 [19], 1907), 130–31.

65. Bir Kürd-Türk [Abdullah Cevdet], "Mekâtib: 20 Mart 1907: *Şûra-yı Osmanî* Gazetesi Müdîri'ne," *İctihad* 2, no. 3 (November 1906), 255–56.

66. H[üsrev] Sami, "Silah Arkadaşlarıma—5," *Şûra-yı Ümmet*, no. 130 (February 15, 1908), 2–3. The CUP organs that praised Mazzini after the revolution also did not comment on that thinker's strong republicanism. See "İnkılâb-ı Osmanî—İtalya," *İttihad ve Terakki*, September 6, 1908.

67. See supra pp. 38, 339.

68. See my *Bir Siyasal Düşünür Olarak Doktor Abdullah Cevdet ve Dönemi* (Istanbul, 1981), 216–20.

69. "Neşriyât-ı Cedîde: Sancak," *İctihad* 2, no. 2 (October 1906), 238–39.

70. Abdullah Cevdet, "Teselsül-ü Saltanat Mes'elesi," *İctihad*, no. 6 (May 1905), 86–90. See also idem, "Hanedân-ı Osmanî," *İctihad* 2, no. 2 (October 1906), 218. All the claims made here were based on Théodule Ribot's essay *Hérédité: Étude psychologique* (Paris, 1882).

71. See, for example, L. Bourat, "Une revue Turque au Caire," *Revue du Monde Musulman* 1, no. 3 (January 1907), 451–52. A strong criticism came from Gaspıralı. See "Japonya'da Müslümanlık," *Tercüman-ı Ahvâl-i Zaman*, no. 114 (October 9 [22], 1906), 1–2.

72. Some Young Turk journals went so far as to claim that "the Turks and the Japanese are from the same origins and from the same race." See "Musahabe–7," *Balkan*, no. 109 [December 9, 1906], 2.

73. See Chapter 4. Supra, p. 67.

74. Mehmed [Dr. Nâzım] to Şövalye [Bahaeddin Şakir], Salonica, undated [late June? 1907], Private Papers of Bahaeddin Şakir. A later British report claimed that Dr. Nâzım had been deeply influenced by Léon Cahun's essay entitled *Introduction à l'Histoire de l'Asie: Turcs et Mongols à 1405*, which focuses on the racial characteristics of Turanians. See "Report on the Pan-Turanian Movement," PRO/F.O. CP. 10950 (Intelligence Bureau, October 1917).

75. Ahmed Şu'ayib, "Avâmil-i İctima'îye: Irk Nazariyesi," *Ulûm-i İktisadiye ve İctima'îye Mecmuası* 2 (1909), 78.

76. See Joseph Denais, *La Turquie nouvelle et l'ancien régime* (Paris, 1909), 76.

77. See the CUP central committee decision dated [June 19, 1909]/no. 323, Private Papers of Bahaeddin Şakir. Cabinet proceedings reveal that the CUP's warning was taken into consideration. See BBA–MV, 129/no. 26 [June 28, 1909]; no. 79 [July 18, 1909]; and BBA–MV, 133/no. 74 [October 31, 1909]. The main goal of the CUP leaders' claims that they did not know until 1909 that there were "Turkish brothers in Central Asia" was to convince the Great Powers that they were not pursuing a policy of Panturkism. See A. Arsharuni and Kh [Hadzi] [Zagidullovich] Gabidullin, *Ocherki panislamizma i pantiurkizma v Rossii* ([Moscow], 1931), 93. Talât Bey's words to Mandel'shtam quoted here were used by many scholars who accepted this peculiar expression at face value. See, for example, Gerhard von Mende, *Der nationale Kampf der Russlandtürken: ein Beitrag zur nationalen Frage in der Sovetunion* (Berlin, 1936), 86. Talât Bey also encouraged various Turkic groups to establish organizations in Istanbul. See Cafer Seydahmet Kırımer, "Bazı Hâtıralar," *Emel* 1, no. 6 (September 1961), 39.

78. See the CUP central committee decision [June 26, 1909]/no. 899–56, Private Papers of Ahmed Rıza (1).

79. Azmi Özcan, *Pan-Islamism: Indian Muslims, the Ottomans and Britain, 1877–1924* (Leiden, 1997), 133.

80. See, for example, Bonham to Barclay, Dráma, July 25, 1908/no. 49, enclosed with Barclay to Grey, Therapia, July 28, 1908/no. 423 (confidential), PRO/F.O. 371/544, file 26956; Noel Buxton, "The Young Turks," *The Nineteenth Century and After* 65, no. 383 (January 1909), 18; and "Mladoturtsii agitatsii," *Mir*, July 31 [August 13], 1908.

81. Accepted as one of the clauses of the secret agreement and not made public by the government since it was a clear violation of the constitution. The original agreement in Arabic is in BBA–A.DVN.NMH. 37/1 (1330.S.24/1336), and its Turkish translations are in BBA–HR.SYS. 107/38 (1332.Ca.19) and BBA–A.AMD.MV. 103/64 (1332.S.3). [The draft translation is in BBA/BEO, file 281785].

82. See "İttihad-ı Muhammedî Cemiyeti-*La Turquie* Gazetesi ve Bir Zabit Tehdidnâmesi," *Volkan*, no. 98 (April 8, 1909), 3–4.

83. Foreigners found these interpretations of the Şeyhülislâm very interesting. See, for example, "La costituzione turca e il suo significato scientifico," *Nuova Antologia di Lettere, Scienze ed Arti* 138, no. 888 (December 16, 1908), 678; Charles R. Buxton, *Turkey in Revolution* (London, 1909), 172–74; and Samuel Graham Wilson, *Modern Movements Among Moslems* (London, 1916), 267. Some Muslim jurists agreed with this interpretation [see, for

example, Syed H. R. Abdul Majid, *England and the Moslem Word* (York, 1912), 49; and idem, "The Moslem Constitutional Theory and Reforms in Turkey, Persia, and India," *The Imperial and Asiatic Quarterly Review* 32, nos. 61–62 (January 1911), 80], and some European specialists in Islamic Law described the Ottoman constitution as a "death warrant of Moslem law." [See Jurist, "Western Influence on Mohammedan Law," *Moslem Word* 3, no. 4 (October 1913), 360].

84. For example, Nikola Rizov wrote a pamphlet on the issue and distributed it. The authorities first ordered his arrest but then released him. See BBA–TFR.1.A. 40-A/3976 (1327.7.27).

85. Also, contrary to what is often assumed, theses such as Panturkism were openly promoted before the Balkan Wars and defended by many intellectuals. See, for example, A. A., "Yine Pantürkizm Yâni Akvâm-ı Türkün Birleşmesi," *Teârüf-i Müslimîn* 1, no. 4 [May 26, 1910], 57–58. A good analysis of the Turkist journals published during the second constitutional period can be found in Masami Arai, *Turkish Nationalism in the Young Turk Era* (Leiden, 1992), 24–68. For *Türk Yurdu*, see also Hüseyin Tuncer, *Türk Yurdu (1911–1931) Üzerine Bir İnceleme* (Istanbul, 1990).

86. Yusuf Akçura, *Üç Tarz-ı Siyaset* (Cairo, 1906), 80.

87. "Küstahlık," *Şûra-yı Ümmet*, no. 75 (May 20, 1905), 1. See also Martin Hartmann, "Der Islam 1908," *Mitteilungen des Seminars für orientalische Sprachen*, 12 (1909), 52.

88. Ahmed Rıza's undated note among his scattered notes in AN 17/AS/10/dr 7.

89. Before the first dispute with the Greeks, CUP organs stated that "the non-Turkish elements did not have equality in the sense of having an equal share in sovereignty under the old regime," but they claimed there would be absolute equality under the new regime. See Hüseyin Cahid, "Anâsır-ı Osmaniye," *Tanin*, [August 30, 1908].

90. The minutes of the "emergency meeting" between Greek committee members Zannas, Dingas, and Hatzilazaros, and the CUP leaders Dr. Nâzım, Talât Bey, and Major Enver Bey held on July 17 [30], 1908, and the minutes of the meeting between Greek committee members Lazaros, Zannas, Giannoulis, Theodoridou, and Dingas and the CUP representatives Major Cemal Bey, Mustafa Rahmi, and Âdil Bey held between August 15 and 17 [August 28 and 30], 1908, reveal that the Greek leaders categorically refused to accept the CUP's political program that "aimed at uniting the various ethnic groups of Turkey," and the two sides could not reach an agreement on proportional representation. A report (from Kanellopoulos to Baltatzis, August 20 [September 2], 1908/no. 779-4569, AYE) provides detailed information about these meetings. For Dr. Nâzım's complaints about the Greek demands, see Harris to the Secretary of State, Izmir, September 25, 1908/no. 41, Numerical and Minor Files of the Department of State, # 717, NF 862 (Case numbers 10042-10044/95). For Greek criticism, see "Les événements de Turquie: la dénationalisation de l'Empire," *L'Hellénisme* 6, no. 7 (July 1909), 66–71; N. Casasis, "L'Hellénisme et la Jeune Turquie," *L'Hellénisme* 7, nos. 7–8 (July-August 1910), 325–43; nos. 9–10 (September-October 1910), 433–54; no. 11 (November 1910), 543–58; and no. 12 (December 1910), 639–73; and V. N. Kazasis, *Les Grecs sous le nouveau Régime ottoman* (Paris, 1908), which defends a monarchy similar to that of Austria-Hungary, the most irritating example for the CUP leaders. See also Alfred Berl, "Jeune Turquie," *La Revue de Paris* 15, no. 23 (December 1, 1908), 599 ff; and F. Cayré, "Les chrétiens de Turquie," *Échos d'Orient* 15, no. 92 (January 1912), 72–76. The evidence shows that the negotiations between the CUP and the right wing of the IMRO produced similar results. Like the Greek religious leaders, the Bulgarians also adopted a very hostile stand against the CUP's idea of wholesale Ottomanism. See Belorussov, "Voprosy natsional'nogo mira na Balkanskom poluostrove," *Vestnik Evropy* 2, no. 4 (April 1909), 829. See also F.-Fo., *La vérité sur le Régime constitutionnel des Jeunes Turcs* (Paris, 1911), 11.

91. See, for example, "Türk ve Rum İttihad Kulübü," *Yeni Edirne*, September [16], 1908. Even the Ottoman Greeks, who criticized the separatist Greek organizations and attempted to refute the claim that the majority of the Ottoman Greeks were secessionists, defended the idea of an understanding between Greeks and Turks and not the wholesale Ottomanism of the CUP. See Yorgaki Efimianidi, *Sevgili Türk Kardaşlarımıza Takdim: Rum Kardaşlarınız* (Istanbul, 1324 [1908]), passim.

92. Meram, "Türkiya Osmanlılarındır," *Meram*, no. 3 [December 2, 1908], 66.

93. "Ayrılığın Sebebleri," *Tonguç*, [March 14, 1909].

94. Hüseyin Cahid, "Millet-i Hakime," *Tanin*, [November 7, 1908].

95. Nordau to Wolffsohn, Paris, November 25, 1908, CZA, W 96/I.

96. This interesting comparison was made in 1909, during the early contests between the CUP and the organizations representing various ethnic groups. See Mustafa Bey, "The Future of Parliamentary Life in Turkey," *The International* 5 (1909), 185.

97. The CUP's Turkish opponents, too, made similar accusations. See, for example, *Canlı Tarihler: Ahmet Reşit Rey (H. Nâzım): Gördüklerim-Yaptıklarım, 1890–1922* (Istanbul, 1945), 127: "We named our party Freedom and Entente [Liberal Entente] . . . because our aim was to make an unremitting concord and solidarity possible among various [Ottoman] elements through real harmony . . . instead of the vain illusion of Turkifying various peoples each of whom has begotten a distinct character." For similar accusations, see Chérif Pacha, "La faillite des continuateurs d'Abdul Hamid," *La Revue* 93, no. 21 (November 1, 1911), 40.

98. The second part of the second article of the CPU's internal regulations reads as follows: "To hinder those who work toward creating discord because of their racial and religious desires, too, is among the principal duties of the committee." *Osmanlı Terakki ve İttihad Cemiyeti Teşkilât-ı Dahiliye Nizamnâmesi* ([Paris], 1324 [1908]), 1. This clause was slightly changed when the CUP became a legal organization: "Using legal channels to hinder those who work toward creating discord because of their racial and religious desires . . . is among the duties of the committee." See *Osmanlı İttihad ve Terakki Cemiyeti'nin Nizamnâmesi* (Salonica, 1325 [1909]), 2.

99. Ahmed Rıza, *Vazife ve Mes'uliyet* 2, *Asker*, 6.

100. For example, Albanian nationalists viewed the Grand Vizier, Mehmed Ferid Pasha (Vlorë), in this way. See "Sadrazémi i ri," *Albania*, vol H, 7, no. 1 (January 1903), 57–58.

101. Following the revolution, organizations that were minimally representative of the societies on behalf of which they were speaking, but that allegedly expressed the sentiments prevailing among the Arabs and other non-Balkan ethnic groups, made similar comments. See, for example, Rachid [Rashīd] Moutran [Muṭrān]'s introductory note to the Comité Central Syrien's proclamation, dated December 25, 1908, in PRO/F.O. 371/561. See also Nadra Moutran, *Hatırat: Réflexions d'un vieux Jeune-Turc* (Constantinople, 1908), 42–44; and Martin Hartmann, "Der Islam 1908," *Mitteilungen des Seminars für orientalische Sprachen*, 12, 55–59.

102. For an interesting analysis of the Ottoman Greeks' allegiances, see George Lloyd, "Some Aspects of the Reform Movement in Turkey," *The National Review* 52 (November 1908), 422.

103. See the Deputy of Görice (Korçë), Dr. Filip Mişea's statements in the Ottoman Chamber of Deputies on January 3, 1909, in "Meclis-i Meb'usan'ın Zabıt Ceridesidir, Yirmi İkinci İctima'," *Takvim-i Vekayi'*, no. 117 [January 9, 1909], 7.

104. *Hayye-ale-l-felâh: Osmanlı İttihad ve Terakki Cemiyeti'nin Kardaşlarına Hediyesi* [Salonica, 1910], 3–5, 9. Later, CUP members urged that because of the differences between the customs of the Turks and other peoples living in the empire, a "strong and just government" was needed to unify the different ethnic groups and to compel each of these Ottoman elements that the Turks "dominated" to say "I have a government," thereby acknowledging Ottoman authority. See Mehmed Şeref, *Cemiyet ve Muhalifleri* (Edirne, [1911?]), 47–51 and 59–60.

105. In Ottoman documents too the phrase "Ottoman language, that is to say, Turkish," had been frequently used. See, for example, BBA–İrade-Hususî, Ra 1312/no. 99–929. A CUP member's statement gives us a clear idea: "Our language is Turkish. Because under the banner of evolution there existed various elements, they have gradually gained the title of Ottoman. It is necessary that domination in language belong to the Turk, just as national domination belongs to the Turks, for the sake of union and advancement. Thus the Ottoman elements must unite linguistically and understand that they will render services to the fatherland only through this [linguistic union]." See İlyas Macid, "Kulüb Hatırâlarından: Samimî Temenniler," *Bağçe*, no. 49 [August 10, 1909], 370. These ideas of the CUP leaders were strongly denounced by their old foes. See, for example, Francis de Pressensé, "The

International Situation, as Modified by the Events in Turkey," *The International* 5 (April–July 1909), 173.

106. Ahmed Rıza later authored the severest criticism of European imperialism's alleged moral bankruptcy. See Ahmed Riza, *La faillite morale de la politique occidentale en Orient* (Paris, 1922). It received good reviews only from the positivists. See Émile Corra, "La faillite morale de la politique occidentale en Orient," *La Revue Positiviste Internationale* 28, no. 6 (November 1, 1922), 118–21.

107. "Şundan Bundan," *Şûra-yı Ümmet*, no. 61 (October 10, 1904), 3.

108. "Me'yus Olmalı mı?" *Şûra-yı Ümmet*, no. 62 (October 24, 1904), 1. See also "La Guerre russo-japonaise et l'Opinion turque," *Mechveret Supplément Français*, no. 149 (March 15, 1904), 3–4; O., "Leçons japonaises," *Mechveret Supplément Français*, no. 161 (March 1, 1905), 3–4; Ahmed Riza, "La leçon d'une guerre," *Mechveret Supplément Français*, no. 169, (November 1, 1905), 2; and idem, "La leçon d'une guerre—II [III]," *Mechveret Supplément Français*, no. 175, 8.

109. Michael Gasster, *Chinese Intellectuals and the Revolution of 1911: The Birth of Modern Chinese Radicalism* (Seattle, 1969), 231.

110. See Halil Halid, *Cezair Hatıratından* (Cairo, 1906), 130–31.

111. Eşref, *Deccâl: İkinci Kitab: Gönül Eğlenceleri* (Cairo, 1907), 72.

112. See, for example, Ahmed Rıza's letter to Milholland, in "Le nouveau Régime turc et l'Opinion européenne," *Le Nil*, January 24, 1912.

113. Ahmed Rıza's notebook, p. 46, Private Papers of Ahmed Rıza (1). Another note of Ahmed Rıza stated the following: "The interventions on behalf of the Christians: Are they indeed for the love of Christianity and humanity? No! The real aim is to annihilate the Turkish government." Ahmed Rıza's note, among his scattered notes in AN 17/AS/10/dr 2. See also "Religion ou politique," *Mechveret Supplément Français*, no. 175, 5–6; and Mahmoud, "Fanatismes comparés," *Mechveret Supplément Français*, no. 172 (February 1, 1906). 4–5.

114. Necmeddin Ârif, *Paris'de Tahsil* (Cairo, 1322 [1904]), 7. See also Ahmed Riza, "Informations partiales," *Mechveret Supplément Français*, no. 130 (June 15, 1902), 1–2.

115. See *Société d'Enseignement Populaire Positiviste: Conférences publiques et gratuites, 1906–1907*. The conference schedule is in AF 17/AS/10/dr 1; Ahmed Riza, *La crise d'Orient* (Paris, 1907), 30–33, and idem, "Der Fatalismus," *Das freie Wort* 8 (August 1908), 352–55.

116. M., "La Presse révolutionnaire arménienne et la Jeune-Turquie," *Mechveret Supplément Français*, no. 190 (August 1, 1907), 4.

117. Ahmed Riza, "Le Fanatisme musulman," *Mechveret Supplément Français*, no. 178 (August 1, 1906), 2.

118. Corra to Ahmed Rıza, Paris, October 17, 1907, AN 17/AS/23/dr 2.

119. For a brief history of the initiative, see "Une mosquée à Paris," *Le Temps*, May 8, 1898.

120. Ahmed Rıza to Corra, December 9, 1907, and Corra's response dated December 11, 1907, AN 17/AS/23/dr 2.

121. The CPU organs addressed their most interesting criticism to Pierre Loti's novel entitled *Les désenchantées*. See "A propos des 'Désenchantées,'" *Mechveret Supplément Français*, no. 178, 7; and "Les Harems parisianisés," *Mechveret Supplément Français*, no. 184 (February 1, 1907), 3. See also "Turcophobie," *Mechveret Supplément Français*, no. 200 (June 1, 1908), 2. Surprisingly, Egyptian nationalists defended Loti and his work by criticizing those who had disparaged him and by claiming that Loti understood Islam well. See Mustafa Kamel Pacha, "Loti et l'islam," *Le Figaro*, September 25, 1906. The modern literary critiques, however, state that Loti lacked respect for, and willingness to understand, the Other. See Alec G. Hargreaves, *The Colonial Experience in French Fiction: A Study of Pierre Loti, Ernest Psichari, and Pierre Mille* (London, 1981), 84–85.

122. A[hmed] Agaeff, "Le réveil de l'Orient," *Le Progrès de Salonique*, July 22, 1910. See also Tahsin, "Asya ve Avrupa," *Bağçe*, no. 44 [July 6, 1909], 273–74.

123. In their interview with Sir Edward Grey, Ahmed Rıza and Dr. Nâzım maintained that the Ottoman Empire was the Japan of the Near East. See Grey to Lowther, November 13, 1908

(private), Sir (Viscount) Grey's Private Papers, Turkey 1905–1910, PRO/F.O. 800/79. This idea was common in intellectual circles. See Guglielmo Ferrero, "Die Widersprüche einer Revolution," *März* 2, no. 4 (October 2, 1908), 64. See also M[ax] Beer, "Die Türkei als konstitutionelles Reich," *Die neue Zeit*, no. 52 (September 25, 1908), 937; F. A., "La révolution à Constantinople," *Bulletin du Comité de L'Asie Française* 111, no. 90 (September 1908), 371; and Gabriel Hanotaux, *La politique de l'équilibre, 1907–1911* (Paris, 1912), 148.

124. Makino to Komura, Vienna, March 4, 1904, Gaimushô Gaiko Shiryôkan, 5/2/15/14. I am indebted to Professor Masami Arai, who translated this document from Japanese into Turkish for me. For various Young Turk groups' congratulatory telegrams to the Japanese authorities and the latter's responses, see Haydar Bey to Münir Pasha, Geneva, December 7, 1905/no. 250, Archives of the Turkish Embassy in Paris, D. 287; "Havâdis-i Hariciye," *Türk*, no. 65 (January 26, 1905), 2; "Havâdis-i Mahalliye," *Türk*, no. 62 (January 6, 1905), 2; and "Havâdis-i Mahalliye," *Türk*, no. 63 (January 13, 1905), 2. The impact of the Japanese victory on Ottoman intellectuals is well examined in Klaus Kreiser, "Der japanische Sieg über Russland (1905) und sein Echo unter den Muslimen," *Die Welt des Islams* 21 (1984), 209–39.

125. "Rusya-Japonya," *Türk*, no. 11 (January 14, 1904), 1–2.

126. "Şaşmaz mısınız [?]" *Şûra-yı Ümmet*, no. 123 (October 15, 1907), 1–2.

127. The strength of the Young Turks' faith in the militaristic attitudes of mainstream Darwinism is evident in the fact that even Abdullah Cevdet considered antimilitarism an unrealistic ideal. This was despite his admiration for the pacifistic Darwinist Baronin Bertha von Suttner, and his membership in her society *Friedens Freunde*. See Abdullah Cevdet's preface to his translation of J[acques] [IAkov Aleksandrovich] Novicow, *Harb ve Sözde İyilikleri* (Istanbul, 1927), 8] in which he maintained that antimilitarism was unrealistic. See also Abdullah Cevdet, "Doktor Gustave Le Bon," *İctihad*, no. 8 (July 1905), 120.

128. Ali Fuad, "Felsefe-i Harb," *Asker* 1 (1908), 108–12.

129. A European observer spoke of "Le Comité 'Union et Progrès' formé à l'école du positivisme politique" in order to describe the CUP's dealings with realpolitik. See H. Marchand, "La Turquie nouvelle et l'islam," *Questions Diplomatiques et Coloniales* 26, no. 280 (October 16, 1908), 479.

130. See Ahmed Rıza's letter on behalf of the CUP, dated Paris, August 18, 1908, Nachlaß Fürsten von Bülow, NL 182, Bundesarchiv-Koblenz.

131. See Ahmed Rıza's letter on behalf of the CUP central committee, Paris, August 18, 1908, PRO/F.O. 371/545, file 28993.

132. See Grey to Lowther, November 13, 1908 (private), Sir (Viscount) Grey's Private Papers, Turkey, 1905–1910, PRO/F.O. 800/79.

133. The comments made here refer only to the prerevolutionary era and the first year after the revolution. See also Božidar Samardžiev, "British Policy Toward the Young Turk Revolution, 1908–1909: Some Problems," *Bulgarian Historical Review* 14, no. 3 (1986), 22–43. [For information about and analysis of the relations between the Ottoman Empire and Great Britain during the early years of the second constitutional period, see Joseph Heller, *British Policy Toward the Ottoman Empire, 1908–1914* (London, 1983), passim.] It seems that this characteristic of CUP foreign policy-making continued throughout the period between 1908 and 1914. See Feroz Ahmad, "Great Britain's Relations with the Young Turks 1908–1914," *MES* 2, no. 4 (July 1966), 302–29.

134. During the period between 1902 and 1908 the most significant essays attempting to use religion as a device for modernization were authored by Abdullah Cevdet. See especially Abdullah Cevdet, *Uyanınız! Uyanınız!* (Cairo, 1907), 25 ff.

135. Scheikh Abdul Hagk, "Le dernier mot de l'islam à l'Europe," *La Revue* 40, no. 3 (March 1, 1902), 501–16. A Turkish translation can be found in Şeyh Abdülhak Bağdadî, "İslâmın Avrupa'ya Son Sözü," trans. Şeyh Muhsin-i Fânî [Hüseyin Kâzım Kadri], *İctihad*, no. 38 [December 14, 1911], 951–62; and in Şeyh Muhsin-i Fânî [Hüseyin Kâzım Kadri], *Felâha Doğru: İslâmın Avrupa'ya Son Sözü* (Istanbul, 1331–1328 [1912]), 1–21.

136. "Le dernier mot de l'islam à l'Europe," *Mechveret Supplément Français*, no. 133 (October 1, 1902), 4. Similarly a Russian author quoted a passage from the article maintain-

ing that the Muslims will have a settling of accounts with the European conquerors. See Z. V. Evdokimov, "Panislamizm i pantiurkizm," *Voennyi sbornik*, no. 12 (December 1911), 90.

137. Sabahaddin Bey's appeal to the ulema during the 31 March Incident was the only important exception. It should be remembered that Sabahaddin Bey issued this appeal under extraordinary circumstances. See "Sultanzâde Sabahaddin Beyefendi'nin Ûlema-yı Kirâma Açık Mektubları," *Osmanlı* (*4*), April [14, 1909].

138. Some examples of the Young Turk leaders' defense of Islamic values to appease their readership are quoted in A[rminius] Vámbéry, "The Future of Constitutional Turkey," *The Nineteenth Century and After* 65, no. 385 (March 1909), 368.

139. Ahmed Rıza, *Vazife ve Mes'uliyet* 2, *Asker*, 31.

140. Victor Bérard, *La mort de Stamboul: considérations sur le gouvernement des Jeunes-Turcs* (Paris, 1913), 107–8.

141. See Léon Ostrorog, *The Turkish Problem: Things Seen and a Few Deductions* (London, 1919), 80.

142. See the French police report dated April 27, 1909 (17.194), in Archives de la Préfecture de Police de Paris (Sabahaddine et Loutfoullah).

143. See the testimony of the former *Şeyhülislâm* Musa Kâzım Efendi at the special court martial in 1919. See "8 Mart Sene [1]335 Tarihinde İrade-i Seniye-i Hazret-i Padişahî'ye İktiran Eden Kararnâme ile Müteşekkil Divan-ı Harb-i Örfî Muhakematı Zabıt Ceridesi: Birinci Muhakeme, 3 Haziran 1335," enclosed with *Takvim-i Vekayi*ʿ, no. 3571 (June 10, 1335 [1919]), 133; "Cemiyet-i İttihadiye-i İlmiye," *Tanin*, [August 20, 1908]; and "İttihad ve Terakki," *İttihad ve Terakki*, August 30, 1908.

144. H[enry] Charles Woods, *The Danger Zone of Europe: Changes and Problems in the Near East* (London, 1911), 32. Many foreign observers quote Young Turks making similar comments on religion before and after the revolution. See, for example, Telford Waugh, *Turkey: Yesterday, To-Day, and To-Morrow* ([London], 1930), 102. Many European observers also claimed that a strong atheist tendency had prevailed in the revolutionary circles. See Georges Gaulis, "Force et faiblesse de la Jeune-Turquie," *Bulletin du Comité de L'Asie Française* 4, no. 99 (June 1909), 240.

145. "Let's offer services to this Union Committee . . . this esteemed committee succeeded in finding the straight path. Divine guidance became their counselor. They did not confront any obstacles. This is a great grace of God! This is a great benediction and blessing of God! . . . When God wishes to show the straight path to a people, He creates circumstances that would astonish the entire world." See [Manastırlı İsmail Hakkı], "Meva'iz: Ders 46, 18 Temmuz 324," *Sırat-ı Mustakim* 1, no. 1 [August 28, 1908], 13.

146. See Manastırlı İsmail Hakkı, "Manastırlı Fâzıl-ı Şehîr İsmail Hakkı Efendi Hazretleri Tarafından 10 Ağustos Tarihiyle Aldığımız Mektubu Bervech-i Âti Derc Ediyoruz," *İttihad ve Terakki*, August 30, 1908.

147. For detailed information, see İsmail Kara, *İslâmcıların Siyasî Görüşleri* (Istanbul, 1994), 66–69.

148. See, for example, Musa Kâzım, *İslâmda Usûl-i Meşveret ve Hürriyet* (Istanbul, 1324 [1908]); and Şeyh Sami, *Cemiyet ve Hürriyet: Vatandaşlarımıza Naçizâne Bir Hediyedir* (İzmir, 1324 [1908]).

149. See, for example, "İslâmiyet ve Kanun-i Esasî," *İkdam*, July 26, 1908; "Ûlema-yı İslâm ve Meşrutiyet İdare," *İkdam*, August 2, 1908; Beyazıd Cami'-i Şerifi Mucîz Dersi'amlarından Ahmed Cevdet, "Islahât-ı İlmiye Hakkında," *İkdam*, August 12, 1908; and "Cemiyet-i İttihadiye-i İlmiye," *İkdam*, August 13, 1908. Foreign observers maintained that the ulema who were backing the CUP made a good case. See Francis McCullagh, "Turkey's Future," *The International* 6 (August 1909–November 1910), 236–37.

150. "Asker Kardaşlarımıza Armağan," *Tercüman-ı Hakikat*, August 13, 1908.

151. See, for example, "Âdâb-ı Diniyeye Ri'ayet," *İttihad ve Terakki*, September 29, 1908.

152. See, for example, Manastırlı İsmail Hakkı, "Meva'iz," *Sırat-ı Mustakim* 1, no. 9 [October 22, 1908], 144; idem, "Meva'iz: Ders 51," *Sırat-ı Mustakim* 1, no. 18 [December 24, 1908], 286; "Hüseyin Cahid Bey'e," *Volkan*, no. 1 (December 11, 1908), 3; "Hak," *Volkan*, no. 2 (December 12, 1908), 4; and "Kari'in-i Kirâmdan Rica," *Volkan*, no. 3 (December 13, 1908), 2.

153. "Cemiyetimiz," *Beyan'ül-hak*, no. 1 [November 5, 1908], 11.

154. The then CUP Edirne deputy Rıza Tevfik made the statement. See "Meclis-i Meb'usan'ın Zabıt Ceridesidir: Yirmi İkinci İctima': December 21, 1324 [January 3, 1909]," *Takvim-i Vekayi'*, no. 117 [January 9, 1909], 9. The Islamist press erroneously quoted his statement as "the *sharī'a* has nothing to do here in the parliament." For the reaction, see "Takdir ve Te'essüf," *Mikyâs-ı Şeri'at*, no. 19 [January 11, 1909], 1. European observers wrote in connection with Rıza Tevfik's statement: "Un fait brutal domine le positivisme des Jeunes-Turcs." See H. Marchand, "Les Turcs & l'islam," *Revue Française de l'Étranger et des Colonies* 35 (1910), 467.

155. See, for example, "Cinayet," *Volkan*, no. 98 (April 8, 1909), 4. Later the opponents of the CUP republished Ahmed Rıza's speeches delivered at positivist gatherings in which he had described positivism as a new religion. See Şerif Paşa, *İttihad ve Terakki'nin Sahtekârlıklarına, Denaetlerine Bülend Bir Sada-yı La'netimiz* (Paris [1911]), 48–51.

156. See, for example, accusations made in Sayyid Ṭālib's manifesto against the CUP and Ahmed Rıza, as mentioned in Crow to Marling, Basra, August 30, 1913/no. 52, enclosed with Marling to Grey, Constantinople, September 25, 1913/no. 819, PRO/F.O. 371/1845, file 45368. On various occasions members of the ulema and dervishes went as far as cursing Ahmed Rıza. For example, for an incident in Konya where two Mevlevî dervishes cursed Ahmed Rıza, see Governor Ârifî Pasha to the Grand Vizier's office, Konya [August 20, 1910]/no. 125-110, BBA–BEO/Şifre Telgraf Kayd Defteri, Anadolu, 698-28/9.

157. "[İhtar]," *Beyan'ül-hak*, no. 14 [January 4, 1909], 298.

158. Kara, *İslâmcıların Siyasî Görüşleri*, 73.

159. Ibid., 221–22.

160. See, for example, Osmanlı İttihad ve Terakki Cemiyeti'nin Şehzâdebaşı Kulübü Hey'et-i İlmiyesi, *Mevā'iz-i Dinîye* (Istanbul, 1328 [1910]), passim. In addition to these clubs in the capital, the CUP İkiçeşmelik branch in Izmir organized public seminars conducted by leading ulema and published the lectures. See Şeyh Mehmed Nuri el-Kadirî, *Mev'ize: Osmanlı İttihad ve Terakki Cemiyet-i Muhteremesine Mensub İkiçeşmelik Kulübünde Din Dersleri* 1, *Fezâil-i Ahlâk* (Izmir, 1328 [1910]); and 3, *İlm ü Ma'rifet* (Izmir, 1328 [1910]).

161. See Deniz Müzesi Arşivi, MKT. II, 1664 G/2 [February 23, 1909]; and Daireler I, 44/2 [May 8, 1909]. The second issue has appeals to the soldiers. See *Işık*, no. 2 (1909), 37 ff.

162. See *Işık*, no. 1 (1909), 10 ff. For instance, the constitution was described as follows: "You know that these are things which are ordered by our *sharī'a*. The *sharī'a*, however, is very comprehensive and endless. In addition, it is written in Arabic. The necessary things taken from the *sharī'a* are written in Turkish and these are called laws. Look! In the constitution the things ordered by our *sharī'a* for government business are gathered, compiled, and written in Turkish. Dear compatriots! Our Prophet worked by depending on his companions' and disciples' opinions. Therefore, the constitutional regime would fit us more than any other country" (p. 20).

163. The prayer leaflet issued by the CUP Sultan Ahmed Club with the heading *Hādhā ḥirz mujarrab li'-l-ḥifẓ min al-rīḥ al-aṣfar wa-min al-ṭā'ūn* ([Istanbul], n.d. [1910?]).

164. See, for example, the CUP Arabgir branch's letter to the sultan dated [June 13, 1909]/no. 49, BBA–İrade-Hususî, Ca 1327/no. 21-200.

165. Ahmed Rıza to Corra, Constantinople, March 20, 1924, AN 17/AS/ 2/dr 1.

166. The State Council's memorandum and the cabinet's subsequent decision were based on the *Mecelle*; however, the imperial decree obviously strengthened the power of the civil courts. See "Mahakim-i Nizamiyede Bilrü'ye İlâma Rabt Edilen Hukuk-u Şahsiye Da'valarının Mahakim-i Şer'iyede İstima' ve Rü'yetinin Memnu'iyeti Hakkında İrade-i Seniye [April 3, 1909]," *Düstûr*, 2nd Series, 1 (Istanbul, 1329 [1911]), 192–94.

167. "Bilumum Mahakim-i Şer'iye ile Merbutatının Adliye Nezareti'ne Tahvil-i İrtibatı Hakkında Kanun," March 12, 1917, *Düstûr*, 2nd Series, 9 (Istanbul, 1928), 270–71.

168. See Hanioğlu, *The Young Turks*, 206.

169. See Ö[mer] Naci, "İnkılâba Dair," *Şûra-yı Ümmet*, October 26, 1908.

170. Enver Bey to a German woman with whom he frequently corresponded, 'Ayn al-Manṣūr, September 2, 1912, Ernst Jäckh Papers, Yale University, MS 466, Box 1, Folder 40.

171. [İsmail] Hakkı Hafız, *Bozgun* (Istanbul, 1330 [1914]), 20–21, 51.

172. See Gustave Le Bon, *Ruh'ül-akvâm*, tr. Abdullah Cevdet (Cairo, 1907). This was a translation of Le Bon's *Les lois psychologiques de l'évolution des peuples*.

173. Abdullah Cevdet's preface to his translation. Ibid., 7.

174. "Küstahlık," *Şûra-yı Ümmet*, no. 75, 1–2.

175. See Hanioğlu, *The Young Turks*, 23.

176. See ibid., 207; and Şerif Mardin, *Continuity and Change in the Ideas of the Young Turks* (Istanbul, 1969), 23.

177. "Abdülhamid'in Hal'i," *Şûra-yı Ümmet*, no. 25, 3.

178. See, for example, "Vazife-i Şahsiye," *Şûra-yı Ümmet*, no. 76 (June 4, 1905), 2.

179. Türkmen, "Şark'a Bir Nazar," *Türk*, no. 61 (December 29, 1904), 1.

180. See, for example, "Cinnet," *Şûra-yı Ümmet*, no. 44 (December 21, 1903), 1–2; "Mektub: İntizar," *Şûra-yı Ümmet*, no. 53 (May 17, 1904), 3; and "Şâyân-ı İmtisâl Bir Fi'il," *Şûra-yı Ümmet*, no. 68 (February 6, 1905), 3: "We do not want to excuse the masses while criticizing the elite." See also "Abdülhamid'in Şürekâ-yı Cinayâtı," *Şûra-yı Ümmet*, no. 83 (September 30, 1905), 1.

181. "Ahmed Rıza Bey'e Paris'den Gönderilen Bir Mektubdan," *Türkçe İstanbul*, March 24, 1919.

182. "Mütalâat," *Şûra-yı Ümmet*, no. 134 (May 15, 1908), 5–7.

183. For an interesting comparison, see Paul Farkas, *Staatsstreich und Gegenrevolution in der Türkei* (Berlin, 1909), 12.

184. M. Âlî, "*Tanin*'i Hakka Da'vet," *Volkan*, no. 58 (February 27, 1909), 2–3; and idem, "İzhar-ı Hakikat," *Volkan*, no. 57 (February 26, 1909), 3.

185. Another interesting comparison was made in Russia. During the press campaign against the Octobrists in 1908 and 1909, the Young Turks and the CUP leaders were described as the "Octobrists of Turkey." See Geoffrey A. Hosking, *The Russian Constitutional Experiment: Government and Duma, 1907–1914* (Cambridge, 1973), 94.

186. Hasan Sabri Ayvazof, "Rusya İnkılâb-ı Kebîri: Genc Türklere!" *İctihad* 2, no. 5 (January 1908), 294. For a veiled attack by *Tercüman* asking the Young Turks to stop wandering around Europe and go back to Anatolia, see "Devlet-i Aliyye ve İdare-i Meşruta," *Tuna*, no. 400 [January 22, 1907], 2.

187. A[li] Hüseyizâde, "Teklifimiz Mu'ayyen Olmalıdır," *Hayat*, no. 58 (September 6 [19], 1905), 2.

188. [Colmar] von der Goltz, *Der jungen Türkei Niederlage und die Möglichkeit ihrer Wiedererhebung* (Berlin, 1913), 7.

189. Catulle Mendès, *Le Roman rouge* (Paris, [1885]).

190. The CPU Internal Headquarters advocated the translation and distribution of this book. See Sâî [Talât Bey] to [Bahaeddin Şakir], January 6, [1]907 [1908], in "Osmanlı İttihad ve Terakki Cemiyeti: Vesâik-i Tarihiyeden," *Şûra-yı Ümmet*, no. 212 [March 17, 1910], 2; and Sâî [Talât Bey] to [Bahaeddin Şakir], October 19, [1]907/no. 1, in "Osmanlı İttihad ve Terakki Cemiyeti: Vesâik-i Tarihiyeden," *Şûra-yı Ümmet*, no. 204 [January 20, 1910], 2.

191. "Kâmil Paşa," *Şûra-yı Ümmet*, no. 109 (February 15, 1907), 1.

192. See "Osmanlı İttihad ve Terakki Cemiyeti'nin Dün Gazetelere Tebliğ Etdiği Beyan-nâme," *Tanin*, [August 8, 1908]; and "Osmanlı İttihad ve Terakki Cemiyeti'nin Beyannâme-sidir," *Tanin*, [August 10, 1908].

193. Şerif Mardin, "Ideology and Religion in the Turkish Revolution," *IJMES* 2, no. 3 (July 1971), 198–99. A Russian observer addressed the same point when he stated that the revolutionary tactics employed by the Young Turks were considerably different from those of the European revolutionaries. See "Khronika: inostrannoe obozrenie," *Vestnik Evropy* 5, no. 9 (1908), 405.

194. The only exception to this general rule is İbrahim Temo's founding of the short-lived Osmanlı Demokrat Fırkası (Ottoman Democratic party) in 1909. For Temo's description of being a democrat, see Bir Muhibb, "Terakkiyât-ı Fikriye," *Muhibban*, no. 3 [November 28, 1909], 19; and, for the articles of the party organs defending a populist program see, for example, "Bir İki Söz," *Hukuk-u Beşer*, no. 1 [January 9, 1910], 1; "Yolumuz," *Selâmet-i*

Umumiye, no. 1 [June 2, 1910], 1–2; and "Kavliyat ve Fiʿliyat," *Genc Türk*, [December 26, 1910]).

195. Enver Bey to a German woman with whom he frequently corresponded, ʿAyn al-Manṣūr, September 2, 1912, Ernst Jäckh Papers, Yale University, MS 466, Box 1, Folder 40.

196. The European press attributed such a character to the Young Turk movement during the revolution. See, for example, "Die Jungtürken," *Freie Zeitung*, July 23, 1908; and "Sachen und Bedeutung der jungtürkischen Bewegung," *Neue freie Presse*, July 22, 1908.

197. Ahmed Rıza's notebook. This page has no number, Private Papers of Ahmed Rıza (1).

CHAPTER 11

1. Muhittin Birgen, "İttihad ve Tarakkide [*sic*] On Sene: İttihad ve Tarakki [*sic*] neydi?" *Son Posta*, October 16, 1936.

2. See, for example, Rizof [Rizov], *Türkiya Nasıl Teceddüd Edebilir* [*?*] *Ahmed Rıza Bey'e Açık Mektub* (Istanbul, 1325 [1909]), 5; and Rıza Nur, *Cemiyet-i Hafiye* (Istanbul, 1330 [1912]), 544.

3. Halil Halid, "The Origin of the Revolt in Turkey," *The Nineteenth Century and After* 65, no. 387 (May 9, 1909), 755.

4. See, for example, Ahmed Rıza's announcement maintaining that the intervention of the Great Powers stemmed from the "maladministration of the absolutist regime" and that, since the CUP provided "justice and freedom," no intervention would ever occur again. See "Ahmed Rıza Bey," *İkdam*, September 28, 1908.

5. See "Rumeli Islahatında İslâm," *Şûra-yı Ümmet*, no. 53 (May 17, 1904), 4.

6. See, for example, A[kçura] Y[usuf], "Son İnkılâb ve Sevâbıkı ile Netâyici," *İctihad* 2, no. 9 (March 1909), 322.

7. For more information, see Esther Benbassa, *Un grand rabbin sepharde en politique, 1892–1923* (Paris, [1990]), 27–28.

8. A[li] H[üseyinzâde], "İntikad Ediyoruz, İntikad Olunuyoruz," *Füyûzat*, no. 27 (September 26 [October 9], 1907), 372.

9. Babanzâde Ahmed Naʿim made the best Islamist intellectual critique of the CUP program, arguing that Islam and nationalism could never be reconciled. See his *İslâmda Daʿva-yı Kavmiyet* (Istanbul, 1332 [1916]).

10. Ziya Gökalp, *Türkleşmek, İslâmlaşmak, Muʿasırlaşmak* (Istanbul, 1918). This essay was first published in *Türk Yurdu* 3 (1913), 331 ff.

11. Foreign observers noticed the development of Turkism during the last days of the Hamidian regime and commented that after its fall a strong Turkism would emerge. See, for example, N. Freiherr von Stetten, "Das hamidianische System; türkische Studie," *Neue Revue* 1, no. 9 (March 1908), 686: "Mit dem Fall des hamidianischen Systems wird Europa mit einem ganz neuen Faktor im nahen Osten zu rechnen haben, mit dem erwachenden, im Kern gesunden und starken Türkentum."

12. The phrase "constitutional rights" quickly replaced "the will of the sultan," the standard locution of the old regime. Even conflicting tribal groups accused each other and local authorities of not "taking [their] constitutional rights into account." See, for example, ʿAbd al-ʿAzīz ʿAbbās's telegram to the speaker of the Ottoman Chamber of Deputies, Medina, April 3, 1910 in BBA–DH.MUİ. 17-4/22 (1328.Ca.29). Likewise officials began to use phrases such as "compatibility with the constitutional regime." For example, when discussing the ways to suppress a local revolt in ʿAsīr, a commander and a subgovernor used the phrase "the restoration of peace and order through a method compatible with the constitutional regime." See Necib Bey, subgovernor of al-Ḥudayda, and Commander Behçet Bey to the Grand Vizier's office [September 2, 1909], BBA–BEO/Dahiliye Giden, 108-3/57; 2382 [September 9, 1909]/ 272255.

13. See, for example, "Τουρκικός και Ελληνικός Στρατός," *Χρόνος*, July 26 [August 8], 1908.

14. Basil Thompson, *The Allied Secret Service in Greece* (London, 1931), 31. Although the fact that some Greek officers took part in the Greek coup tends to suggest that the Young Turk Revolution had an impact on them, some scholars have maintained that this was not really so. See, for example, Gregor Manousakis, *Hellas-Wohin? Das Verhältnis von Militär und Politik in Griechenland seit 1900* (Godesberg, 1967), 36–37.

15. For the Greek coup d'état and the impact of the Young Turk Revolution on this venture, see S. Victor Papacosma, *The Military in Greek Politics: the 1909 Coup d'état* (Kent, Ohio, 1977), 38 ff; and Μιλτ[ιάδης] I. Μαλαίυος, *Η Επανάστασις του 1909* (Athens, 1965), 18 ff.

16. For a general overview, see "The Ottoman Constitution and Its Effect on the Orient," *The American Review of Reviews* 38 (November 1908), 609–10.

17. See "Cemiyet-i İttihad ve Terakki-i İraniyân," *İkdam*, September 9, 1908.

18. The Persian expatriates who gathered in Switzerland were given the CPU regulations and used them as their guideline for organizing their secret organization. Ahmed Rıza and Dr. Nâzım, who were portrayed as the Voltaire and Rousseau of the Ottoman Empire by Persian constitutionalists, required the latter group not to give this document to untrustworthy people. See *Mubārazah bā Muḥammad 'Alī Shāh: asnādī az fa 'āliyat'ha-yi azādīkhvāhan-i Irān dar Urūpā va Istanbūl*, ed. Iraj Afshār (Tehran, 1359 [1980-81], 74–75 and 175, for a copy of the regulations on which Doctor Ismā'īl Marzbān wrote the following note: "Please read these regulations because they are essential as a guideline for our actions."

19. See Azmi Özcan, *Pan-Islamism: Indian Muslims, the Ottomans and Britain, 1877-1924* (Leiden, 1997), 157.

20. See Seymour Becker, *Russia's Protectorates in Central Asia: Bukhara and Khiva, 1865–1924* (Cambridge, Mass., 1968), 205.

21. "Möldir bulak zhane öli su," *Sotsialistik Qazaqstan*, November 21, 1988.

22. See his letter to the president of the CUP in Salonica, dated Charleville, November 9, 1908, and his pamphlet entitled *Le Congo ou secret d'état*, enclosed with that letter in BBA–TFR.1.M. 22/2199-1 (1326.10.22).

Select Bibliography

For the sake of brevity this select bibliography omits much material used in preparing this book and many items cited in the endnotes. The archival material is listed under major categories without a full breakdown. All manuscripts, official publications, and published documents used in preparing this book are given. All works of the Young Turks used in this book, except for their translations of European books, are also listed, although neither this list nor that of the Young Turk journals is by any means a complete compilation of the Young Turks. The list of the works of Young Turks includes memoirs that provide information on the events that took place before or during the revolution. Appeals issued by various Young Turk organizations before and after the revolution are not included. Dates of publication have been converted into the Gregorian calendar. A list of secondary journals and newspapers is also included. This list does not include the journals and newspapers that published contemporary articles with relevant information. No secondary work published either during the Young Turk movement or afterward is mentioned. Full details of such secondary works, as well as of Young Turk appeals, used in preparing the book can be found in the endnotes.

I. ARCHIVES

Albania

Arkivi Qendror Shtetëror (Tirana)
Fondi Dr. I. Temo : 19

Files:

31	106–2
58	106–5
59	106–6
60	

Austria

Allgemeines Verwaltungsarchiv (Vienna)

K.u.k. Innenministerium Präsidiale, zl. 6842/1903, zl. 7304/1903.

Haus-, Hof- and Staatsarchiv (Vienna)

Akten des k.u.k. Ministeriums des Äußeren, 1848–1918 (Politisches Archiv).

VIII 141, England, Berichte 1908.
XII 190, Türkei, Varia 1907.
XII 351, Türkei, Liasse XXXIX/1b (Verhandlungen anläßlich der Annexion Bosniens und der Herzegowina mit dem jungtürkischen Komité in Saloniki, 1908–1909).
XIII 195, Türkei, Berichte 1908 VI–VII 1908.
XIII 196, Türkei, Berichte 1908 VIII–IX 1908.
XIII 197, Türkei, Varia 1908.
XXXVIII 395, Konsulat Monastir, 1908.
XXXVIII 409, Konsulat Saloniki, Berichte 1908 I–VIII.
XXXVIII 410, Konsulat Saloniki, Berichte 1908 IX–XII.

Österreichisches Kriegsarchiv (Vienna)

Kriegsministerium Präsidial Register (1908).

Bosnia and Hercegovina

Arhiv Bosne i Hercegovine (Sarajevo)

Zajedničko ministarstvo finansija, odjeljenje za Bosnu i Hercegovinu, prezidialna, 1656/1900.

Bulgaria

TSentralen Dŭrzhaven Arkhiv (Sofia)

3K Monarkhicheski institut.
176K Ministerstvo na vŭnshnite raboti i izpovedaniiata.
321K Bŭlgarska legatsiia v TSarigrad.
331K Bŭlgarsko konsulstvo v Bitolia.
334K Bŭlgarsko konsulstvo v Solun.
336K Bŭlgarsko generalno konsulstvo v Odrin.
339K Bŭlgarska legatsiia v TSetina.

Bŭlgarski Istoricheski Arkhiv (Sofia)

317 S. Paprikov.

Egypt

Dār al-Wathā'iq al-Qawmiyya (Cairo)

Sijillāt ʿĀbidīn-Turkī-Ṣādir talagrāfāt, S/5/52/10.

France

Archives nationales (Paris)

Fonds Émile Corra; Archives positivistes

17/AS/2/dr 1.
17/AS/10/dr 7.
17/AS/23/dr 2.

Police générale
F7
Sociétés et associations du département de la Seine
F7/12366–12376/B

Archives de la Préfecture de Police de Paris (Paris)

Kémal Ismail Bey, B. A (1699)-216.335.5119.
Sabaheddin et Loutfullah, B. A (1653)-171154.

Archives du Ministère de la Guerre (Château de Vincennes)

E.M.A et Attachés militaires, 7 N 1635.

Archives du Ministère des Affaires étrangères (Paris)

Nouvelle Série-Turquie

3   (1899–1901).

4   (1902–1904).

5   (1905–1907).

6   (1908–1909).

Turquie: Politique Intérieure: Arménie, Anatolie, Cilicie XII (1905–1907): 82.
Turquie: Politique Intérieure: Macédoine, 38 (Juin–Sept., 1908).

Germany

Bundesarchiv (Koblenz)

NL. 182.

Bundesarchiv-Militärarchiv (Freiburg im Breisgau)

RM 5 (Admiralstab der Marine)/1598: Türkei Politisches, Bd. 3–4.
RM 5 (Admiralstab der Marine)/ 5868: Türkei: Unruhen im Jahre 1909, Bd. 1, 197.

Politisches Archiv des Auswärtigen Amtes des Bundesrepublik Deutschland (Bonn)

495/2, Allgemeine Angelegenheiten der Türkei, 134 (Bd. 22–23).
626/3, Mazedonien, 156 (Bd. 140–41).
630/2, Das Verhältnis der Türkei zu Deutschland, 158 (Bd. 9–10).
638/3, Der Sultan und seine Familie, 159/1 (Bd. 11–12).
641/3, Türkische Staatsmänner, 159/2 (Bd. 9–10).
733/3, 734/1, Die Jungtürken, 198 (Bd. 4–5) and (Bd. 5–6).
943/5, Diverse Personalien, 159/4 (Bd. 1–2).

Greece

Αρχείον Υπουργείο Εξωτερικών (Athens)

Ιστορικό Αρχείο Μακεδονίας (Salonica)
Selânik Vilâyeti Meclis-i İdare Kalemi, Mazbata Müsvedde Paketi, 1/1324.

Israel

Central Zionist Archives (Jerusalem)
A 119: Personal Papers of Max Nordau.
H VIII: Personal Papers of Theodor Herzl.
W 94: Personal Papers of David Wolffsohn.
Z 2: Zionistisches Centralbureau.

Israel State Archives (Jerusalem)
RG. 83–1/ט.

Italy

Archivio Storico del Ministero degli Affari Esteri (Rome)
Affari Politici, Serie P. Politica (1891–1916)
    pacco 121
    pacco 123–24
    pacco 172

Japan

Gaimushô Gaiko Shiryôkan (Tokyo)
Section 5/2/15/14.

The Netherlands

Algemeen Rijksarchief (The Hague)
Tweede Afdeling: Kabinetarchief van het Ministerie van Buitenlandse Zaken betreffende
politieke rapportage door Nederlandse diplomatieke vertegenwoordigers in het buitenland,
1871–1940: 50.

Sweden

Rijksarkivet (Stockholm)
Utrikesdepartementet, 1902 ars dossieringssystem, vol. 7, Redogörelsen fran Beskickningen
i Konstantinopel 1908.

Switzerland

Archives de la Justice et Police (Geneva)
Dossier: Abdullah Djevdet.

Archives d'État-Genève (Geneva)
Chancellerie: B.8.

Bundesarchiv (Bern)
E. 21/14'248.
E. 21/14'252.

Turkey

Archives of the Turkish Embassy in London (London)
Boxes
362   (4)
372   (2)
373   (2)
377   (1)
383   (1)
395   (1)

Archives of the Turkish Embassy in Paris (Paris)
Dossiers
D.   228
D.   244
D.   277
D.   283
D.   287
D.   290

Archives of the Turkish Embassy in Rome (Rome)
Box 71 (1).
Box 81 (7).

Başbakanlık Arşivi (Istanbul)
1. Âmedî Evrakı

   a. A.AMD.MV. (Meclis-i Vükelâ).
   b. A.AMD.NMH. (Nâme-i Hümayûn).
   c. A.DVN.MV. (Divan-ı Hümayûn Kalemi).

2. Bâb-ı Âli Evrak Odası

  a. Nezaret ve Devâir
     Adliye Gelen (Âmed).
     Adliye Giden (Reft).
     Bulgaristan Hülâsası.
     Bulgaristan Komiserliği Gelen.
     Bulgaristan Komiserliği Giden.
     Bulgaristan Komiserliği Muharrerat Defteri.
     Dahiliye Gelen.
     Dahiliye Giden.
     Harbiye Gelen (Serasker Âmed).
     Harbiye Giden (Serasker Reft).
     Hariciye Gelen.
     Hariciye Giden.
     Hidiviyet-i Celile-i Mısriyenin Tahrirat Defteri.
     İrade-i Hususiye.
     Maliye Gelen.
     Maliye Giden.
     Mısır Fevkâlâde Komiseri Gazi Ahmed Muhtar Paşa'dan Vürûd Eden.
     Mısır Hidiviyet-i Celilesinin Muharrerat Defteri.
     Mısır Hidiviyet-i Celilesinin Tezâkir Defteri.
     Mısır Hülâsa Defteri.
     Mısır Komiserliği Âmed.
     Posta ve Telgraf Nezareti Gelen.
     Posta ve Telgraf Nezareti Giden.
     Re'sen İrade-i Seniye.
     Sadaretden Giden Şifre. (Each volume bears a distinct title).
     Sadarete Gelen Şifre. (Each volume bears a distinct title).
     Umum Muhaberat.
     Vilâyât-ı Muhtare ve Mümtaze Kalemlerine Mahsus Yevmiye Defteri.
     Zabtiye Gelen.
     Zabtiye Giden.

  b. Vilâyetler Gelen-Giden (2)
     Âmedî Kalemi: Marûzat-ı Hususiye Hülâsa Kayd Defteri: 290.
     Anadolu Mutasarrıflığı Reft: 80.
     Anadolu [Telgrafı] Defteri: 909.
     Anadolu Vilâyâtı Telgrafı Gelen: 910 and 911.
     Ankara Vilâyeti Gelen: 103.
     Ankara Vilâyeti Reft: 98.
     Dersaadet Giden: 424.
     Diyar-ı Bekir Reft: 121.
     Edirne Giden: 483.
     Erzurum Reft: 129.
     Erzurum Vilâyeti Gelen: 126.
     Haleb Giden: 297 and 298.
     Kastamoni Gelen: 153.
     Kastamoni Reft: 157.
     Ma'muret el-Azîz Vilâyeti Giden: 173.
     Manastır Giden: 552.
     Müşiriyet 1324 Sadrası: 651.
     Müşiriyet [1]324 Vâridesi: 639.
     Müsted'iyat 1324: 830/1.
     Müteferrika 1323: 878.
     Rumeli Müteferrikası: 445.

Rumeli Vilâyâtı Giden: 465.
Selânik Giden: 566.
Takdim Evrakına Mahsus Defter: 1171.
Trabzon Giden: 193.
Umum Defteri: 880.
Van Reft: 198.
Van Vilâyeti Âmed: 195.
Vâride: Kosova Vilâyeti: 512.
Yemen Âmed: 367 and 368.
Yemen ve Trablusgarb Giden: 371.

c. Mümtaze Kalemi: Bulgaristan Tasnifi Evrakı I-II.
d. Mümtaze Kalemi: Mısır.
e. Mahremâne Müsveddat:

168
209

3. Dahiliye Nezareti Evrakı

a. DH.HMŞ. (Hukuk Müşavirliği).
b. DH.MUİ. (Muhaberât-ı Umumiye).
c. DH.SYS. (Siyasî).

4. Hariciye Nezareti Evrakı

a. HNA-TDA. (Hariciye Nezareti Arşivi-Osmanlı Belgelerinde Ermeniler Tasnifi).
b. HR.MTV. (Mütenevvia Kısmı Evrakı).
c. HR.SYS. (Siyasî).

5. Hatt-ı Hümayûn Tasnifi (HH)

6. İrade Tasnifi

DUİT (Dosya Usûlü İrade Tasnifi).
İrade-Adliye ve Mezâhib.
İrade-Askerî.
İrade-Bulgaristan.
İrade-Dahiliye.
İrade-Hariciye.
İrade-Hususî.
İrade-Kavânin ve Nizâmât.
İrade-Maliye.
İrade-Mısır Mesâlihi.
İrade-Ticaret ve Nafiʿa.

7. MV (Meclis-i Vükelâ Mazbataları)

Vol. 107
Vol. 108
Vol. 110
Vol. 111
Vol. 115
Vol. 119
Vol. 129
Vol. 133
Vol. 149

8. Rumeli Müfettişliği Evrakı

a. TFR.1.A. (Sadaret ve Başkitabet Evrakı).
b. TFR.1.AS. (Jandarma Müşiriyet ve Kumandanlık Evrakı).

c. TFR.1.İŞ. (İşkodra).
d. TFR.1.KNS. (Konsolosluk Evrakı).
e. TFR.1.KV. (Kosova).
f. TFR.1.M. (Müteferrik Evrak).
g. TFR.1.MN. (Manastır).
h. TFR.1.SFR. (Sefaret Evrakı).
i. TFR.1. ŞKT. (Arzuhaller).
j. TFR.1.SL. (Selânik).
k. TFR.1.UM. (Umum Evrakı).

9. Yıldız Evrakı

a. YEE (Yıldız Esas Evrakı).

Sections:

5
9
15
23
30
31
36

b. Yıldız Esas Evrakı-Kâmil Paşa Evrakına Ek I–II.
c. Yıldız Marûzat Defterleri:

No. 11488
No. 14452
No. 14925
No. 15158

d. YMGM (Yıldız Mütenevvî-Günlük Marûzat).
e. YP (Yıldız Perâkende).
f. Y.PRK.GZT. (Yıldız Perâkende Gazete).
g. YSHM (Yıldız Sadaret Hususî Marûzat).
h. YSRM (Yıldız Sadaret Resmî Marûzat).

10. Şûra-yı Devlet Evrakı
    Dersaadet XXI-30.

Deniz Müzesi Arşivi (Istanbul)

Sections:
Daireler I and II.
Gemiler, Erkân-ı Harbiye, Tersane, Limanlar, Daireler.
Mektubî.
Müteferrik-Divan-ı Harb.
Şûra-yı Bahrî.
Umumî Evrak.

Dışişleri Bakanlığı Hazine-i Evrak Arşivi (Istanbul)*

Dossiers:

İdarî. Box   198

Siyasî.   225

                226

* This used to be an independent archive and was recently acquired by the Başbakanlık Archives.
Recataloging is currently in progress.

İstanbul Üniversitesi Bedî N. Şehsuvaroğlu Tıp Tarihi ve Deontoloji Arşivi (Istanbul)
Dossier: 6/59.

İstanbul Üniversitesi Cerrahpaşa Tıp Fakültesi Tıp Tarihi ve Deontoloji Arşivi (Istanbul)
Dossier: *İttihad ve Terakki* (İ.4).

Tercüman Gazetesi Arşivi (Istanbul)
Dossier: 157 (1317).

Türk İnkılâp Tarihi Enstitüsü Arşivi (Ankara)
Section 82.

Türkiye Büyük Millet Meclisi Arşivi (Ankara)
Dossier 239/31: "Ankara İstiklâl Mahkemesi'nin İzmir Suikastına ait (239/31) No:lu Dosyası."

United Kingdom

British Library: India Office (London)

IOR: R/20/A : Aden: Records of British Administration, 1839–1967: Settlement of Aden, 1839–1937, and Protectorate Affairs, 1878–1928.
IOR: L/P&S/10: Political and Secret Department: Departmental Papers: Political and Secret Separate (or Subject) Files, 1902–1931.

Public Record Office (London)

CAB
37/63
38/2
38/8
38/11

F.O.

a. General Correspondence
78/5140
78/5142
78/5187
78/5191
78/5192
78/5193
78/5209
78/5211
78/5212
78/5224
78/5226
78/5229
78/5230
78/5240
78/5259
78/5267
78/5392

78/5422
78/5958
120/248
371/152
371/153
371/155
371/156
371/157
371/344
371/346
371/356
371/534
371/540
371/544
371/545
371/546
371/548
371/551
371/559
371/577
371/659
371/768
371/1845

b. Embassy and Consular Archives
195/2124
195/2129
195/2131
195/2154
195/2171
195/2187
195/2222
195/2250
195/2251
195/2283
195/2290
195/2292
195/2297
195/2298
195/2300
195/2328
294/35
294/45
294/46
294/49
295/19
297/2

c. Confidential Print
424/192
424/205
424/210
424/212
424/213
424/215
424/217

United States

Papers of the American Board of Commissioners for Foreign Missions (ABCFM), Harvard University, Houghton Library (Cambridge, Mass.)
vol. 15.
vol. 30.

U.S. Archives (Washington D.C.)
Dispatches from U.S. ministers to Turkey, 1818–1906, vols. 70, 73, and 74.
Notes from the Turkish Legation in the United States to the Department of State, 1867–1908, vols. 8–9 (July 2, 1895–July 2, 1906).
Numerical and Minor Files of the Department of State, # 717, NF 862 (case numbers 10042–10044/95).

II. PRIVATE PAPERS

a. Young Turks
Private Papers of Abdullah Cevdet (Gül Karlıdağ's private collection-Istanbul).
Private Papers of Ahmed Rıza (1) (the author's private collection).
Private Papers of Ahmed Rıza (2) (Faruk Ilıkhan's private collection—Istanbul).
Private Papers of Bahaeddin Şakir (the author's private collection).
Papiers du Prince Sabahaddine, Bibliothèque nationale (Paris), Supplément turc, no. 1599: Boxes 1–2.
Sabahaddin Bey's uncataloged papers in European languages, in Manuscrits Occidentaux, Bibliothèque nationale (Paris).
Private Papers of Yusuf Akçura (the late Emel Esin's private collection—Istanbul).
Miscellaneous letters of Hakkı Baha Pars, Reşid Sadi, and Colonel Sadık Şehreküştü.

b. Other
Abbas II Papers, Durham University.
The Private Papers of Sir (Lord) Francis Bertie, Confidential Series A (1899–1919), PRO/F.O. 800/180.
Blowitz Papers, *The Times* Archives (London).
Nachlaß Fürsten von Bülow, Bundesarchiv–Koblenz, NL. 182.
Crewe Papers, University Library, Cambridge, C. 14.
Cromer Papers, PRO/F.O. 633.
Gladstone Papers, British Museum, Add. MS 44537.
Sir (Viscount) Grey's Private Papers, Turkey 1905–1910, PRO/F.O. 800/79.
Harrison Papers, British Library of Political and Economic Science, London School of Economics (London).
Aubrey Herbert Papers, Somerset Record Office (Taunton), DD/DRU 47.
Ernst Jäckh Papers, Yale University Sterling Memorial Library, MS. 466.
Lansdowne Papers, Turkey, PRO/F.O. 800/143; and Lansdowne Papers, India Office Library, MSS Eur D 558.
E. J. Monson Papers, 1900–1905, MS English History c. 1200, Bodleian Library, Oxford.
Private Papers of Athanasios-Souliotis-Nicolaides (Αρχείο Σουλιώτη), Gennadion Library (Athens).
O'Conor Papers, Churchill College, Cambridge.
Correspondance de Joseph Reinach, Bibliothèque nationale (Paris), MS Occ. XXXVIII.
Private Papers of Salih Münir Pasha (the author's private collection).
Lord Sanderson's Private Papers, PRO/F.O. 800/1–2.
Nachlaß Süssheim, Staatsbibliothek Preußicher Kulturbesitz: Orientabteilung.
Vambéry Papers, PRO/F.O. 800-33.
Yusuf İzzeddin Efendi Evrakı, BBA–DUİT, 86-1 and 86-2.

III. MANUSCRIPTS

Bahaeddin Sâî, *Güldeste-i Hatırât-ı Ahrar ve Eslâf-Refuge [Réfugié] Turc à Paris,* Istanbul
   Hakkı Tarık Us Library, MS D. 38/1.
[Câmi Baykut], *Câmi Baykut'un Anıları Defteri* 1–2, Türk Tarih Kurumu Arşivi, no. 1082.
*İttihad ve Terakki Cemiyeti'nin 15 Teşrin-i sânî 1907–28 Mart 1908 Senelerine Ait
   Muhaberatının Kayıt Defteri,* Türk Tarih Kurumu Yazmaları, no. 130.
M[ehmed] Sabri, *Adem-i Merkeziyet Cemiyeti Beyannâmesi* (1908), Türk Tarih Kurumu
   Yazmaları, no. 129.
Osmanlı İttihad ve Terakki Cemiyeti Merkezi'nin 1906–1907 Senelerinin Muhaberat Kopyası,
   Atatürk Library, Belediye Yazma, O. 30.

IV. PUBLISHED DOCUMENTS, OFFICIAL PUBLICATIONS

Albania

Akte të rilindjes kombëtare Shqiptare 1878–1912 (*memorandume, vendime, protesta, thirrje*),
   ed. Stefanaq Pollo and Selami Pulaha (Tirana, 1978).

Austria-Hungary

Austro-Hungarian Documents Relating to the Macedonian Struggle, 1896–1912, ed. E. F.
   Bridge (Thessaloniki, 1962).
Borba Muslimana: Bosne i Hercegovine za vjersku i vakufsko-mearifsku autonomiju, ed. Ferdo
   Hauptmann (Sarajevo, 1967).
*Österreich-Ungarns Aussenpolitik von der bosnischen Krise 1908 bis zum Kriegsausbruch
   1914: Diplomatische Aktenstücke des österreichisch-ungarischen Ministeriums des Äussern*
   1, ed. Ludwig Bittner et al. (Vienna, 1930).

Belgium

*Amtliche Aktenstücke zur Geschichte der europäischen Politik, 1885–1914: Die belgischen
   Dokumente zur Vorgeschichte des Weltkrieges* 4, *Die Balkanprobleme, die bosnische Krise/
   Albanien, der Panthersprung nach Agadir, 1908–1911,* ed. Bernhard [Heinrich] Schwertfeger
   and Alfred Doren (Berlin, 1925).

Bulgaria

*Dokumenti po obiaviavane na nezavisimostta na Bŭlgariia 1908 godina: iz tainiia kabinet
   na kniaz Ferdinand,* ed. TSv. Todorova and El. Statelova (Sofia, 1968).

France

Chambre des Députés, 9ᵉ législature-session ordinaire (1909). Enclosed with *Journal Officiel.*
Documents diplomatiques français, 2ᵉ Série (1901–1911), 4 (Paris, 1932); 11 (Paris, 1950).

Germany

Die geheimen Papiere Friedrich von Holsteins 4, *Briefwechsel,* ed. Norman Rich and M. H.
   Fisher (Göttingen, 1963).
*Die Große Politik der europäischen Kabinette, 1871–1914: Sammlung der diplomatischen
   Akten des Auswärtigen Amtes,* ed. Johannes Lepsius, Alfred Mendelssohn Barthold, and
   Friedrich Thimme:
1, *Der Frankfurter Friede und seine Nachwirkungen, 1871–1877* (Berlin, 1922).
4, *Die Dreibundmächte und England* (Berlin, 1922).

6, *Kriegsgefahr in Ost und West: Ausklang der Bismarckzeit* (Berlin, 1922).
13, *Die europäischen Mächte untereinander, 1897–1899* (Berlin, 1924).
18/2, *Zweibund und Dreibund, 1900–1904* (Berlin, 1924).
21/1, *Die Konferenz von Algeciras und ihre Auswirkung* (Berlin, 1925).
25/1–2, *Die englisch-russische Entente und der Osten* (Berlin, 1925).
27/2, *Zwischen den Balkankrisen, 1909–1911* (Berlin, 1925).
28, *England und die deutsche Flotte, 1908–1911* (Berlin, 1925).
39, *Das Nahen des Weltkrieges, 1912–1914* (Berlin, 1926).

Italy

I Documenti Diplomatici Italiani, (3rd. ser., 1896–1907), vol. 4 (Rome, 1972) and vol. 6 (Rome, 1985).

Macedonia

Dokumenti za borbata na makedonskiot narod za samostojnost i za nacionalna država 1 (Skopje, 1981).

Ottoman Empire

Düstûr 2nd Ser., vol. 1 (Istanbul, 1911) and vol. 9 (Istanbul, 1928).
Meclis-i Meb'usan Zabıt Ceridesi (Istanbul, 1908 and 1909). Enclosed with *Takvim-i Vekayi'*.
Salnâme-i Devlet-i Aliyye-i Osmaniye:
    62 (Istanbul, 1906).
    64 (Istanbul, 1908).
    65 (Istanbul, 1910).

Russia

Au service de la Russie: Alexandre Iswolsky, Correspondance Diplomatique, 1906–1911 (Paris, 1937).
Konstantinopol' i prolivy: po sekretnym dokumentam b. ministerstva inostrannykh del 2, ed. E[vgenii] A[lexandrovich] Adamov (Moscow, 1926).
Krasnyi arkhiv 6/43 (1930): *Turetskaia revoliutsiia 1908–1909 gg.* (Moscow, 1931).
Razdel aziatskoi Turtsii: po sekretnym dokumentam b. ministerstva inostrannykh del, ed. E[vgenii] A[lexandrovich] Adamov (Moscow, 1924).

Turkey

1925–1926 Türkiye Cumhuriyeti Devlet Salnâmesi (Istanbul, 1926).

United Kingdom

A & P (Accounts and Papers—State Papers)
Egypt 3 (1906): *Correspondence Respecting the Attack on British Officers at Denshawai.*
Egypt 4 (1906): *Further Paper Respecting the Attacks on British Officers at Denshawai.*
Turkey 1 (1908): *Further Correspondence Respecting Proposals by His Majesty's Government for Reforms in Macedonia.*
Turkey 2 (1908): *Further Correspondence Respecting Proposals by His Majesty's Government for Reforms in Macedonia.*
Turkey 3 (1908): *Further Correspondence Respecting the Affairs of South-Eastern Europe.*
British Documents on the Origins of the War, 1898–1914
    1, *The End of the British Isolation* (London, 1927).
    5, *The Near East* (London, 1928).

Command Paper:
"Report on the Pan-Turanian Movement," PRO/F.O. CP. 10950 (Intelligence Bureau, October 1917).
Hansard's Parliamentary Debates 4th series, volumes 103(1902), 160(1906), 184(1908).

V. THE WORKS OF THE YOUNG TURKS

Abdülhakim Hikmet, *Külliyat-ı Hikmet* 3: *Rüya veya Hudâ-negerde Hakikat-ı Müstakbele* (Geneva, 1904).
Abdullah Cevdet, *Cihan-ı İslâma Dair Bir Nazar-ı Tarihî ve Felsefî* (Istanbul, 1922).
———, *Dimağ ve Melekât-ı Akliyenin Fizyolociya ve Hıfzısıhhası* (Istanbul, 1919).
———, *Droit d'asile en Suisse* (Geneva, 1905).
———, *Hadd-ı Te'dib: Ahmed Rıza Bey'e Açık Mektub* (Paris, 1903).
———, *Kafkasya'daki Müslümanlara Beyannâme* (Geneva, 1905).
———, *Magyar-Turc* ([Budapest, 1901?]).
———, *Réponse au Journal de Genève* (Geneva, 1904).
———, *Uyanınız! Uyanınız!* (Cairo, 1907).
Ahmed Niyazi, *Hatırât-ı Niyazi yahud Tarihçe-i İnkılâb-ı Kebîr-i Osmanîden Bir Sahife* (Istanbul, 1908).
Ahmed Refik, *İnkılâb-ı Azîm* (Istanbul, 1908).
Ahmed Rıza, *La crise de l'Orient* (Paris, 1907).
———, *Échos de Turquie* (Paris, 1920).
———, *La faillite morale de la politique Occidentale en Orient* (Paris, 1922).
———, *Vazife ve Mes'uliyet*, 1, *Mukaddime, Padişah, Şehzâdeler* (Cairo, 1902); 2, *Asker* (Cairo, 1907).
Ali Fahri, *Emel Yolunda* (Istanbul, 1910).
———, *Yine Kongre* (Paris, [1900]).
Ali Haydar Midhat, *Hatırâlarım, 1872–1946* (Istanbul, 1946).
———, *The Life of Midhat Pasha* (London, 1903).
———, *Menfa-yı İhtiyarî Hatıratı* (Geneva, 1905).
Avnullah el-Kâzımî, *Son Müdafaa* (Istanbul, 1908).
Bekir Fikri, *Balkanlarda Tedhiş ve Gerilla: Grebene* (Istanbul, 1976).
Mithat Şükrü Bleda, *İmparatorluğun Çöküşü* (Istanbul, 1979).
Le congrès des libéraux Ottomans (Paris, 1902).
Döküntüler [pseud.], *Uçurum* (Cairo, 1905).
Kâzım Nami Duru, *"İttihad ve Terakki" Hatıralarım* (Istanbul, 1957).
Enver Paşa'nın Anıları, ed. Halil Erdoğan Cengiz (Istanbul, 1991).
Eşref, *Deccâl: İkinci Kitab: Gönül Eğlenceleri* (Cairo, 1907).
Ethem Ruhi Balkan Hatıraları-Canlı Tarihler 6 (Istanbul, 1947).
Hafız Cemal, *Kıbrıs Cemiyet-i Hayriye-i İslâmiyesine Mahsus Ta'limatnâme* ([Nicosia], 1906).
———, *Kıbrıs Cemiyet-i Hayriye-i İslâmiyesi'nin Yeni Ta'limatnâmesi* (Nicosia, 1912).
———, *Kıbrıs Osmanlılarına Mahsus Son Hediye-i Âcizânem veyahud Kıbrıs'da Geçen Dört Senelik Tarih-i Hayatım ile Kıbrıs Osmanlılarına Mahsus Parlak İstikbâl Programı* ([Nicosia], 1909).
———, *Sevgili İslâmlarım! Artık Uyanalım!* ([Nicosia], 1906).
Halil Ganem, *Les Sultans ottomans* (Paris, 1901).
Halil Halid, *Cezair Hatıratından* (Cairo, 1906).
Halil Paşa, *İttihat ve Terakkî'den Cumhuriyet'e: Bitmeyen Savaş: Kütûlamare Kahramanı Halil Paşa'nın Anıları*, ed. Taylan Sorgun (Istanbul, 1972).
İbrahim Temo, *İttihad ve Terakki Cemiyetinin Teşekkülü ve Hidemati Vataniye ve İnkılâbi Milliye Dair Hatıratım* (Medgidia, 1939).
İmamet ve Hilâfet Risâlesi (Cairo, 1898).
İsmail Hakkı, *Cidâl yahud Ma'kes-i Hakikat* (Cairo, 1907).
İsmail Kemal, *The Memoirs of Ismail Kemal Bey*, ed. Somerville Story (London, 1920).

Kâzım Karabekir, *İttihat ve Terakki Cemiyeti, 1896–1909* (Istanbul, 1982).
Doktor Lütfi, *L'État politique de la Turquie et le Parti Libéral* (Paris, 1903).
———, *Millet ve Hükûmet* (Paris, 1906).
Mehmed Cemil, *Tarihçe-i Ahrardan Birkaç Yaprak: Ali Şakir, Kendim, Edhem Ruhi* (Ruse [1908]).
Mehmed Kadri Nâsıh, *Sarayih* (Paris, 1910 [1911?]).
Giridli Bir Türk [Mehmed Macid], *Firak* (Cairo, 1906).
Mehmed Ramih, *Berrî ve Bahrî Silah Arkadaşlarıma* ([Paris], 1908).
Cevrî [Mehmed Reşid], *İnkılâb Niçin ve Nasıl Oldu*[*?*] (Cairo, 1909).
Mehmed Sabahaddin, *İttihad ve Terakki Cemiyeti'ne Açık Mektublar: Mesleğimiz Hakkında Üçüncü ve Son Bir İzah* (Istanbul, 1911).
———, *Mémoire des libéraux Turcs relatif à la Question d'orient* (Paris, 1906).
———, *Teşebbüs-i Şahsî ve Adem-i Merkeziyet Hakkında İkinci Bir İzah* (Istanbul, 1908).
———, *Teşebbüs-i Şahsî ve Tevsiʿ-i Meʾzuniyet Hakkında Bir İzah* (Istanbul, 1908).
———, *Türkiye Nasıl Kurtarılabilir? Meslek-i İctimaʿî ve Programı* (Istanbul, 1918).
M[ehmed] Sabri, *Vatandaşlarımıza* (Paris, 1908).
Mehmed Ubeydullah, *Geçid* (Cairo, 1905).
[Halil Menteşe], *Osmanlı Mebusan Reisi Halil Menteşe'nin Anıları*, ed. İsmail Arar (Istanbul, 1986).
Necmeddin Ârif, *Paris'de Tahsil* (Cairo, 1906).
Neler Olacak! . . . (Cairo, 1896).
Osmanlı Terakki ve İttihad Cemiyeti Umur-i Dahiliye [Ömer Naci], *Hayye-ale-l-felâh* ([Paris], 1907).
Osmanlı İttihad ve İnkılâp Cemiyeti'nin Nizamnâme-i Dahilisi ([Cairo], 1904).
Osmanlı İttihad ve Terakki Cemiyeti'nin Nizamnâmesi (Salonica, 1909).
Osmanlı Terakki ve İttihad Cemiyeti Nizamnâme-i Esasî (Egypt [Cairo], 1906).
Osmanlı Terakki ve İttihad Cemiyeti Teşkilât-ı Dahiliye Nizamnâmesi ([Paris], 1908).
Bir Diplomat [Reşid Sadi], *Usûl-i İdare ve Islahat* ([London], 1902).
Şerafeddin Mağmumî, *Düşündüm ki* (Cairo, 1913).
[Süleyman Nazif], *Gizli Figanlar* (Cairo, 1906).
Şûra-yı Ümmet-Ali Kemal Daʾvası (Istanbul, 1909).
[Talât Paşa?] *Talât Paşa'nın Hâtıraları*, ed. Enver Bolayır (Istanbul, 1958).
[Tarsusîzâde Münif], *Türk Sözü Anadolu Ağzı* ([Cairo, 1904?]).
Tunalı Hilmi, *Makedonya: Mazi-Hâl-İstikbâl* (Cairo, 1898).
———, *Murad* (Geneva, 1899).
———, *Onbirinci Hutbe: Türkiyalılık Osmanlılıkdır; Osmanlılık Türkiyalılıkdır* (Geneva, 1901).
———, *Un projet d'organisation de la souveraineté du peuple en Turquie* (Geneva, 1902).
———, *Rezalet: Dördüncü Fasıl-Portekiz* (Ihsanbol [Geneva], 1900).
Youssouf Fehmi, *La Révolution ottomane* (Paris, 1909).
Yusuf Akçura, *Eski Şûra-yı Ümmet'de Çıkan Makalelerimden* (Istanbul, 1913).
———, *Midhat-Pacha, la Constitution ottomane et l'Europe* (Paris, 1903).
———, *Türk Yılı 1928* (Istanbul, 1928).
———, *Üç Tarz-ı Siyaset* (Cairo, 1907).

VI. UNPUBLISHED THESES

Merwin Albert Griffiths, "The Reorganization of the Ottoman Army under Abdülhamid II, 1880–1897," Unpublished Ph.D. diss., University of California (Los Angeles, 1966).
J. Michael Hagopian, "Hyphenated Nationalism: The Spirit of the Revolutionary Movement in Asia Minor and the Caucasus, 1896–1910," Unpublished Ph.D. diss., Harvard University (Cambridge, Mass., 1942).
Nader Sohrabi, "Constitutionalism, Revolution and State: The Young Turk Revolution of 1908 and the Iranian Revolution of 1906 with Comparisons to the Russian Revolution of 1905," Unpublished Ph.D. diss., University of Chicago (Chicago, 1996).

VII. YOUNG TURK JOURNALS

Ahali (Plovdiv)
Anadolu (Cairo)
Balkan (Ruse)
Curcuna (Cairo)
Doğru Söz (Cairo)
Efkâr-ı Umumiye (Ruse, Sofia)
Ezan (Geneva)
La Fédération Ottomane-İttihad-ı Osmanî (Geneva)
Feryad (Sofia)
Hilâfet-Khilāfa (London)
İctihad (Idjtihad-İçtihat) (Geneva, Cairo, and Istanbul)
İntibâh (Paris)
İntikam (Geneva)
Islahat (The Piraeus)
İstirdat (Geneva)
Lâklâk (Cairo)
Kanun-i Esasî (Cairo)
Kürdistan (Geneva)
Mechveret Supplément Français (Paris)
Mecmua-i Kemal (Cairo)
Mizan (Geneva, Istanbul)
Muvazene (Plovdiv, Varna, and Geneva)
Neyyir-i Hakikat (Monastir)
Osmanlı (Folkestone, Cairo, and Geneva)
Osmanlı (2) (Cairo)
Osmanlı (3) (The Pireaus)
Rumeli (Plovdiv)
Sada-yı Girid (Canea)
Sancak (Cairo)
Şûra-yı Osmanî (Cairo)
Şûra-yı Ümmet (Cairo, Paris, Istanbul, and Salonica. It also appeared as *Haftalık Şûra-yı Ümmet* and *Selânik'de Şûra-yı Ümmet*.)
Terakki (Paris)
Tuna (Ruse)
Türk (Cairo)
Uhuvvet (Ruse)
Yeni Fikir (Alexandria)

VIII. THE JOURNALS SUPPORTING THE YOUNG TURK CAUSE

Füyûzat (Baku)
Hayat (Baku)
İrşad (Baku)
Kaspii (Baku)
Tercüman-ı Ahvâl-ı Zaman (Bağçesaray-Bakhchysaray/Crimea)

IX. OTHER NEWSPAPERS AND JOURNALS

Where confusion is likely to arise, I have provided the place of publication in parentheses.

a. Newspapers

al-Ahrām
L'Aurore
Basler Nachrichten
Berliner Börsen-Courrier
Berliner Tageblatt
Budapesti Hírlap
Der Bund (Bern)
Constanţa
The Daily Chronicle
The Daily Graphic
The Daily Mail
The Daily News
The Daily Telegraph
Deutsche Zeitung
Dobrogea Jună
Écho de Paris
L'Éclair
L'Express (Istanbul)
Le Figaro
Frankfurter Zeitung
Freie Zeitung
Genc Türk (Istanbul)
Le Genevois
Gil Blas
Il Giornale d'Italia
The Globe
The Guardian
Hukuk-u Beşer (Istanbul)
Hukuk-u Umumiye
L'Humanité
İfham
İkdam
L'Intransigeant
L'Italie (Rome)
İttihad ve Terakki (Salonica)
Journal de Genève
Journal de Marseille
Journal de Nyon
Le Journal d'Orient (Istanbul)
Le Journal du Caire
Journal Officiel (Paris)
Χρόνος (Athens)
Le Matin
Il Messagero
Metin (Istanbul)
Mir (Sofia)
Le Monde Hellénique (Athens)
Münchner allgemeine Zeitung
al-Nafīr

Neue freie Presse
Neue Zürcher Zeitung
The New York Times
The New York Tribune
Le Nil (Cairo)
Nov zhivot (Sofia)
Osmanlı (4) (Istanbul)
Le Paris Nouvelles
Le Petit Marseilles
Le Petit Parisien
Le Petit Temps
La Petite République
Le Peuple de Genève
Peyâm
Preußische Zeitung
Le Progrès de Salonique
Les Pyramides (Cairo)
Le Radical
Reichswehr
Sabah
Schweizer freie Presse
Selâmet-i Umumiye
Serbest İzmir
Serbestî
Le Siècle
Le Soir (Paris)
The Standard
La Suisse
Svobodno slovo (Sofia)
Der Tag
Tägliche Rundschau
Täglicher Anzeiger
Takdirat
Takvim-i Vekayiʿ
Takvimli Gazete
Tanin
Le Temps
Tercüman-ı Hakikat
Thurgauer Zeitung
The Times (London)
Tonguç (Istanbul)
The Tribune (London)
Tribune de Genève
Türkçe İstanbul
Vakit
Vecherna poshta (Sofia)
Vossische Zeitung
Die Welt
Wiener Morgen Zeitung
The World
Yeni Asır (Salonica)
Yeni Edirne
Yeni Gazete (Istanbul)

b. Journals

Albania (Brussels, London)
Albania (2) (Rome)
The American Magazine
Annales des Sciences Politiques
Archives Diplomatiques
Archives Israélites
Armenia (Boston)
The Armenian Herald
Armenian Review
Arnaud (Istanbul)
Arnavudluk Gazetesi
Asia
Asien
Asker
Athenæum
The Atlantic Monthly
Bağçe (Salonica)
Berliner Monatshefte für internationale Aufklärung
Beyan'ül-Hak
Blackwood's Edinburgh Magazine
Bulletin de la Société Endjouman Terekki-Islam
Bulletin de la Société Internationale de Science sociale
Bulletin du Comité de L'Asie Française
The Bystander (London)
Ceride-i Mahakim-i Adliye
Ceride-i Vakfiye (Istanbul)
Çocuk Bağçesi (Salonica)
The Contemporary Review
Correspondance d'Orient
Le Correspondant (Paris)
Cosmopolitan Magazine
Courrier de la Conférence de la Paix
Le Courrier Européen (Paris)
Deutsche Monatsschrift für das gesamte Leben der Gegenwart
Droshak
The Dublin Review
Échos d'Orient
The Eclectic Magazine
The Economist
The Edinburgh Review
The English Review
Études
L'Européen
Feyz-i Hürriyet (Istanbul)
The Fortnightly Review
Das freie Wort
Geist des Ostens
Guguss
Ḥabl al-Matīn
Hakayık-ı Tarihiye ve Siyasiye
L'Hellénisme (Paris)
The Hindustan Review
Hürriyet (London)

Hürriyet (2) (Istanbul)
Ilinden (Sofia)
L'Illustration (Paris)
Illustrirte Zeitung (Leipzig)
The Imperial and Asiatic Review
L'Indépendance Arabe (Paris)
The Independent
The Indian Review
İnkılâb (Istanbul)
The Institute of Bankers (London)
The International
Das Interview (Berlin)
Işık (Istanbul)
İslâm (Nicosia)
İstikbâl (Canea)
La Jeune Turquie (Paris)
The Jewish Chronicle
The Jewish Review
Jüdische Rundschau
Juhayna (Cairo)
Kambana (Sofia)
Küçük Mecmua (Diyar-ı Bekir)
The Living Age
Majlis
al-Manār
März
Mècheroutiette (Paris)
Le Mémorial Diplomatique
Menschheitsziele
Meram
Mercure de France
Mihrab (Istanbul)
Mikyâs-ı Şeri'at (Istanbul)
The Missionary Review of the World
Mitteilungen des Seminars für orientalische Sprachen
The Modern Review
Moslem Word
Muhibban
al-Muqtataf
Musāvāt
Musavver Salnâme-i Servet-i Fünûn
The Nation (London)
The National Geographic Magazine
The National Review
The Near East
Der neue Orient
Neue Revue
Die neue Zeit
The New Europe (London)
The Nineteenth Century (*and After*)
Nord und Süd
The North American Review
Novo vreme (Sofia)
Nuova Antologia di Lettere, Scienze ed Arti
Odrisnki glas (Sofia)

Der Orient
L'Orient (Paris) (it also appeared as *L'Orient et L'Agence Ottoman*)
The Orient Review (London)
Peyman (Diyar-ı Bekir)
The Positivist Review
Preußische Jahrbücher
Pro Armenia
The Quarterly Review (London)
Questions Diplomatiques et Coloniales
The Review of Reviews
Revoliutsionnyi vostok
La Revue
Revue Bleue
La Revue de L'Islam
La Revue de Paris
La Revue des Deux Mondes
La Revue du Mois
Revue du Monde Musulman
Revue Française de l'Étranger et des Colonies
La Revue Occidentale
La Revue Politique Internationale
La Revue Positiviste Internationale
Rivista d'Italia
Russkaia mysl'
Rūznāma-i Rasmī-i Kishvar-i Shāhinshahī-i Irān
Sabah'ül-Hayr (Van)
Science sociale
Servet-i Fünûn
Silâh (Salonica)
Sırat-ı Mustakim (Istanbul)
Sovremennyi mir
Srpski Književni Glasnik
Tarih-i Osmanî Encümeni Mecmuası
Teârüf-i Müslimîn
Terakki (2) (Baku)
Top (Skopje)
Türk Yurdu
Ulûm-i İktisadiye ve İctima'îye Mecmuası
La Vara
Vestnik Evropy
La Vie Politique dans les Deux Mondes
Voennyi sbornik
La Voix de l'Arménie
Volkan
Die Welt des Islams
The Westminster Review
Die Woche
The World To-day
The World's Work
Zeitschrift für Politik

Index

Muslim Ottomans did not have family names. An individual was known by his personal name (as in "Ali"), by a combination of his birth-name and personal name (e.g., "Ahmed Rıza"), by a combination of an adjective indicating his place of birth and his personal name (e.g., "Mekkeli Sabri"), by a combination of an honorific and his personal name (e.g., Uzun Osman), and by a combination of a patronymic indicating the genealogy of his family and his family name (e.g., Tarsusîzâde Münif or Akçuraoğlu Yusuf). Muslim Ottoman names are therefore alphabetized by personal name—"Ahmed Rıza," and not "Rıza, Ahmed;" "Sabri, Mekkeli," and not "Mekkeli, Sabri;" "Osman, Uzun," and not "Uzun Osman;" and "Münif, Tarsusîzâde," and not "Tarsusîzâde Münif." An exception is made for those individuals who survived long enough into the Republican period to adopt a family name in accordance with the "Surname Law" of June 21, 1934. This law required all citizens of the Turkish Republic to adopt a family name by January 1, 1935. Such individuals are alphabetized by family name, e.g., "Akgöl, Eyüb Sabri," and not "Eyüb Sabri."